WILLIAM HARVEY

BENJAMIN FRANKLIN

HIPPOCRATES

LOUIS PASTEUR

MICHAEL FARADAY

THOMAS A. EDISON

SOME BOOKS ON SCIENCE
BY ISAAC ASIMOV

Inside the Atom

Building Blocks of the Universe

The Clock We Live On

Words of Science

Realm of Number

The Living River

The Kingdom of the Sun

Realm of Measure

The Wellsprings of Life

Realm of Algebra

Life and Energy

Fact and Fancy

The Genetic Code

The Human Body

The Human Brain

View From a Height

A Short History of Biology

Quick and Easy Math

Adding a Dimension

A Short History of Chemistry

Of Time and Space and Other
   Things

The New Intelligent Man's Guide to
   Science

An Easy Introduction to the Slide Rule

The Noble Gases

The Neutrino

Understanding Physics (3 volumes)

The Universe

From Earth to Heaven

Is Anyone There?

Science, Numbers and I

Photosynthesis

Twentieth Century Discovery

The Solar System and Back

The Stars in Their Courses

The Left Hand of the Electron

More Words of Science

Today and Tomorrow and—

Jupiter, the Largest Planet

The Tragedy of the Moon

Asimov on Astronomy

Our World in Space

Asimov on Chemistry

Of Matters Great and Small

Science Past—Science Future

Eyes on the Universe

The Ends of the Earth

Asimov on Physics

The Planet that Wasn't

Alpha Centauri, the Nearest Star

The Collapsing Universe

The Beginning and the End

Mars, the Red Planet

Quasar, Quasar, Burning Bright

Life and Time

Saturn and Beyond

Extraterrestrial Civilizations

The Road to Infinity

A Choice of Catastrophes

Venus, Near Neighbor of the Sun

Views of the Universe

The Sun Shines Bright

ASIMOV'S BIOGRAPHICAL ENCYCLOPEDIA
OF
SCIENCE AND TECHNOLOGY

◆——

Second Revised Edition

ASIMOV'S BIOGRAPHICAL ENCYCLOPEDIA *of* SCIENCE *and* TECHNOLOGY

The Lives and Achievements of 1510 Great Scientists from Ancient Times to the Present Chronologically Arranged

by ISAAC ASIMOV

Second Revised Edition

Doubleday & Company, Inc., Garden City, New York
1982

PICTURE CREDITS

LIBRARY OF CONGRESS CATALOG CARD NUMBER 81–47861

TO MY DAUGHTER, ROBYN,
FOR HER PATIENCE AND
FOR HER GOODNESS OF HEART

HOW TO USE THIS BOOK

The 1510 biographical entries are arranged in chronological order, not alphabetical. They are numbered from 1 to 1510 and this numbering system I consider more significant than the page numbers. It is, in my opinion, the individual biography and not the page that should be taken as the unit of reference. For this reason the index references at the end are by biography number and *not* by page number. In a very few cases, this means searching through several pages; in most, it means a glance through less than one page.

To help find individual scientists to begin with, I have supplied a table of contents at the start in which all the biographical entries are listed in alphabetical order, with the biography number given for each.

In the body of each biography I have inserted numerous cross references (again to biography number rather than page number). It may be that some readers dipping into the book at random, or with the purpose of looking up a particular individual, will be lured into looking up the cross references, then into chasing after the new cross references. If they do so assiduously enough, they will find that, no matter where they start, they are likely to end by reading the whole book.

But then, science is a complex skein, intricately interknotted across the artificial boundaries we draw only that we may the more easily encompass its parts in our mind. Pick up any thread of that skein and the whole structure will follow.

And so it is with this book.

ISAAC ASIMOV

PREFACE TO THE SECOND REVISED EDITION

This time I have introduced no changes in the format of the Encyclopedia; I have merely enlarged it.

I have added 310 additional biographies, about half of them taken from contemporary scientists and half distributed through time. The total is now 1510. Of the biographies that were present in the previous edition, most have been slightly enlarged as I gathered additional information about each scientist. This edition is, therefore, substantially larger than the previous one.

Nevertheless, it is still entirely a one-man job. No one else but myself (and my good editor) has touched it. This means that, although I have corrected a number of errors and misstatements in the earlier editions, I am very likely to have overlooked some and to have introduced others. I take the full responsibility for that and, as always, I welcome corrections and comments from my readers.

ISAAC ASIMOV

New York, New York
April 1981

PREFACE TO THE FIRST REVISED EDITION

The differences between this revised edition and the first are as follows:

(1) Almost every biography has been enlarged and, when necessary, altered, in accordance with the findings of my continuing researches over the last five years.

(2) Nearly two hundred new biographies, including recent Nobel Prize winners and a number of earlier individuals (even a few ancient Greeks), have been added.

(3) I have abolished the system of main biographies and "footnote" biographies as an element of artificiality and now list all entries, without exception, in strict chronological order according to birth.

(4) I have added a contents section at the front of the book in which all entries are listed alphabetically, with their biography number, for easy reference.

I must now repeat what I said in the preface to the first edition, to the effect that I alone am responsible for the choice of those to include and for the decision as to how much space to give each person—and, of course, for all errors, omissions, and infelicities.

The "alone" part is stronger than some people realize, I think, for from a number of comments I have received in connection with the first edition, I have detected some tendency to take it for granted that the book is a community endeavor and that I have headed a sizable team engaged in research and in writing.

This is not so! I alone have done every bit of the necessary research and writing; and without any assistance whatever, not even that of a typist. This is not because of any parsimony on the part of Doubleday & Company, my esteemed publishers. They have been generous in their offers to finance research and secretarial assistance but I have—quite deliberately—refused those offers.

It means, of course, that, as a lone worker, I am incomplete in places where some help might have brought matters to completion; and wrong outright, in some places where a little help might have righted me. On the other hand, because the book is the product of one mind and two hands and no more (except for the invaluable editing the manuscript received at Doubleday) it has its own particular flavor, style, and point of view—whether for good or ill—throughout.

And besides, the book is a labor of love, and I loved it far too much to want to share it in the slightest.

ISAAC ASIMOV

New York, New York
August 1971

FROM THE PREFACE TO THE FIRST EDITION

It is not likely that anyone will be overcome by the novelty of a history of science. There are any number of such histories. Therefore I had better explain just how this one differs and why I feel justified in adding it to the list.

First: In this book the history of science is told through biographies (biographies that concentrate on the subjects' scientific labors, of course, rather than their private lives). This has its shortcomings, for it makes it easy to leave gaps and to become repetitious. Yet it has the great merit, in my opinion, of stressing the fact that scientific knowledge is the painfully gathered product of thousands of wonderful, but fallible, human minds.

Nor are these scientists more than human. In writing of them I have tried to stress this fact and to show that even the greatest among them went wrong on occasion or stubbornly lost step.

Second: There is no attempt to divide the sciences into separate categories and devote chapters to each, as is often done in histories of science. When this is done, the sense of the panorama is easily lost. The scientists included in this book are listed in chronological order of birth. You will encounter what might seem a bewildering succession of chemists, mathematicians, inventors, explorers, physicists, astronomers, biologists, and physicians. But in real life, after all, that is precisely how science advances, and a chemist does his work in a world in which not only chemistry has reached a certain point but all other branches of science as well. There is interaction among the branches, as I hope this book will show, and the nature of the interaction depends upon the point which all the branches, and not only one, have reached.

Third: I have resisted, to a greater extent than is usual, the temptation to fade off as modern times are approached. The foundations of modern science were laid in the days of ancient Greece during the five centuries from 600 B.C. to 100 B.C. and in early modern times from A.D. 1600 to 1800. Since foundations are extremely important, these centuries are stressed in most histories of science and it is not uncommon to give them more than half the total space.

On the other hand, the period after 1800, and particularly after 1900, witnesses so remarkable an increase in the complexity of science and in its rate of growth that it is quite impractical to attempt to deal with all of it. The temptation is to grow sketchier as the present is approached, and I have had to do this to a certain extent. It is said, after all, that ninety percent of all scientists who have ever lived are alive now. It is also said that as many scientific papers have been published in the years since 1950 as were published in all the centuries before 1950. Clearly I could not devote nine-tenths of this book to living scientists and half of it to post-1950 developments.

I have, however, done my best to give recent decades as much room as is reasonable, after giving all due space to the foundations. This means that the book ends by being considerably longer than either my publishers or I had expected.

All decisions as to whom to include or exclude, to whom to devote much space and to whom little, were made by me. And, of course, for all errors of fact I am likewise responsible.

Naturally the book cannot help but reflect my own intellectual shortcomings. While I try to acquaint myself with as much of science as I can, it is not possible for the human mind to encompass all of it. There are some segments of science I understand less than others, and I'm sure the book will show which those are.

During the many months I have lived with this book, I gained a feeling of continuity in the steady progression of scientists and technologists. The references back and forth across space and time gave me the illusion that all was happening at once, that across the centuries as well as the oceans there was a brotherhood of the mind.

This brotherhood is a small one, to be sure. If it is true that five percent of all the human beings who have ever lived are now alive—as I have heard said—then sixty billion men and women have lived and died upon this planet since our species arose. Out of the sixty billion more than one thousand have biographies in this book.

Certainly my listing is not complete. Though I believe I have included most of the major contributors to scientific advance, I am willing to admit that the total number who have contributed significantly may be ten times as great. Even so, this would mean that the advance of science throughout history has depended on the eagerly working minds of no more than one man in six million!

ISAAC ASIMOV

West Newton, Massachusetts
March 1964

ALPHABETICAL LIST OF
BIOGRAPHICAL ENTRIES

(Numbers in brackets are entry numbers, not page numbers.)

ABBE, Cleveland [738]
ABEGG, Richard Wilhelm Heinrich [978]
ABEL, Sir Frederick Augustus [673]
ABEL, John Jacob [877]
ABEL, Niels Henrik [527]
ABELARD, Peter [88]
ABELSON, Philip Hauge [1383]
ABNEY, Sir William de Wiveleslie [765]
ACHESON, Edward Goodrich [863]
ADAMS, John Couch [615]
ADAMS, Walter Sydney [1045]
ADDISON, Thomas [482]
ADELARD OF BATH [89]
ADLER, Alfred [984]
ADRIAN, Edgar Douglas, Baron [1137]
AGASSIZ, Jean Louis Rodolphe [551]
AGRICOLA, Georgius [132]
AHMOSE [2]
AIRY, Sir George Biddell [523]
ALBATEGNIUS [83]
ALBERTI, Leone Battista [117]
ALBERTUS MAGNUS [96]
ALCMAEON [11]
ALCUIN [77]
ALDER, Kurt [1254]
ALDEROTTI, Tadeo [101]
ALFONSO X [100]
ALFRED THE GREAT [81]
ALFVÉN, Hannes Olof Gösta [1335]
ALHAZEN [85]
AL-KHWARIZMI, Muhammed ibn Musa [79]
ALLBUTT, Sir Thomas Clifford [720]
ALPINI, Prospero [160]

ALVAREZ, Luis Walter [1363]
AMAGAT, Émile Hilaire [751]
AMBARTZUMIAN, Victor Amazaspovich [1338]
AMICI, Giovanni Battista [447]
AMONTONS, Guillaume [244]
AMPÈRE, André Marie [407]
AMUNDSEN, Roald Engelbregt [1008]
ANAXAGORAS [14]
ANAXIMANDER [4]
ANAXIMENES [5]
ANDERSON, Carl David [1292]
ANDERSON, Philip Warren [1458]
ANDREWS, Roy Chapman [1091]
ANDREWS, Thomas [580]
ANFINSEN, Christian Boehmer [1403]
ÅNGSTRÖM, Anders Jonas [585]
APIAN, Peter [133]
APOLLONIUS [49]
APPERT, Nicolas [359]
APPLETON, Sir Edward Victor [1158]
AQUINAS, Saint Thomas [102]
ARAGO, Dominique François Jean [446]
ARBER, Werner [1485]
ARCHER, Frederick Scott [577]
ARCHIMEDES [47]
ARCHYTAS [25]
ARGELANDER, Friedrich Wilhelm August [508]
ARISTARCHUS [41]
ARISTOTLE [29]
ARKWRIGHT, Sir Richard [311]
ARMSTRONG, Edwin Howard [1143]
ARMSTRONG, Neil Alden [1492]
ARNOLD OF VILLANOVA [103]

ARREST, Heinrich Ludwig d' [639]
ARRHENIUS, Svante August [894]
ARTSIMOVICH, Lev Andreevich [1343]
ASTBURY, William Thomas [1210]
ASTON, Francis William [1051]
AUDUBON, John James [443]
AUER, Karl, Baron von Welsbach [890]
AVERROËS [91]
AVERY, Oswald Theodore [1054]
AVICENNA [86]
AVOGADRO, Amedeo, count of Quaregna [412]
AXELROD, Julius [1374]

BAADE, Walter [1163]
BABBAGE, Charles [481]
BABINET, Jacques [486]
BACON, Francis [163]
BACON, Roger [99]
BAEKELAND, Leo Hendrik [931]
BAER, Karl Ernst von [478]
BAEYER, Johann Friedrich Wilhelm Adolf von [718]
BAFFIN, William [178]
BAILY, Francis [406]
BAKER, Henry [265]
BALARD, Antoine Jérôme [529]
BALBOA, Vasco Núñez de [128]
BALFOUR, Francis Maitland [823]
BALMER, Johann Jakob [658]
BALTIMORE, David [1508]
BANKS, Sir Joseph [331]
BANTING, Sir Frederick Grant [1152]
BÁRÁNY, Robert [1040]
BARDEEN, John [1334]
BARGHOORN, Elso Sterrenberg [1399]
BARKHAUSEN, Heinrich [1079]
BARKLA, Charles Glover [1049]
BARNARD, Christiaan Neethling [1452]
BARNARD, Edward Emerson [883]
BARRINGER, Daniel Moreau [905]
BARTHOLIN, Erasmus [210]
BARTLETT, Neil [1499]

BARTON, Sir Derek Harold Richard [1427]
BASOV, Nikolai Gennadievich [1453]
BATES, Henry Walter [656]
BATESON, William [913]
BAUMANN, Eugen [786]
BAWDEN, Sir Frederick Charles [1337]
BAYER, Johann [170]
BAYLISS, Sir William Maddock [902]
BEADLE, George Wells [1270]
BEAUMONT, William [444]
BECHER, Johann Joachim [222]
BECQUEREL, Alexandre Edmond [623]
BECQUEREL, Antoine Henri [834]
BEDE [75]
BEEBE, Charles William [1050]
BEER, Wilhelm [499]
BEGUYER DE CHANCOURTOIS, Alexandre-Émile [622]
BEHRING, Emil Adolf von [846]
BEIJERINCK, Martinus Willem [817]
BEILSTEIN, Friedrich Konrad [732]
BÉKÉSY, Georg von [1220]
BELL, Alexander Graham [789]
BELLINGSHAUSEN, Fabian Gottlieb von [426]
BELON, Pierre [148]
BENACERRAF, Baruj [1442]
BENEDEN, Édouard Joseph Louis-Marie van [782]
BERG, Paul [1470]
BERGER, Hans [1014]
BERGIUS, Friedrich Karl Rudolf [1098]
BERGMAN, Torbern Olof [315]
BERING, Vitus Jonassen [250]
BERLINER, Émile [819]
BERNARD, Claude [578]
BERNOULLI, Daniel [268]
BERT, Paul [702]
BERTHELOT, Pierre Eugène Marcelin [674]
BERTHOLLET, Claude Louis, Comte [346]
BERZELIUS, Jöns Jakob [425]

BESSARION, John [116]
BESSEL, Friedrich Wilhelm [439]
BESSEMER, Sir Henry [575]
BEST, Charles Herbert [1218]
BETHE, Hans Albrecht [1308]
BICHAT, Marie François Xavier [400]
BIELA, Wilhelm von [434]
BINET, Alfred [878]
BIOT, Jean Baptiste [404]
BITTNER, John Joseph [1277]
BJERKNES, Jacob Aall Bonnevie [1205]
BLACK, Davidson [1096]
BLACK, Joseph [298]
BLACKETT, Patrick Maynard Stuart [1207]
BLAKESLEE, Albert Francis [1029]
BLANCHARD, Jean Pierre François [362]
BLOCH, Felix [1296]
BLOCH, Konrad Emil [1369]
BLOEMBERGEN, Nicolaas [1436]
BLUMBERG, Baruch Samuel [1467]
BLUMENBACH, Johann Friedrich [357]
BODE, Johann Elert [344]
BODENSTEIN, Max [994]
BOERHAAVE, Hermann [248]
BOETHIUS, Anicius Manlius Severinus [71]
BOHR, Aage Niels [1450]
BOHR, Niels Henrik David [1101]
BOK, Bart Jan [1302]
BOLTWOOD, Bertram Borden [987]
BOLTZMANN, Ludwig Edward [769]
BOLYAI, Janos [530]
BOND, George Phillips [660]
BOND, William Cranch [464]
BONDI, Sir Hermann [1433]
BONNET, Charles [291]
BOOLE, George [595]
BORDEN, Gail [524]
BORDET, Jules Jean Baptiste Vincent [986]
BORELLI, Giovanni Alfonso [191]
BORN, Max [1084]

BOSCH, Karl [1028]
BOSE, Sir Jagadischandra [893]
BOSE, Satyendranath [1170]
BOTHE, Walther Wilhelm Georg Franz [1146]
BOUCHER DE CRÈVECOEUR DE PERTHES, Jacques [458]
BOUGAINVILLE, Louis Antoine de [303]
BOUGUER, Pierre [264]
BOUSSINGAULT, Jean Baptiste Joseph Dieudonné [525]
BOUVARD, Alexis [392]
BOVERI, Theodor [923]
BOVET, Daniele [1325]
BOYD, William Clouser [1264]
BOYLE, Robert [212]
BRACONNOT, Henri [430]
BRADLEY, James [258]
BRAGG, Sir William Henry [922]
BRAGG, Sir William Lawrence [1141]
BRAHE, Tycho [156]
BRAHMAGUPTA [73]
BRAID, James [494]
BRAND, Hennig [216]
BRANDT, Georg [260]
BRATTAIN, Walter Houser [1250]
BRAUN, Karl Ferdinand [808]
BRAUN, Wernher Magnus Maximilian von [1370]
BRETONNEAU, Pierre Fidèle [419]
BREUER, Josef [755]
BREWSTER, Sir David [433]
BRIDGMAN, Percy Williams [1080]
BRIGGS, Henry [164]
BRIGHT, Richard [465]
BROCA, Pierre Paul [653]
BRONSTED, Johannes Nicolaus [1061]
BROOM, Robert [959]
BROUNCKER, William, 2d Viscount [202]
BROUWER, Dirk [1258]
BROWN, Herbert Charles [1373]
BROWN, Robert [403]
BRUNO, Giordano [157]
BUCH, Christian Leopold von [405]

BUCHNER, Eduard [903]
BUCHNER, Hans Ernst Angass [813]
BUDD, William [570]
BUFFON, Georges Louis Leclerc, comte de [277]
BUNSEN, Robert Wilhelm Eberhard [565]
BURBANK, Luther [799]
BURIDAN, Jean [108]
BURNET, Sir Frank Macfarlane [1223]
BURT, Sir Cyril Lodowic [1086]
BUSH, Vannevar [1139]
BUTENANDT, Adolf Friedrich Johann [1265]
BUTLEROV, Alexander Mikhailovich [676]
BYRD, Richard Evelyn [1129]

CAILLETET, Louis Paul [698]
CALLINICUS [74]
CALLIPPUS [32]
CALVIN, Melvin [1361]
CANDOLLE, Augustin Pyrame de [418]
CANNIZZARO, Stanislao [668]
CANNON, Annie Jump [932]
CANNON, Walter Bradford [998]
CANO, Juan Sebastián del [124]
CANTON, John [290]
CANTOR, Georg [772]
CARDANO, Girolamo [137]
CARNOT, Nicolas Léonard Sadi [497]
CARO, Heinrich [706]
CAROTHERS, Wallace Hume [1190]
CARREL, Alexis [1016]
CARRINGTON, Richard Christopher [667]
CARROLL, James [849]
CARVER, George Washington [937]
CASSINI, Giovanni Domenico [209]
CAUCHY, Augustin Louis, Baron [463]
CAVALIERI, Bonaventura [186]
CAVENDISH, Henry [307]
CAVENTOU, Joseph Bienaimé [493]
CAYLEY, Arthur [629]
CELSIUS, Anders [271]
CELSUS, Aulus Cornelius [57]

CHADWICK, Sir James [1150]
CHAIN, Ernst Boris [1306]
CHALLIS, James [535]
CHAMBERLAIN, Owen [1439]
CHAMBERLAND, Charles Edouard [816]
CHAMBERLIN, Thomas Chrowder [766]
CHANCE, Britton [1384]
CHANDRASEKHAR, Subrahmanyan [1356]
CHAPTAL, Jean Antoine Claude, comte de Chanteloup [368]
CHARCOT, Jean Martin [662]
CHARDONNET, Louis Marie Hilaire Bernigaud, comte de [743]
CHARGAFF, Erwin [1291]
CHARLEMAGNE [78]
CHARLES, Jacques Alexandre César [343]
CHARPENTIER, Johann von [449]
CHÂTELET, Gabrielle Émilie le Tonnelier de Breteuil, marquise de [274]
CHERENKOV, Pavel Alekseyevich [1281]
CHEVREUL, Michel Eugène [448]
CHLADNI, Ernst Florens Friedrich [370]
CLAIRAUT, Alexis Claude [283]
CLAPEYRON, Benoit Pierre Émile [507]
CLARK, Alvan Graham [696]
CLAUDE, Albert [1222]
CLAUDE, Georges [989]
CLAUS, Carl Ernst [495]
CLAUSIUS, Rudolf Julius Emmanuel [633]
CLAVIUS, Christoph [152]
CLEVE, Per Teodor [746]
COBLENTZ, William Weber [1021]
COCKCROFT, Sir John Douglas [1198]
COHN, Ferdinand Julius [675]
COLOMBO, Realdo [140]
COLUMBUS, Christopher [121]
COMPTON, Arthur Holly [1159]

CONON [44]
COOK, James [300]
COOLIDGE, William David [1020]
COOPER, Leon N. [1489]
COPE, Edward Drinker [748]
COPERNICUS, Nicolas [127]
CORI, Carl Ferdinand [1194]
CORI, Gerty Theresa Radnitz [1192]
CORIOLIS, Gustave Gaspard de [480]
CORMACK, Allan MacLeod [1461]
CORNFORTH, Sir John Warcup [1417]
CORRENS, Karl Franz Joseph Erich [938]
COSTER, Dirk [1135]
COULOMB, Charles Augustin [318]
COUPER, Archibald Scott [686]
COURNAND, André Frédéric [1181]
COURTOIS, Bernard [414]
COUSTEAU, Jacques-Yves [1353]
COWAN, Clyde Lorrain [1434]
CRAFTS, James Mason [741]
CRAIG, Lyman Creighton [1305]
CRICK, Francis Harry Compton [1406]
CRONIN, James Watson [1497]
CRONSTEDT, Axel Fredrik [292]
CROOKES, Sir William [695]
CROSS, Charles Frederick [862]
CTESIBIUS [46]
CURIE, Marie Sklodowska [965]
CURIE, Pierre [897]
CURTIS, Heber Doust [1007]
CUVIER, Georges Léopold Chrétien Frédéric Dagobert, Baron [396]
CYSAT, Johann [180]

D'ABANO, Pietro [106]
DAGUERRE, Louis Jacques Mandé [467]
DAIMLER, Gottlieb Wilhelm [708]
DALE, Sir Henry Hallett [1034]
D'ALEMBERT, Jean le Rond [289]
DALTON, John [389]
DAM, Carl Peter Henrik [1177]
DANIELL, John Frederic [470]
DART, Raymond Arthur [1162]
DARWIN, Charles Robert [554]

DARWIN, Erasmus [308]
DARWIN, Sir George Howard [777]
DAUBRÉE, Gabriel Auguste [584]
DAUSSET, Jean [1411]
DAVISSON, Clinton Joseph [1078]
DAVY, Sir Humphry [421]
DEBIERNE, André Louis [1026]
DE BROGLIE, Louis Victor Pierre Raymond, Prince [1157]
DEBYE, Peter Joseph Wilhelm [1094]
DEDEKIND, Julius Wilhelm Richard [688]
DE DUVE, Christian René [1418]
DE FOREST, Lee [1017]
DELAMBRE, Jean Baptiste Joseph [350]
DE LA RUE, Warren [589]
DELBRÜCK, Max [1313]
D'ELHUYAR, Don Fausto [367]
DELISLE, Joseph Nicolas [255]
DEL RIO, Andrès Manuel [382]
DEMARÇAY, Eugène Anatole [825]
DEMOCRITUS [20]
DE MOIVRE, Abraham [246]
DE MORGAN, Augustus [549]
DEMPSTER, Arthur Jeffrey [1106]
DENIS, Jean Baptiste [227]
DESAGULIERS, John Théophile [253]
DESCARTES, René [183]
DESMAREST, Nicolas [296]
DE VRIES, Hugo Marie [792]
DEWAR, Sir James [759]
D'HÉRELLE, Félix Hubert [1012]
DICAEARCHUS [33]
DICKE, Robert Henry [1405]
DIDEROT, Denis [286]
DIELS, Otto Paul Hermann [1039]
DIESEL, Rudolf [886]
DIOCLES [34]
DIOPHANTUS [66]
DIOSCORIDES [59]
DIRAC, Paul Adrien Maurice [1256]
DÖBEREINER, Johann Wolfgang [427]
DOBZHANSKY, Theodosius [1224]
DOISY, Edward Adelbert [1169]
DOLLOND, John [273]

DOLOMIEU, Dieudonné de Gratet de [353]

DOMAGK, Gerhard [1183]

DONATI, Giovanni Battista [671]

DONDERS, Franciscus Cornelis [605]

DOPPLER, Christian Johann [534]

DORN, Friedrich Ernst [795]

DOUGLASS, Andrew Ellicott [963]

DRAKE, Edwin Laurentine [614]

DRAKE, Frank Donald [1491]

DRAPER, Henry [723]

DRAPER, John William [566]

DUBOIS, Marie Eugène François Thomas [884]

DU BOIS-REYMOND, Emil Heinrich [611]

DUBOS, René Jules [1235]

DU FAY, Charles François de Cisternay [266]

DUGGAR, Benjamin Minge [1010]

DUJARDIN, Félix [517]

DULBECCO, Renato [1388]

DULONG, Pierre Louis [441]

DUMAS, Jean Baptiste André [514]

DUNNING, John Ray [1330]

DÜRER, Albrecht [126]

DUTTON, Clarence Edward [753]

DU VIGNEAUD, Vincent [1239]

DYSON, Freeman John [1459]

EASTMAN, George [852]

ECCLES, Sir John Carew [1262]

ECKERT, John Presper, Jr. [1431]

EDDINGTON, Sir Arthur Stanley [1085]

EDELMAN, Gerald Maurice [1486]

EDISON, Thomas Alva [788]

EDLÉN, Bengt [1316]

EHRENBERG, Christian Gottfried [491]

EHRLICH, Paul [845]

EIGEN, Manfred [1477]

EIJKMAN, Christiaan [888]

EINSTEIN, Albert [1064]

EINTHOVEN, Willem [904]

EKEBERG, Anders Gustaf [391]

ELSASSER, Walter Maurice [1279]

ELSTER, Johann Philipp Ludwig Julius [858]

ELVEHJEM, Conrad Arnold [1240]

EMPEDOCLES [17]

ENCKE, Johann Franz [475]

ENDERS, John Franklin [1195]

EÖTVÖS, Roland, Baron von [794]

EPICURUS [35]

ERASISTRATUS [43]

ERATOSTHENES [48]

ERICSSON, John [533]

ERLANGER, Joseph [1023]

ERLENMEYER, Richard August Carl Emil [661]

ESAKI, Leo [1464]

EUCLID [40]

EUDOXUS [27]

EULER, Leonhard [275]

EULER-CHELPIN, Hans Karl August Simon von [1011]

EUPALINUS [8]

EUSTACHIO, Bartolomeo [141]

EWING, William Maurice [1303]

FABRICIUS AB AQUAPENDENTE, Hieronymus [151]

FABRICIUS, David [167]

FABRY, Charles [962]

FAHRENHEIT, Gabriel Daniel [254]

FALLOPIUS, Gabriel [149]

FALSE GEBER [107]

FARADAY, Michael [474]

FECHNER, Gustav Theodor [520]

FERDINAND II OF TUSCANY [193]

FERMAT, Pierre de [188]

FERMI, Enrico [1243]

FERNEL, Jean François [134]

FERRIER, Sir David [761]

FESSENDEN, Reginald Aubrey [958]

FEYNMAN, Richard Philips [1424]

FIBONACCI, Leonardo [95]

FIELD, Cyrus West [621]

FINSEN, Niels Ryberg [908]

FISCHER, Emil Hermann [833]

FISCHER, Ernst Otto [1429]

FISCHER, Hans [1076]
FISHER, Sir Ronald Aylmer [1142]
FITCH, John [330]
FITCH, Val Logsden [1454]
FITZGERALD, George Francis [821]
FITZROY, Robert [544]
FIZEAU, Armand Hippolyte Louis [620]
FLAMMARION, Nicolas Camille [756]
FLAMSTEED, John [234]
FLEMING, Sir Alexander [1077]
FLEMING, Sir John Ambrose [803]
FLEMMING, Walther [762]
FLEROV, Georgii Nikolaevich [1381]
FLOREY, Howard Walter, Baron [1213]
FLORY, Paul John [1354]
FOLKERS, Karl August [1312]
FONTENELLE, Bernard le Bovier de [239]
FORBES, Edward [590]
FORD, Henry [929]
FORSSMAN, Werner [1283]
FOUCAULT, Jean Bernard Léon [619]
FOURCROY, Antoine François, comte de [366]
FOURIER, Jean Baptiste Joseph, Baron [393]
FOX, Sidney Walter [1371]
FRAENKEL-CONRAT, Heinz [1355]
FRANCK, James [1081]
FRANK, Ilya Mikhaylovich [1340]
FRANKLAND, Sir Edward [655]
FRANKLIN, Benjamin [272]
FRANKLIN, Kenneth Linn [1455]
FRANKLIN, Rosalind Elsie [1440]
FRASCH, Herman [824]
FRAUNHOFER, Joseph von [450]
FREDERICK II [97]
FREGE, Friedrich Ludwig Gottlob [797]
FREMY, Edmond [582]
FRERE, John [324]
FRESNEL, Augustin Jean [455]
FREUD, Sigmund [865]
FRIEDEL, Charles [693]
FRIEDMAN, Herbert [1407]

FRIEDMANN, Alexander Alexandrovich [1125]
FRISCH, Karl von [1110]
FRISCH, Otto Robert [1284]
FRONTINUS, Sextus Julius [62]
FUCHS, Leonhard [136]
FULTON, Robert [385]
FUNK, Casimir [1093]

GABOR, Dennis [1230]
GADOLIN, Johan [373]
GAFFKY, Georg Theodor August [805]
GAGARIN, Yuri Alekseyevich [1502]
GAHN, Johann Gottlieb [339]
GAJDUSEK, Daniel Carleton [1456]
GALEN [65]
GALILEO [166]
GALL, Franz Joseph [371]
GALLE, Johann Gottfried [573]
GALOIS, Evariste [571]
GALTON, Sir Francis [636]
GALVANI, Luigi [320]
GAMOW, George [1278]
GASCOIGNE, William [195]
GASSENDI, Pierre [182]
GASSER, Herbert Spencer [1126]
GATLING, Richard Jordan [609]
GAUSS, Johann Karl Friedrich [415]
GAY-LUSSAC, Joseph Louis [420]
GEBER [76]
GEGENBAUR, Karl [669]
GEIGER, Hans Wilhelm [1082]
GEISSLER, Heinrich [583]
GELLIBRAND, Henry [184]
GELL-MANN, Murray [1487]
GEMMA FRISIUS, Reiner [138]
GERARD OF CREMONA [90]
GERBERT [84]
GERMAIN, Sophie [410]
GESELL, Arnold Lucius [1070]
GESNER, Konrad von [147]
GIAEVER, Ivar [1484]
GIAUQUE, William Francis [1178]
GIBBS, Josiah Willard [740]
GILBERT, Walter [1498]
GILBERT, William [155]

GILL, Sir David [763]
GLASER, Donald Arthur [1472]
GLASHOW, Sheldon Lee [1500]
GLAUBER, Johann Rudolf [190]
GMELIN, Johann Georg [280]
GMELIN, Leopold [457]
GODDARD, Robert Hutchings [1083]
GÖDEL, Kurt [1301]
GOEPPERT-MAYER, Marie [1307]
GOETHE, Johann Wolfgang von [349]
GOLD, Thomas [1437]
GOLDBACH, Christian [256]
GOLDBERGER, Joseph [1027]
GOLDHABER, Maurice [1362]
GOLDMARK, Peter Carl [1319]
GOLDSCHMIDT, Johann (Hans)
  Wilhelm [909]
GOLDSCHMIDT, Victor Moritz [1123]
GOLDSTEIN, Eugen [811]
GOLGI, Camillo [764]
GOMBERG, Moses [950]
GOODRICKE, John [381]
GOODYEAR, Charles [516]
GORGAS, William Crawford [853]
GOUDSMIT, Samuel Abraham [1255]
GRAAF, Regnier de [228]
GRAEBE, Karl James Peter [752]
GRAHAM, Thomas [547]
GRAM, Hans Christian Joachim [841]
GRAMME, Zénobe Théophile [666]
GRANIT, Ragnar Arthur [1232]
GRASSMAN, Hermann Günther [556]
GRAUNT, John [201]
GRAY, Asa [562]
GRAY, Stephen [262]
GREENSTEIN, Jesse Leonard [1345]
GREGOR, William [377]
GREGORY, David [240]
GREGORY, James [226]
GREW, Nehemiah [229]
GRIGNARD, François Auguste Victor
  [993]
GRIMALDI, Francesco Maria [199]
GROSSETESTE, Robert [94]
GROVE, Sir William Robert [568]
GUERICKE, Otto von [189]

GUETTARD, Jean Étienne [287]
GUILLAUME, Charles Édouard [910]
GUILLEMIN, Roger [1460]
GULDBERG, Cato Maximilian [721]
GULLSTRAND, Allvar [919]
GUTENBERG, Beno [1133]
GUTENBERG, Johann [114]
GUTHRIE, Samuel [435]
GUYOT, Arnold Henry [552]
GUYTON DE MORVEAU, Baron
  Louis Bernard [319]

HABER, Fritz [977]
HADFIELD, Sir Robert Abbott [892]
HAECKEL, Ernst Heinrich Philipp
  August [707]
HAFFKINE, Waldemar Mordecai
  Wolfe [901]
HAHN, Otto [1063]
HALDANE, John Burdon Sanderson
  [1160]
HALE, George Ellery [974]
HALES, Stephen [249]
HALL, Asaph [681]
HALL, Charles Martin [933]
HALL, Granville Stanley [780]
HALL, Sir James [374]
HALL, Marshall [469]
HALLER, Albrecht von [278]
HALLEY, Edmund [238]
HALSTED, William Stewart [830]
HAMILTON, Sir William Rowan [545]
HAMPSON, William [851]
HANNO [12]
HARDEN, Sir Arthur [947]
HARE, Robert [428]
HARKINS, William Draper [1022]
HARRISON, John [259]
HARTLINE, Haldan Keffer [1276]
HARTMANN, Johannes Franz [940]
HARVEY, William [174]
HASSEL, Odd [1197]
HATCHETT, Charles [383]
HAUKSBEE, Francis [245]
HAÜY, René Just [332]
HAVERS, Clopton [237]

HAWKING, Stephen William [1510]
HAWKINS, Gerald Stanley [1481]
HAWORTH, Sir Walter Norman [1087]
HAYFORD, John Fillmore [970]
HEAVISIDE, Oliver [806]
HECATAEUS [9]
HEEZEN, Bruce Charles [1462]
HEISENBERG, Werner Karl [1245]
HELLRIEGEL, Hermann [689]
HELMHOLTZ, Hermann Ludwig
  Ferdinand von [631]
HELMONT, Jan Baptista van [175]
HENCH, Philip Showalter [1188]
HENDERSON, Thomas [505]
HENLE, Friedrich Gustav Jakob [557]
HENRY THE NAVIGATOR [111]
HENRY, Joseph [503]
HERACLEIDES [28]
HERACLITUS [10]
HERMITE, Charles [641]
HERO [60]
HEROPHILUS [42]
HÉROULT, Paul Louis Toussaint [925]
HERSCHEL, Caroline Lucretia [352]
HERSCHEL, Sir John Frederick
  William [479]
HERSCHEL, Sir William [321]
HERSHEY, Alfred Day [1341]
HERTZ, Gustav Ludwig [1116]
HERTZ, Heinrich Rudolf [873]
HERTZSPRUNG, Ejnar [1018]
HERZBERG, Gerhard [1286]
HESS, Germain Henri [528]
HESS, Harry Hammond [1304]
HESS, Victor Francis [1088]
HESS, Walter Rudolf [1073]
HEVELIUS, Johannes [194]
HEVESY, György [1100]
HEWISH, Anthony [1463]
HEYROVSKÝ, Jaroslav [1144]
HILBERT, David [918]
HILL, Archibald Vivian [1108]
HILLARY, Sir Edmund Percival [1432]
HILLIER, James [1401]
HINSHELWOOD, Sir Cyril Norman
  [1200]

HINTON, Christopher, Baron [1238]
HIPPARCHUS [50]
HIPPOCRATES [22]
HISINGER, Wilhelm [390]
HITTORF, Johann Wilhelm [649]
HITZIG, Julius Eduard [731]
HJELM, Peter Jacob [342]
HOAGLAND, Mahlon Bush [1447]
HODGKIN, Alan Lloyd [1387]
HODGKIN, Dorothy Crowfoot [1352]
HOFMANN, August Wilhelm von [604]
HOFMEISTER, Wilhelm Friedrich
  Benedikt [651]
HOFSTADTER, Robert [1395]
HOLLEY, Robert William [1449]
HOLMES, Arthur [1138]
HOLMES, Oliver Wendell [558]
HONDA, Kotaro [985]
HOOKE, Robert [223]
HOPKINS, Sir Frederick Gowland [912]
HOPPE-SEYLER, Ernst Felix
  Immanuel [663]
HORROCKS, Jeremiah [200]
HOUSSAY, Bernardo Alberto [1115]
HOWE, Elias [616]
HOYLE, Sir Fred [1398]
HUBBLE, Edwin Powell [1136]
HUGGINS, Charles Branton [1242]
HUGGINS, Sir William [646]
HUMASON, Milton La Salle [1149]
HUMBOLDT, Friedrich Wilhelm
  Heinrich Alexander, Baron von [397]
HUTTON, James [297]
HUXLEY, Andrew Fielding [1419]
HUXLEY, Thomas Henry [659]
HUYGENS, Christiaan [215]
HYATT, John Wesley [728]
HYPATIA [69]

IMHOTEP [1]
INGENHOUSZ, Jan [306]
INNES, Robert Thorburn Ayton [915]
IPATIEFF, Vladimir Nikolaevich [966]
ISIDORE OF SEVILLE [72]
IVANOV, Ilya Ivanovich [988]
IVANOVSKY, Dmitri Iosifovich [939]

JACKSON, Charles Thomas [543]
JACOB, François [1438]
JACOBI, Carl Gustav Jacob [541]
JAMES, William [754]
JANSKY, Karl Guthe [1295]
JANSSEN, Pierre Jules César [647]
JEANS, Sir James Hopwood [1053]
JEFFERSON, Thomas [333]
JEFFREYS, Sir Harold [1147]
JENNER, Edward [348]
JENSEN, Johannes Hans Daniel [1327]
JOHANNSEN, Wilhelm Ludwig [872]
JOLIOT-CURIE, Frédéric [1227]
JOLIOT-CURIE, Irène [1204]
JONES, Sir Harold Spencer [1140]
JOSEPHSON, Brian David [1509]
JOULE, James Prescott [613]
JUNG, Carl Gustav [1035]
JUSSIEU, Antoine Laurent de [345]

KAMEN, Martin David [1385]
KAMERLINGH ONNES, Heike [843]
KANT, Immanuel [293]
KAPITZA, Peter Leonidovich [1173]
KAPTEYN, Jacobus Cornelius [815]
KARMAN, Theodore von [1075]
KARRER, Paul [1131]
KASTLER, Alfred [1252]
KATZ, Sir Bernard [1359]
KEELER, James Edward [879]
KEESOM, Willem Hendrik [1042]
KEILIN, David [1113]
KEKULÉ VON STRADONITZ,
   Friedrich August [680]
KELVIN, William Thomson, Baron
   [652]
KENDALL, Edward Calvin [1105]
KENDREW, John Cowdery [1415]
KENNELLY, Arthur Edwin [916]
KEPLER, Johann [169]
KERST, Donald William [1367]
KETTERING, Charles Franklin [1044]
KHORANA, Har Gobind [1448]
KIDD, John [409]
KIDDINU [37]

KING, Charles Glen [1193]
KIPPING, Frederic Stanley [930]
KIRCHER, Athanasius [187]
KIRCHHOF, Gottlieb Sigismund
   Constantin [380]
KIRCHHOFF, Gustav Robert [648]
KIRKWOOD, Daniel [586]
KITASATO, Baron Shibasaburo [870]
KJELDAHL, Johann Gustav Christoffer
   [801]
KLAPROTH, Martin Heinrich [335]
KLEIN, Christian Felix [800]
KLEIST, Ewald Georg von [269]
KOCH, (Heinrich Hermann) Robert
   [767]
KÖHLER, Wolfgang [1112]
KOLBE, Adolph Wilhelm Hermann
   [610]
KOLLER, Carl [882]
KÖLLIKER, Rudolf Albert von [600]
KOPP, Hermann Franz Moritz [601]
KORNBERG, Arthur [1422]
KOSSEL, (Karl Martin Leonhard)
   Albrecht [842]
KOVALEVSKI, Alexander Onufriyevich
   [750]
KOVALEVSKY, Sonya [804]
KOZYREV, Nikolai Alexandrovich
   [1336]
KRAFFT-EBING, Baron Richard von
   [749]
KREBS, Sir Hans Adolf [1231]
KROGH, Shack August Steenberg
   [1030]
KRONECKER, Leopold [645]
KUHN, Richard [1233]
KÜHNE, Wilhelm (Willy) Friedrich
   [725]
KUIPER, Gerard Peter [1297]
KUNDT, August Adolph Eduard
   Eberhard [744]
KURCHATOV, Igor Vasilevich [1261]

LACAILLE, Nicolas Louis de [284]
LA CONDAMINE, Charles Marie de
   [270]

LAËNNEC, Théophile René Hyacinthe [429]

LAGRANGE, Joseph Louis, comte de [317]

LALANDE, Joseph Jérôme Le Français de [309]

LAMARCK, Jean Baptiste Pierre Antoine de Monet, chevalier de [336]

LAMBERT, Johann Heinrich [299]

LAMONT, Johann von [546]

LAND, Edwin Herbert [1344]

LANDAU, Lev Davidovich [1333]

LANDSTEINER, Karl [973]

LANGERHANS, Paul [791]

LANGEVIN, Paul [1000]

LANGLEY, Samuel Pierpont [711]

LANGMUIR, Irving [1072]

LAPLACE, Pierre Simon, marquis de [347]

LARSON, John Augustus [1161]

LARTET, Édouard Armand Isidore Hippolyte [519]

LASSELL, William [509]

LAUE, Max Theodor Felix von [1068]

LAURENT, Auguste [553]

LAVERAN, Charles Louis Alphonse [776]

LAVOISIER, Antoine Laurent [334]

LAWES, Sir John Bennett [588]

LAWRENCE, Ernest Orlando [1241]

LAZEAR, Jesse William [955]

LEAKEY, Louis Seymour Bazett [1268]

LEAVITT, Henrietta Swan [975]

LEBEDEV, Pyotr Nicolaievich [952]

LE BEL, Joseph Achille [787]

LEBLANC, Nicolas [328]

LE CHÂTELIER, Henri Louis [812]

LECOQ DE BOISBAUDRAN, Paul Émile [736]

LEDERBERG, Joshua [1466]

LEE, Tsung-Dao [1473]

LEEUWENHOEK, Anton van [221]

LEGENDRE, Adrien Marie [358]

LE GENTIL, Guillaume Joseph Hyacinthe Jean Baptiste [295]

LEIBNIZ, Gottfried Wilhelm [233]

LEISHMAN, Sir William Boog [948]

LELOIR, Luis Frederico [1314]

LEMAÎTRE, Abbé Georges Édouard [1174]

LENARD, Philipp Eduard Anton von [920]

LENOIR, Jean Joseph Étienne [635]

LENZ, Heinrich Friedrich Emil [536]

LEONARDO DA VINCI [122]

LEUCIPPUS [15]

LEUCKART, Karl Georg Friedrich Rudolf [640]

LEVENE, Phoebus Aaron Theodor [980]

LEVERRIER, Urbain Jean Joseph [564]

LEWIS, Gilbert Newton [1037]

LEXELL, Anders Johan [326]

LEY, Willy [1315]

LI, Choh Hao [1382]

LIBAVIUS [162]

LIBBY, Willard Frank [1342]

LIEBIG, Justus von [532]

LILIENTHAL, Otto [793]

LIND, James [288]

LINDBERGH, Charles Augustus [1249]

LINDBLAD, Bertil [1185]

LINDE, Karl Paul Gottfried von [758]

LINDEMANN, Carl Louis Ferdinand von [826]

LINNAEUS, Carolus [276]

LIOUVILLE, Joseph [555]

LIPMANN, Fritz Albert [1221]

LIPPERSHEY, Hans [168]

LIPPMANN, Gabriel Jonas [778]

LIPSCOMB, William Nunn, Jr. [1435]

LISTER, Joseph, Baron [672]

LISTER, Joseph Jackson [445]

LOBACHEVSKI, Nikolai Ivanovich [484]

LOCKYER, Sir Joseph Norman [719]

LODGE, Sir Oliver Joseph [820]

LOEB, Jacques [896]

LOEWI, Otto [1015]

LÖFFLER, Friedrich August Johannes [828]

LOMONOSOV, Mikhail Vasilievich [282]

LONDON, Fritz Wolfgang [1226]
LONG, Crawford Williamson [594]
LORENTZ, Hendrik Antoon [839]
LORENZ, Konrad [1271]
LOSCHMIDT, Johann Joseph [628]
LOVE, Augustus Edward Hough [926]
LOVELL, Sir Alfred Charles Bernard [1386]
LOWELL, Percival [860]
LOWER, Richard [219]
LUCRETIUS [53]
LUDWIG, Karl Friedrich Wilhelm [597]
LURIA, Salvador Edward [1377]
LWOFF, André Michael [1253]
LYELL, Sir Charles [502]
LYNEN, Feodor [1360]
LYOT, Bernard Ferdinand [1196]
LYSENKO, Trofim Denisovich [1214]

MACH, Ernst [733]
MACLAURIN, Colin [263]
MÄDLER, Johann Heinrich [488]
MAGELLAN, Ferdinand [130]
MAGENDIE, François [438]
MAIMAN, Theodore Harold [1479]
MAIMONIDES, Moses [92]
MALPIGHI, Marcello [214]
MALTHUS, Thomas Robert [387]
MALUS, Étienne Louis [408]
MANSON, Sir Patrick [771]
MANTELL, Gideon Algernon [468]
MARCONI, Marchese Guglielmo [1025]
MAREY, Étienne Jules [683]
MARGGRAF, Andreas Sigismund [279]
MARIGNAC, Jean Charles Galissard de [599]
MARIOTTE, Edmé [203]
MARIUS, Simon [171]
MARKOVNIKOV, Vladimir Vasilevich [729]
MARSH, Othniel Charles [690]
MARTIN, Archer John Porter [1350]
MASKELYNE, Nevil [310]
MATTHIAS, Bern Teo [1425]
MAUCHLY, John William [1328]

MAUNDER, Edward Walter [818]
MAUPERTUIS, Pierre Louis Moreau de [267]
MAURY, Matthew Fontaine [548]
MAXIM, Sir Hiram Stevens [745]
MAXWELL, James Clerk [692]
MAYER, Julius Robert [587]
MAYOW, John [230]
McADAM, John Loudon [369]
McCOLLUM, Elmer Verner [1062]
McMILLAN, Edwin Mattison [1329]
MECHNIKOV, Ilya Ilich [775]
MEDAWAR, Sir Peter Brian [1396]
MEITNER, Lise [1060]
MELA, Pomponius [58]
MELLONI, Macedonio [504]
MENAECHMUS [30]
MENDEL, Gregor Johann [638]
MENDELÉEV, Dmitri Ivanovich [705]
MENZEL, Donald Howard [1237]
MERCATOR, Gerardus [144]
MERSENNE, Marin [181]
MESMER, Franz Anton [314]
MESSIER, Charles [305]
METON [23]
MEYER, Julius Lothar [685]
MEYER, Viktor [796]
MEYERHOF, Otto Fritz [1095]
MICHAELIS, Leonor [1033]
MICHAEL SCOT [98]
MICHELL, John [294]
MICHELSON, Albert Abraham [835]
MIDGLEY, Thomas, Jr. [1132]
MIESCHER, Johann Friedrich [770]
MILLER, Dayton Clarence [953]
MILLER, Jacques Francis Albert Pierre [1494]
MILLER, Stanley Lloyd [1490]
MILLER, William Hallowes [518]
MILLIKAN, Robert Andrews [969]
MILNE, Edward Arthur [1186]
MILNE, John [814]
MINKOWSKI, Hermann [935]
MINKOWSKI, Rudolph Leo B. [1179]
MINOT, George Richards [1103]
MITCHELL, Maria [608]

MITCHELL, Peter Dennis [1441]
MITSCHERLICH, Eilhardt [485]
MÖBIUS, August Ferdinand [471]
MOHL, Hugo von [542]
MOHOROVIČIĆ, Andrija [871]
MOHS, Friedrich [401]
MOISSAN, Ferdinand Frédéric Henri [831]
MONDINO DE' LUZZI [110]
MONGE, Gaspard [340]
MONIZ, Antonio Caetano de Abreu Freire Egas [1032]
MONOD, Jacques Lucien [1347]
MONTGOLFIER, Jacques Étienne and Joseph Michel [325]
MOORE, Stanford [1379]
MORGAGNI, Giovanni Battista [251]
MORGAN, Thomas Hunt [957]
MORGAN, William Wilson [1298]
MORGENSTERN, Oskar [1248]
MORLEY, Edward Williams [730]
MORSE, Samuel Finley Breese [473]
MORTILLET, Louis Laurent Gabriel de [630]
MORTON, William Thomas Green [617]
MOSANDER, Carl Gustav [501]
MOSELEY, Henry Gwyn-Jeffreys [1121]
MÖSSBAUER, Rudolf Ludwig [1483]
MOTT, Sir Nevill Francis [1294]
MOTTELSON, Ben Roy [1471]
MOULTON, Forest Ray [1003]
MUELLER, Erwin Wilhelm [1364]
MULDER, Gerardus Johannes [531]
MÜLLER, Franz Joseph [323]
MULLER, Hermann Joseph [1145]
MÜLLER, Johannes Peter [522]
MÜLLER, Otto Friedrich [304]
MÜLLER, Paul Hermann [1216]
MULLIKEN, Robert Sanderson [1191]
MURCHISON, Sir Roderick Impey [477]
MURDOCK, William [363]
MURPHY, William Parry [1154]
MUSSCHENBROEK, Pieter van [257]

NAGAOKA, Hantaro [946]
NÄGELI, Karl Wilhelm von [598]
NANSEN, Fridtjof [914]
NAPIER, John [159]
NATHANS, Daniel [1482]
NATTA, Giulio [1263]
NECKAM, Alexander [93]
NEEDHAM, John Turberville [285]
NÉEL, Louis Eugène Félix [1285]
NE'EMAN, Yuval [1465]
NEF, John Ulric [921]
NEISSER, Albert Ludwig Sigismund [859]
NERNST, Hermann Walther [936]
NEUMANN, John von [1273]
NEWCOMB, Simon [713]
NEWCOMEN, Thomas [243]
NEWLANDS, John Alexander Reina [727]
NEWTON, Sir Isaac [231]
NICHOLAS OF CUSA [115]
NICHOLSON, Seth Barnes [1151]
NICHOLSON, William [361]
NICOL, William [394]
NICOLLE, Charles Jules Henri [956]
NIEPCE, Joseph Nicéphore [384]
NIEUWLAND, Julius Arthur [1058]
NILSON, Lars Fredrik [747]
NIRENBERG, Marshall Warren [1476]
NOBEL, Alfred Bernhard [703]
NODDACK, Ida Eva Tacke [1187]
NODDACK, Walter Karl Friedrich [1166]
NORDENSKIÖLD, Nils Adolf Erik [700]
NORMAN, Robert [161]
NORRISH, Ronald George Wreyford [1206]
NORTHROP, John Howard [1148]

OBERTH, Hermann Julius [1172]
OCHOA, Severo [1293]
OCKHAM, William of [109]
OENOPIDES [18]
OERSTED, Hans Christian [417]
OHM, Georg Simon [461]

O'KEEFE, John Aloysius [1412]

OKEN, Lorenz [423]

OLBERS, Heinrich Wilhelm Matthäus [372]

OLIPHANT, Marcus Laurence Elwin [1244]

OMAR KHAYYÁM [87]

O'NEILL, Gerard Kitchen [1475]

ONSAGER, Lars [1272]

OORT, Jan Hendrik [1229]

OPARIN, Alexander Ivanovich [1171]

ÖPIK, Ernst Julius [1168]

OPPENHEIMER, J. Robert [1280]

OSBORNE, Thomas Burr [900]

OSTWALD, Friedrich Wilhelm [840]

OTIS, Elisha Graves [569]

OTTO, Nikolaus August [694]

OUGHTRED, William [172]

OWEN, Sir Richard [539]

PACIOLI, Luca [120]

PALADE, George Emil [1380]

PALMIERI, Luigi [550]

PANDER, Christian Heinrich [489]

PANETH, Friedrich Adolf [1118]

PAPIN, Denis [235]

PAPPUS [68]

PARACELSUS [131]

PARÉ, Ambroise [139]

PARKER, Eugene Newman [1478]

PARKES, Alexander [581]

PARKINSON, James [365]

PARMENIDES [13]

PARSONS, Sir Charles Algernon [850]

PASCAL, Blaise [207]

PASCHEN, Louis Carl Heinrich Friedrich [941]

PASTEUR, Louis [642]

PAULI, Wolfgang [1228]

PAULING, Linus Carl [1236]

PAVLOV, Ivan Petrovich [802]

PAYEN, Anselme [490]

PEACOCK, George [472]

PEANO, Giuseppe [889]

PEARSON, Karl [875]

PEARY, Robert Edwin [866]

PELLETIER, Pierre Joseph [454]

PENZIAS, Arno Allan [1501]

PEREGRINUS, Petrus [104]

PERKIN, Sir William Henry [734]

PERRIN, Jean Baptiste [990]

PERRINE, Charles Dillon [964]

PERUTZ, Max Ferdinand [1389]

PETIT, Alexis Thérèse [476]

PETRIE, Sir (William Matthew) Flinders [838]

PETTENKOFER, Max Joseph von [612]

PEURBACH, Georg von [118]

PFEFFER, Wilhelm [773]

PHILOLAUS [19]

PHILON [45]

PIAZZI, Giuseppe [341]

PICARD, Jean [204]

PICCARD, August [1092]

PICKERING, Edward Charles [784]

PICKERING, William Henry [885]

PICTET, Raoul Pierre [783]

PIERCE, John Robinson [1351]

PINCUS, Gregory [1266]

PINEL, Philippe [338]

PLANCK, Max Karl Ernst Ludwig [887]

PLANTÉ, Gaston [709]

PLASKETT, John Stanley [949]

PLATO [24]

PLINY [61]

PLÜCKER, Julius [521]

POGSON, Norman Robert [679]

POINCARÉ, Jules Henri [847]

POISEUILLE, Jean Léonard Marie [500]

POISSON, Simeon Denis [432]

POLHEM, Christopher [242]

POLO, Marco [105]

PONCELET, Jean Victor [456]

PONNAMPERUMA, Cyril [1457]

PONS, Jean Louis [376]

POPE, Sir William Jackson [991]

POPOV, Alexander Stepanovich [895]

PORTA, Giambattista della [150]

PORTER, George [1443]

POSEIDONIUS [52]
POULSEN, Valdemar [983]
POWELL, Cecil Frank [1274]
PRAXAGORAS [36]
PREGL, Fritz [982]
PRELOG, Vladimir [1310]
PRÉVOST, Pierre [356]
PRIESTLEY, Joseph [312]
PRIGOGINE, Ilya [1414]
PROCLUS [70]
PROCTOR, Richard Anthony [724]
PROKHOROV, Alexander Mikhailovich [1409]
PROUST, Joseph Louis [364]
PROUT, William [440]
PRZHEVALSKY, Nikolay Mikhaylovich [742]
PTOLEMY, Claudius [64]
PUPIN, Michael Idvorsky [891]
PURCELL, Edward Mills [1378]
PURKINJE, Jan Evangelista [452]
PYTHAGORAS [7]
PYTHEAS [39]

QUETELET, Lambert Adolphe Jacques [496]

RABI, Isidor Isaac [1212]
RAINWATER, Leo James [1420]
RAMAN, Sir Chandrasekhara Venkata [1130]
RAMÓN Y CAJAL, Santiago [827]
RAMSAY, Sir William [832]
RANKINE, William John Macquorn [625]
RAOULT, François Marie [684]
RAWLINSON, Sir Henry Creswicke [559]
RAY, John [213]
RAYLEIGH, John William Strutt, 3d Baron [760]
RÉAUMUR, René Antoine Ferchault de [252]
REBER, Grote [1368]
REDFIELD, William C. [462]
REDI, Francesco [211]

REED, Walter [822]
REGIOMONTANUS [119]
REGNAULT, Henri Victor [561]
REICH, Ferdinand [506]
REICHSTEIN, Tadeusz [1201]
REID, Harry Fielding [898]
REINES, Frederick [1423]
REINHOLD, Erasmus [143]
REMAK, Robert [591]
REMSEN, Ira [781]
RETZIUS, Anders Adolf [498]
RHAZES [82]
RHETICUS [145]
RHINE, Joseph Banks [1182]
RICCIOLI, Giovanni Battista [185]
RICHARDS, Dickinson W. [1184]
RICHARDS, Theodore William [968]
RICHARDSON, Sir Owen Willans [1066]
RICHER, Jean [217]
RICHET, Charles Robert [809]
RICHTER, Burton [1493]
RICHTER, Hieronymus Theodor [654]
RICHTER, Jeremias Benjamin [378]
RICKETTS, Howard Taylor [992]
RICKOVER, Hyman George [1225]
RIEMANN, Georg Friedrich Bernhard [670]
RIGHI, Augusto [810]
RINGER, Sydney [717]
RITTER, Johann Wilhelm [413]
ROBBINS, Frederick Chapman [1410]
ROBERTS, Richard Brooke [1357]
ROBINSON, Sir Robert [1107]
ROCHE, Édouard Albert [627]
ROEMER, Olaus [232]
ROENTGEN, Wilhelm Konrad [774]
ROOZEBOOM, Hendrik Willem Bakhuis [854]
RORSCHACH, Hermann [1099]
ROSE, William Cumming [1114]
ROSS, Sir James Clark [512]
ROSS, Sir Ronald [876]
ROSSE, William Parsons, 3d earl of [513]
ROSSI, Bruno Benedetto [1289]

ROUS, Francis Peyton [1067]
ROUX, Pierre Paul Émile [844]
ROWLAND, Henry Augustus [798]
RUBNER, Max [848]
RUDBECK, Olof [218]
RUMFORD, Benjamin Thompson, Count [360]
RUSKA, Ernst August Friedrich [1322]
RUSSELL, Bertrand Arthur William, 3d Earl [1005]
RUSSELL, Henry Norris [1056]
RUTHERFORD, Daniel [351]
RUTHERFORD, Ernest [996]
RUTHERFURD, Lewis Morris [596]
RUŽIČKA, Leopold Stephen [1119]
RYDBERG, Johannes Robert [857]
RYLE, Sir Martin [1428]

SABATIER, Paul [856]
SABIN, Albert Bruce [1311]
SABINE, Sir Edward [459]
SABINE, Wallace Clement Ware [972]
SACCHERI, Girolamo [247]
SACHS, Julius von [699]
SAGAN, Carl [1504]
SAINTE-CLAIRE DEVILLE, Henri Étienne [603]
SAKHAROV, Andrey Dmitriyevich [1444]
SALAM, Abdus [1468]
SALK, Jonas Edward [1393]
SANCTORIUS, Sanctorius [165]
SANDAGE, Allan Rex [1469]
SANGER, Frederick [1426]
SAUSSURE, Horace Bénédict de [322]
SAVERY, Thomas [236]
SCALIGER, Joseph Justus [154]
SCHAEBERLE, John Martin [836]
SCHAEFER, Vincent Joseph [1309]
SCHALLY, Andrew Victor [1474]
SCHAUDINN, Fritz Richard [997]
SCHEELE, Karl Wilhelm [329]
SCHEINER, Christoph [173]
SCHIAPARELLI, Giovanni Virginio [714]
SCHLEIDEN, Matthias Jakob [538]

SCHLIEMANN, Heinrich [634]
SCHMIDT, Bernhard Voldemar [1065]
SCHMIDT, Maarten [1488]
SCHOENHEIMER, Rudolf [1211]
SCHÖNBEIN, Christian Friedrich [510]
SCHÖNER, Johannes [129]
SCHRIEFFER, John Robert [1495]
SCHRÖDINGER, Erwin [1117]
SCHULTZE, Max Johann Sigismund [657]
SCHWABE, Heinrich Samuel [466]
SCHWANN, Theodor [563]
SCHWARZSCHILD, Karl [1019]
SCHWEIGGER, Johann Salomo Christoph [422]
SCHWINGER, Julian Seymour [1421]
SCOTT, Robert Falcon [971]
SEABORG, Glenn Theodore [1372]
SECCHI, Pietro Angelo [606]
SEDGWICK, Adam [442]
SEEBECK, Thomas Johann [398]
SEFSTRÖM, Nils Gabriel [451]
SEGRÈ, Emilio [1287]
SELEUCUS [51]
SEMENOV, Nikolay Nikolaevich [1189]
SEMMELWEISS, Ignaz Philipp [607]
SERTÜRNER, Friedrich Wilhelm Adam Ferdinand [437]
SERVETUS, Michael [142]
SHANKS, William [572]
SHANNON, Claude Elwood [1404]
SHAPLEY, Harlow [1102]
SHARPEY-SCHÄFER, Sir Edward Albert [807]
SHEMIN, David [1358]
SHERMAN, Henry Clapp [1036]
SHERRINGTON, Sir Charles Scott [881]
SHKLOVSKII, Iosif Samuilovich [1408]
SHOCKLEY, William Bradford [1348]
SIDGWICK, Nevil Vincent [1013]
SIEBOLD, Karl Theodor Ernst von [537]
SIEGBAHN, Karl Manne Georg [1111]
SIEMENS, Sir William [644]
SILLIMAN, Benjamin [424]

SIMON, Sir Franz Eugen Francis [1165]
SIMPSON, Sir James Young [567]
SITTER, Willem de [1004]
SLIPHER, Vesto Melvin [1038]
SMITH, Hamilton Othanel [1496]
SMITH, Philip Edward [1090]
SMITH, Theobald [899]
SMITH, William [395]
SNELL, George Davis [1275]
SNELL, Willebrord van Roijen [177]
SNOW, John [576]
SOBRERO, Ascanio [574]
SOCRATES [21]
SODDY, Frederick [1052]
SOLVAY, Ernest [735]
SOMMERFELD, Arnold Johannes
  Wilhelm [976]
SØRENSEN, Søren Peter Lauritz [967]
SOSIGENES [54]
SPALLANZANI, Lazzaro [302]
SPEDDING, Frank Harold [1259]
SPEMANN, Hans [981]
SPENCER, Herbert [624]
SPERRY, Elmer Ambrose [907]
SPITZER, Lyman, Jr. [1390]
SPRENGEL, Christian Konrad [354]
STAHL, Georg Ernst [241]
STANLEY, Wendell Meredith [1282]
STARK, Johannes [1024]
STARLING, Ernest Henry [954]
STAS, Jean Servais [579]
STAUDINGER, Hermann [1074]
STEFAN, Josef [715]
STEIN, William Howard [1365]
STEINMETZ, Charles Proteus
  (originally Karl August) [944]
STEPHENSON, George [431]
STENO, Nicolaus [225]
STERN, Otto [1124]
STEVINUS, Simon [158]
STEWART, Balfour [678]
STOCK, Alfred [1043]
STOKES, Sir George Gabriel [618]
STONEY, George Johnstone [664]
STRABO [56]
STRASBURGER, Eduard Adolf [768]

STRASSMAN, Fritz [1251]
STRATO [38]
STROHMEYER, Friedrich [411]
STRUVE, Friedrich Georg Wilhelm von
  [483]
STRUVE, Otto [1203]
STURGEON, William [436]
STURTEVANT, Alfred Henry [1153]
SUESS, Eduard [687]
SUMNER, James Batcheller [1120]
SUTHERLAND, Earl Wilbur, Jr. [1402]
SUTTON, Walter Stanborough [1047]
SVEDBERG, Theodor H. E. [1097]
SWAMMERDAM, Jan [224]
SWAN, Sir Joseph Wilson [677]
SYDENHAM, Thomas [208]
SYLVIUS, Franciscus [196]
SYNGE, Richard Laurence Millington
  [1394]
SZENT-GYÖRGYI, Albert [1167]
SZILARD, Leo [1208]

TAKAMINE, Jokichi [855]
TALBOT, William Henry Fox [511]
TAMM, Igor Yevgenyevich [1180]
TARTAGLIA, Niccolò [135]
TATUM, Edward Lawrie [1346]
TAYLOR, Frederick Winslow [864]
TEISSERENC DE BORT, Léon
  Philippe [861]
TELLER, Edward [1332]
TEMIN, Howard Martin [1505]
TENNANT, Smithson [375]
TESLA, Nikola [867]
THABIT IBN QURRA [80]
THALES [3]
THEAETETUS [26]
THEILER, Max [1217]
THÉNARD, Louis Jacques [416]
THEOPHRASTUS [31]
THEORELL, Axel Hugo Teodor [1267]
THOMSEN, Christian Jurgensen [460]
THOMSEN, Hans Peter Jørgen Julius
  [665]
THOMSON, Sir Charles Wyville [682]
THOMSON, Elihu [837]

THOMSON, Sir George Paget [1156]
THOMSON, Sir Joseph John [869]
THOMSON, Robert William [637]
TINBERGEN, Nikolaas [1326]
TING, Samuel C. C. [1507]
TISELIUS, Arne Wilhelm Kaurin [1257]
TITIUS, Johann Daniel [301]
TODD, Alexander Robertus, Baron [1331]
TOMBAUGH, Clyde William [1299]
TOMONAGA, Shin'ichiro [1300]
TORRICELLI, Evangelista [192]
TOSCANELLI, Paolo [113]
TOWNES, Charles Hard [1400]
TRAVERS, Morris William [1001]
TREVITHICK, Richard [399]
TRUMPLER, Robert Julius [1109]
TSAI LUN [63]
TSCHERMAK VON SEYSENEGG, Erich [999]
TSIOLKOVSKY, Konstantin Eduardovich [880]
TSVETT, Mikhail Semenovich [1006]
TURING, Alan Mathison [1375]
TWORT, Frederick William [1055]
TYNDALL, John [626]

UHLENBECK, George Eugene [1234]
ULUGH BEG [112]
URBAIN, Georges [1002]
UREY, Harold Clayton [1164]

VALENTIN, Gabriel Gustav [560]
VAN ALLEN, James Alfred [1392]
VAN DE GRAAF, Robert Jemison [1246]
VAN DE HULST, Hendrik Christoffell [1430]
VAN DE KAMP, Peter [1247]
VAN DER WAALS, Johannes Diderïk [726]
VAN'T HOFF, Jacobus Henricus [829]
VAN VLECK, John Hasbrouck [1219]
VAUQUELIN, Louis Nicolas [379]
VAVILOV, Nikolay Ivanovich [1122]
VEKSLER, Vladimir Iosifovich [1324]

VENETZ, Ignatz [453]
VENN, John [710]
VERNADSKY, Vladimir Ivanovich [924]
VERNIER, Pierre [179]
VESALIUS, Andreas [146]
VESPUCIUS, Americus [123]
VIETA, Franciscus [153]
VILLARD, Paul Ulrich [906]
VIRCHOW, Rudolph Carl [632]
VIRTANEN, Artturi Ilmari [1176]
VITRUVIUS [55]
VIVIANI, Vincenzo [206]
VOGEL, Hermann Carl [757]
VOIT, Karl von [691]
VOLTA, Alessandro Giuseppe Antonio Anastasio, Count [337]
VOLTAIRE [261]
VON EULER, Ulf Svante [1288]
VONNEGUT, Bernard [1391]

WAAGE, Peter [701]
WAGNER VON JAUREGG, Julius [874]
WAKSMAN, Selman Abraham [1128]
WALD, George [1318]
WALDEN, Paul [928]
WALDEYER-HARTZ, Heinrich Wilhelm Gottfried von [722]
WALDSEEMÜLLER, Martin [125]
WALLACE, Alfred Russel [643]
WALLACH, Otto [790]
WALLIS, John [198]
WALTER, William Grey [1349]
WALTON, Ernest Thomas Sinton [1269]
WARBURG, Otto Heinrich [1089]
WASSERMAN, August von [951]
WATSON, James Dewey [1480]
WATSON, John Broadus [1057]
WATSON-WATT, Sir Robert Alexander [1155]
WATT, James [316]
WEBER, Ernst Heinrich [492]
WEBER, Wilhelm Eduard [540]
WEGENER, Alfred Lothar [1071]

WEIERSTRASS, Karl Theodor Wilhelm [593]

WEINBERG, Steven [1502]

WEISMANN, August Friedrich Leopold [704]

WEISS, Pierre [942]

WEIZMANN, Chaim [1031]

WEIZSÄCKER, Carl Friedrich, Baron von [1376]

WELLER, Thomas Huckle [1397]

WENDELIN, Godefroy [176]

WERNER, Abraham Gottlob [355]

WERNER, Alfred [960]

WESTINGHOUSE, George [785]

WHEATSTONE, Sir Charles [526]

WHEELER, John Archibald [1366]

WHEWELL, William [487]

WHIPPLE, Fred Lawrence [1317]

WHIPPLE, George Hoyt [1059]

WHITEHEAD, Alfred North [911]

WHITNEY, Eli [386]

WIECHERT, Emil [917]

WIELAND, Heinrich Otto [1048]

WIEN, Wilhelm [934]

WIENER, Norbert [1175]

WIGNER, Eugene Paul [1260]

WILDT, Rupert [1290]

WILKINS, John [197]

WILKINS, Maurice Hugh Frederick [1413]

WILKINS, Robert Wallace [1320]

WILKINSON, Sir Geoffrey [1445]

WILLIAMS, Robert Runnels [1104]

WILLIAMS, Robley Cook [1339]

WILLIAMSON, Alexander William [650]

WILLIS, Thomas [205]

WILLSTÄTTER, Richard [1009]

WILSON, Charles Thomson Rees [979]

WILSON, Edmund Beecher [868]

WILSON, Robert Woodrow [1506]

WINDAUS, Adolf [1046]

WINKLER, Clemens Alexander [739]

WISLICENUS, Johannes [716]

WITHERING, William [327]

WITTIG, Georg Friedrich Karl [1199]

WÖHLER, Friedrich [515]

WOLF, Maximilian Franz Joseph Cornelius [927]

WOLFF, Kaspar Friedrich [313]

WOLLASTON, William Hyde [388]

WOODWARD, Robert Burns [1416]

WOOLLEY, Sir Charles Leonard [1069]

WREN, Sir Christopher [220]

WRIGHT, Orville [995]

WRIGHT, Thomas [281]

WRIGHT, Wilbur [961]

WROBLEWSKI, Zygmunt Florenty von [779]

WUNDERLICH, Carl Reinhold August [592]

WUNDT, Wilhelm Max [697]

WURTZ, Charles Adolphe [602]

WYCKOFF, Ralph Walter Graystone [1202]

XENOPHANES [6]

YALOW, Rosalyn Sussman [1446]

YANG, Chen Ning [1451]

YERKES, Robert Mearns [1041]

YOUNG, Charles Augustus [712]

YOUNG, Thomas [402]

YUKAWA, Hideki [1323]

ZEEMAN, Pieter [945]

ZENO [16]

ZEPPELIN, Ferdinand Adolf August Heinrich, Count von [737]

ZERNICKE, Fritz [1127]

ZIEGLER, Karl [1215]

ZINN, Walter Henry [1321]

ZOSIMUS [67]

ZSIGMONDY, Richard Adolf [943]

ZWICKY, Fritz [1209]

ZWORYKIN, Vladimir Kosma [1134]

ASIMOV'S
BIOGRAPHICAL ENCYCLOPEDIA
OF
SCIENCE AND TECHNOLOGY

[1] **IMHOTEP** (im-hoh'tep)
    Egyptian scholar
    Born: near Memphis
    Flourished 2980–2950 B.C.

Imhotep is remarkable for being the first historic equivalent, known by name, of what we would today call a scientist. There was not to be another for over two thousand years.

The one definite feat that is attributed to him is that of being the architect of the "step pyramid" at the modern village of Sakkara (near the site of ancient Memphis) in Egypt. This was the earliest of the Egyptian pyramids, and if Imhotep was indeed the architect, he may be credited with a literally monumental first.

The memory of Imhotep was saddled with all sorts of other achievements, the tales certainly not dwindling in the telling as generations passed. Most of all, he was remembered for his powers of healing, which the tales eventually magnified to the point of magic. In fact, by Ptolemaic times, he had come to be deified as the son of the great god Ptah and as himself the god of medicine. His tomb at Sakkara became a shrine where people came in search of cures as today they come to Lourdes. A ruin thought to be this shrine was uncovered in 1965. Our first scientist is thus unique in another way, for no scientist since has been made into a god.

The Greeks identified Imhotep (whom they called Imouthes) with Asklepios, their own god of medicine, and his leg-end may also have influenced their own tales of Daedalus, who, if he did not build a pyramid, was at least supposed to have built the Cretan labyrinth.

Some ancient manuscripts speak of Imhotep as having counseled Zoser (the Pharaoh for whom the step pyramid had been built) as to the methods of appeasing the gods after a succession of seven consecutive failures of the Nile floods had brought a seven-year famine. Might not this have influenced the later Hebrews in their legends of Joseph?

[2] **AHMOSE** (ah'mose)
    Egyptian scribe
    Lived about 1650 B.C.

Ahmose is known only because his name is on a mathematical treatise headed "Directions for Attaining Knowledge of All Dark Things." It was discovered in Egypt in the mid-nineteenth century and is now in the British Museum.

Ahmose is merely the copyist of the papyrus, which deals with the solution of various types of simple equations, with devices for handling fractions with unit numerators, with finding areas and volumes and so on. The actual authors are lost in the past.

The papyrus attests to the ancientness of Egyptian mathematics. It also lacks any sign that the Egyptians generalized their methods. Each problem discussed is treated as a special case, with a detailed description of the method of handling the particular numerical values contained

1

in the problem. No rules are given for solving a particular *type* of problem for all possible sets of conditions.

Perhaps it is assumed that the reader will work out the rule for himself from the cases given. Perhaps the rules are given on some other papyrus not yet found, or possibly forever lost. Perhaps the priestly caste kept the general rules a secret, just as the followers of Pythagoras [7] many years later were to keep certain mathematical discoveries secret. Certainly, considering the technical proficiency of the Egyptians in mathematics (for the builders of the pyramids could by no means have been mathematical novices) it is hard to believe that generalization did not exist.

Nevertheless the fact remains that there is no documentary sign of generalization in mathematics until the time of Thales [3], who lived a thousand years after Ahmose.

[3] **THALES** (thay'leez)
    Greek philosopher
    Born: Miletus, 624 B.C.
    Died: Miletus, 546 B.C.

The later Greeks considered Thales the founder of Greek science, mathematics, and philosophy, and they credited to him the origin of almost every branch of knowledge. It is hard to say how much of this is later embroidery.

He is supposed to have been born of a Phoenician mother, though this is doubted by some. Perhaps the legend only signifies that he was educated in Eastern science. Certainly he visited Egypt and probably Babylonia. It may be that what seemed to the Greeks a multiplicity of achievement was simply the lore of the more ancient peoples.

For instance, the single deed that most secured his reputation, according to the tale told a century and a half later by the Greek historian Herodotus, was his prediction of an eclipse of the sun, an eclipse which then proceeded to take place in the very year for which it was predicted. (When it occurred it frightened the Medes and Lydians, who were on the point of advancing into battle, and convinced them of the beauties of peace. They signed a treaty and the armies returned home.) Modern astronomical research showed that the only eclipse that took place in Asia Minor in Thales' time was on May 28, 585 B.C., so that the aborted battle is the first human historical event that can be dated with certainty to the exact day.

Nevertheless Thales' feat seems not so miraculous when we consider that the Babylonians had worked out systems for the accurate prediction of lunar eclipses at least two centuries before his time. His ability to predict this solar eclipse, and to the year rather than to the day, was, therefore, almost certainly acquired in the East. Thales was the first Greek to maintain that the moon shone by reflected sunlight and this, too, may represent Babylonian lore.

Thales also borrowed Egyptian geometry, but here he made a fundamental advance. He converted it into an abstract study, being the first man we know of to consider it as dealing with imaginary lines of zero thickness and perfect straightness, rather than with actual lines, thick and imperfect, scraped in the sand or scratched on wax. (If the Egyptians or Babylonians had already made this advance, it is still true that Thales was the first to place such views on record in a form that has reached us, via the works of later philosophers.)

Thales seems also to have been the first to go about proving mathematical statements by a regular series of arguments, marshaling what was already known and proceeding step by step to the desired proof as inevitable consequence. In other words, he invented deductive mathematics, which was to be systematized and brought to a high polish two and a half centuries later by Euclid [40].

Certain specific geometric theorems were later supposed to have been discovered by him; for instance, that the diameter of a circle divides it into two equal parts, that vertical angles are equal, and that the base angles of an isosceles triangle are equal.

He was also supposed to have measured the height of an Egyptian pyramid by comparing the length of its shadow to that of the shadow of a stick of known size—which represents the concept of trigonometry.

In the physical sciences, he was the first to study magnetism. More important, he is the first man we know of who asked the question: Of what is the universe made? and to answer it without introducing gods or demons.

His own answer was that the fundamental stuff (the "element," we would now say) of the universe was water, and the earth was only a flat disc floating on an infinite ocean. This answer was a most reasonable guess for the times, since it was clear that life, at least, depended on water. But the question itself was far more important than the answer, for it inspired later philosophers, who flourished in the same region, near Miletus, among them Anaximander [4], Anaximenes [5], and Heraclitus [10], to speculate on the same subject. It was this line of thought that led eventually, after two thousand years of painful intellectual struggle, to modern chemistry.

Thales in addition to being a philosopher was, according to later tradition, a practical man of affairs. In politics he shrewdly urged a political union of the various Greek cities of Ionia (the modern southwest coast of Turkey), of which Miletus was one, for self-defense against the encroaching non-Greek kingdom of Lydia. This, the following centuries amply demonstrated, was the only way the Greeks could defend themselves against the surrounding nations. However, the Greek passion for disunity rose triumphant over all and was the cause of the country's ruin.

Aristotle [29] said that Thales, stung by jibes to the effect that if he were so wise, it was strange that he wasn't rich, quietly bought up the olive-presses in Miletus and surrounding territory in a year when his knowledge of weather told him the olive crop would be a good one. Charging monopoly prices for the use of the presses, he grew rich in one season. Then, having proved his point, he abandoned business and returned to the world of the mind.

This may have been invented merely to point a moral. If so, Plato [24] invented another tale to point another moral. While walking along and studying the stars, Plato said, Thales fell into a well. An old woman coming in response to his cries, helped him out, but said with contempt, "Here is a man who would study the stars and cannot see what lies at his feet."

Already in the time of Plato and Aristotle, two and a half centuries after Thales, the old philosopher's views were remembered imperfectly and made the subject of legend.

In valuing philosophical speculation over the practical applications of science, Thales set the tone for later Greek thinking. As a result the work of Greek engineers and inventors was largely ignored by later Greek writers and badly underestimated, in consequence, by all later generations. We have only very slight information about Thales' younger contemporary, Eupalinus [8], who in his way may have been as accomplished a sage.

In later centuries, when the Greeks made up lists of the "seven wise men," Thales was invariably placed first.

[4] ANAXIMANDER (a-nak'si-man-der)
    Greek philosopher
    Born: Miletus, 610 B.C.
    Died: Miletus, about 546 B.C.

Like Thales, whose pupil he was, Anaximander helped introduce the science of the ancient East to Greece. He was the first Greek to make use of the sundial, for instance, which had been known for centuries both in Egypt and Babylonia. No better timekeeper was to be found until the days of Ctesibius [46], over three centuries later. Anaximander was also the first to attempt to draw a map of the whole earth as he knew it.

He recognized that the heavens revolved about the Pole star and so he pictured the sky as a complete sphere and not merely as a semispherical arch over the earth. For the first time the notion of spheres invaded astronomy; this was to culminate eventually in the sophisticated (but erroneous) picture of the universe drawn up by Ptolemy [64].

He also recognized that the earth's surface must be curved, to account for the change in the position of the stars as one traveled. He felt a north-south curvature was enough, however, so he pictured the earth as a cylinder about an east-west axis with a height one-third its diameter. The notion of a spherical earth had to wait several decades for Pythagoras [7] and his followers.

Anaximander's idea of the basic element of the universe was far more mystical than Thales' plain and undramatic notion that it was water. Anaximander envisaged a formless mass that was both the source and the destination of all material things. He called this unobservable substance *apeiron,* meaning infinite. Nevertheless, he conceded this much to water—he thought life originated there. In this he was quite correct.

The treatise Anaximander wrote describing his views is thought to be the first work of consequence in Greek prose. His works are now lost.

[5] **ANAXIMENES** (an'ak-sim'ih-neez)
Greek philosopher
Born: Miletus, about 570 B.C.
Died: about 500 B.C.

Little is known about Anaximenes except that he may have been a pupil of Anaximander [4], and that he believed air to be the fundamental element of the universe. By compression, he supposed, it could take on the form of water and, eventually, earth. By rarefaction, it heats and becomes fire. He is supposed to have been the first Greek to distinguish clearly between planets (such as Mars and Venus) and stars and to have maintained that the rainbow was a natural phenomenon rather than a goddess.

[6] **XENOPHANES** (zee-nof'uh-neez)
Greek philosopher
Born: Colophon, Ionia, about 570 B.C.
Died: about 480 B.C.

Like Pythagoras [7], his contemporary, Xenophanes left Ionia after 545 B.C. when Persia had conquered the region. He settled in the town of Elea. He wrote on Pythagorean doctrine, but was less mystical than most of the school. He did not believe in transmigration of souls or in the primitive Greek gods but in a monotheism not at all characteristic of Greek thought.

He guessed that earth might be the fundamental element of the universe, but he is best known for his theory, derived from the fact that seashells were sometimes found on mountain heights, that the physical characteristics of the earth changed with time. Mountains, he maintained, must have originally been covered by the sea and, with time, risen to their present heights.

This was a remarkable forecast of later geologic thinking, but it remained an isolated ray of light until Hutton [297], twenty-three centuries later, founded geology and made sober sense of Xenophanes' seemingly wild guess.

[7] **PYTHAGORAS** (pih-thag'oh-rus)
Greek philosopher
Born: Samos (an Aegean island), about 560 B.C.
Died: Metapontum (in southern Italy), about 480 B.C.

Pythagoras, like the other early sages of Greece, was reputed to have traveled widely in Egypt and the East, and he may well have done so. He is also reported to have studied under Anaximander [4] or even under Thales [3] himself.

However, the first event in his life that seems reasonably certain is his departure from Samos in 529 B.C. and his emigration to Croton in southern Italy. (By that time the coasts of southern Italy and eastern Sicily had been colonized by the Greeks and the region remained Greek in culture well into the Middle Ages.) Pythagoras' move, according to tradition, was brought about by the harsh, one-man rule over Samos on the part of the tyrant Polycrates. Whatever the cause, the move extended the philosophic and scientific tradition—begun by Thales at the eastern rim of the Greek world—to the far west of the Greek world.

In Croton, Pythagoras broke with the rationalism of the east-Greek tradition and founded a cult marked by secrecy, asceticism, and mysticism. The cult, Pythagoreanism, forbade, for instance, the poking of fire with an iron poker and the eating of beans. It also taught the doctrine of the transmigration of souls. There is a story, for instance, that Pythagoras ordered a man to stop beating a dog, claiming he recognized the voice of a dead friend of his. This may merely have been a humane impulse on Pythagoras' part—or it may have been invented by the cult's many enemies to cast ridicule upon it.

In many ways Pythagoreanism was like the mystery cults prevalent in Greece then and afterward, but it differed from them in the interest the followers of Pythagoras had in mathematics and astronomy. The cult achieved important political power in Pythagoras' later years and was usually to be found on the side of the aristocrats. Even during the lifetime of Pythagoras, however, the democrats had started to gain the upper hand in southern Italy and the cult began to suffer persecution. Pythagoras was exiled from Croton about ten years before his death. Pythagoreanism survived as an active cult for only a century after its founder's death.

The unpopularity it brought upon itself by its political activity resulted in a violent wave of persecution that spread over all the Greek world. By 350 B.C. Pythagoreanism was wiped out. The influence of its ideas, however, has lasted into modern times, and Pythagoras remains the most famous of the earlier Greek philosophers. It is he, indeed, who is supposed to have coined the word "philosopher."

Because of the secrecy shrouding the beliefs of Pythagoreans, it isn't always easy to tell what they were, or how much of what was attributed to them by later Greek writers is correct. In particular, it is hard to say for what Pythagoras himself was responsible, and what was

originated by his many disciples, especially Philolaus [19].

The greatest scientific success attributed to Pythagoras was in his study of sound. He found that the strings of musical instruments delivered sound of higher pitch as they were made shorter. Furthermore he found that the relationship of pitch could be simply correlated with length. For instance, if one string was twice the length of another, the sound it emitted was just an octave lower. If the ratio of the strings was three to two, the musical interval called a fifth was produced, and if it was four to three, the interval called a fourth was produced. Increasing the tension of the strings also raised the pitch. Thanks to these observations, the study of sound was the one branch of physics in which Greek views remained unaltered in modern times.

This study may have led Pythagoras to the belief that the whole universe rested on numbers and their relationship, for he (or his followers) proceeded to invest numbers with all sorts of mystic significance. Today these notions seem foolish, but they did encourage the investigation of the mathematical properties of the numbers. For instance, it was the Pythagoreans who discovered that the square root of two (that is, the number which, multiplied by itself, gives a product of exactly two) could not be expressed as the ratio of two numbers. No conceivable fraction, however complicated, will give the product of two when multiplied by itself.

Here was a very simple concept that could not be put into whole numbers. How then could numbers account for something as complicated as the whole universe? The Pythagoreans were supposed to have vowed themselves to secrecy concerning such "irrational numbers" lest outsiders scoff. It slipped out anyway and there is a story that the Pythagoreans executed one of their fellows whose tongue had wagged too freely on the subject, though this may be another slander circulated by the anti-Pythagoreans.

Pythagoras is most famous, perhaps, for having been the first to work out the proposition (by strict mathematical deduction) that the square of the length of the hypotenuse of a right triangle is equal to the sum of the squares of the lengths of its sides. This is still known as the Pythagorean theorem.

Pythagoras was the first Greek to recognize that the morning star (Phosphorus) and the evening star (Hesperus) were in fact one star. After his time it was called Aphrodite, and we know it now as the planet Venus. He was also the first to note that the orbit of the moon is not in the plane of the earth's equator but is inclined at an angle to that plane.

He was the first man known to us who taught that the earth was spherical. He was also the first Greek philosopher to point out that the sun, moon, and various planets did not partake of the uniform motion of the stars, but that each had a path of its own and was at a different distance from the earth. Thus began the notion that in addition to the heavenly sphere that Anaximander had postulated, separate spheres had to be provided for the various planets. For seven hundred years thereafter, the number of spheres necessary to account for the planetary movements was to multiply, and over twenty-one hundred years passed before Kepler [169] wiped them out.

[8] EUPALINUS (yoo-puh-ly'nus)
Greek architect
Born: Megara (20 miles west of Athens); flourished in the sixth century B.C.

It is obvious that the ancients possessed their share of great engineers, for some of their feats of construction were as great as anything we can do today, considering the primitive nature of the tools and techniques available to them. It is a pity that we know so little of them. Except for the semilegendary Imhotep [1], nothing is known about individual pre-Greek engineers, and very little is known about engineers in Greece's golden age. An exception is Eupalinus, whose name is at least attached to a

specific accomplishment. He specialized in water systems, building one for his native city in Megara about 530 B.C. Later, he was engaged by Polycrates, the tyrant of the Aegean island of Samos, to build an aqueduct there. For this project, Eupalinus had to tunnel through a hill for over half a mile. The ancients were profoundly impressed that Eupalinus started the tunnel at both ends and the two halves met only a couple of feet off center.

[9] HECATAEUS (hek-uh-tee'us)
Greek traveler
Born: Miletus, about 550 B.C.
Died: about 476 B.C.

Hecataeus carried on the rationalist tradition of Thales [3] and applied it particularly to the surface of the earth. He traveled widely through the Persian Empire (which in his time dominated Asia Minor) and wrote a book on Egypt and Asia which, however, has not survived. In Egypt he is supposed to have become aware of the true stretch of previous history when the Egyptians showed him records going back hundreds of generations.

Hecataeus continued the work, begun by Anaximander [4], of attempting to map the world. He divided the land area into a northern half (Europe) and a southern half (Asia) with the east-west structures of the Mediterranean Sea and the Caucasus Mountains forming the dividing line. Both continents were drawn as semicircles and the whole was encircled by Oceanus, the "ocean river." The Greeks, however, were not the outstanding travelers and explorers of the time. That honor was held by the far less articulate (and therefore less advertised and less remembered) Phoenicians, of whom Hanno [12] bears off the palm, if the vague remnants of his tale are to be credited.

Hecataeus rationalized history as well as geography, writing the first Greek account of the deeds of men which did not accept gods and myths at face value. In fact, Hecataeus took a skeptical and downright scornful view of myths. His

history did not survive but undoubtedly
served as an inspiration for his greater
successor, Herodotus, a couple of generations later. Because Herodotus' history
did survive (and deservedly so, for it
remains one of the greatest of all times,
in sheer charm of style, if not always in
accuracy), it is the later historian, who
is known as the father of history, though
Hecataeus may better deserve the title.

Like Thales, Hecataeus was a shrewd
politician, and he opposed the revolt of
the Greek cities of Asia Minor against
Darius I of Persia in 499 B.C. His advice
was not followed, the revolt was disastrously suppressed, and the scientific
pre-eminence of the Greek cities of Asia
Minor, which had lasted a century and a
half, came to an end.

[10] **HERACLITUS** (her-uh-kly'tus)
Greek philosopher
Born: Ephesus (about 30 miles
north of Miletus), about 540 B.C.
Died: about 475 B.C.

The work of Heraclitus survives only
in fragments. His pessimistic view of life
and the universe led to his being called
the "weeping philosopher." To him the
most permanent thing about the universe
seemed to be impermanence, and the one
fact that was unchangeable was that
change was certain. For instance, he
thought so little of the unchangeability
of even so glorious an object as the sun,
as to suggest it was made fresh each
morning so that every day saw a different sun.

It made sense to him, then, that fire,
itself ever-changing and capable of
bringing about change in other things,
should be the fundamental element of
the universe.

[11] **ALCMAEON** (alk-mee'on)
Greek physician
Born: Croton (in southern Italy),
about 535 B.C.
Died: date unknown

Alcmaeon, born in the center of Pythagoreanism and living during the height

of its power, was naturally a Pythagorean. He had some mystical notions,
such as that the human body was a
microcosm, reflecting in small the universe or macrocosm. This, however, did
not prevent him from being an accurate
and careful observer.

He is the first individual known to
have conducted dissections of the human
body. He recorded the existence of the
optic nerve and the tube connecting the
ear and mouth (which are now called
Eustachian tubes after Eustachio [141],
their rediscoverer, who lived two thousand years later). Alcmaeon distinguished arteries from veins, though he
did not recognize the former as blood
vessels, since in cadavers the arteries are
empty.

He felt that the brain was the center
of intellectual activity and so did Democritus [20] and Hippocrates [22] two
generations later. This view, however,
was not accepted by Aristotle [29] and it
did not come into its own until modern
times.

[12] **HANNO**
Carthaginian navigator
Born: Carthage (near the site of
modern Tunis), about 530 B.C.
Died: date unknown

The Phoenicians (of whom the Carthaginians were a branch) were the great
navigators and explorers of the ancient
world but only a dim tale of Hanno,
with sixty vessels and thirty thousand
men and women (numbers undoubtedly
exaggerated) and his explorations down
the African coast survives. Herodotus,
the Greek historian, describes the voyage
and declares that Hanno claimed to have
circumnavigated Africa. Concerning this,
Herodotus expresses his doubts, because
the Carthaginians reported that in the
far south the noonday sun was in the
northern half of the sky. This Herodotus
felt to be impossible. Nevertheless, this *is*
the case in the southern hemisphere and
it is unlikely that anyone would make up
so ridiculous a tale unless he had actually witnessed the phenomenon. Thus,
the very point at which the ordinarily

credulous Herodotus balks is the point that is most convincing to moderns. It may be, then, that Hanno the Carthaginian was the first man of the Mediterranean world to have crossed the equator.

[13] **PARMENIDES** (pahr-men'ih-deez)
Greek philosopher
Born: Elia (modern Velia), Italy, about 515 B.C.
Died: after 450 B.C.

Parmenides was a follower of those notable Ionian exiles Pythagoras [7] and Xenophanes [6] and was the first major philosopher native to Italy. He opposed the notions of Heraclitus [10] and, far from accepting change as the universal truth, denied the possibility of change since one object, he held, could not turn into another object fundamentally different. It was more reasonable, he insisted, to suppose that creation (something from nothing) and destruction (nothing from something) were impossible.

Since change was all about us despite this reasoning, Parmenides had to choose between the senses and reason; he chose reason. The senses were untrustworthy, in his opinion, and not to be used as guides. This view was the cornerstone of the Eleatic school, which he founded and of which the best-known member, Zeno [16], was to carry the distrust of the senses into a set of famous paradoxes.

Plato [24] entitled one of his dialogues "Parmenides" and in it describes a meeting between the aged Parmenides and the youthful Socrates [21].

[14] **ANAXAGORAS** (an-ak-zag'oh-rus)
Greek philosopher
Born: Clazomenae (75 miles north of Miletus), about 500 B.C.
Died: Lampsacus (modern Lâpseki, Turkey), about 428 B.C.

As is the case for almost all the early Greek philosophers, tradition states that Anaxagoras, the son of wealthy parents, traveled widely during his youth. He is sometimes said to have studied under Anaximenes [5] but this is probably in order to maintain an Ionian continuity. Anaximenes is almost sure to have been dead before Anaxagoras was old enough to be a student.

About 462 B.C., Anaxagoras migrated to Athens from his Asia Minor homeland. Athens at the time was at the height of its golden age and the pinnacle of Greek culture. By his move Anaxagoras, the last of the Ionians, carried to Athens the scientific tradition of Thales [3] as, two generations earlier, Pythagoras [7] had carried it to Italy. However, whereas Pythagoras had emphasized mysticism, Anaxagoras was a rationalist. He explained—accurately—the phases of the moon and eclipses of both moon and sun in terms of the movements of those bodies.

To him the universe originated not through the creative act of any deity, but through the action of abstract Mind upon an infinite number of "seeds." These seeds were a form of the atoms whose existence was being postulated simultaneously by Leucippus [15].

The result, according to Anaxagoras, was that the heavenly bodies were brought into existence by the same processes that formed the earth, and therefore heavens and earth were composed of the same materials. The existence of a stony meteorite that fell on the north shore of the Aegean in 468 B.C. may have helped him come to this conclusion. The stars and planets were flaming rocks, and the sun he believed to be an incandescent rock about the size of the Peloponnesus (which is roughly as large as Massachusetts). As for the moon, he regarded it as an earthlike body and possibly even inhabited. These were irreligious views that shocked conservative Athenians.

Anaxagoras taught in Athens for thirty years and his school was the beginning of the philosophic pre-eminence of Athens in the Greek world, a pre-eminence that was to be maintained for nearly a thousand years. (Even in late Roman times, when Athens' early military and political glory was a faded and ancient dream, it kept the scholarly aura of the University town, much as Oxford does today in England.) He is supposed to have written one book, some time after 467 B.C.

Anaxagoras was not, however, allowed to pursue his studies and teachings in peace. The Athens of his day was not yet ready to accept his rationalism (as the Greeks of Italy had not been ready to accept Pythagoras' aristocratic mysticism). Anaxagoras was accused of impiety and atheism and brought to trial, the first scientist we know to have had this kind of legal conflict with a state religion. Anaxagoras was a friend of the most respected Athenian citizens, including Euripides, the great playwright, and even Pericles, the uncrowned king of the city. This hurt rather than helped Anaxagoras, for the enemies of Pericles, unable to strike at the leader himself, eagerly attempted to hurt him through his friend the philosopher. Pericles faced the court in his friend's defense and managed, with difficulty, to secure his acquittal of the charge of impiety (a happier fate than was to befall Socrates [21] on a similar charge a generation later).

Anaxagoras believed the atmosphere of the city to be unsafe, however, and in 434 B.C. he retired to Lampsacus on the Hellespont, where he died six years later. The mark of the trial endured. To be sure, a younger contemporary, Meton [23], continued astronomical researches at Athens, but the city's thinkers turned away from natural philosophy to take up moral philosophy.

[15] **LEUCIPPUS** (lyoo-sip'us)
Greek philosopher
Born: Miletus, about 490 B.C.
Died: date unknown

Almost nothing is known of Leucippus, not even that he really lived. If he did, he represented the final flash of the old tradition of Asia Minor, somehow surviving the destruction of the coastal cities by Persia. He is supposed to have been a pupil of Zeno [16]. He was, apparently, the inventor of atomism, the teacher of Democritus [20], and the first to state the rule of causality,

that is, that every event has a natural cause.

[16] **ZENO**
Greek philosopher
Born: Elea (modern Velia), southern Italy, about 490 B.C.
Died: Elea, about 425 B.C.

Zeno is the chief of the Eleatic school of philosophy (the name being taken from the town of Elea, where it was centered). He may have been a student of Parmenides [13]. He appears to have lived in Athens for a time according to Plato [24] and is supposed to have taught Pericles, among others. His life ended, according to one account, when he was on the wrong side of a political argument and was executed for treason.

The Eleatic school denied the usefulness of the senses as a means of attaining truth. In fact the Eleatics attempted to demonstrate that by reason they could show that the message of the senses must be ignored.

Zeno presented the Greek thinkers with four famous paradoxes, all of which seemed to disprove the possibility of motion as it was sensed. The best known is that of Achilles and the tortoise. Suppose Achilles can run ten times as fast as a tortoise and the tortoise has a ten-yard head start. It follows then that Achilles can never overtake the tortoise because while he covers the ten yards' difference, the tortoise will have moved ahead one yard. When Achilles covers that one yard, the tortoise will have moved on a tenth of a yard and so on. Since our senses, however, clearly show us a fast runner overtaking and passing a slow runner, our senses must be false.

These paradoxes, although all based on fallacies, were of the utmost importance to science, for they stimulated thought. Aristotle [29], for instance, presented arguments against them, and down to our own day, others have taken up positions either for or against the Eleatic view.

Since Zeno's paradoxes were all based on the assumption that space and time are infinitely divisible, it encouraged men like Democritus [20] to avoid the paradoxes by searching for indivisibility and finding it in the atoms of which they claimed matter to be composed. This view did not win general favor in Greek times, but it did win out twenty-two centuries later with Dalton [389]. The notion of infinite divisibility was further erased, a hundred years after Dalton, by the theories of Planck [887] concerning the ultimate particles of energy.

In pure mathematics, it was shown almost twenty-one centuries later, by James Gregory [226], that such things as converging series existed, in which an infinite number of terms nevertheless added up to a finite sum. The Achilles-and-the-tortoise paradox involved (without Zeno's knowledge) such a converging series. Then, too, methods for handling the infinitely divisible (even were that supposed to exist) were not developed until Newton [231] and his invention of the calculus.

Zeno was completely defeated in the end, but he deserves a chorus of thanks just the same for the values that grew out of more than two millennia of intellectual struggle required to defeat him. (Zeno of Elea is sometimes confused with another Zeno, Zeno of Citium, who founded the Stoic school of philosophy almost two centuries after the time of the earlier Zeno.)

[17] **EMPEDOCLES** (em-ped'oh-kleez)
Greek philosopher
Born: Akragas (modern Agrigento), Sicily, about 492 B.C.
Died: Mount Etna (?), about 432 B.C.

Empedocles was one philosopher who, at least in younger life, did not hesitate to immerse himself in politics. He was a moving spirit in the overthrow of a tyranny in his native town of Akragas. The grateful citizens offered him the tyrant's seat in reward but, in a self-denial not often found among Greeks of the time, Empedocles refused. He preferred to spend his time on philosophy.

Empedocles was, to a considerable extent, under the influence of the teachings of Pythagoras [7]. This is shown in the strong vein of mysticism in his teachings. He had no objection to being looked upon as a prophet and miracle-worker and was even supposed to have brought dead people back to life. According to one tradition, he let it be known that on a particular day he would be taken up to heaven and made a god. On that day he is supposed to have jumped into the crater of Mount Etna in order that, by disappearing mysteriously, he might be thought to have made good on his prediction. (It is also possible he believed his own story and jumped into the crater in despair when the heavenly chariot failed to appear. It is even more possible the whole story is false, for there are some who say he traveled to Greece in later life and died there.)

Some of Empedocles' views were rational enough. He believed the moon shone by reflected light from the sun. He believed the heart was the center of the blood-vessel system (which is true) and therefore the seat of life (which is certainly not an unreasonable guess). This notion was passed on to Aristotle [29], from whom it has descended to our day. We still speak of "not having the heart to do it" when we mean not having the will. We say we are "lion-hearted" when we mean brave, "broken-hearted" when we mean disappointed, and so on. He also had a dim notion of an evolutionary process through natural selection and felt that some creatures, ill-adapted to life, had perished in the past. This was a foretaste of Darwin [554].

Another influential notion arose when Empedocles combined some of the views of the Asia Minor school. Where Thales [3] had thought the basic element of the universe was water, Anaximenes [5] air, Heraclitus [10] fire, and Xenophanes [6] earth, Empedocles hit on merging all these. All things, he believed, were made up of various combinations and arrangements of these. Substances changed in nature when the elements broke apart and recombined in new arrangements under the action of forces akin to what humans recognize as "love" and "strife."

The notion was taken up and improved by Aristotle and remained the basis of chemical theory for more than two thousand years. It lasts in the common language even today, for we speak of the "raging of the elements" when we mean that air and water are being lashed into fury by a storm.

[18] **OENOPIDES** (ee-nop'ih-deez)
Greek philosopher
Born: Chios (an Aegean island), about 480 B.C.
Died: date unknown

Nothing is known about Oenopides except for mentions in the surviving works of other Greeks.

Pythagoras [7] probably knew that the path marked out by the sun was at an angle to the celestial equator, something called the obliquity of the ecliptic. In modern terms, this means that earth's axis of rotation is at an angle to a line perpendicular to its plane of revolution about the sun. The Babylonians knew this before Pythagoras.

It may be, though, that Oenopides was the first actually to put a figure to the amount of tipping, and that he placed it at about 24°, which is only a half-degree greater than the true value.

He may also have fixed the length of the year at 365⅛ days, which is a trifle longer than the actual length, which is nearly 365¼.

[19] **PHILOLAUS** (fil-oh-lay'us)
Greek philosopher
Born: Tarentum or Croton (in southern Italy), about 480 B.C.
Died: date unknown

Philolaus was the most eminent (after Pythagoras [7] himself) of the Pythagorean school and was the first, apparently, to publish Pythagorean views for the general public. He suffered in the course of the persecutions to which the Pythagoreans were subjected in southern Italy and had to flee (at least temporarily) to Thebes, on the Greek mainland. Later he returned to Tarentum, the last stronghold of Pythagoreanism.

The majority of the contributions of Philolaus were highly mystical. One thought, however, was of particular interest, for within the Pythagorean nonsense there were occasional shrewd (or lucky) guesses, as was the case with Xenophanes [6].

In Philolaus' case the shrewd guess was that the earth was not the center of the universe but that it moved through space. The earth, he thought, along with the sun, moon, Mercury, Venus, Mars, Jupiter, Saturn, and the stars circled in separate spheres about a central fire, of which the visible sun was only a reflection.

This meant nine circling spheres, so Philolaus invented a tenth, occupied by a counter-earth, a planet always hidden from us on the other side of the sun. This whole scheme was designed merely to take advantage of the magical powers of the number 10 (magical because it was the sum of 1, 2, 3, and 4).

Whatever the motivation, however, this was the first known speculation that the earth moves through space. When, two thousand years later, Copernicus [127] was to advance his theory of the universe, in which the earth and planets were pictured as moving about the sun, it was branded by some of his opponents a Pythagorean heresy.

[20] **DEMOCRITUS** (de-mok'rih-tus)
Greek philosopher
Born: Abdera, Thrace, about 470 B.C.
Died: perhaps as late as 380 B.C.

Like Thales [3] and Pythagoras [7] before him, Democritus is supposed to have traveled widely in Egypt and the East before settling down to philosophy at home in Greece. He also picked up the rationalist world view of Asia Minor through his teacher, Leucippus [15], who was of Miletus, as Thales himself had been. Like all the early rationalists, he had some startlingly modern-sounding notions. He maintained, for instance, that the Milky Way was a vast conglomeration of tiny stars and that the moon was an earthlike world with mountains and valleys.

Democritus was, indeed, the most successful of the Greek natural philosophers in the uncanny accuracy of his ideas (at least from our present viewpoint), but he lived in the shadow of his contemporary, Socrates [21], whose disciples rejected Democritus' notion of the universe. Almost none of Democritus' work, some seventy-two books in all, has survived and we know of him entirely as a result of references (often unfriendly) in the works of others.

Democritus was widely known as the Laughing Philosopher, either because his philosophy was an essentially cheerful one, or because he was viewed as laughing at the follies of mankind.

He is best known for his atomic theory. He believed that all matter consisted of tiny particles, almost infinitesimally small, so small that nothing smaller was conceivable. Hence they were indivisible; the very word "atom" means "indivisible." The atoms, he held, were eternal, unchangeable, indestructible. Besides themselves only the void—that is, the space between the atoms—existed. Even the human mind and the gods (if any) were made up of atom combinations.

The atoms, said Democritus, differed from each other physically, and in this difference was to be found an explanation for the properties of various substances. The atoms of water were smooth and round so that water flowed and had no permanent shape. The atoms of fire were thorny, which was what made burns so painful. The atoms of earth were rough and jagged, so that they held together to form a hard and stable substance. Apparent changes in the nature of substances consisted merely in the separation of joined atoms and their rejoining in a new pattern. These views were reminiscent of the *apeiron* of Anaximander [4].

The motions and behavior of the atoms, according to Democritus, are imposed upon them by definite and unbreakable laws of nature and are not the result of the whims of gods or demons. Democritus was thus one of the earliest of the thoroughgoing mechanists, believing that the workings of the universe were as mindless and determinate as those of a machine. To Democritus, even the creation of the universe was the blind result of swirling motions set up in great numbers of atoms. These motions ended in the clumping together of atoms, forming worlds.

In all this, there is a recognizable similarity to modern theories of the structure of matter and of cosmogony, but there is also a key difference. The conclusions of Democritus were born of introspection and intuition. Modern theories which seem similar are based on quantitative experiment and on orderly mathematical reasoning. Democritus' views, being merely intuitive, could be opposed by other views, equally intuitive, and the choice would then be a matter of personal predilection. The ancient philosophers, by and large, chose to follow Socrates and his disciples rather than Democritus and his.

That atomism did not die out completely was to the credit of Epicurus [35] who, over a century later, made use of atomism in his own popular teachings.

[21] **SOCRATES** (sok'ruh-teez)
Greek philosopher
Born: Athens, about 470 B.C.
Died: Athens, 399 B.C.

All that is known of Socrates is through the words of others, for he left no writings of his own. The man pictured in those reports was a sort of pagan saint. In personal appearance he was ugly: short and stout with a broad face, prominent eyes, a wide pug nose. He won over nearly everyone, however, with his good humor, his wit, and the fascination of his conversation.

He was fearless in battle and in politics. Neither an armed foe nor the Athenian government could compel him to act against his judgment. He was interested only in his quest for knowledge, living a life of poverty in utter content, and scorning luxury, though he could be a *bon vivant* when it suited him. He is even renowned for his bad-tempered

wife, Xanthippe, who has become pro-
verbial as a shrew and whom he bore
with patience (although, considering
what a poor provider Socrates was, she
had some reason for complaint). She
had three children by Socrates, none of
whom amounted to anything.

Socrates in his discussions pretended a
disarming ignorance (Socratic irony)
and then by shrewd questioning forced
his listeners, disciples, and opponents to
admit their own ignorance and the
wrongness of their casually accepted in-
tuitions. He was the gadfly of Athens,
and no less an institution whom the
oracle at Delphi proclaimed to be the
wisest of the Greeks (to which Socrates
replied that if he were the wisest it was
only because he alone knew that he knew
nothing). His methods also made him
enemies, for no one actually likes to be
proved wrong and least of all out of
one's own mouth.

Although Socrates was trained in the
rational science of Asia Minor (he may
have been a pupil of Anaxagoras [14] or
of one of Anaxagoras' disciples) he
questioned the importance of knowledge
concerning the universe. He was far
more interested in questions of ethics, in
the right code of behavior. He wished to
understand the workings of virtue rather
than of the heavenly bodies.

This had a profound effect on the history of science. It is rather surprising
that the Greeks failed in science after
having made such an excellent start with
Thales [3], having available the astonishing guesses of Democritus [20], the
shrewd views of Eratosthenes [48] and
Aristarchus [41] and the inventiveness
of Archimedes [47]. There are indeed
many factors involved in the failure, but
one, at least, lay in the views of Socrates. The larger part of Greek intellect
was, through admiration of him and of
his chief disciple Plato [24], channeled
into the field of moral philosophy, while
natural philosophy (what we now call
science) was allowed to wither.

In the end Socrates was too sharp a
gadfly to be left to himself. He was
brought to trial in 399 B.C. on charges of
atheism and treason—and, it seems, cor-

ruption of the young. Both charges were,
in a sense, justified. He certainly did not
believe in the Greek gods according to
the ancient fashion (few of the Greek
intellectuals of the time did). As for
treason, he never approved of the Athenian democracy and several of his favorite pupils, notably Alcibiades and Critias,
proved to be active traitors. Others, such
as Xenophon and Plato, were an-
tidemocratic and pro-Spartan.

Even so, Socrates would have been acquitted if he had made the least attempt
to defend himself rationally. He deliberately goaded on the jury of five hundred
men until they voted the death sentence
in spite of themselves, and then only by
a small majority of 280 to 220.

Socrates spent a month between sentence and execution, refusing to escape
although escape could easily have been
arranged. With utter calmness, dying as
courageously as he had lived, he drank
the poison hemlock. He was seventy
years old and had lived what was in his
own eyes a good life.

[22] **HIPPOCRATES** (hih-pok'ruh-teez)
         Greek physician
         Born: Cos (an Aegean island),
         460 B.C.
         Died: Larissa (now Larisa), Thes-
         saly, about 370 B.C.

Virtually nothing concrete is known
about Hippocrates. He was, it was said,
born of a family who were members of a
hereditary guild of magicians on the island of Cos and who were reputedly descended from Asklepios, the Greek god
of medicine. According to tradition, he
visited Egypt early in life, and there studied medical works attributed to Imhotep
[1]. Some traditions make him a student
of Democritus [20].

Hippocrates is supposed to have
taught at various places, including
Athens, but eventually he founded a
school of medicine on Cos that was the
most rational the ancient world had to
offer. It is because of his founding of
this school, and not because he was the
"first" physician, that he is properly

13

known today as the father of medicine. As a matter of fact, he was not the first physician, for there were able individual students of the human body before his time, as, for instance, Alcmaeon [11].

More than fifty books (called the Hippocratic collection) have been attributed to him, but it is more than doubtful that these are really his. They are rather the collected works of several generations of his school, brought together at Alexandria in the third century B.C., and attributed to him that they might be the more impressive. But the writings are certainly in his tradition, and in the best of them there is a high order of rationalism, careful observation, and honorable standards of conduct. Among the rule-of-thumb comments in the Hippocratic collection are a number that have become famous adages. Included are "desperate diseases require desperate remedies," for instance, and "one man's meat is another man's poison."

The Hippocratic school believed in moderation of diet, in the efficacy of cleanliness and rest for a sick or wounded man (and cleanliness for the physician too). They thought that the physician should interfere as little as possible with the healing processes of nature (and in view of how little was then known about the human body and its disorders, this was excellent advice).

Disease was looked upon as a purely physical phenomenon, something not to be ascribed to the arrows of Apollo or to possession by demons. Epilepsy, for instance, was considered by the men of the times to be a "sacred disease" because the patient in a fit seemed to be in the grip of a god or demon. The Hippocratic school ascribed even epilepsy to natural causes and considered it curable by physical remedies, not exorcism. In general, the Hippocratic school believed disease to result from an imbalance of the vital fluids ("humors") of the body, a notion first advanced by Empedocles [17]. These were eventually listed as four in number: blood, phlegm, black bile, and yellow bile.

As for Hippocratic ethics, this is reflected in the oath (ascribed to Hippocrates) that is still taken by medical students upon completing their course of training.

A statue discovered on Cos in 1933 is thought to be a representation of Hippocrates.

[23] **METON** (mee'ton)
Greek astronomer
Born: Athens, about 440 B.C.
Died: date unknown

Meton's great achievement was his discovery in 432 B.C. that 235 lunar months made up just about 19 years. This meant that if one arranged to have 12 years of 12 lunar months and 7 years of 13 lunar months, every 19 years, the lunar calendar could be made to match the seasons. This is the Metonic cycle, named in the astronomer's honor, although the cycle was undoubtedly known to the Babylonian astronomers long before Meton's time.

The Greek calendar was based on the Metonic cycle, since it had an arrangement of lunar years that repeated itself every 19 years. This remained the calendar of the ancient world until 46 B.C., when the Julian calendar was established by Julius Caesar with the help of Sosigenes [54]. The Jews have retained the Greek calendar and so the Metonic cycle is in use even today for religious purposes. In fact, there are traces in Christianity as well, for the date of Easter is calculated through the use of the Metonic cycle.

[24] **PLATO**
Greek philosopher
Born: Athens, about 427 B.C.
Died: Athens, about 347 B.C.

The original name of this Athenian aristocrat was Aristocles, but in his school days he received the nickname Platon (meaning "broad") because of his broad shoulders. (He is not the only great man to be known universally by a nickname. The Roman orator Cicero is another.)

14

In early life Plato saw war service and had political ambitions. However, he was never really sympathetic to the Athenian democracy and he could not join wholeheartedly in its government. He was a devoted follower of Socrates [21] whose disciple he became in 409 B.C., and the execution of that philosopher by the democrats in 399 B.C. was a crushing blow. He left Athens, believing that until "kings were philosophers or philosophers were kings" things would never go well with the world. (He traced his descent from the early kings of Athens and perhaps he had himself in mind.)

For several years he visited the Greek cities of Africa and Italy, absorbing Pythagorean notions, and then in 387 B.C. he returned to Athens. (En route, he is supposed to have been captured by pirates and held for ransom.) There, for the second half of his long life, he devoted himself to philosophy. In the western suburbs he founded a school that might be termed the first university. Because it was on the grounds that had once belonged to a legendary Greek called Academus, it came to be called the Academy, and this term has been used for schools ever since.

Plato remained at the Academy for the rest of his life, except for two brief periods in the 360s. At that time he visited Syracuse, the chief city of Greek Sicily, to serve as tutor for the new king, Dionysius II. Here was his chance to make a king a philosopher. It turned out very badly. The king insisted on behaving like a king and of course made the Athenian democrats look good by comparison. Plato managed only with difficulty to return safely to Athens. His end was peaceful and happy, for he is supposed to have died in his sleep at the age of eighty after having attended the wedding feast of one of his students.

Plato's works, perhaps the most consistently popular and influential philosophic writings ever published, consist of a series of dialogues in which the discussions between Socrates and others are presented with infinite charm. Most of our knowledge of Socrates is from these dialogues, and which views are Socrates'

and which are Plato's is anybody's guess. (Plato cautiously never introduced himself into any of the dialogues.)

Like Socrates, Plato was chiefly interested in moral philosophy and despised natural philosophy (that is, science) as an inferior and unworthy sort of knowledge. There is a famous story (probably apocryphal and told also of Euclid [40]) of a student asking Plato the application of the knowledge he was being taught. Plato at once ordered a slave to give the student a small coin that he might not think he had gained knowledge for nothing, then had him dismissed from school. To Plato, knowledge had no practical use; it existed for the abstract good of the soul.

Plato was fond of mathematics because of its idealized abstractions and its separation from the merely material. Nowadays, of course, the purest mathematics manages to be applied, sooner or later, to practical matters of science. In Plato's day this was not so, and the mathematician could well consider himself as dealing only with the loftiest form of pure thought and as having nothing to do with the gross and imperfect everyday world. And so above the doorway to the Academy was written, "Let no one ignorant of mathematics enter here."

Plato did, however, believe that mathematics in its ideal form could still be applied to the heavens. The heavenly bodies, he believed, exhibited perfect geometric form. This he expresses most clearly in a dialogue called *Timaeus* in which he presents his scheme of the universe. He describes the five (and only five) possible regular solids—that is, those with equivalent faces and with all lines and angles, formed by those faces, equal. These are the four-sided tetrahedron, the six-sided hexahedron (or cube), the eight-sided octahedron, the twelve-sided dodecahedron, and the twenty-sided icosahedron. Four of the five regular solids, according to Plato, represented the four elements, while the dodecahedron represented the universe as a whole. (These solids were first discovered by the Pythagoreans, but the fame of this dialogue has led to their being called the Platonic solids ever since.)

Plato decided also that since the heavens were perfect, the various heavenly bodies would have to move in exact circles (the perfect curve) along with the crystalline spheres (the perfect solid) that held them in place. The spheres were another Pythagorean notion, and the Pythagorean preoccupation with sound also shows itself in Philolaus' [19] belief that the spheres of the various planets made celestial music as they turned—a belief that persisted even in the time of Kepler [169] two thousand years later. We still use the phrase "the music of the spheres" to epitomize heavenly sounds or the stark beauty of outer space.

This insistence that the heavens must reflect the perfection of abstract mathematics in its simplest form held absolute sway over astronomical thought until Kepler's time, even though compromises with reality had to be made constantly, beginning shortly after Plato's death with Eudoxus [27] and Callippus [32].

In the dialogue *Timaeus*, by the way, Plato invented a moralistic tale about a thoroughly fictitious land he called Atlantis. If there is a Valhalla for philosophers, Plato must be sitting there in endless chagrin, thinking of how many foolish thousands, in all the centuries since his time, down to the very present day—thousands who have never read his dialogue or absorbed a sentence of his serious teachings—nevertheless believed with all their hearts in the reality of Atlantis. (To be sure, recent evidence of an Aegean island that exploded volcanically in 1400 B.C. may have given rise to legends that inspired Plato's fiction.)

Plato's influence extended long past his own life and, indeed, never died. The Academy remained a going institution until A.D. 529, when the Eastern Roman Emperor, Justinian, ordered it closed. It was the last stronghold of paganism in a Christian world.

Plato's philosophy, even after that date, maintained a strong influence on the thinking of the Christian Church throughout the early Middle Ages. It was not until the thirteenth century that the views of Aristotle [29] gained dominance.

[25] **ARCHYTAS** (ahr-ky'tus)
  Greek mathematician
  Born: Tarentum (now Taranto), Italy, about 420 B.C.
  Died: about 350 B.C.

Archytas was a Pythagorean who lived in Tarentum when it was the last remaining center of Pythagoreanism. He labored, as a number of Greek scholars did in the fourth century B.C. to persuade the Greek cities to unite against the increasing strength of the non-Greek world. As was true of all the others, Archytas failed, and the Greeks persisted in suicidal strife among themselves to the last possible moment.

Archytas was interested in one of the three great problems of the Greek mathematical world; the duplication of the cube. Given a cube, in other words, the problem was to construct another cube with just twice the volume of the first, making use of a compass and straightedge only. Under those conditions, the solution is impossible (as was discovered in later times) but in making the effort, Archytas evolved theorems concerning means; that is, lines or values midway between two extremes. He solved the problem by means of an ingenious three-dimensional construction, making use of somewhat more liberal devices than the strictest interpretations of the rules of the game would allow.

He was the first Greek mathematician who tried to apply his pure art to mechanics, when he worked out a theory of sound and pitch based on his means. He invented the notion of harmonic progression $(1, \frac{1}{2}, \frac{1}{3}, \frac{1}{4} \ldots)$ as opposed to arithmetic progression $(1, 2, 3, 4 \ldots)$ and geometric progression $(1, 2, 4, 8 \ldots)$ and maintained that the pitch of sound depended on the speed of vibration of air. He was right, but he did not quite have the concept of wave motion. He believed that sounds of high pitch traveled faster through the air, bodily, than sounds of low pitch, which was wrong.

He is also supposed to have invented the pulley.

[26] THEAETETUS (thee'uh-tee'tus)
Greek mathematician
Born: Athens, about 417 B.C.
Died: Athens, 369 B.C.

Theaetetus was the son of a rich Athenian whose money was apparently squandered by those in charge of it before it could reach the young heir. Despite that, he had apparently the advantage of the kind of education and upbringing that wealth could bring, studying at Plato's Academy. Plato [24] thought enough of him, apparently, to make him a character in two of his dialogues, one of them called "Theaetetus." He died in action in battle against the city of Corinth in one of the endless stupid wars the Greek cities fought against each other in those days.

The Pythagoreans had discovered the irrationality of the square root of two. Theaetetus apparently systematized the study of these irrationals to show that there were large numbers of them and, apparently, an infinite number. That rather drew the fangs of their mystery. One is an anomaly; many are normal.

He studied the five regular solids of Plato and may have been the first to demonstrate that there were, in fact, only those five and that no other regular polygons could exist.

[27] EUDOXUS (yoo-dok'sus)
Greek astronomer and mathematician
Born: Cnidus (on what is now the Turkish coast), about 400 B.C.
Died: Cnidus, about 347 B.C.

Eudoxus studied under Archytas [25] and also at Plato's [24] Academy under difficult circumstances. Being poor, he lived in Piraeus, Athens' port city, where quarters could be obtained more cheaply. This meant he had to walk five miles to school every morning and five miles back every evening.

After graduating, he traveled to Egypt for what we would today call postgraduate work in astronomy. Thereafter he established a school of his own in Cyzicus on the northwestern coast of what is now Turkey. Eventually he transferred it to Athens, where he taught for many years. As a now successful and established philosopher, he visited his old teacher Plato again and was rewarded with a banquet in his honor. (He may even have served as active head of the Academy while Plato was in Sicily in 367 B.C.)

During those years he introduced many geometric proofs that later found their way into the summarizing work of Euclid [40]. He also began to work with systematic approximations of lengths and areas that could not be determined directly, something developed further a century later by Archimedes [47].

Eudoxus accepted Plato's notion that the planets moved in perfect circles as a matter of necessity, but, having observed the motions of the planets, he could not help but realize that the *actual* planetary motions were *not* those of objects moving evenly in perfect circles.

He was the first to try to adjust Plato's theory to actual observation to "save the appearances" as it was called. He suggested that the sphere into which a planet was set had its poles set into another sphere which had its poles set into still another sphere and so on. Each sphere rotated evenly, but the combination of speeds and the inclination of the poles of one sphere to those of the next resulted in the overall motion of the planet being the irregular one that was actually observed. Thus, by combining perfect regularities, the observed imperfection of irregularity was achieved. The appearances were saved, and so was Plato.

Eudoxus also drew a new map of the earth, better than that of Hecataeus [9] and was the first Greek to attempt a map of the stars. He divided the sky, for this purpose, into degrees of latitude and longitude, a notion eventually transferred to the surface of the earth itself. In later centuries, Cicero considered Eudoxus the greatest of the Greek astronomers, though this may be unjust to Hipparchus [50].

Unfortunately, none of the writings of Eudoxus survive.

[28] **HERACLEIDES** (her-uh-kly'deez)
   Greek astronomer
   Born: Heraclea Pontus (modern Bander Eregli, on Black Sea shore about 150 miles east of Istanbul, Turkey), about 388 B.C.
   Died: Athens, 315 B.C.

Heracleides (often called Heracleides Ponticus after his birthplace) traveled to Athens as a young man, for it was then the center of the philosophic universe, and studied in Plato's Academy. He must have done well, for there is a story that when Plato [24] went to Sicily in his ill-fated venture to make a king a philosopher, Heracleides was left in charge of the school (other stories say Eudoxus [27] was).

Heracleides wrote a good deal on astronomy and geometry, but little of his work survives. He is known today only for certain suggestions in astronomy that were very important, although they remained uninfluential in his own time.

The heavenly objects generally, and in particular the fixed stars, take part in an even rotation about the earth from east to west. It had always been assumed that this apparent rotation was a real one, that the vault of heaven actually turned. Heracleides pointed out that the same effect would be observed if the heavens stood still and if the earth rotated about its axis from west to east once every day. Heracleides was the first man we know of to suggest the rotation of the earth, but the idea was not to become dominant in the world of astronomy until the time of Copernicus [127], eighteen hundred years later.

Against the background of the stars (considered as unmoving points), the sun, moon, and five known planets— Mercury, Venus, Mars, Jupiter, Saturn— moved from west to east in rather erratic fashion. It was this erratic west-to-east

motion superimposed on the motion of the starry vault that Eudoxus had tried to explain by assigning each body a number of separate spheres.

Of these various bodies, the motions of two, Mercury and Venus, were peculiar in that they were never very far from the position of the sun. The spheres of Eudoxus could explain this, at least approximately, but it seemed to Heracleides that a more straightforward explanation was the supposition that Mercury and Venus revolved about the sun and therefore could not depart very far from that body.

Heracleides kept the earth in the center of the universe but was nevertheless the first to suggest the revolution of one heavenly body about another. He differed from Philolaus [19] in suggesting a revolution about a visible and actual body, the sun, and not about a mystical and unseen one such as the "central fire."

This beginning of a heliocentric theory was carried further by Aristarchus [41] a century later but lost out to the contrary views of Hipparchus [50]. This portion of Heracleides' concept had also to await Copernicus for vindication.

[29] **ARISTOTLE** (ar'is-totl)
   Greek philosopher
   Born: Stagira (in northern Greece), 384 B.C.
   Died: Chalcis (on the Aegean island of Euboea, now Evvoia), 322 B.C.

Inland from Stagira was the semi-Greek kingdom of Macedon, with which Aristotle's family was closely connected. Aristotle's father, for instance, had been court physician to the Macedonian king, Amyntas II. Aristotle lost both parents while a child and was brought up by a friend of the family. He is supposed to have spoken with a lisp and to have been something of a dandy.

At the age of seventeen Aristotle traveled to Athens for a college education and after Plato [24] returned from Syracuse, the young man joined Plato's Academy, where he studied assiduously.

Eventually he was to become by far the most renowned of all the pupils of Plato. Plato called him "the intelligence of the school."

When Plato died in 347 B.C., Aristotle left the school. The reason he gave was that he disapproved of the growing emphasis on mathematics and theory in the Academy and the continuing decline in natural philosophy. However, it is possible that he may have been displeased that Plato, on his deathbed, designated his nephew, an undistinguished person, as his successor, passing over the merits of Aristotle. It is also true that Athens and Macedon were enemies at the time and Aristotle may have felt uneasily conscious of being considered pro-Macedonian.

In any case Aristotle found it expedient to set out upon a journey that carried him to various parts of the Greek world, particularly to Asia Minor. While there he married and engaged in the study of biology and natural history, always his chief love.

In 342 B.C. he was called to Macedon. The son of Amyntas II had succeeded to the throne of Macedon as Philip II while Aristotle was at the Academy, and now the king wanted the son of his father's physician back at court. The purpose was to install him as tutor for his fourteen-year-old son, Alexander. Aristotle held this position for several years. Since Alexander was to become Alexander the Great, the conqueror of Persia, we have the spectacle of the greatest soldier of ancient times being tutored by the greatest thinker.

In 336 B.C. Philip II was assassinated and his son succeeded as Alexander III. Alexander had no further time for education so Aristotle left Macedon the next year and went back to Athens, while Alexander went on to invade the Persian Empire in a great conquering campaign. Aristotle's nephew, Callisthenes, accompanied Alexander, but Aristotle's influence over his erstwhile pupil was not very great for in 327 B.C. Callisthenes was executed by the increasingly megalomaniac monarch.

Meanwhile, in Athens, Aristotle founded a school of his own, the Lyceum, so called because Aristotle lectured in a hall near the temple to Apollo Lykaios (Apollo, the Wolf-God). It was also called the "peripatetic school" ("walk about") because Aristotle, at least on occasion, lectured to students while walking in the school's garden. He also built up a collection of manuscripts, a very early example of a "university library." It was this which eventually served as the kernel for the great Library at Alexandria.

The school continued under Aristotle's directorship quite successfully, emphasizing natural philosophy. In 323 B.C., however, the news arrived of the death of Alexander the Great in Babylon. Since Aristotle was well known to have been Alexander's tutor, he feared that an anti-Macedonian reaction in Athens might lead to trouble. And, indeed, the accusation of "impiety" was raised. Aristotle had no mind to suffer the fate of Socrates [21]. Saying he would not allow Athens to "sin twice against philosophy" he prudently retired to Chalcis, his mother's hometown, and died there the next year.

Aristotle's lectures were collected into nearly a hundred and fifty volumes and represent almost a one-man encyclopedia of the knowledge of the times, much of it representing the original thought and observation of Aristotle himself. Nor was it confined entirely to science, for Aristotle dealt with politics, literary criticism, and ethics. Altogether, of the volumes attributed to him, some fifty have survived (not all of which are certainly authentic), a survival record second only to that of Plato.

This survival came about through a fortunate chance. Many of his manuscripts were found in a pit in Asia Minor about 80 B.C. by men in the army of the Roman general Sulla. They were then taken to Rome and recopied.

The one field for which Aristotle is not noted is mathematics, but even here he may be credited with a glancing blow, for he is the virtual founder of the systematic study of logic, which is allied to mathematics. He developed, in great and satisfying detail, the art of reasoning from statement to necessary conclusion and thereby demonstrating the validity of a line of thought. His system stood without major change until the nineteenth-century development of symbolic logic by Boole [595], which converted logic into a branch of mathematics in form as well as spirit.

Aristotle's most successful scientific writings were those on biology. He was a careful and meticulous observer who was fascinated by the task of classifying animal species and arranging them into hierarchies. He dealt with over five hundred animal species in this way and dissected nearly fifty of them. His mode of classification was reasonable and, in some cases, strikingly modern. He was particularly interested in sea life and observed that the dolphin brought forth its young alive and nourished the fetus by means of a special organ called a placenta. No fish did this, but all mammals did, so Aristotle classed the dolphin with the beasts of the field rather than with the fish of the sea. His successors did not follow his lead, however, and it took two thousand years for biologists to catch up to Aristotle in this respect. It was J. Müller [522] who finally confirmed Aristotle in this respect. Aristotle also studied viviparous sharks, those that bear live young—but without a mammalian placenta.

He also noted the odd ability of the torpedo fish to stun its prey though, of course, he knew nothing of the electric shock with which it managed it. He was also wrong on occasion, as when he denied sexuality in plants. Nineteen centuries were to pass before Alpini [160] was to correct this particular error.

His formation of a hierarchy of living things led him irresistibly toward the idea that animals represented a chain of progressive change, a sort of evolution. Other Greek philosophers groped similarly in this direction. However, barring any knowledge as to the physical mechanism whereby evolutionary changes could be brought about, such theories invariably became mystical. A rational theory of evolution had to await Darwin [554], twenty-two hundred years after the time of Aristotle.

Aristotle studied the developing embryo of the chick and the complex stomach of cattle. He decided that no animal had both tusks and horns, and that no single-hooved animal had horns. But his intuition sometimes led him astray. He believed the heart was the center of life and considered the brain merely a cooling organ for the blood.

In physics Aristotle was far less successful than in biology, perhaps because he was too Platonic. He accepted the heavenly spheres of Eudoxus [27] and Callippus [32] and even added further to them, reaching a total of 54. He seemed to think of the spheres as having an actual physical existence whereas Eudoxus probably thought of them as imaginary aids to calculation, as we consider the lines of latitude and longitude we draw on a map. Aristotle also accepted the four elements of Empedocles [17] but restricted them to the earth itself. He suggested a fifth element, "aether," of which all the heavens were composed. (We still use phrases such as "ethereal heights" today.)

This line of reasoning led him to agree with the Pythagoreans that earth and heaven were subjected to two different sets of natural law. On the earth all things were changeable and corrupt, while in the heavens all was permanent and unchanging. On earth the four elements each had its own place, and motion was an attempt to reach that place. Earth was in the center, water above it, air above that, and fire highest of all the earthly substances. Therefore an object composed largely of earth, such as a rock, would, if suspended in air, fall downward, while bubbles of air trapped underwater would move upward. Again, rain fell, but fire rose.

It also seemed to Aristotle that the heavier an object was, the more eagerly it would strive to achieve its proper place, since the heaviness was the manifestation of its eagerness to return. Hence a heavier object would fall more rapidly than a lighter one. (Nineteen centuries later, a reconsideration of this problem by Galileo [166] was to lead to momentous consequences.)

The motion of heavenly objects, on the other hand, was no attempt to get anywhere. It was a steady, permanent motion, even and circular.

Aristotle, apparently, was not an experimentalist for all that he was a close observer. He observed that rocks fell more quickly than feathers, but he made no attempt to arrange an observation of the falling of rocks of graded weight. Furthermore, neither he nor any other ancient scholar properly appreciated the importance of precise, quantitative measurement. This was not mere perversity on their part, for the state of instrumentation was rudimentary indeed in ancient times and there were few clear methods of making accurate measurements. In particular, they could not measure small intervals of time accurately, a deficiency that was to remain for two thousand years until the time of Huygens [215].

Aristotle rejected Democritus' atomism, dooming that concept through ancient and medieval times. On the other hand, he accepted the Pythagorean notion of the roundness of the earth, presenting his reasoning in a fashion that remains valid today. The most telling argument was that as one travels north, new stars appear at the northern horizon while old ones disappear at the southern. If the earth were flat, all stars would be equally visible from all points on its surface. It was Aristotle's championing of this view that kept it alive through the darkest days that were to follow.

Upon Aristotle's retirement, leadership of the Lyceum fell to his friend and pupil Theophrastus [31] and after him to Strato [38], under whom the Lyceum continued to be a vital and progressive force.

Aristotle's system of philosophy was never as influential in ancient times as Plato's. Indeed, Aristotle's works may not have been published for some centuries after his death. After the fall of Rome, his work was largely lost to Europe (only *Organon*, his work on logic, was saved) while Plato's works were, for the most part, retained. However, Aristotle's books survived among the Arabs, who valued them highly.

Christian Europe regained Aristotle from the Arabs, translating his books into Latin in the twelfth and thirteenth centuries. From that time Aristotle replaced Plato as *the* Philosopher. His views came to be regarded as possessing an almost divine authority, so that if Aristotle said it was so, it was *so*. By a queer fatality, it almost seemed as though his statements were most accepted when they were most incorrect.

This cannot be blamed on Aristotle, who was himself no believer in blind obedience to authority. Nevertheless, following the era of over-adulation, he became the very symbol of wrongness, and when the Scientific Revolution took place in the sixteenth and seventeenth centuries, its first victories involved the overthrow of Aristotelian physics. In the centuries since, Aristotle has, as a consequence, too often been viewed as an enemy of science, whereas actually he was one of the truly great scientists of all time and even his wrongness was rational. No man should be blamed for the stubborn orthodoxy of those who many centuries later insist they speak in his name.

[30] **MENAECHMUS** (mih-nek′mus)
Greek mathematician
Born: about 380 B.C.
Died: date unknown

Nothing is known of Menaechmus' life except that he may have been a student of Eudoxus [27].

He seems to have been the first to take up the geometry of the cone systematically and to show that ellipses, parabolas and hyperbolas are all curves produced by the intersection of a cone and a plane. This work was continued by Archimedes [47] and Apollonius [49] and was to be given startling and profound application to the real universe by Newton [231].

[31] **THEOPHRASTUS** (thee-oh-fras′-tus)
Greek botanist
Born: Eresus, Lesbos (an Aegean island), about 372 B.C.
Died: Athens, about 287 B.C.

21

Theophrastus came to Athens at an early age to study under Plato [24]. Aristotle [29] first met Theophrastus on Lesbos, during the period after Plato's death, and a lifelong friendship ensued. In fact, Theophrastus ("divine speech") is really a nickname bestowed upon the man by Aristotle because of the latter's delight in his conversation. His real name was Tyrtamus.

Theophrastus conducted the Lyceum after Aristotle's retirement and served as guardian of his old teacher's children. He inherited Aristotle's library and remained in charge of the school until his own death thirty-five years later. The school was at its peak of prosperity under him and is supposed to have had as many as two thousand students.

Theophrastus carried on the Aristotelian tradition of biology, concentrating chiefly on the plant world and describing over five hundred and fifty species, some from as far away as India, for the conquests of Alexander the Great had opened wider horizons to Greek science.

Theophrastus is usually considered the founder of botany, as Aristotle was the founder of zoology. Two botanical works are all that have survived of some two hundred scientific volumes he produced, one of which was a general history of science that would have been priceless if but one copy had survived.

As it is, he is best known for no scientific work at all, however, but for a delightful series of character portraits that bear the mark of universality. The human "types" satirized by Theophrastus are easily recognized today.

[32] **CALLIPPUS** (kuh-lip'us)
    Greek astronomer
    Born: Cyzicus, about 370 B.C.
    Died: about 300 B.C.

Callippus, having studied under Eudoxus [27], improved on his master. His observations of planetary movements showed him that the spheres of Eudoxus, even though they numbered twenty-six in all, did not exactly account for reality no matter how their movements were adjusted. He added eight more spheres, making thirty-four in all.

He also measured the length of the seasons accurately and obtained a measure of the year that was closer to the true value than was that of Oenopides [18].

[33] **DICAEARCHUS** (dy-see-ahr'kus)
    Greek geographer
    Born: Messina, Sicily, about 355 B.C.
    Died: about 285 B.C.

As a young man Dicaearchus went to Athens, studying at the Lyceum under Aristotle [29] and becoming a close friend of Theophrastus [31]. Interested mostly in moral philosophy he nevertheless wrote a history of Greece and a geography in which he described the world in words and maps, being the first to consider such a map as part of a sphere.

He estimated the heights of Greek mountains and showed they did not upset the notion of the sphericity of the earth by arguing that their height was very small compared to the width of the terrestrial sphere.

He had the advantage of being able to use the descriptions brought back by the far-ranging officers of Alexander the Great. Dicaearchus' most notable contribution was that of being the first to draw a line of latitude from east to west across his maps, this marking the fact that all points on that line saw the noonday sun (on any given day) at an equal angle from the zenith.

[34] **DIOCLES** (dy'uh-kleez)
    Greek physician
    Born: Carystus, Euboea, about 350 B.C.
    Died: date unknown

Diocles, the son of a physician, was held in great esteem by the ancients as second only to Hippocrates [22] himself. He studied at the Lyceum under Aristotle [29].

He may have been the first to assemble the writings of the Hippocratic school, and he made use of them in his own works, of which fragments survive. He is thought to have been the first person to write a book on anatomy and the first to use the word itself to describe the study. He became prominent enough to treat some of the Macedonian princes and generals of the time of Alexander the Great.

He seems also to have been the first Greek to write a manual on how to recognize different plants, and on how they might be used nutritionally and medically. This book served as the basic authority on pharmacy until it was replaced by that of Dioscorides [59] nearly four centuries later.

[35] EPICURUS (ep-ih-kyoo'rus)
Greek philosopher
Born: Samos, 341 B.C.
Died: Athens, 270 B.C.

Epicurus was the son of an Athenian schoolmaster and, after teaching in various places in the Greek world, he settled in Athens in 306 B.C. There he founded an enormously popular school and established the philosophy known as Epicureanism. This maintained an unbroken tradition for seven centuries until the tide of Christianity in the late Roman Empire washed out all the pagan philosophies. His school was the first to admit women students, which both shocked and titillated the scholarly world of the time.

Epicurus' philosophy was mechanistic and found pleasure the chief human good. Epicurus himself held that the highest pleasure consisted of living moderately and behaving kindly and in removing the fear of the gods and of death. His later followers were more self-indulgent in their definition of pleasure and Epicureanism is nowadays unjustly used as a synonym for hedonism. Epicurus may have been the student of Nausiphanes who was himself a student of Democritus [20]. In any case, Epicurus adopted the atoms of Democritus as a satisfactorily mechanistic explanation of the universe.

Although of his voluminous writings (consisting, supposedly, of three hundred treatises), practically nothing survives, they lasted long enough to convert the Roman Lucretius [53] some two and a half centuries later, and, in turn, Lucretius' writings lasted into modern times. Democritus' atoms, though voted down by philosophers, were never wholly forgotten.

Epicureanism, as a philosophy, endured till nearly the end of the Roman Empire, but then perished with the rise of Christianity.

[36] PRAXAGORAS (prak-sag'oh-ras)
Greek physician
Born: Cos, about 340 B.C.
Died: date unknown

Praxagoras, the son and grandson of physicians, was supposed to have been the teacher of Herophilus [42] and to have been a strong defender of the humoral theory of Hippocrates [22].

Praxagoras distinguished between veins and arteries, recognizing that there were two different kinds of blood vessels, though some attribute this discovery to Alcmaeon [11]. The arteries, however, he thought carried air (they are usually empty in corpses) and the name of these vessels is derived from that belief. He thought moreover they tapered into very fine vessels (which they do) that led into the nerves (which they do not).

He also noted the physical connection between the brain and spinal cord but thought the heart was the seat of the intellect.

[37] KIDDINU
Babylonian astronomer
Born: Babylonia, about 340 B.C.
Died: date unknown

It is certain that Babylonian astronomy was flourishing at a time when Greek astronomy was merely in its beginnings. If the Babylonians did not, to our knowledge, work out the intricate (and often terribly mistaken) theories of the Greeks, they at least had centuries of careful observations to their credit. Their names and individual accomplishments are shadowy indeed, however, so that they are unjustly neglected in a biographical work such as this.

There is mention of Kiddinu in Strabo [56] and Pliny [61], where he is called Kidenas or Cidenas. He was the head of the astronomical school at the Babylonian city of Sippar and worked out the precession of the equinoxes, paving the way for Hipparchus' [50] more accurate work.

He also devised, apparently, complicated methods of expressing the irregular movement of the moon and other planetary bodies, departing from the assumption that they must move at constant velocities (something the Greeks insisted upon) and consequently getting close approximations of their actual movements.

[38] **STRATO** (stray'toh)
Greek physicist
Born: Lampsacus, about 340 B.C.
Died: Athens, about 270 B.C.

Born in the city where two centuries earlier Anaxagoras [14] had died in exile and where Epicurus [35] had taught before moving on to Athens, Strato carried on in the tradition of Asia Minor. In youth, he studied at the Lyceum, then traveled to Alexandria, an Egyptian city founded by Alexander the Great. While there, he is supposed to have tutored the son of Ptolemy I, the Macedonian general who had become Egypt's king. He also helped establish Alexandria as a scientific center, a position it was to hold through the remainder of ancient times.

Strato returned to Athens on the death of Theophrastus [31] to become third director of the Lyceum. Strato was a more advanced physicist than Aristotle [29], was favorable to Democritus' [20] atomic theory, and apparently conducted experiments. He was called Strato Physicus in ancient references.

He described methods for forming a vacuum although he agreed with Aristotle that no vacuum existed in nature. He also agreed that heavier bodies fell faster than lighter ones, and he was the first to argue that, in falling, a body accelerated; that is, moved more quickly with each successive unit of time. (It was the measurement of this acceleration by Galileo [166] that was to mark the birth of the new physics nineteen centuries later.)

Strato also seems to have understood the law of the lever, but he did not work it out as Archimedes [47] was to do later in the century. Where Aristotle had felt that sound traveled by a succession of impacts on air and that sound could not be conducted in the absence of air (he was right), Strato went further and seemed to be on the point of recognizing sound as a wave motion.

After Strato's death the Lyceum declined. Primacy in philosophy remained in Athens with the Platonic Academy, but scientific endeavor was making its home increasingly in Alexandria.

[39] **PYTHEAS** (pith'ee-us)
Greek geographer and explorer
Born: Massalia (modern Marseille, France), about 330 B.C.
Died: date unknown

Pytheas lived in a time of great outflowing of Greek energies. His contemporaries led Greek culture as far east as what are now the nations of Afghanistan and Pakistan.

Pytheas, dwelling in Massalia, westernmost of the Greek-colonized cities of the Mediterranean, turned in the other direction, not at the head of armies, but on board a ship. He sailed westward through the Pillars of Hercules (now the Strait of Gibraltar) and up the northwestern coast of Europe.

His accounts, which have not survived directly but reach us through references in later writers, seem to show that he explored the island of Great Britain and then sailed northward to "Thule," which was possibly Norway. There fog stopped the intrepid navigator and he turned back to explore northern Europe and penetrate the Baltic Sea as far as the Vistula.

Pytheas' accounts, in the main truthful, as nearly as we can tell, were disbelieved by contemporaries, who were much readier to believe fantasies. Even Pliny [61] some centuries later, who routinely swallowed five or six new impossibilities each morning before breakfast, balked at Pytheas' tales and the geographer, Strabo [56] was particularly abusive. A similar fate had befallen Hanno [12] two centuries before Pytheas and was to befall Marco Polo [105] fifteen centuries after Pytheas.

Pytheas was a scientific geographer as well as an explorer. Following the teachings of the contemporary Dicaearchus [33], he determined the latitude of his hometown, Massalia, by careful observations of the sun, and did so with praiseworthy accuracy. He was also the first to point out that the North Star was not exactly at the pole and that it therefore shifted position, making a small circle in the course of a day. He improved on Eudoxus [27] in this respect.

His voyages beyond Gibraltar led him into the open ocean, where he could observe the tides, which in the land-locked Mediterranean were almost nonexistent. What was most amazing was that, being the first Greek to observe real tides, he also produced the correct explanation for them, attributing them to the influence of the moon. In this, however, he was even further ahead of his time, for it was to be two thousand years before this explanation was accepted and then only when Newton [231] had managed to explain lunar attraction as part of a grand scheme of the universe.

[40] **EUCLID** (yoo'klid)
   Greek mathematician
   Born: about 325 B.C.
   Died: Alexandria, about 270 B.C.

Euclid, who may have studied at Plato's [24] Academy in Athens, is another who marks the passage of scientific pre-eminence from Athens to Alexandria. After the death of Alexander the Great, his generals snatched at portions of his empire, fighting among themselves bloodily and inconclusively for a generation. One general, Ptolemy, seized Egypt and established his capital at the new city of Alexandria. He founded a line of kings, all named Ptolemy, that lasted for two and a half centuries. (The last monarch of the line was the famous queen Cleopatra.)

Ptolemy and his immediate successors were patrons of science and labored to establish Alexandria as the intellectual capital of the world. In this, they succeeded. They built a splendid library and a famous university called the Museum, because it was a kind of temple to the Muses, who were the patron goddesses of science and the fine arts. Among the earliest scholars to be attracted to the new establishment was Euclid.

Euclid's name is indissolubly linked to geometry, for he wrote a textbook (*Elements*) on the subject that has been standard, with some modifications, of course, ever since. It went through more than a thousand editions after the invention of printing and it was not so long ago that the phrase "I studied my Euclid" was synonymous with "I studied geometry." Euclid is, therefore, the most successful textbook writer of all time.

And yet, as a mathematician, Euclid's fame is not due to his own research. Few of the theorems in his textbook are his own. What Euclid did, and what made him great, was to take all the knowledge accumulated in mathematics since the days of Thales [3] and codify the two and a half centuries of labor into a single work. In doing so, he evolved, as a starting point, a series of axioms and postulates that were admirable for their brevity and elegance. He then arranged theorem after theorem in a manner so logical as almost to defy improvement. The only theorem that tradition definitely ascribes to Euclid himself is the proof he presented for the Pythagorean theorem.

Although most of his great treatise dealt with geometry, it also took up ratio and proportion and what is now known as the theory of numbers. It was Euclid who proved that the number of primes is infinite. He also proved that the square root of two was irrational (the fact first discovered by Pythagoras [7] and his followers) by a line of argument so neat that it has never been improved upon.

He made optics a part of geometry, too, by dealing with light rays as though they were straight lines.

Of course Euclid does not include all of Greek mathematics, or even all of Greek geometry. Greek mathematics remained vital for a considerable time after Euclid, and such men as Apollonius [49] and Archimedes [47] added a great deal.

Yet Euclid as an individual remains an impenetrable mystery. It is not known where or just when he was born or when he died. The figure given here, 325 B.C. is a pure guess, but he did work at Alexandria during the reign of Ptolemy I (305–285 B.C.).

About the only personal aspect of Euclid's life that reaches us is his reported remark to King Ptolemy when the latter, studying geometry, asked if Euclid couldn't make his demonstrations a little easier to follow. Euclid said, uncompromisingly, "There is no royal road to geometry." There is also a doubtful legend that gives him a shrewish wife.

For many centuries it was considered that there was something objectively and eternally true about the principles of mathematics and, in particular, about the axioms on which Euclid's work was based: that the whole is equal to the sum of its parts, for instance, or that a straight line is the shortest distance between two points. It was only in the nineteenth century that it came to be realized that axioms are merely agreed-upon statements rather than absolute truths. Mathematics was broadened by men such as Lobachevski [484] and Riemann [670], and non-Euclidean geometries, on which the theories of Einstein [1064] came to be based, were developed.

[41] **ARISTARCHUS** (ar-is-tahr′kus)
      Greek astronomer
      Born: Samos, about 310 B.C.
      Died: Alexandria, about 230 B.C.

Virtually nothing is known about the personal life of Aristarchus except that he must have come to Alexandria, then the Mecca for scientists, in his youth and

may have studied under Strato [38]. Enough is known about his work, however, to stamp him as the most original and, from the modern view, successful of the Greek astronomers.

Aristarchus combined the Pythagorean view of the moving earth with the contention of Heracleides [28] that some planets moved about the sun. Aristarchus pointed out, about 260 B.C., that the motions of the heavenly bodies could easily be interpreted if it were assumed that all the planets, including the earth, revolved about the sun. Since the stars seemed motionless, except for the diurnal motion due to the rotating earth, they must be infinitely far away.

Because of this view, Aristarchus has been known as the Copernicus of Antiquity and, indeed, Copernicus [127] seems to have known of Aristarchus' views, mentioning them in a passage he later eliminated, as though not wishing to compromise his own originality.

Aristarchus' heliocentric hypothesis was too revolutionary to be accepted by the scholars of his time and his book on the subject did not survive. His theory would be forgotten today but for the mention of it in the writings of Archimedes [47] and of Plutarch, the Greek historian.

The age was sufficiently enlightened, however, to protect Aristarchus from the dangers that had befallen Anaxagoras [14] two and a half centuries earlier for much less radical views. Yet, at least one important philosopher of the time, Cleanthes the Stoic, accused him of impiety and believed he should be made to suffer for it.

From Aristarchus' own writings we know of work he did to determine the size and distance of the moon and sun. At the moment when the moon is exactly half-illuminated, the earth, moon, and sun must occupy the apices of a right triangle. By geometry one can then determine the relative lengths of the sides of the triangle and determine the ratio of the distance of the sun from the earth (the hypotenuse of the triangle) to the distance of the moon from the earth (the short leg of the triangle). In theory this method is correct, but unfortunately

Aristarchus had no instruments capable of measuring angles accurately and his estimates of what those angles must be were rather off. He concluded that the sun was about twenty times as far as the moon, whereas in fact it is about four hundred times as far.

Aristarchus then worked out the actual size of the moon by noting the size of the shadow thrown by the earth during an eclipse of the moon. By a correct line of argument, again marred by the inaccuracy of his measurements, he concluded that the moon had a diameter one-third that of the earth. This is only a slight overestimate. If the sun were twenty times as distant as the moon, and yet the same size in appearance, it must be twenty times the diameter of the moon or about seven times the diameter of the earth.

Actually we now know the sun is over a hundred times the diameter of the earth, but even Aristarchus' too-small value was enough to make it seem illogical, to him, that the sun revolved about the earth. It seemed to him that the smaller object should revolve about the larger.

Unfortunately this logic, which seemed so solid to him (and which seems so solid to us), did not impress his contemporaries.

[42] **HEROPHILUS** (hee-rof'ih-lus)
Greek anatomist
Born: Chalcedon (the modern Kadiköy, a suburb of Istanbul, Turkey), about 320 B.C.
Died: date unknown

The biological sciences as well as the physical ones reached new heights in Alexandria's early days. Working there, Herophilus, who may have studied under Praxagoras [36], established himself as the first careful anatomist and the first to perform dissections in public, perhaps as many as six hundred altogether. He labored hard to compare the human mechanism with that of animals. There was no serious objection among the Greeks to anatomical dissections in those pre-Christian days and indeed the Platonic view was that the body of man meant very little in comparison with his soul. The dead body was then a mere lump of flesh that could be cut with impunity. To the Egyptian natives, however, human dissection was a serious impiety. (Some centuries later the early Christian Fathers held it as an example of pagan cruelty that vivisections—the dissections of living bodies—were performed. This was taken from statements by Celsus [57] and was probably exaggeration. It seems quite certain that deliberate vivisection was not practiced. Even ordinary dissection of dead bodies was all too limited, or the ancients wouldn't have made some of their anatomical errors.)

Herophilus was particularly interested in describing the brain. He divided nerves into sensory (those which received sense impressions) and motor (those which stimulated motion). He also described the liver and spleen. He described and named the retina of the eye and he named the first section of the small intestine, the duodenum. His investigation of the genital system led to a description of the ovaries and of the tubes leading to the ovaries from the uterus. He also observed and named the prostate gland.

He noted that arteries, unlike veins, pulsate and timed the pulsations with a water clock, but he failed to see the connection between this arterial pulse and the heartbeat. He held that the arteries carried blood and he also felt that bloodletting had therapeutic value. This emphasis on bleeding was to have a deleterious effect on medicine for two thousand years. His work was worthily carried on by his successor Erasistratus [43], but thereafter the Alexandrian school of anatomy declined.

[43] **ERASISTRATUS** (er-uh-sis'tra-tus)
Greek physician
Born: Chios (now Khios; an Aegean island), about 304 B.C.
Died: Mycale, about 250 B.C.

Erasistratus, according to tradition, was trained in Athens, then traveled to Asia where he served as court physician for Seleucus I, who controlled the major portion of what had once been the Persian Empire.

Erasistratus then moved west, where he continued the work of Herophilus [42] at Alexandria. In later life, Erasistratus devoted himself to research and, according to tradition, committed suicide when afflicted with an incurable ulcer in the foot.

He, too, paid particular attention to the brain, which he described as being divided into a larger (cerebrum) and smaller (cerebellum) part. He compared the convolutions in the brain of man with those of animals and decided (correctly) that the complexity of the convolutions was related to intelligence.

He noticed the association of nerves with arteries and veins and imagined that each organ of the body was fed by all three, each of them, nerve, artery, and vein, bringing its own fluid to the organ.

The nerve, which he and others of the time believed to be hollow, carried "nervous spirit," according to this view; the artery, "animal spirit"; and the vein, blood. He took a step backward from Herophilus' views by denying that the arteries carried blood. On the other hand, he believed that air was carried from the lungs to the heart and changed into the "animal spirit" that was carried in the arteries. If we remember that it is oxygen that is carried by the blood and relate oxygenated hemoglobin with "animal spirit" and ordinary hemoglobin with blood, his views are not so wrong. The difference is mainly one of semantics.

In fact, Erasistratus came near to grasping the notion of the circulation of the blood, but not quite. That concept had to wait two millennia for Harvey [174]. He also refused to accept the erroneous humor theory of disease which had been made popular by Hippocrates [22]. Unfortunately, Galen [65] returned to it and that proved decisive for the next fifteen centuries.

Tradition makes Erasistratus a grandson of Aristotle [29] and a pupil of Theophrastus [31]. If so, he broke with his grandfather's views and accepted the atomism of Democritus. Indeed, Erasistratus believed that all body functions were mechanical in nature. Digestion, for instance, he thought to result from the grinding of food by the stomach. Two thousand years later Borelli [191] was to revive this notion.

Egyptian objections to human dissection prevailed, however, and after the promising start made by Herophilus and Erasistratus, the study of anatomy declined, not to be revived until the time of Mondino de' Luzzi [110], fifteen centuries later.

[44] CONON (koh'non)
    Greek mathematician
    Born: Samos, about 300 B.C.
    Died: Alexandria, date unknown

Conon was a pupil of Euclid [40], according to tradition, and a teacher of Archimedes [47]. It is possible that the mathematical curve usually ascribed to Archimedes and called, therefore, the "spiral of Archimedes" was actually first studied by Conon.

Conon is best known for a piece of conscienceless flattery. It seems that about 245 B.C., Ptolemy III, king of Egypt, was off to the wars and Berenice, his queen, dedicated her hair at the temple of Aphrodite in order to persuade that goddess to bring him home safe and victorious.

The hair disappeared, undoubtedly stolen by souvenir hunters, but Conon smoothly assured the sorrowing queen that Aphrodite had snatched the hair up to heaven where it now hung as a brand-new constellation. He pointed out a group of dim stars not previously honored by the attention of astronomers and that group is known as Coma Berenices ("Berenice's Hair") to this day.

[45] PHILON (figh'lon)
    Greek engineer
    Born: Byzantium, about 300 B.C.
    Died: date unknown

Like Hero [60], Philon experimented with air in a decidedly modern fashion and came to conclusions that were remarkable but were ignored by the philosophers of the time.

He found that air expanded with heat, and he may even have groped toward the beginnings of an air thermometer as Galileo [166] was to do thirteen centuries later. He also found that some air in a closed vessel was consumed by a burning torch, an observation from which Lavoisier [334] was to draw revolutionary conclusions fifteen centuries later.

He studied catapults carefully and since these were war weapons, those researches were given more notice. He also wrote on the art of besieging a city and of defending it against siege. A book he wrote on secret messages and cryptography is lost.

[46] CTESIBIUS (teh-sib′ee-us)
Greek inventor
Born: about 300 B.C.
Died: date unknown

Ctesibius founded the engineering tradition at Alexandria, a tradition which was to reach its peak with Hero [60] one century later. In the intellectually arrogant Greek world, Ctesibius came by his practical interests legitimately, for he was the son of a barber and his first invention was for his father's benefit. He supplied the barber's mirror with a lump of lead as a counterweight so that it could more easily be raised and lowered. The lead counterweight was concealed in a pipe, and when it moved rapidly through the pipe a squeaking noise was made. It occurred to Ctesibius that a musical instrument could be built on this basis. He therefore constructed a water organ in which air was forced through different organ pipes not by a falling lead weight, but by the weight of water. He made use of weights of water and of compressed air in other ways as well, to construct an air-powered catapult, for instance. He undoubtedly had the "feel" of a mechanical age, but he lacked the proper inanimate power to work with. Hero was to discover steam power but by then the moment had passed, not to return until the time of Newcomen [243]

and Watt [316] some seventeen centuries later.

The most famous invention of Ctesibius, however, was his improvement of the ancient Egyptian clepsydra, or water clock. In this, water dripping into a container at a steady rate raised a float which held a pointer that marked a position on a drum. From that position the hour could be read. The drum was ingeniously adjusted so that it could be used at various times of the year. (The day and night were each divided into twelve equal hours at all times, which meant that in summer the hours of day were long and those of night were short, while in winter it was the other way around.)

The water clock was the best of the ancient timepieces. The mechanical clocks of the Middle Ages, run by falling weights, were more convenient, but no more accurate. It was not until the pendulum clock of Huygens [215], eighteen centuries after the time of Ctesibius, that the clepsydra was finally outclassed.

None of Ctesibius' writings have survived and we know of him only through references in Vitruvius [55] and Hero.

[47] ARCHIMEDES (ahr-kih-mee′deez)
Greek mathematician and engineer
Born: Syracuse, Sicily, about 287 B.C.
Died: Syracuse, about 212 B.C.

Archimedes, the son of an astronomer, was the greatest scientist and mathematician of ancient times, and his equal did not arise until Newton [231] two thousand years later. Archimedes studied in Alexandria, where his teacher Conon [44] had, in his own time, been a pupil of Euclid [40]. In an unusual move for those days, Archimedes chose not to remain there but to return to his native town. This may have been the result of his relationship with the Syracusan king, Hieron II. Archimedes was an aristocrat and a man of independent means and did not require the support of the Egyptian royal house for his work.

No scientist of ancient times, not even

Thales [3], had so many stories told about him; and all the stories are so good that it seems cruel to question their authenticity. As a small example, tales of his absent-mindedness were lovingly retailed and it was said that in concentrating on his thoughts, he could not remember whether he had eaten or not. (Similar stories are told of more recent mathematicians, such as Newton and Wiener [1175]).

To pass on to something of importance, however, Hieron was supposed to have asked his bright relative to determine whether a crown just received from the goldsmith was really all gold, as it was supposed to be, or whether it contained a grafting admixture of silver. Archimedes was strictly warned to make the determination without damaging the crown.

Archimedes was at a loss as to how to proceed until one day, stepping into his full bath, he noted that the water overflowed. In a flash it occurred to him that the amount of water that overflowed was equal in volume to that portion of his body which was inserted into the bath. Well, then, if he dipped the crown into water, he could tell by the rise in water level the volume of the crown. He could compare that with the volume of an equal weight of gold. If the volumes were equal, the crown was pure gold. If the crown had an admixture of silver (which is bulkier than gold), it would have a greater volume.

Excited beyond measure by the discovery of this "principle of buoyancy," Archimedes dashed out of the bath and, completely naked, ran through the streets of Syracuse to the palace, shouting, "I've got it! I've got it!" (In connection with this story, it is important to remember that the ancient Greeks were not as disturbed by nakedness as we are.) Since Archimedes shouted in Greek, what he said was "Eureka! Eureka!" and that has been used ever since as the appropriate remark with which to announce a discovery. (The conclusion of the story is that the crown turned out to be partly silver and that the goldsmith was executed.)

Archimedes also worked out the prin-

ciple of the lever. Strato [38] had made use of the principle, but it was Archimedes who worked it out in full mathematical detail. He showed that a small weight at a distance from a fulcrum would balance a large weight near the fulcrum and that the weights and distances were in inverse proportion. (Thus, he founded the science of "statics" and developed the notion of a center of gravity. In thus applying the notion of quantitative measurement of weights and distances to scientific observations, he was two thousand years ahead of his time. In fact, it was the translation of his works into Latin in 1544 that helped inspire renewed efforts in that direction by men such as Stevinus [158] and Galileo [166].)

The principle of the lever explained why a larger boulder could be pried up by a crowbar. The force at the end of the long portion of the crowbar (which is just a form of lever) balanced the force of the large weight at the end of the short portion. Archimedes made another famous remark in this connection by saying: "Give me a place to stand on and I can move the world." (Provided, of course, he also had a lever long enough and rigid enough.)

Hieron is supposed to have questioned this remark and dared him to move something startlingly large, even if not as large as the whole world. Archimedes thereupon hooked up a system of compound levers in pulley form, seated himself comfortably, and without undue effort (the story goes) singlehandedly pulled a fully laden ship out of the harbor and up onto the shore.

Archimedes defied the tradition of art for art's sake made popular by Plato [24] and indulged himself in intensely practical interests. He is supposed to have invented a hollow, helical cylinder that, when rotated, could serve as a water pump. It is still called the "screw of Archimedes" (though, to be sure, the Egyptians are supposed to have had the device long before the time of Archimedes). Archimedes is also supposed to have designed a planetarium in which the motions of the heavenly bodies could be imitated. However, it seems that Archimedes was not exactly proud of his mechanical triumphs, feeling that perhaps they were not the proper work of a philosopher. He therefore published only his mathematical work.

In that field, he calculated a value for pi (the ratio of the length of the circumference of a circle to its diameter) which was better than any other obtained in the classical world. He showed that it lay between $223/71$ and $220/70$. To do this, he used a method of calculating the circumferences and diameters of polygons described inside and outside a circle. As the polygons were given more and more sides, they approached the circle in shape and area. The circumference of the inner polygon grew longer and that of the outer polygon grew shorter while the circumference of the circle was "trapped" between the two. This is very like some of the methods used in calculus much later, and it is often stated that Archimedes would have discovered calculus nearly two thousand years ahead of Newton if he had only had a decent system of mathematical symbols to work with.

Archimedes is also famous for a treatise in which he calculated the number of grains of sand required to fill the entire universe (making some guesses as to what the size of the universe was). He did this mainly to make the point that nothing real existed that was too large to be measured; or, in other words, that nothing finite was infinite. To do so, he made use of a system for expressing large numbers that is almost equivalent to our own exponential notation.

Archimedes did not, however, end his days in peace. In fact, he achieved his greatest fame as a warrior. Rome had, during Archimedes' old age, been at war with Carthage (a city of North Africa) for the second time. The Carthaginian leader was Hannibal, one of the greatest generals of history. He invaded Italy in 218 B.C. and began to enjoy remarkable success.

Hieron II had a treaty of alliance with Rome and remained faithful to that treaty. He died, an extremely old man, and a grandson, Hieronymus, ruled in his place. Rome suffered a disastrous defeat at Cannae and for a time seemed about to be crushed. Hieronymus, anxious to remain on the winning side, switched to that of Carthage. The Romans, however, were not quite through. They sent a fleet, under the general Marcellus, against Syracuse and thus began a strange three-year war of the Roman fleet against one man, Archimedes.

According to tradition the Romans would have taken the city quite quickly had it not been for the ingenious devices brought against their fleet by the great scientist. He is supposed to have constructed large lenses to set the fleet on fire, mechanical cranes to lift the ships and turn them upside down, and so on. In the end, the story goes, the Romans dared not approach the walls too closely and would flee if as much as a rope showed above it, for they were convinced that the dreaded Archimedes was dooming them with some new and monstrous device.

Much of this was undoubtedly exaggerated in the telling, for the later Greeks (such as Plutarch, from whom the story mainly stems) were only too eager to describe how Greek brains held off Roman brawn. Still, the siege *was* a long one and it was not until 212 B.C. that Syracuse was beaten down. (In 202 B.C. came the final victory of Rome over Carthage; the too-clever Hieronymus had guessed wrong after all.)

During the sack of the city, Archimedes, with a magnificent and scholarly disregard for reality, engaged himself in a mathematical problem and was bent over the geometrical figures he had marked in the sand. A Roman soldier ordered him to come along, but Archimedes merely gestured imperiously, "Don't disturb my circles."

The Roman soldier, apparently a practical man with no time for fooling, at once killed Archimedes and went on. Marcellus, who had given orders for Archimedes to be taken alive and treated with distinction (an unusual spirit of generosity for that time—or for any time, perhaps), mourned his death and directed that an honorable burial be given him. He also went out of his way to treat Archimedes' relatives kindly.

Archimedes' tomb was lost track of with time. In 75 B.C., Cicero, the Roman orator, then governing Sicily, reported having found it. Since then, it has been lost to sight once more, though in 1965, Italian archaeologists report a find that possibly is the tomb.

[48] **ERATOSTHENES** (er-uh-tos'-theh-neez)
Greek astronomer
Born: Cyrene (now Shahat, on the Libyan coast), about 276 B.C.
Died: Alexandria, about 196 B.C.

Eratosthenes, who was educated in Athens, was a friend of Archimedes [47] and a man with interests as universal as those of Aristotle [29]. He was not only an astronomer and geographer, he was also a historian. He attempted to set up a scientific chronology in which all events were dated from the Trojan war; he was the first man in history to concern himself with the matter of accurate dating. He was even a literary critic and wrote a treatise on Greek comedy. In fact, he was known by the nickname of Beta, the second letter of the Greek alphabet, for in several of the directions in which he chose to exert his talents, he proved the second best in all the world.

He was the ideal scholar to put in charge of the Library at Alexandria, and after he had graduated from the Athenian schools and had turned out some well-regarded writings, he was summoned to Alexandria by Ptolemy III, about 225 B.C., for precisely that post. He served also as tutor for Ptolemy's son.

In mathematics Eratosthenes worked out a system for determining prime numbers that is still called the "sieve of Eratosthenes." He suggested the introduction of an extra day every fourth year to keep the Egyptian solar calendar in line with the seasons. Egyptian conservatism would not accept that sensible notion and it was not acted upon till the time of Sosigenes [54] a century and a half later.

In geography he made a map of the known world, from the British Isles to Ceylon and from the Caspian Sea to Ethiopia, that was better than any drawn before him, though it was to be succeeded by the still better work of Hipparchus [50] and Strabo [56] in the course of the next two centuries. In astronomy he worked out the angle of the earth's axis to the plane of the sun's apparent motion in the sky and got an almost exact value. This is the determination of the obliquity of the ecliptic. He also prepared a star map that included 675 stars.

However, the astonishing achievement for which Eratosthenes is best known, and for which he remained insufficiently appreciated until modern times, was that of determining the size of the earth about 240 B.C. To do this, he made note of the fact that on the day of the summer solstice, the sun was directly overhead in Syene (the modern Aswan) in southern Egypt at the same time that it was seven degrees from the zenith in Alexandria. This difference could only be due to the curvature of the earth's surface between Syene and Alexandria. Knowing the actual north-south distance between Syene and Alexandria, it was possible to calculate the diameter of the earth, if one assumed it were a sphere with equal curvature on all parts of its surface.

Eratosthenes carried through the calculation and obtained his results in Greek units of distance ("stadia"). We are not certain how long a stadion is in our units. Taking the most probable length, however, it would seem that Eratosthenes calculated the circumference of the earth at a little over twenty-five thousand miles, which is almost correct. From this large figure and the comparatively small area of known land, he suspected the various seas to form a single interconnected ocean, a suspicion that proved true but was not verified till the voyage of Magellan [130] eighteen centuries later.

Unfortunately this figure seemed too large to the ancients. It meant that the known world occupied only a small portion of the earth's total surface, not more than a quarter, and much of that quarter was sea. The other three quarters either contained other lands, unknown and unheard of, or were entirely water. Both alternatives seemed hard to accept, and the smaller value for the earth's circumference, worked out by Poseidonius [52], was accepted by the ancients in preference.

At the age of eighty, Eratosthenes, blind and weary, died of voluntary starvation.

[49] **APOLLONIUS** (ap-uh-loh′nee-us)
Greek mathematician
Born: Perga (on what is now the southern coast of Turkey), about 262 B.C.
Died: Alexandria, Egypt, about 190 B.C.

Apollonius was educated at the Museum, possibly studying under Archimedes [47], and, in the tradition of Euclid [40], wrote an eight-book treatise (of which the first seven books survive) on the "conic sections." These books, which gained him the title of the Great Geometer, include three curves, ellipse, parabola, and hyperbola, with which Euclid did not deal. All of these can be produced by cutting through a cone at particular angles (hence, "conic section").

For many centuries Apollonius' conic sections seemed merely the play of mathematical ingenuity without practical application. In the time of Kepler [169] and Newton [231], however, eighteen centuries later, it was found that the orbits of heavenly bodies were not necessarily circles at all but could follow a path described by any of the conic sections. The most familiar heavenly bodies, the various planets and satellites, including the moon and the earth itself, travel in ellipses.

Apollonius may have tried to compromise the views of Aristarchus [41] and Eudoxus [27] by supposing the planets to revolve about the sun, and the sun with its attendant planets to revolve about the earth. This was similar to the compro-

mise of Tycho Brahe [156] eighteen centuries later, and was just as unsuccessful.

Late in life, Apollonius left Alexandria for Pergamum, a city in western Asia Minor which at this time had a library second only to that of Alexandria.

He was the last topflight mathematician of the ancient world.

[50] **HIPPARCHUS** (hih-pahr′kus)
Greek astronomer
Born: Nicaea (now Iznik, in northwest Turkey), about 190 B.C.
Died: about 120 B.C.

Hipparchus was the greatest of the Greek astronomers as Archimedes [47] was the greatest of the Greek mathematicians, and, like Archimedes, Hipparchus was unusual in that he did not work at Alexandria, although he may have been educated there. He set up his observatory at Rhodes, an island in the southeastern Aegean, and invented many of the instruments used in naked-eye astronomy for the next seventeen centuries.

Hipparchus carried on the work of Aristarchus [41] measuring the size and distance of the sun and moon. He not only made use of Aristarchus' lunar eclipse method, but also determined the moon's parallax. We all experience parallax when we note the apparent shift of the position of a near object compared with a far one when we change our own position. (From a train window we can see the trees nearby move against the background of the trees farther off.)

The angle through which the near object shifts depends both upon the size of your own change of position and upon the distance of the near object. If you know the amount by which you have shifted, you can calculate the distance of the object. To do this, you must know the ratios of the sides of a right triangle for the various angles the sides make with the hypotenuse. The theory was known and some mathematicians managed to work with such ratios. Hipparchus, however, was the first to work out an accurate table of such ratios

33

and is therefore usually considered the founder of trigonometry.

By measuring the position of the moon against the stars under appropriately changing conditions, the moon's parallax can be determined and its distance calculated. He found that distance to be thirty times the diameter of the earth, which is correct. If anyone had used the value for the earth's diameter as determined by Eratosthenes [48], the moon would be shown to be about a quarter million miles from the earth.

Unfortunately no other heavenly body is as close to the earth as the moon, and none, therefore, shows so large a parallax. Before the invention of the telescope, no other heavenly body showed a parallax large enough to be measured. The moon, therefore, remained the only heavenly body with a known distance from the earth for nineteen centuries after Hipparchus.

In 134 B.C. Hipparchus observed a star in the constellation Scorpio of which he could find no record in previous observations. This was a serious matter. Nowadays we know that stars, ordinarily too faint to be seen with the naked eye, do occasionally explode, increase in brightness, and become visible, but in Greek times no such thing was imagined. Instead there was the definite belief that the heavens were permanent and unchangeable. Hipparchus could not easily tell whether this star was an example of the contrary because of the unsystematic nature of previous observations. He decided then that future astronomers would not suffer similar difficulties if a new star should appear and proceeded to record the exact positions of a little over a thousand of the brighter stars. This was the first accurate star map and far outclassed the earlier efforts of Eudoxus [27] and Eratosthenes.

In order to make his map he plotted the position of each star according to its latitude (angular distance north or south of the equator) and longitude (angular distance east or west of some arbitrary point). It was an easy analogy to plot positions on the earth's surface in the same way. Latitude and longitude had been used on maps before, notably by Dicaearchus [33] a century and a half before, but with Hipparchus they became the organized gridwork that they have remained to this day.

Hipparchus' star map led to another important discovery, for in comparing his observations with those he could find among the reports of his predecessors, he found a uniform shift from west to east. He could account for this by supposing that the north celestial pole moved in a slow circle in the sky, completing one cycle in 26,700 years. This meant the equinox arrived a trifling bit earlier each year and the effect was called the "precession of the equinoxes." It was not until the time of Copernicus [127] that it was shown that the reason for this motion was a slow wobble of the earth upon its axis, rather than the star's movement. And it required Newton [231] eighteen centuries after Hipparchus to explain the cause of the precession.

Hipparchus was also the first to divide the stars into classes depending on their brightness. The twenty brightest stars of the sky are of "first magnitude." Then, in order of decreasing brightness there are second, third, fourth, and fifth magnitudes, while those of the sixth magnitude are just visible to the naked eye. This system has been kept (although refined and extended) to the present day.

Hipparchus' most ambitious achievement, however, was to work out a new scheme of the universe, replacing that of Eudoxus. The work of Callippus [32] and Aristotle [29] had filled the heavens with a large number of spheres and the system had become unwieldy. Hipparchus therefore tackled the matter from a fresh viewpoint, one that had been suggested, but not developed, by Apollonius [49] a half century before.

Hipparchus reduced the number of heavenly spheres within the outermost starry celestial vault to seven, one for each of the planets. The individual planet, however, was not actually part of the sphere. It was part of a smaller sphere and it was the center of that smaller sphere that was on the main sphere. The planet moved in a circle as the small sphere turned, and it also moved along in a larger circle as the center of the small sphere turned as part of the large sphere. The large sphere was the "deferent," the small sphere the "epicycle."

By adjusting the speeds of the two spheres, by piling smaller epicycle upon larger epicycle, the actual motion of the planet could be duplicated. Hipparchus also helped matters by introducing the notion of the eccentric; that is, the suggestion that a planet did not move about the earth's center, but about a fictitious point in space that was near the earth's center, and this fictitious point in turn revolved about the earth's center.

The Hipparchian scheme of the universe was highly complicated but it preserved the axioms of Plato and Aristotle, to the effect that the earth was the unmoving center of the universe, and that the planets moved in combinations of circles.

Actually it might seem as though the Aristarchean view of the planets revolving about the sun was much simpler in concept and that it ought to have won out. This is not so. In the first place it was hard to think of the whole earth flying through space (unless you are taught it is so when you are a child and will believe anything). In addition the Hipparchian scheme was useful and the Aristarchean was not. The changing position of the planets was important for ritualistic reasons and in astrology, and what Hipparchus had done was to produce a mathematical system for calculating the positions of the planets at any given future time.

His scheme of epicycles, deferents, and eccentrics helped him perform his calculations, like the construction lines drawn on geometric figures to help arrive at the proof of a theorem. Looking back at it now, we realize there was no reason to think the "construction lines" were real, but for some sixteen centuries astronomers insisted on thinking they were. Whether the construction lines were real or not, however, Hipparchus' methods of calculating planetary positions worked.

On the other hand, the views of Aristarchus in which the planets circled the sun were merely a pretty picture. The system was not, to our knowledge, worked out mathematically to yield predictions of planetary positions. Therefore the scheme was not useful.

When Copernicus finally did work out the mathematics of the Aristarchean universe, the Hipparchian universe was doomed.

[51] SELEUCUS (see-lyoo'kus)
    Greek astronomer
    Born: Seleucia (on the Tigris River), about 190 B.C.
    Died: date unknown

A contemporary of Hipparchus [50], Seleucus was far the inferior, but he was the one astronomer of note who championed the notions of Aristarchus [41] concerning the position of the sun at the center of the planetary system. Hipparchus, with his earth-centered system, won out temporarily (if eighteen centuries can be considered temporary), but it was Seleucus who was right just the same.

Seleucus groped toward an explanation of the tides, feeling that the moon was responsible and noting that the tides did not come at the same time or in the same manner in different parts of the world. He was hampered here by his refusal to accept Eratosthenes' [48] view that the earth's oceans formed a single, interconnected body of water. In this case, he joined Hipparchus in being wrong.

Because Seleucus lived in Babylonia, he was commonly called a Chaldean or Babylonian, but he was probably part Greek in descent at least.

[52] POSEIDONIUS (pos-ih-doh'nee-us)
    Greek philosopher
    Born: Apamea, Syria, about 135 B.C.
    Died: about 50 B.C.

Poseidonius was a Stoic philosopher who studied at Athens, later headed a school at Rhodes and had great and influential friends among the Romans.

Cicero and Pompey were among his pupils. Some of his scientific researches were valuable, for he, like Pytheas [39] two and a half centuries earlier, believed the moon caused the tides and he traveled west to the Atlantic Ocean to study them. He also worked out a size for the sun that was larger (and therefore closer to the truth) than that proposed by any other ancient astronomer, even Aristarchus [41], and was the first astronomer to take into account the refraction of the atmosphere in making his observations. He tried, like Aristotle [29] and Eratosthenes [48] before him, to take all knowledge for his province but was less successful, partly because of the accumulation of knowledge in the two centuries since Aristotle.

However, his real importance in history lies in an erroneous determination he made. He repeated the work of Eratosthenes in determining the size of the earth. He used the position of the star Canopus in place of the sun, which was, indeed, an improvement over Eratosthenes. Poseidonius, however, apparently neglected, in this case, to allow for the shift in the star's position with atmospheric refraction of light and he therefore obtained the too-low figure of eighteen thousand miles for the earth's circumference. (It is also possible that Strabo [56], the only source we have for this, for Poseidonius' own works have not survived, misquoted him a half century later.)

However that might be, Ptolemy [64] accepted the lower figure in preference to Eratosthenes' value, and the world of scholarship went along with that decision until the beginning of modern times. Columbus [121], for instance, was encouraged to sail westward from Spain because he believed the lower value and thought Asia lay only three or four thousand miles westward. Had he known that Eratosthenes was correct and that it lay twelve thousand miles westward, he would probably never have dreamed of sailing, and if he had, he would certainly have got no one to finance him.

In addition Poseidonius helped popularize the doctrines of astrology (that planetary positions influence human affairs) and make them respectable. Plato [24] was mystical enough to lean in that direction, but astronomers such as Eudoxus [27] had opposed it. With Poseidonius, astrology won and its pernicious influence over true astronomy was to endure seventeen centuries, into the time of Kepler [169].

[53] **LUCRETIUS** (lyoo-kree′shee-us);
in full, TITUS LUCRETIUS
CARUS
Roman philosopher and poet
Born: Rome, about 95 B.C.
Died: Rome, about 55 B.C.

From 200 B.C. onward, Rome dominated the Mediterranean world politically, militarily, and economically, but never intellectually. Leadership in science was left in Greek hands to the very end of ancient times. When Roman thinkers did concern themselves with science, it was as transmitters rather than as originators.

Lucretius was the best of these. He was a convinced and ardent follower of Epicurus [35]. In his book *De Natura Rerum* ("On the Nature of Things"), published in 56 B.C., he expounded a mechanistic Epicurean view of the universe in a long poem.

Lucretius held that all things were composed of atoms, quite in line with the theories of Democritus [20], and this he carried to the ultimate extreme. Even such immaterial objects as the mind and soul, said Lucretius, are made up of atoms, which are, however, finer than the atoms making up gross material things.

Lucretius did not deny the existence of gods, but held that they too were composed of atoms and that they did not concern themselves with the affairs of men. Nor did he believe in a life hereafter, but considered death the prelude to peaceful nothingness and therefore not to be feared.

Lucretius envisaged an evolutionary universe, one that developed slowly to its present state, physically, biologically, and sociologically—quite a modern view. He was the first to divide human history, for instance, into a Stone Age, a Bronze Age, and an Iron Age.

Nothing is known of his life except what is drawn from a small handful of references from later writers. From Saint Jerome, writing four and a half centuries later, we learn that he had intervals of insanity, and he is supposed to have died a suicide during one of them, brought on perhaps by a love philter given him by his wife.

It is doubtful whether we ought to accept this, although it is constantly being cited. There is no reference to this earlier and it may have been a tale invented out of distaste for the man and out of a kind of glee that his end should have been so un-genteel. After all, Lucretius was the boldest spokesman in the ancient world of antireligious views. His book was specifically intended to lift what he considered the burden of religious fears from the backs of mankind. He was indeed a lonely voice crying in the wilderness in this respect and the pious of ancient times viewed him much as those of later times viewed Voltaire [261].

Lucretius' poem barely survived. It was lost throughout the Middle Ages. A single surviving manuscript was discovered and popularized in 1417 and soon after Gutenberg's [114] invention of printing, the poem was printed in full and sown broadcast. In this way, Lucretius acted as the transmitter of the notion of atomism from Democritus to Dalton [389] by way of Gassendi [182].

[54] **SOSIGENES** (soh-sij'ih-neez)
Greek astronomer
Born: about 90 B.C.
Died: date unknown

Although the Greeks developed marvelous mathematical interpretations of a geocentric universe, thanks to Hipparchus [50], their calendar remained a primitive one, based on the lunar month and the cycle of Meton [23].

The Egyptians had early abandoned the lunar calendar in favor of a solar calendar based on twelve 30-day months plus five extra days. The overall length of such a year, 365 days, was a quarter day less than the true year, so that the Egyptian year fell one day behind the sun every four years and made a complete cycle in 1460 years. In Ptolemaic times, the Alexandrian astronomers tried to establish a 365¼-day year, but Egyptian conservatism rebelled.

The chance came with the Romans. The Roman lunar calendar had fallen into complete chaos because the priests in charge had manipulated it for political reasons, in order to alter the time in office of various functionaries. Julius Caesar accepted the advice of Sosigenes and in 46 B.C. established the Julian Calendar, which consisted of a 365-day year three times in a row to be followed by a 366-day leap year. With minor modifications, this has lasted until now.

Nothing else is known of Sosigenes except that he wrote some treatises on astronomy which are now lost and that he mentioned the belief that Mercury revolved about the sun.

[55] **VITRUVIUS** (vi-troo'vee-us); in full, MARCUS VITRUVIUS POLLIO
Roman architect
Born: about 70 B.C.
Died: about 25 B.C.

Virtually all that is known of Vitruvius' life is that he served as a military engineer in Africa under Julius Caesar.

The Romans are renowned as a "practical" people, more interested in engineering and applied science than in high-flown speculations of the Greek type. It is interesting, then, that Vitruvius, who put out a large volume on architecture, refers constantly to Greek science and scientists, recognizing apparently that engineering rests on science. Nor did he underestimate the Greek engineers, for he speaks highly of Ctesibius [46], for instance.

Vitruvius' book remained the chief reference on architectural matters well into the Italian Renaissance. What's more, he went beyond a mere consideration of architecture in his book. He discussed astronomy, dealt with acoustics, described the construction of various sundials and water wheels, and discussed theories that Mercury and Venus went about the sun, without, however, mentioning the name of Heracleides [28] in that connection. Where the Greek astronomers might conceivably have viewed the planetary spheres as abstractions, Vitruvius' intensely practical mind considered them real and material. He envisaged the earth's axis as set in bearings.

On the other hand, he treated the discovery of fire from the scientific rather than the mythological standpoint and recognized the prime importance of that discovery in the history of mankind.

Yet, even though Vitruvius' appreciation of Greek science was great and his transmission thereof unusually accurate for a Roman writer, he did make mistakes. He gave 3⅛ as the value of pi, and this was less accurate than the value worked out by Archimedes [47] two centuries earlier.

[56] **STRABO** (stray'boh)
Greek geographer
Born: Amasya, Pontus (about 75 miles south of what is now the Black Sea coast of Turkey), about 63 B.C.
Died: about A.D. 25

Strabo, the son of wealthy parents, traveled widely and, in fact, boasted that no geographer had traveled more widely than he. For instance, he traveled up the Nile to the borders of Nubia in 25 B.C.

He based his geography (in seventeen volumes, all but one of which is preserved) on Eratosthenes [48], to whom, however, he was inferior in mathematics. Because of this, his descriptions quickly become distorted as he leaves the Mediterranean area, for his manner of converting from a sphere to a plane is inaccurate. His work also suffered because he insisted on considering Homer to be accurate and disregarded the better data to be found in Herodotus.

His work represents the first attempt to collect all geographical knowledge into a single treatise and possesses particular value because it is the only geography that survives from antiquity and we know of earlier work chiefly through his book.

He recognized Vesuvius as a volcano. (It did not erupt in the memory of man until the time of Pliny [61] about half a century after Strabo's death.) Strabo also discussed the land-forming activity of rivers. He accepted Eratosthenes' view of the size of the globe and was impressed by the small portion of the earth's globe covered by the known world. He suggested the existence of unknown continents, therefore, and this suggestion was to haunt the world for fifteen centuries, till the time of Columbus [121].

He divided the known world into frigid, temperate, and tropic zones, a division we still use.

In middle age he settled in Rome, which, after the destruction of Carthage, was rapidly becoming all-powerful in the Mediterranean area. He wrote a long history of Rome but this work has not survived.

[57] **CELSUS**, Aulus Cornelius (sel'sus)
Roman encyclopedist
Born: about 10 B.C.
Died: date unknown

Celsus, a member of one of the most blue-blooded of the Roman families, gathered together the knowledge and learning of the Greeks and epitomized them for the delectation of the Roman audience. He did so in eight books of elegant Latin that eventually earned him the title of the Cicero of Medicine.

The "of medicine" comes about because, by chance, all that has survived of his writings are those concerned with medicine. His books contain a good description of tonsillectomy and a number of other operations. His books are also the first to discuss heart attacks and insanity in recognizable fashion. He also wrote on dentistry and described the use of the dental mirror. He also described the "cataract," a condition in which the lens of the eye grows opaque. Celsus' book was probably drawn for the most part from the collection of writings of the school of Hippocrates [22]. In fact, he has also been called the Roman Hippocrates.

Celsus and his book had an odd echo in early modern times. After being snubbed as a mere popularization in ancient times and being totally lost in the Middle Ages, a copy of the medical portion of his book was discovered in 1426 and an edition was printed in 1478, just at the time when medicine was reviving under the humanistic impact of the Renaissance. Its Latin terminology made use of numerous anatomical terms, such as cartilage, abdomen, tonsil, vertebra, anus, and uterus. In addition Celsus gained a sudden reputation as a physician of extraordinary merit (the men of the Renaissance regarded the ancient thinkers with an exaggerated veneration).

As a result, some half century after the edition appeared, an eccentric alchemist with new theories of medicine adopted the nickname of Paracelsus, which means "beyond Celsus" or "better than Celsus." There is no question that the name of Celsus remains in the modern consciousness almost entirely as the result of being a part of the name of Paracelsus [131].

[58] **MELA,** Pomponius (mee'luh)
Roman geographer
Born: Tingentera, Spain, about 5 B.C.
Died: date unknown

Mela is known only for a small geography book, written A.D. 43 or 44, which was probably intended for popular reading among the general Roman public. It borrowed from the Greek geographers but left out all the mathematics. However, since it was the one ancient book of geography that was written in Latin, it was particularly important throughout medieval times. In fact, its ideas remained in force until the beginning of the age of exploration some thirteen centuries after the time of Mela.

Mela divided the earth into five zones, following Strabo [56], a division we keep right down to the present: North Frigid, North Temperate, Torrid, South Temperate, and South Frigid. Of these, Mela considered only the Temperate zones to be habitable. The known world of the time was located in the North Temperate Zone and Mela believed, by analogy (always a dangerous route to a conclusion), that a similar world must exist in the South Temperate Zone. This southern land area, though habitable, was forever barred to the men of the north by the burning impenetrable heat of the Torrid Zone.

After the Torrid Zone was found to be passable in early modern times, the southern world of Mela was persistently searched for down to the days of Captain Cook [300].

(*Note: From this point on, all dates are* A.D. *unless specifically noted to be otherwise.*)

[59] **DIOSCORIDES** (dy-os-kor'ih-deez)
Greek physician
Born: Anazarbus (near Adana, in what is now Turkey), about 20
Died: date unknown

Dioscorides was a surgeon who served with the Roman armies under Nero. His chief interest lay in the use of plants as a source of drugs.

In this connection he wrote *De Materia Medica* in five books, and this was the first really systematic pharmacopeia. It at once replaced the work of Diocles [34] which was primitive in comparison.

Dioscorides was an objective observer and both his botanical and pharmacological details are accurate and free of superstition.

The work, which deals with about six hundred plants and nearly a thousand drugs, was preserved by the Arabs and when translated into Latin served as an inspiration for later botanical research. It finally appeared in a printed edition in 1478.

Dioscorides reported the condensation of mercury on the underside of the lid of the container holding it. Some think this observation eventually led to the technique of distillation, in which a liquid is heated and the vapors condensed and stored separately.

[60] HERO
Greek engineer
Born: about 20
Died: date unknown

After 150 B.C. Ptolemaic Egypt fell into decay and by 30 B.C. it had become a Roman province. The great days of Alexandria—and, indeed, of Greek science—were over. Nevertheless the curtain did not go down abruptly. There were fitful flashes of genius for some centuries.

One of those flashes was that of Hero, who displayed an almost modern aptitude for mechanics. Almost nothing, however, is known of his personal life, not even, until recently, the century in which he lived. It has been pointed out, however, that a lunar eclipse referred to in his writings was visible in Alexandria in 62. We might guess then that he was born about 20.

He is most famous for his invention of a hollow sphere to which two bent tubes were attached. When water was boiled in the sphere, the steam escaped through the tubes and as a result of what we now call the law of action and reaction (not stated explicitly until Newton [231]) the sphere whirled rapidly about. This was an early method of converting steam power to motion and it is often called a steam engine. The device is still used as a rotating lawn sprinkler, in which jets of water, rather than of steam, are the motivating force.

The principle of steam power was established, but it was put to use only in the automatic workings of doors and statues (by means of which priests might impose on gullible worshipers), in toys to amuse children, and so on. The idea of utilizing the energy implicit in inanimate nature as a substitute for strained and aching slave muscle seemed to occur to no one. The idea was not to arise for seventeen centuries after Hero and then only in regions where slave labor did not exist and nonslave labor was getting more expensive.

Hero wrote on mechanics, describing the various simple machines (lever, pulley, wheel, inclined plane, screw, wedge) by which effort could be properly channeled and magnified. He made it quite clear that when a force was magnified it was at the expense of exerting that magnified force through a correspondingly shortened distance. This was an extension and generalization of Archimedes' [47] law of the lever.

In constructing his ingenious devices, he made use of syphons, syringes, and gears. He used gears, for instance, in converting wheel revolutions of a chariot to the revolutions of a pointer—a primitive taximeter.

Hero wrote a book on air that was far in advance of his time. He demonstrated air was a substance by showing that water would not enter a vessel already filled with air unless the air was allowed to escape. He also maintained, from the fact that air was compressible, that it must be made up of individual particles separated by space. Here was the atomism of Democritus [20] again. This matter of the compressibility of air made no impression on scholars generally in Hero's time, but it was to come up again, more forcefully, fifteen hundred years later with Boyle [212] and his successors.

Hero also wrote a book on mirrors and on light. He felt that vision resulted from the emission of light by the eyes and that these light rays traveled at infinite velocity. These conclusions were incorrect, but he also said that the angle at which a light ray struck a reflecting surface was equal to the angle at which it was reflected, and that was correct.

[61] PLINY (plih'nee); in full, GAIUS PLINIUS CECILIUS SECUNDUS, the Elder
Roman scholar
Born: Novum Comum (modern Como), Italy, 23
Died: near Mount Vesuvius, Italy, August 25, 79

Pliny was a man of universal interests and universal curiosity. He had ample opportunity for indulging these in the Rome of his day, for the empire was in its full flush of power. In military service he commanded troops in Germany and had a chance to explore various regions of Europe. He returned to Novum Comum in 52, studied law, and settled down to writing and scholarship.

He was an intimate friend of Vespasian, who became Roman emperor in 69. In 70 Pliny was appointed governor over a section of Gaul, and in 73 over a section of Spain. Finally he was placed in charge of the Roman home fleet and this, indirectly, proved fatal to him. The fleet was stationed at the naval base at Misenum, just northwest of the Bay of Naples, when in 79 the nearby volcano of Vesuvius erupted, burying Pompeii and Herculaneum. In his eagerness to witness the eruption, Pliny went ashore and delayed too long in retreating from the ashes and vapor. He was found dead afterward.

Pliny is the very model of the compulsive worker. If he wasn't reading or having books read to him, he was taking notes or writing. He hated sleeping and he considered walking a waste of time, because, if he drove, he could write at the same time. Even in the army he managed to find time to write a history of the Germanic wars and to put down observations on the manner of hurling weapons while on horseback. He scribbled voluminously, and his major work, *Natural History,* included in thirty-seven volumes a complete summary of ancient knowledge concerning the world. It was first published in 77 and was dedicated to the Emperor Titus, son of Vespasian.

Pliny's *Natural History* was secondary —a digest drawn from two thousand ancient books by nearly five hundred writers. In preparing his digest, Pliny was completely credulous and undiscriminating. If anything interested him, it went in, regardless of its plausibility, though occasionally he did draw the line. He refused to accept the possibility of immortality, for instance. And sometimes the implausible was correct, like Pytheas' [39] theory that the moon was responsible for the tides, which Pliny refused to accept. Again, he described the origin of amber correctly, but only after he had also included all the wrong and fanciful theories on the subject that had been advanced.

The book dealt with astronomy and geography, where he accepted the sphericity of the earth, but its major concern was zoology and it was here that he went hog-wild. His tales of monsters and wonders lingered on through the Middle Ages under the guise of sober science. He described men without mouths who lived by inhaling the perfumes of flowers; men with large feet, which they used as umbrellas to shade themselves from the heat of the sun; unicorns; mermaids; flying horses; and so on. (In *Othello,* Othello charms Desdemona with tales of wonders taken straight out of Pliny.)

The unifying thread throughout Pliny's work was that of anthropocentrism. Man was the measure of everything; all was designed for the use of men. A plant had to be useful as a food or as a drug; an animal as a food or as a servant. If a plant or animal seemed of no material use to man (or even a danger) then its life and habits taught a moral lesson.

To this view the early Christians were sympathetic and this helps to explain the survival of the work. And although Pliny contains more errors per square foot than any other ancient author, he did perform the very useful service of maintaining, through medieval times, a sense of the wonder and majesty of the natural world. After all, while food for curiosity is supplied, there is always the hope that observation and research will rise anew and that error will be corrected.

[62] **FRONTINUS,** Sextus Julius (fron-
ty'nus)
Roman administrator
Born: about 30
Died: 104

Frontinus served as governor of Britain, and during his term of service subdued the hardy tribes of what is now southern Wales. His military career over, he wrote on many branches of applied science—on land surveying and military science, for instance. These books do not survive. In 97 the Emperor Nerva put him in charge of the water system of Rome. As a result, he published a two-volume work describing the Roman aqueducts, probably the most informative work we possess on ancient engineering. He proudly pointed out the superiority of these useful aqueducts as compared with the useless engineering feats of the Egyptians and the Greeks. However, Roman engineering had already peaked and the long, slow decline was beginning, with a new period of advance not slated to begin for sixteen weary centuries.

[63] **TSAI LUN** (tsy loon)
    Chinese inventor
    Born: Kueiyang, Kweichow,
    China, about 50
    Died: about 118

Tsai Lun was a eunuch; the only one, perhaps, who can claim a key position in the history of science.

Only one deed is recorded of him in the ancient Chinese histories, but that one deed is enough, for in 105 he is supposed to have invented the making of paper from such substances as tree bark, hemp, and rags. Slowly, in the centuries afterward, the secret of papermaking spread westward. It reached Baghdad by A.D. 800 and Europe after the Crusades. It was in time to serve as the material of which to make the flood of books produced by the printing press invented by Gutenberg [114], thirteen centuries after Tsai Lun's time.

No substance, in the nineteen centuries since Tsai Lun's time, has come along to supplant paper.

[64] **PTOLEMY** (tol'uh-mee; Latin
    name), CLAUDIUS
    PTOLEMAEUS
    Greek astronomer
    Born: Ptolemais Hermii (?),
    about 100
    Died: about 170

Ptolemy may have been an Egyptian rather than a Greek. He was not a member of the royal family of the Ptolemies that ruled Egypt a half century before his birth but may have attained his name from his supposed birthplace. Some traditions place him at Alexandria over a forty-year period, others say that he died at the age of seventy-eight. As you see, nothing is known of his private life, even his nationality, that goes beyond conjecture.

As in the case of Euclid [40], Ptolemy is not important for his own work, but rather for the grand synthesis he produced.

He drew principally on the work of Hipparchus [50], but since virtually none of the latter's writings survive, the system of the universe that he obtained from Hipparchus is universally referred to now as the Ptolemaic system. (Some, in fact, go so far as to suppose that Ptolemy was little more than a copyist of Hipparchus. This is probably too extreme, however.)

In the Ptolemaic system, the earth is at the center of the universe and the various planets revolve about it. The planets, in order of increasing distance from the earth, are the moon, Mercury, Venus, the sun, Mars, Jupiter, and Saturn. To account for their actual motions as seen in the sky, Hipparchus' epicycles and eccentrics are used, and Ptolemy very likely added a few refinements of his own.

The Ptolemaic system could be used to predict the positions of the planets for some time into the future and with an accuracy that was good enough for reasonable naked-eye observation. It was not until the time of Tycho Brahe [156], fourteen centuries later, that observations of the planets were made with sufficient accuracy to require a theory better than Ptolemy's.

In his book Ptolemy also included a star catalogue based on Hipparchus, listed forty-eight constellations to which he gave the names we still use today, and preserved and extended the work of Hipparchus on trigonometry. He even described instruments to be used in astronomic observations. His book was called by the admiring generations that followed *Megale mathematike syntaxis* ("Great mathematical composition"). Sometimes they said *Megiste* ("Greatest") rather than *Megale*.

After the fall of the Roman Empire, Ptolemy's works survived among the Arabs, who adopted the Greek word and called the book "The Greatest" using their own *al,* meaning "the." The book thus became the *Almagest* and has remained so ever since. The Arabic versions of the book were finally translated into Latin in 1175, and dominated European astronomical thinking through the Renaissance.

For instance, Ptolemy accepted Hipparchus' correct estimate of the distance of the moon, and also Aristarchus' [41] incorrect estimate of the distance of the sun. The latter estimate held the field till the time of Kepler [169]. He also treated astrology seriously, following Poseidonius [52] in this respect and this helped that pseudoscience gain a respect it did not deserve.

Ptolemy wrote a book on optics in which he discussed the refraction of light and he also wrote a book on geography based on the marchings of the Roman legions through the known world. He included maps and painstakingly prepared tables of latitudes and longitudes. However, he made a serious error in accepting Poseidonius' rather than Eratosthenes' [48] estimate of the earth's size. The geography was translated into Latin, thirteen centuries later, just in time to persuade Toscanelli [113] and, through him, Columbus [121] of the feasibility of a westward voyage from Europe to Asia.

[65] **GALEN** (gay'len)
Greek physician
Born: Pergamum (now Bergama, in Turkey), about 130
Died: probably in Sicily, about 200

Galen's father had been an architect. Tradition has it that Asklepios, the god of medicine, came to him in a dream and told him to make a physician of his son. He did.

Galen spent his youth traveling about the eastern provinces of the Roman Empire, receiving his education. He even visited the medical school at Alexandria.

About 159 he was appointed physician to the gladiatorial school at Pergamum, which gave him ample opportunity for some rough and ready observations in human anatomy.

In 161 he settled in Rome and spent most of his active life in that city, where for a time he was court physician under the emperor Marcus Aurelius. He was close, also, to two later emperors, Commodus and Septimius Severus.

Galen's best work was in anatomy. The dissection of human beings had fallen into disrepute and Galen's work was confined to animals, including dogs, goats, pigs, and monkeys. What he saw, he described with great and meticulous detail, but of course not everything he saw was applicable to human anatomy. For instance, he carefully described a network of blood vessels under the brain, present in many animals but *not* in man, and assigned it an important role in his scheme of the functioning of the human body.

Nevertheless, he did particularly good work on muscles, identifying many for the first time. He noted they worked in teams. He also showed the importance of the spinal cord by cutting it at various levels (in animals) and noting the extent of the resulting paralysis.

Galen developed an overall system of physiology that was based to a great extent on the three-fluid theory of Erasistratus [43]. Galen recognized that the fluid in the left half of the heart must get to the right half somehow and postulated the presence of tiny holes, too small to see, in the thick muscular wall separating the two halves. In this way he missed the true explanation of the circulation of the blood. On the other hand, he was the first to use the pulse as a diagnostic aid, and he described the flow of urine through the ureters to the bladder.

He was a prolific writer who engaged in polemics with other physicians, thought little of Hippocrates [22], and showed a rather unattractive side to his character in his arrogance, disputatiousness, and pompous self-esteem. He was violently anti-atomist and this helped keep the views of Democritus [20] submerged until modern times.

Galen lived at a time when Christianity was rising in power, and although he was not himself a Christian he developed a form of monotheism. He believed, somewhat as Pliny [61] did, that everything in the universe was made by God for a particular purpose. This search for design and purpose in the universe and particularly in the human body made his works popular with Christians and ensured the survival of many of his books through the Middle Ages.

Galen's works, then, were the ultimate medical authority for Europeans until the time of Vesalius [146] in anatomy and Harvey [174] in physiology.

[66] **DIOPHANTUS** (dy-oh-fan'tus)
　　　Greek mathematician
　　　Born: about 210
　　　Died: about 290

The great glory of Greek mathematics was geometry and its great shortcoming was the lack of algebra. It was only in the late twilight of ancient Greek science that a mathematician erased that shortcoming.

Nothing is known of Diophantus but his work, not even the century in which he lived. The year of birth given here, 210, is one guess. Others have placed it as early as 50. One problem associated with him requires that his age be deduced from data given. If that is autobiographically accurate, he may have lived to be eighty-four.

Diophantus solved problems by means of what we would now call algebraic equations, working out a symbolism of his own. His works were preserved by the Arabs and were translated into Latin in the sixteenth century, when they served as inspiration for the great algebraic advances that began at that time.

He is best known for his work with equations for which solutions in terms of integers are required. Sometimes the equation is indeterminate, that is, has no single set of solutions. It has, instead, more than one or even an infinite number. These are still called Diophantine equations. Diophantus was the first Greek to treat fractions as numbers.

[67] **ZOSIMUS** (zoh'si-mus)
　　　Greek alchemist
　　　Born: Panopolis (modern
　　　Akhmim), Egypt, about 250
　　　Died: date unknown

While the Greeks excelled in mathematics and in abstract schemes of the universe, the Egyptians dealt in a practical way with materials. This interest in what we would today call chemistry arose, perhaps, out of their efforts to preserve the human body after the death through mummification.

After the time of Alexander the Great, Egyptian practice fused with Greek theory to form the science of "khemia." (Some people find the source of this word in *khem*, the Egyptian word for land. It means "black" and refers to the fertile black soil watered by the Nile floods, as compared with the tawny soil of the desert areas beyond.) The Arabs eventually inherited this science and placed *al* ("the") before the name, so that it became "alchemy."

Very little of the original Greek or Egyptian writings on alchemy survive, but about three hundred, the entire range of alchemical knowledge, were summarized by Zosimus (concerning whose personal life nothing is known) in an encyclopedia made up of twenty-eight books.

These books are a riot of mysticism. This is perhaps understandable. If alchemy was indeed born of Egyptian mummification procedures, then it began in close association with religion. It was a form of knowledge that would naturally be considered sacred and of peculiar interest to the priestly class. It would become habitual to discuss it in a jargon that would exclude the uninitiated.

It is possible to find, among the obscure references of Zosimus, passages that indicate he may have known of arsenic. Also, he seems to have described the formation of lead acetate and to have known of its sweet taste. (It is called "sugar of lead" even today.)

The Greek theories of the four elements led alchemists to think that it was possible to rearrange the elements in a base metal such as lead to form the noble metal gold. This is transmutation. The will-o'-the-wisp of transmutation combined with the tradition of mysticism and obscure symbolism in alchemical writings held back the development of chemistry until the time of Lavoisier [334], who, fifteen centuries after Zosimus, finally completed the breaking of the spell.

[68] **PAPPUS** (pap'us)
Greek mathematician
Born: Alexandria, about 260
Died: Alexandria, date unknown

Pappus, like Zosimus [67] and Diophantus [66], brought up the rear guard of Greek science. Like Zosimus, he was primarily an encyclopedist, summarizing in eight rather masterly books (of which major parts of all but the first survive) all of Greek mathematics.

He contributed little himself but his collection is of first importance, nevertheless, for it contains almost all we know of Greek mathematicians. Pappus also commented in detail on Ptolemy's astronomical system and helped keep it popular for the next millennium and a half.

[69] **HYPATIA** (hy-pay'shee-uh)
Greek philosopher
Born: Alexandria, about 370
Died: Alexandria, 415

Hypatia, the daughter of Theon, who was the last recorded member of the great Museum at Alexandria, is remark-

able as the only noted woman scholar of ancient times. This, combined with reports as to her beauty and virtue and the skill and popularity of her lectures, has led to her idealization in later times. Like her father, she contributed nothing original to science but produced useful commentaries on a number of earlier scholars such as Ptolemy [64] and Diophantus [66].

She was a pagan, and, although Christian bishops were among her pupils, she was the subject of violent antagonism on the part of zealots. In the end she was brutally murdered. Her story was greatly romanticized by Charles Kingsley, in his novel *Hypatia,* published in 1853.

[70] **PROCLUS** (proh'klus)
Greek mathematician
Born: Constantinople (the modern Istanbul, Turkey), 410
Died: Athens, April 17, 485

Proclus, the son of a lawyer, was virtually the last pagan scientist of any consequence. He was a devotee of Neoplatonism, a system of philosophy that stemmed from the work of Plotinus, a Roman philosopher. Plotinus, two centuries before, had modified the system of Plato, adding mysticism in order to make it more capable of competing with the salvationist Eastern religions then beginning to dominate the Roman Empire. In this, Plotinus failed, but Neo-Platonist elements entered into the thinking of Christianity, which was the ultimate victor in the battle of ideas.

By Proclus' time it had become dangerous (though not yet fatal) to be a pagan. Proclus, who was the last neo-Platonist of importance and who taught at the Academy in the last century of its existence and served as its head eventually, found that out. About 450 he was driven into a year's exile from Athens.

Among his writings Proclus included commentaries on Ptolemy [64] and Euclid [40] and it is there that his importance to the history of science lies. The flame of science had dimmed to such a feeble flicker that any commentary, however primitive, was important, for it added one more book that might be seen and that might survive.

[71] **BOETHIUS,** Anicius Manlius Severinus (boh-ee'thee-us)
Roman philosopher
Born: Rome, about 480
Died: Ticinum (modern Pavia), Italy, 524

Boethius, who represented the last spark of the old Greco-Roman world, came of a noble Roman family. One of that family was Olybrius who, for a few months in 472–73, reigned as puppet emperor of Rome. In Boethius' time, no emperor reigned at Rome, for the last had been deposed in 476, the date usually taken as the fall of Rome.

Boethius, however, was befriended by Theodoric, ruler of the Ostrogoths, and the supreme power in Italy and the lands immediately surrounding. It was a fatal friendship, as it turned out, for Boethius, who was given high office and who, in 522, had the pleasure of seeing his two sons simultaneously raised to the honorable office of consul, was tactlessly vocal concerning the abuses visited by the Ostrogothic overlords upon the Roman populace. Eventually his attitude was unjustly translated, by an increasingly suspicious Theodoric, into treasonable correspondence with the Eastern emperor at Constantinople. Boethius was imprisoned, tortured, and finally executed without trial.

Boethius' chief work (written in prison) was a philosophic treatise, *On the Consolation of Philosophy*. It is a great work, rather pagan in its discussion of virtue and free will, although Boethius is considered to have been a Christian. He was the last Roman writer who understood Greek, and his service to science lies in his having prepared translations of and commentaries on Aristotle [29] and summaries on various scientific subjects. His works were the only source from which the Europeans of the early Middle Ages could draw for information on Greek science until Arabic works were translated into Latin about six centuries after the time of Boethius.

[72] **ISIDORE OF SEVILLE**
Spanish scholar
Born: Seville, about 560
Died: Seville, April 4, 636

Isidore was a great controversialist, defending Christianity against the Jews, and Catholicism against the heresy of Arianism. In 609 he was made Archbishop of Seville. Between 622 and 633 Isidore published an encyclopedia in which, like Bede [75] a few decades later, he salvaged all he could of the learning of the Greeks, borrowing, again like Bede, from Pliny in particular. This book, called *Etymologies* in English, was very influential in early medieval times. It was so popular that a thousand medieval manuscripts of the book still survive.

Isidore accepted the validity of astrology and this contributed to its acceptance in medieval Europe, even though Biblical verses could be quoted against it. He also dealt with the mystic significance of numbers after the fashion of Pythagoras [7]. His work, on the whole, tended to darken the intellectual world rather than enlighten it; but like Pliny he kept alive a sense of wonder, and that is important, too.

[73] **BRAHMAGUPTA** (brah'muh-goop'tuh)
Hindu astronomer and mathematician
Born: about 598
Died: about 665

When Greek learning was spreading eastward, during and after the time of the Arabic conquest of the Near East, it penetrated as far as the Indian subcontinent. The men of science who arose there had little influence on subsequent developments in the West but Brahmagupta, as perhaps the best among them, ought to be mentioned.

He worked at Ujjain, in west-central India, which, for several centuries before and after him, was the center of Hindu science. Brahmagupta's astronomy was summarized in a book written in 628 and in it he denied the rotation of the earth, which a few Hindu astronomers supported.

The most notable feature of the book is the application of algebraic methods to astronomical problems. Hindu mathematicians were indeed of prime service to the world, for sometime within the next two centuries some nameless mathematician devised the notion of a symbol for "zero." This made positional notation practical, and a number system based on such notation was adopted. It spread to Arabs such as al-Khwarizmi [79] and from them was introduced (as the "Arabic numerals" we use today) to Europe by men such as Fibonacci [95].

[74] **CALLINICUS** (kal-ih-ny′kus)
Born: Heliopolis, Egypt (?),
about 620
Died: date unknown

Actually, nothing at all is known about the personal life of Callinicus. The birth date given above is not more than an educated guess, and some think he was born in Syria rather than in Egypt or that he was Jewish rather than Christian. Whether Syrian or Egyptian, Jewish or Christian, he fled to Constantinople ahead of the conquering Arabian armies and in Constantinople invented Greek fire.

This was a mixture containing an inflammable petroleum fraction, plus potassium nitrate to supply oxygen, plus quicklime perhaps to supply further heat through reaction with water. The exact secret of the composition is lost, but because of the nature of modern war weapons, Greek fire is not important to rediscover, except out of historical curiosity. It burned on water and therefore could be used to destroy a wooden fleet.

The Greeks of the Byzantine Empire used Greek fire in 670 to repel the ships of an Arabic naval onslaught on Constantinople and in this way, this one invention, an authentic "secret war weapon," may well have radically changed the course of history. It may be that Constantinople would have fallen without the use of Greek fire. If so, it is possible that the Muhammadan faith would have swept Europe.

[75] **BEDE** (beed)
English scholar
Born: Jarrow, Durham, 673
Died: Jarrow, May 26, 735

When the Germanic invaders had submerged Roman civilization in the West, those scraps of ancient learning remained that were preserved by the monkish copyists and summarizers. One of the most notable of these was Bede.

He received an ecclesiastical training from childhood, having entered the monastery at Jarrow, where he was to spend his life, at the age of seven. He was finally ordained priest at thirty and might eventually have become an abbot, but he refused higher office in order to write. This he did, spending a quiet and idyllic life immersed in his writing and his religious duties, never traveling more than fifty miles from home.

He is commonly called the Venerable Bede, this being an old-fashioned ecclesiastical title. Some, taking the word in its later meaning, have thought it referred to extreme age and put forth the notion that he lived a hundred years or more. This is not so.

In his writings Bede gives an account of the history of the early centuries of Anglo-Saxon England, and also all the knowledge he has managed to accumulate. This consisted largely of bits of Pliny [61]. He also deals with such astronomy as was necessary for the proper dating of Easter, concerning which there was much controversy in his time.

He noted that the vernal equinox had slipped to a point three days earlier than the traditional March 21. This imperfection of Sosigenes' [54] Julian calendar was to lead to a reform and a slight adjustment of the number of leap years per millennium. The reform did not come in a hurry, though; it came nine centuries after Bede's observation.

He maintained that the earth was a sphere, and even this much was valuable at a time when scholarship in western Europe was close to bottom. Nor was it only the most primitive bits of knowledge he preserved. He revived the suggestion of Pytheas [39] that the tides were governed by the phases of the moon, an effect that was to escape the great Galileo [166] nine centuries later. He also realized, like Seleucus [51], eight centuries before, that high tide did not occur everywhere at once and that tide tables had to be prepared separately for each port.

This is considered the only original scientific contribution in western Europe, during some eight centuries after the end of Greek learning.

A more trivial point, but one that affects us all very intimately, is that in his historical works he dated events from the birth of Jesus rather than from the creation of the world. In this respect, we have all come to follow him.

Bede worked to the last, completing his translation of St. John on his deathbed.

He was canonized in 1899 by Pope Leo XIII and is a Doctor of the Church.

[76] **GEBER** (jee'ber); Arabic name, ABU MUSA JABIR IBN HAY-YAN
Arabian alchemist
Born: possibly in Al-Kufah (in what is now Iraq), about 721
Died: possibly in Al-Kufah, about 815

After the coming of the prophet Muhammad, the Arabian tribes, in a great burst of expansionist energy, swept over western Asia and northern Africa. They disrupted, but did not destroy, the Eastern Roman Empire, which had survived the barbarian onslaughts that had wiped out the empire in the West. The Eastern Empire, particularly after the Arabian conquests, came to be known as the Byzantine Empire after its capital, Byzantium.

The Arabs occupied Syria in the 630s and Egypt in the 640s. In so doing, they fell heir to much of Greek science, and this proved of importance and even benefit to the history of science. The advance of science in what remained of Roman dominions came to a complete halt. For a thousand years of Byzantine history the only name worth mentioning is Callinicus [74]. Western Europe was in

darkness. It was the Arabs alone who were in a position to preserve and transmit the accumulated knowledge of the ancients.

They not only preserved but also, in some cases, made advances, notably in alchemy. The first of the important Arabian alchemists was Geber (as he was known to Europeans after his works were translated into Latin) and he was also the best. He carried the science far beyond the point it had reached in the time of Zosimus [67].

Geber's lifetime corresponded with the very height of Arabic power, falling as it did at the time of the reign of the celebrated Harun al-Rashid, the famous Caliph of the Thousand and One Nights.

Geber, the son of a druggist, was a personal friend of Harun's vizier Ja'far al-Sadiq, and was also an adherent, it would seem, of the sect of the Sufis, which gave rise to the notorious Assassins (who fed on hashish—hence their name—and performed political assassinations on command). The sect was never popular with outsiders, and small wonder. Then, to make matters worse, Ja'far fell from power and was executed. On both scores, Geber felt his life insecure. He went into retirement in his native village and there died in peace.

Meanwhile, though, he had written numerous works on alchemy. It is doubtful that all the books attributed to him are really his, for later alchemists often attempted to gain greater respect for their work by attributing them to an earlier man of renown. This remained true as long as the publication of books was a matter of arduous hand labor so that only comparatively few could appear in any numbers at all. It was only after the invention of printing, when almost anyone could see his book appear in large editions, that the habit of surrendering credit died out.

The older habit seems saddest when a great man of science retreats into undeserved anonymity by his own choice. Thus, a much later alchemist wrote under Geber's name and is now known only as the "false Geber" [107].

Geber's most influential contribution to alchemy was his modification of the

48

Greek doctrine of the four elements. Geber felt that these combined to form two different kinds of solid substances—sulfur and mercury. The former was the idealized principle of combustibility, the latter that of metallic properties. By the appropriate combination of the two any metal could be formed. Therefore, lead could be separated into sulfur and mercury, which could then be recombined in new proportions to form gold. This transmutation could be brought about through a mysterious substance that he, or later Arabs, called *al-iksīr* from a Greek word for a dry, medicinal powder. This came down in Latin as "elixir."

Following Geber's initial impulse, alchemists for a thousand years sought this "philosopher's stone," as the dry material was popularly termed. Since any substance capable of forming gold must also have other miraculous properties, alchemists surmised it could cure all disease, restore youth, confer immortality. It was therefore also named the "elixir of life."

Among these mistaken theories, however, Geber published accurate descriptions of valuable chemical experiments. He described ammonium chloride and showed how to prepare white lead. He prepared weak nitric acid and he also distilled vinegar to obtain strong acetic acid. He worked with dyes and varnishes and dealt with methods for refining metals. Most important, he described various chemical operations with great care.

Unfortunately, later alchemists followed Geber's mistaken theories into wilder and deeper morasses. For the most part they abandoned Geber's system of practical, straightforward descriptions of worthwhile experiments.

[77] **ALCUIN** (al′kwin)
English scholar
Born: York, about 732
Died: Tours, France, May 19, 804

Alcuin's teacher had been a pupil of Bede [75] and Alcuin carried on the earlier scholar's tradition. The school at York, where he studied, was the most re-

nowned in its time, in western Europe, and in 778, Alcuin became its head. However, he never rose beyond the status of deacon.

Alcuin visited Rome in 781 and there he met Charlemagne [78]. The latter, having established a strong rule over most of western Europe, aspired to culture. He therefore invited Alcuin to serve as head of an educational system for his empire. Alcuin accepted and brought English learning (little enough, but better, at the moment, than anything available in Charlemagne's dominions) to the continent.

Charlemagne himself learned to read under Alcuin's tutelage, though writing remained beyond his powers. Alcuin was installed at Tours as abbot and there established a school where scribes were trained for the careful copying of manuscripts. In order to crowd as much writing as possible onto a piece of parchment, yet leave it legible, Alcuin designed a way of writing in condensed fashion ("Carolingian minuscule" from Carolus [Magnus], the Latin name of Charlemagne) which is the ancestor of our "small letters."

Under Alcuin's influence, there was a brief graying (the Carolingian Renaissance) of the darkness, which, however, soon returned. The first slow glimmers of the actual dawn were still more than two centuries in the future.

[78] **CHARLEMAGNE** (shahr-luh-main′)
Frankish emperor
Born: Aachen, Germany, about 742
Died: Aachen, January 28, 814

Charlemagne is one of the great monarchs of Western tradition and one about whom myths have clustered with almost the same fantastic concentration that they cling to the legendary Arthur of Britain.

For our purposes, however, his importance lay in his realization that his realm lay under a barbarous blanket of ignorance that was both disgraceful and dangerous to any state aspiring to prosperity and greatness. In 789 he began to establish schools in which the elements of mathematics, grammar, and ecclesiastical subjects could be taught, and Alcuin [77] was made the educational coordinator of the empire.

Charlemagne himself undertook to learn to read and write, and managed the former. There are touching tales of his unsuccessful efforts to force his fingers, in mature life, to shape the tiny letters properly and his failure to do so.

The Carolingian Renaissance did not outlast the great Charles, but no spark of light truly dies, perhaps, and his work left dim traditions that were to be carried onward a few centuries later.

[79] **AL-KHWARIZMI,** Muhammad ibn
Musa (al-khwah'riz-mee)
Arabian mathematician
Born: Khwarizm (modern Khiva, in the Uzbek SSR of the Soviet Union), about 780
Died: about 850

Al-Khwarizmi's best claim to immortality lies in a word in the title of a work in which he preserved and extended the mathematics of Diophantus [66]. The title of his book was *ilm al-jabr wa'l muqabalah,* which means "the science of transposition and cancellation." The Arabic word *al-jabr* ("transposition") became "algebra" in the Latin transliterations of the title and that in turn became the name of the entire branch of mathematics that Diophantus had founded. It is the branch that involves the solution of equations by such devices as transpositions and cancellations.

Al-Khwarizmi's own name was distorted into "algorism," which came to mean "the art of calculating," something we now call "arithmetic." ("Arithmetic" when used in ancient times is what we now call "theory of numbers.")

A more important contribution attributed to al-Khwarizmi rests on the fact that he drew on Hindu sources as well as Greek, for he picked up the Hindu numerals, including the zero. When his work was translated into Latin, those numerals (miscalled "Arabic numerals") were transmitted to Europe via the work of Fibonacci [95]. Their slow adoption revolutionized mathematical manipulations, making long division, for instance, a technique for children, rather than for experts only.

While an improved symbolism does not directly advance science it does free men from undue preoccupation with mere techniques and makes possible further advances in theory by simply giving them more time to think.

Al-Khwarizmi was supported by the Caliph Mamun, under whom the power of Baghdad reached its height. (Mamun ruled from 813 to 833.) With that support, al-Khwarizmi prepared a world geography based largely on Ptolemy [64]. In contrast to Ptolemy, al-Khwarizmi overestimated the size of the earth, giving it a circumference of forty thousand miles.

[80] **THABIT IBN QURRA**
Arabian mathematician
Born: Harran, in what is now southeastern Turkey, 836
Died: Baghdad, February 18, 901

Although Thabit lived in a Muslim society, he was not a Muslim but was a member of a Sabian sect that traced back to the pre-Muslim Babylonian society. He was to the Muslims what the Neo-Platonists were to the Christians.

He came of wealthy parents; he was himself a money changer; and he was apparently an accomplished linguist, being fluent in both Greek and Arabic, in addition to his native Syriac. An Arabic mathematician, encountering him and admiring his knowledge and obvious intelligence, invited him to come to Baghdad where he would have the chance to obtain a thorough education.

This he did and to such good effect that he became a great scholar; this meant that when he returned home, he was greeted with the utmost hostility by his own sect, which accused him as having left the fold. He was condemned by their religious court and it seemed only prudent to him to return to Baghdad, where he remained the rest of his life.

There he advanced rapidly and was in the retinue of the Caliph al-Mutadid. He translated many of the works of the Greek scientists; and wrote commentaries on them as well, thereby becoming a powerful factor in making Greek science available to the Muslim world.

He himself also did work of his own, particularly in mathematics and, for instance, considered the matter of Euclid's parallel postulate, something that nearly a thousand years later, at the hands of Bolyai [530] and Lobachevski [484] would lead to non-Euclidean geometry.

[81] ALFRED THE GREAT
English monarch
Born: Wantage, Berkshire, 849
Died: Winchester, Hampshire,
October 28, 900

In the deepest Dark Ages, Alfred the Great, like Charlemagne [78], offered a spark of light, an earnest of things to come in the slowly developing west European civilization that was arising out of the ruins of the classical world.

Alfred is best known for his indomitable battles against the Danish invaders, battles through which his persistence, bravery, and skill finally saved half the island and kept it firmly in Saxon hands. Both for his accomplishments and his character, Alfred was clearly the best of the Anglo-Saxon rulers of England.

Alfred was not merely interested in learning for himself but felt a deep concern that his subjects have learning available to them. For that reason he made every effort to have worthwhile Latin books translated into Anglo-Saxon. He did much of the work himself, translating the works of Boethius [71] and Bede [75].

[82] RHAZES (ray'zeez); Arabic name,
ABU-BAKR MUHAMMAD IBN
ZAKARIYYA AR-RAZI
Persian physician and alchemist
Born: Rhages (now Rai near Teheran, in what is now Iran), about 845
Died: Rhages, about 930

Rhazes (the Latinized version of his name) had no such close connection with the caliph's court as Geber [76], but he at least had the distinction of being born in Harun al-Rashid's hometown.

In 880 or thereabouts Rhazes visited Baghdad and there, so we are told, came across an old apothecary who fascinated him with stories of medicine and disease. Rhazes decided to study medicine and ended as chief physician of Baghdad's largest hospital. He is supposed to have been the first to differentiate clearly between smallpox and measles.

Rhazes, like Geber, described his experiments so carefully that modern chemists can repeat them and check on his work. He prepared what we now call plaster of Paris, for instance, and described the manner in which it could be used to form casts holding broken bones in place. He also studied and described metallic antimony.

He shared with Aristotle [29] a delight in classifying and was the first, so far as is known, to divide all substances into the grand classification of animal, vegetable, and mineral. He also subclassified minerals into metals, volatile liquids (spirits), stones, salts, and so on; a division that was much the most useful up to his time.

He went along with Geber's notions concerning mercury and sulfur as the basic ingredients of solid substances and added to it salt as a third.

He was a thoroughgoing rationalist, by the way, who dismissed miracles and mysticism. He thought religion harmful as the cause of hatred and wars. He accepted a materialist atomism as his view of the universe. Naturally, he was greatly vilified for these views.

[83] ALBATEGNIUS (al-buh-teg'nee-us); Arabic name, ABU-'AB-DULLAH MUHAMMAD IBN JABIR AL-BATTANI
Arabian astronomer
Born: Haran (in what is now southeastern Turkey), about 858
Died: near Samarra, Iraq, 929

Greek astronomy as finally refined by Ptolemy [64] was preserved by the

Arabs, but little more. The only advances, minor ones, were made by Albategnius, the son of a builder of astronomical instruments and the greatest of Islamic astronomers.

Albategnius went over Ptolemy's calculations carefully and inserted a few improvements. He noticed, for instance, that the point at which the sun was smallest in apparent size (a point now called the aphelion) was no longer located where Ptolemy said it was. From this he deduced that the position moved slowly and obtained a fairly correct value for that motion.

He used better instruments than the Greeks did (the advantage of being the son of his father) and so got more accurate results for the length of the year. (This value was used in the Gregorian reform of the Julian calendar seven centuries later.) He also determined the time of equinox to within an hour or two and got an excellent value for the angle at which the earth's axis was tipped to its plane of revolution.

He introduced new types of mathematical computations in astronomy, being the first to make use of a table of sines for the purpose. The greatest contribution of Arabic astronomy was the perfecting of spherical trigonometry.

In medieval Europe he was to be the most respected of the Arabian astronomers.

[84] GERBERT (zhare-bare')
French scholar
Born: Aurillac, Auvergne, about 945
Died: Rome, Italy, May 12, 1003

As a scholar, Gerbert tutored the son of Hugh Capet, king of France, and gained the admiration of the Holy Roman emperor, Otto II.

As a churchman he reached the pinnacle, becoming archbishop and finally pope (the first French one), in 999, under the name of Sylvester II. (It was a ticklish time to be pope, for there was strong feeling in Europe that the world was coming to an end in 1000.) Gerbert was for his time a famous scholar, fa-

mous enough to be suspected of wizardry, despite his eminence in the church. He reintroduced the use of the abacus in mathematical calculation and may have picked up the use of Arabic numerals (without the zero) from al-Khwarizmi [79]. He built clocks, organs, and astronomical instruments out of his consultation of Arabic works, which he procured in translation. The rebirth of European learning may be dated from Gerbert.

[85] ALHAZEN (al'ha-zen); Arabic name, ABU-'ALI AL-HASAN IBN AL-HAYTHAM
Arabian physicist
Born: Basra (Al Basra, in what is now Iraq), about 965
Died: Cairo, Egypt, 1039

Alhazen, in an attempt to obtain a sinecure for himself, put forth the claim that he could devise a machine that would regulate the flooding of the Nile.

As he hoped, this attracted the attention of the Egyptian caliph, who hired him to do the job. Unfortunately for Alhazen, the Egyptian caliph was al-Hakim, the most dangerous crowned madman between the times of Caligula and Ivan the Terrible. It dawned on Alhazen that al-Hakim was not joking about his request that the machine should be built at once and that he would see that Alhazen was put to death in some complicated fashion if the machine was not built.

There was nothing for Alhazen to do but pretend to have gone mad. He had to keep it up for years, until al-Hakim died in 1021.

At the times when Alhazen could afford to be sane, he proved himself the most important physicist of the Middle Ages. His field of particular interest was optics. This science had been fumblingly begun by Hero [60] and by Ptolemy [64], who felt that men saw by means of rays of light issuing from the eye and reflecting from the objects seen. Alhazen held the correct view that light issued from the sun or from some other luminous source and was reflected from the object seen into the eye.

He also explained, correctly, how a lens worked, attributing its magnifying effect to the curvature of the surface and not to any inherent property of the substance making it up.

He was interested in the reflection and refraction of light, discussed the rainbow, studied the focusing of light through lenses and constructed a pinhole camera. He also constructed parabolic mirrors, a type now used in telescopes. Like Ptolemy he assumed the atmosphere had a finite depth, and estimated that depth to be about ten miles.

His work was published in Latin translation in the sixteenth century and exerted an important influence on such men as Kepler [169]. It was not until Kepler, six centuries later, in fact, that work on optics progressed beyond the point to which Alhazen had brought it.

[86] **AVICENNA** (av-ih-sen'uh); Arabic name, ABU-ALI AL-HUSAIN IBN ABDULLAH IBN SINA
Persian physician
Born: Kharmaithen, near Bukhara (in what is now the Uzbek SSR of the Soviet Union), 980
Died: Hamadan (in what is now northwest Iran), June 1037

Avicenna, the son of a tax collector, was an infant prodigy able to recite the entire Koran at the age of ten. He received all the education the cultivated Arab world of the time could offer. Unfortunately the once-great Arabian empire, although still highly cultured, had fallen apart into warring pieces and there was no safe place even for the greatest physician of medieval times, which Avicenna was. Avicenna was in the employ of several Muslim rulers but political instability was such that although this brought him fame, money, and a chance to do research, it also placed his life in danger more than once.

In Hamadan, he served as vizier for a while and for his pains was nearly put to death during a military coup. He remained in hiding until a medical emergency on the part of the shah made his presence necessary and his person safe. When Hamadan fell to a neighboring ruler, Avicenna was one of the spoils of war and served a new master. In the end he died on the march with the army of that new master when it was heading for another attack on Hamadan. Avicenna apparently had a tendency to work hard at his pleasures as well as his studies, for it was of indigestion (or colic) that he died.

More than two hundred and fifty books are attributed to Avicenna (many are probably really his) and of these the most important are his works on medicine. His theories were based on those of Hippocrates [22] and Galen [65], and once his books were translated into Latin in the twelfth century, they became Europe's most important medical textbooks, remaining so until the time of Harvey [174].

Avicenna also dealt with alchemy, and he was unusual in being one of the few who intuitively felt that transmutation was impossible. In his philosophical works he helped preserve the views of Aristotle [29] for western Europe, but his importance in this respect is less than that of Averroës [91].

[87] **OMAR KHAYYÁM** (oh'mar ky-ahm')
Persian astronomer
Born: Nishapur (in what is now Iran), May 15, 1048
Died: Nishapur, December 4, 1131

The two things known about Omar Khayyám to the average well-educated modern are that he was a tentmaker, which is what "Khayyám" means, and that he wrote clever quatrains. His father was a tentmaker, and he himself was a tentmaker in early life, it is true, but he was recognized as a gifted scholar and spent most of his life pensioned by, first, the vizier of the Seljuk sultan, Alp Arslan, and then by the sultan's successor, Malik Shah. (Under these two rulers, the Seljuk Turkish Empire reached its height.) Omar's poetry came into prominence in English only in 1859 when Edward FitzGerald produced his translation of the *Rubáiyát.* However, the lines we admire are far more the work of FitzGerald than of Omar.

Omar Khayyám wrote a book on algebra that was the best of its time, and he also prepared improved astronomical tables. His most spectacular feat was that of reforming the Muslim calendar in 1074 and producing one that would better fit the astronomical facts of life. This was comparable with the Gregorian reform in Europe five centuries later. He could handle quadratic equations neatly but was stumped by cubic equations. He suspected that a general solution for the cubic equation did not exist, but Cardano [137] was to publish one four and a half centuries later.

After the death of Malik Shah and the assassination of his vizier, Omar Khayyám fell into disfavor in 1092, partly because of his free-thinking attitudes (which show up in his quatrains). However, he was allowed to live out his life in peace.

[88] **ABELARD**, Peter (ab'uh-lahrd, or a-bay-lahr′ in French)
French scholar, French name, PIERRE ABÉLARD
Born: Le Pallet or Palais, Brittany, 1079
Died: near Chalon-sur-Saône, April 21, 1142

Abelard was the son of a landowner, and it would have been natural for him to train for a military career; but he entered the field of scholarship and theology, although his attitude toward it was that of a fighter and polemicist.

He studied with competing masters and developed contempt, to a greater or lesser degree, for all, since they taught on the basis of what authorities had said and did not use reason—or, rather, they distrusted it as leading to pitfall and error.

It was Abelard's service to the cause of science that he fought hard for the use of reason and praised the ancient pagans for it. What is more, in his most famous book, *Sic et Non* ("Yes and No") he carefully quoted the most respected authorities on a variety of important theological questions and showed them, in every case, to be hopelessly at odds with each other. It needed no comment from Abelard to show the bankruptcy of appeals to authority.

Naturally, Abelard, who was a magnificent and popular lecturer, (and is usually considered the founder of the University of Paris) incurred the wrath of less intelligent, but more orthodox, scholars (particularly the wrathful Bernard of Clairvaux, an abbot more powerful than the pope) and he was in constant danger of condemnation for heresy. Indeed, when he died he was preparing his defense against such a charge.

The best-known aspect of Abelard's life, however, is his affair with his beautiful and intelligent student Heloise. It was apparently a case of deep love on both sides. They were secretly married (It had to be secret or Abelard's career in the church would have come to an end.) and a son was born to them. Heloise's uncle, Fulbert, the powerful canon of Notre Dame, was furious at all this, and hired thugs to castrate Abelard in 1121. That prevented any advancement in the church just as surely as marriage would, since no eunuch could be a priest. He continued his studies and his writings, however.

[89] **ADELARD OF BATH**
English scholar
Born: Bath, about 1090
Died: about 1150

Adelard was a tutor of the English prince who later became Henry II. He is supposed to have traveled widely during his youth through the lands of ancient learning, Greece, Asia Minor, northern Africa. He learned Arabic and upon his return to England translated Euclid [40] from Arabic into Latin. This was the first time Euclid became available to Europe. He also translated al-Khwarizmi [79], and made use of "Arabic numerals," something that Fibonacci [95] was to establish firmly a century later. For popular consumption Adelard also wrote a book called *Natural Questions* which contained a summary of all he had learned of Arabic science.

[90] GERARD OF CREMONA (jerard')
Italian scholar
Born: Cremona, about 1114
Died: Toledo, Spain, 1187

The twelfth century is unique in the history of science as being the time when it was possible for translation to be the most important scientific work. The books of the Arabic scholars, who for centuries had preserved the works of the Greek philosophers by translation and commentary, began to be rendered into Latin. One of the earliest men to encourage the task was Gerbert [84], an important churchman.

Over the space of three centuries, however, the most important translator was Gerard of Cremona. He spent much of his life in Toledo, Spain, working under church auspices. Toledo had been a center of Muslim learning and had been reconquered by the Spaniards in 1085. It was a good place to find learned Arabic works, and learned Arabs too, who could help with the translation and with clearing up uncertain points.

Gerard translated (or supervised the translation of) ninety-two Arabic works, some extremely long. These included portions of Aristotle [29] and all of the *Almagest* of Ptolemy [64], as well as the works of Hippocrates [22], Euclid [40] and Galen [65].

[91] AVERROËS (uh-ver'oh-eez); Arabic name: ABU-AL-WALID MUHAMMAD IBN AHMAD IBN RUSHD
Arabian philosopher
Born: Córdoba, Spain, 1126
Died: Marrakesh, Morocco, December 10, 1198

Averroës, the son of a judge in Córdoba, had, like Avicenna [86] and Alhazen [85], both the benefit and the difficulties involved in being patronized by powerful Muhammadan rulers. The rulers of those portions of Spain still under Muhammadan control set him up as a judge, first in Seville and then, like his father, in Córdoba. He was sent on diplomatic missions. Because (apparently) he was suspected of being a scholar, he was imprisoned for a while in 1195. Finally he retired to Morocco for his own safety.

Averroës' importance is not due to any original work, but to his lengthy and thoughtful commentaries on the work of Aristotle [29]. In this only his younger contemporary Maimonides [92] is to be compared to him.

Averroës was at once the peak and the end of Arabic philosophy, for the gathering woes of Muslim disunity were coming to a head. After Averroës' time, the Muhammadans were to feel the blows of the Christians in Spain and the Mongols and Turks in the east. The Muslim world entered a Dark Age, where scientific inquiry was lost, just as the Christian world was emerging from one.

It followed, then, that Averroës' importance was not felt by the Muslims as much as by the Christians of Europe, who read his work in Latin translation and who built on it, this reaching a climax with Thomas Aquinas [102].

In fact, some of Averroës' books are lost in their Arabic original and exist only in their Latin translations.

[92] MAIMONIDES (my-mon'ih-deez); Hebrew name, MOSES BEN MAIMON
Jewish philosopher
Born: Córdoba, Spain, March 30, 1135
Died: Cairo, Egypt, December 13, 1204

As a child, Maimonides left Spain with his family. Córdoba had been taken by a new and barbaric line of rulers from North Africa and Maimonides' family no longer felt comfortable there. He traveled eastward and finally settled in Egypt in 1165. There he served as physician to Saladin himself, the famous ruler who opposed Richard the Lion-Heart during the third Crusade. Indeed, Richard invited Maimonides to come to England but the philosopher preferred to remain in Egypt, then by far the more civilized of the two nations.

Maimonides in his book *Guide for the Perplexed* disdains astrology, tries to reconcile the teachings of Aristotle [29] with the teachings of the Old Testament. He has been the most influential of all Jewish philosophers.

[93] **NECKAM,** Alexander (nek'am)
English scholar
Born: St. Albans, Hertfordshire, September 8, 1157
Died: Kempsey, Worcestershire, early 1217

Neckam was born, according to legend, on the same night as the prince who later became Richard I, the Lion-Heart. Neckam's mother was wet nurse for the prince as well, but if Neckam lacked the stature, gallantry, and derring-do of the prince, he far surpassed him in intelligence.

Neckam traveled to Paris, and studied and later lectured at its renowned university. In 1186 he returned to England and in 1213 became abbot of Circencester. In Paris, Neckam had learned of the mariner's compass, which the Chinese had been using for at least two centuries. In a book he wrote about 1180 was the first reference to the compass as being in use among Europeans.

He must have had his enemies though (as most scholars did in the ferociously polemical philosophical battles of the Middle Ages) for he was often deliberately misreferred to as "Nequam," which is Latin for "useless."

[94] **GROSSETESTE,** Robert (grohs'-test)
English scholar
Born: Stradbroke, Suffolk, about 1168
Died: Buckden, Huntingdonshire, October 9, 1253

Grosseteste's primary fame is that of a theologian and prelate. Of a poor family, he was nevertheless educated at Oxford and rose steadily in the church, becoming bishop of Lincoln in 1235. He did not fear controversy, standing firmly on principle against all authorities. He fought for the inclusion of more science in the university curriculum, defended the Jews against King Henry III and attacked church abuses even against Pope Innocent IV.

He was also pre-eminent in scholarship and was one of the earliest to introduce Aristotle [29] to Europe. In an age when the translation of the Arabic works of science was of crowning importance, he went even further back. Feeling that third-hand Latin translations from Arabic translations of Greek originals were inevitably corrupt, he brought scholars from the remains of the Byzantine Empire (sections of which were under the temporary control of the West at the time) to translate from the original Greek.

Grosseteste was particularly interested in optics, using Alhazen [85] as his guide. He experimented with mirrors and with lenses and advanced an explanation for the rainbow. Indeed, he thought the primal substance of the universe was not any form of matter, but light itself. If, for light, we substitute the more general term of "energy," Grosseteste, like Heraclitus [10] would seem curiously close to the modern conception.

And yet his greatest claim to fame lies not in his own deeds, but in the fact that he was the teacher of Roger Bacon [99].

[95] **FIBONACCI,** Leonardo (fee-boh-naht'chee); also called LEO-NARDO DA PISA
Italian mathematician
Born: Pisa, about 1170
Died: about 1240

Fibonacci, the first great Western mathematician after the end of Greek science, lived in Pisa at a time when it was one of the great mercantile centers of Italy. It had strong commercial ties with Muhammadan North Africa and Fibonacci's father was the head of a warehouse and therefore intimately connected with this commerce. Fibonacci himself was tutored by a Muhammadan in Algeria and, in later life, traveled widely, remaining in North Africa for extended periods and not settling down in Pisa till 1200.

He thus had ample opportunity to become acquainted with Arabic mathematics and, in particular, with the system of arithmetic notation that al-Khwarizmi [79] had learned from the Hindus.

This notation Fibonacci considered so much more useful than any he had met with in Europe that he bent his energies to propagating its value. In his book *Liber Abaci* ("Book of the Abacus"), published in 1202, he explained the uses of "Arabic numerals." He also made clear the values of positional notation, which made the numbers 213, 123, 132, 321, 231, and 312 all have different values. And, of course, he explained the use of zero.

This had been anticipated by Adelard of Bath [89] a century earlier, but it was with the appearance of this book that the old system of notation by letters of the alphabet, which the Greeks and Romans had used, received its deathblow. (However, the old system took several centuries to die, and we still use Roman numerals for ceremonial occasions, part of their impressiveness being that few people can make them out without some study.)

Fibonacci's learning was sufficiently recognized for him to be presented to the Emperor Frederick II [97] in 1225.

[96] ALBERTUS MAGNUS
German scholar
Born: Lauingen (in southern Germany), 1193
Died: Cologne, November 15, 1280

Albertus Magnus' actual name is Albert, Count von Bollstädt (an inherited title), but he was called Albertus Magnus (Albert the Great) because of his learning. He was also called the Universal Doctor. It was a grandiloquent age and Thomas Aquinas [102], a pupil of Albertus Magnus, was called the Angelic Doctor, while Roger Bacon [99], an enemy and reluctant admirer of Albertus Magnus, was called the Admirable Doctor.

Albertus Magnus studied at the University of Padua in Italy, the intellectual center of Europe in those days, and brought the new learning of the translations from the Arabic northward to Paris, where he lectured from 1245 to 1254. He labored to adapt Aristotelian philosophy into a world view fitted to the medieval mind, a work in which he was to be surpassed by Aquinas. He was, however, more concerned with science itself than Aquinas was, being particularly interested in botany, bringing to that science his own observations made in his many travels on church business. (He was sometimes called the Bishop with the Boots.)

He did not consider Aristotle [29] the last word (although his enemies slightingly referred to him as the Ape of Aristotle) and insisted on the value of personal observation.

He conducted alchemical experiments and is equivocal on the possibility of the transmutation of elements. In this connection he apparently found it difficult to swim against the tide; yet he shows extreme skepticism concerning the possibility. He describes arsenic so clearly in his writings that he is sometimes given credit for its discovery, although it was probably known to earlier alchemists in an impure form.

He suspected the spots on the moon to be surface configurations and the Milky Way to be composed of myriads of stars. He compiled a list of a hundred minerals and seems to have taken note of the existence of fossils.

His learning was such that he was suspected of wizardry, but his position in the church and his orthodoxy protected him. He was bishop of Regensburg from 1260 to 1262 after which he retired to a monastery in Cologne to devote himself for the remainder of his life to his studies. Pius XI proclaimed him a Doctor of the Church—thus automatically canonizing him—in 1931.

[97] FREDERICK II
German Emperor
Born: Iesi, central Italy, December 26, 1194
Died: Lucera, southern Italy, December 13, 1250

Frederick II was one of the remarkable monarchs of history, a man of many talents and a "Renaissance man" two centuries before the Renaissance. His reign was a romantic and turbulent one, marked by desperate battles with the papacy and against his own rebellious son. He took over Jerusalem by negotiation, where previous monarchs had failed through the use of force, but he didn't hold it long. He was the last strong ruler of the medieval Empire.

He was unusual also in his tastes. Although he ruled over Germany and was German by descent, he preferred Sicily for his home and under him Sicily had one last period of splendor, one last moment when it might be recognized as the land of Archimedes [47].

Frederick was unusual for his time in another respect too, for he possessed no religious intolerance. This came easily to him for he was a convinced and practicing atheist. He made no distinctions among the religions, delighted in the company of learned Jews and Muslims, as well as Christians, and even employed Muslim mercenaries in his armies. (They were particularly useful in his battles against the pope.)

Frederick II was one of those monarchs who, like Charlemagne [78], Alfred [81], and Alfonso X [100] were interested in learning. Frederick spoke many languages, patronized scholars and corresponded with them, wrote poetry, kept a zoo that, at one time or another, included monkeys, camels, a giraffe and an elephant, and interested himself in every branch of science.

His most important personal contribution was an excellent book on falconry in which he reported his own observations and thrust aside conclusions based on hearsay (an uncharacteristic attitude for a medieval scholar). In the book, he discussed hundreds of kinds of birds, with illustrations, and made numerous valid generalizations concerning their anatomy, physiology, and behavior. It was first-rate natural history, and in it he did not hesitate to refute Aristotle [29].

[98] MICHAEL SCOT
Irish (?) scholar
Born: before 1200
Died: about 1235

The surname "Scot" may indicate Irish birth, but so little is known about the life of Michael that even this cannot be said with any degree of certainty.

He was another of those whose importance lay in his translations. In particular, he translated Averroës [91] from Arabic into Latin; and in this way made the teachings of Aristotle [29] available to European scholars.

He was one of those scholars whom the learned and intellect-admiring Emperor Frederick II [97] gathered round him, and it was Frederick who encouraged him in his work of translation and urged him to disseminate the results through the universities of Europe.

Michael was an astrologer and indulged in the mystical nonsense of the times, with the result that he was feared by the superstitious, and rumors arose of his great wizardry and of his dealings with demons. This was one of the hazards of secular scholarship in those days. Albertus Magnus [96] and Roger Bacon [99] were likewise suspected of wizardry, and that attitude of mind was eventually responsible for the Faust legend brought to its highest pitch of literary excellence by Goethe [349].

[99] BACON, Roger
English scholar
Born: Ilchester, Somerset, about 1220
Died: Oxford, June 11, 1292

Roger Bacon, the son of well-to-do parents in the service of Henry III, studied at Oxford and then traveled to Paris to teach. There he obtained his degree of master of arts by 1241, then resigned his post in 1247 to devote himself to research. He returned to Oxford about 1251. Among those he studied under in the course of his education was Grosseteste [94].

Bacon somewhat resembles Galileo [166]. Like the Italian scientist of three and a half centuries later, Bacon was a man of bold ideas and imperious self-confidence. Like Galileo, he was unsparing in expressing his contempt of those he felt worthy of it and, in so doing, made numerous important enemies. It was the influence of these enemies (one of them the general of the Franciscan order, of which Bacon was a member) that had him imprisoned for fifteen years and ordered his works suppressed. On the other hand the church did not officially condemn him, and much of his work was done at the request of Pope Clement IV, a great admirer of Bacon. Clement IV died in 1268 and Bacon in his later years no longer had papal protection.

Bacon attempted to write a universal encyclopedia of knowledge, but in his time the task had already become impossible. In his works, he denounced magic generally but accepted the value of astrology. He upheld the roundness of the earth and was the first to suggest that man could circumnavigate it (a romantically fantastic thought for his day). Columbus [121] quoted this in a letter to Ferdinand and Isabella of Spain, but it was to be nearly three centuries before Magellan [130] made reality out of the suggestion.

Bacon estimated the outermost of the heavenly spheres, that of the stars, to be one hundred and thirty million miles from earth, or some five hundred times the distance of the moon. This was a daring guess for the times but Bacon's whole universe was, by this estimate, far smaller than we now know the solar system itself to be.

Bacon pointed out that the Julian calendar made the year a trifle long, so that the equinoxes fell earlier by a day every century or so, but it was to be three centuries before the defect was corrected. He followed his teacher, Grosseteste, in his interest in optics, constructing magnifying glasses, suggesting the use of spectacles for those who were farsighted and even made remarks that sound very much like the description of a telescope (to say nothing of others that sounded like the prediction of steamships, automobiles, and airplanes). Like Grosseteste he appreciated the value of Greek and, indeed, compiled a Greek grammar.

He was interested in alchemy, too, which he claimed was essential to medicine, thus foreshadowing Paracelsus [131], and believed in the possibility of making gold. Because he was one of the first to mention gunpowder (in a letter written in 1247), it was long supposed that he had invented it. (How gunpowder came to be introduced to the Western world, whether from China or through independent invention, is uncertain.) In fact, a whole cluster of legends gathered about Bacon in later centuries, most of which—like the tale that he had constructed a mechanical man—can be dismissed.

Bacon's most modern ideas involve his vehement pioneering belief in experimentation and mathematics as the true routes of scientific advance. He even appealed to Pope Clement to change the educational system to allow for more experimentation and he wrote in high praise of Peter Peregrinus [104], a contemporary experimenter of ability. Unfortunately his influence was lessened by the fact that his books were condemned and therefore unread by most scholars. His greatest work, *Opus Majus*, was not published till 1733. It was to be three and a half centuries before experimentation and quantitative measurements were to become all important in science.

[100] **ALFONSO X** of Castile
Spanish monarch
Born: Burgos, November 23, 1221
Died: Seville, April 24, 1284

Alfonso X, who became king of Castile and León in 1252, was victorious over the Muslims, capturing Cádiz in 1262, but was not a success as a king. His visionary schemes resulted in debased currency and revolts among the nobles and he wasted much effort in a futile attempt to become Holy Roman emperor. He suppressed a revolt by one son, but a second revolt, raised by a second son, forced him from the throne in 1282.

He was noted for his scholarship and his encouragement of learning, for the schools he founded, and for the law codes he sponsored. This resulted in his being called Alfonso el Sabio (Alfonso the Wise), a cognomen granted very few other rulers in history.

Under his patronage the first history of Spain was written and Jews of Toledo translated the Old Testament. He prepared a code of laws, wrote poetry, made commentaries on alchemy, and encouraged further translation of scholarly Arabic books.

He is most famous for encouraging the preparation of revised planetary tables. These were published in 1252, on the day of his accession to the throne. These "Alfonsine Tables" proved the best the Middle Ages had to offer and were not replaced by better ones for over three centuries.

Alfonso X is famous for his remark, made during the tedious preparation of those tables on the basis of the complicated Ptolemaic view of the universe, that had God asked his advice during the days of creation, he would have recommended a simpler design for the universe. This touch of impatience with the sacrosanct conclusions of the Greek scientists extended to physics, too, as Buridan [108] was to show, and three centuries after Alfonso's time was to explode in the Scientific Revolution.

An honor the monarch might never have suspected befell him several centuries later when a crater on the moon was named "Alphonsus" in his honor. In 1957 this crater made headlines when possible volcanic activity was noted in it.

[101] **ALDEROTTI,** Taddeo
Italian physician
Born: Florence, 1223
Died: Bologna, about 1295

Alderotti is the bridge between Greek and European medicine. Judging from his own writings, he was brought up in poverty and it was not until he was an adult that he could find his way to an education. He studied at Bologna, which had one of the great medical schools in western Europe, advanced quickly, and by 1260 was lecturing there.

He wrote commentaries on Hippocrates [22], Galen [65], and Avicenna [86] but urged his readers to go to the originals. He collected clinical cases, presented them to his readers along with advice on treatment.

He became a very successful physician, numbering Pope Honorius IV among his patients. Remembering his poverty-stricken childhood, he charged high fees and, presumably, he was worth them.

[102] **AQUINAS,** Saint Thomas (uh-kwy'nus)
Italian theologian
Born: Roccasecca, near Aquino, about 1225
Died: Fossanuova, March 7, 1274

After an education at Monte Cassino and at the University of Naples, which he entered in 1240, Thomas Aquinas, the youngest of nine children, joined the new Dominican order in 1244. His family objected, kidnapped him, and held him in custody. He escaped and made his way to Paris in 1245 where he studied under Albertus Magnus [96], whom he later accompanied to Cologne in Germany. Eventually he began to write commentaries on Aristotle and achieved great fame. He taught at various places in France and Italy but refused all appointments to high posts, including the archbishopric of Naples. Drawing on Averroës [91] and Maimonides [92] and adding his own thought, he tried to build a system that would blend and reconcile

Aristotelian philosophy and Catholic theology. In this he was most successful. He was canonized in 1323, a mere half century after his death, and his philosophic system remains the basis of Catholic teaching to this day, and he is a Doctor of the Church. His importance to science lies in the fact that he was a rationalist. He upheld reason as a respected method for extending the boundaries of human knowledge, and the result was to help make science once again respectable in Christian Europe after a long period of being considered pagan.

[103] ARNOLD OF VILLANOVA
Spanish alchemist
Born: near Valencia, about 1235
Died: at sea, near Genoa, September 6, 1311

Born in Spain of parents who may have been converted Jews, Arnold had the advantage of being physically close to the Arabic heritage. He could speak Arabic and Greek and through him the full tradition of Arabic alchemy entered the stream of European thought.

Arnold traveled widely and wrote voluminously. As a physician of reputation, he became wealthy. Like Alderotti [101] he helped introduce the teachings of Galen [65] and Avicenna [86] to western Europe.

From the grateful royalty he treated (Pedro III of Aragon, for instance), he received castles and a professorship at the University of Montpellier in France.

He was a controversialist, with strong views on theology that led him into occasional conflict with the church. However, he treated Pope Boniface VIII successfully during a papal illness and this got him out of a particularly bad siege of trouble.

Arnold was a strange mixture of mysticism and science. He announced that the world would end in 1378, for instance, with the appearance of the Antichrist.

He accepted transmutation of the elements and modified the mercury-sulfur theory of Geber [76]. He thought mercury alone was sufficient, although he never proved this by actually producing gold out of it.

He was apparently the first to notice that wood burning under conditions of poor ventilation gave rise to poisonous fumes. This amounts to the discovery of carbon monoxide. He was also the first to prepare pure alcohol.

He, like the "false Geber" [107], was one of those later alchemists in whom genuine science was faintly reappearing.

[104] PEREGRINUS, Petrus (per-uh-grine'us)
French scholar
Born: about 1240
Died: date unknown

Little is known of Peregrinus' personal life; he may have been a Crusader, since his cognomen, Peregrinus, means "the pilgrim." His real name was Petrus de Maricourt. A friend of Roger Bacon [99], he was one of the few medieval scholars who practiced experimentation, centuries before Galileo [166] made it the nub of science.

Peregrinus was an engineer in the army of Louis IX and interested himself in mechanics. He began by attempting to construct a motor that would keep the planetarium designed by Archimedes [47] moving for a period of time. To do so without muscular effort, he conceived of using magnetic forces for the purpose. This was the first suggestion that magnetism might be converted to kinetic energy. These speculations, in turn, led him to a deeper consideration of the magnet.

The Greek tradition had it that Thales [3] was the first to observe and study the manner in which certain rocks (lodestone) attracted iron. It was a phenomenon that exercised the ingenuity of philosophers because it seemed to represent "action at a distance." It was hard to understand how one object could exert a force on another without physical contact.

It was somehow learned (by whom is not known) that a magnet in the form of a needle if freely suspended or freely

61

floating would align itself roughly north and south. Some time before 1200, European navigators began to use such a needle (a "compass") to guide them in their voyages. Legend has it that the Chinese made the discovery centuries earlier and the Europeans picked up the knowledge via the Arabs, but this is uncertain.

In any case, in 1269, while taking part in the slow and dull siege of an Italian city, Peregrinus wrote a letter to a friend in which he described his researches on magnets. He showed how to determine the north and south poles of a magnet, pointed out that like poles repelled each other whereas unlike poles attracted. He also explained that one could not isolate one of the poles by breaking a magnet in two, because each half was then a complete magnet with both a north and south pole.

Most important of all, perhaps, he described an improved compass to be formed by placing the magnetic needle on a pivot, rather than allowing it to float on a piece of cork, and surrounding it by a graduated circular scale to allow directions to be read more accurately. Undoubtedly it was this device that made the compass really practical; and it was, in turn, the use of a practical compass that gave European navigators the self-confidence needed to sail into the Atlantic far out of sight of land. Peregrinus thus was another herald of the great Age of Exploration that was to begin in another century and a half.

Where Peregrinus chiefly failed was in his explanation of the reason for the north-south alignment of the needle. He believed the needle pointed to the pole of the celestial sphere, the outermost of the spheres in the Ptolemaic heavens. A better explanation had to await Gilbert [155].

[105] **POLO,** Marco
Italian explorer
Born: Venice, about 1254
Died: Venice, January 9, 1324

Marco Polo came of a family of well-to-do Venetian merchants. While he was still a young boy, his father, Nicolo, and his uncle, Maffeo, set out eastward on a trading mission.

They began in 1260 at an unusual time in history. A half century earlier the Mongol, Genghis Khan, had begun a remarkable career of conquest and now his grandson, Kublai Khan, acknowledged as head of the various Mongol princes, ruled over an immense empire that, for the first time, placed much of Asia and Europe under a single rule and made travel over that whole area practical.

Kublai Khan had the Venetians brought to his summer palace at Shangtu in China (Coleridge, in his famous poem "Kublai Khan" called it Xanadu). The Mongol ruler was fascinated by them and eventually sent them back to Europe to bring missionaries to teach him and his people Christianity. The Polos unfortunately found the papacy in the turmoil of an interregnum. The missionaries were never sent and the great chance to Christianize the Far East never returned.

The Polos returned to China in 1275 and this time Marco was with them. Marco in particular rose to high place and was a trusted diplomat in Kublai Khan's service. In the khan's old age, however, the Polos felt they could not trust in the favor of his successor and, when they were given the mission of escorting a Mongol princess to Persia, they seized the opportunity to continue onward toward home. They finally reached Venice again in 1295. Central Asia was not to be observed by Europeans in such detail for five more centuries.

Marco Polo's stories of the wonders he had seen and of the high civilization of the Far East in the midsummer of Mongol domination was greeted with derision and he was named Marco Milioni (Marco Millions) because he dealt with such large numbers in his descriptions.

In 1298 Venice and Genoa renewed their naval wars and Marco Polo held a command in the Venetian fleet. He was captured. While in a Genoese prison he dictated the story of his travels. He did not deal so much with personal matters as with a description of the portions of Asia and Africa with which he was reasonably familiar. A year later he was released and allowed to return to Venice.

The book was popular, but it was largely disbelieved and considered an entertaining but implausible tissue of tall tales. It was not until five and a half centuries later that European explorers finally penetrated the interior of Asia and found that, on the whole, and barring a few wonder stories, Marco Polo was accurate in his description of such matters as coal, asbestos, and paper currency.

The importance of the book lay in its portrayal of the wealth of the "Indies." Columbus [121] owned a copy of Polo's book and scribbled enthusiastic marginal notes in it. It was Marco Polo's great trek east that drove Columbus west in the hope of arriving at the same destination. Marco Polo therefore contributed his bit toward the intellectual ferment that was to break over Europe within two centuries, broadening horizons both geographically and intellectually.

[106] **D'ABANO,** Pietro (dah'bah-noh)
Italian physician
Born: Abano, near Padua, 1257
Died: Padua, about 1315

D'Abano, after studying at Padua, traveled through Greece and the Near East, visiting Constantinople, absorbing knowledge of Arabic medicine, then completed his formal Western training at Paris. He had apparently met Marco Polo [105] and caught a breath of the world that was still beyond the medieval horizon. As Marco Polo foreshadowed the great Age of Exploration soon to come, so D'Abano foreshadowed the great Age of Science. He wrote a book entitled *Conciliator* in which he tried to weave together the Greek and Arabic schools of medicine and in which he expressed some ideas that were well ahead of his time. For instance, he maintained that the brain was the source of the nerves, and the heart of the blood vessels. He also stated that air had weight, and he made an unusually accurate estimate of the year.

He was, however, convinced of the usefulness of astrology and, like so many of the scholars of the period was suspected of magical practices (particularly by competing physicians less successful in their practice).

He was brought up twice for heresy before the Inquisition because he rejected the miraculous aspects of the gospel tales. He was acquitted the first time and died during the course of the second trial.

[107] **FALSE GEBER**
Born: Perhaps about 1270
Died: Date unknown

Nothing is known of him, not even his name (for he wrote under the pseudonym of Geber [76]), except that he was probably a Spaniard, like Arnold of Villanova [103], and that he wrote about 1300. He was the first to describe sulfuric acid, the most important single industrial chemical used today. The alchemical discovery of sulfuric acid and the other strong acids is, by all odds, the greatest chemical achievement of the Middle Ages. It made possible all sorts of changes that could not be brought about by vinegar, the strongest acid known to the ancients. The discovery was infinitely more important than the preparation of gold would have been, for even if gold could be prepared, the mere fact that it could, would erase its value. Gold, after all, is a comparatively useless metal (although admittedly the most beautiful) and has few values that do not stem from its rarity.

[108] **BURIDAN,** Jean (byoo-ree-dahn')
French philosopher
Born: Béthune, Artois, about 1295
Died: Paris, about 1358

Buridan studied under Ockham [109] and became himself a professor at the University of Paris. He rejected important sections of Aristotle's [29] theories of physics, then in full sway over the minds of Europe's scholars.

Aristotle had felt that an object in motion required a continuous force and reasoned that the air supplied that continuing force after the initial impetus (that of a catapult, for instance) had been spent. Buridan maintained that the initial impetus was sufficient; and that once it was supplied, motion continued indefinitely. The spheres of heaven, for instance, having been put in motion by God, continued so and required no constantly working angels to keep them moving. This was an anticipation of Newton's [231] first law of motion (propounded three centuries later). More generally, he believed the same laws of motion prevailed in the heavens as on earth.

Buridan is most famous for a point he is supposed to have made concerning the impossibility of action by free will under two opposite and exactly balanced impulses. His example was the case of an ass poised exactly between two exactly equivalent bales of hay. Since there would be no reason to choose one bale over the other, the ass would remain in perpetual indecision and would starve to death. However, "Buridan's ass" is nowhere to be found in Buridan's writings, so it is doubtful that he is really the author of it.

[109] OCKHAM, WILLIAM OF (ok'-um)
English scholar
Born: Ockham, Surrey, about 1285
Died: Munich, Germany, 1349

William of Ockham (called the Invincible Doctor) joined the Franciscan order, studied at Oxford, and lectured there from 1315 to 1319. He was among the last of the medieval scholars and led the battle against the views of Thomas Aquinas [102]. Ockham held that much of theology was a matter of faith, not amenable to reason. For this and, even more so, because he was an opponent of papal supremacy, he was tried for heresy in 1324 by Pope John XXII. He fled and was protected by Holy Roman Emperor Louis IV, who as a strong political opponent of the pope automatically favored any antipapal scholar. After Louis' death, Ockham cautiously made his peace with the church.

Ockham battled against the universals that had been introduced by Plato [24], the notion that the only true realities were the ideal objects of which the earthly objects sensible to perception were only imperfect copies. These ideals Ockham considered abstractions, mere names (hence the expression "nominalism" for this philosophy), and held that only the objects perceived were real.

Since the universalists kept adding more and more items to their ideals in order to make their theories work, Ockham laid down the rule that: "Entities must not needlessly be multiplied." This has been interpreted in modern times to mean that of two theories equally fitting all observed facts, that theory requiring the fewer or simpler assumptions is to be accepted as more nearly valid. The rule, now called "Ockham's razor," is of vital importance in the philosophy of science.

[110] MONDINO DE' LUZZI (mon-dee'noh day loot'tsee)
Italian anatomist
Born: Bologna, about 1275
Died: Bologna, 1326

The thirteenth century marked the height of the Middle Ages and thereafter there was a stirring of new viewpoints, particularly in Italy, as was exemplified by Pietro d'Abano [106]. The translations from the Arabic had aroused an interest in the nonscientific works of the Greeks and Romans, which were read anew with great appreciation. They inspired imitation and a resurgence of interest in man and the world (humanism) after the long preoccupation with theology and the afterworld. This was the Renaissance.

Scientifically, an interest in man meant the faint stirrings of biology and medicine. Famous Italian schools of medicine sprang up at Salerno in the ninth century and Bologna in the thirteenth. At Bologna the art of dissection was revived, not specifically for research but for utilitarian work in connection with legal cases or medical postmortems and for demonstrations to confirm the views of Galen [65] and Avicenna [86].

The greatest of the Renaissance anatomists was Mondino de' Luzzi, the son of an apothecary, who studied at the medical school at Bologna, under Alderotti [101] graduating about 1290 and joining its teaching staff in 1306.

He taught anatomy in a very unusual way for the times. Ordinarily the lecturer, mounted on a high platform, lectured loftily from the ancient writers while a menial conducted the actual illustrative dissection. This perpetuated errors, since the lecturer did not himself see what he was talking about, and the anatomist could not understand the talk concerning what he saw.

Mondino, however, did his own dissections, and on the basis thereof wrote, in 1316, the first book in history to be devoted entirely to anatomy. (He is therefore called the Restorer of Anatomy.)

Much of Mondino's terminology is taken from the Arabic and is rather disorderly. The book contains many errors where Mondino remains too much under the influence of the ancients. He describes the stomach as spherical, gives the liver five lobes instead of three, and sticks to Avicenna's description of the heart. However, he made some advances, notably in his description of the organs of the reproductive system.

In any case, Mondino's book was to be the best available until the time of Vesalius [146], over two centuries later, for Mondino's successors reverted to the practice of having somebody else do the dissecting.

[111] HENRY THE NAVIGATOR
Portuguese prince
Born: Oporto (now Porto),
March 4, 1394
Died: Sagres, November 13, 1460

Henry, a younger son of King John I of Portugal, was part English, for his mother's father was John of Gaunt. Henry was thus the great-grandson of Edward III of England.

In Henry's day the tide had turned and the Christians of Portugal were finally recrossing the Strait of Gibraltar to fight the Muslims on African soil. In 1415 Henry took part in a battle at Ceuta, on the northwestern tip of Africa and was knighted for heroism. Although he himself never penetrated deeper into Africa, he fell in love with the continent, or rather with the project of exploring its coasts.

He dedicated himself to that sole purpose, establishing an observatory and school for navigation at Sagres on Cape St. Vincent in 1418. This was in southernmost Portugal, the southwestern tip of Europe. Year after year he outfitted and sent out ships that inched their way farther and farther down the African coast. He even supervised the collection of astronomic data to ensure the greater safety and success of the ships.

It was Henry's ultimate aim to circumnavigate Africa as Hanno [12] had supposedly done two thousand years before, but in his lifetime his ships only reached the area now marked by Dakar, the westernmost point on the western bulge of Africa. He died a full generation before the continent was successfully rounded.

The light he lit did not go out. Portuguese successes inspired other west European nations to send expeditions of their own and the great Age of Exploration was under way, reaching its climax with Columbus [121] and Magellan [130].

[112] ULUGH BEG (oo'loog beg')
Mongol astronomer
Born: Soltaniyeh, Persia, March 22, 1394
Died: Samarkand (now part of the Uzbek S.S.R.), October 27, 1449

Ulugh Beg ("great prince") is the name by which Muhammad Taragay is known. He was a grandson of the Mongol warrior Tamerlane, last of the great barbarian conquerors. He himself governed a portion of the central Asian realm in the lifetime of his father and succeeded to the throne in 1447.

His real fame, however, is as the only

important scientist to be found among the Mongols. In 1420 he founded a university in Samarkand, and in 1424 he built an astronomic observatory there, the best in the world at that time.

Furthermore, he did more than merely fiddle with Ptolemy's [64] tables, as European astronomers were doing throughout the Middle Ages. Ulugh Beg published new tables in the Tadzhik language based on his own observations. They were superior to those of Ptolemy. His star map, containing 994 stars, was the first new one since Hipparchus [50].

Ulugh Beg, however, was doomed to obscurity by the accident of space and time. He had no followers and when he was assassinated by his son in 1449, Mongolian astronomy died with him. His observatory was reduced to ruins by 1500 and it was only in 1908 that its remains were found.

His writings appeared in Arabic and Persian, but the nations of Europe where astronomy was soon to burst into new and gigantic growth did not hear of him.

It was not until 1665 that his tables were translated into Latin and by that time Ulugh Beg had been surpassed by Tycho Brahe [156] and had been made obsolete by the coming of the telescope. Few even today realize that a Mongol prince had once been the greatest astronomer of his time.

[113] **TOSCANELLI,** Paolo (tos-kuh-nel'lee)
Italian physician and mapmaker
Born: Florence, 1397
Died: Florence, May 15, 1482

Toscanelli, the son of a physician, studied medicine and was a friend of Nicholas of Cusa [115]. He was interested in astronomy and made creditable observations of comets.

His lone claim to fame, however, and his chief service to science, consisted of a mistake firmly held. He believed that Asia lay three thousand miles west of Europe and drew up a map of the Atlantic Ocean with Europe on the east and Asia on the west. He showed this to

Columbus [121], and that was all Columbus needed.

[114] **GUTENBERG,** Johann (goo'tenberg)
German inventor
Born: Mainz, Hesse, about 1398
Died: Mainz, about 1468

Little is known of Gutenberg's early life, except that he used his mother's maiden name. (His father's name was Ganzfleisch—"goose meat"—and the change seems an improvement.) About 1430 he had to leave Mainz as a result of being on the losing side of a civic squabble. He went to Strasbourg, a hundred miles to the south. By 1435 he was involved in a lawsuit, and in that suit the word *drucken* (printing) was used. Gutenberg's attempt to make printing practical may have begun as early as that.

Until Gutenberg's time, books were laboriously copied by hand. This meant that they were few and expensive, that only rich men, monasteries, and universities could have libraries of dozens of books, that entire cultures had to be satisfied with only one or two really large libraries. (The one at Alexandria was the most famous in all the centuries before Gutenberg.) Furthermore, errors were bound to infiltrate hand-copied books unless the most heroic precautions were taken. (The Jewish copyists of the Bible counted every letter in an effort to guard against error.)

The mechanical reproduction of lettering—incising it in reverse on wood or metal and then pressing the surface against a soft medium or (after inking) on a blank sheet—was known in ancient times. The Sumerians and Babylonians used small intaglios to serve as signatures when impressed in clay, much as we use inked stamps.

What Gutenberg conceived, however, was not a one-shot stamp, good only for one purpose, but a series of small stamps, each representing a single letter, which could be assembled to form a page of lettering, then broken down and reassembled to form another page. A limited number of such movable type could then be used to print an unlimited number of different books, and, what is more, an unlimited number of identical copies of a particular book could be printed in very little time.

By 1450 Gutenberg was back in Mainz and definitely engaged in working on his invention. Like most crucial inventions, the practical development depended on the concurrent success of other developments. The production of many books required the existence of a cheap and plentiful supply of something on which the printing could be impressed. Fortunately paper, which had been invented by Tsai Lun [63] fourteen centuries earlier, had reached Europe.

Proper inks had to be developed and also proper techniques for forming tiny metal letters all of the same measurements so that they could be interchanged without trouble and so that all would impress themselves on the paper equally. Gutenberg also designed a printing press to make the impression more firmly than could be managed by the unaided biceps. It was not easy; although the concept of printing probably took no more than an instant of time to enter Gutenberg's head, the practical development took at least twenty years.

By 1454 Gutenberg was ready for the big task. He began to put out a Bible, in double columns, with forty-two lines in Latin to the page. He produced three hundred copies of each of 1282 pages and thus produced the three hundred Gutenberg Bibles. It was the first printed book, and many people consider it the most beautiful ever produced—so that the art was born at its height. The Gutenberg Bibles that remain are the most valued books in the world.

Unfortunately, Gutenberg had gone into debt to produce the Bible and was sued for the money. He lost (he was a chronic loser) and was forced to hand over his tools and presses. He did not even get a chance actually to publish his Bible. The winners of the suit, including his ex-partner, did so.

Gutenberg, who never married, died in debt and, apparently, a failure, but printing proved a phenomenal success. It swept Europe and introduced a new method by which propagandists could spread their views. It is probable that Luther's rebellion against the church succeeded where previous rebellions had failed because Luther harnessed the printing press and fought his battle with broadsides of intensely styled pamphlets.

Printing meant cheap books, and cheap books made literacy worthwhile. By 1500 up to nine million printed copies of thirty thousand different works were in circulation. The base of scholarship broadened and the educated community grew in numbers. Furthermore, the views and discoveries of scholars could be made known quickly to other scholars. Scholars began to act as a team, instead of as isolated individuals. The realm of the unknown could more and more be assaulted by concerted blows. Scientists were no longer fists, but arms moving a battering ram.

Printing did not immediately bring on the Scientific Revolution. A century was yet to pass. However, it made the revolution inevitable. And, taken in reverse, the revolution would probably have been impossible without printing.

[115] NICHOLAS OF CUSA
German scholar
Born: Kues, near Treves, Rhineland, 1401
Died: Lodi, Italy, August 11, 1464

Nicholas Krebs, usually known as Nicholas of Cusa from his birthplace, was the son of a fisherman. He studied law at Heidelberg, then at the University of Padua, where he met Toscanelli [113] and where he received his degree in 1423. He abandoned law, however, to enter the church in 1430. He was primarily a philosopher and had the uncanny knack of coming upon notions that are close to those now held.

In opposition to the practical Regiomontanus [119], Nicholas, in a book published in 1440, held that the earth turned on its axis and moved about the sun, that there was neither "up" nor "down" in space, that space was infinite, that the stars were other suns and bore in their grasp other inhabited worlds. These beliefs, however, were not backed by detailed observation, calculation, or theory. They did not affect the course of science, and it is doubtful that Copernicus [121] even heard of them.

In other fields, Nicholas was equally intuitive. He constructed spectacles with concave lenses for the nearsighted, where earlier spectacles had made use only of the more easily ground convex lenses and served only the farsighted. He considered that plants drew their sustenance in part from the air, and he advocated counting the pulse as a diagnostic aid in medicine.

In general, he was anxious to measure physical phenomena, a point of view Galileo [166] was to make popular a century and a half later. Far from getting into trouble for his radical views, Nicholas was appointed a cardinal in 1448. Bruno [157], who shared many of his views in a later and more troubled time, was not to be so fortunate.

[116] **BESSARION,** John (beh-sar'ee-on)
Greek scholar
Born: Trebizond (now Trabzon, Turkey), January 2, 1403
Died: Ravenna, Italy, November 18, 1472

Constantinople, after having been the great Roman capital of the East, had grown weaker and weaker and was in imminent danger of falling to the waxing power of the Ottoman Turks. Repeatedly, the Byzantine Emperors appealed for help to the West. The West wasn't strong enough to help and, in any case, wanted the Eastern Christians to acknowledge the primacy of the pope, which the Eastern Christians would not do even if it meant subjection to the Turks.

In 1437, Emperor John VIII came to Italy, pleading for help. With him was Basil Bessarion, archbishop of Nicaea. Bessarion, at least, favored accepting the pope's terms and when the emperor returned with nothing accomplished, Bessarion stayed on in Italy, took the name

John, and was made a cardinal in 1439 by Pope Eugene IV.

Bessarion was a great scholar who had accumulated many manuscripts of the great Greek books. He spread the knowledge of Greek to western scholars; translated the works of Aristotle [29], which thus reached the West for the first time without having been filtered through the Arabic first.

On his death, he left his library to the Senate of Venice. By that time, Constantinople had fallen to the Turks (in 1453) but, thanks to Bessarion, Greek knowledge was not utterly lost to the West.

[117] **ALBERTI,** Leone Battista (al-ber'-tee)
Italian artist
Born: Genoa, February 18, 1404
Died: Rome, April 25, 1472

In their almost uncritical appreciation of the achievements of the ancients the humanists of the Renaissance failed to see that after those ancients a number of advances had been made in technology, and those later centuries were not simply to be dismissed as "dark." The Dark Ages (a term invented in the Renaissance as a derogatory reference) saw the introduction of the compass, of gunpowder, of windmills, of horseshoes, and horse collars. Nor was the literature, architecture, art, and philosophy of the Dark or Middle Ages to be too easily dismissed. In comparison the men of the Renaissance, who exalted art and literature (the "humanities"), tended to neglect science.

The neglect was not, of course, complete. Even the finest of the fine arts will, in some measure, lead thought in the direction of science, because, in the final analysis, all knowledge is one.

Alberti, the illegitimate son of a wealthy Florentine exile, is an example. He was educated in law at the University of Bologna, receiving his doctorate in 1428, but law did not hold him and could not. He was a "Renaissance man" in the sense of having a broad range of interests, of excelling in many fields and scorning narrow specialization.

Arriving in Rome in 1432, where his talents had full scope, he was prominent in nearly all the arts, in painting and in sculpture. He was an excellent architect (the best since Vitruvius [55]) and designed some notable churches in Mantua and Rimini. He wrote a treatise on architecture that remained authoritative for centuries. He was a musician and organist as well, a writer of tragedies in Latin, and also a mathematician.

Alberti was a developer of the laws of perspective in a book published in 1434 and thus the forerunner of what is today called "projective geometry," a science properly developed by Poncelet [456] four centuries later. He used mechanical aids, such as pinhole cameras, to guide him. The laws of perspective gave Renaissance art its naturalism and distinguished it from the solemn two-dimensionality of medieval art. In the hands of later Renaissance masters, such as Leonardo da Vinci [122], considerations of perspective grew so detailed that art became almost a branch of geometry. The vogue for such "real looking" art has long passed among most artists, but it is still the kind of art most easily appreciated by the untrained eye.

[118] **PEURBACH,** Georg von (poir'-bahkh)
Austrian mathematician and astronomer
Born: Peurbach (near Vienna), May 30, 1423
Died: April 8, 1461

Peurbach studied at the University of Vienna, then traveled to Italy, the intellectual center of Europe at the time. There he met Nicholas of Cusa [115]. He returned to Vienna in 1453 and lectured there on astronomy and mathematics, and was appointed astrologer to King Ladislas V of Hungary and later to the Emperor Frederick III.

Peurbach was an ardent advocate of the use of Arabic numerals, an innovation that was already two hundred and

fifty years old, having been introduced that long ago by Fibonacci [95]. Even so, the infinitely inferior Roman numerals were still doggedly retained by many, a remarkable example of self-damaging conservatism. Peurbach's use of Arabic numerals to prepare a table of sines of unprecedented accuracy, advancing the mechanics of trigonometry past the Greek and Arabic mark, made it very difficult for the reactionaries. He died, however, before he could finish. His pupil Regiomontanus [119] labored at the table too, and also died before he could finish.

Peurbach attempted to polish the Ptolemaic system, but he did not dare change it in essentials. He took a backward step in fact by insisting on the solid reality of the crystalline spheres of the planets, something which Ptolemy [64] had not quite insisted upon in the *Almagest.* These solid spheres only lasted a century, however, and then Tycho Brahe [156] destroyed them once and for all.

[119] **REGIOMONTANUS** (ree-jee-oh-mon-tay'nus)
German astronomer
Born: Königsberg, Franconia, June 6, 1436
Died: Rome, Italy, July 8, 1476

Regiomontanus was the son of a miller and his real name was, appropriately enough, Johann Müller. His high-sounding pseudonym ("king's mountain" in English) is the Latin name of his birthplace, which is not, by the way, the more famous Königsberg (now Kaliningrad), East Prussia.

Regiomontanus was admitted to the University of Leipzig at the age of eleven. In 1450, he was at the University of Vienna, where he gained his bachelor's degree in 1452 and was on the faculty in 1457.

He was a thoroughgoing follower of Ptolemy's [64] astronomy, and learned Greek in order to probe back beyond the Arabs. He studied with Peurbach [118] and labored with him in joint endeavors. Regiomontanus published a revised and corrected version of *Almagest,* making use of the Greek copies Bessarion [116] had brought from Constantinople. However, it was not as good a version as, unknown to him or anyone in Europe, Ulugh Beg [112] was preparing a continent away. Regiomontanus also discovered an uncopied manuscript of Diophantus [66], the only portion of his work ever recovered.

Regiomontanus was conservative in his outlook. He went out of his way to deride the possibility that the earth moved. He insisted that rotation on its axis was a foolish concept and pointed out that the earth's rotation would mean that birds would be blown away, clouds would be left behind, buildings would tumble. This argument had been used before and would continue to be used with powerful effect until the time of Galileo [166].

Regiomontanus made important observations of the heavens and prepared new tables of planetary motions that brought those prepared under Alfonso X [100] up to date. The new tables were widely used by the navigators of the Age of Exploration, which was now in full swing, and were, for instance, used by Columbus [121]. Regiomontanus introduced Germany to the use of Arabic algebraic and trigonometric methods, reproducing the tables by the use of Gutenberg's [114] then newfangled technique of printing.

As might be expected of a Renaissance man, Regiomontanus also lectured on Vergil and Cicero. And, on the other hand, he published books on astrology, of which he was an ardent practitioner.

In 1472 Regiomontanus made observations of a comet (later known as Halley's) and this was the first time that comets were made the object of a scientific study, instead of serving merely to stir up superstitious terror. By 1475 his fame had grown so that he was summoned to Rome by Pope Sixtus IV to help reform the Julian calendar, a project that had been hanging fire for centuries. However, Regiomontanus died in Rome the following year of the plague, and the project dragged on for nearly another century.

[120] **PACIOLI,** Luca (pah-choh'lee)
Italian mathematician
Born: Sansepolcro, Tuscany,
about 1445
Died: Sansepolcro, 1517

Pacioli studied mathematics when he was in the service of a rich Venetian merchant. He became a Franciscan friar about 1470 and wandered from place to place, teaching mathematics and writing books on arithmetic sufficiently successful to net him positions as lecturer at such universities as those at Perugia, Naples, and Rome. At the court of Ludovico Sforza, Duke of Milan, Pacioli met Leonardo da Vinci [122]. Pacioli taught Leonardo mathematics and in return, Leonardo helped illustrate one of Pacioli's books. (Lucky Pacioli!) Pacioli also prepared both Latin and Italian versions of Euclid.

Pacioli's work on mathematics was of minor importance, but there are humble ways, too, in which it can be of use. In 1494, he had published his major work on arithmetic and geometry and it included the first appearance in print of a detailed description of the method of double-entry bookkeeping. It may not seem much but such a device greatly facilitates the ease and accuracy with which business can be conducted and did its bit to contribute to the growth of the merchant states of western Europe on their way to world domination.

[121] **COLUMBUS,** Christopher
Italian explorer
Born: probably Genoa, 1451
Died: Valladolid, Spain, May 20, 1506

Not much is known of Columbus' early life. Although it is generally thought he was born in Italy, there is nothing in his later life to make him seem an Italian. His writing was always in Spanish or Spanish-tinged Latin; he used a Spanish version of his name; and he showed no signs of any Italian sympathies. There is a persistent, but unverified, rumor that he was born of a

Spanish-Jewish family residing in Genoa at the time of his birth.

The son of a weaver, Columbus received an education, though this may have been from reading rather than formal training. About 1465, rather than work as a wool comber like his father, he ran away to sea. While still young he sailed through the Mediterranean and is supposed to have made a trip to Iceland.

In 1479 he married the daughter of a distinguished Italian navigator in the Portuguese service and this intensified his interest in navigation generally.

He gained a knowledge of mapmaking and, very fortunately, gained just enough misinformation to believe with Poseidonius [52] that the earth was no more than eighteen thousand miles in circumference. This was reinforced by a map by Toscanelli [113], with whom he was in contact in 1481. He had read eagerly of the wonders of the Indies in the book by Marco Polo [105] and it seemed to him that a voyage of only three thousand miles west of Europe would bring him to those same Indies.

(It is a common myth that Columbus believed the earth was round while everyone else thought it was flat. The fact is that the earth's rotundity was accepted by all European scholars of the time. The only points of disagreement lay in the distance from Europe to Asia—that is, in the circumference of the earth—and in the feasibility of traveling that distance in the boats of the day.)

In the early 1480s Columbus was, like his father-in-law, sailing in the service of Portugal and his passion for a westward trip finally goaded him into placing the project before the Portuguese king, John II. The king, in turn, referred it to the Portuguese geographers who, very properly, rejected it, for they were sure that Columbus' claim of three thousand miles to Asia was a gross underestimate and that the surest route to Asia was around Africa. In this the experienced Portuguese were quite correct (Africa was successfully circumnavigated fifteen years later) and the Italian dreamer completely wrong. What neither of them knew, however, was that between Europe and Asia lay unknown continents

and that these unknown continents *did* lie three thousand miles distant. (This is one of the more fortunate coincidences of history.)

Columbus then tried to interest the city of Genoa, other Italian city-states, England, and Spain in his visionary plan and, for a while, met failure all around. In 1492, however, the monarchs of Spain, Ferdinand and Isabella, had just wiped out the last remnant of Muslim rule over the peninsula, and in the glow of triumph they agreed to subsidize Columbus.

The subsidy was not a generous one, but on August 3, 1492, Columbus set sail with three small ships and 120 men (mostly from the prisons). On October 12 he landed on a small island of what he thought were the Indies. He explored various regions and returned to Spain and the sort of wild acclamation that these days is accorded an astronaut safely returned to earth.

In the next ten years he made three more voyages to the Indies. He was given office in the new lands, but was as poor an administrator as he was courageous a navigator, and that is very poor indeed. He died in eclipse, still believing that he had reached Asia.

King Ferdinand, having watched with indifference while Columbus ended his life in misery, gave him a splendid funeral. His body was eventually moved to the New World and now rests in the Dominican Republic.

His voyage caught the imagination of Europe far more strongly than any previous ones. There were great explorers before Columbus, but Columbus dramatized exploration and did for ocean-going what Lindbergh [1249] was to do for air-going more than four centuries later.

It was impossible to make a trip of this sort without adding to man's knowledge. Columbus discovered new races of men, new plants, and new phenomena. He was the first to note, on September 13, 1492, the shifting of the direction in which the compass needle pointed as one traveled from place to place on the earth's surface. (He kept this from his men lest they panic at the thought that they were heading into strange regions where the laws of nature were no longer observed.)

The new picture of the globe that followed on Columbus' voyage seemed to emphasize the littleness and insufficiency of ancient knowledge. The fact that huge lands existed of which Aristotle [29] and Ptolemy [64] knew nothing, seemed to lift some of the psychological restraint of intellectual rebellion. The birthpangs of the imminent Scientific Revolution (Copernicus [127] was nineteen when Columbus made his great voyage) were made that much easier.

[122] **LEONARDO DA VINCI** (veen'-chee)
Italian artist
Born: Vinci, near Florence, April 15, 1452
Died: Castle Cloux, near Amboise, France, May 2, 1519

Leonardo was of illegitimate birth, but was acknowledged and raised by his father, a notary. Most of us think of him as an artist, particularly as the painter of the "Mona Lisa" and the "Last Supper," but he was much more than that. Even more than Alberti [117] he was a "Renaissance man," though he lacked a classical education and knew neither Latin nor Greek.

He was a military engineer who visualized devices beyond the scope of his time and drew sketches of primitive tanks and airplanes, using all sorts of elaborate gears, chains, ratchets, et cetera. He was endlessly ingenious in the mechanical gadgetry possible to the level of technology of the time. He is supposed to have designed the first parachute and to have constructed the first elevator, one for the Milan cathedral. In order to design airplanes he studied the flight of birds, and for submarine designs he studied the manner in which fish swam. He also advertised his abilities as flamboyantly as Alhazen [85] five centuries earlier, but more honestly and with better results.

Despite the seeming bloodthirstiness of his war engines, he was a humanitarian who denied himself meat out of an aversion to the killing of animals.

Moreover, the combination of military engineering ability and superlative artistic skill brought Leonardo a succession of powerful patrons in an age that valued war and art equally. These included Lorenzo the Magnificent of Florence, Ludovico Sforza of Milan, Cesare Borgia, the son of Pope Alexander VI, Louis XII of France, Giulio de Medici, brother of Pope Leo X, and, finally, Francis I of France.

In science Leonardo had amazing insight. He had a notion of the principle of inertia, and nearly a century before Galileo [166] he understood that falling bodies accelerated as they fell. He grasped the impossibility of perpetual motion decades before Stevinus [158].

As an artist, he studied the structure of the muscles and bones of the human body, dissecting some thirty cadavers. (This brought on some difficulties with authorities in Rome.) He also studied the structure and working of the heart and its valves and speculated on the circulation of the blood a century before Harvey [174].

He considered the moon to be earthy in nature and to shine by reflected sunlight; and the earth *not* to be the center of the universe, and to be spinning on its own axis. He even considered the possibility of long-continued changes in the structure of the earth two centuries ahead of Hutton [297] and had correct opinions as to the nature of fossils. His close observation and his amazing skill at drawing were such that his pictures of waves and bubbles in water could not be improved on till the coming of the slow-motion camera.

Unfortunately he kept his ideas to himself, writing them in code in voluminous notebooks so that his contemporaries knew nothing of his ideas and remained uninfluenced by them. It is only we moderns who have learned of them, and that only long after the fact.

[123] **VESPUCIUS,** Americus (ves-pyoo'shus)
Italian navigator
Born: Florence, March 1454
Died: Seville, Spain, February 22, 1512

Americus Vespucius is the Latinized version of Amerigo Vespucci. Vespucius was the son of a notary, who worked for Florentine bankers and was sent by them on missions to Spain.

The voyages of Columbus [121] had shaken the world; Asia had presumably been reached, and yet the wealth and civilization of Asia had not become apparent. Between 1497 and 1504, Vespucius took part in voyages to the western shores of the Atlantic to consider the matter.

Vespucius did not make any fundamental physical discoveries, but he did something more important. He had a keen flash of insight. To his dying day, Columbus had been convinced he had reached Asia; but to Vespucius, this was impossible. The new lands extended too far to the south. In 1504, Vespucius said that the new lands were not Asia but represented a new continent totally unknown to the ancients; and that between that continent and Asia there must stretch a second ocean. (Actually, Columbus, too, would have believed this, were it not that he was convinced earth was considerably smaller than it really was.)

It was this concept which really marked the break with the ancient world. If Columbus had simply reached Asia, this was after all in accordance with the Greek notions of the world. It was a new continent unknown to them that turned everything topsy-turvy, and it is only justice that the new continents were named America after Vespucius and *not* Columbia after Columbus.

Vespucius ended his life as official astronomer to Ferdinand II of Spain. Vespucius met Columbus toward the end of the latter's life and their relationship was friendly.

[124] **CANO,** Juan Sebastián del (kah'-noh)
Spanish navigator
Born: Guetaria, about 1460
Died: somewhere in the Pacific Ocean, August 4, 1526

The great moment of Cano's life was his return to Spain with one ship carrying a crew who had circumnavigated the earth. It is he, not Magellan [130], who deserves the title of first circumnavigator. However, it was Magellan whose grit kept the expedition together during the terrible months in the Pacific. Cano died four years later on a second expedition to the far Pacific. The pitcher went to the well once too often.

[125] **WALDSEEMÜLLER,** Martin
(vahlt'zay-myool-er)
German cartographer
Born: Radolfzell or Freiburg, Baden, about 1470
Died: St. Dié, Alsace (now in France), about 1518

Were it not for one thing, Waldseemüller and his maps (competent though they were) would have sunk without a trace as far as the history books were concerned.

In 1507, however, he printed one thousand copies of one particular map in which he decided that Columbus' [121] discovery was indeed a new continent as Americus Vespucius [123] claimed it was, and in the excitement of his sudden conviction, he named that new continent "America" and inscribed the name on the map.

It was the first time the name had appeared in print on a map, and it caught on at once. All but one of the maps of that printing were lost with time. The exceptional one was uncovered in 1901 in the private library of a German nobleman.

Waldseemüller was canon of St. Dié at the time of his death.

[126] **DÜRER,** Albrecht (dyoo'rer)
German artist
Born: Nürnberg, May 21, 1471
Died: Nürnberg, April 6, 1528

Dürer, the son of a goldsmith, worked as his father's apprentice in early life. He is pre-eminently known as one of the great artists of history. He was perhaps the greatest to express himself in the field of engraving and woodcuts, and as the inventor of the art of etching.

Like Leonardo da Vinci [122], Dürer's interest in art drove him to science. In 1525 he published a book on geometrical constructions, using the straightedge and compass. Essentially, it was for use by artists, for this was at the height of the move for naturalism in art, a time when artists strove to present a perfect three-dimensional illusion on a two-dimensional surface. It might, from this standpoint, be considered the first surviving text on applied mathematics.

However, Dürer was not content merely to supply artists with mathematical recipes; he supplied careful proofs to show the validity of his constructions, which included complex curves. The book was published in German (it was unusual in those days to publish learned material in the "vulgar tongue"), but it was quickly translated into Latin so that it might serve the needs of artists and scholars outside Germany. Dürer also wrote on the proportions of the human body.

Dürer was court painter to Emperor Maximilian I and to his successor, Charles V.

[127] **COPERNICUS,** Nicolas (co-per'-nuh-cus)
Polish astronomer
Born: Toruń, February 19, 1473
Died: Frombork, May 24, 1543

Copernicus was the son of a well-to-do copper merchant and, after his father's early death in 1483, was brought up by his uncle, a prince-bishop, so he had the advantage of being able to get a first-class education.

Beginning in 1491, he studied mathematics and painting at Cracow, then and for many years afterward the intellectual center of Poland. In 1496 he traveled to Italy for a decade's stay, during which time he studied medicine and canon law, and after reading the works of Regiomontanus [119], interested himself in astronomy.

In 1500 this interest was intensified when he attended a conference in Rome that dealt with calendar reform, understood to be necessary since the time of Roger Bacon [99] two centuries before but not to come for another seventy years.

The intellectual ferment in Italy was not above questioning established ways. The system of the universe as propounded by Hipparchus [50] and Ptolemy [64], in which all heavenly bodies were considered rotating about the earth, was almost indecently complex and despite all the careful mathematics involved was not very useful for predicting the positions of the planets over long periods. The Alfonsine Tables, of Alfonso X [100], the best the previous centuries had produced, were already far off the mark, and the corrections of Regiomontanus were only of temporary value.

It occurred to Copernicus as early as 1507 that tables of planetary positions could be calculated more easily if it were assumed that the sun, rather than the earth, were the center of the universe. This would mean that the earth itself, along with the other planets, would have to be considered as moving through space and revolving about the sun.

This was not a new idea. Among the ancients, Aristarchus [41] had suggested the notion, and not many years before the time of Copernicus, Nicholas of Cusa [115] had made a similar suggestion.

Copernicus was to do more than suggest, however. Beginning in 1512, he set about working out the system in full mathematical detail in order to demonstrate how planetary positions could be calculated on this new basis. In doing this, he made little use of his own observations, for astronomical observation was not his forte, apparently. He is supposed never to have seen the planet Mercury (which is, however, the most difficult of the planets to observe because of its nearness to the sun). Still, his observations were good enough to enable him to determine the length of the year to within twenty-eight seconds.

As it turned out, the Copernican system explained some of the puzzling motions of the planets rather neatly. The orbits of Mercury and Venus, according to the new system, would naturally never take those planets farther than a certain distance from the sun, as viewed from the earth, because the orbits of those two planets lay closer to the sun than did the orbit of the earth. On the other hand, since the earth would have to be considered as traveling in a smaller orbit than those of Mars, Jupiter, and Saturn, it would periodically overtake those planets and cause them to appear to be moving backward in the sky.

Both the limited motion of Mercury and Venus and the backward ("retrograde") motions of Mars, Jupiter, and Saturn had been thorns in the side of the Ptolemaic theory and vast complications had been introduced to account for them. Now they were easily and simply explained. Furthermore, the phenomenon of the precession of the equinoxes, discovered by Hipparchus, could be explained not by a twisting of the entire celestial sphere, but by a wobbling of the earth as it rotated on its axis. As for the celestial sphere of the stars, Copernicus held it to be a vast distance from the earth, at least a thousand times as distant as the sun, so that the positions of the stars did not reflect the motion of the earth. (The fact that they did not was used as an argument against Copernicus, an argument that was not fully laid to rest until the time of Bessel [439] three centuries later.)

So much was explained so well by the new Copernican system that it grew tempting to consider that system as more than a mere device to calculate planetary positions. Perhaps it described the actual situation, moving earth and all. Copernicus, however, still kept the notion of perfectly circular orbits and had to retain thirty-four of the epicycles and eccentrics associated with the older theory. This was not corrected until the time of Kepler [169] a half century later.

Copernicus described his system in a book, but for years he hesitated to publish it, believing that any suggestion that the earth moved would be considered heretical and might get him into trouble. This view was a natural and perhaps a prudent one in the light of the later troubles of Galileo [166] and Bruno [157].

In 1505 Copernicus returned to Poland, where he served as canon, under his uncle, at the cathedral at Frombork (Frauenberg, in German), though he never became a priest. (He never married, just the same.) He also served as his uncle's doctor and fulfilled a variety of administrative duties, especially after his uncle's death. He was involved in diplomatic negotiations between the Poles and the Teutonic Knights of Prussia, for instance. Then, too, in working on currency reform, he came up with the notion that the appearance of debased currency drives good coins into hiding— something later called "Gresham's law" after an economist who was a younger contemporary of Copernicus.

Meanwhile, by 1530, he had prepared a summary of his notions in manuscript and this circulated among Europe's scholars, creating considerable interest and enthusiasm. Finally, at the urging of the mathematician Rheticus [145], Copernicus permitted publication of his entire book, carefully dedicating it to Pope Paul III. Rheticus volunteered to oversee its publication.

Unfortunately, Rheticus had to leave town since he was involved in some rather uncomfortable doctrinal disputes and since he had a chance to accept a better position at Leipzig. He left a Lutheran minister, Andreas Osiander, in charge. Luther had expressed himself firmly against the Copernican theory, and Osiander played it safe by adding an unauthorized preface to the effect that the Copernican theory was not advanced as a description of the actual facts but only as a device to facilitate computation of planetary tables. This weakened the book and for many years compromised Copernicus' reputation, for it was long thought that he was responsible for the preface. It wasn't until 1609 that Kepler discovered and published the truth.

The book was published in 1543 and the story has long persisted that the first copy reached Copernicus as he lay on his deathbed, suffering from a stroke. A copy of the book, dated four weeks before his death has recently come to light and it may be that Copernicus had a chance to see it.

Only a few hundred copies of this original edition were printed. About two hundred of them still exist, forty-four of them in various American collections. The Vatican Library, ironically enough, has three. The original hand-written draft also exists and we can see in it that Copernicus crossed out an original reference to Aristarchus (in order not to have some suppose, it may be, that his ideas were derivative).

The book began to win converts at once, Reinhold [143] using it within a few years to publish new tables of planetary motion.

Nevertheless it was not a financial success. It was overpriced and was allowed to go out of print. A second edition was not printed till 1566 (in Basel, Switzerland) and a third not until 1617 (in Amsterdam).

With Copernicus began the Scientific Revolution, which was to dethrone Greek science and set man on a new and far more fruitful path. It reached a climax and fulfillment with Newton [231] a century and a half later. Yet it was not until 1835 that Copernicus' book was removed from the list of those banned by the Roman Catholic Church.

In 1807 Napoleon's conquering career had brought him to Poland. He visited the house in which Copernicus was born and expressed his surprise that no statue had been raised in his honor. In 1839 this omission was rectified, but when the statue to Copernicus was unveiled in Warsaw, no Catholic priest would officiate on the occasion.

creditors. He went to America in 1500 for a new start.

In what is now Haiti, he tried to be a planter, went into debt as usual, managed to get onto a ship by hiding in a large barrel that was supposed to be full of provisions, and ended up on the northern coast of South America.

When conditions grew bad there, he suggested in 1510 that the colony be transferred to Darien (what is now Panama). There, in 1513, he received a letter indicating he would be summoned back to Spain to answer certain charges. He decided that the charges would surely be dismissed if he could find gold.

He outfitted an expedition of 190 Spanish soldiers and a thousand Indian warriors and headed inland from the Panama coast to find the gold. He didn't realize he was on a narrow isthmus. On September 7, 1513, he found himself on the other side of the isthmus, facing what seemed to be a huge body of water. Since Panama runs east and west and the Atlantic was on the north shore; Balboa called this new body of water the South Sea.

He didn't quite realize it but for once he had had an amazing stroke of good fortune. He was the first European ever to see the eastern end of the Pacific Ocean. He was standing on the shore of the second ocean that Americus Vespucius [123] had talked of nine years before as lying between Europe and Asia.

But the good fortune wasn't enough; for it wasn't gold. Balboa was replaced as head of the colony and eventually was falsely accused by his enemies, convicted on trumped up charges and perjured testimony, and beheaded.

[128] **BALBOA,** Vasco Núñez de (bal-boh'uh)
Spanish explorer
Born: Jerez de los Caballeros, Badajoz, 1475
Died: Panama, 1517

Balboa was a man for whom misfortune seemed to be a constant companion. He was forever getting into debt and having to go to extremes to elude his

[129] **SCHÖNER,** Johannes (shoi'ner)
German geographer
Born: Karlstadt (now Karlovac, Yugoslavia), January 16, 1477
Died: Nuremberg, Bavaria, January 16, 1547

Schöner studied theology in the University of Erfurt. He did not take a degree but was ordained a Roman Catholic priest.

He was a professor of mathematics at the University of Nuremberg, and is best remembered for the globes he made. The one he constructed in 1515 was the first globe to include the new lands discovered by Columbus [121] and to name those lands "America," as Waldseemüller [125] had suggested.

In later life, Schöner abandoned the priesthood and became a Lutheran.

[130] **MAGELLAN,** Ferdinand (ma-jel'an)
Portuguese explorer
Born: Sabrosa, Trás-os-Montes, about 1480
Died: Philippine Islands, April 27, 1521

Through most of his life, Magellan was a loyal son of Portugal. He served as page at the court of John II, the king who turned down Columbus [121]. He was on expeditions to the East Indies and fought in Morocco, where he was wounded in action and permanently lamed. He was denied a pension, accused of trading with the Moroccans—tantamount to treason—and was dismissed from the armed forces in 1517.

Magellan, bitter at this treatment, joined the Spanish service and offered to show the Spaniards a way to poach on Portuguese preserves. It seems that shortly after the voyage of Columbus, a north-south line had been drawn down the Atlantic under the auspices of Pope Alexander VI. All heathen lands west of the line were to belong to Spain, all east to Portugal. However, the line was not drawn completely around the earth and Magellan pointed out to Emperor Charles V that if the Spaniards continued to sail westward, they would stay on their side of the line and yet find themselves in the East Indies, which the Portuguese were then exploiting. In other words, Magellan was proposing to do what Columbus had intended, but to do it right.

He was placed in command of an expedition, therefore, and set sail on August 10, 1519, with five ships. The ships crossed the Atlantic and sailed down the eastern coast of South America, searching for a sea passage through the continent. They found it finally far to the south, a passage still called the Strait of Magellan. (He called it the Strait of All Saints.)

On this portion of the voyage they also sighted dim luminous clouds in the night sky that looked like detached pieces of the Milky Way. Visible only in the southern hemisphere, they are still called the Magellanic Clouds. Four centuries later, Leavitt [975] was to forge of them a mighty measuring rod for the heavens.

After a stormy and hellish voyage through the strait, Magellan burst into the calm of a great ocean, doing in real life (for a European) what Coleridge's Ancient Mariner was to do in the poem. ("We were the first that ever burst into that silent sea.") The ocean had been discovered at Panama by Balboa [128] seven years before and named the South Sea, but Magellan, because of its calmness after the storms of the strait, called it the Pacific Ocean. Actually it is no more pacific than the Atlantic is.

For ninety-eight days Magellan crossed the Pacific with no sign of land. He seized the occasion to try an ocean sounding, the first on record. He paid out nearly half a mile of rope in the mid-Pacific and did not reach bottom. The empty wastes of waters, calm but terribly blank, reduced the crew to desperation and starvation. On the brink of disaster they reached Guam on March 6, 1521, and were able to take on food and water. They then sailed to the Philippines, where Magellan was killed in a squabble with the natives.

Magellan's expedition was the first to circumnavigate the earth, for one last ship, the *Victoria,* under Cano [124], managed to make its way across the Indian Ocean, around the southern tip of Africa and back to Spain, arriving September 8, 1522. The voyage had lasted three years and cost four ships, but the spices and other merchandise brought back by the surviving vessel were enough to allow a handsome profit.

Magellan's ships had accomplished a heroic task—for the technology of the day—equivalent to the orbital flight of Gagarin [1502]. It proved once and for all that the estimate of Eratosthenes [48] as to the size of the earth was correct and that of Poseidonius [52] and Ptolemy [64] was wrong. It also proved that a single stretch of water girdles the earth. There was one sea, not seven.

[131] **PARACELSUS** (par-uh-sel'sus),
Philippus Aureolus
Swiss physician and alchemist
Born: Einsiedeln, Schwyz, May 1, 1493
Died: Salzburg, Austria, September 24, 1541

Paracelsus' real name was Theophrastus Bombastus von Hohenheim, but in a fit of vainglory he named himself Paracelsus, meaning "better than Celsus" [57], the Roman physician whose works had recently been translated into Latin and had made a great impression on Paracelsus' contemporaries.

His father, a professor at a school of mines, taught him medicine and he himself studied everywhere he could, at the University of Basel which he entered in 1510, in Austrian mines, and wherever his feet carried him. He had to do much wandering (from Ireland to Russia to Turkey, according to his own account), part of it not altogether voluntary, for his life was marked by eccentricity, quarrelsomeness, and a vast army of enemies lovingly manufactured by himself. Despite a mystical obscurity of statement, he marks the beginning of the transition from alchemy to chemistry.

Paracelsus came to one crucial decision about the purpose of alchemy. The purpose of alchemy, he decided, was not to discover methods for manufacturing gold but to prepare medicines with which to treat disease. (These views of his were eventually developed into a system called iatrochemistry.) It was a point of view then coming into fashion, as in the case of Paracelsus' contemporary and fellow physician Agricola [132], but it was Paracelsus' loud mouth

that did most to bring it to general notice.

Before Paracelsus' time, such medicines as were used were from plant sources, but Paracelsus stressed the importance of minerals, although he was the first to use the plant-derived tincture of opium in medical treatment (naming it laudanum). He did not always achieve happy results, for his almost psychotic cocksureness led him to use such medicines as compounds of mercury and antimony even after practice had shown them to be toxic.

Nor did Paracelsus in any way give up the mysticism of alchemy and astrology. He believed wholeheartedly in the four elements of the Greeks and the three principles (mercury, sulfur, and salt) of the Arabs as well as the influence of stars on disease. He sought unceasingly for the philosopher's stone, which he believed to be an elixir of life, and even claimed to have found it, insisting that he would live forever. (To be sure, he died before he was fifty, but that was no real test: He drank heavily and his death was apparently brought about by an accidental fall.)

He had the courage of his convictions. As town physician at Basel, he burned the works of Galen [65] and Avicenna [86] in public in 1527 and found no terms too harsh to denounce the ancients, whose theory of humors he would not accept.

He also insisted on lecturing in German, not Latin, and admitted barber-surgeons to his courses even though they sullied their hands with actual dissections. The result was that he was kicked out of Basel in 1528. That, however, didn't stop him and for the rest of his life he kept furiously inveighing against his enemies and predecessors. He seized medicine by the scruff of its neck, so to speak, and if it wasn't entirely sense that he shook into it, the shaking was beneficial just the same. He wrote intelligently on the problems of mental disease, for instance, scoffing at theories of demonic possession.

He studied lung diseases of miners and associated them with mining. He correctly diagnosed congenital syphilis. He also correctly associated head injury with paralysis, and cretinism (a form of mental and physical retardation) with goiter.

Paracelsus was the first to describe zinc, and he is sometimes considered its discoverer, though zinc, at least in alloy form as brass, was known even in ancient times.

[132] **AGRICOLA,** Georgius (a-grik'-oh-luh)
German mineralogist
Born: Glauchau, Saxony, March 24, 1494
Died: Chemnitz (modern Karl Marx Stadt), Saxony, November 21, 1555

Agricola was the son of a draper and his real name was Georg Bauer but, as was rather the fashion of his time, he Latinized it. Agricola in Latin and Bauer in German both mean "farmer."

Agricola was a physician by profession, having graduated from the University of Leipzig about 1518, then having studied medicine at the University of Ferrara in Italy. In the fashion of his contemporary Paracelsus [131] he became interested in mineralogy through its possible connection with medicines and through the miners' diseases he studied. In fact, the connection between medicine and minerals and the combination of the physician-mineralogist was to remain a prominent feature in the development of chemistry for two and a half centuries.

Agricola began his medical practice in 1527 in Joachimsthal, a mining center where he grew well-to-do through clever mining investments. Later, as his fame grew, he was subsidized by Prince Maurice of Saxony. In 1531 he traveled to Chemnitz where mining was even more important. Here he served as town physician and in 1546 became its mayor.

His most important work, *De Re Metallica*, wasn't published till a year after his death, but in it he summarized all the practical knowledge gained by the Saxon miners. It was clearly written and had excellent illustrations of mining machinery, so that it became popular at once

and indeed remains a worthy classic of science even today. It has been translated into English by Herbert and Lou Henry Hoover. Through this book Agricola earned his title of father of mineralogy. And, incidentally, it is he who may have coined the word "petroleum."

[133] **APIAN,** Peter (ay'pee-an)
German astronomer
Born: Leisnig, April 16, 1495
Died: Ingolstadt, April 21, 1552

Apian, who was also known as Petrus Apianus and Peter Bienewitz, studied mathematics and astronomy at Leipzig and Vienna and prepared maps that were based on the work of Waldseemüller [125]. He wrote books popularizing both mathematics and astronomy and served as professor of mathematics at the University of Ingolstadt, where he remained to his death. He was knighted by Emperor Charles V.

His importance to science rests on a single observation. In 1540, he published a book in which he describes his observations of comets, and in which he describes the appearances of five different comets including the one that was later to be known as Halley's comet. In the course of these descriptions, he mentions the fact that comets have their tails always pointing away from the sun.

This was the first scientific observation concerning comets other than their position in the sky.

[134] **FERNEL,** Jean François (fer-nel')
French physician
Born: Montdidier, Somme, 1497
Died: Fontainbleu, Seine-et-Marne, April 26, 1558.

Fernel, the son of an innkeeper, graduated from the University of Paris in 1519. He went on to obtain his medical degree in 1530 and in 1534 became professor of medicine there. About 1547, after having successfully treated Diane de Poitiers, the king's mistress, he became physician to the king himself, Henry II of France, even though he had failed to prevent the king's father,

Francis I, from dying of syphilis earlier that year. (But then, no one in those days could have.)

Fernel's reputation grew high enough to earn for him the sobriquet of the Modern Galen [65].

Fernel was the first modern physician to make dissection an important part of his clinical duties. He wrote a book on the subject in 1542 and in it did not hesitate to correct Galen's errors. He was the first to describe appendicitis. He also described peristalsis (the waves of contraction of the alimentary canal) and noted the central canal of the spinal cord. He introduced the terms "physiology" and "pathology."

He wrote also on astronomy and mathematics and rejected astrology as possessing no relevance whatever to medicine.

[135] **TARTAGLIA,** Niccolò (tahr-tal´-yah)
Italian mathematician
Born: Brescia, 1499
Died: Venice, December 13, 1557

Tartaglia was brought up in poverty and was largely self-educated. His true name was Fontana and the nickname by which he is now universally known was born of a tragic incident in his childhood. Italy, after several centuries of high civilization, was made the victim of invading armies and was reduced to some centuries of beggary. When Tartaglia was about twelve his native town was sacked and a French soldier slashed his face. He recovered only through the loving care of his mother, and the wound left him with a speech defect and the name Tartaglia ("stutterer"). His mind, however, did not stutter and, as a mature man, he taught mathematics in various universities of northern Italy, coming to Venice at last in 1534.

Tartaglia was the first to work out a general solution for equations of the third degree (cubic equations). In those days, mathematicians posed problems for each other, and upon their ability to solve those problems rested their reputations. Tartaglia could solve problems in-

volving cubic equations and could pose problems of that sort, which others found insoluble. Naturally, he kept his methods secret. Cardano [137] wheedled the method from him under a promise of secrecy and eventually published it, something Tartaglia undoubtedly felt more deeply than ever he did the childhood slash.

In 1537 Tartaglia published the first book on the theory of projectiles. (Leonardo da Vinci [122] had written one that had not been published.) Tartaglia thought the ball began with "violent motion," traveling straight from the cannon's mouth, and ended with "natural motion," falling straight downward, with a region of "mixed motion" between. This did not agree, of course, with the practical experience of gunners, who could not, however, match Tartaglia's theoretical arguments. Ballistics did not receive an accurate foundation until Galileo's [166] time nearly a century later.

[136] **FUCHS,** Leonhard (fyooks)
German botanist
Born: Wemding, Bavaria, January 17, 1501
Died: Tübingen, May 10, 1566

Fuchs obtained his medical degree at the University of Ingolstadt in 1524. In 1528 he became private physician to the margrave of Brandenberg and in 1535, he became professor of medicine at the University of Tübingen. He remained there the rest of his life.

Like Gesner [147], Fuchs interested himself in natural history and wrote books such as *History of Plants* (1542) in which numerous plant species were described in detail. There is a genus of shrubs that was eventually named in his honor because he described them, and the color of its flower has given him a kind of immortality. Not only the genus, but that particular color, a bluish red, is called fuchsia.

Fuchs prepared the first important modern glossary of botanical terms. This represented a clear break from Dioscorides [59] and helped pave the way for modern botany. Fuchs was an active supporter of Vesalius [146].

[137] **CARDANO,** Girolamo or Geronimo (kahr-dah'noh)
Italian mathematician
Born: Pavia, September 24, 1501
Died: Rome, September 21, 1576

Cardano was the illegitimate son of a learned lawyer-mathematician who was a friend of Leonardo da Vinci [122]. The young Cardano was nearly dead when he was born and passed a sickly and very unhappy childhood. The illegitimacy embittered his adult life, too, for after having attained his medical degree, he was denied admittance to the College of Physicians until he had earned that right by a clear demonstration of his excellence in the field. Eventually, his fame as a physician came to be second only to Vesalius [146] and he was admitted in 1539. In 1546, he was appointed professor of medicine at the University of Pavia.

He was the first to write a clinical description of the disease we now know as typhus fever. In 1552 he cured a Scottish cardinal of asthma by forbidding him to use feathers in his bed, and this showed an intuitive understanding of the phenomenon of allergy. He had vague notions of evolution, believing all animals were originally worms. He was also an astrologer, convinced of the validity of the "science" no matter how many times his predictions failed. He even attempted (so some said) to cast the horoscope of Jesus, a deed that resulted in his imprisonment for a time.

He was a thoroughgoing knave and rascal, a gambler, cheat, given to murderous rage, insufferably conceited and yet, withal, a first-class mathematician. He was the first, for instance, to recognize the value of negative numbers and imaginary numbers. He also put his gambling to use by writing a book on the mathematics of chance—a prelude to the complete opening of the subject by Pascal [207] and Fermat [188].

He obtained the method of solving cubic equations from Tartaglia [135] in 1539, then published the method six years later despite having solemnly vowed to keep it secret—an act that has placed a permanent blot on his memory. He did give Tartaglia credit, but the method is still called "Cardano's rule."

The importance of this incident lay in the fact that it aroused controversy on the ethics of scientific secrecy. Eventually the decision was made that secrecy is of great harm to science and that the credit for any finding must go not to the man who first makes the discovery, but to the one who first publishes it. This is now universally accepted. It has led to some injustices, as in the case of Scheele [329] and John Couch Adams [615], but on the whole the rule has served the cause of science well.

In his two hundred works, Cardano contributed useful ideas to science. He was the first to grasp the water cycle: that the seas are evaporated, that the vapor turns to rain, that the rain flows back to the ocean via the rivers.

Cardano's later life was tragic. His favorite son married a worthless woman who was repeatedly unfaithful. The son overreacted by murdering his wife and, despite Cardano's efforts in the defense, was executed in 1560 for the murder. Cardano was brokenhearted over this and the fact that another son was constantly being jailed for various crimes did not help. Cardano himself did not always escape punishment for his knaveries. In 1570 he himself spent some time in prison for debt or heresy or, possibly, both.

There is a persistent story that in old age Cardano predicted (astrologically) the day of his own death. When the day came and found him in good health, he killed himself. This sounds too dramatic to be true.

[138] **GEMMA FRISIUS,** Reiner
Dutch geographer
Born: Dokkum, Friesland, 1508
Died: Louvain, Brabant, 1555

The surname "Frisius" refers to Gemma's birth in Frisia (Friesland). He received his medical degree at the University of Louvain and practiced medicine there.

His interest was in geography, however, and his importance to science rests on an observation he made concerning longitude. The latitude of a particular spot on earth is easily measured by the height of the noonday sun. The longitude is another matter altogether; no measurement of any object in the sky will suffice.

Gemma Frisius pointed out in 1533 that if one had an accurate way of keeping time, it would then be possible to determine longitude. He was perfectly correct; but considering that no accurate timepiece existed or could, at the time, even be conceived as existing, the suggestion has a certain imaginatively science-fictionish air about it.

Nevertheless, the time was to come when Harrison [259] was to convert Gemma Frisius' suggestion into reality two centuries later.

[139] PARÉ, Ambroise (pa-ray')
French surgeon
Born: Bourg Hersent, near Laval,
Mayenne, 1510
Died: Paris, December 20, 1590

Paré belonged to an era in which physicians removed themselves from surgery, considering it to be fit for manual laborers but not for professional men of intellect. In those days, and for two centuries later, surgery was merely one of the specializations of the barbering profession; the flesh was cut as well as the hair. And, indeed, Paré was only a barber's apprentice when he came to Paris as a boy in 1519. He attained the rank of master barber-surgeon in 1536.

Paré attached himself to the army as barber-surgeon, a post for which he qualified in 1541, and his fame grew rapidly. He rose to higher and higher posts until he was surgeon to a series of four kings, Henry II and his three sons, who ruled successively as Francis II, Charles IX, and Henry III. There is a story, possibly a fable, that he turned Protestant and that he was saved during the St. Bartholomew's Day massacre only be-

cause Charles IX needed his services and hid him in his own bedchamber.

Paré's fame was securely founded, for he introduced several important changes in the surgery of the day that could not help but make him popular with any man who felt he might someday be a candidate for surgery. Most surgeons of the time practiced searing heavily. They disinfected gunshot wounds with boiling oil and stopped bleeding by cauterizing the arteries (without anesthetics). Paré followed Hippocrates' [22] principle of interfering as little as possible with nature. He practiced cleanliness and he used soothing ointments for gunshot wounds. (One story is that once, in camp, he ran out of boiling oil and quickly discovered he was better off without it—to say nothing of the poor wounded soldiers.) He also tied off arteries to stop bleeding.

With an infinitesimal fraction of the pain he brought off far more cures. It is no wonder that he is often considered the father of modern surgery.

He wrote a report of his findings in this area in 1545. His lack of education forced him to write it in French rather than Latin. For this, he was scorned by the learned ignoramuses of the day.

He also wrote French summaries of the works of Vesalius [146], so that barber-surgeons might learn something of the structure of the human body before hacking away. He devised clever artificial limbs and improved obstetrical methods.

[140] COLOMBO, Realdo (koh-lohm' boh)
Italian anatomist
Born: Cremona, about 1510
Died: Rome, 1559

Colombo, the son of an apothecary, was educated at Milan and was himself an apothecary until he was apprenticed to a leading Venetian surgeon. He went on to study medicine at Padua and obtained his degree in 1541.

He was appointed professor of anatomy at Padua, replacing Vesalius [146], then went on to teach at Pisa. Although friendly to Vesalius at first, Colombo found he could not make the break with ancient anatomy that Vesalius' teachings required and he became a violent critic of the new anatomy. He went to Rome in 1548 in an effort to enlist Michelangelo as illustrator for a book that would surpass Vesalius'. But Michelangelo was in his seventies and could not take on the task. (Pity!).

Nevertheless, Colombo was not merely a spoiler. He departed from Galen [65] himself by clearly showing in 1559 that blood leaves the heart on its way to the lungs by means of the pulmonary artery and returns by the pulmonary vein, without ever passing through the wall separating the two ventricles (as Galen claimed). He had thus demonstrated the pulmonary circulation of the blood though he stopped short of grasping the general circulation. That was left for Harvey [174] seven decades later, but Colombo was an important forerunner as Harvey himself recognized.

Colombo remained in Rome the rest of his life, serving as papal surgeon.

[141] **EUSTACHIO,** Bartolemeo (ay-oo-stah'kee-oh)
Italian anatomist
Born: San Severino, about 1510
Died: Fossombrone, Urbino, August 27, 1574

Eustachio, the son of a physician, and a physician himself from 1540, was an adversary of Vesalius [146] and an upholder of Galen [65], yet his anatomical studies paralleled those of the former and not those of the latter. Eustachio's work was completed in 1552 but was not published until rediscovered in 1714. For this reason he scarcely influenced his contemporaries.

His illustrations were in some respects even more accurate than those of Vesalius, but they were stiff and clumsy and unworthy, as far as sheer beauty is concerned, to be mentioned in the same breath. Eustachio's most successful work was done on the sympathetic nervous system, the kidney, and the ear. His name has been given to the Eustachian tube, a narrow canal connecting the ear

and throat, although this had been discovered by Alcmaeon [11] two thousand years before. He was also the first to describe the adrenal glands and he pioneered in the study of the detailed structure of the teeth.

In 1562 he was appointed professor of medicine in the Collegio della Sapienza in Rome, a post he held till his death.

[142] **SERVETUS,** Michael (sur'vee'-tus)
Spanish physician
Born: Villanueva de Sixena, September 29, 1511
Died: Geneva, Switzerland, October 27, 1553

Servetus, the son of a notary, was intended for the law, but his interests were much wider. He lectured on astrology (in which he firmly believed) and defended the botanical views of his friend Fuchs [136].

These, however, were the days of the Protestant Reformation and all Europe was convulsed with theological discussions. Servetus developed radical notions that would today be described as Unitarian. He advanced them tactlessly, angering both the Catholics and the Protestants. He went to Paris in 1536 and studied medicine there, meeting his eventual nemesis, John Calvin, one of the most noted and powerful of the early Protestants. Servetus quarreled with the physicians in Paris, went elsewhere, and finally settled down to practice in Vienne, in southeast France. In 1553 Servetus published his theological views anonymously and some years previously he had sent a manuscript version to Calvin, with whom he was carrying on a correspondence. Calvin, however, quickly broke off the correspondence on reading those views. He was not one to appreciate—or forget—Servetus' views.

In the book, Servetus also described the circulation of that part of the blood that went through the lungs. The blood, he held, traveled out of the heart through the pulmonary artery and back through the pulmonary vein; it did not go through the heart muscle itself. This was a good start at breaking with Galen, though it got nowhere until Harvey [174] generalized the matter for all the body, three quarters of a century later.

Servetus' physiological heresy was disregarded, but his theological heresy was not. His authorship was discovered, he was arrested and escaped, making for Italy. Foolishly he went by way of nearby Geneva, then under control of the dark and bitter Calvin. Servetus was not a subject or resident of Geneva and had committed no crime in Geneva for which he could be held. Nevertheless, Calvin insisted on having him condemned to death (a deed that has blackened Calvin's name in the eyes of posterity) and Servetus was burned at the stake, crying out his Unitarian views to the last.

[143] **REINHOLD,** Erasmus (rine′-hold)
German mathematician
Born: Saalfeld, Thuringia, October 22, 1511
Died: Saalfeld, February 19, 1553

Reinhold studied at the University of Wittenberg and was appointed professor of mathematics there in 1536. Although the University was the very center of Lutheran doctrine, and although Lutheranism was profoundly anti-Copernican at the start, Reinhold was nevertheless one of the first converts to the new astronomical theory even before Copernicus' [127] book was published for he had studied it in manuscript.

Reinhold made the practical contribution of calculating the first set of planetary tables based on Copernican theory, and, for the purpose, he went over Copernicus' calculations from stem to stern, correcting where necessary.

The tables were subsidized by Albert, Duke of Prussia, and were therefore called Tabulae Prutenicae (Prussian Tables). Published in 1551, they were rather better than the Alfonsine Tables, and their mere existence was a strong argument in favor of Copernicus. They were not, however, quite as good as the partiality of the author led him to claim

they were, and in three quarters of a century they were to be superseded by the better tables published by Kepler [169].

Reinhold's acceptance of the Copernican theory was not wholehearted. He recognized it as a mathematical device for preparing planetary tables more accurately but did not consider it a representation of reality.

[144] **MERCATOR,** Gerardus (mer-kay′ter)
Flemish geographer
Born: Rupelmonde (in what is now Belgium), March 5, 1512
Died: Duisburg, Germany, December 2, 1594

Mercator's real name was Gerhard Kremer, but he shared in the sixteenth-century predilection for Latinized pen names, and adapted the Latin version (meaning "merchant") when he entered the University of Louvain in 1530, emerging with a master's degree in 1532.

Young Mercator's interest in geography was dictated by both time and place. The great voyages of the Age of Exploration filled the air in his youth, and the ships of the Netherlands were not backward in the exploration of distant islands. Good maps were necessary if navigation was to be more than hit or miss (with lives very likely sacrificed if it was miss).

In 1534, therefore, Mercator, who had studied under Gemma Frisius [138], founded a geographical establishment at Louvain, from whose university he had graduated four years earlier, and began the preparation of a long series of maps, making use of instruments designed by himself and bringing to his task more than a bit of mathematical knowledge. He also prepared a set of such instruments for Emperor Charles V.

The religious unrest of the time placed Mercator, a Protestant in a Catholic region, in some danger. In 1544 he was prosecuted for heresy and although he got off with a whole skin, he eventually decided to play it safe and emigrated to Protestant Germany in 1552. In 1559 he was appointed cartographer to the Duke of Cleves.

At first he remained under the domination of Ptolemy [64], whose rediscovery in the late Middle Ages had had a cramping effect on cartography. So revered was the old Greek that maps built on observation, and therefore showing the Mediterranean Sea at its correct length, were deliberately altered into error in order to make them match Ptolemy's version, which had the Mediterranean several hundred miles too long.

Gradually Mercator adjusted Ptolemy to the facts and then, in 1568, he made his great advance. It had always been a problem to depict a spherical surface on a flat piece of paper. In ancient days the area of immediate geographical interest formed so small a portion of the globe that it could be presented as flat without serious trouble to the coast-hugging mariners. By the sixteenth century, however, the whole world had to be depicted and the change from sphere to plane meant inevitable distortion. The problem was to obtain the least damaging distortion for mariners sailing thousands of miles across the open ocean.

It occurred to Mercator to make use of a "cylindrical projection." Imagine a hollow cylinder encircling the earth and touching it at the equator. A light at the earth's center can then be imagined as casting the shadow of the surface features on the cylinder, and the cylinder when unwrapped carries a map of the world by "Mercator projection."

In this map the meridians of longitude are vertical and parallel. Since on the sphere the meridians of longitude approach each other and meet at the poles, this means that east-west distances are increasingly exaggerated as one travels north and south from the equator. The parallels of latitude run horizontal and parallel. As one goes north and south from the equator, they spread out more widely.

On such a map Greenland and Antarctica are enormously enlarged and neither the North Pole nor the South Pole can be shown. Nevertheless, it was a particularly useful map for navigators (who generally avoided both Arctic and Ant-arctic) because a ship traveling in a constant compass direction followed a route that appeared as a straight line on the Mercator projection, but a curved line on all other projections.

The world map most familiar to us even today is drawn according to the Mercator projection.

The last few years of Mercator's life were devoted to preparing a detailed series of maps of various portions of Europe. It was not published till the year after his death. Because the cover of the book of these maps showed a picture of the Greek Titan, Atlas, holding the world on his shoulders, the book (and all future books of maps) was called an atlas.

With Mercator the influence of Greek geography comes to an end, and the era of modern geography begins.

[145] **RHETICUS** (ray'tih-koos)
German mathematician
Born: Feldkirch, Austria, February 16, 1514
Died: Cassovia, Hungary, now Košice, Czechoslovakia, December 4, 1574

The real name of Rheticus was Georg Joachim von Lauchen, but he named himself after the ancient name (Rhaetia) of the province in which he was born. (His father had been a physician who was beheaded for sorcery when Rheticus was fourteen so that may have made the change of name advisable.)

Rheticus studied at Zürich, where Gesner [147] was a schoolmate and where he met Paracelsus [131]. He went on to Wittenberg and obtained his master's degree in 1536; then began to teach mathematics there. He was a reasonably important mathematician, being the first to relate the trigonometric functions to angles rather than to the arcs of circles and preparing the best trigonometric tables up to his time.

He is best known, however, as Copernicus' [127] first disciple. In 1539 he traveled to Frombork to study Copernicus' manuscript, and received an intense ten-week course in the new view.

He published a summary of its contents in 1540, but was careful not to mention Copernicus by name. He then persuaded the older man to publish his great book.

He wrote a biography of Copernicus but that, unfortunately, is lost. He also drew the first map of East Prussia and that too is lost.

[146] **VESALIUS,** Andreas (veh-say'-lee-us)
Flemish anatomist
Born: Brussels, December 31, 1514
Died: Zante (now Zakinthos), west of Greece, October 15, 1564

Vesalius' mother was English and his father was court pharmacist to Emperor Charles V. He came, in fact, of a long line of physicians who originally dwelt in Wesel—hence his surname. He studied medicine at Louvain (in what is now Belgium) and in Paris, both very conservative centers saturated with the teachings of Galen [65]. He quarreled bitterly with his teacher in Paris, but learned his Galen thoroughly, wrote a graduation dissertation on Rhazes [82], and, as late as 1538, was publishing material largely Galenian in nature.

He was always eager to dissect for himself but found this difficult to arrange in northern Europe where he served for a while as a military surgeon. He therefore traveled to Italy, where in the light of the late Renaissance there was more intellectual freedom than in other parts of Europe. Dissection was improper, to be sure, but the authorities were readier to look the other way and men such as Mondino de' Luzzi [110] had made it almost respectable two and a half centuries earlier. He obtained his medical degree at Padua in 1537.

In Italy, Vesalius taught anatomy at the universities of Pavia, Bologna, and Pisa. Disgusted with slipshod, hacking dissections by assistants, he reintroduced Mondino's important but forgotten habit of conducting anatomical demonstrations in person. He became a popular lecturer, and students, of whom the most important was Fallopius [149], flocked to him.

He managed to make a sensation with something as simple as a demonstration that men and women have equal numbers of ribs. (Because of the story in Genesis that Eve had been created out of Adam's rib, it was widely believed during the Middle Ages that men had one rib fewer than women.)

He put together the result of his researches in one of the great books of scientific history, *De Corporis Humani Fabrica* ("On the Structure of the Human Body"). This was the first accurate book on human anatomy; its great advantage over the ancient books was that it had illustrations which, being printed, could be reproduced exactly in any number of copies. (Before the time of printing, even where words were copied accurately, illustrations degenerated of necessity.) This alone allowed printing to revolutionize biology.

Illustrations in themselves would have been enough, but those in Vesalius' books were outstanding in beauty. Jan Stephen van Calcar, a pupil of the artist Titian, did many of them, and it was chiefly in the illustrations that Vesalius was superior to his rival, Eustachio [141].

The human body was shown in natural positions and the illustrations of the muscles in particular are so exact that nothing since has surpassed them. The book, an astonishing achievement for a man not yet thirty, met with fierce opposition from such anatomists as Colombo [140], but it was the end of Galen. Vesalius' work was not a false dawn, as Mondino's had been. It marked at one stroke the beginning of modern anatomy. By an interesting coincidence it was published in the same year as Copernicus' [127] book, a simultaneous end and beginning in the biological and physical sciences. Together, they were the birth of the Scientific Revolution.

Though he was accurate as an anatomist, Vesalius clung to some of the old ideas in physiology. (Whereas anatomy deals with the structure of the living organism, physiology deals with its functioning.) Vesalius accepted Galen's views on the circulation of the blood and believed that blood must pass from one ventricle of the heart to the other through invisible pores in the wall of muscle separating those ventricles. However, the truth of the matter was beginning to dawn on Servetus [142]. Toward the end of Vesalius' life, he too grew to doubt Galen in this respect.

Vesalius was opposed to the view of Aristotle [29] that the heart was the seat of life, mind, and emotion. Vesalius believed that the brain and nervous system represented that seat, and no one has doubted it since.

Vesalius' work came to a halt with the publication of his book. Perhaps annoyed at the furore it aroused and the opposition to it (led by his old teacher at Paris), he quit research. It had made him enough of a reputation, however, to earn him the post of court physician to Charles V, and later to Charles's son, the Spanish king Philip II. When Henry II of France was fatally wounded in a tournament in 1559, Vesalius attended him, taking precedence over Paré [139].

As he became more prominent his enemies accused him of heresy, body snatching, and dissection, and for a while it looked as though he might be executed. But his royal connections stood him in good stead, and the sentence was commuted to a pilgrimage to the Holy Land. This, however, represented but a short reprieve. On the way back from his pilgrimage, his ship was battered by storms off the coast of Greece and Vesalius died shortly after the ship managed to land at Zante.

[147] **GESNER,** Konrad von (guess'ner)
Swiss naturalist
Born: Zürich, March 26, 1516
Died: Zürich, December 13, 1565

The late Middle Ages brought to the attention of Europeans the zoological and botanical works of Aristotle [29] and Theophrastus [31]. In addition, the explorations of the fifteenth century introduced Europe to hordes of plants and animals of which the ancients had been ignorant. A new group of writers on natural history arose, and among these the most prominent were Gesner and Fuchs [136].

Gesner, the son of a furrier killed in the religious wars, and the protegé of the Protestant reformer, Ulrich Zwingli, was a physician by profession. He obtained his medical degree at the University of Basel in 1541 and served as town physician in Zürich during the last decade of his life. However, he was a Renaissance man with interests ranging from Greek through comparative philology to natural history. He used the collection of rare mountain species of plants as an excuse for indulging in the then newfangled hobby of mountain climbing and it is difficult to say which interested him more. He was the first to present illustrations of fossils, but he had no suspicion that they represented remnants of past life. He considered them simply stony concretions.

In his wide-ranging interests, his credulity, and his absolute compulsion to work, he resembled Pliny [61] and, indeed, has been known as the German Pliny and as a "monster of erudition." He wrote a "Universal Library," for instance, in which he listed all known books in Hebrew, Greek, and Latin, with summaries of each. Between 1551 and 1558 he wrote similarly exhaustive volumes designed to describe all known animals and replace the earlier and less complete work of Aristotle. He also collected at least five hundred plants not known to the ancients. Gesner was still working feverishly when in 1565 a plague struck Zürich. He refused to abandon his patients and died of plague.

Although there is some attempt at classification in his works, Gesner belongs, by and large, to the old school of purely descriptive natural history. Other naturalists, of a more analytical turn of mind, such as Alpini [160] and Belon [148], were oriented more in the direction of the future, but they were less influential in their own time.

The attempt to make deeper sense out of the realm of life through rational classification had to wait another century for Ray [213] and, above all, Linnaeus [276].

[148] BELON, Pierre (be-lohn')
French naturalist
Born: Soultière, 1517
Died: Paris, April, 1564

Belon, the son of poor parents, was recognized as a promising youth by the local bishop, who made it possible for him to study medicine. Belon obtained his medical degree at the University of Paris and had King Francis I as patron. He was sent east in 1546, accompanying diplomatic missions. This gave him a chance to study plant and animal life in countries bordering the eastern Mediterranean and he was the first to notice the similarities of basic plan in the skeletons of the various vertebrates from mammals to fish. These homologies (a first step toward comparative anatomy) were an important impulse in the slow development of evolutionary theories over the next three centuries. He also studied the porpoise embryo and initiated researches, in this way, that were to lead to the science of embryology.

Belon introduced the cedar tree to France and founded two botanical gardens. Having survived his travels without trouble, he was so indiscreet as to go out to gather herbs in the Bois de Boulogne, in the heart of Paris, and there he was waylaid by robbers and killed.

[149] FALLOPIUS, Gabriel (fa-loh'-
pee-us)
Italian anatomist
Born: Modena, 1523
Died: Padua, October 9, 1562

Fallopius entered the church when his father died, leaving the family impoverished. He was canon in the cathedral of Modena for a time, but when the financial situation took a turn for the better, he abandoned the religious life to practice science.

He succeeded his teacher Vesalius [146] as the most important anatomist, rising eventually to a professorship at Padua in 1551 as successor to Colombo [140]. He is best known today for his descriptions of the inner ear and of the organs of generation. He described the tubes that lead the human ovum from the ovary, where it is formed, to the uterus where, if the ovum is fertilized, the embryo develops. It is in these tubes that fertilization takes place.

Fallopius did not know the function of the tubes because the mammalian ova, or egg cells, were not discovered for nearly three centuries after his time. Nevertheless, the organs today are known as the Fallopian tubes.

He coined the term "vagina" and described the clitoris.

He died before his fortieth birthday of that great killer of young people in those days—tuberculosis.

[150] PORTA, Giambattista della
(pawr'tah)
Italian physicist
Born: Vico Equense, near Naples, October 1535
Died: Naples, February 4, 1615

Porta was the son of a small government official and may have been largely self-taught.

His most important work was a quite serious discussion of magic and how it could be used to control the environment —all quite worthless, of course.

Yet he cannot be dismissed. He founded the first of the modern scientific "academies," those associations for the intercommunications of scientific research. This was the Academia Secretorum Naturae in 1560. It was suppressed by the Inquisition, but he then reconstituted it as the Accademia dei Lincei in 1610 and that remained. (Perhaps lynxes, for all their legendary sharpness of sight didn't seem as threatening to the clerics as investigating the secrets of nature would.)

Porta also worked with the camera obscura or pinhole camera, in which light entering an enclosed box through a small hole forms an inverted image inside. It lacked the essentials of a modern camera—the lens and the photosensitive film; but that would come eventually with the work of Niepce [384] and Daguerre [467] a little over two centuries later.

Most important, Porta was the first to demonstrate the heating effect of light. It was a small step, but a step, toward the recognition of the unity of energy.

[151] **FABRICIUS AB AQUAPEN-DENTE,** Hieronymus (fa-brish'-ee-us)
Italian physician
Born: Aquapendente, Papal States, May 20, 1537
Died: Padua, May 21, 1619

Fabricius obtained his M.D. at Padua in 1559 and in 1565 became a professor of surgery there. He has two chief claims to fame. First, he was the teacher of Harvey [174]. Second, he discovered the one-way valves in the veins and described them accurately in a book published in 1603. However, he failed to see their significance.

Fabricius was a pupil of Fallopius [149], whom he had succeeded at Padua, in 1565 so that the line from Vesalius [146] to Harvey, via Fallopius and Fabricius, covers four student generations. Fabricius corrected Vesalius in one respect. Vesalius, for some reason, placed the lens in the center of the eyeball. Fabricius correctly described its location near the forward rim.

Fabricius also published an exhaustive study of the chick embryo in 1612, restoring the subject to the point where Aristotle [29] had left it and paving the way for future advance.

[152] **CLAVIUS,** Christoph (klah'vee-oos)
German astonomer
Born: Bamberg, Bavaria, 1537
Died: Rome, Italy, February 6, 1612

Clavius entered the Jesuit order in 1555 and attended lectures at the University of Coimbra in Portugal. He lectured at the Collegio Romano in Rome beginning in 1565 and remained there for the rest of his life with inconsiderable exceptions.

His contribution to astronomy is the rather negative one of being one of the last important astronomers to be a die-hard opponent of Copernicus' [127] doctrine. He very carefully pointed out the various Biblical quotations that showed that God himself declared Copernicus to be absurd. Somehow that didn't stop the steady shift of scholarly opinion toward Copernicus.

On the other hand, Clavius was the first astronomer since Sosigenes [54] to reform the calendar. The Julian calendar set up by Sosigenes had been gaining three days on the sun every four hundred years, as had been pointed out by Roger Bacon [99]. By Clavius' time, the calendar was eleven days ahead of the sun and it marked the vernal equinox eleven days after the sun did—with serious effects on the calculation of Easter.

An astronomical conference was held in Rome and Clavius' proposal was accepted. Eleven days were dropped so that the day after October 4, 1582, was October 15, 1582, and thereafter, the century years not divisible by 400 were *not* leap years. Pope Gregory XIII established this, so Clavius' reform is the "Gregorian calendar" that is used virtually throughout the world today.

Naturally, the Protestant nations objected and refused for quite a while to accept the reform. Surprisingly, there was opposition from some scientists (Protestant, to be sure) such as Vieta [153] and Scaliger [154].

[153] **VIETA,** Franciscus (vyay'tuh)
French mathematician
Born: Fontenay-le-Comte, Poitou, 1540
Died: Paris, February 23, 1603

Vieta (François Viete), the son of a lawyer, was educated in law at Poitiers and received his degree in 1560. He occupied high administrative office under Henry IV. This may have come about because for a time he was a Protestant as Henry had been before he became king. When Henry turned Catholic, Vieta did likewise.

Perhaps the most dramatic of Vieta's

feats involved his capacity as a skilled cryptanalyst. Working for the French government in 1589, he deciphered the code that Philip II of Spain was using. This worked to the great disadvantage of the Spanish armies then at war with France. Philip II could explain the leakage of what he thought were inviolable secrets by no means other than sorcery and he accused the French of that crime to the pope.

Vieta engaged himself in mathematics only as a hobby and yet accomplished great work in algebra and trigonometry. In fact, it was he who first used letters to symbolize unknowns and constants (vowels for the former and consonants for the latter) in algebraic equations, so that a book he wrote in 1591, *Isagoge in artem analyticam,* is the first that a modern high-school student could look at and recognize at once as a book on algebra. For this reason, he is called the father of modern algebra, although great men in the field such as Cardano [137] preceded him.

Oddly enough Vieta repudiated the word "algebra," which was Arabic and not Latin, and preferred the term "analysis." In fact, the title of his book, in English, is *Introduction to the Analytic Art.* As a result, the term "analysis" is now used for algebraic methods of solving problems, though the term "algebra" is still retained for that branch of mathematics that deals with the rules governing the manipulation of equations.

In one respect, Vieta was formidably geometric. He made use of Archimedes' [47] method for calculating pi through polygons of many sides. Vieta used polygons of 393,216 sides in his calculation and obtained a value of pi accurate to ten decimal places—the best value up to that time.

Scaliger was a monumental scholar who had been inhumanly driven by his scholarly father into an encyclopedic knowledge of Latin and Greek authors at an early age. Young Scaliger took to the task with avidity, but his proficiency in the classics did not blind him to other matters. He studied at Bordeaux first and then, in 1559, traveled to Paris.

He was converted to Protestantism in 1562 and had the good sense to leave France for Geneva in 1572, just before the dreadful St. Batholomew's Day Massacre of Protestants. In 1593 he took a professorial position with the safely Protestant University of Leiden and remained there the rest of his life.

He did not consider Greek and Roman history the only history that counted but urged that the records of the various Oriental empires be studied. In a book published in 1606, he studied every scrap of record he could find and carefully compared the various chronologies in the light of the astronomic learning of the day. His hope was to bring them all into some agreement and to deduce a single line of history. He is the founder of modern chronology.

In addition he founded the system of the Julian Day. He set January 1, 4713 B.C., equal to Day 1 and numbered all the days from that. (Thus, January 1, 1982, is Julian Day, 2,444,970.) This freed astronomers from the vagaries of changing calendars, and the system is still used to this day.

The word "Julian" is Scaliger's homage to his intellectually slave-driving father, Julius Caesar Scaliger. It was an undeserved homage, for the father had filled his son's ears with tales of noble birth that the son innocently boasted about. When the stories were proved lies, Scaliger was utterly humiliated. He wilted and died.

[154] **SCALIGER,** Joseph Justus (skal'-ih-jer)
French scholar
Born: Agen, Lot-et-Garonne, August 5, 1540
Died: Leiden, Netherlands, January 21, 1609

[155] **GILBERT,** William
English physician and physicist
Born: Colchester, Essex, May 24, 1544
Died: London, November 30, 1603

Gilbert took his medical degree at Cambridge in 1569, then traveled through Europe, unhampered by family, since he remained a lifelong bachelor. He settled in London about 1573 and gained considerable renown as a physician, becoming president of the College of Physicians in 1600. In 1601 he was appointed court physician to Queen Elizabeth I, at the usual salary of £100 per year.

The year before, he had published a book, *De Magnete* ("Concerning Magnets"), which established his reputation as a physicist.

Gilbert might be viewed as merely repeating the work done earlier by Peter Peregrinus [104]. Peregrinus' work, however, had been mostly forgotten. Also, Gilbert went much further than Peregrinus. Gilbert, like Galileo [166], was a pioneer of experimentation and refuted many superstitions by direct testing. Indeed, Galileo considered Gilbert the chief founder of experimentalism. Gilbert showed that garlic did not destroy magnetism, as it was believed to do, by smearing a magnet with it and demonstrating that the magnet's powers remained unimpaired.

Gilbert further showed not only that a compass needle points roughly north and south, but also that if it is suspended to allow vertical movement it points downward toward the earth ("magnetic dip"). A compass needle also shows a dip in the neighborhood of a spherical magnet, and at the magnetic poles of the sphere it points vertically. Gilbert's great contribution was to suggest that the earth itself is a great spherical magnet and that the compass needle points not to the heavens (as Peregrinus believed) but to the magnetic poles of the planet. Gilbert believed this situation was fixed—that at any point on the earth the magnetic needle held constant. This idea was corrected a generation later by Gellibrand [184]. (Because Gilbert was a pioneer in the study of magnetism, magnetomotive force is measured now in units called "gilberts.")

Gilbert studied other attractive forces in the universe. It had been known since ancient times that amber, when rubbed, acquired the power of attracting light objects. This differed from magnetism in that magnetism involved iron only, whereas the amber attraction could be felt by any light object and Gilbert was the first to point out this difference clearly. (According to the Greeks it was Thales [3] who first studied this effect of rubbed amber.)

Gilbert extended knowledge in this field by discovering that substances other than amber, as, for example, rock crystal and a variety of gems, showed the same attractive force when rubbed. He grouped all such substances under the name of "electrics," from the Greek word for amber (*elektron*).

He also elaborated notions on the structure of the universe that were both advanced and daring for his time. He accepted the views of Copernicus [127] and was the first important Englishman to do so. Also, he followed Nicholas of Cusa [115] in believing that the stars were at varying, but enormously large, distances from the earth and that they might themselves be circled by habitable planets. Finally, he was the first to speculate on what might keep the planets in their paths if the celestial spheres first invented by Pythagoras [7] two thousand years before his time proved, after all, not to exist. Coming down heavily on his own specialty, Gilbert decided it was a form of magnetic attraction. Galileo and Kepler [169] came to no better conclusion.

When Elizabeth I died, Gilbert was reappointed court physician by James I. He died within the year.

Gilbert left his books, instruments, and other memorabilia to the College of Physicians, but they were destroyed in the Great Fire of London sixty years later.

[156] **BRAHE,** Tycho (ty-ko brah'uh)
Danish astronomer
Born: Knudstrup, Scania (south Sweden, then part of Denmark), December 14, 1546
Died: Prague (in what is now Czechoslovakia), October 24, 1601

Tycho Brahe, the son of a Danish nobleman of Swedish descent, is supposed to have been one of twins. His brother, however, was either stillborn or died soon after birth. When one year old, Tycho was kidnapped by his childless uncle, and Tycho's father accepted the situation.

Tycho (usually known by his first name only, a Latinized version of the Danish, Tyge) was the last and, with the possible exception of Hipparchus [50], the greatest of the naked-eye astronomers. In early life he studied law and philosophy at the University of Copenhagen, which he entered at the age of thirteen. He originally intended to go into politics, but in 1560 he observed an eclipse of the sun and switched to astronomy and mathematics. Later he went to Germany for more training.

In observing a close approach of Jupiter and Saturn in 1563, Tycho noticed that it came a month away from the time predicted for it by the tables prepared under Alfonso X [100]. Consequently he began to buy instruments with which to make observations for the preparation of new tables. He also began to cast horoscopes, and retained a lifelong interest in astrology, as did many astronomers of early modern times. (Astrology was a far more lucrative pursuit than was genuine astronomy, and patrons would far more willingly pay for horoscopes than for scientific findings.)

In 1572, after a period in which alchemy temporarily claimed Tycho's attention, he finally made his mark, on the occasion of the flaring out (on November 11) of a new star. Hipparchus had noted one and used it as an occasion to prepare the first star map of importance. Another appeared in 1054, but it was observed only by Chinese and Japanese astronomers.

These are not new stars but existing ones that explode and increase enormously in brightness. Prior to the explosion they may be too faint to be seen with the naked eye. Before the days of the telescope, they did indeed seem new stars. Tycho, observing the new star of 1572 (now sometimes called "Tycho's star"), described it—and its astrological significance—in a fifty-two-page book of which a short version of the title is *De Nova Stella* ("Concerning the New Star"). Tycho's star grew to be brighter than Venus and remained visible for a year and a half before fading out.

Tycho had at first hesitated to publish the book, for he felt it beneath the dignity of a nobleman to write books, but, fortunately, he overcame this snobbish impulse.

Tycho's book did three things. It established the name "nova" for all exploding stars. It made the young man's reputation as an astronomer. And, finally, since Tycho showed by parallax measurements, using the observations of other astronomers from distant places such as England, that the new star was too far for its distance to be measured, but certainly much farther than the moon, it struck a telling blow against the notion of Aristotle [29] that the heavens were perfect and unchanging.

Tycho stretched his mind to the limit to imagine the size of the universe but, of course, he fell short. He thought the nova was three billion miles from earth, and the farthest star only four million miles beyond the nova. The stars, in other words, only occupied a comparatively thin shell just beyond the planetary system. The whole universe, by Tycho's scheme, was only 6,100,000,000 miles in diameter—which is less than we now know the diameter of the planetary system to be.

The king of Denmark, Frederick II, decided to serve as patron for his remarkable young subject, who had flashed into prominence like a living nova, and to keep him from emigrating to Germany, then the center of astronomical research. (The brain drain is by no means a modern phenomenon only.) To do this, he sponsored astronomical lectures by the young man and, more important still, he subsidized the building of an observatory for Tycho on the island of Hveen (now Ven), three square miles in area between Denmark and Sweden. Tycho built elegant buildings

and outfitted them with the best instruments he could make. Completed in
1580, it was the first real astronomical
observatory in history and cost, it is estimated, about a million and a half dollars of today's money. He spared no expense, even building a five-foot spherical
celestial globe.

Here his reputation continued to grow
and scholars from all over Europe visited
him. So did rulers who fancied themselves scholars, such as James VI of
Scotland, who visited Denmark in 1590
to marry a Danish princess. (Later, he
succeeded to the English throne as James
I.)

In 1577 a great comet appeared in the
sky and Tycho observed it carefully.
Parallax studies showed that this object
also was farther than the moon—an
even worse blow against the perfection
of the heavens. Aristotle, recognizing
that the erratic comings and goings of
comets could not be harmonized with
the permanence and regularity of motion
of other bodies, had insisted that comets
were atmospheric phenomena. He was
wrong. Galileo [166] in this respect
agreed with Aristotle and was therefore
behind Tycho here.

Tycho, in studying the apparent motion of the comet, reluctantly came to
the conclusion that its orbit could not be
circular but must be rather elongated.
This was a daring suggestion because in
that case it must be passing through the
various planetary spheres, and it could
scarcely do that unless the planetary
spheres did not exist.

Such a possibility went much against
Tycho's personal leanings, for he was a
conservative astronomer who would not
abandon the notion of Ptolemy [64] and
his Greek predecessors that the earth
was the center of the universe. He was
the last great astronomer to insist on it
and to reject the heliocentric theory of
Copernicus [127].

His great argument against it was the
lack of stellar parallax, and he used this
argument in his correspondence with
Galileo to wean away the latter from
Copernicanism. In this he failed.

In his book on the comet, published in

1583, Tycho tried to strike a compromise. He was willing to go so far as to
suggest that all the planets *but* the earth
revolved about the sun. Then, he
insisted, the sun with its train of attendant planets revolved about the earth.
This would explain everything Copernicus' theory explained, but it did away
with the celestial spheres of the Greeks,
something Copernicus had not done.
That was bothersome for if the spheres
did not exist, what kept the planets in
their orbits?

This "Tychonic theory" was proposed,
in part, to emphasize Tycho's orthodoxy
against his enemies at the Danish court
—of whom he had many. Reminiscent
of the views of Heracleides [28], it
shared the fate of all halfhearted compromises in an age of desperate antagonism. It went almost entirely disregarded.

(Nevertheless, a half century later,
Riccioli [185] was to give names to the
craters on the moon, which the telescope
of Galileo revealed. Riccioli, at least, admired the Tychonic theory, and so he
gave Tycho's name to the most prominent and spectacular of all the craters
visible from earth. Since he was an admirer of Greek astronomy, the book in
which he did this was named the *New
Almagest,* and he gave the names of
Hipparchus and Ptolemy to two large
craters, centrally located on the moon's
surface. The name of Copernicus was
given to a lesser crater and that of Aristarchus [41] to quite a small one. The
face of the moon still bears these names
—a mark of the reluctance with which
Greek astronomy was abandoned.)

All through the years Tycho kept
making magnificently accurate observations, reaching the limits that could be
expected of the unaided eye. He was one
of those who allowed for changes in the
apparent position of heavenly bodies because of atmospheric refraction, and he
corrected for instrumental errors as well.

Nobody has ever observed more accurately without a telescope. Where Ptolemy's observations were correct to ten
minutes of arc, Tycho's were correct to
two, which is about the theoretical limit

for naked-eye observation. Tycho corrected almost every important astronomical measurement for the better. He observed the motions of the planets, particularly of Mars, with unprecedented accuracy. He prepared tables of the motion of the sun that were far better than anything previously done. He determined the length of the year to less than a second. Even Tycho, however, could not free himself from his times altogether. He estimated the distance of Saturn, then the farthest known planet, at forty-five million miles, which seemed an enormous distance to the astronomers of the age, but was only one-eighteenth the real figure.

The new accuracy in astronomy made calendar reform inevitable, and in 1582, under the sponsorship of Clavius [152] and of Pope Gregory XIII, it finally came to pass. Ten days were dropped, these having accumulated since the time of the Roman Empire because the Julian year was some minutes longer than the real year. To prevent further accumulations in the future, every cycle of four hundred years was to see only ninety-seven leap years rather than one hundred. The even-century years, such as 1700, 1800, and 1900, were not to be leap years, even though divisible by four, unless (like 1600 and 2000) they were also divisible by four hundred.

This "Gregorian calendar" was quickly accepted by the Catholic nations, but only slowly accepted by the Protestant and Greek Orthodox countries. (They preferred to be wrong with Sosigenes [54] than right with the pope.) It is now universally used throughout the civilized world, except where religious ritual demands the use of another.

At about the time of the reform, chronology generally was being put on a scientific basis by Scaliger [154].

But troubles were gathering about Tycho's head, mostly of his own making. Tycho simply could not forget he was a Danish nobleman and insisted on being an extraordinarily quarrelsome and arrogant one. He was harsh to his underlings and fought with everyone. In a foolish midnight duel at Rostock over some point in mathematics (it was 1565 and

he was still only nineteen) his nose was cut off and he wore a false nose of metal for the rest of his life. Some have doubted the story, but a recent exhumation of his skeleton has confirmed it. Tycho's vision of himself as a nobleman even led him to the rather humorous extreme (according to tradition) of making his astronomical observations in court dress.

His patron, Frederick II, had the patience of a saint and endured it all, but he died in 1588 and his successor, Christian IV (who was to rule Denmark for sixty years), had a bit of a temper himself. After a few years he had had enough of the cantankerous and expensive astronomer. He stopped the subsidy and forced Tycho out. (It should be mentioned that despite his haughty aristocratic ways, Tycho married a peasant girl for love and made a good life with her.)

Tycho left for Germany in 1597 and, at the invitation of the Emperor Rudolf II (whose coronation Tycho had witnessed years before), settled in new quarters in Prague. There he made his greatest discovery, for he found an assistant in a young German named Johann Kepler [169].

Tycho gave Kepler his painstakingly gathered observations and set him to working on the preparation of tables of planetary motions. That was the crowning act of his life. When he died in 1601, after a short illness due, perhaps, to a ruptured bladder, he moaned, "Oh, that it may not appear I have lived in vain." Kepler kept control of the data and continued to work with what were to prove to be results of the first importance. Tycho received an elaborate state funeral and Kepler saw to it, in fact, that Tycho had not lived in vain. He even loyally worked on Tycho's scheme of the universe as he promised his teacher he would. Even Kepler, however, could not keep that alive.

As for Tycho's instruments—the glorious equipment with which he had outfitted his Danish observatories—they were never used again. Within a decade of his death, Galileo's telescope had made all of Tycho's instruments obsolete. They gathered dust and were finally burned during the first years of the Thirty Years' War.

[157] BRUNO, Giordano
Italian philosopher
Born: Nola (near Naples), January 1548
Died: Rome, February 17, 1600

Bruno, the son of a soldier, was born of very poor parents, was educated at the University of Naples, and entered a Dominican monastery in 1563. He held unpopular opinions with fearlessness and had the ability to attract huge audiences by his speaking and writing. (He had also developed a system of mnemonics—a memory course, so to speak—which proved most popular.)

Bruno developed mystical religious notions that fit in with the opinions of Nicholas of Cusa [115] concerning the infinity of space, the inhabitability of other worlds, the motions of earth, and so on. He was also an atomist, and a believer in the circulation of the blood but everything was in the service of his dark and obscure mysticism; and it was his obvious and extreme religious heresy that made him *persona non grata* to all sides.

Changing his name to Filippo Giordano for safety, he fled first to Rome, then to Geneva. In Geneva, the Calvinists ejected him and he went to Paris where he was patronized by Henry III, but where the Aristotelians also ejected him. He wandered over Europe, lecturing at Oxford, England, in 1582 and in Germany for some years after 1586. In 1592 he was arrested in Venice by the Inquisition and charged with heresy.

He might have gotten off by recanting as Galileo [166] was to do a generation later. However, no one since the days of Socrates [21] worked quite so hard and with such determination to secure his own conviction. As he said, his judges were more afraid of him than he was of his judges. After a seven-year trial he was burned alive at the stake.

Intransigent to the last, he refused to accept the cross held out to him at the last moment.

[158] STEVINUS, Simon (steh-vee′nus)
Belgian-Dutch mathematician
Born: Bruges, 1548
Died: The Hague, Netherlands, about March 1620

Stevinus was of illegitimate birth. His first position was as tax collector at Bruges, but he left this for broader fields in 1583, when he entered the University of Leiden. As quartermaster in the Dutch army under Maurice of Nassau, Stevinus worked out a system of sluices in the dikes that made it possible to flood the country quickly in case that were needed to stop an enemy. In mathematics he introduced the use of decimal fractions and was the first to translate Diophantus [66] into a modern language. He was also a firm partisan of the Copernican view of the planetary system.

His main contributions to science are three:

First, he showed in 1586 that the pressure of a liquid upon a given surface depends on the height of the liquid above the surface and upon the area of the surface but does *not* depend on the shape of the vessel containing the liquid. He may be said to have founded the science of hydrostatics.

Second, he demonstrated the impossibility of at least one variety of perpetual motion. He used for this purpose an endless chain about two inclined planes joined in a triangle and showed geometrically that the chain would have to remain motionless. In this manner he continued the study of statics where the recently translated Archimedes [47] had left off.

Third, in 1586 he performed the key experiment of dropping two different weights simultaneously and observed that they struck the ground at the same time—the experiment that seems indissolubly, if incorrectly, wedded to the name of his younger contemporary Galileo [166].

Stevinus was also the first (in 1599) to give values of magnetic declination for specific spots on earth—forty-three of them.

In that same year, he published a design for a sail-propelled cart with front wheels that could be used to steer—a novelty. He also worked out the theory of navigating a ship according to a Mercator [144] map.

The fact that Stevinus wrote in Dutch —and did so charmingly—helped mark the beginning of the end of Latin as the universal European language of learning. Other scholars of the era were beginning to use the "vulgar tongue," Alberti [117] and Galileo for instance using Italian and Descartes [183] using French. The change was slow, however. Even a century after Stevinus' time Newton [231] was writing his great works in Latin.

Stevinus married late in life, at sixty-four, but managed to have four children, two of each sex, before dying.

[159] **NAPIER,** John (nay'pee-ur)
Scottish mathematician
Born: Merchiston Castle, near Edinburgh, 1550
Died: Merchiston Castle, near Edinburgh, April 4, 1617

Napier was born into the Scottish aristocracy and was the eighth Laird of Merchiston. During his youth, he traveled through a Europe split into warring camps by the Protestant Reformation. His native Scotland was itself in the process of turning Calvinist. Napier was a wholehearted Protestant and in 1593 he published a bitterly anti-Catholic commentary on the Revelation of St. John, the first Scottish work on biblical interpretation.

As a further sign of the hot passions aroused in those times, Napier spent considerable energy thinking out devices for destroying an invasion by Philip II of Spain, in case it should come. He planned a burning mirror like that ascribed to Archimedes [47], artillery that would destroy almost all life within a radius of over a mile, and armored war chariots and submarines. He did not produce any of these inventions and the only attempt made by the Spanish Armada anywhere near Scotland was destroyed in 1588 by the small, maneuverable English vessels. No new inventions were needed.

It is no wonder, though, that Napier gained the reputation among the common folk of being a black magician. Some considered him unbalanced. Napier's firm belief in astrology and divination certainly did nothing to discourage such beliefs.

Napier's solid reputation rests upon a new method of calculation that first occurred to him in 1594, the year after he wrote on the Bible. The result was a much more fruitful and memorable work. It occurred to Napier that all numbers could be expressed in exponential form. That is, 4 can be written as 2^2, while 8 can be written as 2^3, and 5, 6, and 7 can be written as 2 to some fractional power between 2 and 3. Once numbers were written in such exponential form, multiplication could be carried out by adding exponents, and division by subtracting exponents. Multiplication and division would at once become no more complicated than addition and subtraction.

Napier spent twenty years working out rather complicated formulas for obtaining exponential expressions for various numbers. He was particularly interested in the exponential forms of the trigonometric functions, for these were used in astronomical calculations and it was these which Napier wanted to simplify. His process of computing the exponential expressions led him to call them logarithms ("proportionate numbers") and that is the word still used.

Finally, in 1614, Napier published his tables of logarithms, which were not improved on for a century, and they were seized on with avidity. Their impact on the science of the day was something like that of computers on the science of our own time. Logarithms then, like the computers now, simplified routine calculations to an amazing extent and relieved working scientists of a large part of the noncreative mental drudgery to which they were subjected. This relief was intensified by a slight modification of logarithms introduced almost at once by Briggs [164].

Napier tried to mechanize the use of logarithms by the manipulation of calculating rods. These were called "Napier's bones" and achieved a certain fame but were completely outclassed and replaced by a much more practical device first constructed by Oughtred [172].

Lost in the colossal structure of logarithms is another advance made by Napier, much smaller, almost invisible in fact but familiar to every grammar school student. Napier completed the present form of the decimal fraction, first used by Stevinus [158], by inventing the decimal point.

[160] **ALPINI,** Prospero (ahl-pee'nee)
Italian botanist
Born: Marostica, Venice, November 23, 1553
Died: Padua, November 23, 1616

Alpini earned his medical degree at the University of Padua in 1578. He served as physician to the Venetian consul in Cairo, Egypt. There he was able to study the date palm and to detect, for the first time, that plants, like animals, could exist as male and female. It was the sexual differences among plants that Linnaeus [276], a century and a half later, was to use as the basis for his classification of the plant kingdom.

Alpini was also the first European to describe the coffee plant and the banana. In 1593 he became professor of botany at the University of Padua.

He died of a kidney infection contracted while in Egypt.

[161] **NORMAN,** Robert
English navigator
Born: Bristol, about 1560
Died: date unknown

Norman, a navigator, would naturally be interested in the compass and its workings. He was the first to note that steel did not alter its weight when it was magnetized. This argued against magne-

tism being a fluid which was somehow poured into the steel.

He was also the first, apparently, who allowed a compass needle to swing up and down, showing, in 1576, that its north-seeking end would then point below the horizon. This is "magnetic dip" and was used to good effect by Norman's contemporary, Gilbert [155].

[162] **LIBAVIUS** (lih-bay'vee-us)
German alchemist
Born: Halle, Saxony, 1560
Died: Coburg, Bavaria, July 25, 1616

Libavius is the Latinized name of Andreas Libau, the son of a weaver, who is known almost entirely for the book he wrote. Like Zosimus [67], his contribution to science is that he summarizes an epoch of alchemy.

Libavius obtained his medical degree at the University of Jena in 1581 and was then town physician at Rothenburg from 1591 to 1596. After quarreling with the rector at Jena, where he was lecturing, he founded a school of his own in Coburg in 1605, remaining there till his death.

In 1597 Libavius published *Alchemia,* a summary of the medieval achievements of alchemy that could be considered the first chemical textbook worthy of the name. He was a follower of Paracelsus [131] in that he believed in the importance of the medical applications of alchemy.

He differed from Paracelsus, however, in largely eschewing mysticism. He bitterly attacked the mumbo-jumbo of those he called Paracelsians and also argued against the doctrines of the Rosicrucians. In fact, his writing is quite clear. He was the first to describe the preparation of hydrochloric acid, tin tetrachloride, and ammonium sulfate. He gave clear directions for preparing strong acids such as sulfuric acid and aqua regia. He suggested that mineral substances could be identified from the shape of the crystals produced when a solution is evaporated.

More clearly than Paracelsus a half

century earlier, Libavius foreshadowed the chemistry of the future.

And yet, for all the foreshadowing, Libavius remained firmly immersed in alchemy. He believed in the possibility of transmutation and considered the discovery of practical methods of making gold to be an important end of alchemical study.

[163] **BACON,** Francis
English philosopher
Born: London, January 22, 1561
Died: London, April 9, 1626

Bacon was born of a family prominent at the English court, and he himself took up the court as a career. He was a great success as a courtier, for he had a remarkable facility for choosing the winning side and abandoning it just before it stopped winning.

He studied law at Cambridge where he gained a distaste for Aristotle's [29] philosophy. He entered practice in 1576. After a stay in France with the English ambassador, he entered Parliament in 1584. He became confidential aide to the earl of Essex, Queen Elizabeth I's favorite, but carefully judged the moment when Essex fell out of favor. By 1601 he was one of the judges who tried and convicted Essex for treason, and with Essex executed, he remained in favor with Elizabeth.

Elizabeth died two years later, but Bacon, in ample time, had won the favor of her successor, and under James I his star rose higher than ever, especially since he courted the patronage of the duke of Buckingham, James's favorite. Bacon was knighted in 1603, shortly after James's accession, became solicitor general in 1607, attorney general in 1613, lord chancellor in 1618. In 1618, also, he was raised to the peerage, being made Baron Verulam. Throughout, he bought his preferment by a disgraceful display of obsequiousness to people in authority and an unprincipled willingness to do any dirty work that needed doing.

In 1621 he was made viscount of St. Albans, and at that moment, at the height of his career, he was suddenly dashed down. He was accused of taking bribes in his capacity as judge, and the evidence was overwhelming. Bacon's only defense was that the bribes, although accepted, did not influence his judgment, and that he judged against the bribe-giver when that seemed the just thing to do. (It did not seem to occur to him that to accept a bribe and then cheat the briber was to be doubly dishonest.)

He was not punished severely, as he might have been, because the king intervened to spare him the worst. However, his political career was over. (There are enthusiasts who think Francis Bacon wrote Shakespeare's plays, largely because Bacon was very educated and wrote, as a matter of course, in Latin, while Shakespeare was, apparently, poorly educated.)

Despite his mean character, Bacon was an effective and influential philosopher. In early life he wrote to his uncle that he was taking "all knowledge to be my province," something that in his day, could still reasonably be attempted. And he was the first, perhaps, to see history as the story of developing ideas rather than of conquering kings.

Bacon's great contribution to experimental science was the glow of respectability he gave it. (He was no relation to Roger Bacon [99], however, who had attempted the same thing three and a half centuries before.)

In 1605 Francis Bacon published a book called *Advancement of Learning* in which he argued against mysticism and characterized the dead hand of tradition as the true devil threatening mankind. There was no use, he said, in studying magic and trying to work through spirits. Science should concern itself with the actual world that was apparent to the senses, for its true purpose was not that of bolstering religious faith, but of improving the human condition. (Nevertheless, he accepted astrology, as indeed nearly everyone did up to the time of Newton [231].)

In 1620 came the *Novum Organum*, that is, the "New Organon," the reference being to the *Organon* of Aristotle in which the Greek philosopher had demonstrated the proper method of logic—of reasoning by deduction. Bacon's book, as the title implies, contains a new method of reasoning.

Bacon argued strenuously that deduction might do for mathematics but that it could not do for science. The laws of science had to be induced, to be established as generalizations drawn out of a vast mass of specific observations.

Bacon, however, was no experimentalist himself and, ironically, one of his few attempts to be one brought on his death. In March 1626 he suddenly began to wonder if snow would delay the putrefaction of living tissue. (Substitute "cold" for "snow" and this is an excellent stroke of intuition.) He was in his carriage at the time, staring at heaps of snow outside, and no doubt that set up the train of thought. He jumped out of the carriage, bought a chicken, and then, with his own hands, stuffed it with snow. He caught a chill almost at once, which turned to bronchitis and brought him to his death.

Bacon's concern with theory blinded him to the men who in his generation were practicing experimental science. Two of them, Gilbert [155] and Harvey [174], were in his own country and time. Moreover, his views remained (perhaps due to his intensively classical education) medieval in some respects. For instance, he could not bring himself to accept the views of Copernicus [127], for he could not swallow the notion of the great, solid earth flying through space.

Harvey, unblinded by Bacon's fine words, and seeing the backwardness of some of the thought, stated dryly that Bacon wrote of science "like a lord chancellor."

Nevertheless, Bacon put the theory of experimental science in the most refined of scholarly terms and made it possible for other scholars to accept it. The world of philosophy might easily ignore a Gilbert or even a Galileo [166] as a mere tinkerer and mechanic. (That is undoubtedly the way in which the Greek philosophers of the Alexandrian period viewed Hero [60], for instance.) But when Bacon placed the stamp of philo-

sophic approval on such "tinkering," it became a different matter.

Largely because of Bacon's influence, experimental science became fashionable among English gentlemen. A group of them began to gather to discuss and practice the new intellectual fad, in imitation of the "House of Solomon," a community of investigators and philosophers described by Bacon in his book *The New Atlantis*. This finally developed into the Royal Society, perhaps the most unusual collection of brilliant scientists to forgather in a single city since the great days of Alexandria.

Yet Bacon had had a real-life model to draw on, too; for a similar group, "Accademia dei Lincei," had been established in Rome earlier by Porta [150]. Its membership had included Galileo.

[164] **BRIGGS**, Henry
English mathematician
Born: Warley Wood, Yorkshire, February 1561
Died: Oxford, January 26, 1630

Briggs obtained his master's degree in Cambridge in 1585 and lectured there in 1592. In 1596, he became professor of geometry at Gresham College in London. He is remembered chiefly for his reaction to Napier's [159] publication of logarithms. He was lost in admiration for the beauty of the system and its simplicity (and aghast at his own stupidity in not seeing it until it was shown him).

He went to the considerable trouble of making a trip to Edinburgh to see Napier and talk to him. Napier had written his exponential numbers as e^2, $e^{2.32}$, $e^{3.97}$, and so on, where e is an unending decimal fraction that starts 2.7182818284 . . . There are good mathematical reasons for doing this and such Napierian or "natural" logarithms are still used in calculus. However, Briggs pointed out during his conversation with Napier the convenience of using exponential numbers such as 10^2, $10^{2.32}$, $10^{3.97}$, and so on. Logarithms in this fashion are called Briggsian or "common" logarithms and are almost invariably used for ordinary calculations.

Briggs worked out the first logarithm tables for numbers from 1 to 20,000 and from 90,000 to 100,000 (to fourteen places!) in 1624. Briggs also invented the modern method of long division.

In 1619 he had reached the peak of his academic career when he became professor of astronomy at Oxford.

Unlike Napier, Briggs scorned astrology.

[165] **SANCTORIUS,** Sanctorius (sank-toh'ree-us)
Italian physician
Born: Justinopolis, Venice (now Koper, Yugoslavia), March 29, 1561
Died: Venice, March 6, 1636

Sanctorius obtained his medical degree at the University of Padua in 1582 and later is supposed to have spent fourteen years as physician to King Sigismund III of Poland and then to have returned to Italy.

Along with Harvey [174], Sanctorius subjected the human body to its first quantitative measurements. As a professor of medicine at Padua, a post he took in 1611, he weighed human beings from day to day on a balance he had constructed himself and proved that they lost weight through "insensible perspiration" (perspiration that evaporated as it formed). This marked the beginning of the modern study of metabolism.

Galileo [166] had invented the first thermometer, a rather bulky and clumsy device in which a trapped volume of air changed the level of water in a tube as it expanded with a rise in temperature or contracted with a drop. Scantorius applied this device to measuring the warmth of the body by placing the bulb of air in the mouth. This was the first clinical thermometer. Sanctorius also invented a device to measure the pulse rate.

Sanctorius, who never married, died of a disease of the urinary tract, one, no doubt, of the eighty thousand different diseases which, in a moment of misguided theory, he at one time calculated were possible in human beings.

[166] **GALILEO** (gahl-ih-lay'oh)
Italian astronomer and physicist
Born: Pisa, February 15, 1564
Died: Arcetri (near Florence), January 8, 1642

Galileo is universally known by his first name only, his full name being Galileo Galilei. The form of the name arose from a Tuscan habit of using a variation of the last name for the first name of the oldest son. He was born three days before Michelangelo died; a kind of symbolic passing of the palm of learning from the fine arts to science.

Galileo was destined by his father, a mathematician of a onetime wealthy but now rather run-down family, to the study of medicine and was deliberately kept away from mathematics. In those days (and perhaps in these) a physician earned thirty times a mathematician's salary. Galileo would undoubtedly have made a good physician, as he might also have made a good artist or musician, for he was a true Renaissance man, with many talents.

However, fate took its own turning and the elder Galilei might as well have saved himself the trouble. The young student, through accident, happened to hear a lecture on geometry and then, pursuing the subject further, came upon the works of Archimedes [47]. He promptly talked his reluctant father into letting him study mathematics and science.

This was fortunate for the world, for Galileo's career was a major turning point in science. He was not content merely to observe; he searched for a crucial experiment that would demonstrate his theories. He began to measure, to reduce things to quantity, to see if he could not derive some mathematical relationship that would describe a phenomenon with simplicity and generality. He was not the first to do this, for it had been done even by Archimedes (whom

Galileo extravagantly admired) eighteen centuries before. What's more, Galileo was not really a thoroughgoing experimenter compared with those who were to follow, and he still retained a great deal of the Greek tendency to theorize.

Nevertheless, Galileo made experimentation attractive. For one thing, he had the literary ability (another talent) to describe his experiments and theories so clearly and beautifully that he made his quantitative method famous and fashionable.

The first of his startling discoveries took place in 1581, when he was a teenager studying medicine at the University of Pisa. Attending services at the cathedral of Pisa, he found himself watching a swinging chandelier, which air currents shifted now in wide arcs, now in small ones. To Galileo's quantitative mind, it seemed that the time of swing was the same, regardless of the amplitude. He tested this by his pulsebeat. Then, upon returning home, he set up two pendulums of equal length and swung one in larger, one in smaller sweeps. They kept together and he found he was correct.

(In later experiments, Galileo was to find that the difficulty of accurately measuring small intervals of time was his greatest problem. He had to continue using his pulse, or to use the rate at which water trickled through a small orifice and accumulated in a receiver. It is ironic then, that after Galileo's death Huygens [215] was to use the principle of the pendulum, discovered by Galileo, as the means by which to regulate a clock, thus solving the problem Galileo himself could not. Galileo also attempted to measure temperature, devising a thermoscope for the purpose in 1593. This was a gas thermometer which measured temperature by the expansion and contraction of gas. It was grossly inaccurate and not until the time of Amontons [244] a century later was a reasonable beginning made in thermometry. (It should never be forgotten that the rate of advance of science depends a great deal on advances in techniques of measurement.)

In 1586 Galileo published a small booklet on the design of a hydrostatic balance he had invented and this first brought him to the attention of the scholarly world.

Galileo began to study the behavior of falling bodies. Virtually all scholars still followed the belief of Aristotle [29] that the rate of fall was proportional to the weight of the body. This, Galileo showed, was a conclusion erroneously drawn from the fact that air resistance slowed the fall of light objects that offered comparatively large areas to the air. (Leaves, feathers, and snowflakes are examples.) Objects that were heavy enough and compact enough to reduce the effect of air resistance to a quantity small enough to be neglected, fell at the same rate. Galileo conjectured that in a vacuum *all* objects would fall at the same rate. (A good vacuum could not be produced in his day, but when it finally was, Galileo was proved to be right.)

Legend has it that Galileo demonstrated his views by simultaneously dropping two cannon balls, one ten times heavier than the other, from the Leaning Tower of Pisa. Both were seen and heard to strike the ground simultaneously. This seems to be nothing more than a legend, but a similar experiment was actually performed, or at least described, some years earlier by Stevinus [158].

Nevertheless, the experiments that Galileo did indeed perform were quite sufficient to upset Aristotelian physics.

Since his methods for measuring time weren't accurate enough to follow the rate of motion of a body in free fall, he "diluted" gravity by allowing a body to roll down an inclined plane. By making the slope of the inclined plane a gentle one, he could slow the motion as much as he wished. It was then quite easy to show that the rate of fall of a body was quite independent of its weight.

He was also able to show that a body moved along an inclined plane at a constantly accelerating velocity; that is, it moved more and more quickly. Leonardo da Vinci [122] had noted this a century earlier but had kept it to himself.

This settled an important philosophic point. Aristotle had held that in order to keep a body moving, a force had to be continually applied. From this it followed, according to some medieval philosophers, that the heavenly bodies, which were continually moving, had to be pushed along by the eternal labors of angels. A few even used such arguments to deduce the existence of God. On the other hand, some philosophers of the late Middle Ages, such as Buridan [108], held that constant motion required no force after the initial impulse. By that view God in creating the world could have given it a start and then let it run by itself forever after. If a continuous force *were* applied, said these philosophers, the resulting motion would become ever more rapid.

Galileo's experiments decided in favor of this second view and against Aristotle. Not only did the velocity of a falling ball increase steadily with time under the continuous pull of the earth, but the total distance it covered increased as the square of the time.

He also showed that a body could move under the influence of two forces at one time. One force, applying an initial force horizontally (as the explosion of a gun), could keep a body moving horizontally at a constant velocity. Another force, applied constantly in a vertical direction, could make the same body drop downward at an accelerated velocity. The two motions superimposed would cause the body to follow a parabolic curve. In this way Galileo was able to make a science out of gunnery.

This concept of one body influenced by more than one force also explained how it was that everything on the surface of the earth, including the atmosphere, birds in flight, and falling stones, could share in the earth's rotation and yet maintain their superimposed motions. This disposed of one of the most effective arguments against the theories of Copernicus [127] and showed that one need not fear that the turning and revolving earth would leave behind those objects not firmly attached to it.

(Galileo's proofs were all reached by the geometric methods of the Greeks. The application of algebra to geometry and the discovery of infinitely more powerful methods of mathematical analysis than those at Galileo's disposal had to await Descartes [183] and Newton [231]. Yet Galileo made do with what he had and his discoveries marked the beginning of the science of mechanics and served as the basis a century later for the three laws of motion propounded by Newton.)

In his book on mechanics Galileo also dealt with the strength of materials, founding that branch of science as well. He was the first to show that if a structure increased in all dimensions equally it would grow weaker—at least he was the first to explain the theoretical basis for this. This is what is now known as the square-cube law. The volume increases as the cube of linear dimensions but the strength only as the square. For that reason larger animals require proportionately sturdier supports than small ones. A deer expanded to the size of an elephant and kept in exact proportion would collapse. Its legs would have to be thickened out of proportion for proper support.

The success of Galileo and his successors, particularly Newton, in accounting for motion by pushes and pulls ("forces") gave rise to the thought that everything in the universe capable of measurement could be explained on the basis of pushes and pulls no more complicated in essence than the pushes and pulls of levers and gears within a machine. This mechanistic view of the universe was to gain favor until a new revolution in science three centuries after Galileo showed matters to be rather more complicated than the mechanists had assumed.

Yet Galileo was reluctant to denounce Aristotelian physics too publicly. He waited for a safe opportunity to do so and this came with the nova of 1604 (the one usually associated with Kepler [169]). Galileo used the nova to argue against the Aristotelian notion of the immutability of the heavens and, by implication, against the Aristotelian view generally.

Galileo's work made him unpopular at Pisa and he moved to a better position at Padua, in Venetian territory. (Venice was a region of considerable intellectual freedom at that time.) The new position

paid three times the salary of the old one
—though Galileo lived gaily and generously and was always in debt anyway.
He was always in trouble, too, for he
made himself unpopular with influential
people. He had a brilliant and caustic
wit and he could not resist using that wit
to make jackasses—and therefore bitter
enemies—of those who disagreed with
him. Even as a college student, he had
been nicknamed "the wrangler" because
of his argumentativeness and noncon-
formity. He even refused to wear academic robes, though this cost him several
fines. Besides he was so brilliant a lecturer that students flocked to hear him,
coming in numbers as high as two thousand, according to a possibly exaggerated
report, while his colleagues mumbled
away in empty halls, and nothing will in-
furiate colleagues more than that.

In Padua, Galileo was corresponding
with Kepler, and in this correspondence
he admitted, as early as 1597, that he
had come to believe in the theories of
Copernicus, though he prudently re-
frained for a while from saying so publicly. The execution of Bruno [157] in
1600 must have encouraged Galileo to
continue refraining.

In 1609, however, he heard that a magnifying tube, making use of lenses, had
been invented in Holland. Before six
months had passed, Galileo had devised
his own version of the instrument, one
that had a magnifying power of thirty-
two. He could adjust it in reverse, to
serve as a microscope, and he observed
insects by this means. However, it was
as a telescope that he made best use of
it. He turned it on the heavens. Thus
began the age of telescopic astronomy.

Using his telescope Galileo found that
the moon had mountains and the sun
had spots, which showed once again that
Aristotle was wrong in his thesis that the
heavens were perfect and that only on
earth was there irregularity and disorder.
Tycho Brahe [156] had already done
that in his studies on his nova and his
comet, and Fabricius [167] had done it
in his studies of a variable star, but
Galileo's findings attacked the sun itself.

(Other astronomers discovered the sunspots at almost the same time as Galileo

—for indeed, very large spots can sometimes be made out with the naked eyes,
when the sun's brilliance is dimmed at
the horizon, or by mist—and there was
wrangling over priority, which made
Galileo additional enemies. Galileo, however, whether he had priority in the discovery or not, did more than merely see
the spots. He used them to show that the
sun rotated about its axis in twenty-seven
days, by following individual spots
around the sun. He even determined the
orientation of the sun's axis in that fashion. (Nor did Galileo get off scot-free.
His studies of the sun damaged his eyes,
which had already suffered from infections in his youth, and in old age he
went blind.)

The stars, even the bright ones, remained mere dots of light in the telescope, while the planets showed as little
globes. Galileo deduced from this that
the stars must be much farther away
than the planets and that the universe
might be indefinitely large.

Galileo also found that there were
many stars in existence that could be
seen by telescope but not by naked eye.
The Milky Way itself owed its luminosity to the fact that it was composed of
myriads of such stars.

More dramatically, he found that Jupiter was attended by four subsidiary
bodies, visible only by telescope, that
circled it regularly. Within a few weeks
of observation he was able to work out
the periods of each. Kepler gave these
latter bodies the name of satellites and
they are still known as the Galilean satellites. They are known singly by the
mythological names of Io, Europa, Ganymede, and Callisto. Jupiter with its satellites was a model of a Copernican system—small bodies circling a large one. It
was definite proof that not all astronomical bodies circled the earth.

Galileo observed that Venus showed
phases entirely like those of the moon,
from full to crescent, which it must do if
the Copernican theory was correct. According to the Ptolemaic theory Venus
would have to be a perpetual crescent.
The discovery of the phases of Venus
definitely demonstrated, by the way, the
fact that planets shine by reflected sun-

light. Galileo discovered that the night side (that is, the dark portion) of the moon when the moon was less than full had a dim glow, which he explained as caused by light shining upon it from the earth (earthshine). It had been seen before but had been explained otherwise. Poseidonius [52] thought it was sunlight shining through a partly transparent moon. Reinhold [143] thought the moon's surface was phosphorescent. Earthshine showed that earth, like the planets, gleamed in the sun, and removed one more point of difference between the earth and the heavenly bodies.

All these telescopic discoveries meant the final establishment of Copernicanism more than half a century after Copernicus had published his book.

Galileo announced his discoveries in special numbers of a periodical he called *Sidereus Nuncius* ("Starry Messenger") and these aroused both great enthusiasm and profound anger. Aged Venetian aristocrats clambered to the top of a tower in order to look through one of his telescopes and see ships, otherwise invisible, far out at sea. He was the best lensmaker in Europe at the time and built a number of telescopes. He sent them all over Europe (one reaching Kepler) so that others might confirm his findings. Both Venice and Florence offered him lucrative positions. To the annoyance of the Venetians, Galileo chose to travel to his beloved Florence.

Galileo visited Rome in 1611, where he was greeted with honor and delight, though not everyone was happy. The thought of imperfect heavens, of invisible objects shining there, and, worst of all, of the Copernican system enthroned and the earth demoted from its position as center of the universe was most unsettling. Galileo also rather unwisely ventured to write a book giving his views on the Bible and generally discussing theological subjects to the offense of theologians. Galileo's conservative opponents persuaded Pope Pius V to declare Copernicanism a heresy, and Galileo was forced into silence in 1616.

Intrigue continued. Now Galileo's friends, now his enemies seemed to have gained predominance. In 1632 Galileo

was somehow persuaded that the pope then reigning (Urban VIII) was friendly and would let him speak out. He therefore published his masterpiece, *Dialogue on the Two Chief World Systems,* in which he had two people, one representing the view of Ptolemy [64] and the other the view of Copernicus, present their arguments before an intelligent layman. (Amazingly enough, despite his long friendship with Kepler, Galileo did not mention Kepler's modification of Copernicus' theory, a modification that improved it beyond measure—but then, Kepler's work was appreciated by virtually no one at the time.)

Galileo of course gave the Copernican the brilliant best of the battle. The pope was persuaded that Simplicio, the character who upheld the views of Ptolemy in the book, was a deliberate and insulting caricature of himself. The book was all the more damaging to those who felt themselves insulted, because it was written in vigorous Italian for the general public (and not merely for the Latin-learned scholars) and was quickly translated into other languages—even Chinese!

Galileo was brought before the Inquisition on charges of heresy (his indiscreet public statements made it easy to substantiate the charge) and on June 22, 1633, was forced to renounce any views that were at variance with the Ptolemaic system. Romance might have required a heroic refusal to capitulate, but Galileo was nearly seventy and he had the example of Bruno to urge him to caution. He recanted and was condemned to a penance of psalm recitations each week for three years—and, of course, to refrain from further heresy.

Legend has it that when he rose from his knees, having completed his renunciation, he muttered, "Eppur si muove!" ("And yet it moves," referring to the earth.) This was indeed the verdict given by the world of scholarship, and the silencing of Galileo for the remaining few years of his old age (during which —in 1637—he made his last astronomical discovery, that of the slow swaying or "libration" of the moon as it revolves) was an empty victory for the conservatives. When he died they won an even shallower victory by refusing him burial in consecrated ground.

The Scientific Revolution begun with Copernicus had been opposed for nearly a century at the time of Galileo's trial, but by then the fight was lost. The revolution not only existed, but had prevailed, although, to be sure, there remained pockets of resistance. Harvard, in the year of its founding (1636), remained firmly committed to the Ptolemaic theory.

Galileo's *Dialogue* was not removed from the Roman Catholic Index of prohibited books until 1835. In 1965, Pope Paul VI, on a visit to Pisa, spoke highly of Galileo—an even clearer admission that on this issue the church had been in the wrong.

[167] **FABRICIUS,** David (fa-brish′-ee-us)
German astronomer
Born: Esens, Ostfriesland, March 9, 1564
Died: Osteel, Ostfriesland, May 7, 1617

The surname is a Latinized version of Goldschmidt. Fabricius, a Protestant minister, was a friend of Tycho Brahe [156] and Kepler [169]. He was one of the first to join Galileo [166] in using the telescope for astronomical research but he could never bring himself to accept Kepler's elliptical orbits. He insisted on Plato's [24] circles.

His best-known discovery came in the time of naked-eye astronomy, for in 1596 he observed a star that Bayer [170] later named Omicron Ceti and found to show periodic variations in brightness. Hevelius [194], a half century later, named it Mira ("wonderful"). It was the first variable star to be discovered. The mere existence of a star varying in brightness was another blow to the orthodox Aristotelian view that the heavens were perfect and unchanging.

Fabricius was murdered by one of his parishioners, who was apparently a thief and whom Fabricius had threatened to expose.

[168] **LIPPERSHEY,** Hans (lip′er-shee)
German-Dutch optician
Born: Wesel, Germany, about 1570
Died: Middelburg, Netherlands, about 1619

Lippershey was a lens grinder who sold spectacles, the one device for which lenses were commonly used in those days. One of his apprentices, while passing away an idle moment in 1608, adjusted two lenses before his eyes and found that distant objects seemed closer.

Startled, he told Lippershey, who mounted such lenses in tubes and attempted to sell them (the first telescopes) to the Dutch government. Recognizing the use of the instrument in warfare, the government tried to keep it secret. Hearing rumors of such a device, however, Galileo [166] in Italy quickly constructed one and turned it upon the heavens, revolutionizing astronomy rather than warfare.

[169] **KEPLER,** Johann
German astronomer
Born: Weil der Stadt, Württemberg, December 27, 1571
Died: Regensburg, Bavaria, November 15, 1630

In his youth, Kepler, the son of a professional soldier (who deserted his family) and grandson of a man who had served as mayor of the family's hometown, was cursed with a sickly constitution. An attack of smallpox, when he was three, crippled his hands and weakened his eyes. This made it necessary for him to have a religious education, for he seemed fit for no post more strenuous than that of minister.

He studied at the University of Tübingen, where he was scapegoated by the other students, and where he was converted to Copernicanism. He graduated in 1588 and earned a master's degree in 1591. His brilliance in mathematics was soon recognized, and by 1594 all thought of the ministry was abandoned and he was teaching science at the University of Graz in Austria. In 1597, he married and in this way eventually gained five children and fourteen years of unhappiness.

There was a strong strain of mysticism in Kepler. An astronomy professor in those days was expected to cast horoscopes, and Kepler threw himself into that form of work. He was no faker but studied the Greek astronomers carefully in an attempt to make a real science out of astrology as Cardano [137] had done nearly a century before. In this he failed, as Cardano had.

Again like Cardano, Kepler attempted to use astrological techniques to solve biblical mysteries. He tried to work out the date of creation, for instance, and found it to be 3992 B.C.

In later life Kepler seemed rather apologetic about his ability as an astrologer, but there is no question that it was more valued by his patrons than his achievements in science. He cast horoscopes for Emperor Rudolf and in later years for the imperial general, Albrecht von Wallenstein, earning him their protection, although he was a Protestant and the times were those of the Thirty Years' War, during which religious hatreds were strong.

In 1598 religious disputes (well in advance of the climactic quarrel of the Thirty Years' War) were intense in Graz, and Kepler felt it advisable to leave. He accepted a position at Prague with the aged Tycho Brahe [156], with whom he had been in correspondence for some time. On Tycho's death in 1601 Kepler inherited the invaluable data that the older man had collected over the years, including his careful observations of the apparent motion of the planet Mars.

Kepler set about trying to devise a system of the heavens based on these observations. He was spurred on by the appearance of another nova ("Kepler's star") on September 30, 1604, not quite as bright as Tycho's star, but spectacular enough.

In his work, however, Kepler was sidetracked by his interest in mystic notions dating back to the Greeks. He believed firmly in the "music of the spheres" first propounded by Pythagoras [7] and his

followers and even tried to work out the exact notes sounded by each planet in its motions. (Earth, he said, sounded the notes "mi," "fa," "mi," indicating it to be the abode of *mi*sery, *fa*mine and *mi*sery.)

He also felt the influence of Plato [24], for he tried to fit the five Platonic solids into the planetary scheme of things. The book in which he advanced this notion, published in 1596, was what first interested Tycho Brahe in Kepler.

In working out his regular-solid theory of the planets, he circumscribed an octahedron about the sphere of Mercury and placed the sphere of Venus through its vertices. An icosahedron was circumscribed about the sphere of Venus and the sphere of earth was placed through its vertices. And so on.

He spent a tremendous amount of time working it all out in the hope of accounting exactly for the relative distances from the sun of the various planets. He finally realized by 1595 he couldn't adjust the various solids and spheres properly.

Nevertheless, he did not give up. It occurred to him at last that nothing he could do with spheres would fit Tycho's data, and he began to search for some noncircular curve that would fit. First, he tried an egg-shaped oval without success, and then he settled on the ellipse.

The ellipse, a curve first studied by Apollonius [49], resembles a flattened circle. A circle has a diameter that is fixed in length however it is drawn, but an ellipse's diameter (a straight line drawn through its center) varies in length according to its position. The longest diameter is the major axis, the shortest the minor axis. The flatter the ellipse, the greater the proportionate difference in length between major and minor axis and the greater its "eccentricity." (The eccentricity of a circle is zero; it is not flattened at all.)

Along the major axis are two points called foci at equal distances from the center. The foci have this property: if from each focus a straight line is drawn to the same point on the curve of the ellipse, the sum of the two lines is always equal to the length of the major axis.

This is true no matter to which point on the curve the two lines are drawn.

Kepler found that the positions of Mars, as observed by Tycho, fitted into an elliptical orbit with a high degree of accuracy. It wasn't a very flattened ellipse, but it was most definitely not a circle. Furthermore, the sun was located at one focus of the ellipse.

Kepler found that the orbits of the other planets could also be drawn as ellipses with the sun always at one of the foci. He announced this in *Astronomia Nova*, a book published in 1609, and this is now known as Kepler's first law. The book also contained his second law: "A line connecting the planet and the sun will sweep over equal areas in equal times as the planet moves about its orbit." This meant that the closer a planet was to the sun the faster it would move according to a fixed and calculable rule.

Kepler went on later to apply these laws to the satellites of Jupiter as well. However, he was unable to handle earth's own moon. Its motions were too complicated. This was done in 1638 by Horrocks [200].

Kepler's ellipses put an end to Greek astronomy. They destroyed the sacredness of circular motion and abolished the celestial spheres that Eudoxus [27] had placed in the heavens two thousand years before, and which even Copernicus had retained. Kepler's scheme of the solar system has been followed by astronomers ever since, without significant modification. (Kepler's insight was restricted to the solar system. The stars, he thought, all occupied a thin shell some two miles thick far outside the solar system. Here he was far behind Bruno [157].)

With the abolition of the celestial spheres some other cause had to be found to explain the fact that the heavenly bodies remained in their orbits. The fact that the sun was always at one focus of the elliptical orbit, that it was always in the plane of the orbit, that planetary motion was faster the closer the planet was to the sun, made it obvious to Kepler that the sun somehow controlled the motions of the planets. He followed the notions of Gilbert [155] in thinking that some magnetic force was involved, but the systems he attempted to work out on such a basis were unsatisfactory. It was left for Newton [231] to suggest a satisfactory explanation a half century later.

Kepler published another book in 1619, one that was particularly full of verbose mysticism. Kepler, aware of its difficulty, despondently suspected it might have to wait a century for a reader. In it, however (rather like a pearl in a mass of seaweed), was what is now called Kepler's third law, which stated that the square of the period of revolution of a planet is proportional to the cube of its distance from the sun. Again the sun seemed indicated as the controller of planetary motion.

The book was dedicated to James I of Great Britain, a royal pedant to whom a turgid book was meat and drink and a dedication the dessert to top it with. James invited Kepler to England, but the astronomer refused to leave Germany even though that land was now plunging into the Thirty Years' War.

Kepler and Galileo [166] carried on a friendly correspondence for a time, though they never met, and Kepler communicated his theories to Galileo. Galileo, however, in his book on the Copernican theory made no mention of Kepler's laws. Presumably he felt they were as little to be regarded as Kepler's fantasies about regular solids and the music of the spheres (to say nothing about his horoscopes—although Galileo, on occasion, could cast one too). As a matter of fact, the correspondence had been broken off in 1610, and this may indicate the loss of sympathy between the two.

Nevertheless, when Galileo was constructing telescopes and sending them where he thought they would do the most good, one found its way to Kepler.

Kepler used the telescope to observe Jupiter's moons—which he had refused to accept till he saw them with his own eyes—and promptly described them as "satellites," from a Latin term for the hangers-on of a powerful man. He began to work on the manner in which light

waves were refracted by lenses. He managed to explain in this way how it was
that telescopes (and eyes, too) performed their function.

He described an improved telescope in
1611, using two convex lenses in place
of the one convex and one concave used
by Galileo, and described, in theory, a
compound microscope better than any
then available. He also showed that a
parabolic mirror focused parallel rays of
light, a fact essential to the development
of reflecting telescopes by Newton later
in the century. Thus he founded the science of modern optics. But he was not
able to deduce a general mathematical
relationship to express the refraction of
light. That was left for his younger contemporary Snell [177].

In 1612 Kepler's protector, Rudolf II,
died. (So did Kepler's wife, and a second marriage, to a younger woman,
brought him happiness.) The new emperor, Matthias, maintained Kepler in
his position as court astronomer with a
salary that was usually in arrears. (Rudolf II had not been a prompt payer either. The Holy Roman emperors were
usually strapped for cash.) In 1618
Kepler's mother, who dabbled in the occult, was arrested as a witch and, although not tortured, did not long survive
her release, which was procured through
her son's long-sustained efforts.

Kepler spent these years completing
new tables of planetary motions based
on Tycho's superlative observations and
his own theory of elliptical orbits. He
used the newly invented logarithms of
Napier [159] in his calculations, this
being the first important use to which
logarithms were put. Despite family
troubles, financial difficulties exacerbated
by the fact that Kepler fathered thirteen
children, and continuing war and religious unrest, the tables, called the Rudolphine Tables in honor of Kepler's old
patron, were published in 1627 and dedicated to the memory of Tycho. The
work included tables of logarithms and
Tycho's star map as expanded by Kepler.

Kepler's final service to astronomy was
his calculation of the times of passage of
the inner planets Mercury and Venus
across the face of the sun. Such passages

had never been observed, but according
to Kepler's calculations they had to take
place. In 1631 such a "transit" of Mercury was observed by Gassendi [182] at
the predicted time, but Kepler by then
was dead of a fever, followed by enthusiastic medical bleeding.

Kepler, by the way, wrote a story,
"Somnium," about a man who traveled
to the moon in a dream. For the first
time the lunar surface was described as
it really was, so that "Somnium" may be
considered the first piece of authentic
science fiction, as opposed to fantasy. It
was published after Kepler's death.

Kepler's manuscripts were eventually
bought by Catherine II of Russia over a
century after his death and are preserved
now at the Pulkovo Observatory in the
USSR.

[170] BAYER, Johann (by'er)
German astronomer
Born: Rain, Bavaria, 1572
Died: Augsburg, Bavaria, March
7, 1625

While Kepler [169] was putting the
planetary system into its modern shape,
his countryman Bayer, a lawyer by profession and adviser to the Augsburg City
Council, was adding a modern touch to
the stars themselves.

The constellations and their names
stretch back to antiquity and have always proved a useful means of dividing
the starry vault. The names of the stars
within the constellations were in ancient
times not so well organized. The bright
ones were given names of course and the
present versions of those names are
mostly derived from the Arabic. Betelgeuse, Aldebaran, and Rigel bear witness
to the centuries between the eighth and
the eleventh when it was the Arabs who
preserved Greek astronomy. Some
names, such as Castor, Pollux, and
Sirius, date back to classical times. However, there was no way of associating the
name of a star with the constellation that
contains it except brute memory.

In 1603 and 1627 Bayer published editions of Uranometria, a catalogue of the
heavens (the first one to show the entire

108

1. PYTHAGORAS

2. HIPPOCRATES

3. ARISTOTLE

4. EUCLID

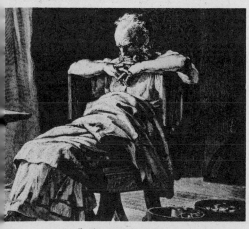

5. ARCHIMEDES

6. PTOLEMY

7. NICOLAS COPERNICUS

8. ROGER BACON

9. GALEN

10. ANDREAS VESALIUS

11. GALILEO GALILEI AND THE DUKE OF PADUA

12. JOHANN KEPLER

13. WILLIAM HARVEY

14. RENÉ DESCARTES

15. ROBERT BOYLE

16. ANTON VAN LEEUWENHOEK

17. ISAAC NEWTON

18. BENJAMIN FRANKLIN

19. HENRY CAVENDISH

20. SIR WILLIAM HERSCHEL

21. ANTOINE L. LAVOISIER

22. EDWARD JENNER

celestial sphere) that corrected this. He described the constellations carefully and located more stars (1,706 altogether) than Tycho Brahe [156] had done in his catalogue.

In addition, and more important, Bayer listed the stars of each constellation by Greek letters in order of brightness. Thus Betelgeuse, the brightest star in Orion, became Alpha Orionis, while Rigel was Beta Orionis, and Bellatrix was Gamma Orionis. This device has been kept to the present. Indeed, some bright stars of the southern skies, which have been observed carefully only since Bayer's day, are known only by this system. Thus the brightest star of the southern heavens and—as Henderson [505] was to show two centuries later—the star that is closest to us is in the constellation Centaurus and is known only as Alpha Centauri. (In later years, as more and fainter stars were studied, Roman letters and numbers, alone and in combination, had to be brought into use.)

Bayer, who was an amateur theologian and an ardent Protestant, did not succeed in another project. Offended by the heathen names of the constellations, he tried to introduce a system whereby the northern constellations were given names from the New Testament, and southern constellations from the Old.

[171] **MARIUS,** Simon
German astronomer
Born: Gunzenhausen, January 20, 1573
Died: Anspach, Bavaria, December 26, 1624

Marius' real name was Mayer but, like many another scholar of the time, he used a Latinized version in his scholarly career. He studied astronomy under Tycho Brahe [156] and medicine in Italy and served as court astronomer for the elector of Brandenburg.

His career is possibly an unsavory one. He seems to have had one of Galileo's [166] works copied and published under another author's name, and he claimed (apparently without justification) to have seen the four satellites of Jupiter in 1609 before Galileo had. We can well imagine that Galileo was furious at this and charged into the fight with all his strength.

Yet one aspect of Marius' work, even if false, remains. Galileo had not named Jupiter's satellites, but Marius did. Marius made use of Greek mythology and chose the names Io, Europa, Ganymede, and Callisto—four individuals who were closely involved with Jupiter (Zeus) in the myths. Those names remain. Marius also prepared tables of their motions before Galileo did.

Marius made one discovery that, apparently, no one disputes as Marius'. In 1612 he was the first astronomer to mention the Andromeda Nebula, the most distant object one can see without a telescope—though that fact was not to be appreciated for three more centuries.

[172] **OUGHTRED,** William (aw'tred)
English mathematician
Born: Eton, Buckinghamshire, March 5, 1574
Died: Albury, Surrey, June 30, 1660

Oughtred, who obtained his master's degree at Cambridge in 1600, was a minister and not a professional mathematician, but that makes little difference since he spent almost all the time he could spare on mathematics, even when it meant sleeping but two or three hours a night.

He published a textbook on mathematics in 1631 in which he introduced the multiplication sign ($\times$) and the abbreviations commonly used today for the trigonometric functions: *sin, cos,* and *tan* for sine, cosine, and tangent.

His greatest innovation, however, came in 1622, and consisted of two rulers along which logarithmic scales were laid off. By manipulating the rulers and sliding one against the other, calculations could be performed mechanically by means of logarithms. We know it now as a slide rule, and, for centuries, engineers carried slide rules at least as lovingly as any physician ever carried his stethoscope and tongue depressor.

He was a pronounced royalist but managed to keep his post during the time of Cromwell and the Commonwealth. There is a story that he died of joy at hearing that Charles II had been recalled and the British monarchy was to be re-established. However, he was eighty-five at the time and undoubtedly the thread of life was sufficiently frayed to require no great drama to bring about death.

[173] **SCHEINER,** Christoph (shigh'-ner)
German astronomer
Born: Wald, Rhine Province, July 25, 1575
Died: Neisse, Silesia (now Nysa, Poland), June 18, 1650

Scheiner taught Hebrew and mathematics, first at Freiburg and then at Ingolstadt (where he had studied). He was appointed professor of Hebrew and mathematics at Ingolstadt in 1600. He observed sunspots on a projection of the sun's disc in March 1611. This was not really very unusual, for some spots are big enough to be seen by the unaided eye and records of their occasional observation dated back to ancient times. Scheiner claimed to have seen them before Galileo [166], however, and that irritated the contentious Italian who plunged eagerly into controversy.

When Scheiner (a Jesuit since 1595) first reported his discovery to his superior, the latter warned him to be careful in his interpretations, for Aristotle [29] had said nothing about spots on the sun. Scheiner therefore judged them to be small bodies, circling the sun but not part of it. (It did not occur to him, apparently, that Aristotle had said nothing about that either.)

This was all Galileo needed. He attacked both Scheiner and Aristotle in his best polemical style, and this helped end the brief popularity of Galileo with the church authorities and began the long road that ended in the inquisitorial chambers.

Scheiner also studied the physiology of vision and showed that the curvature of the lens changes as the eye focuses to different distances. This is called "accommodation."

[174] **HARVEY,** William
English physician
Born: Folkestone, Kent, April 1, 1578
Died: London, June 3, 1657

As a young man, Harvey (the son of a well-to-do businessman and the oldest of nine children) supplemented his education at Cambridge (from which he took his degree in 1597) by courses at the medical school in Padua, Italy, which ever since Mondino's [110] day, three centuries before, had been the world's greatest. There he studied under Fabricius ab Aquapendente [151] among others.

Harvey was in Italy when Galileo [166] was making his mark and it was Harvey's great feat to apply the Galilean view of science to physiology and medicine. One of Galileo's Italian colleagues, Sanctorius [165], made a start in this direction, but Harvey was to outstrip him.

After obtaining his medical degree in 1602 Harvey returned to England, where he married and set up a most successful practice. Francis Bacon [163] was one of his patients, and from 1618 he was court physician for James I and Charles I until the latter was beheaded in 1649.

He was more interested in medical research than in routine practice. By 1616, he is supposed to have dissected eighty species of animals. In particular he studied the heart and blood vessels. Men such as Servetus [142] had groped toward the concept of the circulation of the blood. Harvey, however, was not a speculator but an experimenter. He determined the heart was a muscle and that it acted by contracting, pushing blood out. Through actual dissection he noted that the valves separating the two upper chambers of the heart (auricles) from the two lower (ventricles) were one-way. Blood could go from auricle to ventricle but not vice versa. There were one-way valves in the veins too, these having been discovered by Fabricius. For that reason, blood in the veins could travel only toward the heart and not away from it. In fact, it was the valves in the veins that first put Harvey on the right track, as, late in life, he explained to the young Boyle [212].

When Harvey tied off an artery it was the side toward the heart that bulged with blood. When he tied off a vein the side away from the heart bulged. Everything combined to indicate that blood did not oscillate back and forth in the vessels as Galen [65] had believed but traveled in one direction only.

Furthermore Harvey calculated that in one hour the heart pumped out a quantity of blood that was three times the weight of a man. It seemed inconceivable that blood could be formed and broken down again at such a rate. Therefore it had to be the same blood moving in circles, from the heart to the arteries, from these to the veins, from those back to the heart. The blood, in other words, moved in a closed curve. It circulated.

He began lecturing on the subject in 1616, but it was not until 1628 that he published these conclusions and the evidence backing them in a small book of only seventy-two pages, miserably printed in Holland on thin, cheap paper and full of typographical errors. However, the experiments it described were clear, concise, and elegant, and the conclusions were incontrovertible. The book became one of the great scientific classics. Its short title is *Exercitatio De Motu Cordis et Sanguinis* ("On the Motions of the Heart and Blood").

Harvey was ridiculed at first, for it was no light matter to refute Galen. His practice fell off and learned doctors wrote tomes refuting him (by quoting Galen and not by repeating Harvey's experiments). Harvey was called Circulator, which was a cruel pun, for it was the Latin slang for "quack," the name given to peddlers who hawked medicines at the circus. He did not take much part in the controversy, but let the facts speak. For that matter, Harvey avoided controversy on principle and did not engage in the polemics that delighted the anatomists of the day.

Harvey had led the team of doctors at the bedside of James I on the occasion of his last illness in 1625. James's son, who succeeded as Charles I, had enough faith in Harvey to let him have royal deer with which to experiment, and at the king's command, Harvey performed a postmortem on the body of Thomas Parr ("Old Parr") who died in 1635 at a reputed, but almost certainly exaggerated, age of 152.

Harvey was one of the first to study the development of the chick in the egg, something that had once interested Aristotle [29]. Although in attendance on Charles I during the English Civil War, in which Charles lost throne and head, Harvey did not fall victim to partisan passion, but returned safely to London, though revolutionaries did break into his home and destroy some notes and specimens. (In particular, Harvey is supposed to have been at the battle of Edgehill in 1642 and spent his time there calmly reading a book while waiting for any royal call.)

By the time of Harvey's old age the fact of circulation was accepted by physicians generally. Even in France, where opposition was strongest, the influential Descartes [183] supported Harvey. Harvey was elected president of the College of Physicians in 1654. He declined the privilege, preferring to spend his last years in peace.

The validity of the theory of circulation depended on the blood's passing from the arteries to the veins, but there were no visible connections between those blood vessels. Harvey, noting that both arteries and veins divided and subdivided into finer and finer vessels till they passed out of sight, supposed the connections were simply too fine to see. This was proved correct by Malpighi [214], who had the advantage of the use of a microscope. This final proof was not obtained until four years after Harvey's death.

Since Harvey's small book was the end of Galen and of Greek medicine, the English physician may be considered the founder of modern physiology.

His personal library, which he left to

111

the London College of Physicians, was
destroyed in the Great Fire of 1666.

[175] **HELMONT,** Jan Baptista van
Flemish physician and alchemist
Born: Brussels, January 12, 1580
Died: Vilvoorde (near Brussels),
December 30, 1635, or 1644

Helmont, the scion of a noble family,
obtained his medical degree in 1599 at
the University of Louvain and practiced
without charge. He lived in troubled
times, for Spain was trying to suppress
rebellion in the Netherlands, and was
doing so ruthlessly.

Like Paracelsus [131], by whom he
was much influenced, he was interested
in alchemy and given to mysticism. Helmont searched for the philosopher's
stone and tried to fuse chemistry and
religion into something that was not
quite either. On one occasion, at least,
that got him into difficulties. He maintained that saintly relics displayed their
effects through magnetic influence. For
ascribing earthly causes to divine phenomena, he got into trouble with the Inquisition in 1634.

He was very emphatic about the "philosopher's stone," which he claimed he
had seen and used. He also believed in
"spontaneous generation"; that is, the
development of living organisms from
nonliving surroundings. He declared that
mice could arise from dirty wheat, for
instance. He denied transmutation of
metals, however.

In one respect he was unusually conservative, for he abandoned Paracelsus
and the alchemical notions of mercury,
sulfur, and salt as the basis of solid substances. Instead, he moved all the way
back to Thales [3]. Helmont, like the
Greek philosopher, believed that water
was the basic element of the universe. It
is symptomatic of the new era, however,
with new quantitative methods gaining
favor and the Scientific Revolution well
under way, that Helmont tried to prove
his case by experiment.

He grew a willow tree in a weighed
quantity of soil and showed that after
five years, during which time he added
only water, the tree had gained 164
pounds while the soil had lost only two
ounces. From this he deduced that water
was converted by the tree into its own
substance. Though he was wrong, the experiment is of crucial importance. For
one thing, he was the first to use quantitative methods in connection with a biological problem and is sometimes called
the "father of biochemistry" for that
reason. Also he did at least prove that it
was not from the solid soil that the chief
nourishment of plant life was drawn.

In another respect Helmont the alchemist was unusually advanced. He was
the first to recognize that there is more
than one airlike substance; that some of
the vapors he obtained in his experiments are distinct substances, as different
in properties from ordinary air as water
is. Because vapors, unlike liquids and
solids, have no fixed volume but fill any
container, he considered them examples
of matter in complete chaos and, about
1620, named them so. However, he
spelled "chaos" according to its phonetic
sound in Flemish, which made it "gas."
This word, ignored at the time, was reintroduced by Lavoisier [334] a century
and a half later and has been used by
chemists ever since.

In particular Helmont studied the gas
produced by burning wood. He called
this "gas sylvestre" ("gas from wood")
but we now call it carbon dioxide. Ironically it is this gas, not water, that is
plant life's chief source of nourishment
and Helmont, in interpreting his experiment with the willow tree, had neglected
to consider the air that surrounded it. He
had the right answer in the substance
that he himself discovered, but he did
not know it.

Unfortunately Helmont wrote in a
very obscure style, so that he was not as
influential as he might have been. His
writings were not published till after his
death, when his son, a friend of Leibniz
[233], edited them.

[176] **WENDELIN,** Godefroy
Flemish astronomer
Born: Herken, near Liége, Bel-
gium, June 6, 1580
Died: Gent, 1667

Wendelin was a cleric, as were so many of the astronomers of the time, and was a canon of Tournai.

Despite his position in the church, he was a convinced Copernican. He repeated Aristarchus' [41] attempt to determine the distance of the sun by observing the geometry of the situation at the exact moment of half-moon. His observations were more accurate than Aristarchus' had been nearly two thousand years before, and his estimate of the sun's distance was sixty million miles, which was twelve times greater than the earlier value.

It was still one-third short of the actual distance, but it did give mankind a glimpse at the real size of the solar system, a glimpse that gave way to relatively clear vision with Cassini's [209] work half a century later.

[177] **SNELL,** Willebrord van Roijen
Dutch mathematician
Born: Leiden, 1580
Died: Leiden, October 30, 1626

Snell received his master's degree in 1608 and succeeded his father as professor of mathematics at the University of Leiden in 1613. He is best known for his discovery in 1621 that when a ray of light passes obliquely from a rarer into a denser medium (as from air into water or glass) it is bent toward the vertical.

The phenomenon (refraction of light) was known as long ago as the time of Ptolemy [64], but Ptolemy thought that as the angle to the vertical made by the light ray in air was changed, it maintained a constant relationship to the angle to the vertical made by the light ray in water or glass. Snell showed this was not so. It was the *sines* of the angles that bore the constant relationship. It was only because at small angles the sines are almost proportional to the angles themselves that Ptolemy was deluded.

This key discovery in optics was not well publicized until 1638, when Descartes [183] published it—without giving proper credit to the source. In 1617 Snell had also developed the method of determining distances by trigonometric triangulation and thus founded the modern art of mapmaking.

[178] **BAFFIN,** William
English explorer
Born: Probably London, about 1584
Died: off the island of Qeshm, Persian Gulf, January 23, 1622

For a thousand years after Pytheas [39] the Arctic regions slumbered untouched by the curiosity of men from warmer climes. From the ninth to the eleventh centuries the Vikings of Scandinavia penetrated to Iceland, Greenland, and even North America, but these were isolated ventures with no important consequences for Europe as a whole.

The voyages of Columbus [121] and the subsequent realization that the land he had discovered represented new continents and not old Asia, led to attempts to reach beyond the Americas to the fabled Indies. The route of Magellan [130] south of South America was a kind of Southwest Passage, which worked but was terribly long. The search was on for a shorter Northwest Passage around northern North America.

The effort to find the Northwest Passage reached an early climax with William Baffin. In 1612 he served as chief pilot on a ship that explored the southwestern coast of Greenland. The next year he turned his energies eastward toward Spitzbergen.

In 1615 he was back in Greenland waters and this time he penetrated northward into the large body of water lying to the west of northern Greenland, a body now known as Baffin Bay. The large island west of the bay is Baffin Island. Baffin penetrated to within eight hundred miles of the North Pole and no one else was to get closer for two and a half centuries.

Baffin's explorations caused him to doubt the existence of a Northwest Passage. He was both right and wrong, since the sea passage does exist but is so choked by ice that it is not a practical route, except perhaps for specially designed icebreakers.

Baffin's explorations were accomplished with scientific precision. He determined latitudes and observed tides carefully. His recordings of the orientation of the compass needle led to the first magnetic chart. He was the first to try to determine longitude at sea by observations of the moon.

After these Arctic explorations Baffin made a fatal switch to tropic waters, surveying areas in and about the Red Sea and the Persian Gulf. He was an employee of the East India Company at this time. When the Company allied itself in 1621 with the Shah of Persia against the Portuguese, Baffin found himself in a war. During an attack on Qeshm, an island at the mouth of the Persian Gulf, Baffin was killed.

[179] **VERNIER,** Pierre (vehr-nyay')
French engineer
Born: Ornans, August 19, 1584
Died: Ornans, September 14, 1638

Vernier was the son of a lawyer and a minor government official in a part of France (Franche Comte) that was then ruled by the Hapsburg kings of Spain. Vernier was a military engineer in the employ of the Spanish king.

He was interested in instruments and in particular in devices that would allow one to measure angles or small distances with great precision. Others had worked on the problem before and the idea had existed of dividing a number of intervals of progressively larger size (by small steps) into equal numbers of subdivisions. The measure one wanted would be bound to fall near a subdivision on one of the scales and from that the angle or distance could be calculated quite precisely. The difficulty lay in devising these many scales with the necessary precision in the first place. Clavius [152] was one of those who worked on the problem.

It occurred to Vernier that only two such scales were necessary, if one was made movable. It could be adjusted against the immovable scale to just fit the angle or the linear measure and then the position of the moving subdivisions against the fixed ones would give the measure to an extra decimal point. Vernier announced his device in 1631 and immortalized himself for the device has been known as a "vernier" ever since (pronounced "vur'nyer" in English).

Since one motive force behind the advance of science has been the invention and construction of ever more precise measuring instruments, Vernier deserves mention for that feat alone.

[180] **CYSAT,** Johann
Swiss astronomer
Born: Lucerne, 1586
Died: Lucerne, May 3, 1657

Cysat, a pupil of Scheiner [173], entered the Jesuit order in 1604 and later became a priest. He served as professor of mathematics at the Jesuit college of Ingolstadt in Bavaria.

He was one of the early users of the telescope and surveyed the sky with one as early as 1611. He studied spots on the sun and was the first to use a telescope to observe a comet. His most notable achievement was the discovery of the Orion Nebula in 1619.

[181] **MERSENNE,** Marin (mer-sen')
French mathematician
Born: near Oizé, Sarthe, September 8, 1588
Died: Paris, September 1, 1648

Mersenne was a schoolfellow of Descartes [183] but, unlike the latter, went on to enter the church, joining the Minim Friars, in 1611. Within the church, Mersenne did yeoman work for science, of which he was an ardent exponent. He defended Descartes's philosophy against clerical critics, translated some of the works of Galileo [166], and defended him, too.

Mersenne's chief service to science was the unusual one of serving as a channel for ideas. In the seventeenth century, long before scientific journals, international conferences, and even the establishment of scientific academies, Mersenne was a one-man connecting link among the scientists of Europe. He wrote voluminous letters to regions as distant as Constantinople, informing one correspondent of the work of another, making suggestions arising out of his knowledge of the work of many, and constantly urging others to follow this course of copious intercommunication.

He opposed mystical doctrines such as astrology, alchemy, and divination and supported experimentation. As a practical example of this belief he suggested to Huygens [215] the ingenious notion of timing bodies rolling down inclined planes by the use of a pendulum. This had not occurred to Galileo, and Huygens was to take this idea to fruition in a pendulum clock.

Mersenne is best known today for the "Mersenne numbers," numbers produced by a certain formula which, Mersenne said, would yield primes. His reasons for deciding this are not known, but in any case he was wrong; some of the large numbers he maintained to be prime proved not to be. Nevertheless, the Mersenne primes proved to stimulate research into the theory of numbers.

[182] GASSENDI, Pierre (ga-sahn-dee')
French philosopher
Born: Champtercier, Provence,
January 22, 1592
Died: Paris, October 24, 1655

Gassendi, born of poor parents, studied and taught at the University of Aix, where he obtained his doctorate in theology in 1616, but rebelled against its medieval attitude. His philosophic views served science in two ways. In the first place, like his older contemporary Francis Bacon [163] he strongly advocated experiment in science. He came to understand the importance of experimentation in his reading of Galileo [166] whom he supported even after Galileo's condemnation by the Inquisition.

Secondly he was a convinced atomist and helped bridge the gap between Epicurus [35] and Lucretius [53], whose nineteen-century-old views he strongly supported, and the scientific atomism

that was to come two centuries after his time. More specifically, his views strongly affected those of Boyle [212].

He was interested in astronomy, too, describing the aurora borealis in 1621 and giving it its name. Another of his concrete scientific accomplishments was to observe the transit of Mercury in 1631, within five hours of the time predicted by Kepler [169]. It was the first planetary transit ever observed.

He also dropped a stone from the top of the mast of a moving ship and showed that it landed at the bottom of the mast. The ship did not move from under it. This bore out one of Galileo's "thought experiments" and disproved the Ptolemaic argument against the earth's rotation, the one which maintained that if the earth rotated then someone jumping up into the air would come back to earth far from his starting point.

Gassendi vigorously opposed Descartes's [183] philosophy and Harvey's [174] theory of blood circulation. He made up for that in his study of sound, though. He studied its velocity, which he showed to be independent of pitch, thus refuting Aristotle's [29] contention that high notes traveled more rapidly than low notes.

Gassendi published biographies of Peurbach [118], Regiomontanus [119], Copernicus [127], and Tycho Brahe [156], and it might be mentioned as a link between science and literature that among Gassendi's pupils was the great French playwright Molière.

In 1645 he became professor of mathematics at the Collège Royale at Paris.

[183] DESCARTES, René (day-kahrt')
French philosopher and mathematician
Born: La Haye, now called La
Haye-Descartes (near Tours),
March 31, 1596
Died: Stockholm, Sweden, February 11, 1650

As was common in his day, when Latin was the language of scholarship, Descartes used a Latinized version of his name for his writings, signing them Renatus Cartesius. It is because of this that Descartes's system of philosophy is spoken of as Cartesian and that the common system of plotting the curves represented by equations (a system Descartes originated) involves Cartesian coordinates. Nevertheless, Descartes wrote in French rather than in Latin, another indication of the continuing decline of Latin as the universal language of scholarship in Europe.

Descartes's mother died when he was a year old and he appears to have inherited her ill health. He was troubled with a chronic cough and at school was allowed to remain in bed as long as he wished. (The fact that he was a brilliant student contributed also to the favoritism.) He retained the habit of doing much of his work in bed for the rest of his life and could well pamper himself in this way for he never married and thus avoided family responsibilities.

From the days of his Jesuit education Descartes remained carefully devout. For instance when in 1633 he heard that Galileo [166] had been condemned for heresy, he at once abandoned a book he was writing on the universe in which he accepted the views of Copernicus [127].

Instead, by 1644, he had worked out a theory according to which all space was filled with matter arranged in rotating vortices. He considered the earth at rest in the center of a vortex. It was the vortex, then, that traveled about the sun. This compromise, like that of Tycho Brahe [156], was ingenious but worthless. Nevertheless it was accepted by many scholars until Newton [231] a generation later put all lesser theories to flight with his theory of gravitation. Descartes's vortices, however, were, in some ways, strangely like Weizsäcker's [1376] vortices three centuries later.

After some years in the French army —during which time he was not exposed to actual warfare and found ample time to work out his philosophy—Descartes settled in Protestant Holland. There he remained for almost all his life until at an unlucky moment in September 1649 he succumbed most reluctantly to an invitation to the Swedish court.

The Swedish ruler at the time was Christina, who was anxious to obtain the services of a renowned philosophe. in order to glorify her court. (This desire by European royalty for intellectual luster was to become particularly pronounced during the Age of Reason, as the eighteenth century was to be called.)

Unfortunately Christina was one of the most eccentric rulers ever to grace a throne, and her notion of utilizing Descartes's services was to have him call on her three times a week at 5 A.M. to instruct her in philosophy. Visiting the castle during the coldest part of a Swedish winter night three times a week was too much for Descartes's delicate lungs and he was dead of pneumonia before the winter was over. His body, all but the head, was returned to France. In 1809 Descartes's skull came into the possession of Berzelius [425], who turned it over to Cuvier [396], and thus Descartes came home at last.

Descartes was a mechanist. Out of extension and motion, he would say, the universe could be constructed and he thought it necessary to begin with some incontrovertible fact, something that could be accepted to begin with.

In his *Discourse on Method,* published in 1637, he began by doubting everything; but this very doubt appeared to him to be the incontrovertible fact for which he searched. The existence of a doubt implied the existence of something that was doubting, hence the existence of himself. He expressed this in the Latin phrase "Cogito, ergo sum" ("I think, therefore I am"). The system he built on this was sufficiently impressive to earn the title sometimes bestowed on him: father of modern philosophy.

Descartes applied the mechanistic view even to the human body though not to the human soul, or to God. Basing his conclusions on the work of Vesalius [146] and Harvey [174] (whose work on the circulation of the blood he helped to popularize) he tried to present the purely animal workings of the body as a system of mechanical devices. The mind was outside the body and independent of it, but interacting with it through the medium of the pineal gland, a small structure attached to the brain, which Galen [65] had thought served as a channel and valve to regulate the flow of thought.

Descartes may have been influenced by this, but he also chose the pineal gland because he believed it to be the one organ found only in man and not in the lower animals, which, without the pineal gland, lacked mind and soul and were merely living machines. (In this respect he was shown to be wrong. A few decades later Steno [225] discovered the pineal gland in lower animals, and now we know that there is a species of very primitive reptile in which the pineal gland is far better developed than in man.)

Descartes's most important contributions to science, however, were in mathematics. For one thing, he was the first to use the letters near the beginning of the alphabet for constants and those near the end for variables. This modification of Vieta's [153] system stuck and it is to Descartes therefore that we owe the familiar x's and y's of algebra. He also introduced the use of exponents and the square root sign.

Descartes had grown interested in mathematics while in the army, where his military inactivity gave him time to think. His great discovery came to him in bed, according to one story, while he was watching a fly hovering in the air. It occurred to him that the fly's position could be described at every moment by locating the three mutually perpendicular planes that intersected at the position occupied by the fly. On a two-dimensional surface, such as a piece of paper, every point could be located by means of two mutually perpendicular lines intersecting at that point.

In itself this was not original. All points on the earth's surface can be (and are) located by latitude and longitude, which are analogous, on a sphere's surface, to the Cartesian coordinates on a plane surface.

What was world-shaking, though, was that Descartes saw that through the use of his coordinate system every point in a plane could be represented by an ordered system of two numbers, such as 2, 5, or −3, −6, which can be interpreted as "two units east and five units north from the starting point" or "three units west and six units south from the starting point." For points in space an ordered system of three numbers is required, the third number representing the units up or down.

In any algebraic equation in which one variable y is made to depend on the fluctuations of a second variable x according to some fixed scheme, as, for instance, $y = 2x^2 - 5$, then for every value of x there is some fixed value of y. If x is set equal to 1, y becomes −3; if x is 2, y is 3; if x is 3, y is 13, and so on. If the points represented by the x, y combinations (1, −3; 2, 3; 3, 13; etc.) are converted into points on a plane according to the Cartesian system, a smooth curve is obtained. In this case it is a parabola. Every curve represents a particular equation by this system; every equation represents a particular curve.

Descartes advanced this concept in an appendix of about a hundred pages which was attached to his book (published in 1637) on vortices and the structure of the solar system. It is not the only time in the history of science that a casual appendix proved to be inestimably more important than the book to which it was attached. Another example, two centuries later, involved Bolyai [530].

The value of Descartes's concept was that it combined algebra and geometry to the great enrichment of both. The combination of the two could be used to solve problems more easily than either could be used separately. It was this application of algebra to geometry that was to pave the way for the development of the calculus by Newton, which is essentially the application of algebra to smoothly changing phenomena (such as accelerated motion), which can be represented geometrically by curves of various sorts.

Since a synonym for algebra ever since the days of Vieta is "analysis," Descartes's system of fusing the two branches of mathematics into one has come to be called analytic geometry.

[184] **GELLIBRAND,** Henry (gell'uh-brand)
English astronomer and mathematician
Born: London, November 17, 1597
Died: London, February 16, 1636

Gellibrand was educated at Oxford, obtaining his master's degree in 1623. He became professor of astronomy at Gresham College in 1627. He was a friend of Briggs [164] and finished some of the latter's unfinished manuscripts after Briggs's death. His strongly Puritan tendencies got him into trouble with the Anglican authorities in 1631, but he was acquitted.

Gellibrand noted that the recorded direction of the compass needle in London changed slowly despite Gilbert's [155] contention, and had shifted by more than seven degrees in the previous half century. In 1635 he published his findings. This was the first indication that the earth's magnetic field slowly changes and, indeed, not only the horizontal angle of the needle changes, but also the angle of magnetic dip. The very strength of the field changes and, to the present day, no clear explanation for this has been given.

[185] **RICCIOLI,** Giovanni Battista (reet-choh'lee)
Italian astronomer
Born: Ferrara, April 17, 1598
Died: Bologna, June 25, 1671

Riccioli, a Jesuit from the age of sixteen, did not accept the views of Copernicus [127]. To arguments that the Ptolemaic system was impossibly complicated, he countered with the argument that the more complicated the system, the better the evidence for the greatness of God. He mentioned the ellipses of Kepler [169] but dismissed them out of hand.

It seems natural, therefore, that he should have concentrated on a study of the moon. The moon revolved about the earth in the Copernican system as well as in the older system of Ptolemy [64], and its investigation could raise no embarrassing problems. In connection with the moon, he could produce some useful results. He was the first to maintain there was no water on the moon.

In 1651 Riccioli published a book called *New Almagest* in Ptolemy's honor in which he accepted Tycho Brahe's [156] system and in which he included his own maps of the lunar surface, four years after Hevelius' [194] pioneer effort. On his maps Riccioli named the lunar craters in honor of the astronomers of the past, giving due weight to his anti-Copernican views. Hipparchus [50], Ptolemy, and Tycho Brahe received better craters than Copernicus and Aristarchus [41]. These names are still used today.

Some of those honored now are Albategnius [83], Anaxagoras [14], Apollonius [49], Arago [446], Archimedes [47], Aristotle [29], Bessel [439], Biot [404], Bond [660], Cassini [209], Clavius [152], De la Rue [589], Eudoxus [27], Fabricius [167], Flammarion [756], Flamsteed [234], Gassendi [182], Gauss [350], Geber [76], Guericke [189], Herschel, Caroline [352], Kepler [169], Lalande [309], Messier [305], Meton [23], Olbers [372], Picard [204], Pickering [784], Plato [24], Pliny [61], Poseidonius [52], Rheticus [145], Roemer [232], Stevinus [158], and Riccioli himself. A mountain has been named for Huygens [215] and a mountain range for Leibniz [233]. The basic system has even been extended by astronomers to the other side of the moon.

In 1650 Riccioli had used a telescope to view the star Mizar (the middle star of the handle of the Big Dipper) and found it to be two stars very close together. This was the first observation of a double star and it gave another proof that the telescope could reveal features of the heavens not visible to the naked eye.

He also tried to measure the parallax of the sun and decided it was twenty-four million miles from the earth, a value soon to be more than tripled by Cassini.

He noticed colored bands on Jupiter parallel to its equator and, along with Grimaldi [199], improved the theory of the pendulum and made clearer the conditions under which it would mark time accurately.

[186] **CAVALIERI,** Bonaventura (kah'-vah-lyeh'ree)
Italian mathematician
Born: Milan, 1598
Died: Bologna, November 30, 1647

Cavalieri joined the Jesuit order in 1615, where he was introduced to a thorough study of the Greek mathematicians. He also met Galileo [166], corresponded with him and considered himself a disciple of that man. His various church offices did not prevent him from working at his mathematics and from teaching.

Archimedes [47] had done some of his work in measuring geometric areas by supposing such areas to be made up of very small components. Cavalieri followed that line of reasoning to produce the notion that volumes were made up components that were not exactly lines but thin areas so small as to be no further divisible. Making use of such "indivisibles" he could work out a number of theories involving areas and volumes.

The importance of this is that it was a stepping-stone toward the notion of infinitesimals and the development of the calculus by Newton [231], which is the dividing line between classical and modern mathematics.

[187] **KIRCHER,** Athanasius (kir'kher)
German scholar
Born: Fulda, Hesse-Nassau, May 2, 1601
Died: Rome, Italy, November 28, 1680

Kircher, the youngest of six sons, received a Jesuit education and was ordained a priest in 1628.
Like that other cleric of two centuries before, Nicholas of Cusa [115], Kircher

had an uncanny knack of making intuitive guesses that were eventually proved correct. His early work with the microscope, for instance, caused him to wonder if disease and decay might not be brought about by the activities of tiny living creatures, a fact that Pasteur [642] would demonstrate two centuries later.

He invented a magic lantern, an Aeolian harp, and a speaking tube. Interested in antiquities, he was one of the very first to make an attempt to decipher the Egyptian hieroglyphics, something that was not carried much further till Young's [402] time a century and a half later.

In 1650 Kircher made use of the new methods of producing a vacuum introduced by Guericke [189]. His experiments demonstrated that sound would not be conducted in the absence of air. This supported one of the few theories in physics that Aristotle [29] advanced and that turned out to be correct.

[188] **FERMAT,** Pierre de (fehr-mah')
French mathematician
Born: Beaumont-de-Lomagne, Languedoc, August 20, 1601
Died: Castres, near Toulouse, January 12, 1665

Fermat, the son of a leather merchant, was educated at home and then went on to study law, obtaining his degree in 1631 from the University of Orleans. He was a counselor for the Toulouse parliament and devoted his spare time to mathematics. Considering what he accomplished one wonders what he might have done as a full-time mathematician.

Fermat had the supremely frustrating habit of not publishing but scribbling hasty notes in margins of books or writing casually about his discoveries in letters to friends. The result is that he loses credit for the discovery of analytic geometry, which he made independently of Descartes [183]. In fact, where Descartes's formal analysis involves only two dimensions, Fermat takes matters to three dimensions. Fermat also loses credit for the discovery of some features of the calculus that served later to inspire Newton [231]. (However, he probably would not have cared. He engaged in mathematics for his own amusement and that he achieved.)

He, together with Pascal [207], founded the theory of probability. He also worked on the properties of whole numbers, being the first to carry this study past the stage where Diophantus [66] had left it. Fermat is thus the founder of the modern "theory of numbers."

In that field he left his greatest mark, for in the margin of a book on Diophantus he scribbled a note saying he had found that a certain equation ($x^n + y^n = z^n$, where n is greater than 2) had no solution in whole numbers but that there was no room for the simple proof in the margin. For three centuries mathematicians, including the greatest, have been searching for the proof of what is now called "Fermat's last theorem" (because it is the last that remains unproved) and searching in vain. Modern computers have shown that the equation has no solutions for all values of n up to 2,000, but this is not a *general* proof.

In 1908 a German professor willed a prize of 100,000 marks to anyone who would find a proof, but German inflation in the early 1920s reduced the value of those marks to just about zero. In any case, no one has yet won it. Fermat did not publish his work on the theory of numbers. His son published his notes five years after Fermat's death.

[189] **GUERICKE,** Otto von (gay′rih-kuh)
German physicist
Born: Magdeburg, November 20, 1602
Died: Hamburg, May 11, 1686

Guericke studied law and mathematics as a youth and attended the University of Leiden, where Snell [177] may have been one of his teachers. He then traveled in France and England, and served as an engineer for the German city of Erfurt. Guericke in 1627 returned to Magdeburg and entered politics there. It

was a bad time. The Thirty Years' War was raging and Magdeburg, a Protestant city, was on the side that was, at the moment, losing. In 1631 it was destroyed by the imperial armies in the most savage sack of the war, and Guericke and his family barely managed to escape at the cost of all their possessions. After serving for a time in the army of Gustavus II Adolphus of Sweden (who managed to turn the tide of the war), Guericke returned to a Magdeburg rising again out of ruins, serving as an engineer in this rebirth effort, and in 1646 became mayor of the town, retaining that post for thirty-five years, then retiring to Hamburg in his eightieth year. In 1666, he had been ennobled, gaining the right to add "von" to his name.

He grew interested in philosophic disputations concerning the possibility of a vacuum. Numerous arguments denying its existence were advanced. Aristotle [29] had worked out a theory of motion in which a body impelled by a certain continuing force would move faster as the surrounding medium grew less dense. In a vacuum it would move with infinite speed. Since Aristotle did not accept the possibility of infinite speed he decided that a vacuum could not exist. This, like almost all of Aristotle's views, was accepted uncritically by later philosophers and was expressed in the catch phrase "Nature abhors a vacuum."

Guericke decided to settle the question by experiment rather than argument and in 1650 constructed the first air pump, a device something like a water pump but with parts sufficiently well fitted to be reasonably airtight. It was run by muscle power and was slow, but it worked and Guericke was able to put it to use for pieces of showmanship of quite Madison Avenue proportions. And he spared no expense, either, for he spent $20,000 on his experiments, a tremendous sum for those days.

He began with an evacuated vessel. He showed that a ringing bell within such a vessel could not be heard, thus bearing out Aristotle's contention that sound would not travel through a vacuum, though it would travel through liquids and solids as well as through air. Guericke also showed that candles would not burn and that animals could not live in a vacuum, but the true significance of these observations had to await Lavoisier [334] a century and a quarter later.

Guericke grew more dramatic. He affixed a rope to a piston and had fifty men pull on the rope while he slowly drew a vacuum on the other side of the piston within the cylinder. Air pressure inexorably pushed the piston down the cylinder despite the struggles of the fifty men to prevent it.

Guericke prepared two metal hemispheres that fitted together along a greased flange. (They were called the Magdeburg hemispheres, after his town.) In 1657 he used them to demonstrate the power of a vacuum to Emperor Ferdinand III. When the hemispheres were put together and the air within evacuated, air pressure held them together even though teams of horses were attached to the separate hemispheres and whipped into straining to their utmost in opposite directions. When air was allowed to reenter the joined hemispheres, they fell apart of themselves.

It was about this time that Guericke heard of Torricelli's [192] experiments, and he saw that the results of his more dramatic demonstrations were due to the fact that air had weight. His demonstrations added nothing to what Torricelli had established, but they had flair and forced the world of scholarship to understand and accept the basic discovery. Furthermore, he saw the application of the barometer to weather forecasting and in 1660 he was the first to attempt to use it for this purpose.

Guericke also made important advances in another field. Gilbert [155] had worked with substances that could be "electrified" by rubbing and made to attract light objects. Guericke mechanized the act of rubbing and devised the first frictional electric machine. This was a globe of sulfur that could be rotated on a crank-turned shaft. When stroked with the hand as it rotated, it accumulated quite a lot of static electricity. It could be discharged and recharged indefinitely.

He produced sizable electric sparks from his charged globe, a fact he reported in a letter to Leibniz [233] in 1672.

Guericke's sulfur globe initiated a full century of experimentation—with other and better frictional devices—which reached its height with the work of Franklin [272].

Guericke was also interested in astronomy and felt that comets were normal members of the solar system and made periodic returns. This notion was to be successfully taken up by Halley [238] some twenty years after Guericke's death.

[190] **GLAUBER**, Johann Rudolf
(glow'ber)
German chemist
Born: Karlstadt, Lower Franconia, 1604
Died: Amsterdam, Netherlands, March 10, 1670

At an early age the self-taught Glauber, the son of a barber, lived in Vienna, then in various places in the Rhine Valley. Some time during this interval, perhaps about 1625, he noted that hydrochloric acid could be formed by the action of sulfuric acid on ordinary salt (sodium chloride). This was the most convenient method yet found for the manufacture of hydrochloric acid, but what interested Glauber most was the residue (today called sodium sulfate).

Glauber fastened on to this substance, studying it intensively and noting its activity as a laxative. Its action is mild and gentle and throughout history there have always been those who place great value on encouraging the bowels. Glauber, enamored of his discovery, labeled it *sal mirabile* ("wonderful salt") and advertised it as a cure-all in later years. He believed its use had once cured him of typhus. (The fact that his only source of income was the sale of his chemical products forced him into a heavy sell, of course.)

We don't consider it a cure-all these days, but the common name of sodium sulfate is still "Glauber's salt."

121

Glauber made a number of discoveries that mark him as a legitimate "dawn-chemist," even if his interest in cure-alls was an alchemical hangover. He prepared a variety of compounds of the metals then known. These included tartar emetic, an antimony salt which has some medical use.

In 1648 he moved to Amsterdam, where he took over a house that had once belonged to an alchemist. He made out of it the best chemical laboratory of the day, with special furnaces and equipment that he himself had designed. One furnace had a chimney, the first ever to be so equipped. This was all symbolic of the passage from alchemy to chemistry taking place in the seventeenth century.

Glauber prepared a variety of chemical compounds by secret methods and sold them for medicinal purposes. In working with vinegar, oils, coal, and other substances, he obtained organic liquids such as those we now call acetone and benzene. He did well and, at one time employed five or six workmen in his laboratories. He always modeled himself on Paracelsus [131], whom he greatly admired and to whose grave he made a pilgrimage.

Glauber was ahead of his time in his clear-sighted view of how a country's natural resources could be exploited for the betterment of living conditions, and he published a book suggesting what Germany should do in this respect. He objected, for instance, to the overexport of raw materials to Austria and France. The political fragmentation of seventeenth-century Germany made his ideas impractical, however.

Glauber's concern with medicinal compounds carried a penalty. What is useful at one dose may be toxic at a larger one, and what is harmless in a single administration may be dangerous in several. Glauber's death was hastened, it is believed, by poisoning during the slow and tedious work over his compounds and he died poor and discouraged. Other chemists since Glauber's time have been gradually killed by their work, the most notable case perhaps being that of Madame Curie [965].

[191] **BORELLI,** Giovanni Alfonso
(boh-rel'lee)
Italian mathematician and physiologist
Born: Naples, January 28, 1608
Died: Rome, December 31, 1679

Borelli, the son of a Spanish soldier stationed in Naples, was a professor of mathematics at Messina in 1649 and at Pisa in 1656. He returned to Messina in 1667.

His life was not entirely smooth. In 1674 he was suspected of political conspiracy against the occupying Spaniards and had to leave Messina again and retire to Rome, where he remained under the protection of Christina, former queen of Sweden. (This was the queen whose eccentric habits had brought on the death of Descartes [183]. She abdicated in 1654 and was received into the Roman Catholic Church the following year, after which she settled in Rome.)

Borelli corrected some of Galileo's overconservatism. Galileo had neglected Kepler's [169] elliptical orbits, but now Horrocks [200] had extended them even to the moon, and Borelli rescued the ellipses, publicizing and popularizing them.

He tried to extend the vague notions of Galileo and Kepler concerning the attractive forces between the sun and the planets but was not successful. He tried also to account for the motion of Jupiter's satellites by postulating an attractive force for Jupiter as well as for the sun. In this he (and Horrocks also at about this time) made a tentative step in the direction of universal gravitation, but that had to wait a generation for Newton [231].

Borelli suggested (under a pseudonym) that comets traveled in parabolic orbits, passing through the solar system once and never returning. (The parabola, like the ellipse, was first studied by Apollonius [49]. A parabola is an open curve something like a hairpin.) Any body following a parabolic path would approach the sun from infinite space, round it, and recede forever. Such an orbit would explain the erratic behavior of comets without completely disrupting the orderliness of the universe.

Borelli understood the principle of the balloon, pointing out that a hollow copper sphere would be buoyant when evacuated, if it were thin enough, but that it would then collapse under air pressure. It did not occur to him that collapse could be avoided if a lighter-than-air gas were used to fill the sphere as, in essence, the Montgolfier brothers [325] were to do a century and a half later.

Borelli grew interested in anatomy through his friendship with Malpighi [214]. He tried to apply the mechanistic philosophy to the working of the body after the style of Descartes and here he achieved his greatest fame. In a book entitled *De Motu Animalium* ("Concerning Animal Motion"), he successfully explained muscular action on a mechanical basis, describing the actions of bones and muscles in terms of a system of levers. In it, also, he made careful studies of the mechanism of the flight of birds as Leonardo da Vinci [122] had done a century and a half earlier.

He attempted to carry these mechanical principles to other organs such as the heart and lungs with somewhat less success and to the stomach with (as we now understand) no success at all. He considered the stomach a grinding device and did not recognize that digestion was a chemical rather than a mechanical process.

This tendency to overmechanization of the body was in part neutralized by the labors of contemporaries such as Sylvius [196], who interpreted the body in purely chemical terms.

[192] **TORRICELLI,** Evangelista (tor-rih-chel'lee)
Italian physicist
Born: Faenza (near Ravenna), October 15, 1608
Died: Florence, October 25, 1647

Torricelli, left an orphan at an early age, received a mathematical education in Rome. He was profoundly affected when in 1638 he first read Galileo's [166] works. A book he himself wrote on mechanics in turn impressed Galileo, who invited him to Florence. Torricelli went gladly to meet the blind old man and served as his secretary and companion for the last three months of his life. He then succeeded him as court mathematician to Grand Duke Ferdinand II of Tuscany [193] and learned how to make the best lenses for telescopes yet seen.

Galileo suggested the problem through which Torricelli was to gain fame.

The ability to pump water upward was attributed to the supposed fact that "Nature abhors a vacuum." When a piston was raised, a vacuum would be produced unless the water within the cylinder lifted with the piston. Since a vacuum could not occur in nature, it was thought, the water *had* to lift. But in that case it ought to lift upward indefinitely as long as the pump worked. Water, however, could only be raised about thirty-three feet above its natural level.

Galileo, who accepted the vacuum-abhorrence of nature (despite his many revolutionary deeds he was surprisingly conservative in many ways), could only suppose that this abhorrence was limited and not absolute. He suggested that Torricelli look into the matter.

It occurred to Torricelli that this was no matter of vacuum-abhorrence, but a simple mechanical effect. If the air had weight (according to Aristotle [29] it didn't but tended rather to have "levity" and to rise but Galileo had shown that a full balloon weighed more than an empty one) then this weight would push against the water outside the pump. When the piston was raised, that push would force the water up with the piston. However, suppose the total weight of the air would only balance thirty-three feet of water. In that case, further pumping would have no effect. The weight of the air would push water no higher.

In 1643, to check this theory Torricelli made use of mercury, whose density is nearly thirteen and a half times that of water. He filled a four-foot length of glass tubing, closed at one end, stoppered the opening and upended it (open end down) into a large dish of mercury. When the tube was unstoppered, the mercury began to empty out of the tube as one might expect, but it did not do so altogether. Thirty inches of mercury remained in the tube, supported by the weight of the air per unit area, or "pressure," pressing down on the mercury in the dish. The weight of the air could easily be used to account for the mercury column's remaining in place in defiance of gravity.

Above the mercury in the upended tube was a vacuum (except for small quantities of mercury vapor). It was the first man-made vacuum, and, thanks to the publicity given the experiment by Mersenne [181], is called a Torricellian vacuum to this day. (Seven years later Guericke [189] produced a vacuum on a far larger scale by pumping and did dramatic things as a result.)

Torricelli noticed that the height of the mercury in the tube varied slightly from day to day and this he correctly attributed to the fact that the atmosphere possessed a slightly different pressure at different times. He had invented the first barometer.

(The pressure of the atmosphere is equivalent to that of a column of mercury 760 millimeters high. The pressure exerted by one millimeter of mercury is sometimes defined as one torricelli, in honor of the physicist.)

The fact that air had a finite weight meant it could only have a finite height, a view confirmed by Pascal [207] a few years later. This was the first definite indication (aside from philosophical speculation) that the atmosphere does not extend indefinitely upward and that the depths of space must be a vacuum. Thus, far from a vacuum being an impossibility, it is undoubtedly the natural state of most of the universe.

Questions concerning the existence of a vacuum may have seemed rarefied and philosophical, but the proof of its existence led by a chain of events and reasoning to the development of the steam engine, the advent of the Industrial Revolution, and the making of our own technological society. All resulted from the upending of a tube of mercury.

124

Torricelli died of typhoid fever only four years after his great experiment.

[193] **FERDINAND II OF TUSCANY,**
Grand Duke
Italian ruler
Born: July 14, 1610
Died: May 24, 1670

Ferdinand II was of the famous family of the Medici, who were, in his time, past their best days.

Ferdinand succeeded to the ducal throne in 1621 when he was only eleven, and his reign was largely disastrous for Tuscany, which became and remained a cipher in the European arena from then on.

He is remarkable, however, for the eager and liberal patronization of men of science, including Steno [225] and Galileo [166] and for helping support the foundation of the Accademia del Cimento in 1657.

He was a deeply religious man, and though he was a political antagonist of the pope, he could not bring himself to challenge the church on matters of heresy. He did not, therefore, come to Galileo's defense and for this the world of science blamed him severely.

He made a personal contribution to technology. In 1654 he devised a sealed thermometer which, unlike Galileo's open one, was not affected by changes in air pressure. This led, eventually, to the perfected instruments of Fahrenheit [254] sixty years later.

[194] **HEVELIUS,** Johannes (heh-vay'-lee-oos)
German astronomer
Born: Danzig (now Gdańsk, Poland), January 28, 1611
Died: Danzig, January 28, 1687

Hevelius was one of ten children of a prosperous brewer. As a young man, he toured Europe and, having obtained his education en route, returned to Danzig at the age of thirty. An eclipse of the sun, which he had observed in 1639, had turned his attention to astronomy, so he established an astronomical observatory, the best in Europe at that time, atop his house.

He concentrated on the moon, studying its features with a succession of telescopes of greater and greater power. The manufacture of these telescopes was made easier by Hevelius' construction of a lathe to be used in the grinding of large lenses.

Galileo [166], the first to study the moon by telescope, was also the first to try to draw its features. His drawings, however, were only crude sketches. Hevelius, a generation later, was the first to make drawings containing features of the lunar surface as we recognize them today.

In 1647 he published a magnificent volume called *Selenographia,* an atlas of the moon's surface, using hand-engraved copper plates for his illustrations. He titled the features systematically, using names taken from earth's geography, in line with the notion that had become widespread after Galileo's time that the moon was but a smaller earth. Thus, he named the lunar mountain chains Alps, Apennines, and so on, and these names persist.

The dark, relatively flat areas of the moon, he called "seas" (*maria* in Latin), so that there is a Mare Serenitatis ("Pacific Ocean") on the moon as on the earth. The *maria* retain their name to the present time, even though it is now known that they are but dry stretches of dust.

Hevelius' names for the individual craters, however, did not last. For this, his older contemporary Riccioli [185] can take credit.

In 1644 he made out the phases of Mercury, a necessary accompaniment to Galileo's discovery of the phases of Venus a generation before.

Next to his work on the moon, Hevelius is best known for his two large volumes on comets. He listed what information he could find on all the comets recorded in the past and discovered four more. The best he could do in connection with cometary orbits was to suggest like Borelli [191] that they might be parabolas.

Although he observed the physical features of the moon with telescopes, he refused to use them for measuring the positions of the stars. He was the last important astronomer to insist on naked-eye observations, and there was reason to it, considering the imperfections of the telescopes of the day.

Hevelius got into an acrimonious debate on the subject with the ever quarrelsome Hooke [223], and in 1679 he entertained for two months a young Englishman named Halley [238] who had come to make peace between him and Hooke. Unfortunately Hevelius' observatory burnt down shortly afterward. The tragedy embittered him and made him intransigent and not inclined to accept peace.

Hevelius also prepared a star catalogue of 1,564 stars, which was at least as accurate as that of Tycho Brahe [156]; but it was not published till 1690, after his death.

[195] **GASCOIGNE,** William (gas'koin)
English astronomer
Born: Middleton, Yorkshire,
about 1612
Died: Marston Moor, Yorkshire,
July 2, 1644

Gascoigne did not have much of an education but picked up enough knowledge of astronomy to engage in competent correspondence on the subject and to make two important advances.

The telescope, first used to study the astronomical objects by Galileo [166] was scarcely suitable for determining the exact position of those bodies. It was for that reason that Hevelius [194] scorned it and depended on the eye alone. To convert the telescope to such use, Gascoigne devised cross hairs in the focal plane so that an object in view could be accurately centered at the intersection, and a micrometer with which to measure accurately small angular separations of one star from another. It was this that began the conversion of the telescope from a mere viewing toy to an instrument of precision.

Gascoigne fought for King Charles I in the English Civil War and died at the Royalist defeat at Marston Moor.

[196] **SYLVIUS**, Franciscus
Dutch physician
Born: Hanau, Prussia, March 15, 1614
Died: Leiden, Netherlands, November 19, 1672

Sylvius' name is a Latinized version of his real name, Franz de la Boë (duh-lah-boh-ay'). He was born of Dutch parents who had sought refuge in Germany from the Spanish armies that were trying to subjugate their homeland. Sylvius obtained his medical degree in Basle, Switzerland and then, after some years, returned to the Netherlands, which had won a hard-earned independence. In 1658 he became professor of medicine at the University of Leiden. His contemporary Borelli [191] followed Descartes [183] in viewing the body as a mechanical device, but Sylvius followed Paracelsus [131] and Helmont [175] in viewing it as a chemical device, bringing the former's "iatrochemistry" to a peak of systematization.

Sylvius strongly supported Harvey's [174] view of the circulation of the blood and was the first to abandon the theory that the health of the body depended on the relative proportions of the four chief fluids or "humors" that it contained (blood, phlegm, black bile, and yellow bile), a theory dating back to Greek medicine. Instead, he stressed the opposing properties of acids and bases and their ability to neutralize each other. Viewing the body as a balance of acid and base, though insufficient, is certainly far nearer to what we now believe than was the old notion of the four humors. Sylvius and his followers studied digestive juices (pointing out that saliva was one of them) and correctly believed digestion to involve a fermenting process.

He is credited with having developed the alcoholic drink gin and having used it to treat kidney ailments. He may also have organized the first university chemistry laboratory.

[197] **WILKINS**, John
English scholar
Born: Fawsley, Northamptonshire, 1614
Died: London, November 19, 1672

Wilkins, the son of a goldsmith, entered Oxford in 1627, obtaining his master's degree in 1634, and was ordained a few years later. Eventually, he married the sister of Oliver Cromwell, who controlled England with a firm hand during the 1650s.

Wilkins spent most of his time on theology but he contributed to science in two ways. First, he was a powerful spokesman for the Copernican view, in books written for the intelligent layman. He laid great stress on the fact that the astronomical bodies, the moon in particular, were worlds, and that therefore they might be inhabited. In 1640 he even speculated that methods might be discovered whereby the moon could be reached. In this he may have been inspired by the appearance in 1638 of a very popular work of fiction *Man in the Moone* by Francis Godwin, which dealt with such a flight (though by the romantic notion of having geese hitched to a chariot after which they fly to the moon).

Wilkins' book reinforced the impression of the earlier one and gave rise to thoughts of space flight, both in fiction and fact, that have continued to this day.

Second, Wilkins was one of the moving spirits behind the founding of the Royal Society.

[198] **WALLIS**, John
English mathematician
Born: Ashford, Kent, December 3, 1616
Died: Oxford, November 8, 1703

Wallis was the son of a rector who died when Wallis was six. Wallis was himself ordained in 1640. By then he had obtained both a bachelor's and a master's degree from Cambridge, having aimed at medicine as his profession.

England was in turmoil. The English

Civil War had broken out and Wallis, who had a keen sense of the prevailing wind, threw in his lot with the Parliamentarians against King Charles I. Like Vieta [153] he made a name for himself by applying his mathematical training to deciphering code messages captured from Royalists.

Because of this—and despite the fact that he voted against execution of the king—he received a professorial appointment at Oxford in 1649 under the Parliamentarian regime. The fact that he had been against execution, however, counted in his favor when in 1660 the son of Charles I came to the throne as Charles II. Wallis then became the king's chaplain.

Wallis wrote voluminously on mathematics and was one of those who could serve as "calculating prodigies." He is reported to have worked out the square root of a fifty-three-digit number in his head, getting it correct to seventeen places. He was the first to extend the notion of exponents to include negative numbers and fractions, so that x^{-2}, for instance, was defined as $1/x^2$, while $x^{1/2}$ was equivalent to $\sqrt{x}$ and he was also the first (in 1656) to use ∞ as the symbol for infinity. In addition, also he was the first to interpret imaginary numbers geometrically (though he wasn't entirely successful at this). Two centuries later Steinmetz [944] was to make this representation fundamental to his theoretical treatment of alternating current circuits. Wallis was one of the first to write a serious history of mathematics.

Wallis took steps toward calculus, but it was his misfortune to be overshadowed by his younger contemporary Newton [231], soon to bring calculus into being.

He was a vain and quarrelsome man, and an extremely nationalistic Englishman, eager to enter into disputes with foreigners such as Descartes [183]. He was among the first, therefore, to back Newton's priority in calculus and to accuse Leibniz [233] of plagiarism, in what was the bitterest scientific quarrel in history. He also used his influence against the adoption of the Gregorian calendar by Great Britain on the ground that it implied subservience to Rome (and,

hence, foreigners). The inevitable adoption was delayed half a century as a result.

Wallis's greatest contribution to science, perhaps, was his role, along with his close friend Boyle [212], as one of those who, in 1663, founded the Royal Society. He accepted the challenge of the Society to investigate the behavior of colliding bodies and, in 1668, was the first to suggest the law of conservation of momentum. This was the first of the all-important conservation laws. His findings were extended by Wren [220] and Huygens [215].

[199] **GRIMALDI,** Francesco Maria
       (gree-mahl'dee)
       Italian physicist
       Born: Bologna, April 2, 1618
       Died: Bologna, December 28, 1663

Grimaldi was the son of a silk merchant of aristocratic lineage. He entered the Jesuit order at fifteen and became a professor at the University of Bologna after obtaining his doctoral degree there in 1647. He served as an assistant to Riccioli [185] for some time and drew the lunar map on which Riccioli placed his names.

Grimaldi published his own most important discovery in a book that only appeared some two years after his death. He had let a beam of light pass through two narrow apertures, one behind the other, and then fall on a blank surface. He found that the band of light on that surface was a trifle wider than it was when it entered the first aperture. Therefore he believed that the beam had been bent slightly outward at the edges of the aperture, a phenomenon he called diffraction.

This was clearly a case of light bending about an obstacle, as would be expected of waves but not of particles, and Grimaldi therefore accepted light as a wave phenomenon. More unusual still was the fact that he observed the band of light to show one to three colored streaks at its extremities. This he could not explain and it was not until the time

of Fraunhofer [450] a century and a half
later that the phenomenon was taken out
of cold storage and put to work.

[200] **HORROCKS,** Jeremiah
English astronomer
Born: Toxteth Park, near Liver-
pool, 1618
Died: Toxteth Park, January 13,
1641

Horrocks (sometimes spelled Horrox)
was the son of a watchmaker. He attended Cambridge from 1632 to 1635
but did not get a degree. He served as a
curate at Hoole in Lancashire from 1639
and practiced astronomy (in which he
was self-taught) in his spare time.

In his short life of twenty-three years
he accomplished an amazing number of
things. He corrected the Rudolphine
Tables of Kepler [169] with regard to
the transit of Venus across the face of
the sun and predicted an occurrence on
November 24, 1639. This was a Sunday
and he just got away from church in
time to view it—the first transit of
Venus to be observed. He suggested that
observations of such a transit from
different observatories might set up a
parallax effect that could be used to calculate the distance of Venus and therefore the scale of the solar system. This
eventually was done.

He was the first astronomer to accept
the elliptical orbits of Kepler wholeheartedly. By observing the motions of
the moon he was able to extend Kepler's
work by showing that the moon moved
in an elliptical orbit about the earth and
that the earth was at one focus of that
ellipse. This completed the Keplerian
system by applying it to the one known
heavenly body that Kepler himself could
not manage.

Horrocks thought that some of the irregularities of the moon's motion might
be due to the influence of the sun and
that Jupiter and Saturn might exert an
influence on each other. This was a
foretaste of the theory of universal gravitation, which Newton [231] was to develop a generation after Horrocks' early
death.

[201] **GRAUNT,** John (grant)
English statistician
Born: London, April 24, 1620
Died: London, April 18, 1674

Graunt was the son of a draper and,
entering the family business, did well
until his business was destroyed in the
Great Fire of 1666.

More or less by accident, he found
himself studying the death records in
London parishes and beginning to notice
certain regularities. As a result, in 1662
he published a book on the matter; it
served to found the science of statistics
and of demography, which is the branch
of statistics that deals with human populations. This is not bad for a businessman without training in mathematics.

He noted things for the first time that
anyone might have seen if he had
looked, and it is to Graunt's credit that
he looked. He noted that the death rate
in cities was higher than that in rural
areas; that while the male birth rate was
distinctly higher than the female birth
rate, a smaller percentage of boys survived the early years, so that the proportion evened out. He tried to detect the
influence of occupation on the death rate
and was perceptive enough to consider
overpopulation as itself a cause of a rise
in the death rate.

He was the first to try to establish life
expectancy and to publish a table indicating the percentage of people who
might be expected to live to a certain
age, and how much longer they might,
on the average, live, having reached a
certain age.

As a result of this book, Graunt was
elected to the Royal Society at the suggestion of Charles II himself.

[202] **BROUNCKER,** William, 2d Vis-
count (brung′ker)
English mathematician
Born: 1620
Died: Westminster, London,
April 5, 1684

Brouncker was born into the nobility
and inherited a viscount's title in 1645.
He received a doctor's degree from Ox-

ford in 1647 and cut a minor figure in the history of mathematics of the time. In particular, he popularized the use of continued fractions (first introduced in 1613 by the Italian mathematician P. A. Cataldi) when he made use of such fractions to evolve an expression for pi, which enabled him to calculate its value to ten decimal places.

He is best known, however, for the fact that he was the first president of the Royal Society nominated to that post by Charles II and elected without opposition. He was then reelected year after year till he resigned in 1677.

[203] **MARIOTTE,** Edmé (ma-ryut')
French physicist
Born: Dijon, 1620
Died: Paris, May 12, 1684

Mariotte's life was strangely parallel to that of Boyle [212]. The two lives spanned the same decades and Mariotte was as devout as Boyle; Mariotte was, indeed, a Roman Catholic priest. As Boyle was an early member of the Royal Society in London, so Mariotte was an early member of the Academy of Sciences in Paris.

In 1676, fifteen years after Boyle, Mariotte discovered Boyle's law independently and with an important qualification. He noticed that air expands with rising temperature and contracts with falling temperature. The inverse relationship of temperature and pressure therefore holds well only if the temperature is kept constant. This was a point Boyle had neglected to make. There is thus some justification for using the phrase Mariotte's law.

Mariotte also made important studies of rainfall and put forth modern views concerning the circulation of the earth's water supply. He discovered the "blind spot" of the eye—the point where the optic nerve interrupts the retinal film.

[204] **PICARD,** Jean (pee-kahr')
French astronomer
Born: La Flèche, Sarthe, July 21, 1620
Died: Paris, July 12, 1682

Picard, who eventually became a Roman Catholic priest, studied astronomy under Gassendi [182] and, in 1655, succeeded him as a professor of astronomy at the Collège de France and was one of the charter members of the French Academy of Sciences. He also helped to found the Paris Observatory and scoured Europe for men to serve in it worthily; among them, Cassini [209] from Italy and Roemer [232] from Denmark.

Picard was the first to put the telescope to use not merely for simple observations but for the accurate measurement of small angles. This innovation made use of an improvement of the micrometer invented by Gascoigne [195] and then reinvented by Huygens [215]. He also popularized the use of Huygens' pendulum clock to record times and time intervals in connection with astronomic observations.

The feat for which Picard is most renowned is the measurement of the circumference of the earth, the first measurement more accurate than that of Eratosthenes [48] nineteen centuries earlier. Picard made use of Eratosthenes' principle, substituting a star for the sun. The use of a point instead of a large body made greater accuracy of measurement possible.

In 1671 he published the figure for the length of a degree of longitude at the equator as 69.1 miles, giving the earth a circumference of 24,876 miles and a radius of 3,950 miles (close to the values accepted today). According to one story it was the use of Picard's values in place of somewhat smaller ones that in 1684 gave Newton [231] the correct answer to the moon's motion, replacing the incorrect answer of 1666.

[205] **WILLIS,** Thomas
English physician
Born: Great Bedwyn, Wiltshire, January 27, 1621
Died: London, November 11, 1675

Willis, the son of a steward of a manor, obtained his master's degree from Oxford in 1642. He was a member of the losing Royalist cause during the Civil War and decided not to enter the embattled church. He turned to medicine instead, getting his license to practice in 1646. After the Restoration, of course, his activity in the Royalist cause worked in his favor and in 1666 he set up a practice in London, which was profitable indeed and he quickly became the most fashionable physician in the land.

He was, however, a capable practitioner. He studied epidemic disease and was the first great epidemiologist. He gave the first reliable clinical description of typhoid fever, was the first to describe myasthenia gravis, and childbed fever. It was he who named the latter "puerperal fever," from the Latin phrase for "childbearing." In 1664, he wrote a treatise on the brain and nerves that was the most complete and accurate up to that time.

Most interesting of all, perhaps, was his discovery (or rediscovery in case it was known to some of the Greek physicians) of the sugar content in urine among some people with diabetes. In this way he distinguished diabetes mellitus, the most serious form, from other varieties.

He died of pneumonia and was buried in Westminster Abbey.

[206] **VIVIANI,** Vincenzo (vih-vee-ah'-nee)
Italian mathematician
Born: Florence, Tuscany, April 5, 1622
Died: Florence, September 22, 1703

Viviani was introduced to Galileo [166] by Ferdinand II of Tuscany [193]. He worked with Galileo and later with Torricelli [192]. He was a mathematician primarily and was perhaps the leading geometer of his time. He was also a practical engineer and succeeded Galileo as superintendent of the rivers of Tuscany.

It might be argued that his most important accomplishment, however, was his founding of the Accademia del Cimento, one of the first great scientific societies and a forerunner of the Royal Society soon to be established in England.

[207] **PASCAL,** Blaise (pas-kal')
French mathematician and physicist
Born: Clermont-Ferrand, Auvergne, June 19, 1623
Died: Paris, August 19, 1662

Fortunately, in view of his short life and the fact that the last decade of it was devoted to theology and introspection, Pascal managed to accomplish a good deal. He was a sickly child whose mother died when he was three; and in infancy his life was, on one occasion, believed to have ended. Nevertheless, he was, mentally, a prodigy. His father, himself a mathematician and a government functionary, supervised his child's education and was determined that he study ancient languages first. He denied him, therefore, any books on mathematics.

When the young Pascal inquired as to the nature of geometry and was told it was the study of shapes and forms, he went on, at the age of nine, to discover for himself the first thirty-two theorems in Euclid in the correct order. (This story, told by his sister, appears too good to be true.) The awe-struck father then gave in and let the boy study mathematics.

When he was only sixteen Pascal published a book on the geometry of the conic sections that for the first time carried the subject well beyond the point at which Apollonius [49] had left it nearly nineteen centuries before. Descartes [183] refused to believe that a sixteen-year-old could have written it, and Pascal, in turn, would not admit the value of Descartes's analytic geometry. In 1642, when he was only nineteen, Pascal had invented a calculating machine that, by means of cogged wheels, could add and subtract. He patented the final version in 1649 and sent one model to that royal patron of learning, Queen Christina of Sweden. He hoped to profit from it but didn't. It was too expensive to build to be completely practical. Nevertheless, it was the ancestor of the mechanical devices that reached their culmination in the pre-electronic cash register.

Pascal corresponded with the lawyer-mathematician Fermat [188] and together they worked on problems sent them by a certain gentleman gambler and amateur philosopher who was puzzled as to why he lost money by betting on the appearance of certain combinations in the fall of three dice. In the course of settling the matter, the two men founded the modern theory of probability.

This had incalculable importance for the development of science because it lifted from mathematics (and the world in general) the necessity of absolute certainty. Men began to see that useful and reliable information could be obtained even out of matters that were completely uncertain. The fall of a particular coin can be either heads or tails, but which one, in any particular instance, is unpredictable. However, given a vast number of falls, separately unpredictable, conclusions as to the general nature of the falls (such as that the number of heads would be approximately equal to the number of tails) can be drawn with considerable confidence.

Two centuries later, mathematical physicists such as Maxwell [692] were applying such considerations to the behavior of matter and producing great results out of the blind, random, and completely unpredictable movements of individual atoms.

Pascal also applied himself to physics. In studying fluids he pointed out that pressure exerted on a fluid in a closed vessel is transmitted undiminished throughout the fluid and that it acts at right angles to all surfaces it touches. This is called Pascal's principle and it is the basis of the hydraulic press, which Pascal described in theory.

If a small piston is pushed down into a container of liquid, a large piston can be pushed upward at another place in the container. The force pushing up the larger piston will be to the force pushing down the small one, as the cross-sec-

tional area of the large is to the cross-sectional area of the small. This multiplication of force is made up for by the fact that the small piston must move through a correspondingly greater distance than the large. As in the case of Archimedes' [47] lever, force times distance is equal on both sides. In fact the hydraulic press is a kind of lever.

Pascal also interested himself in the new view of the atmosphere initiated by Torricelli [192]. If the atmosphere had weight, then that weight should decrease with altitude, since the higher you went, the less air would remain above you. This decrease in the weight of the atmosphere should be detectable on a barometer.

Pascal was chronically sick, suffering continuously from indigestion, headaches (a postmortem investigation showed he had a deformed skull), and insomnia, so he contemplated no mountain climbing for himself. However, on September 19, 1648, he sent his strong, young brother-in-law carrying two barometers up the sides of the Puy-de-Dôme (the mountain near which Pascal was born). The brother-in-law climbed about a mile and found the mercury columns had dropped three inches. The brother-in-law must have enjoyed mountain climbing for he repeated the experiment five times. This established the Torricellian view quite definitely, even against the persistent doubting of Descartes. It showed, moreover, that a vacuum existed above the atmosphere against Descartes's denial of the existence of a vacuum and his contention that all space is filled with matter. (Pascal also repeated Torricelli's original experiment, using red wine instead of mercury. Because red wine is even lighter than water, Pascal had to use a tube forty-six feet long to contain enough fluid to balance the weight of the atmosphere.)

In the year of the mountain climb Pascal came under the influence of Jansenism (a Roman Catholic sect marked by strong anti-Jesuit feeling). In 1654 he had a narrow escape from death when the horses of his carriage ran away. He interpreted this as evidence of divine displeasure and his conversion became sufficiently intense to cause him to devote the remainder of his short life to meditation, asceticism, religious writings (including the famous *Pensées*), and illness. The writings were brilliant and served to inspire Voltaire [261] but Pascal worked on science and mathematics no more, except for one week in 1658 when he lived through a toothache by distracting his mind with a geometric problem, which he dispatched with great neatness. In his last years, in fact, Pascal declared reason an insufficient tool for understanding the physical universe, thus retreating beyond Thales [3].

His best-known remark had nothing to do with science. It was to the effect that had Cleopatra's nose been differently shaped, the history of the world would have been altered.

[208] **SYDENHAM,** Thomas (sid'num)
English physician
Born: Wynford Eagle, Dorset,
September 10, 1624
Died: London, December 29,
1689

Sydenham came of a family of the gentry that fought on the side of the Parliament in the English Civil War. Two of Thomas's brothers died in the course of it and his oldest brother became an associate of Cromwell and an important figure in the Commonwealth. Thomas himself fought, and reportedly narrowly escaped death on two occasions. All the fighting interrupted his education, and he did not get his master's degree till 1648.

He began practicing medicine in 1656. The restoration of Charles II meant there was no chance of public life for Sydenham with his Parliamentary record so he turned entirely to medicine and made a huge success of it. Like Willis [205] he studied epidemics and the textbook he wrote on the subject remained standard until the development of the germ theory of disease by Pasteur [642].

In the course of his practice, he insisted on detailed clinical observations and accurate records. He was the first to differentiate scarlet fever from measles,

and it was he who first called it scarlet fever. He was the first to use opium derivatives (laudanum) to relieve pain and induce rest. He popularized the use of cinchona (quinine) to treat malaria. He also used iron in the treatment of anemia. He produced careful descriptions of gout and of Saint Vitus's dance (still called "Sydenham's chorea").

Before he died, he was being called the English Hippocrates.

[209] **CASSINI,** Giovanni Domenico
(ka-see-nee': French) (ka-see'-
nee: Italian)
Italian-French astronomer
Born: Perinaldo (near Nice),
June 8, 1625
Died: Paris, September 14, 1712

Cassini made his reputation in Italy, where he studied under Riccioli [185] and Grimaldi [199] and where, from 1650, he taught astronomy at the University of Bologna, succeeding to Cavalieri's [186] position. The story is that he originally studied astronomy in order to gather data to disprove the follies of astrology.

In 1665 and 1666 he measured the periods of rotation of Mars as twenty-four hours, forty minutes. In 1668 he issued a table of the motions of Jupiter's moons, which was later to serve Roemer [232] in his discovery of the velocity of light. He also established Jupiter's period of rotation as nine hours, fifty-six minutes, and was the first to study the zodiacal light. (This last is a faint illumination of the night sky, stretching outward from the sun along the line of the ecliptic. We know now that it is sunlight reflected from dust particles in interplanetary space.)

Picard [204] of the Paris Observatory, who was always on the lookout for foreign talent, persuaded Louis XIV of France to invite Cassini to Paris in 1669. The observatory was being elaborately rebuilt at the time. Cassini took one look and demanded changes in design so that the buildings would be less ornamental and more useful. King Louis pouted, but agreed, and there at the Paris Observatory Cassini remained for the rest of his life, becoming a French citizen in 1673. He is often considered a French astronomer, and his first names are often given as Jean Dominique.

In Paris, Cassini continued his discoveries. He located no fewer than four new satellites of Saturn using telescopes over one hundred feet long: Iapetus in 1671, Rhea in 1672, and Dione and Tethys in 1684. Then, having outdone his younger contemporary Huygens [215] in the matter of the Saturnian satellites (Huygens discovered only one), he went on to improve on Huygens' most spectacular discovery, the rings of Saturn. In 1675 Cassini noted that the ring was actually a double one, the two rings being divided by a dark gap that is still called Cassini's division.

Cassini suspected the rings might consist of myriads of small particles, but most astronomers, including Herschel [321], refused to accept that notion. They considered the rings solid, with Cassini's division a dark marking upon it. Finally Maxwell [692] proved Cassini to have been right all along, a century and a half after the latter's death.

Outside the solar system, Cassini discovered several stars to be double, including the bright star Castor.

His most valuable piece of work lay in his determination of the parallax of Mars in 1672 through his observations of the planet in Paris and Richer's [217] simultaneous observations in French Guiana. This gave him a value for the distance of Mars. The relative distances of the sun and planets had been known quite accurately since the days of Kepler [169], so it was only necessary to determine any one of those distances accurately to be able to calculate all the rest. From his value for the distance of Mars, Cassini calculated that the sun was eighty-seven million miles from the earth, a value confirmed that same year by Flamsteed [234].

This is too low a value by 7 percent, but it was the first determination ever made that was nearly right. Aristarchus [41] had placed the sun a mere five million miles from the earth, while Poseidonius [52] had estimated forty million miles and Kepler had actually cut that down to a guess (it was nothing more) of fifteen million miles.

Cassini founded a dynasty of five successive generations of astronomers that dominated French astronomy for over a century. This was not altogether fortunate. Cassini himself was an opinionated, self-important person who was not nearly as good as he thought. Furthermore he was amazingly conservative for his times. He was the last of the great astronomers to refuse to accept the heliocentric views of Copernicus [127].

His descendants gradually adopted the new view of the universe but always a couple of generations too late. Thus the second of the line accepted Copernicus but rejected Kepler. The third of the line insisted that the earth was flattened at the equator when other astronomers were satisfied that it was flattened at the poles. And it was only the fourth of the line who could finally bring himself, a century after the fact, to accept Newton [231]. Eighteenth-century France suffered a decline in astronomy because of the dead hand of the first Cassini, as eighteenth-century England was to suffer a decline in mathematics because of slavish adherence to Newton.

[210] **BARTHOLIN,** Erasmus (bahr-
        too′lin)
        Danish physician
        Born: Roskilde, August 13, 1625
        Died: Copenhagen, November 4,
        1698

Bartholin was a member of a Danish medical dynasty. His father, brother, and son were all physicians, as he was himself. In 1654 he obtained a medical degree at the University of Padua, and was professor of medicine at the University of Copenhagen from 1656 to his death.

His fame, however, did not arise from anything connected with medicine. In 1669 he received a transparent crystal from Iceland (now called Iceland spar) and he noted that objects viewed through it were seen double. He assumed that the light traveling through the crystal was refracted in two different angles, so that

133

two rays of light emerged where one had entered. This phenomenon he therefore called double refraction.

Furthermore he noted that if he rotated the crystal, one of the images remained fixed while the other rotated about it. The ray giving rise to the fixed image he called the ordinary ray, the other the extraordinary ray. These terms are still used today.

Bartholin was unable to explain these observations. Greater men than himself attempted it too, recognizing that any theory of light, if it were to be successful, must explain double refraction. After all, why should some light refract through one angle, and the rest through another?

Isaac Newton [231] developed a particle theory of light which did not explain double refraction, and Huygens [215] developed a wave theory that did not explain it. The whole matter of double refraction remained in a kind of cold storage where physicists refused to look at it until Young [402] finally established a new variety of wave theory a century and a half after Bartholin. Then and only then was double refraction explained and put to use in chemistry.

[211] **REDI**, Francesco (ray'dee)
Italian physician and poet
Born: Arezzo, Tuscany, February 18, 1626
Died: Pisa, March 1, 1697

Redi obtained his medical degree at the University of Pisa in 1647, and was personal physician to two Medici grand dukes of Tuscany, Ferdinand II [193] and Cosimo III. As a poet, he is known chiefly for *Bacco in Toscana* written in 1685; but in the world of science he is known for reasons far more enduring. Or perhaps for one reason: a famous experiment involving flies and their manner of breeding.

It had long been held by many men, from casual observers up to careful thinkers such as Aristotle [29] and Helmont [175], that some species of animals arose spontaneously from mud, decaying

grain, or in general from corrupting matter. The living things that arose through such spontaneous generation were usually vermin such as insects, worms, frogs, and so on. One of the best attested cases was that of maggots, which appeared in decaying meat, apparently out of the substance of the meat itself.

In the small book on the circulation written by Harvey [174] about the time Redi was born, there was a speculation to the effect that small living things that appeared to be born spontaneously, might actually arise from seeds or eggs that were too small to be seen. Redi read this and in 1668 determined to test it.

He prepared eight flasks with a variety of meats in them. Four he sealed and four he left open to the air. Flies could land only on the meat in the vessels that were open and only the meat in those vessels bred maggots. The meat in the closed vessels was just as putrid and smelly, but without maggots. To test whether it was the absence of fresh air that did it, Redi repeated the experiment without closing any flasks, but covering some with gauze instead. The air was not excluded, but flies were, and that was sufficient. There were no maggots in the gauze-covered meat. This was the first clear-cut case of the use of proper controls in a biological experiment.

Redi concluded that maggots were not formed by spontaneous generation but from eggs laid by flies. This finding might have been extended to all forms of life but that would have been premature. Leeuwenhoek [221] had just demonstrated the existence of a new world of minute animals invisible to the eye. These appeared to breed in any drop of stagnant water, and the question of the spontaneous generation of these microorganisms raged for two centuries.

[212] **BOYLE**, Robert
British physicist and chemist
Born: Lismore Castle, County Waterford, Ireland, January 25, 1627
Died: London, December 31, 1691

134

Robert Boyle was born into the aristocracy (as the fourteenth child and seventh son of the earl of Cork) and was an infant prodigy. He went to Eton at eight, at which time he was already speaking Greek and Latin, traveled through Europe (with a tutor) at eleven, and at fourteen was in Italy studying the works of Galileo [166], who had just died, and finding himself also influenced by his reading of Descartes [183]. His private tutoring saved him from exposure to the didactic Aristotelianism that still victimized most universities.

While in Geneva he was frightened by an intense thunderstorm into a devoutness that persisted for the rest of his life. He never married.

Back home in 1645, Boyle found his father dead and himself with an independent income. He kept out of the English Civil War and eventually settled at Oxford in 1654 and took part in the periodic gatherings of scholars tackling the new experimentalism made fashionable by Francis Bacon [163] and dramatic by Galileo. It was called the Invisible College, but in 1663 after King Charles II had been restored to the throne the association of scholars received official recognition and a charter and became known as the Royal Society. Its motto was "Nullius in verba" ("Nothing by mere authority").

Boyle's interest in experimentation still represented an odd innovation in science. Most scholars were still suspicious of this. The Dutch-Jewish philosopher Benedict Spinoza corresponded with Boyle and tried to convince him that reason was superior to experiment. Fortunately Boyle disregarded the gentle Spinoza.

In 1657 Boyle heard of the experiments of Guericke [189] and set about devising an air pump of his own. This he accomplished successfully with the help of a brilliant assistant, Robert Hooke [223]. His pump was an improvement upon Guericke's and for a while a vacuum produced by an air pump was called a Boylean vacuum.

Boyle was one of the first to make use of an evacuated, hermetically sealed thermometer. He also made use of an evacuated cylinder to show, for the first time, that Galileo was actually correct in maintaining that in a vacuum all objects fall at the same velocity. A feather and a lump of lead, in the absence of air resistance, land together.

Then, too, he was able to demonstrate that sound (the ticking of a clock) could not be heard in a vacuum but that electrical attraction could be felt across one.

All this led him to experiment with gases. He was the first chemist to collect a gas. Further, he discovered in 1662 that air was not only compressible but that this compressibility varied with pressure according to a simple inverse relationship. If a quantity of gas was put under doubled pressure (by trapping it in the closed end of a seventeen-foot tube shaped like a J and adding more mercury in the long open end) its volume halved. If pressure was tripled the volume was reduced to a third. On the other hand if pressure was eased off the volume expanded. This inverse relationship is still referred to as Boyle's law in Great Britain and America; in France it is credited to Mariotte [203]. Because the compressibility and expansibility of air in response to the force upon it was reminiscent of the coiled metal springs then being studied by Hooke, Boyle referred to it as the "spring of the air."

The most significant conclusion drawn from this experiment was that since air was compressible, it must be composed of discrete particles separated by a void. The compression consisted of squeezing the particles closer together. Hero [60] had suspected this fifteen centuries earlier, but where Hero faced hordes of theoretical philosophers who scorned experiment, Boyle was part of a growing experimentalist school. Boyle was influenced by the writings of Gassendi [182] and his experiments made him a convinced atomist. Atomism was to gain momentum steadily from that time on; after two thousand years the views of Democritus [20] prevailed.

Boyle's experiments on gases were also important because he here initiated the practice of thoroughly and carefully describing his experiments so that anyone

135

might repeat and confirm them—a habit which became universal in science, and without which progress would have remained at a creep.

Boyle had much of the alchemist about him. He believed in the transmutation of gold and, indeed, was instrumental in persuading the British government in 1689 to repeal the law against the manufacture of gold, not because it was a useless law (which it was) but because he felt the government should take advantage of any gold that was formed and should encourage scientists to form it.

Even so, Boyle transformed alchemy into chemistry in 1661 with the publication of *The Sceptical Chemist*. In it he abandoned the Greek view that made the elements mystical substances of a nature deducible from first principles. Instead he suggested that an element was a material substance and that it could be identified only by experiment. Any substance that could not be broken down into still simpler substances was an element. Furthermore two elements could be combined into a compound and then obtained once again out of that compound. This does not mean he abandoned the old elements. He just wanted them established experimentally rather than intuitively. With this book, Boyle divorced chemistry from medicine and established it as a separate science.

Boyle was the first to distinguish between acids, bases, and neutral substances, studying them by means of the color changes of what we would now call acid-base indicators. He showed that water expanded when it froze and, indeed, began to expand a little before it froze.

He also came within a hair of being the first discoverer of a new element (in the modern Boylean sense). In 1680 he prepared phosphorus from urine. However, some five to ten years before that, Brand [216] had preceded Boyle in the discovery. There was fierce controversy (*not* including Boyle) about just who had first discovered phosphorus, largely because investigators held discoveries secret. Boyle maintained strongly that all experimental work should be clearly and quickly reported so that others might repeat, confirm, and profit. This has been an accepted tenet of scientific research ever since, and when industrial or military security interferes with publication it cannot help but harm the cause of science.

In the sense that Boyle applied the philosophy of experimentalism to the study of material substances and the changes they could be made to undergo, he might be considered the father of chemistry. The reform was not thoroughgoing, however, and was not to become so until the time of Lavoisier [334] a century later; and it is the latter who more properly deserves the honor of paternity.

Boyle's interest in religion grew with age. He learned Hebrew and Aramaic for his biblical studies. He wrote essays on religion and financed missionary work in the Orient. In 1680 he was elected president of the Royal Society but could not accept because he disapproved of the form of the oath. He also repeatedly refused offers of a peerage. Through his will he founded the Boyle Lectures, not on science but on the defense of Christianity against unbelievers.

[213] **RAY,** John
English naturalist
Born: Black Notley, Essex, November 29, 1627
Died: Black Notley, January 17, 1705

The son of a blacksmith, Ray nevertheless made his way through Cambridge, obtaining his master's degree in 1651. He stayed on as a lecturer.

He had a passion for natural history and would ride for many miles through the countryside, observing and collecting plants. In 1660 he published a scientific description of plants growing near Cambridge. But then Charles II was restored to the British throne, the land's religious climate changed, and Ray had to leave the university in 1662 because of his refusal to take the proper oaths.

He then conceived the notion of engaging in travel and preparing a description of all living species of both plants and animals. He was to do it in company with a younger man who was to finance the effort. The friend died soon after but left money in his will for the purpose.

In 1667 Ray published a catalogue of plants in the British Isles and was elected a member of the Royal Society. He refused to serve as secretary, however, as that would take time from his work. Toward the end of his life he had generalized his catalogue into a three-volume encyclopedia of plant life, published between 1686 and 1704. He described 18,600 different plant species and laid the groundwork for systematic classification, which was to be brought into modern form by Linneaus [276].

Ray also tried to systematize the animal kingdom and in 1693 he published a book that contained the first logical classification of animals, based chiefly on hoofs, toes, and teeth. His descriptions finally destroyed the fanciful stories of animals inherited from Pliny [61], sixteen centuries earlier.

His views on fossils were rather enlightened for the time. In 1691 he published an account in which he declared fossils were the petrified remains of extinct creatures. This was not accepted by biologists generally until a century later.

[214] **MALPIGHI,** Marcello (mahl-pee'-gee)
Italian physiologist
Born: Crevalcore, near Bologna, March 10, 1628
Died: Rome, November 30, 1694

When Galileo [166] invented the telescope he well realized that an arrangement of lenses could also be used to magnify objects. In a sense he was inventor of the microscope as well. The optical theory of the microscope was further advanced by his friend Kepler [169] and by his young assistant Torricelli [192]. In the mid-seventeenth century microscopy became all the rage and a number of first-rate investigators took it up.

First by a hair and therefore entitled to be called the father of microscopy

was Malpighi. He was a physician by training, obtaining his medical degree at the University of Bologna in 1653 after an interruption caused by the death of his father. He then lectured at various Italian universities, though chiefly at Bologna, and associated with Redi [211] and Borelli [191] among others. In 1691 he finally retired to Rome, rather reluctantly, to become private physician to Pope Innocent XII.

Malpighi began his work in microscopy in the 1650s by investigating the lungs of frogs. In 1660 he showed that the blood flowed through a complex network of vessels over the lungs and this discovery led to important conclusions. In the first place it explained a key step in the process of respiration, for it was easy to see that air could easily diffuse from the lungs into the blood vessels and that the blood stream would then carry it to all parts of the body. Soon Swammerdam [224] was to detect the structures within the blood stream that were eventually found to carry the essential portions of the air and Lower [219] was to arrive at the first suspicions of the true details of the process.

Malpighi's observations of the wing membranes of a bat showed him the finest blood vessels, which were eventually named capillaries ("hairlike"). Invisible to the eye, these were clearly visible in the microscope. They connected the smallest visible arteries with the smallest visible veins. With this discovery Malpighi supplied the key factor lacking in the theory of blood circulation advanced a generation earlier by Harvey [174], who died a few years too soon to witness this triumph. At about this time, too, Rudbeck [218] added his final touch to the circulatory system.

He disproved the impression that there were two varieties of bile, yellow and black, thus disposing of a mistaken belief that dated back to the school of Hippocrates [22] two thousand years before.

Malpighi went on to study other minute aspects of life—chick embryos and insects, for instance. He devoted a volume to the internal organs of the silkworm, the first treatise to deal with an invertebrate. Without quite realizing what he had discovered he found traces of gill structures in the developing chick, attesting to its descent from fishlike creatures. (One of Malpighi's contemporaries, Graaf [228], unwittingly went even further back than the embryo in his investigations.)

Malpighi studied the respiratory vessels in insects—tiny, branching tubes that filled the body and opened to the outer world through tiny apertures in the abdomen. In the stems of plant structures he found tiny tubes that possessed a spiral structure. Because of their resemblance to the tubes in insects, he wrongly believed them to be used in respiration. He described the small openings (stomata) on the underside of leaves. These, whose function he could not guess, *were* concerned with respiration. This interest in plant microscopy was shared by his younger contemporary Grew [229].

Malpighi's researches were so famous that in 1667 the Royal Society in London suggested he send them his scientific communications.

The work of Malpighi and his fellow microscopists showed that living tissue was far more complex in structure than the eye alone could tell and that the world of the very small was as grand and worthy of study as the world of astronomy.

[215] **HUYGENS**, Christiaan (hoy′genz or hy′genz)
Dutch physicist and astronomer
Born: The Hague, April 14, 1629
Died: The Hague, June 8, 1695

Huygens' father was an important official in the Dutch government. Young Christiaan was given a good education at the University of Leiden and had the benefit of friendship with Descartes [183]. Huygens' early training was in mathematics and he might have made a great mark in that field had he not been diverted to astronomy and physics. In 1657, for instance, he published a book on probability, the first formal book on the subject to appear, and applied the

subject to the working out of life expectancy.

In 1655, when he was helping his brother devise an improved telescope, he hit upon a new and better method for grinding lenses. (He had the help here of the Dutch-Jewish philosopher Benedict Spinoza.) At once he incorporated these improved lenses into telescopes and began to use one, twenty-three feet long, to discover new glories in the heavens, such as (in 1656) a huge cloud of gas and dust, the Orion Nebula. Another discovery, that same year, was a satellite circling Saturn, one as large as any of the satellites of Jupiter that Galileo [166] had discovered nearly half a century before. Huygens named it Titan. At that moment six planets (including the earth) and six satellites (including the moon) were known and this seemed such a neat picture that Huygens declared no more of either remained to be discovered. He lived to see Cassini [209] discover four more satellites of Saturn.

Huygens' mysticism was a momentary aberration and his real achievements continued. Galileo had, in 1610, noted a peculiarity about Saturn: it seemed triple. His primitive telescope could not make out the nature of the tripleness, but Huygens' improved instrument made it out clearly. In 1656 he was able to see that Saturn was surrounded by a thin ring which nowhere touched the planet. He announced his discovery in a cipher, protecting his priority while making certain he was correct through further observations. Cassini was to improve on Huygens, for he discovered the ring was a double one. Huygens recognized that the plane of the ring was tipped to that of earth's orbit and that they would be seen edge-on, and therefore be briefly invisible, every fourteen years.

Huygens was the first to note surface markings on Mars. In 1659 he detected the V-shaped Syrtis Major ("large bog"), whose name proved to be a mistake, for there is nothing boggy about it.

He was the first to make a specific guess at the distance of the stars. By assuming Sirius to be as bright as the sun, he estimated its distance at 2.5 trillion miles. (This is about one-twentieth the actual distance and Huygens' error lay in his assumption, for Sirius is actually much brighter than the sun and must be correspondingly farther to appear as dim as it does.) Huygens believed, as Nicholas of Cusa [115] had, that stars were uniformly distributed through infinite space, each with its complement of planets.

Huygens struggled to reduce telescopic observations to a quantitative basis. This he did in two ways: in the measurement of space and the measurement of time. For the former, Huygens devised a micrometer in 1658 with which he could measure angular separations of a few seconds of arc. In this form of quantitative observation his work rather paralleled that of his contemporary Picard [204].

In the measurement of time, however, was to be found his greatest achievement. The best device the ancients had with which to measure time was the water clock of Ctesibius [46], but this was only accurate to rather large fractions of an hour. The late Middle Ages developed mechanical clocks in which the pointer was made to indicate the hour through the action of a slowly falling weight rather than slowly rising water. The elimination of water made the clocks more rugged, less in need of care, and therefore more suitable for installation in church towers, but they were insufficiently accurate for scientific use.

What was really needed was some device that kept a constant periodic motion to which a clock could be geared, but no such motion was known until Galileo discovered the isochronicity of the pendulum. Galileo did not fail to recognize the possibility of hitching a pendulum to the gears of a clock and in his old age even had a design for such a clock drawn up.

It was Huygens who put the possibility into practice in 1656, over a decade after Galileo's death. He showed that a pendulum didn't swing in exactly equal times unless it swung through an arc that wasn't quite circular. He devised attachments at the pendulum's fulcrum that made it swing in the proper arc and then

attached that to the works of a clock, using falling weights to transfer just enough energy to the pendulum to keep it from coming to a halt through friction and air resistance.

It was with Huygens' first "grandfather's clock," which he presented to the Dutch governing body, the estates general, that the era of accurate timekeeping may be said to have begun. It is difficult to see how physics could have advanced much further without such an invention.

Huygens extended Wallis' [198] findings on the conservation of momentum (mass times velocity, or mv). Huygens showed that mv^2 was also conserved. This quantity is twice the kinetic energy of a body and this was the first step in the direction of working out the law of conservation of energy, which was to be brought to the attention of science by Helmholtz [631] a century and a half later.

Huygens' reputation spread throughout Europe. In 1660 he visited England and in 1663 was elected a charter member of the Royal Society. Louis XIV lured him to France in 1666 in line with his policy of collecting scholars for the glory of his regime. There, Huygens helped found the French Academy of Sciences.

Huygens, like Cassini might have remained in Paris for the rest of his life, but he was Protestant. Louis was gradually moving in the direction of nontoleration for the Protestants, and in 1681 Huygens returned to the Netherlands.

As he corrected Galileo on the question of Saturn, so he endeavored, in 1690, to correct Newton [231] on the subject of light. To Huygens it seemed quite possible that light could be interpreted as a longitudinal wave, a wave that undulated in the direction of its motion, as a sound wave did.

The chief objection to such a wave theory was that most people, through their experience with water waves and sound waves, believed that waves would bend around obstacles. Only a stream of particles, they thought, would travel in absolutely straight lines and throw sharp shadows, as light rays did.

Huygens tried to show that there were

conditions under which waves would indeed travel a straight line and would follow the laws of reflection and refraction which were observed in the case of light. In addition Grimaldi [199] showed that light had a slight tendency to bend about obstacles after all.

However, Newton's theory that light consisted of particles remained the more popular throughout the eighteenth century, mainly because of Newton's immense prestige. The wave theory remained disregarded for a full century until the time of Young [402].

[216] **BRAND,** Hennig
German chemist
Born: Hamburg, about 1630
Died: date and place unknown

Brand was a military officer who called himself a physician though he had never earned a degree. He is sometimes called the last of the alchemists (which he wasn't really), though he might better be called the first of the element discoverers.

He was the first man known to have discovered an element that was not known in any form before his time. The date of the discovery is disputed, but it must have been somewhere between 1669 and 1675. Brand was searching for the philosopher's stone and it occurred to him that he could find it in urine. He did not succeed, but he obtained a white, waxy substance that glowed in the dark. He therefore called it phosphorus ("light-bearer"). The glow was the result of the slow combination of the phosphorus with air, but that was not to be understood for another century. The glow, however, served the purpose of making the discovery mysterious and glamorous.

Several men quarreled over who had first made this brilliant find, but the quarrels were less important than the fact that another step had been taken away from the mysticism of alchemy toward the rationality of chemistry.

What happened to Brand after his discovery is utterly unknown.

[217] **RICHER,** Jean (ree-shay')
French astronomer
Born: 1630
Died: Paris, 1696

Richer was elected to the French Academy of Sciences in 1666 and in 1671 led an expedition to Cayenne in French Guiana (quite near the equator). There he made careful observations of Mars while Cassini [209], his superior, did the same in Paris. Together, these measurements supplied the first adequate parallax of Mars and the first notion of the scale of the solar system.

Richer also found that a pendulum beat more slowly in Cayenne than in Paris, so that a clock, correct in Paris, lost two and a half minutes a day in Cayenne. The conclusion was that the force of gravity was weaker in Cayenne because the spot was farther from the center of the earth. (The rate of beat of a pendulum varies with the size of the force of gravity acting upon it.)

If Cayenne had been on a mountaintop that would not have been surprising, but it was at sea level. Consequently Newton [231] deduced that the surface of the sea itself was farther from the center of the earth in the equatorial regions than in more northerly regions. This would be true if the earth was an oblate spheroid as the theory of gravitation required. (Actually it is now known that the equatorial surface is thirteen miles farther from the center of the earth than the polar surfaces.)

Richer returned to Paris in 1673 to such acclaim as to rouse the jealousy of Cassini. Since Richer was a military engineer as well as an astronomer, Cassini arranged to have him bundled off to the provinces to erect fortifications. The rest of his life was spent in obscurity.

[218] **RUDBECK,** Olof (rood'bek)
Swedish naturalist
Born: Westerås, December 12, 1630
Died: Uppsala, September 17, 1702

Rudbeck, the son of a science-minded bishop and the tenth of eleven children, was a man of encyclopedic interests. He taught at the medical school at the University of Uppsala, Sweden, and there took anatomy, botany, chemistry, and mathematics as his subjects. He built up a beautiful botanical garden. He was a well-read classical scholar and was made chancellor of the university at the age of thirty-one.

In science his best-known discovery is the lymphatic vessels, which he demonstrated to Queen Christina of Sweden in 1653, using a dog for the purpose. The lymphatics resemble the veins and capillaries but have thinner walls and carry the clear, watery fluid portion of the blood (lymph). This fluid portion is forced out of the thin-walled capillaries and into the spaces around the cells, forming the interstitial fluid. The interstitial fluid is connected in the lymphatics and carried back into the blood vessels. In various regions of the body, lymphatic vessels gather in small knots (lymph glands or lymph nodes), which are now known to be important in developing immunity to disease. These were first noted by Malpighi [214] in 1659. Rudbeck quarreled with Bartholin [210] over priority in this discovery.

Outside the world of science Rudbeck is known for a curious quirk. He thoroughly believed the fictional tale of Plato [24] concerning the supposedly-lost continent Atlantis and wrote a large treatise, in several volumes, attempting to prove that Atlantis was really Scandinavia and that Sweden particularly was the fount of human civilization.

[219] **LOWER,** Richard
English physician
Born: near Bodmin, Cornwall,
about 1631
Died: London, January 17, 1691

Lower obtained his bachelor's degree from Oxford in 1653 and his medical degree there in 1665. He was elected to the Royal Society in 1667 after being nominated by Boyle [212]. He made two dis-

coveries involving blood that had to await future centuries for proper understanding. He discovered that dark venous blood was converted to bright arterial blood on contact with air. Something, he believed, was absorbed from air, but what that might be had to wait a century for Lavoisier's [334] explanation of the nature of air.

In 1665 he transfused blood from one animal to another, at the suggestion of Christopher Wren [220], and demonstrated that this technique might be useful in saving lives. However, the transfusion of animal blood into a man or even one man's blood into another was too often fatal. Landsteiner [973], two and a half centuries later, demonstrated the existence of different types of human blood, and it was only in the twentieth century that transfusion became practical.

Lower disproved Galen's [65] notion that phlegm originated in the brain by showing that it was manufactured in the nasal membranes. He also showed that the heartbeat was caused by the contraction of the heart's muscular walls.

[220] **WREN,** Sir Christopher
English architect
Born: East Knoyle, Wiltshire,
October 20, 1632
Died: London, February 25, 1723

Wren was the son of a clergyman (and royal chaplain). He obtained his master's degree at Oxford in 1654, and in 1657 became professor of astronomy at Gresham College. Although he and his family were royalists, he was left undisturbed by Cromwell.

He is best known as an architect, having designed the new St. Paul's Cathedral, constructed in London after the disastrous fire of 1666. He designed other churches as well and was knighted for his services in 1673. He would have deserved even more from his nation had he been allowed to carry through his orderly design for a new, rationally planned London. The interests of those who owned London land prevented it.

The fame of his architecture has completely obscured the fact that Wren was one of the coterie of scientists who made Restoration England a brilliant spot in the history of science. He was a charter member of the Royal Society and rose to its presidency in 1681. He was a notable geometer, having studied mathematics under Oughtred [172]. He lectured in astronomy, first at Gresham College, then at Oxford, and was one of those whose speculations on the nature of gravity laid the groundwork for Newton's [231] work.

Wren is buried in St. Paul's and on the commemorative tablet is one of the best-known epitaphs in history: "Si monumentum requiris, circumspice" ("If you would see his monument, look about you").

[221] **LEEUWENHOEK,** Anton van
(lay'ven-hook)
Dutch biologist and microscopist
Born: Delft, October 24, 1632
Died: Delft, August 26, 1723

Of all the seventeenth-century microscopists, Leeuwenhoek was the most remarkable. He was not the first, for Malpighi [214] preceded him. Nor were his microscopes marking the way of the future, for Hooke [223] was developing a compound microscope, one made up of more than one lens, and this was the true path of advancement. However, Hooke's compound microscopes, with their still imperfect lenses, were quite limited in their clarity and powers of magnification. Leeuwenhoek, on the other hand, retained the simple microscope based on a single lens ground with such delicacy and perfection that they could magnify up to nearly two hundred times. They were tiny and short-focus, some being no larger than the head of a pin, but through them Leeuwenhoek saw what no other man in his century could.

He had had little schooling. His father, a basketmaker, died when young Leeuwenhoek was sixteen and the youngster became a clerk in a dry-goods store in Amsterdam, then opened a drapery shop of his own in Delft. As a sinecure he was appointed janitor at the Delft City Hall, a position he held for the rest of his life.

His business and his appointment kept him comfortably off, and he lived only for his hobby, grinding lenses. This had begun because drapers used magnifying glasses to inspect cloth and Leeuwenhoek wanted to see more and better.

He began feeding his mania (which is what it became) in 1674. In his lifetime he ground a total of 419 lenses, many of which were focused on some permanently mounted object and through some of which no man other than himself looked. He worked alone and since he could read only Dutch, he could see the illustrations but could not read the writings of the great contemporary microscopists such as Hooke and Malpighi.

Leeuwenhoek, with a passion for peering at the small, looked at everything from tooth scrapings to ditch water. He noted the fine structure of muscle, skin, hair, and ivory. He also reported a great deal of accurate detail on the development of tiny insects. He found tiny creatures parasitic on fleas and inspired the English author Jonathan Swift to write a famous quatrain:

So naturalists observe, a flea
Has smaller fleas that on him prey;
And these have smaller still to bite 'em;
And so proceed ad infinitum.

Leeuwenhoek was the first to discover the one-celled animals now called protozoa and in 1677 opened up a whole world of living organisms as alive as the elephant and whale yet compressing all that life into a space too small to see without mechanical help. He observed human capillaries and red blood cells with more care and detail than had the original discoverers, Malpighi and Swammerdam [224], and was the first to describe spermatozoa. He reported this last discovery rather nervously, fearing it might be considered obscene.

Beginning in 1673 he wrote voluminously to the British Royal Society, in Dutch, with his letters sometimes long enough to be respectable pamphlets. The Society received the communications from this unknown Dutchman with considerable reservations. However, in 1677

Hooke built microscopes according to Leeuwenhoek's specifications and confirmed the Dutchman's observations. Leeuwenhoek sent twenty-six of his tiny microscopes to the Society so that members could see for themselves. In 1680 the Royal Society elected the Dutch draper to membership—and did so unanimously.

In all he sent 375 communications to the Royal Society (to whose attention his work had been brought by Graaf [228]) and 27 to the French Academy of Science (to which he was elected in 1680).

His discoveries were dramatic enough to make him world-famous. The Dutch East India Company sent him Asian insects to put under his lenses. The queen of England paid him a visit, as did Frederick I of Prussia and Peter the Great, tsar of all the Russias, when he was visiting the Netherlands "incognito" to learn shipbuilding.

It was in 1683 that Leeuwenhoek made his most remarkable discovery. He described structures that could only be bacteria. These tiny things were just at the limit of what his lenses could make out. In fact, no one else was to see bacteria again for over a century.

Leeuwenhoek continued true to his passion and his hobby almost to the end of his long life of ninety years, cared for always by a devoted daughter, his sole surviving child. He was little interested in anything but observing and describing, but in that he was unexcelled. After his death, a number of his microscopes were sent to the Royal Society, in accordance with his last will.

He competes with Malpighi for the title of father of microscopy. Even though Malpighi preceded him in time, Leeuwenhoek did more to dramatize and popularize the field.

[222] **BECHER**, Johann Joachim
(bekh'er)
German chemist
Born: Speyer, Palatinate, May 6, 1635
Died: London, England, October 1682

Becher was the son of a Lutheran minister who had become impoverished in the Thirty Years' War. The necessity of helping to support his family slowed his education.

Becher was a curious mixture of sense and nonsense. He was a successful physician, serving as court physician at Mainz in Germany in 1666. (Germany at the time was broken up into several hundred independent political units so that there was room for many court physicians.)

He was also an economist with intelligent notions concerning the regulation of trade, notions which got him into trouble with conservative merchants who considered any change subversive. As economic adviser to Holy Roman Emperor Leopold I, he suggested a Rhine-Danube canal, cutting across from headwaters to headwaters, to facilitate trade between Austria and the Netherlands.

He was also convinced that transmutation was possible and tried to turn the sands of the Danube into gold. His failure, though not quite as dangerous to personal safety as Alhazen's [85] had been, was dangerous enough. At least, he felt it wise to leave Austria, first for the Netherlands and then for England.

In a book published in 1669 he tried to adapt the alchemical elements to the growing chemical knowledge of the seventeenth century. To do so he divided solids into three kinds of earth. One of these he called *terra pinguis* ("fatty earth"), and saw this as a principle of inflammability, like the alchemical sulfur. His notions on the behavior of this principle were to be refined into the phlogiston theory by his follower Stahl [241] a generation later.

Among his more immediately practical suggestions was one to the effect that sugar was necessary for fermentation and another that coal be distilled to obtain tar.

There is a statement attributed to Becher that goes as follows: "The chemists are a strange class of mortals, impelled by an almost insane impulse to seek their pleasure among smoke and vapor, soot and flame, poisons and poverty, yet among all these evils I seem to live so sweetly, that may I die if I would change places with the Persian King."

Surely, with appropriate changes in phrasing, this is applicable to all those who find in the attainment of knowledge the greatest good.

[223] **HOOKE**, Robert
English physicist
Born: Freshwater, Isle of Wight,
July 18, 1635
Died: London, March 3, 1703

Hooke, the son of a clergyman, was a sickly youngster, scarred by smallpox, who showed himself an infant prodigy in mechanics and who managed to get into Oxford in 1653. There he supported himself by waiting on tables, and apparently never got over the humiliation. At Oxford he attracted the attention of Robert Boyle [212], with whom he got his start. The association was one of mutual advantage for it was Hooke's mechanical skill that made a success of Boyle's air pump.

Hooke became a member of the Royal Society in 1663 and was secretary from 1677 to 1683. Moreover, from 1662 to the end of his life he held the post of "curator of experiments" to the Society. This post, the only paid one in the Society, gave him a kind of bureaucratic power he never hesitated to use against those he conceived to be his enemies.

He was on the one hand a most ingenious and capable experimenter in almost every field of science, and on the other a nasty, argumentative individual, antisocial, miserly, and quarrelsome. Since he investigated in a wide variety of fields, he frequently claimed (with some justice) that he had anticipated the more thorough and perfected ideas of others. His malignant pleasure in controversy could rarely be matched by others. He fought with Huygens [215], for instance, but his particular prey was the transcendent genius (but moral coward) Isaac Newton [231], whom he more than once reduced to distraction and finally drove to nervous breakdown.

In theory Hooke half accomplished much. He worked out an imperfect wave theory of light (which contradicted Newton and anticipated Huygens); he worked out an imperfect theory of gravitation (which anticipated Newton); he speculated on steam engines, toward which the work of Papin [235], Savery [236], and Newcomen [243] was pointing. He speculated on the atomic composition of matter, anticipating Dalton [389].

He ventured into astronomy, too, and in 1664 discovered Gamma Arietis to be a double star. Only Riccioli [185] preceded him in the discovery of such objects. Hooke suggested, too, that earthquakes were caused by the cooling and contracting of the earth and that Jupiter rotated on its axis.

His concrete accomplishments were in two fields: physics and biology. In physics he studied the action of springs and in 1678 enunciated what is now called Hooke's law. This states that the force tending to restore a spring (or any elastic system) to its equilibrium position is proportional to the distance by which it is displaced from that equilibrium position. Earlier he had discovered that spiral springs will expand and contract about an equilibrium position in equal periods regardless of the length of the in-and-out swing. It was this discovery of what we now call the hairspring that made small and accurate timepieces possible and, by eliminating the bulky pendulum, led ultimately to wristwatches and ship's chronometers.

In the field of biology Hooke was one of the most eminent microscopists. In 1665 he published a book, *Micrographia,* written in English rather than Latin. In it are to be found some of the most beautiful drawings of microscopic observations ever made. His studies of microscopic fossils led him to speculate on evolutionary development.

His studies of insects are unrivaled by anyone but Swammerdam [224] and he studied feathers and fish scales with an eye to beauty as well as to accuracy. At least some of the figures were supposedly drawn by Wren [220], the famous architect.

The discovery for which Hooke is best remembered, however, is that of the

144

porous structure of cork. Under the microscope, a thin sliver of cork was found to be composed of a finely serried pattern of tiny rectangular holes. These Hooke called cells. The name was a good one when applied to empty structures for it is used to signify a small room.

These cells turned out to be the dead remnants of structures that in life are filled with a complex fluid. Living structures retained the name of cells, however, and Hooke's word has become as important to biology, thanks to the insight of Schleiden [538] and Schwann [563] a century and a half later, as Democritus' [20] word "atom" has become to chemistry and physics.

Shortly after the publication of *Micrographia*, London burned down in the Great Fire of 1666. Hooke was busily engaged in rebuilding projects and never returned to his microscopy.

[224] **SWAMMERDAM,** Jan (svahm'-er-dahm)
Dutch naturalist
Born: Amsterdam, February 12, 1637
Died: Amsterdam, February 17, 1680

Swammerdam was the son of a pharmacist whose hobby was a museum of curiosities. Young Swammerdam helped his father and acquired a devouring interest in natural history. He studied medicine at Leiden University, where Steno [225] and Graaf [228] were fellow students. He obtained his medical degree in 1667 but never practiced, preferring instead to engage in microscopy.

His father, who had originally intended him for the priesthood, cut off support, but that did not stop Swammerdam's work, although he allowed himself to become sickly and undernourished. He spent the last half of his short life in fits of melancholia, weakened by malaria, and devoted to a religious cult. In the useful portion of his life he collected some three thousand species of insects and produced excellent studies of insect microanatomy. Some of his figures are as good as anything produced after his time, and he may be considered the founder of modern entomology. He showed that muscles changed shape but not volume, thus demonstrating that they did not contract through an influx of animal spirits by way of the nerves—one of Galen's [65] notions. He also demonstrated the detail of the reproductive organs of insects, which tended to support Redi's [211] disproof of their spontaneous generation.

The discovery for which Swammerdam is most famous is that of the red blood corpuscle, which, we now know, is the oxygen-carrying structure of the blood. He announced this discovery in 1658, when he had barely reached his majority. His work was largely neglected until it was resurrected a half century later by Boerhaave [248].

[225] **STENO,** Nicolaus (stay'noh)
Danish anatomist and geologist
Born: Copenhagen, January 11, 1638
Died: Schwerin, Germany, December 5, 1686

Steno is the Latinized form of the Danish name Stensen, and the change is but a symptom of a more general one. Steno, the son of a well-to-do goldsmith, was brought up a Lutheran and trained as a physician, obtaining his medical degree from Leiden in 1664. Eventually he became court physician to the Grand Duke Ferdinand II [193] of Tuscany. The change from Lutheran Denmark to Roman Catholic Italy resulted in a personal conversion to Catholicism and in that faith Steno rose to the position of bishop in 1677, after which, like Pascal [207] and Swammerdam [224], he abandoned science for religion.

Steno's most important concrete discoveries were in anatomy. He recognized that muscles are composed of fibrils and described the duct of the parotid gland (the salivary gland located near the angle of the jaw)—still called the duct of Steno. Also he demonstrated the existence of the pineal gland in animals other than man. In a way this was an embarrassing discovery, since he was a follower of the philosophy of Descartes [183] and his discovery of nonhuman pineals knocked out an important portion of the Cartesian system of physiology.

Steno made a promising beginning in a completely different field. Fossils (a name invented by Agricola [132] to represent anything dug out of the earth) were still a geological mystery. Many of them resembled living things in every detail (and, in fact, the word "fossil" is now applied only to these objects) and an explanation was needed. The easiest explanations for the religion-centered medieval mind were that these fossils were deceiving products of the devils, or "practice-creations" of God before he buckled down to the real business of creation, or the remains of animals drowned in Noah's Flood. Steno, however, reverted to the speculations of a few Greek philosophers and suggested that they were ancient animals who had lived normal lives and in death were petrified, a point in which his contemporary Hooke [223] agreed with him. No supernatural forces were brought into the explanation. Steno also described rock strata in anticipation of William Smith [395] and held that tilted strata were originally horizontal.

Steno also set forth what is now called the first law of crystallography: that the crystals of a specific substance have fixed characteristic angles at which the faces, however distorted they themselves may be, always meet.

[226] **GREGORY,** James
Scottish mathematician and astronomer
Born: Drumoak (near Aberdeen), November 1638
Died: Edinburgh, late October 1675

Gregory, the son of a minister, graduated from Marischal College in Aberdeen.

In 1663 he published the design of a perfectly good reflecting telescope. An attempt to have it constructed ended in failure, however, largely because the art of grinding glass into accurate curves had not yet been perfected, and Newton [231] constructed his, of somewhat different design, first.

Gregory was an ardent astronomical observer and went blind, supposedly through the eyestrain involved in peering through his telescopes. He died young but lived to see Hooke [223], Newton's inveterate enemy, build a reflecting telescope of the Gregorian variety and present it to the Royal Society.

In mathematics Gregory was the first to study systematically the convergent series. (The word "convergent" in this connection is drawn from the lenses with which Gregory was accustomed to work.) Such a series has a finite sum although it is made up of an infinite number of members (which, to be sure, steadily decrease in size). This broke the back of "Achilles and the Tortoise," the twenty-one-century-old paradox of Zeno [16].

[227] **DENIS,** Jean Baptiste (duh-nee')
French physician
Born: Paris, 1640
Died: Paris, October 3, 1704

Denis was the son of one of the engineers working for Louis XIV at Versailles. He himself may have studied medicine at the University of Montpellier.

The establishment of the circulation of the blood by Harvey [174] had set off new interest in anything related to blood. In particular the question arose as to whether blood could be transferred from one organism to another and whether blood from a healthy organism might not be beneficial to one that was sick. Richard Lower [219], for instance, attempted the transfer of blood from one dog to another.

Denis, on hearing of this work, was the first to involve human beings in such transfusion. On June 15, 1667, he transfused the blood of a lamb (about twelve ounces' worth) into an ailing young man, who seemed much the better for it.

Another man also survived transfusion from a sheep.

Two other subjects died, however, and Denis was brought into court on the charge of murder. He was acquitted of that and the court decided that Denis was engaged in a legitimate medical effort to help people. Nevertheless (and wisely) they forbade such transfusions in future, and Denis quit the practice of medicine.

It was not until the time of Landsteiner [973] over two centuries in the future that enough was learned about blood to make transfusion a safe and beneficial procedure.

[228] **GRAAF**, Regnier de
Dutch anatomist
Born: Schoonhoven, July 30, 1641
Died: Delft, August 17, 1673

Graaf was a student of Sylvius [196] at the University of Leiden and obtained his medical degree from the University of Angers, France, in 1665. One of his fellow students was Swammerdam [224] with whom, in later life, he had disputes over priority.

Graaf studied the pancreas and gall bladder and is notable for having collected the secretions those organs discharge into the intestine, work he did without a microscope.

He is better known, however, for his studies of the reproductive system. In 1668 he described the fine structure of the testicles and in 1673 of the ovary (a word he was the first to use). He described particularly certain little structures of the ovary that are still called Graafian follicles in his honor, the name having been given them by Haller [278]. As he suspected, he had penetrated to the beginning of life, for within those structures the individual ova or egg cells (not actually to be discovered until the time of Baer [478] a century and a half later) are formed.

It was Graaf who first appreciated Leeuwenhoek [221] and introduced his work to the Royal Society. He died, still a young man, of the plague.

[229] **GREW**, Nehemiah
English botanist and physician
Born: Mancetter Parish, Warwickshire, September 1641
Died: London, March 25, 1712

Grew was the only son of a clergyman who placed himself on the side of Parliament in the English Civil War. With the return of Charles II, the father lost his income and young Nehemiah's studies at Cambridge were interrupted. He finally obtained his medical degree at the University of Leiden in the Netherlands in 1671. He was one of the early members of the Royal Society, serving as secretary in 1677 along with Hooke [223].

He turned his microscope on plants, studying their sexual organs in particular, including the pistils (feminine) and stamens (masculine). He observed the individual grains of pollen produced by the latter, which were the equivalent of the sperm cells in the animal world. He wrote a book on the stomachs and intestines of various creatures in 1681 and, in a lecture before the Royal Society in 1676, was the first to use the term "comparative anatomy."

He also isolated magnesium sulfate from springs at Epsom, Surrey, and this compound has been called "Epsom salts" ever since.

[230] **MAYOW**, John (may'oh)
English physiologist
Born: Bray, Berkshire, December 1641
Died: London, September 1679

Mayow was educated at Oxford, getting his bachelor's degree in 1665 and a doctorate in civil law in 1670. He also studied medicine. He may have worked for a time with Hooke [223].

He was one of the early investigators of gases. He wondered if there might not be some substance held in common by air and by saltpeter, since both encouraged combustion.

Mayow compared respiration to combustion. He suggested that breathing was something like puffing air at a fire; that the blood carried the combustive principle in air from the lungs to all parts of the body (and to the fetus by way of the placenta). He held that it was this combustive principle that turned dark venous blood into bright arterial blood.

He was right, completely right, but he died young and there was no one to take up his theories and carry on. Furthermore, Stahl's [241] phlogiston theory took the stage shortly after Mayow's death and carried all before it—in the wrong direction.

It was Lavoisier [334], a century after Mayow's death, whose work established principles like those of Mayow firmly and permanently.

[231] **NEWTON**, Sir Isaac
English scientist and mathematician
Born: Woolsthorpe, Lincolnshire, December 25, 1642
Died: London, March 20, 1727

Newton was a Christmas baby by the Julian calendar, but by the Gregorian (which we now use) he was born on January 4, 1643.

Newton, adjudged by many to have been the greatest intellect who ever lived, had an ill-starred youth. He was born posthumously and prematurely (in the year in which Galileo [166] died) and barely hung on to life. His mother, marrying again three years later, left the child with his grandparents. (The stepfather died while Newton was still a schoolboy.) At school he was a strange boy, interested in constructing mechanical devices of his own design such as kites, sundials, waterclocks, and so on. He was curious about the world about him, but showed no signs of unusual brightness. He seemed rather slow in his studies until well into his teens and apparently began to stretch himself only to beat the class bully, who happened to be first in studies as well.

In the late 1650s he was taken out of school to help on his mother's farm, where he was clearly the world's worst farmer. His uncle, a member of Trinity College at Cambridge, detecting the scholar in the young man, urged that he

be sent to Cambridge. In 1660 this was done and in 1665 Newton graduated without particular distinction.

The plague hit London and he retired to his mother's farm to remain out of danger. He had already worked out the binomial theorem in mathematics, a device whereby the sum of two functions raised to a power could be expanded into a series of terms according to a simple rule. He was also developing the glimmerings of what was later to become the calculus.

At his mother's farm something greater happened. He watched an apple fall to the ground and began to wonder if the same force that pulled the apple downward also held the moon in its grip. Kepler's [169] laws had now, after half a century, come to be accepted, and Newton used them in his thoughts about the apple and the moon. (The story of the apple has often been thought a myth, but according to Newton's own words, it is true.)

Now, throughout ancient and medieval times, following the philosophy of Aristotle [29], it had been believed that things earthly and things heavenly obeyed two different sets of natural laws, particularly where motion was concerned. It was therefore a daring stroke of intuition to conceive that the same force held both moon and apple.

Newton theorized that the rate of fall was proportional to the strength of the gravitational force and that this force fell off according to the square of the distance from the center of the earth. (This is the famous "inverse square" law.) In comparing the rate of fall of the apple and the moon, Newton had to discover how many times more distant the moon was from the center of the earth than the apple was; in other words, how distant the moon was in terms of the earth's radius.

Newton calculated what the moon's rate of fall ought to be considering how much weaker earth's gravity was at the distance of the moon than it was on the surface of the planet. He found his calculated figure to be only seven eighths of what observation showed it to be in actuality, and he was dreadfully disappointed. The discrepancy seemed clearly large enough to make nonsense of his theory.

Some have explained this discrepancy by saying that he was making use of a value of the earth's radius that was a bit too small. If this was so, then he would calculate earth's gravity as decreasing with distance a bit too rapidly and he would naturally find that the moon was dropping toward the earth at a rate somewhat less than was actually true. (The dropping of the moon is actually the amount by which its orbit deviates from the straight line. This drop is sufficient to keep it constantly in its orbit but of course not sufficient to make it approach any closer to the earth in the long run.)

Others think Newton retreated because he wasn't sure it was right to calculate the distance from the center of the earth in determining the strength of the gravitational force. Could the earth's large globe be treated as though it attracted the moon only from its center? He was not to be reassured on that point until he had worked out the mathematical technique of the calculus.

This second reason is much more probable, but whatever the reason, Newton put the problem of gravitation to one side for fifteen years.

In this same period, 1665–66, Newton conducted startling optical experiments, inspired in that direction, perhaps, when he read a book by Boyle [212] on color. Kepler's writings on optics had roused his interest. Newton let a ray of light enter a darkened room through a chink in a curtain and pass through a prism of glass onto a screen. The light was refracted, but different parts of it were refracted to different extents, and the beam that fell on the screen was not merely a broadened spot of light, but a band of consecutive colors in the familiar order of the rainbow: red, orange, yellow green, blue, and violet.

It might have been thought that these colors were created in the prism, but Newton showed they were present in the white light itself and that white light was only a combination of the colors. He did this by passing the rainbow or "spectrum" through a second prism oriented in reverse to the first, so as to recombine the colors, and, behold, a spot of white light appeared on the screen. If a second prism were placed so that only one band of color fell upon it, that band of color might be broadened or contracted, depending on the orientation of the prism, but it remained a single color.

(Nobody knows exactly why Newton did not report the dark lines that mark the spectrum. Some of his experiments were so conducted that a few of the lines must have been visible. However, he had an assistant run some of the experiments because his own eyes were insufficiently keen, and it may be that the assistant saw the lines but did not consider them sufficiently important to report. At any rate, the discovery, which turned out to be of first importance, had to wait a century and a half for Wollaston [388] and Fraunhofer [450].)

Newton's prism experiments made him famous. In 1667 he returned to Cambridge and remained there for thirty years. In 1669 his mathematics teacher resigned in his favor and Newton at twenty-seven found himself Lucasian professor of mathematics at Cambridge. (The chair was named after Henry Lucas, who originally provided the money to found the professorship.) A special ruling by the Crown made it unnecessary for him to enter the church to hold his job. He only gave about eight lectures (rather poor ones) a year. The rest was research and thought.

He was elected to the Royal Society in 1672 and promptly reported his experiments on light and color to the Society— and as promptly fell afoul of Robert Hooke [223].

Hooke had performed some experiments with light and prisms but typically had never carried them through to a decent conclusion and had evolved only half-baked explanations. Nevertheless he attacked Newton at once and maintained a lifelong enmity, clearly founded on jealousy.

Even if the greatest intellect that the world has produced, Newton was otherwise a rather poor specimen of man. He never married and except for a mild

149

youthful romance never seemed to show any signs of knowing or caring that women exist. He was ridiculously absent-minded and perpetually preoccupied with matters other than his immediate surroundings. He was also extremely sensitive to criticism and childish in his reaction to it. More than once he resolved to publish no more scientific work rather than submit to criticism. In 1673 he even tried to resign from the Royal Society in a fit of petulance and though the resignation was not accepted, relations between Newton and the Society remained cold.

But Newton's hatred of criticism did not prevent his being just as contentious as Hooke, though in a less forthright manner. He himself avoided controversy, allowing his friends to bear the brunt of the battle, secretly urging them on, making no move either to protect them or to concede a point.

Newton and Leibniz [233] developed the calculus independently and at about the same time. For years this seemed to make no difference and Newton and Leibniz were friendly, but as the fame of both men grew some people substituted "patriotism" for sense. Newton had, as usual, delayed publication, which unnecessarily confused matters. It began to seem a great point as to whether an Englishman or a German had made the discovery and a battle began over which of the two men had stolen the idea from the other.

Neither had stolen the idea. Both were first-rate intellects capable of discovering the calculus, especially since this branch of mathematics was very much in the air and had been all but discovered a half century before by Fermat [188]. But the battle continued with Newton secretly urging his followers on.

The calculus is an indispensable tool in science, but English mathematicians stubbornly continued to utilize Newton's notation even though that of Leibniz was much more convenient. Thus they cut themselves off from Continental advance in mathematics, and English mathematics remained moribund for a century.

Newton's experiments with light and color led him to theorize on the nature of light. Some scientists believed that light, like sound, consisted of a wavelike periodic motion. The ubiquitous Hooke was one and Huygens [215] another. To Newton, however, the fact that light rays moved in straight lines and cast sharp shadows was decisive. Sound, a wave form, worked its way about obstacles so that you could hear around corners. Light does not and you cannot see around corners without a mirror. Newton agreed with Democritus [20], therefore, that light consisted of a stream of particles moving from the luminous object to the eye.

The particle theory of light was by no means cut-and-dried. Grimaldi [199] showed that light did bend around obstacles to a very small extent, and that was hard to explain by particles. Then there was the double refraction of light discovered by Bartholin [210] and that was even harder to explain. In attempting to handle such matters Newton developed thoughts that were quite sophisticated for the time. Actually, the modern theory of light harks back in some interesting ways to Newton. Newton's followers, however, dropped most of the sophistication and revised his theory into a straightforward matter of speeding particles. This maintained its sovereignty over the competing wave theory for a century, thanks to Newton's prestige. (During the eighteenth and even into the nineteenth century Newton's name sometimes carried the deadweight effect that Aristotle's had in the sixteenth and seventeenth.)

It seemed to Newton that there was no way of preventing spectrum formation when light passed through prisms or lenses. It was for this reason that the refracting telescopes of the time were reaching their limits. It was no use making them larger and expecting greater magnification. Light passing through the lenses cast confusing colored rims about the images of the heavenly bodies and blurred out detail—a phenomenon called "chromatic aberration."

Therefore Newton in 1668 devised a "reflecting telescope" that concentrated light by reflection from a parabolic mirror, rather than by refraction through a lens. In this he was anticipated in theory but not in practice by James Gregory [226].

This reflecting telescope had two advantages over the refracting telescope. In Newton's device, light did not actually pass through glass but was reflected off its surface so that there was no light absorption by the glass. Secondly, the use of the mirror eliminated chromatic aberration.

The reflecting telescope was a great advance. Newton's first telescope was six inches long and one inch in diameter, a mere toy, but it magnified thirty to forty times. He built a larger one, nine inches long and two inches in diameter, in 1671 and demonstrated it to King Charles II, then presented it to the Royal Society, which chose this as the occasion for electing him to membership and which still preserves it. Hooke promptly prepared one according to Gregory's somewhat different design, but it wasn't nearly as good as Newton's.

The largest modern telescopes are of the reflecting variety. And yet Newton was wrong just the same. It was possible to have a refracting telescope without chromatic aberration and not long after Newton's death Dollond [273] built one.

The 1680s proved the climax of Newton's life. In 1684 Hooke met Wren [220] and Halley [238] and boasted in his obnoxiously positive way that he had worked out the laws governing the motions of the heavenly bodies. Wren was not impressed by Hooke's explanation and offered a prize for anyone who could solve the problem.

Halley, who was a friend of Newton, took the problem to him and asked him how the planets would move if there was a force of attraction between bodies that weakened as the square of the distance.

Newton said at once, "In ellipses."

"But how do you know?"

"Why, I have calculated it." And Newton told of his theoretical speculations during the plague year of 1666. Halley in a frenzy of excitement urged Newton to try again.

Now things were different. Newton knew of a better figure on the radius of the earth, worked out by Picard [204]. In addition he had worked out the calcu-

lus to the point where he could calculate that the different parts of a spherical body (with certain conditions of density) would attract in such a way that the body as a whole would behave as though all the attraction came out of the center.

As he repeated his old calculations, it appeared that this time the answer would come out right. He grew so excited at the possibility (according to one story) that he was forced to stop and let a friend continue for him.

Newton began to write a book embodying all this, completing it in eighteen months and publishing it in 1687. He called it *Philosophiae Naturalis Principia Mathematica* ("Mathematical Principles of Natural Philosophy") and it is usually known by the last two words of the title. It was written in Latin and did not appear in English until 1729, forty-two years after its original publication and two years after Newton's death. It is generally considered the greatest scientific work ever written. Laplace [347] considered it so, for instance, and Laplace was no more inclined to give credit to others than Newton himself was. Despite his invention of the calculus, Newton proved the propositions in this book by geometrical reasoning in the old-fashioned way. It was the last great work of science written in the Greek style.

In the book Newton codified Galileo's findings into the three laws of motion. The first enunciated the principle of inertia: a body at rest remains at rest and a body in motion remains in motion at a constant velocity as long as outside forces are not involved. This first law of motion confirmed Buridan's [108] suggestion of three centuries before and made it no longer necessary to suppose that heavenly bodies moved because angels or spirits constantly impelled them. They moved because nothing existed in outer space to stop them after the initial impulse. (What produced the initial impulse is, however, still under discussion nearly three centuries after Newton.)

The second law of motion defines a force in terms of mass and acceleration and this was the first clear distinction between the mass of a body (representing its resistance to acceleration; or, in other words, the quantity of inertia it possessed) and its weight (representing the amount of gravitational force between itself and another body, usually the earth).

Finally the famous third law of motion states that for every action there is an equal and opposite reaction. That law makes news today, since it governs the behavior of rockets. Newton considered the behavior of moving bodies both in vacuum and in media that offered resistance. In connection with the latter situation, he foreshadowed modern aeronautics.

From the three laws Newton was able to deduce the manner in which the gravitational force between the earth and the moon could be calculated. He showed that it was directly proportional to the product of the masses of the two bodies and inversely proportional to the square of the distance between their centers. The proportionality could be made an equality by the introduction of a constant. The equation that resulted is a famous one:

$$F = \frac{Gm_1m_2}{d^2}$$

where m_1 and m_2 are the masses of the earth and the moon, d the distance between their centers, G the gravitational constant, and F the force of gravitational attraction between them.

It was an additional stroke of transcendent intuition that Newton maintained that this law of attraction held between any two bodies in the universe, so that his equation became the law of *universal* gravitation. It remained for Cavendish [307] a century later to determine the value of G and, therefore, the mass of the earth, but Newton guessed that mass quite accurately and then estimated the mass of Jupiter and Saturn at nearly the correct value.

It quickly became apparent that the law of universal gravitation was extremely powerful and could explain the motions of the heavenly bodies as they were then known. It explained all of Kepler's laws. It accounted for the precession of the equinoxes. The various irregularities in planetary motions were seen to be the result of their minor attractions (perturbations) for each other superimposed on the gigantic attraction of the sun. It even accounted for the complex variations in the motion of the moon. (This motion, which Kepler had not been able to deal with, was the only problem that Newton used to admit made his head ache.) Newton even included a drawing in his book to illustrate the manner in which gravitation would control the motion of what we today call an artificial satellite.

Newton's great book was published in an edition of only twenty-five hundred copies, but it was well accepted and its value was recognized at once by many scientists. It represented the culmination of the Scientific Revolution that had begun with Copernicus [127] a century and a half earlier. Newton made the Scientific Revolution more than a matter of mere measurement and equations that theoretical philosophers might dismiss as unworthy to be compared with the grand cosmologies of the ancients.

Newton had matched the Greeks at their grandest and defeated them. The *Principia Mathematica* developed an overall scheme of the universe, one far more elegant and enlightening than any the ancients had devised. And the Newtonian scheme was based on a set of assumptions, so few and so simple, developed through so clear and so enticing a line of mathematics that conservatives could scarcely find the heart and courage to fight it. It excited awe and admiration among Europe's scholars. Huygens, for example, traveled to England for the express purpose of meeting the author.

Newton ushered in the Age of Reason, during which it was the expectation of scholars that all problems would be solved by the acceptance of a few axioms worked out from careful observations of phenomena, and the skillful use of mathematics. It was not to prove to be as easy as all that, but for the eighteenth century at least, man gloried in a new intellectual optimism that he had never experienced before and has never experienced since.

Newton's book, however, was not published without trouble. The Royal Society, which was to publish it, was short of funds and Hooke was at his most disputatious in claiming priority and pointing out he had written a letter to Newton on the subject six years earlier. Newton, brought to the extremes of exasperation, was finally forced (much against his rather ungenerous nature) to include a short passage referring to the fact that Hooke, Wren, and Halley had inferred certain conclusions that now Newton was to expound in greater detail. Even so the Royal Society, then under the presidency of none other than Samuel Pepys, the diarist, refused to involve itself in what might be a nasty controversy and backed out of its agreement to publish.

Fortunately Halley, who was a man of means, undertook to pay all expenses of publication, arranged for illustrations, read galley proofs, and labored like a Trojan to keep Hooke quiet and Newton's ever-sensitive nature mollified. When the book appeared, men of science rallied to the new view. David Gregory [240], the nephew of the man who had anticipated the reflecting telescope, was among the first.

But continual controversy was wreaking havoc with Newton, as was the terrific strain of his mental preoccupations. (When asked by Halley how it was he made so many discoveries no other man did, Newton replied that he solved problems not by inspiration or by sudden insight but by continually thinking very hard about them until he had worked them out. This was no doubt true and if there were such a thing as mental perspiration, Newton must have been immersed in it. What's more, he detested distractions and once scolded Halley for making a joking remark.)

As though his work in mathematics and physics were not enough, Newton spent much time, particularly later in life, in a vain chase for recipes for the manufacture of gold. (He was an ardent believer in transmutation and wrote half a million worthless words on chemistry.) He also speculated endlessly on theological matters and produced a million and a half useless words on the more mystical passages of the Bible.

Like Kepler, he calculated the day of creation and set it about 3500 B.C., making the earth five centuries younger than Kepler had done. It was not till Hutton's [297] time, a century later, that science was freed from enslavement to biblical chronology.

Apparently Newton ended with Unitarian notions that he kept strictly to himself, for he could not have remained at Cambridge had he openly denied the divinity of Christ.

In any case in 1692 his busy mind tottered. He had a nervous breakdown and spent nearly two years in retirement. His breakdown, according to a famous tale, may have been hastened by a mishap in which Newton's dog Diamond upset a candle and burned years of accumulated calculation. "Oh, Diamond, Diamond," moaned poor Newton, "thou little knowest the mischief thou hast done." (Alas, this affecting story is probably not true. It is doubtful that Newton ever even owned a dog.)

Newton was never quite the same, though he was still worth ten ordinary men. In 1696, for example, a Swiss mathematician challenged Europe's scholars to solve two problems. The day after Newton saw the problems he forwarded the solutions anonymously. The challenger penetrated the disguise at once. "I recognized the claw of the lion," he said. In 1716, when Newton was seventy-five, a problem was set forth by Leibniz for the precise purpose of stumping him. Newton solved it in an afternoon.

In 1687 Newton defended the rights of Cambridge University against the unpopular King James II, rather quietly, to be sure, but effectively. As a result he was elected a member of Parliament in 1689 after James had been overthrown and forced into exile. He kept his seat for several years but never made a speech. On one occasion he rose and the House fell silent to hear the great man. All Newton did was to ask that a window be closed because there was a draft.

Through the misguided efforts of his friends he was appointed warden of the mint in 1696 with a promotion to master of the mint in 1699. This placed him in charge of the coinage at a generous salary, so that after his death he could leave an estate of over £30,000. It was considered a great honor and only Newton's due, but since it put an end to Newton's scientific labors, it can only be considered a great crime. Newton resigned his professorship to attend to his new duties and threw himself into them with such vigor and intelligence that he revolutionized its workings for the better and became a terror to counterfeiters. He appointed his friend Halley to a position under himself.

In 1703 Newton was elected president of the Royal Society (only after Hooke's death, be it noted) and he was reelected each year until his death. In 1704 he wrote *Opticks,* summarizing his work on light—having carefully waited for Hooke's death here, too. *Opticks,* unlike the *Principia,* was written in English but it was soon translated into Latin so that Europeans outside Great Britain might read it. In 1705 he was knighted by Queen Anne.

He had turned gray at thirty but his faculties remained sound into old age. At eighty he still had all his teeth, his eyesight and hearing were sharp, and his mind undimmed. Nevertheless, his duties at the mint neutralized this maintenance of vigor and prevented him from preparing a second edition of the *Principia* till 1713.

Newton was respected in his lifetime as no scientist before him (with the possible exception of Archimedes [47]) or after him (with the possible exception of Einstein [1064]). When he died he was buried in Westminster Abbey along with England's heroes. The great French literary figure Voltaire [261], who was visiting England at that time, commented with admiration that England honored a mathematician as other nations honored a king. The Latin inscription on his tomb ends with the sentence "Mortals! Rejoice at so great an ornament to the human race!" Even so, national prejudices had their influence and outside Great Britain there was some reluctance to accept the

Newtonian system. It took a generation for it to win final victory.

Newton had the virtue of modesty (or, if he did not, had the ability to assume it). Two famous statements of his are well known. He wrote, in a letter to Hooke in 1676, "If I have seen further than other men, it is because I stood on the shoulders of giants." He also is supposed to have said, "I do not know what I may appear to the world; but to myself I seem to have been only like a boy playing on the seashore, and diverting myself in now and then finding a smoother pebble or a prettier shell than ordinary, whilst the great ocean of truth lay all undiscovered before me."

However, other men of Newton's time stood on the shoulders of the same giants and were boys playing on the same seashore, but it was only Newton, not another, who saw further and found the smoother pebble.

It is almost imperative to close any discussion of Newton with a famous couplet by Alexander Pope:

Nature and Nature's laws lay hid in night:
God said, Let Newton be! and all was light.

and with a verse by William Wordsworth who, on contemplating a bust of Newton, found it to be

The marble index of a mind forever
Voyaging through strange seas of thought, alone.

[232] **ROEMER,** Olaus (roi'mer)
Danish astronomer
Born: Århus, Jutland, September 25, 1644
Died: Copenhagen, September 19, 1710

Roemer, the son of a shipowner, studied astronomy at the University of Copenhagen under Bartholin [210], whom he also served as secretary; but his great achievement came in Paris. It seems that in 1671 the French astronomer Picard [204] traveled to Denmark in order to

visit the old observatory of Tycho Brahe
[156]. He wished to determine its exact
latitude and longitude in order to recal-
culate if necessary Tycho's observations
of a century before. While there he utilized the services of young Roemer as an
assistant and impressed by him brought
him back to Paris.

In Paris, Roemer made his mark by
carefully observing the motions of Jupiter's satellites. Their times of revolution were accurately known, thanks to
Cassini [209], another of Picard's imports. Because of this it was theoretically
possible to predict the precise moment at
which they would be eclipsed by Jupiter
(as viewed from the earth).

To Roemer's surprise the eclipses
came progressively earlier at those times
of the year when the earth was approaching Jupiter in its orbit, and progressively later when it was receding
from Jupiter. He deduced that light must
have a finite velocity (though Aristotle
[29] and, in Roemer's own time, Descartes [183] had guessed the velocity to
be infinite) and that the eclipses were
delayed when the earth and Jupiter were
farthest apart because it took light several minutes to cross the earth's orbit.

All previous attempts to determine the
speed of light had failed. Galileo [166]
had attempted to measure it by station-
ing an assistant on a hill with a lantern
and himself on another hill with a lantern and flashing lights back and forth.
But the time lag between the flashing of
one lamp and seeing the flash of the
other in response seemed entirely due to
the time it took a human being to react
to a stimulus. There was no change in
this lag when hills separated by greater
distances were used.

What Roemer had were two "hills"
that were separated by some half a billion miles (earth and Jupiter) and a
light flash (the moment of satellite
eclipse) that did not involve human reaction times. He calculated the velocity of
light to be (in modern units) 227,000 kilometers per second. Although this value
is too small (the accepted modern value
is 299,792 kilometers per second) it certainly was not bad for a first attempt.

Roemer announced the calculation at
a meeting of the Academy of Sciences in
Paris in 1676. Although nowadays the
velocity of light is considered one of the
fundamental constants of the universe,
this first announcement made no great
splash. Picard backed his young protégé,
as did Huygens [215], but the conservative Cassini was opposed. In England,
Halley [238], Flamsteed [234], and Newton [231] favored it, but on the whole
the matter faded out of astronomical
consciousness until Bradley [258] a half
century later proved the finite velocity of
light in a new and still more dramatic
fashion.

However, Roemer's work in general
was highly regarded. He visited England
in 1679, meeting Newton, Flamsteed,
and Halley, and in 1681 he was called
back to Copenhagen by King Christian
V to serve as astronomer royal and as
professor of astronomy at the University
of Copenhagen. There he reformed the
Danish system of weights and measures
and introduced the Gregorian calendar.
In 1705 he was mayor of Copenhagen.

The record of his extensive observations from Copenhagen was lost in 1728
in a fire that swept the city.

[233] **LEIBNIZ,** Gottfried Wilhelm
(lipe′nits)
German philosopher and mathematician
Born: Leipzig, Saxony, July 1,
1646
Died: Hannover, November 14,
1716

Leibniz, the son of a professor of philosophy who died when the boy was six,
was an amazing child prodigy whose universal talents persisted throughout his
life. Indeed, his attempt to do everything
prevented him from being truly first
class at any one particular thing. He has
been called the Aristotle [29] of the
seventeenth century and was perhaps the
last to take—with reasonable success—
all knowledge for his province.

He began quite young, teaching himself Latin at eight and Greek at fourteen.

He obtained a degree in law in 1665 and, in addition, was a diplomat, philosopher, political writer, and an attempted reconciler of the Catholic and Protestant churches. As a diplomat he tried to distract Louis XIV from a prospective invasion of Germany by suggesting a campaign against Egypt instead. Louis XIV didn't bite, but a century later Napoleon did. Leibniz also acted on occasion as adviser to Peter the Great, tsar of Russia.

He was an atomist after the style of Gassendi [182] and tackled mathematics seriously after his travels brought him into contact with such men as Huygens [215] who introduced him to the mathematical treatment of the pendulum. In 1671 he devised a calculating machine superior to that of Pascal [207], a machine that could multiply and divide as well as add and subtract. He was also the first to recognize the importance of the binary system of notation (making use of 1 and 0 only). (This is important in connection with modern computers.)

Even earlier, in 1667, he had attempted to work out a symbolism for logic. It was imperfect but it anticipated the work of Boole [595] two centuries later, in many ways.

As a result, when Leibniz visited London in 1673, where he met Boyle [212], he was elected a member of the Royal Society.

In that same year he began to think of a system of the calculus, which he published in 1684. This eventually aroused a strenuous controversy between himself and the admirers of Newton [231], with Newton himself participating secretly. In fact, Newton all but accused Leibniz of plagiarism in the second edition of the *Principia*. Leibniz's activity as a diplomat had been (of necessity) shady enough to make his word suspect to the furious Newtonians, and his contact with English mathematicians in 1673 seemed all the proof of plagiarism they needed. However, there seems no doubt now that his work was independent of Newton and, in any case, his line of development of the calculus was the superior. The terminology and form first advanced by

Leibniz is currently preferred to Newton's. Leibniz also introduced the use of determinants into algebra.

In 1693 he recognized the law of conservation of mechanical energy (the energy of motion and of position). A century and a half later this was to be generalized by men such as Helmholtz [631] to include all forms of energy. Leibniz was also the first to suggest an aneroid barometer that would measure air pressure against a thin metal diaphragm without the inconvenience of Torricelli's [192] column of mercury.

In 1700 Leibniz induced King Frederick I of Prussia to match the Royal Society in London and the Academy of Sciences in Paris by founding the Academy of Sciences in Berlin and this has been a major scientific body ever since. Leibniz served as its first president. In 1700 also, he and Newton were elected (admirable neutrality of the French!) the first foreign members of the Parisian Academy of Sciences. For forty years Leibniz served the electors of Hannover.

In 1710 Leibniz published, in French, a book in which he tried to demonstrate that this was the "best of all possible worlds" to use the now popular phrase. Surely, though, Leibniz must have found that hard to believe in his last few years, and after his death this view was mercilessly satirized by Voltaire [261] in his *Candide*.

In 1714 the then elector of Hannover succeeded to the throne of Great Britain as George I, and Leibniz was eager to go with him to London. But the new king had no need of him and perhaps did not wish to offend the Newton partisans in his new kingdom.

Leibniz died in Hannover, neglected and forgotten, with only his secretary attending the funeral. Like his great adversary, Newton, Leibniz had never married and had no family.

[234] **FLAMSTEED,** John
English astronomer
Born: Denby, Derbyshire, August 19, 1646
Died: Greenwich, near London, December 31, 1719

When only fifteen, Flamsteed, the son of a prosperous dealer in malt, was forced by bad health out of school and into the hobby of reading astronomy. He was the gainer thereby, for he grew interested enough to begin to construct instruments and by 1670 had published some astronomical work that attracted attention. In that year he became acquainted with Newton [231] and entered Cambridge.

England more than any other nation was interested in improving navigational procedures, since her merchant fleet was becoming the largest in the world. Any scheme for accurate determination of longitude at sea was of interest to the government.

Flamsteed was one of those called upon to pass on a method for determining longitude that had been suggested, but he shook his head. No method would work, he decided, until such time as a map of the stars more accurate than any existing was prepared. He was among those who petitioned King Charles II for the establishment of a national observatory to take care of that job.

Charles II reacted favorably and had one established at Greenwich, a London suburb, putting Flamsteed in charge. Flamsteed thus became the first astronomer royal, beginning work in 1675.

The job was no sinecure. The king had provided the building but had supplied only a tiny salary, with no provision for assistants or instruments. Flamsteed had to build his own instruments or beg the funds with which to have them built. He had to tutor on the side to support himself.

Fortunately he was a bear for work, making innumerable observations and then performing all the calculations necessary to reduce them to useful values, work that would ordinarily be the routine functions of assistants. He used a clock systematically in his observations, the first astronomer to do so.

On top of low pay (two pounds a week), no help, and poor health Flamsteed's perfectionism brought him into conflict with the great astronomers of the time. Men like Newton felt it was Flamsteed's function to serve as general astronomical flunky, making and handing over any observations that were called for and doing it at once. Flamsteed had with justification a more exalted notion of his position and grew rebellious at Newton's unending demands. Newton was quite incapable of seeing another man's point of view and the two became enemies. Newton took a rather mean revenge by omitting certain credits to Flamsteed in the second edition of the *Principia*.

Flamsteed was pressed to publish his work as quickly as possible, but he refused to do so until he was all finished, and considering the perfectionism with which he worked, the date at which he would be all finished kept receding into the future in exasperating fashion. Finally, in 1708, Newton's friend Halley [238] managed to get his hands on a number of Flamsteed's observations and published them at once with the Prince Consort, George of Denmark, undertaking the cost of printing. Flamsteed was furious. He called Halley violent names, accused him of irreligion and immorality—yet the two had originally been friends and Halley had helped in the design and construction of the observatory. Flamsteed burned every copy of the work he could find (at least three hundred).

This incident spurred him on to completion, however, and eventually his star catalogue came out in full (though part of it appeared only after his death). It was three times as large as Tycho Brahe's [156] and the individual stars were located (thanks to the telescope) with six times the precision. It was the first great star map of the telescopic age.

When two centuries after his time the nations of the world agreed on an international system of marking off meridians of longitude (an offshoot of the problem that got Flamsteed his post in the first place), it was agreed that the meridian of the observatory at Greenwich be the starting place. It is at Longitude 0°0'0" (the Prime Meridian), and that is a kind of monument to the first astronomer royal.

[235] **PAPIN,** Denis (pa-pan')
French physicist
Born: Coudraies, near Blois,
Loire-et-Cher, August 22, 1647
Died: London, England, early
1712

Papin studied medicine in his youth and obtained his medical degree in 1669 at Angers, but that is not the field in which he gained his fame. He served as assistant to Huygens [215] in 1671 and in 1674 helped introduce improvements in Boyle's [212] air pump. Papin corresponded with Leibniz [233] who introduced Papin's work to Boyle. In consequence Papin went to England as Boyle's assistant in 1675.

In 1679 he developed a steam digester, in which water was boiled in a vessel with a tightly fitted lid. The accumulating steam created a pressure that raised the boiling point of water and at this higher temperature, bones softened and meat cooked in quick time. A safety valve was included in case steam pressure got too high. This digester was the forerunner of the modern pressure cooker, and it earned Papin membership in the Royal Society in 1680. He cooked a meal for the Royal Society in his digester and prepared a particularly impressive one for King Charles II.

The steam pressure within the digester must have given Papin the notion of making steam do work. He placed a little water at the bottom of a tube and, by heating it, converted it to steam. This expanded forcibly, pushing a piston ahead of it. Fifteen centuries after Hero [60], men were once again toying with steam, but this time the matter was to be followed up and a century later reach a climax with Watt [316].

Papin never returned to France where, as a Protestant, he would have found the atmosphere unpleasant, thanks to the growing intolerance of Louis XIV. Papin spent some years in Italy, then in Germany, where he built a steam engine in 1698. In his last years, he returned to England, where he died in obscurity and poverty.

[236] **SAVERY,** Thomas
English engineer
Born: Shilstone, Devonshire,
about 1650
Died: London, May 1715

Savery, a military engineer, was a prolific inventor and he lived at a time when one particular invention was badly needed. England was deforested and what trees remained were needed for the navy and could not be used indiscriminately for fuel. Fortunately England could use its deposits of coal. However, water seeps into coal mines and pumping this out by hand (or even by animal power) was arduous and slow.

Guericke [189] had shown that air pressure could do wonders if a vacuum was produced, but producing one by an air pump worked by hand was also arduous and slow. It occurred to Savery that a vacuum could be produced by filling a vessel with steam and then condensing the steam. Burning fuel would then supply all the necessary energy and human muscle could be conserved. He connected such a vessel to a tube running down into the water in the mine. The vacuum produced in the vessel would suck water some way up the tube and then steam pressure, after the principle of Papin [235], could be used to blow the water out altogether.

This instrument, which Savin called the Miner's Friend, was the first practical steam engine and about 1700 it was actually in use in a few places. Its great drawback was that it used steam under high pressure and the technology of the time was insufficient for the manufacture of vessels that could really handle it safely.

[237] **HAVERS,** Clopton (hav'erz)
English physician
Born: Stambourne, Essex, about
1655
Died: Willingale, Essex, April
1702

Havers, the son of a rector, entered Cambridge in 1668 but did not graduate.

He did not get a full license to practice medicine until 1687, after having received a medical education at the University of Utrecht in the Netherlands.

The mark he made in medicine lay in the first full and complete study of bone structure. The text he published in 1691 on the subject remained standard for a century and a half. The Haversian canals in the bone are named for him.

[238] **HALLEY**, Edmund
English astronomer
Born: Haggerston, near London, November 8, 1656
Died: Greenwich, January 14, 1742

Interested in astronomy from his school days, Halley, the son of a wealthy businessman, published work on Kepler's laws when he was nineteen; and then, with Flamsteed's [234] encouragement, set off in 1676 to record the stars of the southern hemisphere. All astronomers until his time had been based in the northern hemisphere and except for the reports of mariners and travelers the southern heavens were virgin territory.

Halley established the first observatory of the southern hemisphere at the island of St. Helena in the South Atlantic (to become famous a century and a half later as the last home of Napoleon Bonaparte). He discovered an object in Centaurus that was eventually found to be a huge globular cluster of stars, Omega Centauri, closest of all such clusters to ourselves.

As it turned out, though, St. Helena had a poor climate for astronomical observations and when Halley returned in 1678 he was only able to publish a catalogue of 341 southern stars. This was nevertheless a new and worthy addition to star lore and made his reputation. He was called the southern Tycho [156], was awarded a master's degree from Oxford despite his not having fulfilled all the requirements, and was elected to the Royal Society.

In England he became a fast and enduring friend of Newton [231] in 1684 and it was through Halley's encouragement and financial help that the *Principia* was published. (Halley's father had been found murdered in 1684 and Halley inherited a tidy sum and was well-to-do thereafter.)

Halley's fame grew and he dined with Peter the Great of Russia during that monarch's visit to England. Halley, according to all reports, had a joyous and riotous time of it.

Newton's principle of gravitation applied easily and well to the various planets and even to the moon, but it was doubtful how well it applied to those outlaws of the skies, the comets, that seemed to come and go as they pleased. Halley (who, in 1703, was appointed professor of geometry at Oxford) addressed himself to this problem and with Newton's help compiled records of numerous comets, working out their paths across the sky. (In 1679 Halley had visited the aged Hevelius [194], then the recognized authority on comets, and this may have inspired his interest in the problem.)

One of the comets Halley dealt with was that of 1682, which he had personally observed. By 1705, when he had listed the movements of two dozen comets, he was struck by the similarity of the path of the 1682 comet with those that had appeared in 1456, 1531, and 1607. These four had come at intervals of seventy-five or seventy-six years and it occurred to Halley that what he was dealing with was a single comet in a closed but very elongated orbit about the sun that was visible only when it was relatively close to the earth. Between appearances it must recede far beyond Saturn, the most distant planet then known.

Halley predicted, in a book written in 1705, that this same comet would return again about 1758, though he was aware that the gravitational interference of the planets might alter the orbit somewhat and change the time of appearance. (Clairaut [283] later showed this to be true.)

Although Halley did not live long enough to witness the return of the comet (he would have had to live to the age of one hundred and two to do so, instead of dying at eighty-six, in the centennial year of Newton's birth), it returned as predicted, allowing for Clairaut's changes. It has been known as Halley's comet ever since. It has returned again in 1835 and in 1910 and, it is confidently expected, will return once more in 1986.

Through Halley's work the comets were tamed once and for all and were shown to be as much subjects of the sun as the earth itself. If cometary motions seemed erratic it was only because cometary orbits were so elongated that some might appear only at intervals of many thousands of years and remain visible during only minute portions of their total orbit.

Halley repeated the suggestion of Kepler [169] that the transit of Venus be used to determine the scale of the solar system and this suggestion bore successful fruit after Halley's death.

He also traveled widely about the turn of the century measuring magnetic variations. And in a completely different field, he was the first (in 1693) to prepare detailed mortality tables. This made it possible to study life and death statistically and led to modern insurance practices.

In 1718 he pointed out that at least three stars, Sirius, Procyon, and Arcturus, had changed their positions markedly since Greek times and had even changed position perceptibly since the time of Tycho Brahe a century and a half earlier. From this he concluded that stars had proper motions of their own which were perceptible only over extended periods of time because of their vast distances from us. The stars, after all, were not fixed.

In 1720 Halley's enemy Flamsteed was dead and the post of astronomer royal was vacant. Halley was appointed. He inherited a virtually instrumentless observatory, since the instruments that had existed had been Flamsteed's personal property and were removed either by heirs or by creditors. Halley reequipped the observatory and devoted his twenty-year tenure largely to careful observations of the moon.

[239] **FONTENELLE,** Bernard le Bovier de (fohnt-nel')
French science writer
Born: Rouen, February 11, 1657
Died: Paris, January 9, 1757

Fontenelle, the son of a well-thought-of but not very well-off lawyer, was educated under the Jesuits in Rouen. He originally planned to be a lawyer, but that didn't work out, and he turned to literature.

At first he tried poetry, operas, dramatic stuff of all kinds, and then found himself with a book entitled *Conversations on the Plurality of Worlds* published in 1686. This was an introduction to the interested and intelligent layman of the new astronomy of the telescope; a careful consideration of each of the planets from Mercury to Saturn, with speculations as to the kind of life that might be found upon them.

He wasn't a scientist, and he was, in any case, a follower of Descartes [183], who never quite caught up with Newton [231]. Still, his book went through numerous editions and he was careful to correct the errors when he could and to bring it up to date.

He was elected to the French Academy in 1691 and became perpetual secretary of the French Academy of Sciences in 1697. He wrote annual summaries of its activities and obituaries for famous scientists as they died. He was perhaps the first person to make a reputation in science on the basis of his popular science writing alone.

He was that rarity; a happy man—calm, equable, doing what he most loved to do and successful at it, loving society and finding himself welcome everywhere, in constant good health and keeping all his faculties into advanced old age. In the end, he died one month before his hundredth birthday. To have lived that final month could surely have been all that remained for him to ask for.

[240] **GREGORY,** David
Scottish mathematician and as-
tronomer
Born: Aberdeen, June 3, 1659
Died: Maidenhead, Berkshire,
England, October 10, 1708

David Gregory was a nephew of
James Gregory [226]. He had just become professor of mathematics at the
University of Edinburgh in 1683 at the
recommendation of Newton [231] and
Flamsteed [234], when Newton's *Principia Mathematica* was published. He
claimed afterward to have been the first
to give public lectures on Newtonian
theory. In 1702, by which time he was a
professor of astronomy at Oxford and a
personal friend of Newton, he published
a book in defense of the theory.

He did not agree with Newton on the
subject of chromatic aberration, however. He noted something that had escaped Newton, that different kinds of
glass spread out the colors of the spectrum to different extents. He suggested
then that a proper combination of two
kinds of glass might produce no spectrum at all. This was realized by Dollond
[273] a half century later.

[241] **STAHL,** Georg Ernst (shtahl)
German chemist
Born: Ansbach, Bavaria, October
21, 1660
Died: Berlin, May 14, 1734

Stahl, the son of a minister, was a
physician by profession (having obtained
his degree at Jena in 1684) and a successful one. He was for a time court
physician at Weimar, even before he was
thirty. He also managed to marry four
times, and his lectures on medicine at
the University of Halle were both famous and well attended. By 1716 he became physician to King Frederick William I of Prussia.

His greatest fame, however, lies in a
chemical theory he adapted from the
views his teacher Becher [222] published
a half century earlier. The matter of

combustion had always interested practical chemists if for no other reason than
that metals could not be formed from
their ores without the action of burning
wood or coal. In the seventeenth century, scientists were beginning to play
with the power of steam, and it led to
the invention of the Savery [236] steam
engine. This made the subject of combustion (the energy of which produced
the steam in the first place) even more
interesting.

Alchemists such as Geber [76] had
tried to establish sulfur as the principle
of combustion and Becher had spoken of
terra pinguis. Stahl, for his part, spoke
of phlogiston (from a Greek word
meaning "to set on fire").

Combustible objects, Stahl held, were
rich in phlogiston and the process of
combustion involved a loss of phlogiston.
What was left behind after combustion
was without phlogiston and therefore
could no longer burn. Thus wood possessed phlogiston, but ash did not.

Stahl recognized that the rusting of
metals was analogous to the burning of
wood (a great and by no means obvious
discovery) and considered that a metal
possessed phlogiston but that a rust (or
"calx") did not.

Air was considered only indirectly useful to combustion, for it served only as a
carrier, holding the phlogiston as it left
the wood or metal and passing it on
sometimes to something else. Thus,
phlogiston could be transferred from
charcoal (considered rich in it) to a
metal ore, which was poor in it. In this
way the charcoal burned and the ore was
converted to metal.

Actually this viewpoint had much to
recommend it about the year 1700,
which was when it was proposed. It did
explain a great deal about combustion,
certainly more than any previous theory
had. It also helped transfer chemical interest from medicine, where it had rested
from the time of Paracelsus [131], to the
preparation of minerals and gases—
which in turn led inevitably to the development of modern chemistry.

The chief difficulty involved in the

phlogiston theory was that it did not take into account changes in weight during combustion or rusting. Thus charcoal in burning lost almost all its weight, leaving only a light ash. Metals, in rusting, actually gained weight, as Boyle [212] had shown a half century earlier. Thus the loss of phlogiston either decreased or increased weight, depending on cases.

Stahl apparently was not perturbed at this because he was still an adherent of the alchemical system of qualitative description only. The science of physics had been stressing the importance of quantitative measurement for over a century, since the time of Galileo [166], but that view had not penetrated the allied science of chemistry. Later, when eighteenth-century chemists, under the influence of the great success of Newton [231], began to feel guilty about ignoring weight considerations they tried to introduce a principle of levity, which was the reverse of gravity. Thus phlogiston, by leaving metal, reduced its levity and made it heavier. This was a foolish notion, however, and did not last long.

Nevertheless phlogiston, with all its contradictions, dominated chemistry for a century until the liberating influence of Lavoisier [334] was felt.

Stahl's influence on physiology was a considerable one, too. He had rational views on mental disease, but on the whole his influence was not an altogether good one from the modern point of view. He did not consider the body either a mechanical system as did Borelli [191], or a chemical system as did Sylvius [196]. Instead he believed it followed laws that were different from those ruling the nonliving universe. This view is called vitalism. It remained prominent until the nineteenth century and is not really dead even yet. Stahl's most prominent contemporary adversary was Boerhaave [248].

[242] POLHEM, Christopher (pool'-
hem)
Swedish inventor
Born: Visby, Gotland Island, December 18, 1661
Died: Tingstäde, August 30, 1751

Polhem, left fatherless at ten, became a clockmaker and entered the University of Uppsala in 1687.

He invented a variety of machines for industrial purposes, particularly in mining. He was an ardent advocate of replacing human muscle with water power and in 1700 built a water-powered factory for the manufacture of tools. He also recognized the value of division of labor, something in which he was two centuries ahead of his time, for it was only at the opening of the twentieth century that Ford [929] really put the notion to work. Outside his native land Polhem built a minting machine for George I of Great Britain. He would not remain in that land, however, nor would he let himself be lured to Russia by Peter I.

He was knighted by Frederick I of Sweden.

[243] NEWCOMEN, Thomas
English engineer
Born: Dartmouth, Devonshire, February 24, 1663
Died: London, August 5, 1729

Newcomen was a blacksmith by profession but an eager and inquiring one, who was supposed to have consulted with Hooke [223] on the workings of vacuums though this may not be so. In 1698 he went into partnership with Savery [236] who had already built a steam engine and who held comprehensive patents. Newcomen devised an improved version in which high-pressure steam was never used and air pressure was made to do all the work. For the purpose he had to construct carefully polished cylinders in which pistons could be made to fit with reasonable airtightness.

By 1712 such a machine was constructed and by 1725 it was coming into general use, where it remained for over half a century until the Watt [316] engine replaced it. Englishmen such as Savery and Newcomen foreshadowed the Industrial Revolution a century later, but there were harbingers outside England, too. Polhem [242], a Swede, is an example.

[244] **AMONTONS,** Guillaume
(a-mohn-tohn´)
French physicist
Born: Paris, August 31, 1663
Died: Paris, October 11, 1705

Amontons, the son of a lawyer, went deaf while still young, but he considered this a blessing because it permitted him to concentrate on his scientific work. (This view was much the same as that held two centuries later by Edison [788], who was similarly afflicted.)

Amontons was interested primarily in the improvement of instruments, particularly barometers and thermometers. In 1687 he invented a new hygrometer, an instrument for measuring the quantity of moisture in the atmosphere. He also designed barometers that did not use mercury and could therefore be used at sea, where the pitching of the waves would ordinarily cause the mercury level to oscillate and destroy the precision of the reading.

As for thermometers, he improved on Galileo [166], who had used air trapped in a tube with a bulb at the end and leading into another tube of water. As the air expanded with a rise in temperature, the water level rose; as the air contracted with a fall in temperature, the water level fell. This thermometer was not at all accurate because changes in air pressure also altered the water level, a point Galileo did not realize.

Amontons used a similar air thermometer, but trapped the air with mercury instead of water. Furthermore the temperature was read by altering the mercury height until the air was held at some fixed volume. In this way temperature was measured by changing air pressure rather than changing air volume. Amontons' thermometer was somewhat more accurate than Galileo's, and he used it to determine that a liquid such as water always boiled at the same temperature (within the limit of precision of his instrument). However, it was still not an instrument for general scientific work; that had to wait two decades for Fahrenheit [254].

In any case, Amontons' interest in thermometers led him to consider the effect of changing temperature on gas volume, which had also interested Mariotte [203]. Amontons went a step beyond Mariotte, however, who had merely shown that the volume of air changed with temperature. Amontons, studying different gases, showed that each gas changed in volume *by the same amount* for a given change in temperature. Out of this he may have gained a vision of an ultimate cold, a kind of absolute zero at which gases contracted to the point where they could contract no farther.

He published his observations on gases in 1699, but they lay fallow for about a century before Charles [343] revived them. Then a half century passed before the important notion of absolute zero was firmly established by Kelvin [652].

[245] **HAUKSBEE,** Francis
English physicist
Born: Colchester, about 1666
Died: London, April 1713

Hauksbee, the son of a draper, became an instrument maker, was a pupil of Boyle [212] and was elected to the Royal Society about 1705. That is virtually all that is known of his private life.

He was the first to study capillary action, effects involving the attractive forces between a liquid and a solid; that causes water, for instance, to rise within thin tubes, and spread out over a flat surface.

He was also one of the earliest investigators of electrical phenomena. His chief advance, made in 1706, was the construction of a glass sphere, turned by a crank, which, through friction, could build up an electric charge. This was something like Guericke's [189] sulfur ball but it was much more efficient.

[246] **DE MOIVRE,** Abraham (duh-mwah´vr)
French-English mathematician
Born: Vitry-le-Francois, Marne, May 26, 1667
Died: London, England, November 27, 1754

De Moivre, the son of a surgeon, was a Protestant and in his youth, France was growing steadily more intolerant of its Protestant (or Huguenot) minority. In 1685, Louis XIV revoked the Edict of Nantes which had granted them toleration, and De Moivre may have been imprisoned for a time. He left France, when he could, and went to England where he remained for the rest of his life, one of the very many talented men whom France lost to its enemies because it could not resist the pleasure of prejudice.

De Moivre got to know Newton [231] and Halley [238] and was elected to the Royal Society in 1697, but he never attained a professorial position and had to make a poor living by tutoring.

He advanced the mathematics of probability well past where it had been left by Pascal [207] and Fermat [188] and made use of factorial numbers in that connection. He was the first to advance some of the fundamental formulas of probability.

He was also the founder of analytical trigonometry. Just as Descartes [183] had converted geometry to algebraic formulas, so did De Moivres do the same for trigonometry.

De Moivres was an early example of what we might call an "industrial mathematician." He supplemented his earnings by serving as a consultant to insurance firms, making use of his probability know-how. (He was also consulted by gamblers, naturally.)

[247] **SACCHERI,** Girolamo (sahk-
        kehr'ee)
        Italian mathematician
        Born: San Remo, September 5,
        1667
        Died: Milan, October 25, 1733

Saccheri was ordained a priest in 1694 and taught mathematics at the Jesuit College of Pavia from 1697 to his death.

He was interested in the fifth postulate of Euclid [40]. the one that assumes (to put it in one of several alternate forms) that through any point not on a given line. one and only one line can be drawn

that is parallel to the given line. It is the only one of the statements with which Euclid starts that cannot be expressed in a few words and that is not intuitively obvious. Many mathematicians, including Omar Khayyám [87] tried to prove the fifth postulate from the remaining axioms and failed. It is quite astonishing and a tribute to Euclid that he saw the difficulty and solved it by accepting it as an assumption and going no further with it.

It occurred to Saccheri to try a novel approach. He would *assume* that the postulate was wrong; that through the point not on a given line, two or more parallels could be drawn to the given line. He would then follow through the consequences and find a contradiction. The existence of the contradiction would prove that more than one parallel could not be drawn and that Euclid was right.

He began a systematic consideration of the consequences, went on and on, failing to find a contradiction and growing very disturbed because he felt somehow that Euclid was a divine truth and to deny it was to deny religion. Eventually, he persuaded himself he had found a contradiction when he had, in fact, not done so and, in 1733, published the results in a book entitled *Euclid Cleared of Every Flaw.* It was one of the outstanding examples of a failure of nerve in science, for Saccheri was on the point of discovering non-Euclidean geometry when he gave up. It had to wait for over a century for Lobachevski [484] and Bolyai [530].

[248] **BOERHAAVE,** Hermann (boor-
        hah'vuh)
        Dutch physician
        Born: Voorhout (near Leiden),
        December 31, 1668
        Died: Leiden, September 23, 1738

Boerhaave was the son of a clergyman and it was originally intended that he study theology. For that purpose he went to the University of Leiden, where he obtained his Ph.D. in 1689. He became interested in medicine, however, obtained his medical degree at Harderwyck in 1693, and returned to Leiden in 1701 as a physician and one who was to accelerate the process by which Leiden became for a time the most famous medical center in Europe. He spent the whole of his professional life there.

He taught medicine by taking his students to the sickbed and was the founder of clinical teaching. Students came to him from all over Europe. Among them was Peter the Great, tsar of Russia, who also took the opportunity of visiting Boerhaave's compatriot Leeuwenhoek [221].

Boerhaave published the neglected drawings of Swammerdam [224] at his own expense. He also published a textbook on physiology in 1708 and one on chemistry in 1724 and each was the most popular of the day and extremely influential. In the former, Boerhaave makes a thoroughgoing mechanistic interpretation of the body in opposition to Stahl [241].

Though famous for his teaching and his writing, Boerhaave made few original advances of his own. He was the first to describe the sweat glands and he established that smallpox is spread only by contact, but there is little else. Nevertheless he is possibly the most eminent European physician during the sixteen centuries between Galen [65] and Koch [767] and is sometimes known as the Dutch Hippocrates [22]. The success of his practice may be attested to by the fact that he died an extremely wealthy man.

[249] HALES, Stephen
English botanist and chemist
Born: Bekesbourne, Kent, September 17, 1677
Died: Teddington, Middlesex, January 4, 1761

Hales studied theology at Cambridge, obtaining his master's degree in 1703, and was a curate at Teddington from 1708 (where the poet Alexander Pope was his neighbor and friend), dabbled in several branches of science and did well

enough to be elected a fellow of the Royal Society in 1717. He was strongly influenced by Newton's [231] work and labored to apply the quantitative experimental approach to biology.

His most important experiments involved plants, for he measured rates of growth, the pressure of sap, and so on. He recognized that it was a portion of the air that contributed to the nourishment of plants, finally correcting Helmont's [175] misconceptions of a century before. For this he is considered the founder of plant physiology. Hales was also the first to measure blood pressure.

He advanced methods for distilling fresh water from the ocean, for protecting grain from weevils by the use of sulfur dioxide, and fish from spoiling. He recognized the value of ventilation and he was the first to collect different gases over water. He experimented with such gases as hydrogen, carbon monoxide, carbon dioxide, methane, and sulfur dioxide, but did not clearly recognize these as distinct gases.

A book on his discoveries, published in 1727, was the last to receive the official *imprimatur* of the aged president of the Royal Society, Isaac Newton.

In 1753 he was elected one of the eight foreign members of the French Academy.

[250] BERING, Vitus Jonassen
(bay'ring)
Danish-Russian navigator
Born: Horsens, East Jutland, Summer 1681
Died: Bering Island, east of Kamchatka (now part of the Soviet Union), December 19, 1741

Bering, the son of an impoverished family, went to sea early. Barely twenty, he went off on a long voyage to the East Indies. When he returned, he was recruited in 1703 into the Russian navy which, under the direction of the tsar, Peter I (the Great) was being rapidly modernized.

Peter wanted Russia's vast new holdings in Siberia mapped, and he chose

165

Bering for the job. In particular Bering was to discover whether Siberia joined North America. In 1725, he crossed Siberia overland and reached the great far eastern peninsula of Kamchatka, which he was the first to map.

From Kamchatka, he set sail northward in 1728 and reached the Arctic ice without sighting land. He had passed through what is now the Bering Strait and he correctly decided that Siberia and North America were not joined.

In a second expedition from Kamchatka in 1741, he explored the Bering Sea (as it is now called), sighted some of the Aleutian Islands but, weakened by scurvy, died on what is now called Bering Island.

He was the first to bring Siberia and its eastern shores into the sharp focus of geographic knowledge.

[251] **MORGAGNI,** Giovanni Battista (mawr-gah'nyee)
Italian anatomist
Born: Forlì, Papal States, February 25, 1682
Died: Padua, December 5, 1771

Morgagni, an only child, was brought up by his widowed mother. He was a brilliant student at the University of Bologna while in his teens, graduating in 1701. In his early twenties he assisted mightily in the preparation of a book on the anatomy and diseases of the ear, which pointed his own direction, the anatomy of diseased rather than of healthy tissue.

At the age of thirty he became professor of anatomy at the University of Padua and remained in that post for nearly sixty years, dying in his ninetieth year. By the time he reached Padua his book on anatomy had established his fame, but the height of his career came in his eightieth year. It was in 1761 that he published a book on the 640 postmortem dissections he had conducted. He tried to interpret the causes and progress of disease from the anatomical standpoint and is considered the father of pathology.

[252] **RÉAUMUR,** René Antoine Ferchault de (ray-oh-myoor')
French physicist
Born: La Rochelle, Charente-Maritime, February 28, 1683
Died: near St.-Julien-du-Terroux, October 18, 1757

Réaumur was the son of a judge who died when the boy was one year old. Réaumur went to Paris in 1703. There a relative, who was an important official, took him under his wing. He did some work in mathematics that was good enough to get him into the Academy of Sciences in 1708. In 1710 he was commissioned by Louis XIV to prepare a description of the various useful arts and manufactures of France, thus giving his active mind the opportunity of exploring many branches of science. He prepared a kind of opaque white glass still known as Réaumur porcelain, he showed that certain so-called turquoises found in southern France were really fossil teeth of extinct animals, and he did work on new methods for steel manufacturing, becoming the first to demonstrate the importance of carbon to steel. For the last, which was the first attempt to make a science out of what was almost a secret art, he earned a considerable cash award, which he turned over to the Academy of Sciences. He wrote a six-volume work on insects, applying his observations on the nest-making habits of wasps to the improvement of paper manufacture, and was also the first (in 1750) to design an egg incubator. What's more, he was the first to demonstrate that corals were animals and not plants.

He interested himself in developing a thermometer, anxious to improve on that of Amontons [244], devised a generation before. He apparently did not know of the work of Fahrenheit [254] in the previous decade but went on independently. He abandoned the air thermometer used by Galileo [166] and Amontons and in 1731 measured temperature by the expansion and contraction of a liquid, using a mixture of alcohol and water for the purpose. The mixture he used expanded with temperature in such a fashion that it proved convenient to divide the volume change between the freezing point and boiling point of water into eighty divisions. On the Réaumur scale, then, the freezing point of water is 0° and the boiling point is 80°. For a while the Réaumur scale held its own against the superior thermometers of Fahrenheit and of Celsius [271], but slowly it lost ground and is now virtually out of use.

Réaumur's most significant work was on the process of digestion. For a century scholars had been divided on the question of whether digestion was a mechanical process, a sort of grinding as Borelli [191] had held, or a chemical process, a sort of fermentation, as Sylvius [196] supposed. Réaumur devised an experiment that settled the matter.

In 1752 he experimented with a hawk. He placed meat in small metal cylinders open at both ends, the ends being covered by wire gauze, and persuaded the hawk to swallow them. Ordinarily a hawk swallows its food in large pieces, digests what it can, and regurgitates the remainder. Réaumur waited for the hawk to regurgitate the cylinders and found the meat partially dissolved.

He concluded that the meat could not have been affected by grinding or by any mechanical action since the metal cylinder protected it from that. Therefore the stomach juices must have had a chemical action on the meat.

He checked this by collecting a quantity of the stomach juice by allowing the hawk to swallow a sponge and, after regurgitation, squeezing the juice out. This fluid, he found, did indeed slowly dissolve meat placed in it. He experimented with dogs, too, and obtained the same results. Digestion, then, is a chemical process and no one has had occasion to doubt this in the two centuries since Réaumur's time.

[253] **DESAGULIERS,** John Théophile
French-English physicist
Born: La Rochelle, France,
March 12, 1683
Died: London, England, March
10, 1744

La Rochelle had been the center of French Protestantism in the seventeenth century. It had been taken by the French Catholic monarchy under the guidance of Richelieu in 1628, but it was not till 1685 that the repressive attitude of Louis XIV made life entirely impossible for the Protestants.

In that year, Desaguliers' family, who were Protestants, fled to England and there they remained.

Desaguliers was educated at Oxford, was ordained a deacon in 1710, and even served as chaplain to Frederick, Prince of Wales. (He never reigned himself, but he was the father of George III.)

Desaguliers was an ardent experimenter in many fields and a strong exponent of the Newtonian point of view. He was particularly interested in electricity and repeated and extended the experiments of Stephen Gray [262] in that field. It was he who first used the word "conductor" to describe those substances that could conduct a flow of electricity. Nonconductors he called "insulators" from the Latin word for "island" since nonconductors could pen up the electric fluid as the sea penned up an island.

[254] **FAHRENHEIT,** Gabriel Daniel
(fah'ren-hite)
German-Dutch physicist
Born: Danzig (now Gdańsk, Poland), May 24, 1686
Died: The Hague, Netherlands, September 16, 1736

In 1701 Fahrenheit, the son of a wealthy merchant, emigrated to Amsterdam after the sudden death of both parents; there he became a manufacturer of meteorological instruments. Obviously one of the chief devices that can be used for studying climate is a thermometer. The thermometers of the seventeenth century, however, such as the gas thermometer of Galileo [166] or of Amontons [244], were insufficiently exact for the purpose.

Fluid thermometers had come into use, but they used either alcohol or alcohol-water mixtures. Alcohol alone boiled at too low a temperature to allow high temperatures to be measured, and alcohol-water mixtures, which did a bit better in this respect, changed volume with changing temperature in too uneven a way.

In 1714 Fahrenheit made the key advance of substituting mercury for alcohol. He made this practical by inventing a new method for cleaning mercury so that it wouldn't stick to the walls of the narrow tube of the thermometer. The use of mercury meant that temperatures well above the boiling point of water as well as below its freezing point could be recorded. In addition, mercury expanded and contracted at a more constant rate than most other substances and a mercury thermometer could be marked off more accurately into finer subdivisions.

In 1701, for instance, Newton [231] had suggested that the temperature of freezing water and of the body be used as fixed points on the thermometer scale and that the difference in fluid level at these points be marked off into twelve equal divisions.

Fahrenheit, however, added salt to water to get the lowest freezing point he could and called that zero. (He wanted to avoid negative temperatures on winter days that were well below the freezing point of pure water.) He then divided the difference in level between that point and that reached at body temperature not into twelve parts but into eight times that many (in line with the high precision of his instrument) or ninety-six "degrees." He later adjusted that slightly in order to make the boiling point of water come out to 212°, exactly 180 degrees above the freezing point of pure water, set at 32°. On this Fahrenheit scale, body temperature is 98.6°.

This was the first really accurate thermometer, and Fahrenheit used it to expand Amontons' finding that the boiling point of water was fixed. He checked other liquids and found that each had a fixed and characteristic boiling point under ordinary conditions. He also noticed that this boiling point changed with changes in pressure.

Fahrenheit's report on his thermometer in 1724 earned him election that year to the Royal Society. The Fahrenheit scale was adopted at once in Great Britain and the Netherlands.

Most of the civilized world, and scientists everywhere, however, use the scale invented by Celsius [271] a quarter century after Fahrenheit's first mercury thermometer.

[255] **DELISLE**, Joseph Nicolas (duh-leel')
French astronomer
Born: Paris, April 4, 1688
Died: Paris, September 11, 1768

Delisle was the ninth child of a historian and geographer. He was educated at the Collège Mazarin, with no anticipation of a scientific career, but a solar eclipse in 1706 imbued him with a fascination for astronomy. He began studying it avidly and found work, almost any work, to do at the Paris Observatory.

He showed enough talent to get a professorial appointment at the Collège Royal in 1718. Then Peter I (the Great) of Russia, who was anxious to modernize Russia in his own lifetime, felt the need of a modern astronomical observatory in the land and invited Delisle to do the job. In 1725 Delisle was in St. Petersburg to see what he could do in four years and, as it turned out, he stayed twenty-two years. In the process, though, he established the observatory and trained a whole generation of astronomers so that while Russia remained backward in some branches of science, she developed an astronomical tradition equal to that in western Europe. He returned to Paris in 1747.

He was the first astronomer to take seriously the possibility of utilizing a transit of Venus as a way of determining the scale of distances in the solar system. In 1761, the year of such a transit he organized a worldwide study of the phenomenon, the first such to be attempted. It was the prelude for more serious and sophisticated efforts in the next century.

[256] **GOLDBACH,** Christian
(gold'bahkh)
German-Russian mathematician
Born: Königsberg, Prussia (now
Kaliningrad, Soviet Union),
March 18, 1690
Died: Moscow, Russia, November 20, 1764

Goldbach, the son of a minister, studied medicine and mathematics at the University of Königsberg. In 1710, he made a grand tour of Europe (a common way of attaining an education for those who could manage it). In 1725, he settled down in Russia, becoming professor of mathematics at the Imperial Academy of St. Petersburg; in 1728 he served as tutor to the short-lived Peter II (grandson of Peter the Great).

Goldbach is most famous in mathematics for "Goldbach's conjecture," something Goldbach mentioned in 1742 in a letter to Euler [275]. (Goldbach was a voluminous correspondent with the mathematicians of the time.)

The conjecture is this: "Every even number greater than 2 can be expressed as the sum of two prime numbers." Thus $4 = 2 + 2$; $6 = 3 + 3$; $8 = 3 + 5$; $10 = 3 + 7$; $12 = 5 + 7$; and so on. Mathematicians have found it to be true by actual testing for all even numbers up to 10,000 and for some beyond; and no one really expects to find any exceptions. The catch is, though, that in over two centuries, no mathematician has managed to *prove* his conjecture. How can something so simple and so apparently true avoid proof? It is one of the frustrations of mathematics.

[257] **MUSSCHENBROEK,** Pieter van
(mois'en-brook)
Dutch physicist
Born: Leiden, March 14, 1692
Died: Leiden, September 19, 1761

Musschenbroek was born into a family of instrument makers who by the time of his birth had turned to the manufacture of scientific instruments such as tele-scopes, microscopes, and air pumps. Pieter studied at the University of Leiden and received his medical degree in 1715, and a Ph.D. in 1719. From 1721, he held professorial positions first at Duisberg, then at Utrecht, and finally at Leiden.

Musschenbroek is most famous for his invention of the first truly efficient device for storing static energy. Until then, there were such things as the sulfur ball of Guericke [189] which could be charged with enough electricity to produce interesting phenomena, but not with enough to be truly startling.

Musschenbroek, however, placed water in a metal container suspended by insulating silk cords and led a brass wire through a cork into the water. He built up a charge in the water but had not the slightest idea of how great a charge until an assistant happened to pick up the container and then touch the brass wire outside the cork. The container promptly discharged through the assistant's body and gave him a fearful shock; the first good-sized artificial electric shock anyone had ever received. (The lightning stroke is a natural one, of course.)

This happened at the University of Leiden, also spelled Leyden, in January 1746. The news spread rapidly and soon "Leyden jars" were being prepared and improved everywhere. For the first time, physicists had a way of preparing an intense electric charge and studying its properties. Within six years, Franklin [272] was to make astonishing use of it.

[258] **BRADLEY,** James
English astronomer
Born: Sherborne, Gloucestershire,
March 1693
Died: Chalford, Gloucestershire,
July 13, 1762

Bradley was educated at Oxford and received his master's degree in 1717. He was introduced to astronomy through the interest taken in him by his uncle, the Reverend James Pound, himself an astronomer. The young man's aptitude in mathematics gained him the friendship of Newton [231] and Halley [238] and he was elected to the Royal Society in 1718. Not really expecting to make a living as an astronomer, he became a vicar in the Church of England in 1719 but resigned in 1721 in order to teach at Oxford. As it happened, astronomy supported him the rest of his life, though he labored hard in return.

His major astronomical concern was to measure the parallax of the stars. When Copernicus [127] first suggested that the earth moved about the sun, it seemed inevitable that because of this motion the nearer stars would be displaced—compared with the more distant ones—because they would be viewed at varying angles as the earth moved. No such parallax was, in fact, observed. Copernicus declared this was because the stars were so distant that the parallax was too small to measure. His opponents said that the parallax was not observed because the earth was not moving. Although by Bradley's time the Copernican position was accepted by all astronomers, it would still have been satisfying to measure the parallax and obtain some idea of the distance of the stars that was more exact than the phrase "very distant."

Bradley's close observations, with a telescope 212 feet long, did, indeed, indicate to him that the stars showed a tiny displacement through the year, moving in a small ellipse. However, the motion did not jibe with the earth's motion in exactly the way expected of a parallactic displacement. It was not until 1728 that the true explanation occurred to him, during a boat ride on the Thames River when he noticed the wind vane on the mast shift direction whenever the boat put about.

The usual explanation advanced to account for Bradley's effect, however, involves the rain. If rain falls vertically, a man holds an umbrella directly over his head. If he walks he must angle the umbrella in the direction in which he walks. The faster he walks the more he must angle the umbrella. In the same way, to observe light from a moving earth the telescope must be angled very slightly. The angling of the telescope makes the

star appear in a slightly different position as the year moves on.

From the amount of angling, the amount of the "aberration of light," it was possible for Bradley to tell the ratio between the velocity of the earth about the sun and the velocity of light. In this way he was able to produce a second method of estimating the velocity of light, which had first been reported by Roemer [232] a half century before. He succeeded in confirming Roemer's results and rescuing them from oblivion, although Bradley's figure was the more accurate and very much like the currently accepted value for the velocity of light.

To be sure, Bradley did not detect the parallax of the stars and could not tell how distant they were. That had to wait for Bessel [439] a century afterward. However, his main purpose was solved. Light would not undergo aberration if the earth were not moving, and his discovery was the first direct evidence that the earth was not at rest and that Copernicus' view was more than merely a matter of simplifying the basis of calculations. The phenomenon of aberration also tended to support the Newtonian theory of light as a shower of particles (like rain).

In his careful positioning of stars Bradley also discovered that the earth's axis underwent small periodic shifts, which he called "nutation." This was due to changes in the direction of the gravitational attraction of the moon as our satellite moved on its rather complicatedly irregular orbit. To detect nutation Bradley had to determine differences of two seconds of arc. Since he could not detect stellar parallax, that must involve position shifts that were smaller still. Hence, stars had to be very far off. He didn't publish his discovery till 1748, testing it first by a careful nineteen-year study of stellar positions.

In 1733 he measured the diameter of Jupiter and, for the first time, astronomers began to realize just how much larger some of the planets were than our own earth—for so long regarded as the massive center of the universe.

In 1742, upon the death of Halley,

Bradley was appointed the third astronomer royal and in 1748 he was awarded the Copley medal. He finally managed to get a decent appropriation out of the government and with it bought instruments. He is supposed to have turned down a salary increase, however, observing that if the position of astronomer royal were made too lucrative, astronomers would not be appointed to it.

He devoted himself to preparing a star map that was even more extensive and accurate than that of Flamsteed [234]. He had the same industry and application as Flamsteed, and also the advantage of being able to correct for the tiny errors introduced by aberrations and nutation, of which Flamsteed, of course, had been unaware.

He strongly supported the adoption of the Gregorian calendar by Great Britain in 1752, a view that brought upon him the displeasure of much of the unthinkingly conservative public.

[259] **HARRISON,** John
English instrument maker
Born: Foulby, Yorkshire, March 24, 1693
Died: London, March 24, 1776

The eighteenth century saw the British government still deeply concerned with the problem of determining longitude at sea, the problem that on the advice of Flamsteed [234] had inspired the founding of the Greenwich Observatory.

One way was for the navigator to know the Greenwich time accurately wherever he might be on the face of the earth. From the difference between Greenwich time and the local time, as established astronomically, the longitude could be calculated. For this, though, an accurate timepiece was needed, and one that could be used on board ship. An ordinary pendulum clock could not, because the swaying upset the periodic motion of the pendulum.

In 1707 a British fleet miscalculating its position came to grief on rocks off Cornwall. In 1713, therefore, the British government offered a series of prizes of up to £20,000 for an accurate ship's

chronometer. A century earlier, in 1598, Philip III of Spain had offered a prize, never claimed, for the same thing. Now, however, the problem was tackled by John Harrison, a Yorkshire mechanic and the son of a carpenter, self-trained and equipped with nothing but an almost supernatural mechanical sense.

Beginning in 1728 he built a series of five clocks, each better than the one before. Each clock was so mounted that it could take the sway of a ship without being adversely affected. He designed a pendulum of different metals so that temperature changes expanded both metals in such a way as to leave the overall length the same, and the period of beat, in consequence, unaltered. He also inserted a mechanism that allowed the clock to continue to keep time undisturbed while it was being wound.

Any one of Harrison's clocks met the demands of the prize conditions. In fact they were more accurate at sea than any other clock of the time was on land. One of them was off by less than a minute after five months at sea.

To be sure, the first four clocks were heavy (one weighed sixty-six pounds) and complicated and expensive, but the conditions of the prize said nothing about size or complexity or expense. The fifth clock, moreover, was no bigger than a large watch and it was even better than the others.

However, the British Parliament put on an extraordinary display of meanness in this connection. It wore Harrison out with its continual delays in paying him the money he had earned. It repeatedly demanded ever greater perfection, and although Harrison always met those demands it would pay him only niggardly sums. Possibly this was because Harrison was a provincial mechanic and not a gentleman of the Royal Society.

Finally the young King George III took a personal interest and announced that he himself would serve as Harrison's counselor—one of the shining acts of that well-intentioned but stubbornly wrongheaded monarch. Harrison finally received his money in 1765.

Harrison's chronometer introduced the modern era of ship navigation and was not really displaced until a century and a half later when radio communications made the whole world one, and a single clock could be made to do for everybody everywhere.

[260] **BRANDT,** Georg
Swedish chemist
Born: Riddarhyttan, Västman-
land, July 21, 1694
Died: Stockholm, April 29, 1768

Brandt was the son of an apothecary who had gone into metallurgy. From the time of Agricola [132], minerals and medicines were grouped and the difference between the apothecary and the chemist was to remain nearly invisible well into the nineteenth century, reaching its climax with Scheele [329].

Brandt helped his father both in chemical and metallurgical work and then went on to study medicine and chemistry under Boerhaave [248]. He obtained a medical degree in 1726 but did not practice. However, by 1751 his fame had grown so that he was one of the doctors called in to attend the dying Swedish king, Frederick I.

Brandt's metallurgical experience was useful to him, for in 1727 he was placed in charge of the Bureau of Mines at Stockholm, and three years later was made assay master of the Mint.

He did considerable work on arsenic, but the deed for which he is best known was in connection with a particular mineral that had been used for a couple of centuries to make a deep blue pigment. The mineral resembled a copper ore in some of its properties but it yielded no copper, so German miners of the day had named it kobold after an earth spirit which, they believed, had bewitched the copper ore.

About 1730 Brandt was able to treat the dark blue pigment in such a manner as to obtain out of it a new metal. It wasn't copper, and it much resembled iron. Brandt gave it the name of the earth spirit, spelling it "cobalt," and that is still the name of the metal. Brandt was the first man to discover a new element since Brand's [216] discovery of phos-

phorus three quarters of a century earlier, but from his time on the pace of discovery of new elements never lagged. He was the first man to discover a metal entirely unknown to the ancients.

Brandt differed from his predecessors such as Brand, Becher [222], and Stahl [241] and even from such great dabblers in chemistry as Boyle [212] and Newton [231] in that he was the first to be completely free of any alchemical taint.

In his later years, in fact, Brandt made almost a hobby out of combating alchemy, much as men today might make one of exposing fortune-telling frauds. He showed that gold could be dissolved in hot nitric acid and made to precipitate out when the acid was cooled and shaken. Gold would then seem to appear out of nowhere, and this explained one of the ways knaves imposed on fools.

When Brandt died, chemistry was about to reach full maturity under Lavoisier [334]. The end of alchemy for all but the most eccentric faddists, he did not live to see.

[261] **VOLTAIRE** (François Marie
Arouet)
French author
Born: Paris, November 21, 1694
Died: Paris, May 30, 1778

Voltaire was the son of a minor government functionary and his real name was François Marie Arouet. Voltaire was blessed, and cursed, with one of the sharpest wits of modern times. It was a blessing in that he could win any argument, for there is no one on record who ever involved himself in a controversy with Voltaire without coming out shredded and a laughingstock.

It was a curse in that he could not resist lampooning and satirizing the most respected beliefs of the nation and the most highly placed individuals. This led to his being imprisoned in the Bastille now and then, and on at least one occasion of being beaten up by thugs hired by a gentleman who, smarting under ridicule, thought that sticks were more striking arguments than words.

In 1726 Voltaire was sent off to England for his own protection, where he remained three years. While there he made friends in the highest literary circles. He also studied the Newtonian theory and was present at the funeral of Newton [231].

After returning to France (where he was to experience a continual series of ups and downs at the court of Louis XV, according to the manner in which he exercised his sharp tongue) he had one of his mistresses, the marquise de Châtelet [274], translate *Principia Mathematica* into French and he himself in 1737 wrote a commentary on the book. Newton was fortunate in his interpreter, for to find anyone who could write more charmingly than Voltaire was a task for a long summer's day indeed.

It was Voltaire, more than anyone, who made Newton fashionable among nonscientists. This was particularly important in France where the pre-Newtonian views of Descartes [183] still dominated. Voltaire, in fact, was the living embodiment of the Age of Reason, the most shining light of the last period in history in which it was chic for a man of humanistic culture to understand and admire science and for a scientist to love the humanities.

Voltaire died on the eve of the French Revolution, which his writings had done much to bring about. The quiet twilight of the feudal aristocracy of Europe, with its condescending patronage of things scientific, was broken in that holocaust. Science itself, after 1800, expanded in so many directions that it became no longer possible to study it as a mere minor adjunct to a humanistic education. It required a specialist to learn as much of science as was necessary to advance research.

The Age of Reason died with Voltaire. The Age of Specialized Science took its place and is still with us, now more than ever.

[262] **GRAY,** Stephen
English electrical experimenter
Born: about 1696
Died: February 25, 1736

Gray, the son of a dyer, may have received instruction from Flamsteed [234].

He grew avidly interested in the infant study of electricity and made his key discovery in 1729. He found that when a long glass tube was electrified by friction, the corks at the end (which were not touched) were also electrified. The electric fluid, whatever it was, had traveled from the glass to the corks and he thus discovered electrical conduction.

He experimented further, conducting electricity through long stretches of twine and, eventually, found that not everything would suffice for the purpose. Some substances would not conduct electricity. Desaguliers [253] soon categorized the situation by speaking of "conductors" and "insulators."

[263] **MACLAURIN,** Colin (mak-law'-rin)
Scottish mathematician
Born: Kilmodan, February 1698
Died: Edinburgh, January 14, 1746

Maclaurin, the son of a minister, lost his father six weeks after his birth and his mother when he was nine years old. He was brought up by an uncle, also a minister. In 1709, at age eleven, Maclaurin entered the University of Glasgow intending to study for the ministry but grew interested in mathematics instead, and obtained his master's in that discipline in 1715. In 1717, when he was still not yet twenty, he was appointed professor of mathematics at Marischal College, Aberdeen, and two years later was elected to the Royal Academy.

He met Newton [231] in London, and in 1724, moved on to a professorial chair with Newton's strong recommendation. Maclaurin was probably the greatest mathematician in the British Isles in the generation following Newton and did much to tighten and extend the calculus. In particular, in 1742 he wrote in defense of Newton against the criticisms (well-based) of the foundations of calculus by the philosopher George Berkeley. In so doing, he did much to improve matters so as to make the criticisms less trenchant. In a way this contributed to the British idolatry of Newtonian mathematics, so that after Maclaurin mathematics vegetated in Great Britain and made no further progress, Babbage [481] and his friends stirred things up again.

In 1745 a Highland army, supporting Charles Stuart ("Bonnie Prince Charlie," the Stuart Pretender) marched on Edinburgh. Maclaurin supervised the defense with remarkable energy for a mathematician but was forced to flee when the Highlander Jacobites took the city. The Jacobite ascendancy was short-lived and Maclaurin soon returned to Edinburgh, but his health had been undermined and he died soon after.

[264] BOUGUER, Pierre (boo-gair′)
French mathematician
Born: Le Croisic, Loire-Inférieur,
February 16, 1698
Died: Paris, August 15, 1758

Bouguer's father was a hydrographer (that is, a geographer of the waters of the earth, both fresh and salt) and mathematician who brought his son up in the same profession. By 1730 Bouguer was a professor of hydrography at Le Havre, succeeding his father, and he was one of the foremost on the La Condamine [270] expedition. He wrote a useful book about the expedition.

He also invented a heliometer, to measure the light of the sun and other luminous bodies. With it he was the first to attempt a quantitative measurement of the comparative luminosities of the sun and moon and is considered a founder of photometry, the measurement of light intensities.

[265] BAKER, Henry
English naturalist
Born: London, May 8, 1698
Died: London, November 25,
1774

Baker, the son of a law clerk, was apprenticed to a bookseller where (like Faraday [474] a century later) he took the opportunity to read books, including some on microscopy. He later stayed with a relative whose daughter had been born deaf. Baker undertook to teach her to speak and to read, and was successful —so successful that he made a profession out of teaching those with a variety of speech defects and made a good living out of it. He kept his methods secret for the natural reason that only so could he continue to command high fees. Through work of this sort he attracted the interest of the novelist Daniel Defoe (the author of *Robinson Crusoe*), and in 1729 Baker married the youngest of Defoe's daughters.

Baker was also a science writer, and in particular he wrote on the microscope and introduced it to the general lay public, describing its construction and its uses. Like Leeuwenhoek [221], he used the microscope to observe everything he could and reported on all of it. Of particular importance was his observation of the shapes of various kinds of crystals.

[266] DU FAY, Charles François de
Cisternay
French physicist
Born: Paris, September 14, 1698
Died: Paris, July 16, 1739

Du Fay served in the army from the age of fourteen, but after his retirement became the superintendent of gardens for King Louis XV in 1732, a post that gave him security plus time for experimentation. He repeated the experiments of Gray [262] on electrical conduction, and noted that damp twine was a conductor while dry twine was an insulator.

In 1733 Du Fay experimented with suspended bits of cork, which he electrified by touching them with an already electrified glass rod. He found the pieces of cork repelled each other. This effect of repulsion had been noted by Guericke [189] but Du Fay now studied it in detail.

He found that two electrified objects sometimes attracted and sometimes repelled each other. A cork ball electrified by means of a glass rod attracted another which had been electrified by means of a resinous rod. If both were electrified in the same way, either both by glass or both by resin, they repelled each other.

Du Fay postulated the existence of two different electrical fluids: "vitreous electricity" and "resinous electricity." Each repelled itself but attracted the other. It remained for Franklin [272] to introduce the modern convention of calling them "positive" and "negative."

Du Fay, who never married, died of smallpox at forty.

[267] **MAUPERTUIS,** Pierre Louis Moreau de (moh-pehr-tyoo-ee′) French mathematician
Born: St. Malo, Ille-et-Vilaine, September 28, 1698
Died: Basel, Switzerland, July 27, 1759

Maupertuis, the spoiled child of well-to-do parents, spent part of his youth as a musketeer in the army, joining in 1715 but leaving in 1723 to become an instructor in mathematics at the French Academy of Sciences. In 1728 he visited England, was elected to the Royal Society, and became an extravagant admirer of Newton [231], who had just died. He leaped at the chance in 1736 to head an expedition to Lapland, in conjunction with the expedition of La Condamine [270] to the equator, to measure the curvature of the earth. After all, a successful result would help establish Newton's theory. Maupertuis' group completed its task far more quickly than La Condamine's, but not nearly so precisely.

In 1743 Maupertuis was elected to the French Academy and in 1744 yielded to the blandishments of Frederick II of Prussia. He went to Berlin and was appointed head of the Academy of Sciences there in 1746. He was, however, a quarrelsome and unlikable man and conducted a loud argument with Voltaire [261] (who had befriended him, but whose witty comments Maupertuis found insupportable) over the principle of least action. This principle, first advanced by Maupertuis in 1744 (and sharpened a century later by Hamilton [545]),

seemed to show that nature chose the most economical path for moving bodies, rays of light, and so on. Maupertuis worked out theological implications from this and, though Euler [275] supported him, Voltaire scoffed.

Maupertuis lost the argument of course, since one could not bandy words with Voltaire and come out the winner. Voltaire's ridicule drove Maupertuis to Basel, where he took the side of Newton against Leibniz [233] in the argument over which man had priority in the calculus. On the continent he was in the minority. This argument is supposed to have hastened his death.

[268] **BERNOULLI,** Daniel (ber-nool′-ee) Swiss mathematician
Born: Groningen, Netherlands, February 8, 1700
Died: Basel, March 17, 1782

Daniel Bernoulli came of an amazing line of Swiss mathematicians and physicists descended from a Flemish family, driven out of the Netherlands in the late sixteenth century because of their Protestant beliefs. His uncle Jacob (or Jacques), a contemporary of Newton [231] and Leibniz [233], was a mathematician nearly in their class. His father, Johann (or Jean), was almost as capable and was a professor at Groningen when Daniel was born, though the family returned to Switzerland in 1705. Both uncle and father extended the calculus to new applications. Two brothers, a cousin, and a couple of nephews (not to mention other relations) were also mathematicians or scientists.

As for Daniel, he began as a mathematician, despite his father's desire that the young man follow a business career. Daniel's older brother taught him geometry, and though he studied medicine and obtained a medical degree in 1721, it was as a professor of mathematics that he began teaching in St. Petersburg, Russia, in 1725. He returned to Switzerland in 1733 and grew interested in science. In doing so, he became the first non-English scientist to accept without reservation the Newtonian view of the universe.

His book on the flow of fluids (hydrodynamics) in 1738 showed that, as the velocity of fluid flow increases, its pressure decreases. This is still called Bernoulli's principle and is used in producing vacuums in chemical laboratories by connecting a vessel to a tube through which water is running rapidly.

Bernoulli was the first to attempt an explanation of the behavior of gases with changing pressure and temperature. The changes had been observed by men such as Boyle [212], Mariotte [203], and Amontons [244], but none of them had attempted an explanation.

Bernoulli began by assuming that gases were made up of a vast number of tiny particles, a suggestion that was at least as old as Hero [60]. Bernoulli proceeded to treat the situation mathematically, using the probability techniques of Pascal [207] and Fermat [188]. He obtained fair results although his methods were not rigorous. The mere fact that he could do so would have given a powerful boost to the concept of atomism if his work had been paid more attention. A century later Joule [613] improved the treatment and still later Maxwell [692] and Boltzmann [769] were to complete it, but by then atomism was well established.

[269] **KLEIST,** Ewald Georg von (kliste)
German physicist
Born: Pomerania, about 1700
Died: Köslin, Pomerania (now
Koszalin, Poland), December 11,
1748

Kleist was the son of a district magistrate. He was educated at the University of Leiden where he picked up an interest in science then returned home to become dean of the cathedral of Kamin in Pomerania.

Kleist's contribution to science consisted of his attempt to store an electric charge and the accidental invention of an efficient means of doing so. He had, in fact, invented Musschenbroek's

[257] Leyden jar, independently of Musschenbroek and at just about the same time. He had discovered what he had done in the same way, too, by giving himself an accidental shock that all but jarred his teeth loose.

[270] **LA CONDAMINE,** Charles
Marie de (la-kohn-duh-meen')
French geographer
Born: Paris, January 27, 1701
Died: Paris, February 4, 1774

La Condamine, born into the wealthy nobility, joined the army at the age of seventeen but left it to engage in a scientific career.

In La Condamine's time most of the world, except for the polar regions and some of the empty stretches of the Pacific, had been opened up, but much was left to do. Areas had been crossed without having been carefully studied by a scientific eye. La Condamine endeavored to correct that with trips along the coasts of Africa and Asia and in 1730 had, as a result, been elected to the Academy of Sciences.

His great adventure, however, lay in an expedition to South America. It had, as its purpose, nothing less than the determination of the shape of the earth. The earth was, roughly speaking, a sphere, of course, but Newton [231] had pointed out that the speed of rotation of the earth's surface increased steadily from zero at the poles to a bit over a thousand miles an hour at the equator. Centrifugal force increased correspondingly and, in theory, the earth should then be an oblate spheroid, bulging at the equator and flattened at the poles.

The pendulum data reported by Richer [217] seemed to back Newton's views. However, Cassini [209] and his son, with their usual wrongheadedness, insisted on the basis of inadequate surveys in France that the earth's surface curved more and more as one traveled north. Therefore the earth was flattened at the equators and bulged at the poles and was a prolate spheroid. If the Cassinis were right, then the theory of universal gravitation was wrong. It became more and more important to check the matter.

It was decided to survey regions of the earth accurately to determine differences in surface curvature. To get the greatest differences in curvature, one expedition under La Condamine was sent in 1735 to Peru, almost on the equator. Another expedition, under Maupertuis [267], was sent to Lapland in the far north of Sweden. These expeditions were gatherings of giants, for included were Bouguer [264], Clairaut [283], and others of like caliber.

The results were quite conclusive. The earth's curvature was distinctly higher at the equator than at the poles. The earth was therefore an oblate spheroid, bulging at the equator and flattened at the poles. Newton, as was to be expected, was right, while the Cassinis, as was even more to be expected, were wrong.

La Condamine used his stay in South America to go off on an exploratory jaunt. He was the first European to explore the Amazon territory with any thoroughness, and he sent home quantities of a peculiar tree sap called caoutchouc, thus introducing what we now call rubber to Europe. He also discovered and brought back curare, the original of the mysterious South American poisons so beloved by mystery writers, which, however, is also used clinically as a muscle relaxant.

The expeditions to Peru and Lapland had made it quite plain that the delicate measurements being undertaken in the eighteenth century were being hampered by the lack of internationally accepted standard units of measure. La Condamine was in the forefront of the fight to establish such a system of measure but did not live long enough to see it accomplished in the 1790s, with the introduction of the metric system. He was also one of those who speculated on the feasibility of inoculation against smallpox but died twenty-two years before Jenner [348] introduced such inoculation successfully.

[271] **CELSIUS,** Anders (sel'see-us)
Swedish astronomer
Born: Uppsala, November 27, 1701
Died: Uppsala, April 25, 1744

Celsius was of a famous scientific family. His father and grandfather were mathematicians, his uncle a botanist. He studied the aurora borealis and, in his report in 1733, was the first to associate it with changes in the earth's magnetic field. He also took part in the expedition to Lapland under Maupertuis [267].

In 1730 he became professor of astronomy at Uppsala and in 1740 was placed in charge of a large new observatory there, which, however, he was not to enjoy for long, for he died at an early age. He was the first to try to determine the magnitude of stars by measuring the intensity of their light by a device other than the human eye.

His greatest accomplishment, as it happened, had nothing to do with astronomy. It concerned the temperature scale he devised, which divided the temperature difference between the boiling point and freezing point of water into an even hundred degrees. He first described this in 1742 when he placed the boiling point at 0° and the freezing point at 100°, but the next year this was reversed. This is the centigrade scale ("hundred steps") and is used by scientists everywhere. In 1948 it was decided by general agreement to begin to refer to it as the Celsius scale.

[272] **FRANKLIN,** Benjamin
American statesman and scientist
Born: Boston, Massachusetts, January 17, 1706
Died: Philadelphia, Pennsylvania, April 17, 1790

Benjamin Franklin was the fifteenth child of seventeen, born to a poor candlemaker. He was printer, writer, politician, diplomat, and scientist, quite a phenomenon in the New World in the eighteenth century, yet he only had two years of formal schooling. He was the only

American of colonial days to achieve a European reputation. He is best known to Americans, of course, as one of the founding fathers of the nation, but his fame in his own time, at least in Europe, was that of a natural philosopher. He founded America's first scientific society, the American Philosophic Society, in 1743.

His ingenuity showed itself in numerous inventions, notably the Franklin stove and bifocal glasses. However, it was in the field of electricity that he achieved his greatest results.

Static electricity had become a fascinating toy in the century since Guericke [189] had produced the first electric machine and Musschenbroek [257] his Leyden jar in 1745. The latter was actually a "condenser," a name coined by Volta [337] a half century later. It could store large quantities of static electric charge poured into it from a machine in which the charge was produced through friction. The Leyden jar could then be discharged when a hand was brought near the center rod, and if enough electricity had been stored in the first place, the owner of the hand would be given a shock he was not likely to forget. If the jar was brought near metal, a tiny jagged spark would leap across the air gap and this would be accompanied by a sharp crackle.

Many scientists were experimenting with Leyden jars, and Franklin was one of them. He noted the spark of light and the crackle and wondered whether these might not be a very miniature lightning and thunder. Or perhaps, looking at it from another standpoint, might not the majestic thunder and lightning of the heavens be but the interplay of electricity, with earth and sky making up the halves of a gigantic planetary Leyden jar?

Benjamin Franklin decided to attempt an experiment—one for which he lives dramatically in the minds of posterity. He flew a kite in a thunderstorm in 1752. The kite carried a pointed wire to which Franklin had attached a silk thread that could be charged by the electricity overhead; that is, if there was electricity overhead.

As the storm clouds gathered and lightning flickered, Franklin put his hand near a metal key tied to the silk thread and the key sparked just as a Leyden jar would have. Moreover, Franklin charged a Leyden jar from the key just as easily as he would have from a man-made electrical machine. Franklin's kite electrified the scientific world, and he was made a member of the Royal Society.

Franklin's luck was extreme, for the experiment is a killer. The next two men who tried to duplicate his feat were both killed. (At about the same time, however, Canton [290], in observations that involved no danger, pointed up another and more subtle connection between electricity and the sky.)

Franklin was able to put his experiment to practical use at once. His experimentation with the Leyden jar had shown him as long before as 1747 that it discharged more readily and over greater gaps of air if it came near a pointed surface. It was as if the pointed surface attracted the electricity. Franklin therefore suggested that pointed metal rods be placed above the roofs of buildings, with wires leading to the ground. Such lightning rods would discharge the clouds safely and protect the buildings themselves. They did indeed prove efficacious and by 1782 there were four hundred lightning rods in use in Philadelphia alone. Franklin had averted the artillery of Zeus.

When a quarter century later the aged Franklin represented the infant United States during the Revolutionary War at the court of France, he proved the ideal man for the job. Not only did his carefully affected Republican simplicity perversely appeal to the aristocrats at Versailles, but it was the Age of Reason, and educated Frenchmen fell all over the man who had tamed the lightning of the sky and brought it to earth. How much of America's successful birth can be traced back to a kite flying in a thunderstorm?

Franklin also performed an inestimable theoretical service to the science of electricity, with one accidental flaw. It was known that there were two kinds of electric charge. Two amber rods repelled each other if both were rubbed and electrified. Similarly two electrified glass rods repelled each other. An electrified amber rod, however, attracted an electrified glass rod. It seemed a case of "opposites attract and likes repel," as in magnetism, where the north pole of a magnet attracts the south pole of another, while two north poles repel each other and two south poles repel each other.

Franklin reasoned that this could be explained by supposing electricity to consist of a subtle fluid that could be present either in excess or in deficiency. Two substances containing an excess of the fluid repelled each other, as did two substances containing a deficiency. An object with an excess, however, would attract one with a deficiency; the excess would flow into the deficiency (over an air gap and accompanied by thunder and lightning sometimes) and the two electrifications would be neutralized.

Franklin suggested that an excess of the fluid be called positive electricity and a deficiency be called negative electricity.

A century and a half after Franklin's day, electricity came to be associated with subatomic particles, particularly with the electron, discovered by J. J. Thomson [869]. However, if static electricity is considered an accumulation of electrons or a deficiency of them, the situation as we understand it today is exactly what Franklin proposed.

Unfortunately the objects Franklin guessed contained the excess of electricity actually contain a deficiency of electrons. (He took an even-money stab in the dark and missed.) The electrician in setting up his circuits even today assumes that the electric current flows from the positive terminal to the negative, but the physicist knows that electrons flow from the negative terminal to the positive. It doesn't matter, however, which convention is followed as long as whoever is working with the circuit sticks to the same convention throughout.

Franklin's busy mind concerned itself with other matters as well. While in France he watched with extreme interest the early attempts at ballooning and involved himself in the medical theories of

Mesmer [314], coming to some remarkably sound conclusions as to psychoneuroses as a result.

He worked out (as well as he could) the course of storms over the North American continent and was the first to study the circulating belt of warm water in the North Atlantic that we now call the Gulf Stream.

In 1900 Franklin was selected as one of the charter members of the Hall of Fame for Great Americans.

[273] **DOLLOND**, John
English optician
Born: London, June 10, 1706
Died: London, November 30, 1761

Dollond was the son of a Huguenot refugee from France. (Louis XIV, because of his measures against the French Protestants in the 1680s, lost thousands of useful subjects to surrounding nations. Adolf Hitler was to make a similar mistake two and a half centuries later.)

Dollond began work in his father's trade of silk weaving but educated himself in his spare time, teaching himself Latin, Greek, mathematics, and science. In middle life he joined his own son in manufacturing optical instruments. Their work was unsurpassed until the time of Fraunhofer [450] over half a century later.

He followed the suggestions of David Gregory [240] and others and tried to develop lenses that in spite of Newton's [231] theories would not show chromatic aberration. Actually this feat had been accomplished in 1733, it is now known, but the results had not been published. Even so, Dollond had to fight the matter through the courts before he was awarded a patent.

In any case Dollond succeeded in 1758 and announced his results to the Royal Society, which awarded him the Copley medal and three years later elected him a member. In 1761 (the year of his death) he was even appointed optician to King George III.

Dollond solved the problem by using two different kinds of glass, which refracted the various colors of light in different ways and combined them in such a fashion that the action of one glass just counterbalanced the action of the other.

The invention of such an achromatic telescope kept the refracting instruments in the race with reflectors, though by the twentieth century the reflecting telescope was definitely the winner, thanks to the energy and enterprise of Hale [974]. Dollond's work also led to the invention of achromatic microscopes, a more important consequence, for in microscopy there was no easy substitute for refraction. Furthermore Dollond showed that Newton was definitely wrong in his contention that chromatic aberration could not be avoided, and it was a healthy thing for science to be shown that even Newton could be wrong.

[274] **CHÂTELET,** Gabrielle Émilie le
Tonnelier de Breteuil, marquise
du (shah-tlay')
French science writer
Born: Paris, December 17, 1706
Died: Luneville, Meurthe-et-
Moselle, September 10, 1749

Of noble birth, Gabrielle Émilie married the marquis de Châtelet in 1725. She bore him three children, after which he grew quite serious about his military career and saw her but infrequently. She didn't seem to take that much to heart but pursued her own life with the greatest of satisfaction.

She had been well educated in all the subjects deemed necessary to a cultured existence, including science, and from 1733 on she established a liaison with the leading intellectual figure of the age, Voltaire [261]. She was also a close friend of Maupertuis [267] who taught her mathematics and who encouraged her to continue with her science education and, later on, with Clairaut [283].

Because Voltaire was a great admirer of Newton [231], he urged the brilliant marquise to undertake the task of translating the *Principia Mathematica* from Latin into French. She began the task in 1745 and continued it till her death (in

childbirth) and did a masterly job of it. Voltaire wrote a preface and it appeared, complete, in 1759. Since most of Europe's intellectuals in those days could manage to make themselves understood in French and could read the language, her translation (still the only one in French) opened the meaning of the Newtonian universe to those continentals who were not at home in either Latin or English.

[275] **EULER,** Leonhard (oi'ler)
Swiss mathematician
Born: Basel, April 15, 1707
Died: St. Petersburg, Russia, September 18, 1783

Euler, the son of a Calvinist minister who dabbled in mathematics, studied under the Bernoullis and was a friend of Daniel Bernoulli [268]. Euler received his master's degree at sixteen from the University of Basel.

When the Bernoullis went to St. Petersburg, Russia, they persuaded Euler (in 1727) to follow, for there the Empress Catherine I (widow of Peter the Great) had recently founded the Petersburg Academy and there he succeeded Bernoulli as professor of mathematics in 1733.

In St. Petersburg in 1735 Euler lost the sight of his right eye through too-ardent observations of the sun in an attempt to work out a system of time determination.

In 1741, at a time when the young Ivan VI succeeded to the throne and times in Russia grew troubled, Euler went to Berlin. There he was to head and revivify the decaying Academy of Sciences, founded by Leibniz [233] at the invitation of the new king, Frederick II. He didn't get along with Frederick, a king who demanded approval of his wretched poetry and who had no appreciation for pure mathematics. Euler was remembered in Russia, however, and in 1760, during the Seven Years' War, when Russian troops occupied Berlin, Euler's house was given special protection.

In 1766, at the invitation of the new

empress, Catherine II (the Great), he returned to St. Petersburg and remained there for the rest of his life. During his second stay in Russia he challenged the visiting Diderot [286] to a debate on atheism. Euler, a religious man who in his youth had contemplated entering the ministry like his father, advanced his own argument in favor of God in the form of a simple and completely irrelevant algebraic equation. Poor Diderot, who knew no mathematics whatever, was speechless. Feeling a fool, he left Russia.

Euler was the most prolific mathematician of all time, writing on every branch of the subject and being always careful to describe his reasoning and to list the false paths he had followed. He lost the sight of his remaining eye in 1766 but that scarcely seemed to stop him or even slow him down, for he had a phenomenal memory and could keep in mind that which would fill several blackboards. He published eight hundred papers, some of them quite long, and at the time of his death, left enough papers behind to keep the printing presses busy for thirty-five years.

He applied his mathematics to astronomy, working out the nature of some perturbations, being in this respect the precursor of Lagrange [317] and Laplace [347]. He began to replace the geometric methods of proof used by Galileo [166] and Newton [231] with the algebraic, a tendency carried to its conclusion by Lagrange. In particular he worked on lunar theory, that is, on the analysis of the exact motion of the moon, the complications of which have been the despair of astronomers and mathematicians since the time of Kepler [169]. Although his results were far from perfect, they represented an improvement on what had gone before.

He also held that light was a wave form and that color depended on wavelength. A generation later, Young [402] demonstrated this conclusively.

Euler published a tremendously successful popularization of science in 1768, one that remained in print for ninety years. He died shortly after working out certain mathematical problems in con-

nection with ballooning, inspired by the successful flight of the Montgolfier brothers [325]. He introduced the symbol "e" for the base of natural logarithms, "i" for the square root of minus one, and "f( )" for functions.

[276] **LINNAEUS**, Carolus (lih-nee'us)
Swedish botanist
Born: Södra, Råshult, Småland,
May 23, 1707
Died: Uppsala, January 10, 1778

Linnaeus' name is the Latinized form of Carl von Linné. As a child he seemed rather dull, but his father, a pastor, sent him to medical school, first at Lund, then at Uppsala, a bit against his will. Fortunately, put to the test, young Linnaeus made out well scholastically. Financially, though, he came close to disaster at this time. Luckily for him, Celsius [271], then teaching at Uppsala, took the young man into his home.

Linnaeus had always been interested in plants and even as an eight-year-old he had gained the affectionate nickname of "the little botanist." This interest continued at college and he studied, in particular, the stamens and pistils.

Linnaeus wrote a paper on the subject and this led him to feel that he could introduce a new and better classification of plants based on their sexual organs. In 1732 the University of Uppsala (where he was already lecturing on botany as Rudbeck [218] had done before him) asked him to visit Lapland to examine its flora. This he did, traveling forty-six hundred miles throughout northern Scandinavia, discovering a hundred new species of plants and carefully observing the animal life as well. His interest in sex led to an interesting by-product: he was the first to use the symbols ♂ and ♀ for "male" and "female."

He followed this up by traveling through England and west Europe. In 1735 *Systema Naturae* was published. In this famous book Linnaeus established the classification of living things in a particularly methodical way, completely overshadowing the prior work of Ray

[213] and emerging as the founder of modern taxonomy.

In the first place he developed a clear and concise style of describing species that pointed out exactly how each differed from other species. In the second place he popularized binomial nomenclature, in which each type of living thing is given first a generic name (for the group to which it belongs) and then a specific name for itself. Linnaeus' book, published originally in seven large pages, had expanded to twenty-five hundred pages by the tenth edition.

Linnaeus' passion for classification amounted almost to a disease. He was not content merely to list the species and collect them into related groups, or genera. He grouped related genera into classes, and related classes into orders. (Later Cuvier [396] was to extend this notion by grouping related orders into phyla.) Linnaeus, despite his conservative piety, dared even to include man in his classification, giving the human species the name of Homo sapiens ("Man, wise") though he confined this classification to man's body alone. He considered his soul to be outside the animal kingdom.

He included the orangutan in the same genus with man as Homo troglodytes ("Man, cave-dwelling"), but this did not endure. He also classified whales and related species as mammals, thus finally establishing a point of view first advanced by Aristotle [29] two thousand years earlier.

While classification is perhaps not the highest function of science, it can be indispensable in a diverse and amorphous field of study. It was only after Linnaeus had imposed order (somewhat artificially, to be sure) upon life, that biologists could search confidently for great generalizations. The manner in which the classification began with large groups, divided into smaller groups, then still smaller groups, ending finally with individual species, gave the system of living organisms the appearance of a tree. The very existence of such a tree of life helped activate and sharpen the hazy notions of an evolution of living things from simple beginnings to modern complexity. Such thoughts can be traced back to the ancient Greeks, but after Linnaeus the search for some way to systematize those thoughts began in earnest.

Linnaeus himself fought the whole idea of evolution stubbornly, insisting that all species were created separately in the beginning, that no new species had ever been formed since Creation and that none had ever become extinct.

He may have begun to waver toward the end of his life, but in any case his opposition could not stem the tide. His own view had affected his philosophy of classification, for he was not concerned in ordering the world of living things to show family relationships that he did not believe existed. He wanted only to differentiate the various species in the clearest way he could, so his classification was an artificial one based on the external characteristics most obvious to the eye.

Men who followed him, like Cuvier, Jussieu [345], and Candolle [418], kept the principles of Linnaean classification but changed the details to make it a natural one showing relationships. Once that was done, more followed inevitably. Linnaeus had begun a train of thinking that led inexorably to Darwin [554], and the rigidly orthodox Swedish botanist could have done nothing to stay that.

When Linnaeus finally returned to Sweden he entered medical practice and in 1741 was appointed to the chair of medicine at Uppsala. One year later he exchanged it for the chair of botany. He spent the remainder of his life in teaching. He was an excellent teacher, inspiring his students with the same ardor that had moved him, for he sent them out (and they went gladly) through the world in search of new forms of life. It is estimated that one out of three died in the search.

In 1761—by an act antedated to 1757—he was ennobled and given the right to call himself Carl von Linné and was appointed a member of the Swedish House of Nobles. He died in Uppsala Cathedral, where he is interred.

After his death, his books and collections were bought by the rich English naturalist Sir J. E. Smith, who took them to England. There they served as the basis of the famous English biological association called the Linnaean Society, which was founded in 1788, ten years after Linnaeus' death. There is a famous story (dramatic, but untrue) that the Swedish navy sent a warship to try to capture the ship that was carrying these Swedish treasures to England.

In 1866, changes were reported in the lunar crater named for him; these changes have not yet been satisfactorily explained.

[277] **BUFFON,** Georges Louis Leclerc, comte de (byoo-fohn')
French naturalist
Born: Montbard, Burgundy, September 7, 1707
Died: Paris, April 16, 1788

Buffon came of a well-to-do family. He traveled extensively and was able to indulge his taste for learning. He studied both law at Dijon and medicine at Angers, obtaining a degree in the former in 1726. A duel he fought in Angers made it seem wise to him to get out of town. He fell in with a young Englishman at Nantes and they traveled together, including a trip to England.

Buffon was strongly impressed by England's upsurge of science and translated Newton's [231] work on the calculus in order to practice his English. He was interested in the work of Stephen Hales [249] on plants and this too he translated. He also conducted experiments to see if Archimedes [47] could really have burned Roman ships with lenses focusing the sun's rays; he decided it was possible.

He was elected to the Royal Society in 1730, while he was in England, to the Academy of Sciences in 1733, and in 1739 became keeper of the Jardin du Roi, the French botanical gardens, and was thus led into a permanent interest in natural history. Beginning in 1752 and continuing for fifty years, volume after volume of his *Natural History* appeared. There were forty-four volumes altogether, written with various collaborators, the last eight volumes being published after his death.

The treatise was written clearly and attractively for the general public and was the first modern work to attempt to treat the whole of nature. It was deservedly popular but was nevertheless better as popular writing than as science, for Buffon wanted to see grand designs in nature even when it meant doing violence to details. As a result he had a tendency to superficiality and too-easy generalization. In short, there was rather a touch of the Pliny [61] in him.

Buffon was groping toward a concept of evolution in his work. He was temperamentally unsuited to the painstaking work of a Linnaeus [276], which made it all the easier for him to see life as a grand movement. He noted that some creatures had parts that were useless to them (such as the lateral toes of the pig) and from this deduced that parts might degenerate and whole animals do the same. An ape might be considered, then, an imperfect or corrupted man, a donkey an imperfect horse, and so on. These ideas were carried further by Erasmus Darwin [308].

Buffon also advanced generalized notions, more rhetoric than reasoned science perhaps, concerning the slow development of the earth. He suggested, in 1745, that the earth might have been created by the catastrophic collision of a massive body (he called it a comet) with the sun. The view was outdistanced by the nebular hypothesis of Kant [293] and Laplace [347], but a form of it was to make a strong showing in the first half of the twentieth century. Buffon also felt the earth might have been in existence for as much as seventy-five thousand years, with life itself having come into existence perhaps forty thousand years ago. This was the first attempt in Christian Europe to probe back beyond the six-thousand-year limit apparently set by the Book of Genesis, something soon to reach a climax with Hutton [297]. Buffon also felt that the earth might last ninety thousand years before cooling completely.

These evolutionary views concerning earth and man, although cautiously phrased, were daring in an epoch when the view was that earth and man were created whole and at once some six thousand years before. Nevertheless Buffon was a diplomatic person who knew when to recant any views that aroused too much opposition. He had only minor difficulties with authority and was eventually made a count by Louis XV.

His son was less fortunate and was guillotined during the French Revolution.

[278] **HALLER,** Albrecht von (hahl'er)
Swiss physiologist
Born: Berne, October 16, 1708
Died: Berne, December 17, 1777

Haller, the son of a lawyer, was forced into quiet amusements as a child, because of ill health, and quickly showed himself to be a prodigy. He began writing on scholarly subjects at the age of eight, prepared a Greek dictionary at ten, and kept right on going. He studied under Boerhaave [248], whose favorite student he was, and eventually became a physician with wide-ranging tastes, beginning his practice in 1729 when he was only twenty-one.

He was interested in botany, among other things, and collected plants, eventually writing a large book on the flora of Switzerland. For seventeen years, from 1736 to 1753, he taught at the University of Göttingen as professor of medicine, anatomy, surgery, and botany. Then he retired to his hometown to write an encyclopedic summary of medicine, and various romances in addition, to say nothing of didactic poetry (rather better than that of Erasmus Darwin [308]) and works on politics.

His most important contribution to science was his research on muscles and nerves, published in 1766. Until his time it was believed that nerves were hollow and carried a mysterious spirit or fluid, which was never demonstrated. Even Boerhaave, a great rationalist otherwise, made this concession to mysticism.

Haller, however, believing in no spirit that could not be seen or worked with, stuck to the experimental observations. He recognized that muscles were irrita-

ble, that is, that a slight stimulus to the muscle would produce a sharp contraction. He also showed that a stimulus to a nerve would produce a sharp contraction in the muscle to which it was attached. The nerve was the more irritable and required the smaller stimulus. Haller judged that it was nervous stimulation rather than direct muscular stimulation that controlled muscular movement. He also showed that tissues themselves do not experience a sensation but that the nerves channel and carry the impulses that produce the sensation.

Furthermore Haller showed that nerves all led to the brain or the spinal cord, which were thus clearly indicated as the centers of sense perception and responsive action. He experimented by stimulating or damaging various parts of the animal brain and then noting the type of action or paralysis that resulted. Haller may therefore be considered the founder of modern neurology.

In later life, Haller seems to have become an opium addict, as a result of using opium to counteract insomnia.

[279] **MARGGRAF,** Andreas Sigismund (mahrk'grahf)
German chemist
Born: Berlin, March 3, 1709
Died: Berlin, August 7, 1782

Marggraf was the son of the apothecary to the Prussian court, and he himself had a kind of itinerant education studying under apothecaries, chemists, and metallurgists in various parts of Germany.

Eventually he returned to Prussia, was elected to the Royal Academy of Sciences there, and made the director of its chemical laboratory by Frederick II.

Among Marggraf's achievements in chemistry was the fact that in 1754 he distinguished alumina from lime. That discovery was a harbinger of the time when each would be found to contain a different chemical element: alumina is aluminum oxide and lime is calcium oxide.

He also studied the oxidation of phosphorus in 1740 (which of course he didn't understand as an oxidation, since oxygen and its significance had to await Lavoisier [334]). He recorded the fact that phosphorus gained weight when it was oxidized, which did not fit in with Stahl's [241] phlogiston theory, which Marggraf wholeheartedly accepted. (He was the last important German chemist to do so.) The gain in weight, which Marggraf reported but did not attempt to explain, was important to Lavoisier later on.

Marggraf's greatest achievement, however, was the extraction of a crystalline substance from various common plants, including beets, which, on investigation, turned out to be identical to cane sugar. This finding, made in 1747, laid the foundation of Europe's important sugarbeet industry.

[280] **GMELIN,** Johann Georg (guh-may'lin)
German explorer
Born: Tübingen, Württemberg, August 10, 1709
Died: Tübingen, May 20, 1755

Gmelin, the son of an apothecary, obtained his medical degree in 1727. He followed a couple of his teachers to St. Petersburg, and by 1731 held a professorial appointment in chemistry there.

In 1733, he joined one of the expeditions that Russia was sending out to study and explore the Siberian wilderness in the wake of Bering's [250] important explorations.

Among the interesting observations Gmelin made in the course of his explorations were the barometric pressure readings he took in Astrakhan, at the mouth of the Volga River where it flows into the Caspian. He was thus able to show for the first time that the shores of the Caspian lie below sea level.

In 1735, at the Siberian town of Yeniseysk, he recorded the lowest temperature recorded up to that time. It was the first indication that the earth could, in spots, be far colder than home-bound Europeans realized.

In eastern Siberia, he was the first to note that though the frost in the upper-most layer of soil melted under the summer sun, the ground a little way beneath remained solidly frozen all summer long. He thus discovered the existence of permafrost, a very important feature of the polar regions.

At home in Tübingen, where he became professor of medicine, botany, and chemistry in 1749, he reported on the appearance of five or six new plant forms in his St. Petersburg garden. He couldn't explain this in terms of the fixity of species which Linnaeus [276] believed in and which the Biblical account of creation made orthodox. The explanation awaited De Vries [792] a century and a half later.

[281] **WRIGHT,** Thomas
English astronomer
Born: Byers Green, near Durham, September 22, 1711
Died: Byers Green, February 25, 1786

Wright did not exactly have an easy youth. He was the son of a carpenter, and he had little schooling because a speech impediment made life difficult for him. When he grew interested in astronomy and began to study it feverishly, his unsympathetic father burned his books, holding them to be frivolous and time-wasting. Wright was apprenticed to a clockmaker but at eighteen some sort of scandal impelled him to flee home.

He continued to study and, away from his father's influence, he suffered no further book burning. In the course of a continued unsettled life he studied navigation and astronomy; and, speech impediment notwithstanding or surmounted, he began to teach these subjects. By 1742, he was even offered a formal teaching position in St. Petersburg, but that fell through.

Wright was a religious man who tried to build a model of the universe, with God and heaven at the center and a region of darkness and doom at the rim, and with the stars (including the solar system) circling the center inside the outer region of doom. This notion, first advanced in 1750, was the first indication that the sun was no more the center of the universe than the earth was, but that all the stars including the sun moved in orbit.

Furthermore, he reasoned from the existence of the Milky Way that the system of stars was not symmetrical in all directions but was flattened. The Milky Way was the appearance of the stars viewed through the long axis of the flattened system. Stripped of its mysticism, Wright was the first to see the stars as existing in a flattened, rotating galaxy.

[282] **LOMONOSOV,** Mikhail Vasilievich (luh-muh-noh′suf)
Russian chemist and writer
Born: Denisovka (near Archangel), November 19, 1711
Died: St. Petersburg (modern Leningrad), April 15, 1765

Lomonosov was the bookish son of a well-to-do shipowner. He made his way to Moscow when he was seventeen (partly to escape a stepmother) and managed to secure admission to school by pretending to be the son of a nobleman.

His excellent progress resulted in his being sent first to St. Petersburg and then to the University of Marburg in Germany (advanced education in chemistry was not to be had in Russia in those days). He returned to St. Petersburg and was appointed a professor of chemistry at the university in 1745.

In the course of his work he published antiphlogistic views during the 1740s and 1750s and suggested the law of conservation of mass. In important ways he anticipated Lavoisier [334]. He also held atomist views, which he thought were too revolutionary to publish. He espoused the theory of heat as a form of motion as Rumford [360] was to do and the wave theory of light as Young [402] was to do. In all these cases, he was ahead of his time.

He was the first to record the freezing of mercury. (This took place during a very cold Russian winter, for mercury freezes at forty degrees below zero.) He and a friend tried to repeat the kite experiment of Franklin [272]. The friend was killed and Lomonosov barely escaped.

In astronomy he was the first to observe the atmosphere of Venus, during its transit across the sun in 1761, though the fact of his discovery remained unknown outside Russia for a century and a half. Lomonosov was the founder of Russian science, and he would be universally recognized as a great pioneer of science had he only been born a West European. He was famous also for his literary works, including poems and dramas. In 1755 he wrote a Russian grammar that reformed the language and in the same year he, along with Euler [275], helped found the University of Moscow. In 1760 he published the first history of Russia; he was also the first to prepare an accurate map of that country. And yet Russian scientists were looked down upon, even inside Russia, by the men of German extraction who monopolized Russian science through the nineteenth century. Lomonosov quarreled with his German colleague, grew embittered, and in his last years took to drink.

Virtually unknown to the Western nations, he is amply honored by the Soviet Union now. His birthplace of Denisovka had its name changed to Lomonosov in 1948. In 1960, when a Soviet satellite circled the moon and photographed part of its hidden side, one of the craters revealed was named for him.

[283] **CLAIRAUT,** Alexis Claude (klay-roh′)
French mathematician
Born: Paris, May 7, 1713
Died: Paris, May 17, 1765

Clairaut, who was tutored by his mathematician father, was a prodigy, studying the calculus at ten, writing mathematical papers at thirteen, publishing a book of mathematics at eighteen. The last earned him a membership in the French Academy of Sciences in 1731 even though he was below the legal age. (He had a brother who wrote on mathematics at the age of nine, but that brother died at sixteen.)

Clairaut accompanied Maupertuis

[267] to Lapland, where he helped determine the length of the meridian. This led in 1743 to his writing a book on the shape of a rotating body like the earth, acting under the influence of gravity and centrifugal force. He went far beyond Newton [231] in his analysis and produced what is virtually the last word on the subject. He also showed how the shape of the earth could be calculated experimentally by measuring the force of gravity at different points through the timing of pendulum swings.

Clairaut was one of those who did much work on the motions of the moon (lunar theory), a popular pastime among eighteenth-century astronomers. He calculated the effects of the gravitational pull of Venus on earth as compared with the pull of the moon. Combining this with some of the observations of Lacaille [284], he obtained in 1757 the first reasonable figure for the mass of Venus ($\frac{2}{3}$ that of the earth) and a new figure for the mass of the moon ($\frac{1}{67}$ that of the earth). The former estimate is now known to be somewhat too small, the latter too high, but both were the best obtained up to that time. For a while, his studies on celestial mechanics created a particular stir for they seemed to disprove Newton's theories. On the advice of Buffon [277], he extended his observations and found Newton to be right after all.

As the year approached during which —as Halley [238] had predicted a half century before—Halley's comet would return, Clairaut with the assistance of Lalande [309] worked out the effect of the gravity of Jupiter and Saturn upon the comet. He found that the two giant planets would slow it to the point where it would not reach the point closest the sun in its orbit (perihelion) until April 13, 1759. It was spotted on Christmas Day 1758 and reached perihelion within a month of the predicted time.

[284] **LACAILLE,** Nicolas Louis de (la-kah′yuh)
French astronomer
Born: Rumigny, Marne, May 15, 1713
Died: Paris, March 21, 1762

Lacaille, the son of a gendarme, intended to enter the Roman Catholic priesthood, but, with the help of Cassini [209], his interests drifted toward astronomy and mathematics and the church lost out. He was commonly referred to by the title "abbé," however.

He attained professorial rank at Mazarin College in 1739.

The most important event of Lacaille's life was directing an expedition to the Cape of Good Hope from 1750 to 1754. His purpose was to obtain an accurate figure for the moon's parallax in combination with observations by Lalande [309] in Berlin.

From his observations in South Africa he prepared a catalogue of nearly two thousand southern stars plus a star map which was much more extensive and accurate than Halley's [238]. He discovered Alpha Centauri, our nearest stellar neighbor, to be a double star and he filled the southern heavens with constellations named for astronomical instruments.

In 1757 he prepared 120 copies of a small but very accurate catalogue of 400 of the brightest stars, more accurate, in fact, than any work except that of Bradley [258], which was then being issued. Despite his poverty Lacaille gave away copies of his chart to any who asked. In 1761 he made a new and more accurate estimate of the distance of the moon, using calculations that for the first time took into account the fact that the earth was not a perfect sphere.

His unremitting labor at his star charts, singlehanded, is supposed to have shortened his life.

[285] **NEEDHAM,** John Turberville
English naturalist
Born: London, September 10, 1713
Died: Brussels, Belgium, December 30, 1781

Needham was ordained a Roman Catholic priest in 1738, and to get an education for that purpose in those days, he had to leave England. He finally settled in Brussels in 1768.

His most notable contribution to science was his experimentation in 1748, in collaboration with Buffon [277], on spontaneous generation. He boiled mutton broth and sealed it in glass containers. When the containers were opened a few days later, there were numerous microorganisms present. These, he concluded, had arisen from nonliving matter. It was twenty years later that Spallanzani [302] showed that Needham simply hadn't boiled his broth long enough and that some spores had survived the short boiling period.

In 1768, he was elected to the Royal Society, the first Roman Catholic to acquire the distinction. When he died, he was the director of the Academy of Sciences at Brussels.

[286] **DIDEROT**, Denis (dee-droh')
French encyclopedist
Born: Langres, Haute-Marne, October 5, 1713
Died: Paris, July 31, 1784

As a youngster Diderot, the son of a master cutler, was educated at a Jesuit school, but the education did not take in certain ways, although he received a master's degree from the University of Paris in 1732. He might have been a doctor or a lawyer, but he preferred to make a precarious living by small writings of all sorts, fiction, essays, translations, anything and to teach himself science, as well. He produced some valuable material, too. He wrote a pamphlet, for instance, that represented the first serious study of deaf-mutes. He developed notions on religion, despite his training, that seemed heretical, even atheistic, and spent three months in jail in 1749 possibly because in one of his essays he speculated on the possibility that evolution might take place through a form of natural selection. In this there was an interesting anticipation of Charles Darwin [554] and the theory he was to propound a century later.

Life really began for Diderot when he emerged from prison. A bookseller suggested to him that he translate an English encyclopedia into French. Diderot agreed and quickly decided to make it a different and better project, to commission the best scholars in France to write articles on every facet of the new learning of Newton [231] and his followers. The mathematician D'Alembert [289] became his colleague and the first volume was published in 1751. For twenty years thereafter, additional volumes, first of text, then of plates, were produced, the Encyclopedia being completed in 1772 in twenty-eight volumes.

It was a superhuman labor, for the authorities from the beginning frowned on a work that, while not openly subversive, was riddled with views that ran counter to the accepted theories of monarchic absolutism and religious orthodoxy. It was legally suppressed in 1759, when it was half done.

Diderot continued working on it clandestinely. Many of his collaborators and commissioned writers, including D'Alembert, quit, not wishing to risk imprisonment. Diderot continued virtually alone, performing prodigies of self-education and composition, ending by writing many major articles himself. In the end the bookseller who was publishing the volumes turned prudent and eliminated many passages he believed too risky to include.

The work, when done, accomplished a great deal. It was the first of the great encyclopedias, and it brought all the scientific views of the Age of Reason into one place where the general public might reach them.

The Encyclopedia may have made Diderot famous, but it did not make him rich. Over a period of twenty years it had earned him perhaps twelve dollars a week. Once it was completed he decided to sell his library, out of financial necessity, in order to supply a dowry for his daughter. The empress of Russia, Catherine II (the Great) intervened. She bought it for five thousand dollars, then asked him to keep it for her and serve as her librarian at an annual salary. He was even invited to St. Petersburg in 1773 for some months of philosophizing with the empress. (She was even more oppressive in her country than Louis XV was in France, but she fancied herself a liberal, as long as that liberality was confined to high philosophy and never had to be put into practice.)

Diderot died just five years too soon to see the beginning of the French Revolution. The Encyclopedia had done much to rouse the emotions that were to explode in violence in 1789 and thereafter, so perhaps the old French government had been right to fear the industrious scribbler.

[287] **GUETTARD,** Jean Étienne (geh-tahrd')
French geologist
Born: Étampes, Seine-et-Oise, September 22, 1715
Died: Paris, January 6, 1786

Guettard studied medicine at the University of Paris and like other physicians of the day was keenly interested in natural history, botany in particular. He kept the natural history collections of the duke of Orléans.

Guettard observed the rocks of central France and, although he had never seen a volcano, he had read enough descriptions of eruptions and their results to decide that the rocks he saw had been formed at high temperatures. He was not quite ready to suppose the existence of a volcanic past, but others, notably Desmarest [296], took this logical final step.

[288] **LIND,** James
Scottish physician
Born: Edinburgh, October 4, 1716
Died: Gosport, Hampshire, England, July 13, 1794

Lind, the son of a merchant, began his medical career as surgeon's mate in the British navy and was promoted to surgeon in 1747. He left the navy in 1748 and obtained a medical degree at the University of Edinburgh in that year.

It was natural for him to become interested in scurvy, a disease that attacked men on long sea voyages. Great Britain, as a maritime nation and dependent for its national security on the efficiency of its fleet, was most threatened by this disease, which killed far more sailors than enemy action did. (Its most eminent victim, perhaps, was Bering [250].)

Lind believed scurvy to be caused—and curable—by diet, after reading of the disease in besieged towns and exploring expeditions, wherever the diet was limited and monotonous, without fresh fruits and vegetables.

In 1747, he treated scurvy-ridden sailors with various foods and found that citrus fruits worked amazingly well in effecting relief. When he was placed in charge of the naval hospital at Haslar in 1758 he began attempts to get the navy to adopt citrus fruit as a dietary staple. Unfortunately, brass hats are notoriously conservative and progress was slow. Captain Cook [300] kept off scurvy by this means in his great expedition in the 1770s, losing only one man in three years, and still the navy hesitated. Lind became physician to King George III in 1783 and still could not carry his point.

In 1795, British sailors mutinied against vile treatment of all sorts. The British suppressed the mutiny brutally, but they were engaged in a desperate war with the French revolutionaries and they could not afford to keep the sailors sullen and disaffected. They therefore instituted reforms. One of the sailors' demands had been to make use of Lind's findings, so the navy adopted the practice of feeding lime juice to the sailors. Scurvy was wiped out, and British sailors have been called "limeys" ever since. It was to be a century before the work of Eijkman [888] and others showed that Lind unknowingly was treating a vitamin-deficiency disease by supplying vitamins in the diet.

Lind also strove for the establishment of hospital ships in tropic waters, for cleanliness and good ventilation in sick bays, and is generally considered the father of naval hygiene. He also suggested that sea water be made a source of shipboard fresh water, through distillation, a matter now of world importance.

[289] **D'ALEMBERT,** Jean le Rond
(dah-lahn-bear')
French mathematician
Born: Paris, November 16, 1717
Died: Paris, October 29, 1783

D'Alembert was brought up by a glazier and his wife, after having been found abandoned at the church of St. Jean-le-Rond, from which he derived his name. He was the illegitimate son of an aristocrat who did, however, contribute to his support. In later years, when his talents were clearly evident, his mother tried to claim him, but D'Alembert proudly refused her. "The glazier's wife is my mother," he said. He never married and lived with his foster parents till he was forty-seven.

He graduated from Mazarin College in 1735 and was admitted to the Academy of Sciences in 1741, becoming its perpetual secretary in 1772. He worked on gravitational theory, particularly on the precession of the equinoxes, and sponsored both Lagrange [317] and Laplace [347], who completed the job. For a time, he aided in the preparation of the great Encyclopedia of Diderot [286], writing the introduction to it, yet despite the "anti-establishment" character of this work, he received a pension from Louis XV.

As was true of many of the great minds of the time D'Alembert was invited to Berlin by Frederick II and to St. Petersburg by Catherine II, but he refused both invitations. Rather out of character for D'Alembert is the fact that he bitterly disputed with Clairaut [283], apparently driven by jealousy of the latter's work on Halley's comet.

[290] **CANTON,** John
English physicist
Born: Stroud, Gloucestershire, July 31, 1718
Died: London, March 22, 1772

Canton, the son of a weaver, had little formal schooling, since his father took him out of school to work at the family business. Canton persisted in studying at

night and a minister in the neighborhood, recognizing the young man's talent, offered to take charge of him.

With this help, Canton eventually learned enough to become a schoolmaster. He made a number of minor discoveries in physics and chemistry. He prepared artificial magnets in 1749 and was elected to the Royal Society as a result. In 1762 he demonstrated the fact that water was slightly compressible. He invented a number of devices in connection with electricity.

His most interesting observations were made between 1756 and 1759, when he noted that on certain days the compass needle was more irregular than usual and that on those same days the aurora borealis was sometimes very conspicuous. This was the first observation of what are now called magnetic storms and led to the discovery of electric charges in the sky far higher than the clouds, by such men as Appleton [1158], a century and a half later.

[291] **BONNET,** Charles (boh-nay')
Swiss naturalist
Born: Geneva, March 13, 1720
Died: Genthod, near Geneva, May 20, 1793

Bonnet, born of a wealthy French family, was not a good student in his youth. It didn't help him that he was afflicted with increasing deafness. A private tutor was engaged and eventually he studied law and obtained his degree in 1743.

His hobby was natural history, however, and in the pursuit of that hobby he spent his quiet life, during the course of which he never left Switzerland.

His most interesting discovery was that the tiny insects called aphids could reproduce parthenogenetically—the female eggs could develop without the fertilizing action of the sperm. He also studied the respiration of insects and found in 1742 they breathed through pores which he named "stigmata." He noted the capacity of a very simple animal, the freshwater hydra, to regenerate lost parts. The result was that at the age of twenty-three, when he received his law degree, he was also elected to the Royal Society.

In the 1750s his eyes began failing him, and to concentrate on tiny life-forms came to be beyond his powers. He turned to speculation. The fact that aphids produced parthenogenetically made him feel that every creature already existed, preformed, in the egg, and somewhere within that creature was a smaller egg with another creature, pre-formed, within it, and so on without end. Generation nested within generation.

This made it seem that species were fixed and could not change and this, in turn, made it necessary to explain those fossils that resembled no living creatures. This explanation Bonnet found by postulating periodic catastrophes involving all the earth. The fossils were remnants of creatures that dwelt before a catastrophe. Bonnet believed that after each catastrophe all forms of life stepped a notch upward, and he predicted a future catastrophe after which apes would be men and men would be angels.

The principle of catastrophism dominated geological thinking for a generation after Bonnet's death, thanks to its adoption by Cuvier [396]. It was Bonnet who first made use of the term "evolution."

[292] **CRONSTEDT**, Axel Fredrik
(kroon'stet)
Swedish mineralogist
Born: Stroepsta, Södermanland,
December 23, 1722
Died: Stockholm, August 19,
1765

Cronstedt was the son of a high army officer and received a good education. As a youngster he grew interested in mining and mineralogy and studied under Brandt [260]. His career was interrupted by army service between 1741 and 1743 when Sweden was at war with Russia.

Cronstedt's researches paralleled those of his teacher. Brandt had discovered cobalt in an ore that resembled copper ore but was not copper ore. Well, there was a second type of ore that resembled copper ore without being copper ore, and this, too, received a name that testified to the belief of the miners that the false ore was bewitched. It was called Kupfernickel ("Old Nick's copper," in reference to the devil). On the other hand, this false copper ore was not a cobalt ore either and did not impart a blue color to glass as cobalt ore did.

In 1751 Cronstedt tackled this ore and obtained green crystals that, when heated with charcoal, yielded a white metal that certainly was not copper. It resembled iron and cobalt, though it was different from both. Cronstedt discovered that, like iron but much less strongly, the new metal was attracted by a magnet—the first time anything but iron had been found subject to magnetic attraction since the days of Thales [3] twenty-three centuries before.

In 1754 Cronstedt gave the new metal a shortened form of the old miners' name and called it nickel. There followed twenty years of controversy as to whether nickel was really a new metal or just a complex mixture of old ones, but Cronstedt's view won out, though he did not live to see it.

Cronstedt was one of those who reformed mineralogy and initiated a classification of minerals not only according to their appearance, but also according to their chemical structure. A book detailing this new form of classification was published in 1758.

Cronstedt introduced the blowpipe into the study of minerals. By directing a thin jet of air into a flame, it increased the heat of the flame. When this hot flame impinged on minerals, much information could be learned from the color of the flame, the vapors formed, the color and nature of the oxides or metallic substances formed out of the mineral, and so on. He thus systematized and sharpened the technique of observing color changes as a means of chemical analysis—a technique which had been foreshadowed a century earlier by Glauber [190].

For a century the blowpipe remained the most useful instrument in the armory of the chemical analyst, but its use called for a great skill that not all chemists possessed. It was rendered obsolete by the invention of the system of spectral analysis by Kirchhoff [648].

[293] **KANT**, Immanuel
German philosopher
Born: Königsberg, East Prussia (now Kaliningrad, Soviet Union), April 22, 1724
Died: Königsberg, February 12, 1804

Kant, the son of a saddlemaker of Scottish descent, spent all his life in his obscure home town, never traveling more than sixty miles from it in his eighty years of life, following a regime so time-bound that his neighbors could almost set their clocks by him.

He is best known as a profound philosopher and as the author of *Critique of Pure Reason,* published in 1781, a comprehensive scheme of philosophy of most Teutonic thoroughness. In his youth, however, he had studied mathematics and physics at the University of Königsberg and in 1755, the year he obtained his doctor's degree, he had published his physical view of the universe in *General History of Nature and Theory of the Heavens.*

This book contained three important anticipations. First, he described the nebular hypothesis, anticipating Laplace [347]. Second, he suggested the Milky Way was a lens-shaped collection of stars and that other such "island universes" existed, an anticipation of Herschel [321] and of twentieth-century astronomy. Finally he suggested that tidal friction slowed the rotation of the earth, a suggestion that was correct but could not be demonstrated for another century.

In 1770 he became professor of mathematics at the University of Königsberg, but in 1797 he shifted his attention to metaphysics and to logic. His daring speculations were made possible by the fact that he was patronized and protected by the freethinking Frederick II of Prussia. After Frederick's death, Kant had to be more cautious.

[294] **MICHELL**, John (mich'el)
English geologist
Born: Nottinghamshire, 1724
Died: Thornhill, Yorkshire, April 21, 1793

Michell obtained a master's degree at Cambridge in 1752. He was appointed rector of St. Michael's Church in Leeds and held the post till his death.

He presented solid reasons for thinking the stars were light-years distant in 1784, half a century before Bessel [439] and others demonstrated the fact. He also preceded Herschel [321] in suspecting the existence of binary stars.

He invented a torsion balance similar to that which Coulomb [318] later invented. With it he was going to measure the strength of the gravitational constant, but he died before he had the chance and it was Cavendish [307] who carried it through.

Michell is remembered for another accomplishment. In 1760, five years after an earthquake at Lisbon that was so sudden and destructive that Europe was nearly panicked, Michell suggested that earthquakes set up wave motions in the earth. He noted the frequency of earthquakes in the vicinity of volcanoes and suggested that the quakes started as the result of gas pressure produced by water boiling through volcanic heat. He felt that earthquakes might start under the ocean floor and argued that the Lisbon earthquake was an example of that. He further pointed out that by noting the time at which the motions were felt, one could calculate the center of the earthquake. A century and a quarter later, this was brought to pass by Milne [814]. Michell is rightly considered the father of seismology.

[295] **LE GENTIL**, Guillaume Joseph Hyacinthe Jean Baptiste (luh-zhahn-teel')
French astronomer
Born: Coutances, Manche, September 12, 1725
Died: Paris, October 22, 1792

Le Gentil, the son of a good-family-come-down-in-the-world, studied theology at the University of Paris and grew interested in astronomy there. Soon, he involved himself in work at the Paris Observatory, and the stage was set for an almost unbelievable set of astronomical misfortunes.

He was commissioned to go to India in order to observe the transit of Venus in 1761. He was to view it from Pondicherry on India's southeastern coast. The Seven Years' War was raging and Great Britain was fighting France in India. Just as Le Gentil reached India he found the British had taken Pondicherry and he was forced to remain on board ship during the transit. No decent observations were possible.

However, another transit was due in 1769. There were no airplanes then and Le Gentil did not wish to go back to France and then back to India in long, long voyages on the miserable ships of the day. He decided to remain in India for eight years. There were no electric communications in those days and no easy way to inform the people back home of this decision.

In 1769, he had to choose between Manila and Pondicherry for the observation. He decided on Manila but Pondicherry was again a French possession and political decisions on the spot forced him to remain there. Came the crucial day: In Manila, the sun shone out of a cloudless sky. In Pondicherry, where Le Gentil was observing, clouds obscured the sun just during the time of transit.

He returned to France to find himself considered dead and his heirs in possession of his property. —Oh, well, he straightened things out as best he could, married, had a daughter, and wrote a monumental and highly regarded two-volume book on India, so all was not lost.

[296] **DESMAREST,** Nicolas (day-muh-rest′)
French geologist
Born: Soulaines, Aube, September 16, 1725
Died: Paris, September 28, 1815

Just before the French Revolution, Desmarest, the son of a schoolteacher, was appointed inspector general and director of manufactures of France. As a royal appointee, he could not help but be under suspicion, and at the worst of the eventual Terror he was imprisoned. He survived, however, to be recalled to government service.

A contemporary of Hutton [297], Desmarest dealt with changes on the earth's surface in similar fashion. Desmarest was the first to maintain that valleys had been formed by the streams that ran through them. He also carried forward Guettard's [287] ideas, maintaining that basalt was volcanic in origin and that large sections of France's rocks, for instance, consisted of ancient lava flows. Unfortunately, A. G. Werner's [355] erroneous theories that almost all rocks were formed by sedimentation from water held sway for a while, though the volcanic theories of Guettard and Desmarest eventually won out.

[297] **HUTTON,** James
Scottish geologist
Born: Edinburgh, June 3, 1726
Died: Edinburgh, March 26, 1797

Hutton, the son of a merchant, was left fatherless at three. He became a lawyer's apprentice, but grew interested in chemistry and returned to school to study medicine. He obtained his medical degree at Leiden in 1749, but he never practiced. Instead, he worked on various agricultural projects and set up a factory to manufacture ammonium chloride. From chemistry he went on to mineralogy and geology, interest in which was stimulated by his journeys on foot to different parts of England. Hutton's interest in this direction, which was heartily encouraged by his good friend Black [298], absorbed him more and more and in 1768 he retired on the proceeds of his factory and devoted himself to geology.

By that time he had already founded the science, for until then geology did not really exist as an organized field of study. Isolated scholars such as Steno [225] and Buffon [277] had speculated on the past history of the earth and commented on rock strata, but there were no overall generalizations in the subject. A strong inhibiting factor was the conventional belief in an earth created six thousand years before according to the description in the Book of Genesis. Any countering argument seemed irreligious and offended the more conservative.

Hutton's careful studies of the earth's terrain convinced him—as it had convinced others before him—that there was a slow evolution of the surface structure. Some rocks, it seemed clear to him, were laid down as sediment and compressed; other rocks were molten in the earth's interior and were then brought to the surface by volcanic action; exposed rocks were worn down by wind and water.

His great intuitive addition to all this was the suggestion that the forces now slowly operating to change the earth's surface had been operating in the same way and at the same rate through all earth's past. This is the "uniformitarian principle" and it was countered by those like Bonnet [291] who maintained that the history of the earth was one of sharp, catastrophic changes ("catastrophism").

He also felt that the chief agent at work here was the internal heat of the earth. The planet, in short, was a gigantic "heat-engine," a not-unnatural conclusion, perhaps, for one who was a friend of Watt [316] as well as of Black.

To Hutton it seemed as though the earth's history must be indefinitely long, since, although the actions involved were creepingly slow, vast changes had nevertheless had time to take place. There seemed no sign of a beginning, he wrote, and no prospect of an end.

Hutton summarized his views in a book called *Theory of the Earth*, published in 1785. Since it first advanced the general principles upon which geology is now based, he is often called the "father of geology." In the book Hutton also dealt with rainfall and reached essentially modern conclusions, to wit: the amount of moisture that the air could hold rose with temperature. Consequently when a warm air mass met a cold one so that the temperature of the former dropped, some of the moisture could no longer be held in vapor form and precipitated as rain.

Hutton's geological views met with strong resistance and objection from those who held to the biblical account of creation. It was the time of the French Revolution and England was going through a strong conservative reaction. Anything smacking ever so faintly of going against establishment views was suspect. It was not until the popularizing work of Lyell [502] a half century later and well after Hutton's death that the view of the *Theory of the Earth* came into its own.

At the time of his death, Hutton was working on a book in which he expressed a belief in evolution by natural selection, a view to be made famous by Charles Darwin [554] six decades later. However, Hutton's manuscript was not examined till 1947, so that his anticipation of Darwin remained unsuspected for a century and a half.

[298] **BLACK,** Joseph
Scottish chemist
Born: Bordeaux, France, April 16, 1728
Died: Edinburgh, December 6, 1799

Black's father, a Scots-Irish wine merchant living in France, sent young Joseph (one of thirteen children) back to the British Isles in 1740 for his education. Black studied medicine at Glasgow, then, after 1750, at Edinburgh and eventually held professorial positions at each of these institutions and proved an excellent and popular lecturer. While still a medical student he grew interested in kidney stones and from these moved on to minerals that were similar. His thesis for his medical degree—obtained in 1754—proved to be a classic in chemistry. The work was published in 1756 (the year in which he became professor of chemistry at Glasgow) and in it Black reported that the compound we now call calcium carbonate was converted to calcium oxide upon strong heating, giving off a gas that could recombine with the calcium oxide to form calcium carbonate again. Black called the gas "fixed air" because it could be fixed into solid form again. We call it carbon dioxide.

Carbon dioxide was studied by Helmont [175] a century and a quarter before, but Black was the first who showed that it could be formed by the decomposition of a mineral as well as by combustion and fermentation. Furthermore, by involving a gas in a chemical reaction he divested it of its mystery and made it not so very different, from the standpoint of chemistry, from liquids and solids. And since calcium oxide could be converted to calcium carbonate simply by exposure to the air, it followed that carbon dioxide was a normal component of the atmosphere. He also recognized the existence of carbon dioxide in expired breath.

In studying the properties of carbon dioxide, Black found that a candle would not burn in it. A candle burning in ordinary air in a closed vessel would go out eventually and the air that was left would no longer support a flame. This might seem reasonable since the burning candle formed carbon dioxide. However, when the carbon dioxide was absorbed by chemicals, the air that was left and was *not* carbon dioxide would still not support a flame. Black turned this problem over to Daniel Rutherford [351], his young student, and within a decade chemistry was in part revolutionized by just such experiments.

In studying the effect of heat on calcium carbonate, Black measured the loss of weight involved. He also measured the quantity of calcium carbonate that would neutralize a given quantity of acid. This technique of quantitative measurement, as applied to chemical reactions, was to come into its own a few decades later with Lavoisier [334].

Black's work in physics was equally important. In 1764 he grew interested in the phenomenon of heat and was the first to recognize that the *quantity* of heat was not the same thing as its *intensity*. It was the latter only that was mea-

sured as temperature. Thus, he found that when ice was heated, it slowly melted but did not change in temperature. Ice absorbed a quantity of "latent heat" in melting, increasing the amount of heat it contained but not the intensity. An even larger quantity of latent heat was involved in the conversion of water to vapor by boiling.

Furthermore, when water vapor condensed to water, or when water froze to ice, an amount of heat was given off equal to that taken up by the reverse change. Yet the act of condensation or freezing involved no temperature change either. The fact that the heat taken up in one change was given off in the reverse change was a step in the direction of understanding the great generalization called "conservation of energy," which was to be clearly established some three quarters of a century later with the work of such men as Mayer [587], Joule [613], and Helmholtz [631].

The heat taken up by water in boiling was a clue to the far greater energy content of steam at the boiling point temperature as compared with an equal weight of liquid water at the same temperature. This fine theoretical point was known to James Watt [316], who was aware of Black's work, and Watt used it in developing his steam engine. (It is never sufficiently realized, particularly in the United States, how much the "down-to-earth" inventor is indebted to the "ivory tower" theoretician.)

Black also showed that when equal weights of two different substances at different temperatures are brought together and allowed to come to temperature equilibrium, the final temperature is not necessarily at the midway point. One substance might lose 30°, for instance, while the second was gaining only 20°. The same quantity of heat, in other words, might effect a temperature change 50 percent greater in one substance than in another. This characteristic temperature change resulting from the input of a particular amount of heat is now called the specific heat.

Black had trouble accounting for all this. He, in common with other chemists of his time, believed heat to be an imponderable fluid, like light, electricity, or the phlogiston postulated by Stahl [241]. In terms of an imponderable fluid pouring from one substance to another, the concept of specific heat and latent heat could be explained only by troublesome and implausible arguments. When the kinetic theory of heat was finally developed by men such as Maxwell [692], Black's experiments fell neatly into place.

[299] **LAMBERT,** Johann Heinrich
(lahm'behrt)
German mathematician
Born: Mulhouse, Alsace, August 26, 1728
Died: Berlin, September 25, 1777

Lambert was the son of a poor tailor. He had to quit school at twelve to help his father and was forced thereafter to scrimp what education he could out of life. Fortunately, men of great talent can make do even under difficulties. He began to earn his living as a tutor until he attracted the attention of Frederick II of Prussia who saw to it, in 1764, that the final decade of his life was passed in reasonable comfort. In mathematics Lambert, in 1768, proved pi to be an irrational quantity (though a century later Lindemann [826] was to give it an even more subtle distinction) and introduced hyperbolic functions into trigonometry. In 1760 he published his investigations of light reflection. His book was in Latin and his word for the fraction of light reflected diffusely by a body was *albedo* ("whiteness"). The term is still commonly used in astronomy to represent the reflectivity of planetary bodies. He was the first to devise methods for measuring light intensities accurately, and the unit of brightness is the lambert, in his honor. In 1761 he speculated that the stars in the neighborhood of the sun made up a connected system and that groups of such systems made up the Milky Way. He suspected that there might be other conglomerations like the Milky Way in the far reaches of space. The accuracy of his guesses was con-

firmed by the careful work of Herschel [321] a generation later.

[300] **COOK,** James
English navigator
Born: Marton village, Cleveland, Yorkshire, October 27, 1728
Died: Kealakekua Bay, Hawaii, February 14, 1779

Cook's reputation as a seaman is proved by the fact that he is hardly known by any name other than Captain Cook. His first name is all but forgotten.

He was the son of a farmhand and his first job was in a haberdasher's shop. While still young he was apprenticed to a firm of shipowners and worked his way up to mate. In 1755 he joined the Royal Navy and by 1759 had qualified as a master and took part in Wolfe's expedition against Quebec in the French and Indian War.

The expeditions in which he engaged were intended for sounding and surveying, for gaining knowledge of the ocean and of the geographical nature of the earth. Thus he spent several years in the sixties surveying the coasts of Labrador and Newfoundland. He observed a solar eclipse on August 5, 1766, near Cape Ray, Newfoundland. He was the first of the really scientific navigators.

In 1768 he made the first of three voyages into the Pacific that were to make him the most famous navigator since Magellan [130], two and a half centuries earlier. Under the auspices of the Royal Society (through the Admiralty) he was sent to the South Pacific to observe the transit of Venus from the newly discovered island of Tahiti. In the course of that expedition he discovered the Admiralty Islands and the Society Islands, named for his sponsors. He also circumnavigated New Zealand, explored its shores, and landed in Australia, being the first to gain a notion of the size and position of this last of the inhabited continents to be opened to the Europeans. Accompanying him as ship's botanist was Banks [331].

In a second expedition, from 1772 to

1775, perhaps the greatest single sea voyage ever made, Cook took his ship throughout southern waters down to the Antarctic circle and proved the nonexistence of any vast southern continent other than Australia, or rather proved that any that did exist had to be confined to the Antarctic regions. This expedition outlined the southern hemisphere, except for Antarctica itself, in approximately the form in which it is now known to exist. Except for the polar regions the oceans of the earth had been entirely opened.

It was on this voyage, too, that Cook tested the dietary theories of Lind [288] and found them to be sound. He received a medal from the Royal Society for this.

In his third and last voyage, from 1776 to 1779, he was commissioned to explore the far northern Pacific. He sailed the full north-south length of the ocean, discovering the Hawaiian Islands on the way. After following the Alaskan and Siberian coasts as far as the ice would permit, he returned to Hawaii. There, after one of the ship's boats was stolen by the natives, a scuffle took place in which he was killed, and at the spot today an obelisk stands in his memory. Since the natives practiced cannibalism he was presumably eaten. For his last voyage, which took place during the American Revolutionary War, Benjamin Franklin [272], who fully appreciated the scientific importance of Cook's work, arranged that he should not be molested by American privateers.

[301] **TITIUS,** Johann Daniel (tish'us)
German astronomer
Born: Konitz, Prussia (now Chojnice, Poland), January 2, 1729
Died: Wittenberg, Saxony, December 16, 1796

Titius, the son of a draper who was also a city councillor, was brought up by his uncle after his father's death. His uncle, a naturalist, encouraged the youngster's interest in science. He obtained his master's degree from the University of Leipzig in 1752. In 1756, he

was appointed to a professorial position at the University of Wittenberg, where he remained for the rest of his life.

The one thing for which he is remembered in the history of science is his suggestion in 1766 that the mean distances of the planets from the sun very nearly fit a simple relationship of $A = 4 + (2^n \times 3)$, where the value of n is, successively, $-\infty$, 0, 1, 2, 3 and so on.

This works out to the series: 4, 7, 10, 16, 28, 52, 100, . . . which fits the relative distance of Mercury, Venus, earth, Mars, ———, Jupiter and Saturn. The dash between Mars and Jupiter was not filled by any planet.

The relationship was not noted when first advanced and only came to the attention of astronomers generally when Bode [344] publicized it in 1772. And then it was called Bode's law, with poor Titius ignored. It turned out, however, that once Neptune was discovered seven decades later the "law" was only a coincidence with no actual scientific significance. Nevertheless, it did encourage Olbers [372] and others to search for the planetary objects in the empty spot and to discover the asteroids.

[302] **SPALLANZANI,** Lazzaro (spahl-lahn-tsah'nee)
Italian biologist
Born: Scandiano, Modena, January 12, 1729
Died: Pavia, Lombardy, February 11, 1799

Spallanzani, the son of a successful lawyer, attended the University of Bologna, where his cousin, Laura Bassi, was a singular anomaly for that time—a woman professor of physics who managed to have twelve children in her spare time. It is thought she influenced him in the choice of a scientific career.

He obtained his Ph.D. in 1754 and then became a priest in order to help support himself. He taught at several Italian universities, visited Naples in 1788 while Vesuvius was in eruption, and, unlike Pliny [61], survived. He had made trips along the shores of the Mediterranean and even into Turkey in 1785 to collect natural history specimens for the museum at Pavia, where Maria Theresa of Austria had placed him in charge.

His most dramatic work is in connection with the question of spontaneous generation. By the eighteenth century the matter of the spontaneous generation of animals visible to the naked eye was a closed one. Thanks mainly to the experiments of Redi [211] a century before, even insects were known to arise only from eggs. But regarding the microorganisms discovered by Leeuwenhoek [221] at about the time of Redi's experiments, the question remained open.

Needham [285] had conducted experiments that seemed to show microorganisms *did* appear through spontaneous generation. Spallanzani tackled the problem in 1768, determined to be thorough. He not only boiled solutions that would ordinarily breed microorganisms, he boiled them for between one half and three quarters of an hour. Then he sealed the flasks. No microorganisms appeared in the solutions however long they stood. His conclusion was that microorganisms appeared in such solutions only because they already existed in it in spore form, or were on the inner walls of the flask or in the air within the flask. Some of these organisms were resistant to brief boiling, but all succumbed to prolonged boiling. Spallanzani believed his own procedure killed all the microorganisms in the solution, in the air above it or on the inner walls about it. Sealing the flask prevented new spores from entering. The fact that no microorganisms appeared in such flasks meant that there was no spontaneous generation. This made possible Appert's [359] advance in food preservations.

But the battle was not over. Those who favored spontaneous generation maintained that by long boiling, Spallanzani had destroyed some "vital principle" in the air and that without this principle microorganisms could not breed. It was another century before that objection was finally taken care of by Pasteur [642].

At the request of his friend Bonnet [291], Spallanzani studied the mechanics of the development of eggs. He showed in 1779 that sperm cells had to make actual contact with egg cells if fertilization was to take place. He also carried through artificial insemination on a dog in 1785.

In the last decade of his life Spallanzani grew interested in the problem of how nocturnal animals found their way. Bats flew easily in the most complete darkness. He blinded some bats and found them still capable of flying with perfect ease. Some days later he caught several and dissected them. Their stomachs were crammed with insect remains. Not only could they fly while blinded, but also they could catch insects. In his usual thorough manner he tackled the other senses (for he could not believe that the ability was what we would today call "extrasensory"). He found that when he plugged the bats' ears, they were helpless.

He had no explanation for this and the experiment seemed so bizarre—could an animal see with its ears?—that it was forgotten. It was only with developing knowledge of ultrasonic sound vibrations a century and more later that an answer to the problem became possible.

[303] **BOUGAINVILLE,** Louis Antoine de (boo-gan-veel')
French navigator
Born: Paris, November 11, 1729
Died: Paris, August 31, 1811

Bougainville was the son of a notary and, to avoid becoming a notary himself, he enlisted in the French army. He fought in North America as an aide-de-camp to General Louis Joseph de Montcalm in the battles that lost French Canada to the British. After the war was over in 1763, Bougainville joined the navy and led an expedition to the Falkland Islands off the shore of southern Argentina, but failed to establish a colony in that rather forbidding territory.

He was commissioned by the French government to set sail on a voyage of exploration and with this end in mind, he sailed in December 1766. The voyage took him around the world, and he led the first French ships to accomplish the feat. He lost only seven men to scurvy, even though he did not have Cook's [300] preventive of lime juice.

He almost reached Australia but turned north too soon to sight its shores. He did sail along the Solomon Islands, the largest of which is Bougainville Island, named in his honor since, in 1768, he was the first European to sight it. He confirmed the existence of marsupials in the eastern islands of Indonesia, something Buffon [277] had refused to believe. His voyage and those of Captain Cook finally completed the geography of the Pacific Ocean.

After the voyage he became secretary to Louis XV, and then fought against the British in the course of the American Revolutionary War. Despite his royalist connections, he managed to avoid the guillotine in the French Revolution, and lived to be honored as a senator and count by Napoleon Bonaparte.

[304] MÜLLER, Otto Friedrich
Danish biologist
Born: Copenhagen, March 2, 1730
Died: Copenhagen, December 26, 1784

Müller, the son of a court trumpeter, studied theology and law at the University of Copenhagen, then served an aristocratic family for twenty years as tutor. In 1773 he married a wealthy widow, retired, and devoted his remaining years to science.

Müller was one of the early microscopists and concentrated on the tiny bacteria first dimly seen by Leeuwenhoek [221].

These were at just about the limits of resolution of the primitive microscopes that antedated the modern achromatic varieties introduced by J. J. Lister [445], and Müller was the first who saw them well enough to divide them into categories. He introduced the terms "bacillum" and "spirillum" to describe two of the categories.

He was also the first to classify microorganisms, generally, into genera and species after the fashion of Linnaeus [276].

[305] MESSIER, Charles (meh-syay')
French astronomer
Born: Badonviller, Meurthe-et-Moselle, Vosges, June 26, 1730
Died: Paris, April 11, 1817

Messier, the tenth of twelve children, was left fatherless when he was eleven. He went to work as an assistant to Delisle [255] in 1755 and became an accomplished astronomical observer.

Messier was the first in France to spy Halley's comet on the famous 1758 return that Halley [238] had predicted. This inspired him to become a comet hunter and his greatest pleasure was to track down those fuzzy creatures at their first appearance. Louis XV referred to him, with patronizing affection, as "my little comet ferret." In his systematic searchings, however, he was constantly being fooled by fuzzy nebulosities that occurred here and there as permanent heavenly objects. In 1781 he made a compilation of a little over a hundred such objects in order that neither he nor any other comet hunter would be fooled by them. If a suspected comet were to be spotted, its position would first be checked against Messier's list before being announced as a discovery.

The objects in Messier's list are still frequently known as Messier 1, Messier 2, or just M1, M2, and so on. They cover a wide variety of objects. Some are indeed nebulosities. Others are collections of stars that, to Messier's weak telescope, showed up simply as blurs. Thus Messier 13, first noted by Halley in 1714, is a huge cluster of stars, perhaps a million of them, all told, that is now known as the Great Hercules Cluster because it occurs in the constellation Hercules. About a hundred such clusters exist in our galaxy and all were noted down by Messier. Herschel [321] resolved them into stars. It was these clusters that were used by Shapley [1102] a century and a quarter after Messier's time to demonstrate the true size of the Milky Way.

199

In addition, some of Messier's listed objects are systems of stars as large as or larger than the entire Milky Way. Thus, Messier 31 is the great Andromeda galaxy, which, a century and a half later, Hubble [1136] was to resolve, at least partly, into stars.

As a comet hunter Messier was as good as could be expected, discovering twenty-one, but none of the comets he discovered are of any particular interest. The miscellany of objects he recorded in order to clear the way for his comets, however, have immortalized his name. He could not have predicted this, for in his time the true grandeur of the universe was unknown, though some, like Lambert [299] and Kant [293], were beginning to suspect a bit of the truth.

[306] **INGENHOUSZ,** Jan (ing'en-hows)
Dutch physician and plant physiologist
Born: Breda, December 8, 1730
Died: Bowood Park, Wiltshire, England, September 7, 1799

Ingenhousz, the son of a leather merchant, got his medical training at the universities of Louvain and Leiden, receiving his medical degree in 1752. He traveled to England in 1764, where he eventually grew expert in the technique of smallpox inoculation. He went on to Vienna to inoculate the royal house and to become personal physician to Empress Maria Theresa in 1772. In 1779 he returned to England and became a member of the Royal Society.

In that year he published experiments clarifying the previous work of Hales [249] and Priestley [312]. He showed that green plants take up carbon dioxide and give off oxygen, but *only in the light* (hence "photosynthesis"—formation in light—is the name we now give the process). In the dark, they, like animals, give off carbon dioxide and absorb oxygen. This was the first indication of the role of sunlight in the life activities of green plants. Ingenhousz had thus demonstrated the broad scheme of balance in nature. Plants, in the presence of light,

consume the carbon dioxide produced by animals, and give off the oxygen that is in turn consumed by animals. The activity of both plants and animals brought about a balance in which oxygen and carbon dioxide were, in the long run, neither used up nor overproduced.

It remained to fill in the details of these processes, of course, and those details after over a century and a half are only now falling into place.

[307] **CAVENDISH,** Henry
English chemist and physicist
Born: Nice, France, October 10, 1731
Died: London, February 24, 1810

Cavendish, of an aristocratic English family, was born in Nice because his mother was there on a trip to improve her health in the salubrious climate of the Riviera. In this she did not succeed, and died when her son was two.

Cavendish was educated in England and eventually spent four years at Cambridge, but he never took his degree, partly because he would not participate in the obligatory religious exercises. He also seems to have thought he could not face the professors during the necessary examinations. In all his life, he had difficulty facing people.

Mad scientists are many in fiction, few in real life. Yet certainly Cavendish comes as near to qualifying as any one of the truly first-class scientists of history.

He was excessively shy and absent-minded. He almost never spoke and when he did it was with a sort of stammer. He might, in an emergency, exchange a few words with one man, but never with more than one man, and never with a woman. He feared women to the point where he could not bear to look at one. He communicated with his female servants by notes (to order dinner, for instance) and any of these female servants who accidentally crossed his path in his house was fired on the spot. He built a separate entrance to his house so he could come and leave alone, and his library in London was four miles from his house, so that people who had to use it would not trouble him. In the end he even literally insisted on dying alone.

This eccentric had one and only one love, and that was scientific research. He spent almost sixty years in exclusive preoccupation with it. It was a pure love, too, for he did not care whether his findings were published, whether he got credit, or anything beyond the fact that he was sating his own curiosity. He wrote no books and published only twenty articles altogether. As a result, much of what he did remained unknown until years after his death.

His experiments on electricity in the early 1770s anticipated most of what was to be discovered in the next half century, but he published virtually none of it. It was only a century afterward that Maxwell [692] went through Cavendish's notes and published his work. There is no way of estimating what that unnecessary secrecy cost the human race in scientific progress. His electrical experiments also proved his superhuman devotion to science. He had no talent for inventing instruments and he measured the strength of a current in a very direct way, shocking himself with the current or the charge and estimating the pain. Nevertheless he managed to live to be nearly eighty.

Fortunately he suffered few economic pressures. He came of a noble family that included the dukes of Devonshire and he had a comfortable allowance. At the age of forty he inherited a fortune of over a million pounds but paid no particular attention to it; he continued living as before. On his death, the fortune, virtually untouched, went to relatives, and his unpublished notes remained a rich mine for later scientists.

In 1766 he communicated some early researches to the Royal Society, describing his work with an inflammable gas produced by the action of acids on metals. This gas had been worked with before—for instance, by Boyle [212], who had collected some, and by Hales [249]—but Cavendish was the first to investigate its properties systematically and he is usually given the credit for its dis-

covery. Twenty years later the gas was named hydrogen by Lavoisier [334].

Cavendish was the first to measure the weight of particular volumes of different gases to determine the density. He found hydrogen unusually light, with only one-fourteenth the density of air. The lightness of the gas and its easy inflammability led him to believe he had actually isolated the phlogiston postulated by Stahl [241], a view quickly adopted by another well-known phlogistonist, Scheele [329].

On January 15, 1784, he was able to demonstrate that hydrogen, on burning, produced water. In this way water was shown to be a combination of two gases and if the Greek notion of the elements still required a deathblow, this was it.

As was fashionable at the time, Cavendish experimented with air. In 1785 he passed electric sparks through air, forcing the nitrogen to combine with the oxygen (to use modern terminology) and dissolving the resulting oxide in water. (In doing so, he worked out the composition of nitric acid.) He added more oxygen, expecting to use up all the nitrogen in time. However, a small bubble of gas, amounting to less than 1 percent of the whole, remained uncombined no matter what he did. He speculated that air contained a small quantity of a gas, then, that was very inert and resistant to reaction. As a matter of fact, he had discovered the gas we now call argon. This experiment was ignored for a century, however, until Ramsay [832] repeated it and followed it up.

Cavendish's most spectacular experiment involved the vast globe of the earth itself. The law of gravitation as worked out by Newton [231] placed the mass of the earth in the equation representing the attraction between the earth and any other body (say, a falling object). However, the mass of the earth could not be calculated from the mass of the falling object, its rate of fall, and its distance from the earth's center because the equation also contained G, the gravitational constant, of which the value was not known.

If the value of the gravitational constant were known, then all the quantities in the equation but the earth's mass would be known and the earth's mass could be calculated.

It was assumed that the gravitational constant was the same for all bodies and that it could, in theory, be determined if only the gravitational attraction between two objects, each of known mass, could be measured. The trick was to measure this attraction, for gravitational force is very weak and it takes a very large body, far too large to work with in a laboratory, to pile up enough of it to measure easily.

Cavendish tackled the problem in 1798. Using a method suggested by Michell [294], he performed what is now commonly referred to as the Cavendish experiment.

Cavendish suspended a light rod by a wire attached to its center. At each end of the rod was a light lead ball. The rod could twist freely about the wire and a light force applied to the balls would produce such a twist. Cavendish measured how large a twist was produced by various small forces.

He brought two large balls near the two light balls, one on either side. The force of gravity between the large balls and light ones twisted the wire. From the extent of twist, Cavendish calculated the gravitational force between the two pairs of balls. He knew the distance between them, center to center, and the mass of each. This meant he had all the figures required for Newton's equation, except for the gravitational constant, and he could now solve for that.

Once the constant was determined, it could be put into the equation representing the attraction between the earth and some object of known mass upon its surface. Again all quantities were known with one exception—the mass of the earth, and now *that* could be calculated for. The earth turned out to have a mass of 6,600,000,000,000,000,000,000,000 tons and to have a density of about five and a half times that of water. (Newton with his clear intuition had guessed it might come to that a century before.)

The Cavendish Physical Laboratory at Cambridge—which a century after Cavendish's time was to produce work of

unparalleled excellence in nuclear physics—is named in his honor.

[308] **DARWIN**, Erasmus
English physician
Born: Elton, Nottinghamshire, December 12, 1731
Died: Breadsall Priory, near Derby, April 18, 1802

Darwin, the son of a prosperous lawyer, studied at Cambridge and obtained his medical degree at the University of Edinburgh in 1754. He was one of the foremost physicians of his day so that George III asked him to become his personal physician in London. Darwin, however, refused.

He was a man of decided opinions, radical, freethinking, and a prohibitionist. He was a member of the Lunar Society, as were Watt [316] and Priestley [312].

He had the deplorable habit of writing long, didactic poems that had some interest as far as scientific content was concerned but no discernible poetic value. His early poems dealt largely with botany and in them he backed the classification system introduced by Linnaeus [276].

His second most famous accomplishment is his last book, *Zoonomia,* written 1794–1796, in which he elaborated on Buffon's feelings about evolution and anticipated some of the suggestions of Lamarck [336] on the subject. Darwin argued that evolutionary changes were brought about by the direct influence of the environment on the organism.

The accomplishment for which he is most famous, however, is his being the grandfather (by his first wife) of Charles Darwin [554], who a little over half a century later was to advance the theory of evolution, which, with necessary modifications, is now believed to be the correct one. In addition Erasmus Darwin became the grandfather (by his second wife) of Francis Galton [636].

Erasmus Darwin's reputation has suffered partly by his being overshadowed by his more famous grandson and partly by a campaign of ridicule set in motion by the conservative British government during the French revolutionary era against Darwin and others who sympathized with the French revolutionaries.

[309] **LALANDE,** Joseph Jérôme Le Français de (la-lahnd´)
French astronomer
Born: Bourg-en-Bresse, Ain, July 11, 1732
Died: Paris, April 4, 1807

Lalande, the son of a post office official, had studied law as a young man, but he happened to lodge near an astronomical observatory, and this caught his fancy. He completed his legal education, but did not practice. Instead, in 1751 he went to Berlin to take observations on the parallax of the moon, as Lacaille [284] was sent to southern Africa for the purpose.

He became professor of astronomy at the Collège de France in 1762 and in 1795 became director of the Paris Observatory. In the hectic decade of the 1790s, he was openly anti-Jacobin and did what he could to save some who were threatened by the Reign of Terror. Later, he did not hesitate to indicate his opposition to the war policies of Napoleon Bonaparte.

He devoted much of his time to preparing a catalogue of forty-seven thousand stars which he published in 1801. One of the stars, listed Lalande 21185, turned out eventually to be the third nearest to the sun and to be one of those which in the mid-twentieth century was discovered by Van de Kamp's [1247] observatory to possess a planet. He was also one of those who observed Neptune and recorded its position (but without realizing it was a planet and not a star) a full half century before its discovery by Leverrier [564].

He was a great popularizer of astronomy and wrote all the astronomical articles in Diderot's [286] Encyclopedia. In 1798 he made a balloon ascension and later suggested improvements in the parachute.

[310] **MASKELYNE,** Nevil (mas´kuh-line)
English astronomer
Born: London, October 6, 1732
Died: Greenwich, London, February 9, 1811

Maskelyne, born into an upper-class family, graduated from Cambridge University in 1754 and was ordained as a clergyman in 1755. However, he had done well in mathematics and in science, and an eclipse he had viewed in 1748 had interested him permanently in astronomy.

Someone was needed to head an expedition to St. Helena to view the transit of Venus in 1761 and Bradley [258] recommended Maskelyne. The transit observation as a method of determining the distance of Venus and, therefore, of other bodies of the solar system, was a failure because of clouds and other problems. On the way there, however, Maskelyne worked on methods of determining longitude by lunar observations, and this method competed with that of the use of the chronometer devised by Harrison [259].

Harrison won out for the prize that had been offered, but Maskelyne went on to produce lunar tables and the *Nautical Almanac*, which remained a useful navigational aid for well over a century. He was appointed fifth astonomer royal, succeeding Nathaniel Bliss, in 1765.

He was the first man to make time measurements that were accurate to a tenth of a second.

[311] **ARKWRIGHT,** Sir Richard
English inventor
Born: Preston, Lancashire, December 23, 1732
Died: Cromford, Derbyshire, August 3, 1792

Arkwright, the youngest of thirteen children, was a barber and wigmaker in his youth. A secret process for dyeing hair was the foundation of his fortune. He had little formal education, but in mechanical invention this is not necessarily a handicap. By 1769, with help from others and with guidance from the work of previous inventors, he patented a device that would spin thread by mechanically reproducing the motions ordinarily made by the human hand. At first, this was powered by animals, then by falling water, and finally, in 1790, by steam. Arkwright invented (or promoted) machinery that would replace handwork in other steps of textile manufacture and became the first "capitalist" of the newborn industrial age. The machines not only replaced handwork; they produced so rapidly and efficiently that handworkers were permanently out of business. Popular rage against his machines put his mills and himself in danger more than once, but the progress of mechanization was too obviously profitable for society in general and for a small group of hard-driving men in particular.

In 1782, Arkwright was employing five thousand men. He was appointed high sheriff of Derbyshire in 1783 and was knighted in 1786. At his death his fortune amounted to two and a half million dollars, an enormous sum for those days.

[312] **PRIESTLEY,** Joseph
English chemist
Born: Birstal Fieldhead,
Yorkshire, March 13, 1733
Died: Northumberland, Pennsylvania, February 6, 1804

Priestley's mother died when he was six and he was brought up by a pious aunt. The boy was slight, rather sickly, and suffered from an impediment in his speech. In his youth he studied languages, logic, and philosophy and showed himself a prodigiously good student in all these, learning a variety of languages, including Hebrew and Arabic, rather like Hamilton [545] seventy years later. He never studied science formally, yet it was in science that he made his name.

He was the son of a Nonconformist preacher and was himself even more radical in religion, despite his aunt's upbringing, for he eventually became a Unitarian minister. He was radical in politics as well, openly supporting the American colonists when they were revolting against George III. He was also against the slave trade and against religious bigotry of all sorts. One of his books seemed radical enough to be officially burned in 1785. It was his sympathy for the French Revolution that eventually got him into the most serious trouble.

In 1766, on one of his periodic visits to London, Priestley met Benjamin Franklin [272], who was then in England in a vain attempt to adjust the dispute with the American colonies over taxation. That apparently was what influenced him to take up a scientific career. Shortly after, he took over a pastorate in Leeds; there was a brewery next door, and this was another piece of scientific good fortune. Under Franklin's influence, Priestley did some research on electricity, becoming the first to discover that carbon was an electrical conductor. He then wrote an important history of electrical research in 1769, and later one on the history of optics. He was the first to suggest that electricity would prove of importance to chemistry, and eventually he turned to chemistry itself.

Fermenting grain produces a gas, the properties of which Priestley took to studying with interest and curiosity. He noted that it put out flames, was heavier than air, and dissolved to a certain extent in water. It was, in fact, carbon dioxide, the "fixed air" of Black [298].

When Priestley dissolved carbon dioxide in water he tasted the solution and found that he had created a pleasantly tart and refreshing drink, the one we call seltzer or soda water today. The Royal Society awarded him the Copley medal for this. Since it required only flavoring and sugar to produce soda pop, Priestley may be viewed as the father of the modern soft-drink industry.

Priestley's interest in gases grew. Only three gases were known at the time he began work—air, carbon dioxide, and hydrogen, the last having just been discovered by Cavendish [307]. Priestley changed that drastically for he went on to isolate and study a number of them, such as nitrous oxide, in 1772. He collected gases over mercury and thus was able to isolate ones that cannot be collected over water—such as ammonia, sulfur dioxide, and hydrogen chloride, which are water soluble. His experiments earned him membership in the French Academy of Sciences in 1772 and a lucrative post as librarian and companion to Lord Shelburne, who had lost a government post because of his own liberal tendencies. (He, too, sympathized with the rebellious American colonies.)

During his eight years with Lord Shelburne, Priestley did his most interesting work. In 1774, for instance, the mercury he used in his work with gases was the occasion of his most important discovery. Mercury, when heated in air, will form a brick-red "calx," which we now call mercuric oxide. Priestley heated some of this calx in a test tube with a lens that he had just obtained and was yearning to use. This concentrated sunlight upon the calx. It broke down to mercury again, this appearing as shining globules in the upper portion of the test tube.

In addition, a gas was given off that possessed most unusual properties. Combustibles burned more brilliantly and rapidly in it than in air. Priestley, who accepted the phlogiston theory of Stahl [241], reasoned that the new gas must be particularly poor in phlogiston and therefore accepted the phlogiston of wood so eagerly that the combustion that accompanied phlogiston loss was hastened. Priestley called the new gas "dephlogisticated air," since a couple of years earlier D. Rutherford [351] had named a gas of opposite properties "phlogisticated air."

A few years later, Lavoisier [334] killed the phlogiston theory and named the gas oxygen, which is the name it is still known by. Priestley, however, as conservative in chemistry as he was liberal in politics and religion, remained a convinced phlogistonist to the end of his life.

(Actually Scheele [329] had isolated oxygen a couple of years earlier than Priestley had. Through no fault of Scheele, news of the discovery was not published until after Priestley had reported on his own experiments. For that reason Priestley is usually given the credit for the discovery.)

Priestley experimented enthusiastically with his "dephlogisticated air." He found that mice were particularly frisky in it and he himself felt "light and easy" when he breathed it. He imagined that breathing "dephlogisticated air" might some day become a fashionable minor vice among the rich. He also recognized the fact that plants restored used-up air to its original freshness by dephlogisticating it. (We say the plants release oxygen into the air.) This observation was sharpened by Priestley's contemporary, Ingenhousz [306].

It is almost anticlimactic to add that Priestley also gave the modern name "rubber" to the product of the South American tree sap which La Condamine [270] had introduced to Europe. He used that name simply because the substance could be used to rub out pencil marks.

Priestley's scientific achievements were not sufficient to make him popular with his neighbors. A Unitarian is not popular among people of more orthodox religion, since Unitarianism denies the divinity of Jesus. Add to that Priestley's sympathetic views toward the French revolutionaries, whose activities were shocking British conservative opinion, and it is not surprising that the populace of Birmingham (where he had settled in 1780 after retiring on a small pension) viewed him with suspicion.

In Birmingham he joined the Lunar Society, which included Watt [316] and Erasmus Darwin [308], who had been its founder. The name of the society was derived from the fact that the meetings were held near the night of the full moon so that members would have something to light their way home.

On July 14, 1791, some Birmingham pro-French Jacobins held a celebration in honor of the second anniversary of the fall of the Bastille. An angry mob retaliated against the best-known Jacobin in the city and burned down Priestley's house. The next Sunday, Priestley took as the text for his sermon, "Father, forgive them for they know not what they do." He managed, eventually, to escape with his family to London. He wasn't much better off there, for people avoided him as a dangerous radical, particularly after France became a republic, cut off the head of its ex-king, Louis XVI, and went to war with Great Britain. Nor did it help him that the French Republican government made Priestley a French citizen. (Of course, attitudes toward Priestley changed after he was safely dead. In 1875, at the centenary of the discovery of oxygen, Birmingham raised a statue to Priestley.)

In 1794 Priestley gathered some money and left Great Britain forever just one week before his French colleague Lavoisier was executed by the intolerants of France. Priestley crossed the sea to the land of his old friend Benjamin Franklin, the now independent nation of the United States, where the populace was at that time anti-British and pro-French, and where he was welcomed gladly and where he gained the friendship of Thomas Jefferson [333]. The last ten years of his life were spent in peace, and he did much to further the cause of Unitarianism in the new nation. He turned down offers of a Unitarian ministry in New York and of a professorship of chemistry at the University of Pennsylvania. He wanted only a chance to write quietly.

[313] **WOLFF,** Kaspar Friedrich
German physiologist
Born: Berlin, January 18, 1734
Died: St. Petersburg (now Leningrad), Russia, February 22, 1794

In 1759, when Wolff, the son of a tailor, had just obtained his medical degree from the University of Halle and was serving as army surgeon during the Seven Years' War, he published a booklet on the development of living things that was revolutionary in its implications. Until his time many biologists, for example, Bonnet [291], were of the opinion that a living creature existed preformed and perfect in every miniature detail in the egg or sperm. Textbooks even had diagrams showing these tiny

"homunculi" within sperm cells, these having been seen, described, and drawn by microscopists with enthusiasm and imagination.

Wolff, however, reported that specialized organs arose out of unspecialized tissue. Thus, the tip of a growing plant shoot consists of undifferentiated and generalized cells. As these divide and subdivide, however, specialization develops and some bits of tissue develop into flowers, while other bits, originally indistinguishable, develop into leaves.

Even more important (from our human-centered view) was the fact that he could show that this same principle held for a developing animal, such as a chick, within the egg. Undifferentiated tissue gave rise to the different abdominal organs, he showed, through gradual specialization.

Wolff may thus be considered the founder of modern embryology, although unfortunately his work was largely neglected for over half a century. Nevertheless, it made enough of an impression on the new Empress Catherine II of Russia (that collector of scholars and lovers) to cause her to invite him to St. Petersburg in 1764, when the Seven Years' War had ended.

He became professor of anatomy and remained there until his death. His name is preserved in several anatomic terms, notably in the Wolffian body, an early form of kidney in embryonic animals preceding the true kidney.

[314] **MESMER,** Franz Anton
German physician
Born: Iznang am Bodensee, Baden, Germany, May 23, 1734
Died: Meersburg, Germany, March 5, 1815

Mesmer, the son of a forester, entered the University of Vienna in 1759. He began by studying law but shifted to medicine and obtained his medical degree in 1766.

He was a mystic, very much interested in astrology. He was a follower of Paracelsus [131] and believed in the existence of cosmic forces permeating the earth and affecting the lives of human beings. In any age he would have been interested in whatever ill-understood phenomenon was claiming the attention of scholars. In the late eighteenth century this meant electricity and magnetism, and as a physician he naturally attempted to turn these forces to the curing of disease.

He began by passing magnets over the bodies of his patients and managed to effect cures in some cases. Later he discovered that magnets were unnecessary and that the same happy results could be achieved by the simple passing of hands. He decided that in the latter case he was making use of "animal magnetism."

His practice in Vienna was not without troubles. His undoubted cures (well advertised by doctor and patient alike) were mixed with failures. The patients who suffered these failures naturally felt aggrieved, and charges of malpractice multiplied. The unsympathetic police ordered Mesmer to move on.

He went to Paris in 1778 and there became the rage. The volatile French society of the day, in the twilight of the Age of Reason, was ready for any novelty expressed in scientific-sounding words. Orthodox Parisian doctors were naturally enraged, and eventually a commission of experts investigated Mesmer's methods. Among the experts was Benjamin Franklin [272], who was then in Paris representing the brand-new United States, Lavoisier [334], and Joseph Guillotin, the inventor of the guillotine. The experts reported unfavorably and in 1785 Mesmer was forced to leave Paris. He retired to Versailles, then to Switzerland, then to his native region, and obscurity. (Franklin, by the way, although denying the validity of Mesmer's work, made it clear he felt that cures could be effected by suggestion and went on to discuss psychosomatic ailments in almost modern terms.)

Although Mesmer was 90 percent gobbledygook, he was in earnest and there is no reason to doubt that his cures were genuine. His followers raised the gobbledygook percentage to 100, but it remains clear, in retrospect, that Mesmer was curing psychosomatic ailments by suggestion. His methods, refined and freed of some of their mumbo-jumbo, became respectable once more a half century later when Braid [494] reintroduced what he called hypnotism. An accepted synonym for hypnotism is, even today, mesmerism, in honor of the Austrian doctor.

[315] **BERGMAN,** Torbern Olof
Swedish mineralogist
Born: Katrineberg, Västmanland, March 9, 1735
Died: Medevi, July 8, 1784

Bergman, the son of a tax collector, obtained his doctor's degree at the University of Uppsala in 1758. Though a physicist and mathematician as well as a chemist, he was chiefly interested in mineral classification, which is not surprising, considering that he had studied under that great classifier Linnaeus [276].

Bergman based his classification on chemical characteristics rather than on appearance alone, as his older contemporary Cronstedt [292] was also doing. Bergman evolved a theory to explain why one substance reacted with a second but not, perhaps, with a third, by supposing the existence of "affinities" (that is, attractions) between substances in varying degrees. He prepared elaborate tables listing affinities, and they were very influential during his lifetime and for a few decades after.

He also attempted to produce exact determinations of mineral composition ("quantitative analysis") by producing precipitates and weighing them accurately ("gravimetric determinations").

Yet neither these things nor such specific discoveries as the fact that carbon dioxide possessed acidic properties in solution is what he is best remembered for. His greatest discovery was a human being, Scheele [329], the apothecary of genius whom Bergman helped and encouraged.

Bergman was forced into retirement in 1780 because of bad health, and died of tuberculosis before he was fifty.

[316] **WATT,** James
Scottish engineer
Born: Greenock, Renfrew, January 19, 1736
Died: Heathfield, near Birmingham, England, August 19, 1819

Watt was a rather sickly child who could not go to school and was taught to read and write by his mother. He suffered from chronic migraine headaches and was suspected of being mentally retarded. His mother died while he was in his teens and his father, originally a prosperous merchant, experienced hard times that grew progressively worse. Watt traveled to England, reaching London eventually, and there went through a hard year of apprenticeship, during which he learned the use of tools and the craft of instrument maker.

In 1756 he returned to Scotland and tried to establish himself as an instrument maker in Glasgow. However, he did not meet the municipal requirements, for he lacked a sufficient period of apprenticeship, so he obtained a position at the University of Glasgow, which was outside municipal jurisdiction.

There he met Joseph Black [298] and learned of the matter of latent heat. Undoubtedly this set him to thinking how steam engines might be improved. Savery [236] and Newcomen [243] had devised engines that were in use as power sources for water pumping. However, such machines were terribly inefficient. This had been brought forcibly to Watt's attention when in 1764 the university gave him a model of a Newcomen steam engine to repair after a London instrument maker had failed. Watt could repair it without trouble, but that was not enough for him. He wanted to improve it.

During the course of a thoughtful Sunday walk, it seemed to him that he perceived the chief source of inefficiency. In the Newcomen engine, the steam chamber was cooled to condense the steam and produce the vacuum. It then had to be filled with steam again, but, since it had been cooled, a great deal of steam was first necessary just to heat up the chamber. All that steam was wasted. At

every cycle, immense quantities of fuel were required to undo the work of the cold water.

Watt introduced a second chamber (a "condenser") into which the steam could be led. The condenser could be kept cold constantly while the first chamber (the "cylinder") was kept hot constantly. In this way the two processes of heating and cooling were not forced to cancel each other. By 1769 Watt had a steam engine working with greater efficiency than the Newcomen variety. Furthermore, since there was no long pause at each cycle to heat up the chamber, Watt's engine did its work much more quickly. So impressed was Black with this development that he lent him a large sum of money to keep the project in operation.

Watt introduced other ingenious improvements, such as allowing steam to enter alternately on either side of a piston. Previously air pressure had driven the piston rapidly in only one direction as a vacuum was produced when steam was condensed. It was only mounting steam pressure, then, that slowly moved it back in the other direction. With steam entering and condensing on both sides, air pressure drove the piston rapidly in both directions alternately. In 1774 Watt went into partnership with a businessman and began to manufacture steam engines for sale. (In 1784 he used steam pipes to heat his office, so he also invented "steam heat.")

By 1790 the Watt engine had completely replaced the older Newcomen variety and by 1800 some five hundred Watt engines were working in England. In fact so superior was the Watt engine that the very existence of the Newcomen engine was all but forgotten and Watt began to be looked upon as the inventor of *the* steam engine.

In a sense, however, this was justified, for Watt not merely improved the Newcomen engine, he was the first to make such an engine more than a pump. In 1781 he devised mechanical attachments that ingeniously converted the back and forth movement of a piston into the rotary movement of a wheel, and by one type of movement or the other, the steam engine could then be made to power a variety of activities. Soon iron manufacturers were using it to power bellows to keep the air blast going in their furnaces and to power hammers to crush the ore.

The now-versatile steam engine had thus become the first of the modern "prime movers," the first modern device, that is, to take energy as it occurred in nature (in fuel) and apply it to the driving of machinery. It was just at this time, too, that the textile industry, England's most important, was being mechanized by men such as Arkwright [311]. The steam engine proved to be the right invention at the right time.

The consequences were incalculable. Steam engines, powered by burning coal, could deliver large quantities of energy constantly, at any needed spot. Manufacturing locations were not confined to rapid streams where water power might be used. Large and massive machinery, powered by steam, could be constructed and housed in factories. Large-scale production in such factories made handwork at home uneconomical. The artisan was replaced by the factory worker. Cities mushroomed; slums boomed; farming withered. All the benefits and evils of the factory system blossomed. In short, the Industrial Revolution began.

Watt started another revolution, which, however, was not to bloom for a century and a half. He invented a "centrifugal governor" that automatically controlled the engine's output of steam. The steam output whirled the governor about a vertical rod. The faster it whirled, the farther outward were thrown two metal spheres (through the action of centrifugal force). The farther outward the balls were thrown, the more they choked off the steam outlet. The steam output thus decreased, the governor whirled more slowly, the spheres dropped and the outlet was widened. In this way the steam output hovered between two limits and was never allowed to grow too large or too small.

In this is the germ of automation, since the centrifugal governor was a device that controlled a process by means of the variations in the process itself.

Automation has not come into its own until recent decades, but it began with James Watt, and the word governor, via the Greek, has given us the modern term "cybernetics."

Watt enjoys one honor that arose out of his efforts to measure the power (that is, the rate of doing work) of his steam engine. In 1783 he tested a strong horse and decided it could raise a 150-pound weight nearly four feet in a second. He therefore defined a "horsepower" as 550 foot-pounds per second. This unit of power is still used. However, the unit of power in the metric system is called the watt, in honor of the Scottish engineer. One horsepower equals 746 watts.

In 1800, prosperous, successful, and respected, Watt retired. He received an honorary doctorate from Glasgow University and was elected to the Royal Society. He refused the offer of a baronetcy and lived to be the last survivor among the founders of the famous Lunar Society of Birmingham, to which Priestley [312] and Erasmus Darwin [308] had belonged.

[317] LAGRANGE, Joseph Louis, comte de (la-grahnzh')
Italian-French astronomer and mathematician
Born: Turin, Piedmont, January 25, 1736
Died: Paris, France, April 10, 1813

Lagrange was of French ancestry, though born and raised in the Italian kingdom of Piedmont. His parents were wealthy but his father had speculated his fortune into oblivion. He was the youngest of eleven children and the only one to survive to adulthood. His father intended him for the law, but at school he came across an essay by Halley [238] on the calculus and was at once converted to mathematics. By the age of eighteen he was teaching geometry at the Royal Artillery School in Turin. There he organized a discussion group that became the Turin Academy of Sciences in 1758.

Lagrange's mathematical ability was

recognized by Euler [275], who at that time headed the Berlin Academy of Sciences under Frederick II (a monarch who rifled all Europe for scientific talent). In 1755 Lagrange had sent Euler a memorandum on the "calculus of variations" on which Euler himself had been working. So impressed was Euler that he deliberately held back his own work to allow Lagrange to publish first. (However, Euler and Lagrange never met.)

In 1766 Euler moved to St. Petersburg, Russia (where Catherine II was also bidding for scientific talent—it was the royal fashion to do so during the Age of Reason). At the recommendation of Euler and D'Alembert [289], the young Lagrange, aged forty, was appointed head of the Berlin Academy. As Frederick II put it, rather vaingloriously, the "greatest king in Europe" ought to have the "greatest mathematician in Europe" at his court.

Lagrange applied his mathematical ability to a systematization of mechanics, which had begun with Galileo [166]. His interest in the subject was aroused when he read Wallis's [198] treatise on the subject. Using the calculus of variations, he worked out very general equations from which all problems in mechanics could be solved. He summarized his methods in his book *Analytical Mechanics*, published in Paris in 1788 by a most reluctant publisher. The book was purely algebraic or, to use the term of Vieta [153], analytic, as the title proclaimed. There was not one geometric diagram in it.

In astronomy Lagrange addressed himself to a general problem left open by Newton [231]. (Lagrange once said that Newton was the luckiest man in the history of the world, for the system of the universe could only be worked out once and Newton had done it; however, in this he was too pessimistic, for there was to be room for Einstein [1064] a century and a half later, and Lagrange himself proceeded to make significant additions to the knowledge of the universe.)

Newton's law of universal gravitation could deal with two bodies if they were alone in the universe, but the solar system consists of many bodies. To be sure,

the sun's influence is supreme, but the minor bodies affect each other in minor ways called "perturbations" and these could not be ignored.

Lagrange worked out mathematical treatments of the motions of systems containing more than two bodies, such as the earth-moon-sun system and the system of Jupiter and its four moons. He included a study of situations in which three bodies might form a stable configuration as at the apices of an equilateral triangle (provided one body was very small). Such a system (now called a "Trojan system"), including the sun, Jupiter, and certain asteroids, was actually discovered a century and a half later.

Lagrange thought there might be two kinds of perturbations, periodic and secular. The periodic type causes a planet's orbit to vary first in one direction, then in the opposing direction, leading to no permanent change in the long run. The secular type caused an accumulating variation in one direction only so that the orbit is completely disrupted eventually. Lagrange tackled the problem of determining whether any of the observed perturbations in the solar system were indeed secular. In this he was joined by his younger contemporary Laplace [347], and together they answered, "No!"

After Frederick the Great's death, Lagrange moved to Paris in 1787 at the invitation of Louis XVI and was there lionized by Marie Antoinette, though he had then entered a period of deep depression that made the final decades of his life largely unproductive. With the coming of the French Revolution it might have been better for Lagrange to depart, in view of his friendship with the royal family. He remained, however, and lived through the Terror, partly because of the general respect for his accomplishments and partly because of his foreign birth.

The revolution gave him the opportunity for one last service to science. He was appointed in 1793 to head a commission to draw up a new system of weights and measures. Laplace and Lavoisier [334] were among the other members. Out of the deliberations of that commission came, in 1795, the metric system, the most logical system of measurement ever devised. It is now the universal language of scientists, although (to our shame, be it said) the United States, almost alone, clings to the illogical English system of measurement in daily life.

Napoleon delighted to honor Lagrange in the evening of his life and eventually made him a senator and a count.

[318] COULOMB, Charles Augustin
(koo-lome')
French physicist
Born: Angoulême, Charente,
June 14, 1736
Died: Paris, August 23, 1806

Coulomb was a military engineer in his younger days, serving in the West Indies for nine years beginning in 1764. There, he supervised the building of fortifications in Martinique. He returned to Paris in 1776, with his health impaired, and his search for a quieter life drew him toward scientific experimentation. When the disturbances of the French Revolution began he combined discretion with inclination and retired to the provincial town of Blois to work in peace. He rode out the Terror handily and was eventually restored to those posts he had lost, by an appreciative Napoleon.

By then he had made his name. In 1777 he invented a torsion balance that measured the quantity of a force by the amount of twist it produced in a thin, stiff fiber. Weight is a measure of the force of gravity upon an object, so a torsion balance can be used to measure weight. A similar instrument had been invented earlier by Michell [294], but Coulomb's discovery was independent and in 1781 he was elected to the French Academy.

Coulomb put the delicacy of his instrument at the service of electrical experiments. In a course of experimentation that began out of a desire to improve the mariner's compass, he placed a small electrically charged sphere at different distances from another small electrically charged sphere and measured the force of attraction or repulsion (depending on whether the charges were opposite or similar) by the amount of twist produced on his torsion balance. In this way he was able to show in 1785 that the force of electrical attraction or repulsion is proportional to the product of the charges on each sphere and inversely proportional to the square of the distance between the spheres, center to center. (Priestley [312] had come to this conclusion a few years earlier on the basis of indirect evidence.) This meant that electrical forces obeyed a rule similar to that of gravitational forces as worked out by Newton [231]. This is still called Coulomb's law. In his honor, an accepted unit for quantity of electric charge is the coulomb.

Cavendish [307] had actually discovered Coulomb's law before Coulomb, but Cavendish never published his results, and they were not discovered until half a century after his death.

[319] GUYTON DE MORVEAU,
Baron Louis Bernard (gee-ton'
duh mawr-voh')
French chemist
Born: Dijon, Côte d'Or, January
4, 1737
Died: Paris, January 2, 1816

Guyton de Morveau, the son of a lawyer, was himself a lawyer by profession and served in the Dijon parliament before the French Revolution. Science was his hobby and, in 1782, when he retired from his legal position, he turned to chemistry.

Already, in 1772, he had as an amateur demonstrated by careful weighing that rusted metals were indeed heavier than the metals themselves as earlier chemists had maintained on the basis of cruder observations all the way back to Boyle [212]. This fit Lavoisier's [334] new chemistry when that was developed.

His problems with chemical nomenclature led to a fruitful collaboration with Lavoisier. With the revolution in full swing, he turned to politics again, on the side of the revolutionists, and lived through the period—which is more than Lavoisier did. Sadly enough, Guyton de Morveau was another of Lavoisier's associates who, like Fourcroy [366], made no move to save the great man.

Guyton de Morveau suggested to the French revolutionaries that balloons be used for military reconnaissance and so he may be considered the great-grand-father of aerial warfare. He served as master of the mint under Napoleon, and in 1811 he was made a baron.

[320] **GALVANI,** Luigi (gahl-vah'nee)
Italian anatomist
Born: Bologna, September 9, 1737
Died: Bologna, December 4, 1798

Galvani studied theology in early life but turned to medicine and received his medical degree in 1759 from the University of Bologna. In 1762, he began lecturing on medicine there and in 1775 he became professor of anatomy. It was his good fortune that electrical machines, such as Leyden jars, were the scientific rage of the time. They could be found in most laboratories, including the one in which Galvani carried on his anatomical and physiological researches.

Galvani noticed, in 1771, that the muscles of dissected frog legs (some say they were in the laboratory because they were about to be used in the preparation of soup) twitched wildly when a spark from an electric machine struck them, or when a metal scalpel touched them while such a machine was in operation, even though the spark made no direct contact. This was, in itself, not too surprising. Electric shocks made living muscles twitch, why not dead ones too?

Since Franklin [272] had shown lightning to be electrical in nature a generation before, the frog muscles might be expected to twitch during a thunderstorm. This would be independent confirmation of the electrical nature of lightning. Galvani therefore laid frog muscles out on brass hooks outside the window so that they rested against an iron latticework.

The muscles did indeed twitch during the thunderstorm, but they also twitched

in the absence of it. In fact, they twitched whenever they made contact with two different metals.

Apparently electricity was involved, but where did it come from—the metals or the muscle? Being an anatomist he had a natural predilection toward living tissue, and he decided on the muscle. He declared there was such a thing as animal electricity and clung to that view fiercely. He was proved wrong some years later by Volta [337] and ended his life in disappointment. Even his university appointment was lost, for in 1797 he refused to swear allegiance to a new government set up in northern Italy by the young French general, Napoleon Bonaparte—so that he died in poverty, too.

In the last decade of his life, however, Galvani had succeeded in making his name a household word. The steady electricity set up by two metals in contact was called galvanic electricity, as opposed to the static electricity set up by rubbing amber or glass. A person stung into sudden action by an electric current (or by any attack of strong emotion) is galvanized. Iron on which crystals of zinc are layered by means of an electric current (or even, eventually, by means other than an electric current) is said to be galvanized iron. Finally an instrument designed to detect electric current was invented in 1820 and, at the suggestion of Ampère [407], was named a galvanometer.

[321] **HERSCHEL,** Sir William
German-English astronomer
Born: Hannover, Germany, November 15, 1738
Died: Slough, Buckinghamshire, England, August 25, 1822

At the time of Herschel's birth, Hannover was a possession of King George II of England (though it was not actually part of the British realm). Herschel's father was a musician in the Hannoverian army and Herschel himself was headed toward the same profession. The coming of the Seven Years' War, however, and the occupation of Hannover by the French made army life somewhat unattractive, and Herschel's parents managed in 1757 to spirit him out of the service and smuggle him into England.

Herschel stayed in England for the rest of his life and adapted himself thoroughly to his new home, changing his German name of Friedrich Wilhelm to the English "William." His musical talents brought him success in England. He arrived in Leeds in 1757 and by 1766 he was a well-known organist and music teacher at the resort city of Bath, tutoring up to thirty-five pupils a week.

Economic security gave him a chance to gratify his fervent desire for learning. He taught himself Latin and Italian. The theory of musical sounds led him to mathematics and that to optics. Optics led him to a book about Newton's work and suddenly he was filled with a desire to see the heavens for himself. Since he could not afford to buy good telescopes, he decided to grind lenses and make his own instruments for viewing the heavens. He tried two hundred times before he made one that satisfied him. In 1772 he returned to Hannover long enough to collect his sister Caroline [352] and take her to England.

This proved an exceedingly fortunate move, for Caroline proved as fanatic a lens grinder and amateur astronomer as Herschel himself, and it is not likely that Herschel could have accomplished as much without the heroically single-minded help of his sister. (She became the first important woman astronomer.)

Together the Herschels ground excellent lenses. Caroline read aloud to William and fed him meals a bit at a time, while he ground for hours. They ended with the best telescopes then in existence.

Herschel made up his mind to look in systematic fashion at everything in the sky. By 1774 he had not only made himself the best reflector in the world but the first that was actually more efficient than any refractor then existing, so he certainly had the tool for the job. He began to bombard the scientific world with papers describing his observations of the mountains of the moon, on variable stars, on the possibility that changes in sunspot activity might affect agriculture on earth, and so on.

In 1781, while systematically moving from star to star with his excellent telescope, Herschel came across an object that appeared as a disc instead of a mere point of light. He made the natural assumption that he had discovered a new comet and reported it as such. However, additional observations showed that the disc had a sharp edge like a planet and not fuzzy boundaries like a comet. Furthermore, when enough observations had been made to calculate an orbit, he and others, notably Laplace [347], found that orbit to be nearly circular, like a planet's, rather than elongated, as a comet's would be. And to top it off, the orbit of the object lay far outside that of Saturn.

The conclusion Herschel came to, with great wonder and delight, was that he had discovered a new planet and had doubled the extent of the known solar system. It was the first new planet to be discovered in historic times.

Actually the planet is just barely visible to the naked eye and it had been observed a number of times earlier. It was even included in the star map prepared by Flamsteed [234], who noted it a century earlier in the constellation Taurus and recorded it as 34 Tauri. In 1764 it had been spotted near Venus and it was reported as a satellite of that planet. However, it was Herschel's telescope that showed the disc and Herschel that finally recognized the object as a planet.

Herschel tried to name the planet Georgium Sidus ("George's Star") after George III, then king of England. Some astronomers, at the suggestion of Lalande [309], named it Herschel in his honor. In the end, it was decided to stick to mythological names for planets. Bode [344] had suggested the new planet be named Uranus after the father of Saturn (in Greek "Cronos") and by the mid-nineteenth century this was universally accepted.

The news of the discovery of Uranus made a tremendous sensation. Astronomers had thought that Newton [231] left them nothing to discover, and Frederick II of Prussia (no scientist, to be sure, though a patron of scientists) believed all scientific findings had already been made. Herschel's announcement was like a breath of fresh air, indicating that there yet remained portions of the unknown. (The same false complacency and sharp awakening was to take place a century later in Michelson's [835] time.) Herschel was elected to membership in the Royal Society in 1781 and awarded the Copley prize. George III, who was of Hannoverian extraction and who was pleased with the achievement of a fellow countryman, pardoned Herschel's youthful desertion from the Hannoverian army and appointed him his private astronomer at a salary of three hundred guineas a year.

Herschel started astronomical observations in earnest. For a while he had to continue to manufacture and sell telescopes (the king's subsidy was not much), but in 1788 he married a wealthy widow and became a full-time observer. (Caroline remained unmarried and continued to devote herself to her now-famous brother and to astronomy.)

Herschel became the most important and successful astronomer of his time. No one else could have been mentioned in the same breath. Like Bradley [258], Herschel tried to observe the parallax of stars and failed. However, he used a method first suggested by Galileo [166], which was to concentrate on pairs of stars in close proximity (such pairs having first been discovered by Riccioli [185] nearly a century and a half before). At the time it was thought that these stars were close together only through the accident of happening to lie in nearly the same line of sight, and that one might, in actuality, be very many times farther away than the other. If that were so, the nearer star ought to show a parallactic shift in position in comparison with the farther one.

This is undoubtedly the situation on occasion, but in a number of cases that Herschel tried, he found that neither showed a parallactic shift in position. They moved, but from the manner in which they were moving he could only conclude that they were close to each other not only in appearance, but also in

actuality. By 1793 he was convinced that they were circling each other. In the course of his career he discovered some eight hundred such double stars or "binary stars," as he called them.

This was the first indication that double stars might really be just that. Furthermore, by studying them it was possible to show that their motions were in accord with Newton's law of gravity. Until then the validity of the law could only be tested within the solar system. Now, a century after the establishment of the law, it was traced out in the motions of incredibly distant stars and the theory first truly earned its title of Universal. Herschel was as thorough in observing stars whose luminosity varied and was the first systematic reporter on variable stars.

In 1801, during a short lull in the Napoleonic Wars, Herschel visited Paris and met Laplace and Napoleon himself. Herschel was unimpressed with Napoleon, detecting the latter's way of affecting to know more than he really did know.

Herschel's voluminous observations of the stars gave him an overall view of the starry universe that no predecessor had had. In fact, Herschel was the first to present an astronomical picture in which the solar system was reduced to what, in point of fact, it really was, a tiny and inconsiderable speck in the vast universe of the stars. For instance, in analyzing the proper motions of a large number of stars, he believed, by 1805, that he could explain the regularities he observed by assuming that the sun itself was moving toward a point in the constellation Hercules, a matter studied more thoroughly by Argelander [508]. Just as Copernicus [127] had dethroned the earth as the motionless center of the universe, so Herschel dethroned the sun.

By studying the Milky Way and counting stars in various directions, Herschel prepared a picture of the starry system as a whole. He viewed the visible universe as representing a gigantic collection of stars arranged roughly in the shape of a grindstone. Our own sun, he believed, was located somewhere near the center of the system and when we looked out in the directions of the long axis of the grindstone, we saw a vast multiplicity of stars that faded (through distance) into the general faint glimmer of the Milky Way. (The sun's apparent position in the center of this system was to be shown an illusion a century later by Shapley [1102].)

Herschel also viewed various cloudy objects in the skies, cataloguing some twenty-five hundred of them. His own better telescopes resolved into stars some of the objects viewed and recorded by Messier [305], so that he discovered the large "galactic cluster," like the one in Hercules. Other objects remained unresolved, and Herschel speculated that they might be other huge star collections (or "galaxies") like our own. He also observed dark areas in the Milky Way which we now know to be clouds of dust. Herschel believed they were empty gaps and said, "Surely this is a hole in the heavens."

Nor did he entirely neglect the solar system after his discovery of Uranus. He returned to Uranus with improved telescopes and in 1787 discovered two of its satellites, Titania and Oberon. (He had become more English than the English and abandoned classic mythology for Shakespeare.) He reported four other satellites, but those proved to be mistakes.

He built a brand-new telescope, forty feet long with a 48-inch reflector. George III contributed £4,000 toward its construction and took proprietary delight in showing the instrument to visitors. On the first night of observation Hershel turned the telescope on Saturn and discovered two new satellites, Enceladus and Mimas, which, added to the one discovered by Huygens [215] and the four by Cassini [209], made a total of seven for the ringed planet. Herschel also timed the period of rotation of Saturn and showed that its rings rotated as well.

He was not without an occasional peculiar idea, however. He thought the moon and the planets were inhabited. He also suggested that the luminosity of the sun might be confined to its atmosphere and that under its belt of fire was a cold, solid body that might even be inhabited. The sunspots, he speculated, were holes in the atmosphere through which the cold surface could be seen. No one took this notion seriously except cranks and faddists, who were pleased to use the great name of Herschel to cover their own follies.

Herschel also extended man's view in a direction that had nothing directly to do with astronomy. In 1800 he tested various portions of the sun's spectrum by thermometer to see if he could find interesting differences in the amount of heat the different colors delivered. He did, but in a rather unexpected way, for he found that the temperature rise was highest in no color at all, at a spot beyond the red end of the spectrum. He concluded that sunlight contained invisible light beyond the red. This is now called infrared radiation. The following year Ritter [413] was to extend the visible spectrum in the other direction.

Herschel was knighted in 1816 and died in the fullness of years and fame, working almost to the end and making his last observations in 1819 when he was in his eighty-first year. He lived eighty-four years, which is Uranus' period of revolution about the sun. Herschel left a son, John Herschel [479], who was likewise a renowned astronomer.

[322] SAUSSURE, Horace Bénédict de (soh-syoor')
Swiss physicist
Born: Geneva, February 17, 1740
Died: Geneva, January 22, 1799

Saussure was the son of a noted agricultural scientist. He earned his Ph.D. at the University of Geneva in 1759 and in 1762 he obtained a professorial position there, on the recommendation of Haller [278].

He was an enthusiastic mountaineer and was among those who helped create the mountain-climbing craze that has continued ever since. Certainly, he was the first to climb mountains with the notion of making scientific observations in the process. For the purpose, he devised an electrometer, the first device used to measure electric potential. He also constructed a hygrometer for measuring humidity, the first to use a human hair for the purpose. His investigations produced useful data in both meteorology and geology. (In fact, Saussure was the first to use the word "geology," in 1779.)

In 1787 Saussure climbed Mont Blanc, the highest peak of the Alps, and led the second expedition to do so successfully. His own thoughts of the development of the earth were in line with those that Hutton [297] was just publishing, and, in fact, some of the data Saussure gathered was used by Hutton in his book.

[323] MÜLLER, Franz Joseph (myoo'-ler)
Austrian mineralogist
Born: Nagyszeben, Transylvania, (now Sibiu, Romania), July 1, 1740
Died: Vienna, October 12, 1825

Müller, the son of a treasury official, studied law and philosophy in Vienna, but he attended a school of mines, too, and became most interested in mineralogy. Emperor Joseph II appointed him chief inspector of mines in Transylvania and, on his retirement in 1818, Emperor Francis I raised him to the nobility as Baron von Reichenstein.

In 1782, while working with a gold ore, he obtained a substance that he decided was a new element. He sent a specimen to Bergman [315], who died before he could complete his investigation. Müller then sent a sample to Klaproth [335], who confirmed the finding, gave due credit to Müller, and named the element "tellurium."

[324] FRERE, John (freer)
English archaeologist
Born: Westhorpe, Suffolk, August 10, 1740
Died: East Dereham, Norfolk, July 12, 1807

Frere, the son of a landowner, entered Cambridge in 1758 and attained his master's degree there in 1766. He was a

practicing lawyer and was a Member of Parliament in 1799.

He was elected a member of the Royal Society in 1771. This was for his antiquarian interests.

In 1790 he discovered shaped flints which, he suggested, were tools formed by people who did not have the use of metal, and which, he thought, were very old. What's more, the site seemed to be the source of a great many such tools.

He reported this in 1797, but the matter roused no interest since the orthodoxy of the time insisted that humanity (and, indeed, the whole universe) was less than six thousand years old. The clear indication of human tools many times older than this was therefore simply ignored. It was not until similar finds were made by Boucher [458] a half century later, that the matter could no longer be set aside.

[325] MONTGOLFIER, Joseph Michel (mohn-gohl-fyay')
French inventor
Born: Vidalon-les-Annonay, August 26, 1740
Died: Balaruc-les-Bains, June 26, 1810
MONTGOLFIER, Jacques Étienne
French inventor
Born: Vidalon-les-Annonay, January 6, 1745
Died: Serrières, August 1, 1799

These brothers were two of the sixteen children of a well-to-do paper manufacturer, a family trade of romantic antecedents. An ancestor at the time of the Crusades was supposed to have discovered the process while a prisoner in Damascus and to have brought Tsai Lun's [63] invention to France.

The Montgolfiers were first inspired to aeronautics by observing the manner in which the smoke of fire caught up light objects and sent them flying into the air. (A less romantic story has it that Joseph, the elder brother, had his mind turned toward ballooning by reading Priestley's [312] account of his experiments with various gases.)

Hot air seemed clearly lighter than

cold air, and floated on cold air as wood floated on water. It seemed natural to suppose that if a light bag were held, opening downward, over a fire, it would fill with hot air and be carried upward. This proved to be the case.

On June 5, 1783, in the market place of their home town, the brothers filled a large linen bag, thirty-five feet in diameter, with hot air. It lifted fifteen hundred feet upward, and floated a distance of a mile and a half in ten minutes. By November they went to Paris, where they managed a flight of six miles before a crowd of three hundred thousand that included Benjamin Franklin [272].

Hot air, however, has very little buoyancy and as soon as it cools down it has none. With Charles's [343] suggestion that hydrogen be used, balloons that could lift men came into fashion. Mankind had always filled its myths and legends with flying men, flying horses, flying carpets, and so on. Leonardo da Vinci [122] had even tried to design flying machines two centuries before the Montgolfier brothers. However, 1783 was the first year in which men were actually lifted off the ground for prolonged periods. The scientific exploration of the upper atmosphere became a possibility.

[326] **LEXELL,** Anders Johan
Swedish astronomer
Born: Äbo, Sweden (now Turku, Finland) December 24, 1740
Died: St. Petersburg (now Leningrad), Russia, December 11, 1784

The son of a city councillor, Lexell graduated from the University of Äbo in 1760 and gained a professorial position at Uppsala in 1763. Invited to St. Petersburg by the Academy of Sciences, he accepted a post there in 1769 and remained there for the rest of his life. In St. Petersburg, he was a close associate of Euler [275].

In 1770 Lexell worked out the orbit of a comet observed in that year and determined its period of revolution to be five and a half years. It was the first shortterm comet to have its orbit calculated. In 1781 he studied the object discovered

by Herschel [321] who himself thought the object must be a comet. It was Lexell's observations that proved the orbit of the object to lie everywhere outside the orbit of Saturn and therefore to be a new planet—eventually called Uranus. What is more, Lexell eventually pointed out that the difficulties of establishing an accurate orbit might be the result of the gravitational interference of a hitherto unknown planet beyond Uranus—a suggestion that was borne out a half century later with the work of Adams [615] and Leverrier [564] and the discovery of Neptune.

[327] **WITHERING,** William
English physician
Born: Wellington, Shropshire, March 1741
Died: Birmingham, October 6, 1799

Withering, the son of a surgeon, obtained his medical degree from the University of Edinburgh in 1766. In 1775, he moved his practice to Birmingham where he prospered and where he joined the Lunar Society, whose members included Priestley [312] and Watt [316].

He had an interest in botany, which caused him to listen with more patience than might otherwise have been possible to "old wives' tales" concerning the folk remedies used by herb-gatherers. He picked up the use of foxglove, learned of its efficacy in the case of certain cases of edema (caused by heart failure) and of the doses safe to use. In 1785 he published a careful report of his findings that added the very useful drug digitalis to the pharmaceutical armory of physicians.

[328] **LEBLANC,** Nicolas (luh-blank')
French chemist
Born: Ivoy-le-Pré, Indre, December 6, 1742
Died: St.-Denis (near Paris), January 16, 1806

Leblanc, who was orphaned at an early age, was apprenticed to an apothecary by his guardian, a physician. He studied surgery and in 1780 became physician to the future duke of Orleans, who during the early days of the French Revolution gained a dubious fame as Philippe Égalité, an aristocrat who voted for the death of the king but who was himself guillotined in 1793.

In 1775 the French Academy of Sciences had offered a prize for a practical method of manufacturing sodium hydroxide and sodium carbonate out of salt (sodium chloride). Leblanc developed what is now called the Leblanc process which, together with the work of Chevreul [448], made soap manufacture on a large scale possible for the first time with important effects on personal hygiene. In 1783 he was awarded the prize, which, however, was not paid. It was the first chemical discovery that had an immediate commercial use.

During the revolution the government (which definitely *did* need scientists regardless of the comment to Lavoisier [334]) needed soda badly for a variety of industrial chemical industries and forced Leblanc to make his process public without remuneration after the execution of his patron, Philippe Égalité. Leblanc was reduced to poverty in this fashion. He received his factory back in 1802 but lacked the capital to start things rolling. In 1806 he killed himself. On the whole the revolution had been kinder to Lavoisier. In 1855, Napoleon III made restitution to Leblanc's heirs.

The Leblanc process was ultimately replaced by that of Solvay [735].

[329] **SCHEELE,** Karl Wilhelm (shay'-luh)
Swedish chemist
Born: Stralsund, Pomerania, December 9, 1742
Died: Köping, Västmanland, May 21, 1786

Pomerania has been part of Germany through most of its history (it is now part of East Germany). At the time of Scheele's birth it belonged to Sweden, because of that country's participation in the Thirty Years' War a century earlier. Scheele can therefore be considered German by ancestry; he usually wrote in German. But he did all his adult work in Sweden and is generally considered a Swedish chemist.

He was the seventh child of eleven, and with children the only form of wealth in that family young Karl Wilhelm could not be supported in idleness. At fourteen he was apprenticed to an apothecary. In those days this, for a boy with an active mind, was as good as a university education in chemistry, for apothecaries were profoundly interested in minerals and usually prepared their own drugs.

Scheele taught himself chemistry and became an apothecary extraordinary, passing periodically to more and more famous establishments, till finally he was working at Stockholm and at Uppsala. (Later in life, he had ample opportunity to obtain a university position and all its prestige, but he preferred to remain an apothecary and concentrate on research. As a professor, he would have been one of many. As an apothecary, he was the greatest the world has seen. He also refused to serve Frederick II of Prussia as court chemist and turned down the offer of a similar position in England.)

In 1770 he met the Swedish mineralogist Bergman [315], who sponsored and encouraged him. This meeting was arranged through another chemist, Gahn [339], who was a friend, as was another excellent chemist, Hjelm [342]. (Sweden, in proportion to its population, has probably produced more first-rate chemists in the last two centuries than any other nation in the world.)

In the course of his research career Scheele probably discovered or helped discover more new substances in greater variety than any other chemist in a like period of time.

He discovered a number of acids, including tartaric acid, citric acid, benzoic acid, malic acid, oxalic acid, and gallic acid in the plant kingdom; lactic acid and uric acid in the animal; and molybdic acid and arsenious acid in the mineral. He prepared and investigated three highly poisonous gases, hydrogen fluoride, hydrogen sulfide, and hydrogen cyanide and managed to avoid killing himself. (He even recorded the taste of hydrogen cyanide—a report one would swear could only be made posthumously.)

He was involved in the discovery of the elements chlorine, manganese, barium, molybdenum, tungsten, nitrogen, and oxygen, and yet he is undoubtedly the unluckiest chemist in history, for despite his phenomenal labors in uncovering new elements, he does not receive undisputed credit for having discovered a single one. In some cases chemists independently made the same discovery a little sooner. In others Scheele did not quite carry matters far enough and chemists such as Hjelm, Gahn, and d'Elhuyar [367] took the last step and got the credit. In the case of chlorine, Scheele prepared it in the 1770s but did not recognize it as an element. He thought it an oxygen-containing compound. It was Davy [421], over thirty years later, who recognized the elementary nature of chlorine and he is the one usually given credit for its discovery.

The most tragic case of all was that of oxygen, which, from the standpoint of chemical history, was the most significant of all his discoveries. He prepared it in 1771 and 1772 by heating a number of substances that held it loosely, including the mercuric oxide used by Priestley [312] a couple of years later. This was a clear "first" for Scheele, who described his experiments carefully in a book, which, however, through the negligence of his publisher, did not appear in print until 1777. By that time Priestley had reported his own experiments, and it is Priestley who gets the credit for oxygen.

(Scheele called oxygen "fire air." Like Priestley, Scheele was a confirmed phlogistonist and did not interpret the role of oxygen in combustion correctly. That was left for Lavoisier [334].)

However, copper arsenite, which Scheele studied, is still called Scheele's green, while a calcium tungstate mineral is called scheelite. He also discovered the effect of light on silver compounds, which, half a century later, Daguerre [467] and others were to use in the development of photography.

Scheele's private life had its share of misfortune. He suffered poor health and agonizing pain from rheumatism, which was aggravated by his long hours of work. He eschewed virtually all social life in favor of science, his only passion, and when he decided to marry he found he had time for it only on his deathbed. When he died he was only forty-three, and his death may have been hastened by his habitual tasting of the new compounds he prepared. His final symptoms resembled those of mercury poisoning.

[330] **FITCH,** John
American inventor
Born: Windsor, Connecticut, January 21, 1743
Died: Bardstown, Kentucky, July 2, 1798

It is hard to find a man so beset by misfortune as John Fitch. He had little schooling, a harsh father, and a nagging wife, whom he deserted. He made some money during the Revolutionary War when he was in charge of a gun factory, but the colonial currency became worthless. He passed the last part of the war as a British prisoner.

In Pennsylvania in 1785 Fitch thought of building a steamship. With superhuman effort he obtained the capital and the necessary grants of monopoly from five states. In 1790 his fourth and best steamship traveled from Philadelphia to Trenton and back on a regular schedule. However, there were few passengers, the ship operated at a loss, his backers quit, and finally the ship was destroyed in a storm in 1792.

He tried to begin again in France in 1793 but could obtain no funds. He returned to America in deep depression and died (perhaps a suicide) nine years before Fulton [385] repeated his work and received credit for the invention of the steamship.

[331] **BANKS,** Sir Joseph
English botanist
Born: London, February 13, 1743
Died: Isleworth, near London,
June 19, 1820

Banks was that convenient but rare phenomenon, a scientist of great independent wealth (which he inherited from his father in 1761) who spends that wealth liberally in the support of science.

His interest in botany arose at the age of fifteen, when he became entranced with the flowery beauty of a country lane. While still a student at Oxford he financed a lectureship in botany, which is how the subject came to be taught there for the first time.

In 1766 he made his first trip abroad, accompanying an expedition to Newfoundland, where he gathered new varieties of plants and insects and earned a membership in the Royal Society.

It became fashionable at about that time for sea expeditions intent on scientific exploration to carry naturalists who could make appropriate studies of the flora and fauna encountered. (This was to reach its peak some three quarters of a century later, when Charles Darwin [554] made his first reputation on such a voyage.)

Banks had his chance in 1768 on Cook's [300] first expedition to the Pacific. He not only accompanied the expedition around the world but paid for all the necessary equipment. He hired a pupil of Linnaeus [276] as assistant and four artists as well. (Those were the days before photography.)

The whole thing is supposed to have cost him £10,000 but at least he had an unparalleled chance to explore, for Cook landed on Australia. There Banks could browse through an isolated continent with life forms unlike those of any other. In fact the first point of landing, in 1770, near what is now Sydney, was named Botany Bay because of the delight of Banks in the prospect of exploration. (A quarter century later, Botany Bay became a penal establishment.) A peninsula just south of the present city of Christchurch in New Zealand was

named Banks Peninsula by Cook in honor of his botanist.

Banks was the first to show that almost all the Australian mammals were marsupials and were more primitive than the placental mammals inhabiting the other continents. A century later Wallace [643] was to draw far-reaching conclusions from this.

After Banks returned from the South Pacific, he had a personal audience with George III, who wanted to know about his discoveries. He then accompanied an expedition to the North Atlantic, in 1772. In Iceland he discovered great geysers.

In 1778 he was elected president of the Royal Society, thanks to the influence of George III. He kept that post until his death, forty-one years later. This long tenure was not entirely good. Banks grew lax with age and while the membership of the Society grew, the standards declined and it became nearly moribund.

In 1781 Banks was made a baronet. He remained a philanthropist to the end, supporting young men of talent, notably Robert Brown [403] and making his home a gathering place for men of science.

Banks was interested in helping found colonies in the far regions of the world, and it was largely through his efforts that the first colonies were established in Australia. He is sometimes called the father of Australia. He also labored to transplant plants from their native regions to other lands where they might be useful. It was through his efforts that the breadfruit plant was brought from Tahiti to the West Indies.

One ship transporting these breadfruits, in 1788, was the *Bounty* under William Bligh, who had been a ship's master under Cook on the latter's final voyage to the Pacific. The crew of the *Bounty* mutinied against harsh treatment by the captain and against having to leave Tahiti (and thus supplied Charles B. Nordhoff and James N. Hall with a good theme).

Banks was impressed with Franklin's [272] action in persuading the American rebels to leave Cook unmolested.

Through the Napoleonic Wars he labored to follow this precedent and keep scientists above national angers and prejudices. It was an enterprise doomed to failure in later wars as nationalism grew more heated and as science began to play a greater and greater role in war-making technology.

[332] HAÜY, René Just (a-yoo-ee′)
        French mineralogist
        Born: St.-Just-en-Choisée, Oise,
        February 28, 1743
        Died: Paris, June 1, 1822

Haüy, the son of a poor weaver, trained for the church and became a priest in 1770. He grew interested in natural history and mineralogy only after he was thirty, through the circumstance of making friends with an old priest whose hobby was botany.

In 1781 Haüy had a fortunate accident. He dropped a piece of calcite and it broke into small fragments. It had been part of the collection of a friend and Haüy was mortified. His embarrassment was assuaged somewhat when he noticed that the fragments clove along straight planes that met at constant angles, something Steno [225] had casually noted a century before but had not followed up.

Haüy broke more pieces of calcite and found that no matter what the original shape, the broken fragments were rhombohedral (that is, slanted "cubes").

He hypothesized that each crystal was built up of successive additions of what we now call a "unit cell" to form—in the absence of external interference—a simple geometric shape with constant angles and with sides that could be related by simple integral ratios. He maintained that an identity or difference in crystalline form implied an identity or difference in chemical composition.

This was the beginning of the science of crystallography, which was to attain maturity over a century later with the development of X-ray techniques by Laue [1068] and Bragg [922].

Haüy was involved in the labors that went into the establishment of the metric system. With Lavoisier [334] he determined the density of water in order to set up a standard of mass.

During the French Revolution, however, Haüy, as a priest, was in considerable danger. Scientific friends, who were in better standing with the government, kept him alive, though he was imprisoned for a time. Despite his own insecurity, Haüy tried, unsuccessfully, to intercede for Lavoisier, which was more than a few other friends of Lavoisier, more favorably situated, dared do.

Haüy survived to become a professor of mineralogy at the Museum of Natural History under Napoleon and wrote the first important texts on crystallography at Napoleon's specific request. After Napoleon fell, however, Haüy was deprived of his post, and spent his few remaining years in retirement.

[333] JEFFERSON, Thomas
        American statesman and scholar
        Born: Shadwell, Virginia, April
        13, 1743
        Died: Monticello, Virginia, July 4,
        1826

The chief events of the life of Jefferson are known to every well-read American. He was educated at William and Mary College and was admitted to the bar in 1767. He served in the Virginia legislature, took an active part in the American revolution and wrote the Declaration of Independence.

During the War of Independence he was governor of Virginia and after its end he succeeded Franklin [272] as minister to France. He was secretary of state under Washington, the first President; and Vice-President under John Adams, the second. In 1800 he was elected third President and served two terms. After retiring in 1809 he remained a revered elder statesman until his death on the fiftieth anniversary of the adoption of the Declaration he wrote.

What is not so well known is that Jefferson was an accomplished scholar and gentleman-scientist of the last decades of the Age of Reason. He knew many languages, interested himself deeply in scientific research (was intimately acquainted with Priestley [312] for instance), studied agriculture and experimented with new varieties of grain. He also studied and classified fossils unearthed in New York state at a time when the investigation of these objects was in its infancy. He was also an architect of considerable excellence.

He was the closest approach to scientist-in-office among all the Presidents of the United States.

[334] **LAVOISIER,** Antoine Laurent
(la-vwah-zyay')
French chemist
Born: Paris, August 26, 1743
Died: Paris, May 8, 1794

Lavoisier was born of a well-to-do family, was loved and pampered to an extreme, first by his mother and then, after her early death in 1748, by an adoring aunt, and was given an excellent education. This good fortune was not wasted, for the young man, suffering from chronic dyspepsia, devoted himself to his studies by both inclination and necessity, and proved a brilliant student. His father, a lawyer, hoped his son would follow in that profession, but young Lavoisier, who obtained his license in law in 1764, attended lectures on astronomy by Lacaille [284] and grew interested in science. After dabbling in geology, and doing creditable work in that field, he veered toward chemistry, and that became his life work.

From the very beginning of his chemical researches he recognized the importance of accurate measurement. Thus his first important work, in 1764, lay in an investigation of the composition of the mineral gypsum. This he heated to drive off the water content, and he measured accurately the water given off. There were chemists before Lavoisier, notably Black [298] and Cavendish [307], who devoted themselves to measurement, but it was Lavoisier who pounded away at it until, by his very successes, he sold the notion to chemists generally. He did for chemistry what Galileo [166] had done for physics two centuries earlier and the

effect on chemistry was just as fruitful. It is partly for this that Lavoisier is often called the father of modern chemistry and sometimes the Newton [231] of chemistry.

Lavoisier was a most public-spirited citizen, joining numbers of boards and commissions designed to improve the lot of the people. In the 1760s he worked on improved methods of lighting towns (making a splash as a twenty-year-old with an essay on the subject), while in the 1770s he designed new methods for preparing saltpeter, a substance needed in the manufacture of gunpowder. These new methods made it unnecessary for government officials to ransack cellars and barns for crystals of the stuff, an invasion of privacy that was sometimes brutally carried out and was strongly resented by the populace. In the 1780s he worked on the modernization of agriculture, and his researches involved a model farm he had established in 1778.

All this public spirit was not to help him in the end, because of two mistakes. In the first place, he invested half a million francs in the Ferme Générale in 1768 in order to earn money for his researches. The Ferme Générale was a private firm engaged by the French government, at a fixed fee, to collect taxes. Anything they collected over and above the fee they could keep. Naturally the "tax-farmers" gouged every last sou, and no group was more hated in eighteenth-century France than those same tax-farmers. Lavoisier himself was not engaged in active tax-collecting, of course, but he worked busily in an administrative capacity. Nor did he use the money earned for selfish purposes but plowed it back into chemical research, setting up a magnificent private laboratory in which the scientific leaders of France regularly gathered. The envoys from the new republic across the sea, Thomas Jefferson [333] and Benjamin Franklin [272], were particularly welcome there.

Nevertheless, Lavoisier *was* a tax-farmer and earned one hundred thousand francs a year out of it. What's more, in 1771 he married Marie-Anne, the daughter of an important executive of the Ferme Générale. She was young (only fourteen at the time), beautiful, and intelligent, and she threw herself wholeheartedly into his work, taking his notes, translating from English, illustrating his books, and so on. In general it was a splendid love-match, but she *was* the daughter of an executive tax-farmer.

Lavoisier's second mistake involved the French Academy of Sciences, to which honored association he was elected in 1768, when only twenty-three. In 1780 a certain Jean-Paul Marat, a journalist who fancied himself a scientist, applied for membership and Lavoisier was active in blackballing him, for the very good reason that the papers he offered the academy (containing some foolish home-grown notions on the nature of fire) were worthless. Marat, however, was not the man to forget, and the time came when he was to take a fearful revenge.

Lavoisier in the early, happy days was busily engaged in breaking down, one by one, the antique chemical notions that still cobwebbed the thinking of eighteenth-century chemists.

There were still some who maintained the old Greek notion of the elements and said that transmutation was possible because water could be turned to earth on long heating. This seemed so, for water heated for many days developed a solid sediment.

Lavoisier decided, in 1768, to test the matter and boiled water for one hundred and one days in a device, called a "pelican," that condensed the water vapor and returned it to the flask so that no water was lost in the process. And, of course, he employed his method of careful measurement. He weighed both water and vessel before and after.

Sediment appeared, but the water did not change its weight during the boiling. Therefore, the sediment could not have been formed out of the water. However, the flask itself had lost weight, a loss just equal to the weight of the sediment. In other words, the sediment was not water turning to earth, it was material from the glass, slowly etched away by the hot water and precipitating in solid frag-

ments. Here was a clear-cut example of the manner in which observation without measurement could be useless and misleading.

Lavoisier's interest in street lighting introduced him to the whole problem of combustion. The phlogiston theory of Stahl [241] had been in existence for a century now, and there were many things it could not explain. The resulting confusion among chemists was clarified by Lavoisier's work and only after that clarification could chemistry move forward (a second reason he is called the father of modern chemistry).

Lavoisier began heating things in air in 1772. For instance, he and some other chemists bought a diamond and placed it in a closed vessel under the focused sunlight of a magnifying glass. The diamond disappeared. Carbon dioxide gas appeared within the vessel, proving the diamond to be carbon or, at least, to contain carbon. Lavoisier also took particular note of the fact that the diamond would not burn in the absence of air. Burning diamonds may seem pretty steep, just to prove a scientific point, but a prominent Parisian jeweler had made the claim that diamonds would not burn without air, and so confident was he of this and so anxious to prove himself right that he supplied the diamonds for the experiment and was willing to have one burned in the presence of air.

Lavoisier went on to burn phosphorus and sulfur and to prove that the products weighed more than the original, so that he suspected some material had been gained from the air. (He didn't believe phlogiston could have negative weight.)

In 1774, to test this point, he heated tin and lead in closed containers, with a limited supply of air. Both metals formed a layer of calx on the surface. The calx was known to be heavier than the metal it replaced, but Lavoisier found that the entire vessel (metal. calx, air, and all) was no heavier after the heating than before. This meant that if the calx represented a gain in weight, there must be a loss in weight elsewhere, possibly in the air. If that was so, then a partial vacuum must exist in the vessel.

Sure enough, when Lavoisier opened the vessel, air rushed in and *then* the vessel and its contents gained in weight.

Lavoisier was thus able to show that the calx consisted of a combination of the metal with air, and that rusting (and combustion) did not involve a loss of phlogiston but a gain of at least a portion of the air.

When this notion finally made its way through the ranks of the chemists, it killed the phlogiston theory and established chemistry on its modern basis. Furthermore, Lavoisier's demonstration that mass was never altogether gained or lost but was merely shifted from one point to another in the course of chemical changes, is the law of conservation of mass, a bulwark of chemistry throughout the nineteenth century (and a third reason why he is proclaimed father of modern chemistry). Einstein [1064] extended and refined the concept.

In October 1774 Priestley [312] went to Paris. He visited Lavoisier and discussed his experiments with "dephlogisticated air." Lavoisier repeated the experiments and realized at once that the dephlogisticated-air notion was nonsense. Here instead was the portion of the air that combined with metals to form calxes. The very reason that objects burned so readily in the new gas was that it was undiluted by that portion of the air in which objects did not burn.

By 1778 Lavoisier's ideas were clear. He was the first to announce what other great chemists of the time, particularly Scheele [329], had only dimly suspected: that air consisted of two gases, one of which supported combustion and one of which did not. In 1779 he called the former "oxygen" (from Greek words meaning "to give rise to acids," because he believed that all acids contained this element, in which belief he was, for once, wrong). The latter he called azote (from Greek words meaning "no life"), but in 1790 it was named nitrogen by Chaptal [368] and that is the name it now bears.

In one respect Lavoisier displayed a deplorable infirmity of character, for he avoided mentioning the help he had received from Priestley and, without actu-

ally saying so, did his best to give the impression that he, himself, had discovered oxygen. To be sure, Priestley's help was not great and Lavoisier looked down upon Priestley as a mere tinkerer. Lavoisier saw the true significance of Priestley's work which Priestley himself did not, so that Lavoisier deserves full marks for everything but the actual discovery of oxygen. However, it was the last bit of credit that he most coveted; he wanted to discover an element. He would do more for chemistry than any man before or since, but he would never discover an element.

Lavoisier also studied the behavior of animals in air, in oxygen, and in nitrogen. He measured the amount of heat they produced and was able to show that life was very like combustion in that respect.

In 1783 Cavendish had shown that water could be formed by burning his inflammable gas in air. Cavendish, a convinced phlogistonist, insisted on interpreting this in terms of phlogiston. Lavoisier promptly repeated the experiment in an improved manner and named the inflammable gas hydrogen (from Greek words meaning "to give rise to water"). This fitted in well with his new view of chemistry. He could see that when animals broke down foodstuffs (composed very largely of carbon and hydrogen), they did it by adding the oxygen they breathed and forming carbon dioxide and water, both of which appeared in the expired breath.

Here, too, Lavoisier implied that the experiment of burning hydrogen was original with him. In fact, Lavoisier has such a dubious reputation as a credit snatcher that when it was discovered that a Russian chemist, Lomonosov [282], had published views like those of Lavoisier a quarter century *before* the Frenchman, some people began to wonder if Lavoisier had read Lomonosov's works and didn't bother to mention the matter. However, this is doubtful.

The new chemistry began to catch on at once. In England, Hutton [297], Cavendish, and Priestley refused to abandon phlogiston, but Black [298] became a follower of Lavoisier. In Sweden, Bergman [315] went along with the new view, and in Germany, Klaproth [335].

At about this time, Guyton de Morveau [319] was trying to write an article on chemistry for an encyclopedia. He was having a miserable time trying to summarize the knowledge of centuries and turned to Lavoisier for help. Lavoisier gave the problem some thought and decided that the difficulty was a matter of language. (Guyton de Morveau had not accepted the new views of Lavoisier but, after collaborating with him for a while, he became another convert.)

Having put chemistry on a new foundation, Lavoisier went to work to give it a sensible language. The alchemists and early chemists had no fixed standard for naming the various chemical substances, and the alchemists, indeed, went out of their way to use obscure and fanciful names. The result was that no chemist could be sure exactly what another chemist was talking about.

In collaboration with other chemists, including Berthollet [346] and Fourcroy [366], Lavoisier published a book, *Methods of Chemical Nomenclature*, in 1787. In this book were established the principles whereby every substance was assigned a definite name based on the elements of which it was composed. The idea was that the name should indicate the composition. The system was so clear and logical that it was adopted by chemists everywhere after some short-lived opposition on the part of a few phlogistonists. It still forms the basis of chemical nomenclature (a fourth reason why Lavoisier can be considered the father of modern chemistry).

In 1789 Lavoisier went on to publish a textbook, *Elementary Treatise on Chemistry*, which served to present a unified picture of his new theories and in which he clearly stated the law of conservation of mass. It was the first modern chemical textbook (a fifth reason for his paternity of modern chemistry) and, among other things, it revived Boyle's [212] notion of an element, and contained a list of all the elements then known; that is, all the substances that had not yet been broken down into still simpler substances.

For the most part the list was quite accurate, and no material substance was listed that is not recognized today as either an element or the oxide of an element. However, Lavoisier listed light and heat as elements, though we now recognize them to be nonmaterial. Lavoisier believed heat consisted of an "imponderable fluid" called "caloric." He had eradicated one imponderable fluid, phlogiston, but it was partly through his influence that caloric, just as false, remained in existence in the minds of chemists for a half century.

Lavoisier extended his interest in combustion into biology. From 1782 to 1784, with the assistance of the young Laplace [347], he tried to measure heats of combustion and work out some of the details of what went on in living tissue. In connection with these experiments, he made the first crude attempts at the analysis of compounds characteristic of living tissue, something that was to be developed successfully by Liebig [532] a half century later.

But in the same year that his textbook appeared the French Revolution broke out. By 1792 the radical antimonarchists were in control, France was declared a republic, and the tax-farmers began to be hunted down. Lavoisier was first barred from his laboratory and then arrested. When he objected that he was a scientist and not a tax-farmer (not quite true), the arresting officer is supposed to have responded with the famous remark, "The republic has no need of scientists." (The republic quickly found out how wrong it was, as in the case of Chaptal and Leblanc [328].)

The trial was a farce, with Marat—now a powerful revolutionary leader and eager for revenge—accusing Lavoisier of all sorts of ridiculous plots, such as that of "adding water to the peoples' tobacco," and wildly demanding his death.

Marat was assassinated in July 1793, but the damage had already been done. Lavoisier (along with his father-in-law and other tax-farmers) was guillotined on May 8, 1794, and buried in an unmarked grave. Two months later the radicals were overthrown. His was the most deplorable single casualty of the revolution.

Lagrange [317] mourned: "A moment was all that was necessary to strike off his head, and probably a hundred years will not be sufficient to produce another like it." Within two years of Lavoisier's death, the regretful French were unveiling busts of him.

[335] **KLAPROTH**, Martin Heinrich
(klap′rote)
German chemist
Born: Wernigerode, Prussian Saxony, December 1, 1743
Died: Berlin, January 1, 1817

When Klaproth, the son of a tailor, was eight his family was impoverished as a result of a fire. At the age of sixteen he was apprenticed to an apothecary, which was, as Scheele [329] showed, an excellent route to chemistry. Like Scheele, Klaproth rose from shop to shop and reached eminence, entering chemical research on his own in 1780. (It didn't hurt that in that year he gained economic security by marrying the well-to-do niece of Marggraf [279].

He was one of the early converts to the new theories of Lavoisier [334] and this was important. Stahl [241], whose phlogiston theory Lavoisier had overthrown, had been a German and there was a nationalistic resistance to the new "French chemistry." Klaproth helped break that down with conclusive experiments in 1792.

He made his own mark, however, mainly in the discovery of new elements. His first adventure in this direction proved to be the most meaningful. In 1789 he investigated a heavy black ore called pitchblende. He obtained a yellow compound from it that he was quite certain contained a hitherto unknown element. He obtained the oxide of the metal—thinking it was the metal itself—and named it uranium after the fashion of the old alchemists who named metals after planets. The planet Uranus had been discovered eight years before by Herschel [321] and it seemed to Klaproth fitting to have a new metal named for a new planet. (A century and a half

later, uranium, in the hands of Fermi [1243] and Hahn [1063], was to achieve an unexpected and grisly fame.)

In that same year Klaproth also obtained a new oxide from the semiprecious jewel the zircon, and named the new metal contained in the oxide "zirconium." In 1795 he isolated the oxide of a new metal he named titanium (after the Titans of Greek mythology). Klaproth, unlike Lavoisier, was not covetous of honor and gave full credit to Gregor [377] for the initial discovery of this metal. On January 25, 1798, he was one of those instrumental in recognizing tellurium to be a new element, but again he pointed out he was not the first to do so and in reporting on it he was careful to give credit to the original discoverer, F. J. Müller [323].

Klaproth was hard on the heels of Berzelius [425] and Hisinger [390] in the discovery of cerium in 1803 and he was one of those who early showed the unexpected complexity of the rare earth minerals discovered by Gadolin [373]. This portion of his work was to be carried further by Mosander [501].

Klaproth was one of the outstanding analytical chemists of his age and is sometimes referred to as the father of analytic chemistry. He was meticulous in his analytical work, publishing all his figures and making no attempt to adjust them in order to have them come out neatly, as even Lavoisier did on occasion.

Klaproth was a pioneer in analytic chemistry and in the application of chemistry to archaeological objects, studying coins, glass, and ancient metal objects. When the University of Berlin was founded in 1810, Klaproth, although sixty-seven years old, was named its first professor of chemistry and served in that post until his death seven years later.

[336] **LAMARCK**, Jean Baptiste Pierre Antoine de Monet, chevalier de
French naturalist
Born: Bazentin-le-Petit, Somme, August 1, 1744
Died: Paris, December 28, 1829

Lamarck took a long time finding himself. He was the eleventh child of a family of impoverished aristocrats who recognized no honorable profession (assuming that money had to be made somehow) but the army and the church. Young Lamarck was marked for the church very much against his will. His father died in 1760, however, and that event left him free to turn soldier.

He did well enough, fighting with some distinction in the Seven Years' War, where he received an officer's commission for bravery. By 1766 illness, resulting from overrough horseplay, had forced his resignation and he resumed civilian life. He tried his hand at several occupations and finally went into medicine, writing a couple of overambitious books.

An interest in plant life had been stirred when he was stationed in the army on the Mediterranean coast. Eventually this interest led to a book on French flora in 1778, and, with help from Buffon [277], he found himself on the road of natural history. In 1781 he was appointed botanist to the king, which meant a salary and the chance of traveling; then, in 1793, he became professor of invertebrate zoology at the Museum of Natural History in Paris. Here, at last, at the age of nearly fifty, he came into his own.

Linnaeus [276] had left the invertebrates rather in a mess from the standpoint of classification. It was as though, having expended unbelievable energy and pains on the vertebrates, he had grown tired and thrown a bunch of the most diverse creatures into a single pigeonhole and called them "worms."

Lamarck tackled the miscellany and began to make order out of them. He differentiated the eight-legged arachnids (spiders, ticks, mites, and scorpions) from the six-legged insects. He established a reasonable category for the crustaceans (crabs, lobsters, and so on) and for the echinoderms (starfish, sea urchins, and so on). He summarized his findings in publications that appeared between 1801 and 1809 and finally produced a gigantic seven-volume work between 1815 and 1822 entitled *Natural History of Invertebrates* which founded modern invertebrate zoology. (It was Lamarck who first used the terms "vertebrate" and "invertebrate." He also popularized the word "biology."

More important in the memory of posterity than the very real and fruitful labors summarized in these volumes is a theory of evolution advanced in his book *Zoological Philosophy*, published in 1809. It is very difficult to classify living species without thinking in terms of evolution. Linnaeus had refused to face the possibility, and Cuvier [396] avoided it by adopting Bonnet's [291] catastrophism. Erasmus Darwin [308] was an evolutionist a half century before Lamarck, but he was a minor figure and rather a dilettante.

Lamarck was the first biologist of top rank to devise, boldly and straightforwardly, a scheme rationalizing the evolutionary development of life, and maintaining that the species were not fixed but that they changed and developed.

Unfortunately the scheme was wrong. Organisms, Lamarck suggested, made much use of certain portions of their body in the course of their life and underused others. Those portions that were used, such as the webbed toes of water birds, developed accordingly, while the others, such as the eyes of moles, withered. This development and withering were passed on to descendants.

Lamarck used the recently discovered giraffe for his most often quoted example of this. A primitive antelope, he said, fond of browsing on the leaves of trees would stretch its neck upward with all its might to get all the leaves it could. It would stretch out its tongue and legs as well. In the process, neck, tongue, and legs would become slightly longer than they would have been otherwise. These longer body parts would be passed on to the young and when these had grown to adulthood, they would have a longer neck, tongue, and legs to begin with, would stretch them more, pass on still longer ones to their young and so on. Little by little the antelope would turn into a giraffe. This is an example of the "inheritance of acquired characteristics."

The theory foundered on the rock of fact, however. In the first place, Lamarck visualized evolution as the product of attempts by the animal to change. This might be imagined in the case of long necks since necks can be stretched voluntarily. But how would it work in the development of protective coloration? Surely a creature couldn't *try* to become striped or splotched. Secondly there was no reason to think that acquired characteristics could be inherited. In fact all available experimental evidence pointed in the opposite direction, that acquired characteristics could *not* be inherited.

Mistaken or not, Lamarck moved evolutionary theory into the forefront of biological thinking and for this deserves full credit. However, in his lifetime (during which he married three times and had eight children) he was overshadowed by the greater renown of the nonevolutionist Cuvier and died blind, penniless, and largely unappreciated. Cuvier had taken a strong dislike to Lamarck, as a matter of fact, owing to Lamarck's sarcastic references to Cuvier's theories of catastrophism. Cuvier was powerful at the time and those he opposed simply did not do well.

Lamarck's reputation was not helped by the fact that he was a vociferous opponent of Lavoisier's [334] new chemistry. Then, thirty years after his death, when evolutionary views finally won out, it was Charles Darwin [554] with his superior mechanism of evolution by natural selection who gained the fame.

Every once in a while Lamarckism (that is, the inheritance of acquired characteristics) comes to the fore in one form or another. The most recent example is that of Lysenko [1214] in the Soviet Union.

[337] **VOLTA,** Alessandro Giuseppe Antonio Anastasio, Count (vole′-tah)
Italian physicist
Born: Como, Lombardy, February 18, 1745
Died: Como, March 5, 1827

Volta was born into a noble family that had come down in the world. Most of his brothers and sisters (he was one of nine children) entered the church. Not so, young Alessandro.

He was not an infant prodigy by any means. He did not talk until he was four and his family was convinced he was retarded. By seven, however, when his father died, he had caught up with other children and then began to forge ahead. When he was fourteen, he decided he wanted to be a physicist.

Volta was interested in the phenomenon of the age, electricity, that interest having been aroused by Priestley's [312] history of the subject. He even wrote a long Latin poem (considered rather good) on the subject. In 1774 he was appointed professor of physics in the Como high school and the next year he invented the electrophorus, describing it first in a letter to Priestley. This was a device consisting of one metal plate covered with ebonite and a second metal plate with an insulated handle.

The ebonite-covered plate is rubbed and given a negative electric charge. If the plate with a handle is placed over it, a positive electric charge is attracted to the lower surface, a negative charge repelled to the upper. The upper negative charge can be drawn off by grounding and the process repeated until a strong charge is built up in the plate with the handle. This sort of charge-accumulating machine replaced the Leyden jar and is the basis of the electrical condensers still used today.

Volta's fame spread as a result. In 1779 he received a professorial appointment at the University of Pavia, where he continued his work with electricity. He invented other gadgets involving static electricity and received the Copley medal of the Royal Society in 1791. He was elected to membership in the Society.

The major feat of his life involved not static electricity, but dynamic electricity —the electric current. He had followed the experiments of Galvani [320], who was a friend of his and who sent Volta copies of his papers on the subject. Volta took up the question of whether the electric current resulting when muscle was in contact with two different metals arose from the tissue or from the metals.

To check this he decided in 1794 to make use of the metals alone, without the tissue. He found at once that an electric current resulted and maintained that it therefore had nothing to do with life or tissue. This sparked a controversy between the two Italians with the German Humboldt [397], the chief of Galvani's supporters, and the Frenchman Coulomb [318], the chief of Volta's. The weight of evidence leaned more and more heavily toward Volta, and Galvani died embittered.

In 1800 Volta virtually clinched the victory by constructing devices that would produce a large flow of electricity. He used bowls of salt solution that were connected by means of arcs of metal dipping from one bowl into the next, one end of the arc being copper and the other tin or zinc. This produced a steady flow of electrical current. Since any group of similar objects working as a unit may be called a battery, Volta's device was an "electric battery"—the first in history.

Volta made matters more compact and less watery by using small round plates of copper and zinc, plus discs of cardboard moistened in salt solution. Starting with copper at the bottom, the discs, reading upward, were copper, zinc, cardboard, copper, zinc, cardboard, and so on. If a wire was attached to the top and bottom of this "Voltaic pile" an electric current would pass through it if the circuit was closed. Within a short time the voltaic cell was put to practical use by William Nicholson [361] and this led directly to the astonishing work of Davy [421].

The invention of the battery lifted Volta's fame to the peak. He was called to France by Napoleon in 1801 for a kind of "command performance" of his experiments. He received a stream of medals and decorations, including the Legion of Honor, and was even made a count and, in 1810, a senator of the kingdom of Lombardy.

Throughout his life, though, Volta, like Laplace [347], had the ability to shift with the changing politics of the time and to remain in good odor with whatever governments were in power. After Napoleon fell and Austria became dominant in Italy once more, Volta continued to do well and to receive posts of honor.

Volta received his greatest honor, however, at the hands of no potentate, but of his fellow scientists. The unit of electromotive force—the driving force that moves the electric current—is now called the "volt."

The energy of moving charged particles produced by modern atom-smashing machines is measured in electron-volts. A billion electron-volts is abbreviated "bev," and when we speak of the particular atom-smasher called the bevatron, the "v" in the name stands for Volta.

Volta was also the first, in 1778, to isolate the compound methane, a major constituent of natural gas.

[338] **PINEL**, Philippe (pee-nel')
French physician
Born: Saint-André, Tarn, April 20, 1745
Died: Paris, October 26, 1826

Pinel took his doctor's degree at the University of Toulouse in 1773, and went to Paris in 1778. He supported himself first by teaching mathematics and translating scientific books. Under the influence of Linnaeus [276] he classified diseases into species, genera, orders, and so on. The labor was useless, but he became interested in the problem of mental disease after a friend of his had gone violently mad.

Until his time the insane in most cultures were believed to be possessed of demons and were often treated with a certain reverence. While this may seem fine for the insane, it was not treatment. If they grew violent, the only remedy was to put them in chains.

Hospitals for the insane were dreadful nightmares of howling, demented people, imprisoned and often subjected to the most brutal treatment. It was even a form of amusement for presumably sane

229

people to visit the hospitals for a look at the antics of the unfortunates.

In 1791 Pinel published his views on "mental alienation," referring to a mind alienated from its proper function (and even today, especially in connection with courtroom evidence, a psychiatrist is sometimes called an alienist). Pinel advocated considering them as people, sick in mind, to be treated with the same consideration as the sick in body; and he advocated talking to patients, rather than manhandling them.

The French Revolution was in full swing then and it was the time for upsetting encrusted tradition. In 1793 Pinel was placed in charge of an insane asylum and there he struck off the chains from the insane and began to adopt systematic studies. He was the first, for instance, to keep well-documented case histories of mental ailments.

His methods were slow to be accepted, but within half a century they were dominant in medicine, reaching a climax with the work of Freud [865].

[339] **GAHN,** Johann Gottlieb
Swedish mineralogist
Born: Voxna, South Hälsingland, August 19, 1745
Died: Falun, Kopparburg, December 8, 1818

Gahn was born in an iron-mining town and began life as a miner (a practical, if not very easy, introduction to mineralogy). He worked himself upward not only in science but in business as well, for he ended life owning and managing mines. He also took part in Swedish politics, serving in the legislature for a time.

He studied under Bergman [315] and became especially proficient in the use of the blowpipe, the convenient analytical tool that had been introduced by Cronstedt [292]. It was Gahn who trained Berzelius [425] in this technique. Gahn's proficiency in mineralogy is marked by the fact that a zinc aluminate mineral is still called gahnite, but his best-known achievement is the isolation of metallic manganese in 1774. He gets the credit as

discoverer of the metal although his friend Scheele [329] had done much of the preliminary spadework. In collaboration with Scheele, Gahn discovered about 1770 that phosphorus was an essential component of bone.

Gahn had a connection with American history: during the Revolutionary War, copper was needed by the young nation for sheathing ships, and it was one of his companies that filled the rush order.

[340] **MONGE,** Gaspard (mohnzh)
French mathematician
Born: Beaune, Côte d'Or, May 9, 1746
Died: Paris, July 28, 1818

Monge, the son of a merchant, showed remarkable mathematical ability in his early years. At sixteen he made a large-scale plan of Beaune, using original methods that impressed a military officer, who hired him as a draftsman. Monge's methods of using geometry to work out quickly constructional details that ordinarily required complicated and tedious arithmetical procedures was the foundation of what is called "descriptive geometry." It was so important in connection with fortress construction that for a couple of decades it was guarded as a military secret.

With the French Revolution, Monge became increasingly involved in public affairs. He was on the committee that worked out the metric system. He founded the École Polytechnique and was its first director. He worked out further details of descriptive geometry which showed how to describe a structure fully by plane projections from each of three directions and finally received permission to publish and teach his methods in 1795.

He was a close friend of Napoleon Bonaparte and accompanied him on his campaign in Egypt in 1798, returning in 1801. Having supported both the revolution and Napoleon, he was appropriately rewarded. He was made president of the senate in 1806 and comte de Péluze in 1808. After the fall of Napoleon, he was deprived of all his honors by the new

230

government of Louis XVIII and harassed in many ways. He did not long survive.

In chemistry, Monge was the first to liquefy a substance that ordinarily occurs as a gas. In 1784 he liquefied sulfur dioxide, the normal boiling point of which is −72.7°C.

[341] **PIAZZI,** Giuseppe (pyah'tsee)
Italian astronomer
Born: Ponte de Valtellina (now located in Switzerland), July 16, 1746
Died: Naples, July 22, 1826

Piazzi was a Theatine monk and priest, having entered the order in 1764. He received his early training in philosophy but later in life took up mathematics and astronomy. The government of Naples (then an independent kingdom), having decided to establish observatories in its two largest cities, Naples and Palermo, put Piazzi in charge in 1780. He traveled to the observatories in France and England as preparation and in England visited Herschel [321]. There he had the doubtful privilege of falling off the ladder at the side of Herschel's great reflector and breaking his arm.

Piazzi established his observatory at Palermo and by 1814 had mapped the position of 7,646 stars. He showed that the proper motions first detected by Halley [238] were the rule among stars and not the exception. He also discovered a dim star called 61 Cygni with an unusually rapid proper motion, a star that was to play an important role a generation later when Bessel [439] came to observe it.

Piazzi's chief accomplishment did not, however, involve the stars at all. After Herschel's discovery of Uranus, the astronomical world was abuzz with plans for the discovery of additional planets. Uranus was in the position predicted for it by a mathematical rule popularized by Bode [344] and therefore called Bode's law. Following this same rule, astronomers suspected a planet to be lying between the orbits of Mars and Jupiter. (Even Kepler [169] had commented on the unusual size of the gap between the

orbits of those two planets.) A group of German astronomers, of whom the most distinguished was Olbers [372], made preparations for a thorough survey of the heavens to locate this planet, if it existed.

While preparations were under way, Piazzi, on January 1, 1801, in the course of his systematic observation of the stars, came across one in the constellation Taurus that changed its position over a period of several days between observations. He began to follow its course. It appeared to be a planet lying between Mars and Jupiter, since it moved more slowly than Mars and more quickly than Jupiter. He wrote about this to Bode, but before its orbit could be determined, Piazzi fell sick and when he returned to the telescope the object was too near the sun to be observed.

At this point Gauss [415] worked out a new method for calculating an orbit from only three reasonably spaced observations. Piazzi's observations were sufficient, the orbit was calculated, the planet relocated, and it proved indeed to lie between the orbits of Mars and Jupiter. The new heavenly object was named Ceres after the Roman goddess most closely associated with Sicily. However, the planet was so dim, considering its distance, that it had to be very tiny. Herschel estimated a diameter of two hundred miles, and the modern figure is 485 miles. In any case it scarcely seemed a respectable planet.

The search for additional bodies took place therefore (since the German astronomers were all prepared for it) and in the next few years three more planets were discovered, each even smaller than Ceres. They were named the asteroids ("starlike"), a name suggested by Herschel because they were too small to show as discs in the telescope but appeared as starlike points of light. (Some have suspected that Herschel wanted to reserve planetary discoveries for himself and therefore moved to refuse the tiny new worlds the name of planet.) "Asteroids" is, however, a poor name, for the bodies are not really starlike and the alternate names "planetoids" or "minor planets" are usually considered preferable, though "asteroids" may always remain more popular.

Over sixteen hundred planetoids are now known, so that Piazzi's discovery was not that of a planet merely, but of a whole zone of planets. At the time of Piazzi's death, however, the number of known planetoids was still only four. When the thousandth planetoid was discovered in 1923, it was named Piazzia in his honor.

[342] HJELM, Peter Jacob (yelm)
Swedish mineralogist
Born: Sunnerbo Härad, October 2, 1746
Died: Stockholm, October 7, 1813

Hjelm was a friend of Scheele's [329] who gets credit for discovering a metal on which Scheele worked. In 1781 at the suggestion of Scheele, Hjelm used methods similar to Gahn's [339] in isolating manganese. The result was the isolation of still another metal, and new element, molybdenum.

[343] CHARLES, Jacques Alexandre César (shahrl)
French physicist
Born: Beaugency, Loiret, November 12, 1746
Died: Paris, April 7, 1823

Teaching at the Sorbonne, Charles, who held a minor government post and was granted a small pension by Louis XVI, popularized Franklin's [272] one-fluid theory of electricity. He proved a skillful and popular lecturer on science for the layman.

Upon hearing of the experiments of the Montgolfier brothers [325] on balloons, he realized at once that hydrogen, the lightness of which had been discovered fifteen years earlier by Cavendish [259], would be a far more efficient buoyant force (though much more expensive) than hot air. On August 27, 1783, he constructed the first hydrogen balloon, inventing, in the process, all the

devices used to handle and manipulate balloons.

He himself went up several times, reaching a height of over a mile, and helped establish an aeronautic craze, exemplified by such men as Blanchard [362].

Louis XVI, who was fascinated by balloons, continued to patronize Charles, which made him unpopular to the revolutionaries. During the French Revolution he might have been killed by a mob, had he not won them over by reciting his ballooning achievements.

His most important discovery was really a rediscovery. He repeated the work of Amontons [244] about 1787 and showed that different gases all expanded by the same amount with a given rise in temperature. Charles's advance lay in his being the first to make an accurate estimate of the degree of expansion. For each degree (Centigrade) rise in temperature, he found, the volume of a gas expanded by $1/273$ of its volume at $0°$. For each degree of fall, the volume contracted by $1/273$ of that volume.

This meant that a temperature of $-273°C$ the volume of a gas would reach zero (if the law held good) and that there could be no lower temperature. It was two generations later that Kelvin [652] was to crystallize this notion of an absolute zero.

Charles did not publish his experiments, and about 1802 Gay-Lussac [420], also a balloon-ascensionist, published his own observations in this matter, duplicating those of Charles. The rule that the volume of a given quantity of gas is proportional to the absolute temperature where pressure is held constant is sometimes called Gay-Lussac's law and sometimes Charles's law.

[344] BODE, Johann Elert (boh'duh)
German astronomer
Born: Hamburg, January 19, 1747
Died: Berlin, November 23, 1826

Bode, the son of a teacher, was self-educated in astronomy and was writing astronomy texts in 1766, while he was still a teenager. In 1777 he took a position as assistant to Lambert [299] and advanced rapidly. He became director of the Berlin Observatory in 1786, and was the author of a vast catalogue of star positions, issued in 1801.

Nevertheless he is best known for popularizing a relationship that he did not originate. It had been pointed out in 1772 by Titius [301] that one might start with the series 0, 3, 6, 12, 24, 48, 96, 192, . . . each number (after the first two) double the one before. If one added 4 to each, then the series became 4, 7, 10, 16, 28, 52, 100, 196. . . . If one sets the earth's distance from the sun at 10, then Mercury is, in proportion, at distance 4 and Venus at distance 7 (at least roughly). Similarly Mars is at 16, Jupiter at 52, and Saturn at 100 (roughly). This relationship is still known as Bode's law, though lately quite often as the Bode-Titian law.

At the time it was popularized, no planet was known for position 28, though even Kepler [169], nearly two centuries before, had felt the gap between Mars and Jupiter to be too large, and had suggested that a small planet might exist there.

When Uranus was discovered and found to be at position 196 (roughly), astronomers could no longer resist. The search began for the planet at position 28, which Ceres filled nicely. However, when Leverrier [564] discovered Neptune, it was found in a position quite far from that predicted by Bode's law, although Leverrier had made use of it in his calculations, and the law's importance vanished.

[345] **JUSSIEU,** Antoine Laurent de
   (zhyoo-syuh′)
   French botanist
   Born: Lyon, April 12, 1748
   Died: Paris, September 17, 1836

Jussieu was a member of a distinguished family of botanists. An uncle, Bernard, had first identified sea anemones and related creatures as animals rather than as plants, which they resemble. Another uncle, Joseph, had been a

member of the Peruvian expedition of La Condamine [270].

Antoine Laurent himself began his work in 1765 under his uncle Bernard and obtained his doctorate in 1780. He popularized a system of natural classification of plants in 1789 that was the base upon which Cuvier [396] and Candolle [418] built, a generation later.

Jussieu was placed in charge of the hospital of Paris during the French Revolution and in 1793 was appointed professor of botany at the Jardin des Plantes, a post he held till his retirement in 1826.

[346] **BERTHOLLET,** Claude Louis,
   Comte (ber-toh-lay′)
   French chemist
   Born: Talloires, Haute Savoie,
   December 9, 1748
   Died: Arcueil, near Paris, November 6, 1822

Berthollet was born of poor French parents in what was then part of Italy. He obtained his medical degree at the University of Turin in 1768 and moved to Paris in 1772. He was one of the first to accept Lavoisier's [334] new theories, and he joined with him in devising the new chemical nomenclature.

On his own, Berthollet continued Scheele's [329] research on chlorine, showing in 1785 how it could be used for bleaching, but like Scheele he was convinced that it was a compound and contained oxygen. He continued Priestley's [312] investigation of ammonia and was the first to show its composition (of nitrogen and hydrogen) with reasonable precision. He discovered potassium chlorate and Lavoisier thought its explosive qualities might make it a substitute for gunpowder. However, it was too explosive. Two men died in a potassium chlorate explosion and Lavoisier abandoned the project.

In 1781 he was elected to the Academy of Sciences against the opposition, for some reason, of Fourcroy [366], and in 1794 was appointed professor at the École Normale. Unlike Lavoisier, he got along well with the revolutionaries. In

1798, while in Egypt on a business trip, he met Napoleon and attached himself to the rising star, teaching him chemistry. Napoleon eventually made him a senator and a count. Later, Berthollet voted for the deposition of Napoleon and the returning Bourbons made him a peer.

His great service to chemistry was his realization in 1803 that the manner and rate of chemical reactions depended on more than just the attraction of one substance for another. The "affinities" of Bergman [315] were not enough. Substance A would react with Substance B and not with Substance C, though its affinity for Substance C was greater, if Substance B was present in sufficiently greater quantity. This was a foreshadowing of the extremely important law of mass action. Here, however, Berthollet's views were ignored and they did not enter the mainstream of chemistry until the rise of the physical chemists, three quarters of a century later.

Berthollet also maintained that the composition of the products of a reaction varied with the relative masses of the substances taking part in the reaction, but in this respect he was proved wrong by Proust [364]. This, unfortunately, helped discredit his sound views on mass action. He was wrong, also, in his views on the nature of heat, which he considered a fluid, in opposition to the more accurate view of men such as Rumford [360].

[347] **LAPLACE,** Pierre Simon, marquis de (la-plahs′)
French astronomer and mathematician
Born: Beaumont-en-Auge, Calvados, March 28, 1749
Died: Paris, March 5, 1827

Not much is known of Laplace's early life, because he was one scientist who was a snob and, ashamed of his origins, spoke little of them. It is usually stated that he came of a poor family and that well-to-do neighbors helped the obviously bright boy get an education. Recent researchers, however, indicate he may have been of comfortable middle-class birth.

At eighteen he was sent to Paris with a letter of introduction to D'Alembert [289], who refused to see him. Laplace sent him a paper on mechanics so excellent that D'Alembert was suddenly overjoyed to act as his sponsor. He obtained for the young man a professorship in mathematics.

Early in his career Laplace worked with Lavoisier [334], determining specific heats of numerous substances. In 1780 the two men demonstrated that the quantity of heat required to decompose a compound into its elements is equal to the heat evolved when that compound is formed from its elements. This can be considered the beginning of thermochemistry and as another pointer—following the work of Black [298] on latent heat—toward the doctrine of conservation of energy, which was to come to maturity six decades later.

However, Laplace turned his chief powers to a study of the perturbations of the members of the solar system and to the question of the general stability of that system, the problem that was already exercising Lagrange [317].

In 1787 Laplace was able to show the moon was accelerating slightly more than could earlier be explained. This he attributed to the fact that the eccentricity of the earth's orbit was very slowly decreasing as a result of the gravitational influence of other planets. This meant a slightly changing gravitational influence of the earth upon the moon, which was not earlier allowed for and which could account for the moon's trifling quantity of extra acceleration. He also studied certain anomalies in the motions of Jupiter and Saturn and, by building on some of Lagrange's work, showed that they could be accounted for by the gravitational attraction of each planet upon the other.

Laplace and Lagrange, working separately but cooperatively, managed to generalize matters and show, for instance, that the total eccentricity of the planetary orbits of the solar system had to stay constant, provided all planets revolve about the sun in the same direction (which they do). If the orbit of one planet increases its eccentricity, that of others must decrease in eccentricity sufficiently to strike a balance. The same sort of constancy holds for the inclination of a planet's orbit to the plane of the ecliptic. The total stock of either eccentricity or inclination in the entire solar system is so small that no one planet could change its orbital characteristics very much even if it drew upon the entire supply.

This showed that as long as the solar system remained effectively isolated, and as long as the sun did not change its nature drastically, the solar system would remain much as it is now for an indefinite period in the future.

In this way Laplace rounded off the work of Newton [231], at least as far as planetary astronomy is concerned, and he is sometimes called the French Newton in consequence. Further refinements had to wait for men such as Leverrier [564] fifty years later and Poincaré [847] fifty years later still.

Laplace summed up gravitational theory in a monumental five-volume work called *Celestial Mechanics,* which appeared over the time interval from 1799 to 1825. His work was not interrupted significantly by the political changes that swept France in that period, including the rise and fall of Napoleon, even though he dabbled in politics. His prestige protected him and so did his ability to apply his mathematics to problems involving artillery fire. He also displayed a not-altogether-admirable ability to change his political attitude to suit changing circumstance.

Another unattractive facet of Laplace's personality was that he (like Lavoisier) was reluctant to give credit to others. He did less than justice to Lagrange's contributions to their joint work on celestial mechanics, something the gentle Lagrange didn't seem to mind.

Napoleon made Laplace minister of interior, and when the astronomer proved incompetent in that post, he was promoted to the purely decorative position of senator. Yet when Louis XVIII came to the throne after Napoleon's fall, Laplace was not penalized for attaining

office under Napoleon, as Haüy [332] and Chaptal [368] were, but was made a marquis. Other honors were his. He had been elected to the Academy of Sciences in 1785, but that was rather to be expected. In 1816 he was elected to the far more exalted and exclusive literary society, the French Academy, and in 1817 became president of that body.

Celestial Mechanics, by the way, is notorious for its habit of stating that from Equation A "it is obvious" that Equation B follows—except that students must often spend hours and days determining just why it is so obvious. Napoleon is supposed to have remarked, on leafing through this book, that he saw no mention of God. "I had no need of that hypothesis," said Laplace. When Lagrange heard this, he said, "Ah, but it is a beautiful hypothesis just the same. It explains so many things."

In pure mathematics Laplace wrote a treatise on the theory of probability between 1812 and 1820 that gave this portion of mathematics its modern form.

Oddly enough Laplace is best known for a speculation he published as a note at the end of later editions of a non-mathematical book on astronomy meant for the general public, a speculation that he did not himself take any too seriously. Since all the planets revolve about the sun in the same direction and in just about the same plane, Laplace suggested that the sun originated as a giant nebula or cloud of gas that was in rotation. As the gas contracted, the rotation would have to accelerate and an outer rim of gas would be left behind (by centrifugal force). The rim of gas would then condense into a planet. With continued contraction, this would happen over and over until all the planets were formed, still moving in the direction of the original nebular rotation. The core of the nebula finally would condense into the present-day sun.

This nebular hypothesis caught the fancy of astronomers and remained popular throughout the nineteenth century as the favored explanation of the origin of the solar system. After a period of eclipse in the first few decades of the twentieth, it returned about mid-century in Weizsäcker's [1376] modified form to greater popularity than ever.

Possibly unknown to Laplace, a similar suggestion, not quite as thoroughly worked out, had been advanced forty years earlier by Kant [293].

[348] **JENNER**, Edward
English physician
Born: Berkeley, Gloucestershire, May 17, 1749
Died: Berkeley, January 26, 1823

Jenner was the son of a clergyman and lost his father and mother when he was only five. Under the guardianship of an elder brother, he had some schooling and was then apprenticed to a surgeon in 1762. He eventually obtained his medical degree from St. Andrew's in 1792. His interests ranged far beyond medicine, however, into music, poetry, and natural history. He was sufficiently competent in the last to be given the job of preparing and arranging zoological specimens collected by Captain Cook [300] after his first voyage to the Pacific. He was even offered a post as naturalist on the second voyage, but he refused, preferring to remain in practice at home.

In medicine Jenner's chief interest was smallpox, one of the most dreaded diseases of its time. Almost everyone got it, in varying degrees of virulence, and in bad epidemics as many as one out of three died. The survivors were usually pockmarked, their skin pitted and scarred. The disfiguration at its worst almost robbed a face of any appearance of humanity. Many feared such disfiguration worse than death.

A very mild case of smallpox was far better than none at all, for once the patient recovered he became immune to all future attacks. In Turkey and China there were attempts to catch the disease from those with mild cases. There was even deliberate inoculation with matter from the blisters of such cases. Unfortunately one could not always guarantee that the disease would be mild in the new host, so that this sort of inoculation was a rather grisly form of Russian

roulette. Nevertheless, the notion was making an impression on western Europe. Diderot [286], for instance, supported it ardently.

In the early eighteenth century that Turkish habit of inoculation had been introduced into England. It did not catch on, but inoculation was much in the air and as early as 1775 it set Jenner thinking. There was an old wives' tale current in Gloucestershire that anyone who caught cowpox (a mild disease of cattle resembling smallpox) was immune not only to cowpox but also to smallpox. Jenner wondered if it might not be true. He observed a disease of horses called the grease, in which there was a swelling and blistering in part of the leg. People working in stables and barnyards might get some blisters of their own this way, and they too seemed rarely to get smallpox.

It was something that had to be tested and the test was a fearsome one. On May 14, 1796, Jenner found a milkmaid, Sarah Nelmes, who had cowpox. He took the fluid from a blister on her hand and injected it into a boy, named James Phipps, who of course got cowpox. Two months later he inoculated the boy again, this time with smallpox. Had the boy died or even been badly sick, Jenner would clearly have been a criminal. The boy did not die; the smallpox did not touch him; and Jenner was a hero.

Jenner wanted to try it again to make sure, but it took him two years to find someone else with active cowpox. In 1798 he was able to repeat his experiment with equally happy results and finally he published his findings. The Latin word for cow is *vacca* and for cowpox, *vaccinia*. Jenner coined the word vaccination to describe his use of cowpox inoculation to create immunity to smallpox. He had, in this way, founded the science of immunology.

So widespread was the dread of smallpox that the practice of vaccination was accepted quickly and spread to all parts of Europe. The British royal family was vaccinated, and the British Parliament, never noted for wild generosity, voted Jenner £10,000 in 1802 (and another

£20,000 in 1806). A Royal Jennerian Society, headed by Jenner, was founded in 1803 to encourage vaccination. In eighteen months, twelve thousand people were vaccinated in England and the number of deaths from smallpox was reduced by two thirds. A hundred thousand were vaccinated the world over by 1800.

In parts of Germany, Jenner's birthday was celebrated as a holiday and in 1807 Bavaria led the way in making vaccination compulsory. Even backward Russia adopted the practice. The first child to be vaccinated there was named Vaccinov and was educated at the expense of the nation.

Jenner's name even transcended wartime passions. After the short Peace of Amiens ended and Great Britain resumed its war with Napoleonic France, some British civilians were held prisoners. They were released because Jenner's name was included on the petition addressed to Napoleon on their behalf and Napoleon, alive to the advantages of the gesture, freed them for the physician's sake. He even had a medal struck in Jenner's honor and made vaccination compulsory in the French army.

English medicine, however, did not hasten to honor Jenner. In 1813 he was proposed for election to the College of Physicians in London. The college wanted to test him in the classics, that is, in the theories of Hippocrates [22] and Galen [65]. Jenner refused, being of the opinion that his victory over smallpox was qualification enough. The gentlemen of the college did not agree and Jenner was not elected.

It was a small loss to Jenner, who died knowing that for the first time a major disease had been completely conquered. And it is true that smallpox has never been a problem for the medically advanced portions of the earth since Jenner's time and has, in the 1970s, been declared by the World Health Organization to have been eradicated.

Jenner's discovery was a purely pragmatic one, of course. Neither he nor anyone else knew why vaccination worked. The fact that it did was cer-

tainly satisfying enough, but more knowledge was required for further progress. Smallpox remained the *only* disease to be conquered for another half a century until the causes of disease came to be known as a result of the work of Pasteur [642].

[349] **GOETHE,** Johann Wolfgang von (ger'tuh)
German poet
Born: Frankfurt-am-Main, Hesse-Nassau, August 28, 1749
Died: Weimar, Thuringia, March 22, 1832

Goethe, the son of a lawyer, took a degree in law himself in 1771 at the University of Strasbourg, but he never practiced.

The fact that Goethe was one of the super-figures in literature, and perhaps the only German man of letters who can be mentioned in the same breath with Shakespeare, tends to obscure the fact that he had wide-ranging intellectual interests and wrote ably (if usually wrongly) on scientific matters.

He wrote a large volume on the nature of light, in which he opposed Newton's [231] views on the formation of colors out of white light. His own view that white light was not a mixture of colors was based on intuition alone and the whole book is worthless. He was also a convinced neptunist in geology after the fashion of A. G. Werner [355].

Then, too, he concerned himself with biology in the years between 1790 and 1810 and held, for instance, that all plant structures were modified leaves, that plants and animals originated as separate archetypes which were differentiated and specialized through the ages to their present forms (a clear expression of the evolutionary view). He studied bone structure in competent fashion, except that, following his own theory of archetypes, he involved himself in the fallacious theory of the vertebral structure of the skull, which Oken [423] was later to popularize.

It was Goethe who coined the word

"morphology" to represent the systematic study of the structure of living things.

[350] **DELAMBRE,** Jean Baptiste
Joseph (duh-lahm'br)
French astronomer
Born: Amiens, Somme, September 19, 1749
Died: Paris, August 19, 1822

Delambre was born into poverty and gained an education under great difficulties. For a time he lived, literally, on bread and water. He attracted the attention of Lalande [309] in 1780 and it was then only that he began seriously to interest himself in astronomy. He was skilled at computation and, in 1786, produced new tables of the planetary motions of Jupiter, its satellites, Saturn, and the newly discovered planet Uranus.

Just before the French Revolution, the Academy of Sciences decided to work on a new system of measures based on some natural phenomena. The revolutionaries pushed for this enthusiastically as another break with the past. It was decided to make the fundamental measure of length the "meter" (from a Greek word for "measure"), which was to be one ten-millionth of the distance from the North Pole to the equator. For this reason it was decided to make an accurate measure of at least a portion of the meridian, a large enough portion to give the meter an accurate length.

The task fell to Delambre and Pierre F. A. Mechain, who measured the distance from Dunkerque to Barcelona, across the full north-south distance of France. Under the conditions of revolution and war, the task was an enormous one that took six years. It was only when the final figure was attained and brought to the French government that the metric system was formally adopted, in June 1799.

In 1807, Delambre became professor of astronomy at the Collège de France, succeeding his old patron, Lalande. He spent the last decade of his life writing a monumental history of astronomy.

238

[351] **RUTHERFORD,** Daniel
Scottish chemist
Born: Edinburgh, November 3, 1749
Died: Edinburgh, November 15, 1819

Rutherford, the son of a professor of medicine, was a step-uncle of Walter Scott, the writer. He studied medicine at the University of Edinburgh, where Black [298] was one of his teachers. Black set him the problem of working with the portion of the air that would not support combustion, and Rutherford reported on it in his doctor's thesis in 1772. (He received his medical degree in 1777.)

He let a mouse live in a confined quantity of air till it died, then burned a candle and then some phosphorus in that same air as long as they would burn. He presumed the air contained carbon dioxide as a result and removed it by passing the air through strong alkali. What was left contained no carbon dioxide and yet was still "mephitic" and "noxious." A candle would not burn in it and a mouse would not live.

Rutherford, following the phlogiston theory of Stahl [241], believed that the air had accepted all the phlogiston it could carry and that such "phlogisticated air," being unable to accept more, could no longer support respiration and combustion, two processes that depended on the giving off of phlogiston. Rutherford's phlogisticated air is now called nitrogen and he is usually given the credit for its discovery, although it remained for Lavoisier [334] a few years later to describe its real nature.

Rutherford was appointed professor of botany at the University of Edinburgh in 1786 and in 1794 he designed the first maximum-minimum thermometer.

[352] **HERSCHEL,** Caroline Lucretia
German-English astronomer
Born: Hannover, Germany, March 16, 1750
Died: Hannover, January 9, 1848

Caroline Herschel joined her brother, William Herschel [321], in England in 1772. He was an organist and she was training to be a concert singer. Both were successful and both gave up their musical careers for the sake of their all-consuming interest in astronomy. Caroline never married and submerged herself almost completely in her brother's career.

In what spare time she could find she observed the heavens on her own with a small telescope her brother made for her. She did good work and became the first woman astronomer of note. She searched for comets particularly and discovered eight of them.

After her brother's death she returned to Hannover, enjoyed the astronomical success of her nephew (William's son), John Herschel [479], and died at nearly ninety-eight.

[353] **DOLOMIEU,** Dieudonné de Gratet de (doh-loh-myoo')
French geologist
Born: Dolomieu, Dauphiné, June 23, 1750
Died: Châteauneuf, Saône-et-Loire, November 28, 1801

Dolomieu, the son of an aristocrat, was enrolled in the Order of the Knights of Malta when only two years old and rose to the rank of commander in 1780, although he seemed to be in perpetual trouble with his superiors.

He was interested in science as a hobby, and particularly in geology. His military travels enabled him to study minerals in various places and to make an excellent mineralogical collection. Despite his aristocratic heritage, Dolomieu was strongly in favor of the French Revolution when it broke out and only turned against it at the time of the Terror.

He accompanied Napoleon Bonaparte to Egypt in 1798, but on his return was forced into Taranto by a storm and there underwent imprisonment and solitary confinement for nearly two years through the machinations of enemies in

the Knights of Malta. He died not long after his release.

Dolomieu was particularly interested in volcanoes and studied them more thoroughly than anyone before him. He could not bring himself to go against Werner's [355] neptunism, however, and tried to work out the activity of volcanoes without making volcanic action responsible for the power that lay behind the geologic changes of the earth. The common mineral dolomite, a calcium magnesium carbonate, is named in his honor.

He is supposed to have begun his treatise on mineralogy, published in 1801, while he was in prison, using a pen he had made out of wood, soot from his lamp, and the margins of his Bible as writing paper.

[354] **SPRENGEL,** Christian Konrad (shpreng'el)
German botanist
Born: Brandenburg, Prussia, September 22, 1750
Died: Berlin, April 7, 1816

Sprengel was the fifteenth and last child of an archdeacon and was himself educated for the clergy. He graduated from Halle University in 1774 and in 1780 was appointed rector of a school where he taught languages and science.

Botany was his hobby. His theological training led him to think that every part of the flower was created for a reason and this included the fact that some flowers had markings that seemed to point the way to the nectar. This he felt had to be for the purpose of attracting and guiding insects.

He began, in 1787, to study the phenomena of plant fertilization in detail, and he published his findings in a book in 1793. He clearly described the role of insects in plant fertilization and pointed out that in other cases, plants were fertilized by the wind. He also noted that in some plants, stamens and pistils developed at different times so that self-pollination was made impossible.

His absorption in his work caused him

to neglect his school and he was pensioned off in 1794 and spent his last years in Berlin as a private tutor. His book attracted no attention at first and was brought before the eyes of scientists only through the enthusiastic praise of Darwin [554] a half century after its publication.

[355] **WERNER,** Abraham Gottlob
(vehr'ner)
German geologist
Born: Wehrau, Silesia (modern Osiecznica, Poland), September 25, 1750
Died: Dresden, Saxony, June 30, 1817

Werner's life was impregnated with minerals, so to speak, from the start. His father was an inspector at an ironworks and he himself entered mining school at Freiburg, a Saxon mining center. By 1775 he was a teacher at the mining school and stayed there the rest of his professional life. He devoted himself to establishing a language for mineralogy, classifying minerals as Linnaeus [276] had classified life forms a half century earlier.

Like Hutton [297] he recognized the fact that strata occurred in a definite succession and were evolved rather than created, with the deepest stratum the oldest. Unlike Hutton, who believed in the overriding importance of heat and volcanic action in geologic history (and was therefore a vulcanist), Werner believed that virtually all strata had been laid down as sediment through the action of water (and was therefore a neptunist). Werner believed that volcanic action was very much the exception.

Whereas Hutton accepted processes that were visibly taking place in the present and asked nothing more of the past, Werner found it necessary to suppose that there had been a primeval ocean covering all the earth, although there was no evidence of this. After the continents had been laid down through sedimentation, most of this primeval ocean had to disappear in some fashion, which Werner left unexplained. As for vol-

canoes, they were merely the manifestation of burning coal seams near the surface—and of no geologic importance. At least so Werner maintained.

Werner was almost a caricature of the stage Teuton, self-satisfied and self-assured. He did not travel at all and knew only the rocks of Saxony, but he calmly assumed that what was true for Saxony was true for the whole world. He resolutely refused to accept any evidence or even to listen to any that went counter to his theories. He paid no attention to the experimental work of James Hall [374] and blissfully ignored the clearest observations that large tracts of Europe gave every sign of having once consisted of lava flows. He considered volcanoes recent phenomena.

Nevertheless he was an electrifying teacher, who attracted students from all over Europe and who left behind him a whole generation of evolutionary geologists, some of whom eventually broke away from neptunism. During his lifetime and for some years after his death his views completely overshadowed those of Hutton, partly perhaps because neptunism was at least reminiscent of the biblical story of the Flood and therefore seemed more reconcilable with Genesis. The coming of Lyell [502] was to be the defeat of Werner and neptunism.

[356] **PRÉVOST,** Pierre (pray-voh')
Swiss physicist
Born: Geneva, March 3, 1751
Died: Geneva, April 8, 1839

Prévost, the son of a minister, studied first theology and then law, receiving his doctor's degree in 1773. He went to Berlin for a while at the invitation of Frederick II, returned to Geneva on his father's death in 1784, and in 1793 was appointed professor of philosophy and of physics at the University of Geneva.

There he clearly established the fact that cold was not a second "imponderable fluid" opposed to caloric, the existence of which Lavoisier [334] had postulated to explain heat, but showed that all the observed facts concerning heat could be interpreted by means of a single fluid, much as Franklin [272] had interpreted electrical observations by means of a single fluid.

In 1791 Prévost pointed out that cold did not flow from snow to a hand, but that heat flowed from the hand to the snow. It was the loss of heat, not the gain of cold that gave rise to the sensation of cold. In fact, he held that all bodies of all temperatures radiated heat. The hotter the body, the more heat was radiated so that heat always flowed from the hot body to the cold. A body that was not changing temperature was still radiating heat. It was, however, receiving heat from its surroundings at a rate that just matched its heat loss.

In all this, he was perfectly right. Nevertheless, although it all fitted in with the caloric theory and was held to confirm that theory, it also proved to fit in with the heat-as-motion of "kinetic" theory, as Maxwell [692] was to make perfectly plain, seven decades later.

Prévost lived through the perilous revolutionary and Napoleonic period, during which Geneva was annexed to France, with only a brief arrest in 1794. After Geneva regained its freedom in 1814, he served on its legislature.

[357] **BLUMENBACH,** Johann Friedrich (bloo'men-bahkh)
German anthropologist
Born: Gotha, Saxony, May 11, 1752
Died: Göttingen, Saxony, January 22, 1840

Blumenbach was the son of a well-to-do headmaster. He studied at the universities of Jena and of Göttingen and received his medical degree from the latter institution in 1775. His doctoral thesis dealt with his thoughts on the origin of the different human races and is considered one of the basic works on anthropology. In fact, he is the founder of scientific anthropology and was the first to view the human being as an object of study in the same fashion that other animals were.

Blumenbach used comparative anatomy as a guide to early human history,

trying to show by cranial measurements how groups of men migrated from one place to another. He was the first to attempt a rational division of human beings into divisions. He coined the term "Caucasian" for what we ordinarily refer to as the "white race" because he thought that the cranial measurements of some of the Caucasian tribes were perfect examples of that division. Similarly, he coined "Mongolian" and "Ethiopian" for the "yellow race" and the "black race," as well as "American" and "Malayan" for the "red race" and "brown race."

The division was far too simple and gave a false impression to the general public of airtight divisions, making it a little more possible to speak racist nonsense in what sounded like scientific terms. This was certainly not in Blumenbach's mind; for one thing, he spoke out strongly against beliefs that blacks were somehow less human than whites.

[358] **LEGENDRE,** Adrien Marie (luh-zhahn'dr)
French mathematician
Born: Paris, September 18, 1752
Died: Paris, January 9, 1833

Legendre was born into a well-to-do family and had enough money to allow him to dedicate himself to mathematics. He made important contributions to the theory of numbers and to a branch of calculus that dealt with what are called elliptical integrals, though in the latter case he was quickly surpassed by the work of Abel [527] and Jacobi [541]. Legendre rejoiced in these new discoveries regardless of the fact that they overshadowed his own years of labor.

Legendre recast the textbook of Euclid [40] into a simpler and better-ordered form so that from his day students study "Legendre" rather than "Euclid." He showed that not only pi but the square of pi was irrational and conjectured that pi was transcendental, something that Lindemann [826] was to show was so a century later.

In number theory, he was the first to work out the method of least squares as a way of calculating orbits, something that Gauss [415] was soon to perfect.

The upheaval of the French Revolution cost him his financial independence, but by that time he was sufficiently well known to be able to support himself by teaching and by accepting government positions. He never did as well as he deserved, apparently because of the enmity of Laplace [347], a small-minded man.

[359] **APPERT,** Nicolas (François)
(a-pair')
French inventor
Born: Châlons-sur-Marne, October 23, 1752
Died: Massy, near Paris, June 3, 1841

Appert, the son of an innkeeper, was a cook and confectioner, working in his father's establishment at first and then for several noblemen in the days before the French Revolution.

Self-educated, he was interested in devices for preserving food, for professional purposes. So was Napoleon, for economic and military purposes. Napoleon offered a prize in 1795 for practical preservation methods, and Appert spent fourteen years working out a system in which by first heating the food and then sealing it from air, putrefaction was prevented. He opened a factory to produce such sealed products in 1804. (This was an application, whether Appert knew it or not, of Spallanzani's [302] experiment and depended for its efficacy on the fact that spontaneous generation of microorganisms did not take place. It foreshadowed pasteurization a half century later, as Pasteur [642] himself freely admitted.)

Napoleon gave him 12,000 francs in 1809 and Appert then published his discovery—which served as the foundation of the vast canning industry of today and, with Borden's [524] work a half century later, altered the food habits of man.

Appert, who also developed the bouillon cube, did well for a while but was financially ruined after Napoleon's fall and died poor. The commercial cannery he founded—the first in the world— remained in business, however, and did not close its doors till 1933.

[360] **RUMFORD,** Benjamin Thompson, Count
American-British physicist
Born: Woburn, Massachusetts, March 26, 1753
Died: Auteuil (near Paris), France, August 21, 1814

Benjamin Thompson (better known as Count Rumford) was born the son of a farmer, only two miles from the birthplace, a half century before, of that other Benjamin, Benjamin Franklin [272].

He began life quietly as an apprentice to a storekeeper in Salem, but in 1766 he was nearly killed in the explosion of some fireworks he was making to help celebrate the repeal of the Stamp Act. After recovery, he returned to Boston to become an assistant in another store. At nineteen he married a rich widow considerably older than himself and lived with her in Rumford (now Concord), New Hampshire. All would have gone well were it not that the Revolutionary War broke out and young Thompson's sympathies were with the king. Indeed, he served the British troops by spying on his countrymen.

When the British troops left Boston, Thompson went with them (leaving wife and child behind) and spent the war in minor government offices in England, ending with a short stay in the still embattled colonies as a lieutenant colonel in the king's forces. When the Revolutionary War was over and the colonials had won their independence, Thompson knew himself to be in permanent exile.

Thompson's character did not improve in England. He took bribes and was suspected of selling war secrets to the French. In 1783, with the permission of George III, he found it safer to go to the Continent in search of adventure.

There he fell in with Elector Karl Theodor of Bavaria, for whom he worked as an intelligent and capable administrator. He established workhouses for Munich beggars, for instance, and had them turn out army uniforms with an efficiency that helped both the beggars and the army. He also introduced Watt's [316] steam engine and the potato to the Continent.

The elector expressed his gratitude in 1790 by making Thompson a count, and Thompson chose Rumford as his name, for that was the town in which his wife was born and near which he had had an estate. In the Bavarian service he grew interested in the problem of heat and that was the occasion for his most important contribution to science.

In the eighteenth century, heat was looked upon as an imponderable fluid, like phlogiston. Lavoisier [334], who demolished phlogiston, continued to think of heat as a fluid that could be poured from one substance to another and called it caloric.

Rumford, however, while boring cannon in Munich in 1798 noticed that the blocks of metal grew hot as blazes as the boring tool gouged them out, so that they had to be cooled constantly with water. The orthodox explanation was that caloric was being loosened from the metal as the metal was broken down into shavings by the boring. Rumford noticed that the heating continued as long as the boring did, with no letup, and that enough caloric was removed from the brass to have melted the metal if it were poured back in. In other words, more caloric was being removed from the brass than could have been contained in it. In fact, if the boring instruments were dull so that no metal was ground to shavings, the caloric did not stop pouring out of the metal. On the contrary, the metal heated up more than ever.

Rumford's conclusion was that the mechanical motion of the borer was being converted to heat and that heat was therefore a form of motion, a view that had been groped toward for a century and more by such men as Francis Bacon [163], Boyle [212], and Hooke [223]. And in this, they and Rumford are now considered to have been right.

Rumford even tried to calculate how much heat was produced by a given quantity of mechanical energy. He was thus the first to set a figure for what we now call the mechanical equivalent of heat. His figure was far too high, however, and a half century passed before Joule [613] reported the correct value.

Rumford, through his arrogance and the general unpleasantness of his character, finally outwore his welcome in Bavaria too, particularly after the death of the elector. That, and the pressure of Napoleon's victories, made it advisable for Rumford to return to England in 1799, and there his achievements were recognized and he was admitted into the Royal Society. In that year he weighed a quantity of water both as water and as ice and could detect no change in weight with the most delicate balance. Since water lost heat when it froze and gained it when it melted, as had been demonstrated by Black [298], it followed that caloric, if it existed, must be weightless. The fate of phlogiston made weightless fluids suspect and this experiment weakened the caloric theory, too.

Rumford, with the encouragement of that scientific Maecenas, Sir Joseph Banks [331], founded the Royal Institution in 1799 and obtained young men such as Young [402] and Davy [421] as lecturers. Rumford was a little dubious about the latter until he heard him give a lecture. That resolved all doubts, and indeed Davy was to grow famous through his lectures. In addition, Davy had just conducted some experiments that led him to the same conclusions as Rumford. Davy had arranged for ice to be rubbed mechanically, the entire system being kept one degree below the freezing point. There was insufficient caloric in the whole system, according to the orthodox view, to melt the ice, and yet it melted. Davy decided that the mechanical motion was converted to heat. Certainly this experiment didn't hurt Davy in Rumford's regard. (Historians of science doubt that the experiment could have worked as described by Davy, but Davy believed it worked and described the results in his first publication.)

In any case, neither Rumford's nor Davy's experiment was convincing to physicists. The caloric theory, which seemed to be substantiated by the work

243

of Prévost [356], and was strongly backed by such men as Berthollet [346], lived on for another half century until Maxwell [692] killed it once and for all.

In 1804 Rumford went to Paris, though Great Britain and France were at war and France was threatening an invasion. (Political passions were milder then, it would seem.) While he was in Paris, his path crossed that of the dead Lavoisier a second time. Having produced evidence against Lavoisier's theory of heat, he (having outlived his first wife) proceeded to marry Lavoisier's widow (who was rich and who kept the famous name of her martyred first husband). It was a late marriage—he being slightly over fifty, she slightly under— and an unhappy one, their first quarrel coming the day after their marriage. After four years they separated and Rumford was so ungallant as to hint that she was so hard to get along with that Lavoisier was lucky to have been guillotined. However, it is quite obvious that Rumford was no daisy himself.

In 1811 his American daughter by his first wife joined him and cared for him in his last years.

Incidentally, despite all the unpleasant messes of Rumford's character, there was a strong streak of idealism in him. He believed it better to make people happy first as a way of making them virtuous later (rather than the reverse, which has been the seemingly hopeless tactic of religions for so long). Then, too, like Franklin he refused to patent his inventions, which included a double boiler, a drip coffeepot, and a kitchen range. He even attempted a reconciliation with the United States in the end, and though he died, as he had lived, in exile, he left most of his estate to the United States and endowed a professorship in applied science at Harvard.

[361] **NICHOLSON,** William
English chemist
Born: London, 1753
Died: London, May 21, 1815

Nicholson, the son of an attorney, left school at sixteen and became a midship-

man in the service of the East India Company. He made two or three voyages to the East Indies while so employed. Then he worked in a lawyer's office and finally as a waterworks engineer. He never married.

He became a science writer, turning out a successful *Introduction to Natural Philosophy* in 1781. Oddly enough, though, it was in connection with water (a natural subject of interest for an ex-midshipman) that he had his opportunity of doing as well as writing.

In 1790 he invented a hydrometer for measuring the density of water, but his most significant work was in 1800.

On March 20 of that year Volta [337] wrote to Banks [331], president of the Royal Society, informing him of his construction of an electric battery. Nicholson heard of this and with the aid of a friend built his own Voltaic pile by May 2, making no attempt, apparently, to point out that Volta had priority. It was the first in England. Nicholson's great contribution was to place wires attached to the two ends of the pile in water. He found that with the current flowing, bubbles of gas (hydrogen and oxygen) were given off. He had "electrolyzed" water, breaking up the molecules into the individual elements. He thus reversed the demonstration of Cavendish [307], that hydrogen and oxygen could unite to form water. This was the first demonstration that an electric current could bring about a chemical reaction—the reverse of Volta's demonstration that a chemical reaction could bring about an electric current.

Nicholson edited a chemical journal, which he founded in 1797 and in which he reported his own work with the Voltaic pile even before Volta himself got a chance to publish. It was the first independent scientific journal. In 1808 he compiled a *Dictionary of Practical and Theoretical Chemistry*.

[362] **BLANCHARD,** Jean Pierre François (blan-shahr′)
French aeronaut
Born: Les Andelys, Eure, July 4, 1753
Died: Paris, March 7, 1809

Blanchard, born of poor parents, had a natural mechanical ability. When he was sixteen, he constructed a kind of bicycle. Then, in the 1770s, he tried to construct a flying machine, but once he heard of the Montgolfier [325] balloons, equipped with hydrogen, that was enough for him.

He began to make daring flights in both England and France in 1784 and on March 2, 1784, he and an American physician, John Jeffries, were the first to float across the English Channel, carrying the first airmail in history. They landed near Calais.

He went to the United States in 1793 and made balloon ascensions there, with President George Washington among the spectators on one occasion. He suffered a heart attack in the course of his sixtieth balloon ascension (this one in the Netherlands), fell from it, was badly hurt, and died not long after.

His great contribution was the invention of the parachute. In 1785 in London he became the first man in history to make use of a parachute, dropping a dog (or cat) in a basket attached to one. But despite all the feats of daring of men such as Blanchard the balloon remained a dead end for aeronautics, even after it was powered by Zeppelin [737] a century later. The true road was to be found by the Wright brothers [961, 995].

[363] **MURDOCK,** William
Scottish inventor
Born: Auchinleck, Ayrshire, August 21, 1754
Died: Birmingham, Warwickshire, England, November 15, 1839

Murdock, largely uneducated, cut his eyeteeth in 1777 in James Watt's [316] firm near Birmingham when Watt was beginning to sell his steam engines. Murdock went down to Cornwall to supervise the installation of engines in the mines there and by 1800 had risen to be a partner in the concern.

He joined the Lunar Society, a group of Birmingham scientists that included Watt, Priestley [312], and Erasmus Darwin [308], among others. This society

was politically liberal and was brought to an end in the disorders in 1791 that burned down Priestley's house.

Murdock invented various devices in connection with the steam engine, but his great feat was in another direction. He was the first to see in coal something more than a simple solid fuel. In 1792 he began to heat coal (also peat and wood) in the absence of air, and to store the gases that were driven off. These gases were, like the materials from which they came, inflammable, but being gases they possessed certain conveniences. They could be piped from place to place and required no strenuous transport. They could easily be set alight and the flame could easily be controlled by adjusting the rate of gas flow. Although the idea was ridiculed by many (including the poet and novelist Walter Scott), Murdock persisted.

By 1800 Murdock had set up an experimental gas light, using coal gas. In 1802 he celebrated the temporary Peace of Amiens with Napoleon by setting up a spectacular display of gas lights, and by 1803 he was routinely lighting his main factory with them. In 1807 some London streets began to use gas lighting. It was the first new form of lighting of the industrial age, and gas lighting was to expand in importance for nearly a century, until superseded by Edison's [788] electric light. Gas flames are of course still used in heating and cooking.

As in the case of Whitney's [386] cotton gin, gas lighting proved too simple an invention for the inventor's peace of mind. Others exploited it and Murdock had to expend considerable effort to maintain his own claims for priority.

[364] **PROUST,** Joseph Louis (proost)
French chemist
Born: Angers, Maine-et-Loire, September 26, 1754
Died: Angers, July 5, 1826

The son of an apothecary, Proust had the opportunity of passing his youth in an atmosphere saturated with chemistry. He went to Paris while still a young man and established himself there as an apothecary-chemist. He was one of the first to take part in the balloon rage of the 1780s, making an ascension in 1784.

He avoided the upheaval of the French Revolution since he traveled to Spain shortly before it began. There he spent two decades in fruitful labor in Madrid under the patronage of the Spanish king, Charles IV, who supplied him lavishly, for instance, with platinum vessels. In 1808 Charles IV was ousted from his throne by Napoleon, and Proust, his laboratory looted by the French soldiers, lost his position. He returned to France and lived out his life in retirement. Napoleon offered him a grant to enable him to continue his research, but he was in poor health and turned it down. After Napoleon's fall, Proust was made a member of the French Academy and was given a pension by Louis XVIII.

Proust investigated different sugars and distinguished between different varieties. He was the first to study the sugar in grapes, which we now call glucose.

However, the great event of his life was an eight-year running controversy of epic proportions with his contemporary Berthollet [346]. (This did not prevent Berthollet from greeting Proust cordially on the latter's return to France.)

Berthollet believed that the course of reactions depended on the mass of the reacting materials present and that this dictated both the rate of action and the nature of the composition of the final products. He was right in the first conclusion but, as Proust showed, wrong in his second.

Using painstakingly careful analysis Proust showed in 1799 that copper carbonate contained definite proportions by weight of copper, carbon, and oxygen no matter how it was prepared in the laboratory or how it was isolated from nature. The preparation was always 5 of copper to 4 of oxygen to 1 of carbon. He went on to show a similar situation for a number of other compounds and formulated the generalization that all compounds contained elements in certain definite proportions and no others, regardless of conditions of production.

This is called the law of definite proportions, and sometimes Proust's law.

Proust also showed that Berthollet, in presenting evidence that certain compounds varied in composition according to the method of preparation, was misled through inaccurate analyses and through the use of products he had insufficiently purified. Proust's victory in this battle was quite clear and was to be made conclusive a generation later by Berzelius [425].

Proust's law went a long way toward persuading Dalton [389] that elements must occur in the form of atoms and thus paved the way for the final and long-delayed victory of atomism.

[365] **PARKINSON,** James
English physician
Born: Hoxton Square, London,
April 11, 1755
Died: London, December 21, 1824

Parkinson, the son of a surgeon, was a practicing surgeon himself by 1784. He was a political and social liberal who wrote pamphlets in favor of parliamentary reform and for better treatment of mental patients.

He was the first to write a medical report on a perforated appendix (in 1812) and to recognize it as a cause of death. In 1817 he wrote a medical description of a condition he called "the shaking palsy," but which others have called Parkinson's disease ever since.

Geology and the study of fossils was an avocation of his. He was correct in thinking that coal was of plant origin, but he favored Werner [355] over Hutton [297] and accepted Cuvier's [396] catastrophism.

[366] **FOURCROY,** Antoine François, comte de (foor-krwah')
French chemist
Born: Paris, June 15, 1755
Died: Paris, December 16, 1809

Fourcroy, the son of an apothecary, worked as a clerk early in his life. He was fortunate enough to interest an anatomist in his obvious intellect, and that man arranged to have him receive a medical education.

Fourcroy obtained his degree in 1780, but found his interest in chemistry. He became a professor of chemistry at the Jardin du Roi in 1784. An excellent and successful teacher, he obtained his chief fame in connection with others. He was one of the first converts to the theories of Lavoisier [334], with whom he collaborated in establishing the new chemical nomenclature.

During the French Revolution he was a violent partisan of the radicals, succeeding to the seat that had been held by the assassinated demagogue Marat. He helped engineer the temporary suppression of the Academy of Sciences, which was suspected of being an aristocratic organization. Nor did he use his influence to save Lavoisier. Indeed, his testimony was damaging to his old associate—perhaps deliberately so. Later, however, he used his influence to save other scientists.

Under Napoleon he served as Minister of Public Instruction and in later life he was the patron of Vauquelin [379].

He died on the day Napoleon made him a count.

[367] **D'ELHUYAR,** Don Fausto (del-oo'yahr)
Spanish mineralogist
Born: Logroño, northern Spain, October 11, 1755
Died: Madrid, January 6, 1833

D'Elhuyar and his older brother, Juan José, studied mineralogy in Germany and became disciples of the theories of Werner [355]. They visited Sweden in 1782, studied with Bergman [315], and visited Scheele [329]. They analyzed a mineral called wolframite, which had been obtained from a tin mine, and in 1783 obtained a new metal from it, called wolfram. The same metal is also called tungsten from the Swedish words meaning "heavy stone." Scheele had investigated tungsten-containing minerals but had missed spotting the new metal.

The D'Elhuyar brothers were eventually sent to Latin America (then under Spanish domination) to supervise mining there. Fausto's older brother died in what is now Colombia, but Fausto, having served in Mexico with distinction, lived to return to Spain after Mexico gained its independence.

[368] **CHAPTAL,** Jean Antoine Claude, comte de Chanteloup (shap-tal')
French chemist
Born: Nogaret, Lozère, June 4, 1756
Died: Paris, July 30, 1832

Chaptal, the son of a small landowner, had a rich physician as an uncle, which was helpful. The young man studied medicine, receiving his medical degree at Montpellier in 1777. Against his uncle's will, he grew interested in chemistry, though, and obtained a professorship at the University in 1781. He was one of the first to adopt Lavoisier's [334] new view of chemistry.

He was particularly interested in the application of chemistry to industry and, having inherited a large sum from his uncle and having married a wife with a large dowry besides, he had the wherewithal to establish a plant at Montpellier in 1781 for the first commercial production of sulfuric acid in France. His usefulness was such that both Spain and the infant United States bid for his services (both without success).

After the French Revolution broke out he was arrested, in 1793, but he was soon liberated and put in charge of a plant manufacturing gunpowder. The republic *did* have need of scientists, after all (though they had thought otherwise in the case of Lavoisier), for without the development of new chemical methods France (which was at war with all the surrounding nations) could not have produced the gunpowder she needed and the republic would have been crushed.

Under Napoleon, Chaptal was placed in charge of education and was a strong advocate of the writing of science for the layman. He supervised the introduction of the metric system and was eventually made a count. When Napoleon fell, and the old monarchy returned with Louis XVIII, Chaptal was relieved of his title but was done no other harm. He lost much of his wealth, however, paying the debts his son ran up when he conducted the family firm in a slipshod manner.

It was Chaptal, by the way, who, in 1790, suggested the name "nitrogen" for the element Lavoisier had called "azote."

His most important book was *Chemistry Applied to the Arts,* published in 1807. This was the first book to be devoted specifically to industrial chemistry.

[369] **McADAM,** John Loudon
Scottish engineer
Born: Ayr, Ayrshire, September 21, 1756
Died: Moffat, Dumfriesshire, November 26, 1836

In 1770, after his father died, McAdam traveled to New York to work for his uncle, who during the war was a well-to-do Tory. McAdam, naturally, was a Tory too and made a comfortable living as agent for the sale of war prizes. Once the peace treaty was signed and the colonies established as an independent power, he returned to Scotland, in 1783.

His true fame began in 1806, when he became paving commissioner in Bristol. He began to push energetically for new and rational principles of paving: making roads out of crushed rock, with proper allowance for drainage, instead of the alternating ruts and mud (depending on whether the weather was dry or wet). There was strong economic motivation for this since the first third of the nineteenth century was the golden age of stagecoaches.

After McAdam's death, Stephenson's [431] locomotive—traveling on iron rails rather than on paving—killed the coaches. Nevertheless the time was to come when paved roads would carry automobiles on rubber tires and that in turn was to send the railroad into decline. To macadamize is still sometimes used to mean the paving of a road, in honor of McAdam.

[370] **CHLADNI,** Ernst Florens Friedrich (klahd'nee)
German physicist
Born: Wittenberg, Saxony, November 30, 1756
Died: Breslau, Silesia (modern Wrocław, Poland), April 3, 1827

Chladni, the son of a lawyer, found his own education directed to the law, much against his will. He received his degree from the University of Leipzig in 1782, but when his father died Chladni was able to consult his own interests more freely, and these lay in the direction of science.

Since he was interested in music and was himself an amateur musician, he began to investigate sound waves mathematically in 1786. He was the first to work out the quantitative relationships governing the transmission of sound and is therefore called the father of acoustics.

Chladni set thin plates, covered with a layer of sand, to vibrating. The plate vibrated in a complex pattern, with some portions (nodal lines) remaining motionless. The nodal lines retained sand shaken onto them by the neighboring areas that were vibrating. In this way the plates came to be covered with characteristic sand patterns from which much could be deduced concerning vibrations. The patterns (which are still called Chladni figures) fascinated the audience when they were exhibited before a gathering of scientists at Paris in 1809. Napoleon had the demonstration repeated for himself.

The velocity of sound had already been measured in air by Gassendi [182] and others two centuries earlier, but Chladni went a step further. He filled organ pipes with different gases and from the pitch of the note sounded on those pipes was able to calculate the velocity of sound in each of those cases. The free vibration of a column of gas determines its pitch, and that vibration depends on the natural mobility of the molecules making it up. The velocity of sound through the gas also depends on the natural mobility of those molecules, so that the velocity of sound in a particular gas can be calculated from the pitch sounded by an organ pipe filled with gas.

Chladni invented a musical instrument called the euphonium, made of glass rods and steel bars that were sounded by being rubbed with the moistened finger, and traveled about Europe performing on this instrument and giving scientific lectures. He also had a collection of meteorites and was one of the first scientists to insist that these fell from the heavens, as a number of peasants, who claimed they had seen it happen, had reported. In 1794 he wrote a book on the subject and suggested the meteorites to be the debris of an exploded planet. In the very reasonable Age of Reason of the late eighteenth century, scientists were reluctant to believe such obviously tall tales, until Biot [404] settled matters at the turn of the century.

[371] GALL, Franz Joseph (gahl)
German physician
Born: Tiefenbrunn, Baden, March 9, 1758
Died: Montrouge, near Paris, France, August 22, 1828

Gall, the son of a merchant who was of Italian descent, studied medicine at Baden, Strasbourg, and Vienna, obtaining his medical degree in the last-named city in 1785. He was particularly interested in the physiology of the nerves and the brain.

He pointed out, quite correctly, that the gray matter was the active and essential part of the brain and that the white matter was connecting material.

Gall believed that the shape of the brain had something to do with mental capacity and that different parts of the brain were involved with different parts of the human body. In this there was considerable truth. Modern neurologists map the brain in detail, finding one region in control of finger movement, another in control of jaw movements, and so on.

Gall imagined he could correlate the shape of the brain with all sorts of emotional and temperamental qualities and that the shape of the brain could, in turn, be deduced from the superficial unevennesses of the skull.

This marks the beginning of the pseudoscience of phrenology, in which a man's character is supposedly analyzed by feeling the bumps on his head. Gall lectured in Vienna on the subject (charging admission) until 1802, when he was stopped by Emperor Francis I because his materialistic philosophy seemed subversive of religion. (If one reduces evil impulses to the presence of a particular bump on the skull, what becomes of free will?)

Like Mesmer [314], a generation before him, Gall traveled to Paris (having first made a tour of northern Europe in 1807). In 1808 he presented his theories to the Institut de France. The French, as in the case of Mesmer, appointed a committee to look into the matter, and the committee reported unfavorably. Emperor Napoleon I acted to limit his influence in France. (Gall was about the only thing France and Austria agreed on in these years.)

This did not stop the favorable reception of phrenology among the general public any more than it had earlier stopped the appeal of mesmerism. After Gall's death his disciples increased the nonsense in phrenology and reduced it to utter folly. As a result the stigma of the quack clings to Gall, and the valuable work done by him tends to be forgotten, as in the case of Mesmer.

Gall became a French citizen in 1819.

[372] OLBERS, Heinrich Wilhelm Matthäus (ohl'bers)
German astronomer
Born: Arbergen (near Bremen), October 11, 1758
Died: Bremen, March 2, 1840

Olbers, the eighth of sixteen children of a minister, was trained as a physician at Göttingen, graduating in 1780. He practiced medicine in Bremen, but spent his nights in astronomical observations, having converted the upper portion of his house into an observatory. His first love was the pursuit of comets. He worked out a method in 1797 for determining their orbits that is still used, and

249

he discovered five. One of these, discovered in 1815, is still called Olbers' comet. In 1820, after the death of his second wife and of his daughter, he retired from ordinary pursuits and devoted himself completely to astronomy.

He was one of the guiding spirits in the team dedicated to the discovery of the planet in the gap between Mars and Jupiter. Although he lost out in the initial discovery to Piazzi [341], he rediscovered the planet after Gauss [415] had calculated the orbit. He went on to discover the asteroid Pallas in 1802 and the asteroid Vesta in 1804. He was the first to suggest that the asteroids had originated through the explosion of a moderately sized planet once moving in an orbit in the asteroid zone—a suggestion that is considered valid by many to this day. The 1002d asteroid to be discovered was named Olbería in his honor.

Olbers is best known nowadays for the "Olbers's paradox." He pointed out, in 1826, that if there were an infinite number of stars evenly distributed in space, the night sky should be uniformly light. He believed that the stars *were* infinite in number and that the reason the night sky was dark was that dust obscured most of the light. It is true that dust exists in interstellar space, but its existence is not an adequate explanation of Olbers's paradox. Astronomy had to await the discovery of the expanding universe by Hubble [1136] for the realization that a "red shift" weakened the light of distant stars and kept the night sky dark—to say nothing of the fact that the universe is so large (and growing larger through expansion to such a degree) that the light pouring out of the stars has not, in any case, had time to fill it.

[373] **GADOLIN,** Johan (gah′doh-leen)
Finnish chemist
Born: Åbo, now Turku, June 5, 1760
Died: Wirmo, August 15, 1852

Gadolin's father was himself an astronomer and physicist (and bishop, too), so that the young man's education began at home. Gadolin received his formal training in Sweden (Finland was part of the Swedish realm in the eighteenth century) and studied under Bergman [315]. He was a phlogistonist to begin with, but was converted to Lavoisier's [334] views. Gadolin's textbook on chemistry, published in 1798, was the first in the Swedish language to teach the new chemistry.

The great opportunity of a long and useful life as a professor of chemistry at Åbo University came when on a trip to Sweden in 1794 he was shown a new mineral that had been obtained at the Ytterby quarry.

It seemed to Gadolin as he tested the mineral that it contained a new "earth." In those days, the word "earth" was applied to any oxide that was insoluble in water and resistant to the action of heat. Lime, magnesia, silica, and iron oxide were examples of very common earths. This new earth that Gadolin had located was clearly much less common than those others. It became known as a rare earth.

In the next century the rare earth located by Gadolin (and minerals similar to it) was found to contain over a dozen different elements, now called the rare earth elements. These amused three generations of chemists. In 1886, a generation after Gadolin's death, one of the rare earth elements was named gadolinium in his honor by Lecoq de Boisbaudran [736].

[374] **HALL,** Sir James
Scottish geologist and chemist
Born: Haddington, January 17, 1761
Died: Edinburgh, June 23, 1832

Hall, who succeeded to his father's baronetcy in 1776, sat in Parliament from 1807 to 1812. He was an amateur geologist, attended lectures by Black [298] and, after making Hutton's [297] acquaintance threw himself wholeheartedly on the side of Hutton's theories. He was also one of the first in England to adopt Lavoisier's [334] new chemistry.

Hutton supposed the chief agent of geological change to be the planet's internal heat. Werner [355] and his followers held out for the action of water. The neptunists, as Werner's followers were called, pointed out that if rock had really been heated to high temperatures and had liquefied, it would cool into a glassy substance and would not become crystalline, whereas substances precipitating from water solution make their appearance in crystalline form. This, they held, argued for water and against heat as the agent of change. Furthermore, said the neptunists, stones like limestone would decompose under strong heat; the vast deposits existing had never been heated, nor had the earth generally.

It occurred to Hall that he might test these objections in the laboratory. At a glass factory he noticed that molten glass need not cool to ordinary glass. If it were cooled very slowly, it became opaque and crystalline. He therefore had rock melted in a furnace and showed that if it was allowed to cool quickly, it would form a glassy solid, but if allowed to cool slowly, it would form a crystalline solid. He further showed that if limestone was heated in a closed vessel, it would not decompose but would melt and then cool again to marble.

Hall may be considered the founder of experimental geology and of geochemistry. Although every one of his experiments strongly backed Hutton's views and demolished Werner's, Hutton himself disapproved. Hutton believed that one could not study vast planetary changes by little experiments in furnaces. For that reason Hall did not publish his results until after Hutton's death in 1797.

Nevertheless the neptunists maintained their ascendancy until Lyell [502] published a book supporting Hutton's views at just about the time that Hall died.

[375] **TENNANT,** Smithson
English chemist
Born: Selby, Yorkshire, November 30, 1761
Died: Boulogne, France, February 22, 1815

Tennant was the son of a clergyman and lost both parents as a youngster, his

mother dying from an accident while horseback riding. For the most part he was self-educated through his teens and was interested in chemistry as a hobby. He had attended lectures given by Black [298] in 1781.

During a trip to Sweden he met Scheele [329] and later was to make friends with another Swede, Berzelius [425]. He finally undertook medical studies, obtaining his doctor's degree in 1796 from Cambridge, but he never practiced medicine.

He maintained his interest in chemistry and in 1796 undertook, as Lavoisier [334] had done a quarter century before, the rather expensive experiment of burning a diamond. By measuring the carbon dioxide produced in the process, he was able to show that the diamond did not merely contain carbon but was *all* carbon. He did not complete the experiment himself, but went out horseback riding as was his daily custom. His assistant, however, was Wollaston [388], who was quite reliable.

In 1803 he (as well as Wollaston) was working with platinum minerals. Tennant discovered two metals something like platinum, yet with distinct properties and even less reactive. One he named iridium, from the Greek word for "rainbow" because of the different colors of its compounds. The other he named osmium, from the Greek word for "smell" because of the odor of one of its compounds.

Tennant also experimented with the fertilizing of soil with lime. In 1813 he was appointed professor of chemistry at Cambridge but did not teach long. In 1815, on a visit to France (just in time to witness the return of Napoleon from Elba), a small drawbridge gave under him and he and his horse were catapulted into the ditch. Horseback riding finished him as it had his mother.

[376] **PONS,** Jean Louis (pohns)
French astronomer
Born: Peyres, Hautes Alpes, France, December 24, 1761
Died: Florence, Italy, October 14, 1831

Pons, born of poor parents, received a rather sketchy education. He joined the observatory in Marseille in 1789, but only as janitor. Eventually he earned a position as observer. In 1819 he left for Italy, where he spent his last years as director of an observatory in Florence.

He was an ardent hunter of comets, as ardent as ever Messier [305] had been. Indeed, he was called the comet-chaser. He discovered thirty-seven comets and several bear his name to this day, notably the Pons-Brookes and the Pons-Winnecke.

His most interesting discovery was made in 1818 when he detected a comet that proved to have the shortest period of any discovered before or since. However, it does not bear his name, but that of Encke [475], who worked out its orbit the following year.

[377] **GREGOR,** William
English mineralogist
Born: Trewarthenick, Cornwall, December 25, 1761
Died: Creed, Cornwall, July 11, 1817

Like Priestley [312], Gregor was a minister who discovered an element. He graduated from Cambridge in 1783 and entered his ministerial duties in 1787, becoming rector of Creed in 1793.

He attended some lectures on science and grew interested in mineralogy, abandoning, like his American contemporary Fulton [385], a promising artistic ability. Thereafter he analyzed as many odd minerals as he could find and in 1791 discovered the new element that four years later was named titanium by Klaproth [335].

[378] **RICHTER,** Jeremias Benjamin
(rikh'ter)
German chemist
Born: Hirschberg, Silesia (now Jelenia Góra, Poland), March 10, 1762
Died: Berlin, April 4, 1807

Richter joined the Prussian army in 1778 but studied chemistry in his spare time. When he left the army in 1785, he went to the University of Königsberg, where he studied mathematics and may have attended lectures by Kant [293]. He received his Ph.D. in 1789. He made a small living as a chemist but never held an academic position. He died of tuberculosis when he was forty-five, just when Prussia had been catastrophically defeated by Napoleon and was at a low point in its history.

Richter was powerfully influenced by Kant's contention that science is applied mathematics and spent his time trying to find mathematical relationships in chemistry. He was convinced that substances reacted with each other in fixed proportions, a sort of offshoot of the ideas of Proust [364].

He was most successful in demonstrating, in 1791, that acids and bases, in neutralizing each other to form salts, do so in fixed proportions. Such reaction in fixed proportions is called stoichiometry, and Richter was the first to establish it, making it the basis of quantitative chemical analysis for some two and a half centuries.

[379] **VAUQUELIN,** Louis Nicolas
(voh-klan')
French chemist
Born: St. André, Hébertôt, Calvados, May 16, 1763
Died: St. André, Hébertôt, November 14, 1829

The son of a peasant, Vauquelin labored in the fields. His aptitude for studies was noted by the village priest, who helped him to obtain a post in an apothecary's shop and later go to Paris. Through one of the Paris apothecaries for whom he worked, he was brought to the attention of Fourcroy [366], who made him an assistant. Vauquelin never forgot this and in later years provided the same sponsoring kindness for Thénard [416], another peasant's son.

Vauquelin left France temporarily during the worst of the Terror in 1793 and 1794. This was a prudent move, for he had rescued a soldier from a rioting mob and might well have been guillotined if he had stayed.

23. John Dalton

24. Georges L. Cuvier

25. Dalton collecting marsh gas

26. Thomas Young

27. André M. Ampère

28. Sir Humphry Davy

29. Jöns J. Berzelius

30. Michael Faraday

31. Joseph Henry

32. Friedrich Wöhler

33. Justus von Liebig

34. CHARLES DARWIN

35. THEODOR SCHWANN

36. CLAUDE BERNARD

37. JAMES P. JOULE

38. HERMANN L. F. VON HELMHOLTZ

39. ABBÉ GREGOR J. MENDEL

40. Louis Pasteur

41. Gustav R. Kirchhoff

42. Lord William Thomson Kelvin

43. Friedrich A. Kekulé von Stradonitz

44. James Clerk Maxwell

45. Dmitri I. Mendeléev

In 1797 Vauquelin made the discoveries for which he is most famous. In a Siberian mineral he located a new metal, which was named chromium, a name suggested by Fourcroy from the Greek word for color because of the many colors of its compounds. Vauquelin just beat out Klaproth [335] with this discovery, for Klaproth repeated the work independently within months.

Vauquelin also recognized the existence of the element beryllium in the gems beryl and emerald, although he did not actually isolate it. His interest in that direction had been sparked by studies on the two crystal forms by Haüy [332] and it was Wöhler [515], a generation later, who actually isolated the metal.

In another direction, Vauquelin isolated the compound asparagine from asparagus in 1806. Eventually it proved to be one of the amino acids that occur in proteins, the first to be discovered.

In 1811 Fourcroy died and Vauquelin succeeded to his post as professor of chemistry. Fourcroy's maiden sisters remained with Vauquelin, who never married, and he returned their care for him when he was young by taking care of them when they were old. In 1827 he was elected to the French legislature.

[380] **KIRCHHOF**, Gottlieb Sigismund
Constantin (kirkh′huf)
German-Russian chemist
Born: Teterow, Mecklenburg-Schwerin, February 19, 1764
Died: St. Petersburg (now Leningrad), Russia, February 14, 1833

Kirchhof, the son of a pharmacist, worked with his father and then at other pharmacies, qualifying as an apothecary. In 1792 he moved to St. Petersburg, working in that capacity.

Kirchhof developed methods of use in industrial chemistry, working out a method for refining vegetable oil, for instance, and established a large factory for the purpose that prepared two tons of refined oil a day, and that prospered.

His most important work, however, consisted of the treatment of starch with sulfuric acid, something that brought

about the hydrolysis of the large molecule into its small glucose units. (Glucose is the commonest of the "simple sugars.") This amounted to the discovery of glucose and was also the first use of a controlled catalytic reaction, since sulfuric acid brought about the hydrolysis of starch without being consumed in the process, something Berzelius [425] was to name "catalysis."

Kirchhof's work laid the foundation for the scientific study of the processes of brewing and fermentation.

[381] **GOODRICKE**, John
English astronomer
Born: Groningen, Netherlands, September 17, 1764
Died: York, England, April 20, 1786

Goodricke, the son of an English diplomat serving in the Netherlands, is a most unusual case. He was a deaf-mute from birth, or possibly as the result of a very early illness, and barely lived past his twenty-first birthday. Yet, with that disability and with so short a life, he managed to make a first-rate discovery.

Goodricke studied the star Algol, the brightest star to show noticeable variations in its light. (It is a "variable star.") To those who followed Aristotle's [29] dictum that the heavenly bodies were changeless, this variation in light was unsettling. Perhaps the variation accounted for the fact that its name, which is Arabic, means "the ghoul" and that the Greeks built the constellation of Perseus about it, making Algol represent the head of the demon Medusa.

The young deaf-mute studied the light variations without mystic uneasiness. He was the first to show that the variations were quite regular and, in 1782, when he was not quite eighteen, he suggested that an invisible companion star periodically eclipsed Algol and diminished the light we could see. It was a daring suggestion for so young a man to make and an "invisible star" was indeed an anomaly; but Goodricke's idea, in the end, turned out to be entirely right, as Vogel [757] was to show a century later.

[382] **DEL RIO,** Andrès Manuel (del-ree′oh)
Spanish-Mexican mineralogist
Born: Madrid, November 10, 1764
Died: Mexico City, March 23, 1849

Del Rio graduated from the University of Alcalá de Henares in 1781, and went on to study at the Academy of Mines at Almadén with a subsidy from the enlightened Charles III, who was trying (vainly) to bring Spain into the mainstream of European science.

Del Rio's aptitude for study and interest in mining and mineralogy was such, during his Spanish school days, that he was sent to study in France, England, and Germany at government expense. He studied under Werner [355], the neptunist, and there made friends with young Humboldt [397].

During the worst of the French Revolution he was in Paris and was nearly marked off for the guillotine because of his too-close association with Lavoisier [334]. In 1794 the Spanish government sent him to Mexico City to take up a professorship at the School of Mines that had been established by D'Elhuyar [367]. He was to remain there for half a century, staying on, unlike D'Elhuyar, after Mexico had gained its independence.

In 1801 he discovered what he thought was a new metal in a lead ore and named it erythronium. However, other chemists thought erythronium was really chromium, which had been discovered three years earlier by Vauquelin [379]. Del Rio let himself be persuaded and abandoned his claim of having discovered a new metal. When Sefström [451] discovered vanadium, Wöhler [515] showed it to be identical with Del Rio's erythronium, but by then it was too late. Sefström is now usually given the credit for the discovery.

[383] **HATCHETT,** Charles
English chemist
Born: London, January 2, 1765
Died: Chelsea, March 10, 1847

In 1801 Hatchett, the son of a prosperous coach builder, analyzed an unusual mineral that had originally been found in the colony of Connecticut and had been sent to England by the colonial governor. Hatchett reported a new metal in the mineral and named it columbium in honor of its having been found in Columbia, the poetic synonym for the new nation of the United States. In 1809 Wollaston [388] analyzed another portion and declared columbium to be identical with Ekeberg's [391] tantalum. The Wollaston view won out and Hatchett retired from research, either out of anger or out of sheer uninterest. In 1846 it was finally proved that the metal Hatchett had discovered was truly a new metal and not identical with tantalum. Wollaston and Ekeberg were both dead by then, but Hatchett was still alive—and vindicated. Columbium in its rediscovery was, however, given the name niobium (after Niobe, the daughter of Tantalus), though for a century Americans stubbornly clung to columbium. An international agreement in recent years has established the name officially as niobium, so in the long run poor Hatchett lost out.

After his father died, Hatchett, no longer a chemist, took over the family business and was coach builder to the king.

[384] **NIEPCE,** Joseph Nicéphore (nyeps)
French inventor
Born: Chalôns, Saône-et-Loire, March 7, 1765
Died: Saint-Loup-de-Varennes, near Chalôns, July 5, 1833

Niepce was the son of a wealthy lawyer suspected of royalist sympathies. The family fled the French Revolution but young Niepce returned to serve in Napoleon's army till ill health forced his discharge.

In 1813 he grew interested in lithography, a form of art that involved the placing of greased designs on stone. Niepce had no artistic talent of his own and his son made the designs. When that son was called up for military service,

Niepce began to try to produce designs automatically. His interest shifted to such automatic production as an end in itself.

He tried, at first, to have the sun darken silver chloride, so that reflected sunlight could produce an imitation of the design it formed itself in the process of reflection. Essentially he was trying to produce a light-dark pattern that imitated nature; i.e. a photograph.

He produced the first object we might call a primitive photograph in 1822 (and it is now in a collection at the University of Texas). In 1827 he submitted one to the Royal Society, one which had required an eight-hour exposure. He tried to interest George IV in this, but anything that required so much time had to remain no more than a curiosity, and Niepce's efforts merely drove him toward bankruptcy. That process was accelerated by the fact that his brother, who was in partnership with him, was insane and had wasted money on imaginary projects.

Daguerre [467] was doing similar work and in 1829 economic necessity forced Niepce into partnership with him. Daguerre eventually succeeded but Niepce died of apoplexy too soon to see that success.

[385] **FULTON**, Robert
American inventor
Born: Little Britain (now Fulton), Pennsylvania, November 14, 1765
Died: New York, New York, February 24, 1815

Fulton, the son of a farmer, was left fatherless at three. He began life as a jeweler's apprentice and then as an artist. Franklin [272] sat for a portrait by him in Philadelphia. In 1786 he traveled to England to study. There he made friends with engineers and his own interest in engineering and invention was stimulated, so that, though he was reasonably successful in art, he abandoned it for civil engineering. It was the great age of canal building in England (an age to which the coming of the railroad a half

century later was to put an end) and Fulton investigated methods of improving canal navigation.

From this his mind naturally traveled to the possibility of powering water transportation by steam. In 1797 he went to France where he made friends with Laplace [347] and where for seven years he attempted to devise a workable submarine. (His best submarine, built in 1801, he called the *Nautilus,* a name that was to inspire Jules Verne seventy years later and, via Verne, the American navy a century and a half later.)

For a while the French government was interested in these attempts, thinking that submarines might offer a way of destroying the British navy. However, tests were disappointing and the French lost interest. The British hired Fulton, and they were disappointed too, although on the advice of men such as Cavendish [307] and Banks [331] they subsidized him handsomely.

Meanwhile Fulton had tried to launch a surface vessel that was propelled by a paddle wheel powered by a steam engine, but experiments on the Seine with such a vessel failed. When he returned to the United States in 1806 he resumed tests and in 1807 built the *Clermont,* 150 feet long. This vessel performed well, steaming up the Hudson from New York to Albany in thirty-two hours, so that it maintained an average speed of nearly five miles an hour. Soon he had a fleet of steamships in operation.

Fulton's fortune was made but most of it was spent on patent litigation, on submarine projects and so on.

Steam was not quite up to helping the United States in the War of 1812, but it was in the minds of American naval men. Fulton died of pneumonia after working in bad weather on the open decks of a steam warship he was constructing, and was given a state funeral. The War of 1812 had ended two months before.

Fulton is generally considered the inventor of the steamship and when the Hall of Fame for Great Americans was established in 1900 he was included. Actually the *Clermont* was not the first workable steamship. John Fitch [330] more nearly deserves credit for the invention. However, Fulton was the first to make steamships profitable and a permanent feature of the world scene.

Nor was the feat a minor one. By freeing sea travel from the tyranny of the wind and the brutality of the oar, Fulton carried through the first of several revolutions in transportation that were to end by making no part of the earth more than a few hours away from any other part.

[386] **WHITNEY**, Eli
American inventor
Born: Westboro, Massachusetts,
December 8, 1765
Died: New Haven, Connecticut,
January 8, 1825

Whitney, the son of a farmer who served as a justice of the peace, was the model of the ingenious Yankee gadgeteer. He might indeed have been the very Connecticut Yankee Mark Twain invented a century later and sent to King Arthur's court. Whitney's skill at making and patching contrivances kept him in pocket money and helped him through Yale University.

After graduation in 1792 he traveled to Savannah, Georgia, as a teacher, with the intention of studying law. There he met the widow of the Revolutionary War general Nathanael Greene and lived on her plantation while studying law. She recognized young Whitney's ability, which he had demonstrated by working out a few household gadgets for her, and introduced him to some gentlemen who were concerned about the South's cotton industry.

Cotton was a valuable substance that could mean wealth for the South, but it was difficult to pluck the cotton fibers off the seeds to which they were attached. It seemed to Whitney that it would be easy to devise metal projections to do this. In April 1793 he invented the cotton gin ("gin" being short for "engine"). Metal wires poked through slats, entangled themselves in the cotton fibers and pulled them free. One gin could produce fifty pounds of cleaned cotton per day.

Rarely has such a device had such grave and even catastrophic effects. Slavery was dying out in the United States, even in the South, because slavery is no match economically for free labor plus machinery. The cotton gin, however, made cotton growing big business and slavery seemed eminently suitable for the cotton plantations. Slavery revived, grew, and strengthened, and the South went to war rather than give up its "peculiar institution" peaceably. The American Civil War might never have been fought but for the cotton gin.

Fortified by a $50,000 grant awarded him by the legislature of South Carolina, Whitney returned to New England to manufacture the gin. However, the device was so simple to manufacture and the principle so easy to copy that he spent the grant and all profits on protecting his patent and in the end he reaped no financial reward.

In 1798 he obtained a contract to manufacture ten thousand muskets for the government and in the process of fulfilling it he produced a second invention, more subtle than the first and just as important.

Up to that time, every musket (and, indeed, every device consisting of more than one part) had to be made by hand, with each part adjusted to fit the adjoining part. If a part was broken, a new one had to be manually adjusted. A corresponding part from a similar device would not necessarily (and, in fact, virtually never did) replace the broken part without adjustment.

Whitney, however, machined his parts with such precision that a particular part could replace any other one of that type. The story is that in 1801 he brought some muskets disassembled and threw them down at the feet of the government official. "There are your muskets," he said and, picking out parts at random, put together a working musket. This time he made a fortune and kept it.

He introduced division of labor in his factories and was thus the grandfather of mass production, something that Henry Ford [929] was to make a living reality a century later. Whitney was one of the charter members of the Hall of Fame

for Great Americans when it was established in 1900.

[387] **MALTHUS,** Thomas Robert
    (malt'hus)
    English economist
    Born: near Guildford, Surrey,
    February 13, 1766
    Died: Haileybury, Somersetshire
    December 23, 1834

Malthus' father, a man of property,
was a product of the Age of Reason and
believed in the goodness of man and in
his progress toward an ideal society.
Malthus, as an undergraduate at Cambridge (from which he graduated in
1788), observed England's population
beginning to increase rapidly with the
onset of the Industrial Revolution and
was less optimistic. He believed that
progress toward a better society was impossible because of the rapid increase in
human numbers that invariably accompanied such progress.

His father, hearing his argument,
urged him to put his theories into writing. In 1798, after he had been ordained
in the Church of England (despite the
handicap of a cleft palate that interfered
with his speech), Malthus published his
Essay on Population anonymously. He
maintained that population would always
outrun the food supply and that in the
end human numbers would have to be
kept down by famine, disease, or war.
This was an idea that had been earlier
mentioned by Franklin [272].

Malthus was greeted with a storm of
abuse and published a second and enlarged edition in 1803. In the second edition he admitted that moral restraint
(delayed marriage and sexual con-
tinence) might counter the increase in
population. In 1805 he received a professorial appointment in political economy
at East India Company's College at Hai-
leybury (the first professor of this subject in England) and wrote books on this
subject that stirred up far less controversy. He first formulated what is called
the law of diminishing returns, for instance.

Malthus was one of the first to attempt
a systematic study of human society; he
was a pioneer sociologist, in other words.
More specifically, his book inspired both
Darwin [554] and Wallace [643] to a
working out of the theory of evolution
by natural selection, a theory that would
undoubtedly have appalled Malthus.

[388] **WOLLASTON,** William Hyde
    (wool'us-tun)
    English chemist and physicist
    Born: East Dereham, Norfolk,
    August 6, 1766
    Died: London, December 22,
    1828

Wollaston was the son of a clergyman
and one of seventeen children. He studied languages at Cambridge, then
switched to medicine and obtained his
medical degree in 1793. After seven
years of practice as a physician, however, deteriorating eyesight led him to retire and devote himself to research.

In particular he dedicated himself to
platinum, in connection with which he
worked for a while as Tennant's [375]
assistant. Platinum was the glamour metal
of the late eighteenth century, heavier,
rarer, and more inert than gold. Only
in beauty did it fall short. Wollaston
developed a method for working platinum, allowing it to be hammered and
molded into shape for laboratory apparatus. He kept his method secret (no
one was ever allowed in his laboratory)
and earned a fortune of thirty thousand
pounds, enough money to make himself
financially independent and to make his
early retirement possible. He arranged to
have a description of the method published after his death.

In working with platinum he isolated
from its ores two platinum-like metals in
1804. One of these he named palladium
after the planetoid Pallas, just discovered
by Olbers [372], thus continuing Klaproth's [335] device of naming a new
metal after a new planet. The other he
named rhodium (from the Greek for
rose) after the rose color of some of its
compounds. In 1810 he discovered cys-

tine (from the Greek word for bladder) in a bladder stone. It was the second of the amino acid building blocks of protein to be discovered, though its identification as such was not to come for nearly a century.

His successes bore the fruit of fame as well as wealth. In 1793 he was elected to membership in the Royal Society with Cavendish [307] and William Herschel [321] as his sponsors. In 1806 he was made secretary of the Society and in 1820, when Banks [331], the long-time president, died, it was expected that Wollaston would succeed. At least, it was known that Banks had wanted Wollaston to be his successor. Wollaston, however, stepped back modestly in favor of his good friend Davy [421].

Nor was it only in chemistry that Wollaston left his mark. He invented a goniometer, a device to measure the angles between crystal faces, which greatly advanced mineralogical research. In fact, by using it, he was able to correct points concerning which Haüy [332] had been in error. A calcium silicate mineral is named wollastonite in his honor. In his will he bequeathed the interest on £1,000 as an annual award (the Wollaston medal) for researches into the mineral structure of the earth. He also introduced the chemical concept of "equivalent weight."

Wollaston was a superb experimentalist and technician but he often did not go far enough and scored several important near misses. He was interested in the discovery of Oersted [417] that an electric current produced a magnetic field and he tried to bring about the reverse, having a magnet produce an electric current. He failed, but the notion was a good one. He discussed the matter with Humphry Davy [421]. Davy's assistant, Michael Faraday [474], who was also present and was thus introduced to the subject, succeeded where Wollaston had failed. That success was to have the greatest consequence.

In studying the spectrum, Wollaston was one of the first to observe ultraviolet light, though here the credit is usually given to the more thorough research of Ritter [413]. More important, Wollaston

in 1802 was the first to note that dark lines crossed the spectrum, an observation that Newton [231] had unaccountably missed. To Wollaston, however, it seemed that they were merely the natural boundaries between the various colors of the spectrum and he let the matter rest, a classic example of a missed opportunity. Fraunhofer [450] was to carry it further a dozen years later, and a half century after Wollaston's death those lines were to roll back the curtains of the heavens even more astonishingly than the telescope had done.

Wollaston foresaw the necessity of considering molecular structure in three dimensions but left it at that. It was Van't Hoff [829] three quarters of a century later who developed that notion properly.

In 1809 Wollaston was responsible for a piece of deplorable confusion. He analyzed a mineral in which Hatchett [383] had claimed to have found a new metal, columbium. Wollaston denied this and his greater authority carried the day. But Wollaston was wrong and the error was not righted for a generation.

Even more unfortunate was the fact that he was a strong force against British adoption of a decimal system of weights and measures. The royal commission of which he was a member submitted its disapproving report in 1819, and as a result Great Britain and the United States as well (for it followed Britain's lead) have been infinitely hampered for generations through use of the irrational English, or common, systems of weights and measures. (Britain and the Commonwealth of Nations have in recent years made the switch to the metric system, but the United States blindly holds out.)

Wollaston could also stand firmly on the side of what we now believe to be right. He supported Young's [402] wave theory of light, an unpopular stand in England, and withstood the abuse this brought down upon his head.

Though Wollaston was generous to a fault, he was, like Cavendish, cold, withdrawn, unsociable, and interested only in his work. He died of a brain tumor.

[389] **DALTON,** John
English chemist
Born: Eaglesfield, Cumberland,
about September 6, 1766
Died: Manchester, July 27, 1844

Dalton, the son of a weaver, came of a
Quaker family and was a practicing
Quaker all of his life. As Quakers, his
parents did not register the boy's birth,
and the day of that birth is uncertain,
being given by the perhaps fallible memories of neighbors.

Dalton left school at the age of eleven
and a year later, in 1778, at the age of
twelve he returned to begin teaching at a
Quaker school. This had its difficulties,
for some of his pupils were as old as he
was and presented disciplinary problems.
However, it was there that he grew interested in science.

His first love was meteorology and, beginning in 1787, he studied the weather
with instruments he built himself. In
1793 he wrote a book on the subject,
Meteorological Observations and Essays,
which qualifies him as one of the pioneers in meteorology. Though he passed
on to chemistry, he never abandoned
meteorology, keeping careful daily records
of the weather for fifty-seven years altogether, to the day he died. (Benjamin
Franklin [272] had also kept a "weather
diary.") He recorded some two hundred
thousand observations. It is not surprising that, as he always maintained, he
could never find time for marriage.

He was the first to describe color
blindness, in a publication in 1794. He
was color-blind himself and the condition is sometimes called daltonism. Color
blindness is not exactly an advantage to
a chemist, who must be able to see color
changes when he works with chemicals.
Perhaps that was one reason why Dalton
was a rather clumsy and slipshod experimenter.

Dalton was a poor speaker and could
not make money by lecturing in a day
when such things were the rage. However, it is upon neither fine talk nor experiments that his fame rests but upon
his successful interpretation, beginning
about 1800, of a century and a half of

the experimentation and fine talk of
others.

His meteorological observations led
Dalton to study the composition of the
air and from that it was but a step to
thinking about the properties of gases. In
considering those properties, beginning
with the experiments of Boyle [212],
Dalton could not help supposing that
gases were made up of tiny particles, as
other scientists, including Boyle himself
and Newton [231], had believed. (In
fact, Dalton contributed to the theory of
gases by promulgating what is now
known as Dalton's law of partial pressures in 1801. This states that each component of a mixture of gases exerts the
same pressure that it would if it alone
occupied the whole volume of the mixture, at the same temperature. He was
also the first to measure the rise in temperature of air when it was compressed
and to show that the amount of water
vapor the air could hold rose with temperature.)

But Dalton went on to consider that
all matter and not gases alone must consist of these small particles. The law of
definite proportions as enunciated by
Proust [364] in 1788 made it appear that
a compound might contain two elements
in the ratio of 4 to 1, perhaps, but never
4.1 to 1 or 3.9 to 1. This could easily be
explained by supposing that each element was made up of indivisible particles. If the particle of one element
weighed four times the weight of a particle of the other, and the compound was
formed by uniting a particle of one with
a particle of the other, the ratio by
weight would always be 4 to 1 and never
4.1 to 1 or 3.9 to 1.

Sometimes elements might combine in
different proportions to produce different
compounds, but then each compound
obeys the law of definite proportions,
and the two compounds are closely related in this respect. This can best be explained by an example. Carbon dioxide
is made up of carbon and oxygen in proportions by weight of 3 to 8. The compound carbon monoxide is made up of
carbon and oxygen in proportions by
weight of 3 to 4. Carbon dioxide has just
twice the proportion of oxygen that car-

bon monoxide has. Dalton found such cases in connection with methane (carbon:hydrogen = 3:1) and ethylene (carbon:hydrogen = 6:1) and with various oxides of nitrogen.

Examples like this illustrate the law of multiple proportions, first clearly enunciated by Dalton in 1803. It seemed to Dalton that carbon monoxide might be composed of one particle of carbon united with one particle of oxygen (where the oxygen particle was four thirds as heavy as the carbon particle) while carbon dioxide was composed of a particle of carbon combined with two oxygen particles. (He was later proved correct.)

Dalton recognized the similarity of this theory to that advanced by Democritus [20] twenty-one centuries earlier and therefore called these tiny particles by Democritus' own term, "atoms."

However, Democritus' notions had been pure deduction, pure speculation, and designed to fill out some grand scheme of the universe. Dalton's notions, on the other hand, were based on a century and a half of chemical experimentation and were designed only to organize and explain a specific set of observations. Dalton's theory was a chemical theory and not a philosophical one.

Dalton held that all elements were composed of extremely tiny, indivisible, and indestructible atoms and that all the substances we know are composed of combinations of these atoms. One substance could be turned into another by breaking up a particular combination and forming a new one. All the atoms of one element, Dalton held, were exactly alike, but the atoms of each element were different from the atoms of every other.

This sounds very much like Democritus, but then Dalton veered off from the speculations of all other atomists. He maintained that atoms differed from each other only in mass. This was something that could be measured and so Dalton was the first to advance a *quantitative* atomic theory. It was a wedding of Democritus and Lavoisier [334].

From the proportions by weight of the elements in particular compounds Dalton even tried to work out the relative weights of the different atoms. He was the first to prepare a table of atomic weights.

Thus, since water was made up of eight parts of oxygen to one part of hydrogen (by weight) and assuming that water contained one oxygen atom for every hydrogen atom, it is necessary to conclude that the atomic weight of oxygen is eight times that of hydrogen. If the atomic weight of hydrogen is arbitrarily set at 1, then the atomic weight of oxygen is 8. (Dalton was wrong. Water contains two atoms of hydrogen for every atom of oxygen so that the individual oxygen atom is eight times as heavy as two hydrogen atoms or sixteen times as heavy as a single hydrogen atom. However, his principle was correct.) Nowadays a rarely used name for the measure of atomic weight is the dalton. It is just one-sixteenth the mass of the oxygen atom, which therefore weighs 16 daltons.

Dalton first advanced his atomic notions in 1803, and in 1808 he published a book, *New System of Chemical Philosophy*, in which he spelled out his theories in detail.

Once explained, Dalton's atomism was so inevitable that it was accepted by most chemists with surprisingly little opposition, considering its revolutionary nature. Wollaston [388] accepted it at once. Davy [421] held out bitterly for a few years (out of jealousy, most likely, for poor Davy suffered agonies from that disease) but then came round. Dalton, like a good Quaker, responded to all criticism gently, speaking highly of Davy at all times. Opposition didn't die down for a century, however, for Ostwald [840] objected to atoms well into the twentieth century. However, in general, one might say that chemistry became atomist with Dalton and has remained atomist.

Dalton's Quaker beliefs led him to shun any form of glory. He refused to let Davy nominate him for membership in the Royal Society in 1810, and he had to be quietly elected in 1822 without his knowledge. As the importance of the atomic theory came to be appreciated more and more, further honors from foreign scientific societies broke upon his quiet Quaker simplicity. Distinguished foreign chemists, such as Pelletier [454], came to Manchester to see him, and when he visited Paris, Laplace [347] and Humboldt [397] were eager to greet and lionize him.

In 1831 he helped found the British Association for the Advancement of Science. In 1832, when he received a doctor's degree from Oxford, the opportunity was seized to present him to King William IV. He had resisted such a presentation because he would not wear court dress, but Oxford robes were sufficient. The only trouble was that the Oxford robes were scarlet and a Quaker could not wear scarlet. Fortunately Dalton's color blindness came to his rescue. He calmly announced that he could see no scarlet. He received his degree and was presented to the king in scarlet, which he saw as gray. In 1833 he received a £150 annual pension from the king, a pension that was doubled in 1836.

When he died and was helpless to prevent it, his funeral was turned into an elaborate and giant tribute to him.

Dalton's records, carefully preserved for a century, were destroyed during the World War II bombing of Manchester. It is not only the living who are killed in war.

[390] **HISINGER,** Wilhelm (hee'sing-er)
Swedish mineralogist
Born: Skinnskatteberg, Västmanland, December 23, 1766
Died: Skinnskatteberg, June 28, 1852

Hisinger, the son of a wealthy ironworks owner, was born Hising, but adopted the ending after he was ennobled. He came of a wealthy family and was interested in mineralogy as a hobby. He befriended and supported the young Berzelius [425], and the mineral in which the two discovered cerium was from Hisinger's own estate.

[391] **EKEBERG,** Anders Gustaf (ay'-kuh-berg)
Swedish chemist
Born: Stockholm, January 15, 1767
Died: Uppsala, February 11, 1813

Ekeberg graduated from the University of Uppsala in 1788, and after traveling through Germany returned to Uppsala where in 1794 he began teaching chemistry. He helped introduce Lavoisier's [334] new chemistry to Sweden but was rather badly treated by the science in return, for an exploding flask in 1801 blinded him in one eye. He was also partly deaf as a result of an infection in childhood. However, neither handicap affected hand or brain.

In 1802 he began the analysis of minerals from Finland and from that wonderland of mineralogy, Ytterby, where Gadolin [373] had found his rare earth. He located a new metal, one that was not a rare earth, and named it tantalum because, according to one suggestion, it had been such a tantalizing task to track down. According to another, he named it so because it was resistant to the action of acid and did not dissolve in it though it was surrounded by it, as Tantalus in the Greek myths could not drink though he stood up to his chin in water.

In one of his later pieces of research Ekeberg was assisted by the young Berzelius [425], who eventually took Ekeberg's side in a controversy with Hatchett [383].

[392] **BOUVARD,** Alexis (boo-vahr')
French astronomer
Born: Contamines, Haut Faucigny, June 27, 1767
Died: Paris, June 7, 1843

Bouvard was born into a poor family. When he got to Paris in 1785, he could not afford schooling and was forced to attend free lectures. He was good at mathematics and found employment at the Paris Observatory where Laplace [347] was willing to give him the job of carrying through the tedious computations necessary for his *Mécanique céleste*.

Computations became his whole life. He observed eight new comets and calculated their orbits, but the climax of his life came with his attempt to calculate the orbit of the newly discovered planet Uranus.

In 1821 he made use of not only the observed positions since Herschel's [321] discovery in 1781, but all the earlier positions noted before the "star" was recognized to be a planet. He found to his dismay that the orbit he calculated from the observations after 1781 did not quite fit the prediscovery observations, so he was forced to ignore the latter. However, the orbit he calculated from the postdiscovery observations did not suit either. Uranus began to drift away from it. Something was wrong and for twenty years, astronomers labored and puzzled over the discrepancy until Adams [615] and Leverrier [564] solved the problem with the discovery of a new planet, which Bouvard died three years too soon to see.

[393] **FOURIER,** Jean Baptiste Joseph, Baron (foor-yay′)
French mathematician
Born: Auxerre, Yonne, March 21, 1768
Died: Paris, May 16, 1830

Fourier was an orphan by the age of eight. As a youth he was headed for the priesthood, rather against his will. He wanted to be in the army, but as the son of a tailor he could serve only as cannon fodder in the ranks. And then came the French Revolution.

Fourier set his heart on becoming an artillery officer, so he could use the mathematics in which he was interested —much as did another man, Napoleon Bonaparte, who was born a few months after Fourier. Fourier did not have Bonaparte's success, however, for he showed too much ability at mathematics. He tried to play a moderate role in the French Revolution and came close to the guillotine, but the fall of Robespierre saved him. A while later he was arrested by the conservatives who succeeded Robespierre, and who accused Fourier of being pro-radical. Again he was released.

After his graduation from military school he was offered a professorship by the school in 1795 and accepted it.

Nevertheless his career remained linked with Napoleon's. He accompanied Napoleon to Egypt in 1798 and was governor of a portion of it during the French occupation, using the opportunity to explore the upper Nile. In 1808, after he had made his great mathematical discoveries, he was made a baron by Napoleon. He survived Napoleon's downfall to receive new honors under the restored Bourbons. In 1822 he became joint secretary of the Academy of Sciences, along with Cuvier [396].

After Fourier returned to France from Egypt in 1801, he was charged with organizing the accumulated mass of data gathered in Egypt and of arranging its publication. This he did, and thereafter busied himself with science (his adventure in military affairs in Egypt had not been a happy one and he had had enough). The problem that interested him chiefly was the manner in which heat flowed from one point to another through a particular object. This depended on the temperature difference between the two points, the heat conductivity of the material making up the object, the shape of the object, and so on. The matter was quite complex.

Fourier summoned all his mathematical ingenuity and discovered what is now called Fourier's theorem. This states that any periodic oscillation (that is, any variation which, sooner or later, repeats itself exactly, over and over), however complex, can be broken up into a series of simple regular wave motions, the sum of which will be the original complex periodic variation. It can be expressed, in other words, as a mathematical series in which the terms are made up of trigonometric functions. It was the announcement of this in 1807 that brought Fourier scientific fame and earned him his baron's title. When Napoleon returned to France in 1815, after his first abdication and exile to Elba, Fourier rejoined him. After Napoleon's second fall at Waterloo, Fourier was consequently out of favor in France for a while.

It was not until 1822 that Fourier, using his theorem, completed his work on the flow of heat in a book entitled *Analytic Theory of Heat,* a work that inspired Ohm [461] to similar thoughts on the flow of electricity. In this book Fourier was the first to make clear the point that a scientific equation must involve a consistent set of units. Thus began dimensional analysis.

Fourier's theorem has a very broad value. It can be used in the study of sound and of light and, indeed, of any wave phenomenon. The mathematical treatment of such phenomena, based on Fourier's theorem, is called harmonic analysis.

Even great scientists can have their irrational beliefs. Fourier believed heat to be essential to health so he always kept his dwelling place overheated and swathed himself in layer upon layer of clothes. He died of a fall down the stairs.

[394] **NICOL,** William
Scottish physicist
Born: Scotland, 1768
Died: Edinburgh, September 2, 1851

In 1828 Nicol, who lectured at the University of Edinburgh, made use of the phenomenon of double refraction discovered by Bartholin [210] to produce a single beam of what is now called polarized light. He did this by placing two crystals of Iceland spar together and cementing them with Canadian balsam.

Light entering the first half of the crystal was refracted into two rays. One of them was reflected out of the crystal altogether at the layer of balsam. The other, striking the balsam at a slightly different angle, passed through. This beam could also pass through a second "Nicol prism" if the second prism was lined up parallel to the first. If the second prism was then rotated, less and less of the light would pass through until, when the second prism was at right angles to the first, none of the light got

through. When a solution of organic substance was placed between the prisms, the second prism had to be placed at a certain angle (sometimes) to allow all the light to pass through it. This angle represented the degree of the twisting of polarized light that Biot [404] had first observed. The Nicol prism made it easy to observe this twisting and opened up the technique of polarimetry, which was to have great consequences in connection with theories of molecular structure.

Also notable was Nicol's development of methods for preparing thin slices of minerals and of fossil wood in order to make microscopic studies feasible.

[395] **SMITH,** William
English geologist
Born: Churchill, Oxfordshire, March 23, 1769
Died: Northampton, August 28, 1839

Smith's father, a village blacksmith, died when the child was but eight. In consequence, young Smith got nothing but the barest of a grammar school education.

He began his career when, in 1787, a surveyor came to town to do a job and needed a bright young man to help him. Smith eagerly applied and did so well that the surveyor took him into the business.

It was the era when England was lacing the countryside with canals, and Smith had to do with laying routes for them. Observing the earth in cross section at excavation sites, he was impressed by the way rocks of different types and forms were arranged in parallel layers, or strata.

In 1793 he was put in charge of surveying the Somerset coal canal and he toured England to observe other canals. This further increased his interest in and knowledge of strata, and his friends took to calling him Strata Smith.

By 1799 he was writing on the subject, but did not publish for a number of years. Others had observed strata before him, but Smith was making a new point. Each stratum had its own characteristic form of fossils, not found in other strata. No matter how the strata were bent and crumpled—even when one sank out of view and cropped up again miles away—this fact did not change. The characteristic fossils bent, crumpled, sank out of view, and cropped up again with the stratum. In fact it was reasonable to identify a stratum by its fossil content, a point Smith made in a book published in 1816. This was a beautifully colored geologic map of England, the first of its kind. It was dedicated to Banks [331] who, with his usual generosity to the poor in science, had helped him.

Since it could reasonably be assumed that a stratum nearer the surface was younger than one farther away, the strata offered a method for working out the history of life forms from the fossils. (Over a century before, Hooke [223] had suggested this in one of his inspired guesses.) For the first time it was possible to arrange the fossils in order of age. And since the oldest fossils were the ones that differed most from present-day life, with similarities growing stronger as the fossils grew younger, an evolutionary view became almost inevitable. Cuvier [396] was compelled to labor hard to resist it.

In 1831 Smith was the first recipient of the Wollaston medal, funds for which had been set up in the will of Wollaston [388]. The presentation was made by Sedgwick [442], retiring president of the Geologic Society. The money award involved was most welcome, for Smith's travels in search of geologic data had pauperized him (not a really difficult task, to be sure) and had forced him to such shifts as selling his fossil collection to the British Museum.

[396] CUVIER, Georges Léopold Chrétien Frédéric Dagobert, Baron
(kyoo-vyay')
French anatomist
Born: Montbéliard, Doubs, August 23, 1769
Died: Paris, May 13, 1832

Cuvier was descended from French Huguenots who had been forced into Switzerland after Louis XIV's suspension of toleration. His father, although a Swiss national, was serving in the French army at the time of Cuvier's birth. In 1793 Cuvier's birthplace was annexed to France by the revolutionaries, and it has remained French ever since. Cuvier became a French citizen automatically with that.

Cuvier remained an active Protestant all his life, but he received constant honor and advancement in predominantly Roman Catholic France under a variety of forms of government. This was not altogether surprising, for in his lifetime he became the most eminent European scientist and virtually an intellectual dictator in the field of biology.

For a time in his youth Cuvier seemed to be headed for the ministry, but as a precocious child he had been fascinated by Buffon's [277] books and while tutor to a Protestant family of the French aristocracy he grew seriously interested in science. At that time, too, he met a zoologist who in 1795 obtained for him a post at the Museum of Natural History in Paris, where he engaged in his researches to such good effect that he became permanent secretary of physical and natural sciences of the Institut National in 1803.

While at the museum he refused, in 1798, an offer to accompany Napoleon Bonaparte on his expedition to Egypt, which was just as well for him, because on the whole it was a disastrous adventure. It was in that period, too, that he became interested in anatomy and, in particular, in the comparison of the anatomy of one species with another, a study that he brought to a high pitch of excellence. In fact he came to understand the necessary relationship of one part of a body with another so well that from the existence of some bones he could infer the shape of others and so, little by little, reconstruct the entire animal (a process that even today strikes laymen with amazement and incredulity). He can thus be considered the founder of the science of comparative anatomy. Cuvier's appreciation of how one part of an organism made other qualities necessary is exemplified in a famous story. One of his students dressed up in a devil's costume and, with others, invaded Cuvier's room in the dead of night and woke him with a grisly "Cuvier, Cuvier, I have come to eat you." Cuvier opened one eye and said, "All creatures with horns and hooves are herbivores. You can't eat me." Then he went back to sleep.

It seems natural that a comparative anatomist should be interested in the classification of species, and Cuvier most certainly was. He extended and perfected the classificatory system of Linnaeus [276] by grouping related classes (Linnaeus' broadest classification) into still broader groups called phyla. Cuvier divided the animal kingdom into four phyla: Vertebrata, Mollusca, Articulata (including all jointed animals), and Radiata (everything else). In doing so he laid stress on the internal structures of animals, which most clearly indicate relationship, rather than on surface superficialities. Modern classification is more complex than Cuvier's—some two dozen animal phyla are now recognized, for instance—but Cuvier's principles have guided biologists in their classifications ever since. Cuvier's younger associate, Candolle [418], applied those principles to the classification of plants, completing what had been begun by Jussieu [345].

Cuvier was the first to extend the system of classification to fossils. It seemed to his anatomical eye that every fossil he found, although not quite like any living forms, clearly belonged to one of the four phyla he had established. He could even classify them in subgroups and include them generally in his classification of life along with living forms. He began in 1796, with a fossil that was clearly an elephant, though neither of the two living species. He showed that an extinct South American animal, the *Megatherium*, was a ground sloth, related to the much smaller sloths of today. In 1812 he exhibited the much more spectacular fossil of a flying creature, with true wings, which was nevertheless clearly a reptile. He named it a "pterodactyl" ("wingfinger") because the membrane of its wing was stretched out along one enormous finger. For these discoveries Cuvier

is called the founder of paleontology. He missed identifying the true dinosaurs, however. When the teeth of such creatures—the first to be discovered—were submitted to him in 1822, he judged them to be mammalian rather than reptilian and to belong to an extinct species of rhinoceros.

Yet Cuvier had a blind spot, and this was his devotion to the literal words of Genesis. He saw with his own eyes that the fossils must be ancient, buried as they were deep in rocky strata. He saw also that the deeper the fossil and the older the rock, the more that fossil differed in structure from modern life forms. It would seem, from the superior wisdom of our hindsight, that it would be an easy leap to some evolutionary theory, and indeed Cuvier's older contemporary Lamarck [336] advanced one.

Nevertheless Cuvier was a firm antievolutionist. To account for the fossils and their gradations with time, he adapted the catastrophism of Bonnet [291]. The earth, he suggested, was periodically inundated in a world-wide flood. After each flood, life would be created anew. The fossils would then be remnants of ages before the most recent catastrophe. Needless to say, Cuvier was a neptunist after the fashion of Werner [355].

The last catastrophe, Cuvier believed, was the Flood described in Genesis, through which, by divine intervention, some living things had survived. In this way the vast age of the earth (as revealed by a study of the strata) could be squared with the biblical account by supposing the Bible to deal only with the latest postcatastrophic age, that being the only era of importance to man in the story of salvation.

In 1808 Napoleon put Cuvier in charge of investigating the state of education in France. His eminence was such that the returning Bourbons made no attempt to penalize him but used him instead. He was made chancellor of what had been the Imperial University and was now again the University of Paris, and also served in the cabinet of Louis XVIII, who had had enough of exile and wanted matters to last his lifetime. (They did.)

In 1818 Cuvier was elected to the French Academy and by that time he was wealthy (and grossly obese, too).

In 1824 Louis was succeeded by his archreactionary brother, Charles X, and Cuvier fell out with him. In 1831, after Charles X had been once more driven into exile, the new king, Louis Philippe, made Cuvier a baron and, the next year, minister of interior, a post he did not live to accept.

All of Cuvier's eminence, however, could not keep the theory of catastrophism alive very long. Increasing knowledge of paleontology made more and more unlikely any world-wide catastrophe that had wiped out all life. There were many animals whose life spans as closely related groups of species stretched across any boundary lines that could be drawn between eras.

Cuvier had suggested only four catastrophes, but under his followers after his death the number grew to as many as twenty-seven. Nevertheless, even as Cuvier was dying in the cholera epidemic of 1832, Lyell [502] was forcing catastrophism into a catastrophe of its own and was establishing the dominance of the uniformitarian doctrine of Hutton [297].

Cuvier was another of the monsters of erudition who are to be found here and there in the history of science. He is supposed to have virtually memorized the contents of the nineteen thousand volumes in his library.

[397] **HUMBOLDT,** Friedrich Wilhelm Heinrich Alexander, Baron von
German naturalist
Born: Berlin, September 14, 1769
Died: Berlin, May 6, 1859

Humboldt, the son of a military officer who served as an official at the court of Prussia's Frederick II, was, on his mother's side, descended from those Huguenots driven from France by Louis XIV. He was an incredible personality. His life of feverish activity, broad interests, and large accomplishments seems

too much to be squeezed into even the ninety years he lived, though it must be said that he remained unmarried and was therefore spared the distractions of a wife and children.

His education was sporadic but a year at Göttingen in 1789 was sufficient to inspire him with a vast interest in science, particularly botany. In 1790 he began the first of many journeys; this one, modestly, merely through western Europe where he had the occasion of meeting various men of science. Back home he enrolled in the school of mines at Freiburg and absorbed, at the source, the fallacious neptunism of Werner [355].

Humboldt decided to be a geologist and mining engineer and for several years was inspector of mines at Bayreuth. He filled the post admirably and also found time to experiment with the electrical currents in muscles and nerves, a phenomenon recently discovered by Galvani [320]. Humboldt backed Galvani in his dispute with Volta [337] and was on the losing side.

Humboldt's mother died in 1796 and Humboldt's share of the inheritance set him free of any need to earn a living. He could indulge his passion for travel to its fullest extent. In 1799 he set sail on what was to be a five-year visit to the American continents, beginning this particular journey by having to elude British warships, for the Napoleonic Wars were beginning.

His voyage consisted of exploration— for he navigated the length of the Orinoco and verified its connection with the Amazon drainage system—and scientific investigation, for he collected reams of botanical material and geological specimens. (By the end of his life, he had collected sixty thousand plants, including thousands of species never described before.) He studied the ocean currents off the western coast of South America (and the current there is still called the Humboldt Current in his honor). He also studied the American volcanoes and noted their occurrence in straight lines as though they were following some deep-buried flaw in the earth's crust. He measured the decline in magnetic intensity as one passed from the poles toward the equator and, also, the rate of temperature drop with altitude. He observed a rich meteor shower and his report helped increase scientific interest in the phenomenon, paving the way for Chladni [370] and Biot [404]. He also reported on Indian antiquities, and introduced Europe to the fertilizing powers of the Peruvian guano. He was the first to see the practicality of a canal through Panama—something that would not become an actuality until the work of Gorgas [853] a century later. In Ecuador he even climbed the volcano Chimborazo, which is nineteen thousand feet high, and that set a record that no one was to better for a generation afterward.

He stopped off in the new nation of the United States on his way back to Europe, visiting President Thomas Jefferson [333].

Back in Paris, Humboldt wrote of his travels to America in most engaging fashion (he was an excellent writer and had artistic talents as well) and founded an international society for the study of terrestrial magnetism. He conducted experiments on the composition of the atmosphere with Gay-Lussac [420]. By some, he was considered the most spectacular man in Europe next to Napoleon himself. (Humboldt and Napoleon were born only a month apart, but Napoleon lived only half as long and came to a bad end.)

After the fall of Napoleon, Humboldt served the Prussian king, Frederick William III, as a diplomat and, eventually, his money running out at last, he accepted a salaried post in Berlin, in which he was the titular head of the Prussian school system. He retained the privilege of frequent visits to Paris, where he was happiest, and where he could serve Prussia as liaison man with King Louis Philippe of France (a personal friend of his).

Throughout his life, he retained a liberal, democratic attitude, quite at variance with the growing conservatism in Prussia. He applauded the French Revolution, inveighed against human slavery in the Americas and was an influence for the better on young Simón Bolívar who eventually led Latin America in its struggle for freedom from Spain. Humboldt's purse, like that of Banks [331], a generation before, was always at the service of poor but promising scientists.

His restless mind kept him busy. He suggested the use of isothermal lines (lines marking equal temperature levels) on the world map as one method of understanding the geography of our planet and the life upon it.

In 1829 he was invited by the Russian tsar Nicholas I to explore the vast Asian dominions over which he ruled, and this Humboldt did in a kind of whirlwind trek.

Finally, in his seventies Humboldt began to organize the gathered knowledge of his life into a book called *Kosmos* in which he tried, as the name implied, to give a truly cosmic view of the earth; to see it whole, all in one piece. Certainly, no man before him, with so active a mind, had seen so much of the world, and no man before him was so well equipped to write such a book. Fortunately he lived long enough to complete it despite his late start, though the fifth and last volume did not appear until after his death.

It was a florid production, rather overblown, but it is one of the remarkable books in scientific history and was the first reasonably accurate encyclopedia of geography and geology. In this book Humboldt might almost be said to have founded the science of geophysics.

When he died, in his ninetieth year, he was given a state funeral, and all of scholarly Europe mourned.

[398] **SEEBECK,** Thomas Johann (zay′-bek)
Russian-German physicist
Born: Revel, Estonia (now Tallinn, Estonian SSR), April 9, 1770
Died: Berlin, Germany, December 10, 1831

Seebeck, born of a well-to-do merchant of German descent, studied medicine at the universities of Berlin and Göttingen, receiving his M.D. from the latter institution in 1802. He was a friend of Goethe [349] and worked with him on his wrongheaded theories about color.

More fruitfully, in the long run, Seebeck was the first to observe, in 1821, that if two different metals were joined at two places, and the two points of junction were kept at different temperatures, an electric current would flow continuously round the circuit.

This conversion of heat into electricity ("thermoelectricity") was not properly interpreted by Seebeck himself and it was not followed up. The "Seebeck effect" lay in abeyance for over a century, therefore, though it is now fruitfully used, particularly in connection with the semiconductor devices first produced by Shockley [1348] and his co-workers.

[399] **TREVITHICK,** Richard (treh'vih-thik)
English inventor
Born: Illogan, Cornwall, April 13, 1771
Died: Dartford, Kent, April 22, 1833

Trevithick had a father who was professionally involved in coal mining. The young man grew interested in steam engines early (his father was one of the first to install the Watt [316] engines) and developed a model that made use of higher pressures than those of Watt. This was a retreat to Savery [236] a century and a quarter before, in a sense. However, metallurgical techniques were improving and machinery was now adequate to handle high-pressure steam.

In 1796 Trevithick was designing steam locomotives and in 1801 an engine of his pulled passenger trains. It was Trevithick who proved that smooth metal wheels on smooth metal rails would supply sufficient traction to pull trains. Trevithick, encouraged by men such as Rumford [360] and Davy [421], had many novel and ingenious ideas—too many, for he tried to act on them all. He did not concentrate sufficiently on any one of them and he could make no one of them succeed thoroughly, not

even his locomotives. Then, too, like Fitch [330], Trevithick was plagued by incredibly bad luck. His locomotives worked but he had to face broken axles, insufficient steam, fire, public hostility. In the end, he had to see credit go to a later and more fortunate man. Where Fitch had his Fulton [385], Trevithick had his Stephenson [431].

In South America, where he had gone to introduce his steam engines, he built pumps for the silver mines of Peru but was stranded as a result of the revolt of the Spanish colonies. He was forced to take part in the fighting; and he returned to England only by borrowing money from Stephenson's son, who happened to be in South America at the time and whose money came from the dividends of a successful railroad.

Trevithick continued to the end of his life to have more ideas than he could handle, and he died in poverty, having been unable to persuade Parliament to vote him a grant in return for his inventive achievements. He had a pauper's burial and an unmarked grave.

[400] **BICHAT,** Marie François Xavier (bee-shah')
French physician
Born: Thoirette, Jura, November 14, 1771
Died: Lyon, July 22, 1802

Bichat was the precocious son of a physician and eagerly entered a medical career. He began work in Lyon but the tumult of the French Revolution (he was a moderate republican) drove him out of that city and into Paris in 1793 (though Paris was entering the Terror at the time). Like Morgagni [251] nearly a century earlier, Bichat's advances arose out of the numerous postmortems he conducted. There were as many as six hundred of these in the final year of his short life, during which he never married. He was the classical biological observer, with the eye (unaided even by a microscope, which he distrusted) as his chief tool. Nor did he seek to probe deeper, for he was an extreme vitalist who denied that physics or chemistry could possibly aid in the understanding of life.

He was the first to draw the attention of the anatomist and the physiologist to the organs of the body as a complex of simpler structures, but he gave due credit to Pinel [338] who had moved in this direction. Though working without benefit of microscope he was able to show that each organ was built up of different types of "tissues" (a term he himself introduced, using it because they were generally flat and delicately thin layers). Furthermore, different organs might possess some tissues in common. All told, he identified twenty-one types of tissues, published his book on the subject, *General Anatomy*, in 1800, and may be considered the founder of histology.

This was an important step in the direction of the cell theory of life, which was to come with the work of Schleiden [538] and Schwann [563] a generation later. Bichat might well have lived to see this ordinarily, but he died at the age of thirty, shortly after fainting and falling down the stairs in his laboratory. Had he lived longer, it might not have been so easy to decide that Laënnec [429] was the most distinguished French physician of the early nineteenth century.

[401] **MOHS,** Friedrich (mose)
German mineralogist
Born: Gernrode, Anhalt-Bernburg, January 29, 1773
Died: Agardo, Italy, September 29, 1839

Mohs, a student of Werner [355], taught in Austria and Germany and is best known today for the fact that he devised the Mohs scale in 1822. This is a standard by which the hardness of minerals can be expressed.

To make use of the scale, the smooth surface of the mineral to be tested is scratched by the sharp edge of a series of substances of graded hardness. A substance can be scratched by one harder than itself and can in turn scratch one softer than itself. The scale ranges from 1 for the soft mineral, talc, to 10 for diamond. The numbers do not, in actual

fact, measure equal differences in hardness.

He died on a journey to southern Italy, where he planned to study the volcanic areas.

[402] **YOUNG,** Thomas
English physicist and physician
Born: Milverton, Somerset, June 13, 1773
Died: London, May 10, 1829

Young, the son of a Quaker banker, was an infant prodigy who could read at two and who had worked his way twice through the Bible at six. During his youth, he learned a dozen languages including not only Greek, Latin, and Hebrew, but also Arabic, Persian, Turkish, and Ethiopian. He could also play a variety of musical instruments, including the bagpipes. He was the best kind of infant prodigy, the kind that matures into an adult prodigy. He was called Phenomenon Young at Cambridge and there became financially independent on the death of a rich uncle in 1797.

Young took up medicine and studied at the University of Edinburgh under the aged Black [298]. He went to Germany and obtained his degree at the University of Göttingen in 1796, then opened his practice in London in 1799. Between 1801 and 1803 he lectured on science at the Royal Institution, newly founded by Rumford [360], and in 1802 he was appointed foreign secretary of the Royal Society.

As a physician he was unsuccessful because he lacked a suave bedside manner.

He was interested in sense perception. He was the first to discover (while still a medical student) the manner in which the lens of the eye changes shape (accommodation) in focusing on objects at differing distances. In 1801 he described the reason for astigmatism: the fuzziness of vision arose from the irregularities of the curvature of the cornea.

It was an easy step from the eye to light itself. For more than a century now there had been a controversy as to whether light consisted of particles or of waves, particle supporters having much the best of it. The most important evidence against waves was the fact that light cast sharp shadows and did not make its way around corners as sound waves did. Some had suggested that the smaller the size of waves, the less bending they did and that the wavelengths of light might be so small that the bending was exceedingly minute. Grimaldi [199] had, in actual fact, detected this minute bending a century and a half before, but his observations had been neglected. It fell to Young to demonstrate the wave nature of light in more dramatic fashion.

Young accomplished this in 1803 by sending light through very narrow openings and showing that separate bands of light appeared where there should have been nothing but the sharply shadowed boundary of the edge of the opening. These bands of light arose from the kind of diffraction around corners that Grimaldi had noted, and it could not be explained by the particle theory.

Young had a more conclusive piece of evidence. From his study of sound he grew interested in the phenomenon of beats, in which two different pitches of sound produced periods of intensified sound separated by periods of silence. This was easily explained, since the two pitches had different wavelengths and therefore did not keep step. At first the two waves might be temporarily in step and the two wave peaks would reinforce each other to produce doubled sound. They would then fall out of step and the molecules of air would be pushed in one direction by one wave and in the opposite direction by the other, with a net effect of motionlessness and—no sound.

Now, then, would two light waves add up to produce darkness? If they were particles, they couldn't; if they were waves, they could. Young introduced light beams through two narrow orifices. They spread out and overlapped. The overlapping region was not a simple area of intensified light but formed a striped pattern of alternating light and darkness, a situation (interference) exactly analogous to beats in sound.

At first Young's work met with considerable hostility in England, particularly as the result of the enmity of a personal antagonist, Henry Brougham, a baronet and an influential literary reviewer. Young's mathematics was, besides, difficult and his exposition rather fuzzy. For another thing, the particle theory was particularly "English" since it had been introduced by Newton [231] and there were psychological difficulties concerning its rejection by English physicists though Wollaston [388] supported him vigorously. (National pride often plays a role in science—almost always a deleterious one.) It therefore fell to Frenchmen, Fresnel [455] and Arago [446], to do the necessary follow-up work that was to establish Young's work and to strike down the particle theory (if not forever, then at least for nearly a century).

From his diffraction experiment, Young was able to calculate the wavelength of visible light, for it was only necessary to figure out what wavelength would allow the observed degree of small bending. The wavelengths turned out to be very small indeed, being less than a millionth of a meter.

Young's interest in light also led him to consider the manner of color perception. He was the first to suggest that it was not necessary to see each color separately by some different physiologic mechanism. It was enough to see three colors: say red, green, and blue. Combinations of these in various proportions would give the effect of all the myriads of shades of different colors. This theory was further refined by Helmholtz [631] a half century later and is usually referred to as the Young-Helmholtz three-color theory. The color photography and color television of the twentieth century make use of this three-color theory.

There remained an important question concerning light, even if the existence of waves were allowed. What type of waves would light waves be? They might be transverse waves, like the waves on a water surface, undulating at right angles to the direction of movement of the wave train as a whole. Or they might be longitudinal, like sound waves, undulating in the same direction as the movement of the wave train. All the early proponents of the wave theory of light, notably Huygens [215], had taken longitudinal waves almost for granted and so did Young at first. However, longitudinal waves could not explain the double refraction first noted by Bartholin [210]. In 1817 Young wrote to Arago that the light waves must be transverse and that this would explain double refraction. In this he was correct.

Young was interested in forms of energy other than light. In 1807 he was the first to use the word energy in its modern sense—as the property of a system that makes it capable of doing work and as proportional to the product of the mass of a body and the square of its velocity. In that year also he argued against the caloric theory of heat, citing Rumford's experiments. Here, however, it was the French physicists who found it difficult to abandon the "French" theory of Lavoisier [334] and a half century passed before the caloric idea was demolished by Maxwell [692], an Englishman.

Young also contributed to an understanding of surface tension of liquids and reported on the nature of elastic substances. A constant, used in equations defining the behavior of elastic substances, is still called Young's modulus.

And as though this varied activity were not enough, Young contributed many and varied articles to the Encyclopaedia Britannica. He also reached beyond the physical and biological sciences altogether and in 1814 took up the problem of the Rosetta Stone. This had been discovered while Napoleon was in Egypt, and was the key to the ancient hieroglyphic language of the Egyptians.

He gave up his medical practice to do so and was the first to make progress in deciphering it.

In 1818 this physician and physicist was able to write an authoritative article on Egypt that outshone the efforts of contemporaries who were merely historians, thus laying the groundwork for the definitive work to be done later by Champollion.

[403] **BROWN**, Robert
    Scottish botanist
    Born: Montrose, Angus, December 21, 1773
    Died: London, June 10, 1858

Brown was the son of an Anglican priest and studied medicine at the University of Edinburgh. He did not take a degree, however. As a young man he served in the army and spent his spare time (he was a medical officer and therefore had spare time) collecting plants. While stationed in Ireland, where he had been sent in 1795, he met Banks [331], (in 1798), who promptly took Brown under his wing.

In 1801, through Banks's influence, Brown obtained the post of naturalist on a voyage to the still-new and largely unknown continent of Australia, duplicating the feat of his sponsor, Banks, a generation earlier. The ship returned in 1805 with some four thousand species of plants.

In classifying the new plants, Brown made use of the microscope and, for the first time in England, made use of the natural system of Jussieu [345] and Candolle [418] and not the artificial one of Linnaeus [276]. This completed the victory of the natural system. Brown was the first to separate the higher plants into gymnosperms and angiosperms.

He worked on a huge treatise on his Australian plants, but only the first volume ever appeared. That was in 1810, and the next year he was elected to the Royal Society.

As a consequence of his work Brown was also appointed librarian of the Linnaean Society in 1810. He also served as librarian to Banks and when Banks died in 1820, his will left Brown in charge of his house, his library, and his collection of plants. Brown transferred the whole to the British Museum in 1827 but remained in charge of it.

Brown is remembered particularly for two discoveries. In his botanical researches he, like others before him, was aware of a small body within the cells that composed the plant tissues. Brown, unlike his predecessors, recognized this as a regular feature of cells and in 1831 gave it the name by which it has been known ever since: "nucleus," from the Latin word meaning "little nut."

The second discovery had startling repercussions quite outside the field of the life sciences, a development that Brown himself could scarcely have foreseen. It resulted from his rather routine investigations of plant pollen.

In 1827 as he was viewing a suspension of pollen in water under the microscope, he noted that the individual grains were moving about irregularly. This, he thought, was the result of the life hidden within the pollen grains. However, when he studied dye particles (indubitably nonliving) suspended in water, he found the same erratic motion.

This has been called Brownian motion ever since and Brown could merely report on the observation. He had no explanation for it. Nor had anyone else until the development of the kinetic theory of gases by men such as Maxwell [692] a generation later.

It seemed plain, after Maxwell and especially after the work of Einstein [1064] and Perrin [990] a half century after Maxwell, that the Brownian motion was actually a visible effect of the fact that water was composed of particles. It was the first evidence for atomism that was primarily an observation rather than a deduction.

[404] **BIOT,** Jean Baptiste (byoh)
French physicist
Born: Paris, April 21, 1774
Died: Paris, February 3, 1862

Biot, the son of a treasury official, served a year in the artillery in 1792, fighting the British. Then he entered the École Polytechnique, studying under Lagrange [317] and Berthollet [346]. He and Malus [408] took part in a street riot in 1795, one which was easily put down, marking the end of the French Revolution. The man who put it down was Napoleon Bonaparte, who thus took the first step on his rise to prominence. Biot suffered imprisonment for a while as a result. In later life, he remained consistently anti-Napoleon and he was awarded the Legion of Honor by Louis XVIII who succeeded the fallen emperor.

Biot obtained an appointment as professor of mathematics at the University of Beauvais, and in 1800 moved on to the Collège de France through the sponsorship of Laplace [347], whose self-centered soul he had pleased by offering to read proof on the colossal *Mécanique Céleste* and then actually doing it. He proved himself no disappointment in the post.

In 1803 he investigated a reported sighting of material falling from heaven and his findings finally convinced a skeptical scientific world that meteorites existed. His first real fame, however, came not so much in science itself as in a stroke of adventure.

In 1804 there seemed a heaven-sent opportunity to study the atmosphere with a balloon left over from Napoleon's Egyptian campaign. Biot and Gay-Lussac [420] loaded themselves down with instruments, plus an assortment of small animals, and made an ascension on August 23, 1804, showing that terrestrial magnetism remained undiminished at the heights they reached. It was a tentative groping of science toward the upper atmosphere, a move that was to reach its climax in the rocketry of the mid-twentieth century.

Biot and Gay-Lussac ran a number of experiments and collected many observations between heights of one and three miles. The descent was dangerous and tricky and Biot panicked. Gay-Lussac made another ascension later in the year to a height of four miles but Biot did not accompany him.

Biot and Arago [446] traveled to Spain in 1806 on a meridian-measuring expedition and remained close friends for a decade, until Thomas Young's [402] sudden revival of the wave hypothesis of light threw the world of physics into turmoil. At first, both Arago and Biot strongly favored the old particle hypothesis and Biot worked out an ingenious mathematical treatment of it that greatly pleased his old sponsor, Laplace. Arago, on the other hand, defected and became one of the prime movers in favor of the wave hypothesis. A bitter dispute arose between the two friends and they were friends no more.

Biot's most important work was in connection with what we now call polarized light. Bartholin [210] had discovered the phenomenon of double refraction a century and a half before, and it was shown that the two rays of light that emerged from Iceland spar differed in properties, a difference that was usefully taken advantage of by Nicol [394].

This phenomenon could only be explained properly by a wave theory of light and Fresnel [455] produced such an explanation. However, one doesn't have to explain a phenomenon to work with it, and though Biot did not accept Fresnel's theories, he nevertheless worked fruitfully with polarized light.

In 1815 he showed that organic substances might, in effect, rotate polarized light either clockwise or counterclockwise, when the organic compounds were liquid or in solution. He suggested that this was due to an asymmetry that might exist in the molecules themselves. By 1835 he showed how the hydrolysis of sucrose could be followed by changes in optical rotation, thus founding the science of polarimetry. In 1840 he was awarded the Rumford medal.

He lived long enough to see Pasteur [642] prove asymmetry in organic crystals that had this twisting effect on polarized light, but (despite his longevity) not long enough to see the molecular asymmetry he had predicted become an important facet of organic chemistry through the work of Van't Hoff [829] and Le Bel [787].

Though an atheist most of his adult life, he returned to Catholicism in 1846.

[405] **BUCH,** Christian Leopold von
(bookh)
German geologist
Born: Stolpe, Prussia, April 25, 1774
Died: Berlin, March 4, 1853

Buch was one of thirteen children of a wealthy Prussian landowning family. He studied mineralogy and chemistry at Berlin, and then went on to be a student of Werner [355] the great neptunist, from 1790 to 1793.

Buch did not have to work for a living and engaged himself in traveling about Europe in order to study volcanic regions, sometimes in the company of Humboldt [397].

His studies quickly showed him that Werner's theories were quite wrong and that they could only be held by someone who, like Werner, had never actually seen the volcanic regions he theorized about. For instance, Buch's investigations at the turn of the century and shortly after, showed that the Italian volcanoes rested on granite and there was no sign of any coal beds the burning of which, according to Werner, supplied the heat.

Instead, Buch became more and more certain that both basalt and granite were formed by volcanic action and had crystalized out of the molten state rather than settling out of a watery suspension as Werner had claimed. In 1826 he prepared a huge geologic map of Germany, the first of its kind.

With Buch, vulcanism triumphed over neptunism, and the stage was set for the great geologic synthesis of Lyell [502].

[406] **BAILY,** Francis
English astronomer
Born: Newbury, Berkshire, April 28, 1774
Died: London, August 30, 1844

Baily was a prosperous stockbroker who had received only an elementary education. He retired in 1825, at last able to devote himself to his intellectual mistress, astronomy. He had been one of the founders of the Royal Astronomical Society and was a perennial president or vice president of the organization. On May 15, 1836, during an eclipse of the sun, he described an effect whereby just before the last glowing sliver of sun disappeared behind the moon, it broke into a line of shining bits and pieces, as the sunlight made its way between the jutting mountains on the moon's horizon. The same phenomenon appeared on the other side when the sunlight first broke through between the mountains, then quickly joined into an intact curve of sun. The broken bits of sunlight are still called Baily's beads.

This discovery fired new astronomical

interest in eclipses and began the custom of outfitting long-distance expeditions to observe eclipses in far corners of the world; something which has been going on ever since.

[407] **AMPÈRE,** André Marie (ahm-pare´)
French mathematician and physicist
Born: Lyon, January 22, 1775
Died: Marseille, June 10, 1836

Young Ampère was privately tutored and proved to be quite a phenomenon, devouring the encyclopedic works of Buffon [277] and Diderot [286] and mastering advanced mathematics by the age of twelve. He even learned Latin in order to read the works of those like Euler [275] who wrote in that language. The even tenor of his youth was, however, interrupted by the coming of the French Revolution.

In 1793 Lyon revolted against the revolutionaries and was taken by the republican army. Ampère's father, who was a well-to-do merchant and one of the city's officials, was guillotined. Ampère went into a profound depression as a result, out of which, with the encouragement of the sympathetic Lalande [309], he struggled with difficulty. In 1803 his beloved wife of but four years died and this again hit him hard. Indeed, he never recovered from that blow. (In 1818 he married a second time, and this time the marriage was unhappy.)

At Napoleon's insistence, Ampère continued a fruitful career as a professor of physics and chemistry at Bourg, and then in 1809 as a professor of mathematics in Paris.

He was, like Newton, the classic example of an "absent-minded professor." Many stories (not necessarily true) are told of him, including one in which he forgot to keep an invitation to dine with the Emperor Napoleon, probably the only occasion on which the emperor was ever disappointed in this manner—and with impunity, for Napoleon appointed him inspector general of the national university system in 1808.

When the discovery of Oersted [352]—that a wire carrying an electric current deflected a compass needle—was announced to the French Academy of Sciences in 1820, French physicists burst into activity. (Nothing like it was seen until the announcement of nuclear fission a century later.)

Ampère and Arago [417] were in the forefront. Within one week after Oersted's work had been reported, Ampère showed that the deflection of the needle could be expressed by what is now known as the "right-hand screw rule." The right hand is imagined as grasping the wire through which the current runs, with the thumb pointing in the direction of the current. The fingers then indicate the direction in which the north pole of a magnet will be deflected. The magnet will be deflected in the direction of the curling fingers at any point around the wire, so that one might imagine a magnetic force circling the wire. This was the beginning of the concept of lines of force that Faraday [474] was to generalize and that was eventually to advance the picture of the universe beyond the purely mechanical concepts of Galileo [166] and Newton [231].

Of course, in setting up this right-hand screw rule, one had to decide in which direction the current was traveling. There was no clear indication of that from the wire itself. It was a matter of convention only whether the current was flowing from the positive pole to the negative pole or vice versa—at least this was true in Ampère's time. It seemed natural to take the flow from positive to negative, using the concept of Franklin [272] that the positive pole had the excess of "electrical fluid" and the negative pole the deficiency.

That convention has been used ever since, but Franklin had guessed wrong and Ampère had gone wrong with him. We now know that the electric current is a movement of electrons flowing from the negative pole to the positive. However, taking things in reverse does no damage as long as one remains *consistently* wrong.

Ampère showed that visualizing the attractions and repulsions set up by a current-carrying wire did not require either a magnet or iron filings. He set up two parallel wires, one of which was freely movable back and forth. When both wires carried current in the same direction, the two wires clearly attracted each other. If the current flowed in opposite directions, they repelled each other. If one wire was free to rotate about an axis perpendicular to itself and to the other wire, then, when the currents flowed in opposite directions, the movable wire rotated through a semicircle, coming to rest in such a position that the currents flowed in the same direction in both.

Ampère also worked with the magnetic fields set up by currents flowing through a circular wire, and he recognized, as did Arago, that from a theoretical standpoint a helix of wires (a wire curved into bedspring shape) would behave as though it were a bar magnet. He called such a helix a solenoid. This notion was put into practice by Sturgeon [436] and was then refined to a startling degree by Henry [503].

It was Ampère's experiments that founded the science of electric currents in motion, which Ampère named electrodynamics. He also introduced the term "electrostatics" for the older study of stationary electric charges in which Franklin's work had been so important.

Meanwhile, Oersted's discovery had led to the quantization of electrical experimentation. If a magnetized needle could be deflected by an electric current, the needle could be made to move against a marked-off background and by the extent of the deflection, the amount of current could be measured.

Ampère was attuned to this quantization, for he was the first to try to apply advanced mathematics to electrical and magnetic phenomena. In 1823 he advanced a theory that the magnet's properties arose from tiny electrical currents circling eternally within it. In this he was ahead of his time, for the existence of tiny electrically charged particles circling eternally was not to be known for three quarters of a century. Ampère's contemporaries received his theories with great skepticism.

In Ampère's honor it is now conventional to measure the quantity of electric current passing a given point in a given time in amperes, a usage originated by Kelvin [652] in 1883. This is justified since he was the first to differentiate the rate of passage of current from the driving force behind it. The latter is measured in volts in honor of Volta [337].

Ampère died of pneumonia, and his judgment of his own life is indicated by the sorrow-laden epitaph he chose for his own gravestone—"Tandem felix" (Happy, at last).

[408] MALUS, Étienne Louis (malyoos')
French physicist
Born: Paris, July 23, 1775
Died: Paris, February 24, 1812

Malus was the son of a government official, so his youth was filled with a variety of difficulties. Attending a military engineering school during the French Revolution, he was dismissed without a degree because his father had served the monarchy, which meant that he himself was suspected of undesirable political activity. He switched to the newly founded École Polytechnique, where he was a classmate of Biot [404] and was involved with Biot in the street riot of 1795 that was put down by the young Napoleon.

Malus was not as marked by anti-Napoleonic feelings as Biot was, perhaps because, as a military engineer, he would naturally approve a successful general. He went on to serve in Egypt with Napoleon in 1798 and barely survived that disastrous campaign.

Malus worked in optics as a hobby. The Paris Academy of Sciences had offered a prize for the best mathematical theory accounting for double refraction and Malus was interested in it. One day in 1808 he idly pointed his doubly refracting crystal of Iceland spar at the sunlight reflected from a window and found that only one ray of light was emerging from the crystal. Through a mistaken theory that he had of the nature of light, he believed the two refracted rays ordinarily passing through the Iceland spar represented different poles of the light (analogous to magnetic poles). He called the rays "polarized light," therefore, a name it bears to this day. He concluded from his observation of the reflected sunlight that light could be polarized by reflection.

He also concluded that the two refracted rays emerging from the Iceland spar were polarized perpendicularly to each other, for it was possible to arrange matters so that as the crystal turned, one ray would fade out while the other strengthened, the two fading out completely but alternately with each ninety-degree turn of the crystal. All this was neatly explained by Fresnel's [455] theory of transverse waves.

In 1811 he was informed by Young [402] (despite the war that was at that time existing between Great Britain and France) that he had been awarded the Rumford medal. Malus died in his thirty-seventh year of tuberculosis.

[409] **KIDD,** John
British chemist and physician
Born: London, September 10, 1775
Died: Oxford, September 17, 1851

In 1803 Kidd, the son of a ship's captain, was appointed professor of chemistry at Oxford after having obtained his M.D. there two years before.

His most important discovery came in 1819, when he obtained naphthalene from coal tar. Murdock [363] a quarter century earlier had pioneered the use of coal as a source of gaseous fuel, but Kidd pointed the way toward the use of coal as a source for chemicals. The substances in coal tar were important not only in themselves but, as Perkin [734] was to show a generation later, they were even more important as the starting material for synthetics that would put the naturally occurring compounds in the shade.

[410] **GERMAIN,** Sophie, (zher-mang')
French mathematician
Born: Paris, April 1, 1776
Died: Paris, June 27, 1831

Germain was the daughter of a well-to-do merchant and managed to find books in the library at home out of which to teach herself Latin, Greek, and mathematics. It was enormously difficult for a woman to receive any kind of education, however, for the opinion was that women's minds were too limited for education. And by refusing them an education and by hammering inferiority into them, their minds were *made* limited.

Germain was forced to study the notes of other students who attended the École Polytechnique that she was not allowed to attend, then sent in a report under a male pseudonym. Lagrange [317] was astonished at its worth, discovered the author was a woman and, to his credit, sponsored her thereafter.

She did important work on Fermat's [188] last theorem. Euler [275] had proved it for $n = 3$ and Legendre [358] for $n = 5$. Germain proved it for any prime under 100 where certain conditions are met. She also worked out a mathematical model that explained the vibrations of a flat plate, such as that Chladni [370] used to work out his figures.

Germain even impressed the self-centered Gauss [415] with her worth. Gauss arranged to have her receive an honorary doctor's degree from Göttingen, but Germain died before it could be awarded.

We can only wonder how many marvelous feminine brains were stultified and prevented from fulfilling themselves and serving humanity because of the cruel and stupid male chauvinism that has permeated so much of society for so long a time.

[411] **STROHMEYER,** Friedrich
(shtroh'my-er)
German chemist
Born: Göttingen, Hannover, August 2, 1776
Died: Göttingen, August 18, 1835

Strohmeyer, the son of a professor of medicine, began his education in Göttingen, his father's school, but the final touch was added in Paris, where he studied under Vauquelin [379]. He followed in the footsteps of Vauquelin as to his field of specialization and remained a mineralogist throughout his career. (This contagion of specialty is by no means a general rule. Strohmeyer's own most prominent pupil, Gmelin [457], developed much wider interests.)

In 1802 he joined the faculty of the University of Göttingen and by 1810 was a full professor of chemistry. He was one of the first to offer laboratory instruction in chemistry, though he was soon to be overshadowed in this respect by Liebig [532]. The most important discovery of his life did not come about through his strictly academic work, however.

He also doubled as inspector general of apothecaries in Hannover. In 1817, fulfilling the duties of this office, he came across an apothecary's shop in which a bottle labeled zinc oxide contained zinc carbonate. Following this up, Strohmeyer found himself interested in zinc carbonate, which turned yellow on strong heating as though it contained iron as an impurity, yet it contained no iron. He traced the yellow to an oxide not of zinc but of a hitherto unknown metal rather like it chemically. He named it cadmium from the Latin name for a zinc ore in which it is usually found accompanying the zinc.

[412] **AVOGADRO,** Amedeo, count of Quaregna (ah-voh-gah'droh)
Italian physicist
Born: Turin, Piedmont, August 9, 1776
Died: Turin, July 9, 1856

Avogadro was born into a family of lawyers and succeeded to his father's title in 1787. In 1796 he received a doctorate in law and practiced for three years before turning to science. A professor of physics at the University of Turin in later life, Avogadro suffered the not-too-uncommon fate of neglect in his lifetime and success after death.

Avogadro considered the discovery made by Gay-Lussac [420] that all gases expand to the same extent with rise in temperature and decided that this must signify that all gases (at a given temperature) contain the same number of particles per unit volume. This is Avogadro's hypothesis, which he advanced in a paper published in 1811. He was careful to specify that the particles need not be individual atoms, but might be combinations of atoms (which we now call molecules, a word Avogadro coined). Avogadro was the first to distinguish between atoms and molecules in this way.

On this basis he could easily explain Gay-Lussac's law of combining volumes. Furthermore, when water was electrolyzed and the hydrogen and oxygen collected separately, as Ritter [413] had first done a decade earlier, the volume of hydrogen produced was twice the volume of oxygen. Avogadro could then use his hypothesis to maintain that the water molecule contained two hydrogen atoms for each one of oxygen. Then, if the oxygen as a whole weighed eight times as much as the hydrogen, the individual oxygen atom was sixteen times as heavy as the individual hydrogen atom (not eight times, as Dalton [389] insisted).

But Avogadro's suggestion, loudly and repeatedly proclaimed by him, was little regarded in the following decades. Ampère [407] was one of the few who upheld it but Dalton rejected it with vigor and Berzelius [425], the most prominent chemist of his time, ignored it. Partly this was because Avogadro did not support it with a convincing body of experimental evidence.

The result was that there was great and continuing confusion in differentiating atoms from molecules, and atomic weights from molecular weights. It was not until Avogadro's countryman Cannizzaro [668] took up the cudgels on his behalf (half a century after the hypothesis was published and, alas, shortly after Avogadro's death) that the hypothesis finally took its rightful place.

Now, of course, Avogadro is famous. His name is applied to the number of atoms or molecules present in an amount of substance that has a mass of its atomic (or molecular) weight in grams. Thus carbon dioxide has a molecular weight of 44. Forty-four grams of carbon dioxide contains "Avogadro's number" of molecules, and in Arabic figures that number comes out to 602,600,000,000,000,000,000,000.

[413] **RITTER,** Johann Wilhelm
German physicist
Born: Samitz, Silesia, (now Chojnów, Poland), December 16, 1776
Died: Munich, Bavaria, January 23, 1810

Initial advances in current electricity moved quickly. In early 1800 Volta [337] had constructed the first battery, and within months Nicholson [361] had used the electric current to break up water into hydrogen and oxygen.

Within months after that, still in 1800, Ritter, the son of a minister and an apothecary by profession, who had studied at the University of Jena and taught there as well, was able to repeat Nicholson's experiment with electrodes placed in such a way that the hydrogen and oxygen produced from the water could be collected separately. He also announced that if a current was passed through a solution of copper sulfate, metallic copper could be made to plate out. This was the beginning of electroplating. Ritter attempted to use his experiments to revive the dying phlogiston theory, which had been mortally wounded by Lavoisier [334], and he failed, of course.

Ritter made a startling advance in connection with light in 1801. It was well known that silver chloride broke down in the presence of light, liberating finely divided metallic silver, the presence of which turned the originally white silver chloride black. (This is the key chemical reaction involved in photography.) Ritter found, as Scheele [329] had reported a generation earlier, that the blue end of the spectrum was far more efficient in bringing this about than the red end was. He went on to discover, however, to his amazement, that the region beyond the violet end, where nothing was present to the eye, was more efficient in this respect than any visible region of this spectrum. Like Herschel [321] the year before, Ritter was forced to conclude that radiation

existed that was invisible to the eye. The section of the spectrum immediately adjacent to the violet end is now called ultraviolet ("beyond the violet") radiation. Because of its action on silver chloride, it was sometimes referred to as chemical rays.

Toward the end of his short life, Ritter grew interested in dowsing and other mystical practices. Nothing came of it, of course.

[414] **COURTOIS,** Bernard (koor-twah')
French chemist
Born: Dijon, Côte d'Or, February 8, 1777
Died: Paris, September 27, 1838

Courtois's father had once served as assistant to Guyton de Morveau [319] at Dijon University and was a manufacturer of saltpeter (potassium nitrate), a compound of importance in the manufacture of gunpowder. Courtois assisted him in the factory and served an apprenticeship to an apothecary. He was admitted, with Guyton de Morveau's recommendation, to the École Polytechnique, where he studied under Fourcroy [366] and Thénard [416].

After a period in the army as a pharmacist, Courtois returned to the saltpeter business. His father had done poorly, but Courtois kept doggedly at the job, particularly since France (now revolutionary) was at war and needed saltpeter badly.

Courtois had, in his early researches, isolated morphine from opium extract. It was the first alkaloid to be obtained in pure form. He is better known, however, for another discovery, which came about as follows.

The method of manufacturing potassium nitrate in those days used potassium carbonate (potash) as one of the starting materials. To get the potassium carbonate, it was Courtois's practice to burn seaweed. The ash contained the potassium carbonate and, of course, a number of other things as well. There were sulfur compounds, for instance, which were undesirable and which Courtois got rid of by heating in acid.

One day in 1811 he added too much

acid and on heating obtained a beautiful violet vapor. On condensing, it produced dark, lustrous crystals. He investigated the new substance but conscious (or perhaps overconscious) of his own shortcomings as a chemist passed it on to others. By 1814 Davy [421], who was shown the new material on the occasion of his tour of Europe, and Gay-Lussac [420] had shown it to be a new element and Davy suggested the name iodine, from the Greek word for violet. Seaweed still remains one of the prime sources of iodine.

The discovery gave Courtois a measure of fame and in 1831 he received a prize of 6,000 francs from the Academy of Sciences. However, he had no better luck in business than his father. The saltpeter factory failed when the Napoleonic Wars ended and the need for gunpowder abated. He eked out a living, but not much of one, by preparing and selling iodine; and in the end, died in poverty.

[415] **GAUSS,** Johann Karl Friedrich (gowss)
German mathematician
Born: Braunschweig (Brunswick, in English), April 30, 1777
Died: Göttingen, Hannover, February 23, 1855

Gauss, the son of a gardener and a servant girl, had no relative of more than normal intelligence apparently, but he was an infant prodigy in mathematics who remained a prodigy all his life. He was capable of great feats of memory and of mental calculation. There are those with this ability who are of only average or below-average mentality, but Gauss was clearly a genius. At the age of three, he was already correcting his father's sums, and all his life he kept all sorts of numerical records, even useless ones such as the length of lives of famous men, in days. He was virtually mad over numbers.

Some people consider him to have been one of the three great mathematicians of all time, the others being Archimedes [47] and Newton [231]. His unusual mind was recognized and he was educated at the expense of Duke Ferdinand of Brunswick. In 1795 Gauss entered the University of Göttingen and in 1799 received his doctor's degree in absentia.

While still in his teens he made a number of remarkable discoveries, including the method of least squares, advancing the work of Legendre [358] in this area. By this the best equation for a curve fitting a group of observations can be made. Personal error is minimized. It was work such as this that enabled Gauss, while still in his early twenties, to calculate an orbit for Ceres from Piazzi's [341] few observations so that the first asteroid might be located once more after it had been lost. (The 1001st asteroid discovered was named Gaussia in his honor.) He also worked out theories of perturbations that were eventually used by Leverrier [564] and John C. Adams [615] in their discovery of the planet Neptune.

While still in the university he also demonstrated a method for constructing an equilateral polygon of seventeen sides (a 17-gon) using only straightedge and compass. Here was a construction all the ancient Greeks had missed. Gauss went further: he showed that only polygons of certain numbers of sides could be constructed with straightedge and compass alone. (These two tools were the only ones thought suitable for geometric constructions by Plato [24].) A polygon with seven sides (a "heptagon") could *not* be constructed in this fashion. This was the first case of a geometric construction being proved impossible. From this point on, the proof of the impossible in mathematics grew in importance, reaching a climax with Gödel [1301] nearly a century and a half later.

Gauss was quickly recognized as the greatest mathematician of his time, even by Laplace [347] who was not likely to be overgenerous in his estimate of others. (For that matter, Gauss in later life was not overgenerous to younger mathematicians either. The case of Niels Abel [527] is an example.)

Gauss did important work on the theory of numbers, the branch of mathematics that Fermat [188] had founded, and on every other branch of mathematics. He also worked out a non-Euclidean geometry—a geometry based on axioms different from those of Euclid [40]—but hesitated to publish, for he had the habit, in any case, of keeping some of his results secret for periods of time. Lobachevski [484] and Bolyai [530] published first and obtained the credit.

In 1799 Gauss proved the fundamental theorem of algebra, that every algebraic equation has a root of the form $a + bi$, where a and b are real numbers and i is the square root of minus one. Numbers of the form $a + bi$ are called complex numbers, and Gauss showed that these can be represented as analogous to the points on a plane. This was the work that earned for him his doctorate. In 1801 he went on to prove the fundamental theorem of arithmetic: that every natural number can be represented as the product of primes in one and only one way.

All this was not without a price, for his intense concentration on the great work that poured from him withdrew him sometimes from contact with humanity. There is a story that when he was told, in 1807, that his wife was dying, he looked up from the problem that engaged him and muttered, "Tell her to wait a moment till I'm through."

Outside the realm of pure mathematics it was his work on Ceres that gained Gauss fame. In 1806 Gauss's sponsor, Ferdinand of Brunswick, was dead, fighting against Napoleon, and Gauss had to have some way of making a living. Through the influence of Humboldt [397], a great admirer of Gauss, and the mathematician's own record in connection with Ceres, he was appointed director of the Göttingen Observatory in 1807. Even then, war conditions kept him on a bare subsistence level for some years.

During his years at Göttingen, Gauss devised a heliotrope, an instrument that reflected sunlight over long distances, so that light rays could be put to work as straight lines marking the face of the earth, and more precise trigonometric determinations of the planet's shape could be made.

He worked also on terrestrial magnetism and instituted the first observatory designed specifically for work in that field. He calculated the location of the magnetic poles from geomagnetic observations and his calculations proved remarkably accurate. In 1832 he devised a logical set of units of measurement for magnetic phenomena. The unit of magnetic flux density was eventually named the gauss. He pointed out that once a few fundamental units were established (as, for instance, those for length, mass, and time) many other derived units (such as those for volume, density, energy, viscosity, power, and so on) could be expressed in terms of those fundamental units. In 1833 he even constructed an electric telegraph, as Henry [503] was doing in the United States. His agile mind never seemed to cease. At the age of sixty-two he taught himself Russian.

He remained on the faculty at Göttingen all his working life but hated teaching and had few students. Each of his two wives died young and only one of his six children survived him. His life was filled with personal tragedy, and though he died wealthy, he also died embittered.

After his death, a medal was struck in his honor by the king of Hannover. A statue of him, raised by the city of his birth, stands on a pedestal in the shape of a 17-pointed star, celebrating his discovery of the construction of the 17-gon.

[416] THÉNARD, Louis Jacques (tay-nahr')
French chemist
Born: La Louptière, Aube, May 4, 1777
Died: Paris, June 21, 1857

Thénard's was a true rags-to-riches story. He was the son of a poor peasant who, in the best tradition of such things, struggled hard to obtain an education for his son. Thénard went to Paris and studied chemistry for three years under conditions of semistarvation until he was befriended by Vauquelin [379], who, himself the son of a peasant, had not forgotten his own early life.

Thénard eventually grew well-to-do by responding to a demand by Chaptal [368] for the development of a color as bright as ultramarine but capable of withstanding the heat of furnaces used in preparing porcelain. Thénard obliged with what is now known as "Thénard's blue" (which contains an aluminum-cobalt oxide).

Thénard's greatest fame came in his collaboration with his lifelong friend Gay-Lussac [420], but he also did much on his own. In 1818 he discovered hydrogen peroxide and between 1813 and 1816 he published an important four-volume text on chemistry.

He was made a baron in 1832 by Charles X, after having become a member of the Chamber of Deputies in 1828 (thus pointing the way in which his collaborator, Gay-Lussac, was to follow in the next reign).

Eight years after Thénard's death, his native village was renamed La Louptière-Thénard.

[417] **OERSTED,** Hans Christian (er'-sted)
Danish physicist
Born: Rudkøbing, Langeland, August 14, 1777
Died: Copenhagen, March 9, 1851

The young Hans worked in his father's apothecary shop, but this early training, which in most cases would have led straight to a career in chemistry, led to physics instead. He studied at the University of Copenhagen, where he obtained his Ph.D. in 1799 for a dissertation on Kant's [293] philosophy. He then traveled through Europe, and in 1806 was appointed professor of physics and chemistry at his alma mater. He became an ardent adherent of the school of "nature philosophy" of which Oken [423] was an outstanding member. He accepted, with great gullibility, foolish theories and faked experimental work by

men he admired and for a while his scientific reputation lay under a cloud.

His brother Anders, younger by a year and a half, took to law, became attorney general of Denmark, and eventually the prime minister. He was a very unpopular prime minister and underwent impeachment proceedings after a forced resignation. It would seem, then, thanks to a single experiment, that Hans Oersted had taken the better road to fame.

It was in 1819 that Hans Oersted's great day came. He too was experimenting with the electric current, as half of Europe's scholars were doing. As part of a classroom demonstration, he brought a compass needle near a wire through which a current was passing. Scientists had long suspected there might be some connection between electricity and magnetism and Oersted may have felt that the current in the wire might have some effect on the needle.

It did indeed. The compass needle twitched and pointed neither with the current nor against it, but in a direction at right angles to it. When he reversed the direction of the current, the compass needle veered and pointed in the opposite direction, but still at right angles. The astounded Oersted remained after class to repeat and continue his experiments.

This was the first demonstration of a connection between electricity and magnetism, and Oersted's experiment may be considered the foundation of the new study of electromagnetism.

Oersted's discovery (published in Latin, in the old-fashioned way) was announced in 1820, and it set off an explosion of activity. Coulomb [318] had developed views indicating that electricity and magnetism could not interact, and he had been very persuasive; but now it was clearly seen that he had been wrong. Arago [446] and Ampère [407] charged into the fray. Later, in the hands of Faraday [474] and Henry [503] especially, electromagnetism was to grow into an entity that was eventually to change the world as drastically as the steam engine had changed the world a century before and as the internal combustion engine was to change it half a century later.

Oersted did not keep up with the whirlwind of activity his experiment had stirred up. He did show that the force of the current on the needle made itself felt through glass, metals, and other nonmagnetic substances, but except for that, he did nothing further to follow up his own momentous discovery. Nevertheless, the unit of magnetic field strength was officially named the "oersted" in his honor in 1934.

Outside electromagnetics, Oersted was the first to isolate the organic compound piperidine (1820) and the first to prepare metallic aluminum (1825).

[418] **CANDOLLE,** Augustin Pyrame de (kahn-dole')
Swiss-French botanist
Born: Geneva, February 4, 1778
Died: Geneva, September 9, 1841

Candolle was a member of a Huguenot family that had fled France at the time of the religious wars to escape persecution. Once the French Revolution ended religious disabilities, young Candolle settled in Paris in 1796 and there obtained his medical degree at the University of Paris in 1804. He was appointed professor of botany at the University of Montpellier in 1808.

He began working on a large plant encyclopedia, which attracted the favorable attention of Lamarck [336] and Cuvier [396]. It turned out to be enormous and more than a lifetime of work. Candolle published seven volumes before his death (his son saw to the publication of the remaining fourteen). His reputation was firmly established by the early volumes and he spent six years making a botanical and agricultural survey of France at the express request of the French government.

Candolle introduced Jussieu [345] and Cuvier's system of classification by deeplying similarities into the plant kingdom. He spent the rest of his life extending and perfecting this system. It was he who invented the word "taxonomy" in 1813 to describe the science of classification. His system of plant classification is largely in use today.

In 1819 he accepted a professorship in botany at the University of Geneva and there remained for the rest of his life.

Like Cuvier, Candolle was firmly antievolutionary.

[419] **BRETONNEAU,** Pierre Fidèle (breh-tuh-noh')
French physician
Born: St.-Georges-sur-Cher, April 3, 1778
Died: Passy, February 18, 1862

Bretonneau was the son of a master surgeon, but his education was very haphazard indeed. Nevertheless, he finally managed to obtain his M.D. degree in 1815.

He did some important medical work. From 1818 to 1820 an epidemic of diphtheria ravaged Tours. Bretonneau worked hard during that time and examined carefully. He was the first to study the symptoms of the disease thoroughly and, indeed, gave it its present name, "diphtheria," in 1826. He took the name from the Greek word for "leather" or "parchment" because of the parchmentlike membrane that formed in the course of the disease. To prevent the fatal asphyxia that that membrane produced, Bretonneau performed a tracheotomy on a four-year-old girl in July 1825, cutting an opening into the windpipe through the skin and muscles of the neck. It was the first operation of its kind and it was successful.

Bretonneau also distinguished between typhus fever and typhoid ("typhuslike") fever. His speculations on the communicability of disease foreshadowed the germ theory of Pasteur [642] a generation later.

[420] **GAY-LUSSAC,** Joseph Louis (gay'lyoo-sak')
French chemist
Born: St. Léonard, Haute Vienne, December 6, 1778
Died: Paris, May 9, 1850

As a young man, Gay-Lussac, the son of a judge who was imprisoned for a time because of royalist sympathies during the French Revolution, studied at the École Polytechnique under Berthollet [346], Guyton de Morveau [319] and Fourcroy [366]. He graduated in 1800.

While in school, Gay-Lussac was particularly befriended and encouraged by Berthollet, and for a while he worked along with Berthollet's son in a factory where chlorine was used to bleach linen. Gay-Lussac proved himself worthy of the friendship soon enough.

In 1802 he showed that different gases all expanded by equal amounts with rise in temperature. Charles [343] had made the same discovery some years earlier but had not published it; the credit therefore belongs to Gay-Lussac at least as much, and probably more and the phenomenon is frequently called Gay-Lussac's law. This was an extremely important discovery, which Avogadro [412] was to use within the decade to formulate his long-neglected hypothesis that equal volumes of different gases at equal temperatures contained equal numbers of particles.

In 1804 the young Gay-Lussac made a balloon ascension with Biot [404] and later made one on his own. These were among the first ascents for scientific purposes. Gay-Lussac reached a height of four miles, higher than the tallest peak of the Alps, in one of these flights. He found no change either in the composition of the air or in the earth's magnetic force. In 1805 and 1806, he traveled with Humboldt [397] measuring terrestrial magnetism.

At this time England was the spearhead of continued attempts on the part of various European powers to unseat Napoleon. England was also the center of astonishing chemical advances made by Davy [421], who in 1807 and 1808 was isolating a number of new elements through the action of electricity.

In the wake of the French Revolution, nationalism had become strong enough for governments to wish to make deliberate attempts to harness science to the cause of national prestige. Napoleon pro-vided Gay-Lussac and his long-time friend and co-worker Thénard [416] with funds for building a powerful battery as a source of a large electric current in order that France might close the "element gap."

The battery proved unnecessary. Gay-Lussac and Thénard made use of one of Davy's own elements, potassium, to do the job without electricity. By treating boron oxide with potassium, they liberated boron, for the first time, in elementary form. They announced this on June 21, 1808. Davy was beaten by nine days: He announced the independent isolation of boron on June 30. Napoleon had his scientific victory, and Gay-Lussac was appointed professor of physics at the Sorbonne, a post he held till 1832.

Gay-Lussac went on to make more important discoveries. In 1809 he found that in forming compounds, gases combined in proportions by volume that could be expressed in small whole numbers. For instance, two parts of hydrogen united with one part of oxygen to form water; one part of hydrogen united with one part of chlorine to form hydrogen chloride; and three parts of hydrogen united with one part of nitrogen to form ammonia. This law of combining volumes was worked out, in part, with the help of the universally talented Humboldt [397].

This relationship by volume of the elements in a compound could be used most fruitfully in the determination of atomic weights, and this Berzelius [425] went on to do. However, Dalton [389] refused to accept Gay-Lussac's results and stuck firmly to the principle of composition by weight only and his atomic weights continued to be wrong. Avogadro's hypothesis came along within two years to explain Gay-Lussac's law, but it was ignored for half a century.

Gay-Lussac then began a series of researches on cyanides, which ended with the conclusive proof that prussic acid, or hydrogen cyanide, contained no oxygen. This finally showed that acids could be acids without the presence of oxygen and demonstrated that in this respect at least, Lavoisier [334] was wrong.

(As it turned out, hydrogen is the essential element of acids.)

Gay-Lussac also followed up Courtois's [414] discovery of iodine and showed it to be a new element (entering into a dispute with Davy over priority in this matter). He added new techniques to the armory of the analytical chemist through the use of titrations (careful addition of exact volumes) involving alkali and chlorine. As early as 1811 he and Thénard used their analytical skill to determine the elementary composition of sugar for the first time.

In 1831 Gay-Lussac was elected to the French Chamber of Deputies under the new regime of Louis-Philippe and spent his later years as a lawmaker, entering the upper house, the Chamber of Peers in 1839.

[421] DAVY, Sir Humphry
English chemist
Born: Penzance, Cornwall, December 17, 1778
Died: Geneva, Switzerland, May 29, 1829

Davy, the son of a woodcarver, spent his youth in poverty. His father died leaving a £1,300 debt as legacy—one that young Davy and his mother eventually paid off in full. He did not enjoy school and was soon apprenticed to an apothecary. At the apothecary's he began a course of self-education and was discharged when this led him into conducting chemical reactions that ended in explosions.

His interests were, at first, rather wide-ranging. He was an enthusiastic fisherman and wrote a book on the subject. He was interested in philosophy and is considered to have displayed considerable talent as a poet; later in life he was befriended and respected by such literary lights as Wordsworth and Coleridge.

However, in 1797 he read Lavoisier's [334] textbook on chemistry and thereafter he was a chemist. Upon completing his apprenticeship, Davy was recommended to a physician who had just established an institution for the study of the therapeutic properties of gases. At the age of twenty, Davy became superintendent of the institution.

Within a year he had experimented with heat and had disagreed with Lavoisier's caloric theory, maintaining instead that heat was a form of motion. He also experimented with gases, using instruments made for him by Watt [316] and nearly killing himself with the more poisonous ones. He felt something was to be gained by breathing his products and observing the results. He breathed four quarts of hydrogen, for instance, nearly to the point of his own suffocation and tried to breathe pure carbon dioxide. (The connection with Watt, by the way, was not accidental. Davy was born in Cornwall, where Watt's steam engine first gained fame. Watt's second son, Gregory, lodged with Davy's mother.)

At least once, Davy's foolishly risky inhalation experiments paid off. He studied nitrous oxide in 1800 and reported upon its unusual properties. On being inhaled, it gave rise to a giddy, intoxicated feeling. Inhibitions were lowered so that subjects would laugh easily, cry, or go into other emotional exhibitions when those were suggested. (Hence, it is often called laughing gas.) For a while, nitrous oxide parties were all the rage among those who could think of nothing more worthwhile to do. It was almost the LSD of its day and Davy's poet friend Robert Southey was one of those who tried it and then wrote up his experiences of being "turned on."

Much more important was the fact that nitrous oxide was to serve as the first chemical anesthetic (and it is still sometimes so used in dentistry).

In 1801 Rumford [360] needed a lecturer at the newly founded Royal Institution in London. Doubtfully he tested Davy, but upon hearing the young provincial lecturer he hired him at once, and by the next year Davy was a professor. Rumford soon quarreled with others backing the institution (which had financial problems) and left England. Davy took over. He prepared and polished his talks to the last syllable and proved a delightful lecturer, with the poise and charm of a born showman. Some historians of science maintain him to have been the handsomest of all the great scientists.

The Napoleonic Wars were keeping the English gentry at home and London society, particularly the ladies, flocked to hear the handsome young man talk about the new principles of chemistry. The institution began to do famously and soon no longer had financial difficulties.

During this time he worked on agricultural chemistry. While not entirely successful in the field, he eventually published (in 1813) the first textbook dealing with the applications of chemistry to agriculture. He was also interested in mineralogy and in 1807 was one of the charter members of the newly founded Geological Society of London. It was the first society of its kind in the world.

His true fame was in electricity. After Nicholson [361] had broken up the water molecule by means of an electric current, Davy began to wonder about the effect of electricity on other compounds. A number of substances such as lime, magnesia, potash, and soda were strongly suspected of possessing metallic elements as part of their structure—metals that had never been isolated. The trouble was that these metals held on so tightly to oxygen that neither strong heat nor the counterattractions of other metals for the oxygen could liberate them.

Davy began his own electrical experiments, producing an electric arc in 1805, and in 1806 was awarded a prize established by Napoleon for the best work of the year in electricity. Since England was at war with Napoleonic France at the time, there was some doubt as to whether Davy should accept the medal. Davy, however, accepted, saying stoutly that the governments might be at war but the scientists were not.

He then proceeded to construct a battery with over two hundred and fifty metallic plates, the strongest ever built at that time, and began running electric currents first through solutions of these metal-containing materials and then through the molten substances themselves.

The results were spectacular. On October 6, 1807, the current passing through molten potash liberated a metal, which Davy called potassium. The little globules of shining metal tore the water molecule apart as it eagerly recombined with oxygen and the liberated hydrogen burst into lavender flame. Davy danced about in a delirium of joy. A week later he isolated sodium from soda.

In 1808, by using a somewhat modified method suggested by Berzelius [425], he isolated barium, strontium, calcium, and magnesium. He also isolated boron, but here he was beaten by nine days by Gay-Lussac [420] and Thénard [416]. His path and Gay-Lussac's crossed at several other places. Both he and Gay-Lussac disproved Lavoisier's contention that all acids had oxygen and did it at about the same time, Davy showing that hydrochloric acid had no oxygen and Gay-Lussac that prussic acid had none. Both Gay-Lussac and Davy showed that poor Courtois's [414] iodine was indeed an element.

Davy's work with hydrochloric acid was the most impressive of these conflicts, for not only was hydrochloric acid one of the common strong acids (so that the absence of oxygen was astonishing) but it led to his proof that chlorine was an element and contained no oxygen, despite the opinion of Scheele [329] a generation earlier. It was Davy who suggested the name chlorine —from a Greek word for "green"— because of the greenish color of the gas. He discovered, furthermore, that chlorine could support combustion as oxygen could. It was the first indication that oxygen was not unique in this and that there were other chemically active gases. Davy further detracted from oxygen's importance by suggesting (correctly) that it was the content of hydrogen that was characteristic of acids.

Despite his great work in chemistry, Davy could not bring himself to accept Dalton's [389] atomic theory, even though his own close friend Wollaston

[388] was a convinced atomist and tried to convert him.

In 1812 he resigned his lectureship, was knighted, promptly married a rich Scottish widow, and, the next year, was off on a tour of Europe in a blaze of fame. England and France were still at war, but the French chemists greeted him warmly. He met Rumford there once more, shortly before the latter's death.

In a way, he needed the vacation badly. Thanks to his habit of sniffing and tasting new chemicals, he was an invalid from 1811 on, undoubtedly as a result of chemical poisoning. Then, in 1812, he damaged his eyes in a nitrogen trichloride explosion. It is not surprising he died in middle life.

In 1815 he invented the Davy lamp, in which an open flame is surrounded by a cylinder of metallic gauze. Oxygen can get through the gauze and feed the flame. The heat of the flame, however, is dissipated by the metal and explosive gases outside the lamp are not ignited. For the first time, miners were reasonably safe from explosion. Davy refused to patent the invention and profit from so humanitarian a discovery. However, he burst into a jealous fury when Stephenson [431]—justifiably, in the opinion of many—claimed priority in the invention. In 1818 Davy was made a baronet for this service to the mining industry.

He turned his electric arc to service too, converting it into an arc lamp, the first attempt to turn electricity to the task of illumination (a task that was to reach a climax in the time of Edison [788]). Davy was also the first to take note of the catalytic ability of platinum, a phenomenon that Döbereiner [427] was to make spectacular.

In 1820 Davy became president of the Royal Society, succeeding Banks [331]. Davy campaigned openly for the office, which might otherwise have gone to the more diffident Wollaston, and this is another example of Davy's avidity for scientific honors.

After 1823 Davy spent most of his time abroad and died in Switzerland. In his will he left funds to establish a medal to be given annually to chemists who

had made the most important discovery of the year. Awarded in 1877 for the first time, Bunsen [565] and Kirchhoff [648] received it. Considering that those two men discovered a new way to locate new elements, as Davy had done, and in particular discovered two close relatives of Davy's sodium and potassium, this first award was most appropriate.

Davy's chief accomplishment may not have been material. A young man named Michael Faraday [474] attended Davy's lectures and applied for and eventually got the post of assistant, which he filled most wonderfully. It was Faraday, for instance, who skillfully prepared that most dangerous explosive, nitrogen trichloride, which Davy, less skillful, then allowed to explode, nearly losing his eyesight as a result.

In later years Faraday was considered the greatest of all Davy's discoveries, and greater in science than his patron.

Davy could sense that this would happen and grew jealous. In 1824 he tried to block Faraday's election to the Royal Society but fortunately was unsuccessful. Faraday was never seduced into responding to Davy's ungenerosity in kind. He was the better man in more than science.

[422] **SCHWEIGGER,** Johann Salomo Christoph (shvigh'ger)
German physicist
Born: Erlangen, Bavaria, April 8, 1779
Died: Halle, Prussian Saxony, September 6, 1857

Schweigger, the son of a professor of theology, received his Ph.D. in 1800 at the University of Erlangen. He taught at a succession of German schools and was at the University of Halle in 1820 when the news of Oersted's [417] experiment reached him.

He quickly saw that the deflection of the needle could be used to measure the strength of the current, since the stronger the current the greater the deflection. He made the effect more sensitive by winding the wire many times in a coil around the magnetic needle.

In this way he invented the first galvanometer.

[423] **OKEN,** Lorenz (oh'ken)
German naturalist
Born: Bohlsbach, Baden, August
1, 1779
Died: Zürich, Switzerland,
August 11, 1851

Oken (whose real name was Ock-
enfuss) was the son of a poor farmer.
He was much influenced by the philosophy of Kant [293], and in 1803 he grew
interested in and eventually became the
most important member of the Na-
turphilosophen ("nature philosophers")
who flourished in early-nineteenth-cen-
tury Germany and who had, on the
whole, a deleterious effect on the development of biology.

Goethe [349] had announced a theory
that the skull of vertebrates had originally been formed out of vertebrae. In
1807 when Oken was appointed a professor of natural science at the University of Jena, he elaborated on this
theory. It was later carried to extremes,
as when the notion arose that the original vertebrate had had a skeleton that
looked like a centipede, with ribs and
limbs attached to each vertebra. When
the first several vertebrae fused to form
the skull, the limbs attached fused to
form the jaw.

This whole notion was false, as was
finally demonstrated in 1858 by Huxley
[659], but it served science well in one
way: It included the idea of evolution. If
a portion of a backbone could change
into a skull, it went without saying that
one species could slowly change into another.

Oken's views were quite mystical and
obscure, and rather repellent to the rationalist. He considered man the summit
of creation, a microcosm reflecting the
macrocosm, or universe. His speculations
seemed to foreshadow the cell theory
and the protoplasmic basis of life, but
mere speculation is easy enough and is
no substitute for generalizations based on
careful observation and experiment.

In 1816 Oken founded an important
biological journal, *Isis,* that not only
published worthwhile papers on biology
but also served as a vehicle for Oken's
nationalist views (and in those days Ger-

man nationalism was a liberal movement). He was forced out of Jena as a
result, giving up his position rather than
submit to censorship of *Isis.* Eventually,
though, he found a haven in Switzerland.

He performed an even greater service
by founding an important German
scientific society of which Humboldt
[397] became a leading light. He also advocated annual meetings of biologists,
physicians, and natural historians, so
that views on the life sciences could be
made public and communicated throughout the world of scholarship. Such meetings in virtually all branches of science
are now a common (and, indeed, indispensable) feature of the scientific
way of life.

[424] **SILLIMAN,** Benjamin
American chemist
Born: North Stratford (now
Trumbull), Connecticut, August
8, 1779
Died: New Haven, Connecticut,
November 24, 1864

Silliman studied at Yale and obtained
a degree in law in 1796. In 1802, however, the president of Yale asked the
young lawyer to accept a post as professor of chemistry. This was not because
Silliman was qualified, but because there
were no chemists to appoint.

Silliman accepted and went to the
University of Pennsylvania for training.
There he met Hare [428]. He then completed his training by studying in England, where he met Davy [421], among
others. He returned in 1804 to serve half
a century at Yale, and established its
graduate school, which awarded its first
Ph.D. in 1861. He was never a great experimental chemist, but he was an inspiring teacher who made chemists out of
others and who by public lectures popularized science generally in the young nation.

In 1806 he introduced Priestley's [312]
soda water into America. In 1807 he and
a colleague observed a meteorite fall. At
the time the general scientific opinion
was that tales of stones from heaven
ranked with ghost stories. In fact,

Thomas Jefferson [333], then president of the United States and an amateur scientist, observed, concerning Silliman's report, that it was easier to believe that two Yankee professors would lie than that stones would fall from heaven. Biot [404] had already demonstrated the existence of meteorites four years earlier, and a gigantic meteor shower a quarter century later was to make the whole scientific world meteor-conscious.

In 1818 Silliman founded the *American Journal of Science and Arts,* which was an influential factor in the development of American science and which was popularly known as "Silliman's Journal."

[425] **BERZELIUS,** Jöns Jakob (bur-zee′lee-us)
Swedish chemist
Born: Väversunda Sörgård,
August 20, 1779
Died: Stockholm, August 7, 1848

Berzelius lost his father, a clergyman-schoolmaster, when four years old, and his mother when nine. During his mother's widowhood, she had married again, however, and the stepfather, another clergyman, saw to the young man's education. Berzelius attended medical school at Uppsala, where he studied under Ekeberg [391], among others. However, he was an indifferent student, at least as far as medicine was concerned. Chances are he would have flunked out had it not been for his unusual proficiency in physics. At any rate, he obtained his medical degree in 1802 and was so proficient in chemistry as well (he had been introduced to that subject by his stepbrother) that he dominated the field in his later years. He was a full professor by 1817.

About 1807, working with Hisinger [390] to begin with, he determined the exact elementary constitution of various compounds. By running two thousand analyses over a period of ten years, he advanced so many examples of the law of definite proportions first announced by Proust [364] that the world of chemistry could no longer doubt its validity.

This in turn helped place Dalton's [389] atomic theory (which Berzelius was among the first to accept) on a firm footing and Berzelius next devoted himself to investigating the one key property of atoms that was then appreciated—the atomic weight. In this task he had the help of generalizations advanced by his contemporaries Dulong [441] and Petit [476] and by Mitscherlich [485]. These generalizations, combined with the law of combining volumes advanced by Gay-Lussac [420], gave him enough to go on. He was able to prepare a list of atomic weights that can be considered the first reasonably accurate one in history.

This table, published in 1828, is in fair agreement in all but two or three cases with the accepted values of today. Unfortunately, Berzelius did not appreciate the value of Avogadro's [412] hypothesis and he remained in some confusion as to the distinction between atoms and molecules. This spoiled some of the usefulness of his table and atomic weights did not come into their own until Cannizzaro [668] had had his say at the Congress of Karlsruhe in 1860, more than a decade after Berzelius' death.

Berzelius, while working with atomic weights, was made painfully aware of the tedium of forever speaking about the elements by their full names. It seemed clear to him that some sort of symbols were necessary to represent the elements, particularly in attempting to give the formulas of compounds. Dalton had used symbols composed of circles with different markings, but these were difficult to draw and to reproduce, and it was an unnecessary effort of memory to have to tie up a particular symbol with an element.

Berzelius suggested, therefore, in 1813, that the initial letter of the Latin name (or the initial letter plus a second letter from the body of the name) be used as symbol. Thus, oxygen could be O, nitrogen N, hydrogen H, carbon C, sulfur S, calcium Ca, chlorine Cl, copper (cuprum) Cu, gold (aurum) Au, and so on.

The makeup of a compound could be expressed by such letters, together with subscripts where more than one atom of a given variety was present in the molecule. Thus ammonia would be NH_3, calcium carbonate $CaCO_3$, and so on. Dalton opposed this new suggestion, preferring his own system of pictographs, but he stood virtually alone. Berzelius' system was eventually adopted and now forms the international, and indispensable, symbolic language of chemistry.

Meanwhile, Berzelius was also engaged in dealing with the new wonder of the age, electricity. Shortly after Volta [337] had demonstrated how to produce a continuous electric current by means of a battery, Berzelius began, in 1803, to experiment with the effects of electric currents upon solutions of chemicals. In this he had the collaboration of his good friend Hisinger [390]. Davy [421] was to produce the more startling results in this field, but Berzelius used his experiments as a basis for certain interesting theories. He held, for instance, that atoms formed stable combinations that moved as intact groupings from larger combination to larger combination during the course of a chemical reaction. These stable combinations he called radicals. This view has proved correct in many ways, although Berzelius' attempt to carry it over into organic chemistry went too far. Berzelius also developed electrical theories of molecular structure that have proved wrong but that maintained a hold on chemical thinking for decades because of Berzelius' great prestige. Yet it was in the attempt to explain this theory clearly that Berzelius experienced the final impetus to work out the chemical symbols of the elements—so perhaps it was all worth it.

With Hisinger, back in 1803, Berzelius had been among the first to recognize the new element cerium but was just beaten out by Klaproth [335]. Berzelius went on to discover other new elements: selenium in 1818, silicon in 1824, and thorium in 1829.

By 1830 Berzelius was the great chemical authority of the world. His textbook of chemistry, first published in 1803 and going through five editions before his death, was considered the last word. When he visited France he was presented to King Louis Philippe. In Germany, Goethe [349] was proud to have lunch with him.

Between 1821 and 1849 he published a yearly review of chemical progress in which he editorialized on the work of others; and when he condemned a new suggestion or experiment, it was as good as dead. This was not altogether good, for Berzelius grew conservative in his old age and held to his own ideas fiercely, all the more so when they were under attack. He was on the wrong side in almost all the controversies of his old age, though it wasn't till the old dictator was dead that the right side could finally establish itself. Berzelius' wide-ranging interests placed him in the midst of every branch of chemistry and many of the words that are most commonly in use now—catalysis, isomer, polymer, allotrope, halogen, protein—were introduced at his suggestion.

His later life was made miserable by sickness but in 1835, at the age of fifty-six, he finally married, taking to himself a fine-looking, twenty-four-year-old wife, with whom his last decade was spent in complete happiness. On his wedding day his gift from the Swedish king, Charles XIV, was that of being made a baron.

[426] **BELLINGSHAUSEN**, Fabian Gottlieb von (bel'lingz-how'zen) Russian explorer
Born: Arensburg on the island of Oesel, Russia (now Kingisepp, Sarema, Estonian SSR), August 30, 1779
Died: Kronstadt (now Kronshlot, USSR), January 25, 1852

Bellingshausen was born in the Baltic provinces where people of German descent were still the landowners, the Germans having conquered and dominated the region in the Middle Ages. His name, to the Russians, is Faddei Fadeevich Bellinsgauzen.

He entered the Russian navy in 1789 as a cadet, when he was only ten years old, and between 1803 and 1806 he participated in the first Russian cruise that circumnavigated the world.

In 1819 he was commissioned to explore the Antarctic and it is on those exploits that his fame rests. In 1820 he was one of three people (the other two being an American, Nathaniel B. Palmer, and an Englishman, Edward Bransfield) who first sighted the continent of Antarctica. Of the three, only Bellingshausen did so south of the Antarctic Circle. Bellingshausen also discovered the first islands south of the Antarctic Circle, naming them Peter I Island and Alexander I Island (now known as Alexander Island). The portion of the ocean he sailed through is called the Bellingshausen Sea in his honor.

With Bellingshausen's voyage, the world's ice-free ocean may be considered to have been completely explored. Only the frozen polar wastes and the continental interiors remained.

In later life, Bellingshausen became an admiral and was commander of the Kronstadt naval base at the time of his death.

[427] **DÖBEREINER,** Johann Wolfgang
(der'buh-ry-ner)
German chemist
Born: Hof, Bavaria, December 13, 1780
Died: Jena, Thuringia, March 24, 1849

Döbereiner was the son of a coachman and received very little formal education. He was apprenticed to an apothecary and read widely, however. He attended any learned lecture he could get to, and somehow managed to display sufficient ability to attract the attention of a nobleman, who used his influence to obtain a position for him in 1810 as professor of chemistry and physics at the University of Jena. He obtained a doctor's degree in that year as well. He held that position worthily for the rest of his life. He taught chemistry to Goethe [349]. A more material accomplishment was his discovery of furfural.

Of his two most important contributions, one involved platinum. In 1816 Davy [421] had noted that a heated plat-

inum or palladium wire seemed to bring about the oxidation of organic vapors mixed with air. In the 1820s Döbereiner found the effect was sharpened if the platinum was powdered (platinum sponge). He obtained supplies of that expensive and hard-to-get material through the generosity of the grand duke who sponsored the university.

Döbereiner went on to invent an automatic lighter called Döbereiner's lamp that was based on this principle. This was an arrangement whereby a jet of hydrogen could be played at will upon platinum sponge, at which point the hydrogen would catch fire at once. It didn't last long, for the platinum (too expensive to begin with) was quickly fouled by the impurities in the hydrogen and stopped working. Some money might have been made out of the device but Döbereiner refused to patent it saying he loved science more than he loved money.

The device, however, like the steam engine of Hero [60], foretold great things. The action of platinum was what Berzelius [425] was to name catalysis and during the course of the nineteenth century platinum was to become important in industrial chemistry for bringing about certain reactions easily and quickly. A new and better method for the production of the crucial chemical, sulfuric acid, based on platinum catalysis, was devised. (He also discovered the catalytic effect of manganese dioxide on the decomposition of potassium chlorate—a favorite demonstration of oxygen production in elementary chemistry courses.)

Another of Döbereiner's discoveries also seemed trivial to his contemporaries. It involved the fact that by the beginning of the nineteenth century the number of elements that had been discovered was over fifty. Furthermore, they were of all sorts and varieties, and chemists despaired of finding order among them.

In 1829 Döbereiner noted that the element bromine, discovered three years before by Balard [529], seemed just halfway in its properties between chlorine and iodine. Chlorine, bromine, and iodine, it seemed to him, possessed a smooth gradation of properties as far as color, atomic weight, reactivity, and many other matters were concerned. Even earlier he had found the same to be true of the elements calcium, strontium, and barium, and of sulfur, selenium, and tellurium. With the matter of bromine he thought himself ready to announce a law of triads.

Unfortunately few other clear-cut cases could be found among the list of elements and for a generation Döbereiner's triads were shrugged off as interesting coincidences that were of no real value, though Gmelin [457] was one of those impressed. Nevertheless they foreshadowed the periodic table of Mendeléev [705], a crucial chemical advance of the mid-nineteenth century which Döbereiner did not live to see.

[428] HARE, Robert
American chemist
Born: Philadelphia, Pennsylvania,
January 17, 1781
Died: Philadelphia, May 15, 1858

Hare's father was a brewer and much of Hare's life was spent in managing the brewery till it failed in 1815. His early education was achieved by reading at home. In his late teens he was able to attend lectures on chemistry. In the course of those lectures he grew interested in the possibility of attaining great heat by which to study certain chemical reactions. He thought of hydrogen as a possible fuel. Using materials borrowed from the brewery, he set up a keg as a two-compartment container of hydrogen and oxygen, worked up a sheet of tin into two tubes and, in 1801, prepared the first oxy-hydrogen blowpipe. He had grown friendly with Priestly [312] and it was to him that Hare gave the first demonstration of his device.

This blowpipe was the ancestor of our welding torches of today. With his blowpipe Hare was the first to be able to melt sizable quantities of platinum. Later it was discovered that a blowpipe flame played upon a block of calcium oxide (lime) produced a brilliant white light. This was used to illuminate theater stages and we still speak of someone who faces the glare of publicity as being in the limelight.

In 1809 Hare, with the backing of Silliman [424], tried to break away from the brewery and become a professor of chemistry at the University of Pennsylvania Medical School. Since he lacked a proper medical education he was only appointed professor of natural philosophy. The course was not a required one for medical students, so no one attended and Hare had to resign.

The War of 1812 ruined the brewery business and Hare spent some years in an unsuccessful attempt to recoup his fortunes. In 1818 he finally obtained the position he wanted at the medical school. He was a successful teacher and one of the few strictly American products who in those days could be considered within hailing distance of the great European chemists.

After his retirement he wrote a novel and grew interested in spiritualism. He invented a device by which he thought he could communicate with spirits and wrote a fat volume on the subject in 1854.

[429] LAËNNEC, Théophile René Hyacinthe (lah-en-nek')
French physician
Born: Quimper, Finistère,
February 17, 1781
Died: Kerbouarnec, Brittany,
August 13, 1826

Laënnec, the son of a lieutenant, was left motherless at an early age and was placed in the care of his uncle, a physician. He was introduced to medical work and earned his medical degree in 1804. His distinction as a physician was deservedly great in his own time but he is remembered today chiefly for an invention so simple that Hippocrates [22] might have thought of it as easily as Laënnec.

Physicians could gain important information by listening to the sound of the heart, but when Laënnec, in 1816, was faced with a plump young girl with a heart condition, he thought it would be indelicate (and ineffective) to try to hear the heart through the insulating breast tissue by direct application of the ear. So he rolled up a paper notebook into a cylinder, placed one end to the chest and the other to his ear. He was pleased to find that the heart sounds were actually louder. He constructed further cylinders out of wood and, in short, invented what he named the stethoscope ("to view the chest"), the instrument the general public most closely associates with the medical profession. He is supposed to have got the idea of the stethoscope by watching children listening to one end of a long stick that was being tapped at the other end.

In 1819 he published the details of his discovery and described his methods of diagnosis by listening to sounds ("auscultation"). Laënnec fought against the then prevalent medical practice of bleeding (usually by the application of leeches). This was so common that "leech" came to mean physician. The pernicious practice killed many in its time (including George Washington in 1799) and as the mid-nineteenth century approached, it faded.

Laënnec was appointed to a professorial post at the Collège de France in 1822. He did not die at so young an age as Bichat [400] but his death of tuberculosis (probably contracted from his patients) at forty-five may fairly be said to be too soon.

[430] **BRACONNOT,** Henri (bra-kuh-noh')
French naturalist
Born: Commercy, Meuse, May 29, 1781
Died: Nancy, January 13, 1855

Braconnot was the son of a lawyer who died when Henri was seven. The boy did not enjoy the school he was placed in, nor did he like his stepfather. At fourteen he was apprenticed to an apothecary and eventually he gained enough prominence as a self-taught naturalist to be recommended by Fourcroy [366] for the position of director of the Botanic Garden in Nancy. He was ap-

pointed to the job and with that, things improved for him.

He grew interested in the chemical constitution of plants. In 1819 he boiled various plant products such as sawdust, linen, and bark with acid and from the process obtained glucose, a simple sugar. This had previously been obtained by the boiling of starch with acid.

It was easy to decide that the molecule of starch was built up out of glucose units and that in many plants there must be some nonstarch material that was also built up out of glucose units, presumably in different fashion. It was the nonstarch material that Braconnot was breaking down. Some fifteen years later, this was isolated and studied by Payen [490], who named it cellulose.

Braconnot never married and, after the death of his stepfather, lived with his mother till she died in 1843. He was painfully shy and, mistrusting doctors (not without reason in those days), suffered agonies from untreated stomach cancer—which carried him off eventually.

[431] **STEPHENSON,** George
English inventor
Born: Wylam, Northumberland, June 9, 1781
Died: near Chesterfield, Derbyshire, August 12, 1848

Born in humble circumstances Stephenson nevertheless had the advantage of a father who was fireman for a steam engine that was used to pump water at a coal mine. At the age of fourteen he was helping his father and by seventeen he was going it alone. This exposed him to mechanical contrivances and he was fascinated. However, he so completely lacked an education that he had to attend a night school in his late teens to learn to read in order to study the work of Watt [316] and to read the news reports of the Napoleonic Wars. Then, he was called up to the army but he hired a substitute to report for him. This was legal at that time but it consumed his savings and kept him from emigrating to the United States as, after the death of his wife and daughter in 1805, he had been planning to do. But he had a son, whom he sent to school. As the son studied, Stephenson did the homework along with the young man so that he, too, could get at least the beginnings of an education.

By 1815 he had learned to manufacture engines and was ingenious enough to devise a miner's safety lamp at about the same time that Davy [421] was devising his. Stephenson received £1,000 for this feat.

Stephenson put his ingenuity to work to devise a traveling steam engine, one that could turn wheels that would carry itself and cargo overland, as Fulton [385] had demonstrated could be done on the water. In this he was not first in the field, for others, notably Trevithick [399], had preceded him, as Fitch [330] had preceded Fulton. It was Stephenson, however, whose devices caught on and became profitable and so it is he who is usually considered the inventor of the steam locomotive ("self-moving"). Stephenson was the first to make use of flanged wheels.

On September 27, 1825, one of his locomotives pulled passenger cars along rails, the first practical passenger railway ever built. Thirty-eight cars were drawn at speeds of twelve to sixteen miles an hour; and for the first time in the history of the world, land transportation at a rate faster than that of a galloping horse became possible.

By 1830 a railway using eight engines built by Stephenson and his co-workers was opened between Liverpool and Manchester. This was the beginning of a vast flowering of railways that put horse-drawn coaches out of business, restricted the use of canals, and opened the interiors of continents, making land areas as traversible in all directions as the sea itself.

Stephenson, having retired in 1840, lived to see the beginning of this revolution in transportation. However, a less spectacular advance in land transportation, pioneered by McAdam [369] and seemingly defeated at the time, was to come into its own a century later.

[432] **POISSON**, Simeon Denis, (pwah-sohn')
French mathematician
Born: Pithiviers, Loiret,
June 21, 1781
Died: Paris, April 25, 1840

Poisson, the son of a retired soldier, was marked for the medical profession by his father, but had very little aptitude for it, and he turned to mathematics instead, qualifying for the École Polytechnique in 1798. There he studied under Laplace [347] and Lagrange [317] and impressed both of them with his ability.

On his graduation in 1800, he was instantly offered a teaching position there, thanks to the strong backing of Laplace and by 1806 had replaced Fourier [393] in an important professorial position.

Poisson labored to refine the earlier work of Laplace and Lagrange in celestial mechanics, and the work of Fourier on heat. He also applied mathematics to the study of electricity and magnetism.

He is best known for his work on probability and on something called Poisson's distribution, which deals with events that are in themselves improbable but that take place because of the large number of chances for them to occur (like automobile deaths, for instance.) This is now central to any serious consideration of such events.

Like Laplace, Poisson adjusted himself without difficulty to political changes, and in 1837 was made a baron by Louis Philippe.

[433] **BREWSTER**, Sir David
Scottish physicist
Born: Jedburgh, Roxburghshire,
December 11, 1781
Died: Allerly, Roxburghshire,
February 10, 1868

Brewster, the son of a schoolmaster, was educated for the ministry but hated to preach and in his twenties gave up the calling for science and became editor of the Edinburgh Encyclopaedia.

In 1815 he found that a beam of light could be split into a reflected portion and a refracted portion, at right angles to each other, and that both would then be completely polarized. This is still called Brewster's law and earned him the Rumford medal in 1819. The law can be neatly explained by supposing light to consist of transverse waves. Neither the longitudinal wave theory nor the particle theory could explain it.

Nevertheless, Brewster remained an ardent adherent to the particle theory all his life, refusing to accept the ether. This seemed at the time to be an example of scientific ultraconservatism, but a half century after his death he was to be vindicated by Einstein [1064].

Brewster, by the way, invented the kaleidoscope in 1816, a scientific toy that has never ceased to amuse the young— and the old. He patented it and although thousands were sold in a few days, it was so easy to pirate, he earned virtually nothing from it. He also invented the stereoscope, through which one views two slightly different pictures, one with each eye, giving the illusion of three-dimensionality.

Brewster wrote a biography of Newton [231] and helped found the British Association for the Advancement of Science in 1831. He was knighted in 1832. At the age of 75, he married a second time and had a daughter some years later.

[434] **BIELA,** Wilhem von (bee′luh)
Austrian astronomer
Born: Rossla, March 19, 1782
Died: Venice, Italy (but then under Austria), February 18, 1856

Biela, born into the Bohemian aristocracy, served as an officer in the Austrian army. He achieved a captain's rank and was wounded at the battle of Leipzig in 1813, fighting against Napoleon. He retired from the army in 1846 with the rank of major.

While in the army, Biela studied astronomy and eventually amused himself by becoming a comet-hunter. This is a useful task for an amateur since professional astronomers, by and large, had other things to do.

As a comet-hunter Biela gained unexpected fame, for in 1826 he observed "Biela's comet," which had been observed before. His own name became attached, however, because he worked out its orbit, which had not been done before and which turned out to be a short one. The comet had a period of less than seven years, which made it the second short-period comet to have been discovered, the first having been pinned down the previous decade by Encke [475].

Biela then passes from scientific history, leaving his name, as did the contemporary English amateur astronomer Baily [406], firmly fixed to an astronomic phenomenon, without doing much more of note. However, Biela's comet did something more. It turned out to be mortal, something Kepler [169] had suspected of comets generally three centuries earlier, and it is that which gave Biela's name its immortality.

In 1846 Biela's comet split in two. When it showed up next time round in 1852, the two parts were widely separated. Before its next scheduled return, Biela himself died, which was perhaps just as well in one respect, for Biela's comet never returned. It was the first time a member of the solar system had died before the eyes of watching astronomers.

When Biela's comet should appear, a crowd of meteors often appears instead. These, first observed in 1872, are called the Bielids and they offered the first concrete evidence of a close connection between comets and meteors.

[435] **GUTHRIE,** Samuel
American chemist and physician
Born: Brimfield, Massachusetts, 1782
Died: Sackets Harbor, New York, October 19, 1848

Guthrie obtained his medical degree from the University of Pennsylvania and began practice in Sherburne, New York. He was one of the pioneers in the introduction of Jenner's [348] vaccination procedure into the United States.

He served as surgeon in the army during the War of 1812. One of his warlike inventions was percussion powder, which would explode on impact and without use of a flame.

More important he discovered chloroform in 1831. This compound was shortly to come into prominence in connection with anesthesia, one of the few advances in nineteenth-century science (as opposed to technology) that can be associated mainly with the United States.

[436] STURGEON, William
English physicist
Born: Whittington, Lancashire,
May 22, 1783
Died: Prestwich, Lancashire, December 4, 1850

Sturgeon was a shoemaker's apprentice in early life. He was educated in the army with the help of his officers, who apparently recognized his ability.

Sturgeon grew interested in electricity while observing a severe thunderstorm in Newfoundland, and after he returned to civilian life in 1820 he put Ampère's [407] notion of a solenoid into practice (in about 1823). His own addition, perhaps accidental to begin with, was to wrap the wire about an iron core, making eighteen turns or so. The wires themselves, when a current was running through them, became magnetic. Each coil reinforced all the rest, since they formed a set of parallel wires with the current running in the same direction through all. The magnetic force seemed to be concentrated in the iron core. Sturgeon varnished the core to insulate it and keep it from short-circuiting the wires, and used one that was bent in the shape of a horseshoe.

His device could lift nine pounds—twenty times its own weight—while the current was running. When the current was turned off the magnetic properties ceased. Sturgeon had invented the first electromagnet, a device soon to be greatly improved by Henry [503].

In later life Sturgeon invented a new and improved galvanometer and founded the first English journal to be devoted entirely to electricity. He died, however, as he had begun, in poverty.

[437] SERTÜRNER, Friedrich Wilhelm
Adam Ferdinand (sehr-tyoor'ner)
German chemist
Born: Neuhaus, Westphalia, June
19, 1783
Died: Hameln, Saxony, February
20, 1841

Sertürner, whose father was Austrian, was apprenticed to an apothecary in 1798. In 1809, at which time Westphalia was part of Napoleon's French Empire, Sertürner qualified to open his own pharmacy.

Sertürner was interested in opium and tried to isolate that portion of the juice that induced sleep. In doing so, he discovered morphine and laid the groundwork for alkaloid chemistry.

He was entirely self-taught and had some peculiar notions, a few mystical and useless, a few with some merit. He seems, in fact, to have been mentally disturbed in later years. However, his discovery of morphine was a remarkable job and, after some delay, its importance was recognized in his lifetime.

[438] MAGENDIE, François (ma-zhahn-
dee')
French physiologist
Born: Bordeaux, October 6, 1783
Died: Sannois, Seine-et-Oise, October 7, 1855

Magendie was the son of a surgeon of radical philosophic views, who was active among the French revolutionaries. In 1799, the young Magendie was apprenticed to a surgeon who was a friend of the elder Magendie. In 1803 Magendie entered his formal medical studies and obtained his M.D. at the University of Paris in 1808, studied anatomy at first, but then turned to physiology, where he was strongly antivitalist. Obsessed with a desire to experiment, he did so almost uncritically, to the extent that he gained a rather unpleasant reputation as a vivisector. However, he established experimental physiology and this, in the more analytical hands of his disciples, particularly in that of his most famous pupil, Claude Bernard [578], grew steadily in importance.

Magendie was particularly interested in the nervous system and in 1825 was the first to deal in detail with the cerebrospinal fluid. Working with puppies, he showed that the anterior nerve roots of the spinal cord were motor; that is, carried impulses to the muscles and led to motion. The posterior nerve roots were sensory; that is, carried impulses to the brain that were interpreted as sensation. This was confirmed by J. P. Müller [522].

In 1815 Magendie had served as chairman of a commission investigating whether a nourishing food could be made out of the gelatinous extract of meat. (France had just undergone twenty years of revolution and war, and the plight of the poor was bad.) It was found that no nourishing food could be formed in this manner. Magendie's experiments continued in this field for a quarter century after the commission had done its work, and he was able to show that life could not be sustained in the absence of nitrogen-containing foodstuffs (that is, protein) and that even some proteins, such as gelatin, were insufficient. Magendie thus laid the groundwork for the modern science of nutrition and, in particular, for the work on essential amino acids which culminated in the researches of Rose [1114] a century later. Despite Magendie's failure, the age of modern food technology was fast approaching, with Borden [524] an early exemplar.

Magendie also experimented with the action of various drugs on the human system. He introduced into medical practice the use of strychnine and morphine as well as compounds containing bromine and iodine. He may therefore be considered the founder of experimental pharmacology.

In 1830 he succeeded Laënnec [429] as professor of medicine at the Collège de France and established the first medical-school laboratory, something that rather disturbed his colleagues, who retained a bit of the old notion that it demeaned a physician to dissect with his

296

own hands. In 1837 he became president of the Academy of Sciences.

He was not always right. He maintained (wrongly) that cholera was not contagious, and he objected to the use of ether as an anesthetic.

And yet in 1839 he noted the suddenly heightened sensitivity to serum on a second injection, something Richet [809] was to bring out in the full light of day six decades later.

[439] **BESSEL,** Friedrich Wilhelm
German astronomer
Born: Minden, Prussia, July 22, 1784
Died: Königsberg, Prussia (now Kaliningrad, Soviet Union), March 17, 1846

Bessel, the son of a civil servant, began life as an accountant in Bremen but taught himself astronomy and mathematics and quickly did well at it. In 1804, at the age of twenty, Bessel recalculated the orbit of Halley's comet and sent the results to Olbers [372], who was sufficiently impressed to obtain a post at an observatory for the young man in 1806. (In later years, Olbers would say that his discovery of Bessel was his greatest astronomic achievement.) By 1810 Bessel had grown prominent enough to attract the attention of King Frederick William III of Prussia, who appointed him to superintend the construction of an observatory at Königsberg. He remained as director of that observatory until his death. In order to qualify for the post, by the way, and for the professorial dignity that went with it, Bessel needed a doctor's degree and he was awarded it for the astronomical work he had already done.

At the new observatory, Bessel worked industriously on the observations of James Bradley [258], in 1818 producing a new and excellent star catalogue containing fifty thousand stars—later outdone by his pupil Argelander [508]. Bessel introduced numerous refinements into astronomical calculations and worked out a method of analysis involving what are still called Bessel's functions, applicable to the solutions of many problems both in and out of astronomy.

His most renowned feat was that of being the first to achieve a three-century dream of astronomers, the determination of the parallax of a star. He fixed on the dim star 61 Cygni (discovered by Piazzi [341] a generation earlier), which he assumed to be unusually near the earth, despite its dimness, because of its rapid proper motion, the most rapid, in fact, then known. After careful observations of its position in comparison with two still fainter (and presumably quite distant) stars nearby, he was able to indicate that it had a definite parallax, though a very tiny one.

Judging by its parallax, 61 Cygni turned out to be some 35,000,000,000,000 miles away. Since light, even at its velocity of 186,282 miles a second, travels less than six trillion miles in a year, 61 Cygni can be said to be approximately six light-years (a term that thus entered astronomy) from the earth. The size of the universe was, in this way, greatly enlarged in the mind of man. Kepler [169], after all, had suspected the entire starry sphere to be perhaps 0.1 light-year away and Newton [231] had dared expand that figure to perhaps two light-years.

Bessel's announcement of his discovery in 1838 put the finishing touch to the Copernican theory, for the parallax of a star, like the aberration of light, discovered by Bradley, was visible evidence of earth's motion through space.

The discovery of parallax was "in the air." It often happens in science that a problem defeating all scientists for a long period of time is solved by several almost simultaneously. Within two years Henderson [505] and Struve [483] had independently measured the parallax of a star. By the mid-twentieth century, nearly six thousand stars had had their parallaxes determined and distances up to one hundred light-years had been directly measured in this manner.

Bessel used an instrument of his own design, a heliometer, in measuring the tiny displacements of 61 Cygni. He had Fraunhofer [450] make it for him. In 1844 he used the instrument for a discovery almost as striking. He noted, in 1834, that the stars Sirius and Procyon showed tiny displacements that were not parallactic in nature but were like tiny waves in their proper motion. This he attributed, in 1841, to their revolutions about unseen companions, a theory later proved correct by Clark [696].

Bessel's discovery marked the beginning of the shift of astronomers' attention from the solar system, which had been so neatly and (it almost appeared) so finally put into shape by Laplace [347], to the outer universe of the stars. However, this did not mean that the solar system was exhausted. Schwabe [466] proved this before Bessel's death by a remarkable discovery concerning the sun itself. Beer [499] even did yeoman work in so prosaic a job as mapping the moon.

And, indeed, Bessel's last few years were concerned with the solar system, for he took up the question of the anomalous motion of Uranus and the possibility that an undiscovered planet might exist beyond it. He calculated the masses of Jupiter and Saturn with greater precision than ever before and showed that the irregularities in the motion of Uranus could not be explained by the gravitational attractions of those two giant planets. He died of cancer, however, before he could carry the search farther and too soon to witness the success of Leverrier [564] and John C. Adams [615] in solving this problem.

[440] **PROUT,** William
English chemist and physiologist
Born: Horton, Gloucestershire, January 15, 1785
Died: London, April 9, 1850

Prout, the son of a farmer, was a practicing physician who had obtained his medical degree at Edinburgh in 1811. He interested himself in organic chemistry, that is, the chemistry of living or once-living tissue. This was part of the trend of the times. The first few decades of the nineteenth century saw an acceleration of the shift from the emphasis on the substances of the inorganic world.

which had occupied the attention of the medieval alchemists and of the early chemists. More and more chemists turned toward the more fragile and complex compounds associated with living organisms. Men like Pelletier [454], Guthrie [435], and Kidd [409] were discovering important organic substances at a pace that was to swell the organic sections of Gmelin's [457] textbook from one volume to six in a quarter century. After the mid-century mark, organic chemistry almost inundated inorganic.

Oddly enough, one of Prout's major discoveries was that what had been considered a strictly inorganic substance was actually intimately involved in the process of digestion. In 1824 he identified the acid in stomach secretions as hydrochloric acid. This was rather a stunner for the chemists of the time, for to have the powerful metal-corroding, flesh-burning hydrochloric acid in intimate contact with the delicate stomach lining seemed unbelievable. (The safety of the stomach lining is still not entirely explained, but the hydrochloric acid is there all right.)

Prout's interest in nutrition and digestion, particularly, made him one of the early leaders in the field, outshone perhaps only by Magendie [438]. It was Prout who in 1827 was the first to divide the components of foodstuffs into the familiar groups that today we call carbohydrates, fats, and proteins.

However, Prout's present fame is in neither medicine nor biochemistry. In 1815 he published an anonymous article in which he pointed out that the atomic weights of the elements were all integral multiples of that of hydrogen, which was the lightest known element. Thus, if hydrogen is given an atomic weight of 1, then (using modern values of atomic weights as examples) carbon has an atomic weight of 12, nitrogen of 14, oxygen of 16, sodium of 23, and so on. Prout therefore suggested that the atoms of all the elements were made up of conglomerates of varying numbers of hydrogen atoms. When his authorship became known, this suggestion was called Prout's hypothesis.

Prout's daring hypothesis (with Dalton's [389] atomic theory but a decade

old) spurred on the determination of accurate atomic weights and, before long, facts seemed to rule it out. Thus, the atomic weight of chlorine was definitely shown to be about 35½, that of magnesium about 24¼, and so on. Prout's hypothesis seemed dead, and for a century, if mentioned at all, it was merely as an idea that had misfired.

It was not until the twentieth century that new views of the atom, arising out of the Second Scientific Revolution of the 1890s, revitalized the notion. As a result of the work of Soddy [1052] and Aston [1051], a new form of Prout's hypothesis was established and Prout was found to be not wrong, but merely a century premature.

[441] DULONG, Pierre Louis (dyoo-lawng')
French chemist
Born: Rouen, Seine-Marne, February 12, 1785
Died: Paris, July 18, 1838

Dulong's parents were dead before he was five and he was brought up by an aunt. He practiced as a physician who conceived it his duty to hand out medicine without charge and to treat the poor without asking for payment. Naturally he was a failure as a physician.

He was an equally dedicated chemist, beginning as an assistant to Berthollet [346] and eventually impoverishing himself to buy equipment. In 1811 he had the bad fortune to discover nitrogen trichloride, an extremely touchy and powerful explosive, and during his investigations he lost an eye and nearly a hand in two explosions; nevertheless he continued his investigations of the compound. Davy [421] also worked on the substance, once he heard of its existence, also nearly killed himself, also continued working.

In 1820 Dulong became professor of physics at the École Polytechnique and finally director of the school in 1830.

His most important work was on heat, in collaboration with the physicist Petit [476]. In 1818 they showed that the specific heat of an element was inversely related to its atomic weight. Thus if the specific heat of a new element could be determined (which was easy) a rough idea was at once obtained of its atomic weight (which, to determine otherwise, might be difficult). This law of Dulong and Petit was very useful in determining atomic weights, and Berzelius [425] (under whom Dulong, as a young man, had studied), after early doubts, came round to using it. In 1826 Dulong was elected a foreign member of the Royal Society.

Dulong also collaborated with Thénard [416] in the study of catalysis and with Arago [446] in the study of high-pressure steam.

[442] **SEDGWICK,** Adam
English geologist
Born: Dent, Yorkshire, March 22, 1785
Died: Cambridge, January 27, 1873

Sedgwick, the son of a vicar, was involved in religion and science, donning the cloth and becoming a professor of geology at Cambridge in the same year, 1818. Two years with Werner [355] marked the beginning of his geologic career.

In his geologic investigations he studied ancient Welsh rocks, which, as it turned out, were of the type of the oldest fossil-bearing rocks. He gave the name Cambrian (from an ancient name for Wales) to the geologic era they represented. He studied and worked out the rocks of the Devonian era along with Murchison. Lyell [502], Murchison [477], Sedgwick, and some lesser personalities represent what is sometimes called the heroic age of geology. Certainly they hammered out modern geology among them.

An unfortunate disagreement over priority eventually broke up the fruitful partnership of Sedgwick and Murchison, however.

In 1851 Sedgwick was awarded the Wollaston medal, the award being presented by Lyell. Unlike Lyell, Sedgwick remained strongly opposed to Darwin's

[554] theory of evolution. This had its elements of irony, for the young Darwin had won his scientific spurs during a geologic field trip to North Wales along with Sedgwick, and Sedgwick had been the first to recognize the young man's genius.

[443] **AUDUBON,** John James (aw'doo-bon)
French-American ornithologist
Born: Les Cayes, Santo Domingo (now Haiti), April 26, 1785
Died: New York, New York, January 27, 1851

Audubon was the illegitimate son of a French sea captain and a servant girl who traveled aboard his ship. This captain, however, had fought at Yorktown in alliance with George Washington, and so Audubon began life as American as a foreigner could be.

Audubon's mother died soon after his birth and his father cared for him, adopted him officially in 1794 and took him to France. The captain's legal wife, herself childless, cared for him lovingly. In France young Audubon happened to live near a famous naturalist. His natural love of living things was there well fostered. He had some training in art, too (some say), under Jacques Louis David, one of the best-known painters in France though this tale seems doubtful.

At the age of eighteen he was sent to America to take charge of his father's American properties near Philadelphia and, incidentally, to avoid being drafted into Napoleon's armies. He remained in America for the rest of his life except for occasional trips abroad. While at Philadelphia, he banded some birds and found that they returned to the region in following years. This initiated the study of bird migrations.

Audubon was a failure in business because no necessity could prevent him from spending most of his time observing nature. In 1819 he was jailed for debt. This might seem to put a strain upon his marriage as well, but his marriage was successful.

In 1820, out of jail, Audubon traveled

west to the wilderness and began his life's work of painting birds, while his wife supported the family. In 1826 he had enough paintings to take to England in search of a publisher, and there his worth was recognized. By 1838 he had completed 435 paintings, among the most beautiful natural history studies ever done. The collection of colored plates of those paintings sold at $1,000 a set.

Audubon was one of the first American conservationists, and modern conservationists are organized into Audubon societies named in his honor. In 1900, when the Hall of Fame for Great Americans was established, he was one of those honored.

[444] **BEAUMONT,** William
(boh′mont)
American surgeon
Born: Lebanon, Connecticut, November 21, 1785
Died: St. Louis, Missouri, April 25, 1853

Beaumont, the son of a farmer, studied medicine in a rather haphazard way and gained a license in time to serve as an army surgeon in the War of 1812. He might have lived out his life in obscurity but for an unusual accident.

In 1819 he was appointed post surgeon at a frontier post in northern Michigan. While he was there, on June 6, 1822, a nineteen-year-old French-Canadian, Alexis St. Martin, was accidentally shot in the side. It was a shotgun blast at close range and he received a terrible wound.

Beaumont treated him with great care and skill and the young man recovered and enjoyed good health, even though he retained an opening (or "fistula") nearly an inch across which led into his stomach. In fact, the accident victim, who seemed at the point of death, lived to be eighty-two. Through this opening Beaumont, beginning in May 1825, was able to observe the changes in the stomach under different conditions and to extract samples of gastric juice, which he sent all over the world. (In the process, he so

bullied his subject that poor St. Martin eventually ran away from him.)

Beaumont published his careful, detailed studies in 1833, listing no fewer than 238 experiments, and this work not only served as a source for much early information on the process of digestion but also stirred up interest in the field and suggested to Bernard [578] the use of artificial fistulas in animals for further research.

Beaumont resigned from the army in 1840 and practiced medicine as a private citizen in St. Louis for the rest of his life.

[445] **LISTER,** Joseph Jackson
English optician
Born: London, January 11, 1786
Died: West Ham, Essex, October 24, 1869

J. J. Lister, a wine merchant, was the father of the more famous Joseph Lister [672]. The elder Lister was self-taught and devoted his efforts to the development of a proper lens for the microscope.

Dollond [273] had developed an achromatic lens for the telescope about seventy years earlier and one was needed desperately for the microscope. Without one, there was a limit to the clarity with which objects could be seen, for colored "ghosts" blurred everything. Finally, in 1830, Lister succeeded and only from that day can modern microscopy be said to date.

In 1834, for instance, Lister succeeded in seeing the true biconcave form of red blood corpuscles for the first time.

[446] **ARAGO,** Dominique François Jean (a-ra-goh′)
French physicist
Born: Estagel, Pyrénées-Orientales, February 26, 1786
Died: Paris, October 2, 1853

Arago, the son of a minor government official, contributed to half a dozen fields and the spread of his talents kept him from first-rank accomplishments in any one of them. He intended to enter the army but his excellence in science diverted him to a post at the Paris Observatory, which he obtained with the help of Laplace [347]. He was making accurate surveys in France and Spain with Biot [404] from 1806 on. Spain was then engaged in a bitter guerrilla war against Napoleon, so that these surveys involved hairbreadth escapes that would have read well in a thriller.

He became a professor at the École Polytechnique in 1809, succeeding Lalande [309]. As it happened, he was an excellent lecturer and a good observer, too. He discovered the solar chromosphere. He also began to study the physics of light. First he supported the particle theory but was converted to the wave theory and lost Biot's friendship.

He pointed out to Fresnel [455], who was working on the mathematics of wave theory—and whom he had joined —that Young [402] had performed important experiments in this connection. However, when Fresnel adopted Young's suggestion of transverse light waves, rather than longitudinal, Arago did not dare go along and withdrew.

When Arago heard of Oersted's [417] experiment he checked the magnetic properties of an electric current further. He ran a current through a copper wire and showed that it would attract unmagnetized iron filings as easily as a magnetized needle and that the current could make a magnet out of unmagnetized iron. This showed the wire became a true magnet when current flowed through it. Since it was copper that developed this magnetism, the experiment further showed that iron was not necessary to the development of the magnetic force. In 1825 Arago became the first Frenchman to receive the Royal Society's Copley medal.

Arago also expended his energies on politics. He was a fiery republican, participating in the revolutions of 1830 and 1848. In the Second Republic (1848–1852) he served in the cabinet and was instrumental in having slavery abolished in the French colonies. He promptly resigned his post in 1852 when

President Louis Napoleon made himself Emperor Napoleon III and demanded an oath of allegiance. However, the new emperor refused to accept his resignation and did not press for an oath.

[447] **AMICI,** Giovanni Battista
(ah-mee′chee)
Italian physicist
Born: Modena, March 23, 1786
Died: Florence, April 10, 1868

Amici, the son of a government official, graduated from the University of Bologna in 1807 and promptly took a position as a teacher of mathematics in a school in Modena. In 1831 he was invited to Florence by its grand duke to head the observatory and museum of natural history there.

Amici worked primarily in the field of scientific instrumentation, particularly that of the microscope. The achromatic microscope had finally come into use through the labors of many people, culminating in that of J. J. Lister [445], but Amici, in making further ingenious adjustments to the lens system improved the clarity and magnification of microscopes to the point where they could enlarge an object up to six thousand times. In 1840, he also invented the oil-immersion microscope in which the lowermost lens is immersed in a drop of oil thus removing some of the sources of imperfection in focusing.

He also built lenses, mirrors, and spectroscopic prisms for use in telescopes, and in each case made advances in the art.

[448] **CHEVREUL,** Michel Eugène
(sheh-vruhl′)
French chemist
Born: Angers, Maine-et-Loire,
August 31, 1786
Died: Paris, April 9, 1889

Chevreul was the son of a surgeon. His mighty life span of 103 years made it possible for him to watch a guillotining during the French Revolution when he was a seven-year-old, and the construction of the Eiffel Tower when he was a centenarian. (Both his father and mother had lived to be over ninety, which shows the value of carefully choosing one's parents.)

In 1803 he went to Paris to study under Vauquelin [379] and Fourcroy [366], and his first investigations were upon indigo. On Vauquelin's death, Chevreul succeeded to his post at the Jardin des Plantes. His chief fame, however, rests upon his studies of the chemical nature of fats, which branch of chemistry he initiated. In 1809 he was set to working on soap (which is ordinarily produced from fat). He treated this with hydrochloric acid and found that insoluble organic acids rose to the top of the watery solution. He isolated stearic acid, palmitic acid, and oleic acid, the three most common and important constituents of fats and oils. He also showed that spermaceti so treated did not behave similarly and was a wax rather than a fat.

In 1825 Chevreul, along with Gay-Lussac [420], took out a patent on the manufacture of candles from these fatty acids. In our own days, when candles are little more than curiosities, the importance of the Chevreul-Gay-Lussac advance is easy to miss. However, the fatty acid candles were harder than the old tallow candles, gave a brighter light, looked better, needed less care while burning, and didn't smell as bad. To the men of the mid-nineteenth century, the improvement was a major one and the next year Chevreul was elected to the Academy of Sciences.

Fats were not Chevreul's only concern, however. In 1815 he isolated sugar from the urine of a diabetic and showed that it was identical with grape sugar (glucose). This was the first step in the direction of recognizing diabetes as a disease of sugar metabolism, but a century remained before Banting [1152] and Best [1218] were to place the finishing touch on this line of research.

Chevreul was a pioneer in the analysis of organic substances, writing a book on the subject in 1824. Shortly after, he became director of dyeing at a famous tapestry establishment and grew interested

in the psychology of color. He tried to establish reasonable standards in the field and ended by strongly influencing the Impressionist school of painting.

In the 1850s he worked to expose fakery in spiritualism, which was then quite a popular fad, having ensnared Hare [428] in the United States, for instance.

He was a pioneer in gerontology, a study for which he was peculiarly qualified, and in his nineties studied the psychological effects of old age. His hundredth birthday was celebrated by the chemical world with terrific enthusiasm, including a torchlight parade through the streets of Paris; and he remained a lively participant in chemical affairs to the end, publishing his last scientific paper at the age of 102.

He was one of those fortunates who live into extreme old age without ever living long enough to retire, and his funeral at the Cathedral of Notre Dame was attended by thousands.

[449] CHARPENTIER, Johann von
(shahr-pahn-tyay')
German-Swiss geologist
Born: Freiberg, Saxony, December 7, 1786
Died: Bex, Vaud, Switzerland, September 12, 1855

Charpentier was the son of a mining engineer, and followed his father's profession. He entered the Mining Academy at Freiberg and studied under Werner [355]. He did excellent work in copper mines in the Pyrénées and salt mines in western Switzerland, but it was not in mining that he did his most significant service to science.

In 1818 a glacier dammed a lake, which eventually broke through and drowned many people. That turned his attention to glaciers. A friend of his, Venetz [453], believed that glaciers had at one time been more extensive than at present, but Charpentier at first refused to believe that. Upon studying the Alpine regions closely, however, he was astonished to find that the evidence seemed to support that seemingly wild notion.

He found that there were boulders strewn where the geologic evidence showed they had no business being, and it seemed possible they had been brought there by glaciers that now no longer existed.

He wasn't quite sure how the glaciers had formed in the first place; how they moved; why they disappeared. However, a younger naturalist, Louis Agassiz [551] visited Charpentier and was convinced by the latter's arguments against his initial skepticism, and it was he who carried the matter to a satisfactory conclusion.

[450] **FRAUNHOFER,** Joseph von (frown'hoh-fer)
German physicist and optician
Born: Straubing, Bavaria, March 6, 1787
Died: Munich, June 7, 1826

Fraunhofer, the eleventh and youngest child of a glazier, was apprenticed to an optician in Munich, after having been left an orphan at eleven. Three years later, the rickety tenement he lived in collapsed, and he was the only survivor.

The elector of Bavaria, Maximilian I, hearing of this, gave the now homeless orphan eighteen ducats out of pity. With this as capital, Fraunhofer launched himself on an optician's career. He taught himself doggedly and went on to make glassworking into a fine art by studying the manner in which the properties of glass varied with the method of preparation. He made improvements in various optical instruments and ground prisms of excellent quality. His instruments helped Bessel [439] and Struve [483] determine stellar parallax. He was visited by Tsar Alexander I and by Gauss [415] when they were in search of instruments.

He was interested in determining the refractive index of various types of glass since one of his specialties was the manufacture of achromatic lenses, in which, thanks to the pioneering work of Dollond [273], glasses of different refractive index could be combined to eliminate spectrum formation. Naturally the refractive indices of the glasses had to be known accurately if they were to be combined properly.

In testing prisms of his glass for the purpose, Fraunhofer found in 1814 that the solar spectrum was crossed by numerous dark lines. Even slight imperfections in the prism would have reduced the sharpness of the image sufficiently to fuzz out the lines, and that may perhaps explain the puzzling fact that Newton [231] had not observed them in his pioneering studies a century and a half before.

Wollaston [388], twelve years earlier, had observed such lines, but where Wollaston had observed only seven, Fraunhofer detected nearly six hundred (and modern physicists can find ten thousand).

Fraunhofer went on to do more than observe. He measured the position of the more prominent lines, which he indicated by the letters from A to K (letters by which they are still known), determining their wavelength, and showed that they always fell in the same portion of the spectrum, whether it was the direct light of the sun that he studied or the reflected light from moon and planets. Eventually he mapped the position of several hundreds of these lines, which are called Fraunhofer lines.

He even went so far as to place a prism at the focal point of a telescope in order to pass the light of a star through it and he observed that the dark lines in its spectrum did not have quite the pattern of those in sunlight. He had a great discovery in his grasp, but it eluded him. It eluded the world of science as well, for Fraunhofer's reports on the subject were ignored and it remained for Kirchhoff [648] a half century later to forge of those lines a mighty instrument for chemists, physicists, and astronomers.

Fraunhofer was the first to use gratings (closely spaced thin wires) to serve as a refracting device that would form a spectrum out of white light. Since his time, much more delicate gratings (of fine, parallel scratches on glass or metal) have virtually replaced the prism for spectral purposes.

Despite all his findings, scientific snobbery scorned him as a mere technician, and though he might attend scientific meetings he was not allowed to address them.

He never married and he died of tuberculosis before he was forty. On his tombstone is engraved *Approximavit sidera* ("He approached the stars"), and so he did, as Kirchhoff was to demonstrate by means even more remarkable than those of the great telescopes.

[451] **SEFSTRÖM,** Nils Gabriel (sehv'-strerm)
Swedish chemist
Born: Ilsbo, Hälsingland, June 2, 1787
Died: Stockholm, November 30, 1845

Sefström obtained his medical degree in 1813. Studying under Berzelius [425], he became fascinated by mineralogy, but first he practiced for four years as a physician. Then he accepted an appointment as professor of chemistry at a medical institute, and finally in 1820 he began to teach chemistry at a newly opened school of mines.

At the school of mines, he became interested in a process by which the manager of an iron mine insisted he could tell whether a batch of iron was brittle or not. The iron was treated with hydrochloric acid, and the appearance of a black powder implied brittleness.

Sefström investigated the process in 1831 and found that on some occasions iron was not brittle, though giving the same kind of powder. He examined and analyzed the powder and found a small quantity of metal that resembled uranium or chromium and yet seemed to be neither. Closer study proved it to be a new metal, which he named vanadium after a Norse goddess.

Eventually vanadium turned out to be identical to a metal reported by Del Rio [382] a generation earlier. Del Rio had called it erythronium, from the red color of some of its salts, but unfortunately he lacked confidence in his own discovery and let himself be talked out of considering it a new element.

[452] **PURKINJE,** Jan Evangelista (poor'kin-yay)
Czech physiologist
Born: Libochovice, Bohemia (now in Czechoslovakia), December 17, 1787
Died: Prague, July 28, 1869

In Purkinje's lifetime, what is now Czechoslovakia was a part of the Austrian Empire, with German the language of the ruling groups. Consequently, Purkinje is usually known by this German version of his name. In Czech, however, it is Jan Evangelista Purkyne.

Purkinje, the son of an estate manager, was quietly studying for the priesthood when he felt a call to medicine. He made the necessary educational switch and obtained his medical degree in 1819. His Czech nationality stood in his way, but Goethe [349] approved of Purkinje's thesis on vision, and he befriended him and used his influence to get him a post. Purkinje taught physiology at the University of Breslau in Germany from 1823 to 1850, and there, in 1839, he established the world's first independent department of physiology. He then taught at Charles University in Prague. He first described what is known as the Purkinje effect—that dim light appears bluer to the eye than it really is.

He specialized in microscopy, making many improvements in technique. For instance, he was one of the first to use a mechanical microtome to prepare thin tissue slices for the microscope, instead of a simple razor wielded by a simple hand. (He was the first to give college courses in microscopy, doing so in the 1830s.) He was very aware of the cellular makeup of skin and other animal organs (a type of makeup that some men at the time thought far more typical of plants than animals), but he stopped short of announcing a cell theory. That was left for Schleiden [538] and Schwann [563] a few years later.

In Czechoslovakia, Purkinje is known as a poet (he translated the works of Goethe and Friedrich von Schiller) and as a vigorous Czech nationalist. To the rest of the world, however, his greatest fame depends upon a single word, which he used partly because of his theological training. Adam, the first man, can be termed protoplast, for instance, because this comes from Greek words meaning "first formed" and in the Bible, Adam is described as just that.

Purkinje, thinking of this, no doubt, referred in 1839 to the living embryonic material in the egg as the protoplasm. As far as the eventual animal was concerned, this material was indeed the "first formed." The word was next used by Mohl [542] in a slightly different sense, but eventually it came to mean quite generally the living material within the cell.

[453] **VENETZ,** Ignatz (veh-nets')
      Swiss geologist
      Born: Visperterminen, Valais,
      March 21, 1788
      Died: Saxon-les-Bains, Valais,
      April 20, 1859

Venetz was the son of a poor carpenter, who was intended by his parents for the priesthood, but he evaded that and studied science and mathematics instead. He became chief engineer of Valais when Switzerland was part of the Napoleonic Empire, but he was unable to avert disaster when a glacier dammed a lake. He knew the glacier was bound to thaw and release the dammed water; but his effort to allow the water to leak away in controlled fashion failed, and the flood that followed inundated a valley and destroyed life and property.

It turned his attention to glaciers, and he found that typical striations left in rock by glaciers extended for many miles beyond the limits of glaciers. This made him think that glaciers had in the past covered far more territory than they did now. He published these thoughts of his in 1821, but they were generally ignored. However, his friend Charpentier [449] was convinced and made additional observations of his own (always careful to preserve Venetz's priority). These were also ignored but served to convert Agassiz [551].

[454] **PELLETIER,** Pierre Joseph (pel-tyay')
      French chemist
      Born: Paris, March 22, 1788
      Died: Paris, July 19, 1842

Pelletier, who came of a family of apothecaries, earned his doctorate at the Paris School of Pharmacy in 1812. In 1815 he was given a professorial appointment at the school and by 1832 was its assistant director.

Few can have had the opportunity to discover so many pharmaceutically interesting natural products.

In 1820 with another chemist, Caventou [493], he isolated such alkaloids as brucine, cinchonine, quinine, and strychnine. These had powerful effects on the animal body, and Magendie [438] introduced some of them into medical practice. This marked a shift in pharmacology from the use of infusions and extracts to that of known chemical entities, first of natural occurrence and later of synthetic ones (not necessarily known in nature).

Earlier, in 1817, Pelletier and Caventou had isolated a plant substance of no obvious value to medicine but of infinitely greater value in the scheme of life. This was a green compound, the compound in fact that makes plants green. They called it chlorophyll (from Greek words meaning "green leaf"). It supervised the chemical processes whereby green plants convert sunlight into chemical energy (photosynthesis), supporting thereby themselves and the entire animal kingdom, including man.

[455] **FRESNEL,** Augustin Jean (fray-nel')
      French physicist
      Born: Broglie, Eure, Normandy,
      May 10, 1788
      Died: Ville-d'Avray, near Paris,
      July 14, 1827

Fresnel was destined to complete Young's [402] work on the wave theory of light, but, unlike Young, Fresnel, the son of an architect, was the very reverse of an infant prodigy. He was eight before he could read. Nevertheless his intelligence shone out with the passing years and he became a civil engineer, working for the government for most of his professional life. There was a short break in 1814, when Fresnel opposed the return of Napoleon from exile in Elba, was taken prisoner, and so lost his post. However, Napoleon's return lasted only a hundred days and ended with Waterloo; it was then Fresnel's turn to return.

About 1814 Fresnel grew interested in the problem of light and independently conducted some of the experiments that Young had conducted a decade before. Arago [446] read Fresnel's reports and was converted to the wave theory. He called Fresnel's attention to Young's work and Fresnel's similar work was accelerated. The Frenchman began to construct a thorough mathematical basis for the wave theory.

Huygens [215] had constructed part of such a mathematical basis a century and a half before, but Fresnel went beyond him. For one thing Huygens and all the wave theorists after his time (except for Hooke [223], whose freewheeling conjectures hit the mark a number of times) had felt that light waves, if they existed, were longitudinal, with oscillations taking place along the line of propagation, as in sound waves. Young eventually suggested that light waves might be transverse, with oscillations at right angles to the line of propagation, as in water waves. Fresnel adopted the transverse wave view with alacrity and built up the necessary theoretical basis for it.

The greatest victory of the transverse wave theory was the explanation of the phenomenon of double refraction through Iceland spar, discovered by Bartholin [210]. Neither the particle theory nor the longitudinal wave theory could explain it. The transverse wave theory, however, could, and Fresnel showed that light could be refracted through two different angles because one ray would consist of waves oscillating in a particular plane, while the other ray consisted of waves oscillating in a plane perpendicular to the first plane. The two

rays would therefore be expected to have different properties under certain conditions and to be refracted differently by certain solids.

Ordinary light, according to Fresnel's views, consisted of waves oscillating equally in all possible planes at right angles to the line of propagation, but light with oscillations unequally distributed among the planes was polarized light, a rather poor term introduced by Malus [408]. When the oscillations were restricted to a single plane, as in the case of the light rays passing through Iceland spar, the light was said to be plane-polarized.

Fresnel used his new view of light to design lenses for lighthouses, and they were more efficient than the mirrors they replaced. An understanding of polarized light, moreover, came to have an important application to organic chemistry, through the work of Pasteur [642] a generation later.

Arago, after a period of collaboration with Fresnel, backed out nervously when the transverse waves were adopted by the latter. Later he came round, but Fresnel had published his work alone and got credit alone.

The difficulty that frightened Arago was this. If light consisted of waves, something must be waving. Early wave theorists postulated an "ether" filling space and all transparent substances. Light consisted of waves in this ether, which thus carried light even through an apparent vacuum and could be called a luminiferous ("light-carrying") ether. (The word "ether" is taken from Aristotle's [29] name for the fifth element that he considered to make up the heavens.)

If light waves were longitudinal the ether could be looked on as a very fine gaslike substance, indetectable to ordinary instruments, and there would have been no difficulty in accepting that, or at least no more difficulty than there was in accepting Dalton's [389] indetectable atoms. However, transverse waves can be transmitted through solids only, and if light waves were transverse, the ether would have to be viewed as a solid, and a very rigid one at that, considering the velocity of those waves. In that case how was it planets could move through the ether without any detectable interference? Men such as Brewster [433] refused to accept the wave theory if it meant accepting such an ether and it was only the work of Cauchy [463] that enabled others to swallow it at all.

But Fresnel's work was accepted by physicists generally and Melloni [504] carried it beyond the visible spectrum.

A half year before his death Fresnel received the Rumford medal from the Royal Society for his work.

[456] **PONCELET,** Jean Victor (pohns-lay′)
French mathematician
Born: Metz, Moselle, July 1, 1788
Died: Paris, December 23, 1867

Poncelet was of illegitimate birth, though he was later legitimized by his father, a well-to-do landowner and lawyer. He studied military engineering at the École Polytechnique, where he studied under Ampère [407] among others, graduating in 1810. He then joined the French army in 1812 as a lieutenant of engineers, just in time to take part in Napoleon's grand offensive into Russia and (as is the habit with offensives into Russia) the grim retreat that followed.

Poncelet was left for dead at the battle of Krasnoi on November 17, 1812, during the retreat. Brought back to life by those who noted he was not quite dead, he was taken to prison through a four-month march in the depth of winter to Saratov on the Volga River and kept there till June 1814. He returned to France only after Napoleon's fall, and he was then promoted to captain.

Poncelet spent the long months of imprisonment meditating on geometry. The fruits appeared in 1822 when he published a book on projective geometry. It was a new look at an old field (roughly, the study of shadows cast by geometric figures) and previously knotty problems now yielded easily.

Although Poncelet's views were at first vigorously opposed by Cauchy [463], his book is usually considered to be the foundation of modern geometry. Poncelet also brought back the abacus (a simple computing device consisting of counters strung on wires) from Russia. It had been used in the West in medieval times, but it had long since been entirely forgotten and was now treated as a great novelty. After the war he taught mathematics at Metz and at Paris, gaining professorial status in 1838.

[457] **GMELIN,** Leopold (guh-may′lin)
German chemist
Born: Göttingen, Hannover, August 2, 1788
Died: Heidelberg, Baden, April 13, 1853

Gmelin was a member of a dynasty of scientists. His father, uncle, and grandfather were all noted chemists, and his nephew was to be another. His great-uncle was J. G. Gmelin [280]. After spending a year with Vauquelin [379] in Paris, Gmelin received his doctorate at Göttingen in 1812 and the next year accepted a post on the faculty of Heidelberg and eventually became its first full professor of chemistry. He was the discoverer of potassium ferrocyanide in 1822 and of Gmelin's test for bile pigments. He studied the digestive juices of the stomach and pancreas.

His best-known accomplishment is the publication of an encyclopedic textbook, *Handbook of Chemistry,* that represented the first systematization of the field after the Lavoisier [334] revolution. The book demonstrates the growth of organic chemistry in the early nineteenth century. In the first edition (1817) there were three volumes, one of which, the smallest, was devoted to the substances of living or once-living tissue, substances to which Berzelius [425] had given the name organic a decade earlier. In 1843 Gmelin put out the fourth edition in nine volumes. Six of these nine volumes were devoted to organic substances. Gmelin was the first to use the terms "ester" and "ketone" as names for two common classes of organic compounds.

The organic portion was eventually

abandoned by Gmelin's successors in the sixth edition and that part of the task was then taken up by Beilstein [732].

[458] **BOUCHER DE CRÈVECOEUR DE PERTHES,** Jacques (boo-shay' duh krehv-keur' duh pehrt) French archaeologist
Born: Rethel, Ardennes, September 10, 1788
Died: Abbeville, Somme, August 5, 1868

Boucher was the son of a botanist who had influence with Napoleon. The young man was therefore employed by Napoleon on various diplomatic missions to Germany and Austria. After the fall of Napoleon and the return of the Bourbons, Boucher quietly withdrew to the provincial town of Abbeville, where, beginning in 1825, he served as controller of customs.

His interests were wide. Mainly he aspired to be a literary figure, but he also made a hobby of archaeology. In 1837 he dug up crude axes near Abbeville, which from their position in the strata he judged could only be many thousands of years old like those found half a century before by Frere [324]. Furthermore, they were clearly artifacts and could only have been made by man. The axes, however crude, were as much evidence of the existence of man, he said, as the discovery of an entire Louvre would have been. In 1846 he published a book on his findings, together with his most careful observations and conclusions.

The book created a furor. The views of Cuvier [396], though displaced in England by the work of Lyell [502], were still all-powerful in France. The followers of Cuvier were catastrophists and might admit that fossils in general were extremely ancient, but man himself, they held, could not be. Man was a creature of the most recent age, and to suppose him to be more than six thousand years old was to fly in the face of Cuvier and the Bible. Boucher found he could not get a hearing or persuade anyone to come and look for himself. What he had done was to find the first evidence of

Stone Age man, who, we now believe, came into existence a million years ago and more; but the discovery merely brought him a decade of frustration.

During the 1850s archaeologists began to turn up more ancient tools, and the evidence piled up despite all the Cuvierists could do. Several English scientists, including Lyell, had traveled to France and visited the spots where Boucher had found his axes. They declared themselves on his side and the Royal Society officially accepted the antiquity of man as established. Lyell was shortly to write a book on the subject and the way was clear for the discovery not only of ancient tools but also of fossils of ancient men of species and genera other than that of modern man. This line of research was to establish evolutionary theory at its most sensitive spot—the descent of man.

[459] **SABINE,** Sir Edward (say'bin)
British physicist
Born: Dublin, Ireland, October 14, 1788
Died: Richmond, Surrey, England, June 26, 1883

Sabine served as an artillery officer in the army, eventually reaching the rank of major-general. He went on Arctic expeditions in the years following the conclusion of the Napoleonic Wars and, it occurred to him that in traveling the world over, he could study earth as an astronomical body.

Thus, in 1821 and 1822 he sailed hither and yon in the Atlantic making measurements of the period of a pendulum swing in order to measure the pull of gravity and determine the exact shape of the earth.

He was a person who roused great enmities among other scientists through his political maneuverings. He was even accused by some of falsifying data, though he may only have been naïve in using numbers. However, he did make one important discovery. In 1852, he was able to demonstrate that the frequency of disturbances in earth's magnetic field paralleled the rise and fall of sunspot numbers on the sun. This was the first example of a phenomenon linking earth and sun by some means other than the sun's radiation of light and of its gravitational effect.

He was president of the Royal Society from 1861 to 1871 and was knighted in 1869.

[460] **THOMSEN,** Christian Jurgensen
Danish archaeologist
Born: Copenhagen, December 29, 1788
Died: Copenhagen, May 21, 1865

Thomsen was the son of a merchant and managed his father's business till 1840. His real interest, however, was in archaeology, and his position as curator of the Danish National Museum from 1816 on gave him scope for that activity.

He studied the characteristics of the tools from different periods of prehistory and, in 1834, on the basis of the predominant materials of which those tools were made, he divided early human history into the Stone Age, the Bronze Age, and the Iron Age. It is a division that is still used (with refinements) and is well known even to the average nonscientist.

This division agreed with the suggestion of Lucretius [53], which had been advanced on a far more intuitional basis.

[461] **OHM,** Georg Simon (ome)
German physicist
Born: Erlangen, Bavaria, March 16, 1789
Died: Munich, Bavaria, July 6, 1854

Ohm was the son of a self-taught master mechanic who was interested in science and who went to some pains to see that the youngster received a scientific education. Young Ohm entered the University of Erlangen and obtained his Ph.D. there in 1811. Science was not, however, to deal kindly with Ohm.

He taught in high schools, but his ambition was to achieve a university appointment. To do this he had to produce some important research work and he tackled the new field of current electricity that had been opened by Volta [337]. But he was poor and equipment was hard to get, so he made his own. In particular he drew his own wires, and the influence of his mechanic father stood him in good stead.

Ohm decided to apply to the flow of electricity some of the discoveries made by Fourier [393] concerning the flow of heat. Just as the rate at which heat flowed from point A to point B depended in part on the temperature difference between those two points and in part on the ease with which heat was conducted by the material between, so the rate of flow of electric current should depend on the difference in electrical potential between points A and B and on the electrical conductivity of the material between.

By working with wires of different thicknesses and lengths, he found the quantity of current transmitted was inversely proportional to the length and directly proportional to the cross-sectional area of the wire. He was in this way able to define the resistance of the wire and in 1827 to show that there was a simple relation between that resistance, the electric potential, and the amount of current carried. This came to be called Ohm's law and can be expressed: "The flow of current through a conductor is directly proportional to the potential difference and inversely proportional to the resistance." (Nearly half a century earlier Cavendish [307] had discovered this relationship, but he had never published.)

This was Ohm's only first-class contribution to science, but one first-class contribution is quite enough, and he deserved his university appointment. He did not get it, however. His work stirred up a good deal of opposition and resentment, apparently because Ohm tried to base his results on theory and some of his audience did not understand that good, thorough experimental work was also involved. In any case Ohm met with so much criticism that he was forced to resign even his high school position.

For six years he lived in poverty and bitter disappointment, while very slowly his work became known and appreciated outside Germany. He found himself, probably to his own surprise, coming to be held in honor. The Royal Society gave him its Copley medal in 1841 and made him a member in 1842. Finally, prophet Ohm, with some help from Ludwig I of Bavaria, came to be honored even in his own country and he was appointed to a professorship at the University of Munich in 1849 so that the last five years of his life were spent in the sun of ambition realized at last. What's more, a statue was raised to him in Munich after his death and a street was named in his honor (for dead men, as always, are easy to appreciate).

His name is further immortalized in the fact that the unit of resistance is the ohm. Thus, when a current of one ampere passes through a substance under a potential difference of one volt, that substance has a resistance of one ohm. Furthermore, the unit of conductance (which is the reciprocal of resistance) is the mho—Ohm's name spelled backward —a whimsical device introduced by Kelvin [652].

[462] **REDFIELD,** William C.
American meterologist
Born: Middletown, Connecticut,
March 26, 1789
Died: New York, New York,
February 12, 1857

Redfield was the son of a seafarer and was apprenticed to a saddlemaker in 1803. On a trip from Connecticut to Massachusetts soon after a hurricane had ripped through New England on September 3, 1821, he noticed the manner in which trees had fallen. From this, he deduced that the storm spiraled and that it was, in fact, what he called a gigantic "progressive whirlwind." He confirmed this in connection with violent storms he noted in New York.

In 1831 he published his evidence to the effect that storm winds whirl counterclockwise about a center that moves in the normal direction of the prevailing winds.

His frequent trips made him interested

in transportation; in steam engines and railroads. He laid out the routes of the Harlem and the Hartford-New Haven railroads, for instance. He helped found the American Association for the Advancement of Science and served as president at its first meeting in September 1848.

[463] **CAUCHY,** Augustin Louis, Baron
(koh-shee')
French mathematician
Born: Paris, August 21, 1789
Died: Sceaux, Seine,
May 23, 1857

Cauchy was the son of a government official who fled with his family to a small village to escape the Terror. There young Augustin first met Laplace [347] and Berthollet [346].

In 1805, Cauchy entered the École Polytechnique where Ampère [407] was one of his teachers. He intended to be a civil engineer and for a while served in Napoleon's army, but his health failed and his friends Lagrange [317] and Laplace persuaded him in 1813 to turn to the less physically demanding pursuit of pure mathematics.

In 1816, when Monge [340] was expelled from the Academy of Sciences, Cauchy replaced him.

In one important respect his mathematical work impinged upon physics. He was the first to attempt to work out a mathematical basis for the properties of ether, that solid-but-gas that let both light waves and planets pass through itself. His work made it possible for scientists to accept the ether without loss of respectability, but the theory was not entirely satisfactory. Nor were the later attempts to improve it by such men as Maxwell [692] thoroughly successful. In fact, no theory was ever successful, and the experiment of Michelson [835] and Morley [730], a generation after Cauchy's death, made matters worse. Physicists were for a century caught in a cruel dilemma between the apparent necessity of an ether to explain the nature of light and the apparent impossibility of an ether with such contradictory properties. It required the work of Einstein [1064] to set them free at last.

Cauchy's later life was beleaguered by political controversy for he was aggressively ultraconservative both in politics and in religion. He was an ardent adherent of the Bourbons. When Charles X (who made Cauchy a baron), the last French king of the Bourbon line, went into exile in 1830, Cauchy also went into exile in Italy to avoid swearing allegiance to the new king, Louis Philippe. He taught at the University of Turin while there.

Cauchy returned to France in 1838 but would not swear allegiance to Louis Napoleon when that nephew of the first Napoleon came to power in 1848 as president of the Second Republic and later made himself Emperor Napoleon III. He got away with it, as Arago [446] did, and indeed received a professional appointment at the Collège de France.

[464] **BOND,** William Cranch
American astronomer
Born: Portland, Maine, September 9, 1789
Died: Cambridge, Massachusetts, January 29, 1859

Bond, who came from a poor family, was self-educated. His early profession was that of a watchmaker, but a solar eclipse in 1806 fascinated him and astronomy came to be his hobby. He established a private observatory that was the best in the country. When he was fifty his worth was recognized by Harvard, which invited him to move his observatory to the university (where he was kindly allowed to serve as its first director without pay) and this he did. His son, G. P. Bond [660], succeeded him as director of the Harvard College Observatory after his death.

In 1850 the elder Bond photographed the bright star Vega—the first star to have its picture taken. In 1851 a photograph he took of the moon was a sensation at the Great Exhibition in London. In 1850 he had detected a third, dim ring within Saturn's two bright ones. (The existence of several rings about

Saturn, rather than one only, was explained by Kirkwood [586] during the course of the next decade.) This third ring was called the crape ring because of its dimness. Stars could be seen through it, indicating it was not solid, a situation Maxwell [692] had suggested was true for the bright rings as well, from purely theoretical considerations. Lassell [509] discovered the crape ring independently only a few days after Bond.

[465] **BRIGHT,** Richard
English physician
Born: Bristol, Gloucestershire, September 28, 1789
Died: London, December 16, 1858

Bright was born into a well-to-do banking family and had no economic insecurities. He received his medical degree from the University of Edinburgh in 1813, having interrupted his education in a carefree manner to go off on expeditions to Iceland as the naturalist of the party.

He was an important clinician and wrote an important textbook of medicine with Addison [482], in which is the first good account of appendicitis.

He was interested in a wide variety of diseases, studying them meticulously and making careful postmortem investigations. His name is particularly associated, however, with the clinical symptoms of a serious kidney disorder that is now called "Bright's disease." This he reported on in 1827.

[466] **SCHWABE,** Heinrich Samuel
(shvah'buh)
German astronomer
Born: Dessau, Anhalt, October 25, 1789
Died: Dessau, April 11, 1875

Schwabe was a pharmacist who attended lectures at the University of Berlin between 1810 and 1812, and these drew his interest to astronomy. He needed some phase of the science that would occupy him in the daytime since he worked by day, and had to sleep at

311

night. It occurred to him that he might find a new planet in the neighborhood of the sun, catching it as it passed before the sun's disc.

He began to watch the sun in 1825 with a small two-inch telescope and could not help but note the sunspots. After a while he forgot about the planet and started sketching the sunspots.

In 1829 he sold the family business so he could spend his full time on his hobby of sun-watching. For seventeen years, he sketched sunspots on every sunny day—an incredible monument to patience—and in the end he was rewarded. By 1843 he was able to announce that the sunspots waxed and waned in number according to a ten-year cycle (actually eleven, astronomers have since found).

The announcement was ignored until Humboldt [397] mentioned it in his book *Kosmos* in 1851. This discovery may be considered as initiating modern solar studies. Nor was it long before the work of men such as Lamont [546] showed that the sunspot cycle had its effect on the earth.

Despite his preoccupation Schwabe apparently had time to look elsewhere—occasionally, at least. In 1831 he drew a picture of Jupiter on which the "great red spot" is clearly shown for the first time.

[467] **DAGUERRE,** Louis Jacques
        Mandé (dah-gair')
        French artist and inventor
        Born: Cormeilles-en-Parisis,
        Seine-et-Oise, November 18, 1789
        Died: Petit-Brie-sur-Marne, near
        Paris, July 12, 1851

Daguerre's artistry was intimately concerned with the theater, for he specialized in painting scenic backdrops. To make the backdrops more entertaining, he created dioramas, consisting of optical effects in which real objects were made to blend in with a painted background and in which different scenes might be displayed successively—to give an effect, for instance, of changing seasons.

Optical effects have always interested

mankind. The *camera obscura* (Italian for "dark room") or pinhole camera, had been a much-used device. Sunlight entering such a room or chamber through a small opening could be made to fall on a screen in such a way as to present a sharp image of whatever was outside the room. It wasn't difficult to insert a lens in the pinhole in order to make possible a larger opening and more light without affecting the sharpness of the focus.

Daguerre grew interested in the possibility of making the image produced in the camera a permanent one. It was known that light could darken silver compounds, and in fact Ritter [413] had discovered ultraviolet light a quarter century earlier through that effect. In 1829 Daguerre went into partnership with Niepce [384], who had managed to produce images by the action of light some three years earlier but had failed to make the process really practical since exposures took hours. Daguerre carried on and began to use copper plates on which silver salts were deposited. Light was made to focus on that and an image was formed. The light portions of the image darkened the salts, while the shadowy portions left them unaffected. The unchanged salt was dissolved away by sodium thiosulfate (a process that had been suggested by John Herschel [479]) and a permanent image of sorts was left behind.

The new advance was reported to the Academy of Sciences in 1839 by Arago [446] and Daguerre was at once appointed an officer of the Legion of Honor.

The process was tedious (exposures still took twenty minutes) and the results were dim but the notion of a picture painted by sunlight and without the imperfections introduced by human fallibility caught on everywhere. The photograph produced was known as a daguerrotype, and in the United States, Morse [473] was one of the first to try his hand at the new art. By the 1840s the new technique was being used to record heavenly objects, and men such as Secchi [606] were to make it a recognized tool of astronomy.

[468] **MANTELL,** Gideon Algernon
(man-tel')
English geologist
Born: Lewes, Sussex, February 3,
1790
Died: London, November 10,
1852

Mantell, the son of a shoemaker, studied medicine, obtained his degree in 1811 and began a thriving practice in his hometown. His hobby, however, was geology and, little by little, that hobby ousted everything else—his medical practice, his home, his family.

In 1822 his wife noticed some teeth and scattered bones in a pile of stones by the road they were walking along. Mantell studied them and was puzzled by them until, in 1825, he came across teeth of the iguana (a kind of lizard). He then recognized that the fossil teeth he had found were just like those of the iguana, but larger. He named the animal to which the fossils belonged iguanodon ("iguana teeth").

In succeeding years, he found fossil bones of other large animals and described them accurately. It was Owen [539] who, in 1854, reconstructed the ancient animals (more imaginatively than accurately) and named them dinosaurs ("terrible lizards"). It turned out that Mantell had discovered no less than four of the broad divisions of these magnificent animals.

It was the dinosaurs that, more than anything else in the long past, caught the imagination of the world, convinced people that great animals had existed long before the dawn of humanity, and made them ready to accept the fact of evolution despite the thunders of the religious fundamentalists.

[469] **HALL,** Marshall
English physiologist
Born: Basford, Nottinghamshire,
February 18, 1790
Died: Brighton, August 11, 1857

Hall, the son of a cotton manufacturer, was apprenticed to an apothecary, went on to study medicine, and obtained his medical degree in 1812 from the

University of Edinburgh. After additional education on the Continent, he practiced in Nottingham, moving to London in 1826.

Beginning in 1832, Hall studied the quick involuntary motions that result when one touches something unexpectedly hot—the instant withdrawal that follows even before a conscious perception of heat—and other actions of that nature. This "reflex" action, as he termed it, he attributed, in the 1830s, to nerve impulses to and from the spinal cord.

In 1830 he denounced bloodletting as a medical cure-all and helped wipe out that most pernicious practice.

[470] **DANIELL,** John Frederic
English chemist
Born: London, March 12, 1790
Died: London, March 13, 1845

Daniell, the son of a lawyer, was educated privately and began his career by working in a relative's sugar-refining factory. His early researches were sufficiently impressive to procure him election to the Royal Society when only twenty-three. In 1831 he was appointed the first professor of chemistry at King's College in London.

He invented several scientific instruments, including (in 1820) a hygrometer for measuring humidity. He was interested in the physics of the atmosphere and greatly improved hothouse management by stressing the importance of moisture. In 1831, he devised a pyrometer for the measurement of heat.

He is best known, however, for his work in electrochemistry, his interest having been aroused by the work of his good friend Faraday [474]. Volta's [337] battery had the defect of rapid diminution in current. In 1830 Sturgeon [436] had amalgamated the zinc used (he alloyed it with mercury) and produced a battery of longer life. What was needed, however, was a battery yielding a constant current over a considerable length of time.

In 1836 Daniell succeeded, producing the Daniell cell, of copper and zinc. This was the first reliable source of electric current, though great work had been done by men such as Davy [421] with the rickety electrical sources of Volta's time. Daniell died while attending a meeting of the council of the Royal Society.

[471] MÖBIUS, August Ferdinand
(moi'bee-oos)
German mathematician
Born: Schulpforte, Saxony,
November 17, 1790
Died: Leipzig, Saxony, September 26, 1868

Möbius was the son of a dancing teacher and, through his mother, was a descendant of Martin Luther. He studied at the universities of Leipzig, Göttingen, and Halle, and was at first intent on entering law. Under the influence of Gauss [415], however, he turned to mathematics and astronomy. In 1816 he joined the faculty of the University of Leipzig and in 1844 he was appointed director of the Leipzig Observatory. He is more famous for his mathematical work.

In particular he is remembered for the Möbius strip, a paradoxical figure constructed by joining the two ends of a flexible strip after giving it a half twist. The resulting construction has but one edge and one side. This made Möbius, who presented the construction in 1865, one of the founders of topology, the branch of mathematics that deals with those properties of figures that are not altered by deformations without tearing.

[472] PEACOCK, George (pee'kok)
English mathematician
Born: Denton, Durham, April 9, 1791
Died: Ely, November 8, 1858

Peacock, the son of a curate, was educated at home. He entered Cambridge in 1809 and took second place in mathematics on his graduation. He obtained his master's degree in 1816.

His chief claim to fame is that he, along with Babbage [481] and John Herschel [479] finally broke the hold of

the nomenclature of Newton [231] on English mathematics. Because of a foolish nationalist distaste for the nomenclature of Leibniz [233], which was superior, English mathematics had lagged and decayed for over a century.

Peacock also wrote a text on algebra, published in 1830, which went partway at least toward the establishment of an abstract algebra, divorced from the common algebra that was the servant of arithmetical calculations.

[473] MORSE, Samuel Finley Breese
American artist and inventor
Born: Charlestown (now part of Boston), Massachusetts, April 27, 1791
Died: New York, New York, April 2, 1872

Morse, the son of a minister, graduated from Yale in 1810 and went to England to study art, rather against the wishes of his parents. He remained there during the War of 1812, a matter that in those easygoing days didn't seem to bother anyone. At home he achieved considerable fame as an artist, but little wealth. He was disappointed when Congress rejected his offer to beautify the Capitol.

He unsuccessfully entered politics as a member of the Native American party (a group of bigoted anti-Catholics and anti-immigrants).

During the 1830s he caught the fever of electrical experimentation from C. T. Jackson [543], a fellow passenger on an ocean voyage. Morse decided to build an electrical telegraph but found he could not, for he had little knowledge of electricity. He met Henry [503] by accident and Henry helped him without stint, answering all his questions. Morse then began to try to enlist support for the construction of a telegraph, and here, as a man of pertinacity and bulldog determination, he displayed his real talents.

He obtained a patent in 1840, then managed to persuade and bully a most reluctant Congress into appropriating $30,000 in 1843—by a margin of six votes—to build a telegraph line over the forty-mile stretch from Baltimore to Washington. It was built in 1844, and it worked. Morse's first message was "What hath God wrought?" sent in a code of dots and dashes that he had originated and that is still called the Morse code.

Morse went on to reveal a meanness of soul, for he never acknowledged Henry's help and, indeed, during prolonged litigation with Jackson over priority, tried to maintain that Henry had never helped him. Henry, testifying at the trial, was easily able to prove the contrary. Nevertheless, Morse grew rich and Henry did not.

During the Civil War, Morse, though a Northerner, sympathized with the South, thanks to his racist principles and his belief that Negro slavery was justified. However, he met with great fame, and many honors during his lifetime and when the Hall of Fame for Great Americans was first opened in 1900 on the campus of New York University, Morse was made a charter member. The authentically great American, Henry, was not elected until 1915.

[474] **FARADAY**, Michael
       English physicist and chemist
       Born: Newington, Surrey, September 22, 1791
       Died: Hampton Court, Middlesex (now part of Greater London), August 25, 1867

Faraday was one of the ten children of a blacksmith who moved with his brood to London. It is a rare laboring family with ten children that is affluent, so there was no question of an education beyond reading and writing for young Faraday and he was apprenticed to a bookbinder in 1805.

This, as it happened, was a stroke of luck, for he was exposed to books. Officially he was concerned only with the outside, but he could not help opening the books as well, working his way through the electrical articles in the Encyclopaedia Britannica, for instance, and reading Lavoisier's [334] great textbook of chemistry.

Faraday's second stroke of luck was that his employer was sympathetic to the young man's desire for learning and allowed him to read the books and to attend scientific lectures.

In 1812 a customer gave Faraday tickets to attend the lectures of Humphry Davy [421] at the Royal Institution. Young Faraday took careful notes, which he further elaborated with colored diagrams. He ended with 386 pages, which he bound in leather and sent to Banks [331], president of the Royal Society, in the hope of getting a job that would bring him into closer contact with science. Getting no answer he sent others to Davy himself, along with an application for a job as his assistant. Davy was enormously impressed, as much by the flattery implicit in the gesture as by the clear ability of the youngster. He did not oblige the young man at once but when he fired his assistant for brawling, he offered Faraday the job. In doing so, he followed the advice of a trustee of the Royal Institution who said, "Let him wash bottles. If he is any good, he will accept the work; if he refuses, he is not good for anything."

Faraday accepted the offer in 1813, at the age of twenty-two—at a salary smaller than the one he had been earning as a bookbinder—and washed bottles.

Almost at once Davy left for his grand tour of Europe and took Faraday with him as secretary and valet. This gave Mrs. Davy a chance to treat Faraday with scorn, as a servant; something Davy, to his discredit, did not prevent but which Faraday bore with humility. The trip also gave Faraday the chance to see Napoleon (now rapidly losing to the rest of Europe) at a distance, for what that was worth. More important, he met such men as Volta [337] and Vauquelin [379].

Faraday proved himself more than worthy of his master. He virtually lived in and for the laboratory, then and later, never using a collaborator or assistant. Little by little Davy came to realize that his protégé would eventually outshine himself and he grew bitter and resentful. This was particularly so after Faraday pointed out some flaws in Davy's invention, the miner's safety lamp, though he did so under oath in a court of law where equivocation was impossible—at least for a man like Faraday.

Faraday became director of the laboratory in 1825 and in 1833 the onetime bookbinder's apprentice became professor of chemistry at the Royal Institution.

He concentrated on his lone researches, refusing an ample income for continuing services as an expert witness in court, and turning down a call to the greater distractions of the University of London.

In chemistry Faraday made his first mark in 1823, when he devised methods for liquefying gases such as carbon dioxide, hydrogen sulfide, hydrogen bromide, and chlorine under pressure. He was the first to produce temperatures in the laboratory that were below the zero mark on the Fahrenheit [254] scale. He may thus be viewed as a pioneer in the modern branch of physics called cryogenics (the study of extreme cold). Here he gave Davy further cause for resentment, for in Faraday's reports on gas liquefaction, he did not (in Davy's opinion) give due credit to Davy's prior work in the field.

In 1825 occurred his greatest single contribution to organic chemistry. He discovered benzene, a compound that was to play a key role in Kekulé's [680] development of a means of representing molecular structure.

In addition Faraday carried on Davy's great work in electrochemistry. Davy had liberated a number of new metals by passing an electric current through molten compounds of those metals. Faraday named this process electrolysis. He named a compound or solution that could carry an electric current an electrolyte. The metal rods inserted into the melt or solution he called electrodes, the positive electrode being an anode, the negative one a cathode. All these names, suggested to him by the British scholar, Whewell [487], who also coined the word "scientist" in the 1840s, still exist unchanged and are used constantly in science.

In 1832 Faraday further reduced the matter of electrolysis to quantitative terms by announcing what are now called Faraday's laws of electrolysis. These are (in modern terminology):

1. The mass of substance liberated at an electrode during electrolysis is proportional to the quantity of electricity driven through the solution.

2. The mass liberated by a given quantity of electricity is proportional to the atomic weight of the element liberated and inversely proportional to the valence of the element liberated.

By valence is meant the combining power of an element. For instance, an atom of sodium or silver will each combine with only one atom of chlorine, whereas a copper atom will combine with two atoms of chlorine. Sodium and silver are therefore said to have a valence of one, while copper has a valence of two. Now, sodium has an atomic weight of 23, silver of 108, and copper of 64 (using whole numbers). The quantity of electricity that will liberate 23 grams of sodium will suffice to liberate 108 grams of silver. It will, however, liberate only 32 grams of copper (the atomic weight divided by the valence).

These laws, which established the intimate connection between electricity and chemistry, against diehard opposition by people such as Hare [428] and Fechner [520], are easily interpreted in atomic terms; but Faraday, oddly enough, was never an enthusiastic atomist and ignored atoms whenever possible. The laws also strongly favor the proposition that the electric current was composed of particles (something that Franklin [272] had suggested nearly a century earlier). This particle theory of electricity was not fully developed until the work of Arrhenius [894] a half century later.

Faraday's laws put electrochemistry on its modern basis. In his honor the quantity of electricity required to liberate 23 grams of sodium, or 108 grams of silver or 32 grams of copper (that is, to liberate an "equivalent weight"—a concept named and elaborated by Wollaston [388]—of an element), is called a faraday. Like Coulomb [318], then, Faraday lends his name to a unit measuring quantity of electricity. The two are linked by the fact that 96,500 coulombs make one faraday. (Also, the unit of electrostatic capacitance is the farad, in his honor.)

Faraday, like almost every contemporary scientist, was struck by the experiment of Oersted [417] showing that an electric current is capable of deflecting a magnetic needle. In 1821, the year after this announcement, Faraday constructed a device consisting of two vessels of mercury, each attached to a battery by a metal rod entering the mercury liquid from the bottom of each vessel. The upper levels of the mercury were bridged by a curved metal bar dipping into the mercury in both containers. Thus there was a completed circuit. One end of the curved bridge was fixed in the container, while to the lower rod a small movable magnet was attached—one that could rotate about the fixed upper rod. In the other container a fixed magnet extended upward into the mercury from the lower rod, while the bridge on that side ended in a hinged wire that dipped into the mercury and was free to rotate about the fixed magnet.

When Faraday turned on the current the movable wire began to pivot about the fixed magnet, while the movable magnet pivoted about the fixed wire. In this way Faraday successfully converted electrical and magnetic forces into continual mechanical movement.

(It was at this point, it would seem, that Davy's jealousy of Faraday broke into the open. He implied that Faraday had got his idea for the experiment from a conversation between himself and Wollaston that Faraday had overheard. Faraday protested that the conversation may have turned his attention in the direction of electrical experimentation but that his device was nothing like the one discussed. And, to be sure, experiments that Davy and Wollaston had conducted had failed. Moreover, Wollaston had expected the wire to rotate on an axis rather than to revolve about another wire. These days it is accepted that Faraday was correct and that his work was independent. Unlike Davy, Wollaston exhibited no resentment at all but was always friendly to Faraday.)

Although Faraday's whirling wires and magnets were interesting and novel, his simple electric motor was only a scientific toy, on a level with Hero's [60] steam engine. He was after much bigger game. Since Oersted had produced magnetic attraction out of an electric current, Faraday wanted to reverse matters and produce an electric current out of magnetic attraction.

To bring this about, he wound a coil of wire around one segment of an iron ring. This coil was attached to a battery. The circuit could be opened or closed by a key. If he closed the circuit a magnetic field would be set up in the coil as Ampère [407] had shown and it would be concentrated in the iron ring as Sturgeon [436] had shown.

Suppose, then, that a second coil is wrapped around another segment of the iron ring and connected to a galvanometer. The magnetic field created in the iron ring by the first coil might set up (by reverse action) a current in the second coil, and the galvanometer would indicate that induced current.

The experiment worked and Faraday had invented the first transformer, but it did not work in the manner Faraday had expected. There was no steady flow of electricity in the second coil to match the steady magnetic force set up in the iron ring. Instead, there was a momentary flash of current, marked by a jerk of the galvanometer's needle when he closed the circuit; and a second flash, in the opposite direction, when he broke the circuit. (Ten years before, Ampère had observed the same fact, but it did not fit his theories and he dismissed it.)

To Faraday, this observation required explanation. Because Faraday was uneducated, he was completely innocent of mathematics (perhaps the greatest scientist in history of whom this was true). He made up for this through his intuitive ability to pictorialize, an ability perhaps unequaled in scientific history.

He had dropped iron filings on a paper under which a magnet was located and noticed the regular patterns they took up when the paper was tapped. (So had Peter Peregrinus [104] six centuries before.) Faraday was also aware of Ampère's demonstration that a magnetic force circled a wire carrying a current.

He began to visualize the magnetic force, then, as stretching out in all directions from the electric current that served as its starting point. It filled space as a kind of magnetic field. Lines could be drawn through that field representing all points where the strength of the magnetic force was equal. These Faraday called lines of force, and it was along these lines, it seemed to him, that the iron filings aligned themselves, thus making them "visible." It was possible to work out the form of the lines of force for wires, for bar magnets, for horseshoe magnets, even for globular magnets such as the earth. This was the beginning of a picture of the universe as consisting of fields of various types, one that was more subtle, flexible, and useful than the purely mechanical picture of Galileo [166] and Newton [231]. The field universe was to be recognized with Maxwell [692] a half century later and with Einstein [1064], after an interval of another half century.

Faraday's pictorial and nonmathematical imagination visualized these lines of force as real lines. When a circuit was closed and electricity was set to flowing, the lines sprang outward into space. When the circuit was broken they collapsed inward again. Faraday decided then that an electric current was induced in a wire only when lines of force cut across it. In his transformer, when the current started in the first coil of wire, the expanding lines of force cut across the wire of the second coil and accounted for the short burst of electric current. Once the original current was established, the lines of force no longer moved and there was no current in the second coil. When the circuit was broken, the collapsing lines of force cut across the second coil in the opposite direction and a burst of electric current resulted again, but in the direction opposite to that of the first.

Faraday, at the time, was giving enormously popular lectures in science for the general public, quite after the fashion of his old master, Davy. Indeed, after the popular Davy had resigned, the

Royal Institution nearly went bankrupt, as before Davy's time. It was only with Faraday's lectures that the Institution recovered.

Faraday's new career began when he was forced to give an impromptu lecture after a regularly scheduled lecturer, Wheatstone [526], was unable to appear. Faraday proved so excellent a lecturer that the novelist Charles Dickens, no mean lecturer himself, was among Faraday's admirers, while Prince Albert, the husband of Queen Victoria, and Prince Edward, her son (and later Edward VII), attended them too. Faraday always included special Christmas lectures for youngsters on his schedule and one of these, *The Chemical History of a Candle*, in book form proved an imperishable classic. (It was the first complete book to be converted into "basic English.")

In any case, it was during one of these lectures that Faraday demonstrated the theory involving the lines of force both to himself and to the audiences by inserting a magnet into a coil of wire attached to a galvanometer. While the magnet was being inserted or removed, current flowed through the wire. If the magnet was held stationary and the coil moved over it one way or the other, there was current in the wire. In either case the magnetic lines of force about the magnet were cut by the wire. If the magnet and coil were both held motionless, whether the magnet was within the coil or not, there was no current.

Faraday had thus discovered electrical induction, a discovery made independently and at about the same time by the American physicist Henry [503]. It was to lead to great things, but this was not at once apparent.

Faraday was an inspiring teacher who caught the interest of men such as Daniell [470] and Perkin [734]. His theory of the lines of force (which he published in 1844) was not taken too seriously at first. However, when Maxwell came to tackle the matter of electromagnetism with precise mathematical tools, he was to end with the same picture, mathematically phrased, that Faraday had drawn in simple words.

Once Faraday had demonstrated that electricity could be induced by magnetism, the next step was to do so continuously and not in short spurts. He accomplished this by adapting in reverse an experiment first described by Arago [446]. Arago had shown that a rotating copper wheel could deflect a magnet suspended over it because (Faraday now saw) the wheel was cutting through the magnetic lines of force so that electric currents were being set up in it, these in turn setting up a magnetic field that deflected the magnet. But Faraday did not want an electric current setting up a magnetic field; he wanted a magnetic field setting up an electric current.

Faraday therefore turned a copper wheel in such a fashion that its edge passed between the poles of a permanent magnet. An electric current was set up in the copper disc then, and it continued to flow as long as the wheel continued to turn. That current could be led off and put to work and Faraday had invented the first electric generator. This was accomplished in 1831 and was probably the greatest single electrical discovery in history.

It was only necessary to set a steam engine or water power to turning the copper disc and the energy of burning fuel or of falling water could be converted into electricity. Until Faraday's time the only source of electric current was the chemical battery, which was expensive and small-scale. Now there was for the first time the possibility of a large and cheap supply of electric current. It took a half century and more for subsidiary inventions to make this entirely practical and the generators that eventually did the work look nothing at all like Faraday's turning wheel. But the line of descent is clear and the results of the final development we all know.

In later years Faraday made more discoveries in connection with electromagnetism and its interaction with light.

In 1839, however, he suffered a mental breakdown and, like Newton, he was never quite the same again. Failing memory drove him out of the laboratory (he refused to work when he could no longer trust himself to work capably, nor would he use an assistant) and saddened his last years. It is possible that this is another case, like those of Scheele [329] and Davy, of a chemist suffering from chronic, low-grade poisoning.

Faraday was an extremely religious man who, after his marriage in 1821, joined his wife's church, the splinter sect of Sandemanians, a sect that no longer exists. This sect eschewed worldly vanity, and Faraday accepted the dozens and dozens of honors, medals, degrees, and miscellaneous embroidery with polite distaste. When Lord Melbourne offered him a pension in what seemed an offensively patronizing fashion, Faraday quietly left and would not return until Melbourne apologized. It was not his own honor for which Faraday was concerned (he explained) but that of science.

The only honor he valued was membership in the Royal Society, to which he had been elected in 1824 against Davy's embittered opposition. Davy, in fact, cast the only negative vote.

Faraday strongly favored a more important role for science in education, but he could not bring his gentle soul into alliance with the more radical Babbage [481] in the latter's violent attacks on the Royal Society and on Great Britain's scientific policy generally.

When, in 1857, Faraday was eventually offered the presidency of the Society by Tyndall [626], he declined, and he also declined an offer of knighthood. He was intent on being plain Michael Faraday and on loving only science. He turned down chances for more money even when the duke of Wellington himself suggested he engage in more practical—and profitable—labors.

In 1844 Faraday was invited to dinner with Queen Victoria on a Sunday, when he was due at the small church he attended. After an agonizing period of uncertainty he decided it was necessary for him to obey the queen, but the inflexible congregation excommunicated him and he could not be reinstated until he had undergone considerable penance.

His religious beliefs enabled him, however, to solve without fear or uncertainty a problem that agonizes many scientists of our day—the conflict between the demands of country and of human idealism. During the Crimean War of the 1850s (in which Great Britain was at war with Russia) Faraday was asked by the British government if there was any possibility of preparing quantities of poison gas for use on the battlefield and if he would head a project to perform the task, supposing it to be feasible. Faraday answered at once and with finality that the project was certainly feasible, but that he himself would have absolutely nothing to do with it.

He kept a meticulous day-by-day record of his forty-two years of scientific labors (1820–62). This was published in 1932 in seven volumes.

Faraday began to lose his ability to think clearly after 1855, perhaps because (some think) of chronic mercury poisoning. He retired, uncomplainingly, from his work and waited patiently for death.

He requested during life that he be buried under "a gravestone of the most ordinary kind" and that only a few relatives and friends attend his funeral, and this was done. His true memorial, of course, is our electrified world of today.

[475] **ENCKE,** Johann Franz (enk'uh)
German astronomer
Born: Hamburg, September 23, 1791
Died: Spandau (near Berlin), August 26, 1865

Encke, the son of a minister, entered Göttingen in 1811 and studied under Gauss [415], then served as an artillery officer at the tail end of the Napoleonic Wars.

Back in civilian life he took up astronomy and in 1819 computed the orbit of a comet that had been observed the year before by Pons [376]. The comet proved to have a period of only three and a third years. Encke's comet, as it has been called ever since, was the second comet whose return was predicted, the first being Halley's [238]. Encke's comet was the first short-period comet to be discovered, and no comet has ever been found with a shorter period. In 1835 Encke's comet passed close enough to Mercury

to allow the mass of that planet to be determined for the first time—from the effect of its gravity upon the comet's orbit.

In later life Encke calculated the distance of the sun (from data on past transits of Venus) to be 95,300,000 miles. This is over 2 percent too high a figure, but it was the most accurate value obtained at that time.

In 1825 Encke was made director of the Berlin Observatory, which in ten years he transferred to a larger, magnificently equipped building.

[476] **PETIT,** Alexis Thérèse (puh-tee')
French physicist
Born: Vesoul, Haute-Saône, October 2, 1791
Died: Paris, June 21, 1820

Petit obtained his doctorate in 1811, then taught at École Polytechnique. Although he did much work on heat, Petit is remembered almost exclusively for the work he did with Dulong [441] and for the law of Dulong and Petit. He was also the brother-in-law of Arago [446].

He was another of the scientists of the period to be victimized by that killer of young adults, tuberculosis.

[477] **MURCHISON,** Sir Roderick Impey (mur'ki-son)
Scottish geologist
Born: Tarradale, Ross-shire, February 19, 1792
Died: London, October 22, 1871

Murchison, the descendant of a landowning family, was left fatherless at four. He had a military education and took part in the campaign in Spain against the forces of Napoleon. Afterward, as befitted a retired officer, he became a renowned fox hunter. He was lured by Davy [421] into attending scientific lectures, became enamored of geology and sold his hunting dogs. He began as a neptunist but was soon converted to vulcanism.

He explored Great Britain and then with Lyell [502] and Sedgwick [442] extended his curiosity to the rocky features of much of western Europe. He studied the rocks of what he called the Silurian era (named for an old Celtic tribe in Wales that had lived in the area where Murchison found the rocks) and for this received the Copley medal of the Royal Society. With Sedgwick he next studied rocks of the Devonian era (from Devon, in southwest England).

In the 1840s he headed a geologic survey to the Ural Mountains in Russia. This resulted in the naming of the Permian era, from the city of Perm in the Urals. In 1846 he was knighted.

[478] **BAER**, Karl Ernst von (bare)
German-Russian embryologist
Born: Piep, Estonia, February 28, 1792
Died: Dorpat, Estonia (now Tartu, Estonian SSR), November 28, 1876

As was usually the case with nineteenth-century Russians, the need for higher education made a trip to Germany necessary. This was easier for Baer since he was of German descent, as were most of the landowners in the Baltic provinces of Russia in those days. He obtained a medical degree at Dorpat in 1814, but then obtained further training in Berlin and Vienna. After achieving that education he eventually returned to Russia. His greatest discoveries, however, took place in Germany, where he served as a professor at the University of Königsberg from 1817 to 1834.

In 1827 he published his findings in connection with the mammalian egg. The mammalian ovary contains certain structures called follicles, which had been discovered by Graaf [228] a century and a half before. Since that time the follicle had been taken to be the mammalian egg. Baer opened the follicle of a dog and examined a small yellow point within. It was this much smaller structure, seen only in a microscope, that was the mammalian egg—and so it was finally clear that mammalian development (including human development, of course) was not fundamentally different from that of other animals.

Between 1828 and 1837 he published a two-volume textbook on embryology, which may be considered, along with the work of Pander [489], as founding the subject. Building on Pander's observations, Baer pointed out that the developing egg forms several layers of tissue, each of which is undifferentiated but out of which various specialized organs develop, a given set of organs from a given layer. These he called germ layers— germ being a general term for any small object that contains the seed of life. (Nowadays there is too great a tendency to think that by germ is meant only bacterium.) Baer thought there were four such germ layers, but later Remak [591] pointed out that the two middle layers really form a single structure, so that a total of three layers exist, and that has remained the view ever since.

In his doctrine of germ layers, Baer was taking up the cause of epigenesis, which had first been enunciated by Wolff [313] three quarters of a century before. With Baer the victory of that doctrine was complete.

Baer's studies of embryos also supplied new ammunition for those biologists who believed in the evolutionary development of life. Baer pointed out that the early stages of the development of vertebrate embryos were quite similar even among creatures that in the end were quite dissimilar. Small structures in different embryos, scarcely distinguishable from each other at first, might develop into a wing in one case, an arm in another, a paw in a third and a flipper in still a fourth. Baer believed that relationships among animals could be deduced more properly by comparing embryos than by comparing adult structure (so that he is also the founder of comparative embryology).

Baer pointed this up dramatically when he was able to show that the early vertebrate embryo possessed a notochord for a short while. The notochord is a stiff rod running the length of the back, and there are very primitive fishlike creatures that possess such a structure throughout life. In vertebrates this is quickly replaced by a spinal cord, but the temporary existence of the notochord in the vertebrate embryos shows their relationship to the primitive prevertebrate creatures. Nowadays the vertebrates are lumped together with all creatures that possess a notochord at some stage in their life cycle and the whole group makes up the phylum Chordata.

Baer resisted any suggestion that the development of the embryo followed the line of evolutionary development of the species, a doctrine later made famous by Haeckel [707]. Instead he followed the evolutionary theories of the nature-philosophers and thought that creatures evolved from some primitive archetype, each following its own course of development. Darwin [554] made use of Baer's discoveries to bolster his own theory of evolution, but Baer in his old age remained adamant against Darwinism.

[479] **HERSCHEL,** Sir John Frederick William
English astronomer
Born: Slough, Buckinghamshire, March 7, 1792
Died: Collingwood, Hawkhurst, Kent, May 11, 1871

The only son of William Herschel [321], the greatest astronomer of his time, John Herschel, perhaps naturally, moved into other fields at first.

During his stay at Cambridge, Herschel was chiefly interested in mathematics, finishing first in his class and joining Babbage [481] and Peacock [472] in a successful attempt to revitalize mathematics. Yet mathematics did not serve him as a profession. After graduating from Cambridge in 1813, he tried chemistry, then law. It did not work. In 1816, with the encouragement of Wollaston [388], John turned to his father's profession at last and became an astronomer.

After his father's death, Herschel devoted years to the rounding out of the older man's work, using a telescope he and his father had constructed. He catalogued the double stars and nebulae observed by the elder Herschel and discovered some himself. In 1831 he was knighted. In 1833 Herschel decided to do for the southern hemisphere what his father had done for the northern.

He went south in January 1834, and for four years his base of operations was at Cape Colony, South Africa. There he completed the work first begun by Halley [238] and published the results in a great treatise in 1847. While at it he was the first to measure the brightness of stars with real precision.

He discovered that the Magellanic Clouds were thick clusters of stars, as Galileo [166] had shown the Milky Way itself to be, two and a quarter centuries before. His work at the Cape of Good Hope, by the way, inspired a famous series of hoax articles in the New York *Sun* to the effect that living beings were detected on the moon.

On Herschel's return to England he was made a baronet by Queen Victoria at her coronation in 1837. Herschel was profoundly interested in the new technique of photography as developed by Talbot [511] and was one of the first to attempt to apply it to astronomy. He introduced the use of sodium thiosulfate ("hypo") to dissolve silver salts and he first made use of the terms "photographic negative" and "photographic positive."

In 1848 he was elected president of the Royal Astronomic Society and in 1850, like Newton [231] before him, he was appointed master of the mint. He was not happy at the job and in 1854 (again like Newton) suffered a nervous breakdown.

His old age was spent in writing and his text *Outlines of Astronomy,* which first appeared in 1849 and which reached its twelfth edition shortly after his death, was enormously successful. He also labored in the humanities, producing a verse translation of the *Iliad,* for instance. He was buried in Westminster Abbey, close to the tomb of Newton.

[480] **CORIOLIS,** Gustave Gaspard de (koh-ryoh-lees')
French physicist
Born: Paris, May 21, 1792
Died: Paris, September 19, 1843

Coriolis, a professor of mechanics at the École Polytechnique was limited in his productivity by chronic ill health. Even so, he left his name indelibly marked in physics.

In 1835 he took up the matter of motion on a spinning surface, both mathematically and experimentally. The earth rotates once in twenty-four hours. A point at the surface on the equator must travel 25,000 miles in that time, hence move eastward at about a thousand miles an hour. A point on the surface at the latitude of New York need travel only 19,000 miles during a day, and move eastward at a speed of only some eight hundred miles an hour. Air moving from the equator northward retains its faster velocity and therefore moves eastward in comparison with the more slowly moving surface under it. The same is true of water currents.

The forces that seem to push moving air and water eastward when moving away from the equator and westward when moving toward the equator are therefore called Coriolis forces. (The word is given the Anglicized pronunciation of *kawr'ee-oh'lis*.) It is these forces that set up the whirling motions of hurricanes and tornadoes. In technology they must be taken into account in artillery fire, satellite launchings, and so on.

Coriolis was the first to give the exact modern definitions to kinetic energy and work in a textbook published in 1829. The kinetic energy of an object he defined as half its mass times the square of its velocity, while the work done upon an object is equal to the force upon it multiplied by the distance it is moved against resistance.

[481] **BABBAGE,** Charles
English mathematician
Born: Teignmouth, Devonshire,
December 26, 1792
Died: London, October 18, 1871

Babbage was the son of a banker and inherited money (which he was to spend on his work). He taught himself mathematics and entered Cambridge in 1810.

While still at Cambridge, Babbage along with John Herschel [479] and Peacock [472] founded the Analytic Society in 1815. This was designed to emphasize the abstract nature of algebra, to bring Continental developments in mathematics to England and to end the state of suspended animation in which British mathematics had remained since the death of Newton [231] a century before. It succeeded and Babbage was elected to the Royal Society in 1816. British mathematicians could thereafter participate in the radical advances initiated by mathematicians such as Möbius [471], Lobachevski [484], and Cantor [772].

In 1830 Babbage wrote a controversial book in which he denounced the Royal Society as having grown moribund (which was true). In it, he also deplored the unfavorable climate for science in England, as compared with that in France, much in the manner that a century and a quarter later some Americans compared science in the United States with that in the Soviet Union. He cited the case of Dalton [389], who had to make a precarious living as a teacher after services that in other nations might have earned him a good pension. He fought desperately to effect the reforms he wanted by campaigning to have a man sympathetic to them put in as president of the Royal Society. He lost, however.

Babbage worked on what would now be called "operations research" and advocated extreme division of labor in factories, something Ford [929] was to show could be made practical. Specifically, Babbage showed that the cost of collecting and stamping a letter for various sums in accordance with the distance it was to travel cost more in labor, time, and money than would be the case if some small, flat sum were charged independent of distance. This seemed to go against "common sense" (so many logical conclusions do), but the British government managed to see the point and in 1840 established a modern postage system. Since then, such systems have spread over the world.

Babbage worked out the first reliable actuarial tables (the sort of thing that is now the insurance company's bread and butter), worked out the first speedometer, and invented skeleton keys and the locomotive cowcatcher.

Babbage invented an ophthalmoscope in 1847 by means of which the retina of the eye could be studied. He gave it to a physician friend for testing, but the friend laid it aside and forgot it. Four years later Helmholtz [631] invented a similar instrument, and it is he who now generally gets the credit for it.

But there was a much larger disappointment for Babbage. Most of his life was spent on a vast failure that seems a success only by hindsight. He was very conscious of the errors that littered tables of logarithms and various astronomical data and applied himself to the correction of those errors. As early as 1822 he began to speculate on the possibility of using machinery for purposes of computation. Calculating machines had been built by Pascal [207] and Leibniz [233] but Babbage had in mind something far more complicated.

Somehow he persuaded the British government to invest large sums in the project (a good mechanical computer would have been infinitely useful in both peace and war, but it is rather surprising that a government—any government —of the nineteenth century could have been made to see this) and began work. Unfortunately by the time he was nearly done, he had evolved a much more intricate scheme, so that in 1834 he scrapped everything and began over.

He conceived of a machine that could be directed to work by means of punched cards, that could store partial answers in order to save them for additional operations to be performed upon them later, that could print the results. In short, he thought out many of the basic principles that guide modern computers, but he had only mechanical devices with which to put them into action. His machine aroused the interest of Ada Augusta, countess of Lovelace and daughter of Lord Byron. It is her description of the machine that has preserved the knowledge of it for posterity.

He could get no more help from the government. (It obviously didn't help that he was markedly eccentric almost to the point of madness in some ways. For instance, he carried on an immoderate campaign against organ-grinders, whom he intensely detested.) Nevertheless he continued, spending most of his life and most of his own resources on the machine, which grew ever more complicated. It is preserved still unfinished in the Science Museum in London. In his later years, with his money gone and the demands of the machine unending, Babbage and Lady Lovelace tried to work up an infallible system for winning at horse races, but failed, of course. Winning at the track is far more difficult than designing a computer.

A century later Norbert Wiener [1175] worked out the mathematical principles behind such computers and men such as Bush [1139] constructed them with the help of electronic devices far more delicate, responsive, and rapid than the gears and levers available to Babbage.

Babbage is thus the grandfather of the modern computer, and although this was not understood by his contemporaries, Babbage himself was probably aware of it.

[482] ADDISON, Thomas
English physician
Born: Longbenton, Northumberland, April 1793
Died: Bristol, Gloucestershire, June 29, 1860

Addison received his medical degree from the University of Edinburgh in 1815, then went on to practice in London. His work at Guy's Hospital made it famous as a medical school.

He described pernicious anemia in 1849 and in 1855 was the first to give an accurate description of the hormone deficiency disease resulting from the deterioration of the adrenal cortex. The condition is commonly called Addison's disease to this day.

Addison's disease was the first case in which a disease was shown to be associated with pathological changes in one of the endocrine glands.

[483] **STRUVE,** Friedrich Georg Wilhelm von (shtroo'vuh)
German-Russian astronomer
Born: Altona, Schleswig-Holstein, April 15, 1793
Died: Pulkovo, near St. Petersburg (now Leningrad), Russia, November 23, 1864

In 1808 young Struve, who came of a peasant family, in an effort to escape being forced to serve in the armies of Napoleon, then master of Germany, fled first to Denmark, then to the Baltic provinces of Russia.

He entered the University of Dorpat (now Tartu, in the Estonian SSR), obtaining a degree in philology in 1810. He then turned to science and spent the remainder of his life in Russia. For over twenty years he was director of the observatory at Pulkovo, ten miles south of St. Petersburg, an observatory built to his specifications at the order of Tsar Nicholas I. For the observatory, which opened in 1839, he obtained what was then the largest and best refracting telescope in the world—manufactured by Fraunhofer [450].

Struve spent most of his career in studying double stars, preparing a catalogue of 3,112 of them (three-fourths of them previously unknown), published in 1827, and surveying the Baltic provinces of Russia. His great feat was determining the parallax of Vega, the fourth brightest star in the sky. He was behind both Bessel [439] and Henderson [505], but not far behind, in this respect. Struve was the first of four generations of well-known astronomers. The fourth of the line, Otto Struve [1203], was an ornament of American astronomy. In 1964 an observatory named in his honor was established at Tartu.

[484] **LOBACHEVSKI,** Nikolai Ivanovich (luh-buh-chayf'skee)
Russian mathematician
Born: near Nizhni Novgorod (now Gorki), December 2, 1793
Died: Kazan, February 24, 1856

Lobachevski was the son of a peasant of Polish extraction who died when the boy was six. His widowed mother moved to Kazan and managed to get him schooling on public scholarships. In 1807 he entered the newly established University of Kazan and proceeded to show remarkable mathematical talent. He received his master's degree in 1812 and in 1814 was placed on the faculty. He quickly rose to important professorial and administrative positions. By 1827 he was president of the university.

As such, he was a one-man phenomenon. He organized the faculty, library, and laboratories. He even studied architecture so as to supervise the building program. He led an effective fight against cholera in 1830 and against a great fire in 1842, saving the university in each case.

He wrote many papers on mathematics but his chief fame was as a mathematical "heretic," and a colossally successful one. For twenty centuries Euclid [40] and his system of geometry had remained supreme. It was widely assumed by scholars that mathematics, and geometry in particular, consisted of fundamental truths that existed independently of man. Two and two had to equal four and the sum of the three angles of a triangle had to be equal to 180°.

Nevertheless there was one irritating little imperfection in Euclid. His fifth axiom can be stated in a number of ways, of which the simplest is: "Through a given point, not on a given line, one and only one line can be drawn parallel to the given line."

Unlike Euclid's other axioms, this one was not at all self-evident and it involved the notion of parallelism, which implied the existence of lines of infinite length. All in all it was a tough nut philosophically. Many mathematicians, notably Saccheri [247], believed that it was too complicated to be an axiom and that it could be proved by means of Euclid's other and *really* simple axioms. They all failed. (Mathematicians have come to admire Euclid more for the fifth axiom than anything else. How was it he knew it could not be proved by the other axioms and had to be assumed to begin with?)

Lobachevski took a daring step. He didn't wonder if the fifth axiom could be proved. He wondered if it was necessary at all and whether a geometry (perhaps not Euclid's but *a* geometry) might not be built without it. The thought occurred to him at least as early as 1826, for he referred to it in his lectures then. He showed if one began with an axiom that stated that through a given point not on a given line, *at least two lines,* parallel to the given line, could be drawn, then that and the remaining axioms of Euclid could be used to draw up a new, non-Euclidean geometry. In the Lobachevskian geometry the sum of the three angles of a triangle had to be *less* than 180°. It was a strange geometry, but it was self-consistent.

Lobachevski published his ideas in 1829 and was first in the field. Bolyai [530] worked out a similar geometry independently but did not publish until 1832. Gauss [415] had designed such a geometry before either Lobachevski or Bolyai but had not quite had the courage to publish such a defiance of the sainted Euclid.

Lobachevski's geometry, which he introduced in the West by publishing elementary accounts in French and German, was not intended to represent anything "real"; it was simply a self-consistent mathematical system. However, a Lobachevskian geometry is to be found on the surface of a curve called a pseudosphere, which is shaped somewhat like a pair of trumpets joined at the flaring ends and with the thinning ends stretching out infinitely.

A second type of non-Euclidean geometry was invented a quarter century later by Riemann [670]. Riemann's geometry was similar to that found on the surface of a sphere. The old-fashioned Euclidean geometry is the geometry found on a plane and is a sort of boundary geometry lying between the two varieties of non-Euclidean geometry. And even that familiar old geometry underwent a sea change in the hands of Poncelet [456].

Philosophically the development of a non-Euclidean geometry shattered the notion of self-evident truth in its most secure stronghold, mathematics. It was made clear that there were a number of truths, depending on the arrangement of axioms one chose to select. One particular truth might be more useful than another under a particular set of circumstances, but it could not be truer. Hamilton [545] did something of the same sort in algebra.

So firm was the hold of Euclid on the minds of men generally, however, (and even on the minds of mathematicians) that the work of Lobachevski and the other non-Euclideans was downgraded and overlooked as much as possible until, three quarters of a century after Lobachevski, Einstein [1064] was able to show that the universe was non-Euclidean in structure and that these theoretical concepts had a very practical application.

To be sure, the universe is so gently non-Euclidean that over the small segments with which scientists ordinarily deal the Euclidean geometry was close enough. (In the same fashion, though the surface of the earth is spherical, a small section of that surface can be treated well enough if it is assumed to be flat.)

Lobachevski married a wealthy woman in 1832 and he was ennobled in 1837—but thereafter his life took a downward turn.

His reward for revolutionizing mathematics and the philosophy of science, and for all he had done for the university, was dismissal from his post in 1846. No reason was given.

That, together with his worsening eyesight (he was blind in his last years) embittered his final decade.

[485] **MITSCHERLICH,** Eilhardt
(mich'er-likh)
German chemist
Born: Neuende, Oldenburg (now part of Wilhelmshaven), January 7, 1794
Died: Schönberg, near Berlin, February 28, 1863

Mitscherlich, the son of a minister, was interested in Oriental languages and decided to study medicine because doctors could travel freely in the East. He began the study of medicine with a course in chemistry, fell under the influence of Strohmeyer [411] and made up his mind to stay home and become a chemist.

By 1819 he had discovered that compounds of similar composition tend to crystallize together, as though the atoms of one intermingled with the atoms of the other, through the similar design of their structure. This is the theory of isomorphism. In reverse, one could say that if two compounds crystallize together, they are of similar structure. Then, if the structure of one is known, that of the other can be surmised.

Berzelius [425] made use of this notion in his atomic weight determinations, and Mitscherlich went to Stockholm to study under him. On his return to Germany in 1821 he was elected to the Berlin Academy of Sciences and given a professorial appointment at the University of Berlin holding a position held a few years earlier by Klaproth [335].

In 1828 he was elected a foreign member of the Royal Society and the next year received the Royal Medal of the Society for his discovery of isomorphism. Mitscherlich went on after that to do considerable work in organic chemistry. In 1834, for instance, he synthesized nitrobenzene.

Mitscherlich was an excellent lecturer and incorporated his lectures into a successful and highly regarded textbook of chemistry, first published in 1829.

[486] **BABINET,** Jacques (bab-ih-nay')
French physicist
Born: Lusignan, Vienne, March 5, 1794
Died: Paris, October 21, 1872

Babinet, the son of the town mayor, was aimed for the law but chose science. In 1820 he was a professor of physics at a college in Paris. He proved to be an excellent popularizer of science, writing and lecturing on a wide variety of topics.

He invented a number of scientific instruments, notably a device for measuring the angles of crystals. He is best remembered, however, for a suggestion he made in 1827 concerning standards of measurement.

Until then, men had used trivial objects as standard measures, the lengths of arms or feet, the weights of ears of grain, and so on. Even the metric system, first established at about the time of Babinet's birth, made use of the earth's circumference for establishing the unit of measure, a standard that could not be certainly measured and was in any case not the expression of natural law.

Babinet suggested a true standard that was indeed tied to unalterable natural properties—the wavelength of some particular kind of light ray.

In 1960, a century and a third after the suggestion was made, technology had advanced to the point where wavelength measurements were sufficiently precise for the purpose. The unit of length is now tied to the unalterable behavior of a particular kind of xenon atom.

[487] **WHEWELL,** William (hyoo'ul)
English scholar
Born: Lancaster, May 24, 1794
Died: Cambridge, March 6, 1866

Whewell was the son of a master carpenter. Whewell's father assumed his son would follow in the business, but the boy's intelligence was clearly such that it seemed best to send him to school. Whewell entered Cambridge in 1812 and remained there the rest of his life, getting his master's degree in 1819 and becoming an Anglican clergyman.

He interested himself in the philosophy and history of science. He did some direct work in science himself, adding significantly to the understanding of tides, and inventing an anemometer for measuring direction and pressure of the winds one which, with some modification, is still used today. Whewell also labored with Peacock [472], John Herschel [479] and Babbage [481] to reform British mathematics.

He is best known, however, for the scientific terms he coined. He corresponded with Faraday [474] and, in discussing Faraday's findings, he suggested such words as "ion," "anode," and "cathode." He also invented the terms "Eocene," "Miocene," and "Pliocene" as names for geologic eras. Most important of all, perhaps, he was the first to use the terms "scientist" and "physicist."

[488] **MÄDLER,** Johann Heinrich
(med'ler)
German astronomer
Born: Berlin, May 29, 1794
Died: Hannover, March 14, 1874

Mädler was a seminary teacher, who grew interested in astronomy when the great comet of 1811 appeared in the sky. He met Beer [499], who was rich enough to maintain a private observatory, and that gave Mädler his chance. He worked with him in the preparation of his map of the moon, and his ability became so obvious that he was allowed to work at the Berlin Observatory under Encke [475].

In 1841, Mädler published *Popular Astronomy,* a book intended for the layman; it proved a success and went through six editions in his lifetime. He also wrote a massive two-volume history of astronomy.

[489] **PANDER,** Christian Heinrich
(pahn'der)
Russian zoologist
Born: Riga, Latvia, July 24, 1794
Died: St. Petersburg (now Leningrad), September 22, 1865

Pander was from the Baltic provinces of Russia, where the ruling classes were of German descent. He was the son of a wealthy banker and entered the University of Dorpat (largely German in faculty and student body) in 1812. In 1814 he went on to Berlin and then to Göttingen for further studies and there he met Baer [478].

In his discussions with Baer and others the problem of the chick embryo arose. Unlike mammalian embryos, hidden within the mother's body, chick embryos could easily be studied within the egg. Pander took his M.D. at Wurzburg in

1817 and then proceeded to study the chick embryo. He discovered and described the three layers that formed in the early development of the embryo and described them in a paper published in 1817.

Pander, in this paper, is considered to have founded the science of embryology; but he never continued his researches, spending most of his later life in travels through western Europe and through Russia. However, Baer, who read Pander's paper, carried on magnificently.

[490] **PAYEN,** Anselme (pie-ohn')
French chemist
Born: Paris, January 6, 1795
Died: Paris, May 12, 1871

Payen was the son of a lawyer turned industrialist who established factories for the production of chemicals, particularly ammonium chloride. Payen studied first under his father and then, in the chaotic days following the fall of Napoleon, under Vauquelin [379] and Chevreul [448].

At the age of twenty he was put in charge of a borax-refining plant by his father. Borax was virtually a monopoly of the Dutch, who obtained it from the East Indies. Payen devised a cheaper method, preparing borax from boric acid (a mineral available in Italy), and broke the monopoly, selling borax at one-third the Dutch price.

In 1820 his father died and Payen took full charge. He turned his attention to a factory engaged in the refining of sugar from sugar beets, and in 1822 introduced the technique of decolorization through the use of animal charcoal. This has been a popular device among chemists for removing large-molecular impurities ever since. Charcoal, the adsorptive properties of which were first put to use by Payen, was eventually to find a place in the gas masks of World War I.

Through the sugar beet Payen grew interested in agricultural chemistry. In 1833 he separated a substance from malt extract that had the property of hastening the conversion of starch to sugar. He called it diastase. This was an example of the organic catalysts within living tissue, which eventually came to be called enzymes—a name invented half a century later by Kühne [725].

Diastase was the first enzyme to be prepared in concentrated form and its name set the fashion for using the suffix "-ase" to name enzymes generally.

The next year he began a series of researches during the course of which he separated a substance from wood that seemed to have the same general constitution as starch. He obtained it from all sorts of wood, and because it existed in the cell walls he named it cellulose. This set the fashion of the "-ose" suffix in the naming of carbohydrates.

In 1835 Payen abandoned business and accepted a post as professor of industrial and agricultural chemistry at the École Centrale des Arts et Manufactures, and spent the rest of his life in research.

In his old age he had the sorrow of witnessing the disastrous end of the rule of Napoleon III in the flames of the Franco-Prussian War. Despite his age he refused to leave Paris as the Prussians approached and exerted his specialized knowledge to help feed the besieged and starving city. He died shortly after the final French defeat, just in time to avoid the final humiliation of the crushing of the Paris Commune, when the French army, unable to defend France against the Prussian invaders, contented itself with shooting down Parisians.

[491] **EHRENBERG,** Christian Gottfried (ay'ren-berg)
German naturalist
Born: Delitzsch, Saxony, April 19, 1795
Died: Berlin, June 27, 1876

Ehrenberg, the son of a magistrate, was another one of those who, intended for a clerical life by his parents began a course of study to that effect and then switched to science. He obtained his medical degree in 1818 and in his doctoral dissertation dealt with fungi and their reproductive processes, showing their origin in spores.

In 1820 he took part in an archaeological expedition through Egypt and neighboring countries, and collected enormous numbers of specimens of plants and animals. It was a harrowing and ill-organized expedition and Ehrenberg was, in fact, the only survivor. As a result he was appointed to professorial status in zoology at the University of Berlin.

In 1829 he joined Humboldt [397] in the exploration of Siberia under the sponsorship of Tsar Nicholas I, and again he did excellent work in natural history. He made a special study of protozoa, of coral, of the one-celled plankton in the surface layers of the ocean. He was the first to study fossils of microorganisms in the rocks.

Ehrenberg pioneered the detailed study of the invertebrates, particularly the smaller ones, but he was hampered by his belief that even the smallest organisms had systems of organs analogous to those of large organisms. He therefore did not accept the cell theory in full and, of course, he did not accept evolution.

[492] **WEBER,** Ernst Heinrich (vay'-ber)
German physiologist
Born: Wittenberg, Saxony, June 24, 1795
Died: Leipzig, Saxony, January 26, 1878

Weber, the son of a professor of theology, grew interested in science through contact with Chladni [370], a family friend. Weber obtained a medical degree from the University of Wittenberg in 1815 and was a professor of anatomy at the University of Leipzig from 1818, but he was primarily interested in physiology. In the 1830s he found that the minimum difference in intensity that could be distinguished between two sensations of identical kind bore a constant relationship to the total intensity of sensation.

For instance, suppose a person could just distinguish between a 9-ounce weight and a 10-ounce weight. This would seem to indicate that he could sense the added weight of one ounce and could therefore distinguish between a 90-ounce weight and a 91-ounce weight.

This is not so. He will be able only to distinguish between a 90-ounce weight and a 100-ounce weight. It is not a difference of 1 gram or 10 grams that is important, but the difference of 10 percent of the total weight.

In the same way, in telling the difference between intensities of light or sound, difference in temperature or pressure, it is the percentage difference and not the absolute difference that counts. This is widely known as the Weber-Fechner law because it was Fechner [520] who popularized Weber's discovery.

The law is not exact but it served as the groundwork for all kinds of experimentation into the manner in which the human being senses the environment about him and how he interprets his sense impressions. Weber by his observation may be said to have founded experimental psychology and introduced the workings of the mind into the realm of the natural sciences. This did not, of course, rob these workings of their mystery or make psychology as objective a science as physics. Indeed, Weber's contemporary Braid [494] was, in his work, laying the groundwork for a treatment of the mind that was far removed from the experimental methods of the physical sciences.

Weber had a younger brother, Wilhelm Eduard Weber [540], who was as noted as himself, but in the field of physics rather than physiology.

[493] **CAVENTOU,** Joseph Bienaimé (ka-vahn-too´)
French chemist
Born: Saint-Omer, Pas de Calais, June 30, 1795
Died: Paris, May 5, 1877

Caventou was the son of a pharmacist and followed in his father's profession. His education was interrupted when, in an outburst of patriotism, he joined Napoleon's army after the latter had returned from Elba. However, the defeat at Waterloo quickly followed and Caventou returned to his studies.

In 1817 Caventou formed his partnership with Pelletier [454], and together they isolated chlorophyll, strychnine, quinine, caffeine and many other substances.

Caventou did not accomplish much after Pelletier's death, but he held a post as professor of toxicology at the École de Pharmacie.

[494] **BRAID,** James
Scottish surgeon
Born: Rylawhouse, Fifeshire, 1795
Died: Manchester, England, March 25, 1860

Braid was educated at the University of Edinburgh and practiced surgery in Manchester. In 1841 he attended some exhibitions of mesmerism, the phenomenon discovered by Mesmer [314], which had been discredited for its elements of mysticism. Braid was very skeptical of the whole matter but he tried some experiments of his own and began to think the phenomenon was real. A person could indeed be put into a trancelike state resembling sleep but differing in that he was quasi-conscious and extraordinarily open to suggestion.

Braid recognized that it was not induced by animal magnetism but was rather a suspension of the conscious mind, induced by its having been forced into weariness through repetitive stimuli. He called the state "hypnotism," from the Greek word for "sleep."

Despite the fact that he damaged his reputation by going too far in his newborn enthusiasm for the pseudosciences by also taking up Gall's [371] phrenology, Braid eventually managed to convince others of the reality and usefulness of hypnotism. Broca [653] in particular took the notion favorably.

Hypnotism can be used to make the conscious mind unresponsive to pain, but the coming of Morton's [617] chemical anesthesia decreased the importance of hypnotism in this respect. Hypnotism, by putting aside the conscious mind, revealed poorly understood and almost frightening depths beneath. and a generation later, neurologists up to and including Freud [865] were to use it to treat mental disorders. Freud was to replace it with other methods but hypnotism still has its medical uses, and (shades of Mesmer) will always be popular as a theatrical demonstration designed to amaze and amuse.

[495] **CLAUS,** Carl Ernst (klowz)
Russian chemist
Born: Dorpat, Estonia (now Tartu, Estonian SSR), January 23, 1796
Died: Dorpat, March 24, 1864

Claus was a Balt of German descent, who was apprenticed to a pharmacist in 1810 after he had been left an orphan. In 1815 he entered the University of Dorpat, passed his examination, and in 1826 established practice as a pharmacist in Kazan.

In these early years, he was particularly interested in botany and the plant forms of the Russian steppes but he grew interested in chemistry, returned to Dorpat, received his master's degree in chemistry, was appointed to the first professorship in chemistry at the University of Kazan in 1838.

Four decades before, men such as Tennant [375] and Wollaston [388] had identified dense, inert metals related to platinum in properties, and five, including platinum were now known: platinum, osmium, iridium, palladium and rhodium. One and only one remained to be discovered and Claus managed the job in 1844. From 900 grams of residue out of which these known metals had been extracted, Claus isolated six grams of the sixth. He named it "ruthenium" from the Latin name of Russia.

[496] **QUETELET,** Lambert Adolphe Jacques (ket-lay')
Belgian astronomer and statistician
Born: Gent, February 22, 1796
Died: Brussels, February 17, 1874

Quetelet studied mathematics under Laplace [347]. In 1814 he was appointed professor of mathematics at Gent University and later supervised the construction of the Royal Observatory in Brussels. From 1828 until his death he was director of the observatory.

His greatest contribution was in the application of statistical methods (with which, as a physical scientist and mathematician, he felt at home) to the study of human beings. He recorded the chest measurements of Scottish soldiers, the height of French army draftees, and other such items and found these varied from the average in the same manner one would expect if one were plotting the fall of dice or the scatter of bullet holes about a bull's-eye. He noted this first in 1835. Later he used the 1846 Belgian census for his statistical analysis. In doing so, he worked out many of the rules that govern modern census-taking.

He graphed the results, plotting the measurements against frequency of occurrence, and got a bell-shaped curve. (This sort of curve was used so often by Gauss [415] that it is often called a Gaussian curve.)

Randomness invaded the human realm, and in one more way life (and humanity in particular) was shown to follow the same laws that govern the inanimate universe. The concept of the "average man" grew out of Quetelet's work, as well as the "vital statistics" that govern the size of insurance premiums.

Nevertheless humanity as a whole did not form a homogeneous group centering on the average, but could be divided into subgroups, as Retzius [498] demonstrated.

[497] **CARNOT,** Nicolas Léonard Sadi (kahr-noh')
French physicist
Born: Paris, June 1, 1796
Died: Paris, August 24, 1832

Carnot came of a distinguished French family. His father had been a leading government figure under the First Republic and under Napoleon I. He had been called the Organizer of Victory because of the manner in which he managed to train and equip the raw recruits called to arms against the circling hostile powers of Europe. Carnot's younger brother was a politician of liberal views who was later to oppose Napoleon III.

His brother's son was eventually to serve as one of the presidents of France's Third Republic.

Among this group of politicians was Nicolas, a scientist. He was educated by his father to begin with, entered the École Polytechnique in 1812 and graduated in 1814. He had been trained as a military engineer and fought against the armies invading France in 1814. With Napoleon's fall his father was exiled and his own advancement was out of the question. He remained an army officer, however.

In 1824 he published his only work, a partial title of which is *On the Motive Power of Fire*. The book was enough to secure his place in the history of science. In it he defined work as "weight lifted through a height." (This is now made more general by defining it as "force acting through a distance against resistance," a definition advanced by Coriolis [480].)

Carnot was interested in the amount of work that could be obtained from a heat engine. The steam engine invented by Watt [316], although far better than any previous model, was quite inefficient. In Carnot's time an efficiency of 5 to 7 percent was all that could be expected, meaning that 93 to 95 percent of the heat energy of the burning fuel was wasted. Carnot was interested in determining how far this mark might be improved.

He was able to demonstrate that the maximum efficiency depended upon the temperature difference in the engine. In the case of the ordinary steam engine, the temperature of the steam (T_1) was the hottest part of the engine, the temperature of the cooling water (T_2) the coldest. The maximum fraction of the heat energy that could be converted into work, even if the machine operated with perfect efficiency, would then be:

$$\frac{T_1 - T_2}{T_2}$$

(T_1 and T_2 in this equation represent absolute temperature, a concept that was to be made clear and explicit by Kelvin [652] some fifteen years after Carnot's death. Indeed it was Kelvin who brought Carnot's till-then-neglected work to the attention of science in 1848.)

Carnot was the first to consider quantitatively the manner in which heat and work are interconverted. He was thus the founder of the science of thermodynamics ("heat movement"). He was not correct in his views as to the nature of heat flow, for he held to the caloric theory of Lavoisier [334]. This, however, did not affect the validity of his results.

Carnot's equation makes it clear that what counts in maximum work production are the maximum and minimum temperatures. It does not matter what happens to the temperature in between, whether it drops slowly, quickly, smoothly, or in stages. The dependence on two extreme points only and independence of the path between is characteristic of thermodynamic function. G. H. Hess [528] a decade later showed this to be true about the heat accompanying chemical reactions.

It is possible from Carnot's equation to deduce what is now called the second law of thermodynamics and Carnot was the first to be vouchsafed a glimpse of that great generalization. He might well have gone on to bring it into the full light of day. Unfortunately, he died in a cholera epidemic at the age of thirty-six and his work was neglected. It was left to such men as Clapeyron [507] and Clausius [633], a generation later, to develop Carnot's notions.

[498] **RETZIUS,** Anders Adolf (ret′-see-us)
Swedish anatomist
Born: Stockholm, October 13, 1796
Died: Stockholm, April 18, 1860

Retzius, the son of a professor of natural history, studied at the University of Copenhagen under Oersted [417] among others. He obtained a medical degree in 1819 from the University of Lund and in 1824 was appointed professor of anatomy at the Caroline Institute in Stockholm.

His most important contribution was in anthropology. Mankind has always been aware of differences between groups of human beings—skin color, for instance. In 1842 Retzius attempted to impose an objective and measurable criterion by using the skull. The ratio of skull width to skull length, multiplied by 100, he called the cranial index. A cranial index of less than 80 was dolichocephalic ("long head"); one of over 80 was brachycephalic ("wide head"). In this way Europeans could be divided into Nordics (tall and dolichocephalic), Mediterraneans (short and dolichocephalic), and Alpines (short and brachycephalic).

This was not a satisfactory criterion of race, but it set the stage for other attempts to deal objectively with this extraordinarily difficult subject, attempts that only today through the careful analysis of blood groups are beginning to yield results. The evils of racism—such as slavery in America and the infamies of Nazi Germany—were given a pseudo-scientific justification by men who made use of anthropological terms like those of Retzius to serve their own purposes.

[499] **BEER**, Wilhelm (bayr)
German astronomer
Born: Berlin, January 4, 1797
Died: Berlin, March 27, 1850

Beer was a banker by profession and came of a Jewish family. One of his brothers was a composer who wrote under the name of Giacomo Meyerbeer. Beer's hobby was astronomy. He built an observatory and, with the help of Mädler [488], spent eight years locating the principal features of the moon with great accuracy and measuring the heights of a thousand mountains after the fashion of Galileo [166].

The final map, published in 1836, and based on six hundred nights of careful observation, showed the moon a meter in diameter and was a far cry from Riccioli's [185] map of two centuries before. Through all the eight years, no change was observed in any lunar feature, dramatic evidence that the moon was, at least for the most part, a dead and static world. In his discussion of the map, Beer speculated on the usefulness of an astronomic observatory on the moon which

now—a century and a quarter later—appears on the horizon of the possible.

In 1830 Beer proceeded to the mapping of the planet Mars and was the first to make a definite picture of lighter and darker areas. On his map there was no sign of the canals that, thanks to Schiaparelli [714], were to make such a stir a half century later.

[500] **POISEUILLE**, Jean Léonard Marie
(pwah-zoy'yuh)
French physician
Born: Paris, April 22, 1797
Died: Paris, December 26, 1869

Poiseuille, the son of a carpenter, studied at the École Polytechnique and gained his doctor's degree in 1828.

He was particularly interested in blood circulation and improved on Hales's [249] method of measuring blood pressure by using a mercury manometer for the purpose, instead of allowing the blood to rise in a long tube.

In order to study the manner in which blood made its way through the fine capillaries, Poiseuille studied flow of water in such tubes. He found that the rate of flow depended on diameter and length of the tubes and the pressure difference between the two ends. He worked out an equation, including these values and the temperature, and this was eventually termed Poiseuille's law.

Flow depends on the viscosity of the liquid, too, and the unit of viscosity is the poise, named for Poiseuille.

[501] **MOSANDER**, Carl Gustav (mohsawn'der)
Swedish chemist
Born: Kalmar, September 10, 1797
Died: Ångsholm, October 15, 1858

Mosander was first apprenticed to an apothecary, went on to study medicine, and obtained his medical degree in 1825. He served as an army surgeon for some years. His lifework began as assistant to Berzelius [425], in whose house he lived for a long time and to whose teaching duties he succeeded when Berzelius retired in 1832. Mosander held the post till his death.

As was natural for a Swedish chemist, he interested himself in the rare earth minerals discovered in Sweden by Gadolin [373]. It was Mosander more than anyone else who revealed the complexity of the rare earths.

In 1839 he studied a compound of cerium, an element already discovered in those minerals by Berzelius and others, including Klaproth [335]. In the compound he discovered a new element, which he named lanthanum from a Greek word meaning "hidden" because it had been hidden so effectively in the minerals.

He did not publish at once but, suspecting that he was not through, continued his investigations. In the early 1840s he isolated four other rare earth elements, yttrium, erbium, terbium, and didymium. The first three were named after Ytterby, the quarry in which the minerals were first located, and the last from the Greek word for "twin" because it was so like lanthanum. (In the end, didymium proved to be a mixture of two elements, which were not separated until Auer [890] turned the trick four decades later.)

By the time Mosander was done there was no question but that there was a whole series of very similar rare earth elements. These were to remain a puzzle to chemists for three quarters of a century until Bohr [1101] and others worked out the electronic structure of the atom well enough to account for the properties of the rare earth elements.

[502] LYELL, Sir Charles
Scottish geologist
Born: Kinnordy, Forfarshire (now Angus), November 14, 1797
Died: London, February 22, 1875

At Oxford, from which he graduated in 1819, Lyell, the son of well-to-do parents, went on to study law and, in 1827, was finally accepted for the bar. Lectures on geology fascinated him, however, and he gave more and more of his time to the subject. His Oxford teacher had been

a neptunist after the fashion of Werner [355], but Lyell's own investigations during· trips to the Continent inclined him more and more to vulcanism and to the principle of uniformitarianism that, unknown to him, Hutton [297] had expounded a generation earlier. In a trip to Paris in 1833, he was further stimulated by meeting Cuvier [396] and Humboldt [397]. He also read Lamarck's [336] book and was impressed.

When he finally encountered Hutton's book, he recognized that it paralleled his own views. Furthermore his travels in France and Italy made it possible for him to bring together a large collection of data as confirmation of Hutton's view that the slow processes of heat and erosion (still proceeding today) had gradually brought about all the changes on earth without the necessity of supposing any catastrophes. Indeed, Lyell was, if anything, too extreme in his uniformitarianism and was unready even to admit the possibility of mild and limited catastrophes. (Nowadays geologists believe that something drastic occurred at the end of the Cretaceous, something that killed off the dinosaurs—something as dramatic perhaps as the strike of an asteroid that nearly sterilized the earth.)

Lyell did not contribute anything fundamentally new to geology, though it was he, applying the suggestions of the classical scholar William Whewell [487], who first named a number of the geologic eras, such as the Eocene, Miocene, and Pliocene. He also estimated the age of some of the oldest fossil-bearing rocks at the then-unheard-of figure of 240,000,000 years—but that is still less than half the currently accepted figure.

His most important deed was to popularize and amplify the Huttonian view in a book called The Principles of Geology, which appeared in three volumes between 1830 and 1833 and went through twelve editions in his lifetime. In 1834 he received a medal from the Royal Society for his work.

Some of Lyell's conservative colleagues refused at first to accept his theories, since they seemed to lead inevitably to some form of evolutionary doctrine. That, after all, was the bugaboo of the time for conservative scientists, as Copernicanism had been the bugaboo two and a half centuries before. And indeed the conservatives were right to fear it, for among the scholars who accepted Lyell quite early was the young Charles Darwin [554].

Lyell's book, clearly and attractively written, sold well. Noted geologists like Murchison [477] and Sedgwick [442] began to study the crust of the earth along Huttonian lines. The principle of uniformitarianism became popular, particularly in England, and in the 1840s Lyell visited the United States and lectured to enthusiastic crowds. Before long the catastrophism of Cuvier [396] was dead, though it maintained itself in France into the 1850s.

Lyell formed a close friendship with Darwin (who was himself something of a geologist in his younger days) and when Darwin's great book on evolution came out, Lyell was one of the first converts to his friend's views.

In fact, Lyell carried Darwin's evolutionary views into the most sensitive field of all, that involving the development of man, and this at a time when even Darwin himself was not prepared to do so. In 1863 Lyell wrote *The Antiquity of Man,* basing his evidence for man's antiquity on old artifacts of the type that had been uncovered by Boucher de Perthes [458]. As another example of his unconventionality, Lyell was one of the strong proponents of the North during the American Civil War, when the English "better classes" were largely pro-Southern.

Lyell was knighted in 1848 and created a baronet in 1864. He died while working on the 12th edition of his great book. Despite his unsettling views with regard to the evolution of earth and man, he was buried in Westminster Abbey in appreciation of his services to science.

[503] **HENRY,** Joseph
American physicist
Born: Albany, New York, December 17, 1797
Died: Washington, D.C., May 13, 1878

The life of Joseph Henry paralleled that of Faraday [474] in many ways. Henry, like Faraday, came of a poor family. He was the son of a day laborer, had little schooling, and was forced to go to work while young. Faraday was apprenticed to a bookbinder, and Henry, at thirteen, was apprenticed to a watchmaker. Henry was the less fortunate, since he didn't have Faraday's association with books. At least he might not have had, except for an odd happening.

The story goes that at sixteen while Henry was on vacation at a relative's farm, he chased a rabbit under a church building. He crawled underneath, found some of the floorboards missing and promptly abandoned the rabbit to explore the church. There he found a shelf of books. One was a book called *Lectures on Experimental Philosophy,* which he began leafing through. Before that, he had been playing with the notion of becoming a writer, but now he was fired with curiosity and a new ambition. The owner of the book let the young man keep it and Henry returned to school.

He entered the Albany Academy, teaching at country schools and tutoring privately on the side to earn his tuition, and eventually graduated. He was set to study medicine when an offer of a job as surveyor turned him toward engineering. By 1826 he was teaching mathematics and science at Albany Academy.

Like Faraday he grew interested in the experiment of Oersted [417], and he became the first American to experiment with electricity in any important way since Franklin's [272] pioneer work three quarters of a century earlier.

Sturgeon [436] had put Oersted's work to use in the form of an electromagnet. In 1829 Henry heard of this in the course of a visit to New York and thought he could do better. The more coils of conducting wire one could wrap around an iron core, the greater the reinforcement of the magnetic field and the stronger the magnet. The only trouble was that when one started to wrap more and more wires about the coil, they touched and short-circuited.

It was necessary, therefore, to insulate the wires. Insulation would not interfere with the magnetic field setup, but it would prevent short-circuiting. Insulation was not easy to come by in those pre-electrical days, so Henry tore up one of his wife's silk petticoats for the purpose (a sacrifice to science she could scarcely have been overjoyed with). In the years to come a great deal of Henry's time was put into the brutally boring task of slowly wrapping insulation about wire.

The electromagnet he made was far more powerful than Sturgeon's. He made others, more powerful still, and by 1831 had developed one that could lift 750 pounds as compared with the 9 pounds that was the best Sturgeon could ever do. The same year, in a demonstration at Yale University, another of his electromagnets, using the current from an ordinary battery, lifted more than a ton of iron. In 1832 he reaped his reward in the form of a professorial appointment at Princeton.

But electromagnets were more than a matter of brute strength. Henry built small, delicate ones that could be used for fine control. Imagine a small electromagnet at one end of a mile of wire, with a battery at the other end. Suppose you could send a current through the wire by pressing a key and closing the circuit. With the current flowing, the electromagnet, a mile away, could be made to attract a small iron bar. If the key were then released, the current would be broken, the electromagnet would lose its force, and the small iron bar would be pulled away by a spring attached to it. By opening and closing the key in a particular pattern, the iron bar a mile away could be made to open and close, clicking away in that same particular pattern. By 1831 Henry was doing just this.

However, the longer the wire, the greater its resistance and, by Ohm's [461] law, the smaller the current flowing through it. There is a practical limit, then, to the distance over which such a pattern can be sent. To circumvent that, Henry invented the electrical relay in 1835. A current just strong enough to activate an electromagnet would lift a small iron key. This key when lifted would close a second circuit

with a current (from a nearby battery) flowing through it. This in turn could activate another relay. In this way the current would travel from relay to relay and could cover huge distances without weakening. The opening and closing of a key could then impress its peculiar pattern through any distance.

In effect Henry had invented the telegraph. However, he did not patent any of his devices for he believed that the discoveries of science were for the benefit of all humanity. As a result, it was Morse [473] who worked out the first telegraph put to practical use (in 1844) and it is Morse who usually gets credit as the inventor. In tackling the technical end of the problem, Morse, who was completely ignorant of science, was helped freely by Henry. In England, Wheatstone [526], after a long conference with Henry, worked up a telegraph in 1837. Henry, an idealist, did not mind not sharing in the financial rewards of the telegraph. It bothered him, however, that neither man ever publicly acknowledged Henry's help.

Henry missed the credit for a more important discovery and did so in a more heartbreaking way. At the Albany Academy, Henry's teaching duties were so heavy that he could turn to research only in the vacation month of August. In August of 1830 he discovered the principle of induction; that is, how an electric current in one coil may set up a current in the other through the development of the magnetic field. He had not quite finished his work at the end of the month so he put it aside for the next August.

Well before the next August he read Faraday's preliminary note concerning his discovery of induction. Henry rushed back to his experiments and published his own work, but by then it was too late. Henry had done the key experiments ahead of Faraday, but Faraday had published first. Henry was not one to feel bitter and always freely admitted Faraday's priority.

In Henry's paper, however, he explained that the electric current in a coil can induce another current not only in another coil but in itself. The actual current observed in the coil is, then, the combination of the original current and the induced current. This is called self-induction, and the discovery is credited to Henry. Faraday discovered it independently by 1834, but this time he was second. A third man, Lenz [536], was also to discover this independently, and he was to go further in this connection than either Henry or Faraday.

In 1831 Henry published a paper describing the electric motor. This, in a sense, is the opposite of the electric generator. In a generator, mechanical force turns a wheel and produces electricity. In a motor, electricity turns a wheel and produces mechanical force.

The importance of the motor cannot be overemphasized. A motor can be made as large or as small as can be desired. It can be run by electricity brought to it over a distance of many miles. It can be started in a moment and stopped in a moment.

The supply of cheap, abundant electricity made possible (at least potentially) by Faraday's discovery of the generator would have been useless without some means of putting it conveniently to work. It is Henry's motor in vacuum cleaners, refrigerators, shavers, typewriters, and a hundred other electrical appliances that puts it to work.

Henry made an interesting contribution to astronomy, too. He projected the image of the sun on a white screen in 1848 and, by sensitive measurements of heat, showed sunspots to be cooler than the rest of the sun.

In 1846 Henry was elected first secretary of the newly formed Smithsonian Institution and proved himself a first-class scientific administrator. He made the Smithsonian a clearing house of scientific knowledge and encouraged scientific communication on a worldwide scale. He was one of the founders of the National Academy of Sciences of the United States and one of the early presidents of the body.

He also encouraged the growth of new sciences within the United States. For instance he was interested in meteorology and used the resources of the Smithsonian Institution to set up a system of obtaining weather reports from all over the nation, the telegraph's first scientific use. The United States Weather Bureau was eventually founded upon the system he devised.

During the American Civil War, Joseph Henry headed the nation's scientific mobilization, playing the role that, eight decades later, Bush [1139] was to play. He recommended the construction of ironclads and was eventually listened to.

When Henry died, honor was his in full measure. His funeral was attended by high government officials, including Rutherford B. Hayes, then President of the United States. When the International Electrical Congress met in Chicago in 1893 they agreed on having the unit of inductance named the henry.

[504] MELLONI, Macedonio
    Italian physicist
    Born: Parma, April 11, 1798
    Died: Portici (near Naples), August 11, 1854

As was true later of Cannizzaro [668], Melloni, who was granted a professorship in physics at the University of Parma in 1824, took part in an unsuccessful Italian revolution (in 1830) and had to leave the country for a time for France, reversing Cauchy's [463] simultaneous exile. He returned when the furor died down and began research on infrared radiation in Naples where he was appointed director of the Cabinet of Arts and Trades.

Herschel [321] had discovered infrared radiation a generation before, but tools were lacking with which to investigate it. In 1830, however, a thermopile was invented—a series of strips of two different metals that produced electric currents when one end was heated. Very weak electric currents, and therefore very weak heating effects, could be detected.

Melloni improved the thermopile and used it to trace the presence of infrared radiation. In 1846 he even measured the heating effect of moonlight from a spot high on Mount Vesuvius. He showed also that rock salt is transparent to infrared. He made lenses and prisms out of rock salt and by 1850 showed that infra-red light behaves just as ordinary light does as far as reflection, refraction, po-larization, and interference are con-cerned. Fresnel's [455] mathematics ap-plied to it, therefore, and infrared light is thus different from ordinary light only in its longer wavelength and in the fact (ir-relevant to the physicist) that the human eye happens to be insensitive to it.

The groundwork was thus laid for Maxwell's [692] theoretical uncovering of an entire forest of radiation on either side of the visible spectrum far beyond any that had yet been detected.

[505] **HENDERSON,** Thomas
Scottish astronomer
Born: Dundee, Angus, December 28, 1798
Died: Edinburgh, November 23, 1844

Henderson, the son of a tradesman, began as a lawyer, but he made a hobby of astronomy. As happens often, the hobby took over. In 1831 he was ap-pointed director of the observatory at the Cape of Good Hope. This gave him the chance to observe the unusual star Alpha Centauri, which is the third brightest in the skies but is located so far south that it was never observed by Europeans until after the Age of Exploration began.

Henderson succeeded in measuring its parallax, which turned out to be about three quarters of a second. This placed its distance at just over four light-years. It is therefore closer than 61 Cygni and, indeed, the system of stars represented by Alpha Centauri (it is made up of three stars altogether) is the closest known to this day. The closest of the three components, discovered in 1915, is a very small and feebly luminous star, called Proxima Centauri.

Henderson actually completed his cal-culations before Bessel [439] did, but his results were published only in January 1839, two months after Bessel's an-nouncement, and priority goes to the first to publish. Henderson was ap-pointed the first astronomer royal of Scotland and ended his days as professor of astronomy at Edinburgh.

[506] **REICH,** Ferdinand (rikhe)
German mineralogist
Born: Bernburg, Anhalt, Febru-ary 19, 1799
Died: Freiberg, Saxony, April 27, 1882

Reich studied at Göttingen under Strohmeyer [411]. In 1823 he went to Paris and returned filled with enthusiasm for the metric system, which he intro-duced into Saxony. He taught at the Freiberg School of Mines throughout his professional life.

After the spectroscopic discovery of cesium and rubidium by Bunsen [565] and Kirchhoff [648] and of thallium by Crookes [695], Reich would have liked to go in for spectroscopic analysis him-self. Here, however, he suffered under a peculiar handicap which he shared with Dalton [389]: He was color-blind. He therefore entrusted his assistant Richter [654] with the color part of the job.

In 1863 Reich thought that a yellow precipitate he had obtained from a zinc ore might contain a new metal. Richter, examining it spectroscopically, found an indigo-colored line different from any produced by the known elements. This was proof of a new element, and it was named indium.

[507] **CLAPEYRON,** Benoit Pierre
Émile (clap-ih-rone')
French engineer
Born: Paris, February 26, 1799
Died: Paris, January 28, 1864

Clapeyron graduated from the École Polytechnique in 1818. He spent the decade of the 1820s in Russia teaching in St. Petersburg and returned to France following the July Revolution of 1830.

He was particularly interested in steam engines, and he was the first to pay no-table attention to the work of Carnot [497]. Making use of Carnot's principles, Clapeyron found an important rela-tionship involving the heat of vapor-ization of a fluid, its temperature, and the increase in volume involved in its va-porization. This relationship, which he advanced in 1834, was related to what later came to be called the second law of

338

thermodynamics. It was made more general by Clausius [633], and it is usually known as the Clapeyron-Clausius equation.

As an engineer, Clapeyron was notable for his work in designing and constructing locomotives and metal bridges.

[508] **ARGELANDER,** Friedrich Wilhelm August (ahr′guh-lahn-der)
German astronomer
Born: Memel, East Prussia (now Klaipeda, USSR), March 22, 1799
Died: Bonn, Rhenish Prussia, February 17, 1875

Argelander was born of a wealthy Finnish father and a German mother. Two Prussian princes lived for a while in the Argelander household when the Prussian royal family fled before the conquering Napoleon. The elder prince succeeded to the throne as Frederick William IV in 1840.

Argelander was a student of Bessel [439] and obtained his Ph.D. at Königsberg in 1822. He was head of Finnish observatories, first at Turku then at Helsinki from 1823 to 1836, then transferred to Bonn in Germany. At Bonn his personal friendship with Frederick William IV, made it possible for him to build a new observatory, something his predecessor had failed to obtain funds for.

Argelander spent most of his professional life at Bonn locating stars, sacrificing some precision for the sake of quantity. From 1859 to 1862 he published the giant *Bonner Durchmusterung* (Bonn Survey) in four volumes. It located the positions of 457,848 stars, a far cry from the first star map of Hipparchus [50] with its fewer than a thousand entries. It was the last star map to be compiled without the aid of photography but was good enough to be reprinted as late as 1950, by popular demand.

Argelander was the first to begin the detailed study of variable stars, of which only six were known when he started. He introduced the modern system of naming them, using letter prefixes beginning with the letter R for *rot* ("red") because so many variable stars were red.

In 1863 he founded the *Astronomische Gesellschaft,* the first large international organization of astronomers. He also followed up Herschel's [321] notion that the sun was moving and gained the first rough notion of its direction of motion.

[509] **LASSELL,** William
English astronomer
Born: Bolton, Lancashire, June 18, 1799
Died: Maidenhead, Berkshire, October 5, 1880

Lassell's life was something like that of a muted Herschel [321]. Lassell was a successful brewer (as Herschel had been a successful musician) who, like Herschel and Lord Rosse [513], took up astronomy as a hobby, grinding his own lenses and adding valuable improvements in design that he devised himself.

His first important discovery, in 1846, was that of Triton, Neptune's large satellite. Its name was suggested by Flammarion [756]. In 1848 he discovered an eighth satellite of Saturn (later named Hyperion), a discovery made simultaneously by G. P. Bond [660].

Finally, in 1851, he duplicated one of Herschel's feats of half a century before by discovering two satellites of Uranus (making four altogether). The new satellites Lassell named Ariel and Umbriel. He made these last discoveries in Malta, where he moved to escape the increasingly smoky atmosphere of the industrializing English midlands, which was making astronomical observations just about impossible.

He returned to England in 1864.

[510] **SCHÖNBEIN,** Christian Friedrich (shoin′bine)
German-Swiss chemist
Born: Metzingen, Württemberg, October 18, 1799
Died: Sauersberg, Baden, August 29, 1868

Schönbein, the son of poor parents, could not afford a formal education and was largely self-taught. He worked at a pharmaceutical factory and visited the universities of Tübingen and Erlangen when he could. He obtained some teaching assignments, which included time in England, where he attended the lectures of Faraday [474], and in France, where he heard Gay-Lussac [420], Ampère [407], and Thénard [416]. He received an honorary Ph.D. at the University of Basel in 1828, joined its faculty and reached the position of full professor by 1835.

In 1840 he studied the peculiar odor that had been noticed for about half a century and more in the neighborhood of electrical equipment and that was particularly noticeable in Schönbein's own poorly ventilated laboratory. Schönbein showed that he could produce the same odor by electrolyzing water or by allowing phosphorus to oxidize. He traced that odor to a gas, which he named ozone, from the Greek word for "smell." Andrews [580] proved it to be a high-energy form of oxygen, its molecule containing three oxygen atoms where ordinary oxygen molecules contain but two.

Still more exciting things awaited Schönbein. The story goes that in 1845 he was toying with a mixture of nitric and sulfuric acids in the kitchen of his house. He was strictly forbidden to experiment there, but his wife was absent. However, he spilled some of the acid. In a panic he seized the first thing at hand, his wife's cotton apron, and sopped up the mixture, then hung it over the stove to dry before his wife came home and caught him.

It dried all right and when it got dry enough, it went poof! and was gone.

Whether Frau Schönbein had much to say on her return, history does not relate, but Schönbein at least was not too astonished or too browbeaten to experiment further. He found that the acid mixture had added nitro groups (NO_2) to the cellulose in the apron, forming nitrocellulose, and that this was excessively inflammable, burning without smoke or residue.

Schönbein recognized the potential use of nitrocellulose in warfare and gave the substance a name that was the German equivalent of guncotton.

Ordinary gunpowder was so smoky that it blackened the gunners, fouled the cannon, and raised a dark cloud that hid the battlefield. Here was something that might be used as a smokeless powder. Schönbein peddled the recipe to several governments, and guncotton factories sprang up. However, guncotton was a bit too unpredictable. It had the bad habit of exploding while still in the factory, which then "sprang up" in a more drastic fashion. In 1847, for instance, a factory run in part by Schönbein himself blew up, killing twenty-one people. By the early 1860s guncotton seemed too hot to handle and the boom was over.

However, methods were found to tame it and Dewar [759] and Abel [673] were soon to use it in the manufacture of cordite, the first practical smokeless powder. The reign of gunpowder, which had begun in the time of Roger Bacon [99] six centuries earlier, was over, only to be replaced by something more efficiently destructive.

Schönbein had a queer streak of conservatism in him. Almost to his death he refused to admit that Scheele [329] had been wrong in thinking chlorine a compound, or that Davy [421] had been correct in proving it an element. He also firmly rejected the atomic theory. Even quite competent scientists can insist on being half a century out of date.

[511] **TALBOT,** William Henry Fox
English inventor
Born: Melbury House, Dorsetshire, February 11, 1800
Died: Lacock Abbey, Wiltshire, September 17, 1877

Talbot, the son of an army officer, obtained his master's at Cambridge in 1825, then, in 1833, entered Parliament. The political life was not for him, however. He retired the next year and began experimenting with photography as (unknown to him) Daguerre [467] was doing across the Channel.

By 1841 Talbot had patented the Talbotype. It was analogous to the daguerreotype but it introduced important improvements, including the production for the first time of a photographic negative, from which any number of positive prints could be made on paper. He received the Rumford medal for this in 1842. In 1844 he published the first book illustrated with photographs. By 1851 he had developed methods by which the length of posing was drastically cut down, so that those who sat for photographs no longer had to be clamped in place to prevent motion.

Talbot was also interested in archaeology and in the 1850s was one of the first to decipher the cuneiform tablets fished out of the ruins of Nineveh, capital of ancient Assyria.

[512] **ROSS,** Sir James Clark
Scottish explorer
Born: London, England, April 15, 1800
Died: Aylesbury, Buckinghamshire, England, April 3, 1862

Ross joined the Royal Navy in 1812. Over a period of twenty years, he accompanied his uncle on several expeditions to the Canadian Arctic where, in those years, some practical waterway was searched for that would allow one to sail from the Atlantic to the Pacific (the Northwest Passage). On June 1, 1831, Ross sledged along the northern coast of North America and located the North Magnetic Pole.

In 1839 Ross was given a command of his own and set out to explore the Antarctic region. On January 1, 1841, he crossed the Antarctic Circle. He discovered Mt. Erebus (named for one of his ships) the southernmost active volcano known. He sailed into the large oceanic inlet that cuts into Antarctica and that is now known as the Ross Sea in his honor. The southern portion of this sea is covered with a vast overhang of ice from the continental area behind and that is known as the Ross Ice Shelf.

He was knighted in 1844.

[513] **ROSSE,** William Parsons, 3d earl of
Irish astronomer
Born: York, England, June 17, 1800
Died: Monkstown, Cork, Ireland, October 31, 1867

An authentic member of the aristocracy, William Parsons graduated from Oxford in 1822, sat in Parliament for a dozen years thereafter, resigning in 1834, and in 1841 succeeded to his father's earldom. In 1845 he was chosen to sit as an Irish representative in the House of Lords.

Rosse's love, indeed his obsession, was the construction of a giant reflecting telescope. He taught himself to polish metal mirrors and, beginning in 1827, worked at it for years. He cut his eyeteeth on a 36-inch telescope and finally built his dream instrument, a 72-inch telescope, called "Leviathan," in 1845. It is supposed to have cost him £30,000. The work was particularly quixotic because weather conditions were so poor on his home estate in Ireland that it was rarely possible to use the clumsy instrument. (It took four men to run it.) Even so, Lord Rosse managed to make some important observations.

For one thing, he was the first to make out the spiral shapes of cloudy objects that some three quarters of a century later were recognized as independent galaxies like our Milky Way, and millions of light-years away. He detected the first in 1845 and fourteen were discovered by 1850. He also studied the irregular foggy patch that Messier [305] had listed first in his catalogue of nebulae. For some reason he thought it resembled a crab, and in 1848 he gave it the name of Crab Nebula, which it has kept ever since. In that year he was elected to the Royal Society.

Rosse was a humane man who considered his Irish tenants human beings. During the potato famine of 1846 he turned back a major portion of his rents to the farmers. Four thousand of his tenants gathered twenty years later to mourn his death.

In 1908 a grandson took apart the large telescope, which had grown rickety and dangerous. It had never really done much but give Lord Rosse a reason for living. It was still the largest telescope ever built when it was dismantled, but soon Hale [974] was to have still larger ones built.

[514] **DUMAS,** Jean Baptiste André
(dyoo-mah′)
French chemist
Born: Alais (now Alès), Gard,
July 14, 1800
Died: Cannes, Alpes-Maritimes,
April 10, 1884

Dumas, the son of a town clerk, was in his youth apprenticed to an apothecary in his native town but found the work dull and traveled to relatives in Geneva. There he studied under Candolle [418] among others. His work attracted the favorable attention of Humboldt [397], who brought the young man to Paris where he first worked as assistant to Thénard [416].

He became professor of chemistry at the Athenaeum and was the first French chemist to offer laboratory instruction. He developed a method for determining the molecular weight of a vapor from its density, which would have worked better if he had understood the distinction between an atom and a molecule and been able to apply Avogadro's [412] hypothesis. However, it was to be another generation before chemists became clear on that point.

His real leap to fame came in 1830 when he dared criticize the "radical" theory of chemical structure that Berzelius [425] had advanced, with its atoms and groups of atoms of different electrical nature. Dumas showed that there existed families of organic compounds and that atoms and groups of atoms, supposedly of opposite electrical charge, could substitute one for the other without seriously altering the properties of the compound. His "type" theory of organic structure was more nearly correct in the light of later developments.

Unfortunately Dumas' courage flagged in the face of Berzelius' anger and he retreated, leaving his more stubborn student, Laurent [553], to bear the brunt of the Swedish lightning. Later, when the type theory gained strength, Dumas changed step again and, rather indecently, tried to appropriate full credit at Laurent's expense.

In 1833 Dumas devised an analytical method for the determination of nitrogen in organic compounds which helped make organic analysis quantitative. In 1851, he tried to find regularities among the properties of elements, something Mendeléev [705] was to prove successful in doing, twenty years later.

During the time of Napoleon III, Dumas more or less abandoned science. From 1848 on, he was high in government circles, serving as minister of agriculture, as senator, as master of the French mint, as the equivalent of the mayor of Paris, and so on. His political career, however, ended with the fall of Napoleon.

[515] **WÖHLER,** Friedrich (voi′ler)
German chemist
Born: Eschersheim (near Frankfurt-am-Main), July 31, 1800
Died: Göttingen, September 23, 1882

Wöhler, the son of a veterinary, studied medicine and surgery and took his degree as a physician in 1823, at Heidelberg, specializing in gynecology but was persuaded by his teacher, Gmelin [457], to take up chemistry. He therefore visited Sweden to study with Berzelius [425], forming a lifelong friendship with him. After that he returned to teach in a trade school in Berlin.

Wöhler's primary interest was inorganic chemistry, and he worked out methods of isolating metallic aluminum and beryllium in 1827 and 1828. He also discovered calcium carbide, a substance that reacts readily with water to yield the inflammable gas acetylene and he almost beat out Sefström [451] in the discovery of vanadium.

In those years, however, he performed a much more important deed when quite accidentally he broke down one of the cherished theories of his friend Berzelius.

Berzelius divided chemicals into two kinds, organic and inorganic, depending on whether they had their origin in living tissue or not. Organic chemicals, he believed, required a "vital force" for their manufacture, something not found in the laboratory, so that no chemist could synthesize an organic compound out of an inorganic one without the assistance of living tissue. He felt that different laws might hold for inorganic and organic compounds; that the law of definite proportions did not hold for organic compounds, for instance. Gmelin, Wöhler's old teacher, believed this too. Chevreul [448], on the other hand, was one of those who doubted that the distinction between organic and inorganic could be so absolute.

In 1828 Wöhler settled the matter. He was interested in cyanides and related compounds and was heating ammonium cyanate while on the trail of something or other. To his amazement he found that the ammonium cyanate formed crystals resembling those of urea, and these, on test, proved to be urea. Now urea is the chief nitrogenous waste of the mammalian body, is found in urine, and is definitely organic. Wöhler had formed an organic compound out of an inorganic one and this was a blow against the concept of vitalism that Stahl [241] had set in motion a century and a quarter before (although vitalism was to survive to receive a number of additional blows—and somehow manage to survive those too).

Wöhler announced his discovery to Berzelius on February 22, 1828, and the great Swede (a hard man to argue out of an opinion) eventually conceded the point. Actually the importance of Wöhler's experiment has been exaggerated, for there are grounds for arguing that ammonium cyanate was an organic compound to begin with, and Berzelius did so. However, the formation of urea did inspire other chemists to tackle the problem of synthesizing organics out of inorganics, and a quarter century later the feats of Berthelot [674] in that connection removed all doubts.

Wöhler also showed that when benzoic acid is taken by mouth, hippuric acid (benzoic acid combined with a compound called glycine) appeared in the urine. This was the beginning of the study of chemical changes within the body (metabolism).

Wöhler formed a close friendship with Liebig [532], and after the death of Wöhler's young wife of two years he threw himself into collaborative work with Liebig. Together they worked out the chemistry of a series of substances related to benzene and showed that a collection of atoms, forming the benzoyl group, was transferred intact through a great variety of chemical reactions.

After the death of Strohmeyer [411] in 1836 Wöhler was appointed to fill the former's professorial position at the University of Göttingen, being chosen in preference to many other candidates, including Liebig. The friendship did not suffer as a result. Wöhler built up an inspiring record of teaching at Göttingen, as Liebig was to do at the University of Giessen.

Wöhler did not stick with organic chemistry. He always preferred the inorganic and remained particularly interested in cyanides and in aluminum.

He also noted the similarity of carbon and silicon and was the first to prepare silane (SiH_4), the silicon-analog of methane (CH_4).

[516] GOODYEAR, Charles
American inventor
Born: New Haven, Connecticut, December 29, 1800
Died: New York, New York, July 1, 1860

Goodyear was the son of an inventor of farm implements. He was one of those men who have indomitable perseverance combined with a talent for failure, and there is no surer formula for frustration. As a young man he entered the hardware business with his father and the two went bankrupt in 1830. Thereafter life was a continuous race with creditors and consisted of grinding poverty broken up by frequent visits to debtors' prisons.

In 1834 he grew interested in rubber. At the time, it was recognized that rubber could be a valuable waterproofing material (in fact it had already been used in the manufacture of raincoats). Unfortunately in cold weather rubber got stiff as a plank and in hot weather it became soft and sticky.

Goodyear decided to discover a way of correcting these shortcomings. He was no chemist and hadn't the slightest notion of what one might do, but in the usual tradition of America's nineteenth-century tinkerers he determined to try everything until he hit on something. His first experiments were conducted while in a debtors' prison.

Some people had been trying to mix rubber with sulfur and Goodyear tried it too, with only limited success. Then, in 1839, some of the mixture came accidentally into contact with a hot stove. To Goodyear's astonishment, those portions that weren't scorched too badly had become dry flexible rubber that didn't lose its flexibility in the cold or its dryness in the warmth. He began to heat the rubber-sulfur mixtures at higher temperatures than anyone else had tried and thus discovered vulcanized rubber (after Vulcan, the Roman god of fire). Goodyear patented the process in 1844.

Unfortunately the process was too simple. As in the case of Whitney's [386] cotton gin, anyone could do it and everybody did. Goodyear had to spend all his time contesting infringements on his patent—about sixty in number, all told. It was not until 1852 that he won his case in the courts (no less a person than Daniel Webster, taking part in his last important trial, was his lawyer).

Even then Goodyear's talent for failure won out. He traveled to London and Paris to promote vulcanized rubber, and although Napoleon III awarded him the Legion of Honor, that meant nothing in terms of money. Goodyear was forced to spend large sums of money, which he had to borrow, in the hope of vast returns. (He passed some time in a French debtors' prison.) Eventually of course wealth might indeed have poured in. However, he died too soon, more in debt than he had ever been in his life, the estimated total being not less than $200,000 and perhaps as high as $600,000.

His name lives on in an automobile tire brand name. It was automobile tires that, half a century after Goodyear's death, came to represent the major use of the improved rubber he had invented.

[517] **DUJARDIN,** Félix (dyoo-zhahr-dan′)
French zoologist
Born: Tours, Indre-et-Loire, April 5, 1801
Died: Rennes, Ille-et-Vilaine, April 8, 1860

Dujardin was the son of a watchmaker. His interest in science was aroused when a family friend, who happened to be a surgeon, lent him books on anatomy and chemistry. He was largely self-educated, having lost out in an attempt to enter the École Polytechnique through failure in mathematics.

He attempted to find himself in chemistry, in mineralogy (and in art, too) but finally made his mark in zoology, particularly in the study of protozoa.

In his careful studies, Dujardin failed to see any of the organ systems that Ehrenberg [491], with the support of Cuvier [396], had insisted were to be found in protozoa. There were no complete digestive systems with oral and anal orifices, merely vacuoles that could form and disappear. In this, he was perfectly right, though he did not succeed in persuading Ehrenberg of it.

Dujardin studied other invertebrate groups, too, and in particular, his studies of flatworms laid the foundation for later work on parasitology.

[518] **MILLER,** William Hallowes
English mineralogist
Born: Llandovery, Carmarthenshire, Wales, April 6, 1801
Died: Cambridge, May 20, 1880

Miller, the son of an army officer who served in the American Revolutionary war, graduated from Cambridge in 1826.

His chief contribution to science was his book *A Treatise on Crystallography*, published in 1839. In it he set up a system of reference axes for crystals in which the different systems of crystal forms could be expressed in terms of three whole numbers, for each crystal face. These Millerian indices have been used ever since.

In 1843 Miller undertook the responsibility for preparing new standards for length and weight, the old ones having been destroyed in the fire in 1834 that destroyed the Parliament buildings.

[519] **LARTET,** Édouard Armand Isidore Hippolyte (lahr-tay′)
French paleontologist
Born: Saint Guirauld, Gers, April 15, 1801
Died: Seissan, Haute Garonne, January 28, 1871

Lartet, the son of a landowner, studied law at the University of Toulouse, receiving his license in 1820, but became fascinated with the fossils that Cuvier [396] was making famous. He made diggings of his own, finding fossils of primitive apes and, in particular, exploring caves in southwestern France. All in all, this nonpracticing lawyer became one of the founders of modern paleontology. Not long before his death he received the academic recognition of being appointed professor of paleontology at the Museum of the Jardin des Plantes.

His most spectacular discovery (about 1860) was of a mammoth tooth, which he found in a cave. On it had been scratched an excellent drawing of a mammoth by someone who, clearly, had seen it in life. There was no way of getting round this demonstration that creatures at least intelligent enough to be artists had been coexistent with the mammoth. It was the most powerful blow yet against the traditionally interpreted chronology of the Bible.

[520] **FECHNER,** Gustav Theodor (fekh′ner)
German physicist
Born: Gross-Särchen, Saxony, April 19, 1801
Died: Leipzig, Saxony, November 18, 1887

Fechner, the son of a minister, was precocious, learning Latin by the age of five, when his father, who was also his teacher, died. He obtained his medical degree at Leipzig in 1822 and spent the rest of his life there, never actually practicing medicine. Originally a physicist, he was among the first to apply Ohm's [461] law to electric circuits.

He passed through a long siege of illness and in 1840 suffered partial blindness from too much gazing at the sun through colored glasses in an attempt to study afterimages. He therefore turned to the less demanding (at least, physically) subjects of philosophy, poetry, literature, and experimental psychology in later life. He even wrote humorous poems and satires under the pseudonym of Dr. Mises and achieved some success in this way.

He popularized Weber's [492] law, to which his own name came to be attached. He attributed more accuracy to it than it possessed and attempted to found upon it a science he called psychophysics. He published a book on the subject in 1860. For all his mysticism and overenthusiasm, he gave a healthy boost to experimental psychology.

[521] **PLÜCKER,** Julius (plyoo′ker)
German mathematician and physicist
Born: Elberfeld (now Wuppertal), Rhenish Prussia, June 16, 1801
Died: Bonn, Rhenish Prussia, May 22, 1868

Plücker, the son of a merchant, obtained his doctorate from the University of Marburg in 1825.

The first half of his life was spent on pure mathematics, and he did notable work in analytic geometry. In 1834 he

345

was professor of mathematics at Halle and in 1836 at Bonn. Beginning in 1847 he turned his attention to physics and in his studies of spectroscopy all but anticipated the advance made by Kirchhoff [648] in the following decade.

When Geissler [583] tubes became available he began to force an electric current through a vacuum and in 1858 wrote a paper describing the fluorescent effects in detail.

His key discovery was that when placed in the field of an electromagnet, the fluorescent glow shifted its position. The shift altered its direction diametrically when the poles of the magnetism were shifted. Whatever the fluorescence was, an electrical charge was involved in its production. This was the first tentative move in the direction of subatomic particles.

In 1865 Plücker found his interest in physics waning, and at the urging of friends, he returned to mathematics.

[522] MÜLLER, Johannes Peter (myoo'-ler)
German physiologist
Born: Koblenz, Rhenish Prussia, July 14, 1801
Died: Berlin, April 28, 1858

Müller, the son of a shoemaker, turned to biology after an initial temptation to become a priest. He studied medicine at the University of Bonn and obtained his degree in 1822. He contributed to almost every branch of biology, served on the faculty first of Bonn then, after 1833, at the University of Berlin. He shared with Magendie [438] credit for founding the modern science of physiology.

His most dramatic discovery was made in 1826, when he was able to show that sensory nerves could interpret an impulse in but one way. The optic nerve, however stimulated, records a flash of light, whether light is really involved or not. He was an old-fashioned biologist in some ways, with vitalist leanings, but logic forced him away from vitalism willy-nilly.

During the 1830s he published a large textbook on physiology in which the sci-

ence was interpreted in the new experimental fashion of himself and Magendie and in opposition to the vague mysticism of men such as Oken [423] and his disciples. Man was viewed as a machine rather than as some sort of microcosmic mirror of the universe. Müller was an inspiring teacher and many first-rate nineteenth-century German biologists, such as Schwann [563], Virchow [632], and Helmholtz [631], were among his students. He was extremely neurotic, suffering several nervous breakdowns, one of them after he tried to control student unrest during the Revolution of 1848. He may have died a suicide.

[523] AIRY, Sir George Biddell
English astronomer and mathematician
Born: Alnwick, Northumberland, July 27, 1801
Died: Greenwich (now part of London), January 2, 1892

Airy, the son of a farmer, was a snobbish, self-seeking youngster, who preferred his well-to-do uncle to his father. At the age of 12 he persuaded that uncle to carry him off and bring him up. He entered Cambridge in 1819 and graduated in 1823 at the head of his class in mathematics. He went on to teach both mathematics and astronomy at the university.

He advanced himself with ruthless intensity and although everyone disliked him, he was successful in his aims. In 1835 he was appointed seventh astronomer royal, a post he was to hold for over forty-five years, retiring in 1881 at the age of eighty.

He modernized the Greenwich Observatory, equipping it with excellent instruments and bringing it up to the level of the German observatories, which since Herschel's [321] heyday had, under the leadership of such men as Gauss [415] and Bessel [439], been forging ahead of those in Great Britain. Airy also organized data that had been put aside to gather dust. He was a conceited, envious, small-minded man and ran the observatory like a petty tyrant, but he made it hum.

A strange fatality haunted Airy, causing him to be remembered for his failures. For instance, he committed himself loudly and firmly against the notion of "lines of force" proposed by Faraday [474], and he was to see Faraday's intuition established on a firm mathematical foundation by Maxwell [692].

He played the role of the villain of the piece in the failure of J. C. Adams [615] to carry through the discovery of Neptune. In fact, Airy is far better known as the man who muffed the discovery of that planet, than for any of the actual accomplishments for which he was deservedly knighted in 1872.

But the most heartbreaking of his failures came in the 1870s and 1880s. With the approach of the nineteenth-century transits of Venus across the face of the sun in 1874 and 1882, Airy was determined to organize vast expeditions to observe the phenomena with unexampled accuracy. In this way he hoped to obtain a measurement of the scale of the solar system still more accurate than that of the recently dead Encke [475]. No effort was spared. Airy's obsessive thoroughness was exercised to the full. He personally trained the observers and even built a model of the Venus transit so that all the motions might be gone through in advance in a kind of dry run.

The expeditions were a failure, for Venus's atmosphere made the moment of contact with the solar disc uncertain. He might have done better to listen to Galle [573], who in 1872 suggested that asteroids, which showed no visible disc, be used for parallax measurements. It was this suggestion that bore fruit under H. Spencer Jones [1140], another astronomer royal, half a century later. In fairness to Airy it must be stated that in his time no asteroid was known to be close enough to the earth to allow a parallax to be made with the necessary accuracy.

Characteristically, he had one success in a matter involving his personal health. In 1827 he was the first to design eyeglass lenses to correct for astigmatic vision—which he himself had.

In 1855 he anticipated Dutton's [753] theory of isostasy to some extent.

[524] **BORDEN,** Gail
American inventor and food technologist
Born: Norwich, New York, November 9, 1801
Died: Borden, Texas, January 11, 1874

Borden's family and later he himself moved continuously westward during the first three decades of his life. By 1829 he had settled in Texas (then part of Mexico). During the War of Texan Independence, he published the one newspaper in the territory. He served as a surveyor, too, producing the first topographical map of the Texas territory and surveying the land upon which the city of Galveston was to be founded.

In 1849, because of the discovery of gold in California, the westward migratory tide became a flood and Borden grew interested in preparing some form of concentrated food that would be nourishing and easily preserved. He produced a dried beef product called pemmican (after a similar Cree Indian product) that won a gold medal at the London Fair of 1851 and that was useful not only for pioneers crossing the western lands, but also, later, for Arctic explorers. Borden failed to sell his pemmican to the army, however, and so it proved a financial failure. In the early 1850s he moved back to New York State and turned his attention to making an easily preserved milk concentrate. In 1853 he produced evaporated milk, used extensively by the armed forces during the Civil War. Later he prepared concentrates of fruit juices and of various beverages and, what with all this, gained a large fortune. He gave birth to the movement that now supplies all the instant-this-and-thats filling our food markets today.

[525] **BOUSSINGAULT,** Jean Baptiste Joseph Dieudonné (boo-sang-goh')
French agricultural chemist
Born: Paris, February 2, 1802
Died: Paris, May 12, 1887

Boussingault was a mineralogist to begin with, having graduated from the mining school of St. Étienne, in Paris, in 1832. In the employ of a mining company, he traveled to South America. He arrived there in time to be involved with the wars of independence of the Spanish colonies, and actually served under Simón Bolívar. For a while he was in charge of the mines of the newly independent nation of Colombia.

Back in France he grew interested in agricultural chemistry and may be considered the founder of the experimental aspect of that subject. One of the tasks he set himself in the 1840s was tracing the source of the nitrogen in the compounds of living organisms. In the case of plants he was able to show that legumes (peas, beans, etc.) obtained their nitrogen from the air, for when he grew such plants in nitrogen-free soil and watered them with nitrogen-free water, they nevertheless gained nitrogen. It could only come from the air. (It was not till half a century later that it was shown that it was not the plant itself that "fixed" the nitrogen, but bacteria growing in nodules about the roots.)

On the other hand, he was also able to show that animals could not use atmospheric nitrogen at all. Boussingault was the first to try to feed animals on a scientifically restricted diet, inadequate for the organism's needs, in order to measure the loss of weight. He showed that the only nitrogen incorporated into the body came from the nitrogen of the food. He was also able to measure the nutritive values of different foods in this manner by checking the quantities necessary to prevent loss of weight. He established a precedent in this respect that, suitably refined, was to be of inestimable value a half century later in studies of vitamins, trace minerals, and other food factors.

Acting on a statement by Humboldt [397] that South American Indians believed certain salt deposits to be capable of curing goiter, a young doctor obtained samples of those deposits and sent them to Boussingault for analysis. Boussingault found iodine in them and suggested that iodine compounds might be the cure for goiter. The suggestion was ignored for over half a century, but Boussingault was right just the same.

His work culminated in the production between 1860 and 1874 of an eight-volume treatise on agricultural chemistry.

[526] **WHEATSTONE**, Sir Charles
English physicist
Born: Gloucester, February 6, 1802
Died: Paris, France, October 19, 1875

Wheatstone was primarily interested in acoustics in his younger days and in the manufacture of musical instruments (a family involvement). In 1829 he invented the concertina, a small accordionlike instrument. He had no formal scientific training but was sufficiently self-educated to gain a professorship in experimental philosophy at King's College, London, in 1834.

He grew interested in electricity and invented a form of the telegraph, in which he somewhat anticipated Morse [473] and which he constructed only after a long visit from Henry [503]. Wheatstone was knighted in 1868 for this and for an improvement (in 1841) of the electric generator that caused it to deliver a less varying current.

His name is best known, however, in connection with the Wheatstone bridge, a device that can measure the resistance of a circuit very delicately by balancing a number of currents against each other. Although his use of this device was what brought it into prominence, he was not its inventor and, indeed, openly admitted he was not.

[527] **ABEL**, Niels Henrik (ah-bel′)
Norwegian mathematician
Born: Finnøy Island, near Stavanger, August 5, 1802
Died: Froland, April 6, 1829

Abel, the son of an alcoholic pastor, lived his life in poverty and suffered professionally from being in Norway, out of the mainstream of scientific advance in France and Germany. He had to support the family when his father died, but he managed to attend the University of

Christiania (now Oslo) in Norway's chief city. There a teacher recognized his talent, encouraged him, and helped him financially.

During this period he tackled the solution to the general equation of the fifth degree. Equations of the third and fourth degree had been solved generally in the time of Cardano [137] but the fifth degree had withstood all attacks in the nearly three centuries since. For a time, Abel thought he had it, but then he found his mistake and went on, in 1824, to prove the *impossibility* of solving it by algebraic methods.

This was a first-rate discovery and Abel was certain it would prove his passport to the intellectual and academic world. He sent a copy to Gauss [415] who, however, mistakenly thought it to be another crackpot effort at solving the problem and tossed it to one side.

Abel finally managed to get to France and Germany in 1825 and did much important work. The binomial theorem, which had been developed by Newton [231] and Euler [275], was extended by Abel in a completely general form. He also did brilliant work in certain branches of higher math.

Recognition came at last, and in April 1829 news of his forthcoming appointment to a professorial position at the University of Berlin came through. Two days earlier, however, poor Abel had died of tuberculosis at the age of twenty-six.

[528] **HESS,** Germain Henri
Swiss-Russian chemist
Born: Geneva, August 8, 1802
Died: St. Petersburg (now Leningrad), Russia, December 13, 1850

Hess, the son of an artist, was taken to St. Petersburg when he was three because his father had obtained a position as tutor to a rich Russian family. He studied medicine at the University of Dorpat from 1822 to 1825 and pored over chemistry and geology in his spare time. After a month with Berzelius [425] in 1828, he stayed for a period of time in Irkutsk, Siberia. Then in 1830 he went on to a professorial appointment at

the University of St. Petersburg in Russia.

A half century earlier Lavoisier [334] and Laplace [347] had measured heats of combustion, but the subject had remained untouched since then. Hess took up the matter once again and in far greater detail. He measured the heats evolved in various reactions and was able to demonstrate that the quantity of heat produced in going from Substance A to Substance B was the same no matter by what chemical route the reaction proceeded or in how many stages.

This, now called Hess's law, was announced in 1840. By this law Hess made himself the founder of thermochemistry. The evolution of a fixed quantity of heat independently of the nature of the route taken by the reaction was a clear hint that thermodynamics might apply to chemical reactions as well as to heat engines and paved the way for the climactic development of chemical thermodynamics by Gibbs [740] a generation later.

Hess also wrote a chemistry textbook that was the standard Russian work in the science till it was superseded by Mendeléev's [705].

[529] **BALARD,** Antoine Jérôme (ba-lahr′)
French chemist
Born: Montpellier, Hérault, September 30, 1802
Died: Paris, March 30, 1876

Balard was born of poor vine-growers, and it was his godmother who saw to his education as an apothecary. He came to Paris to study at the École de Pharmacie and there he served as assistant to Thénard [416]. He graduated in 1826. He was interested in the chemistry of the sea, particularly, and did considerable searching for new sources of iodine, the element that Courtois [414] had discovered the previous decade in the ashes of seaweed.

In his own researches among the ashes he noted that at times the liquid with which he was extracting his ashes turned brown. In 1826 he tracked this color to a substance that seemed to be intermediate in its properties between chlorine and io-dine. At first he thought he had a com-pound of those two elements, an iodine chloride, so to speak, but further investi-gation convinced him it was a new ele-ment, which came to be called bromine.

(Liebig [532] had come across the same element some years before, had considered it iodine chloride, and had put it away in a bottle with that name on its label. After Balard's announcement, he rushed back to it and found it to be bromine.)

The fact that bromine was an element helped confirm the opinion (just about accepted by then) that chlorine and io-dine were elements. The fact that bro-mine was intermediate in its properties between chlorine and iodine was also the final proof to Döbereiner [427] that his law of triads was correct. And though Döbereiner's triads were ignored for a generation, they remained an important step in the direction of the periodic table.

Balard remained interested in sea water and devised methods for extracting various salts, such as sodium sulfate, from it. In 1858 deposits of potassium salts were discovered at Stassfurt, Ger-many (the remains of a long-since dried-up arm of the ocean), and the existing oceans were abandoned as a source. In the mid-twentieth century, chemists re-turned to the ocean, which is now the prime source of magnesium metal and of Balard's bromine. No doubt the ocean will serve more and more as a source of mineral wealth.

In 1842, when Thénard left his post at the Sorbonne, Balard succeeded him, and in 1851 he was appointed to a professorial position at the Collège de France.

[530] **BOLYAI**, Janos (boh'lyoy)
Hungarian mathematician
Born: Kolozsvár, Hungary (now Cluj, Romania), December 15, 1802
Died: Marosvásárhely, Hungary (now Târgu-Mures, Romania), January 17, 1860

Janos Bolyai was the son of a mathe-matician who as a young man became a good friend of Gauss [415]. The elder Bolyai had been interested in trying to prove Euclid's [40] parallel axiom but of course had failed and had warned his son in dramatic terms against wasting his time on the problem. That merely served to entice his son into working on it when the time came.

Bolyai went to engineering school in Vienna at fifteen and at twenty joined the army. In addition to his proficiency in mathematics he had the romantic Hungarian attributes of being a skillful violinist and an excellent duelist. He is once supposed to have measured swords with thirteen men, one after the other, playing the violin between duels and beating them all.

By 1823 he had worked out the same ideas that Lobachevski [484] was work-ing out in Russia. In 1831, when the elder Bolyai published a book on mathe-matics, he included a twenty-six-page ap-pendix written by his son that was worth several times the rest of the book put to-gether. It explained the non-Euclidean geometry that Lobachevski, unknown to the Bolyais, had already published three years earlier.

Gauss praised the paper but could not resist the pettiness of saying he had done the work himself earlier (without publishing—presumably because, though he had the genius to do the work, he lacked the courage to withstand the criti-cism so revolutionary a publication might bring down upon himself). The embarrassed Bolyai, equally petty, re-fused to do any additional work in the field.

[531] **MULDER**, Gerardus Johannes (moil'der)
Dutch chemist
Born: Utrecht, December 27, 1802
Died: Bennekom, April 18, 1880

Mulder obtained his medical degree from the University of Utrecht in 1825.

He was particularly interested in the albuminous substances characteristic of living tissue, which seemed more complicated in constitution than the fats and carbohydrates, and which altered properties radically on even mild heating.

His researches led him to believe that these substances were made up of a basic building block containing atoms of carbon, hydrogen, oxygen, and nitrogen and that to these were added varying numbers of sulfur and phosphorus atoms. He called the basic building block protein from a Greek word for "first" since that was the foundation of substances that seemed, in turn, to be of first importance in living tissue.

Mulder's theories of the structure of albuminous substances proved to be wrong. Their structure was much more complicated than he supposed. Nevertheless, the word he used for the building block came to be attached to the albuminous substances themselves. This invention of a word is Mulder's only important contribution to science—but it is a very important word and suffices.

[532] **LIEBIG,** Justus von (lee′bikh)
German chemist
Born: Darmstadt, Hesse, May 12, 1803
Died: Munich, Bavaria, April 18, 1873

Liebig's father dealt in salts and pigments and conducted amateur chemical experiments with them. That was Liebig's introduction to chemistry. In 1818 he was apprenticed to an apothecary, but he did not rest until he could go to a university for formal instruction. He went to Bonn for this purpose but the post-Napoleonic period was a time of reaction and repression in Central Europe. Liebig was arrested for political activity on the side of liberalism and had to leave Bonn. He made his way to Paris with the financial help of the Hessian government and there was befriended by Humboldt [397] and Thénard [416]. In 1822 his influential friends obtained for him the award, *in absentia,* of the doctor's degree he had earned. Then, through Humboldt's recommendation, he

worked in the laboratory of Gay-Lussac [420].

In 1824 he completed his investigation of a series of compounds called fulminates. At the same time Wöhler [515] was studying the cyanates (out of one of which he would be preparing urea in a few years, and revolutionizing chemistry). When both papers were published in a journal of which Gay-Lussac was editor, Gay-Lussac noticed that the formulas of the two sets of compounds were the same.

Berzelius [425], informed of this, was astounded that different compounds should have the same formula. At first, in fact, he flatly refused to believe it. He investigated and found it to be true in other cases. He referred to such compounds of similar formula as isomers (from Greek words meaning "equal parts"). This was the beginning of the realization that the molecule of a compound was more than a collection of particular atoms; these atoms had to be arranged in a particular way and different arrangements meant different properties. In this way the notion of a structural formula was born and came to maturity with Kekulé [680] a generation later.

As a result of this interconnection of their work, Liebig and Wöhler became fast friends and conducted a series of researches together.

Liebig was as opinionated and as quarrelsome as Berzelius and as apt to take up the wrong side in a controversy. Of the great chemists of the time, only Wöhler (whose disposition was as sweet as Liebig's was caustic) escaped his sharp tongue and pen. In fact, Wöhler tried, gently, to keep Liebig's temper within bounds.

Liebig entered the new field of organic chemistry (given such a new aspect by his friend Wöhler) with great enthusiasm. Organic compounds generally had molecules of far more complicated structure than those of inorganic ones, and methods for analyzing the former quantitatively lagged. Gay-Lussac and Thénard had worked out a way of burning organic compounds and measuring the quantity of carbon dioxide and water that was formed. By 1831 Liebig had taken this technique in hand and perfected it to the point where, from the figures on carbon dioxide and water formed, accurate measurements of the carbon and hydrogen in the original compound could be obtained. Dumas [514] added a satisfactory method for determining nitrogen, and the Liebig-Dumas method of quantitative organic analysis remained in effect, almost untouched, until the development of micromethods of analysis by Pregl [982] some three quarters of a century later.

In 1824 Liebig had begun to teach at the university in the small Hessian city of Giessen and there he proved himself one of the great chemistry teachers of all time. He established a laboratory for general student use (an innovation) and was the intellectual father and grandfather of most of the chemists since his time. Giessen became the chemical center of the world for a quarter century, and helped make Germany chemically supreme in the latter half of the nineteenth century.

In 1845 Liebig was created a baron. In 1852, his health having worsened, he accepted an appointment at the University of Munich on condition that he need not be expected to teach, and remained there for the rest of his life.

In the latter half of his career Liebig became interested in biochemistry. He applied his analytic abilities to the examination of tissue fluids such as blood, bile, and urine. He maintained and helped establish the view that body heat and vital activity arose out of the energy derived from the oxidation of foodstuffs within the body, and declared carbohydrates and fat—rather than carbon and hydrogen as Lavoisier [334] had thought—the fuel of the body. In this he was proved correct. He also believed, as Berzelius did, that fermentation was a purely chemical phenomenon, not involving life. He engaged in a long dispute with Pasteur [642] on this subject and here Liebig was proved to be wrong.

He also concerned himself with agricultural chemistry, after the British Association for the Advancement of Science had happened to ask him to prepare a report on the subject. He maintained (correctly) that the chief factor in the loss of soil fertility was the consumption by the plant of the mineral content of the soil; that is, of compounds containing elements essential to life, such as sodium, potassium, calcium, and phosphorus.

He was the first to experiment with fertilization through the addition of chemical fertilizers in place of natural products such as manures. Unfortunately, he was of the opinion that plants generally obtained their nitrogen from the atmosphere, as Boussingault [525] had shown that peas and beans did. Therefore, Liebig did not add nitrogen compounds to his chemical fertilizers and they did not succeed in promoting fertility.

Eventually though, this mistake was rectified. The use of chemical fertilizers has not only greatly multiplied the food supply of those nations making use of scientific agriculture but also helped reduce epidemics through the elimination of the ubiquitous manure pile.

[533] **ERICSSON**, John
Swedish-American inventor
Born: Långbanshyttan, Värmland, Sweden, July 31, 1803
Died: New York, New York, March 8, 1889

After a six-year hitch as an engineering officer in the Swedish army, Ericsson, the son of a mines inspector, resigned and devoted himself to inventions. In 1826 he went to England and tried his hand at devising a steam locomotive. In this he was beaten by Stephenson [431], but in 1836 he devised the screw propeller, which replaced the huge paddle wheel as a propulsive device for steamships. For the first time it was practical to apply steam propulsion to war vessels, since the paddle wheel had till then made entirely too large and vulnerable a target.

In 1839 he came to the United States and built a screw-propelled vessel for the American navy. One of the guns on this vessel, the U.S.S. *Princeton,* exploded while government officials were inspecting it and a number were killed. President John Tyler himself had a narrow escape. This damaged Ericsson's reputation for a while, though the explosion was in no way his responsibility.

He stayed in this country and became an American citizen in 1848. This was fortunate, for in 1861 he built the *Monitor*, an ironclad vessel, the plans of which Napoleon III of France had turned down. It was launched just in time for it to sail south to battle to a draw the Confederate navy's ironclad *Merrimac*. Without the *Monitor*, the South would have broken the Northern blockade and, with English help, might have gone on to win the Civil War. The battle of the *Monitor* and the *Merrimac* at Hampton Roads, Virginia, ended at a stroke the supremacy of the wooden vessel and introduced the era of the modern navies of metal (even though both ships were, in essence, destroyed in the battle).

A year after his death his body, at the request of the Swedish government, was sent back to the land of his birth. He was buried there.

[534] **DOPPLER,** Christian Johann
(dohp'ler)
Austrian physicist
Born: Salzburg, November 29, 1803
Died: Venice, Italy (then under Austria), March 17, 1853

Doppler, the son of a master mason, was lost to America by a hair. In 1835, despairing of getting an academic appointment, he made ready to emigrate to the United States. At the last moment he received word of the offer of a professorship in mathematics at a school in Prague and abandoned his plans for emigration. After the revolutionary turmoils of 1848 and 1849, Doppler in 1850 took a position in Vienna where he felt more secure.

His name is forever associated with the Doppler effect, that phenomenon in which a moving sound source seems more highly pitched to someone whom it is approaching than to someone moving with the source; and more deeply pitched to someone from whom it is moving away than to someone moving with the source. The most familiar everyday example is the behavior of the sound of the locomotive whistle as the train passes by someone standing at a station. From a high pitch it drops suddenly to a low one.

Doppler explained the phenomenon correctly by pointing out that the sound waves partake of the motion of the source and reach the ear at shorter intervals when the source is approaching—hence higher pitch. When the source recedes, the waves reach the ear at longer intervals—hence lower pitch.

In 1842 he worked out a mathematical relationship, relating the pitch to the relative motion of source and observer. This was tested by a rather bizarre experiment in Holland a couple of years later. For two days a locomotive pulled a flat car back and forth at different speeds. On the flat car were trumpeters, sounding this note or that. On the ground, musicians with a sense of absolute pitch recorded the note as the train approached and as it receded. Doppler's equations held up.

Doppler predicted that a similar effect would hold for light waves but his explanation of the behavior of light from a moving source was not quite accurate. This portion of the theory was worked out properly a few years later by Fizeau [620] and turned out to be of great importance to astronomy.

[535] **CHALLIS,** James
English astronomer
Born: Braintree, Essex, December 12, 1803
Died: Cambridge, December 3, 1882

Challis graduated from Cambridge in 1825 and became director of the Cambridge Observatory in 1836. In 1845 he was asked by Airy [523] to check the position predicted by J. C. Adams [615] as one in which a possible trans-Uranian planet might be found.

Challis did not wish to do this, feeling

that it was a waste of time and that it was much more important that he continue his work of hunting for comets. He therefore put off the job as long as he could, and then when procrastination could be continued no longer, he did the job in so dilatory a manner that he never bothered to compare the observations of one day with those of another to see if one of the stars had shifted position and was a planet.

The result was that Galle [573] sighted the new planet, Neptune, first, and only after that did Challis, making use of hindsight, discover that he had observed Neptune twice, before Galle's announcement, but had failed to know that through his own stupidity. In fact, Challis is only remembered in astronomy for this stupidity. That he himself lost credit for the discovery is of no account; that he helped lose Adams the credit is a tragedy.

[536] **LENZ,** Heinrich Friedrich Emil (lents)
Russian physicist
Born: Dorpat, Estonia, (now Tartu, Estonian SSR), February 24, 1804
Died: Rome, Italy, February 10, 1865

Lenz, the son of a magistrate, had originally studied theology but grew interested in science. Between 1823 and 1826, he accompanied a scientific ocean voyage around the globe as Darwin [554] was to do a few years later. He then spent most of his life as professor of physics at the University of St. Petersburg.

Lenz was investigating electrical induction at about the same time as Faraday [474] and Henry [503] and was third in the field. He made a generalization in 1834 to the effect that a current induced by electromagnetic forces always produces effects that oppose those forces. This is Lenz's law and is a general description of the phenomenon of self-induction. Lenz's law must be taken into account in the design of electrical equipment.

In 1833 Lenz also reported his discovery of the manner in which the resistance of a metallic conductor changes with temperature, increasing with rise of temperature, decreasing with its fall.

[537] **SIEBOLD,** Karl Theodor Ernst von (zee'bohlt)
German zoologist
Born: Würzburg, Bavaria, February 16, 1804
Died: Munich, Bavaria, April 7, 1885

Siebold was a member of a scientific dynasty, for his brother, father, uncle, and grandfather were all engaged in one or another of the biological sciences. Siebold himself received his medical degree in 1828, practiced medicine briefly, then, with the advantage of a recommendation from Humboldt [397], served as professor of zoology at various German universities, ending at Munich.

In 1845 he published a book on comparative anatomy in which he dealt in detail with protozoa. He made it quite clear that these consisted of single cells, thus supporting Dujardin [517] against Ehrenberg [491], and decisively so. The cell theory, which had recently been advanced by Schleiden [538] and Schwann [563], would therefore have to state that organisms were composed of "one or more cells" rather than merely "of cells."

Siebold was also the first to study cilia. He showed that unicellular creatures could use these for locomotion, whipping themselves through the water with these numerous hairlike projections. In higher animals, cilia, by their whipping, set up water currents.

[538] **SCHLEIDEN,** Matthias Jakob (shly'den)
German botanist
Born: Hamburg, April 5, 1804
Died: Frankfurt, June 23, 1881

Schleiden, the son of a prosperous physician, was trained as a lawyer, obtaining his degree in 1822. At this work he was most unhappy, even attempting suicide. He found refuge in botany, working under J. Müller [522], and this became first his hobby, then his profession. He rebelled against the occupation of most botanists, which consisted of the ever more painstaking classification and subclassification of plants. Instead, he placed plant tissue under the microscope.

This led him in 1838 to the elaboration of the cell theory for plants, which Schwann [563] was to extend, more systematically, to animals the next year. Schleiden particularly recognized the importance of the cell nucleus, discovered earlier that decade by Robert Brown [403]. He sensed its connection with cell division but imagined (wrongly) that new cells budded out of the nuclear surface. Schwann went along with Schleiden in this mistaken belief.

Schleiden received a doctoral degree at the University of Jena in 1839. Although under the influence of the "nature philosopher" school, which in the persons of Baer [478], Owen [539], and others, led the fight against Darwin [554], Schleiden was among the first of the German biologists to accept Darwinian evolution.

He was a very successful science popularizer, both in lectures and in articles.

[539] **OWEN,** Sir Richard
English zoologist
Born: Lancaster, July 20, 1804
Died: Richmond Park, London, December 18, 1892

Owen, the son of a merchant, obtained his medical degree in 1826 at the University of Edinburgh, after having served an apprenticeship to a surgeon. After graduation, however, he accepted a post as assistant to the conservator of the museum of the Royal College of Surgeons, which introduced him to the joys of zoological classification. This was sharpened and directed through a meeting with Cuvier [396], who visited London in 1830. Owen went on to study in Paris and caught the contagion of comparative anatomy. In 1856 he was appointed superintendent of the Natural History Department of the British Museum. He was

Cuvier's true successor through most of the nineteenth century.

He dissected as many animals as he could. In 1852, while dissecting a rhinoceros, he discovered the parathyroid glands. Another generation passed before they were discovered in man. In particular he was interested in comparing tooth structure, on which he wrote a large treatise in the early 1840s. This is by no means as odd as it might sound, for teeth are the hardest parts of the body and the most easily preserved in fossil form. From the teeth, moreover, a great deal can be learned about the feeding habits and the mode of life of a creature.

Owen, through his interest in teeth, was directed to a study of fossils and extinct animals (paleontology), particularly those of Australia and New Zealand. He was the first to describe the giant and recently extinct moas of New Zealand. At the other end of the scale, he was also the first to describe the parasite (anything but extinct, alas) that Leuckart [640] was to show causes trichinosis in man.

He was the first of the great dinosaur-hunters, having coined the very word ("terrible lizard") in 1842. In 1854 he prepared the first full-sized reconstructions of dinosaurs for display at the Crystal Palace in London. The reconstructions were quite inaccurate, we now know, because of the limited information that had been obtained, but they were very dramatic just the same and aroused enormous interest in the subject.

He refused a knighthood in 1842 but accepted in 1884 at the time of his retirement. The latter half of his career was marked by a violent hostility to the notion of evolution through natural selection as advanced by Darwin [554], a hostility that caused him to go to the extreme of writing anonymous articles in which were included deliberate distortions and misquotations, and of feeding rabble rousers with antievolutionary arguments. In this, he may have been motivated by personal jealousy of Darwin's increasing fame, despite the fact that they had previously been good friends for twenty years.

It was not so much that he was against

evolution itself but that he was the last of the major "nature philosophers," the school initiated by Oken [423] a half century earlier. Owen, therefore, had vitalistic notions of evolution's taking place through internal forces within the cells. Evolution through natural selection was too rationalistic and seemed too much the product of blind chance to suit him.

[540] **WEBER,** Wilhelm Eduard (vay'-ber)
German physicist
Born: Wittenberg, Saxony, October 24, 1804
Died: Göttingen, June 23, 1891

Weber, the younger brother of Ernst Weber [492], was appointed professor of physics at Göttingen in 1831. Young Weber had met Gauss [415] through the good offices of Humboldt [397] and it was at Gauss's recommendation that the appointment was made. For most of his professional life, Weber then worked in collaboration with Gauss on the study of magnetic phenomena.

In 1837 he and a number of other professors lost their posts because of their open opposition to the autocracy of the king of Hannover. Eventually he was reinstated.

Gauss introduced a logical system of units for magnetism, related to the fundamental units of mass, length, and time. Weber did the same for electricity in 1846. These units were officially accepted at an international congress in Paris in 1881, at which Helmholtz [631] was a prominent delegate. The magnetic unit, weber, is named in his honor. With Gauss, Weber also constructed a practical telegraph in 1834, even before Henry [503] had managed to do so.

In conjunction with his brother, Ernst, he studied the flow of liquids through tubes—knowledge that could be applied usefully to the human circulatory system. Then, toward the end of his life, he grew interested in spiritualism, a weakness of aged scientists at the turn of the century.

[541] **JACOBI,** Carl Gustav Jacob (yah-koh'bee)
German mathematician
Born: Potsdam, Prussia, December 10, 1804
Died: Berlin, February 18, 1851

Jacobi, the son of a Jewish banker, was a precocious youth who was ready for university training at the age of twelve but was held back till the minimum entrance age of sixteen. He then went to the University of Berlin and obtained his Ph.D. in 1824 and was qualified for a teaching position at an important school despite the disadvantage of his religion.

He gained a professorial position at the University of Königsberg in 1827, thanks in part to the praise of Legendre [358] for Jacobi's work on elliptical functions, a subject Legendre had pioneered. Jacobi went on to develop the subject in full, independently of Abel [527] who was doing the same thing. He also pioneered in the development of determinants, a useful technique in the manipulation of simultaneous equations.

In 1848, during the revolutionary upheavals of that year, Jacobi fell under suspicion as a possible liberal. (His religion was undoubtedly of no help to him.) He had almost left for Vienna when Frederick William IV of Prussia decided the loss to Prussia would be too great and persuaded him to remain.

However, Jacobi, who had developed diabetes, was not a well man and died not long after of smallpox.

[542] **MOHL,** Hugo von (mole)
German botanist
Born: Stuttgart, Baden-Württemberg, April 8, 1805
Died: Tübingen, Baden-Württemberg, April 1, 1872

Mohl obtained his doctorate in 1828 at the University of Tübingen and then became a professor of botany there in 1835. He held the post till his death.

He studied plant cells assiduously. In 1846 he felt it important to distinguish between the watery, nonliving sap in the center of the cell and the granular, colloidal material rimming the cell. This latter portion, which he recognized as living, he called protoplasm, adapting Purkinje's [452] word.

It was an easy step from that to using the word for the granular colloidal material within all cells generally, something Remak [591] was soon to do.

He was the first to propose that new cells sprang from cell division and provided the first clear explanation of osmosis, whereby liquid moves from a less concentrated side across a membrane to a more concentrated side.

[543] **JACKSON,** Charles Thomas
American chemist
Born: Plymouth, Massachusetts,
June 21, 1805
Died: Somerville, Massachusetts,
August 28, 1880

Jackson could trace his ancestry to the *Mayflower* and was a brother-in-law of the philosopher, Ralph Waldo Emerson. He obtained his medical degree from Harvard in 1829, but after 1836 practiced no more. Like the far greater Hooke [223] a century and a half earlier, he was a man with a restless mind, given to starting jobs and not finishing them, and a bear for controversy besides.

He was interested in geology as well as medicine and chemistry and he made geological surveys of various parts of New England between 1837 and 1844. He experimented with ether, breathing himself into insensibility, and instructed Morton [617] in the proper method of administering it. He was enraged when Morton went ahead and achieved fame. Jackson began a long and pertinacious quarrel over priority.

He engaged in a similar quarrel over priority with Morse [473] in connection with the telegraph and also insisted on claiming himself the true discoverer of the explosive, guncotton. Madness was never far below the surface with him, and in 1873 it took over completely. He remained insane for the rest of his life.

[544] **FITZROY,** Robert (fits-roy')
English meteorologist
Born: Ampton Hall, Suffolk, July
5, 1805
Died: Upper Norwood, London,
April 30, 1865

Fitzroy was a descendant of an illegitimate child of Charles II, and his family had a seafaring tradition. He entered the Royal Naval College in 1819 and was commissioned a lieutenant in 1824.

In 1828 he was put in command of the *Beagle* and ordered to undertake the surveying of the southern coasts of South America. On a second voyage for the purpose, beginning in the summer of 1831, Fitzroy chose as his scientific aide, the young Charles Darwin [554]. Because of this, the second voyage of the *Beagle,* which lasted five years and involved the circumnavigation of the world, became possibly the most important voyage (from the scientific standpoint) in history, and Fitzroy is known, almost exclusively, for his relationship to Darwin.

Fitzroy, a moody man, and given to deep depressions, was a hard man to get along with and even the equable and gentle Darwin couldn't manage to do it. What's more, Fitzroy, ardently religious, was pained by Darwin's interpretations of his discoveries on the voyage and was horrified by his theory of evolution when it was announced.

Fitzroy was a more than competent navigator and surveyor, however, who fulfilled his task magnificently, and in 1837 fully deserved the gold medal voted him by the Royal Geographic Society.

During the voyage he grew interested in meteorology and, in 1855, was placed in charge of the Meteorologic Office with instructions to gather weather information for the use of shipping. Fitzroy made barometers available to ships' captains, gathered information from them, issued weather forecasts which were printed daily in the London *Times.* (He was the first to do this and even popularized the term.) He was always involved in controversy, however (much of it his own doing), and in the end killed himself.

357

[545] **HAMILTON,** Sir William Rowan
Irish mathematician
Born: Dublin, August 4, 1805
Died: Dunsink Observatory, near
Dublin, September 2, 1865

Hamilton, the son of a solicitor, was a child prodigy who attended no school and was largely self-taught. He force-fed himself a vast number of languages, fourteen of them to be exact, including such useless ones—for an Irishman who was not to become an Orientalist—as Persian, Malay, and Sanskrit. He was also, like Davy [421], an amateur poet, numbering Samuel Taylor Coleridge and William Wordsworth among his friends.

He grew interested in Newton's [231] *Principia* at twelve and began to feel himself devoured by a growing interest in mathematics. He taught himself the subject and at the age of seventeen astonished the royal astronomer in Ireland by communicating to him his discovery of a mathematical error in Laplace's [347] *Celestial Mechanics.*

This paid off, for at twenty-two he was appointed professor of astronomy at Trinity College in Dublin (after having finally entered the school for his first bit of formal education and graduating with highest honors in classics and mathematics). He accepted the position on the understanding that he could work freely in mathematics. This was worthwhile too, for he soon produced an important mathematical work on optics that helped establish the wave theory of light.

His most important work, however, was in 1843 on what are called quaternions. The idea for this came to him in a flash of inspiration during a walk to town with his wife.

It seems that Gauss [415] had treated imaginary numbers in combination with real ones as representing points on a plane and showed the methods by which such complex numbers could be manipulated. Hamilton tried to extend this to three dimensions and found himself unable to work out a self-consistent method of manipulation, until it occurred to him that the commutative law of multiplication need not necessarily hold. It is taken for granted that A times B is equal

to B times A (that is, if 8×6 is 48, so is 6×8) and this is an example of what seems to be an eternal and inescapable truth. Hamilton, however, showed that he could build up a logical algebra for his quaternions only when B times A was made to equal—A times B.

This seems against common sense but, like Lobachevski [484], Hamilton showed that truth is relative and depends on the axioms you choose to accept. The time was to come, three quarters of a century later, when a noncommutative algebra was to form the basis for quantum mechanics and for the proper understanding of the internal structure of the atom. Hamilton was knighted in 1835, while he was still young and full of promise. However, he remained poor, his marriage was unhappy, and his wife was an invalid. The last third of his life was wasted through alcoholism.

[546] **LAMONT,** Johann von (lah'-mohnt)
Scottish-German astronomer
Born: Braemar, Aberdeenshire,
Scotland, December 13, 1805
Died: Munich, Germany, August
6, 1879

At the age of twelve, Lamont was sent to Bavaria for an education at a Scottish Benedictine monastery and he remained there the rest of his life, adopting Bavarian nationality. In 1827 he began working in a new observatory at Bogenhausen. He prepared a star catalogue containing nearly thirty-five thousand stars, but his main interest was in the earth's magnetic field.

He measured the intensity of that field all over Europe and from these and previous records decided that this intensity rose and fell in a ten-year period, a result he published in 1862. It was easy to see that this period coincided roughly with Schwabe's [466] sunspot cycle. The connection between the two cycles remained completely mysterious, however, until the discovery of charged subatomic particles and the investigation of the earth's ionosphere half a century later brought a new view of earth-sun interaction.

He also determined the mass of Uranus as well as the orbital details of several of the satellites of Saturn and Uranus.

[547] **GRAHAM, Thomas**
Scottish physical chemist
Born: Glasgow, December 21, 1805
Died: London, September 16, 1869

Graham was headed for the ministry by his father, a prosperous manufacturer, but at the University of Glasgow he was converted to science. When his angry father withdrew his financial support, Graham, nothing daunted, supported himself by teaching and writing and continued right on. He graduated in 1826 and by 1830 was professor of chemistry at that institution. In 1837 he accepted a similar post at University College in London. In 1841, the Chemical Society of London was founded (the first such organization formed on a national basis) and Graham became its first president.

Graham's early interest was in the diffusion of gases. Thus, if hydrogen is placed in the top half of a container and oxygen in the bottom half, the two gases are eventually thoroughly mixed even though the oxygen, being heavier, should stay at the bottom if gravity is the only force to be considered. (The kinetic theory of gases, eventually established by Maxwell [692], showed quite well that a second force arose from the rapid, random motion of the gas molecules, which moved in highly zigzag bouncy fashion in all directions, so that some hydrogen eventually made its way downward and some oxygen upward in defiance of gravity.)

In the 1820s, when Graham began his studies on diffusion, the kinetic theory was still a generation in the future. However, he came across an observation by Döbereiner [427] that a cracked bottle with hydrogen in it, inverted and with its mouth submerged in water, lost hydrogen faster than it gained air so that the water level rose. Graham followed this up. He worked empirically and measured the rate at which gases diffused through a plaster of Paris plug, through fine tubes, and through a tiny hole in a platinum plate. In this way he cut down the rate of diffusion and made it easily measurable, as once Galileo [166] had cut down the rate of free fall by using an inclined plane.

By 1831 he found that the rate of diffusion of a gas was inversely proportional to the square root of its molecular weight. Thus since oxygen molecules are sixteen times as massive as hydrogen molecules, hydrogen diffuses four times as quickly as oxygen. This is still called Graham's law. Through this discovery Graham may fairly be reckoned one of the founders of physical chemistry.

In 1854 he left teaching to become master of the mint (as Newton [231] and John Herschel [479] had done before him; in fact he succeeded Herschel on the occasion of the latter's nervous breakdown). Graham continued his researches, however.

His early studies on diffusion led eventually to something of still greater importance. Graham was interested in the manner in which molecules diffused through a solution. A crystal of copper sulfate at the bottom of a cylinder of water will dissolve, and the blue color of the copper sulfate will slowly spread upward through the cylinder. Graham noticed that here too some substances diffused more slowly than others.

In 1861 he tried the same device as before and put a blocking substance in the way of the diffusing materials. In this case it was a sheet of parchment. He found that substances like salt, sugar, and copper sulfate, which diffused comparatively rapidly, would pass through the parchment and be detectable on the other side. On the other hand, materials such as gum arabic, glue, and gelatin, which diffused exceedingly slowly, would not pass through the parchment.

He distinguished, therefore, two classes of substances. The materials that diffused through the parchment were easily crystallizable materials, so he called them crystalloids. Those that did not diffuse through were not known, in Graham's time, to exist as crystals. He took glue (in Greek, *kolla*) to be a typical member of this second group, which he therefore called colloids.

He further showed that a colloidal material could be purified and crystalloidal contamination removed by placing the material inside a container made of a porous membrane, which is in turn placed in running water. The crystalloids pass through and are washed away, while the colloids remain behind. This process he termed dialysis, and the passage through such a membrane he named osmosis.

As we now know, the difference between the crystalloids and colloids is largely a matter of particle size. The diffusing crystalloids are made up of relatively small molecules, while colloids are made up of relatively large molecules, or of relatively large aggregates of small molecules. This has turned out to be of particular importance to biochemists since the most important molecules of living tissue, such as proteins and nucleic acids, are of colloidal size. The study of protoplasm is, therefore, a foray into colloid chemistry, a science of which Graham is considered the founder.

Between these two journeys into the world of diffusion, Graham in 1833 studied the various forms of phosphoric acid and showed that they differed in hydrogen content. In metaphosphoric acid, one hydrogen atom per molecule can be replaced by a metal; in pyrophosphoric acid, two can be replaced; and in orthophosphoric acid, three. This introduced chemists to the existence of polybasic acids; that is, those with molecules in which more than one hydrogen atom could be replaced by metals.

Graham also studied the presence of water molecules in crystals of various compounds (water of crystallization) and the manner in which the metal palladium absorbed large quantities of hydrogen.

He was also the first to suggest that alcohol intended for nondrinking use be adulterated with poison ("denatured alcohol") to prevent unauthorized drinking—or to punish it.

[548] MAURY, Matthew Fontaine
American oceanographer
Born: near Fredericksburg, Virginia, January 14, 1806
Died: Lexington, Virginia, February 1, 1873

Maury, the son of a small planter, following in the footsteps of an older brother, entered the navy as a midshipman at the age of eighteen and by 1830 had circumnavigated the world. He might not have been heard of in the world of science had he not in 1839 been permanently lamed in a stagecoach accident. He was retired from active duty and given the sinecure of superintendent of the Depot of Charts and Instruments.

A sinecure, however, is never a sinecure without the consent of the man who holds the post, and Maury did not give his consent. He threw himself into the study of ocean winds and currents and distributed specially prepared logbooks to captains of ships so that he might collect further data. Out of his work there grew the United States Naval Observatory. He was also one of the founders of the American Association for the Advancement of Science.

In particular he studied the course of the Gulf Stream (which had been studied by Benjamin Franklin [272] as early as 1769) and gave it a description that has become classic: "There is a river in the ocean." His researches received international recognition when ocean voyages were shortened as captains learned how to take advantage of the currents instead of fighting them. In 1850 he worked up a chart of ocean depths to facilitate the laying of the transatlantic cable, so that both on the surface and in the deep he may be considered among the founders of oceanography. In the course of this project, he noted the Atlantic was shallower in the center than on either side. This was the first indication of the Mid-Atlantic Ridge whose true nature was to become apparent a century later. Maury called the shallow region "Telegraphic Plateau."

It quickly became apparent that a proper study of the earth's vast ocean required international cooperation and Maury was the moving figure behind an international conference held in Brussels on the subject in 1853. In 1855 he published the first textbook in oceanography, *Physical Geography of the Sea*. It was extremely successful in its own time but was marred by Maury's refusal to consider evolutionary aspects of oceanography because of his insistence on accepting the literal words of the Bible.

The coming of the American Civil War interrupted Maury's researches. As a Virginian he followed his state out of the Union and became the head of coast, harbor, and river defenses for the Confederacy. He invented an electric torpedo and went on missions to England for supplies.

With the war over and the Confederacy defeated, Maury thought it wise to go into voluntary exile. For a while he was in Mexico with the Emperor Maximilian trying to establish a colony of Virginians; but Maximilian too was a doomed cause and Maury went to England. By 1868 emotions had cooled to the point where Maury could return to the United States, accept a professorship of physics at the Virginia Military Institute, and pass his last years in peace.

His forgiveness by the United States is total. At the Naval Academy at Annapolis there stands Maury Hall, named in his honor, even though for four years, following his own concept of patriotism, he would have destroyed the American navy if he could. He was elected to the Hall of Fame for Great Americans in 1930.

[549] **DE MORGAN**, Augustus
English mathematician
Born: Madura, Madras, India, June 27, 1806
Died: London, March 18, 1871

De Morgan was the son of an English colonel serving in India and was taken to England when he was seven months old.

De Morgan entered Cambridge in 1823 and graduated in 1827. The following year, with the strong recommendations of Airy [523] and Peacock [472] under whom he had studied, he was granted a professorial position at University College, London.

De Morgan labored to strengthen the logical bases of mathematics, for since ancient Greek times mathematics had rested on a foundation of unspoken assumptions that were not necessarily wrong but were not examined either. De Morgan began a process that was to continue through Bertrand Russell [1005] in which as many formal definitions of things that *seem* self-evident are given, and in which undefinable assumptions are clearly stated.

His greatest work was in logic, for he began the process of extending Aristotle's [29] work in the field. He pointed out that Aristotle dealt clearly with *all* and with *none* but was shaky over statements that made use of *some*. De Morgan worked out a careful set of symbols to be used in such statements of "Some x's are y's." (As, for instance, "some people are wearers of brown trousers.")

De Morgan's work in this field led within a few years to Boole's [595] broader and more systematic development of what came to be known as symbolic logic. Boole admitted his debt to De Morgan.

[550] **PALMIERI**, Luigi (pahl-myeh′ree)
Italian physicist
Born: Faicchio, April 22, 1807
Died: Naples, September 9, 1896

Palmieri obtained his degree in architecture and at first taught at a secondary school, though he eventually became a professor of physics at the University of Naples and worked at the Mount Vesuvius Observatory.

He was particularly interested in earth sciences and invented a number of instruments for the measurement of rainfall. He also invented a device for the detection of minor earthquakes. This consisted of horizontal tubes, turned up at the end and partly filled with mercury.

Even slight quakes would cause the mercury to bob from side to side. Small iron floats were so attached that their movements could be read off on a scale, and the intensity of the quake estimated.

This was the first step to the modern seismograph.

[551] **AGASSIZ**, Jean Louis Rodolphe
(ag'uh-see)
Swiss-American naturalist
Born: Môtier, Canton Fribourg,
May 28, 1807
Died: Cambridge, Massachusetts,
December 12, 1873

Agassiz, the son of a minister, was descended from a Huguenot family that fled France when the hand of Louis XIV grew heavy against them. He obtained a Ph.D. at Munich but went on to a medical degree in 1830 at his parents' insistence. He remained, however, profoundly interested in zoology and had almost succeeded in joining Humboldt [397] in one of the latter's trips. After attaining his degree he went to Paris in 1832 and worked under Cuvier [396] in that scientist's last years. He then took a post as professor of natural history at Neuchâtel in Switzerland and while there worked with Cuvierian enthusiasm and detail on a huge work on fossil fishes. This was published in five volumes between 1833 and 1844 with the sponsorship and financial help (to the tune of 1,000 francs) of the dean of Europe's scientists, Humboldt.

This would have been enough to make his reputation as a naturalist and indeed it won for him the Wollaston Prize, presented to him by Lyell [502], but much more was in store for him, partly through the accident of his Swiss birth. The Swiss are acquainted with glaciers as few other Europeans can be, thanks to their home among the Alps, and, among them Charpentier [449] and Venetz [453], speculating on the boulders that occasionally dotted the North European plains, came to the conclusion that they had been brought there through glacial action. This meant two things: that glaciers had once been far more exten-

sive than they are now, and that glaciers moved.

This notion Agassiz began by doubting, but fortunately he decided to examine matters for himself. He combined pleasure with business by spending his vacations in 1836 and 1837 exploring glaciers. What he saw made it seem most likely that glaciers did move after all. At the ends and sides of glaciers were accumulations of rock; then, too, he found rocks that had been scoured and grooved, as though by the passage of glaciers (and their embedded pebbles) moving over them. He found such grooved rocks also in areas where no glaciers had ever existed in the memory of man.

In 1839 Agassiz found a cabin built on a glacier in 1827 and now located nearly a mile down the glacier from its original site. He drove a straight line of stakes clear across a glacier, driving them deep. By 1841 they had moved a good distance and formed a U—the ones in the center moving faster since the glacier was held back at the edges by friction with the mountain wall.

Agassiz came to the conclusion that glaciers not only moved, but that many thousands of years before, they had grown and moved out over areas to which they were now a stranger. In 1840, for instance, he found signs of glaciation in the British Isles. There had once been an Ice Age. Thus, geology retreated from the extreme uniformitarianism of Lyell in the previous decade, though it was not till 1857 that Lyell himself finally gave in on this point. The minor catastrophes of advancing and retreating ice sheets did seem to take place and it was interesting that this particular catastrophe was a form of neptunism, though very, very far from the extreme form that had been advocated by Werner [355]. Agassiz himself, however, accepted the Ice Age as a full Wernerian catastrophe, imagining repeated creations, perhaps as many as twenty.

In 1846, thanks more to his work on fossil fish than on glaciers, Agassiz was invited to the United States to give a series of lectures in Boston. (Lyell, who had been visiting the United States, had suggested Agassiz for the purpose.) Agassiz came with the financial aid of a grant of 15,000 francs from King Frederick William IV of Prussia and the best wishes of the aged Humboldt.

The success of the lectures plus his intense desire to study the natural history of the North American continent led him to extend his stay, then to decide to remain indefinitely, particularly since a revolution in Prussia in 1848 (an unsuccessful one) cut off his scientific allowance. He spent a quarter century, mostly at Harvard University, where he proved a phenomenally good and popular lecturer, training a whole generation of American natural historians. In 1861 Agassiz became an American citizen as a gesture of pro-Northern sympathy when the Civil War started. Nevertheless, he believed human beings existed in various species and seemed firmly convinced of the inherent inferiority of blacks.

In North America he found signs of ancient glaciation. It, like Europe, had undergone an Ice Age. Eventually he was able to trace out an ancient lake, no longer in existence, that had once covered North Dakota, Minnesota, and Manitoba. It is called Lake Agassiz in his honor. The Museum of Comparative Zoology at Harvard is also named in his honor. It was founded in 1858 around his natural history collection.

The Ice Age, which Agassiz revealed to the world, is now known to exist in the plural. There have been a number of them in the earth's history. The most recent of them, filling the last half million years, was itself plural. Four times the ice advanced and then retreated, the last retreat being not much more than ten thousand years ago.

Though Agassiz drew a spectacular picture of the past, he refused to accept the even more spectacular picture drawn by Darwin [554]. He was the most prominent biologist in the United States —as Owen [539] was in Great Britain— to oppose the notion of evolution by natural selection, though his work, willynilly, helped establish it.

In 1915 Agassiz was elected to the Hall of Fame for Great Americans. By his grave in Mount Auburn Cemetery at Cambridge is a boulder from a Swiss glacial moraine.

[552] **GUYOT,** Arnold Henry (gee'oh)
Swiss-American geographer
Born: Boudevilliers, near Neuchâtel, Switzerland, September 28, 1807
Died: Princeton, New Jersey, February 8, 1884

After an education in Switzerland, Guyot traveled to Germany in 1825. There he abandoned theology for science and obtained his doctoral degree in 1835. In 1838 he met Agassiz [551] and through him eventually grew interested in the study of glaciers.

In 1848, in the aftermath of the revolutionary upheavals of that year, Guyot emigrated to the United States and settled in Cambridge, Massachusetts, where he introduced the teaching of scientific geography. In 1854 he accepted a post as professor of physical geography and geology at Princeton.

He was rescued from obscurity long after his death when the flat-topped seamounts discovered by H. H. Hess [1304] were named for him in 1946.

[553] **LAURENT,** Auguste (loh-rahn')
French chemist
Born: St. Maurice, Haute Marne, November 14, 1807
Died: Paris, April 23, 1853

Laurent, the son of a wine merchant, showed no interest in his father's business, and his teachers urged the disappointed parent to allow his son to enter college. The young man earned a degree as a mining engineer in 1837 and served as assistant to Dumas [514] for a while, then became a professor of chemistry at Bordeaux in 1838.

He was one of those who appreciated the point of view of Avogadro [412] and who fought to have Avogadro's hypothesis accepted as a guide to the determination of atomic weights—a point of view brought to a successful conclusion by Cannizzaro [668].

Laurent also fought against the ideas of Berzelius [425] concerning organic compounds. Berzelius divided all atoms and atomic groupings into positively and negatively charged entities and maintained that organic reactions depended on the manner in which such electric charges were brought together. Laurent, however, showed in 1836 that a supposedly positively charged hydrogen atom could be replaced by a supposedly negatively charged chlorine atom with scarcely any change in essential properties. He defended this view in his doctor's thesis before Dumas and Dulong [441] among others. Dumas had held something of this view, but when the eminent Berzelius retaliated furiously, Dumas backtracked.

Laurent, however, held firm and continued to accumulate evidence. For this he was rewarded by being barred from the more famous laboratories and being forced to remain in the provinces. He is supposed to have contracted tuberculosis as a result of working in poorly heated laboratories, and he died in middle age.

His theories did not. He believed that families of organic compounds were built about certain atomic groupings and that electric charge had nothing to do with it. He classified organic compounds according to the characteristic groupings of atoms within the molecule and this view slowly won out over that of Berzelius. Laurent even tried to present three-dimensional models of molecules. This, too, was ignored in his time but came into its own a generation later with Van't Hoff [829].

Liebig [532] eventually took up the new view though Wöhler [515] held with Berzelius. Gmelin [457] finally adopted the Laurent point of view in his textbook, and Beilstein [732] centered his massive encyclopedia of organic compounds upon it.

As Laurent's theory grew more popular, Dumas, regretting his earlier pusillanimity, attempted to take more than his fair share of the credit and there were lengthy arguments over this.

The essential core of Laurent's theory has persisted to this day. Nevertheless, the concept of positively and negatively charged atoms and groups of atoms rose to prominence again with Arrhenius [894] a half century later, though in connection with inorganic chemistry rather than with organic. The resonance theory of Pauling [1236], a century after Laurent, restored electric charge to its role in organic molecules, too, albeit in a much more sophisticated and subtle form than that envisaged by Berzelius.

Laurent's suggestion for naming organic chemicals formed the basis of the Geneva nomenclature adopted for organic chemistry by a congress held at Geneva in 1892 under the chairmanship of Friedel [693].

[554] DARWIN, Charles Robert
English naturalist
Born: Shrewsbury, Shropshire,
February 12, 1809
Died: Down, Kent, April 19,
1882

Darwin was born on the same day that Abraham Lincoln was born four thousand miles away in Kentucky. Darwin was born in no log cabin, however. He was the son of a well-to-do physician and the grandson of the poet-physician, Erasmus Darwin [308]. His other grandfather was Josiah Wedgwood, famous for his porcelainware.

Darwin showed no particular promise in his youth. At first he studied medicine but found that unlike his father and grandfather he had no aptitude for it. The sight of operations on children (performed without anesthesia) horrified him beyond measure. He thought next that he would make a career in the church but found he had no aptitude for that either. (His father angrily declared he would disgrace the family.) However, he had made natural history his hobby after reading Humboldt [397] and had grown gradually more interested in the subject during his stay at Cambridge. This was his road to fame.

His first scientific work was participating in a geologic field trip led by Sedgwick [442]. Sedgwick recognized the young man's genius, but in later years was to be aggrieved and dismayed by Darwin's theory of evolution.

H.M.S. *Beagle* was about to set out for a voyage of scientific exploration in 1831 and Darwin was offered the post of ship's naturalist, after the fashion of Brown [403] a half century before and Banks [331] a quarter century earlier still. The ship's captain hesitated, for he was not favorably impressed by Darwin. In addition, Darwin's father, larger in bulk (350 pounds) than in judgment, opposed the project as unfitting a future minister, but Darwin's uncle Josiah intervened and talked the elder Darwin out of his opposition.

Darwin accepted, and off he went on a five-year cruise around the world under Robert Fitzroy [544], a cruise that lasted from December 27, 1831, to October 2, 1836. He suffered agonies of seasickness and permanently impaired his health. It is possible that he contracted trypanosomiasis on the trip, for his chronic symptoms in late life resemble those of this disease. Since these symptoms are not dramatic, Darwin has long been considered a hypochondriac and here he may have been done a great injustice. In any case, the voyage was the making of him, and through him it became the most important voyage in the history of biology.

Darwin had already read some of the works of Lyell [502]. He had been introduced to them by someone who felt Lyell's views were ridiculous and thought Darwin would get a good laugh out of them. Darwin didn't laugh. He was converted to uniformitarianism in geology and to a clear realization of the antiquity of the earth and of the long ages through which life had had time to develop.

Now, during the course of the voyage of the *Beagle*, his thoughts on the subject had a chance to sharpen. He noticed how species changed, little by little, as he traveled down the coast of South America. Most striking of all were his observations during a five-week stay of the animal life of the Galápagos Islands, a group of a dozen or so islands about six hundred and fifty miles off the coast of Ecuador. The Galápagos Islands contained unusual giant tortoises, but what

Darwin mainly noticed was a group of birds now called "Darwin's finches."

These finches were closely similar in many ways but were divided into at least fourteen species. Not one of those species existed on the nearby mainland, or, as far as was known, anywhere else in the world. It seemed unreasonable to think that by a special act fourteen different species were created on this small group of islands, fourteen species that existed nowhere else.

Darwin believed that the species of finch on the nearby mainland, a seed-eating variety somewhat similar to the island finches, must have colonized the island eons before and that gradually the descendants of those first finches evolved into different forms. Some came to eat seeds of one sort, some of another; still others came to eat insects. For each way of life a particular species would develop a particular beak, a particular size, a particular scheme of organization. The original finch did not do this on the mainland because a great deal of competition existed in the form of other birds, while on the Galápagos Islands the original finches found a relatively empty land.

But what could cause these evolutionary changes? Lamarck [336] had believed that the inheritance of acquired characteristics was involved and that creatures deliberately *tried* to change in ways advantageous to themselves. Darwin could not accept that.

He returned to England in 1836 with no answer (though he had come to passionate conclusions regarding Negro slavery, which he had witnessed in the Americas and which he detested with all the fire of a gentle, humanitarian soul). He was elected to the Geological Society and kept busy preparing several books on the voyage and the observations he had made. The first of these, now usually known as *A Naturalist's Voyage on the Beagle*, published in 1839, was a great success (impressing Humboldt, for one, as Humboldt had once impressed Darwin) and made him famous. (Darwin always strove for a clear, uncluttered style. He believed "in making the style transparently clear and throwing eloquence to the dogs.") He also announced a theory on the slow formation of coral reefs by the gradual accumulation of the skeletons of corals, which was accepted by naturalists with enthusiasm. This theory was in opposition to one held by Lyell, but so pleased was Lyell with the clearly superior work of Darwin that the two became close friends.

Darwin married his cousin Emma Wedgwood in 1839, and he joined the Geological Society of London, serving as secretary from 1838 to 1844. In this way he had an opportunity for close association with Lyell and discussed with him the problem of evolution—for suddenly he had the key.

On September 28, 1838, he read a famous book entitled *An Essay on the Principle of Population,* written by Malthus [387] forty years earlier. Malthus had maintained that human population always increased faster than the food supply and that eventually population had to be cut down by starvation, disease, or war.

Darwin thought at once that this must hold for all other forms of life as well and that those of the excess population that were first cut down would be those who were at a disadvantage in the competition for food.

For instance, those first finches on the Galápagos Islands must have multiplied unchecked to begin with and would surely have outstripped the supply of the seeds they lived on. Some would have had to starve, the weaker ones first, or those less adept at finding seeds. But what if some could turn to eating bigger seeds or tougher seeds or, better still, turn from the eating of seeds to the eating of insects? Those that could not make the change would be held in check by starvation, while those that could would find a new untapped food supply and could then multiply rapidly until, in turn, their food supply began to dwindle.

In other words, creatures would adapt themselves to different ways of life under the stress of environmental pressure. Every once in a while a change that would allow a better fit to a particular niche in the environment would permit

one group of creatures to swamp another group and to replace them. Thus Nature would select one group over another and by such "natural selection" life would branch out into infinite variety, more efficient groups always replacing less efficient ones in each particular environmental niche. (To be sure, Darwin had been thinking of natural selection before reading Malthus's book, but Malthus had made him aware of just what a powerful force natural selection could be. It made Darwin realize that natural selection was *sufficient* to explain evolution.)

But how did these changes come about? How could a seed-eating finch suddenly learn to eat larger seeds that others could not, or learn to eat insects? Here Darwin was on rough ground. There was no doubt that changes did take place. For one thing, Darwin, a country gentleman, kept pigeons as a hobby and had personal experience with the breeding of odd varieties of domesticated animals.

He could see that in any group of young there were variations from one to another—random variations in size, coloring, abilities. Darwin reasoned that it was through taking advantage of such variations, by deliberately breeding one and suppressing others, that over the generations man had developed larger, stronger, faster horses; cattle to give more milk and beef; sheep to give more wool; hens more eggs; and cats and dogs of odd and amusing shapes.

Could not Nature substitute for man and make the same selection for its own purposes, much more slowly and over a much longer period, fitting animals to their environment rather than to man's tastes and demands? (Empedocles [17] had suggested a very primitive version of this, something of which Darwin was aware.)

By Darwinian notions the giraffe got its long neck not because it tried for one (as Lamarck had it) but because some giraffes were born with naturally longer necks and these got more leaves, lived better, and left more descendants, which inherited the naturally longer necks. A combination of natural variation and natural selection saw to it that the neck continued to get longer very slowly.

This view explained the giraffe's blotched coat just as well. Even Lamarck couldn't have made a case in favor of the giraffe *trying* to be blotched. However, a giraffe that happened to be blotchier by random variation would better blend in with a blotched forest background and would the more likely escape the eyes of prowling predators. It would leave more descendants to inherit its blotchiness.

The chief difficulty about all this was that it was hard to see how the random variations would carry over from generation to generation. There would be matings among creatures that varied differently, and for all Darwin knew these variations should then level out into an undistinguished average.

Darwin never was completely satisfied on this point, but he went on. Some creatures, among whom the male had very conspicuous coloring, did offer a way out, at least with respect to certain prominent characteristics. The female of the species must deliberately select the most flamboyant male she could find as her mate. There it was no question of averaging out. The development of the peacock would be driven constantly in the direction of flamboyance as the result of "sexual selection."

Darwin also collected data on vestiges, that is, the useless remnants of tissues that bespoke full-scale useful organs eons before. For instance whales and snakes have useless scraps of bones that might once have formed parts of hip girdles and hind legs, showing that they were descendants of creatures that had walked on all fours. A horse has a single line of bones down its leg ending in a single hoof, but on either side are two thin splints that come to a dead end, but show that the horse might once have been a three-hooved creature.

Darwin was a painstaking perfectionist, collecting and classifying his information endlessly. In 1844 he started a book on the subject but so ardently did he continue to multiply his examples and tighten his reasoning that in 1858 he was still working at it. Fortunately he was a man of independent means and could work on such a nonremunerative project as slowly and as thoroughly as he liked.

His friends knew what he was doing, and Lyell in particular was constantly urging him to publish or face being anticipated, for evolutionary notions were in the air.

Darwin could not be hurried and Lyell was proved right; Darwin was anticipated. Another naturalist, Wallace [643], wrote a paper embodying Darwin's notions almost to the letter and then sent a copy to none other than Darwin himself for his opinion. When Darwin received the manuscript he was thunderstruck. However, he proceeded to behave like the ideal scientist. He made no attempt to publish quickly in order to reserve the credit for himself. Magnanimously he passed on Wallace's work to other important scientists and might have abandoned his own priority, had not Lyell insisted that he offer to collaborate with Wallace on papers summarizing their combined conclusions. Wallace was equally generous and cheerfully agreed, in view of Darwin's prior claim. The collaboration was carried through and work by both men appeared in the *Journal of the Linnaean Society* in 1858. (How Linnaeus [276] would have turned in his grave if he knew that the society named for him bore so intimate a connection with the Darwinian theory.)

But it was no longer possible to delay. The next year Darwin published his book. It was quite a long one, but it was only a fifth as long as he had been planning and for the rest of his life he referred to it disparagingly as an abstract. The full title of the book (one of the most world-shaking ever published) is *On the Origin of Species by Means of Natural Selection, or the Preservation of Favoured Races in the Struggle for Life*. It is usually known simply as *The Origin of Species*.

The learned world was waiting for the book. Only 1,250 copies were printed and every one was snapped up on the first day of publication. It went through printing after printing, and it is still being reprinted now, a century later. It is one of the classics of science.

(Ironically, within a decade of the publication of the book Mendel [638] was to carry through a course of research that shored up the weakest point in the theory, the manner in which random variations were inherited. Darwin, however, was never to know of this work, nor did the world of science generally until De Vries [792] rediscovered Mendel and his conclusions a generation later.)

Darwin's book started a violent controversy that lasted for generations. It was viewed as contrary to the statements of the Bible by some and many sincerely believed that the Darwinian theory of evolution was destructive of religion. Even among scientists the fight was bitter.

In England, for instance, Richard Owen [539] was a die-hard opponent and in 1865, when Darwin received the Copley medal of the Royal Society, it was for his other achievements, and not for his theory of evolution.

Darwin himself was not temperamentally suited to enter the lists of controversy. For one thing, he was too gentle. He was the kindest of men and incapable of the hurly-burly of polemical warfare. (One of the reasons he spent so many years gathering evidence was in a vain effort to make the case so ironclad as to avoid controversy.) Fortunately, fighting for him was Huxley [659], who called himself "Darwin's bulldog."

In Germany, Haeckel [707] took up the Darwinian struggle against the opposition of Virchow [632], and in America, Asa Gray [562] fought for Darwin against the opposition of Agassiz [551].

Naturally one of the touchiest points about Darwinian evolution was its possible application to man himself. Darwin had skirted that point in *The Origin of Species,* but Lyell, whose geological views had so influenced Darwin a generation before, now returned the compliment. In a book entitled *The Antiquity of Man,* published in 1863, Lyell came out strongly in favor of Darwinism and discussed the many thousands of years during which man, or manlike creatures, must have existed on the earth. He used as his evidence stone tools found in an-

cient strata by men such as Boucher de Perthes [458].

Wallace doubted that evolution could apply to man, but Darwin did not. He took his stand at Lyell's side and in 1871 published *The Descent of Man,* in which he discussed evidence showing man to have descended from subhuman forms of life. For one thing, man contains many vestigial organs. There are traces of points on the incurved flaps of the outer ear, dating back to a time when the ear was upright and pointed, and there are tiny, useless muscles still present that were once designed to move those ears. (Some people still can.) There are four bones at the bottom of the spine which are remnants of a tail, and so on.

The world of science, at least, was won over before long and by the time of Darwin's death the notion of evolution by natural selection had scored a clear victory. The opponents that remained were not scientists but were for the most part members of the more literal word-of-the-Bible sects. These fought a rearguard action that made newspaper headlines on occasion but did not affect the progress of biological science.

Darwin was rated above controversy at his death and buried in Westminster Abbey, among England's heroes and near Newton [231] and Faraday [474], as well as his friend Lyell. However, this burial in Westminster Abbey was the only honor ever granted him by the ultrarespectable government of Great Britain under Queen Victoria. The great British prime ministers William Gladstone and Benjamin Disraeli were both strongly opposed to Darwinism. Disraeli, indeed, coined a famous phrase when he said that, if asked to choose between apes and angels as the forebears of man, "I am on the side of the angels."

[555] **LIOUVILLE,** Joseph (lyoo-veel')
French mathematician
Born: St. Omer, Pas-de-Calais, March 24, 1809
Died: Paris, September 8, 1882

Liouville was the son of an army officer. He was briefly involved in politics after the revolution of 1848, but was defeated for election to the legislature. From 1831 he had been teaching mathematics at the Collège de France in Paris, attaining professorial rank in 1833. He was also the editor of the *Journal de Mathématiques,* so it is just as well that he failed in politics. Mathematics needed him more.

He proved that there were numbers that were transcendental; that is, they could not serve as solutions to any polynomial equation. However, he could not identify any specific number as transcendental. The closest he could come was a conclusion that involved the quantity *e,* an irrational number for which the approximate value is 2.7182818284 . . . Liouville showed, in 1844, that neither *e* nor e^2 could be the solution to any polynomial equation of the second degree.

It was Hermite [641] who went on, a generation later, to show that *e* and expressions containing *e* could not be the solution to any polynomial equation of any degree.

[556] **GRASSMAN,** Hermann Günther (grahs'mahn)
German mathematician
Born: Stettin, Pomerania (now Szczecin, Poland), April 15, 1809
Died: Stettin, September 26, 1877

Grassman was the son of a minister-mathematician and himself studied theology and turned to mathematics. He got a teaching post at the high school level in 1832 and two years later qualified as minister. He did not serve as a clergyman, however, for his teaching posts advanced in importance and mathematics won out. By 1840 he was working entirely on mathematical research.

In 1844, Grassman published a book on mathematics that showed how one might symbolize geometry in more general ways than was made possible by the ordinary analytic geometry of Descartes [183]. Involved was the algebraic manipulation of lines and planes in a field that came to be called vector analysis. What's more, Grassman did not confine himself

to the ordinary three dimensions of the universe but spoke of abstract spaces of any number of dimensions, thus beginning the study of *n*-dimensional geometry.

Unfortunately, Grassman wrote obscurely and invented a novel symbolism of his own. Furthermore, he was soon to be outglittered by the independent and even more general work of Hamilton [545].

Rather disappointed in the failure of the mathematical world to appreciate his work, Grassman turned to Sanskrit and by 1862 worked in that field exclusively, preparing Sanskrit dictionaries, translating Sanskrit classics, and so on. This work met with instant success in its field.

[557] **HENLE,** Friedrich Gustav Jakob (hen'luh)
German pathologist and anatomist
Born: Fürth, Bavaria, July 19, 1809
Died: Göttingen, May 13, 1885

Henle was the son of a Jewish merchant but when he was twelve, the family accepted Protestant Christianity and young Henle thought for a while of becoming a minister. He met Johannes Müller [522] socially, however, and that helped turn his attention to medicine.

He studied medicine at the universities of Heidelberg and of Bonn and obtained his medical degree in 1832, thereafter serving as assistant to Müller in Berlin. He obtained a professorial appointment at Zürich in Switzerland, where he gladly retired for safety after his liberal views had brought him to trial for treason in Berlin and a short period of imprisonment. Later he taught at Heidelberg and at Göttingen.

He made numerous microanatomical discoveries, of which the best known is that of Henle's loop, a portion of the kidney tubule. In 1846 he published a book on pathology, which for the first time unified that study of diseased tissue with the physiology of normal tissue. Virchow [632] was soon to carry this down to the cellular stage.

In 1840 Henle suggested that disease was caused by the activity of microorganisms. However, he had no evidence in favor of this revolutionary notion and it remained only a speculation. When twenty years later Pasteur [642] came to the same conclusion, his work with silkworms had given him strong evidence in its favor and he went on to gather more, so that Pasteur rightly gets the credit for the discovery of the "germ theory."

[558] HOLMES, Oliver Wendell
American author and physician
Born: Cambridge, Massachusetts, August 29, 1809
Died: Boston, Massachusetts, October 7, 1894

Holmes, a Harvard graduate, class of 1829 and the son of a minister, is best known as an essayist and a poet (his most famous poems are "Old Ironsides" and "The Deacon's Masterpiece"; or, "The Wonderful One-Hoss Shay"). This tends to obscure the fact that he was a competent doctor who obtained his medical degree from Harvard in 1836, then served as professor of anatomy first at Dartmouth College and from 1847 at Harvard.

In 1842, between his two professorial stints, he discovered the contagiousness of childbed fever, taking up much the position that Semmelweiss [607] was to take a few years later. Holmes had to withstand much abuse for this, as Semmelweiss would have to do, but Holmes was far more fortunate for he lived to see himself justified.

When ether made its debut as a painkiller it was Holmes—approached for the purpose by a group of Boston doctors—who suggested "anesthesia" as an appropriate term for the process. It is from Greek words meaning "no feeling." In 1910 Holmes was elected a member of the Hall of Fame for Great Americans.

His son and namesake (1841–1935) was one of the great Supreme Court justices and outdid his father—in fields outside science.

[559] RAWLINSON, Sir Henry Creswicke
English archaeologist
Born: Chadlington, Oxfordshire, April 11, 1810
Died: London, March 5, 1895

Rawlinson went to India in 1827 in the employ of the East India Company and in 1833 was sent to Persia where he was assigned to help reorganize the Persian army.

While in Persia he grew interested in one of the great monumental antiquities of the land, a trilingual cuneiform inscription high on a cliffside at Bisitun. As it turned out, it was an inscription placed there by Darius I (who reigned over the vast Persian Empire in 500 B.C.) detailing the circumstances by which he had gained the throne. The same message was given in Old Persian, Assyrian, and Elamitic.

It was not till 1846 that Rawlinson managed to smooth away all the factional infighting and gained permission to investigate the inscription. He scaled the almost unscalable cliff at great personal risk and copied the inscription. He deciphered it, making use of modern Persian as a guide, and thus provided historians with what was, in effect, a dictionary of the earlier languages of Mesopotamia.

Rawlinson's work was steadily expanded and it opened the history of the Near East to modern man as Champollion's similar work on hieroglyphics had done for the history of Egypt.

Rawlinson resigned from the East India Company in 1855 and was knighted. He spent the rest of his life in London, serving in Parliament on two occasions and being made a baronet in 1891.

[560] VALENTIN, Gabriel Gustav
(vah'len-teen)
German-Swiss physiologist
Born: Breslau, Silesia (now Wrocław, Poland), July 8, 1810
Died: Bern, Switzerland, May 24, 1883

Valentin was the son of a silverware merchant who was also an assistant rabbi. Valentin entered the University of Breslau in 1828, studied medicine, and obtained his medical degree in 1833. His father died at about this time and Valentin had to establish a practice to earn a living though his heart was in research.

Purkinje [452] had been one of his teachers at the medical school and with him Valentin stole what time he could for microscopic studies. Thus in 1834 he and Purkinje discovered that certain cells in the inner surface of the oviduct contained cilia, tiny threadlike structures that beat in coordinated fashion independently of the nervous system and thus force the ovum to move along the tube. They investigated the occurrence of ciliated cells elsewhere among vertebrates.

In 1835 Valentin and Purkinje quarreled over the use of a microscope and separated. Valentin's papers had given him enough prestige to receive a post as professor of physiology at the University of Bern in 1836. He was the first Jew to gain a professorial post in a German-language university (even though the university was not in Germany itself). He was also the first Jew to be granted citizenship of the city of Bern.

In 1844 he was the first person to note the digestive activity of pancreatic juice.

[561] **REGNAULT**, Henri Victor (reh-nyoh')
French chemist and physicist
Born: Aix-la-Chapelle, France (now Aachen, West Germany), July 21, 1810
Died: Auteuil, France, January 19, 1878

Regnault's father, an army officer, died in Napoleon's invasion of Russia when the child was two, and his mother died soon after.

Regnault worked in a drapery establishment during his teenage years. He managed to eke out a college education studying under Liebig [532], among others. Among his chemical discoveries was that of carbon tetrachloride, which

he was the first to prepare. In 1840 he succeeded Gay-Lussac [420] at the École Polytechnique, and the following year he succeeded Dulong [441] at the Collège de France.

Regnault was a careful experimenter but no theoretician and the delicate measurements he gathered were left to bear fruit for others. For instance, in 1852 he showed that gases do not quite follow Boyle's [212] law and thus paved the way for Van der Waals [726] to modify that law a generation later. He calculated the exact change of gas volume with temperature so that he could state that absolute zero (the significance of which Kelvin [652] was to elucidate) was at $-273°C$.

He refined Lavoisier's [334] experiments on measuring the oxygen uptake and carbon dioxide production of animals and in 1849 calculated the first good ratios of what came to be called the respiratory quotient. This prepared the way for the work of Voit [691], Pettenkofer [612], and Rubner [848].

He kept measuring to the end but the records of his last voluminous group of measurements on the heat developed by expanding gases were destroyed during the disorders in Paris following the disastrous war with Prussia in 1870. (His son was killed in those same disorders.) Regnault's work was the forerunner of the physical chemistry that came to full life with Ostwald [840].

[562] **GRAY**, Asa
American botanist
Born: Sauquoit, New York, November 18, 1810
Died: Cambridge, Massachusetts, January 30, 1888

Gray obtained his medical degree at Fairfield Academy in 1831 but practiced only briefly. Instead he devoted himself to his hobby of botany. He wrote numerous popular books on the subject and also helped write more elaborate works on North American flora.

He was in correspondence with Darwin [554], whom he had met in 1851.

He boldly supported Darwinism in America against the objections of religious leaders and debated the point vigorously with the antievolutionist, Agassiz [551]. He himself was a prominent religious layman, which gave his point of view added force, since he could not be dismissed as an atheist. He maintained, in fact, that natural selection was not a random force but was guided by God. (Darwin disagreed with him here.)

He was a professor of natural history at Harvard for thirty-one years, beginning in 1842, and there he developed a botanical garden and library almost from scratch.

Between 1863 and 1873 he was president of the American Association for the Advancement of Science. In 1900 he was selected as one of those to be memorialized in the newly established Hall of Fame for Great Americans.

[563] **SCHWANN,** Theodor (shvahn)
German physiologist
Born: Neuss, Rhenish Prussia,
December 7, 1810
Died: Cologne, Rhenish Prussia,
January 11, 1882

After completing his medical training in 1834 Schwann served as assistant to Johannes Müller [522] and almost at once made an important discovery. Ever since the time of Réaumur [252] and Spallanzani [302], it had been known that digestion was a chemical process. When Prout [440] had discovered the presence of hydrochloric acid in the stomach it was naturally thought that the acid was what broke down foodstuffs.

In 1834, however, Schwann prepared extracts of the glandular lining of the stomach and showed that, mixed with acid, it had a meat-dissolving power that was far greater than the acid alone would have had. In 1836, by treating the extract with mercuric chloride, he prepared a precipitate that proved to be the active principle. He called it pepsin, from a Greek word meaning "to digest."

This substance was an example of what was then called a ferment and is

now called an enzyme. Payen [490] had isolated an enzyme from malt extract three years earlier, but pepsin was the first enzyme to be prepared from animal tissue. Its discovery was one of the early turning points in the development of biochemistry.

Schwann devised some experiments at this time that tended to disprove the doctrine of spontaneous generation. In 1838 he showed yeast to be made up of tiny plantlike organisms and held that fermentation of sugar and starch was the result of a life process, a view ridiculed by Berzelius [425], Wöhler [515], and Liebig [532]. The work of Pasteur [642] a generation later was crucial in establishing Schwann's correctness. Putting those to one side, then, what Schwann is best known for is his elaboration in 1839 of the cell theory.

In its simplest form, this is the statement that all living things are made up of cells or of material formed by cells, and that each cell contains certain essential components such as a nucleus and a surrounding membrane. Actually this belief had been held more or less vaguely by a number of men in the preceding century, being one of those ideas that were "in the air." In fact, the year before, Schleiden [538], with whom Schwann was well acquainted, had stated the cell theory in connection with plants as Schwann was doing in connection with animals.

It was Schwann, however, who most clearly stated and summarized the case, and he (usually coupled with Schleiden) is usually credited with establishing the cell theory, as he himself called it. He also coined the term "metabolism" as representing the overall chemical changes taking place in living tissue.

Schwann pointed out that plants and animals alike were formed out of cells, that eggs were cells distorted by the presence of yolk, that eggs grew and developed by dividing and redividing so that the developing organism consisted of more and more cells but always of cells. He refined Bichat's [400] conception of tissues by differentiating these in terms of the types and arrangement of cells that made them up. In this connection, he discovered the "Schwann cells" that make up the nerve sheaths.

The cell theory was extended by Nägeli [598], Siebold [537], Kölliker [600], and Gegenbaur [669], and was neatly summarized by Virchow [632]. It was a landmark in the history of biology comparable to that formed by the atomic theory in chemistry. For one thing, the cell theory succeeded in luring the attention of biologists from the cell boundary (the first portion of the cell to be observed by Hooke [223] and the easiest to study) to the all-important cell contents.

Schwann became professor of anatomy at Louvain in 1838 and at Liège in 1847. In the last forty years of his life he gave way to mysticism and religious meditations and did nothing to match his activities in the one decade of the 1830s, but that is scarcely something of which we have a right to complain.

[564] **LEVERRIER,** Urbain Jean Joseph
(luh-veh-ryay´)
French astronomer
Born: St. Lô, Manche, March 11, 1811
Died: Paris, September 23, 1877

Leverrier's father, a minor civil servant, sold his house in order to put his son through college, and the results justified him. Leverrier began his professional life as a chemist in Gay-Lussac's [420] laboratory and did promising research on the compounds of phosphorus with hydrogen and oxygen. However, in 1836 he had the opportunity of taking a post as an astronomy teacher at the École Polytechnique, where he was working. Quite accidentally, then, he found himself an astronomer.

He occupied himself with questions of celestial mechanics, continuing the work of Laplace [347] and demonstrating with even greater exactness the stability of the solar system.

It was pointed out to him by Arago [446] that the motions of Mercury needed careful analysis, and Leverrier's accurate calculations showed that the planet's perihelion (the point in its orbit at which it most closely approached the sun) did indeed advance forty seconds of arc per century more than could be accounted for by Newton's [231] theory of gravitation, even after the minor perturbing effects of the other planets had been allowed for.

Leverrier decided in 1845 that there must be one planet that was not being taken into account. He postulated an as-yet-undiscovered planet (which he called Vulcan) with a diameter of a thousand miles and a distance from the sun of nineteen million miles. It would just account for the Mercurian anomaly, he believed. Some amateurs, such as Schwabe [466], had been searching for an intra-Mercurian planet even before Leverrier's announcement.

No such planet as Vulcan was found, though the neighborhood of the sun was inspected assiduously at every subsequent eclipse. It is now quite certain that such a planet does not exist.

Others suggested a belt of asteroids while Asaph Hall [681] felt that the force of gravitation varied not quite as the square of the distance but as very slightly more than the square. Both hypotheses raised more difficulties than they solved and were given up.

Nevertheless the worry over Mercury's motion was not entirely fruitless, for in the case of Schwabe the result was the discovery of the sunspot cycle, something more important than a discovery of Vulcan.

Leverrier's work on Mercury gained him admission to the Paris Academy of Sciences in 1846, but he was on the threshold of much greater fame.

The planet Uranus, discovered by Herschel [321] a little over half a century before, was at that time the farthest known planet. Its motion, too, showed anomalies. It was 1.5 minutes of arc away from where it should be, according to the careful computations of Bouvard [392]. Arago urged Leverrier to work on this and in 1846 Leverrier again assumed an undiscovered planet, one beyond Uranus' orbit (something several astronomers such as Bessel [439] and John

Herschel [479] had previously suggested as a possibility).

Such an outer planet would exert a gravitational force that those who calculated Uranus' orbit had not allowed for. Leverrier calculated the size and position the unknown planet would have to occupy in the sky to account for the deviations of Uranus from its calculated orbit.

Unknown to Leverrier, a young English astronomer, J. C. Adams [615], had made the same calculations some months earlier and reached the same result. Leverrier was the more fortunate of the two, however. While Adams's work was neglected at Cambridge University, the Frenchman was able to take action. He wrote to Galle [573] at the Berlin Observatory to thank him for some publications he had sent and asked him to look at a certain spot in the sky for the new planet. As it happened, everything was breaking right for Leverrier. Galle had just received a new and improved star map of the area and was therefore in a position to spot any intruding object easily.

On September 23, 1846, the very first evening of the search, a new planet was discovered very close to the predicted spot, even though both Leverrier and Adams had assumed Neptune to be considerably more distant than it, in fact, proved to be, because they let themselves be guided by Bode's [344] law. In the furor that followed there was a movement among French astronomers, led by Arago, to name the planet "Leverrier" but wiser counsels prevailed and Leverrier himself named it, nonnationalistically, after Neptune, god of the ocean (supposedly because of the green color of the planet). Within a month Lassell [509] had discovered a large satellite of Neptune and named it Triton, after Neptune's (Poseidon's) son in the Greek myths.

This discovery of a giant planet by pure calculation was the most dramatic achievement of Newtonian theory in all its history and removed the last shred of doubt (if any existed) of its validity.

Leverrier participated enthusiastically in the Revolution of 1848 on the side of the republicans, but when Louis Napoleon came to power, Leverrier backtracked (unlike his old friend Arago). He supported Louis Napoleon even after the latter subverted republican principles and announced himself Emperor Napoleon III. After Arago's death Leverrier was appointed director of the Paris Observatory in 1854. As director he tackled all the planets of the solar system and worked out a gravitational accounting of their motions with greater accuracy than ever before. Like Airy [523], Leverrier was an irascible and unpopular director who managed to squeeze a great deal of work out of those under him. He was so hated by those unfortunate enough to have to work for him that he was removed from his position in 1870 by popular demand. When his successor died in 1873, Leverrier was restored, but with restricted powers.

The motion of Mercury's perihelion continued to be an elusive problem for a generation past his death and that remained his one great failure.

And yet this failure was more significant to the future of science than his success in the case of Neptune. The former was to upset Newton's scheme of the universe, which the latter had seemed to establish so firmly. It was Mercury's motion that was to be one of the observational props of Einstein's [1064] general theory of relativity, three quarters of a century after Leverrier's failure.

[565] BUNSEN, Robert Wilhelm
Eberhard
German chemist
Born: Göttingen, March 31, 1811
Died: Heidelberg, August 16, 1899

Bunsen, the son of a professor of philology, obtained his education at the University of Göttingen. He studied under Strohmeyer [411] and earned his doctorate in 1830. After travels through France and Germany he turned to teaching and for a while succeeded to Wöhler's post at the University of Cassell. By 1838 he had a professorial appointment at the University of Marburg. In 1852, when Gmelin [457] died, Bunsen succeeded to his post at Heidelberg.

Bunsen's long life is exclusively the history of his chemical researches, for he was one of those scientists who never married. The excuse he gave was the same as Dalton's [389], that he never had the time. This was certainly not meant entirely humorously for his work was as exacting as any family could have been, and not always kind in its treatment of him, either.

In his late twenties he began his work by studying organic arsenic-containing compounds (a group of substances that were to come into world prominence three quarters of a century later, when Paul Ehrlich [845] successfully developed chemotherapy based on them). In an explosion in 1836, during the course of that work, he lost an eye and twice nearly died of arsenical poisoning through inhalation and slow absorption of the material with which he worked. He finished his researches but never worked in organic chemistry again, nor would he allow it to be taught in his laboratory. Nevertheless, the work that had nearly proved fatal to him inspired his student Frankland [655] to move further in this direction.

His interests in inorganic chemistry, however, were extremely varied. He investigated the gases produced in blast furnaces and suggested methods for cutting down heat loss. In the process he also invented new methods of gas analysis. He invented various calorimeters for the measurement of heat (an interest that led him to a dramatic investigation of the geysers in Iceland in the late 1840s and resulted in his accurate explanation of their workings). He also invented a carbon-zinc battery and a grease-spot photometer for measuring light. He was the first to produce magnesium in quantity and showed how it could be burned to produce an extremely bright light that proved to be of great assistance to photography.

Bunsen is well known for a burner

that he first used in 1855. It was perforated at the bottom so that air was drawn in by the gas flow. The resulting gas-air mixture burned with steady heat and little light, without smoke or flickering. He was not the first to use such a burner (a similar one was used by Faraday [474]), but he popularized it to such an extent that anyone who has ever worked in a high school chemistry laboratory remembers his Bunsen burner even if he has forgotten everything else.

The work for which he was most renowned, however, was the result of the ingenuity and insight of his younger coworker, Kirchhoff [648]. Together, Bunsen and Kirchhoff invented the technique of spectroscopy in 1860 and almost at once discovered two new elements, cesium and rubidium. Other men, such as Draper [566] and Huggins [646], were then to turn that instrument on the heavens.

[566]   **DRAPER,** John William
English-American chemist
Born: Saint Helens, Lancashire, England, May 5, 1811
Died: Hastings-on-Hudson, New York, January 4, 1882

Draper, the son of a minister, studied at the University of London and then in 1833 emigrated to the United States. He obtained a medical degree at the University of Pennsylvania in 1836. There, Hare [428] was one of his teachers. He taught chemistry at New York University in 1838, helped organize a medical school, and taught chemistry and physiology there. Eventually he became president of the medical school.

Under his leadership, New York University became one of the first schools in America to award Ph.D. degrees.

Despite all this, he is best known in fields far removed from the medical. He recognized that light brought about chemical reactions through absorption by the molecules of light energy, thus proving to be a pioneer in photochemistry. He also recognized the fact that all substances at about 525°C glowed a dull red (this is called the Draper point) and that with further rise in temperature more and more of the visible light region was added until the glow was white. He published his experiments in this field in 1847 and this was eventually to lead to the quantitative treatment by Wien [934] a half century later.

From photochemistry his interest moved to photography and spectroscopy. He was one of the earliest photographers and took portraits of human beings, managing to cut the exposure time to under a minute. One of his photographs, taken in 1840, is the oldest surviving photographic portrait.

A little earlier than 1840 he photographed the moon, and this was the first astronomical photograph. When he photographed the solar spectrum soon after, he was the first to show that spectral lines existed in the ultraviolet and infrared as well as in the visible portion of the spectrum. He also showed that some of the lines in the solar spectrum were produced by the earth's atmosphere.

Draper was one of the first to produce photomicrographs, taking photographs of what one could see under a microscope and reproducing them in a book on physiology which he published in 1856.

In 1876 he was elected the first president of the American Chemical Society.

[567] SIMPSON, Sir James Young
Scottish obstetrician
Born: Bathgate, Linlithgow, June 7, 1811
Died: London, May 6, 1870

Simpson, the son of a baker, was a young prodigy, entering the University of Edinburgh at fourteen. He gained his medical degree at twenty-one with a graduation thesis so good that it promptly won him an appointment as assistant to one of the professors at the university.

He was appointed professor in his own right (of obstetrics) in 1840, and was one of the founders of modern gynecology. He conducted a successful practice and, in 1846, upon hearing the news of

anesthesia in America, promptly adopted it. He had a little trouble with ether and used chloroform instead. (Chloroform is much more dangerous and ether won out in the end.) Simpson was the first to use anesthesia in childbirth and this met with considerable criticism from those ardent souls who believed that the pain of childbirth was decreed by God as part of the curse of Eve. Simpson pointed out that God did not rejoice in pain and that when he extracted a rib from Adam to make Eve, he first caused a "deep sleep" to fall upon him. Simpson's victory was clear when he was appointed Queen Victoria's official physician.

In 1853 he utilized chloroform in helping Victoria through the pain of childbed, delivering her seventh child, Prince Leopold, and that stilled all criticism. Simpson was made a baronet in 1866 and would have been buried in Westminster Abbey had not his family refused the honor.

[568] GROVE, Sir William Robert
British physicist
Born: Swansea, Wales, July 11, 1811
Died: London, August 1, 1896

Grove qualified as a barrister in 1835, after an education at Oxford, but he was in poor health and didn't feel up to the rigors of a legal practice. He retired therefore to the quieter and apparently less demanding life of a gentleman experimenter.

In 1839 he devised an electric cell making use of hydrogen and oxygen. Until then (and since, too) the electric cells that have been put into practical use have relied upon more or less expensive metals such as zinc, lead, nickel.

It would be much less expensive to use ordinary fuels such as hydrogen; better yet, natural gas; still better, coal dust. If these were oxidized in an electrical cell, producing electricity directly, small-scale electrical conduction would become unprecedentedly cheap. The "Grove cell" was the first of these fuel cells and earned him a membership in the Royal

Society. To this day, however, fuel cells have remained laboratory curiosities. Intensive research has not yet devised one capable of withstanding the rugged demands of practical use.

Hydrogen and oxygen combine to form water and yield energy. Grove showed the reverse was also true. He demonstrated that water in contact with a strongly heated electric wire would absorb energy and break up into hydrogen and oxygen.

Grove was one of those who ardently supported the notion of conservation of energy in the late 1840s and at that time, too, he served as professor at the London Institution.

In later life, Grove felt sufficiently strong to return to a legal career. He was made a judge in 1871 and knighted the following year.

[569] **OTIS**, Elisha Graves
American inventor
Born: Halifax, Vermont,
August 3, 1811
Died: Yonkers, New York,
April 8, 1861

Otis was the son of a well-to-do farmer. Ill health forced him out of his own business and he became a mechanic for a bedmaker.

His great moment came in 1852 when, in connection with a new factory the firm was building in Yonkers, New York, he invented the first elevator with an adequate safety guard, one that would keep it from falling even if the cable holding it were severed completely. He established a factory in Yonkers to manufacture such devices.

In 1854 he demonstrated one of his elevators in New York City. He got in, had it raised (with himself inside) to a considerable height, and ordered the cable holding it to be cut. He descended safely and was unharmed.

The elevator is, of course, as essential to tall buildings as structural steel is, and Otis's invention is one of the important precursors of the skyscraper, the hallmark of modern cities.

[570] **BUDD,** William
English physician
Born: North Tawton, Devon,
September 14, 1811
Died: Clevedon, Somerset,
January 9, 1880

Budd was the son of a physician and became a physician himself (as did five of his brothers). Budd obtained his medical degree from the University of Edinburgh in 1838, rather late because his schooling was interrupted by serious illnesses. In 1841 he moved to Bristol.

Budd's importance lies in the fact that he recognized the nature of the contagiousness of infectious disease. He felt that the poisons of the disease, whatever those poisons were, multiplied in the intestines and appeared in the excretions. From the excretions they could be carried by water to healthy individuals and cause them to sicken.

Budd particularly alluded to cholera (where he acknowledged the priority of Snow [576]) and typhoid fever. By following his own theory, and adopting measures that would limit the contamination of the town's water supply, he curbed the spread of cholera during an epidemic that hit Bristol in 1866.

While Budd did not take the crucial step of implicating microorganisms as the "poison" associated with the disease, his work was an important precursor to the germ theory of disease that was soon to be advanced by Pasteur [642].

[571] **GALOIS,** Evariste (ga-lwah')
French mathematician
Born: Bourg-la-Reine, near Paris,
October 25, 1811
Died: Paris, May 31, 1832

Galois was the son of a town official. He did not do well at school. He was an ardent liberal during the reigns of Louis XVIII and Charles X, those monarchs who presided over the reaction that followed the final fall of Napoleon. He also rapidly moved forward in his own way in the field of mathematics in which he was an absolute genius, far beyond the ability of his teachers to follow.

377

When he was seventeen, he thought he had solved the general equation of the fifth degree, unaware that Abel [527] had already shown this was impossible. Galois quickly realized his mistake and then moved forward beyond Abel to study the solubility of equations in general, generating his own mathematical techniques for attacking the problem, techniques that were eventually to be named "group theory" and that were to have the greatest significance in twentieth-century mathematics.

Galois ran into an extraordinary series of misfortunes. One mathematical paper he submitted was lost by Cauchy [463], another by Fourier [393]. Poisson [432] dismissed a paper of Galois's as incomprehensible. Galois himself invariably did badly on oral examinations partly because he lacked the ability or patience to explain himself clearly.

His intensifying opposition to Charles X and then to Louis Philippe, who succeeded him in 1830, gained Galois the reputation of a flaming radical (which he was) and he was expelled from school. His father, also an opponent of the regime, committed suicide in 1829.

Finally, Galois somehow got himself involved in a duel over a girl and, feeling himself sure of death, spent his last night scribbling out his explanation of group theory. The next day he was indeed shot and killed. He had not yet reached the age of twenty-one.

[572] SHANKS, William
English mathematician
Born: Corsenside, Northumberland, January 25, 1812
Died: Houghton-le-Spring, Durham, 1882

Shanks's significance to the history of science is a rather odd one. He kept a boarding school and in his spare time engaged himself in laborious and tedious computations, particularly involving pi. This is the ratio of the circumference of a circle to its diameter and is roughly 3⅐. It is impossible to express it exactly for the decimal that results is never end-

ing and never repeating. The first few digits are 3.14159 . . .

To calculate it, not exactly but to as many decimal places as one wishes, one makes use of certain unending series of expressions; each one of which can be calculated from the one before, and the greater the number of expressions used, the more accurate the final value. The catch is that the greater the number of expressions used, the more tedious and lengthy the calculation.

Shanks took many years to calculate pi to 707 places, completing his task in 1873. In a very real sense, Shanks had spent a major portion of his life on the task that had no great significance in theoretical mathematics and no significance at all in applied mathematics. For three quarters of a century, no one did better, and Shanks was granted his footnote in the science history books.

Two ironical notes eventually followed. In 1944, it was discovered that Shanks had made a mistake at the 528th decimal point so that everything that followed was wrong. Then beginning in 1949, computers could be used to calculate the value of pi, in a comparatively short time to far more places than Shanks had achieved. The value of pi is now known to over 100,000 places.

[573] GALLE, Johann Gottfried
(gahl'uh)
German astronomer
Born: Pabsthaus, Saxony, June 9, 1812
Died: Potsdam, Prussia, July 10, 1910

Galle, the son of a turpentine-maker, entered the University of Berlin in 1830. He studied under Encke [475] and obtained his doctorate in 1845. He eventually became director of the Berlin Observatory and was afterward professor of astronomy at the University of Breslau.

His great claim to fame is that he was the first actually to see Neptune and to recognize it as a new planet. He had sent his doctor's thesis to Leverrier [564] among others and Leverrier, in replying, told him of his prediction of the position of a new planet.

Galle's successful search was made possible by the reluctant agreement of his superior Encke, who, like Airy [523], doubted the value of searching for the postulated planet. Nevertheless, the credit for the discovery is given, and rightly so, to Leverrier and to Adams [615] for their pen-and-paper calculations (although Leverrier is supposed never to have got round to actually looking at Neptune in the sky).

Galle also suggested that the parallax of asteroids be used to determine the scale of the solar system. This was finally done, with great success, too, but not till after Galle had been dead for twenty years. This was not due to sheer stubbornness; it was necessary to wait for the right asteroid to be discovered and that took time.

Galle worked assiduously into old age, retiring only at eighty-three. Months before his death, Galle, at the patriarchal age of ninety-eight, glimpsed Halley's comet. He had studied it professionally at its earlier appearance in 1835.

[574] **SOBRERO,** Ascanio (sob-ray'-roh)
Italian chemist
Born: Casale, Monferrato, October 12, 1812
Died: Turin, May 26, 1888

Sobrero studied under Berzelius [425] and Liebig [532]. He was a professor of chemistry at the University of Turin and there made the discovery for which he is famous. In 1847 he added glycerine slowly to a mixture of nitric and sulfuric acids and produced nitroglycerine. He observed and reported the remarkable explosive powers of a single drop heated in a test tube.

Unlike Schönbein [510] who had made the similar discovery of nitrocellulose two years earlier and had at once attempted to put it to war work, Sobrero was horrified at the destructive potentiality of what he had found and made no attempt to exploit it. It was two dec-

ades before Nobel [703] learned how to do so properly.

[575] **BESSEMER,** Sir Henry
English metallurgist
Born: Charlton, Hertfordshire, January 19, 1813
Died: London, March 15, 1898

From youth on, Bessemer, the son of an engineer, expended his ingenuity in a variety of inventions. Before he was twenty he had invented a new method for stamping deeds, which the British government promptly adopted, without, however, granting young Bessemer any compensation. Bessemer was more careful thereafter about seeking patent protection.

During the Crimean War of the early 1850s (in which England, allied to France, battled Russia), Bessemer bent his energies to the invention of a new kind of rifled projectile that would spin in flight, thus keeping a more stable trajectory. A cannon firing such a projectile would shoot farther and more accurately.

The conservative British war office was not interested so Bessemer took his invention to Britain's ally, France. (Bessemer was of French descent, his father having emigrated to England at the outbreak of the French Revolution.)

Napoleon III was interested and encouraged experimentation. However, the projectile would have to fit quite tightly in the cannon or the expanding gas of the burning powder would leak past it and lack the force to set it spinning. The greater pressures that would have to exist within the cannon (as a French artillery expert rather derisively pointed out) would almost certainly explode the weapon and annihilate the gunners without harming the enemy.

Bessemer felt the justice of this criticism and set about devising a form of iron that would be strong enough for high-power cannons. Obviously what was needed was steel, but steel at that time was so expensive that it was virtually a precious metal.

Iron as it came out of the smelting furnaces was "cast iron," rich in carbon. It was exceedingly hard, but brittle. The carbon could be painstakingly removed to form practically pure "wrought iron." This was a tough iron (not brittle at all) that could be beaten into any shape, but it was soft.

However, steel, with a carbon content intermediate between wrought iron and cast iron was both hard and tough. The trouble was that in order to make steel one had to convert cast iron into wrought iron and then add the required carbon.

Bessemer considered the method of converting cast iron to wrought iron. To do this iron ore was added in carefully measured amounts to cast iron. The mixture was heated to the molten stage and the oxygen atoms in the iron ore would combine with the carbon atoms in the cast iron to form carbon monoxide gas which bubbled out and burned off, leaving pure iron behind.

Was there no other way of adding oxygen to burn off the carbon but in the form of iron ore (which was chiefly iron oxide)? Why not add the oxygen directly as a blast of air? The objections seemed to be that the cold air would cool and solidify the molten iron and stop the whole process.

Bessemer tried it anyway and found that just the reverse was true. The blast of air burned off the carbon and the heat of that burning not only kept the iron molten but, indeed, raised its temperature so no external source of fuel was needed. By stopping the process at the right time Bessemer found he had steel ready-made without the wrought iron step and without spending money on fuel. Steel could be made at a fraction of its previous cost.

In 1856 he announced his discovery. Ironmakers were enthusiastic and invested fortunes in "blast furnaces." Unfortunately matters went awry. The steel produced was a very poor grade and Bessemer was damned as a charlatan. He returned to his experimentation.

It turned out that in his original experiments he had used phosphorus-free ore,

but the ironmakers had used phosphorus-containing ore. The Bessemer method would not work if phosphorus was present. Bessemer announced this, but the ironmakers once bitten were twice shy and would not listen. Bessemer borrowed money, therefore, and put up his own steelworks in Sheffield in 1860. He imported phosphorus-free iron ore from Sweden and began to sell high-grade steel for one-tenth the prices of the competition. He grew rich in a very few years and the ironmakers saw the force of that argument.

By 1879 he was accepted as a Fellow of the Royal Society and in that same year he reminded the British government that they were still using his method of stamping deeds without compensation. They did not pay him but they acknowledged the justice of his complaint by knighting him.

With Bessemer, and with those after him, such as Siemens [644], who improved the steelmaking process even further, began the era of cheap steel. It meant the coming of giant ocean liners, of steel-skeletoned skyscrapers, of huge suspension bridges. Bessemer did not invent steel but he did make it available to everyone.

Yet even as he did so, Sainte-Claire Deville [603] was setting in motion a line of action that would end by producing steel's closest metallic competitor.

[576] SNOW, John
English physician
Born: York, March 15, 1813
Died: London, June 16, 1858

Snow was the son of a farmer. He was apprenticed to a surgeon at the age of fourteen and, through his adult life, was a fanatic teetotaler and vegetarian. He gained his medical degree from the University of London in 1844.

The news of the introduction of ether as an anesthetic by Morton [617] in 1846 reached England quickly, and the first operation using it was performed in London before the year was done. Snow studied the procedure, devised an apparatus for administering it, published a book on the technique in 1847, and became the most expert anesthetist in the country. He had a sharp controversy with Simpson [567], who favored the use of chloroform and who administered it rather casually by dropping it on a handkerchief. Snow favored more careful administration that controlled the level of its admixture with air and in this, of course, he was right.

Snow was also interested in the manner of contagion of cholera. When an epidemic struck at London in 1854 he studied the geography of water supply and found a disproportionate incidence of cholera in the area supplied by a company that drew its water from the polluted Thames. Worse yet, he found five hundred cases within a few blocks of a particular water pump used by the public, a water pump drawing water from a well just a few feet from a sewer pipe. He persuaded the local authorities to remove the pump handle and the cholera incidence dropped at once.

Snow maintained that cholera infection was spread by wastes getting into water. His views inspired the work of Budd [570], helped keep the notion of infection in the air until Pasteur [642] completed the job by identifying the actual agents of infection.

[577] **ARCHER,** Frederick Scott
English inventor
Born: Bishop's Stortford,
Hertfordshire, 1813
Died: London, May 2, 1857

Archer, the son of a butcher, began his life as apprentice to a silversmith. He grew interested in photography, however, and worked out a wet collodion process whereby a finely detailed negative could be produced. From this negative, while it was still wet, a series of positive prints could be produced on paper. This was the first time that several identical copies of a photograph could be produced.

Talbot [511] claimed that Archer's process was only an insignificant variation of his own and sued for patent in-

fringement but lost. Archer, however, suffered an all-too-common fate of inventors: He put all his money into research and achieved too many failures. He died impoverished.

[578] **BERNARD,** Claude (ber-nahr')
French physiologist
Born: Saint-Julien, Rhône,
July 12, 1813
Died: Paris, February 10, 1878

Bernard was the son of poor vineyard workers and even after he grew famous, he returned home every fall to participate in the grape harvest.

His youthful ambition was to be a writer. He left the village school where there was not much for a boy to learn and took a position as assistant to a druggist so that he might more effectively write in his spare time. He wrote a fairly successful vaudeville comedy, then composed a five-act play in the grand tradition, entitled *Arthur of Brittany*. In 1834 he traveled to Paris to consult a famous critic, Saint-Marc Girardin. The critic read the play and advised the young man to strike out for medicine, for which the critic well deserves a medal.

Bernard did as he was told, worked his way through medical school, where he did not do very well, finishing twenty-sixth in a class of twenty-nine, and managed to obtain his medical degree in 1843. He then came into his own as an assistant to Magendie [438] in 1847. When Magendie died in 1855 Bernard succeeded him as professor. He was also professor of physiology at the Sorbonne, and Napoleon III, himself, saw to it that Bernard's experimental facilities were adequate, building him a special laboratory in 1868.

Bernard absorbed the philosophy of experimental physiology from Magendie, but unlike his old teacher he planned and integrated his experiments carefully, and under him experimental physiology reached maturity.

His most important discoveries began with a study of digestion. He used animals in which he had artificially created fistulas—openings connecting the digestive tract with the outside of the body. Some of the important early studies on digestion had arisen from the work of Beaumont [444] on a man with an accidentally caused fistula and now Bernard decided not to wait upon accident. (For this he was roundly criticized by the antivivisectionists of the day. Among these were Bernard's wife and two daughters. His wife, whom he had in any case married only for her money, was sincere enough in her anger at him to contribute large sums to antivivisection societies and to obtain a legal separation in 1870.)

He was able to show that the stomach was not the entire seat of digestion as, until his time, it had been assumed to be. Instead, although some digestion did take place there, it was but the anteroom of the process. By introducing foodstuffs directly into the initial portion of the small intestine, where the juices of a gland called the pancreas would impinge upon it, he showed that the main processes of digestion took place through the length of the small intestine and that the pancreatic secretions were an important agent of digestion, breaking down fat molecules in particular.

In 1851 Bernard discovered that certain nerves governed the dilatation of blood vessels and others their constriction. In this way the body was able to control the distribution of heat within itself. On hot days, when heat had to be radiated away efficiently, the blood vessels of the skin were dilated, while on cold days, when heat must be conserved, they were constricted. It is for this reason that individuals flush with heat and turn pale with cold. He also showed that it was the red corpuscles of the blood that transported oxygen from lungs to tissues.

To Bernard this was an example of body mechanisms acting as though they were striving to maintain a constant inner environment despite the changing qualities of the outer environment. To do so, the various organs of the body had to be under a tight and integrated

central control. This is the view now accepted, but in the 1850s, when Bernard advanced it, it was in opposition to a trend of thought that, at the time, would have it that the various organs performed their functions in relative isolation. (As a matter of fact the early proponents of the cell theory, for instance Schwann [563], were sufficiently influenced by "nature philosophy" to suppose that even the individual cells had an almost independent life of their own.)

Bernard went on to show that this careful balance within the body extended to chemical reactions and not merely to physical ones. In 1856 he discovered the presence of a starchlike substance in mammalian liver, which he called glycogen. He showed that it was built up out of blood sugar and acted as a reserve store of carbohydrate that could be broken down to sugar again when necessary. Whether glycogen is built up or broken down depends on the exact state of the body, the energy requirements of the various tissues, the food supply in the intestines, and so on, but the net result is that the glycogen balance is so maneuvered that the sugar content in the blood remains steady.

This was the first clear indication that the animal body did not merely tear down complicated molecules into simple ones (catabolism). It, like the plant organism, could be constructive also, building up a large molecule like glycogen out of small ones like sugar (anabolism).

Of course the body's equilibrium could be upset if pushed too hard. Bernard showed that the poisonous action of carbon monoxide lay in its ability to displace oxygen in its combination with hemoglobin. The body could not counter this quickly enough to prevent death by oxygen starvation. This was the first successful explanation of the specific manner in which a drug acted upon the body.

Bernard was not receptive to Darwin's [554] theory of evolution. French biologists generally, even the great Pasteur [642], were more hostile to Darwinism than were those elsewhere in Europe and

America. This was partly because of the still-remembered teachings of the two great Frenchmen of half a century earlier, Lamarck [336] and Cuvier [396].

In life, Bernard was elected a member of the super-select French Academy in 1869 and served in the French senate under Napoleon III. He escaped from Paris at the last moment when the Prussians were encircling it in 1870. When he died of kidney disease he was given a public funeral, the first scientist upon whom France had bestowed this honor.

[579] **STAS,** Jean Servais
Belgian chemist
Born: Louvain (Leuven),
August 21, 1813
Died: Brussels, December 13,
1891

Stas, the son of a shoemaker, was another one of those who obtained a medical degree but never practiced. He was a professor of chemistry at the University of Brussels and was probably the most skillful chemical analyst of the nineteenth century. Interest in the atomic weights had been sparked by Prout [440] and his famous hypothesis of a half century earlier, Cannizzaro [668] had furthered its importance. Stas had begun work in this direction as a student under Dumas [514], with whom he established the atomic weight of carbon as 12, not 6 as others had persistently claimed.

For a decade centered on 1860 Stas worked assiduously in determining atomic weights more accurately than had ever been done before, even by Berzelius [425]. Stas used oxygen $= 16$ as an atomic weight standard and this became universal practice for a century thereafter. No further advance was to be made until the work of Richards [968] a half century later.

Stas's work showed beyond any doubt that the atomic weight of some elements was far removed from integral values and this seemed to be the deathblow to Prout's hypothesis that all atoms except hydrogen were conglomerations of hydrogen atoms and therefore had integral

atomic weights. However, fifty years later, Soddy's [1052] work was to open this seemingly closed question once more, on a much more sophisticated level.

In 1865 Stas accepted a government position as Commissioner of the Mint, but did not keep it long. His liberal views were too much for the conservative Belgian government, under Leopold II, to accept, and he resigned in 1872.

[580] **ANDREWS,** Thomas
Irish physical chemist
Born: Belfast, December 19,
1813
Died: Belfast, November 26,
1885

Andrews, the son of a linen merchant, attended Glasgow University, then studied under Dumas [514] in Paris and finally went on to receive his medical degree from the University of Edinburgh in 1835. He practiced medicine at Belfast and also taught chemistry. In 1845 he became a professor of chemistry at Northern College in Belfast, a post he held till his retirement in 1879.

Andrews identified ozone, discovered earlier by Schönbein [510] as a form of oxygen but could not determine its constitution.

His most important work was done in the liquefaction of gases. Faraday [474] had pioneered in the field, liquefying certain gases by placing them under pressure. Some, such as oxygen, nitrogen, and hydrogen, had resisted liquefaction despite all the pressure that could be placed upon them. By 1845 these nonliquefying gases were called permanent gases and there was serious suspicion that they might be incapable of liquefaction.

Andrews worked with carbon dioxide, a gas that can be liquefied at ordinary room temperature by pressure alone. Working with a sample of liquid carbon dioxide under pressure, he slowly raised the temperature, noting the manner in which the pressure had to be increased to keep the carbon dioxide liquid. As he did so, however, the boundary line between liquid carbon dioxide and the carbon dioxide vapor above grew fainter and at 31°C it disappeared. The carbon dioxide was all gas and no amount of pressure that Andrews could exert would change it to liquid again.

Andrews therefore suggested that for every gas there was a temperature above which pressure alone could not liquefy it. This temperature he called the critical point. (The Russian chemist Mendeléev [705] had made much the same observation two years earlier while a student in Germany, but his report had gone unnoticed.)

This was a crucial discovery for it pointed the way toward the liquefaction of the permanent gases by demonstrating the necessity of dropping the temperature below the critical point before exerting pressure. This new view led within half a century to the work of Dewar [759] and Kamerlingh-Onnes [843] and the liquefaction of all known gases.

[581] **PARKES,** Alexander
English chemist
Born: Birmingham, December 29, 1813
Died: London, June 29, 1890

Parkes's patents included one, in 1841, for waterproofing fabrics by coating them with rubber and another, in 1843, for an electrometallurgical process that was particularly suited to electroplating delicate objects. He is supposed to have presented to Prince Albert (Queen Victoria's husband, one member of royalty who was consistently interested in science) a silverplated spider web.

In the early 1850s, Parkes discovered that pyroxylin (partly nitrated cellulose), if dissolved in alcohol and ether in which camphor has also been dissolved, will produce a hard solid upon evaporation, which will soften and become malleable when heated. He found no way of successfully marketing this substance, however, and it was left to Hyatt [728], fifteen years later, to place it in the public eye.

Nevertheless, successfully applied or not, Parkes had discovered the first plastic.

[582] **FRÉMY,** Edmond (fray-mee')
French chemist
Born: Versailles, February 28, 1814
Died: Paris, February 2, 1894

Frémy began his chemistry career in 1831 as assistant to Gay-Lussac [420], and gained his first professorial post in 1846. He succeeded Gay-Lussac in his post at the Museum of Natural History when Gay-Lussac died in 1850, and at the retirement of Chevreul [448] in 1879 became the director of the museum.

He worked on a variety of chemical problems and produced synthetic rubies by heating aluminum oxide with potassium chromate and barium fluoride.

He is best remembered today, perhaps, for his work with fluorine compounds. He discovered a number of such compounds, including hydrogen fluoride. Chemists had long known there was an element in the fluorides that resembled chlorine but was even more active. It was so active, however, that it could not be torn away from the other elements with which it had combined so that it was not produced as a free element.

Frémy made a stubborn attempt, but failed. In this, however, he laid the groundwork for Moissan [831], who succeeded.

[583] **GEISSLER,** Heinrich (gise'ler)
German inventor
Born: Igelshieb, Saxe-Meiningen, May 26, 1814
Died: Bonn, Rhenish Prussia, January 24, 1879

Geissler, the son of a burgomaster, was a skillful glassblower and in 1852 opened a shop in Bonn for the manufacture and sale of scientific instruments. His chief fame came in connection with vacuum production.

Two centuries earlier Guericke [189]

had invented the first air pump. With this he could produce a vacuum by pumping air out of a vessel, and with such a vacuum physicists could experiment to their heart's content. Torricelli [192] had created a better vacuum over a column of mercury than an air pump of the time could produce. This remained merely a curiosity, however, for it was a vacuum within a closed container and was not therefore available for experimentation.

In 1855 Geissler took advantage of Torricelli's discovery to devise an air pump without moving mechanical parts. He moved a column of mercury up and down. The vacuum above the column could be used to suck out the air within an enclosed vessel, little by little, until the vacuum within the vessel approached that above the mercury. In this way he evacuated chambers more thoroughly than anyone ever had before. Tubes so evacuated were named Geissler tubes by Geissler's friend Plücker [521].

Geissler tubes made possible an important advance in the study of electricity and of the atom. Physicists had been attempting to send electric discharges through evacuated vessels, and Faraday [474] had noted that a fluorescence was produced as a result. However, the vacuum used by Faraday was not good enough to allow much work to be done. With the Geissler tubes that was changed and a course of research was initiated that led to the discovery of the electron by J. J. Thomson [869] four decades later.

[584] **DAUBRÉE**, Gabriel Auguste
(doh-bray′)
French geologist
Born: Metz, June 25, 1814
Died: Paris, May 29, 1896

Daubrée studied at the École Polytechnique and became a qualified mining engineer in 1834. In 1861 he was appointed professor of geology at the Paris Museum of Natural History. He toured western Europe and Algeria as well. He rose in his profession until, in 1867, he

was appointed inspector general of mines, keeping that position till he retired in 1886.

He applied experimental methods to the study of minerals, investigating methods of origin and formation. He also studied and classified meteorites, building a collection of them. He was struck by the fact that a number of them were almost pure nickel-iron. Since it was well known that the center of the earth was high-density, he suggested in 1866 that nickel-iron was a common component of planetary structure and that earth's core might be formed of that alloy. This suggestion is now accepted as highly probable by geologists generally.

[585] **ÅNGSTRÖM**, Anders Jonas
(ohng′strum)
Swedish physicist
Born: Lögdö, Medelpad,
August 13, 1814
Died: Uppsala, June 21, 1874

Ångström, the son of a lumber mill chaplain, was educated at the University of Uppsala, where he obtained his Ph.D. in 1839 and where he spent his life teaching physics and astronomy, achieving his professorship in 1858. He had anticipated Kirchhoff [648] in seeing that a cool gas absorbs just those wavelengths of light it emits when it is hot. Consequently when Kirchhoff developed this in detail and established spectroscopy, Ångström was not slow to apply it to the heavens.

In 1861 he began to inspect the solar spectrum in this new light—as Huggins [646] was doing independently in England—and, in 1862, announced the discovery of hydrogen in the sun. He soon discovered other elements as well, and in 1868 published a map of the spectrum, locating the wavelength of about a thousand lines with great care. In 1867 he had also been the first to study the spectrum of the aurora borealis.

He did not use an arbitrary measure as Kirchhoff had done, but actually measured the wavelengths in units equal to a ten billionth of a meter. This unit was officially named the Ångström unit in 1905.

Ångström was elected to the Royal Society in 1870 and received the Rumford medal (the first to a Swede) in 1872.

[586] **KIRKWOOD,** Daniel
American astronomer
Born: Harford County, Maryland,
September 27, 1814
Died: Riverside, California,
June 11, 1895

Kirkwood, the son of a farmer, had little formal education in his early years but learned mathematics on his own and finally served as professor of mathematics at Delaware College, then at Indiana University, and finally lectured at Stanford University.

He turned his attention to the asteroids, knowledge of which had been initiated with the work of Piazzi [341] and Olbers [372] a half century before, and was the first to do more than simply discover new ones. In 1857 he proved that the orbits of those already known (about fifty at that time) were not evenly distributed about an average orbit. Instead there were regions that were free of asteroids. He showed in 1866, by which time the number of known asteroids had risen to eighty-seven, that if asteroids did exist in those Kirkwood gaps (as they are now known) they would have annual periods of revolution that would be in simple ratio to that of Jupiter. The perturbations of Jupiter would slowly build up, forcing the asteroids into an orbit closer to or farther from the sun, and the gap would remain a gap.

Kirkwood was further able to show that there were similar gaps in Saturn's rings (which was why they were rings, rather than a ring) owing to the perturbing effect of Saturn's satellites. If there were ring particles in Cassini's [209] gap, for instance, they would circle Saturn in just half the period that Mimas, its innermost satellite, did. Mimas's perturbations would force the ring particles out of that position, renewing the gap that

divided the ring into two major sections. Newton's [231] theory of gravitation thus met another test in explaining the fine details of the structure of the solar system (although in 1980 the Voyager I probe showed the structure of the ring to be too complex to be easily explained by such "resonance" considerations alone).

Kirkwood also maintained that Mercury probably showed a single face to the sun at all times because of tidal effects. Schiaparelli [714] was to report having observed this and it was not till the 1960s that the true rotational period of Mercury (only two-thirds its period of revolution) was to be demonstrated.

Asteroid ⚹1578 has been named in Kirkwood's honor.

[587] **MAYER,** Julius Robert (my′er)
German physicist
Born: Heilbronn, Württemberg,
November 25, 1814
Died: Heilbronn, March 20,
1878

Originally trained as a physician at the University of Tübingen, Mayer, the son of an apothecary, was not a particularly good scholar. He obtained his medical degree in 1838, although the year before he had been expelled for his liberal views. He did not enjoy medical practice.

He served as ship's doctor under conditions which gave him little to do but think; and about 1840, during a trip to Java, he began to interest himself in physics, while considering the problem of animal heat.

In 1842 he presented a figure for the mechanical equivalent of heat, based on an experiment in which a horse powered a mechanism that stirred paper pulp in a caldron. He compared the work done by the horse with the temperature rise in the pulps. His experiments were not as detailed and careful as those by Joule [613] but Mayer saw their significance and clearly presented his belief in the conservation of energy before either Joule or Helmholtz [631] did.

He had some difficulty getting his paper on the subject published but Liebig [532] finally accepted it for the important journal he edited. Though Mayer was five years ahead of Joule his paper aroused no interest, and in the end it was Joule, with his imposing experimental background, who received credit for working out the mechanical equivalent of heat. And it was Helmholtz who received credit for announcing the law of conservation of energy because he announced it so much more systematically. Yet Mayer went further than either of the other two, for he included the tides, the heating of meteorites, and even living phenomena in the realm of energy conservation (a daring step in a decade when vitalism, with its view that the laws of inanimate nature did not apply to living systems, was still a considerable force).

Mayer argued that solar energy was the ultimate source of all energy on earth, both living and nonliving. He further suggested that solar energy was derived from the slow contraction of the sun, or by the fall of meteors into the sun, in either case kinetic energy being converted to radiant energy. Helmholtz and Kelvin [652] got credit for this latter idea.

Mayer's failure to be appreciated and the fact that he was on the losing side in controversies as to priority affected him strongly. The year 1848 saw additional disasters, with the death of two of his children and his brother's involvement with revolutionary activities. Mayer tried to commit suicide in 1849 by jumping from a third-story window but failed in that too, merely injuring his legs severely, and laming himself permanently. In 1851 he was taken to a mental institution where primitive and cruel methods for treating the sick prevailed. He was eventually released but he never fully recovered. He lived in such obscurity that when Liebig lectured on Mayer's views in 1858 he referred to the man as being dead.

That, however, proved a turning point. It was as though the world's conscience smote it. Helmholtz and Clausius [633] referred favorably to his work. Tyndall [626] lectured on his work during the early 1860s and labored to secure him proper recognition. Mayer was granted the right to add "von" to his name, which was roughly the equivalent of an English knighthood. Then, in 1871, he received the Copley medal.

[588] **LAWES,** Sir John Bennett
English agricultural scientist
Born: Rothamsted, Hertfordshire, December 28, 1814
Died: Rothamsted, August 31, 1900

Lawes was educated at Eton and at Oxford, but left without taking a degree. It was not chemistry that he studied, but it was chemistry in which he became interested. Inheriting his father's estate, he began to experiment with artificial fertilizers. In 1842 he patented a method for manufacturing superphosphate and the next year set up a factory for its production (scandalizing his ladylike mother), thus putting into practice the chemical investigations of Liebig [532] in this field.

In 1843 he also organized the Rothamsted Experimental Station, along with Joseph Henry Gilbert (1817–1901), a chemist who had studied briefly under Liebig. This was England's first agricultural laboratory. There in 1854, for instance, he fed pigs protein in either of two forms—lentil meal and barley meal—and found that the pigs retained much more of the nitrogen in barley meal. These were the first "nitrogen balance" experiments and led the way toward the concept of essential dietary components.

Lawes was created a baronet in 1882, and Gilbert was knighted in 1893.

[589] **DE LA RUE,** Warren
British astronomer
Born: Guernsey, Channel Islands, January 15, 1815
Died: London, April 19, 1889

De la Rue, after a college education in Paris, and after having become a close friend of Hofmann [604], entered his father's printing business and invented the first envelope-making machine. He then grew interested in photography.

Like W. C. Bond [464], he was one of the first to photograph the moon. He got a picture that was sharp enough to be magnified twentyfold. This first raised the possibility that photography was more than a permanent record of what the eyes could see and that it offered a method of seeing more than the eyes (even with a telescope).

In 1858 De la Rue devised a photoheliograph, a telescope adapted particularly to solar photography. Thereafter, taking photographs of the sun became a matter of daily routine, something John Herschel [479] had suggested ought to be done.

In 1860 De la Rue observed a total eclipse of the sun in Spain and was able to show that the "prominences" (spurts of red flame) visible about the edge of the moon's disc during the height of the eclipse were from the sun and not from the moon.

This discovery of solar prominences, together with Schwabe's [466] announcement of the sunspot cycle two decades earlier, may be considered as initiating astrophysics (the study of the constitution of stars and of the physical processes within them). This branch of science was carried from the sun to the stars themselves by Secchi's [606] spectroscopy.

[590] **FORBES,** Edward
British naturalist
Born: Douglas, Isle of Man, February 12, 1815
Died: Wardic, near Edinburgh, Scotland, November 18, 1854

Forbes studied medicine at the University of Edinburgh but never completed his courses. Interest in natural history claimed him and by 1833 he was touring Norway and collecting botanical data.

He developed a particular interest in the natural history of the Mediterranean area and perhaps the most noteworthy single incident of his life was the dredging up of a starfish from a quarter-mile depth of that sea. This was the first indi-

cation that life was not, after all, confined to the sunlit topmost portions of the ocean but that living things had colonized the depths. As we now know, the very deepest portions of the ocean have their life forms.

He achieved professorial status in 1851 when he was appointed to the chair of natural history at the Royal School of Mines.

[591] **REMAK,** Robert (ray'mak)
German physician
Born: Posen (now Poznań, Poland), July 30, 1815
Died: Kissingen, August 29, 1865

Remak, the son of a Jewish shopowner, studied at the University of Berlin under Johannes Müller [522] and obtained his medical degree in 1838, specializing in neurology. In 1847 he joined the faculty at Berlin. He was one of the first to make use of an electric current in treating disorders of the nerves and was thus a founder of electrotherapy.

He was also profoundly interested in embryology and in 1845 when he reduced Baer's [478] four germ layers to three, he gave them the names by which they are still known: ectoderm ("outer skin"), mesoderm ("middle skin"), and endoderm ("inner skin").

[592] **WUNDERLICH,** Carl Reinhold August (voon'der-likh)
German physician
Born: Sulz, August 4, 1815
Died: Leipzig, Saxony, September 25, 1877

A professor of medicine at the University of Leipzig, Wunderlich, during the 1840s and 1850s was the first to recognize that fever was not a disease in itself but merely a symptom. He was the first to insist on careful records of the fever's progress and took such records himself.

His advice was not easily followed, however, for in his time the thermometers that were used to record body temperature were bulky and inconvenient and took up to twenty minutes to come to equilibrium. It was not till the invention of small and accurate clinical thermometers by Allbutt [720] that the course of fever could be followed routinely by anyone—even the patient.

[593] **WEIERSTRASS,** Karl Theodor Wilhelm (vy'er-shtras')
German mathematician
Born: Ostenfelde, Westphalia, October 31, 1815
Died: Berlin, February 19, 1897

Weierstrass, the son of a city official, was sent to the University of Bonn in 1834 by his stern father in order that he study law and finance. This Weierstrass did not wish to do so he spent his time in carousing and returned after four years with no degree. However, he came across the work of Abel [527] and Jacobi [541] on elliptical functions and that turned his thoughts to mathematics.

By 1841 he had passed his examinations and took up a rather miserable and underpaid life as a high school teacher. He continued his mathematical work, however, and his extension of previous work on elliptical functions caused him to be recognized as a first-rate mathematician. Indeed, he is called the father of modern analysis. In 1856 he was given a position commensurate with his abilities at the University of Berlin and became a member of the Berlin Academy.

[594] **LONG,** Crawford Williamson
American physician
Born: Danielsville, Georgia, November 1, 1815
Died: Athens, Georgia, June 16, 1878

After obtaining his medical degree from the University of Pennsylvania in 1839, Long opened his practice in Georgia.

On March 30, 1842, he used ether to induce insensibility before removing a tumor from the neck of a patient. This was the first recorded use of an anesthetic in surgery, but Long did not bother to publish an account of it. He performed at least eight other such operations in the next few years but did not publish until 1849 and by then it was too late. Morton [617] had already received the credit and Jackson [543] was already claiming it for his own. The gentle voice of Long, the real discoverer, could not be heard above the din.

[595] **BOOLE,** George
English mathematician and logician
Born: Lincoln, November 2, 1815
Died: Ballintemple, County Cork, Ireland, December 8, 1864

Boole, the son of a shoemaker, pulled himself up by his bootstraps. He thought of entering the church at first but he learned mathematics on his own and by the time he was sixteen he was teaching mathematics at a private school to help support his family. In 1835 he established a school of his own. In 1849 he was appointed professor of mathematics at Queen's College in Cork (despite his lack of degrees) largely because De Morgan [549] admired a pamphlet of Boole's on the subject of logic and mathematics. For the first time he experienced relative security. He remained at the college for the rest of his life.

Boole's great discovery was that one could apply a set of symbols to logical operations, something Leibniz [233] had been groping toward nearly two centuries before. By careful choice, he made symbols and operations resemble those of algebra. In Boolean algebra the symbols could be manipulated according to fixed rules to yield results that would hold water logically.

Boole's predecessors had hesitated to work out the implications of the idea. (It involved an improvement on Aristotle [29] and there was always a certain hesitancy in attempting an improvement on him.)

Boole dared do this, however. In 1847 he published his first, small book on the subject, the one that attracted De Morgan's attention and brought him to Cork. Then in 1854 he published *An Investigation of the Laws of Thought,* which treated the subject in full and founded what is now called symbolic logic.

This mathematicization of logic (Aristotle set to music, so to speak) was slow in making an impression on the mathematicians of the day. It seemed perhaps no more than an intricate game with words. However, it was found that symbolic logic was most useful (and indeed essential) to working out the philosophy of mathematics. The attempt to put mathematics on a rigidly logical basis (fully twenty-one centuries after Euclid [40], who to the ancients and all who followed down to the time of Lobachevski [484] had seemed to have succeeded at this task) was first undertaken by Frege [797] and brought to a climax by Whitehead [911] and Russell [1005]. Boolean algebra was used for the purpose.

Boole died from pneumonia brought on by his insistence on lecturing while wet from a walk through two miles of cold November rain.

[596] RUTHERFURD, Lewis Morris
American astronomer
Born: New York, New York, November 25, 1816
Died: Tranquillity, New Jersey, May 30, 1892

Rutherfurd was born of a wealthy family and could indulge his taste for science freely, even though he had studied law. There was no need for him, after all, to practice at law and he did not. On a visit to Europe, he met Amici [447] and that sharpened his interest in optical instrumentation.

In 1856 he set up a small observatory at his home in New York City, and by 1858 he was working on astronomical photography. He was the first to get the notion that a telescope might be used solely for photographic purposes and might have the optical portions omitted where they were for use of the eyes. He devised the first such telescope, produc-

390

ing what was really a camera in which the telescope served as the lens.

Rutherfurd began to take pictures of star clusters. He devised a micrometer to measure stellar positions on photographs and worked out methods of making the photograhic negatives more stable.

He then turned to the photography of spectrographs and obtained the best such photographs that had yet been obtained. He also devised a machine for ruling gratings that were better and more accurate than anything obtained till the time when Rowland [798] surpassed Rutherfurd's mark. By 1877 Rutherfurd was ruling over 17,000 lines to the inch.

By then, however, his health was beginning to fail and New York City was growing to the point where astronomic observations were becoming difficult and the observatory was dismantled.

[597] LUDWIG, Karl Friedrich Wilhelm (lood'vikh)
German physiologist
Born: Witzenhausen, Hesse, December 29, 1816
Died: Leipzig, Saxony, April 27, 1895

Ludwig, the son of a cavalry officer, was educated at the universities of Erlangen and Marburg, where he was rather a troublemaker and a duelist. He was expelled from school for a while, but finally obtained his medical degree in 1840. He received his first professorial appointment at the latter school in 1846. He proved himself an excellent teacher, second in influence in the field of physiology only to his older contemporary Müller [522].

Ludwig's most important researches were in connection with the circulatory system and here he took up an antivitalist position. In the two centuries following Harvey's [174] discovery of the circulation of the blood, physiologists had been at a loss to account for the mechanical movement of the blood. Consequently, it was tempting to suppose that a "vital force" drove the blood, a force unamenable to ordinary physical experimentation. That, at least, made it unnec-

essary for physiologists to worry about
the matter.

In 1847, however, Ludwig devised a
kymograph, a rotating drum on which
the value of the blood pressure could be
continuously recorded. The detailed
study of blood pressure made possible in
this way showed that blood circulation
could be explained in terms of ordinary
mechanical forces.

This about ended vitalism where the
mechanical portions of the body were involved. In the same decade Du Bois-
Reymond [611] disproved vitalism where
the electrical portions of the body were
involved. Vitalism maintained itself
chiefly in connection with the chemical
aspects of the body and was not laid to
rest there until Buchner's [903] work a
half century later.

Ludwig placed blood under a vacuum
and showed that gases could be made to
bubble out of it. For the first time it became possible to work with the gaseous
components of the body tissues themselves, as well as with the liquid and
solid components.

In 1856 he was the first to remove organs from the animal body and keep
them alive for a period of time by pumping blood through them (perfusion).

[598] **NÄGELI,** Karl Wilhelm von
(nay'guh-lee)
Swiss botanist
Born: Kilchberg, near Zürich,
March 27, 1817
Died: Munich, Germany, May 10,
1891

Nägeli, the son of a physician, decided
not to follow in his father's footsteps but
to become a botanist. He studied under
Candolle [418] at Geneva and graduated
from the University of Zürich in 1840.
He was particularly interested in the
manner of division of plant cells. His
careful microscopic investigations convinced him by 1846 that Schleiden [538]
was wrong about cells budding off the
nuclear surface. This corrected an important flaw in the cell theory, but the
elucidation of the details of the connection of the nucleus with cell division had

to await Flemming [762] a generation
later.

Nägeli did far more harm to biology
than good. He had also studied under
Oken [423], and despite his support of
Darwin's [554] rationalist theory of evolution he retained a large share of mysticism. He could not accept the random
force of natural selection as the only
drive behind evolutionary development
but postulated some inner push that
drove evolutionary changes in a particular direction (such as increased size),
even past the point where the change
benefits the organism. This notion of
orthogenesis served no purpose but to
confuse evolutionary philosophy. In
common with some others, Nägeli suspected that evolutionary change was not
smoothly continuous but proceeded in
jumps, and this notion, a generation
later, was to come to life as De Vries's
[792] mutation theory.

Nägeli's most far-reaching mistake,
however, was his underestimation of a
paper sent him by an obscure monk
named Mendel [638]. Mendel's work was
strictly rationalist and completely non-
speculative and Nägeli wasn't equipped
intellectually to handle it. He dismissed
the work contemptuously and thus
delayed by a full generation the development of genetics.

Twenty years later, in 1884, when he
wrote a textbook on botany, he never
mentioned Mendel.

[599] **MARIGNAC,** Jean Charles
Galissard de (ma-ree-nyak')
Swiss chemist
Born: Geneva, April 24, 1817
Died: Geneva, April 15, 1894

Marignac was descended from a Huguenot family and in 1835 entered the
École Polytechnique in Paris, where he
studied under Dumas [514] among
others. In 1840 he spent some time in
Liebig's [532] laboratory at Giessen. In
1841 he gained a professorial appointment at the University of Geneva and
spent most of his life thereafter, working
without assistants in an ill-appointed laboratory in the basement of the school.

He was generally at the forefront of developments. He supported Guldberg's [721] law of mass action, and readily adopted the views of Avogadro [412] after these had been explained by Cannizzaro [668] in 1860.

He labored to determine atomic weights with great precision and was one of the many who found that Prout's [440] hypothesis did not hold. However, he made the daring speculation that something about the smaller particles of which the atom was made up produced these deviations. Since at that time, it was a basic dogma of chemistry that atoms were fundamental particles and there was nothing smaller, the suggestion was completely ignored but a half century later, it turned out Marignac was right after all.

He also worked with the rare earths separating them by repeated solutions and precipitations designed to take advantage of slight differences in solubilities among them (guided by spectroscopic studies of the different fractions). He is given credit for the discovery of two of the rare earth elements: ytterbium and gadolinium.

Marignac hesitated long, however, before accepting Kekulé's [680] notions of organic molecular structure.

[600] **KÖLLIKER,** Rudolf Albert von (kerl'ih-ker)
Swiss anatomist and physiologist
Born: Zürich, July 6, 1817
Died: Würzburg, Bavaria, November 2, 1905

Kölliker, the son of a bank official, studied under Oken [423], Müller [522], and Henle [557] and obtained his medical degree from Heidelberg in 1842. After a short stay as a professor at the University of Zürich he joined the faculty of the University of Würzburg in 1847 and remained there for half a century.

Kölliker studied tissues by microscope with painstaking care and in 1848 was the first to isolate the cells of smooth muscle. He wrote a textbook in 1852 that might be considered the first good study of histology, the science that had been originated a half century before, without the microscope, by Bichat [400].

In 1861 Kölliker also published an important text on embryology. He was the first to interpret the developing embryo in terms of cell theory and was one of the founders of modern embryology. Kölliker made it quite clear that eggs and sperm might be considered cells and in 1849 he showed that nerve fibers were elongated portions of cells. This was a forerunner of Ramón y Cajal's [827] neuron theory, which in his old age he strongly supported.

He was particularly interested in the cell nucleus and believed it was the key to the transmission of hereditary characteristics. In this he was again a half century ahead of his time. He, like Nägeli [598], believed that evolution proceeded in jumps, and in this too he was half a century in advance.

[601] **KOPP,** Hermann Franz Moritz (kup)
German physical chemist
Born: Hanau, Hesse, October 30, 1817
Died: Heidelberg, Baden, February 20, 1892

Kopp was the son of a physician who occupied himself on occasion with chemistry, so that the youngster was carrying on at least part of the family tradition when he went to the University of Heidelberg in 1836 to study chemistry under Gmelin [457]. He transferred to the University of Marburg a year later and received his Ph.D. there in 1838. He then found himself in Giessen in 1839 drawn by the powerful attraction of Liebig's [532] reputation.

In 1841, when he was twenty-four, he began work on a history of chemistry that was to take six years and to appear in four volumes. It made him famous and he is remembered as a historian of chemistry even more than for his research.

By 1843 he had a professorial position at Giessen, which he kept for twenty years, transferring then to Heidelberg.

392

When Berzelius [425] died in 1848, Liebig and Kopp continued his annual reports on the latest developments in chemistry, broadening the effort to include associated sciences. Kopp continued his share of this labor until 1862.

In research Kopp's chief effort consisted of the association of physical properties with chemical structure. He was the first to make careful measurements of the boiling points of organic substances. He also measured specific gravities and specific heats. He showed the manner in which similar compounds differed by smooth increments in such physical properties when the length of the chain of connected carbon atoms was increased. He was thus a pioneer in the study of physical organic chemistry.

[602] **WURTZ,** Charles Adolphe (vurts)
French chemist
Born: Wolfisheim, near Strasbourg, November 26, 1817
Died: Paris, May 12, 1884

Wurtz, the son of a Lutheran minister (he was born in the German-tinged section of France known as Alsace, which accounts for his last name), was disinclined to follow in his father's footsteps. He embarked on medical studies and gained his doctorate in 1843. By that time, however, it was chemistry that had won his heart. He moved on to Giessen where he studied under Liebig [532] and met Hofmann [604]. He then moved on to the University of Paris, where he gained professorial status in 1853, succeeding Dumas [514].

Wurtz was the first important chemist in France to support the structural views of Laurent [553] in organic chemistry against the older views of Berzelius [425]. Using the new viewpoint, it seemed to him that organic derivatives of ammonia could exist and he prepared the first "amine," as such organic derivatives were called. He also was the first to prepare phosphorus oxychloride and a compound, ethylene glycol, which possessed two alcohol groups, and many other substances.

When the Sorbonne finally established a professorship of organic chemistry, Wurtz was the first one to fill it, in 1875.

Perhaps Wurtz is best remembered for a method of synthesizing long-chain hydrocarbons by reacting hydrocarbon iodides with metallic sodium. This method, which he discovered in 1855, is still called the Wurtz reaction.

Wurtz had the unhappiness of seeing his home province ceded to the new German Empire after France's heavy defeat in the Franco-Prussian War of 1870.

[603] **SAINTE-CLAIRE DEVILLE,**
Henri Étienne (sant-clair duh-veel')
French chemist
Born: St. Thomas, Virgin Islands, March 11, 1818
Died: Boulogne-sur-Seine, France, July 1, 1881

Sainte-Claire Deville was born of a French father (a prominent shipowner) who was serving as French consul on an island that then belonged to Denmark. He was sent to France for an education where lectures by Thénard [416] attracted him to chemistry. In 1843 he obtained doctoral degrees in both medicine and science and in 1845 received a professorial appointment at the University of Besançon. He succeeded Balard [529] at the École Normale in 1851 and then became a professor of chemistry at the Sorbonne, succeeding Dumas [514].

In the 1850s he began an investigation of aluminum. Earlier, Oersted [417] and Wöhler [515] had isolated the metal in small, impure quantities. Sainte-Claire Deville used Wöhler's method of reacting aluminum compounds with metallic potassium but he soon substituted sodium, which was safer and more efficient. After preparing sodium in quantity he was able to do the same for aluminum. A fifteen-pound ingot was prepared in 1855. The price of the metal was reduced from 30,000 francs a kilogram in 1855 to 300 francs in 1859. (In the latter year he became a professor of chemistry at the Sorbonne.)

Even so, aluminum was far too expensive to compete with steel. It required the work of Hall [933] and Héroult [925], a generation later, to bring aluminum into its own. Sainte-Claire Deville, in addition to his work on aluminum, was the first to prepare nitrogen pentoxide and among the first to prepare toluene. He worked on the metallurgy of platinum and demonstrated the manner in which gas molecules broke apart at high temperatures.

He was plagued by ill health and overwork as he aged and, in fit of depression, killed himself when he was sixty-three.

[604] **HOFMANN**, August Wilhelm von (hofe'mahn)
German chemist
Born: Giessen, Hesse, April 8, 1818
Died: Berlin, May 2, 1892

Hofmann, the son of an architect, was another of those who, beginning outside the field of chemistry (he studied law), were lured into the science by the persuasive charm of the teaching of Liebig [532]. Under Liebig, Hofmann worked on coal tar and studied the properties of aniline, obtaining his Ph.D. in 1841 with a thesis on the subject. (He also married Liebig's niece. It was the first of four marriages, he being left a widower three times and having eleven children altogether.)

He was invited to England at the suggestion of Prince Albert, the husband of Queen Victoria. There he taught at the Royal College of Chemistry in London and served as chemist to the British royal mint. He was an excellent lecturer, laying great stress on dramatic demonstrations that he had assistants perform while he talked, for he himself lacked deftness. Many of the demonstrations he devised have remained standards ever since.

Hofmann's interest in coal tar lingered and expressed itself in a remark that set Perkin [734] to work on the analysis of quinine—finding synthetic dyes, instead. Hofmann was not too proud to follow in the course his pupil had charted out and two years after Perkin's discovery he was himself synthesizing new dyes, commonly called Hofmann violets. In 1864, after twenty years in England, he returned to Germany, took a post in Bonn, and within a year moved to the University of Berlin, succeeding Mitscherlich [485].

He founded the German Chemical Society and like Perkin he continued to develop new synthetic methods (the Hofmann degradation reaction is still much used) and to produce new dyes. He wrote numerous obituaries for other chemists in a rather overblown style and these were published in three volumes in 1888. In that same year he was ennobled.

Under his leadership Germany overtook England and France and developed a huge dye industry, for Germany was far ahead in organic chemistry generally. Against Perkin, virtually alone in England, a superlatively capable team of German chemists dominated organic chemistry for half a century after Hofmann's return, until the dislocations of World War I and the British blockade forced other countries, notably the United States, to develop chemical industries of their own and to free themselves of dependence on Germany.

[605] **DONDERS**, Franciscus Cornelis (dawn'derz)
Dutch physiologist
Born: Tilburg, North Brabant, May 27, 1818
Died: Utrecht, March 24, 1889

Donders, who was left fatherless in infancy, was brought up by a mother and eight older sisters. In 1835 he entered the University of Utrecht as a medical student and obtained his degree in 1840 from Leiden University.

In 1842 he returned to Utrecht as assistant to Mulder [531] and interested himself in ophthalmology. He discovered, in 1858, that farsightedness was caused by a too shallow eyeball so that the focus fell behind the retina. In 1862 he found that astigmatism was caused by the uneven curvatures of the cornea or lens. In 1864 he published a book on ophthalmology that was the first important book in the field.

It then became possible to design and manufacture lenses that would correct imperfect vision with much greater accuracy than had been possible before.

[606] SECCHI, Pietro Angelo (sek′kee)
Italian astronomer
Born: Reggio, Emilia, June 18, 1818
Died: Rome, February 26, 1878

Secchi, the son of a cabinetmaker, entered the Society of Jesus in 1833 and his education led him to work as an astronomer. He taught in several Jesuit schools, but then came 1848, when a temporary spasm of liberalism and anticlericalism shot through Europe. Secchi, as a Jesuit, was forced out of Italy and he spent some time in Great Britain and in the United States, teaching at Georgetown University in Washington, D.C., and other places. The spasm ended quickly enough and soon Secchi was back in Rome, where he was appointed director of the Gregorian University Observatory.

He seized early upon new techniques. Along with Huggins [646] he was the first to adapt spectroscopy to astronomy in a systematic manner and he made the first spectroscopic survey of the heavens, studying the spectra of four thousand stars between 1864 and 1868. This made it quite clear that stellar spectra differed among themselves, and so for the first time in history stars were found to differ in more than position, brightness, and color. Since Kirchhoff [648] had established the significance of spectral lines, the difference in stellar spectra meant a difference in chemical constitution.

In 1867 Secchi suggested the establishment of spectral classes and he himself divided the spectra he had studied into four classes. Accumulating data have made a considerably more complex division necessary; however, the classification of stellar spectra begun by Secchi led on to schemes of stellar evolution, as the classification of species by Ray [213] and Linnaeus [276] had led to schemes of the evolution of species.

Secchi was also, along with De la Rue [589] and W. C. Bond [464], among the first to turn the new technique of photography to astronomic use. In 1851 he took photographs of the sun during various phases of an eclipse and by 1859 he had a complete set of photographs of the moon.

He was also the first to make color drawings of Mars and to show the yellow desert areas and the darker (vegetation?) areas.

Secchi's increased reputation in astronomy stood him in good stead in 1870, when the newly unified Kingdom of Italy absorbed the last remnant of the old Papal States. Italy expelled the Jesuits, who were naturally hostile to the new situation, but allowed Secchi to remain at his post this time, his importance as an astronomer outweighing the fact of his membership in the order.

[607] SEMMELWEISS, Ignaz Philipp (zem′el-vise)
Hungarian physician
Born: Budapest, July 1, 1818
Died: Vienna, August 13, 1865

Semmelweiss, the son of a prosperous shopkeeper of German origin, was going to study law at the University of Vienna till he casually accompanied a friend to a lecture on anatomy. He found himself fascinated, tackled medicine, and received his medical degree at the University of Vienna in 1844 (Hungary was at the time part of the Austrian Empire). He interested himself at once in childbed fever. It was a puzzling disease, since women bearing children in Vienna hospitals with the help of superbly educated doctors died of the fever very commonly, while women bearing children at home with the help of ignorant midwives usually survived.

Semmelweiss decided the doctors themselves were somehow carrying the disease from the dissecting rooms and in 1847 began to force doctors under him to wash their hands in strong chemicals before touching any patients. This was unpleasant for the doctors, especially to those older ones who were proud of the "hospital odor" of their hands and who resented being told they were causing disease.

The incidence of childbed fever went down drastically following Semmelweiss's ruling; but when Hungary revolted (unsuccessfully) against Austria in 1849, the Viennese doctors were able to call patriotism to the aid of folly and forced their Hungarian annoyer out. The incidence of childbed fever climbed to record heights as soon as handwashing was stopped but the Viennese doctors did not mind as long as they could keep their pride. Even Virchow [632] turned a deaf ear to a Hungarian.

Semmelweiss retired to a hospital in Budapest where he instituted his antiseptic measures and there the incidence of childbed fever dropped to almost zero. In July 1865 Semmelweiss suffered a nervous breakdown and after a trip to Vienna was committed to a mental hospital there. Two weeks later he was dead of an infection he had been subjected to when he had accidentally wounded himself while working with a sick patient.

Thus, he died of childbed fever himself, just a little too soon to see the principle of antisepsis rise triumphant first in England under Lister [672] (who freely acknowledged Semmelweiss' precedence), then in France under Pasteur [642], and finally even among the foolish doctors of Vienna.

[608] MITCHELL, Maria
      American astronomer
      Born: Nantucket, Massachusetts,
      August 1, 1818
      Died: Lynn, Massachusetts, June
      28, 1889

Maria Mitchell was the first woman astronomer of the United States. She was educated chiefly by her father. She was the librarian at the Nantucket Atheneum but conducted astronomical observations as an amateur. On October 1, 1847, she discovered a comet, which at once brought her to the attention of the world of science.

In 1849 she was employed by the U. S. Nautical Almanac Office where she

engaged in astronomical computations. In 1865 she was appointed professor of astronomy at the newly founded woman's college of Vassar. In 1868, having to choose between a job she enjoyed and her duty to make it possible for women to receive a higher education, she chose the latter, retaining her Vassar position till her death.

Her astronomical achievements were moderate, but they were done without any help from society at large and against all the taken-for-granted assumptions that kept women brainlessly at home. She represented a mark to shoot at for the oppressed half of the American population. She was the first woman member of the American Academy of Arts and Sciences.

[609] GATLING, Richard Jordan
      American inventor
      Born: Maney's Neck, North Carolina, September 12, 1818
      Died: New York, New York,
      February 26, 1903

Gatling spent his whole life putting together devices that would do something better than it had been done before. As a boy he helped his father perfect a machine for planting cotton and, after he moved to St. Louis in 1844, he adapted it to the planting of various grains.

He invented a screw propeller for ships in 1839, but was anticipated here by Ericsson [533].

Rather unexpectedly, he switched to a medical career after an attack of smallpox had concentrated his attention on human disease. He graduated from Ohio Medical College in 1850, but continued to be interested in inventing and does not seem ever to have practiced.

Once the Civil War started, he bent his talents to the development of a rapid-fire gun. By November 1862 he had a model that could fire nearly six bullets per second. The inertia of the military mind kept it from being adopted before the war was over but Gatling had invented the first machine gun.

His name lives today, in a sense, in the use of the slang term "gat" for a gun (not necessarily a machine gun, either).

46. Sir William H. Perkin

47. Robert Koch

48. Wilhelm Konrad Roentgen

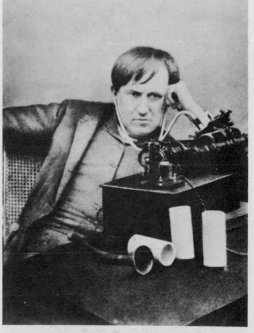

49. Thomas Alva Edison

50. IVAN P. PAVLOV

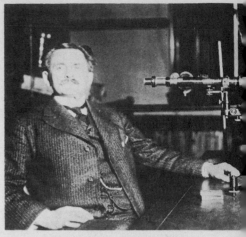

51. ALBERT A. MICHELSON

52. PAVLOV AND HIS STAFF DEMONSTRATING CONDITIONED REFLEX

53. PAUL EHRLICH

54. SIGMUND FREUD

55. Sir Joseph J. Thomson

56. Svante A. Arrhenius

57. Lord Ernest Rutherford

58. Guglielmo Marconi

59. ALBERT EINSTEIN

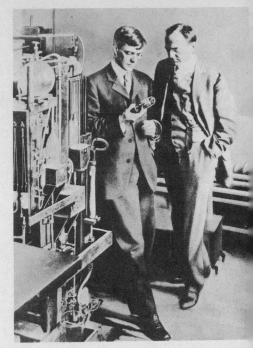

60. IRVING LANGMUIR (LEFT) AND DR. WHITN

61. NIELS BOHR

62. ENRICO FERMI

[610] **KOLBE,** Adolph Wilhelm Hermann (kole′buh)
German chemist
Born: Elliehausen, Hannover, September 27, 1818
Died: Leipzig, Saxony, November 25, 1884

Kolbe, the eldest of fifteen children of a minister, studied at Göttingen under Wöhler [515] and in 1842 served as assistant to Bunsen [565]. In 1845 he studied in London and made the lifelong friendship of Frankland [655]. He received his first professorial appointment at the University of Marburg in 1851, succeeding to the chair that Bunsen had held. He then moved to the University of Leipzig in 1865, remaining there till his death.

He was one of the early synthesizers of organic compounds, for in 1845 he synthesized acetic acid and did so from starting materials that were indubitably inorganic. If anyone wished to quarrel with the significance of Wöhler's synthesis of urea, as starting with something that was organic anyhow, that quarrel was lost.

Kolbe (who introduced the term "synthesis" into chemical usage, by the way) was the first to apply electrolysis to organic compounds, and he obtained interesting organic "double acids" in this fashion. The Kolbe reaction, which he discovered in 1859, made it possible to prepare salicylic acid in quantity and eventually led to the cheap production of the well-known drug, acetylsalicylic acid (aspirin).

Kolbe was a conservative force in chemistry, possibly because the aged Berzelius [425] had once praised Kolbe's work extravagantly, and the younger man retained a sentimental attachment for outmoded Berzelian views. Kolbe was a strenuous opponent of the structural theories of Kekulé [680] and delivered himself in 1877 of an intemperate diatribe against the tetrahedral carbon atom proposed by Van't Hoff [829] and Le Bel [787]. Kolbe was mistaken in both cases. However, he was an outstanding teacher and his good outweighed his bad.

[611] **DU BOIS-REYMOND,** Emil Heinrich (dyoo-bway′ray-mone′)
German physiologist
Born: Berlin, November 7, 1818
Died: Berlin, December 26, 1896

Du Bois-Reymond was of Huguenot stock, hence his French name. He studied biology at the University of Berlin under Müller [522] and for his graduation thesis in 1843 wrote a paper on electric fishes. This was the beginning of a lifelong interest in the electrical properties of animal tissues.

Beginning in 1840 he set about refining old instruments and inventing new ones with which he might detect the passage of tiny currents in nerve and muscle, thus founding scientific electrophysiology. He was able to show that the nerve impulse was accompanied by a change in the electrical condition of the nerve and must have a measurable velocity. This upset vitalism in one of its strongholds, for something as ethereal as the silent, unnoticeable impulse that floods along the nerves and brings about the motions and other responses so characteristic of life, turned out to be interpretable in terms suited to the inorganic environment. The nerve impulse was closely related to the electricity surging along the dead copper wires of the telegraph. And yet this also revived, in a much more sophisticated manner, Galen's [65] notion that the nerves carried a refined and subtle "animal spirit." When Müller died in 1858, Du Bois-Reymond succeeded him as professor of physiology. In later years he became an important early supporter of Darwin's [554] theory of evolution.

[612] **PETTENKOFER,** Max Joseph von
German chemist
Born: Lichtenheim, Bavaria, December 3, 1818
Died: near Munich, Bavaria, February 10, 1901

Pettenkofer, the son of a customs official, was stage-struck early in life, but finally abandoned his attempts at acting since it was clear he lacked talent in that direction.

He turned to medicine instead and obtained his medical degree at the University of Munich in 1843. He became a professor at that university in 1845.

He studied with Liebig [532] and in Liebig's laboratory discovered creatine, a nitrogenous component of muscle tissue. Neither this nor his association with his student Voit [691] was the most significant of his labors, however.

He specialized in hygiene and was one of the first to emphasize the subject as a matter of good health rather than mere good manners. In 1865 he was appointed to a professorship in hygiene at the University of Munich. The fact that the subject was considered worth a professorship is an indication of the importance his work had lent it. He studied the effect of ventilation on health and of the role played by contaminated soil and water in the spread of cholera. Like Virchow [632] he labored to push through public health measures to control such dangers. This sort of work, as much as the great bacteriological studies of Pasteur [642] and Koch [767], wiped out the periodic subjection of Europe to most forms of epidemic disease.

Nevertheless, again like Virchow, Pettenkofer refused to accept the germ theory of disease. To show his contempt for the theory, he deliberately swallowed a virulent culture of cholera bacteria in 1892. It remains a source of amazement that he did *not* get the disease.

In his old age, he mourned the death of his wife and three children. When an infected sore throat caused him more pain than he felt he ought to have to endure—and with only a few worn-out years left him in any case—he bought a gun and shot himself.

[613] **JOULE,** James Prescott (jowl or jool)
English physicist
Born: Salford, Lancashire, December 24, 1818
Died: Sale, Cheshire, October 11, 1889

Joule was the second son of a wealthy brewer, which meant he had the means to devote himself to a life of research. He also suffered poor health as a youngster, having some sort of spinal injury, which meant he could withdraw to his books and studies. His father encouraged him and supplied him with a home laboratory. He had some instruction from the aged Dalton [389], but by and large he was self-educated and, like Faraday [474], remained innocent of mathematics.

Joule was almost a fanatic on the subject of measurement, and even on his honeymoon he took time out to devise a special thermometer to measure the temperature of the water at the top and bottom of a scenic waterfall his wife and he were to visit. (His wife died in 1853, after only six years of marriage.)

In his teens he was publishing papers in which he was measuring heat in connection with electric motors.

Despite the fact that illness forced his father to retire in 1833 and that young Joule had then to do his share toward running the brewery, he continued his scientific labors. By 1840 he had worked out the formula governing the development of heat by an electric current: The heat developed is proportional to the square of the current intensity multiplied by the resistance of the circuit.

He went on to devote a decade to measuring the heat produced by every process he could think of. He churned water and mercury with paddles. He passed water through small holes to heat it by friction. He expanded and contracted gases. Even his honeymoon measurement of the waterfall temperature was based on the thought that the energy of falling water should be converted to heat once it was stopped so that the temperature at the bottom of the waterfall should be higher than that at the top.

In all those cases he calculated the amount of work that had entered the system and the amount of heat that came out and he found, as Rumford [360] had maintained fully half a century before, that the two were closely related. A particular quantity of work always produced a particular quantity of heat. In fact, 41,800,000 ergs of work produced one calorie of heat. This is called the "mechanical equivalent of heat."

Joule's first full description of his experiments and conclusion appeared in 1847. It did not commend itself to most scientists at the time. This may have been due partly to the fact that Joule was a brewer and not an academician. (He never received a professorial appointment though he was proposed for one at least once and was rejected, in part because of his spinal injury.) It may have been due partly, too, to the fact that his conclusions were based on small temperature differences in many cases (he used thermometers that could be read to 0.02°F and, eventually, to 0.005°F), so his experiments were not spectacular.

His original statement of his discovery was rejected by various learned journals as well as by the Royal Society. He was forced to present it at a public lecture in Manchester and then get his speech published in full by a reluctant Manchester newspaper on which his brother was music critic. A few months later he finally managed to present it before an unsympathetic scientific gathering and his presentation would have passed almost unnoticed but for a twenty-three-year-old in the audience. His name was William Thomson, and he was later to be known as Lord Kelvin [652]. His comments on Joule's work were shrewd enough and logical enough to rouse interest and even enthusiasm, and Joule's reputation was made. Later, Stokes [618] also supported Joule's work with enthusiasm. Full recognition came in 1849 when Joule read a paper on his work before the Royal Society, with Faraday himself as his sponsor.

Joule was not the first to determine the mechanical equivalent of heat. Rumford had attempted it but had come out with a value that was far too high. Mayer [587] produced a fairly good value before Joule did, but it was Joule who was most accurate (up to his time), who backed up his figure with a large variety of careful experimental data, and who (with Thomson's help) forced the view on the world of science. He therefore gets the credit; and in his honor a unit of work, equal to 10,000,000 ergs, is called the joule (4.18 joules of work equal 1 calorie of heat).

The determination of the mechanical equivalent of heat led to something very fundamental. Ever since the time of Newton [231] and even of Galileo [166] it was understood that the energy of an object hurtling upward did not really decline as its movement slowed. To be sure, that movement steadily diminished under the pull of gravity, but as the object lost kinetic energy (the energy of movement) it gained potential energy (the energy of position). When the object reached its maximum height, it was momentarily stationary and had no kinetic energy at all, but it had a good deal of potential energy. As it started falling, potential energy was reconverted into kinetic energy and when it reached the ground again, it was with all the kinetic energy with which it had originally been hurtled upward.

Theoretically, potential energy and kinetic energy interchanged without loss and this was the "conservation of mechanical energy." In reality the conservation was not perfect. Some energy was lost through air resistance and friction.

However, if heat is recognized as a form of energy; and if it is further recognized that the loss of mechanical energy through friction or air resistance is balanced by a gain of heat; and if Joule's point is clear, that the loss of other forms of energy is always *exactly* balanced by the gain in heat, then the suspicion arises that total energy is conserved.

This is the law of conservation of energy, which states that energy can neither be created out of nothing nor destroyed into nothing, but that it can be changed from one form to another. This is one of the most important generalizations in the history of science. It is so important in connection with the study of the interactions of heat and work (the thermodynamics first founded as a science by Carnot [497] two decades earlier) that it is frequently called "the first law of thermodynamics."

In the century and a quarter since Joule's time this law has trembled on occasion, notably when radioactivity was discovered and again when the radioactive emission of electrons was studied in detail. Always, through the work of such men as Einstein [1064] and Pauli [1228] the first law has been reestablished more firmly than before—at least so far.

Although Joule recognized the principle of the conservation of energy, and so did Mayer before him, the first to present it to the world as an explicit generalization was Helmholtz [631] and it is usually Helmholtz who is given credit for its discovery.

During the 1850s Joule went on to collaborate with his young friend Thomson. Together the two men showed that when a gas is allowed to expand freely, its temperature drops slightly. This observation, established in 1852, is called the Joule-Thomson effect and it is taken as evidence for the fact that molecules of gases have a slight attraction for their neighbors. It is in overcoming this attraction while moving apart during expansion that individual molecules lose energy and therefore temperature. This turned out to be a very important consideration in obtaining extremely low temperatures toward the end of the nineteenth century. Men such as Dewar [759] took full advantage of it.

Joule also discovered in 1846 the phenomenon of magnetostriction, whereby an iron bar changes its length somewhat when magnetized. This seemed purely academic at the time, but nowadays the effect is used in connection with ultrasonic sound-wave formation.

Joule was elected to the Royal Society in 1850, received its Copley medal in 1866, and was president of the British Association for the Advancement of Science in 1872 and in 1887. That he remained a brewer all his life and was never a professor did not seem to matter in the intellectual democracy of the world of science.

Toward the end of his life he suffered economic reverses, but Queen Victoria granted him a pension in 1878. He was a modest and unassuming man, a sincerely religious one, and toward the end of his life bitterly regretted the increasing ap-

plication of scientific discoveries to the art of warfare.

[614] **DRAKE,** Edwin Laurentine
American petroleum engineer
Born: Greenville, New York,
March 29, 1819
Died: Bethlehem, Pennsylvania,
November 8, 1880

Drake was a railway conductor during the first part of his life, but he had invested in a firm that gathered oil from seepages near Titusville, Pennsylvania, and used it for its presumed medicinal properties.

It occurred to Drake that more oil might be obtained if one drilled for it as, on occasion, people drilled for brine. He studied the methods used for drilling for brine, and in 1859 he set about using those methods at Titusville. He drilled sixty-nine feet into the ground and on August 28, 1859, he struck oil. He had drilled the first oil well and had begun a procedure that was to revolutionize human uses of energy.

In fact, others flew to the site at once and began drilling on their own. Northwestern Pennsylvania became the first oil field in the world and boom towns sprang up. Drake had not patented his methods, however, and he was not a clever businessman. Others were going to grow rich on oil, but Drake was not one of them. He died poor.

[615] **ADAMS,** John Couch
English astronomer
Born: Laneast, Cornwall, June 5,
1819
Died: Cambridge, January 21,
1892

Adams, the son of a poor farmer, was self-taught to begin with, but when he finally attended school showed signs of great precocity. He went on to Cambridge in 1839, entering on a scholarship, and continued to display brilliance there. He was first in his class in mathematics when he graduated in 1843.

He began an investigation of Uranus' motion (since the planet's motion did not fit the orbit calculated by Bouvard [392] twenty years before) while he was an undergraduate. He did the work on his vacation, for during school sessions his spare time was occupied with tutoring (to earn money to send home to his parents). By October 1843 he had a solution, and in 1845 he presented this solution to his superiors.

The incoming astronomer royal, Airy [523], neglected the paper, because he was certain the anomaly of Uranus' motion was the result of imperfections in the theory of gravitation. The matter was not pushed by the unaggressive Adams until it was too late. When Leverrier's [564] figures were published, Airy was finally stirred to action, though even then he neglected to say that similar figures had reached him from Adams first.

The planet itself was still to be located. But Adams had another bad break. Cambridge Observatory lacked a good map of the region of the sky in which the new planet was thought to be located. The Cambridge astronomer James Challis [535], therefore, did not recognize Neptune as an intruder in the area, although later he found he had actually had it twice in his field of vision. (When astronomers checked back, they found the record of an observation of Neptune as far back as 1795.) It was left for Galle [573] with his good map of the area to make the discovery.

Adams eventually received his share of the credit, thanks to enthusiastic labors on his behalf by John Herschel [479]. Adams went on to do good, though less spectacular, work in calculating the orbital motion of the Leonid meteor swarm, showing it to have a cometlike orbit.

In 1851 he became president of the Royal Astronomic Society and by 1858 was a professor of astronomy at Cambridge. In 1860 he succeeded Challis as the director of Cambridge Observatory.

Many years later, after Airy's retirement, Adams was offered the post of astronomer royal, but he refused because of age. He also refused a knighthood.

[616] HOWE, Elias
American inventor
Born: Spencer, Massachusetts, July 9, 1819
Died: Brooklyn, New York, October 3, 1867

Howe, the son of a farmer, gained experience in his father's mill and became a machinist who worked in a factory producing cotton machinery in Lowell, Massachusetts, and later in Cambridge. The fact that every phase of spinning and weaving had come, in the previous century, to be performed by machinery, brought home to him forcefully that sewing in the family was still being done by hand, much as it had been done since before the dawn of civilization.

For five years he worked to devise a practical machine that would sew. The key notion upon which he stumbled was that of placing the eye of the needle near the point instead of at the end opposite, and of using two threads, with stitches made by means of a shuttle. In 1846 he obtained his patent and demonstrated its value by racing against five girls sewing by hand, and winning. However, the impression was unfavorable since the machine seemed complicated and threatened unemployment. He traveled to England in order to get it placed on the market there and sold the English rights for a small sum.

When he returned to the United States he was destitute. He found his wife dying and others marketing sewing machines without paying royalties. He fought the matter through the courts, which took their usual slow and discouraging time about it. Howe's patent was finally confirmed and established in 1854 and he was sensible enough to let his competitors continue their work on payment of a reasonable licensing fee. His competitors went on to dominate the field, but Howe lived out the final decade of his life in security, leaving an estate of two million dollars.

The sewing machine was the first product of the Industrial Revolution that specifically lightened woman's household tasks. In 1915 Howe was elected to a niche in the Hall of Fame for Great Americans.

[617] **MORTON,** William Thomas Green
American dentist
Born: Charlton City, Massachusetts, August 9, 1819
Died: New York, New York, July 15, 1868

Morton may have graduated from the Baltimore College of Dental Surgery, the first dental school in the United States. He opened a dental practice in Boston and devised a new form of dental plate, which required that any remaining teeth be extracted first. Searching for a painless way of doing this (and even investigating the use of mesmerism for the purpose), he approached a chemist and ex-physician, C. T. Jackson [543], in 1844. From him, he heard of the effect of ether inducing unconsciousness and insensibility to pain, and the idea struck him of using it in surgical operations.

Actually, the idea of canceling pain was not new. Nearly half a century earlier Davy [421] had studied nitrous oxide and had speculated on its usefulness as an "anesthetic," a term proposed by Oliver Wendell Holmes [558]. Crawford W. Long [594] had made use of ether in surgery as early as 1842, and Morton's notion came four years after that.

Morton, however, did two things that his predecessors did not do. First, he patented the process in collaboration with Jackson. (Morton accepted this collaboration since Jackson demanded a large fee for his advice and Morton had no money with which to pay.) Secondly, Morton publicized the matter.

In September 1846 he extracted a tooth from a patient under ether and did it successfully. The next month he arranged to have a facial tumor removed from a patient under ether in the Massachusetts General Hospital. The operating doctor, astonished, turned to the assembled physicians when done and solemnly said, "Gentlemen, this is no humbug!" The success of that operation

made anesthesia an essential adjunct of surgery and once and for all divorced the surgeon from the torture chamber. In England anesthesia was introduced by Simpson [567], who used chloroform.

Morton had a great deal of trouble in attaining the fortune and the public gratitude he thought were his due because Jackson began a savage lifelong fight to claim the credit for the discovery of ether-anesthesia. Others made similar claims and Morton, abandoning dental practice, devoted his own life to these controversies.

When a large sum of money was raised for Morton in Great Britain as an award for his discovery of anesthesia, Jackson raised such a fearful fuss that the offer was withdrawn. When a money award was offered by the French Academy of Medicine to both Morton and Jackson, Morton would not accept it. A bill introduced into the Congress of the United States for the purpose of appropriating $100,000 to give to Morton as a testimonial of national gratitude failed of passage in 1852, 1853, and 1854. Finally Morton died in poverty and of a stroke brought on, it is said, by his reading an article supporting Jackson's claims.

There never seems to be much difficulty about handing out posthumous gratitude, however, and Morton was elected to the Hall of Fame for Great Americans in 1920.

[618] **STOKES,** Sir George Gabriel
British mathematician and physicist
Born: Skreen, Sligo, Ireland, August 13, 1819
Died: Cambridge, England, February 1, 1903

Stokes was the youngest child of a clergyman. He graduated from Cambridge in 1841 at the head of his class in mathematics and his early promise was not belied. In 1849 he was appointed Lucasian professor of mathematics at Cambridge; in 1854, secretary of the Royal Society; and in 1885, president of the Royal Society. No one had held all three offices since Isaac Newton [231] a century and a half before. Stokes's vision is indicated by the fact that he was one of the first scientists to see the value of Joule's [613] work.

Between 1845 and 1850 Stokes worked on the theory of viscous fluids. He deduced an equation (Stokes's law) that could be applied to the motion of a small sphere falling through a viscous medium to give its velocity under the influence of a given force, such as gravity. This equation could be used to explain the manner in which clouds float in air and waves subside in water. It could also be used in practical problems involving the resistance of water to ships moving through it. In fact such is the interconnectedness of science that six decades after Stokes's law was announced, it was used for a purpose he could never have foreseen—to help determine the electric charge on a single electron in a famous experiment by Millikan [969].

He also worked on fluorescence (a word he introduced in 1852), on sound, and on light. He studied ultraviolet radiation by means of the fluorescence it produced. He was the first to show that quartz was transparent to ultraviolet radiation, whereas ordinary glass was not.

He also worked with the concept of the luminiferous ether through which light was supposed to travel, a concept that had been vexing physicists during the half century since the time of Fresnel [455]. Stokes tried to explain the apparently contradictory properties of ether by suggesting it was like wax that would be firmly resistant to a hard, sudden blow, but would yield under a slow, steady force. (Thus, light would find the ether rigid, but a planet, moving much more slowly, would find it yielding.) He also suggested that the ether in the neighborhood of a moving planet would be dragged along with it. Such explanations of the properties of the ether served to introduce new difficulties, however, and the whole matter came to a head shortly afterward with the work of Michelson [835].

In his lectures at Cambridge, Stokes announced interpretations of the significance of the Fraunhofer [450] lines, which were in effect anticipations of the later theories of Kirchhoff [648]. Although Stokes never published his views, others tried to award him the credit. Stokes himself (whose character was warm with generosity and modesty) always insisted that he had not seen certain key points that were involved and that he could lay no claim to priority.

In 1896, toward the end of his long life, Stokes was among the first to suggest that X rays, newly discovered by Roentgen [774], were electromagnetic radiation akin to light.

Stokes received the Rumford medal of the Royal Society in 1852 and its Copley medal in 1893. He served as a Conservative member in Parliament, sitting for Cambridge University, as once Newton had done, from 1887 to 1892, and was made a baronet in 1889.

[619] **FOUCAULT**, Jean Bernard Léon (foo-koh')
French physicist
Born: Paris, September 18, 1819
Died: Paris, February 11, 1868

Foucault, the son of a bookseller-publisher, had a sickly childhood and was privately educated. He finally entered on medical studies and began his professional life as a physician but was an utter failure since, like Darwin [554], he couldn't stand the sight of blood. Instead, he became a science reporter for an important newspaper. His articles did not always produce friends, and the cranky Leverrier [564] was, as a result of some of the things Foucault wrote, always hostile to him.

Having met Fizeau [620], Foucault joined him and took up physics as his lifework. He collaborated with Fizeau in the measurement of the velocity of light by means of a toothed wheel, then developed an improved method of his own based on a suggestion advanced a decade earlier by Arago [446].

Imagine a ray of light striking mirror A and reflected at an angle to a second mirror, B, which reflects it in turn back to mirror A. If both mirrors were motionless, then the light would, in theory, bounce back and forth forever. If, however, mirror A is made to revolve rapidly, then when the light returns to it from mirror B, mirror A will have moved slightly and will reflect the light to a new position. From the speed with which mirror A revolves, from the total length of the light path, and from the angle by which the reflected beam of light is moved, Foucault could determine the velocity of light with hitherto unequaled accuracy. His value was more accurate than that of Fizeau and is just a trifle under the value ultimately obtained by Michelson [835].

Foucault went further. He also made use of his mirror method to measure the velocity of light through water and other transparent media. As long before as the time of Huygens [215] and Newton [231], it had been suggested that one way of settling the dispute as to whether light was a wave form or a stream of particles was by measuring its velocity in water. According to the wave theory, light should slow down in water; according to the particle theory, it should speed up. In 1853 Foucault showed that the velocity of light was less in water than in air, a strong piece of evidence in favor of the wave theory. He presented this work as his doctoral thesis.

Foucault's name is most often associated with a spectacular series of experiments that began in 1851. Foucault knew that a pendulum had a tendency to maintain the plane of its oscillation, however the point of its attachment might be twisted. Foucault saw then that if a large pendulum were set in motion it would maintain its plane of oscillation while the earth twisted under it. If the pendulum were at the North Pole the earth would make a complete twist beneath it in twenty-four hours. At more southerly latitudes the earth would seem to twist more slowly, as areas to the north traveled at a slightly slower velocity than areas to the south. This velocity difference would become less as one traveled south and at the equator there would be no twist at all. South of the equator the twist would begin again (but in the opposite direction) and would have a period of twenty-four hours again at the South Pole.

To someone watching the pendulum (and himself partaking of the motion of the earth) it would seem as though the pendulum were slowly changing direction.

Foucault's first experiment was indecisive. A longer pendulum was needed. First Arago offered the use of the observatory building for a second test, and then Napoleon III arranged to have a large Paris church used for the third and most famous test. Foucault suspended a large iron ball about two feet in diameter from a steel wire more than two hundred feet long, under the dome of the church. The pendulum ended in a spike that just cleared the floor but would score a mark in the sand with which the floor of the church was sprinkled.

The iron ball was drawn far to one side and tied to the wall by a cord. Every attempt was made to keep the air and the building free of vibrations that might disturb the steady swing of this tremendous pendulum. When all was quiet, the cord holding the pendulum was set on fire. (If it had been cut by scissors or knives, vibrations would have interfered with the experiment.)

The cord broke, the pendulum began its swing, and a large audience caught and held its breath. As time went on, the mark made by the pendulum spike visibly changed its orientation. It twisted in the direction and at just the rate that was to be expected for the latitude of Paris, one rotation in 31 hours, 47 minutes. The spectators were actually watching the earth rotating under the pendulum.

The experiment caused great excitement at the time. Heracleides [28] had first suggested twenty-two centuries before that the earth was rotating and Copernicus [127] had renewed the suggestion three centuries before. Since the time of Galileo [166] two and a half centuries before, the world of scholarship had not doubted the matter. Nevertheless, all evidence as to that rotation had been indirect, and not until Foucault's experiment could the earth's rotation actually be said to have been demonstrated rather than deduced.

A massive sphere in rotation, like a pendulum, has a tendency to maintain the direction of its axis of spin, as the earth does. Foucault demonstrated this point, which had been established theoretically, by an experimental demonstration. In 1852 he set a wheel with a heavy rim into rapid rotation. It not only maintained its axial direction (and could be used to demonstrate the rotation of the earth) but if it was tipped the effect of gravity was to set up a motion at right angles that was equivalent to the precession of the equinoxes. In doing this, Foucault had, incidentally, invented the gyroscope.

In 1857 Foucault developed the modern technique for silvering glass to make mirrors for reflecting telescopes. This meant glass could be used instead of metal. Mirrors became much lighter, less likely to tarnish and easier to renew if tarnished. For the first time since Newton's invention, reflecting telescopes took a clear lead over refracting ones.

At one point Foucault scored a miss. He saw the significance of the fact that the solar spectrum showed a dark line just where the sodium light showed a bright one. In fact it was upon Foucault's work that Stokes [618] based his lectures on the significance of the Fraunhofer [450] lines. However, neither Foucault nor Stokes carried matters far enough and it was Kirchhoff [648] who, a few years later, was to develop spectroscopy. In the 1840s though, Foucault was one of the first to make microphotographs.

Foucault led an uneventful life, and was interested only in his work (too much so, apparently, for overwork seems to have made him an invalid and contributed to his early death).

[620] FIZEAU, Armand Hippolyte
Louis (fee-zoh')
French physicist
Born: Paris, September 23, 1819
Died: Venteuil, Seine-et-Marne,
September 18, 1896

Fizeau was one of those fortunates born into wealth who can pass their lives in pleasure, and the world is fortunate that there are some of those who find their pleasure in scientific research.

Since his father was an eminent pathologist, it isn't surprising that Fizeau tried at first to study medicine, but like Foucault [619], with whom his name is so often linked, he was not cut out for it and eventually realized his bent was toward physics.

Fizeau's overriding interest was light, and he was the first to measure its velocity by a terrestrial method. Up to the mid-nineteenth century, light's velocity had been measured only by Roemer [232] and Bradley [258], each using an astronomical method. Fizeau, however, refined Galileo's [166] unsuccessful method of flashing lights back and forth from adjacent hills.

In 1849 Fizeau set up a rapidly turning toothed disc on one hilltop and a mirror on another, five miles away. Light passed through one gap between the teeth of the disc to the mirror and was reflected. If the disc turned rapidly enough, the reflected light passed through the next gap. From the speed of revolution at which light was first successfully reflected, the time required for light to travel ten miles could be calculated.

The experiment was a success and the velocity of light was determined to be a value that we now recognize to be some 5 percent too high. This was corrected by the improved method of Foucault the next year.

Fizeau also considered what was to be expected of light from a moving source. Doppler [534] had already done this, since he had worked out matters well for sound, but he had come to erroneous conclusions. In 1848 Fizeau pointed out that the lines in a spectrum ought to shift toward the red if the light source is receding and toward the violet if it is approaching. It was two decades before instrumentation advanced to the point of being able to take advantage of this analysis, but finally Huggins [646] was able to measure the velocity at which a star was approaching toward or receding from the earth.

Fizeau, by the way, had married the daughter of Jussieu [345].

[621] **FIELD,** Cyrus West
American businessman
Born: Stockbridge, Massachusetts, November 30, 1819
Died: New York, New York, July 12, 1892

Field was the younger brother of a famous lawyer who pioneered in the field of international law. He began life as an errand boy and, though he never became in any sense of the word a scientist, he had the vision and daring to carry through a dramatic application of nineteenth-century science, an application that nowadays would be supported by governments rather than single individuals. Over a thirteen-year period Field dissipated his fortune (made in the paper business) and withstood disaster upon disaster in his determined attempt to lay an Atlantic cable. He supplied the money and the drive; Maury [548] supplied the oceanographic know-how, and Kelvin [652] supplied the electrical.

Field's efforts were finally successful and the United States and Europe were united by electrical signals in 1866. Field's reward was a gold medal and a vote of thanks from Congress. Later, Field interested himself in building New York City's elevated railways, where he lost another fortune, particularly through the shady dealings of some financiers. He died poor.

[622] **BEGUYER DE CHANCOUR-TOIS,** Alexandre-Émile (buh-gee-ay' duh shan-koor-twah')
French geologist
Born: Paris, January 20, 1820
Died: Paris, November 14, 1886

Beguyer de Chancourtois, the grandson of a noted artist, was a geologist who had carried his field explorations from Greenland to Turkey. As inspector general of mines in France, he had enforced safety measures over the protests of mine owners.

In 1862 he ventured into chemistry and arranged the elements in order of atomic weights. He plotted them about a cylinder, finding that similar elements fell in vertical lines. He published a paper describing this but was a rather bumbling writer and used geological terms that made little sense to chemists. As if this were not enough to assure oblivion for the paper, the journal publishing it did not see fit to reproduce his diagram of the elements wound about the cylinder or the "telluric helix," as he called it. The diagram might have explained his points; without it, the paper was impossible.

Beguyer de Chancourtois, like Newlands [727], lived to see Mendeléev [705] produce the periodic table and gain the credit. Unlike Newlands, he did not live to see his own vindication. In the 1890s the journal in which his paper originally appeared finally published his diagram.

[623] **BECQUEREL,** Alexandre Edmond (beh-krel')
French physicist
Born: Paris, March 24, 1820
Died: Paris, May 11, 1891

Becquerel was the son of a professor of physics at the Paris Museum of Natural History and worked with him there. He received a doctor's degree from the University of Paris in 1840 and gained a professorial position at the Agronomic Institute of Versailles.

He investigated electricity and magnetism, where his most significant discovery was the magnetic property of liquid oxygen. He showed, in 1840, that light, by inducing certain chemical reactions, could produce an electric current and devised an instrument that measured light intensity by determining the intensity of the electric current produced. He also devised a way of measuring the heat of objects hot enough to give off visible light by determining the intensity of that light.

He was particularly interested in fluorescence, the phenomenon whereby certain substances absorb light of one wavelength and then re-emit light of another. This is particularly marked when the light absorbed is ultraviolet and the light emitted is in the visible range.

Under such circumstances, substances seem to glow in the dark.

Becquerel's son, A. H. Becquerel [834], in carrying on his father's interest in fluorescence was to discover a totally unexpected phenomenon of the very first importance, which Becquerel himself died five years too soon to witness.

[624] **SPENCER,** Herbert
English sociologist
Born: Derby, Derbyshire, April 27, 1820
Died: Brighton, Sussex, December 8, 1903

Spencer, the son of a schoolteacher, remained a lifelong bachelor and had little formal education because of his ill health and was tutored by his father and his uncle, a minister. He was a courageous thinker, however, always ready to speculate and theorize on any subject. The speculations, though always interesting and sometimes valuable, were often superficial and occasionally quite wrong.

In his twenties he was a railway engineer and tried his hand at invention, though not very successfully, and in 1846 or 1848 he moved to London and went in for journalism. He began to write on sociology and psychology, serving as a pioneer in both subjects.

His health continued bad in adult life and it was aggravated by that most incurable of all diseases, hypochondria, but his will to express himself rose triumphant over all and he wrote voluminously.

He was always an evolutionist. Even before Darwin [554] had published his *Origin of Species,* Spencer was speculating that human society and culture had begun at some homogeneous and simple level and evolved to its present heterogeneous and complex state, just as Baer [478] had shown that the homogeneous germ layers of the embryo developed into heterogeneous organs.

Once Darwin's book was published Spencer seized upon it with great delight and applied Darwinian principles to the development of societies and cultures in complete disregard of the fact that this was an application for which the principles were not suited. Spencer popularized the term "evolution" (which Darwin himself hardly ever used) and also the phrase "survival of the fittest."

It seemed to Spencer that human individuals were in continual competition among themselves, with the weaker necessarily going to the wall. Since this ensured the "survival of the fittest," Spencer considered it a good thing. Carrying this notion to its extreme, he argued in 1884 that people who were unemployable or burdens on society should be allowed to die rather than be made objects of help and charity. The same sort of argument would have allowed people suffering from disease or physical imperfections to die (or perhaps be helped over the threshold to avoid a waste of time).

Such Spencerian philosophy was extremely influential outside science. It was used to support the crudest sort of industrial competition, with the winner always justifying himself as the fittest. It led to a brutal form of might-makes-right philosophy in international relations and a glorification of war as a means of weeding out the "unfit." It naturally justified whatever racist views a particular person might have, since other races or nationalities could always be judged inferior and therefore rightly put out of the way as "unfit."

To be sure, Spencer did not invent the evils of war, racism, or even cutthroat competition; he did not even go as far as many of his disciples did. However, Spencerism managed to throw a false glitter of "science" over many abominable practices, and it tended to discredit the Darwinian view among people who felt kindness, pity, and mercy to be virtues.

Spencer's application of Darwinism to social development was, of course, quite unjustified and Darwin himself would have nothing to do with it. Darwinism dealt with changes that required millions of years, while social evolution was a matter of centuries and millennia. Moreover the rules of Darwinism were far too simple to cover the complex changes and manifestations of developing culture.

As a matter of fact the only way Spencer could justify the rapid changes in man's history was to adopt a form of inheritance of acquired characteristics after the fashion of Lamarck [336]. He believed that scions of civilized groups of men inherited the essence of civilization, and the descendants of primitives lacked the capacity for civilization, having failed to inherit its acquired essence. This brought him into conflict with Weismann [704] and while Weismann, representing the opposite extreme, was not entirely right, he was far closer to what now seems the correct state of affairs.

[625] **RANKINE,** William John Macquorn (rang'kin)
Scottish engineer
Born: Edinburgh, July 5, 1820
Died: Glasgow, December 24, 1872

Rankine, the son of an army lieutenant, was first taught by his father. He read Newton's [231] Principia in the original Latin when he was but fourteen. Although trained in physics (but having left the University of Edinburgh in 1837 without a degree), he took up civil engineering and became professor of engineering at the University of Glasgow in 1855. He brought theoretical principles down from the rarefied realm of academic learning and placed them before the earthy practitioners in the field. In particular his Manual of the Steam Engine, published in 1859, introduced working engineers to the realm of thermodynamics for which he introduced much of the modern terminology and notation.

He made use of a temperature scale beginning at absolute zero but counting upward by Fahrenheit degrees rather than centigrade degrees as in the Kelvin [652] scale. The former is called the Rankine scale and is abbreviated ° Rank. It is virtually never used by scientists. He also popularized the use of the term

"energy," which had first been introduced by Young [402] a half century earlier.

Rankine, although handsome, sociable, talented in music, gentle, and popular, never married.

[626] **TYNDALL,** John
Irish physicist
Born: Leighlinbridge, Carlow, August 2, 1820
Died: Hindhead, Surrey, England, December 4, 1893

Tyndall was a descendant of William Tyndale, a sixteenth-century translator of the Bible who was burned at the stake as a heretic in 1536. His education was rather haphazard. After some schooling he became a civil servant and then a railway engineer. However, he had a great drive toward learning, read widely, attended what lectures he could and finally entered the University of Marburg in Germany, where, along with Frankland [655], he studied chemistry under Bunsen [565] and obtained his doctor's degree in 1851. In 1852 he was elected to the Royal Society.

He was chosen professor of natural philosophy at the Royal Institution in 1854 and was a colleague, for over a decade, of Faraday [474], whom he greatly admired. He succeeded to Faraday's post on the latter's death and wrote an admiring biography of him.

Tyndall's most important professional work involved the manner in which gases conducted heat, but he is best known for his analysis of the behavior of a beam of light passing through solutions. If the beam of light passes through pure water or through a solution of the type of substance Graham [547] called crystalloid, the light was not interfered with. Its passage through the water or through the solution when viewed from the side could not be seen.

If, however, the beam of light passed through a solution of a colloid, the particles of the colloid were just large enough to scatter the light. Some of the light "bounced off" the particles in all directions. If the beam of light was viewed from the side, it would therefore be foggily visible. Tyndall's investigation of this phenomenon in 1869 led to its popular name of the Tyndall effect and earned for him the Rumford medal. A generation later Zsigmondy [943] was to develop the ultramicroscope, based on this phenomenon.

Rayleigh [760] was able to show that the efficiency with which light was scattered varied inversely as the fourth power of the wavelength. In other words, a beam of violet light, with half the wavelength of a beam of red light, would be scattered to 2^4 or sixteen times the amount the red light would be.

Tyndall was able to use this to explain the blue of the sky. Sunlight is scattered by the dust particles (of colloidal size) always present in the atmosphere. It is this scattering that makes shadows light enough to read in, for on a world like the moon, which lacks an atmosphere, shadows are pitch black. It is the light waves at the blue end of the spectrum that are most scattered, and the clear sky of day is blue with this scattered light.

When sunlight passes through a greater thickness of atmosphere (as it does at sunset), particularly when the sky is unusually dusty, as after a major volcanic eruption, enough of the longer wavelengths are scattered to give the sky a greenish hue. The sun, which is then seen only by the unscattered light at the red end of the spectrum, turns orange or even red.

Tyndall was also able to show that some of the dust in air consists of microorganisms and this finally explained why broths so easily became riddled with life forms. It was this that so long misled biologists into accepting spontaneous generation. Pasteur [642] was to prevent the infestation of broth by doing no more than keeping out dust.

In middle life, Tyndall grew fascinated with the Alps and began to spend his summers mountain climbing. He married at the age of fifty-six and with his wife spent summers in a house he had built, a mile and a half high in the Alps.

Tyndall was more famous in his own time as a popularizer of science than as a scientist. He was the first to present for popular consumption the theory of heat as molecular vibration according to its new development by Maxwell [692]. This was contained in his book *Heat as a Mode of Motion*, published in 1863. It went through numerous editions. He also popularized Helmholtz's [631] law of conservation of energy. He was one of the first who really appreciated Mayer's [587] work and had the courage to suggest that life, in the beginning, had perhaps evolved out of inanimate matter.

Other books on popular science followed, dealing with water, light, and dust in the air. In 1872 and 1873 he traveled to the United States, where he gave a series of successful lectures, donating the proceeds to a trust for the benefit of American science.

He died of an accidental overdose of sleeping medicine.

[627] ROCHE, Édouard Albert (rohsh)
French astronomer
Born: Montpellier, Hérault, October 17, 1820
Died: Montpellier, April 18, 1883

Roche earned his doctorate at the University of Montpellier in 1844, then worked for three years at the Paris Observatory. He gained a professorial appointment at Montpellier in 1852.

Roche was more a mathematician than an observer, and he worked on the shapes of an astronomical body under the influence of its own gravitational forces, those of near neighbors, and of centrifugal effects. His conclusions are still useful in modern astronomy and are used in studying very closely spaced binaries, especially in binaries where one of the members is a neutron star or a black hole.

Roche is best remembered for his studies of the manner in which the gravitational forces of a large body can impose tidal forces on a smaller circling body that are sufficient to break it up. He showed that if the circling body were held together by gravitational forces only and if chemical bonding could be ignored, it would be torn apart if it approached within two and a half times the radius of the larger body. This is Roche's limit, and Roche advanced this suggestion in 1849. Saturn's rings lie entirely within Roche's limit, for instance, so that they might represent a satellite that has broken up or one that, under tidal influences, could not form in the first place.

[628] **LOSCHMIDT,** Johann Joseph (loh'shmit)
Austrian chemist
Born: Putschirn, Bohemia (now in Czechoslovakia), March 15, 1821
Died: Vienna, July 8, 1895

Loschmidt was the son of poor peasants but showed so much promise that the village priest arranged for his education. By 1839 he was studying at the German University in Prague. He could not obtain a teaching position and his attempts to make a living in business ended in bankruptcy in 1854.

That was a turning point. In 1856 he qualified as a teacher and pretty soon he began publishing papers. He was the first to represent double and triple bonds in organic molecular structures by two and three lines respectively and to show that when a molecule contains more than one alcohol group, each one was attached to a different carbon atom. He also recognized that certain "aromatic compounds" (so-called because they had a pleasant aroma) all had the benzene ring as part of their molecular structure. Thereafter, the term "aromatic" was applied to any organic molecule containing a benzene ring regardless of the nature of its aroma.

Loschmidt was also the first to attempt to work out the actual size of atoms and molecules, using the theoretical equations of Maxwell [692] and Clausius [633] in their work on the kinetic theory of gases. He concluded that the small molecules in air had a diameter of something less than a ten-millionth of a centi-

meter, which was very good for a first estimate, but is a little high.

[629] **CAYLEY,** Arthur (kay'lee)
English mathematician
Born: Richmond, Surrey, August 16, 1821
Died: Cambridge, January 26, 1895

Cayley's father was a merchant living in St. Petersburg. Cayley was born during a short visit of the family to England and he spent most of his childhood in Russia. He entered Cambridge in 1838 and graduated first in his class in mathematics. He was no narrow individual, however, for he proved himself outstanding in languages as well. He studied law so that he might practice it just enough to finance the mathematical researches that were his real interest. He worked on n-dimensional geometry, which had been pioneered by Grassman [556], and further developed the algebra of matrices, which Jacobi [541] had introduced. These were to be of importance, respectively, to Einstein's [1064] relativity and to Heisenberg's [1245] contributions to quantum mechanics some three quarters of a century later.

Cayley finally obtained a professorial position at Cambridge in 1863, and there he not only continued to work on his mathematics but labored to assure the admittance of women to education at the college level.

[630] **MORTILLET,** Louis Laurent Gabriel de (mawr-tee-ay')
French anthropologist
Born: Meylan, Isère, August 29, 1821
Died: St. Germain-en-Laye, Yvelines, September 25, 1898

Mortillet, although he had a Catholic education, became a freethinker. He took part in the Revolution of 1848 and thought it the wiser part of valor to leave France thereafter. He spent sixteen years in Switzerland and Italy, returning to France only in 1864.

While abroad, he had worked on zoology and as a science writer, but once back in France, he turned to anthropology. He studied and gathered together all that was known concerning human "prehistory," a term that came into use only in 1865, and popularized it. He was the first to try to divide the Stone Age into periods based on the level of sophistication of the stone tools uncovered. Such terms as Chellean, Acheulian, Mousterian, Solutrean, and so on (based on the regions in which the tools in question were found) were used right into the twentieth century.

[631] **HELMHOLTZ,** Hermann Ludwig Ferdinand von
German physiologist and physicist
Born: Potsdam, Prussia, August 31, 1821
Died: Charlottenburg (near Berlin), September 8, 1894

Helmholtz, the son of a schoolteacher, was a descendant on his mother's side of William Penn. After a sickly childhood (he continued to suffer from migraine and fainting spells even in adulthood), he studied medicine at his father's insistence, although he himself preferred physics. In medicine, he could qualify for government aid, you see, but not in physics.

He attended the Royal Medicosurgical Institute of Berlin, from which he graduated in 1842. J. P. Müller [522] and Mitscherlich [485] were among his teachers there. In return for the aid he had received, he practiced as surgeon in the Prussian army for some years. In 1848 Du Bois-Reymond [611] obtained a lectureship in anatomy for him at the Berlin Academy of Arts. Then, in 1849, through the interest and influence of Humboldt [397], Helmholtz obtained an appointment as professor of physiology at the University of Königsberg. Later, in 1858, he taught anatomy at Heidelberg and still later, in 1871, physics at Berlin. In his broadness of interests

Helmholtz much resembles Thomas Young [402], another physician-scientist.

Like Young, Helmholtz made a close study of the function of the eye, and in 1851 he invented an ophthalmoscope, with which one could peer into the eye's interior—an instrument without which the modern eye specialist would be all but helpless. (Babbage [481] had invented a similar instrument three years before, but Helmholtz's work was quite independent.) Helmholtz also devised the ophthalmometer, an instrument that could be used to measure the eye's curvature. In addition he revived Young's theory of three-color vision and expanded it, so that it is now known as the Young-Helmholtz theory.

Helmholtz studied that other sense organ, the ear, as well. He advanced the theory that the ear detected differences in pitch through the action of the cochlea, a spiral organ in the inner ear. It contained, he explained, a series of progressively smaller resonators, each of which responded to a sound wave of progressively higher frequency. The pitch we detected depended on which resonator responded.

Moreover, he pointed out, the quality of a tone depended on the nature, number, and relative intensities of the overtones (the overtones being vibrations more rapid than the basic vibration to which the sound source was subjected, the more rapid vibrations being related to the basic vibration by simple ratios). The basic tone plus the overtones caused resonators to react in a specific pattern so that the identical note sounded by two different instruments would be distinguishable by ear because the quality would differ.

He also analyzed the fact that combinations of notes sounded well or discordant on the basis of wavelengths and the production of beats at particular rates. He thus applied the principles of science to the art of music (something he must have particularly enjoyed, for he was an accomplished musician).

Helmholtz was the first to measure the speed of the nerve impulse. His teacher, Müller, was fond of presenting this as an example of something science could never accomplish because the impulse moved so quickly over so short a path. In 1852, however, Helmholtz stimulated a nerve connected to a frog muscle, stimulating it first near the muscle, then farther away. He managed to measure the added time required for the muscle to respond in the latter case.

He was even a mathematician of parts, doing work in the non-Euclidean geometry that had been devised by Riemann [670].

But he is best known for his contributions to physics and in particular for his treatment of the conservation of energy, something to which he was led by his studies of muscle action. (He was the first to show that animal heat was produced chiefly by contracting muscle and that an acid—which we now know to be lactic acid—was formed in the working muscle.)

Mayer [587] had announced the concept of the conservation of energy in 1842, but Helmholtz in 1847 (independently) did so in much greater detail and in more specific fashion, so that he has usually been given the credit, although nowadays the tendency is to divide the credit more or less equally at least three ways among Helmholtz, Mayer, and Joule [613]. Like the others, Helmholtz had difficulties getting his paper printed and finally published it in pamphlet form.

Helmholtz used the notion of the conservation of energy to oppose the vitalists. If there were a "vital force," he said, in living organisms but not in the inanimate universe, then the conservation of energy would not hold for organisms, and they could then be perpetual motion machines—which they were not.

In 1854 Helmholtz considered the possible sources of solar energy. The only source that seemed reasonable at the time was gravitation, as Mayer had earlier pointed out. The nebular hypothesis of Laplace [347] had the sun begin as a vast nebula that gradually contracted. Well, the kinetic energy of the particles falling toward the sun's center could be converted into radiation and that could account for solar energy over long periods of time.

But not long enough. From the amount of radiation energy emitted by the sun, Helmholtz calculated the rate of contraction and then, working backward in time, fixed the period when the sun must have been so voluminous as to include the earth's orbit in its body. By this calculation, the maximum length of time that the earth could have existed was 25 million years. Like Kelvin's [652] calculation of the maximum time required for the cooling of the earth, this gave geologists far too little time for their own theories. Both Kelvin and Helmholtz were misled by ignorance of radioactivity and nuclear energy, and Helmholtz died just a few years too soon to learn his error.

Nevertheless this misconception proved useful in one way. It drove some biologists such as Nägeli [598] and Kölliker [600] to conceive of evolution as proceeding by sudden jumps, thus permitting the squeezing of the entire process into the drastically shortened period allowed by Helmholtz and Kelvin. A generation later De Vries [792] was to develop the theory of mutations out of this and would in this way add the final major touch to Darwin's [554] theory of evolution by natural selection.

Helmholtz began important work that was concluded by others. He was interested in the work of Maxwell [692] on electromagnetic radiation and introduced the problem of locating the radiation well beyond the visible spectrum to his student Hertz [873], whereupon Hertz triumphantly proved the case.

Helmholtz also reasoned that atoms and groups of atoms moving through a solution during electrolysis must carry with them "atoms of electricity." This foreshadowed the work of Arrhenius [894].

To be sure, Helmholtz, despite his excellence and versatility, had his shortcomings. Even the sun has spots, and Helmholtz, it seems, was a poor lecturer.

During his return from a lecture tour in the United States, one of his fainting spells caused him to fall. He suffered a concussion, never recovered, and died eight weeks later.

[632] **VIRCHOW,** Rudolph Carl (fihr'-khoh)
German pathologist
Born: Schivelbein, Pomerania (now Swidwin, Poland), October 13, 1821
Died: Berlin, September 5, 1902

Virchow (the son of a small merchant), like Schwann [563], Kölliker [600], Du Bois-Reymond [611], Helmholtz [631], and Henle [557], studied under J. P. Müller [522]. He obtained his medical degree at the University of Berlin in 1843. He was a man of strong convictions and an even stronger social conscience.

As a young surgeon he was the first to describe leukemia (in 1845), but he also showed too pronounced a sympathy for the revolutionaries that were threatening the stability of the ultraconservative Prussian government in 1848. While investigating a typhus epidemic in Silesia that year he denounced social conditions scathingly and fought on the side of the revolutionaries in the disorders that broke out at this time.

He lost his university position in consequence. This was not entirely a bad thing, for it forced Virchow into semiretirement and steered him into thoughtful consideration of the microscopic structure of diseased tissues.

(He quickly obtained, in 1849, a new professorial post, in any case. It was at Würzburg, in the more liberal atmosphere of Bavaria.)

By the time he returned to Berlin as a professor of pathological anatomy, in 1856, he had worked out his notions in detail. In a book published in 1858 he demonstrated quite conclusively that the cell theory extended to diseased tissue too. He showed that the cells of diseased tissue were descended from normal cells of ordinary tissue. There was no sudden break or discontinuity signifying the disease, but a smooth development of abnormality. Thus he brought the study of disease down to a more fundamental

level than the tissues of Bichat [400] and became the founder of cellular pathology. This permitted molecular biologists a century later to bring the study of disease down to the still more fundamental level of the molecules within the cell.

In 1860 Virchow epitomized his notion of the cell theory by a pithy Latin remark that can be translated as "All cells arise from cells." It was the final knitting together of the cell theory of Schwann and Schleiden [538] and had implicit in it the repudiation of spontaneous generation, a repudiation that Pasteur [642] was about to translate into experimental terms.

Virchow, however, refused to accept Pasteur's germ theory of disease. Perhaps the effect of a germ, in causing a tissue to become diseased, seemed too discontinuous to him. He viewed disease as a civil war between cells, an outbreak of anarchy in the well-ordered cellular society that made up the organism, and not as an invasion from outside. (Of course, as we now know, there are diseases of both varieties, Pasteur's and Virchow's.)

In any case, Virchow found himself part of a rapidly shrinking minority in his views on the germ theory and his reaction was to leave biology and to throw himself into anthropological and archeological research. He was involved in the excavation of Troy, for instance. His anthropological studies convinced him that there were no such things as "superior races."

His medical experience had helped revive (if they needed reviving) the liberal notions of his youth, for in studying poverty-stricken areas he was appalled by the influence of social backwardness on health. He took the position that it was useless to try to treat sick people until one treated a sick society. He went into politics, was on the Berlin city council in 1859, got himself elected to the Prussian Parliament in 1862, and to the Reichstag itself (after the unification of Germany) in 1880. As one of the leaders of the small German Liberal Party, which vigorously opposed Bismarck, he so irritated that statesman that Bismarck challenged him to a duel in

1865. Virchow contemptuously refused to accept this medieval solution to non-medieval problems.

Virchow was no socialist, however, and was one of the German biologists who strongly rejected Darwin's [554] theory of evolution, partly because he considered it "socialist." As a Reichstag member he voted for a law that banned the teaching of Darwin's theory in the schools.

But Bismarck moved in the direction of social reform (to draw the teeth of the gathering opposition) and the edge of Virchow's liberalism gradually blunted with age so that eventually he was unseated by a Social Democrat. Virchow, however, remained active in Berlin city politics and was instrumental in pushing through important improvements in such matters as water supply and the sewage system. (Such improvements were as important in their way in putting an end to the epidemics that had always plagued Europe as were the studies arising out of Pasteur's germ theory, so in a sense Virchow got a little of his own back.)

[633] **CLAUSIUS,** Rudolf Julius Emmanuel (klow′zee-oos)
German physicist
Born: Köslin, Pomerania (now Koszalin, Poland), January 2, 1822
Died: Bonn, August 24, 1888

Clausius, the son of a schoolmaster, studied at the University of Berlin and obtained his doctorate at Halle in 1847. He accepted a professorial position at Zürich in 1855 and at Würzburg in 1867.

Clausius was primarily a theoretical physicist. He did not make his name by conducting experiments but by applying mathematics to the construction of theories that explained the observations and experiments of others. He was one of those who contributed to the working out of the kinetic theory of gases, a project completed by Maxwell [692] and Boltzmann [769]. He also proposed theories concerning the passage of electric current through solutions, being the

first to suggest that the current might pull molecules apart (dissociation) into electrically charged fragments. This notion was not accepted by others at the time and it was only Arrhenius [894] a generation later who managed, with difficulty, to put it across.

Clausius' most fruitful work came in 1850 in connection with the views of Carnot [497] and the suggestions of Kelvin [652] as to the continual degradation of energy. Clausius discovered that if he took the ratio of the heat content of a system and its absolute temperature, this ratio would always increase in any process taking place in a closed system. (A closed system is one that loses no energy to the outside world and gains no energy from it.) With perfect efficiency, which is never realized in the real world, of course, the ratio would remain constant, but it would never, under any circumstances, decrease.

Clausius eventually (in 1865) called this ratio entropy for no clear etymological reason. In 1850, at which time he was a professor in Berlin, he sent a communication to the Berlin Academy of Sciences to the effect that entropy always increased, never decreased.

This was equivalent to Kelvin's notion of energy degradation, and entropy was a measure of the extent to which energy could be converted into work; the higher the entropy, the less the quantity of energy for such conversion. Clausius expressed all this so clearly that he is usually considered the discoverer of this second law of thermodynamics. This inevitable increase of entropy is a generalization second in importance in the field of energy-interconversions only to the first law, that of the conservation of energy. (Oddly enough Clausius was one of those who attacked Helmholtz's [631] enunciation of the first law in the early 1850s.)

The only true closed system in actual practice is the universe as a whole and so the picture arose of a universe in which entropy is steadily rising and the availability of energy for conversion into work steadily falling. Eventually the degradation would be complete, entropy would be at a maximum, and nothing would exist but a universe at complete temperature equilibrium. There would be no more heat flow, no more change, no more time, in fact.

This dramatic picture of the end of all things has been called "the heat-death of the universe." It was a scientific analog of the Last Judgment but its validity is less certain now than it was a century ago. Though the laws of thermodynamics stand as firmly as ever, cosmologists are far less certain that the laws, as deduced in this small segment of the universe, necessarily apply to the universe as a whole and there is a certain willingness to suspend judgment on the matter of the heat-death.

By 1869 Clausius was professor of physics at the University of Bonn, a position he held for the rest of his life. In 1870 he organized a volunteer ambulance corps of Bonn students for service in the Franco-Prussian war and was wounded while leading it—a wound from which he never fully recovered. This is an example of the manner in which the scientific internationalism of the Napoleonic era had withered into chauvinism. As another example, Clausius never hesitated to engage in vitriolic controversies with British scientists in a determined drive to see to it that German scientists got their full share of credit in all scientific advances.

[634] **SCHLIEMANN,** Heinrich (shlee′-mahn)
German archaeologist
Born: Neu Buckow, Mecklenburg-Schwerin, January 6, 1822
Died: Naples, Italy, December 26, 1890

Schliemann, the son of a minister, was caught up in the story of Troy when he was only seven, when he had seen a picture of Troy in flames in a history book he had received as a Christmas present. Unable to afford much of an education, he became a grocer's apprentice at fourteen, then a cabin boy, an office boy, and a bookkeeper. But he had a flair for languages, learned thirteen of them, including Russian and Greek (both ancient

and modern), and his dream drove him. In 1846 he established an indigo business in Russia and it prospered. He traveled to the United States in 1850, went to California, became an American citizen, continued to prosper, and finally had enough money to do what he had wanted to do all along—go to Asia Minor and find Troy.

He went at this with single-minded determination, being guided by the geographical references in the *Iliad* and without the great care that archaeologists have learned to exercise in their excavations since his time.

Nevertheless, he chose the right spot and uncovered a series of ancient cities built one on top of the other, obtained various fascinating artifacts, much of it in gold, and in 1873 announced that one of those cities was Homer's Troy. Later, he dug at the site of Mycenae, which had been Agamemnon's capital, and again found valuable artifacts, which he described in 1878.

Although Schliemann was not the first archaeologist, he made it popular. His findings were sensational, rang through the world, and were the beginning of archaeology in its modern sense.

[635] **LENOIR,** Jean Joseph Étienne (luh-nwahr′)
Belgian-French inventor
Born: Mussy-la-Ville, Belgium, January 12, 1822
Died: Varenne-St. Hilaire (Seine), France, August 4, 1900

Lenoir, who moved to France from his native Belgium in 1838, was self-educated; he taught himself chemistry and put his ingenuity to work in devising a number of inventions. He is best known, however, for his invention in 1859 of the first workable internal combustion engine.

For the previous century and a half the steam engines devised by men such as Savery [236] and Watt [316] had made use of heat outside the cylinder. The steam formed by the heat then entered the cylinder and moved the piston.

415

It had occurred to a number of men that a mixture of some inflammable gas with air could be made to explode within the cylinder and that the energy of combustion would then move the piston directly. In fact Carnot [497] had discussed such a device in his book on heat in 1824. (The difficulty was that the fuel would have to be a gas or at worst an easily vaporized liquid fuel. Such fuels were not really available in large quantity until the petroleum resources of the world were slowly developed in the latter half of the nineteenth century.)

If such an internal combustion engine could be developed it would be much smaller than a steam engine, and much more readily set into motion (since a gas-air mixture will explode at the touch of a spark, while the initial boiling of water over a coal fire is a slow process).

Lenoir was the first to design and build an internal combustion engine that worked, using illuminating gas as the fuel. In 1860 he hitched it up to a small conveyance, which became the first "horseless carriage" to be run by such an engine. (There had been earlier horseless carriages that had been run by ordinary steam engines.) Lenoir also built a boat powered by such an engine. He sold some 300 of these engines in five years.

The Lenoir engine was very wasteful of fuel, however, and the development of a practical automobile had to wait a generation, during which time Otto [694] made the necessary improvements in the internal combustion engine.

Lenoir, despite his inventions and the fact that he was recognized in his own lifetime, died poor.

[636] **GALTON**, Sir Francis
English anthropologist
Born: Birmingham, February 16, 1822
Died: Haslemere, Surrey, January 17, 1911

Galton, born to a wealthy family, was a child prodigy. Tutored by one of his sisters, he could read before he was three and was studying Latin at four. He was first cousin to the far more famous Darwin [554], a fact that is irrelevant but that works against him, for he is always compared to Darwin to his own disadvantage. Galton was merely a good scientist, whereas Darwin was a great one.

Galton's life falls into three segments, in each of which he did very useful work. He underwent initial training as a physician (he graduated from Cambridge in 1844), but when his father died, Galton became financially independent and promptly abandoned his studies. Instead, he spent the late 1840s traveling through Africa. He wrote books on his experiences as an explorer in 1853 and 1855 and, in 1853, entered into what was to prove a long and happy (though childless) marriage.

He then turned his hand to meteorology and in 1863 wrote a book called *Meteorographica* in which he founded the modern technique of weather-mapping. It was he who invented the term anticyclone, signifying the pressure highs, which usually bring fair, calm weather, as opposed to the pressure lows, which bring storms. And, on a much more mundane level, he invented the high-pitched whistle that dogs can hear but humans cannot.

When Darwin's *Origin of Species* came out in 1859 Galton could not help but feel the tug of the biological sciences. In consequence, the last half of his life was spent on anthropology and in particular in the study of heredity.

It was his misfortune that the discoveries of Mendel [638] were not made known to the scientific world, and so the proper basis for genetics did not exist in Galton's time. Thus, Galton believed (as Darwin did) that characteristics would blend when individuals of different types were mated, so that the offspring would represent an intermediate state. Mendel had shown this was not so, a fact Darwin was never to know. Galton, however, was to live long enough to see Mendel's accomplishments brought to light once more by De Vries [792].

Nevertheless, Galton made important advances in the study of heredity. He was the first to stress the importance of applying statistical methods to biology. He was also the first to study identical twins, where hereditary influences might be considered identical so that differences could be attributed to environment only. He also demonstrated the permanence and individuality of fingerprints. These had been studied as early as 1823 by Purkinje [452], but it was Galton who began to work out a thoroughgoing system of fingerprint identification. By the end of his lifetime, spectacular solutions of crime cases through fingerprints had established their use both in Great Britain and the United States.

In 1869 he showed that mental abilities varied among mankind along a bell-shaped curve as Quetelet [496] had shown was true of physical characteristics. By studying the occurrence of high mental ability in families he was able to present evidence in favor of the view that mental ability was inherited and took up a strong position in favor of heredity in the perennial heredity-versus-environment dispute.

However, he had a tendency to go further than the state of the art really permitted. He felt that mental ability could be measured accurately by the techniques of the time. (His faith in measurement went beyond the reasonable. He tried to map the distribution of good looks in England and to test the efficacy of prayer by statistical methods.) He also felt that the incidence of desirable characteristics in humans could be increased by proper breeding and in 1883 he gave the name eugenics to the study of methods whereby this could be brought about.

He was knighted in 1909, and when he died shortly thereafter, working to the end, he left a bequest for the establishment of a laboratory devoted to research in eugenics.

Unfortunately, the mode of inheritance of various human abilities are even now not well understood, and it seems quite certain that the complexities are such that we have no idea of how to breed in one ability without, perhaps, breeding out some others of equal value.

Furthermore, with Mendel's discovery of recessive characteristics and with modern understanding of the incidence of spontaneous mutation, it is further understood that undesirable characteristics can only be bred out of the species after an excessively long period and even then with no guarantee against recurrence.

Nevertheless, the ends of eugenics are so desirable that it cannot be given up entirely and, in later times, men such as H. J. Muller [1145], while recognizing the difficulties, nevertheless presented reasoned programs that would in their opinion achieve some beneficial results. Unfortunately, the loudest contemporary advocates of eugenics are nonscientists who use the language of science to beat their private tom-toms of racism.

[637] **THOMSON**, Robert William
Scottish engineer
Born: Stonehaven, Kincardine, 1822
Died: Edinburgh, March 8, 1873

Thomson was sent to Charleston, South Carolina, as a youth to gain experience as a merchant. He was more interested in engineering, however, and when he returned to Great Britain, he began a program of self-education in which he was encouraged by Faraday [474], the greatest of all the self-educated scientists. For a time Thomson worked with Stephenson [431] on railways.

Thomson's most important invention, in 1845, was the use of a rubber strip intended to fit around wheels; that is, the rubber tire. He intended it for use in carriages to muffle shocks and vibration, but it soon came to be used for bicycles. Indeed, it is difficult to see how bicycles could have become as practical and popular as they did become in the latter part of the nineteenth century without Thomson's rubber tire.

And, of course, the notion came truly into its own well after the inventor's death, when it began to be used on the wheels of automobiles, buses, trucks, and even airplanes.

[638] **MENDEL,** Gregor Johann
Austrian botanist
Born: Heinzendorf, Silesia (now
Hynčice, Czechoslovakia), July
22, 1822
Died: Brünn, Bohemia (now
Brno, Czechoslovakia), January
6, 1884

Mendel entered the Augustinian order,
after a childhood of poverty and hard-
ship, during which, as the son of a peasant, he tended fruit trees for the lord of
the manor. He obtained an education
with difficulty while trying to support
himself by tutoring.

Finally, in 1843 he entered an Augustinian monastery. He assumed the name
Gregor on becoming a monk, and was
ordained a priest in 1847. He lived at
the Abbey of St. Thomas in Brünn.
Since the Augustinians supplied teachers
for the Austrian schools, Mendel was
sent to the University of Vienna in 1851
for training in mathematics and science.
He attended lectures by Doppler [534],
for instance. In 1854 he became a science teacher at the Brünn Realschule,
after having failed three times to pass
examinations (experiencing a nervous
breakdown in the process). As a result,
he did not qualify to teach in more advanced schools.

Particularly interested in mathematics
and continuing his interest in botany
from the days of his tree-tending youth,
Mendel combined the two in a hobby he
made out of botanical research. For
eight years, beginning in 1857, he grew
peas in the monastery garden.

Carefully he self-pollinated various
plants, wrapping them to guard against
accidental pollination by insects, making
sure in this way that if any characteristics were inherited they would be
inherited from only a single parent.
Carefully he saved the seeds produced
by each self-pollinated pea plant, planted
them separately, and studied the new
generation.

He found that if he planted seeds from
dwarf pea plants, only dwarf pea plants
sprouted. The seed produced by this second generation also produced only dwarf

pea plants. The dwarf pea plants "bred
true."

Seeds from tall pea plants did not always behave in quite this way. Some tall
pea plants (about a third of those in his
garden) bred true, producing tall pea
plants generation after generation. The
rest, however, did not. Of these, some
seeds produced tall plants and some
dwarf plants. There were always about
three times as many tall plants produced
by these seeds as dwarf plants.

Apparently, then, there were two kinds
of tall pea plants, the true-breeders and
the non-true-breeders.

Mendel went a step further. He
crossbred dwarf plants with true-breeding tall plants and found that every
resulting hybrid seed produced a tall
plant. The characteristic of dwarfness
seemed to have disappeared.

Next Mendel self-pollinated each hybrid plant and studied the results. They
were all of the non-true-breeding type.
About one quarter of the seeds of each
plant developed into true-breeding dwarf
plants. One quarter developed into true-
breeding tall plants. One half developed
into non-true-breeding tall plants.

Apparently, non-true-breeding tall
plants contained within themselves the
characteristics of both tallness and
dwarfness. When both characteristics
were present, only tallness showed. It
was dominant. Dwarfness, however, although recessive and not visible, was not
eradicated. When the characteristic appeared in some plants in the next generation, unaccompanied by the tallness
characteristic, the plants were dwarfs.

In similar fashion Mendel studied
characteristics other than height. He was
able to show that in every case, mixtures
of characteristics did not blend into in-
termediateness but retained their identity. He showed that pairs of characteristics combined and sorted themselves
out according to fixed and rather simple
rules. Apparently both male and female
parents contributed (equally) a factor
governing each particular trait and the
pairs of factors in the offspring did not
blend but remained distinct.

This was tremendously important (although Mendel did not realize it). Dar-

win's [554] theory of evolution by natural selection had one overwhelming weakness. Darwin envisioned natural variations arising in each generation of a species, and natural selection seized upon those variations to preserve the good and doom the bad. But the action of natural selection was slow and if, in the meantime, through unrestricted and random mating, the varying characteristics melted into intermediacy, upon what would natural selection exert its effect? Mendel's discovery that varying characteristics did *not* blend but remained distinct showed that natural selection could work slowly and still effectively upon natural variation. Mendel might have pointed all this out, for he had read Darwin's *Origin of Species* and was even interested enough to annotate his copy. Nevertheless, when the time came for him to write up his experiments, he never mentioned Darwin.

However, the world was not to know of this. Mendel wrote up the result of his experiments carefully, but when he read them to the local society of natural history, he made no impression at all. There was no discussion and no questions. Conscious of his own status as an unknown amateur, he felt it would be wise to obtain the interest and sponsorship of some well-known botanist. In the early 1860s, therefore, he sent his paper to Nägeli [598], who was the nearest of the prominent botanists of the time. Nägeli glanced through the paper but apparently was repelled by the mathematics. He himself was a biologist of the old school and indulged in rather windy and obscure theorizations. A paper by an unknown monk with no theories but with only painstaking countings and ratios seemed worthless to him. He returned it with brief and cold comments, and this effectively chilled Mendel. To be sure, Nägeli offered to grow some of Mendel's seeds, but he never did and the offer was probably not meant seriously. He did not answer Mendel's later letters, and when Nägeli wrote his major work on evolution twenty years later, he did not mention Mendel.

Those were hard times. The Prussians, under the guidance of Otto von Bismarck, were rising to primacy in Europe and in 1866 they beat Austria in a whirlwind campaign of seven weeks. Not long before Prussian troops occupied Brünn, Mendel published his first paper in 1865 (followed by a second in 1869) in the *Transactions of the Brünn Natural History Society*. He then did no more research for a variety of reasons. In the first place Nägeli's cold reception had undoubtedly disheartened him as did the indifference of the naturalists in Brünn; in the second place he was appointed abbot of the monastery in 1868 and his administrative duties left him little spare time, particularly since he took up the cudgels against what he believed was discriminatory tax legislation concerning religious institutions on the part of the Austrian government. Third, he put on weight and found it difficult to do the bending that was required in cultivating his peas properly. He kept up an amateur interest in meteorology, maintaining careful records of the daily weather, as Dalton [389] had done a half century earlier.

Mendel's work remained ignored and unnoticed. Few people looked through the rather obscure journal in which Mendel's paper appeared and those who did were either at home in botany but not in mathematics, or at home in mathematics but not in botany. In either case, they skipped over the paper.

Darwin died in 1882, never knowing that the greatest weakness in his theory had been patched up. Mendel died in 1884, lonely and saddened, never suspecting that he would someday be famous. Nägeli died in 1891, never dreaming what a terrible mistake he had made.

In 1900 De Vries [792] came across Mendel's paper, and what are now known as the Mendelian laws of inheritance were finally brought to the notice of the scientific world, a full generation after their discovery.

[639] **ARREST,** Heinrich Ludwig d'
(a-reh′)
German astronomer
Born: Berlin, August 13, 1822
Died: Copenhagen, Denmark,
June 14, 1875

Arrest, the son of an accountant of Huguenot descent (which accounts for his French name) entered the University of Berlin in 1839. He was working for his doctorate when Galle [573] undertook to search for the trans-Uranian planet whose position Leverrier [564] had calculated.

Arrest volunteered to help and suggested that Galle use a particular star chart of the region in question, one that had been prepared but had not yet been published. Galle followed the suggestion and that night he called off the stars he observed while Arrest checked each, with its position, against the star chart. That very night, Neptune was discovered, though Arrest's share in the discovery was not officially acknowledged by Galle until 1877.

Arrest received his doctorate in 1850 and the next year published a book on the 13 asteroids then known. He discovered several comets, the 76th asteroid (which he named after the Norse goddess Freia) in 1862 and studied nebulae.

In 1858 he was appointed to a professorial position at the University of Copenhagen and became director of its newly established observatory.

[640] **LEUCKART,** Karl Georg Friedrich Rudolf (loik'ahrt)
German zoologist
Born: Helmstedt, Braunschweig, October 7, 1822
Died: Leipzig, Saxony, February 6, 1898

Leuckart, the son of a printing plant owner, was strongly influenced by his uncle, who was a professor of zoology. He received his education at Göttingen, where he earned his medical degree in 1845. In 1850 he joined the faculty at the University of Giessen. In 1870 he transferred to the University of Leipzig, where he remained thereafter.

Leuckart specialized in the study of the invertebrate phyla, carrying on where Lamarck [336] had left off. He clearly distinguished between the Coelenterata (jellyfish) and Echinodermata (starfish) and showed that the fact that

both displayed radial symmetry was not indicative of a close relationship.

He then turned to the study of parasites and worked out the complicated life histories of tapeworms and flukes, founding the modern study of parasitology. It was made quite clear by his work that there were human diseases (trichinosis, for instance) caused not by bacteria but by multicellular creatures of the various wormlike phyla. He published his studies on the parasites of man (in two volumes) from 1862 to 1876.

[641] **HERMITE,** Charles (ehr-meet')
French mathematician
Born: Dieuz, Merthe, December 24, 1822
Died: Paris, January 14, 1901

Hermite, the son of a cloth merchant, was born lame, a defect that may have hampered him socially, but not intellectually. He did not do well at school, not even in mathematics. However, he was encouraged by Liouville [555], and in the end repaid the courtesy by completing one important aspect of Liouville's work.

This involved the concept of "algebraic numbers"; numbers that could serve as solutions to polynomial equations of which $x^3 + x^2 + x + 1 = 0$ is a very simple example. It was easy to show that any rational number and a great many irrational numbers such as $\sqrt{2}$ and $5 + \sqrt{3}$ could serve as solutions to some such equation or other. The question was whether there were any irrational numbers that could *not* serve as solutions for such equations. Mathematicians were certain there were, but proving it was another matter.

Liouville had made the first step with respect to the important quantity e, with respect to certain polynomial equations. Hermite went on in 1873 to show that e could not be a solution to any conceivable polynomial equation. It was not an algebraic number but a "transcendental number," one that transcended (went beyond) the algebraic. Lindemann [826] was soon to find another and in the end it could be shown that there were infinitely more transcendental numbers than algebraic ones.

In 1876 Hermite became professor of higher algebra at the University of Paris and retained that position till his death.

[642] **PASTEUR,** Louis (pas-teur')
French chemist
Born: Dôle, Jura, December 27, 1822
Died: St.-Cloud (near Paris), September 28, 1895

As a youth Pasteur, the son of a tanner who was a veteran of the Napoleonic Wars, was not a remarkably good student, even though his father drove him on rigorously. He was interested in painting, showing considerable talent, in fact, and did moderately well in mathematics. In chemistry he received the mark of "mediocre." His ambition was to be a professor of fine arts. He struggled against poverty by tutoring but even so underwent semistarvation at times.

However, he attended the lectures of Dumas [514] and Balard [529] and, fired with enthusiasm, decided to enter chemistry. (This is an example of the importance of inspiring teaching, for although Dumas was an important scientist, Pasteur was to be a far greater one, and nothing in Dumas's scientific life was more important than the setting of Pasteur's feet on the proper road.)

As Pasteur studied with increasing interest, his place in class moved up steadily. After completion of his schooling, his first investigations were enough to show his true quality. These involved tartaric acid and related substances, and the manner in which they affected plane-polarized light (the existence of which had been explained by the transverse wave theory of light propounded by Fresnel [455] a generation earlier).

Biot [404] had studied the manner in which the plane of polarized light was twisted when the light passed through quartz or through solutions of certain organic compounds. In some samples of a particular substance, the plane was turned clockwise; in other samples of the same substance, the plane was turned counterclockwise. The reason for this escaped Biot, however.

In 1848—a year of successful revolution in France against King Louis Philippe—Pasteur himself took part on the side of the revolutionaries, although in general he was very conservative in his politics.

Pasteur studied the crystals of tartrates (one of the substances that exhibited the now-clockwise, now-counterclockwise effect) under the microscope and found that the crystals were not all alike. They were rather subtly asymmetric and some of the crystals were mirror images of the others. The two crystals resembled each other as a right-hand glove resembles a left-hand glove.

Pasteur had obtained his crystals from a solution that did *not* rotate the plane of polarized light, and he wondered if that was because the effect of one asymmetric crystal was neutralized by the countereffect of its mirror image. Painstakingly, with tweezers, Pasteur managed to separate the crystals into heaps. He dissolved the two heaps separately and behold, one solution twisted the plane of polarization clockwise and the other solution twisted it counterclockwise. (It was possible to measure the twist very easily by the use of the Nicol [394] prism invented some years before.)

This was a revolutionary discovery and it took some courage to announce it. A few years before, the well-known chemist Mitscherlich [485] had studied the same tartrate crystals and declared them all to be identical. Pasteur was only a twenty-six-year-old unknown. Nevertheless, he announced his findings and went before Biot to repeat his separation of the crystals before the eyes of the aged authority in the field and under his strict supervision. Biot was convinced and Pasteur received the Rumford medal of the Royal Society for this work. Ten years later Pasteur showed that a plant mold, growing in crystals of racemic acid, used only one variety. What was left was optically active. That was the first indication of a fact now accepted. Of two optical isomers, living tissue invariably uses only one.

Pasteur had thus added importantly to

the science of polarimetry in which measurements of the manner in which the plane of polarized light was twisted could be used to help determine the structure of organic substance, to follow various chemical reactions, and so on. He had associated "optical activity" with asymmetry in crystals, but it also showed up in solution where no crystals could exist and where the substance was separated into individual molecules. The most reasonable conclusion was that asymmetry existed in the molecules themselves.

Pasteur lived long enough to see the three-dimensional structure of the carbon bonds worked out by Van't Hoff [829] and Le Bel [787] and once that was done it was quite easy to show that certain molecules were indeed asymmetric and, like the tartrate crystals, existed in mirror-image forms. It was the best evidence in favor of the Van't Hoff-Le Bel theory that just those compounds that ought to exhibit the twisting effect, according to the theory, did exhibit it in actual fact.

It turned out later that Pasteur was lucky in the manner in which he prepared the crystals. In order to have the two types of crystal form separately (instead of in the symmetrical combination that fooled Mitscherlich) the preparation had to be made in just one particular way and Pasteur, by sheer chance, had done it that way and very few have managed, since, to prepare asymmetric crystals as large as Pasteur's. However, as Pasteur himself later said, "Chance favors the prepared mind."

Pasteur's achievement made him famous. He obtained a succession of professorial appointments and was made a member of the Legion of Honor. Yet great as his achievement in chemistry had been, it was to be dwarfed by his accomplishments in biology and medicine.

In 1854, still in his early thirties, the erstwhile indifferent student became dean of the Faculty of Sciences at the University of Lille; but he was rejected for membership in the Academy of Sciences in 1857.

At Lille, he became interested in the problems of France's important wine industry. Wine and beer often went sour as they aged and millions of francs were lost as a result. Wasn't there some chemical that could be added to prevent this? In 1856 a Lille industrialist turned to the famous young chemist and put the problem to him.

Pasteur agreed to tackle the matter and turned to the microscope. He found almost at once that when wine and beer aged properly, the liquid contains little spherical globules of yeast cells. When wine and beer turn sour, the yeast cells are elongated. Clearly there are two types of yeast, one of which produces alcohol (good) and the other lactic acid (bad). Pasteur was the first to show definitely that fermentation does not require oxygen, but that it nevertheless involves living organisms and that it is necessary to supply the correct organism to provide the correct type of fermentation. Here he won out in a long controversy with Liebig [532], who insisted that fermentation was a purely chemical phenomenon that did not involve living organisms.

Pasteur pointed out that the lactic acid yeast must not be allowed to remain in the fermenting wine. In the early 1860s he worked out the remedy. Once the wine or beer is formed, it must be heated gently at about 120°F. That would kill any yeast still left, including the wrong ones that would continue to do their souring work while the wine was aging. After the heating, the wine, if stoppered, would not sour.

The vintners were horrified at the thought of heating wine. Pasteur heated some samples, left others unheated, and told the vintners to wait a few months. When the heated samples were opened they were all fine. A number of the unheated ones had soured.

Ever since, gentle heating, intended to kill undesirable microscopic organisms, has been termed pasteurization. We are most familiar with the pasteurization of milk.

Pasteur's interest in small yeast cells brought him to the study of how microscopic life arose. This was a knotty problem indeed, and the aged Biot warned Pasteur against becoming involved in it.

Berzelius [425] had believed in spontaneous generation and in 1858 there had been reports once more of experiments tending to show that life arose spontaneously out of dead matter. This ran counter to the experiments a century earlier of Spallanzani [302]. Vitalists, however, for example Haeckel [707], maintained that Spallanzani, by heating the air above his broth, had destroyed some vital principle in it.

Pasteur was a very religious man and there was a certain religious value in disproving the doctrine of spontaneous generation, for it left the matter of creation of life in the hands of God. Pasteur was impelled, therefore, to devise an experiment in which air was not heated and yet life did not arise from nonlife. (Pasteur's religious feelings also led him to reject Darwin's [554] theory of evolution by natural selection.)

Pasteur, like Tyndall [626], showed that the dust in air included spores of living organisms and that by introducing dust into nutrient broths he could cause the broth to swarm with organisms. It was next necessary to show that the broth would not develop organisms if dust were kept out. In 1860 he boiled meat extract and left it exposed to air, but only by way of a long, narrow neck bent down, then up. Although unheated air could thus freely penetrate into the flask, any dust particles settled to the bottom curve of the neck and did not enter the flask. The meat extract did not spoil. No decay took place. No organisms developed. And there was no question now of heated air or of a destroyed vital principle. Pasteur announced his results at a gala meeting at the Sorbonne on April 9, 1864, with the leading social and literary luminaries of Paris in attendance. Biot, alas, had not lived to see the triumph, but a committee of scientists, including Pasteur's old teacher, Dumas, studied these experiments and found them decisive. They showed the way to the proper techniques for sterilizing nutrient cultures and thus aided the burgeoning science of bacteriology enormously.

Once and for all, Pasteur had disproved the doctrine of spontaneous generation in the form in which it had been upheld through the nineteenth century. However, the question, in more sophisticated form, was to arise again in the twentieth century.

By now Pasteur was the miracle man of France and had even been admitted into the Academy of Sciences. When, therefore, in 1862, the silk industry in the south was dealt a staggering blow by a disease that was killing the silkworms, the call went out for Pasteur, no one but Pasteur. His old teacher Dumas prodded him to take on the task.

"But I never worked with silkworms," said Pasteur.

"So much the better," said Dumas.

In 1865, then, Pasteur traveled south with his microscope. He located a tiny parasite infesting silkworms and the mulberry leaves that were fed to them. Pasteur's solution was drastic, but rational. All infested worms and infected food must be destroyed. A new beginning must be made with healthy worms and the disease would be wiped out. His advice was followed and it worked. The silk industry was saved.

This turned Pasteur's interest to communicable diseases and he attended the lectures given by Bernard [578]. He began to feel that disease *was* communicable in the first place (something the old Greek physicians had not been willing to allow) and that disease was communicable because tiny organisms caused it and spread from individual to individual. The communication might be by actual bodily contact, by the sprayed droplets of mucus in a sneeze, by infected excreta, and so on.

This "germ theory of disease" of Pasteur's was probably the greatest single medical discovery of all time, for only through an understanding of the nature of infectious disease and the manner of its communication could it be brought under control. Prior to Pasteur's time, men such as Henle [557] had had the same notion but without the necessary backing of observation and experiment. Others, such as Semmelweiss [607], fought disease successfully by chemical disinfection but did not realize that the reason for the success was that dangerous germs were being destroyed. For that reason their advances were abortive. After Pasteur's fermentation experiments and his observations of silkworm disease, Lister [672] was able to introduce chemical disinfection with Pasteur's germ theory as rationale and this time the technique slowly emerged victorious.

With the emergence of the germ theory, moreover, biologists began to turn their attention to bacteria in earnest, Cohn [675] pointing the way. There was almost a tendency to overdo things in the bacteriological enthusiasm that swept the field, but men such as Leuckart [640] were showing that there were other types of parasites, too.

Pasteur himself was almost defeated by circumstance at that time. He had a paralytic stroke in 1868 and for a while was in danger of death. Shortly after, France went to war with Prussia, and Pasteur (almost fifty and still somewhat paralyzed) tried to volunteer for service. Gently Pasteur was conducted home and told to attend to his microscope. All he could do was to return the honorary medical degree he had received from the Prussian University of Bonn.

The experience of that disastrous war (in which France was calamitously defeated) impressed Pasteur with the dangerous conditions in military hospitals. He brought all his prestige to bear on doctors (which was difficult to do, for he had no medical degree and therefore no union card in their business), forcing them to boil their instruments and steam their bandages in order to kill germs and prevent death by infection.

The results were overwhelmingly beneficial, and in 1873 Pasteur was made a member of the French Academy of Medicine. He was still without a medical degree but there was a growing suspicion (and a firm conviction nowadays) that he was the greatest "physician" of all time.

Pasteur, with his new medical prestige, turned his attention to anthrax, a deadly disease that ravaged herds of domestic animals. Some doctors denied that any germ was involved in this disease, but Koch [767] claimed to have detected the

germs responsible in 1876. Pasteur used his microscope and confirmed Koch, showing not only that the germs existed but also that they were sometimes present as heat-resistant spores that could survive long periods in the ground. The very soil trodden by an infected herd could cause healthy animals to sicken thereafter. Pasteur's solution was the same as in the case of the silkworm disease. Kill the infected animals, burn their bodies, bury them deep.

Now he went further. An animal that survived an attack of anthrax was immune thereafter. Half a century before, Jenner [348] had forced immunity to a dangerous disease by inoculation with a mild version of the disease. Unfortunately, there was no mild version of anthrax, so Pasteur made his own. By heating the preparation of anthrax germs he destroyed their virulence, yet found they were capable of bringing about the immune response of the original germs. Thus he could safely establish immunity.

In 1881 he carried through a dramatic experiment. Some sheep were inoculated with his "attenuated" germs; others were not. After a time all the sheep were inoculated with deadly anthrax germs. Every sheep that had not been treated with attenuated germs caught anthrax and died. Every sheep that had been treated with attenuated germs was not affected by anthrax at all.

Pasteur recognized his debt to Jenner by referring to the new type of inoculation as "vaccination" even though in this case the disease vaccinia was not involved.

Similar methods were established by Pasteur in the fight against chicken cholera and against rabies (hydrophobia), the disease caused by the bite of a mad dog. Pasteur showed that an attenuated germ could be manufactured by passing a rabies infection through different species of animals until its virulence had abated. He was puzzled in this investigation by not being able to locate the actual germ. This did not shake his faith in the germ theory, however. He suggested that the germ was too small to be seen in the microscope. In this he was correct, and this observation foreshadowed the study of viruses that Stanley [1282] was to bring to a climax a half century later.

Pasteur in 1885 made the first use of his attenuated rabies preparations to prevent a case of rabies in a boy badly mauled and bitten by a mad dog. The treatment worked and was the most dramatic climax of a most dramatic life. In 1888 the Pasteur Institute was established with the help of donations from all over the world, including grants from the governments of Russia, Turkey, and Brazil. Its purpose was to treat cases of rabies, and it has now become one of the most famous centers of biological research in the world.

(The boy whose life Pasteur had saved from rabies was Joseph Meister, and half a century later he came to a tragic end. He had been made gatekeeper of the Pasteur Institute. In 1940 France was again disastrously defeated, this time by Nazi Germany. The invading Nazis, out of curiosity, ordered Meister to open Pasteur's crypt. Rather than do so, poor Meister killed himself.)

Pasteur died at the height of his glory, recognized both in his lifetime and ever since as one of the greatest scientists in history. In biology it is doubtful that anyone but Aristotle [29] and Darwin can be mentioned in the same breath with him.

[643] **WALLACE,** Alfred Russel
English naturalist
Born: Usk, Monmouthshire,
January 8, 1823
Died: Broadstone, Dorset, November 7, 1913

Wallace, the eighth of nine children of a poor family, had a life that otherwise paralleled that of Darwin [554] in peculiar fashion. Like Darwin he spent his youth fumbling for a profession, trying surveying and architecture at first. Like Darwin he found his opportunity at last as a naturalist, on a ship sailing off on a voyage of scientific exploration. In 1848 he traveled to the Amazon basin and on his return he too wrote a book about his

travels that brought him to the notice of the learned world, even though the ship burned on its return voyage so that many of the records were lost.

In 1854 he sailed to the Malay peninsula and the East Indian islands where he collected over 125,000 specimens. There he was struck by the sharp difference between the animal species of Asia and Australia. In later life, writing on this subject, he drew a line separating the lands in which these species occur. The line (still called Wallace's Line) followed a deep-water channel that ran between the large islands of Borneo and Celebes and between the smaller islands of Bali and Lombok. Out of this grew the notion of dividing the animal species into large continental and supercontinental blocs (something he eventually developed in a book published in 1876).

It seemed to Wallace that the animals of Australia were more primitive than those of Asia and that the reason they survived was that Australia and the nearby islands had split off from the Asian mainland before the more advanced Asian species had developed. Such thoughts led him to speculate on evolution by natural selection. Exactly as in the case of Darwin, these speculations were brought to a head when he happened to read Malthus [387].

Wallace was in Borneo at the time, suffering from malaria, and did not spend many years collecting evidence. Instead, he wrote out the theory in two days and sent the manuscript to Darwin for his opinion. (He had no idea Darwin was working on the same theory.) The two shared publication as a result. Wallace returned to England in 1862.

In later years Wallace never could bring himself to believe that man had evolved from the lower animals and he tried to differentiate between man's body and man's soul. Oddly enough Wallace was also an articulate crusader against vaccination and managed to adopt another minority opinion by espousing spiritualism. He also supported socialism—and even that most difficult doctrine for so many men to understand, feminism

425

[644] **SIEMENS,** Sir William (see'menz)
German-British inventor
Born: Lenthe, Hannover, April 4,
1823
Died: London, November 19,
1883

Siemens was a member of a German inventing dynasty, of which his elder brother was the founder. Their first financial success came in the field of electrical engineering.

Siemens (he was Karl Wilhelm, then) was educated in Germany at Magdeburg and Göttingen, studying under Wöhler [515] and Wilhelm Weber [540], among others. He then went to England in 1842 to introduce a process of electroplating he and his brother had designed. He found that the British patent system was more protective than that in Germany and, eventually, he decided to remain in England. He became a naturalized British subject in 1859 and was elected to the Royal Society in 1862.

Siemens labored to increase the efficiency of steam engines and of the conversion of heat to work, generally, in the light of the new outlook in thermodynamics, resulting from the work of men such as Joule [613]. It occurred to him and to his younger brother, Friedrich, that the heat of the gaseous products of combustion was being wasted. If they could be led round so as to preheat the incoming gaseous fuel, there could be a large saving in efficiency.

Such a "regenerative furnace" was introduced in 1856, and in 1861 Faraday [474] delivered his farewell lecture on the subject. Siemens applied the regenerative furnace to the smelting of steel and achieved unprecedented economy and reliability in what came to be called the open-hearth method. This eventually replaced Bessemer's [575] process.

Siemens also pioneered in the development of the electric locomotive (he opened an electrified railway in Northern Ireland in 1883), in the laying of transoceanic cables (designing a ship named *Faraday* for the purpose), and in improvements in the electric generator. In the last year of his life, he was knighted.

[645] **KRONECKER,** Leopold (kroh'-ne-ker)
German mathematician
Born: Liegnitz, Silesia (now Legnica, Poland), December, 7, 1823
Died: Berlin, December 29, 1891

Kronecker was the son of a Jewish merchant and ran the family business eventually. He did well enough to retire at thirty and turn to mathematics with the assurance of running no danger of starvation. He was converted to Protestant Christianity in the last year of his life.

He obtained his Ph.D. from the University of Berlin in 1845, lectured there from 1861, and by 1883 had gained professorial status despite the fact that he had not yet become Christian. He spent most of his professional career trying to reinterpret all of mathematics in terms of integers alone. This meant trying to do without the irrational, which had been accepted since the time of Pythagoras [7], let alone the imaginary numbers dealt with by such men as Hamilton [545] and the infinities of Cantor [772]. Kronecker was the author of a much-quoted statement: "God made the integers; all else is the work of man."

On the whole, his conservative stand did not win out, but it did force mathematicians to deal with their work with greater rigor. It was not easy to do this as Frege [797] was to find out.

[646] **HUGGINS,** Sir William
English astronomer
Born: London, February 7, 1824
Died: London, May 12, 1910

Huggins, the son of a linen draper, was privately educated. He was interested in microscopy in his younger days but when, in 1856, he was able to dispose of his father's business, he turned to astronomy. It was a case of looking through lenses either way, but in the case of astronomy, he did not have to experiment with animals, something he did not enjoy.

He built a private observatory near

London where he and his wife studied the heavens. After that his interest in astronomy eclipsed all else. He was one of the first to seize upon the notion of spectroscopy as worked out by Kirchhoff [648] and to grasp to the full its application to astronomy.

He studied the spectra of nebulae, of stars, of planets, of comets, and of the sun; of anything, in fact, the light of which he could pass through a telescope and then a prism. In 1863 he announced from a study of spectral lines that the same elements that existed on earth existed in the stars and thus was laid to rest the twenty-one-century-old notion of Aristotle's [29] that the heavens were composed of a unique substance not found on earth.

In 1864 Huggins showed that bright nebulae such as that in Orion consisted of luminous gas, and in 1866 he was the first to study the spectrum of a nova and to show it was enveloped by hydrogen, a gas Ångström [585] had already detected in the sun. (This was the first indication of a fact that has since been amply confirmed: The universe generally—and the stars in particular—consists mainly of hydrogen.)

The spectra of comets had first been studied by Donati [671]. Huggins was able to show that comets are composed at least in part of glowing carbon compounds. His observations of light reflected from planets, however, yielded no clear conclusions. For these, astronomers had to await the improved techniques of the twentieth century.

Huggins was also one of the first to experiment with photography as an adjunct of astronomy and by 1875 had devised methods of photographing spectra. Its importance was that with time exposures, the light from a star or other dim object could be made cumulative and spectra could be developed that had been far too faint to be seen by the naked eye. In addition of course spectra could be recorded permanently by means of photography and measurements upon them conducted at leisure.

His most spectacular feat, however, lay in his application of the effect expounded two decades earlier by Doppler [534] and Fizeau [620]. Huggins realized that if a star was moving toward the earth, there would be a Doppler-Fizeau shift and all its spectral lines would shift slightly toward the violet end of the spectrum when compared with the position of the lines in the spectrum of a source, such as the sun, that was moving neither toward nor away from the earth. If the star was moving away from the earth the lines would shift slightly toward the red end of the spectrum. From the amount of shift the velocity of the star in the line of sight could be determined.

He applied this to the star Sirius in 1868 and found a small "red shift" in one of the hydrogen lines. From this he determined with reasonable accuracy the velocity at which Sirius was moving away from the earth.

This motion in the line of sight (radial velocity) is of exceeding importance in astronomy, for it can be determined by shifts in the position of spectral lines, without regard to the distance of the stars. Even the most distant objects in the universe can be (and are) tested for radial velocity as long as their spectra can be obtained. (Proper motion across the line of sight, however, can be obtained only for the very closest stars.) It was by studying the radial velocity of the vastly distant nebulae that modern notions of the structure of the universe as a whole have been obtained by men such as Hubble [1136].

Huggins was knighted in 1897 and served as president of the Royal Society from 1900 to 1905.

[647] JANSSEN, Pierre Jules César (zhahn-sen′)
French astronomer
Born: Paris, February 22, 1824
Died: Meudon (near Paris), December 23, 1907

Janssen, the son of a musician, was lame from a childhood accident. He obtained a degree from the University of Paris in 1852 and then became a traveling man, in the interests of astronomy. He went to Peru in 1857 to fix the location of the magnetic equator. He visited Italy, the Azores, and Greece to study solar spectra, volcanoes, and so on. In 1865 he gained a professorial post at the University of Paris.

Finally, he met immortality by traveling to India in 1868 to study the total eclipse. It was then that he observed a strange spectral line and forwarded the data to Lockyer [719], who attributed it to a new element he called helium.

Janssen also noted the size of the solar prominences. The day after the eclipse he attempted to take their spectra again and succeeded despite the absence of the obscuring moon. He then announced jubilantly that it was the day after the eclipse that was the real eclipse day for him.

Lockyer also reported this method of studying prominences without an eclipse.

Janssen was the first to note the granular appearance of the sun in those areas where it was clear of spots. He traveled to Japan in 1874 to watch a transit of Venus and in 1875 he was official astronomer on an English expedition to Siam. His most daring voyage of all was by balloon, in 1870, out of the city of Paris, besieged by the Prussians, in order to get to Algeria where he might observe a total eclipse. (Unfortunately, when the time for the eclipse came, the sky was obscured by clouds.)

Like Lockyer, he lived to see his observation of the helium line vindicated by Ramsay's [832] discovery of that element on earth.

In 1904, toward the end of his life, he published a monumental atlas of the sun, including six thousand photographs of its disc.

[648] **KIRCHHOFF,** Gustav Robert
(kirkh'huf)
German physicist
Born: Königsberg, Prussia (now Kaliningrad, Soviet Union), March 12, 1824
Died: Berlin, October 17, 1887

Kirchhoff, the son of a law councillor, studied at the University of Königsberg, graduating in 1847. He was the first to

show that the electrical impulse moved at the velocity of light, and he extended and generalized the work of Ohm [461].

His true fame began in 1854 when he was appointed a professor of physics at Heidelberg and began to deliver meticulous but very dull lectures. There he teamed up with Bunsen [565], with whom he had worked briefly four years earlier at Breslau.

Bunsen was interested in photochemistry (the chemical reactions that absorb or produce light) and he studied the light produced through colored filters. Kirchhoff, with mathematical interests and a strong background of Newton [231], suggested the use of a prism. Once this was done the two developed the first spectroscope by allowing the light to pass through a narrow slit before reaching the prism. The different wavelengths of light were refracted differently so that numerous images of the slit were thrown on a scale in different positions and, of course, with different colors.

The use of a Bunsen burner, first developed by Bunsen in 1857, was helpful. The burner produced so little light of its own that there was no luminous background to drown out and confuse the wavelengths of light produced by the reactions studied or by the minerals heated to incandescence. Previous workers, without Bunsen burners, had been misled by the background of luminous lines and bands produced by heated carbon compounds.

Through the use of a spectroscope it quickly became apparent to Kirchhoff that each chemical element, when heated to incandescence, produced its own characteristic pattern of colored lines. Thus, incandescent sodium vapor produced a double yellow line. In a sense, the elements were producing their "fingerprints" and the elementary composition of any mineral could be determined by spectroscopy.

By 1859 this new analytic method was moving along smoothly and was first publicly reported on October 27 of that year. As was inevitable, a mineral was found displaying spectral lines that had not been recorded for any of the known elements. The conclusion was that a hitherto unknown element was involved. In this way cesium was discovered, the announcement of the fact being made on May 10, 1860. The name of the element (from the Latin for "sky-blue") was derived from the color of the most prominent line in its spectrum. Within a year a second element, rubidium, was discovered and that name (from the Latin for "red") again marked the color of the line that had led to its discovery. This feat was quickly duplicated by Reich [506] and Richter [654] and also by Crookes [695].

Kirchhoff went even further with spectroscopy. He noticed that the bright double line of the sodium spectrum was in just the position of the dark line in the solar spectrum that Fraunhofer [450] had labeled D. He allowed sunlight and sodium light to shine through the same slit in order that the dark line of the first and the bright line of the second might neutralize each other. Instead, the line was darker than ever.

From this and other experiments he concluded that when light passed through a gas, those wavelengths were absorbed which that gas would emit when incandescent. This is sometimes called Kirchhoff's law, although it was discovered by others at about the same time.

If sunlight possessed the D line, then it meant that sunlight passed through sodium vapor on its way to the earth. The only place where the sodium vapor could exist would be in the sun's own atmosphere. Consequently, it was possible to say that sodium existed on the sun. In this way he identified half a dozen elements in the sun, and others such as Ångström [585], Donati [671], and Huggins [646] joined in these spectroscopic endeavors. Thus was blasted the categorical statement of the French philosopher Auguste Comte who, in 1835 had declared the constitution of the stars to be an example of the kind of information science would be eternally incapable of attaining. Comte died (insane) two years too soon to see spectroscopy developed.

Kirchhoff's banker, unimpressed by this ability to find elements in the sun,

asked, "Of what use is gold in the sun if I cannot bring it down to earth?" When Kirchhoff was awarded a medal and a prize in golden sovereigns from Great Britain for his work, he handed it to his banker with the comment, "Here is gold from the sun."

But the gold of the discovery was greater still. Eventually the spectral lines proved to be a guide not only to the great world of the outer cosmos, but to the infra-tiny world within the atom. Balmer [658] made the first steps in this direction.

Kirchhoff also pointed out that a perfect black body—one that absorbed all radiation falling on it, of whatever wavelengths—would, if heated to incandescence, emit all wavelengths. This conclusion had been arrived at independently by Stewart [678]. Although no perfect black body actually existed, one could be constructed by the use of a trick, as Kirchhoff pointed out.

A closed container with blackened inner walls and a tiny hole would serve the purpose. Any radiation, of whatever wavelength, that entered the hole would have only an infinitesimal chance of emerging again through the hole and could therefore be considered as absorbed. Thus, if the box were heated to incandescence, all wavelengths of light ought to emerge from the hole.

The study of this "black-body radiation" was to prove of the utmost importance a generation later, for it was to lead to Planck's [887] quantum theory.

[649] **HITTORF,** Johann Wilhelm
German chemist and physicist
Born: Bonn, Rhenish Prussia,
March 27, 1824
Died: Münster, Rhenish Prussia,
November 28, 1914

Hittorf, the son of a merchant, arrived at physics by way of chemistry and obtained his doctorate in 1846, having studied under Plücker [521]. In 1852 he was appointed to a professorial position at the University of Münster, a position he held for half a century.

Early in his career he worked on

different forms of selenium and phosphorus. It was easy, however, for a chemist to become interested in the chemical changes that took place when an electric current passed through a solution. It was noted, for instance, that the concentration of a dissolved salt in the neighborhood of one electrode grew to be different from that in the neighborhood of the other as electrolysis proceeded. Faraday [474] had explained the passage of electricity through a solution by speaking of ions traveling through the solution under the influence of the current.

Hittorf suggested in 1853 that the ions might travel with unequal speeds so that more would reach one electrode than the other. Thus he evolved the notion of the transport number. This was a valuable concept but nevertheless electrochemistry was not to arrive at maturity until Arrhenius [894] a generation later was to evolve a comprehensive theory of ionization.

Hittorf also studied cathode rays, to which he had been introduced by Plücker [521], and in 1869 he anticipated some of the discoveries that Crookes [695] was soon to make in greater detail. Hittorf retired from his position as professor of chemistry and physics at the University of Münster in 1890 because of ill health.

[650] WILLIAMSON, Alexander William
English chemist
Born: London, May 1, 1824
Died: Hindhead, Surrey, May 6, 1904

As a child, Williamson (born of Scottish parents) lost an arm and the use of an eye. What counted, however—an intelligent mind—remained.

Williamson became interested in chemistry midway through his medical education at Heidelberg, Germany, and, under the influence of Gmelin [457], changed his studies. As a student of chemistry he studied under Graham [547] and eventually worked under Liebig [532]. In 1849 he received an appointment as professor of chemistry at University College in London.

He began a painstaking series of researches on alcohol and ether and succeeded in 1850 in showing the relationship between the two. (This was a problem in which Liebig had been greatly interested.)

He showed, in effect, that in the alcohol molecule an oxygen atom was attached to a hydrogen atom and to a hydrocarbon grouping, whereas in ether it was attached to two hydrocarbon groups. He began to classify organic compounds into types according to structure. His work helped make clearer the nature and structure of molecules—and this was important, for chemists were in a state of confusion about them. (Final clarification came from Cannizzaro [668] and Kekulé [680] a decade later.)

In following the reactions of alcohol and ether Williamson came to understand how a reaction might go in either direction (a reversible reaction). Thus, two substances might react to form products that might themselves react to form the original substances again. At some point the two reactions, forward and backward, might match each other in rates so that there would be no overall change in the concentration of reactants and products with time. There would be a dynamic equilibrium, a concept Williamson was the first to formulate clearly.

This situation, which Williamson observed empirically, was to be an important part of the law of mass action, announced a decade later by Guldberg [721] and Waage [701] and given complete theoretical justification on thermodynamic grounds by Gibbs [740] two decades later.

Williamson suggested in 1854 that the reason sulfuric acid was needed in the formation of ether from alcohol was that first there was a combination of alcohol and sulfuric acid to form ethyl sulfate. The ethyl sulfate thus produced reacted with additional alcohol to form ether, liberating sulfuric acid in the process. The sulfuric acid, first joining the alcohol then being released again, was unchanged and unconsumed at the end of the reaction, yet was necessary to it, and thus acted as a catalyst. For the first time, catalytic action was clearly explained by means of the formation of an intermediate compound. Later, such men as Michaelis [1033] showed how this concept was essential to the explanation of enzyme action.

Williamson was the first to produce a mixed ether—one in which the oxygen atom is attached to two different hydrocarbon groupings. The chemical reaction he used for the purpose is still called the Williamson synthesis.

[651] **HOFMEISTER,** Wilhelm Friedrich Benedikt (hofe′my-ster)
German botanist
Born: Leipzig, Saxony, May 18, 1824
Died: Leipzig, January 12, 1877

Hofmeister was the son of a music publisher who was an accomplished botanist in his off hours. Hofmeister himself eventually ran the business and was a botanist, too, even more seriously and successfully than his father had been.

Hofmeister did not receive an academic education at all, but his work earned him a sufficient reputation to get him a professorial appointment at Heidelberg in 1863.

He was extremely nearsighted and would not wear glasses, so that he was forced to peer very closely at his work. This apparently encouraged him to devote himself to delicate manipulation and microscopic work. Thus, in 1847 he was able to describe in detail the manner in which the plant ovule developed into an embryo. He also examined the process of cell division and showed that the nucleus did not truly disappear in the process. He seems to have been almost on the point of discovering chromosomes and anticipating Flemming [762].

He studied simple plants and was the first to show "alternation of generations" in mosses and ferns, a sexually-reproducing form alternating with an asexually-reproducing one. He also showed the relationship of the gymnosperms (the cone-bearing trees, such as pines) to the other broad groups of plants.

Hofmeister is considered the father of modern botany, but in later life he became intolerant of criticism and, like Berzelius [425], very stubborn in persisting in his errors. His rage at criticism and his attempt to be both a businessman and a botanist each contributed to his early death.

[652] **KELVIN,** William Thomson, Baron
Scottish mathematician and physicist
Born: Belfast, Ireland, June 26, 1824
Died: near Largs, Ayr, December 17, 1907

Lord Kelvin was born William Thomson. He was the son of an eminent mathematician and was an infant prodigy who attended his father's lectures with delight when only eight years old. At eleven he entered the University of Glasgow, where he finished second in his class in mathematics. His first paper on mathematics was written while he was still in his teens, and was read to the Royal Society of Edinburgh by a professor well along in years, since it seemed undignified for the staid assemblage to be lectured to by a schoolboy. In 1841 he went to Cambridge. After graduation, in 1845, Thomson traveled to Paris for postgraduate work and studied under Regnault [561].

Both father and son were in their time professors at the university, the father in mathematics, the son in natural philosophy (the old-fashioned name for science). The younger Thomson held his chair for over half a century. He was one of the first to teach physics in the laboratory (converting an old wine cellar in a professor's house into one for the purpose) as well as the lecture hall. He lectured most dramatically, by the way, even eccentrically.

In 1846, the same year in which he obtained his professorial position, Thomson announced his calculation of the age of the earth from basic physical principles. He assumed that the earth originated from the sun and that it was originally at the sun's temperature, but had been cooling off steadily ever since. Thomson then showed that the time lapse required for the earth to reach modern temperatures had to be between 20 million and 400 million years and was probably about 100 million years.

This horrified the geologists, who, since Lyell [502] made uniformitarian principles popular the decade before, believed they needed more time than that, and earth at more or less present temperatures during all that time. This argument between astronomic and geologic viewpoints was not resolved for over half a century, when the discovery of radioactivity showed that the earth possessed within itself a source of heat independent of the sun, could maintain its temperature for indefinite periods, and might even be heating up.

Meanwhile, however, Thomson's short life-span for the earth together with Helmholtz's [631] equally short span (suggested for other, equally fallacious reasons) prodded biologists such as Nägeli [598] into considering the possibility of evolution by "jumps," speeding evolutionary processes and making the history of life fit into a few million years. This bore fruit eventually in De Vries's [792] mutation theory.

Interested in the phenomenon of heat, Thomson was among the first strenuously to support Joule [613]. Thomson was, in fact, largely responsible for getting Joule a reasonable hearing. Later, they collaborated to work out the Joule-Thomson effect, involving the manner in which gases underwent a drop in temperature when they expanded into a vacuum. This proved a prime factor a generation later in Dewar's [759] liquefaction of the permanent gases and the obtaining of ultra-low temperatures. (Thomson was also among the first to support Faraday's [474] concept of lines of force.)

Thomson further explored the consequences of Charles's [343] discovery that gases lost ½73 of their 0° volume for every drop of one centigrade degree in temperatures. He proposed in 1848 that

not the volume but the energy of motion of the gas's constituent molecules reached zero at −273°C. This, in fact, held true of the molecules of all matter, so that Thomson suggested that −273°C be considered absolute zero, a temperature below which no temperature could be. (The modern figure for absolute zero is −273.18°C.)

Furthermore, he proposed that a new scale of temperature be used with its zero mark at the absolute zero and its degrees equal to those on the centigrade scale. Such a temperature scale is referred to as the absolute scale, or, in honor of Thomson (and using the title conferred on him), the Kelvin scale. Temperatures on that scale are abbreviated as either °A or °K.

The notion of an absolute temperature scale was quickly adopted, for it turned out to be very convenient in thermodynamics. (Rankine [625] introduced a version of it for use by British engineers.) For instance, the demonstration of Carnot [497] that the maximum work to be obtained from a heat engine depended on temperature differences within the engine could be most neatly expressed if the absolute scale was used. It is now universally accepted that at absolute zero the energy of motion (or kinetic energy, a term introduced by Thomson in 1856) of molecules is virtually zero. Maxwell [692] carried this notion of kinetic energy of molecules further, interpreting temperature in terms of that concept and evolving the kinetic theory of gases, in which heat was established as a form of motion.

In 1851 Thomson deduced from Carnot's work the proposition that all energy tends to dissipate itself as heat, that it "runs down" into an unusable form. He pictured this continuous "degradation" of energy as a sign that the whole universe was running down. This is another form of the second law of thermodynamics and was similar to the concept of entropy advanced somewhat more precisely by Clausius [633] at about the same time.

Those were the years when Field [621] was putting his heart and fortune into laying the Atlantic cable, and it was

Thomson who studied the capacity of a cable to carry an electric signal. He invented improvements in cables and galvanometers, without which the Atlantic cable would have been useless. In 1866 he was knighted because of his achievements in this respect. He also introduced Bell's [789] telephone into Great Britain.

In later life he made numerous inventions, including improvements in the mariner's compass, new types of sounding gauges, tide predictors, and so on. From 1890 to 1894 he was president of the Royal Society.

It is sometimes the fate of scientists who in their youth forged new trails and led the way toward new concepts to pass their last days bewildered by still newer developments they cannot accept.

In the 1880s Thomson settled down to immobility, yet within a decade the Second Scientific Revolution burst upon the world and more new aspects of physics have been uncovered in any one decade since than in all the two centuries between Newton [231] and Thomson.

Thomson lived long enough to see the beginning of this revolution but could not appreciate its significance. With almost his last breath, as an old man in his eighties, he, who had been so brilliantly revolutionary in his youth, set his face against novelty and bitterly opposed the notion that radioactive atoms were disintegrating or that the energy they released came from within the atom.

In 1892 Thomson was raised to the peerage as Baron Kelvin of Largs, a title (borrowed from the Kelvin River near Glasgow) that died with him, for he left no heirs. He was buried in Westminster Abbey next to Newton.

[653] **BROCA**, Pierre Paul
French surgeon and anthropologist
Born: Sainte-Foy-la-Grande, Gironde, June 28, 1824
Died: Paris, July 9, 1880

Broca obtained his medical degree from the University of Paris in 1849 and then specialized in brain surgery. He was the first to trepan (cut through the skull) so as to treat an abscess on the brain. He demonstrated in 1861 through postmortems that damage to a certain spot on the cerebrum (the third convolution of the left frontal lobe, or Broca's convolution) was associated with the loss of the ability to speak (aphasia). This was the first clear-cut demonstration of a connection between a specific ability and a specific cerebral point of control. Within twenty years much of the cerebrum was mapped out and associated, piece by piece, with portions of the body. Gall's [371] insight, which had been misdirected into phrenology, was thus put right.

Broca's hobby was anthropology and he founded anthropological societies, anthropological journals, and even an anthropological school. This is not strange, for much of the work done by anthropologists at the time involved skull measurements (craniometry) and followed Retzius' [498] distinction among races on the basis of such measurement. Broca knew more about the skull than anyone else in his time and put his knowledge to practical anthropological use by devising new instruments for craniometric measurements.

Meanwhile in 1856 an old skull had been unearthed in the Neanderthal (a valley near Düsseldorf in the Rhineland). It was clearly a human skull, but it was more primitive and apelike than any modern skull. From the stratum in which it was located, it had to be quite old, and a controversy at once arose. Was it an early primitive form of man that later evolved into modern man? Huxley [659] thought so. Or was it simply an ordinary savage of ancient days with congenital skull malformation, or one who had suffered a bone disease? Virchow [632], himself an amateur anthropologist, maintained the latter.

The publication of Darwin's [554] *Origin of Species* intensified the argument, since if the skull really belonged to a primitive pre-man, then the notion of evolution would be strengthened at its most sensitive point, that of possible human evolution. Not only would there be Boucher de Perthe's [458] ancient tools, but there would be ancient man to make them, and not even a full man, but a creature at an earlier stage of development.

Broca, the most prominent French scientist to become an early supporter of Darwin, insisted that the skull actually represented a primitive Neanderthal man and he carried the day eventually. The dispute was not laid entirely to rest, however, until the discovery by Dubois [884] a generation later of manlike skeletal remains in Java that were far more primitive than the Neanderthal.

Just before his death, Broca was appointed a member of the French senate.

[654] **RICHTER,** Hieronymus Theodor
(rikh′ter)
German mineralogist
Born: Dresden, Saxony, November 21, 1824
Died: Freiberg, Saxony, September 25, 1898

Richter was Reich's [506] assistant at the Freiberg School of Mines, and in 1875, some years after Reich had retired, Richter became director of the school. His great feat was spotting the indigo-colored line in a spectrum that led to the discovery of indium. Although he did this at Reich's direction, Richter later tried to make it seem that indium was his discovery alone.

[655] **FRANKLAND,** Sir Edward
English chemist
Born: near Churchtown, Lancashire, January 18, 1825
Died: Golaa, Norway, August 9, 1899

Frankland, of illegitimate birth, was originally a druggist's apprentice, taught himself chemistry, then managed to enter the field professionally. He went to Germany where he met Kolbe [610] and where Liebig [532] and Bunsen [565] were among his teachers. He obtained his Ph.D. at Marburg in 1849, then became professor of chemistry at Owens College in Manchester and, in 1857 in St. Bartholomew's Hospital in London.

In 1865 he succeeded Hofmann [604] at the Royal College of Chemistry.

He was the first to study those hybrid molecules, the organometallic compounds. Until his time, the known organic substances were composed of nonmetallic elements only: carbon, hydrogen, nitrogen, oxygen, sulfur, phosphorus, and so on, with a few exceptions among the large protein molecules. Bunsen had moved a step onward, studying organic molecules containing the semimetal, arsenic. Frankland went on to prepare small organic molecules of which atoms of true metals such as zinc formed integral parts. This was done in 1850 and was enough to attain for him the professorship at Owens College.

Organometallic compounds were to make possible the important Grignard [993] reactions a half century later. Furthermore, his study of such compounds led Frankland to devise the theory of valence and to announce it on May 10, 1852; the theory, that is, that each type of atom has a fixed capacity for combining with other atoms.

This led not only to the Kekulé [680] structures, but also to the periodic table of Mendeléev [705], since that table was based on the regular change of valence with atomic weight.

Beginning in 1868 Frankland did a great deal of highly practical work on river pollution, a subject gaining great importance in industrial England (and becoming ever more important since). He retired in 1885, received the Copley medal of the Royal Society in 1894, and was knighted in 1897. Two years later he died while on holiday.

[656] **BATES,** Henry Walter
English naturalist
Born: Leicester, February 8, 1825
Died: London, February 16, 1892

Bates, the son of a hosiery manufacturer, did not have much chance at an education before going to work in the hosiery business. Even though he had a thirteen-hour workday, he managed to go to school at night. Entomology was, and remained, his hobby.

In 1844 Bates became friendly with A. R. Wallace [643]. Bates got Wallace interested in entomology and Wallace eventually suggested a trip to tropical forests where they might collect specimens and learn something about the origin of species. (This was before Wallace solved the problem along with Darwin [554].)

In 1848, following up this audacious scheme, the two friends landed in Brazil at the mouth of the Amazon. Wallace returned in 1852 but Bates remained for a total of eleven years, most of it in the virtually unknown upper reaches of the river. He collected over 14,000 animal species, mostly insects, more than 8,000 of which had not hitherto been known to Europeans.

Soon after he returned, Darwin's *The Origin of Species* was published and Bates accepted it wholeheartedly. In fact, Bates presented a great deal of information on insect mimicry, based on his Amazonian collection, that went a great way toward backing Darwinian notions. One cannot suppose that one insect species will imitate another in appearance on purpose; but it is easy to see that if such an imitation is beneficial, then those individuals that come closer to imitation through random variation will survive to have young more readily than those that do not and that in time, through natural selection, the mimicry will become very close and effective.

[657] **SCHULTZE,** Max Johann Sigismund (shool'tsuh)
German anatomist
Born: Freiburg, March 25, 1825
Died: Bonn, January 16, 1874

Schultze studied at the University of Greifswald where his father was an anatomy professor. He also attended lectures by J. P. Müller [522] at the University of Berlin. He obtained his medical degree from Greifswald, then taught at Halle University from 1854. In 1859 he became director of the anatomical institute at Bonn, where he remained the rest of his life.

He was particularly interested in protoplasm, the colloidal matter within the cell, and was able to show that it had nearly identical properties in all kinds of cells. Protoplasm he described, in what became a famous phrase, as the "physical basis of life."

[658] **BALMER,** Johann Jakob
Swiss mathematician and physicist
Born: Lausen, Basel-Land, May 1, 1825
Died: Basel, March 12, 1898

Balmer, the son of a judge, obtained his doctorate at the University of Basel in 1849 and lived a quiet life in Basel, teaching at a girls' school. Relatively late in life he became interested in spectra and reported his first piece of research at the age of sixty.

It had seemed that the lines in the solar spectrum are scattered randomly, but once Kirchhoff [648] called attention to the spectra of individual elements, greater regularity could be found. The spectrum of glowing hydrogen particularly had a series of lines spaced more and more closely with decreasing wavelength. Balmer, applying his mathematical bent to this, devised a formula of rather simple form that could give the wavelengths of all the series. He announced this in 1885.

The formula was purely empirical and Balmer offered no explanation for its existence. A generation later, however, it became of crucial importance when Bohr [1101] (who was born in the year in which the formula was announced) used it as the chief evidence in favor of his theory of the internal structure of the hydrogen atom.

[659] **HUXLEY,** Thomas Henry
English biologist
Born: Ealing, Middlesex, May 4, 1825
Died: Eastbourne, Sussex, June 29, 1895

Huxley, the son of an unsuccessful schoolmaster, had only two years of schooling himself. Nevertheless, he educated himself to the point where he could enter medical school. He obtained his medical degree from London University in 1845 and then traveled as ship's surgeon on a voyage to Australia between 1846 and 1850. As in the case of Darwin [554] and Wallace [643], his interest in natural history became all consuming. It was he who named the phylum Coelenterata, to which jellyfish belong, and in 1851 he was elected to the Royal Society. In 1854 he was appointed professor of natural history at the Royal School of Mines, where he delivered enormously popular lectures that he actively—and successfully—aimed at the lower classes. He thus found his true vocation as a popularizer of science.

In 1858 he finally disproved the theory of the origin of the skull from the vertebrae, a theory that began with Goethe [349] and Oken [423] and that still had its attractions for the nature philosopher Owen [539]. He was a late convert to Schwann's [563] cell theory.

When Huxley read *The Origin of Species* he became at once an ardent exponent of Darwinism. ("Now why didn't *I* think of that?" he is reported to have asked in annoyance.) Since Darwin could not or would not fight, Huxley took to the lecture platform with enthusiasm. In 1860, at a meeting of the British Association for the Advancement of Science at Oxford, he faced the Bishop of Oxford, Samuel Wilberforce (called Soapy Sam because of his unctuous way of speaking), who was primed with "facts" by Owen and who asked sarcastically if Huxley traced his own descent from the apes through his father or mother.

Before an overflow crowd of seven hundred, Huxley answered with deep disdain that if he had to choose as an ancestor either a miserable ape or an educated man who could introduce such a remark into a serious scientific discussion, he would choose the ape. Exit Wilberforce.

Huxley invented a word to describe his religious beliefs. He called himself an "agnostic." He spent the rest of his life as a writer on popular science and on religious questions, and served as president of the Royal Society from 1881 to 1885, but the great feat of his life was the popularization of Darwinism.

[660] **BOND,** George Phillips
American astronomer
Born: Dorchester (now part of Boston), Massachusetts, May 20, 1825
Died: Cambridge, Massachusetts, February 17, 1865

The younger Bond cut his eyeteeth assisting his father, W. C. Bond [464], in the observatory and succeeded to the directorship on his father's death. He specialized in the solar system, discovering a number of comets. In 1848 with his father he discovered Hyperion, an eighth satellite of Saturn. Here, again, as in the crape ring, the Bonds anticipated Lassell [509] by a matter of days.

In 1856 the younger Bond pointed out that the brighter a star the larger the image it made on a photographic plate (through its effect on silver bromide grains over a larger area) and showed that estimates of stellar magnitude could be made from such photographs. In 1857 he photographed the double star Mizar, showing both components on the film. This was the first double-star photography.

Bond succeeded his father as director of Harvard Observatory on the latter's death in 1859, but he himself died at the age of thirty-nine of tuberculosis, having held the position only six years.

[661] **ERLENMEYER,** Richard August Carl Emil (er-len-my′er)
German chemist
Born: Wehen, June 28, 1825
Died: Aschaffenburg, Bavaria, January 22, 1909

Erlenmeyer entered the University of Giessen in 1845, intent on a medical career. However, he heard Liebig [532] lecture and was converted to chemistry.

He then underwent a second kind of conversion when he studied under Kekulé [680], adopting the latter's structural theory of organic compounds.

In his own chemical career, Erlenmeyer was the first to synthesize a number of compounds of organic chemical interest. He synthesized the important amino acid, tyrosine, and the compound guanidine, working out the correct structural formula for the latter, and for the related compounds creatine and creatinine.

In adopting Kekulé's theories, Erlenmeyer used straight lines for bonds, two lines for double bonds and three lines for triple bonds. His constant use of these conventions went far to popularize them throughout chemical writings—and they are still used to this day, although more accurate conventions have been worked out in line with the quantum mechanical modifications of Pauling [1236].

Erlenmeyer also quickly adopted Kekulé's benzene structure and showed that the structural formula of naphthalene was a double benzene ring holding one side of the hexagon in common.

To the chemical student, Erlenmeyer is best known for the conical flat bottomed vessel he invented that is known universally as an Erlenmeyer flask.

[662] **CHARCOT,** Jean Martin (shahr-koh')
French physician
Born: Paris, November 29, 1825
Died: Lake Settons, Nievre, August 16, 1893

Charcot, the son of a wheelwright, received his M.D. in 1853 from the University of Paris. In 1860 he became a professor at the university, and beginning in 1862 he established a major neurological department at La Salpêtrière Hospital. He made extensive investigations into illnesses involving nerve degeneration, and was one of the great clinicians of his time.

In 1872 he began to work on hysteria and as part of the therapy he began to use the techniques of hypnosis that Braid [494] had introduced to medicine. It was in this connection that Charcot made his greatest single mark in the history of medicine; for in 1885 one of his students was Freud [865] who, through Charcot's work, became interested in the treatment of hysteria and in the uses of hypnotism, and then went far beyond that.

[663] **HOPPE-SEYLER,** Ernst Felix Immanuel (hope'uh-zy'ler)
German biochemist
Born: Freiburg-an-der-Unstrut, December 26, 1825
Died: Lake Constance, Bavaria, August 10, 1895

Hoppe-Seyler began life as Ernst Hoppe, the son of a minister. Orphaned at an early age, he was brought up by his brother-in-law, a Dr. Seyler, whose name he adopted as part of his own.

Hoppe-Seyler began as a physiologist, gaining his medical degree at Leipzig in 1851. He served as assistant to Virchow [632] at the University of Berlin in 1856. He prepared hemoglobin in crystalline form in 1862, and his interest shifted to chemistry. His first professorial appointment in 1864 was in applied chemistry. In 1872 he successfully combined the two sciences and was appointed professor of physiological chemistry (now better known as biochemistry) at the University of Strasbourg. He established the first laboratory to be devoted exclusively to biochemistry and in 1877 followed that with the first scientific journal to be devoted entirely to that study.

In 1871 he had discovered invertase, an enzyme that hastens the conversion of table sugar (sucrose) into two simpler sugars, glucose and fructose. He also discovered lecithin, a fatlike substance containing nitrogen and phosphorus. Lecithin is a representative of what are now termed phospholipids, compounds of fundamental importance to life, since no living cell is without them—and yet their function in cells is even yet uncertain.

In 1875 Hoppe-Seyler suggested a system of classifying proteins which is still in use today. Most important of all, his student Miescher [770] discovered the nucleic acids and Hoppe-Seyler began research upon them. Further work in that direction was done by Hoppe-Seyler's onetime assistant, Kossel [842].

[664] **STONEY,** George Johnstone
Irish physicist
Born: Oakley Park, King's County (now County Offaly), February 15, 1826
Died: London, July 5, 1911

Stoney was educated at Trinity College in Dublin, paying his way through by coaching the athletic teams. In 1848 he worked as an assistant to Rosse [513], and in 1852 was appointed professor of natural philosophy at Queen's College in Galway. He worked busily in physical research, yet in the end his prime fame rested on his introduction into the scientific vocabulary of a single word.

From the days that Faraday [474] had elaborated his laws of electrochemistry, it seemed that the logical way of explaining their existence might be to suppose that electricity was not a continuous fluid but consisted of particles of fixed minimum charge. Arrhenius' [894] ionic theory made this seem even more probable, and in 1891 Stoney suggested that this minimum electric charge be called an electron.

When, later that decade, J. J. Thomson [869] finally proved Crookes's [695] contention that the cathode rays were streams of particles and found that each particle carried what was probably Stoney's minimum quantity of negative electric charge, the name was applied to the particle rather than to the quantity of charge.

[665] **THOMSEN,** Hans Peter Jørgen Julius
Danish chemist
Born: Copenhagen, February 16, 1826
Died: Copenhagen, February 13, 1909

Thomsen, the son of a bank auditor, obtained his master's degree at the University of Copenhagen in 1843 and slowly worked his way up the faculty ladder till he became professor of chemistry in 1866. He was also a member of the Copenhagen Municipal Council for thirty-five years and it was his driving civic force that was responsible for the development of Copenhagen's gas, water, and sewage system.

His work on thermochemistry paralleled that of Berthelot [674], and he made about thirty-five hundred calorimetric measurements. Like Berthelot, he wrongly considered the heat evolution of a reaction to be its driving force. He was also the first to measure the relative strengths of different acids, and predicted the existence of a group of inert or "noble" gases (something verified a half century later by Ramsay [832]).

Thomsen shone in applied chemistry. In 1853 he worked out a method of manufacturing sodium carbonate from a mineral called cryolite, which is found only in the Danish island Greenland, and made himself rich. (At the time, cryolite had no other use, but a generation later Hall [933] was to turn it to the still more important task of manufacturing cheap aluminum.)

[666] **GRAMME,** Zénobe Théophile (gram)
Belgian-French inventor
Born: Jehay-Bedegnée, Belgium, April 4, 1826
Died: Bois-Colombes, Hauts-de-Seine, France, January 20, 1901

Gramme was the son of a Belgian government clerk and did not do well at school. To the end of his life, in fact, he remained essentially uneducated. Nevertheless, he was skillful with his hands, and an ingenious tinkerer with electrical equipment.

In 1856 he went to Paris and remained near it the rest of his life. He took a job with a firm specializing in the manufacture of electrical equipment. In 1867 he built an improved dynamo for the production of alternating current, and in 1869 a dynamo for producing direct current.

Faraday [474] and Henry [503] had established the principles that made such dynamos possible but their own versions were laboratory devices. It was Gramme who built the first electrical generating equipment that was truly useful in industry. It was upon Gramme's devices that the electrical industry was built.

[667] **CARRINGTON,** Richard Christopher
English astronomer
Born: London, May 26, 1826
Died: Churt, Surrey, November 27, 1875

Carrington, like Joule [613] was the son of a wealthy brewer. He was privately educated and the original intention was to prepare him for the ministry. It was with that purpose in mind that he entered Cambridge in 1844. However, he attended lectures on astronomy and was fascinated enough to make that his lifework.

He established a private observatory in 1852 and observed both day and night. At night he plotted the positions of the stars in the area circling the north celestial pole. In the day he observed the sun.

Between 1853 and 1861 he observed the sun and its spots almost as assiduously as Schwabe [466] had done two decades earlier. Where Schwabe had merely counted the spots, however, Carrington plotted their position on the sun. In order to do it he had to allow for the rotation of the sun, and he measured that too, by following the spots, as Galileo [166] had done two and a half centuries earlier, but in more detail.

He found that the sun did not rotate all in one piece, or at least that the spots did not circle the sun all at one angular rate. Instead a point on its equator rotated in just about twenty-five days while a point at the solar latitude 45° took twenty-seven and a half days to complete a rotation. The sunspots were therefore not fixed to any solid solar body.

In 1859 he observed a starlike point of light burst out of the sun's surface, last five minutes, and subside. This is the first recorded observation of a solar flare. Carrington speculated that a large meteor had fallen into the sun. It was not until Hale [974] invented the spec-

trohelioscope nearly three quarters of a century later that these flares, which proved to be part of the sun's own turbulence, could be properly studied.

In 1858 Carrington inherited the brewery on his father's death. He sold it in 1865, however, in order that he might continue to devote himself entirely to astronomy, but he died of a stroke before he was fifty.

[668] **CANNIZZARO,** Stanislao (kahn-need-dzah'roh)
Italian chemist
Born: Palermo, Sicily, July 13, 1826
Died: Rome, May 10, 1910

Cannizzaro, the tenth and youngest child of a magistrate, early attracted the favorable attention of Melloni [504]. As for Cannizzaro himself, he was a fiery person who attracted controversy and did not fear a strong line of action.

In his early life this led Cannizzaro into political turmoil, which might have brought him to the end of the road too quickly. In 1848 a series of revolutions shook Europe and one of them affected the inefficient and corrupt government of the Kingdom of Naples, of which Sicily was then a part. Cannizzaro was one of the revolutionaries, but since the revolution failed (as most of them did that year), he had to leave for France in a hurry.

He worked in France under Chevreul [448] while waiting until it was safe to return home. In 1851 he returned to Italy, but not to Naples. Instead, he worked in Sardinia in northwestern Italy, the only truly free portion of the peninsula at that time.

In 1853 he discovered a method of converting a type of organic compound called an aldehyde into a mixture of an organic acid and an alcohol. This is still called the Cannizzaro reaction. But greater things lay ahead.

During the 1850s chemistry was being brought to a distressing pitch of confusion. The atomic theory of Dalton [389] was widely accepted by then, but methods for writing formulas to indicate the structures of substances in terms of molecules and of the atoms making up the molecules was a matter of strong controversy. The trouble was that there was no general agreement on the atomic weights of the different elements, and without such agreement there could be none on the elementary makeup of different compounds. Berzelius [425] had prepared an excellent table of atomic weights and Stas [579] was in the process of preparing a still better one, but there was no agreement on just how these were to be used, as opposed to the more easily measured but less fundamental "equivalent weights."

The net result was that a simple compound like acetic acid (CH_3COOH) was given nineteen different formulas by various groups of chemists.

Finally Kekulé [680] in desperation suggested a conference of important chemists from all over Europe to discuss the matter, and an international scientific meeting was held for the first time in history. It was called the First International Chemical Congress and met in 1860 in the town of Karlsruhe in the little kingdom of Baden, just across the Rhine from France. Among the 140 delegates attending the conference aside from Kekulé were Wöhler [515], Liebig [532], Dumas [514], Bunsen [565], Kopp [601], Kolbe [610], Frankland [655], Mendeléev [705], Beilstein [732], Baeyer [718], and Friedel [693].

Cannizzaro attended too, bursting with a missionary zeal. In 1858 he had come across Avogadro's [412] hypothesis, which had lain disregarded for about half a century. (Avogadro himself had died two years earlier.) He saw that the hypothesis could be used to determine the molecular weight of various gases. From the molecular weight, the constitution of the gases could be determined. From that and the law of combining volumes of Gay-Lussac [420] the atomic weights as determined by Berzelius could be fully justified and clarified. Cannizzaro published a paper on the subject and went to the congress to do more.

He made a strong speech, introducing Avogadro's hypothesis, describing how to use it and explaining the necessity of dis-tinguishing carefully between atoms and molecules. He also distributed copies of a pamphlet in which he explained his points in full.

By the end of the congress he had actually convinced some of the chemists. After the congress further discussions convinced more.

Atomic weights came into their own and chemists moved steadily into total agreement about the chemical formulas of almost all the simpler compounds. Kekulé himself advanced his method of representing these formulas, which greatly clarified matters. Chemistry in general was feeling the impact of heightened precision of measurement—witness the work of Regnault [561]—and many cobwebs were soon to be cleared away. In particular, Cannizzaro impressed both Mendeléev and Lothar Meyer [685], helping start them on the road to the periodic table.

The year 1860 saw a turning point in Cannizzaro's personal life. The small states of the Italian peninsula were being unified, partly by a movement from within Sardinia and partly with the half-hearted help of Napoleon III of France. Cannizzaro joined the small army of Giuseppe Garibaldi in its attack on Naples. Naples fell at once and merged with the rest of the peninsula to form the new kingdom of a united Italy. He received a professorship at Palermo in 1861, and at Rome in 1871 after that city was finally united to the kingdom.

Later in life Cannizzaro entered Italian politics once more, under less turbulent conditions, and finally became vice-president of the Italian senate. As the importance of his service at the Congress of Karlsruhe became apparent in the brilliant light of hindsight, he received the Copley medal of the Royal Society in 1891.

[669] **GEGENBAUR,** Karl (gay'gen-bowr)
German anatomist
Born: Würzburg, Bavaria, August 21, 1826
Died: Heidelberg, June 14, 1903

Gegenbaur studied at the University of Würzburg under men such as Kölliker [600] and Virchow [632]. He obtained his medical degree in 1851 and after some years in Italy joined the faculty of the University of Jena in 1855. In 1873 he transferred to the University of Heidelberg, remaining there until his retirement in 1901.

He specialized in comparative anatomy, particularly as reflected in the embryos. He showed how embryonic structures that in fish eventually come to form gills form other organs, from Eustachian tubes to the thymus gland, in land vertebrates. This point of view was clearly pro-evolution, something Gegenbaur himself stressed, and led to the more radical views of Gegenbaur's pupil Haeckel [707]. Gegenbaur extended the views of his own teacher, Kölliker, to show that not only mammalian eggs and sperm but all eggs and sperm, even the giant eggs of birds and reptiles, were single cells.

[670] **RIEMANN,** Georg Friedrich
Bernhard (ree'mahn)
German mathematician
Born: Breselenz, Hannover, September 17, 1826
Died: Selasca, Italy, July 20, 1866

Riemann was the son of a Lutheran pastor and his original ambition was to follow in his father's footsteps. He studied Hebrew and tried to prove the truth of the Book of Genesis by mathematical reasoning. He failed, but his talent for mathematics was discovered and his ambitions shifted.

He entered the University of Göttingen in 1846, but his college career was interrupted by the Revolution of 1848, during which he served with the Prussian king, Frederick William IV, against the revolutionaries (though he opposed his own king, Ernst August of Hannover). With the danger past and the king victorious, Riemann returned to his studies.

In 1851 his doctor's thesis at Göttingen received the approval of none other than the aged Gauss [415].

In his short life (he died of tuberculosis before he turned forty) Riemann contributed busily to many branches of mathematics. His most famous contribution was a non-Euclidean geometry different from those of Lobachevski [484] and Bolyai [530]. This he advanced in 1854.

Riemann's geometry used in place of Euclid's [40] axiom on parallels the statement that through a given point not on a given line *no* line parallel to the given line could be drawn. He consequently also had to drop the Euclidean axiom that through two different points, one and only one straight line could be drawn. In Riemann's geometry, any number of straight lines could be drawn through two points. Furthermore, in Riemann's geometry there was no such thing as a straight line of infinite length. One consequence of Riemann's axioms was that the sum of the angles of a triangle in his geometry was always more than 180°.

Actually, although this sounds odd to anyone used to Euclid's geometry, it is perfectly reasonable. Riemannian geometry is followed if we consider the surface of a sphere and restrict our figures to that surface. If we define a straight line as the shortest distance between two points, that would be the segment of a great circle on a spherical surface. On the earth's surface, the great circles are never infinite in length; through two points any number of great circles may be drawn; there are no parallel lines since all great circles intersect at two points; a triangle constructed of great circles has angles that add up to more than 180°.

Riemann generalized geometry to the point where he considered geometry in any number of dimensions and situations in which measurements changed from point to point in space but in such a way that one could transform one set of measurements into another according to a fixed rule. At the time, this sounded like a wonderful exercise in pure mathematics but one that was divorced from reality. A half century later Einstein [1064] was able to show that Riemann's geometry represented a truer picture of the universe as a whole than did Euclid's geometry.

[671] **DONATI,** Giovanni Battista (doh-nah'tee)
Italian astronomer
Born: Pisa, December 16, 1826
Died: Florence, September 20, 1873

After obtaining his degree at the University of Pisa, Donati worked at the observatory in Florence, of which he became the director in 1864. He is best known for his work on comets, discovering six. One of them, discovered in 1858, was a brilliant and spectacular one and is still referred to as Donati's comet.

In 1864 he obtained the spectrum of a comet in the neighborhood of the sun. While yet at a distance from the sun a comet glowed only by reflected sunlight, as the spectrum clearly showed. Near the sun its own substance was heated to a glow and the spectrum changed radically. As a result, Donati was appointed a director of the Florence Observatory, with professorial rank.

In 1868 Huggins [646] was able to identify the lines as those belonging to carbon-containing substances. This was the first step leading to the theories of comet structure, finally worked out nearly a century later by Whipple [1317].

[672] **LISTER,** Joseph, Baron
English surgeon
Born: Upton, Essex, April 5, 1827
Died: Walmer, Kent, February 10, 1912

Lister was the son of J. J. Lister [445], who had invented an achromatic microscope. He himself entered medicine, obtaining his degree from the University of London in 1852. As a surgeon he was interested in amputation and the new technique of anesthesia developed by Morton [617].

He was perturbed, however, by the fact that an amputation or other surgery might be painless and successful and yet the patient might die of the subsequent infection. In 1865 he learned of Pasteur's [642] researches in diseases caused by microorganisms and it occurred to him to try to kill any germs in surgical wounds by chemical treatment. He used carbolic acid (phenol) for the purpose in 1867 and deaths by infection stopped.

Eventually chemicals less irritating to tissue and even more effective in killing germs were discovered, but Lister and his carbolic acid had founded antiseptic surgery. Overriding initial resistance to his findings by medical conservatives, he succeeded in converting hospitals into something more than elaborate pauses on the way to the grave.

In 1883 he was made a baronet and in 1897 he was raised to the peerage as Baron Lister of Lyme Regis. He was the first physician to sit in the House of Lords and in 1885 he succeeded Kelvin [652] as president of the Royal Society.

[673] **ABEL,** Sir Frederick Augustus
English chemist
Born: Woolwich (now part of London), July 17, 1827
Died: London, September 6, 1902

After studying chemistry under Hofmann [604], Abel spent his entire career as a kind of military chemist, working with explosives. He pioneered the production of smokeless powders with the invention, in 1889, of cordite, in collaboration with Dewar [759], representing the climax.

Cordite was a mixture of Sobrero's [574] nitroglycerine and Schönbein's [510] nitrocellulose to which some petroleum jelly was added. The mixture was comparatively safe to handle when purified ingredients were used. The resulting gelatinous mass could be squirted out into cords (hence the name of the material) that, after careful drying, could be measured out in precise quantities.

For six centuries—since the time of Roger Bacon [99], once thought to be the inventor of gunpowder—battlefields had lain hidden under a progressively thickening pall of gunpowder smoke, and artillery men had been blackened with it. It may be small comfort to have the scene of carnage relatively clear, but it is important militarily, for then generals can survey the battle's progress instead of losing it in man-made smoke. The Spanish-American War was the last important one fought with gunpowder (although fought seven years after the invention of cordite).

Abel was knighted in 1891 for the invention and created a baronet in 1893.

[674] **BERTHELOT,** Pierre Eugène Marcelin (behr-tuh-loh')
French chemist
Born: Paris, October 27, 1827
Died: Paris, March 18, 1907

Berthelot, the son of a physician, attended the Collège de France, obtaining his doctor's degree in 1854 after having studied under Dumas [514], Regnault [561], and Balard [529]. His doctoral thesis dealt with the synthesis of natural fats, which he formed by combining glycerol with fatty acids, making a crucial step forward in the synthesis of organic compounds and advancing Chevreul's [448] earlier work. Wöhler [515] had synthesized urea, but only by rearranging the atoms in ammonium isocyanate; he had not deliberately combined atoms. Others, notably Kolbe [610], had done so, to be sure, but such syntheses were few and always yielded products that were well known in nature.

Berthelot became professor of organic chemistry at the École Supérieur de Pharmacie in 1859 and moved on to the Collège de France in 1865. He went about the synthesis of organic compounds systematically, and turned them out in hordes, including such well-known and important substances as methyl alcohol, ethyl alcohol, methane, benzene, and acetylene. The theory of a vital force that alone would suffice to form organic compounds had been damaged by Wöhler and a few others. Berthelot ground it to bits.

Berthelot was the first to synthesize organic substances that did not occur in nature, by combining glycerol with fatty acids that did not naturally occur in fats. He thus produced organic compounds that were part of no organism. From that moment on, it became increasingly difficult to talk of organic chemistry as the chemistry of the products of life; gradually, organic chemistry became limited to the chemistry of carbon compounds, Kekulé [680] being the first to advance such a definition formally. Later, when a term was needed for the chemistry of the products of life specifically, the word "biochemistry" ("life chemistry") was introduced.

In some ways Berthelot was conservative. He was one of those who adopted atomic conventions only with reluctance. When Cannizzaro [668] established the matter of atoms and molecules to the satisfaction of most chemists, it was Berthelot who led (unavailingly) the opposition.

In the 1860s Berthelot was done with synthesis and turned to thermochemistry, the study of the heat of chemical reactions. In some of his work he had unknowingly been anticipated by Hess [528], but he went much further. He devised a calorimeter within which he could measure the heat of chemical reactions and ran hundreds of determinations. This work along with that being conducted by H.P.J.J. Thomsen [665] threw the science of thermochemistry into high gear. He invented the terms "exothermic" and "endothermic" for reactions that, respectively, gave off heat and took it up.

Berthelot suggested that the heat evolved by a chemical reaction was its driving force. If he had been right, there would be no such thing as a reversible reaction. Williamson [650] had shown that such reactions, capable of moving in either direction, did exist. It required the more subtle concept of free energy and chemical potential, evolved by Gibbs [740], to settle the matter of the driving force behind chemical reactions.

During the disastrous Franco-Prussian War, Berthelot was in charge of the scientific defense of Paris. After the establishment of the Third French Republic in 1871, he took an active part in public affairs. In 1881 he became a senator, and in 1886 he entered the cabinet. In 1895 he even served a year as foreign secretary. Nor did he lag behind in scientific administration, for in 1889 he succeeded Pasteur [642] as permanent secretary of the French Academy of Sciences.

[675] **COHN,** Ferdinand Julius
German botanist
Born: Breslau, Silesia (now Wrocław, Poland), January 24, 1828
Died: Breslau, June 25, 1898

Cohn, the son of a Jewish merchant, was a child prodigy, beginning to read when he was two years old. He was educated at the universities of Breslau and Berlin, obtaining his doctorate from the latter in 1847, since the former would not grant the doctorate to a Jew.

He sided with the liberals during the revolutionary year of 1848, which, combined with his religion, hampered his subsequent advancement, even though he had studied under J. P. Müller [522] and had done particularly well. He finally obtained a grudging professorial appointment in botany at Breslau in 1857.

He was early interested in algae (that is, one-celled plant life). He had already shown in 1850 that the protoplasm of plant and animal cells were essentially identical and that there was therefore only one physical basis of life.

As the 1860s progressed he became increasingly interested in bacteria, thanks in part to Pasteur's [642] work, and was the first to treat bacteriology as a special branch of knowledge. In 1872 he published a three-volume treatise on bacteria, which may be said to have founded the science. He made the first systematic attempt to classify the bacteria into genera and species. He was also the first to describe bacterial spores and their resistance to even boiling temperatures.

It was Cohn who discovered and encouraged Koch [767] and saw to the publication of the latter's paper on anthrax. Cohn was a successful teacher and an effective popularizer of science.

[676] **BUTLEROV,** Alexander Mikhailovich (boot'lyuh-ruf)
Russian chemist
Born: Chistopol' (in what is now the Tatar Republic of the Soviet Union), September 6, 1828
Died: Butlerovka Kazanskaya, August 17, 1886

Butlerov, the scion of a family of landed gentry, entered the University of Kazan in 1844, and only gradually grew interested in chemistry, obtaining his doctorate in 1854 from the University of Moscow. In that same year he accepted a professorial post at Kazan. In the late 1850s Butlerov traveled through western Europe and met both Kekulé [680] and Couper [686].

He was an eager convert to the new structural theory and in a series of publications in the 1860s he worked out its consequences, particularly in connection with a phenomenon called "tautomerism" in which a compound can possess two structures by the shift of a hydrogen atom.

Butlerov went even further than Kekulé and was the first to speak of the chemical structure of a compound. In later life, like Hare [428] before him and Lodge [820] after him, Butlerov became interested in spiritualism. Among the group of scientists that was organized to investigate his suggestions was Mendeléev [705]. No evidence for the truth of spiritualism was found and Mendeléev was outspokenly critical of the whole matter though he remained friends with Butlerov.

[677] **SWAN,** Sir Joseph Wilson
English physicist and chemist
Born: Sunderland, Durham, October 31, 1828
Died: Warlingham, Surrey, May 27, 1914

Swan spent his youth as a druggist's apprentice but graduated from that to chemistry. In Newcastle he was employed by a firm that manufactured photographic plates. At that time the solution had to be smeared on the plates in liquid form, a process both touchy and messy. Swan, however, showed that heat merely increased the sensitivity of the solution so that the plate could be dried with actual benefit rather than harm. By 1871 he had originated the dry plate method of photography, which greatly simplified the process and led the way to Eastman's [852] further developments fifteen years later.

But even before then, Swan had become involved in the real interest of his life, that of producing light by electricity. Some inventors had tried to produce light by heating a platinum wire to incandescence but such wires didn't last long. Swan realized that carbon would withstand heat better than platinum but carbon would quickly burn, when heated, unless it was enclosed in a vacuum.

In 1848 he began to use thin strips of carbonized paper within an evacuated bulb. By 1860, twenty years in advance of Edison [788], Swan had an electric light with a carbon filament. Unfortunately he could not obtain a vacuum good enough to keep it working a sufficient length of time.

By the late 1870s, when the techniques for producing vacuums had improved to the necessary degree, Edison was already at work and the two finally produced the practical incandescent bulb at approximately the same time. Edison was the more active (as always) in obtaining patents. In addition, he devised a host of subsidiary equipment designed to produce the electricity necessary to keep banks of incandescent lights burning at constant levels despite rapid fluctuations in the extent of their use. Edison therefore rightly receives the lion's share of the credit.

Swan lamps quickly gained popularity in Great Britain. In 1881 the House of Commons was lit by them; in 1882 the British Museum was. Swan's own house was the first private house in Great Britain to be lit by electricity, but Kelvin [652] followed suit by 1884. Edison and Swan settled differences out of court and formed a joint company in Great Britain in 1883, and electrical lighting assumed absolute dominance in the field of illumination by the century's end in the industrialized regions of the world.

Swan continued to try to improve the filaments, devising a plan whereby nitrocellulose could be extruded through holes to form thin threads. The idea was to carbonize them for use in electric light bulbs. That came to nothing, but Swan patented the process in 1883 and this paved the way for Chardonnet [743] and the development of artificial fibers.

Swan was knighted in 1904.

[678] **STEWART,** Balfour
Scottish physicist
Born: Edinburgh, November 1, 1828
Died: near Drogheda, Ireland, December 19, 1887

After an education at the universities of Dundee and of Edinburgh, Stewart, the son of a merchant, joined the staff of the Kew Observatory. He became director in 1859 and in 1870 joined the faculty of Owens College in Manchester.

He interested himself in the theory of heat exchange first enunciated by Prévost [356], extending and generalizing it. He recognized that at constant temperature, radiation and absorption of energy equal each other at all wavelengths; and he was aware of the properties of the "black body" enunciated independently by the more famous Kirchhoff [648]. He collaborated in astronomical research with De la Rue [589] and was also interested in the earth's magnetic field. It was in this last connection that he is now best known.

In 1882 he suggested, on the basis of a theory of Gauss [415], that the daily variations in the orientation of earth's magnetic field might be accounted for by horizontal electric currents in the upper atmosphere. This seemed an outrageous suggestion at the time, but a generation later the work of Kennelly [916] and Heaviside [806] established the validity of the notion in more sophisticated form and revealed the existence of the ionosphere, where electric charges did indeed permeate the thin wisps of upper air.

Stewart was one of those nineteenth-century scientists who saw no conflict in science and religion and who strove to show this in his popular writings.

[679] **POGSON,** Norman Robert
English astronomer
Born: Nottingham, March 23,
1829
Died: June 1891

Pogson worked at observatories in England and in India and discovered nine asteroids in the 1850s and 1860s.

His most fruitful contribution was in connection with Hipparchus' [50] notion of dividing the stars into six magnitudes based on brightness. In 1850 Pogson pointed out that the average first-magnitude star was just about a hundred times as bright as the average sixth-magnitude star. He suggested that this hundredfold difference be defined as representing an exact five-magnitude difference.

This meant that a one-magnitude difference represented a ratio equal to $\sqrt[5]{100}$, or 2.512. This suggestion was adopted and increasingly accurate methods of measuring stellar brightness have made it possible to assign magnitude values to the nearest tenth or, sometimes, hundredth, and to assign magnitude values to the planets, the moon and the sun. Thus, Barnard's Star has a magnitude of 9.5, Sirius one of −1.58, and the sun −26.91.

[680] **KEKULE VON STRADONITZ,**
Friedrich August (kay'koo-lay)
German chemist
Born: Darmstadt, Hesse, September 7, 1829
Died: Bonn, Prussia, July 13, 1896

Kekulé, who was of Czech descent, intended to be an architect but fell under the spell of Liebig [532] and found himself a chemist. He traveled through England and France (meeting Williamson [650] in England and studying under Dumas [514] in France). When he returned to Germany he lectured (in only mediocre fashion) at Heidelberg and set up a private laboratory for his own work. In 1856 he obtained a professorship at Heidelberg.

By that time he was interested in the notions of valence, toward which Cannizzaro [668] and Kekulé's friend Williamson had been groping, and which Frankland [655] was finally to put into clear-cut form. Until the 1850s, chemists had been denoting the atomic composition of molecules by simply listing the numbers of each element in a fixed order. Using symbols for the elements, sodium chloride is $NaCl$, water is H_2O, ammonia NH_3, methane CH_4, ethyl alcohol C_2H_6O, diethyl ether $C_4H_{10}O$, acetic acid $C_2H_4O_2$, and so on. There was little thought of arranging all the various atoms in any particular fashion.

Once Frankland had advanced the thesis that the atom of a particular element might combine with a fixed number of other elements, however, Kekulé got the notion that these fixed combinations might be represented in chemical formulas as specific patterns of atoms making up a molecule.

In 1858, the same year he took up a professorship at the University of Gent in Belgium, through the kindly offices of Stas [579], he presented his theory. His particular contribution was in respect to carbon. It was tetravalent, he suggested; that is, one carbon atom can combine with four others. Moreover he maintained that one, two, or three of the four bonds of a carbon atom could be attached to another carbon atom so that chains of such atoms could be formed. Pretty soon the notion of connecting atoms by little dashes was introduced by Couper [686] and Kekulé structures began to sweep the world of chemistry, although Kolbe [610], for one, poured withering scorn upon the whole notion.

Allowing hydrogen one bond, oxygen and sulfur two each, nitrogen three, and carbon four, it meant that:

water became $H-O-H,$

ammonia $H-\underset{\underset{\displaystyle H}{\vert}}{N}-H,$

methane $H-\underset{\underset{\displaystyle H}{\vert}}{\overset{\overset{\displaystyle H}{\vert}}{C}}-H,$

hydrogen sulfide   H—S—H,

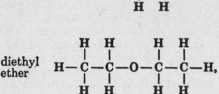

alcohol

diethyl
ether

and acetic acid

One of the strongest supporters of this way of doing things was Butlerov [676] in Russia.

Such structural formulas made sense out of organic compounds (especially since Kekulé allowed for double bonds and triple bonds), gave each a precise and individual representation, and explained how isomers, such as those first discovered by Liebig and Wöhler [515], could exist. Isomers, it could be easily shown, had molecules made up of the same atoms possessing the same valences, but arranged differently. An easy case is

that of ethyl alcohol

and dimethyl ether

The structural formulas offered guides to chemists interested in synthesizing new compounds, as Perkin [734] had just done.

Kekulé was famous enough now to be able to initiate the meeting of the First International Chemical Congress at Karlsruhe, where Cannizzaro starred and where the matter of organic molecular structure began to be put in order.

In 1861 Kekulé published the first volume of a textbook of organic chemistry in which he (mindful of the work of Berthelot [674]) was the first to define organic chemistry as merely the chemistry of carbon compounds. There was no mention of the living or once-living organisms featured in Berzelius' [425] original definition, another blow to vitalism.

There still remained one major problem in the field of organic structural chemistry: the structure of benzene (C_6H_6), a substance which had been discovered in 1825 by Faraday [474] and named by Mitscherlich [485] in 1834. This was most important in connection with the new synthetic dyes that were being built up by Perkin and others. Without a proper idea of its structure, progress could be much impeded.

Again it was Kekulé to the rescue. He had a feeling for building up atomic structures, perhaps because of his early architectural interests. In any case, one day in 1865 (according to his own version of the story), while in a semidoze on a bus, it seemed to him he saw atoms whirling in a dance. Suddenly the tail end of one chain attached itself to the head end and formed a spinning ring. If he had been Archimedes [47], Kekulé might have sprung off the bus and run down the street yelling, "Eureka!" However, he was a dignified German scholar and merely published his suggestions in the accepted manner. He introduced the notion of rings of carbon atoms, and benzene came to be represented thus:

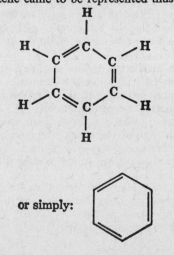

or simply:

(On the centenary of this discovery, in 1965, the Belgian Government issued a commemorative stamp.)

In 1867 Kekulé moved on to the University of Bonn, where he spent the remainder of his life.

Kekulé's structural notions were soon made three-dimensional by Van't Hoff [829] and Le Bel [787], were elaborated into an electronic theory by Lewis [1037], and further elaborated through quantum mechanics by Pauling [1236], but the essence of the Kekulé structure remains. It has guided chemists through the maze of synthesis for a century and despite all modifications still serves to depict the organic molecule and to help predict its reactions.

The last twenty years of his life, during which he was plagued by ill health and an unhappy second marriage, saw little accomplished. He was ennobled by Emperor William II in 1895 so that he could then add "von Stradonitz" to his name.

[681] **HALL**, Asaph
American astronomer
Born: Goshen, Connecticut, October 15, 1829
Died: Goshen, Connecticut, November 22, 1907

Asaph Hall had a hard start. His father, an unsuccessful clock salesman, died when he was thirteen and Asaph had to leave school to support his family as apprentice to a carpenter. After that he was largely self-taught, picking up education wherever he could, a bit here and a bit there.

He married Angelina Stickney, under whom he had studied mathematics and, with her full support, made up his mind to become an astronomer. In 1857, he managed to become an assistant to G. P. Bond [660] at Harvard College Observatory. His salary was three dollars a week. After a year it was raised to eight dollars a week.

In 1863 Hall had proved his worth to the point where he was appointed professor of astronomy at the United States Naval Observatory in Washington. While

there in 1876 he discovered a white spot on Saturn's surface and used it to show Saturn's period of rotation to be 10¾ hours.

In 1877 he made his most dramatic discovery. At the time, eighteen satellites were known to exist in the solar system, four of Jupiter, eight of Saturn, four of Uranus, and one of Neptune. This makes seventeen, but of course the eighteenth is our own moon. No satellites were known for Mercury, Venus, or Mars and if those three planets had any they must be very small. Mercury and Venus were hard to inspect for tiny satellites because they were so often close to the sun. Mars, however, was another matter.

In 1877 Mars was approaching a favorable conjunction and would be only some thirty-five million miles from the earth. All telescopes were turning to it and Hall had at his disposal a 26-inch refractor, then the largest in the world. (It was during this conjunction that Schiaparelli [714] was to start the famous Martian canal controversy.)

Hall began to search the neighborhood of Mars for small satellites at the beginning of August. He worked his way systematically inward toward Mars's surface. By August 11 he was so close to Mars that its glare was beginning to interfere with his observations. He decided to give up, went home, and told his wife of his decision. Mrs. Hall said, "Try it just one more night."

Hall agreed to do so and on that one more night discovered a tiny, moving object near Mars. Unfortunately clouds came in and he had to wait for five agonizingly suspenseful days for another chance to look. On August 16 he could see and definitely observed a satellite. On the seventeenth he found another.

They were small satellites, the larger some fifteen miles in diameter, the smaller seven and a half. What's more they were very close to Mars. The inner satellite revolved about Mars faster than Mars rotated on its axis, so that from the Martian surface it would seem to rise in the west and set in the east. Hall named the satellites Phobos ("fear") and

Deimos ("terror") after the two sons of
the war-god Ares in the Greek myth.

In 1892 Mrs. Hall died, and in 1898
Hall moved to Harvard as a professor of
astronomy, retiring to his home town in
1903.

One sad touch to Hall's great discovery, by the way, was the fact that
Newcomb [713], who was Hall's superior at the time, took an unfair share of
the press coverage that followed. However, he eventually apologized to the
offended Hall for this, and the final
touch came when rocket probes mapped
the surface of the two satellites, for then
the two largest craters on Phobos were
named Hall and Stickney as a well-
earned tribute to the professor and his
wife.

[682] **THOMSON,** Sir Charles Wyville
        Scottish zoologist
        Born: Bonsyde, West Lothian,
        March 5, 1830
        Died: Bonsyde, March 10, 1882

Thomson's name was originally Wyville Thomas Charles, but he changed it
in 1876, when he was knighted, to the
form given above. The son of a surgeon,
he studied medicine at the University of
Edinburgh, but ill health forced him out
in 1850 before he could get his degree.

He grew interested in natural history
and received academic appointments that
culminated, in 1870, in a professorship
in natural history at the University of
Edinburgh.

His chief interest came to be the life
of the ocean depths. It had always been
assumed (by those who thought of it at
all) that ocean life was confined to the
surface layer and that the depths, with
their cold, darkness, and enormous
pressures, were bare of life. However, in
1860 when a cable at the bottom of the
Mediterranean was dredged up, life
forms were found clinging to it though it
had lain at the depth of a mile.

Thomson undertook deep-sea dredging
operations in 1868 and 1869 and found
representatives of all the chief groups of
animal life at considerable depth.

His biggest chance, came with the ex-

pedition of the corvette *Challenger,*
which in 1872 took off on a four-year
combing of the seven seas. Thomson
sailed with it as the head of a staff of six
naturalists in the tradition of Banks
[331] and Darwin [554], everywhere collecting biological samples from great
depths. In the course of the voyage, the
Challenger traveled some 70,000 miles,
took 372 deep-sea soundings, and introduced man to the three-dimensional phenomenon of the ocean.

Life was shown, once and for all, to
inhabit all the ocean, from top to bottom. And, as we know now, life is even
to be found at the bottom-most foot of
the deepest abyss.

[683] **MAREY,** Étienne Jules (muh-ray')
        French physiologist
        Born: Beaune, Côte d'Or, March
        5, 1830
        Died: Paris, May 15, 1904

Marey obtained his doctor's degree in
1857 at the Faculty of Medicine of
Paris. He was professor at the Collège de
France from 1870 to his death.

To begin with he was particularly interested in the mechanism of blood circulation and in the devising of instruments to record the pulse rate and the
blood pressure. He invented the first
sphygmograph for the purpose in 1863,
and his instrument continued, in principle, to be used into our own time.

Marey then became interested in animal locomotion, in the details of just
how a horse moved its legs in order to
walk, run, trot, or canter; and in just
how a bird moved its wings in order to
fly. He realized that this could best be
determined by taking photographs of a
moving animal in rapid succession.

Beginning in 1881 he devoted himself
to animal photography. He succeeded in
modifying cameras so as to produce photographs spaced so closely together that
by viewing them in rapid succession, the
illusion of motion could be obtained.
Not only did Marey, in this way, rationalize animal motion so that old
paintings of galloping horses shown with
two forelegs extended forward and two

hindlegs extended backward as in a rocking horse were seen to be completely wrong, but he was also an important forerunner of the invention of motion pictures.

[684] **RAOULT**, François Marie (rahoo')
French physical chemist
Born: Fournes-en-Weppes, Nord, May 10, 1830
Died: Grenoble, Isère, April 1, 1901

Raoult, after considerable difficulties because of poverty, obtained his doctor's degree at the University of Paris in 1863 and after a stay at the University of Sens joined the faculty of the University of Grenoble, obtaining a professorial position there in 1870. He was one of the founders of physical chemistry along with Van't Hoff [829], Ostwald [840], and Arrhenius [894].

His studies of solutions led him in 1886 to propound what is now known as Raoult's law: the partial pressure of solvent vapor in equilibrium with a solution is directly proportional to the ratio of the number of solvent molecules to solute molecules. This led to a method for calculating molecular weights of dissolved substances and could also be used to show that the freezing point was depressed (and the boiling point elevated) in proportion to the number of particles of solute present in the solution.

It was the anomalous behavior of electrolytes in this respect that led Arrhenius to work out his theory of electrolytic dissociation.

[685] **MEYER**, Julius Lothar
German chemist
Born: Varel, Oldenburg, August 19, 1830
Died: Tübingen, Württemberg, April 11, 1895

Meyer, the son of a physician, was troubled by illness and headaches even as a youth. He earned his degree as a

physician in 1854 at the University of Würzburg, where he attended the lectures by Virchow [632] and obtained his Ph.D. at the University of Breslau in 1858. He began studying the nature and function of blood, but, nearly from the start, chemistry was his main interest.

He studied under Bunsen [565] and Kirchhoff [648]. In 1864 he wrote a text on chemistry and in the course of it considered how the behavior of the elements might depend on their atomic weights. In this respect he, like Mendeléev [705], had been influenced by Cannizzaro's [668] remarks at the Karlsruhe Congress.

Meyer concentrated on the atomic volume (the room taken up by atoms of the individual elements). He found that if he plotted the atomic volume against the molecular weight, the line drawn through the plotted points rose and fell first in two short periods, then in two long periods.

This was exactly what Mendeléev had discovered in connection with valence, but whereas Mendeléev published in 1869, Meyer did not publish until 1870. Furthermore, Meyer, as he himself was later ruefully to admit, lacked the courage to predict the existence of undiscovered elements. Nevertheless, Meyer is often given part credit for the discovery of the periodic table. In 1882, for instance, he and Mendeléev received the Davy medal of the Royal Society, jointly.

Meyer served as an army surgeon during the Franco-Prussian War.

[686] **COUPER**, Archibald Scott (koo'per)
Scottish chemist
Born: Kirkintilloch, Dumbartonshire, March 31, 1831
Died: Kirkintilloch, March 11, 1892

After a childhood in delicate health, during which most of his education was at home, Couper, the son of a mill owner, entered the University of Edinburgh in 1852. There he studied under Hamilton [545], then went on to Berlin and Paris in 1856. In the latter city he studied under Wurtz [602].

He is known for a single paper, published in 1858 under the sponsorship of Dumas [514], in which he paralleled some of Kekulé's [680] thinking and suggested the dash or a dotted line to represent the chemical bond, which Erlenmeyer [661] went on to popularize.

As a result of some delay that was the fault of Wurtz, Couper published two months after Kekulé and there was some controversy over priority as a consequence. Shortly afterward Couper suffered a nervous breakdown, perhaps as a result of the strain of the controversy. Then came sunstroke, and his scientific career was over before he was thirty, though he lived on for thirty years more.

[687] **SUESS,** Eduard (zyoos)
Austrian geologist
Born: London, England, August 20, 1831
Died: Marz, Burgenland, April 26, 1914

Suess was the son of an Austrian who was running a wool business in London at the time the child was born. When Suess was three, the family returned to Austria.

Suess was educated in Vienna and in Prague and was on the side of the liberals during the revolutionary disturbances in 1848, though he missed the worst of them when he stayed with his grandparents in Prague. Nevertheless, he did undergo a short period of imprisonment at the end of 1850.

He grew interested in geology and paleontology. His father, suspecting he would not be able to support himself, endeavored to make Suess work in a leather factory, but a professorial appointment at the University of Vienna (even though he lacked a doctor's degree) saved him from that fate.

Suess's interest in geology led him to advocate the bringing of drinking water into Vienna from mountain springs instead of using disease-laden wells. The aqueduct began operation in 1873. He

also supervised the production of the Danube canal, which was opened in 1876 and which put an end to the flooding of the low-lying sections of Vienna.

Suess did not feel that mountains were formed by the uplifting of the crust, but by thrusting movements that crumpled the crust, and in this he appears to have been right. He also traced the advance and retreat of the coastline, being the first to attempt to describe the panorama of the changing continents through the geologic ages. Here he was plagued by the lack of knowledge of the sea bottom. His ideas were replaced by those of Wegener [1071], Ewing [1303] and others, a half-century and more later.

Beginning in 1873, he spent thirty years as a Liberal in the Austrian legislature.

[688] **DEDEKIND,** Julius Wilhelm Richard (day'deh-kint)
German mathematician
Born: Braunschweig (Brunswick), October 6, 1831
Died: Braunschweig, February 12, 1916

Dedekind, the son of a lawyer, began his college career in the physical sciences but drifted to mathematics and obtained his Ph.D. in 1852 under Gauss [415]. He was Gauss's last student and he was a close friend of Riemann [670]. In 1854 he began to lecture in Göttingen and was the first to introduce Galois's [571] work into the mathematical mainstream.

His best-known work involves the irrationals, first discovered by Pythagoras [7] and his followers and a thorn in the side of mathematicians ever since—to the point where men such as Kronecker [645] wanted to do away with them altogether. Dedekind instead tried to present a logical picture of the irrationals by introducing "cuts." One can picture this by imagining the number series as representing the points on a line. The line may be cut in a certain fashion and by careful mathematical reasoning one can show that the cut may be at a rational number or at an irrational, but that the same rules of manipulation will be valid

451

in either case. In this case, an irrational number is as useful as, and no more mysterious than, a rational number.

Dedekind lived out a quiet, long life. He never married.

[689] **HELLRIEGEL,** Hermann (hel'reegel)
German chemist
Born: Mausitz, Saxony, October 21, 1831
Died: Bernburg, Anhalt-Bernburg, September 24, 1895

Hellriegel studied chemistry at the Forestry Academy near Dresden, and he interested himself in the nutritional requirements of plants. This was the sort of knowledge that would make it possible to fertilize marginally fertile soils with greater efficiency.

He was particularly interested in sugar beets, and their nitrogenous requirements. In the course of these investigations he discovered that certain leguminous plants (e.g., peas, beans) were capable of making use of atmospheric nitrogen, something most plants cannot do. This meant that planting such legumes tended to refertilize soils as far as nitrogen was concerned without the addition of chemical fertilizers. This discovery was announced in 1886.

[690] **MARSH,** Othniel Charles
American paleontologist
Born: Lockport, New York, October 29, 1831
Died: New Haven, Connecticut, March 18, 1899

Marsh, the son of a shoe manufacturer, was brought up by a rich uncle, George Peabody, by whose will he was eventually made independently wealthy. He studied at Yale, graduating in 1860. He grew interested in natural history and persuaded his uncle to endow the Peabody Natural History Museum at Yale in 1866.

In that year Marsh was appointed a professor of vertebrate paleontology (the study of extinct forms of life of past geologic eras) at Yale, the first professorship of the sort to be established in the United States.

Marsh, with William F. Cody ("Buffalo Bill") as a guide, scoured the western United States for fossils, sparing no expense and, in fact, spending a quarter of a million dollars. He never married and had no family who might have needed the money.

He competed with Cope [748] in this task of fossil discovery and between these two paleontologists there grew up a bitter and unforgiving enmity. They raced for fossils almost more to spite each other than to advance science, disputed priority on every possible occasion, and, if that failed, disputed conclusions. It was a rather unedifying spectacle, but on the other hand neither might have accomplished as much without the other's provocation. The net result was that startling fossil evidence was discovered that made particularly dramatic Darwin's [554] theory of evolution.

Marsh, a strong Darwinian, uncovered enough specimens of different forms of ancestral horses to make it quite possible to work out a complete line of descent for the creature. Cope, in the early 1870s, competed desperately in this and between the two such a picture of equine evolution was worked out as virtually to catch Darwinism in action.

In the early 1870s Marsh dug dramatic fossil remnants from the Kansas rocks. He found an extinct bird so primitive that it still retained its reptilian teeth (which no living bird possesses) so that it was clearly marked as a "missing link" between reptile and bird. This lent credibility to the evolution of the latter from the former. This same bird, the Hesperornis ("western bird"), so soon after the first development of feathered flight, had already lost its wings and, penguinlike, returned to the sea.

Marsh also discovered pterodactyls, flying lizards of the Cretaceous era, working out the nature of the first from a single leg bone, together with some of the large land reptiles of the period. This turned his attention to the dinosaurs, which, by all odds, are the most dramatic examples of extinct life. The increasing familiarity of the general public with the bony remnants of these gigantic, small-brained creatures probably did more than anything else to create the necessary atmosphere for the acceptance of evolution. In the end Marsh had described eighty new kinds of saurians and over five hundred new fossil species altogether. He was president of the National Academy of Sciences from 1883 to 1895.

[691] **VOIT,** Karl von
German physiologist
Born: Amberg, Bavaria, October 31, 1831
Died: Munich, Bavaria, January 31, 1908

Voit, the son of an architect, was another man lured to chemistry by the attractions of Liebig [532]. (Wöhler [515] was another of his teachers.) Originally intending to make medicine his profession, and obtaining his medical degree in 1854, Voit veered off course to concern himself with the chemical aspects of the human body, particularly the chemical fate of the various foodstuffs after absorption into the body. He was one of the founders of this branch of biochemistry. In 1863 he became a professor of physiology at the University of Munich and remained there for the rest of his life.

Until his time, chemists, including Liebig himself, thought the various foodstuffs contributed energy for specific functions; that protein, for instance, was the specific source of energy for muscular work. In 1861 Voit showed that this was not so, that the rate at which proteins were broken down in the body did not increase during muscular work.

In 1865 he was able to develop lines of experimentation that indicated foodstuffs did not combine directly with oxygen to form carbon dioxide and water. Rather, they underwent a long chain of reactions during which a succession of intermediate products were evanescently formed. The net result, to be sure, was indeed carbon dioxide and water; but the pathway to those end products was complex indeed.

This was the introduction of biochemists to the concept of intermediary metabolism. Much of the work in biochemistry in the century since has been the slow and patient elucidation of the details in the various chains of reactions.

Some of the details were worked out by Voit himself. For instance, it was known that the starchlike substance glycogen, discovered a generation earlier by Bernard [578], was built up out of glucose units. In 1891 Voit was able to show that mammals stored glycogen not only when they were supplied with glucose but also when sucrose, fructose, or maltose (three other sugars) were in their diet in place of glucose. The logical conclusion was that the mammalian body could convert sucrose, fructose, and maltose into glucose.

It was also Voit who in the 1870s, following one of Liebig's suggestions, developed the test for studying nitrogen intake and output. When protein is broken down, the waste product, urea, is formed and excreted in the urine. By matching the nitrogen contained in the urea excreted with that contained in the protein ingested, Voit could tell the state of the nitrogen balance; that is, whether the body was storing nitrogen, losing nitrogen, or keeping the balance even.

He worked with diets in which one particular protein was the sole nitrogen-containing item in the diet and found that with some the animals would go into negative nitrogen balance; it would excrete more nitrogen than it took in. This particular protein apparently could not be utilized for building tissue and was broken down for energy, the nitrogen portion being excreted. This, added to nitrogen loss through normal wear-and-tear of the proteins constituting the tissues, produced the negative values. In the long run, with such a protein the sole source of nitrogen, the animal must waste away and die, and Voit showed that gelatin was one of these "incomplete proteins." This line of research led eventually to the discovery of the essential amino acids and the climactic work of Rose [1114] a half century later.

Voit studied the human being as a unit in one sense, for with the help of Pettenkofer [612] he devised a calorimeter large enough to enclose a human being. (Previous instruments of the sort could only be used for smaller animals.) In this manner the oxygen consumed, the carbon dioxide liberated, and the heat produced by a human being could all be carefully measured. From 1866 to 1873 he was able to study man's overall rate of metabolism under various conditions. The resting or basal metabolic rate (BMR) could thus be determined for the first time in human beings. This later proved of value in diagnosing abnormal thyroid conditions. Voit's pupil Rubner [848] continued this form of calorimetry, carrying it to an amazing pitch of accuracy.

[692] **MAXWELL,** James Clerk
Scottish mathematician and physicist
Born: Edinburgh, November 13, 1831
Died: Cambridge, England, November 5, 1879

Maxwell, born of a well-known Scottish family, was an only son. His mother died of cancer when he was eight, but except for that, he had a happy childhood.

He early showed signs of mathematical talent. The possession of such talent is, alas, easily mistaken for foolishness by ordinary young men and young Maxwell was nicknamed Daffy by his classmates. At the age of fifteen he contributed a piece of original work on the drawing of oval curves to the Royal Society of Edinburgh. The work was so well done that many refused to believe such a young boy could be the author. The next year Maxwell met the aged Nicol [394], who had invented the polarizing Nicol prism. As a result he grew interested in the phenomena of light generally. Later he was to apply this interest by making use of the Young [402]-Helmholtz [631] theory of color perception in order to suggest methods eventually used in color photography.

At Cambridge, which he entered in 1850, he graduated second in his class in mathematics, as Kelvin [652] had done

before him and J. J. Thomson [869] was to do after him. The student who finished in first place became an eminent mathematician but never achieved Maxwell's fame. Maxwell was appointed to his first professorship at Aberdeen in 1856.

In 1857 Maxwell made his major contribution to astronomy in connection with Saturn's rings. At the time, there was considerable uncertainty as to the nature of those rings. In appearance, they seemed like flat, hollow discs. Maxwell showed, from theoretical considerations, that if the rings were actually solid or liquid, the gravitational and mechanical forces upon them as they rotated would break them up. However, if they consisted of numerous small solid particles, they would give the appearance (from Saturn's vast distance) of being solid and would be dynamically stable, too. Cassini [209] had actually guessed this a century and a half earlier and all evidence since his time had strengthened Maxwell's view. The rings do indeed consist of myriads of small bodies, making a very dense kind of "asteroid belt" about the planet.

About 1860 Maxwell brought his mathematics to bear upon another problem involving many tiny particles, this time the particles making up gases, rather than Saturn's rings. Every gas is made up of molecules in rapid motion in various directions. Maxwell treated the situation statistically as Bernoulli [268] had tried to do a century before. Maxwell had more powerful mathematical tools at his disposal, however, and could go much further than Bernoulli had been able to do. He considered the molecules as moving not only in all directions but at all velocities, and as bounding off each other and off the walls of the container with perfect elasticity. Along with Boltzmann [769], who was also working on the problem at this time, he worked out the Maxwell-Boltzmann kinetic theory of gases.

An equation was evolved that showed the distribution of velocities among the molecules of a gas at a particular temperature. A few molecules moved very slowly and a few very quickly but larger

percentages moved at intermediate velocities, with a most common velocity
somewhere in the middle. A rise in temperature caused the average velocity to
rise, while a drop in temperature caused
it to fall. In fact, temperature, and heat
itself, could be pictured as involving molecular movement and nothing else. This
was the final blow to heat as an imponderable fluid. The notion of Rumford
[360] that heat was a form of motion
was established once and for all.

Maxwell, to emphasize the difference
between the fluid theory of heat and the
moving-molecule theory of heat, invented, in 1871, what is popularly called
Maxwell's demon. In the fluid theory,
heat could flow only from a warm body
to a cold, the reverse flow being inconceivable in the light of Clausius' [633]
second law of thermodynamics.

In the moving-molecule theory, however, individual molecules in a gas at
equilibrium temperature would have a
whole spectrum of velocities from very
slow to very fast. If two containers of
gas at the same temperature were connected by a tiny door guarded by a tiny
demon, one could imagine that door
being opened whenever a slowly moving
molecule was passing to the right, but
not to the left; or whenever a quickly
moving molecule was passing to the left,
but not to the right. In this way the gas
molecules would accumulate in the left
flask, which would thus grow hotter and
hotter while the slow molecules would
accumulate in the right flask, which
would grow colder and colder. Heat
would flow in this fashion continuously
from cold to hot in defiance of the second law.

Of course, Maxwell's demon doesn't
exist, but the random operations of
chance could conceivably bring about
such a situation somewhere, given
enough time. This conversion of the second law of thermodynamics from a certain flow to merely a highly probable
distribution of velocities is important
philosophically. It means, for instance,
that the "heat death" of the universe, in
which entropy reaches its maximum,
might conceivably not be inevitable and,
even if reached, might not be eternal.

The new view of heat did not invali-
date the thermodynamic work of men
such as Carnot [497]. Their conclusions,
based on observation and experiment,
were merely explained on the basis of a
new and better theory and remained as
useful and worthwhile as ever.

In 1871 Maxwell reluctantly allowed
himself to be appointed professor of experimental physics at Cambridge. He
was the first to hold a professorship in
the subject, though it must be admitted
he was not a great success as a lecturer.
He went over the heads of most and usually had an audience of no more than
three or four. A few, who were brainy
enough, J. J. Thomson for one, were inspired by the lectures.

While at Cambridge he organized the
Cavendish Laboratory, named in honor
of the eccentric English scientist Henry
Cavendish [307] of the previous century
and served as its director until his death.
He also contributed considerable sums of
his own to keep it going. A generation
later the Cavendish Laboratory was to
do great work in connection with radioactivity.

The crowning work of Maxwell's life
was carried on between 1864 and 1873,
when he placed into mathematical form
the speculations of Faraday [474] concerning magnetic lines of force. (Maxwell resembled Faraday, by the way, in
possessing deep religious convictions and
in having a childless, but very happy,
marriage.)

In working on the concept of lines of
force, Maxwell was able to work out a
few simple equations that expressed all
the varied phenomena of electricity and
magnetism and bound them indissolubly
together. Maxwell's theory showed that
electricity and magnetism could not exist
in isolation. Where one was, so was the
other, so that his work is usually referred
to as the electromagnetic theory.

He showed that the oscillation of an
electric charge produced an electromagnetic field that radiated outward from its
source at a constant speed. This speed
could be calculated by taking the ratio of
certain units expressing magnetic phenomena to units expressing electrical
phenomena. This ratio worked out to be

just about 300,000 kilometers per second, or 186,300 miles per second, which is approximately the speed of light (for which the best available figure at present is 299,792.5 kilometers per second or 186,282 miles per second).

To Maxwell this seemed more than one had a right to expect of coincidence and he suggested that light itself arose through an oscillating electric charge and was therefore an electromagnetic radiation. In his time, no oscillating charge was known that could possibly give rise to light and it was left for Zeeman [945] a generation later to prove Maxwell's point in this connection.

Furthermore, since charges could oscillate at any velocity, it seemed to Maxwell that there should be a whole family of electromagnetic radiations of which visible light was only a small part.

Over half a century earlier, to be sure, Herschel [321] had discovered infrared light just beyond the red end of the visible spectrum and Ritter [413] had discovered ultraviolet light, just beyond the violet end. Since then, Stokes [618] had shown that ultraviolet light had all the properties of ordinary light and Melloni [504] had done the same for infrared. However, Maxwell predicted radiations far beyond both the infrared and the ultraviolet. This was not to be verified until the time of Hertz [873].

Maxwell believed that not only were the waves of electromagnetic radiation carried by the ether, but the magnetic lines of force were actually disturbances of the ether. In this way he conceived he had abolished the notion of "action at a distance." It had seemed to some experimenters in electricity and magnetism, Ampère [407], for instance, that a magnet attracted iron without actually making contact with the iron. To Maxwell it seemed that the disturbances in the ether set up by the magnet touched the iron and that everything could be worked out as "action on contact." (Not everyone accepted this. Airy [523] strenuously opposed the concept.)

In one respect, however, Maxwell's intuition was at fault. He rejected the notion that electricity was particulate in nature, even though that was so strongly

suggested by Faraday's laws of electrolysis.

Almost the last accomplishment of Maxwell's was his publication of the hitherto unpublished electrical experiments of Cavendish, showing that strange man to have been fifty years ahead of his time in his work. Maxwell was also among the first to appreciate the work of Gibbs [740].

Maxwell died, before the age of fifty, of cancer. Had he lived out what would today be considered a normal life expectancy he would have seen his prediction of a broad spectrum of electromagnetic radiation verified by Hertz. However, he would also have seen the ether, which his theory had seemed to establish firmly, brought into serious question by the epoch-making experiment of Michelson [835] and Morley [730], and he would have seen electricity proved to consist of particles after all. His electromagnetic equations did not depend on his own interpretations of the ether, however, and he had wrought better than he knew. When Einstein's [1064] theories, a generation after Maxwell's death, upset almost all of "classical physics," Maxwell's equations remained untouched—as valid as ever.

[693] FRIEDEL, Charles (free-del')
French chemist
Born: Strasbourg, Bas-Rhin,
March 12, 1832
Died: Montauban, Tarn-et-
Garonne, April 20, 1899

Friedel, who had Pasteur [642] as one of his teachers, became professor of mineralogy at the Sorbonne in Paris in 1876, the year before he and Crafts [741] immortalized themselves by discovering the Friedel-Crafts reaction. (The American pronunciation shifts the accent of Friedel's name to the first syllable.)

He was also interested in mineralogical chemistry, naturally, and was one of those who attempted to make synthetic diamonds, though unlike Moissan [831] he was never under the illusion that he had succeeded.

He also made some observations on silicon-containing organic compounds, which he did not follow up but which were to be taken further, very fruitfully, by Kipping [930]. In 1892 he headed the meeting at Geneva that systematized organic chemical nomenclature.

[694] **OTTO**, Nikolaus August
German inventor
Born: Holzhausen, Hesse-Nassau, June 10, 1832
Died: Cologne, January 26, 1891

After the invention of the Lenoir [635] engine a number of attempts were made to increase its efficiency. In 1862 theoretical studies were published that showed explosions within the cylinder combined with four movements of. the piston would prove adequately efficient. As the piston moved outward (first movement), a mixture of gas and air would be drawn into the cylinder. As the piston moved in (second movement) the mixture would be compressed. At the height of compression a spark would set off the explosion, driving the piston out (the third movement and the power stroke). When the piston moved in (the fourth movement), the exhaust gases would be forced out. The cycle would then be repeated.

In 1876 Otto, a traveling salesman, who was the son of a farmer and who chanced upon a newspaper account of Lenoir's discovery, was the first to build such an internal combustion engine and the four-stroke cycle is sometimes called the Otto cycle in his honor. Otto patented it in 1877 and formed a company that sold 35,000 such engines in a few years, and by 1890 the Otto engines were virtually the only internal combustion engines used. It was the Otto engine that made possible the automobile and the airplane.

[695] **CROOKES**, Sir William
English physicist
Born: London, June 17, 1832
Died: London, April 4, 1919

In 1848 Crookes, eldest of the sixteen children of a tailor who had enriched himself by shrewd real estate investments, entered the Royal College of Chemistry and studied under A. W. von Hofmann [604], but despite this and despite the fact that his first publication, in 1851, concerned organic compounds, he wandered away from organic chemistry with the encouragement of Faraday [474].

Eventually inheriting his father's fortune, he was able to settle down serenely to a life of research and to a marriage that yielded ten children.

The work of Kirchhoff [648] interested him greatly and he threw himself into the study of spectroscopy. The organic compounds he had dealt with were selenium-containing ones, and the ores from which he obtained the selenium were still in his possession. He studied them spectroscopically and in 1861 discovered a beautiful green line in their spectra that fitted no known element. It was a new element therefore and he named it thallium from a Greek word meaning "green twig." He was elected to the Royal Society in 1863 in consequence.

In investigating the atomic weight of thallium, Crookes made delicate weighings in vacuum in order to avoid errors introduced by the buoyant effect of the atmosphere. However, the balance showed erratic swayings at times and Crookes began to study the behavior of objects in vacuum. In 1875 he devised the radiometer, a little affair consisting of a set of pivoted vanes in a vacuum. One side of each vane was blackened to absorb heat and the other side was shiny to reflect it. In the presence of sunlight or other radiation, the vanes turned steadily. This was not due to solar radiation itself for if the container was evacuated particularly well, the motion ceased though the radiation was as strong as ever. It seemed then that the effect was due to air molecules in the partial vacuum that rebounded from the heated side of each vane more strongly than from the shiny side, thus "kicking" it around. Though never more than a toy, the radiometer did provide a new piece of evidence in favor of the kinetic theory of gases and Maxwell [692] himself worked out the theory of radiometer action on that basis.

Crookes's new interest in vacuums led him naturally into the study of the radiation and luminescence that appeared about the cathode (that is, the negative electrode) when it was placed under strong electric potential within an evacuated Geissler [583] tube. Crookes devised methods for producing still better vacuums and by 1875 had devised an improved vacuum tube in which the air pressure was but 1/75,000 that in a Geissler tube and in which the radiation could be more efficiently studied. This has been called a Crookes tube ever since. (The new techniques for producing a vacuum made Edison's [788] incandescent bulb practical for mass production.)

Crookes's careful studies in the 1870s independently covered the ground earlier investigated by Plücker [521] and Hittorf [649], but Crookes presented the results much more systematically and dramatically. He showed that the radiation from the cathode, which Goldstein [811] had just named cathode rays, traveled in straight lines. Small objects placed in the path of the radiation cast a sharp shadow in the fluorescence at the end of the tube. Crookes also showed the radiation could turn a small wheel, when it struck one side. All this could be explained by supposing the cathode rays to be electromagnetic (after all, the electromagnetic radiation of the sun indirectly turned the radiometer), but one experiment remained. Crookes went on to show that the radiation could be deflected by a magnet. He was convinced therefore that he was dealing with charged particles speeding along in straight lines and not with electromagnetic radiation.

Crookes spoke of these charged particles as a fourth state of matter, or an ultra-gas as far beyond the ordinary gas in rarefaction and intangibility as that ordinary gas was beyond the liquid. At the time, this notion was greeted with reservation and even hostility by other scientists, but in less than two decades J. J. Thomson [869] was to show Crookes to be entirely right, and a new word, "electron"—invented by Stoney [664]—was to make its appearance on the scientific scene.

Crookes on several occasions nearly stumbled on great discoveries that were eventually made by others. More than once he fogged photographic plates during the running of his Crookes tube even though those plates were enclosed in their containers. However, he missed the connection and it was Roentgen [774] a decade or so later who, also using a Crookes tube, was to discover X rays and initiate the Second Scientific Revolution. Again, Crookes had views that nearly brought him to the recognition of isotopes but he fell just short, and that great advance was left to Soddy [1052].

Unlike men such as Kelvin [652], Crookes maintained his creative energies and did not let the rapid pace of advancing science leave him behind. The discovery of radioactivity by Becquerel [834] inspired Crookes to investigate on his own into the mysterious uranium. In 1900 he found that a solution of uranium salt could be treated in such a way as to precipitate a small quantity of the material, and that this small quantity contained most of the radioactivity. The uranium left in solution was almost inactive. For a while Crookes maintained that it was not the uranium after all that was radioactive but some impurity.

He was both right and wrong in this. The deactivated uranium regained its activity, as Becquerel pointed out, and so it seemed that uranium in giving off its radiations was converted to something else that was much more radioactive than the parent uranium. This new product could be separated from uranium, leaving the parent much less radioactive, but still by no means entirely nonradioactive.

This was the first indication that radioactivity involved the change of one element into another, something that Kelvin strenuously denied in his own very conservative old age.

In 1903 Crookes showed that the particles of alpha rays (one variety of radiation from radioactive substances) caused zinc sulfide to luminesce and that under the miscroscope this luminescence consisted of numerous individual flashes. It was easy to see that each flash was the result of the impact of a single alpha particle. This spinthariscope (Greek for "spark viewer"), which Crookes had thus invented, was later used most effectively by Rutherford [814] in particularly startling experiments.

Crookes was knighted in 1897, and was president of the Royal Society from 1913 to 1915.

He was one of the occasional important scientists who grow interested in psychic research and spiritualism and was, every once in a while, overgullible in his approach to mediums.

[696] CLARK, Alvan Graham
American astronomer
Born: Fall River, Massachusetts,
July 10, 1832
Died: Cambridge, Massachusetts,
June 9, 1897

Clark was primarily a lens grinder and maker of astronomical instruments, in which profession his father had preceded him. On January 31, 1862, he was at his father's optical shop, testing a new 18-inch lens they had ground, and he pointed it at Sirius. Bessel's [439] observation that Sirius had a small wavy movement had led astronomers to assume that it had a massive dark companion. Clark, however, saw a tiny spot of light near Sirius, which on further study proved to be its companion and not dark at all. For this he received a medal from the French Academy of Sciences.

It was not until well after Clark's death that the most interesting aspect of the companion of Sirius was uncovered, for in 1914 W. S. Adams [1045] showed the companion to be a new kind of star of a nature that would not have seemed possible in Clark's generation.

The telescopes produced by Clark's firm were world famous. In 1859 Clark went to England to demonstrate his telescopes and they came to be used in Europe as well as in the United States. Hall [681] discovered the satellites of Mars through a Clark telescope and Barnard [883] discovered Jupiter's fifth satellite through another. In 1897 shortly before his death Clark crowned his lifework by supervising the construction of the 40-inch Yerkes telescope. This was and is the largest refracting telescope in existence. All larger telescopes built before or since have been reflectors, for large mirrors (used in reflectors) are easier to build and involve fewer mechanical difficulties than the large lenses used in refractors.

[697] WUNDT, Wilhelm Max (voont)
German psychologist
Born: Neckarau, Baden,
August 16, 1832
Died: Grossbathen, near Leipzig,
Saxony, August 31, 1920

Wundt, the son of a minister, having gained both a Ph.D. and an M.D. joined the faculty of the University of Heidelberg in 1854, and spent some time working with J. Müller [522] and Du Bois-Reymond [611].

He grew interested in psychology, which he interpreted in the light of the work of Ernst Weber [492] and Fechner [520].

It seemed to him that there were facets of human behavior that could be measured, in particular, the manner in which man absorbed sense impressions. The work of Helmholtz [631] on vision and hearing seemed an important case in point, and Wundt was enthusiastic enough to initiate, in 1862, the first university course ever given in experimental psychology.

In 1875 he transferred to the University of Leipzig, and there in 1879 he established the first laboratory to be devoted entirely to experimental psychology. He also founded, in 1881, the first journal to be devoted to the subject.

[698] **CAILLETET,** Louis Paul (ka-yuh-tay')
French physicist
Born: Chatillon-sur-Seine, Côte d'Or, September 21, 1832
Died: Paris, January 5, 1913

Cailletet was the son of a metallurgist and as a young man worked in his father's iron foundry. In 1870 he grew interested in the gas laws and made careful measurements to see just how the actual behavior of gases deviated from that predicted by those laws, a matter which Van der Waals [726] was to treat in detail. From that he grew interested in the liquefaction of gases.

He extended Andrews's [580] work and suggested that all gases had a critical temperature. To liquefy gases, he therefore made use of the Joule [613]-Thomson [652] effect. He began by compressing a gas and cooling it as much as he could. He then allowed it to expand, and in expanding, it would cool drastically. In 1877 Cailletet managed in this way to produce small quantities of liquid oxygen, nitrogen, and carbon monoxide. At the same time Pictet [783], working independently, achieved a similar success.

Cailletet was elected to the Academy of Sciences in 1884 and was made an officer in the Legion of Honor in 1889, as a result of his achievement.

The Cailletet-Pictet method is difficult to apply to hydrogen because the Joule-Thomson effect does not work for hydrogen except at temperatures below −83°C. Dewar [759] succeeded in liquefying hydrogen because he cooled his hydrogen gas with liquid nitrogen to reach a very low temperature first, and then began making use of the Joule-Thomson effect.

[699] **SACHS,** Julius von (zahks)
German botanist
Born: Breslau, Silesia (now Wrocław, Poland), October 2, 1832
Died: Würzburg, Bavaria, May 29, 1897

Sachs, the son of an engraver, was orphaned at seventeen and was left without money, but he managed to get an education and began his professional career as assistant to Purkinje [452]. Purkinje recognized his talent and befriended him. Sachs then obtained his Ph.D. at Prague in 1856, became a professor of botany at the University of Freiburg-im-Breisgau, and later established a laboratory at Würzburg.

He showed that plants, like animals, respond to their environment and documented plant tropisms (the manner in which their parts move in response to light, water, gravity, and so on). He also worked out the process of plant transpiration, whereby water travels from the roots, up the stem, and (in vapor form) out the leaves.

He was particularly interested in problems of plant nutrition and his most important discoveries in this connection involved the green pigment, chlorophyll, which had been discovered a generation earlier by Pelletier [454] and a coworker.

Because leaves and other plant parts appear uniformly green, it might seem that chlorophyll is evenly spread throughout the plant. Sachs showed that this was not so. In 1865 he published a comprehensive botanical treatise proving that chlorophyll was confined to certain discrete bodies within the cell, which later received the name of chloroplast. It is within the chloroplast that chlorophyll is formed and that starch grains first appear when the leaf is exposed to light.

This was the final broad brushstroke in the picture of plant nutrition. Helmont [175], Priestley [312], and Ingenhousz [306] had, among them, showed that green plants convert carbon dioxide and water into tissue components, liberating oxygen in the process. Now Sachs showed that the process is catalyzed by chlorophyll, within the chloroplasts, in the presence of light. He also showed that, in addition to this, plants respired as animals do, consuming oxygen and producing carbon dioxide, though it is the reverse photosynthetic effect that predominates.

The working out of the details of the

process had to wait, however, nearly a century for the work with radioisotopes by Calvin [1361] and others.

[700] **NORDENSKIÖLD,** Nils Adolf Erik (noor'den-shuld')
Swedish geologist
Born: Helsinki, Finland, November 18, 1832
Died: Dalbyö, Sweden, August 12, 1901

Nordenskiöld was of an aristocratic Swedish family although he was born in Finland, which had once been part of Sweden but which at the time of his birth was part of Russia. He was educated at the University of Helsinki, but his liberal views got him in trouble with the Russian authorities and in 1858 he left for Sweden, which remained his home thereafter.

He is most famous for his polar explorations and, in particular, for a voyage he made in 1878–1879, on the *Vega*, during the course of which he made his way along the Arctic coast of Siberia from Norway to Alaska (albeit he was icebound for months at a time) then returned to Europe by way of the Pacific Ocean, the Indian Ocean, and the Suez Canal. He was the first person to navigate the so-called Northeast Passage and the first person to circumnavigate Asia.

Nordenskiöld was the first to conduct polar exploration with strict attention to the gathering of scientific data. He published five volumes of material on every aspect of the polar regions of the earth as a result of his *Vega* voyage.

[701] **WAAGE,** Peter (voh'guh)
Norwegian chemist
Born: Flekkefjord, June 29, 1833
Died: Oslo, January 13, 1900

Waage, the son of a ship's captain, was educated at the University of Christiania (Oslo) and became a professor of chemistry there in 1862.

Waage is known entirely because of his association with Guldberg [721], his

brother-in-law, in formulating the law of mass action.

Outside science, he was deeply involved in the temperance movement.

[702] **BERT,** Paul (bair)
French physiologist
Born: Auxerre, Yonne, October 17, 1833
Died: Hanoi, Indochina (now Vietnam), November 11, 1886

Bert, the son of a lawyer, was a student of Bernard [578] in 1868. He had a wide range of interests and although he is chiefly known for his work in physiology, obtaining his M.D. in Paris in 1863, he was also educated in law and engineering and was involved in politics as well.

He became professor of physiology at the University of Bordeaux in 1866, and in 1869 he joined the physiology department at the Sorbonne. In those years men were beginning to dig deep to tunnel under rivers or to lay the foundations for bridges. To do so they had to use compressed air to keep out the water and many workers came down with the agonizing and sometimes fatal condition known as bends. Bert, studying the effect of compressed air on the body, realized that nitrogen under pressure dissolved in tissue fluids more easily and that when the high pressure of the compressed air was released too rapidly as the workers came up to sea level, the nitrogen bubbled out into the blood and tissues. This was the cause of bends, and to prevent it, it was only necessary to lower the air pressure by slow stages. Bert published his views in 1878 and work with compressed air became safe.

Bert served as an ultraliberal member of the French Chamber of Deputies from 1874 to 1886 and in 1881–1882 was a member of the cabinet as minister of public instruction. He fought for free public education and for the separation of church and state.

In 1886, he was appointed governor-general of Indochina and went to his death, for dysentery killed him a few months after his arrival there.

Bert's pioneering work on gas pressure and respiration laid the foundation for a whole branch of medicine involving the effect not of thick air, so much, as of thin air. Bert's studies and Teisserenc de Bort's [861] stratosphere combined, by the 1940s, to produce the study of aviation medicine. Bert's book was translated into English and reprinted in 1943 because of its continuing usefulness in this respect.

[703] **NOBEL,** Alfred Bernhard (noh-bel')
Swedish inventor
Born: Stockholm, October 21, 1833
Died: San Remo, Italy, December 10, 1896

Nobel came by his inventiveness naturally, for his father was a noted (self-educated) inventor. It was an invention of his father, a submarine mine, that brought the family to St. Petersburg, Russia, in 1842, for the Russian government had bought the mine and hired the elder Nobel to supervise its manufacture. Nobel (who, on his mother's side, was a descendant of Rudbeck [218]) therefore grew up in Russia and was educated by private tutors. In 1850 he was sent to the United States, where he spent four years studying under Ericsson [533].

When young Nobel returned to Russia he found his father engaged in a new project, the manufacture of explosives, for Russia was now engaged in the Crimean War against Great Britain and France. There was particular interest in nitroglycerine, which had been discovered a decade earlier by Sobrero [574]. Nobel's stay in the United States had given him the vision of a continent about to be tamed and he could see how roads could be blasted out of mountains, canals dug, foundations laid, by using the directed violence of a shattering explosive such as nitroglycerine instead of the weary muscles of countless human beings. (The vision of peaceful uses for explosives is by no means empty idealism. In the hands of Chardonnet [743] and Hyatt [728], a modified form of

Schönbein's [510] deadly guncotton served to initiate the manufacture of artificial fibers and of plastics.)

The end of the Crimean War led to a decline in the family fortunes. Nobel returned to Sweden in 1859 and began to manufacture nitroglycerine, which proved just as useful as Nobel had expected it to be, but there was no way to make people treat it with the proper respect, and there were numerous accidents. His own factory blew up in 1864, killing his brother. The Swedish government refused to allow the factory to be rebuilt and Nobel came to be looked upon as a mad scientist viciously manufacturing destruction.

Nobel set grimly to work to discover a method of taming nitroglycerine, experimenting on a barge in the middle of a lake to keep danger to a minimum. In 1866 he came across a cask of nitroglycerine that had leaked. The liquid had, however, been absorbed by the packing, which consisted of diatomaceous earth, or "kieselguhr" (made up of the siliceous skeletons of myriads of microscopic diatoms). The earth seemed to remain perfectly dry.

He experimented with the nitroglycerine/diatomaceous earth combination and found that the nitroglycerine could not be set off without a detonating cap. Short of that the mixture could be handled virtually with impunity. Furthermore, once it was set off, the nitroglycerine retained all its shattering power. Nobel called the combination "dynamite" and sticks of dynamite replaced the dangerous free nitroglycerine as a blasting compound.

Nobel also invented blasting gelatin, becoming wealthy in explosives and in the operation of the Baku oil wells in Russia. Dynamite did indeed open the American West, and explosives generally had and still have myriad peacetime uses. However, they remained the backbone of modern war down to the coming of nuclear weapons, and it was as the inventor of horrible tools of war that the humane and idealistic Nobel was seen in the eyes of the world. He was a bachelor, moody, lonely, and unpopular, and people could not be made to realize that the inventor and producer of dynamite actually thought that his explosives would outlaw war by making it too horrible.

At his death Nobel left his entire estate, a fund of $9,200,000, for the establishment of annual prizes (the Nobel Prizes) in five fields: Peace, Literature, Physics, Chemistry, and Physiology and Medicine. (A sixth award, in economics, was begun in 1969, but it is separately funded.) They have become the supreme honor that can be won for achievements in these respective fields, and although they carry a cash award of about $100,000, the money is not to be compared with the honor conferred. The awards were established only after some delay. Nobel had drawn up the will himself and there were numerous loopholes that led to a five-year legal fight. Eventually Nobel's desires won out and the prizes came to be awarded just as the Second Scientific Revolution got under way. The first to be honored with a Nobel Prize in physics was Roentgen [774], whose discovery of X rays began that revolution.

The Nobel Institute in Sweden is named for him; and because element 102 was first isolated there in 1958, it was named nobelium.

[704] WEISMANN, August Friedrich Leopold (vise'mahn)
German biologist
Born: Frankfurt-am-Main, January 17, 1834
Died: Freiburg-im-Breisgau, Baden, November 5, 1914

Weismann, the son of a classics professor, studied medicine and got his degree at Göttingen in 1856. After serving as a surgeon in the Austrian army, during the Austro-Italian War of 1859, he became interested in zoology (Leuckart [640] was one of his teachers) and was appointed professor of zoology at the University of Freiburg-im-Breisgau in 1863. Eye trouble, developing in middle life, made the use of the microscope impossible for him. This forced him to retreat into theory, which in the larger

view served him well for it was in theory that he made his name.

In the 1870s and 1880s he worked out his own notions of evolution. It seemed to him that life itself was continuous and immortal. This was clear in microorganisms that simply divided and divided and divided, without ever growing old and dying (though myriads were killed and eaten, of course). This seemed, however, true of multicellular life as well. Each organism could be traced back to an egg (and sperm) that was a living part of a living organism that could itself be traced back to an egg (and a sperm) and so on for as far back as life existed. At no point, except perhaps at the very beginning, was there a break and the actual start of a new life from nonlife. This is the "continuity of the germ plasm."

This germ plasm, forming the eggs and sperm, can be viewed as the real essence of life. It can then be pictured as periodically growing an organism about itself, almost as a form of self-protection, and also as a device to help produce another egg or sperm out of a piece of the germ plasm carefully preserved within the organism. (Samuel Butler, a contemporary English writer, who attacked Darwin's [554] theories with mystical notions of his own, put this succinctly: "A hen is only an egg's way of producing another egg.")

The organism might itself die, but it is just as evanescent and as inessential to the real life as a flower or a fruit is to a tree. The buffetings of the environment can affect only the nonessential and temporary organism and can have no effect on the permanent and well-protected germ plasm within. Since only the germ plasm is responsible for inheritance, the notions of Lamarck [336] concerning the inheritance of acquired characteristics are false, it seemed to Weismann. This brought him into strenuous conflict with men such as Spencer [624] who depended on a form of Lamarckism for their own sociological theories. Weismann tried to prove his own contention by bringing about a persistent environmental change and showing it was not inherited. He cut the tails off 1,592 mice over twenty-two generations and showed that all continued to bear young with full-sized tails.

Weismann went on to make some suggestions that the next few decades were to prove true. He suggested chromosomes contained the hereditary machinery and that their careful division during cell fission must maintain the machinery intact. This fit well with the observations of Flemming [762]. Weismann further suggested that the quantity of germ plasm was halved in forming egg and sperm and that the process of fertilization restored the original quantity. The new organism had the correct amount of germ plasm, half from the mother and half from the father. The rediscovery of Mendel [638] by De Vries [792] a couple of decades later established Weismann's concept firmly.

Weismann's theories, in attacking the views of Lamarck, seemed to uphold those of Darwin, and indeed Darwin wrote a preface for one of Weismann's books. However, the theory of the continuity of the germ plasm did not resolve the great flaw of Darwinism, which was that the facts of variation among individuals and from generation to generation were not adequately explained. In fact, Weismann's well-protected germ plasm seemed to have no room for variation at all. It went on from generation to generation, perfect and unchanging. If accepted literally, Weismann's theory froze evolution on the spot and left it a mystery how any evolutionary change could ever have come to be.

It was only the theory of mutations of De Vries that unfroze evolution once more. And the time came when Muller [1145] was to show that the germ plasm was not as completely isolated as Weismann had believed. The buffeting of the environment could affect the germ plasm after all, though not predictably, and not by any means as unsubtle as stretching a neck or cutting off a tail.

Weismann was a zealous nationalist and when World War I started, three months before his death, he renounced all his British honors and awards.

[705] **MENDELÉEV**, Dmitri Ivanovich (men-deh-lay'ef)
Russian chemist
Born: Tobol'sk, Siberia, February 7, 1834
Died: St. Petersburg (now Leningrad), February 2, 1907

Mendeléev came of a large family in which there were fourteen to seventeen children, the records not being exactly clear. Dmitri was the youngest, the baby of the lot. He probably had some Asian ancestry, for his mother is supposed to have been part Mongol.

Mendeléev's grandfather had brought the first printing press to Siberia and published the first newspaper. His father was principal of the local high school. Blindness ended his father's career while Mendeléev was still very young. The disability pension his father received wasn't enough to support the large family, so his mother set up a glass factory and with incredible energy and determination managed to make ends meet. Meanwhile, from a political prisoner who had been sent out to Siberia, the young Mendeléev received his first lessons in science.

In 1849, with Mendeléev just finishing high school (where he was but an indifferent student), his father died and his mother's factory burned down. There was no further reason to stay in Siberia. With almost all her children settled into independent life, Mendeléev's mother decided to devote her remaining energies to getting her youngest an education. She set out for Moscow with him and there met failure. She was unable to get him into college.

She went on to St. Petersburg where a friend of her dead husband was able to use his influence to get the young Mendeléev into college. She died soon after.

Mendeléev finished college in 1855 at the top of his class, then went to France and Germany for graduate training. He worked with Bunsen [565] and independently developed the concept of critical temperature for which Andrews [580] usually gets credit. He attended the great Karlsruhe Congress, where he heard Cannizzaro [668] express his views on atomic weight and was profoundly impressed. He also studied under Regnault [561].

He returned to St. Petersburg and in 1866 became a professor of chemistry at the university. He was the most capable and interesting lecturer in Russia and one of the best in all Europe. It was through him that it finally became possible to attain graduate training in chemistry inside Russia. Between 1868 and 1870 he wrote a chemistry textbook called *The Principles of Chemistry* that was probably the best chemistry book ever written in Russian and certainly one of the most unusual anywhere. It had numerous footnotes that took up almost as much space as the book itself.

With Cannizzaro's dictum concerning atomic weights firm in his mind, Mendeléev, like Newlands [727] and Beguyer de Chancourtois [622] before him, began to arrange the elements in the order of atomic weights. At once he found an interesting thing in connection with the property of valence, the concept of which had been worked out some fifteen years earlier by Frankland [655]. The second element in Mendeléev's list was lithium. It had a valence of 1; that is, an atom of lithium would combine with only one other atom. The next element on the list was beryllium; it had a valence of 2; its atoms would combine with as many as two different atoms. Next was boron, with a valence of 3; then carbon with a valence of 4. In fact, the order went 1, 2, 3, 4, 3, 2, 1.

Mendeléev could arrange all the elements known in his time (sixty-three of them) in order of atomic weights and get periodic rises and falls of valence. He could also arrange them in rows, one under the other, so that elements with similar valence would all fall into a vertical column. These elements would also show similarities in many other chemical properties.

Because of the periodic rises and falls of valence, and the equally periodic repetitions of properties in the various rows, such a table was (and still is) called a periodic table.

Mendeléev's table differed from New-lands's in that Newlands tried to force all the elements into equal segments containing seven elements each, whereas Mendeléev recognized that the later periods were considerably longer than the first two. The first two periods did contain seven elements each by Mendeléev's accounting, but the next two contained seventeen each. This fact was also recognized at the same time by Lothar Meyer [685], but Mendeléev published first.

Mendeléev published his first table on March 6, 1869, and for the first time in the history of science a Russian scientist obtained a hearing at once. Ordinarily, as in the case of Lomonosov [282] and Lobachevski [484], Russian thoughts remained buried in the Russian language for a number of years before scientists at the centers of learning in western Europe learned of them. In Mendeléev's case, his paper was translated into German at once and thus was made available to all scholars.

Nevertheless, Mendeléev did not meet with sudden acclamation. The general skepticism that greeted previous attempts in the 1860s to make order out of the chaos of the elements still prevailed. But Mendeléev pushed on, improving and refining his table, not hesitating to put a couple of elements out of what was supposedly the true order of their atomic weight, where that was necessary to put them into the proper columns. (Four decades later this was justified by the work of Moseley [1121].)

Furthermore, in the January 7, 1871, issue of the *Journal of the Russian Chemical Society*, he advanced the crucial notion for which he truly deserves all the credit he gets for the discovery of the periodic table, to the exclusion of his contemporaries and predecessors who also contributed to it. He left gaps in the table in order to make the elements fit into proper columns, and announced that the gaps represented elements not yet discovered. Choosing three gaps in particular, he described the properties the missing elements ought to have, judging by the properties of the elements above and below the gap in the table.

This prediction also was met with considerable skepticism. To Western scientists it may have sounded like typical Russian mysticism. However, in 1875 Lecoq de Boisbaudran [736] discovered an element that matched, to the last property, Mendeléev's prediction for one of the gaps. In 1879 Nilson [747] and Cleve [746] produced another. This one matched another of Mendeléev's elements. And in 1885 Winkler [739] produced still another and this matched the third.

Mendeléev and his periodic table were vindicated in the most dramatic manner possible. Order had been brought into the list of elements and this order was to guide chemists a half century later as they worked out the internal structure of the atoms.

Mendeléev was suddenly the most famous chemist in the world. The Royal Society awarded him the Davy medal in 1882 and other honors were showered upon him. Even the backward Russian government could not help but be proud of its Siberian son. He was sent on a mission to the United States, where he studied the oilfields of Pennsylvania in order to better advise the Russians concerning the development of the Caucasian oilfields. In 1905 his textbook, which he kept carefully up-to-date, was translated into English. His eminence allowed him unusual freedom. In 1876, he divorced his wife and married a young art student. By Russian Othodox doctrine, he had committed bigamy, but he was Mendeléev and the matter was not pursued.

In the tradition of Gay-Lussac [420], Mendeléev went up in a balloon in 1887 to photograph a solar eclipse. Since the balloon would only carry one man, he went alone—and returned safely, though he knew nothing about handling it. A picture taken of him in the gondola shows him standing with regal dignity. His long hair and beard give him the appearance of a biblical patriarch.

Mendeléev was a decided liberal in his views and never feared speaking against the Russian government's oppression of students even though he was scolded more than once and missed election to the Imperial Academy of Sciences as a result, losing out to Beilstein [732]. In 1890 he finally resigned his academic post in protest over the oppression of students. His sympathy for the common people led him to travel third-class on trains in order to be with them. (Maxwell [692] had this same habit.) But he was a patriot who worked diligently for the Russian war effort during the Japanese war in 1904. The war was disastrous for the corrupt Tsarist government, but Mendeléev died a decade before that government finally fell victim to its own blind incapacity to meet the emergency of war. In 1906, just a few months before his death, he almost received the Nobel Prize in chemistry; Moissan [831] was chosen by one vote.

In 1955 a newly discovered element (number 101) was named mendelevium, in belated recognition of his importance to the study of the elements.

[706] **CARO,** Heinrich (kah'roh)
German chemist
Born: Posen (now Poznán, Poland), February 13, 1834
Died: Dresden, October 11, 1910

Caro was the son of a prosperous Jewish grain dealer who moved with his family to Berlin in 1842. He was trained to be a dyer, but he attended lectures on chemistry at the University of Berlin. He was working as a dyer when, in 1857, he was sent to England to learn about the new synthetic dyes that Perkin [734] had developed.

He learned quickly, improved Perkin's synthesis, learned enough to become a thoroughgoing chemist, and returned to Germany in 1866 to work for Bunsen [565]. In 1868 he became director of a chemical firm in Ludwigshafen, which was the prototype of the industrial research organizations that were soon to grow up.

Caro, more than any other single person, was responsible for the vast growth of the dye industry in Germany and for Germany's domination of industrial chemistry for forty years.

[707] **HAECKEL,** Ernst Heinrich
Philipp August (hek'ul)
German naturalist
Born: Potsdam, Prussia,
February 16, 1834
Died: Jena, Thuringia,
August 8, 1919

Haeckel, the son of a government
official, obtained a medical degree in
1857 at the University of Berlin at his
parents' insistence although it was botany that was his passion. He studied
under such men as J. P. Müller [522],
Virchow [632], Kölliker [600], and Gegenbaur [669]. He practiced medicine
for only a year, however, and in 1862
became a professor of comparative anatomy at the zoological institute at Jena.
Haeckel was the first German biologist
to take up the cudgels for Darwinism
(he met Darwin [554] in 1866), and he
went all the way, being actually a little
ahead of Darwin in expounding on the
possibility of sexual selection.

Unfortunately, there remained a trace
of the "nature philosopher" in Haeckel,
and his theories outran his facts in consequence. He took up Baer's [478] observations that early embryos of various
vertebrates resembled each other and
carried this to the extreme of supposing
that each creature recapitulated the
stages of its evolution in its developing
embryo. "Ontogeny recapitulates phylog-
eny" is the phrase he popularized.

There is some truth to this but the re-
capitulation simply cannot be trusted in
too great detail and the best proof is that
Haeckel used his principle to work up
lines of evolutionary descent for various
creatures and these lines are now known
to be far wide of the mark.

Haeckel's extreme views are not entirely indefensible, however. He believed
that life derived evolutionarily from nonlife and that psychology was but a
branch of physiology, so that mind, too,
fitted into the scheme of evolution.
There are many biologists now who
would be willing to argue in favor of
both notions.

Haeckel was the first to use the term
"ecology" to refer to the study of living

organisms in relation to one another and
to the inanimate environment.

[708] **DAIMLER,** Gottlieb Wilhelm
(dime'ler)
German inventor
Born: Schorndorf, Württemberg,
March 17, 1834
Died: Kannstatt, Württemberg,
March 6, 1900

Daimler received a technical education
in Stuttgart, the capital of then independent Württemberg. In the decade of the
1870s (with Württemberg now part of
the newly formed German Empire and
sharing in the explosive development
that followed this political and military
birth) Daimler worked as an assistant to
Otto [694], the inventor who had developed the four-cycle internal combustion
engine.

In 1883 Daimler left Otto and began
to design engines for himself. He was the
first to construct a high-speed engine,
making it lighter and more efficient than
ever before and adapting it for the use
of gasoline vapors as fuel. He fitted such
an engine to a boat in his first attempt to
make practical use of it, in 1883.

It was Daimler's high-speed internal
combustion machine that made the
horseless carriage practical, with the
energy of burning gasoline taking the
place of the horse. Though it is difficult
to select one man as the inventor of the
automobile, since many scientists of the
last three decades of the nineteenth
century were working on it and contributed, certainly Daimler's name is among
those in the forefront.

In 1885 he installed one of his
modified engines on a bicycle (adding a
pair of small guide wheels to prevent tipping over) and drove it over the cobbled
roads of Mannheim, Baden. That was
certainly the world's first motorcycle. In
1887 he was able to power a four-
wheeled vehicle and thus had one of the
first true automobiles.

In 1890 he founded the Daimler
motor company, which produced the
first Mercedes automobile (named for

the daughter of the financier backing him) in 1899. The stage was set for Henry Ford [929], who by applying engineering principles to human beings was to make the automobile not only practical but overwhelmingly popular.

[709] PLANTÉ, Gaston (plan-tay')
French physicist
Born: Orthez, Basses-Pyrénées, April 22, 1834
Died: Paris, May 21, 1889

Planté, in 1854, was a lecturer in physics in a Parisian school and achieved professional rank in 1860. By then, he had already accomplished his great advance in the field of electric batteries.

The chemical batteries constructed during the first half century after Volta's [337] invention of such devices were one-shots. Planté's contribution to technology was the construction of the first battery that could be recharged after discharge and, therefore, could be used over and over again.

This "storage battery," first constructed in 1859, was based on lead plates immersed in sulfuric acid and is, in essence, the same battery used in automobiles and trucks today.

[710] VENN, John
English mathematician and logician
Born: Hull, Yorkshire, August 4, 1834
Died: Cambridge, April 4, 1923

Venn was descended from a family much involved with the church. He himself graduated from Cambridge with a degree in mathematics in 1857 and then took holy orders in 1858. He resigned as cleric in 1883, being out of sympathy with Anglican orthodoxy, but he remained devoutly religious.

The work of De Morgan [549] and Boole [595] inspired him to write works on logic and probability. He is best known for his use of overlapping Venn circles to represent sets, suitably shaded if empty. They are particularly graphic

ways of expressing simple logical statements and are easily used to introduce youngsters to logic.

[711] LANGLEY, Samuel Pierpont
American astronomer
Born: Roxbury, Massachusetts, August 22, 1834
Died: Aiken, South Carolina, February 22, 1906

Although he never went to college, and although he worked as a civil engineer and architect to begin with, Langley, the son of a merchant, was competent enough in astronomy to become an assistant in astronomy at Harvard University in 1865 and eventually to receive professorial appointments in the subject at various schools.

In 1881 he invented a bolometer, an instrument for accurately measuring tiny quantities of heat (amounting to differences of a hundred thousandth of a degree) by way of the size of the minute electric currents set up by that heat in a blackened platinum wire. He used the instrument to make careful measurements of the quantity of solar radiation, both in the visible and in the infrared portion of the spectrum, during an expedition to Mount Whitney, California. In the process, he extended knowledge of the solar spectrum into the far infrared for the first time. A unit of radiation equal to 1 calorie per square centimeter is called 1 langley in his honor.

In 1887 he was appointed secretary of the Smithsonian Institution and thereafter experienced the heartbreak of his near misses in the invention of the airplane (as Fitch [330] missed the steamboat and Trevithick [399] the locomotive). Langley carefully worked out aerodynamic principles, showing how birds soared without appreciable wing movements and how air would support thin wings of particular shapes. (His theories were disputed, however, by no less a person than Kelvin [652] who, in this instance, was in the wrong.)

Langley's work was good, and in 1896 he constructed an unmanned heavier-than-air device that actually flew. The trick was, though, to have it bear the weight of a human being while flying. In principle, it could be done, but in actual practice the failure of the strength of the structural materials he used or of his engines kept his planes from making successful flights. Encouraged by President William McKinley, Langley spent $50,000 of the government's money (granted because the Spanish-American War stimulated interest in the possible military applications of heavier-than-air flight) between 1897 and 1903 on three trials and could get no more. After the last failure, the New York *Times* published a severe editorial castigating what they considered Langley's foolish waste of public funds on an idle dream. They predicted that man would not fly for a thousand years. Nine days after the editorial, the thousand years were suddenly up and Orville and Wilbur Wright [995, 961], following in the footsteps of Lilienthal [793], made the first successful airplane flight.

In 1908 the Smithsonian Institution established the Langley medal for achievements in aeronautics and the first award went to the Wright brothers. In 1914 Langley's last plane was fitted with a more powerful engine and was successfully flown, but Langley was eight years dead by then. Langley Field, Virginia, and the Langley Research Center of NASA are named in his honor.

[712] **YOUNG,** Charles Augustus
American astronomer
Born: Hanover, New Hampshire, December 15, 1834
Died: Hanover, January 3, 1908

Young's father and maternal grandfather were professors of science at Dartmouth College. Young himself entered Dartmouth at fourteen and graduated in 1853 at the top of his class. He then taught at Phillips Academy in Andover, Massachusetts, and in 1856 took a professorial position at Western Reserve College in Hudson, Ohio (now Case Western Reserve University in Cleveland, Ohio). He served briefly in the Civil War but did not see action. Then in

1866, he took the professorship at Dartmouth that his father and grandfather had held.

He was particularly interested in solar spectroscopy. He was a careful observer of solar eclipses in 1869 and 1870 and was the first to note that the dark lines in the spectrum momentarily gleamed brightly at the moment of totality. He thus discovered the "reversing layer" of the sun. He was also the first to photograph the spectrum of the sun's corona.

Young wrote some of the most popular and useful general astronomy textbooks of the period, and all later American texts of astronomy were more or less indebted to his.

[713] **NEWCOMB,** Simon
Canadian-American astronomer
Born: Wallace, Nova Scotia, March 12, 1835
Died: Washington, D.C., July 11, 1909

Newcomb, the son of a country schoolteacher, was rather an infant prodigy but had little formal education as a youth. He was apprenticed, at the age of sixteen, to a herb doctor of dubious reputation, but ran away to join his father in the United States in 1853. There, he educated himself, taught school, and finally graduated from Harvard University in 1858. He joined the navy, was appointed professor of mathematics in 1861 at the Naval Observatory, and eventually rose to the rank of rear admiral. In 1884 he was appointed professor of mathematics and astronomy at Johns Hopkins.

In 1860 he made his first mark in astronomy with a paper powerfully attacking the hypothesis that the bodies of the asteroid zone arose through the breakup of a planet once circling in an orbit between those of Mars and Jupiter, as Olbers [372] had maintained a half century earlier.

For most of his professional career Newcomb, strong in mathematics, engaged in a gigantic task of producing new tables for the motions of the moon and the planets. He improved on Leverrier [564] and all preceding tabulations. He completed this task in 1899. He also worked with Michelson [835] in determining the velocity of light.

Newcomb was a well-known popular writer on astronomy, as well as other subjects. About the turn of the century he wrote a number of articles maintaining with considerable vehemence that the hope of heavier-than-air machines was a vain and foolish one. This view seemed to be supported by the failures of Langley [711]. His arguments were weakened but not stopped by the successful plane flights of Wilbur and Orville Wright [961, 995]. Newcomb did not live to see the airplane come into its own during World War I.

After his death he was buried with military honors in Arlington National Cemetery. In 1935 Newcomb was elected to a niche in the Hall of Fame for Great Americans.

[714] **SCHIAPARELLI,** Giovanni Virginio (skyah-pah-rel'lee)
Italian astronomer
Born: Savigliano, Piedmont, March 14, 1835
Died: Milan, July 4, 1910

After graduating from Turin University in 1854 Schiaparelli studied under Encke [475] in Germany and Struve [483] in Russia. On returning to Italy he joined the staff of the Brera Observatory in Milan, becoming its director in 1860. He held that post till his retirement in 1900.

Schiaparelli was mainly interested in the solar system. In the 1860s he investigated comets and, along with J. C. Adams [615], demonstrated their connection with meteor swarms and in 1861 he discovered the asteroid Hesperia.

This was dramatic enough but in the next decade Schiaparelli inadvertently started something that has never quite lost its hold on the general public. In 1877 Mars and the earth reached those points of their respective orbits that are closest together. At such "favorable oppositions," which take place every thirty years or so, the distance between the two planets is only 35,000,000 miles. In 1877, then, telescopes naturally turned on Mars in an attempt to improve still further Proctor's [724] map of its surface. Schiaparelli also removed one possible source of controversy by removing the names of astronomers with which Proctor had labeled the Martian face and using more objective names instead, which we still use today.

Schiaparelli studied the red planet attentively, making delicate measurements with a micrometer and carefully mapping what he saw. In this opposition Asaph Hall [681] discovered the two small moons of Mars, but Schiaparelli did better. He continued his studies at succeeding (less favorable) oppositions and by 1881 was certain that the features he observed included straight lines that joined in a complicated pattern.

He called these lines *canali,* which means "channels." However, the Italian word was mistranslated into the English word "canals." That, combined with the suspicious straightness of the lines, bespoke artificial structures, and this created a furor. Most astronomers couldn't see the canals, but Schiaparelli stuck to his guns.

He also observed vague streaks on Mercury in the 1880s but these were not thin, straight lines and therefore caused no sensation. He maintained, in 1890, through observations of these streaks, that Mercury always kept one face to the sun. His feat was made possible by the fact that he managed to observe Mercury during the day when it was high in the sky. In 1966, however, he was shown to have misinterpreted his observations. Mercury does not have a "day" as long as its year (which would be required if one face was always to be toward the sun) but one that is only two thirds as long as its year.

But it was Mars really that made the big splash, thanks to the "canals." Speculations concerning the possibility of intelligent life on Mars sprang up in the popular press. Even astronomers felt the pull of that dramatic possibility. Among the latter were Flammarion [756] and the greatest "Martian" of them all, Percival Lowell [860], who carried matters far beyond Schiaparelli.

After his retirement, brought on by deepening blindness, Schiaparelli removed himself from controversy and quietly produced excellent studies in the early history of astronomy, in Babylonia particularly.

[715] **STEFAN,** Josef (shteh'fahn)
Austrian physicist
Born: St. Peter, near Klagenfurt, Carinthia, March 24, 1835
Died: Vienna, January 7, 1893

Stefan, the son of Slovenian shopkeepers, gained his Ph.D. at the University of Vienna in 1858 and joined its faculty with professorial status in 1863. He was director of the Physical Institute in 1866.

He was interested in the rate of cooling of hot bodies. Prévost [356] had made the first qualitative observations a century before, but Stefan carefully observed hot bodies over a wide range of temperature and was able to place matters in quantitative terms. He stated in 1879 that the total radiation of a hot body was proportional to the fourth power of its absolute temperature. If the temperature was doubled, the rate of radiation increased sixteenfold. This is Stefan's fourth-power law and has proved of great importance in the study of stellar evolution.

In 1884 Boltzmann [769] showed that this law could be deduced from thermodynamic principles, so it is sometimes called the Stefan-Boltzmann law.

[716] **WISLICENUS,** Johannes (vis-lih-tsay'noos)
German chemist
Born: Klein-Eichsted, Thuringia, June 24, 1835
Died: Leipzig, Saxony, December 5, 1902

Wislicenus' father was a liberal-minded minister who was ordered arrested in 1853 for his unorthodox Bible studies. The family fled to the United States where Wislicenus attended classes at Harvard University. He returned to Germany in 1856.

Wislicenus completed his studies at the University of Halle and was professor of chemistry at schools both in Germany and in Switzerland.

He was interested in isomers; that is, in pairs of molecules made up of the same atoms in different arrangements and, therefore, possessing different properties. In some cases, the properties were widely different and it was possible to deduce noticeably different arrangements with little trouble. Wislicenus called this geometric isomerism.

In 1863, however, Wislicenus discovered two forms of lactic acid (the acid in sour milk), which differed only in the rather subtle way in which they behaved with respect to polarized light. He decided there must be some subtle difference in their formulas, one that could not be displayed in the ordinary method then used to write formulas.

When, in 1874, Van't Hoff [829] proposed a method for arranging the atoms of organic molecules in three dimensions, Wislicenus saw at once this applied perfectly to substances such as the lactic acid pair. He lent his influence to the theory and thus drew down on his head the scorn of the old and conservative Kolbe [610] on this account. It was Wislicenus who was right, just the same.

[717] **RINGER,** Sydney
English physician
Born: Norwich, Norfolk, 1835
Died: Lastingham, Yorkshire, October 14, 1910

Ringer obtained his M.D. at University College, London, in 1863. He then remained in University College Hospital for the whole of his professional life.

Ringer, an excellent teacher, was particularly interested in the chemical influences on the heartbeat. A heart, while the cells were alive could continue beating even when removed from the body, and Ringer discovered that small amounts of other ions added to the sodium chloride of a salt solution would keep the heart beating for longer. He found that small amounts of potassium and calcium ions in the solution would keep not only hearts, but other isolated organs, functioning for a long time.

As a result, Ringer's solution came to be much in demand in physiological laboratories, and the study of the inorganic content of body fluids was greatly accelerated.

[718] **BAEYER,** Johann Friedrich Wilhelm Adolf von (bay'er)
German chemist
Born: Berlin, October 31, 1835
Died: Starnberg, Bavaria, August 20, 1917

Baeyer was the son of a Prussian general and a Jewish mother who had been converted to Christianity. Baeyer's father was interested in science, had worked for Bessel [439] and had become chief of the Berlin Geodetical Institute in 1870. Young Baeyer, meanwhile, had studied chemistry at Heidelberg under Bunsen [565] and Kekulé [680] and had obtained his Ph.D. in 1858.

In 1863 he discovered barbituric acid, parent compound of well-known "sleeping pills" of today. He is supposed to have named it for a girl friend (Barbara) of the moment. The chemistry of the barbiturate compounds was worked out in further detail a generation later by Emil Fischer [833]. When Hofmann [604] returned to Germany in 1864, Baeyer competed with him in dye research. His student Graebe [752] synthesized alizarin and he himself synthesized indigo. The latter feat led to the synthesis of the dye (very similar to indigo in chemical structure) that the men of Tyre had once manufactured for the use of royalty.

In 1872 he became professor of chemistry at the University of Strasbourg and

472

in 1875 he was called to the University of Munich to succeed Liebig [532], who was now dead. Baeyer then established a laboratory that was to become as famous as Liebig's had been. Working with no less a person than Perkin's [734] son, Baeyer devised new methods for forming small rings of carbon atoms and worked out a theory of such rings that is still called Baeyer's strain theory. This helped explain why rings of five atoms or six atoms were so much more common than those of fewer than five or more than six.

In 1905 Baeyer was awarded the Nobel Prize in chemistry, in recognition of his work in synthetic organic chemistry, which did much to establish Kekulé's structural theories, and, particularly, for his synthesis of indigo.

[719] **LOCKYER,** Sir Joseph Norman
English astronomer
Born: Rugby, Warwickshire, May 17, 1836
Died: Salcombe Regis, Devonshire, August 16, 1920

Lockyer, the son of a surgeon-apothecary, began his career in 1857 as a clerk in the War Office. Astronomy, however, became his hobby after he had met an amateur astronomer and found himself fascinated by what the other had to say. Lockyer obtained a telescope and eventually astronomy became his profession.

He was particularly interested in the sun and in the 1860s pioneered (simultaneously with Huggins [646] and Young [712] but independently of them) in the study of solar spectra. He was the first to study the spectra of sunspots, something he initiated in 1866.

He was also interested in prominences, huge gouts of flaming gas hurled out of the sun's outer layer (which Lockyer named the chromosphere). Ordinarily they were only visible during an eclipse, when the blazing light of the solar disc was obscured and the prominences glowed red beyond the obscuring edge of the moon. In 1868 Lockyer demonstrated that the spectra of the prominences could be observed and studied even without an eclipse by leading light from the very edge of the sun through a prism.

This discovery was announced on the same day by the French astronomer Janssen [647], who was in India observing a total eclipse. As a result, the French government some ten years later struck a medallion showing the heads of both scientists.

By that time, the two men had made a much more dramatic discovery at the same time, this time in cooperation. Janssen, studying the spectrum of the sun during the eclipse, had noted a line he did not recognize. He sent a report on this to Lockyer, an acknowledged expert on solar spectra. Lockyer compared the reported position of the line with lines of known elements, concluding that it must belong to a yet unknown element, possibly not even existing on earth. Frankland [655] agreed with him on this point. Lockyer named the element helium, from the Greek word for the sun.

Lockyer's conclusion was dismissed by other chemists, however, as was not unreasonable, for spectroscopy was new and it still seemed risky to hang a new element in the heavens on a foundation no more substantial than a colored line revealed by a spectroscope. In fact since Lockyer's report, many strange lines have been discovered in the light of heavenly objects and some have been attributed to new elements named coronium, geocoronium, nebulium, and so on. All of these have turned out to be just old elements under unusual conditions. All, that is, but one. The one exception was helium.

Nearly forty years after Lockyer announced the existence of helium in the sun, it was discovered on earth by Ramsay [832]. Lockyer lived long enough to see himself vindicated.

Lockyer, in studying spectra, announced in 1881 that certain lines produced in the laboratory became broader when an element was strongly heated. He believed that at very high tempera-

tures, atoms broke down to still simpler substances and that this accounted for the change in the lines. He was one of the first, after Prout [440], to venture a denial of the concept, as old as Democritus [20], that the atoms were indivisible.

His view was far too simple, but the next two decades showed that atoms had an internal structure and could gain electric charge through the gradual chipping off of electrons with increasing heat. It was these mutilated atoms (and not new varieties of atoms) that gave rise to coronium and all the other false alarms. Lockyer was thus not only instrumental in finding a real new element in the heavens, but contributed to the debunking of false ones.

Lockyer was elected to the Royal Society in 1869 and received its Rumford medal in 1874. He was knighted in 1897, after helium was discovered on earth. He founded the famous British journal Nature in 1869 and edited it for half a century, until his death.

Lockyer was not an academic. He did not receive a university appointment till 1881 and no degree until an honorary doctorate from Cambridge was awarded him in 1904.

[720] ALLBUTT, Sir Thomas Clifford
      English physician
      Born: Dewsbury, Yorkshire, July 20, 1836
      Died: Cambridge, February 22, 1925

Educated at Cambridge, Allbutt served as a physician at Leeds General Infirmary until 1889. In later life he was a commissioner in lunacy and then, from 1892, he was professor of medicine at Cambridge, where he remained for the rest of his long life. He was knighted in 1907.

He did good work on such purely medical problems as syphilis and angina pectoris but his greatest service was undoubtedly the invention of the one medical instrument used most frequently by doctors, nurses, and laymen alike—the clinical thermometer. In 1866 he designed a short thermometer no more than six inches long that reached equilibrium in only five minutes, replacing much longer thermometers that required twenty minutes to reach equilibrium.

Then, and only then, did it become possible to make temperature measurements as a matter of course and to follow the progress of fever, as Wunderlich [592] had maintained it was important to do.

[721] **GULDBERG,** Cato Maximilian
(gool'berg)
Norwegian chemist and mathematician
Born: Christiania (now Oslo), August 11, 1836
Died: Christiania, January 14, 1902

Guldberg, the son of a minister, was a professor of applied mathematics at the University of Christiania, and is known primarily for a pamphlet he published on March 11, 1864, in collaboration with his brother-in-law, Waage [701].

In this pamphlet, in which he extended the work of Berthelot [674], he announced his discovery that the direction taken by a reaction is dependent not merely on the mass of the various components of the reaction, but upon the concentration; that is, upon the mass present in a given volume. Since the pamphlet was published in Norwegian, it escaped the notice of most chemists. It was translated into French in 1867 and still made no impression. Finally Guldberg and Waage published a full translation in Germany in 1879 and Ostwald [840] recognized its importance. By then, Van't Hoff [829] had described this law of mass action at least partially. The priority of Guldberg and Waage was, however, recognized.

When Gibbs's [740] work became known it could be seen how the law of mass action followed naturally from the basic principles of chemical thermodynamics.

[722] **WALDEYER-HARTZ,** Heinrich Wilhelm Gottfried von (vahl'dy-er-hahrts)
German anatomist
Born: Braunschweig (Brunswick), October 6, 1836
Died: Berlin, January 23, 1921

Waldeyer (as he was originally named, without the hyphenation) was the son of an estate manager. He studied at Göttingen and obtained his medical degree from the University of Berlin in 1862.

He is best known for his work on the nervous system. He was the first to maintain that it was built up out of separate cells and their delicate extensions. (The individual cell plus its extensions he called a neuron and his views were named the neuron theory.) He pointed out that the extensions of separate cells might approach closely but did not actually meet, much less join.

Waldeyer is another one of those scientists who contributed a key word to the scientific vocabulary. It was he who in 1888 gave the name "chromosome" to the threads of chromatin material that Flemming [762] had discovered to form during cell division.

[723] **DRAPER,** Henry
American astronomer
Born: Prince Edward County, Virginia, March 7, 1837
Died: New York, New York, November 20, 1882

Draper was the son of John William Draper [566]. The younger Draper was educated at the University of the City of New York (his family having moved to New York when he was two years old) and he obtained his medical degree in 1857. By that time, though he had encountered Rosse [513] during a visit to Ireland, it was astronomy that fascinated him. In 1861 he had set up an observatory on his father's estate at Hastings-on-Hudson and it was in astronomy, which he carried on at his own expense, that he made his fame. He served briefly with the Union army as surgeon until discharged because of poor health.

Draper had begun by trying to polish a metal mirror for his telescope, but John Herschel [479] advised him that glass was much better for the purpose. Draper eventually ground about a hundred glass mirrors. In 1872, once he had a twenty-eight-inch reflector, he tried to photograph the spectrum of the star, Vega. On the second try he succeeded and this was the first time that a stellar spectrum had ever been photographed.

In 1879 Draper learned from Huggins [646] in England of the use of dry plates in photography, these being much more stable than the wet collodion plates Draper had been using. Using the dry plates, Draper was able to get stellar spectra by the score. His study of the spectrum of the Orion Nebula showed it to be a cloud of dust and gas lit by starlight.

Draper died prematurely of double pneumonia, but after his death his widow established the Henry Draper Memorial at the Harvard College Observatory to further research on stellar spectra.

[724] **PROCTOR,** Richard Anthony
English astronomer
Born: Chelsea (London), March 23, 1837
Died: New York, New York, September 12, 1888

At Cambridge it was Proctor's intention to study law, his father's profession, but in 1863 he turned to astronomy and mathematics. His first interest was Mars, whose surface he studied, summarizing his observations in 1867 in a map on which he placed continents, seas, bays, and straits as once Riccioli [185] had done for the moon.

He used English astronomers almost exclusively in naming the Martian features and this roused considerable hostility among astronomers of other nations. Schiaparelli [714] corrected this piece of overenthusiastic nationalism.

Like Beer [499], a generation earlier,

Proctor saw none of the "canals" that Schiaparelli was soon to discover. In 1873 Proctor was the first to suggest that the lunar craters arose through meteoric bombardment. Until then it had been taken for granted that the craters were the result of volcanic action, but since Proctor's time the meteor theory has been predominant even though Proctor weakened in his own support of this theory in later life.

Proctor then turned to the task of popularizing astronomy in lecture tours that led him as far afield as the United States and Australia. In 1881 he settled in the United States where he remained for the last years of his life.

[725] **KÜHNE,** Wilhelm (Willy) Friedrich (kyoo'nuh)
German physiologist
Born: Hamburg, March 28, 1837
Died: Heidelberg, June 10, 1900

Kühne, the son of a prosperous merchant, was a student of Wöhler [515] and Virchow [632] and obtained his doctorate at the University of Göttingen in 1856. He worked also with Du Bois-Reymond [611], Hoppe-Seyler [663] and with Bernard [578] in Paris.

In 1871, he became professor of physiology at Heidelberg, succeeding Helmholtz [631]. He extended Bernard's studies on pancreatic juice by isolating from it the ferment trypsin, which was shown to have a digestive action on protein.

In that same year, 1876, Kühne demonstrated his vitalist position by suggesting that the word "ferment" be restricted to those substances that, within living cells, brought about chemical reactions associated with life. The substances that could be isolated from digestive juice (which performed its work outside cells), like the pepsin of Schwann [563] and like his own trypsin, did not, apparently, deserve the dignity of a word so closely associated with life. He suggested that these substances be called enzymes, from Greek words meaning "in yeast," because they resembled the ferments in living cells, notably in yeast.

The distinction was too fine, and two decades later, after Buchner's [903] demonstrations that the ferments within the yeast cell could work outside the yeast cell and without life, the word "enzyme" was applied to all ferments, inside and outside the cell.

[726] VAN DER WAALS, Johannes Diderik (van der vals)
Dutch physicist
Born: Leiden, November 23, 1837
Died: Amsterdam, March 9, 1923

Van der Waals, the son of a carpenter, was largely self-taught when he entered Leiden University in 1862. His doctor's thesis in 1872 on the nature of the gaseous and liquid phase attracted considerable attention and set the dominant note of his lifelong researches. He was appointed professor of physics at the University of Amsterdam in 1877 and stayed there until his retirement thirty years later.

His lifework represents a crucial improvement on the old classic work of Boyle [212] and Charles [343]. Boyle had discovered the relationship of pressure and volume, while Charles had worked out with considerable accuracy the relationship of temperature and volume. The two relationships could be combined into a single equation:

$$\frac{PV}{T} = R$$

where P represents the pressure of a quantity of gas, V its volume and T its absolute temperature. The symbol R represents a constant. Ideally, in any given sample of gas, if any one of the three variables, pressure, volume, or temperature is varied, the values of the other two adjust themselves to keep the value of R constant.

However, this is not quite true in actual fact. In gases such as hydrogen, nitrogen, and oxygen, it is almost true and becomes more nearly true as the temperature of the gas is raised and the pressure lowered. Chemists thought that for an "ideal gas" or "perfect gas" it would hold exactly, and without qualification.

Van der Waals was interested in determining why the "perfect gas equation" did not hold exactly for real gases. He considered the kinetic theory of gases worked out by Maxwell [692] and Boltzmann [769]. It could be made to yield the perfect gas equation provided two assumptions were made: that there were no attractive forces between gas molecules, and that the gas molecules were of zero size.

Neither assumption is quite correct. There are small attractive forces between gas molecules and though those molecules may be exceedingly small, their size is not zero. Taking this into account Van der Waals in 1873 worked out a somewhat more complicated version of the gas equation, in which two more constants were introduced. These constants were different for each gas and had to be determined by actual observation, since for each different gas, the molecules were of a particular size and exerted their own particular intermolecular attractions.

By using the temperature, pressure, and volume of a gas at its critical point (where the gas and liquid forms become equal in density and cannot be distinguished from each other) Van der Waals worked out another equation, one in which new constants were not needed and which would hold for any gas.

As a result of Van der Waals's work, it was discovered that the Joule-Thomson effect, by which a gas cools when allowed to expand, only holds below a certain temperature, one that is characteristic for each gas. For most gases this characteristic temperature is high enough for physicists cooling gases by the Joule-Thomson effect to work freely. For hydrogen and helium, however, the characteristic temperature is very low. The liquefaction of those gases could not be carried through by gas expansion (the most convenient method) until the temperature was first lowered to the requisite point by other methods. It was only then that Dewar [759] and Kamerlingh Onnes [843] were able to enter the approaches to absolute zero.

In 1910 Van der Waals was awarded

the Nobel Prize in physics for his work on gas equations.

[727] **NEWLANDS,** John Alexander Reina
English chemist
Born: Southwark (London), November 26, 1837
Died: London, July 29, 1898

Newlands, the son of a minister, was educated at home. He entered the Royal College of Chemistry in 1856 and studied under Hofmann [604]. He then answered the call of adventure in 1860 and joined Garibaldi's small army, which was successfully to invade the Kingdom of Naples and join it to the new Kingdom of Italy. This gesture was quasipatriotic, for Newlands was of Italian descent on his mother's side.

After his return to England he worked as an analytic chemist at a sugar refinery and grew interested in the table of elements. On February 7, 1863, he arranged the elements in the order of atomic weights (unaware that Beguyer de Chancourtois [622] had done the same thing two years earlier). Newlands found that properties seemed to repeat themselves in each group of seven elements. He announced this as the law of octaves, referring to the musical scale.

When he announced this discovery at a meeting of chemists, he was laughed at. The importance of atomic weights was still unrecognized by some, despite Cannizzaro's [668] labors, and he was asked derisively by George Carey Foster, a professor of physics, if he might not get better results if he listed the elements in alphabetical order.

Foster was a capable scientist and he pointed out legitimate weaknesses in the law of octaves, but he is known today *only* for his facetious remark and is derided for it—which shows the risk one takes in science in laughing at something that seems silly.

Newlands could not get his paper published and the whole matter was forgotten until five years later, when Mendeléev [705] published his periodic table.

As the periodic table came to be recognized for the fundamental advance it was, Newlands's stock began to rise. In 1887 the Royal Society awarded him the Davy medal for the paper that a quarter century earlier he could not get published. Newlands accepted with grace; he had never grown bitter over the treatment.

[728] **HYATT,** John Wesley
American inventor
Born: Starkey, New York, November 28, 1837
Died: Short Hills, New Jersey, May 10, 1920

In his early life Hyatt worked as a printer and then established a factory in Albany, New York, at which he turned out checkers and dominoes.

In the early 1860s he (and many others) were attracted by a prize of $10,000 offered by the New York firm of Phelan and Collender for the best substitute for ivory for billiard balls. Ivory was ideal but getting it always involved a dispute with an elephant. Hyatt heard of a new English method of molding pyroxylin (a partially nitrated cellulose such as Chardonnet [743] later used in manufacturing rayon) by dissolving it in a mixture of alcohol and ether and adding camphor to make it softer and more malleable.

Hyatt improved the techniques and in 1869 patented a method of manufacturing billiard balls out of this material, which he named celluloid. He did not win the prize, however, for some reason. Celluloid enjoyed a minor boom as the material for baby rattles, shirt collars, photographic film, and so on. It was the first synthetic plastic. However, its great flaw was that it was quite inflammable and it was not until the invention of less inflammable plastics, notably Bakelite by Baekeland [931], that this new class of materials came into its own. Hyatt made other inventions in later life and collected over two hundred patents, but none to match celluloid. It was enough, though, and in 1914 he was awarded the Perkin medal.

[729] **MARKOVNIKOV,** Vladimir
Vasilevich (mahr-kuv'nih-kuv)
Russian chemist
Born: Knyaginino, Gorki Region, December 25, 1837
Died: Moscow, February 11,
1904

Markovnikov, the son of an army officer, graduated from Kazan University in 1860, having studied under Butlerov [676], whose assistant he then became. In 1865 he went to Germany for two years where he studied under Erlenmeyer [661] and Kolbe [610]. Returning to Russia, he succeeded to Butlerov's professorship at Kazan and later taught at Odessa and Moscow.

He interested himself in the structure of organic molecules after the fashion of Kekulé [680] and broadened the view in one important aspect. There was a pronounced impression that carbon atoms could form only six-atom rings, and to be sure these were the rings that were stablest and easiest to form. But they were not the only rings as Markovnikov proved when he prepared molecules containing rings of four carbon atoms in 1879 and of seven carbon atoms in 1889.

He also showed how atoms of chlorine or bromine attached themselves to carbon chains containing double bonds. Such additions are still said to follow the Markovnikov rule, though the reason behind it had to await the development of the resonance theory by Pauling [1236] half a century later.

[730] **MORLEY,** Edward Williams
American chemist
Born: Newark, New Jersey, January 29, 1838
Died: West Hartford, Connecticut, February 24, 1923

Morley graduated from Williams College in 1860 and obtained his master's degree there in 1863. His ambition had been to become a Congregational minister (as his father had been), and for that purpose he attended Andover Theo-

logical Seminary. While waiting for a post, he took up chemistry, which until then had been merely a hobby.

In 1868 it was not only a ministerial post that turned up but the offer of a professorship at Western Reserve College in Hudson, Ohio (now Case Western Reserve University in Cleveland, Ohio). Morley accepted it with the provision that he could preach at the university chapel. In the 1870s Morley was involved in the same endeavor that later was to occupy the attention of T. W. Richards [968]—the relative atomic weights of oxygen and hydrogen. This won him a reputation in the world of chemistry, but it was his collaboration with Michelson [835] in the famous Michelson-Morley experiment that won him immortality—and in physics.

Morley retired in 1906 and lived out the remainder of his life in West Hartford.

[731] **HITZIG,** Julius Eduard (hit'sikh)
German physiologist
Born: Berlin, February 6, 1838
Died: Luisenheim zu St. Blasien,
August 20, 1907

Hitzig was the son of a well-known Jewish architect and was a cousin of Baeyer [718]. He studied law first, then switched to medicine, studying under, among others, Du Bois-Reymond [611] and Virchow [632]. He gained his medical degree in 1862.

He interested himself in mental illness and insanity, but he could not have been extremely stable himself; he was vain and contentious to a degree, was constantly embroiled in polemics and seemed unable to get along with anyone.

He was, however, a skillful experimentalist and, together with Gustav Fritsch (1838–1927), was the first to demonstrate clearly the existence of cerebral localization, in 1870. Working with the brains of living dogs he showed that the stimulation of certain definite portions of the cerebral cortex stimulated the contraction of certain muscles and that the damaging of those portions led to the weakening or paralysis of those same muscles. It was possible to draw a sort of distorted "map" of the body on the brain as Ferrier [761] and others did. Not only did this dramatically demonstrate the nature of at least part of the functioning of the brain but it utterly demolished the phrenological theories that had grown out of the work of Gall [371] three quarters of a century before.

[732] **BEILSTEIN,** Friedrich Konrad
(bile'shtine)
Russian chemist
Born: St. Petersburg (now Leningrad), February 17, 1838
Died: St. Petersburg, October 18, 1906

Beilstein received his higher education in Germany—he was of German descent —and in 1860, after studying under Bunsen [565], Kekulé [680] and Liebig [532], served as assistant to Wöhler [515]. He received his doctorate in 1858 and then did further work in Paris and in Breslau.

He returned to Russia in 1866 chiefly because in Germany the accent was on laboratory research, which was not his forte, although his father's death at this time was also a factor in the decision.

In Russia, he succeeded Mendeléev [705] at the Imperial Technological Institute and there he could surround himself with German students and do armchair work. His labors in that respect were colossal, and made the more possible, perhaps, through the fact that he never married.

Like Gmelin [457] his great service to chemistry was the organization of knowledge. He prepared a giant *Handbook of Organic Chemistry,* in which he attempted to list all the organic compounds with all pertinent information about each. The first edition (1880–1882) was in two volumes and had 2,201 pages. From 1886 to 1889 a second edition of three volumes appeared. He had

only a single assistant in this task and both worked at it incessantly.

In 1900 he turned the task over to the German Chemical Society, which still labors at it.

Beilstein used an orderly system of listing the compounds, following Laurent's [553] notions of organic structure, and in this way helped to establish them. Considering that each year sees thousands of new organic compounds synthesized, it is no wonder that *Beilstein* (as the handbook is commonly known), though now consisting of twenty-seven volumes plus another twenty-seven supplementary volumes, is far out-of-date and is likely to remain so indefinitely.

Beilstein was elected to the Russian Imperial Academy of Sciences in 1881, while Mendeléev, the greater man, was rejected. The reason for this apparently was that Russian science in the nineteenth century had (oddly enough) a strongly pro-German and anti-Russian orientation.

[733] **MACH,** Ernst (mahkh)
Austrian physicist
Born: Chirlitz-Turas, Moravia (now in Czechoslovakia), February 18, 1838
Died: Vaterstetten, Bavaria, February 19, 1916

Mach was the son of a schoolteacher who moved with his family to Vienna while young Ernst was still a baby. His training was in physics, and he obtained his doctor's degree in that subject at the University of Vienna in 1860. He taught at Graz and then at Prague before returning to Vienna in 1895. However, he was strongly influenced by the "psychophysics" of Fechner [520]. In considering the physical side of sensation, as was required by psychophysics, he elaborated the notion in 1872 that all knowledge was a matter of sensation.

He became a philosopher of science at a time when scientific overconfidence had reached its peak. After Newton [231] it had seemed that all could be explained by scientists on a mechanical basis and that laws of nature could be considered as almost having an existence of their own.

Mach insisted that laws of nature were simply man-made generalizations, conveniences invented to cover innumerable observations, but that it was only the innumerable observations themselves that had reality, provided we went so far as to accept the validity of sensation.

He vigorously opposed the use of unseen and insensible objects to explain phenomena, holding out against the atomic theory in particular. The flow of heat was an observed fact and the laws of thermodynamics were interpretations of such observed facts. This was fine, in his view, and nothing further was needed. To seize upon tiny billiard balls to explain the observed facts of gas behavior and of heat flow, à la Maxwell [692], was, he believed, to introduce something that could not be perceived and that was therefore mystical.

Furthermore, he was against the notion that space and time were anything more than generalizations built up from observation. The properties of space had no independent existence but were dependent on the mass content and distribution within it (this is still called Mach's principle, a name first applied to it by Einstein [1064]). Moreover, what we call time was merely the comparison of one set of movements with a standardized movement (that of the hands of a clock, for instance).

Mach's philosophy was not greeted with any enthusiasm in his time. The atomists were in the saddle, and as the decades passed, their influence grew continuously stronger. Thanks to the work of Einstein and Perrin [990] at the turn of the century, atoms seemed more than ever to assume a concrete existence, and even such a staunch Machian as Ostwald [840] had to allow himself to accept atoms as real.

Nevertheless, some of Mach's philosophy, Mach's principle in particular, was to influence Einstein. Moreover, if atoms are now accepted as real by all scientists, Mach's point of view wins out this far:

They are not the mere billiard balls that nineteenth-century scientists had pictured. In fact, mechanical analogies on the atomic level are impossible after all, and scientists have been forced to accept mathematical expressions as symbolizing atoms without making any attempt to illustrate them with objects from our ordinary world.

Mach is best known now for his experiments on airflow, published in 1887, in which he was first to take note of the sudden change in the nature of the airflow over a moving object as it reaches the speed of sound. Consequently, the speed of sound in air, under given conditions of temperature, is called Mach 1. Twice the speed of sound is Mach 2, and so on. In this age of supersonic air travel, Mach numbers (a phrase first used in 1925) fill the public prints but few know where the Mach comes from.

Mach retired in 1901, after suffering a stroke, and was succeeded in his chair by Boltzmann [769]. He remained an active thinker, and served in the Austrian House of Lords, a position of much prestige and few duties. In his last years Mach did not accept Einstein's theory of relativity, though this theory incorporated much of his own views. He was planning to write a book pointing out its flaws when death overtook him.

[734] **PERKIN,** Sir William Henry
English chemist
Born: London, March 12, 1838
Died: Sudbury, Middlesex (now part of London), July 14, 1907

In his school days, Perkin, the son of a carpenter, was enthusiastic in the cause of chemistry. He was greatly inspired by lectures given by Faraday [474] just as Faraday had once been inspired by the lectures of Davy [421].

At the time, however, the science was at a low ebb in England, for all it had been the home of Boyle [212], Cavendish [307], Priestley [312], and Dalton [389]. To establish a reasonable college course in chemistry, it had been necessary to import Hofmann [604] from Germany. This was at the suggestion of Queen Victoria's husband, Prince Albert, who was German.

Perkin, over his father's protests, decided to take up chemistry. He studied under Hofmann, and Perkin's keen mind and burning interest commended itself to the latter. Hofmann made the young Englishman his assistant in 1855. Perkin, only seventeen, fleshed out his school work by doing research on his own in a home laboratory.

One day Hofmann speculated aloud as to whether it might not be feasible to synthesize quinine (the valuable chemical used to combat malaria) in the laboratory, using cheap coal tar chemicals as a starting material. This, he believed, would demolish Europe's dependence on far-off tropical lands for the supply. All on fire, Perkin went home to try to achieve the task.

He failed. The structure of quinine was not known at the time, and even if it had been it would have been far too complex to produce by means of the few synthetic methods then known. It was nearly a century later when Woodward [1416] turned the trick.

Perkin tackled the problem in 1856 during his Easter vacation. One day after he had mixed aniline (one of the coal tar chemicals) and potassium dichromate and was about to pour out the usual seemingly worthless mess in his beaker, his eye caught a purplish glint in the material. He added alcohol and this dissolved something out of the˙ mess and turned a beautiful purple.

Perkin wondered at once if the substance might be useful as a dye. Through all of history mankind had been interested in dyes that could turn the colorless textile materials of cotton, linen, wool, and silk into eye-catching and colorful spectacles. Unfortunately, few materials in nature will add firmly to textiles; most either wash out with water or fade out with sun. The most common and best of those that added firmly were the dark blue indigo and the red alizarin, both from plants. (A purple dye from a Mediterranean shellfish made the ancient city of Tyre rich and famous and was so expensive and desirable that it had been reserved for the use of royalty.)

Perkin sent a sample of his purple compound to a dyeing firm in Scotland and the excited answer came back that it would dye silk beautifully and could it be obtained cheaply?

Perkin now reached a decision that took courage and faith. He patented his process for making the dye (after considerable trouble, because there was some question as to whether an eighteen-year-old boy was old enough to take out a patent) and left school over Hofmann's objections. Perkin's father, despite his initial opposition to chemistry, came through admirably and contributed his life savings to Perkin's capital. So did Perkin's elder brother.

In 1857 the Perkin family started to build a dye factory and found themselves at the bottom indeed. Aniline was unavailable on the open market, so Perkin had to buy benzene and make aniline out of it. For this he needed strong nitric acid, which he had to manufacture for himself. At every step of the game he needed special equipment, which he himself had to design. Nevertheless, within six months, he was producing what he called aniline purple.

English dyers proved rather conservative, despite the Scottish experience, and they hesitated, but the French dyers went for the new material in a big way. They named the color mauve (from the French word for the madder plant, which was the source of the somewhat similarly colored alizarin) and the chemical mauveine. So popular did the dye become that the period is known as the Mauve Decade.

The young chemist was suddenly famous and, when only twenty-three, found himself the world authority on dyes. He lectured on them before London's Chemical Society, and in the audience was none other than the inspiration of his youth, Michael Faraday.

Perkin's discovery initiated the great synthetic dye industry and stimulated the development of synthetic organic chemistry. Kekulé [680] worked out his structural theory, particularly in connection with benzene, and chemists had a guide through the jungle.

Hundreds of new chemicals not found in nature—then thousands, then tens of thousands—were synthesized and studied. The task of men like Beilstein [732], who tried to organize the knowledge gathered about all known organic compounds, was endlessly multiplied.

Other compounds, which were indeed found in nature, could nevertheless be prepared in the laboratory more cheaply than they could be extracted from their native place of occurrence. In 1868, for instance, Graebe [752] synthesized the natural dye alizarin, and in 1879 Baeyer [718] synthesized indigo. Natural dyes went out of business altogether.

In 1874 Perkin, then only thirty-five, was independently wealthy. German competition was proving too much for England's dye industry, so he sold his factory and returned to his real love, chemical research. He joined in the grand search for general methods of synthesizing various combinations of carbon atoms so as to devise newer and ever newer routes for manufacturing new compounds. One important type of chemical reaction is known as the Perkin reaction. Using it, Perkin synthesized coumarin, a white, crystalline substance with a pleasant vanilla-like odor. This discovery marks the beginning of the synthetic perfume industry.

His quiet, retiring nature prevented Perkin from getting the due he deserved. However, he received the Davy medal of the Royal Society in 1889 and in 1906, a year before his death, was finally knighted. In that same year the fiftieth anniversary of the discovery of aniline purple was celebrated and representatives from Europe and America came to London to join in the acclaim. It was the grand climax of Perkin's life.

[735] **SOLVAY,** Ernest (sole-vay')
Belgian chemist
Born: Rebecq-Rognon, April 16, 1838
Died: Brussels, May 26, 1922

Solvay, whose health as a child seemed shaky, had little formal education. However, his father was a salt refiner; and surrounded by the atmosphere of industrial chemistry Solvay read voluminously and experimented to his heart's content in chemistry and electricity.

An uncle directed a gasworks and young Solvay was called in to help. He worked out several methods of purifying gas that were quite successful. In the process he found that the water he used for washing the gas had picked up ammonia and carbon dioxide. He wanted to concentrate this ammonia as a possible useful by-product.

Gentle heating drove off the ammonia, and this he could then dissolve in a small quantity of fresh water. For some reason he decided to use a salt solution instead of water alone and when he did this, the ammonia and carbon dioxide entering the solution produced a precipitate that turned out to be sodium bicarbonate.

Solvay saw the importance of this at once. Sodium bicarbonate was regularly formed from sodium chloride, but the process required considerable heat and therefore considerable expense in the way of fuel. The new Solvay process required much less heat and therefore much less fuel. Solvay took out his first patent in 1861, founded a company for the manufacture of sodium bicarbonate in 1863, and after three years of rocky going, settled down to success. By 1913 he was producing virtually the entire world supply of sodium bicarbonate.

The wealth his chemical inventiveness brought him allowed him to spend his last years in endowing schools so that others might receive the education he had missed and in evolving unusual social theories. He invented a system of economy, for instance, that involved the abolition of money and its replacement by a complex credit system. A generation later, during the Great Depression, the system achieved a certain popularity under the name of technocracy. There was never any danger of its being adopted, however.

Solvay remained in Belgium during World War I and organized a committee that obtained and distributed food. Despite his childhood frailty, he lived well into his eighties and survived to see Belgium liberated from the German invader.

[736] **LECOQ DE BOISBAUDRAN,**
Paul Émile (luh-koke' duh bwah-boh-dran')
French chemist
Born: Cognac, Charente, April 18, 1838
Died: Paris, May 28, 1912

Lecoq de Boisbaudran came of a well-to-do family of distillers (Cognac is the home of the beverage of the same name) and received a good education through the help of his well-educated mother and his own reading.

He set up his own chemical laboratory while working in the family business, and in 1859 began to experiment in the new and glamorous field of spectroscopy that had just been developed by Kirchhoff [648]. For fifteen years he searched through various minerals for signs of any unknown spectral lines and in 1874 found what he was looking for in a sample of zinc ore from the Pyrénées.

He announced his discovery in 1875 and named the new element gallium, from the Latin name for the territory that later became France. (However, Lecoq means "rooster" and the Latin equivalent is *gallus,* so there is some speculation that Lecoq de Boisbaudran was using his own name, too.) By 1875 he had prepared enough of the new element, an easily liquefied metal, to present some to the Academy of Sciences.

Mendeléev [705] read the reports and stated his belief that gallium was one of the elements he had predicted. When the properties of gallium were studied and compared with the undiscovered element Mendeléev had called eka-aluminum, Mendeléev proved to be right. Lecoq de Boisbaudran discovered two more elements in later years: samarium in 1879 and dysprosium in 1886.

[737] **ZEPPELIN,** Ferdinand Adolf August Heinrich, Count von (tsep'uh-lin)
German inventor
Born: Konstanz, Baden, July 8, 1838
Died: Charlottenburg, Prussia, March 8, 1917

As was to be expected of a member of the Central European nobility, Count von Zeppelin received a military education and became a cavalry officer in 1858. In 1863 he served in the United States as an observer with the Northern Army of the Potomac. In America also he received the inspiration for his life's work, for in St. Paul, Minnesota, he engaged in his first balloon ascension.

However, his military career came first. He took part in the Seven Weeks' War of 1866, his state of Württemberg (then independent) fighting on Austria's losing side against Prussia. With Württemberg then allied with Prussia, he took part on the winning side against France in 1870. Finally in 1891 he retired with the rank of lieutenant general in the German Army. Thereafter he was free to spend his time and every cent of his money on aeronautical experiments.

Since the time of the Montgolfier [325] brothers, numerous balloons had risen in the air, but once there they could only drift as the wind blew. It was the dream of many men to mount an engine in the gondola of the balloon so as to direct it according to human will and not according to the wind's whim. Such a powered air vessel would be a "dirigible balloon" (that is, a directable one). In pursuit of this dream, Zeppelin ran through his wealth in no time and had to draw upon public support and the patronage of Kaiser William II.

It was Zeppelin who conceived the notion of confining the balloon itself within a cigar-shaped structure of aluminum. (This could not have been possible until the light metal aluminum could be supplied cheaply and in quantity by the method discovered by Hall [933] and Héroult [925] in the 1880s.)

On July 2, 1900, one of Zeppelin's

beautiful cigar-shaped vessels rose into the air. Beneath it was a gondola bearing an internal combustion engine and propellers. It took off on a stately flight that, despite damage on landing, was the first effective directed flight by man, antedating by three and a half years the first heavier-than-air flight of the Wright brothers [961, 995]. In common speech, the dirigible balloon was frequently called a zeppelin in the count's honor (with the initial pronounced "z" rather than "ts" by English-speaking individuals).

However, the dirigible was doomed to be overtaken by the airplane. The dirigible was stately, silent, and awesome, but it was too weak to withstand bad weather and in wartime it presented so fat and (if hydrogen-filled) so explosive a target as to be useless. There were zeppelin raids on London during World War I, but some forty of the large cigars were reported destroyed and Zeppelin died knowing that his invention would not win the war for Germany.

Nevertheless, between World Wars I and II, dirigibles made a last stand. Italian, British, French, and American dirigibles broke up in a series of disasters, but German vessels remained successful for two decades. The most successful was the *Graf Zeppelin* named for the inventor (*Graf* is German for "count"). This had its maiden flight in 1928 and went around the world in 1929. A larger dirigible, the *Hindenburg,* was launched in 1936, bearing the swastika on its tail fins. It went down in flames over New Jersey in 1937, and since then airships (usually relatively small blimps) have had but limited uses.

[738] **ABBE,** Cleveland (ab'ee)
American meteorologist
Born: New York, New York, December 3, 1838
Died: Chevy Chase, Maryland, October 28, 1916

In 1857 Abbe graduated from the school that is now the College of the City of New York. After teaching for some years at the University of Michigan he undertook a series of longitude determinations for the United States Government. He spent the years 1864 to 1866 in Russia, studying astronomy under the son of Struve [483], who had succeeded his father as director of the observatory at Pulkovo. After his return to America, Abbe was appointed director of the Cincinnati observatory.

It was here he achieved his fame, for, taking advantage of telegraphic reports of storms (as Henry [503] had done at the Smithsonian Institution), he began to put out daily weather bulletins. These dated from September 1, 1869. The service was highly popular and for once the government acted quickly. A national bureau was established under an army general, and Abbe was offered the post of scientific assistant. He accepted in 1871 and began a system of three-a-day weather forecasts. In 1891 the bureau became the United States Weather Bureau. Abbe remained the meteorologist in charge until 1916. He is commonly known as the father of the Weather Bureau.

He taught meteorology at Johns Hopkins and did much research in the field. As the earth shrank (in human terms) with advances in transportation and communication, the importance of weather forecasting increased. To the use of the telegraph was gradually added the use of radio reports, of sounding balloons, of radar, and finally of space satellites designed to view the earth's cloud cover from a vantage point outside the atmosphere.

Abbe was one of those who proposed the establishment of standard time zones. Prior to the late nineteenth century, every locality kept its own local time, more or less adjusted to the position of the sun as seen from its own spot on the earth's surface. When travel was slow, this created no particular problems.

With the coming of the railroad, however, proper scheduling was almost impossible. As a result of a report published by Abbe in 1879, the government accepted for the nation as a whole what the railroads were already using for themselves. In 1883 the United States was divided into four zones of standard time. Within each zone, the time was standardized at some average value. The time zone system now exists throughout the world, and the advent of air travel has made it all the more useful and necessary.

[739] **WINKLER,** Clemens Alexander
(veenk'ler)
German chemist
Born: Freiberg, Saxony,
December 26, 1838
Died: Dresden, Saxony,
October 8, 1904

Winkler's father was a chemist and metallurgist who had studied under Berzelius [425] so Winkler had the proper background for his own lifework. He studied at the Freiberg School of Mines and early in his career developed new techniques for analyzing gases.

Winkler was proud of the neatness and efficiency of his analytic methods and was upset when in 1885 he analyzed a silver ore and found that all the elements he located amounted to only 93 percent of the whole. There was a missing 7 percent he could not find. He searched for it steadily for four months and in 1886 isolated a new element, which he named germanium. It proved to be the third of Mendeléev's [705] predicted elements, one that he had called eka-silicon.

By an odd chance, all three of the elements Mendeléev had successfully predicted had received nationalistic names: gallium for France, scandium for Scandinavia, and germanium for Germany. In each case, the place of discovery and the nationality of the discoverer was honored.

[740] **GIBBS,** Josiah Willard
American physicist
Born: New Haven, Connecticut,
February 11, 1839
Died: New Haven, April 28, 1903

Gibbs, the son of a Yale professor, led a quiet, secluded life in the United States, which during the nineteenth century was as far off the beaten track of science as Russia. He obtained his Ph.D. from Yale in 1863, the first ever awarded by that school for a thesis in engineering, and then continued his studies abroad in France and Germany. He returned to New Haven in 1869 and became professor of mathematical physics at Yale in 1871, retaining that position until his death.

Gibbs displayed practical inventiveness and obtained patents for a railroad brake in 1866. Theory, however, was his forte and he performed few, if any, experiments.

He was a poor teacher, and his fame rests chiefly on a series of papers, totaling some four hundred pages, which he published over the period 1876 to 1878 in the *Transactions of the Connecticut Academy of Sciences.* (The editors of the journal were at first seriously in doubt as to whether to publish the papers.) In these papers, he dealt with the principles of thermodynamics, as worked out by men such as Carnot [497], Joule [613], Helmholtz [631], and Kelvin [652]. He applied them in a thoroughly mathematical fashion to chemical reactions, although they had been worked out from a consideration of heat engines. In doing this, he evolved the modern concepts of free energy and chemical potential as the driving force behind chemical reactions.

In the papers he also considered equilibria between different phases (liquid, solid, and gas) where one or more components of a system were involved. He found that for a given number of phases and components (that is, a system made up of ice, water, and water vapor, which is one component and three phases; or solid salt at the bottom of a salt solution in water, which is two components in two phases), the number of ways ("degrees of freedom") in which temperature, pressure, or concentration could be varied was fixed by a simple equation. This is called the phase rule, probably the most elegant discovery Gibbs made.

Unfortunately, Gibbs worked against disadvantages. The great European scientists bothered little with American journals, particularly those as relatively obscure as that in which Gibbs had published. Secondly, Gibbs's mathematical treatment placed his work over the heads of most of the chemists who did see it. (Though, to be sure, the mathematical foundation of chemical thermodynamics as Gibbs constructed it was so thorough and solid as to leave little for his successors to add.)

One person who did grasp the meaning and importance of Gibbs was Maxwell [692]. Unfortunately Maxwell died soon after the appearance of the papers, and although he did speak of it to Van der Waals [726], who passed it on to Roozeboom [854], he did not get a chance to publicize it as it deserved, or to show how neatly it accounted for empirical discoveries in physical chemistry such as those by Germain Hess [528] and by Guldberg [721].

It was not until the 1890s, therefore, that Europe really discovered Gibbs. In 1892 Gibbs's work was translated into German by Ostwald [840] and in 1899 it was translated into French by Le Châtelier [812]. By that time Van't Hoff [829] had worked out chemical thermodynamics independently. Nevertheless, Gibbs's priority was universally recognized and the American found himself appreciated at last.

In 1901 he received the Copley medal of the Royal Society. In 1950 he was elected a member of the Hall of Fame for Great Americans.

[741] **CRAFTS,** James Mason
American chemist
Born: Boston, Massachusetts,
March 8, 1839
Died: Ridgefield, Connecticut,
June 20, 1917

Crafts, the son of a woolen-goods manufacturer, graduated from Harvard in 1858 and, as was almost essential for American chemists throughout the nineteenth century, went to Germany for postgraduate training. Among other things he spent a year as assistant to Bunsen [565]. In 1861 he met Friedel [693] in Paris.

Back in the United States he obtained a professorial position first at Cornell University in 1868, then at Massa-

chusetts Institute of Technology in 1871. In 1874 he returned to Paris to devote himself to research with Friedel.

In 1877 he and Friedel were studying the effect of metallic aluminum on certain chlorine-containing organic compounds and noticed that a reaction set in only after a period of inactivity and that then hydrogen chloride gas was formed. They found that during the period of inactivity aluminum chloride was formed and that it was the aluminum chloride that initiated the reaction. It turned out that aluminum chloride was a versatile catalyst for reactions tying together a chain of carbon atoms to a ring of carbon atoms. The Friedel-Crafts reaction, as it is called, became an important weapon in the armory of the chemical synthesizers and it still is.

In 1891 Crafts returned to the United States once more and resumed teaching at M.I.T., serving as president of that institution from 1898 to 1900.

The chronic ill health that had plagued him all his life forced him to retire then.

[742] **PRZHEVALSKY,** Nikolay Mikhaylovich (per-zhe-val'sky)
Russian explorer
Born: Kimbarovo, Smolensk region, April 12, 1839
Died: Karakol (now Przhevalsk [renamed in his honor], Kirgiz SSR), November 1, 1888

Przhevalsky, an army officer, taught history and geography at the Warsaw Military School from 1864. Two years later he was assigned to eastern Siberia and he began making major explorations of east-central Asia both within and without the borders of Russia.

Five separate expeditions carried him through Mongolia, Sinkiang, and Tibet, though he never was allowed entry into the Tibetan capital of Lhasa. He discovered mountain ranges unknown to European geographers and located Lob Nor, a lake mentioned by Marco Polo [105] and not heard of since in Europe. It is located in eastern Sinkiang. He described the Gobi Desert and his meteorological observations brought to the world important knowledge concerning the climate of central Asia and its influence on world weather patterns.

He also gathered and recorded numerous species of plants and animals, several hundred of them being new to science. His best-known discovery was that of a wild horse, the last remaining wild subspecies of that animal; one that is now called Przhevalsky's horse in his honor. He also discovered a wild camel.

He died of typhus on his fifth expedition (through the unguarded drinking of river water) and was buried on the shores of Lake Issyk Kul in what is now Soviet territory near the Sinkiang border.

[743] **CHARDONNET,** Louis Marie Hilaire Bernigaud, comte de
(shahr-doh-nay')
French chemist
Born: Besançon, Doubs, May 1, 1839
Died: Paris, March 12, 1924

In the later stages of his education Chardonnet worked as an assistant to Pasteur [642], who was investigating silkworm diseases. Chardonnet's interest in fibers was roused. Later, he worked on guncotton for the French Government.

Since he was independently wealthy, he could devote himself freely to work of his own choosing, and he chose to combine these two interests. He began, in 1878, to produce fibers by forcing solutions of nitrocellulose through tiny holes and allowing the solvent to evaporate. In 1884 he obtained a patent for the process, as Swan [677] had done the year before in England.

At the Paris Exposition of 1891 "Chardonnet silk" was a sensation. It was called rayon, since it was so shiny that it seemed to give forth rays of light. The nitrocellulose used was not fully nitrated so that it was not explosive. Nevertheless, rayon was at first so dangerously inflammable that it came to be called "mother-in-law silk" because (the grisly joke went) a rayon dress and a lighted match were ideal presents for a mother-in-law. Swan showed how the nitro groups could be removed from the rayon after fiber formation to make the

material far less inflammable (though not as strong).

Rayon was the first artificial fiber to come into common use. It was only modified cellulose, to be sure, but it pointed the way toward the completely synthetic fibers developed by Carothers [1190] and others a half century later. In 1914 Chardonnet was awarded the Perkin medal for his development of rayon.

[744] **KUNDT,** August Adolph Eduard Eberhard (koont)
German physicist
Born: Schwerin, Mecklenburg, November 18, 1839
Died: Israelsdorf (near Lübeck), May 21, 1894

Like Helmholtz [631], Kundt (who was educated at the University of Berlin and received his doctor's degree in 1864) was interested in sound. In 1866 he invented an interesting method for studying the velocity of sound in different gases. He did this by dusting the interior of tubes with a finely divided powder, which was then disturbed by traveling waves. From the pattern of disturbance Kundt could calculate the velocity of sound in the material making up the tube or in the gas contained in the tube.

In 1888 he succeeded Helmholtz as professor of physics at the Berlin Physical Institute. He is best known now, however, as the teacher and sponsor of Roentgen [774], whose great discovery he did not quite live to witness.

[745] **MAXIM,** Sir Hiram Stevens American-English inventor
Born: Sangerville, Maine, February 5, 1840
Died: London, England, November 24, 1916

Maxim, the son of a farmer, spent his early life apprenticed to various iron works establishments and devised numerous inventions. His career (which included a period of professional prizefighting) reached one climax when he went to Paris to demonstrate one of his patents at the Paris Exposition in 1881. He received an award for it.

Feeling that there was more opportunity for him in Europe, he went to England, where he remained for the rest of his life, becoming a British subject in 1900.

In 1883 he produced his most important invention, the first fully automatic machine gun. It was an advance over that of Gatling [609] in that it made use of the energy of the recoil of a fired bullet to eject the spent cartridge and load the next. It worked particularly well after the development of smokeless powder, to which he contributed. The British Army adopted the Maxim gun in 1889 and Maxim was knighted in 1901.

The use of automatic machine guns gave European armies a still greater advantage over native levies in Africa and Asia. One popular jingle of the time went:

> Whatever happens, we have got
> The Maxim gun and they have not!

It added its peculiar horror to World War I, when both sides had machine guns; its offensive power was not neutralized till the invention of the tank. Before the tank came along, generals let their soldiers be mowed down by the hundreds of thousands before enemy machine guns. Maxim lived just long enough to see that.

He was afflicted with a tendency to envy, unfortunately, and begrudged the fame of other inventors, including, particularly, Edison [788].

[746] **CLEVE,** Per Teodor (klay'vuh)
Swedish chemist and geologist
Born: Stockholm, February 10, 1840
Died: Uppsala, June 18, 1905

Cleve, the thirteenth child of his parents, studied under Mosander [501] and like him was particularly interested in the rare earth minerals. His doctoral dissertation was on the subject. He obtained his degree in 1863 and in 1868 received a professorial appointment at the University of Uppsala.

In 1879 he demonstrated the identity of Nilson's [747] scandium with Mendeléev's [705] predicted eka-boron, and in the same year discovered two new elements among the rare earth minerals, thulium and holmium.

He was one of the reviewing board who sat in judgment upon the Ph.D. dissertation of the young Arrhenius [894] and disapproved. Twenty years later, when he was serving as chairman of the committee that selected winners of the recently established Nobel Prize in chemistry, he helped pick Arrhenius for the prize—for that very same dissertation.

Cleve was also interested in biology and explored the microscopic ocean life (plankton) of the North Sea. In fact, when he retired he planned to devote himself to the study of plankton but he died a few months later.

[747] **NILSON,** Lars Fredrik
Swedish chemist
Born: Östergötland, May 27, 1840
Died: Stockholm, May 14, 1899

Nilson's chief interest in chemistry was in the study of the rare earth minerals, which had been discovered in Sweden by Gadolin [373].

In 1879 he discovered that one of the minerals contained a hitherto unknown element, which he named scandium in honor of Scandinavia. It had properties that were exactly like those predicted by Mendeléev [705] for an element he called eka-boron, whose existence he had predicted. This was pointed out by Nilson's colleague Cleve [746].

In later years Nilson was most notable for his work on chemical fertilizers.

[748] **COPE,** Edward Drinker
American paleontologist
Born: Philadelphia, Pennsylvania, July 28, 1840
Died: Philadelphia, April 12, 1897

Cope, who was born of a wealthy family, was educated privately in his youth and then attended the University of Pennsylvania. He was quite precocious and was publishing scientific papers while still in his teens.

He served as professor of comparative zoology and botany at Haverford College, then went on to do his major work while on the staff at the University of Pennsylvania. His career paralleled that of his mortal enemy Marsh [690], especially in the collection of fossils in the western United States and in working out the evolutionary history of the horse. All told, he discovered about a thousand species of extinct vertebrates in the rocks of the United States.

Cope was a Quaker and consequently refused to carry a gun during his Western journeys despite the very real danger from Indians. At one point, surrounded by hostile Indians, he flabbergasted them by taking out his false teeth and putting them back, over and over. When all had had a chance to watch this, they let him go.

In his search for a driving force in evolution, he retreated nearly to the position of Lamarck [336] and felt that the natural movements of animals helped alter and develop the moving parts. He called this kinetogenesis. In his efforts to beat out Marsh, Cope went to the lengths of trying to telegraph descriptions of fossils in order to establish priority. In the end, both he and Marsh impoverished themselves in their competition.

In 1889 the drain on his resources produced by his field trips forced him to retire to mere teaching at the University of Pennsylvania.

[749] **KRAFFT-EBING,** Baron Richard von (krahft ay'bing)
German neurologist
Born: Mannheim, Baden, August 14, 1840
Died: Mariagrun, near Graz, Austria, December 22, 1902

Krafft-Ebing began his psychiatric career as a professor of psychiatry at the University of Strasbourg in 1872 and then as director of an insane asylum at Graz.

He published a textbook on psychiatry which went through seven editions in his lifetime. His great work, however, and the one for which he is chiefly remembered today is his study of case histories of sexual abnormality in a book entitled *Psychopathia Sexualis,* first published in 1886. It is mostly descriptive, but it helped initiate the scientific discussion of sexual abnormality, which was to culminate two decades later in Freud's [865] theories. Krafft-Ebing introduced such terms as "paranoia," "sadism," and "masochism."

He served as professor of psychiatry at several Austrian universities, culminating with an appointment at the University of Vienna in 1889 where he remained until his death.

[750] **KOVALEVSKI,** Alexander Onufriyevich (koh-va-lev'skee)
Russian embryologist
Born: Dünaburg (now Daugavpils), Latvia, November 19, 1840
Died: St. Petersburg (now Leningrad), November 22, 1901

Like many Russian scholars, Kovalevski, the son of a landowner of Polish descent, received a good German education. He studied at the universities of Heidelberg and Tübingen and received his doctorate in 1867. He then obtained a professorial appointment at the University of St. Petersburg, teaching later at other schools as well.

He was a student of Haeckel [707] and therefore a strong evolutionist. He, more than anyone else, in fact, introduced Darwinism into Russia. In the 1870s his careful researches bridged the gap between vertebrates and invertebrates. In the first place he studied embryonic development intensively (following Haeckel's belief that the embryo follows the line of evolution), searching for similarities across the wide gaps dividing the main groups of creatures.

Thus, Remak [591] had shown that vertebrate embryos developed three germ layers, each one of which gave rise to a specific group of organs. Kovalevski was able to show that these same three germ

489

layers also appeared among invertebrates as well.

Furthermore, he studied such nonvertebrates as amphioxus and tunicates and showed that the former possessed a notochord and the latter did so at least in its larval stage. A larval notochord was also to be found in the balanoglossus, or acorn worm. Vertebrates possess notochords in the embryonic stage and so Kovalevski suggested the existence of a phylum that consists largely but not entirely of the vertebrates and that also includes related invertebrate forms. Balfour [823], who made the same suggestion independently, suggested the name Chordata for the phylum in question.

Thus another sharp dividing line was broken down and a further impulse was given to the concept of life as a basic unit, differentiated into grander and smaller divisions and subdivisions by slow change over the eons, and not as a series of forever separate and unchangeable species.

[751] **AMAGAT,** Émile Hilaire
French physicist
Born: Saint-Satur, January 2, 1841
Died: Saint-Satur, February 15, 1915

Amagat obtained his doctorate in 1872 and taught first in Switzerland, then in France.

He was particularly interested in working with substances (particularly gases) under high pressure and observing their properties under those conditions. In the 1880s he managed to attain a pressure equal to 3,000 atmospheres. This was a record for the nineteenth century and pointed the way to the further work of Bridgman [1080] a couple of decades later.

[752] **GRAEBE,** Karl James Peter (greh'buh)
German chemist
Born: Frankfurt-am-Main, February 24, 1841
Died: Frankurt-am-Main, January 19, 1927

Graebe, the son of a soldier, graduated from Heidelberg in 1862. At his father's wish, he studied engineering but soon followed his heart into chemistry. He studied under Kolbe [610], served as assistant to Bunsen [565], and then joined Baeyer's [718] laboratory in 1865.

Graebe was working on alizarin in 1868. Baeyer himself suggested a mode of attack and when Graebe proved reluctant to follow the suggestion, he put it in the form of an order, forcing Graebe into fame. Graebe and a fellow student attempted the experiment and the result clearly demonstrated alizarin to have a molecular structure based on anthracene, a compound made up of three joined rings of carbon atoms. It was now comparatively simple to reverse the process and, starting with anthracene from coal tar, make alizarin out of it. By 1869 a practical method for this was evolved, partly by accident (a mixture was inadvertently left over a flame and forgotten until it charred).

Perkin [734] worked out the synthesis of alizarin also and obtained a patent on June 26, 1869, only one day after Graebe and his co-workers obtained theirs. In 1870 Graebe was appointed professor of chemistry at the University of Königsberg, and in 1878 he transferred to the University of Geneva.

Graebe introduced the familiar terms "ortho," "meta," and "para" by which organic chemists describe the structure of aromatic compounds.

Graebe's life had its misfortunes. He suffered a nervous breakdown in 1875. He lost all he had in the inflation that followed World War I. He died, in the end, penniless and disregarded.

[753] **DUTTON,** Clarence Edward
American geologist
Born: Wallingford, Connecticut, May 15, 1841
Died: Englewood, New Jersey, January 4, 1912

Dutton graduated from Yale in 1860, when he was only nineteen, and almost at once faced the enormous fact of the Civil War. He joined the Union army in

1862 as a first lieutenant and remained in the service thereafter, though not always on active duty. In 1890 he reached the rank of major.

After the war he grew interested in geology and joined a governmental survey of the nearly empty West, studying volcanic eruptions and earthquakes. He developed methods for determining the depth of earthquake origin and the velocity with which earthquake waves travel through the earth.

He maintained that the rocks under the continents were less dense than those under the oceans and that the continents were dry precisely because they were light enough to ride high on the rocks making up the outer layers of the planet. The notion that the major slabs of rock found their natural level (through a very slow process), sinking or rising according to their densities, he gave the name "isostasy."

Late in life, in 1906, he suggested that pockets of radioactivity might slowly overheat local areas of the earth's crust and give rise to volcanic action. This was the first realization of the role of the very slow but very steady heat production of radioactive elements in connection with geologic processes.

[754] JAMES, William
American psychologist
Born: New York, New York,
January 11, 1842
Died: Chocorua, New Hampshire,
August 26, 1910

William James was the son of Henry James, the Swedenborgian philosopher, and the brother of Henry James, the novelist. His life was plagued by ill health and by an initial uncertainty as to goals. He dabbled in art in his youth, then studied medicine, but broke that off in 1865 to travel to the Amazon valley as assistant to the naturalist Agassiz [551]. He returned to his medical studies and in 1867 went to Europe, where he studied under men such as Bernard [578], Helmholtz [631], and Virchow [632], these studies arousing his interest in physiology. In 1869 he obtained his

medical degree from Harvard but his health did not permit him to practice.

In 1872 he accepted a faculty post in physiology at Harvard, but in 1876 he took the daring step of switching to psychology, a science then in its barest infancy. He viewed it as an experimental science based on physiology and not as a vague form of philosophy. He prepared a monumental two-volume work *The Principles of Psychology* in 1890, and from this was prepared a shorter textbook that was standard for many years. He was temperamentally unsuited to laboratory work himself but students of his, such as Granville Hall [780], carried on.

Later in life he turned to the psychology of religion (his book *The Varieties of Religious Experience*, published in 1902, proved an enduring success) and to philosophy. He also came to be interested in psychic research, which had grown fashionable at the turn of the century.

[755] BREUER, Josef (broi'er)
Austrian physician
Born: Vienna, January 15, 1842
Died: Vienna, June 20, 1925

Breuer, the son of a Jewish teacher of religion, studied at the University of Vienna and obtained his medical degree in 1867 and soon became one of the most highly regarded physicians in Vienna. In physiology, Breuer, together with the physiologist Ewald Hering, demonstrated the reflexes involved in respiration, in 1868. He went on, in the 1870s, to demonstrate the functioning of the semicircular canals of the inner ear as organs of balance.

In 1880 Breuer moved into a new area, when he studied a patient whom he reported on as "Anna O." She suffered from psychological disturbances, including various disabilities (even occasional paralysis) and a dissociated personality.

Breuer found that if Anna O. could be induced to relate her fantasies, sometimes with the help of hypnosis, her symptoms were alleviated. He decided that important causes of such ailments were embedded in the unconscious mind and that verbalizing them consciously offered a chance of a cure.

This was important in itself and was even more important in that he described his theories to Freud [865], who carried the matter further. Breuer was thus the most important precursor of psychoanalysis. Breuer, himself, did not wish to continue in the field and willingly left its future development to Freud.

Freud quarreled with Breuer in 1896 and they never spoke again, but then Freud was a difficult person who quarreled with many people.

[756] **FLAMMARION**, Nicolas Camille (fla-mah-ree-ohn')
French astronomer
Born: Montigny-le-Roi, Haute Marne, February 26, 1842
Died: Juvisy-sur-Orge, June 3, 1925

As a youngster, Flammarion, the son of a storekeeper, was already caught in the allure of astronomy and wrote a 500-page manuscript on the universe. When Flammarion was ill, the doctor tending him came across that manuscript and was sufficiently impressed to bring it to the attention of Leverrier [564], who helped him get a position at the Paris Observatory in 1858.

There was nothing wrong with either Flammarion's nerve or his imagination. He made numerous balloon ascensions and he threw himself wholeheartedly into the Martian canal controversy that had been initiated by Schiaparelli [714], coming down hard on the side of the existence of the canals and of intelligent life on Mars, a life perhaps more advanced than earth's. Meanwhile, he had also reported detecting changes in one of the craters of the moon and maintained they were the result of growing vegetation. He believed ardently, in fact, that all worlds were inhabited by living beings.

Late in life (perhaps not surprisingly) he took to psychical research. His great service, however, was in science popularization. His book *Popular Astronomy*, published in 1879 and translated into English in 1894, was the best book of its sort produced in the nineteenth century.

He published several science fiction novels as well.

[757] **VOGEL**, Hermann Carl (foh'-gul)
German astronomer
Born: Leipzig, Saxony, April 3, 1841
Died: Potsdam, August 13, 1907

A pioneer of spectroscopic astronomy, Vogel, the son of a high school principal, graduated from his father's school but had trouble going on to college when his father's death left him with financial problems. He accepted help from an older brother, found work, accumulated the necessary funds, and was finally able to get university training in astronomy.

He became an assistant at the Leipzig Observatory in 1867 and director of a private observatory in 1870. He was one of those who, along with Huggins [646] and Janssen [647], tried to analyze the planetary atmospheres by spectroscope in the 1870s.

In 1882 he became the director of the Potsdam Observatory, and about 1890 made his most spectacular discovery. Studying the velocities of stars in the line of sight by the shifting of spectral lines according to Fizeau's [620] principle, he found that in some stars the lines shifted first one way then the other. The star, in other words, was alternately receding from us and advancing. This was interpreted as a revolution with some dimmer companion about a center of gravity. The star was actually two stars, so close that no telescope existing (then or now) could show them separate, yet clearly shown to be double by spectroscope. Thus were spectroscopic binaries discovered.

There are large numbers of them and the component stars of such binaries are sometimes so close as to be almost in contact, colossal whirling dumbbells of flaming gas.

He also showed that Algol was indeed an eclipsing binary as Goodricke [381] had suggested a century before.

[758] **LINDE,** Karl Paul Gottfried von
(lin'duh)
German chemist
Born: Berndorf, Bavaria, June
11, 1842
Died: Munich, Bavaria, November 16, 1934

Linde, the son of a minister, studied engineering at Zürich Polytechnic, where Clausius [633] was one of his teachers.

Beginning in 1870, when he became a professor of theoretical engineering in a Munich school of technology, Linde grew interested in the task of obtaining low temperatures. In 1876 he devised the first practical refrigerator, basing it on liquid ammonia.

In 1895 Linde saw that the Joule-Thomson effect could be made to pull temperature down by its own bootstraps, so to speak. After allowing condensed gas to expand and cool, he led the cool gas back so that it might bathe a container holding another sample of compressed gas. This second sample was thus cooled far below the original temperature of the first sample. When the second sample was now allowed to expand, its temperature dropped lower still and could be used to cool a third sample of compressed gas. This was repeated, with lower temperatures reached at each step. Using this principle he set up a continuous process by which large quantities of liquefied gases (instead of mere cupfuls) could be produced. Liquid air became a commercial commodity instead of a laboratory curiosity. Linde further developed methods of separating the oxygen and nitrogen and producing both in liquid form in quantities large enough for industrial use.

Linde was ennobled in 1897.

[759] **DEWAR,** Sir James (dyoo'er)
Scottish chemist and physicist
Born: Kincardine, Fife, September 20, 1842
Died: London, England, March 27, 1923

Dewar, the son of an innkeeper, was educated at the University of Edinburgh

and studied abroad under Kekulé [680]. In 1875 he obtained a professorial position at Cambridge and, two years later, at the Royal Institution in London, holding both posts throughout his life.

His researches covered a wide field, for he published papers on organic chemistry, on the measurement of high temperatures, on the effect of light upon the retina, and on spectroscopy.

His most important work, however, was in the field of extremely low temperatures. His interest was kindled in the 1870s, when Cailletet [698] and Pictet [783] simultaneously and independently announced the liquefaction of gases such as oxygen, nitrogen, and carbon monoxide and attained temperatures less than eighty degrees above the absolute zero.

In 1891 Dewar constructed a device that produced liquid oxygen in quantity and he was able to study the substance in some detail. He showed that it was attracted by a magnet, as was liquid ozone (a variety of oxygen).

In 1892 he constructed double-walled flasks with a vacuum between the walls. The vacuum would not transmit heat by conduction or by the convection of air currents. It would do so only by radiation. By silvering the walls so that radiated heat would be reflected rather than absorbed, Dewar cut down on that variety of heat transmission as well. In such flasks the extremely low-temperature liquid oxygen could be kept for much longer periods than it could ordinarily, simply because heat entered the interior of the flask from the outside world only very slowly. Such flasks are called Dewar flasks and have been adapted to everyday uses, for keeping hot coffee hot during trips, for instance, or keeping cold milk cold (since heat transfer is barred in either direction). The home variety of the Dewar flask is better known as a Thermos bottle.

Dewar then began to experiment with hydrogen, which still resisted liquefaction. He made use of the Joule-Thomson effect, first discovered by Joule [613] and Kelvin [652] to produce low temperatures, as Cailletet and Pictet had done, but used the system of regeneration that Linde [758] had introduced. He built a large-scale machine in which this process could be carried out more extensively and efficiently than ever before. The result was that hydrogen was liquefied in 1898 and solidified in 1899. In this way Dewar reached a temperature of only fourteen degrees above absolute zero.

At this temperature, all substances were reduced to a solid state, except for a new gas, helium, that had just been discovered by Ramsay [832] and that, at that temperature, was not even liquefied. It resisted all efforts at liquefaction for another decade, when Kamerlingh Onnes [843] finally succeeded.

In 1891, while Dewar was engaged in these projects of importance to basic chemistry and physics, he was also involved in the highly practical study of explosives. Together with Abel [673], he developed cordite, the first practical smokeless powder. The development of cordite did not come about, however, until after long discussions with Nobel [703]. Nobel indignantly protested the patent issued Dewar and Abel and sued. He lost his case, but some justice seems to have been on his side. Dewar was knighted in 1904.

[760] **RAYLEIGH**, John William Strutt, 3d Baron
English physicist
Born: Terling Place, near Malden, Essex, November 12, 1842
Died: Witham, Essex, June 30, 1919

Strutt at the age of thirty-one inherited his father's title, so that he is almost invariably referred to as Lord Rayleigh.

At school, where he attended the lectures of Stokes [618], his mathematical talent was evident and in 1865 he finished at the head of his class in mathematics at Cambridge. He suffered an attack of rheumatic fever in 1871 and on a rest-and-recuperation visit to Egypt, he rested and recuperated by beginning work on a monumental text on sound.

In 1873, the same year in which he became Lord Rayleigh, he was elected to the Royal Society, and in 1879 he succeeded Maxwell [692] as director of the

Cavendish Laboratory at Cambridge, holding the post till 1884.

Through most of his professional life he was interested in wave motion of all varieties. As far as electromagnetic waves were concerned he worked out an equation to account for the variation of light-scattering with wavelength and was able to confirm Tyndall's [626] view of light-scattering by atmospheric dust as accounting for the blueness of the sky. (Dewar [759], who had discovered that liquid oxygen was blue, wrongly suspected that the sky was blue because of the oxygen in the atmosphere.)

Rayleigh also worked out an equation to account for the manner of distribution of wavelengths in black-body radiation, a question that had been raised by Kirchhoff [648]. Rayleigh's equation, however, advanced toward the end of the century, proved to hold only for long-wave radiation, as another equation evolved at about the same time by Wien [934] held only for short-wave radiations. Both equations were soon to be hurled into limbo by the shattering work of Planck [887].

Rayleigh studied sound waves, too, as well as water waves and earthquake waves. His careful work helped to establish the accurate determination of absolute units in electricity and magnetism, the work of Rowland [798] in America also contributing.

And yet Rayleigh's most famous discovery was in chemistry and not in physics at all. It began in a theoretical manner, for he became interested in Prout's [440] hypothesis, according to which all the atoms of the various elements were built up out of hydrogen atoms, so that all atomic weights ought to be exact multiples of that of hydrogen. This had been a dead letter for over half a century, and it was as certain as anything could be, thanks to Stas [579] and others, that atomic weights were *not* exact multiples of hydrogen.

Nevertheless, Rayleigh felt like trying again. He went about it by measuring densities of gases very accurately. In this manner he was able to show in 1882 that the ratio of the atomic weights of oxygen and hydrogen was not 16:1 as the hypothesis would require but 15.882:1. Once again Prout's hypothesis was killed, making perhaps the hundredth time in all. (And yet, by one of the supreme ironies of scientific history, the hypothesis was to undergo a startling resurrection within a generation, in a new and much more sophisticated guise.)

However, in doing all this, Rayleigh came across a curious puzzle. With oxygen, he always obtained the same density, regardless of how the oxygen might be produced, whether from one particular compound, from a second compound, or from the air. The situation was different with nitrogen. The nitrogen he obtained from air consistently showed a slightly higher density than the nitrogen he obtained from any of various compounds.

Rayleigh could think of several ways in which the nitrogen obtained from air might be contaminated but none of the possibilities checked out experimentally. He was so frustrated that he went so far as to write to the journal *Nature* asking for suggestions. Ramsay [832], a brilliant Scottish chemist, asked permission to tackle the problem and received it. The upshot was that a new gas, somewhat denser than nitrogen, was discovered to exist in the atmosphere. Its existence was announced on August 13, 1894. It was named argon and, it was the first of a series of rare gases of unusual properties whose existence had never been suspected.

The year 1904, then, presented the scientific world with a curious spectacle. Rayleigh received the Nobel Prize in physics while Ramsay received the Nobel Prize in chemistry. Rayleigh donated the cash reward that accompanied the prize to Cambridge.

In 1905 Rayleigh was elected president of the Royal Society and in 1908 became chancellor of Cambridge University. Like several other scientists of the time, notably William James [754] and Oliver Lodge [820], he grew interested in psychic research about the turn of the century. The Second Scientific Revolution, after all, was under way then and cherished views were being upset. How far was the iconoclasm to go? How

many more things were there on heaven and earth than were dreamt of in Newton's [231] philosophy?

[761] **FERRIER,** Sir David
Scottish neurologist
Born: Aberdeen, January 13, 1843
Died: London, England, March 19, 1928

Ferrier obtained his medical degree in 1868. He did not like general practice and spent his time on neurological research instead. He worked, of necessity, where the neurological mechanisms were to be found—on living animals. As a result, he was accused of cruelty to animals and suit was brought against him in 1882. In the courtroom he upheld the necessity and value of animal experimentation and won his case.

He followed the work of Hitzig [731] in the stimulation of the cortex, using not only dogs as Hitzig did, but other animals, primates in particular, up to and including apes. He showed that in the brain's cortex there were both motor regions, controlling the responses of muscles and other organs, and sensory regions, receiving sensations from muscles and other organs. He was also able to map out the location of the various parts of the body affected on both regions. He was knighted in 1911.

[762] **FLEMMING,** Walther
German anatomist
Born: Sachsenberg, Mecklenburg, April 21, 1843
Died: Kiel, Schleswig, August 4, 1905

Flemming, who was of Flemish descent, obtained his medical degree in 1868, served as assistant to Kühne [725] the next year, and then did his duty as a physician on the Prussian side of the Franco-Prussian War of 1870.

His first professorial appointment was at the University of Prague in 1872, where he was plagued by the growing resentment of Czech students against German domination. He escaped in 1876 by becoming professor of anatomy at the University of Kiel, a position he held for the rest of his life.

Since the time Schleiden [538] and Schwann [563] had enunciated the cell doctrine a generation earlier, research into the inner workings of cells had lagged. The trouble was that cells are quite transparent so that little inner detail can be made out under the microscope. As the mid-century passed, however, the age of the synthetic dyestuff dawned, thanks largely to Perkin [734], and in the 1870s cytologists learned how to apply these dyes to cells. Flemming and Ehrlich [845] were among the pioneers in this respect.

Parts of the cell were found to absorb some dyes, while other parts did not, so that the transparent cell was converted into a panorama in color. In this way Strasburger [768] was able to observe and describe the changes that went on in plant cells during cell division.

Flemming studied animal cells and produced the classic work on the subject. He found that scattered within the cell nucleus was material that strongly absorbed the dye he was working with. He called this absorptive material chromatin, from the Greek word for color.

When he dyed a section of growing tissue, cells were caught at different stages of cell division and he could sort out the successive stages through which the chromatin material passed. As the process of cell division began, the chromatin coalesced into short threadlike objects, which eventually came to be called chromosomes ("colored bodies"). Because these threadlike chromosomes were so characteristic a feature of cell division, Flemming named the process mitosis, from a Greek word for thread.

As cell division proceeded, the chromosomes doubled in number. After that came what seemed the crucial step. The chromosomes, entangled in the fine threads of a structure which Flemming named the aster ("star") were pulled apart, half going to one end of the cell, half to the other. The cell then divided and the two daughter cells were each left with an equal supply of chromatin material. And, because of the doubling of the chromosomes before the division, each daughter cell had as much chromatin as the original undivided cell.

Flemming summarized his observations in a masterly book, *Cell Substance, Nucleus, and Cell Division,* published in 1882.

At the time, Flemming did not see the genetic significance of all this, for he was unaware of Mendel's [638] work. However, when Mendel was rediscovered by De Vries [792] two decades later, the work of Flemming and of Beneden [782] provided the physical basis for the rules of inheritance Mendel had discovered empirically.

[763] **GILL,** Sir David
Scottish astronomer
Born: Aberdeen, June 12, 1843
Died: London, England, January 24, 1914

Gill, the son of a watchmaker, at first intended to continue his father's business, and did so. At the University of Aberdeen, however, he had attended classes taught by Maxwell [692] and grew more and more interested in astronomy. He turned dreams to reality when he accepted the post of private astronomer to a Scottish lord who was building an observatory.

A great deal of Gill's effort was expended on determining the exact distance of the sun. This is the astronomic unit against which all the remaining distances within the solar system are compared.

In order to determine the astronomic unit, Gill headed an expedition to the Indian Ocean island of Mauritius in 1874 to observe a transit of Venus, and in 1877 he headed another expedition to the Atlantic Ocean island of Ascension to observe Mars at its time of close approach. The place where he did his work is still called Mars Bay. Both expeditions were designed to determine a distance (of Venus in one case, of Mars in the other) from which the astronomic unit could be computed.

The results were not what was hoped for because both Venus and Mars have perceptible discs with boundaries that are fuzzy because of their atmospheres. This makes it difficult to determine the precise time when they make apparent contact with the sun. It occurred to Gill, as it had previously occurred to Galle [573], that observation of the more prominent asteroids, which were starlike points of light, might be more profitable, even though the asteroids were further than either Venus or Mars. By 1889 he had completed such observations with heartening results and obtained the first determination of the sun's distance with modern accuracy in 1901.

Nine years later, the asteroid Eros was discovered and was found to have an unprecedented orbit lying between Mars and the earth. It could approach the earth to within 15 million miles (closer than either Mars or Venus). Gill's initial efforts were therefore improved upon by Jones [1140] a generation later at the time of a close approach of Eros to the earth.

From 1879 to 1907 Gill was astronomer royal at the Cape of Good Hope Observatory. In 1882 he photographed a comet, and the number of stars on the plate convinced him that stellar photography was eminently practical. From his strategically placed post in the southern hemisphere, he swept the heavens photographically—the first to perform this service for the southern stars. With Kapteyn [815] he extended Argelander's [508] star chart to the south celestial pole. He was knighted in 1900.

[764] **GOLGI,** Camillo (gole′jee)
Italian histologist
Born: Corteno (now Corteno Golgi [renamed in his honor] Brescia), July 7, 1843
Died: Pavia, Lombardy, January 21, 1926

Golgi, the son of a physician, entered medicine and obtained his degree in 1865 from the University of Padua, going on to do his research at the University of Pavia. At first he gravitated toward psychiatry, but he came under the influence of Virchow's [632] work and devoted himself thereafter to the study of cells and tissues.

In 1873 he published the key discovery of his life. Cellular staining was being brought into prominence by men such as Flemming [762], Koch [767], and Ehrlich [845], but they used organic dyes. Golgi, on the other hand, introduced the use of silver salts. By staining with this material, cellular components were revealed that are still called by such names as Golgi bodies and Golgi complex. These, first detected in the brain of a barn owl in 1898, have fascinated cytologists ever since, but their functions remain largely unknown.

Eventually Golgi applied his staining methods to nerve tissue in particular and found it well adapted for the purpose. He was able to see details not visible before, to make out the fine processes of the nerve cells in unprecedented detail, to distinguish different types of Golgi cells and to bear out Waldeyer's [722] contention that the apparently joining fibers of different nerve cells did not really join, but left tiny gaps called synapses. Knowledge of the fine structure of the nervous system dates from this work and from that of Ramón y Cajal [827], who carried on the Golgi techniques.

Golgi was appointed professor of anatomy at the University of Siena in 1879 but transferred to the chair of histology and pathology at the University of Pavia the next year. There he ultimately served as president of the university. In the 1880s he turned his attention to malaria, which was making medical headlines as a result of Laveran's [776] discovery that it was caused by a protozoan. Golgi showed the difference between several varieties of the disease. In 1906 he shared with Ramón y Cajal (with whom he disagreed bitterly on points of theory) the Nobel Prize in medicine and physiology for the work he did on the structure of the nervous system.

[765] **ABNEY,** Sir William de Wiveleslie
English astronomer
Born: Derby, July 24, 1843
Died: Folkestone, Kent, December 2, 1920

Abney, the son of a clergyman, graduated from the Royal Military Academy and served with the Royal Engineers in India. He was invalided home, however, and with no military career to occupy him, he grew interested in photography.

In 1874 he invented a dry photographic emulsion (clearly easier to handle than a wet one) and used it to photograph a transit of Venus across the sun in December of that year.

He then devised a red-sensitive emulsion which made it possible to photograph, for the first time, the solar spectrum in the infrared in 1887. This made it possible to determine how sunlight was altered in passing through the atmosphere since some of the infrared was absorbed by air.

Working in the infrared also made it possible to detect absorption region caused by molecules rather than by individual atoms. In 1882, therefore, Abney was the first to try to correlate spectroscopic absorption with the structure of organic molecules (something that was to lead a century later to the determination of molecular structure in distant interstellar clouds of dust and gas).

He was knighted in 1900.

[766] **CHAMBERLIN,** Thomas Chrowder
American geologist
Born: Mattoon, Illinois, September 25, 1843
Died: Chicago, Illinois, November 15, 1928

Chamberlin was the son of a farmer who left North Carolina for Illinois because he disapproved of slavery. Chamberlin graduated from Beloit College in 1866 and did graduate work at the universities of Michigan and Wisconsin. By 1873 he was professor of geology at Beloit and in 1887 he became president of the University of Wisconsin.

As a geologist Chamberlin was particularly interested in glaciers and was one of the first to see that there was not one Ice Age but several. In delving further and further back in time, he found himself speculating not merely on the earth's youth, but on its birth.

In 1900 he revived a notion that Buffon [277] had advanced a century and a half earlier. Chamberlin, together with Moulton [1003], suggested that a star had passed close to our sun, that matter had been raised from both stars by tidal forces, that these cooled into small fragments (planetesimals), which further coalesced into the planets. This planetesimal hypothesis still holds good in part, for many geophysicists such as Urey [1164] believe the planetary bodies were built up at moderate temperatures out of smaller fragments though they consider these fragments were never part of the sun.

Despite its formidable championship a quarter century later by Jeans [1053], the hypothesis of stellar collisions or near collisions steadily lost popularity. The planetesimals are now considered to have arisen out of a turbulent cloud of dust and gas, as suggested by Weizsäcker [1376].

[767] **KOCH,** (Heinrich Hermann) Robert (kokh)
German bacteriologist
Born: Klausthal-Zellerfeld, Hanover (now in Lower Saxony), December 11, 1843
Died: Baden-Baden, Baden, May 27, 1910

Koch, one of thirteen children of a mining official, obtained his medical degree in 1866 at the University of Göttingen, where Wöhler [515] and Henle [557] were among his teachers. He graduated *cum laude* but showed no particular sign that he was destined to be, along with Pasteur [642], the founder of modern medical bacteriology. He dreamed, in fact, of being an explorer, but his wife (less romantic than he) quashed that notion. (Late in life he had his revenge, for he divorced her and married a much younger woman, shocking the Victorian society of the times.) After serving as an army surgeon on the Prussian side during the Franco-Prussian War, Koch settled down to the life of a country doctor near Breslau in Silesia.

An anthrax epidemic struck the cattle

498

in the area, and Koch studied the disease. Painstakingly in 1876 he obtained the bacterium causing anthrax from the spleen of infected cattle and transferred it to mice, carrying the infection from mouse to mouse and recovering the same bacilli in the end. More important still, he learned to cultivate the bacteria outside the living body, using blood serum at body temperature. In this way he was able to follow the entire life cycle of the anthrax bacillus and to study its method of forming resistant spores.

Koch brought his work to the attention of the bacteriologist Cohn [675], who was teaching at the University of Breslau. Cohn invited the young doctor to his laboratory, studied his work, and enthusiastically sponsored the paper that Koch thereafter wrote.

Koch, enjoying a growing fame, transferred his labors to Berlin and developed two points of technique that were all important. First he made use of the aniline dyes that had been synthesized since Perkin's [734] time. These he tested for their possible use in staining bacteria for easier study. (Unstained bacteria are semitransparent and therefore hard to see.)

Furthermore, having made use of liquid media to grow bacteria outside an organism, Koch advanced to the use of solid media such as gelatin in the form of gels. Agar-agar, a complex carbohydrate obtained from seaweed, was a particularly good gel for the purpose. It is not itself edible, but a nutrient broth could be mixed with it. Originally, Koch used flat glass slides for the purpose, but an assistant, Julius Richard Petri, substituted shallow glass dishes with covers in 1887. Such Petri dishes have been used for the purpose ever since.

On such gels, bacteria could not move about, so that if one bacterium happened to be isolated on one spot of the medium, it would, by division and redivision, give rise to a patch of descendent bacteria, a colony consisting of members of one species all clumped together. Bacteria could then be transmitted to animals or allowed to start new cultures in the full knowledge that it was of a particular strain. In liquid media, however,

a number of varieties of bacteria were endlessly mixed and it was a tedious chore to attempt to separate them. Koch's solid media may be said to mark the beginning of a rationalized system of bacterial culturing and to mark the final victory of Pasteur's germ theory.

Koch established rules for properly identifying the causative agent of a disease. The microorganism must be located in the diseased animal. After being cultured, it must be capable of causing the disease in a healthy animal. The newly diseased animal must yield bacteria of the same sort found in the original animal.

Using his rules and his techniques, Koch isolated the specific bacteria of a number of diseases. His most remarkable discovery and the high point of his career was his discovery in 1882 of the tubercle bacillus, the causative factor of the dreaded disease tuberculosis. (This led him eventually to a search for a cure and in 1890 he thought he had one, announced it as such, and, to his intense disappointment, found the announcement had been premature.)

In 1883 he traveled to Asia to study bubonic plague and cholera and to Africa to study sleeping sickness. For his discovery of the cholera bacillus he received a government gift that was the equivalent of $25,000, and was appointed professor of hygiene at the University of Berlin in 1885. He was able to show, between 1897 and 1906, that the bubonic plague was transmitted by means of a flea that infested rats, while sleeping sickness was transmitted by the tsetse fly. This, together with the work of Laveran [776] and Ross [876] on malaria, pointed out new methods for the control of disease. Rather than a frontal attack on the bacteria themselves, the insect vector carrying the disease from person to person could be fought. The germ by itself is helpless (and man is safe) when the insect carrier is destroyed or immobilized.

A generation of bacteriologists received training and inspiration working with Koch. Gaffky [805], who accompanied Koch on his Asian travels, was one, and Kitasato [870] was another. The

Nobel Prize winners Behring [846] and Ehrlich [845] were also among Koch's assistants in their younger days.

In 1905 Koch was awarded the Nobel Prize in medicine and physiology, primarily for his discoveries in connection with tuberculosis.

[768] STRASBURGER, Eduard Adolf (shtrahs'boor-ger)
German botanist
Born: Warsaw, Poland, February 1, 1844
Died: Poppelsdorf, near Bonn, May 19, 1912

Strasburger, born of German parents in what was then Russian territory, studied in Warsaw and at the Sorbonne in Paris. He profited from hearing lectures by Nägeli [598] and Haeckel [707]. He received his doctorate at the University of Jena in 1866 and was appointed professor of botany there in 1869, moving on to the University of Bonn in 1880. He was one of the pioneers of cytology, studying the behavior of the plant cells during mitosis. He observed the union of nuclei when the sex cells of plants joined in the course of fertilization.

In 1882 he invented the terms "nucleoplasm" for the protoplasm within the nucleus and "cytoplasm" for the protoplasm outside it. In 1888 he showed that sex cells have only half the number of chromosomes of body cells, a fact that is crucial for the understanding of sexual reproduction.

In 1891 he demonstrated that fluids moved upward through stems by physical forces such as capillarity, rather than by primarily physiological ones.

[769] BOLTZMANN, Ludwig Edward (bohlts'mahn)
Austrian physicist
Born: Vienna, February 20, 1844
Died: Duino, near Trieste (then in Austria, now in Italy), September 5, 1906

Boltzmann, the son of a civil servant, received his Ph.D. from the University

of Vienna in 1866. His work on the kinetic theory of gases was done independently of Maxwell [692] and they share the credit.

Beginning in 1871, Boltzmann increased the rigor of the mathematical treatment and emphasized the statistical interpretation of the second law of thermodynamics, thus founding "statistical mechanics." He showed that Clausius' [633] concept of increasing entropy could be interpreted as increasing degree of disorder, laying the groundwork for the later achievements of Gibbs [740].

He was a firm proponent of atomism at a time when Ostwald [840] was mounting the final campaign against it. Boltzmann also advanced a mathematical treatment that explained the manner in which, according to the experimental observations of Stefan [715] (whom Boltzmann, in his college years, served as assistant), quantity of radiation increased as the fourth power of the temperature. This is therefore sometimes called the Stefan-Boltzmann law.

Boltzmann turned down a chance to succeed Kirchhoff [648] at Berlin but in 1894 succeeded to Stefan's post in Vienna.

Though Boltzmann lived longer than Maxwell, his life too was cut short. In his case it was suicide, brought on by recurrent episodes of severe mental depression accentuated, perhaps, by opposition to his atomistic notions by Ostwald and others.

His equation relating entropy and disorder was engraved on the headstone of his grave.

[770] MIESCHER, Johann Friedrich (mee'sher)
Swiss biochemist
Born: Basel, August 13, 1844
Died: Davos, August 26, 1895

Miescher was the son of a physician. His great moment came in 1869 when he isolated a substance containing both nitrogen and phosphorus from the remnants of cells in pus.

Hoppe-Seyler [663], who was Miescher's teacher, was much astonished, for lecithin, which he himself had discovered, was the only natural substance known, up to that time, to contain both nitrogen and phosphorus. Hoppe-Seyler refused to allow Miescher's work to be published for two years until he investigated matters himself and discovered a similar substance in yeast. Because the substance seemed to arise from the cell nuclei, it was named nuclein.

The name, later modified to nucleic acid, persists to the present day, although such substances have been found to exist in the cytoplasm as well as in the nucleus.

Later he found that nucleic acid and a simple protein called protamine existed in salmon sperm. He also noted that it was the carbon dioxide concentration in the blood, and not the oxygen concentration, that governs respiration rates.

He was another of those scientists who died prematurely of tuberculosis.

[771] **MANSON,** Sir Patrick
Scottish physician
Born: Old Meldrum, Aberdeen-shire, October 3, 1844
Died: London, England, April 9, 1922

Manson, the son of a bank manager, studied at Aberdeen University, getting his medical degree in 1866. He was stationed a year later in Formosa (now Taiwan) as medical officer to the Chinese Imperial Customs. He settled in Hong Kong in 1883 and founded a school there that eventually became the University of Hong Kong. He stayed in the Far East twenty-three years and helped introduce vaccination to the Chinese. His experiences there roused his interest in tropical medicine, which he established as a distinct specialty, founding a school in that field in London in 1899. (He is sometimes called the father of tropical medicine.)

He studied elephantiasis, for instance, in which there is a gross swelling of legs or other portions of the body resulting from infestation by certain worms. He was also the first to suggest that mosqui-

toes might be the agents for the spreading of malaria, something that was to bear valuable fruit with Ross [876].

His work led to the founding of the London School of Tropical Medicine in 1899, where he taught until his retirement in 1914. He was knighted in 1903.

[772] **CANTOR,** Georg
German mathematician
Born: St. Petersburg (now Leningrad), Russia, March 3, 1845
Died: Halle, Saxony, January 6, 1918

To designate Cantor by nationality is difficult. He was born in Russia, but his father, a well-to-do merchant, had emigrated to Russia from Denmark, and then left Russia for Germany when young Georg was only eleven. And in addition, the family was of Jewish descent, though his mother was born a Roman Catholic and his father was converted to Protestantism.

Even as a schoolboy Cantor showed talent for mathematics and eventually (over his father's objections) he made mathematics his profession. Weierstrass [593] and Kronecker [645] were among his teachers, and in 1867 he obtained his Ph.D. *magna cum laude* from the University of Berlin with a paper dealing with a point Gauss [415] had glossed over. He obtained an academic position at the University of Halle, advancing to a professorial appointment in 1872.

In 1874 Cantor, after an exchange of letters with Dedekind [688], began to introduce his intellect-shaking concepts of infinity. The notion of the infinite (sheer endlessness as exemplified, for instance, by the series of integers 1, 2, 3, . . .) had disturbed thinkers since the time of Zeno [16] twenty-three centuries earlier, and not all their thoughts had yet produced any clear-cut decision.

Cantor decided that to deal with the infinite, one must set up correspondences between two series. For instance, it is possible to match up the integers 1, 2, 3, . . . with the set of even integers 2, 4, 6, . . . in such a way that each integer in the first group is associated with the even integer in the second group that is equal to just twice itself. For every number in the first group there is one and only one number in the second; for every number in the second, one and only one in the first. This is one-to-one correspondence.

In this way one can fairly argue that the number of even integers is equal to the number of all integers, regardless of the fact that common sense would have it that the number of all integers is twice that of the number of even integers. The arithmetic of the infinite is not the same as the familiar arithmetic of the finite.

Galileo [166] had caught a glimpse of this in 1636 when he argued in similar fashion that the number of square integers was equal to the number of all integers. Cantor went on, however, to erect a complete logical structure in which a whole series of transfinite numbers was postulated, representing different orders of infinity, so to speak. Thus, all rational numbers could be set equal to the integers, but rational plus irrational numbers could not be. These together were the "real numbers" and they represented a higher transfinite number than the integers did. The number of points on a line matched all the real numbers and also represented the higher transfinite number. This correspondence between the points on a line and the set of real numbers was rigorously demonstrated by Cantor and Dedekind.

Cantor's views were not accepted by all his colleagues. Though Hermite [641] was sympathetic, Kronecker, who possessed a Zeno-like suspicion of the infinite, attacked Cantor's work with great vigor. Inspired by professional jealousy, Kronecker prevented Cantor's advancement, keeping him from a post at the University of Berlin, for instance. Cantor's mental health broke in 1884 under the strains of the controversy that followed and much of the rest of his life was spent in severe depression. He died in a mental hospital.

With the twentieth century, his work came to be accepted. Kronecker's objections are not taken very seriously by most mathematicians.

[773] **PFEFFER,** Wilhelm (pfef'er)
German botanist
Born: Grebenstein, Hesse, March 9, 1845
Died: Kassel, Hesse, January 31, 1920

Pfeffer, the son of an apothecary, was put to work in the family shop when he was fifteen. Eventually, though, he managed to enter the University of Göttingen and to get his Ph.D. there in 1865. He went on to teach botany at the University of Bonn.

In 1877 Pfeffer became a pioneer in serious work with semipermeable membranes (those with apertures so tiny that small molecules could go through but large ones, like those of proteins, could not). If a protein solution is separated from water by such a semipermeable membrane, water passes more easily across the membrane into the solution than out of it. Fluid, and pressure, accumulate on the solution side of the membrane. The process is osmosis and Pfeffer showed how one might measure the osmotic pressure resulting.

Pfeffer also showed that this osmotic pressure depended on the size of the molecules that were too large to pass through. This meant that, from osmotic pressure, the molecular weight of specific proteins could be determined. In this way Pfeffer was able to make the first reasonably reliable measurements of the size of giant molecules.

His life ended in disaster. There was his nation's shattering defeat in World War I and the death of his only son, killed in action less than two months before the armistice.

[774] **ROENTGEN,** Wilhelm Konrad (runt'gen)
German physicist
Born: Lennep, Rhenish Prussia, March 27, 1845
Died: Munich, Bavaria, February 10, 1923

Roentgen's father was a textile merchant and his mother was Dutch. He was educated in Holland and Switzerland

and his undergraduate degree was in mechanical engineering. (He was expelled from one school for ridiculing a teacher.)

At the University of Zürich, he studied under Clausius [633] and Kundt [744] and decided to make physics his profession.

After obtaining his doctoral degree in 1869, he worked as an assistant to Kundt. Kundt accepted positions in Germany and Roentgen accompanied him, doing solid work in many branches of physics.

The great moment that lifted Roentgen out of mere competence and made him immortal came in the autumn of 1895 when he was head of the department of physics at the University of Würzburg in Bavaria. He was working on cathode rays and repeating some of the experiments of Lenard [920] and Crookes [695]. He was particularly interested in the luminescence these rays set up in certain chemicals.

In order to observe the faint luminescence, he darkened the room and enclosed the cathode ray tube in thin black cardboard. On November 5, 1895, he set the enclosed cathode ray tube into action and a flash of light that did not come from the tube caught his eye. He looked up and quite a distance from the tube he noted that a sheet of paper coated with barium platinocyanide was glowing. It was one of the luminescent substances, but it was luminescing now even though the cathode rays, blocked off by cardboard, could not possibly be reaching it.

He turned off the tube; the coated paper darkened. He turned it on again; it glowed. He walked into the next room with the coated paper, closed the door, and pulled down the blinds. The paper continued to glow while the tube was in operation.

It seemed to Roentgen that some sort of radiation was emerging from the cathode-ray tube, a radiation that was highly penetrating and yet invisible to the eye. By experiment he found the radiation could pass through considerable thicknesses of paper and even through thin layers of metal. Since he had no idea of the nature of the radiation, he

called it X rays, X being the usual mathematical symbol for the unknown. This name persists today even though the nature of the radiation is now known. For a time, there was a tendency to call them Roentgen rays, but the inability of the non-Teutonic tongue to wrap itself about the German *oe* diphthong militated against that. The unit of X-ray dosage is, however, officially called the roentgen.

Roentgen was fully aware of the importance of the discovery and was in a fever to publish before he was anticipated. Yet he recognized the fantastic nature of the discovery, and he dared not publish without as much data as he could find. (Someone, years later, asked him what he thought when he discovered X rays. He answered peevishly, "I didn't think; I experimented.") For seven weeks he experimented furiously and then, finally, on December 28, 1895, submitted his first paper, in which he not only announced the discovery but reported all the fundamental properties of X rays, such as their ability to ionize gases and their failure to respond to electric or magnetic fields.

The first public lecture on the new phenomenon was given by Roentgen on January 23, 1896. When he had finished talking, he called for a volunteer, and Kölliker [600], almost eighty years old at the time, stepped up. An X-ray photograph was taken of his hand—which shows the bones in beautiful shape for an octogenarian. There was wild applause, and interest in X rays swept over Europe and America.

Other physicists quickly confirmed Roentgen's result. In fact, Crookes found he had actually observed X rays before Roentgen without realizing what he had.

X rays offered a new tool for medical diagnosis, for they penetrated the soft tissues of the body easily, but passed through bone only with considerable absorption. A beam of X rays passing through tissue on its way to a photographic plate will therefore cast a shadow of bones in white on black. Metal objects such as bullets, swallowed safety pins, and so on will show up very clearly. Decay in teeth will show up as gray on white. Only four days after news of Roentgen's discovery reached America, X rays were used to locate a bullet in a patient's leg. (It took a few tragic years to discover that X rays were also dangerous and could cause cancer, particularly that form called leukemia.)

Aside from its obvious applications, Roentgen's discovery galvanized the world of physics and led to a rash of further discoveries that so completely overturned the old concepts of the science, that the discovery of X rays is sometimes considered the first stroke of the Second Scientific Revolution. (The First Scientific Revolution is, of course, that which included Galileo [166] and his experiments on falling bodies.)

Within a matter of months, investigations of X rays led to the discovery of radioactivity by Becquerel [834]. Physicists now term all of nineteenth-century physics (with just a faint air of condescension) as classical physics.

The importance of the discovery was recognized in its own time but not always understood. Panicky members of the New Jersey legislature tried to push through a law preventing the use of X rays in opera glasses to protect maidenly modesty—about par, perhaps, for legislative intelligence. Nevertheless there was intelligent interest, too. Within a year of Roentgen's discovery, a thousand papers on X rays were published.

In 1896 Roentgen shared the Rumford medal with Lenard and in 1901, when the Nobel Prizes were set up, the first to be honored with a Nobel Prize in physics was Roentgen.

He had an opportunity to accept ennoblement from the king of Bavaria, with the right of using *von* before his name, but this he refused. He also made no attempt whatever to patent any aspect of X-ray production or to make any financial gain from a discovery that proved infinitely precious to science, medicine, and industry, a fact upon which Edison [788] commented with a kind of tolerant humor. (Still, Edison himself refused to patent a fluoroscope out of humanitarian motives.)

This was not because he could not have used the money. The aftermath of World War I was an inflation that impoverished many Germans, including Roentgen. He died at the worst of it and in quite straitened circumstances.

[775] **MECHNIKOV**, Ilya Ilich (mech'-nih-kuf)
Russian-French bacteriologist
Born: Ivanovka, Ukraine, May 16, 1845
Died: Paris, France, July 15, 1916

Mechnikov was the son of an officer of the Imperial Guard, though his mother was of Jewish descent. He had the best education that the Russian Empire could afford, which, of course, wasn't much. After graduating from the University of Kharkov he traveled to Germany for advanced study. Siebold [537] and Leuckart [640] were among his teachers, and he also worked with Kovalevski [750].

In 1867 he returned to Russia and obtained an academic position at the new university in Odessa. He was troubled by poor eyesight, a violent temper, and the general difficulty of working in tsarist Russia. In 1873, after his wife of five years died of tuberculosis, he even tried suicide by swallowing morphine, but took too large a dose and threw it up.

In 1882 Mechnikov resigned to devote himself to research. He was interested in digestion and while working with simple animals (so simple as to be transparent) he noted that they possessed semi-independent cells, which, although playing no direct part in digestion, were nevertheless capable of ingesting small particles. Any damage to the animals brought these cells to the spot at once.

Mechnikov followed up this lead in more complicated animals and eventually was able to show that the white corpuscles in animal blood (including human blood) corresponded to these cells, that it was their function to ingest bacteria. They flocked to the site of any infection and what followed was a battle between bacteria and what Mechnikov called phagocytes ("eating cells"). When the phagocytes lost heavily, their disintegrated structure made up pus. The white corpuscles, Mechnikov held, were an important factor in resistance to infection and disease. Virchow [632], on having phagocytes demonstrated to him, shook his head; he was not impressed. Mechnikov did not allow that to discourage him.

By 1888 Mechnikov's work had attracted the attention of Louis Pasteur [642], and the Russian was invited to join the Pasteur Institute. This he did, remaining in France till his death. It is for this reason that his name is sometimes seen in its French version, Élie Metchnikoff. On Pasteur's death in 1895, Mechnikov succeeded Pasteur as director of the Institute.

Mechnikov continued studies of the bacteria infesting the large intestine and became fascinated by their possible connection with longevity or the lack of it. He held that the natural life-span of man was one hundred and fifty years and believed that drinking cultured milk would help him attain it.

His work on white corpuscles earned for him, along with Ehrlich [845], the 1908 Nobel Prize in medicine and physiology. His work on longevity, which lent itself unfortunately to exploitation by dietary quacks and food faddists, requires only the comment that Mechnikov died at seventy-one.

[776] **LAVERAN,** Charles Louis Alphonse (la-vrahn')
French physician
Born: Paris, June 18, 1845
Died: Paris, May 18, 1922

The son of a military surgeon, Laveran took his medical degree in 1867 at the University of Strasbourg and eventually took up the role of military surgeon himself and served in Metz when it was under siege in the Franco-Prussian War. Between 1878 and 1883, he was stationed in Algeria and there he had ample opportunity to study malaria. In 1880 he discovered the causative factor of malaria and found it to be not a bacterium but a protozoon. It was the first case in which a protozoon, a one-celled animal, rather than a bacterium, was shown to

cause a disease. The discovery made no particular splash at first, however, and his career was not particularly benefited.

After another decade of service in France itself, Laveran retired from the army, entered the Pasteur Institute in 1896, and devoted the rest of his life to research on tropical disease. In 1907 the splash came at last. He was awarded the Nobel Prize in physiology and medicine for his discovery concerning protozoa and disease.

[777] **DARWIN,** Sir George Howard
English astronomer
Born: Down House, Kent, July 9, 1845
Died: Cambridge, December 7, 1912

George Darwin was the second son of Charles Darwin [554], but he avoided being swamped by his father's biological reputation by going into a different field of science. He studied astronomy and graduated from Cambridge with high honors, including second place in mathematics. In 1883 he was appointed a professor of astronomy at his alma mater.

His best work was done in connection with tides. Although some early scholars had connected the moon with the tides, it remained for Newton [231] to build a satisfactory rationale for them, pointing out the effect of lunar gravitation on earth's ocean cover. After Newton's time, Laplace [347], in his general elaboration of gravitational theory, went into the matter of tides in greater detail. It was left, however, for George Darwin to analyze all the various irregularities of tides created by the interference of land barriers and the frictional effects produced by the ocean bottom.

Darwin carried the consequences of tidal friction further. In a series of papers dating from 1879, he attempted to use it to forecast the far future and reveal the far past. The effect of tidal friction on the earth was to slow its rotation and to decrease its angular momentum. This decrease had to be made up for by an increase elsewhere in the earth-moon system. If the moon were to increase its angular momentum to make up for earth's decrease, this could only mean that the moon would have to increase its distance from the earth.

The effect of the tides would be to force a slow retreat on the moon as the day lengthened. This would continue until the earth's rotation was slowed to the point where its day would be equal to fifty-five times the length of the present day. One side of the earth would then perpetually face the far distant moon and the lunar tides would be frozen in place. Further changes would take place as a result of the lesser action of solar tides.

Working backward, the earth's period of rotation will have been shorter, and its angular momentum greater, in the past. The moon's share of angular momentum would then have to be less, which meant that it would have to be closer to the earth. Darwin carried this back to the point where the earth rotating at six times its present speed would be virtually in contact with the moon. This represented, he believed, the time at which the whirling earth threw off a portion of its outer crust by centrifugal action, losing angular momentum in that way.

This was the first attempt to work out a cosmogony based on known mathematical principles, rather than on vague generalization. Darwin tried to apply the effects of tidal friction to the evolution of stellar systems, including multiple stars. A generation later, Jeans [1053] was to continue and extend Darwin's work.

There were attractive points to all this, at least as far as the earth-moon system was concerned. It explained why the moon was less dense than the earth, since it was supposedly produced out of earth's outer layers, and it also explained why the granite layer that made up the continents was not continuous over the earth's surface. Some even suggested that the Pacific Ocean, which is free of granite, is the vast hole that marks the place where the moon was lost.

However, although tidal friction and the slowing of earth's rotation are matters that are still accepted, there is considerable doubt whether it can be extrapolated backward in time in such a way as to prove that the moon was ever part of the earth. The feeling is currently more general among astronomers that earth and moon developed independently, although the details are as yet very much in dispute.

In 1899 Darwin was made president of the Royal Astronomical Society and in 1905 he was knighted.

[778] LIPPMANN, Gabriel Jonas (leep-man')
French physicist
Born: Hollerich, Luxembourg, August 16, 1845
Died: aboard ship on the Atlantic Ocean, July 13, 1921

Lippmann, though born in Luxembourg, was born of French parents and the family settled in Paris while he was yet a boy.

In 1875 he received his Ph.D. from the Sorbonne, but by then he had already developed a capillary electrometer, which was capable of detecting as little as a change of a thousandth of a volt in the electromotive force.

He invented a number of other ingenious devices, but the one that made the biggest splash at the time was that of color photography. By using a thick emulsion over a mercury surface that reflected the incident light, he had the incoming light and the reflected light producing stationary waves that reproduced the original colors of the object photographed.

It was not really a practical method since a long exposure is required and no copies could be made, and it has no relation to modern methods of color photography. Nevertheless, the impression it made was such that Lippmann received the 1908 Nobel Prize for physics for it.

[779] WROBLEWSKI, Zygmunt Florenty von (vroo-blef'skee)
Polish physicist
Born: Grodno, Russia, October 28, 1845
Died: Cracow, Poland, April 19, 1888

Wroblewski, although a Pole by language and culture, was born and lived in that part of Poland which was then part of the Russian Empire. He entered the University of Kiev in 1862 and within a year was banished to Siberia for taking part in an unsuccessful Polish rebellion against Russian rule.

He was pardoned in 1869 and allowed to go to Germany to treat an eye condition. He continued his education there obtaining his Ph.D. in 1874 at the University of Munich, and did some postdoctorate work under Sainte-Claire Deville [603] in Paris. He finally received a professorial appointment at the Jagiellonian University in Cracow in 1882.

He is best known for his work on the liquefaction of the difficult-to-liquefy gases. Following the method of Cailletet [698] and improving on it, he produced liquid oxygen, nitrogen, and carbon monoxide in greater quantities than the former was able to. He was even able, for the first time, to get a fine mist of liquid hydrogen, the last known gas (at that time) to remain unliquefied.

He seemed to have a hint of strange electrical properties at very low temperatures but was prevented from carrying on his research when he died of burns in a fire that resulted when he accidentally overturned a kerosene lamp in his laboratory. It was Kamerlingh Onnes [843] who carried on the work of both liquefaction and the study of low temperature electrical properties to a climax.

[780] **HALL**, Granville Stanley
American psychologist
Born: Ashfield, Massachusetts,
February 1, 1846
Died: Worcester, Massachusetts,
April 24, 1924

Hall, the son of a state legislator, graduated from Williams College in 1867 and then did graduate work at Harvard under William James [754], obtaining his Ph.D. in 1878. After further studies in Germany, under Helmholtz [631] among others, he was given a special lectureship in 1882 at Johns Hopkins and was made professor of psychology and pedagogics in 1883.

At Johns Hopkins he established a laboratory in experimental psychology inspired by his reading of the work of Wundt [697]. It was the first of its type in the United States. He also pioneered in the study of child psychology. In 1889 he became president of the newly formed Clark University in Worcester and remained in that post until his retirement in 1919.

[781] **REMSEN**, Ira
American chemist
Born: New York, New York,
February 10, 1846
Died: Carmel, California, March 4, 1927

Remsen obtained his medical degree in 1867 from Columbia University's College of Physicians and Surgeons, but decided to make chemistry rather than medical practice his lifework. He went to Germany for postdoctorate work and caught some of the lectures of Liebig [532] then in the twilight of his career, and worked with the German chemist, Rudolf Fittig (1835–1910). He earned his Ph.D. in chemistry in 1870.

Back in the United States, he received a professorial appointment at Williams College in 1872, then in 1876 went on to the newly established Johns Hopkins University in Baltimore, Maryland. There he introduced German methods of advanced laboratory instruction. In 1901 he became the second president of Johns Hopkins, one of whose buildings is still called Remsen Hall.

He is best remembered for the fact that in 1879 he and a student, Constantine Fahlberg, working under his direction, first synthesized orthobenzoyl sulfimide. Fahlberg accidentally discovered its intensely sweet taste (he put his fingers to his lips without knowing that a few grains had adhered to them) and patented the compound which is today known as saccharin.

[782] **BENEDEN,** Édouard Joseph
Louis-Marie van (beh-nay'den)
Belgian cytologist
Born: Louvain, March 5, 1846
Died: Liège, April 28, 1910

Beneden, the son of a biologist, became a professor of zoology at the University of Liège in 1870. He expanded
on Flemming's [762] work and in 1887
was able to demonstrate two key facts
about chromosomes. First, their number
was constant in the various cells of the
body and this number was characteristic
for a particular species. (It is now
known, for instance, that each human
cell contains forty-six chromosomes.)
Furthermore, he discovered that in the
formation of the sex cells, ova and spermatozoa, the division of chromosomes
during one of the cell divisions was not
preceded by a doubling. Each egg and
sperm cell has only half the usual count
of chromosomes.

This fitted in exactly with Mendel's
[638] theories of inheritance. If the chromosomes occurred in pairs, and if every
genetic factor existed in duplicate (one
on each of a particular chromosome
pair), then each parent would contribute
one such factor to a sex cell. When
ovum and sperm united in fertilization,
the chromosomes would reach their normal number and the offspring would
have a pair of factors again, one from
the mother and one from the father. As
soon as De Vries [792] rediscovered
Mendel, all this became clear.

[783] **PICTET,** Raoul Pierre (peek-
tay')
Swiss chemist
Born: Geneva, April 4, 1846
Died: Paris, July 27, 1929

Pictet, the son of a military officer, became professor of physics at the University of Geneva in 1877, moved to Berlin
in 1886, and later on went to Paris. He
was originally interested in the very
practical problem of the artificial production of ice (which had its value of

course as a refrigerant and, therefore,
food preserver) and from this his attention shifted to the production of extremely low temperatures.

His method was quite similar to that
of Cailletet's [698], but Pictet made use
of more elaborate equipment and was
able to produce greater quantities of the
liquefied gases.

[784] **PICKERING,** Edward Charles
American astronomer
Born: Boston, Massachusetts,
July 19, 1846
Died: Cambridge, Massachusetts,
February 3, 1919

Pickering was a descendant of an old
New England family. His great-grand-
father had served in George Washington's cabinet. He graduated *summa cum
laude* in 1865 from Harvard, taught
mathematics there for a couple of years,
then became professor of physics at
Massachusetts Institute of Technology.
There he established a laboratory which
was the first in the United States where
students could actually work with physical instruments. In 1876 he was appointed professor of astronomy at Harvard and became the director of its observatory.

He made important advances in spectroscopy. In 1882 he had a notion of
how to speed the study of spectra. Instead of trying to focus the stars one at a
time, through a small prism, he placed a
large prism in front of the photographic
plate. In this way every star in the field
was presented not as a sharp point but as
a tiny spectrum. Spectra in wholesale
numbers could be studied, and much
could be learned by way of statistical astronomy, after the fashion of Kapteyn
[815].

Much of the work was done by dedicated women such as Annie J. Cannon
[932] and Antonia C. Maury.

With his younger brother, William
Henry Pickering [885], he established an
astronomical observatory in Peru, in
1891.

In 1903 Pickering published a photographic map of the entire sky, the first such map ever published.

[785] WESTINGHOUSE, George
American engineer
Born: Central Bridge, New York, October 6, 1846
Died: New York, New York, March 12, 1914

Westinghouse's father, a manufacturer of agricultural implements, had a machine shop, and there Westinghouse had a chance to develop his inventiveness. After an interlude during which he served in the Union army in the Civil War, he made his fortune with the invention of the air brake in 1868 (which he improved to a pitch of true practicality in 1872). In this device it was compressed air, rather than muscle power, that applied the brakes.

When Westinghouse first took his invention to Cornelius Vanderbilt, the great railroad magnate, Vanderbilt called the whole notion of stopping a train by air sheer nonsense and would not listen. However, it quickly turned out that Vanderbilt's objections were the real nonsense and the Westinghouse air brake caught on like wildfire.

Westinghouse later took on the alternating current side of the electrical controversy, manufacturing equipment designed by Tesla [867] and fighting Edison [788] hard. In 1893 Westinghouse won the crucial victory by obtaining for his electrical company the contract to develop the Niagara Falls power on an alternating current basis.

He also developed a practical system for transporting gases through pipes under controlled conditions and over long distances. This made gas ovens and gas furnaces practical.

His fortune was more or less destroyed in the Panic of 1907, and his life ended with its aura of success tarnished. But money is no real measure, and in 1955 he was elected to the Hall of Fame for Great Americans.

[786] BAUMANN, Eugen (bow'mahn)
German chemist
Born: Cannstatt, Württemberg, December 12, 1846
Died: Freiburg, November 3, 1896

Baumann, who taught in Strasbourg, Berlin, and Freiburg, made his most important discovery in the last year of his life.

In 1896 he found that the thyroid gland was rich in iodine, an element not known before that to occur naturally in animal tissue. The thyroid was unique in being the only tissue to possess iodine. This led to the discovery of the iodine-containing thyroid hormone and to its use in the treatment of thyroid disorders.

[787] LE BEL, Joseph Achille
French chemist
Born: Merkwiller-Péchelbronn, Bas-Rhin, January 24, 1847
Died: Paris, August 6, 1930

Le Bel, a nephew of Boussingault [525], was more fortunate than most scientists, for he was well off financially because of family holdings in petroleum workings. When he inherited the fortune, he established his own laboratory.

He was educated in Paris where he studied under Balard [529], among others. He met Van't Hoff [829] briefly on the latter's visit, as a student, to Paris. In 1874, two months earlier than Van't Hoff, and quite independently, he announced the theory of the relationship of optical activity to molecular structure. His analysis was not quite as precise as Van't Hoff's, however, but it is customary to allow him an equal share of the credit.

Unlike Van't Hoff, Le Bel, who never married, retreated into isolation and did not go on to still greater things. In 1891 he tried to show that the spatial distribution of bonds about the nitrogen atom could also produce optical activity. Although the thought is correct, Le Bel's demonstration was faulty. The completion of this task had to await Pope [991].

[788] **EDISON,** Thomas Alva
American inventor
Born: Milan, Ohio, February 11, 1847
Died: West Orange, New Jersey, October 18, 1931

Edison was the son of a Canadian whose grandfather was an American Tory who had fled to Canada after the Revolutionary War. Edison's father fled back to the United States after the Canadian rebellion of 1837.

Young Thomas himself represents the classic tale, so beloved by Americans, of the self-made man—of the poor boy who, without schooling or influence, made his way to fame and fortune by hard work and intelligence.

He was a puzzling boy from the start. His curious way of asking questions was taken for queerness by the neighbors, and his schoolteacher told his mother he was "addled." Edison's mother, furious, took him out of school. She was in any case concerned for his delicate health and, being a schoolteacher by profession, could easily supervise his education herself. Edison also turned to books for an education. His unusual mind then began to show itself, for he remembered almost everything he read, and he read almost as quickly as he could turn the pages. He devoured nearly everything, though he found Newton's *Principia* too much for him—but then he was only twelve years old at the time.

When he began to read books on science, he turned to experimentation in a chemical laboratory he built in the house, as Perkin [734] was doing in England. In order to get money for chemicals and equipment he began to work. At the age of twelve he got a job as a newsboy on a train between Port Huron and Detroit, Michigan. (During the stop at Detroit, he spent his time in the library.)

Selling newspapers wasn't enough for Edison. He bought secondhand printing equipment and began to publish a weekly newspaper of his own, the first newspaper ever to be printed on a train. With his earnings he set up a chemical laboratory in the baggage car. Unfortu-

nately, a chemical fire started at one time and he and his equipment were thrown off the train. On another occasion, according to one story, which may not be true, while trying to board a freight train, he was helped in by the conductor, who used his ears as a handle. This resulted in his permanent deafness. (It should be pointed out that his son, Charles, who was one day to be governor of New Jersey, also suffered from deafness, so the condition may be organic and not externally imposed.)

In 1862 young Edison, in true Horatio Alger fashion, rescued a small boy on the train tracks and the grateful father, who had no money, offered to teach Edison telegraphy. Edison was eager to learn and quickly became the best and fastest telegrapher in the United States. He also earned enough money to buy a collection of the writings of Faraday [474], which solidified his interest in electrical technology.

In 1868 Edison went to Boston as a telegrapher and that year patented his first invention. It was a device to record votes mechanically. He thought it would speed matters in Congress and that it would be welcomed. However, a Congressman told him there was no desire to speed proceedings and that sometimes a slow vote was a political necessity. After that, Edison decided never to invent anything unless he was sure it was needed.

In 1869 he went to New York City to find employment. While he was in a broker's office, waiting to be interviewed, a telegraph machine broke down. Edison was the only one there who could fix it, and he was promptly offered a better job than he had expected to get. In a few months he decided to become a professional inventor, beginning with a stock ticker he had devised during his stay in Wall Street. He offered it to the president of a large Wall Street firm, wanting to ask $5000 but lacking the courage to do so. So he asked the president to make an offer and the president offered $40,000.

Edison, still only twenty-three, was in business. He founded the first firm of consulting engineers and for the next six years worked in Newark, New Jersey, turning out such inventions as waxpaper and the mimeograph, to say nothing of important improvements in telegraphy. He worked about twenty hours a day, sleeping in catnaps, and developed a group of capable assistants. Somehow he found time to get married.

In 1876 Edison set up a laboratory in Menlo Park, New Jersey, the first industrial research laboratory. It was to be an "invention factory." Eventually he had as many as eighty competent scientists working for him. It was the beginning of the modern notion of the "research team."

He hoped to be able to produce a new invention every ten days. He didn't fall far short of that, for before he died, he had patented nearly 1,300 inventions, a record no other inventor has ever approached. In one four-year stretch, he obtained 300 patents, or one every five days. He was called the Wizard of Menlo Park and in his lifetime it was already estimated that his inventions were worth twenty-five billion dollars to humanity—surely a conservative estimate. Needless to say, he himself profited far less than humanity generally.

In Menlo Park in 1877 Edison improved the telephone, invented earlier by Alexander Graham Bell [789], and made it practical. He also invented what proved to be his own favorite accomplishment—the phonograph. He put tin foil on a cylinder, set a free-floating needle skimming over it as the cylinder turned, and connected a receiver to carry sound waves to the needle. The needle, vibrating in time to the sound waves, impressed a wavering track on the tin. Afterward, following that track, it reproduced the sound waves (distorted but recognizable).

The device has been improved in detail since then (by Edison himself, to begin with). The cylinder has become a flat disc, thanks to Berliner [819], and the sound is magnified electronically and much improved in quality, but the basic principle remains the same.

With the invention of a machine that could talk, Edison finally convinced the world he could do anything. In 1878, still only thirty-one, he announced that he would tackle the problem of producing light by electricity. Now, inventors had been attempting this for many years, and several like Nernst [936] and Swan [677] had constructed devices for producing electrically generated light. Swan, indeed, had devised an incandescent bulb much like the one that Edison was later to construct, but he could not make the necessary vacuum within it sufficiently good for long life. Each had attained but a qualified success and no one had yet produced anything that could really be used cheaply and in quantity outside the laboratory, with a quality of light that could compete with burning gas. Nevertheless, when Edison announced that he would try, illuminating gas stocks tumbled at once in value in New York and London, so absolute was the faith in his ability.

This time, however, Edison had bitten off almost more than he could chew. What he was looking for was some sort of wire that could be heated to incandescence by an electric current. The wire would have to be kept within an evacuated glass chamber, of course, for in the presence of air it would simply burn up in the oxygen once it was heated hot enough to glow. It was hard to get a wire that would withstand the intense heat over a long period of time even in a vacuum and for a while it looked as though Edison would fail altogether. It took him $50,000 and a year of experimentation to find that platinum wires would not work.

After thousands of experiments, Edison found what he wanted: a wire that would warm to white heat in a vacuum without melting, evaporating, or breaking. No metal was needed after all —only a scorched cotton thread. Independently he had reached the same solution that Swan had arrived at in England.

On October 21, 1879, Edison set up a bulb with such a filament. It burned for forty continuous hours. The electric light was at last a reality and it received patent number 222,898. On the next New Year's Eve, the main street of Menlo Park was illuminated by electricity in a public demonstration before three thousand people who had come out of New York City to watch. Newspaper reporters from all the world came to cover the event and to marvel at one who was easily the greatest inventor since Archimedes [47] and very possibly of all time.

In a way, this was the climax of Edison's life, for nothing quite so dramatic ever happened again, although he worked on for more than half a century, and effectively, too. For instance, in order to make the electric light practical, Edison had to develop an electric generating system that would supply electricity as needed and in varying amounts, as lights were switched on and off. This required more ingenuity, if anything, than the electric light itself and was the greater feat, but by 1881 Edison had built such a generating station and within a year he was supplying about four hundred outlets divided among 85 customers. Edison might not have had the profundity of a Newton [231] or a Maxwell [692], but for sheer ingenuity he had no master.

In the business of producing electricity, Edison came into conflict with men such as Tesla [867] and Westinghouse [785] and here the hard-driving Edison sometimes showed the less attractive side of his nature.

In 1889 Edison tackled the problem of taking a series of photographs in rapid succession and then projecting them on a screen one after the other to give the illusion of motion. This too had been attempted, one way or another, for many years, with varying success, and no one man can clearly be credited with the invention of the motion picture. However, Edison made a crucial discovery. He used a strip of "film" of the sort invented by Eastman [852] and took a series of photographs along its length. These could be flashed on the screen in rapid succession by means of perforations along the sides of the film through which sprocket wheels could be used to move the pictures before the flashing light at a carefully regulated speed. In 1903 his company produced *The Great Train Robbery,* the first movie to tell a story. Once he had done all this,

Edison's interest flagged and others went on to develop the device further.

Edison had no patience with slow and analytical thought. His favorite method of working was to read everything and try everything in an all-devouring attack on every phase of a problem. He often conquered by sheer weight of effort. When eight thousand attempts to devise a new storage battery failed, he said, "Well, at least we know eight thousand things that don't work."

"Genius," he said, scorning those who spoke of insight, "is one percent inspiration and ninety-nine percent perspiration." This worked for him, to be sure, but there are few human beings with Edison's capacity for perspiration.

He was not always successful, however. At the turn of the century, he lost all he had in an attempt to work out a new method of dealing with iron ore. But he just went on to succeed in new directions.

Edison did record one purely scientific discovery. In 1883, in one of his experiments looking toward improving the electric light, he sealed a metal wire into a light bulb near the hot filament. To his surprise, electricity flowed from the hot filament to the metal wire across the gap between them. Edison wrote it up in his notebooks, patented it in 1884, and described it in the technical literature. It had no immediate utility for his purposes, so he did not follow it up with his accustomed intensity.

However, the Edison effect became very important indeed when the electronic structure of matter came to be understood in the next decade, thanks to the more scientific approach of men such as J. J. Thomson [869]. Fleming [803] put the Edison effect to use and out of his work arose the great electronics industry, including, of course, radio and television.

Although Edison was not, in the usual sense of the word, a scientist, he, more than anyone else, introduced the practical by-products of scientific advance to the public. He also helped foster the confusion (particularly in the United States) between science and invention, a confusion that has inhibited public support and understanding of basic science until the mid-twentieth century.

In 1960 Edison was elected as a member of the Hall of Fame for Great Americans.

[789] **BELL,** Alexander Graham
Scottish-American inventor
Born: Edinburgh, Scotland,
March 3, 1847
Died: Beinn Bhreagh, Nova Scotia, August 2, 1922

Bell was born into a dynasty interested in the problems of speech. Both father and grandfather had studied the mechanics of sound and Bell's father had been a pioneer teacher of speech to the deaf.

Between 1868 and 1870 Alexander, who was largely family-trained and self-taught, worked along with his father in studying speech and in teaching deaf children in Edinburgh. Two brothers, however, died of tuberculosis and he himself was threatened. What was left of the family moved to Canada in August 1870 and Alexander's health improved.

The next year he went to the United States and in 1873 was appointed professor of vocal physiology at Boston University. He fell in love with one of his deaf pupils, which helped drive him on even more furiously in his studies. He married her in 1877. He became interested in the mechanical production of sound and labored to improve the telegraph, basing his work on the theories of Helmholtz [631], and received the strong encouragement of the aged Henry [503]. When Bell referred ruefully to his own lack of electrical know-how, Henry said, "Get it!"

It seemed to Bell that if the sound wave vibrations could be turned into a fluctuating electric current, that current could be reconverted into sound waves identical with the original at the other end of the circuit. In this way, sound could be carried across wires at the speed of light.

One day, having spilled battery acid on his pants while working with an instrument designed to carry sound, he automatically cried out to his assistant, "Watson, please come here. I want you." Thomas Watson, at the other end of the circuit on another floor, heard the instrument speak and ran downstairs, beside himself with joy. It was the first important telephonic communication.

On March 7, 1876, Bell patented the telephone. Others disputed Bell's priority as absolute inventor, but Bell was certainly the first to commercialize the instrument successfully. In 1882 he became a citizen of the United States.

Edison [788] went on to devise a mouthpiece containing carbon powder, which transmitted electricity with greater or less efficiency as it was compressed or not compressed by the fluctuating air vibrations set up by sound. This created a current that fluctuated in perfect time to sound waves and greatly increased the ease with which the sounds could be made out. The device was so beautifully simple even without the improvement that it disappointed the great Maxwell [692], who expected something far more subtle of a device that could carry a voice.

However, simple or not, the telephone was a feature of the Centennial Exposition held at Philadelphia in 1876 to celebrate the hundredth anniversary of the Declaration of Independence. It was the great hit of the occasion, and the visiting Brazilian emperor, Pedro II, was greatly impressed, dropping the instrument to say, "It talks!" a fact that made headlines. The next to try was a British visitor, no less a person than Kelvin [652], who was equally impressed. In almost no time the telephone was introduced onto the American scene. In 1877 Queen Victoria herself acquired a telephone. Bell was famous and rich at thirty.

Bell continued his inventive career, working out improvements on Edison's phonograph, for instance. In 1881 he dramatically invented a metal-locating device to find the bullet in the body of President Garfield, who was slowly dying of an assassination attempt. The device was a workable one but was frustrated on this occasion because no one thought of removing the steel-springed mattress,

513

the metal of which interfered with the search.

Bell built a summer home in Nova Scotia, founded the American journal *Science* in 1883, and subsidized it generously in its first few years. He grew interested in aeronautics and supported Langley [711] financially, experimented with air conditioning and even with animal breeding. He received many honors during his life and in 1915 when the first transcontinental telephone line opened, Bell (in the East) spoke once again to his old assistant Watson, who was now in the Far West. Once again he said, as he had forty years before, "Watson, please come here. I want you." And the words spread, not from one room to another, but from one coast to another.

In 1950 Bell was elected to a niche in the Hall of Fame for Great Americans.

[790] **WALLACH,** Otto (vahl'ahkh)
German organic chemist
Born: Königsberg, Prussia (now Kaliningrad, USSR), March 27, 1847
Died: Göttingen, February 26, 1931

In 1867 Wallach entered the University of Göttingen for his graduate work. There he obtained his Ph.D. in 1869, studying under Wöhler [515], and Hofmann [604]. He went on to the University of Bonn in 1870, where he served as assistant to Kekulé [680]. He stayed at Bonn for nineteen years, becoming a professor of chemistry in 1876. In 1879 he had to undertake instruction in pharmacy, which was an untried field to him, but he threw himself into it with vigor.

For one thing, he found that he now had to deal with natural products, which were important as pharmaceuticals, and his chemist's instinct made him want to determine their molecular structure. Kekulé advised him against this, pointing out they formed mixtures that were too complex to be separated. Wallach was not to be deterred so Kekulé let him have, as a starter, some bottles of essential oils that had been standing on his shelves, unopened, for fifteen years.

These essential oils contained a group of substances called terpenes, of which such examples as menthol and camphor are best known to the general public. (The realization of their importance has grown steadily since Wallach's time, as it has turned out that vitamin A and related compounds, as well as the various steroids of which vitamin D and the sex hormones are examples, are related to the terpenes.) In 1884 Wallach began a line of research that was to last some twenty-five years. In that time he painstakingly separated one terpene from another and established the structure of each. The feat was difficult, as Kekulé had warned, but not impossible. Many of the terpenes have pleasant odors and Wallach's work did much to develop the modern perfume industry.

In 1889 Wallach received a professorial appointment at Göttingen, where he succeeded Viktor Meyer [796], and in 1910 he was awarded the Nobel Prize in chemistry for his work on terpenes.

Throughout his life, he was interested in art and, to the end, maintained an impressive art collection.

[791] **LANGERHANS,** Paul
German physician
Born: Berlin, July 25, 1847
Died: Funchal, Madeira, July 20, 1888

Langerhans, the son of a physician, got his medical degree in 1869 from the University of Berlin where he studied under Virchow [632] among others. While still a student, he worked in Virchow's laboratory and it was there that he began to specialize in microanatomy, studying tissues under the microscope.

For his doctoral dissertation in 1869 he prepared the first careful description of the microscopic structure of the pancreas. In the process he noted the numerous groups of cells that differed from the cells in the body of the pancreas. These groups have since been called the islets of Langerhans. It was not till considerably later that the function of the islets in secreting insulin was discovered and it was Banting [1152] who first showed how to prepare insulin from them.

In 1874 Langerhans was forced to interrupt his career because of tuberculosis. Eventually he retired to the island of Madeira in an attempt to find a cure. He practiced medicine there till his death.

[792] **DE VRIES,** Hugo Marie (duh vrees)
Dutch botanist
Born: Haarlem, February 16, 1848
Died: Lunteren, May 21, 1935

De Vries, the son of a government official, studied botany under Julius Sachs [699], earned his M.D. in 1870, and in 1878 became a professor of botany at the University of Amsterdam. In 1883 he studied the effect of salt solutions of different concentrations on plant cells, work that was to inspire Van't Hoff [829] to go on to do theoretical analyses of the properties of solutions. This work was to win the latter a Nobel Prize.

De Vries devoted a great deal of thought to Darwin's [554] theory of evolution and saw that the great flaw in it was that there was no explanation for the manner in which individuals might vary; yet it was only on that unexplained manner of variation that the changes of evolution could in turn be explained. De Vries devised a theory of how different characteristics might vary independently of each other and recombine in many different combinations. This, in fact, amounted to a rediscovery of Mendel's [638] theories.

In 1900 he had done enough work on plants to feel sure that the rules he had worked out were correct. Before publishing, he went back over the literature to see what, if anything, existed on the subject. Imagine his amazement when he came across the papers of Mendel and found his own laws worked out in full detail a generation earlier.

In the same year of 1900, Correns [938] in Germany and Tschermak [999] in Austria, both unknown to De Vries and to each other, had separately worked out the laws of inheritance. Each had then searched through the literature and had come across Mendel's papers.

It is one of the most glorious chapters in scientific history that not one of the three men made any effort to claim credit for a discovery that, intellectually at least, was independently their own and which would have meant great fame. Each man, with the ideal integrity of the true scientist, announced Mendel's discovery and introduced his own work only as confirmation. The laws of inheritance are therefore still known as Mendelian.

De Vries was able to go beyond Mendel in one respect, thanks to an accidental discovery made in 1886. The American evening primrose had been introduced to the Netherlands some time before, and De Vries, out on a walk, came across a colony of these plants growing in a waste meadow. It did not take the sharp eye of a botanist to see that some were widely different from others.

He brought them back and bred them separately and together and found the same results that Mendel had found. But he also found that every once in a while, a new variety, differing markedly from the others, would grow and that this new variety would perpetuate itself in future generations.

Evolution ceased to be an infinitely slow process that could be theorized about but not observed. Here it went on under De Vries's very eyes. The forming of new varieties could be expected and experimentation with evolution could proceed. Bateson [913] was also moving in this direction.

De Vries evolved a new doctrine of evolution by sudden jumps or mutations (from a Latin word meaning "to change"). Actually, this sort of thing had always been known to herdsmen and farmers, who had frequently seen the production of freaks, or "sports." Some freak characteristics had even been put to use, as for instance the short-legged breed of sheep (a mutation) in 1791 that could not jump over fences and was therefore useful and was preserved. Furthermore, several nineteenth-century evolutionists such as Huxley [659] and

Nägeli [598] had suggested evolution by jumps, but without evidence.

Unfortunately, herdsmen do not usually draw theoretical conclusions from their observations or tell scientists about them, nor do scientists involve themselves with the mechanics of herding to test their theories (at least, not often enough in the nineteenth century). So it was not until 1901 that theory and observation met in the person of De Vries.

In any case, De Vries, by rediscovering the Mendelian laws of inheritance and adding to them his own theory of mutation, plugged the hole in Darwinian theory and successfully completed its structure. The mutation theory also modified the theories of Weismann [704] by showing that the germ plasm could be altered after all, although the nature of the alterations remained to be worked out over the succeeding half century.

[793] **LILIENTHAL,** Otto (lil'een-thal)
German aeronautical engineer
Born: Auklam, Prussia, May 23, 1848
Died: near Rhinow, Germany, August 10, 1896

Like many another man of the time, Lilienthal dreamed of human flight. In his case, the dream began at the age of thirteen, but it was not until he had grown and had completed his service in the Franco-Prussian War that he could begin to try to turn his dream to reality.

He concentrated on imitating the engineering of birds but was satisfied to achieve a gliding flight without any attempt to make the wings flap (a pitfall for many other inventors).

In 1877 he built his first device, one with arched wings like a bird, and was able to show that these were superior to flat wings. (Modern airplane wings are still curved, though not exactly after the fashion of birds.)

By 1891 Lilienthal launched himself on his first glide. Gliding became the great aeronautical sport of the 1890s as ballooning had been just a century earlier, but none outdid Lilienthal in this respect. He launched himself into the air

successfully more than two thousand times. Then in 1896 he launched himself unsuccessfully once, while testing a new rudder design, and died of injuries sustained in the crash. He might otherwise have lived an additional seven and a half years, to see the Wright brothers [961, 995], also gliding enthusiasts, demonstrate that by mounting an engine on a glider it could be converted into an airplane.

[794] **EÖTVÖS,** Roland, Baron von (oit'voish)
Hungarian physicist
Born: Budapest, July 27, 1848
Died: Budapest, April 8, 1919

Eötvös was the son of a renowned Hungarian statesman and writer. He studied at the University of Heidelberg where he obtained his Ph.D. *summa cum laude* in 1870. By 1872 he had a professorial appointment at the University of Budapest.

His most important work dealt with gravity. He worked with the torsion balance of the kind used by Cavendish [307] to measure the mass of the earth, but increased its sensitivity to unprecedented heights. This he used for geophysical purposes. From tiny variations in gravitational pull from place to place on earth's surface, he could make deductions as to the nature of the structure beneath the surface.

Secondly and far more important, Eötvös used it to determine the rate of gravitational acceleration of falling bodies (a problem that had originally exercised Galileo [166]) and did so, again, with unprecedented precision. In the process, he showed that gravitational mass and inertial mass (which have no obvious connection) are identical to less than five parts per billion. This very close identity encouraged Einstein [1064] to assume an actual identity and develop from it his general theory of relativity.

Eötvös helped found the Hungarian Mathematical and Physical Society and served as its first president. He was an ardent mountain climber in addition and he climbed a number of European peaks that had not been climbed before.

63. MARIE S. CURIE

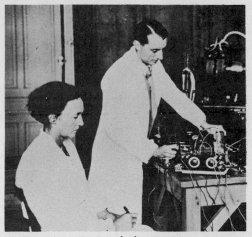

64. IRÈNE AND FRÉDÉRIC JOLIOT-CURIE

65. WERNER HEISENBERG

66. ROBERT H. GODDARD BESIDE HIS LIQUID-
FUELED ROCKET, MARCH 16, 1926

67. WALLACE H. CAROTHERS

68. FRANCIS H. C. CRICK

69. JOHN F. ENDERS

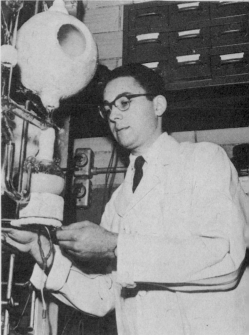

70. STANLEY L. MILLER

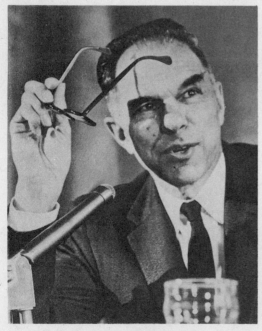

71. GLENN T. SEABORG

72. HIDEKI YUKAWA AND ISIDOR I. RABI

73. HAROLD UREY

74. SIR FREDERICK G. BANTING

75. CHAIM WEIZMANN

76. OTTO F. MEYERHOF

77. Robert B. Woodward

78. Linus Pauling

79. Edward Teller

[795] **DORN,** Friedrich Ernst
German physicist
Born: Guttstadt (now Dobre
Miasto, Poland), East Prussia,
July 27, 1848
Died: Halle, June 13, 1916

Dorn was educated at the University of Königsberg and taught physics at the universities of Darmstadt and Halle. He turned to the study of radioactivity in the wake of Madame Curie's [965] discoveries and in 1900 showed that radium not only produced radioactive radiations, but also gave off a gas that was itself radioactive.

This gas eventually received the name radon and turned out to be the final member of Ramsay's [832] family of inert gases. It was the first clear-cut demonstration that in the process of giving off radioactive radiation, one element was transmuted (shades of the alchemists!) to another. This concept was carried further by Boltwood [987] and Soddy [1052].

[796] **MEYER,** Viktor
German organic chemist
Born: Berlin, September 8, 1848
Died: Heidelberg, August 8, 1897

Meyer, who came of a wealthy Jewish family in the textile trade, had an early ambition to be an actor. His family persuaded him to go to Heidelberg where his older brother was a student. The chemistry lectures there converted him to a chemist.

He studied under Bunsen [565], Kirchhoff [648], and Kopp [601], and obtained his Ph.D. *summa cum laude* in 1867 under Baeyer [718] at the University of Berlin. He was not yet nineteen at that time.

Meyer received his first professorial appointment at the University of Stuttgart in 1871 but by 1889 had returned to Heidelberg, to succeed his old teacher, Bunsen, as professor of chemistry and held that post till his death.

Meyer found, in 1871, that the molecules of bromine and iodine, made up of two atoms each, broke up into single atoms on heating.

He synthesized a number of new classes of organic compounds and in 1882 discovered a compound called thiophene under dramatic circumstances. He was accustomed to demonstrate to his class a color test for benzene. One time, instead of using benzene obtained from petroleum, he used a sample that had been synthesized from benzoic acid. The test did not work. He turned the battery of his high-powered research ability upon the recalcitrant material and discovered the test was not for benzene after all, but for the very similar thiophene. When benzene was isolated from petroleum, thiophene always accompanied it; when it was formed from benzoic acid, however, no thiophene accompanied it. Experiments that fail are sometimes useful.

Meyer also pointed out the manner in which a large atom-grouping on a molecule might interfere with reactions at some nearby point in that molecule. This is called steric hindrance and Meyer introduced the term "stereochemistry" for the study of molecular shapes.

While still in the prime of life, Meyer, in a fit of depression over ill health and the continuing pain of neuralgia, drank prussic acid and killed himself in a chemist's suicide. He was buried in the Heidelberg cemetery where, nearby, lay his old teachers, Bunsen and Kopp.

[797] **FREGE,** Friedrich Ludwig Gottlob
(fray'guh)
German mathematician
Born: Wismar, Mecklenburg, November 8, 1848
Died: Bad Kleinen, Mecklenburg, July 26, 1925

Frege, the son of a school principal, obtained his Ph.D. from Göttingen in 1873. He joined the faculty of the University of Jena, gained a professorship in 1879, and remained there all his working life.

He was interested in symbolic logic and improved on Boole [595] by refusing to restrict himself to those symbols already used in mathematics. He evolved a set that would be suitable for logic even where the analogy to ordinary mathematics was not close. Thus, there could be a symbol for "or," one for "if—then —," and so on.

Although this is now standard in the field, Frege is better known for a colossal and unique intellectual catastrophe. In the 1880s he began the preparation of a gigantic work applying symbolic logic to arithmetic and attempting to build up the entire structure of mathematics, including the very concept of number, on a rigorous and contradiction-free basis. The first volume of his tremendous work appeared in 1893 and the second in 1903.

While the second volume was yet in galleys, the young Bertrand Russell [1005] addressed a query to Frege. How would Frege's system, asked Russell, deal with the particular paradox that we can here explain as follows: " 'Classes' are groups of similar objects. Some classes are themselves members of the class they describe. For instance, 'the class of all phrases' is itself a phrase. On the other hand there are classes that are not themselves members of the class they describe. Thus, 'the class of all cats' is not itself a cat. So one might speak of 'the class of all classes that are members of themselves' and 'the class of all classes that are not members of themselves.' "

Well, then, asked Russell of Frege, is the "class of all classes that are not members of itself" a member of itself or not? If it *is* a member of itself then it is one of those classes that are *not* members of themselves. On the other hand, if it is *not* a member of itself then it must be a member of the other class of all classes that *are* members of themselves. But if it *is* a member of itself— You can go on forever, you see, and get nowhere. On consideration Frege realized his system was helpless to resolve it and was forced to add a final paragraph to the second volume of his lifework, admitting that the very foundation of his reasoning was shattered and the books therefore worthless. He published no more after that.

Frege was an extreme nationalist, who hated Frenchmen, Catholics, and Jews and was embittered by Germany's loss of World War I. One can suspect that he might have been a Nazi sympathizer had he lived long enough.

[798] **ROWLAND,** Henry Augustus (roh'land)
American physicist
Born: Honesdale, Pennsylvania, November 27, 1848
Died: Baltimore, Maryland, April 16, 1901

Rowland, the son of a minister, was educated at first for the ministry but became an engineer. He graduated from the Rensselaer Polytechnic Institute in 1870 and obtained a professorial position there in 1874. After graduate studies in Germany under Helmholtz [631], he returned to America to become the first professor of physics at Johns Hopkins University in 1876, a post he held till his death.

He was one of the few important nineteenth-century American physicists, and his careful work in electromagnetism, though unappreciated at home, was greeted with enthusiasm by Maxwell [692] in England. Maxwell had wondered if a piece of electrically charged matter, moving rapidly, might not behave like an electric current and, for instance, set up a magnetic field. Helmholtz suggested an experiment which in 1876 Rowland carried out. He attached pieces of tin foil to a glass disc, placed an electric charge upon the tin, and had the disc rotated rapidly. The system deflected a magnet in the proper fashion and Maxwell's question was answered in the affirmative.

Two decades later, the experiment gained added significance with final confirmation that (as had long been suspected) an electric current was, after all, accompanied by electrically charged matter in motion.

Rowland's chief fame, however, came out of a bit of applied science. The prisms used to create spectra from the days of Newton [231] onward were giving way to the ruled gratings of the type Fraunhofer [450] had begun to use. As spectroscopy grew more and more important in chemistry and astronomy, attempts were made to prepare more and more accurate gratings, with the scratched lines more closely and evenly spaced.

Toward the end of the 1870s, Rowland devised a method for preparing gratings on concave metal or glass far finer than any formed previously. He scored almost 15,000 lines per inch. A new precision was thus brought to the studies of stellar spectra, and since the telescope was now becoming little more than a handmaiden of the spectroscope, this was a matter of considerable importance. Between 1886 and 1895 Rowland himself prepared a map of the solar spectrum in which the precise wavelength of some 14,000 lines was given.

One story about Rowland is that when testifying at a trial, he answered a question as to the name of the greatest living American physicist by calmly giving his own. When asked how he, usually so modest, could bring himself to make such a seemingly egotistic remark, he replied, "What could I do? I was under oath."

He died, comparatively young, of diabetes, for it was before the day of Banting [1152].

[799] **BURBANK**, Luther
American naturalist
Born: Lancaster, Massachusetts,
March 7, 1849
Died: Santa Rosa, California,
April 11, 1926

If anyone ever had a green thumb, it was Burbank. He was the thirteenth of fifteen children and he had only the equivalent of a high school education, but for his unique talent even so much was superfluous.

As a youngster he was interested in gardening and in growing plants. He had a knack for noting small differences between plants and for developing and extending these by a variety of techniques including hybridization and grafting.

He read Darwin's [554] book and was aware of the importance of variation. The work of Mendel [638], however, was unknown to him during most of his life, and he never accepted the doctrine that variations were gene-determined at the moment of the fertilization of the egg or seed. He held out in favor of inheritance of acquired characteristics, something after the fashion of Lamarck [336], and lectured to that effect at Stanford University in his later years.

In this erroneous viewpoint, he was encouraged by the fact that he worked with plants, whose form and structure are less standardized and more variable than those of animals, and by the fact that his skill at detecting and nurturing differences almost made it seem as though he were creating the changes himself by suitably adjusting the environment. This same belief was to be upheld by another plant breeder, Lysenko [1214], over half a century later, with less excuse and with more serious consequences.

Burbank began his botanical work in 1870, when he bought a plot of ground near Lunenburg, Massachusetts. In a year or so he developed the Burbank potato. His three older brothers had moved to California, and in 1875 Burbank followed, using $150 obtained by selling his rights to the potato, settling near Santa Rosa in an Eden-like garden spot. He remained there fifty years and made it world famous. The Burbank potato meanwhile traveled in the other direction, for it was introduced into Ireland, to minimize the chances of a blight like the one in the 1840s that killed or drove into exile half of Ireland's population.

As might be expected in the great fruit-growing state of California, Burbank made the development of new varieties of fruit a specialty. He developed no fewer than sixty varieties of plum through work that stretched over forty years. Over a period of thirty-five years he developed ten new commercial varieties of berry. He worked on pineapples, walnuts, and almonds. Nor was he concerned only with the edible, for he developed numerous varieties of flowers that could serve no other use than to delight the eye in new and previously unknown fashion. These include such examples as the Fire poppy, the Burbank rose, the Shasta daisy, and the Ostrich-plume clematis.

For Burbank it was all a labor of love, but he did demonstrate that living nature, given enough care and trouble, can be modified as effectively as the inanimate world to the needs of man.

[800] **KLEIN,** Christian Felix
German mathematician
Born: Düsseldorf, April 25, 1849
Died: Göttingen, June 22, 1925

Klein received his doctorate at the University of Bonn in 1868. After service in the Franco-Prussian War, he received a professorial appointment in 1872 at the University of Erlangen. He married a granddaughter of the German philosopher, G.W.F. Hegel.

Klein's most important mathematical work was the systematization of the non-Euclidean geometries worked out by Lobachevski [484], Bolyai [530], and Riemann [670]. By using projective geometry, he showed how forms of both non-Euclidean geometry and Euclidean geometry itself could be viewed as special cases of a more general view.

This brought non-Euclidean geometry into the mainstream of mathematical thinking, since it made it no more an esoteric curiosity and put it on the same level with "ordinary" geometry.

[801] **KJELDAHL,** Johann Gustav
Christoffer (kel'dal)
Danish chemist
Born: Jagerpris, August 16, 1849
Died: Tisvildeleje, July 18, 1900

Kjeldahl, the son of a physician, studied at the Technological Institute in Copenhagen. He was particularly interested in chemical analysis. When the owner of the Carlsberg brewery set up the Carlsberg Laboratory, a scientific research institution, Kjeldahl was appointed director in 1876 and held that position till his death.

Kjeldahl's most important achievement was his devising, in 1883, a method for the analysis of the nitrogen content of organic material. Dumas [514] had already worked out a method but one that was long and complicated. Kjeldahl's was much simpler and faster. By using concentrated sulfuric acid, all the nitrogen bound in organic molecules was released in the form of ammonia, the quantity of which could be easily determined. This Kjeldahl determination could be carried out in a specially designed Kjeldahl flask, which first came into use in 1888.

[802] **PAVLOV,** Ivan Petrovich (pa'vluf)
Russian physiologist
Born: Ryazan', September 26, 1849
Died: Leningrad, February 27, 1936

Pavlov came of a family rich in priests, and originally his education was intended to make him a worthy follower of the family tradition. At the theological seminary, however, he read Darwin's [554] *Origin of Species* and found that his call was for natural science and not for the priesthood. He left the seminary in 1870 and studied at St. Petersburg University under Mendeléev [705] and Butlerov [676]. He obtained his Ph.D. at the St. Petersburg Military Medical Academy in 1883 and spent the years 1884 to 1886 in further study in Germany, where he studied under Ludwig [597].

Back at the academy, he became interested in the physiology of digestion and worked out the nervous mechanism controlling the secretion of the digestive glands, particularly of the stomach. In 1889 he carried on rather impressive experiments in which he severed a dog's gullet and led the upper end through an opening in the neck. The dog could then be fed, but the food would drop out through the open gullet and never reach the stomach. Nevertheless, the stomach's gastric juices would flow. It seemed plain to Pavlov that nerves stimulated in the mouth carried their message to the brain, which, in turn, via other nerves, stimulated the gastric secretion. Pavlov capped the experiment by showing that, with appropriate nerves cut, the dog might eat as heartily as before, but now there would be no gastric flow.

Pavlov was rewarded for this work with a professorial position at the academy in 1890 and, as his researches were crucial in establishing the importance of the autonomic nervous system and in laying bare the details of the physiology of digestion, he received the Nobel Prize in medicine and physiology for 1904.

Oddly enough, this was after the central core of his work had been rendered partly obsolete by the work of Bayliss [902], who showed the importance of chemical stimulation over nervous stimulation. Bayliss's work was confirmed in Pavlov's own laboratory, and with Pavlov's work on nerve stimulation reduced to secondary importance, the Russian physiologist lost interest in digestion and moved on to other things, which turned out to be even more important than that for which he earned the Nobel Prize.

The manner in which stimulation of nerves in the mouth by food elicited a response in the stomach is an unconditioned reflex. It is brought about by the construction of the nerve network with which the organism is born. Pavlov began work to see if he could impose a new pattern upon such inborn ones.

Thus, a hungry dog that is shown food will salivate. That is an unconditioned reflex. If a bell is made to ring every time he is shown food, he will eventually salivate when the bell rings even though food is not shown him. The dog has associated the sound of the bell with the sight of food and reacts to the first as though it were the second. This is a conditioned reflex.

(Pavlov's studies of conditioned reflexes marked an early climax to the new physiologically oriented psychology that had begun in Germany with Weber [492]. In Pavlov's own time, the "new psychology" was being introduced to the United States by men such as William James [754] and Granville Hall [780].)

Studies of the conditioned reflex led to the theory that a good part of learning and of the development of behavior was the result of conditioned reflexes of all sorts picked up in the course of life.

Such behaviorist theories of psychology, popularized in the United States by Watson [1057], were opposed to the theories of Freud [865] and those who followed him, who considered the mind more as a thing in itself. Pavlovian psychology is far more popular in the Soviet Union today than it is elsewhere.

Pavlov remained in Russia after the revolution and, although he was an outspoken anti-Communist, the Soviet government sensibly left him alone and patiently endured his opposition. It even built him a laboratory in 1935. To the end of his life, he remained an ornament of Russian science and a showpiece of Soviet toleration.

[803] **FLEMING,** Sir John Ambrose
English electrical engineer
Born: Lancaster, Lancashire, November 29, 1849
Died: Sidmouth, Devonshire, April 18, 1945

Fleming, the son of a Congregational minister, graduated from University College, London, in 1870. In 1877 he entered Cambridge and worked for Maxwell [692], repeating Cavendish's [307] electrical experiments, which Maxwell had recently uncovered. He held the post of professor of electrical engineering at University College from 1885.

In the 1880s he served as consultant to Edison's [788] London office in connection with the developing electric light industry and in the 1890s he worked with Marconi [1025]. He proceeded to combine the two masters. He took up the Edison effect (the passage of electricity from a hot filament to a cold plate within an evacuated bulb) and found it to be due to the passage of the newly discovered electrons boiling off the hot filament. He found that the electrons would travel only when the plate was attached to the positive terminal of a generator, for then the plate would attract the negatively charged electrons. This meant that in alternating current (where the charge on the plate was perpetually shifting from negative to positive, as the charge on the filament shifted from positive to negative) the current would pass only half the time, when filament was negative and plate positive, and not the other half. Alternating current would enter the device but direct current would leave.

In 1904 he had thus developed a rectifier. He called it a valve, since it turned on for current in one direction and off for the current in the other. In the United States, for some reason, it came to be called a tube. De Forest's [1017] addition of a grid that would make the tube an amplifier, as well as a rectifier, was the final touch needed to make electronic instruments practical.

Fleming was knighted in 1929 and his long life of nearly a century made it possible for him to see the consequences of his little rectifier to the full.

[804] **KOVALEVSKY,** Sonya (kov-uh-lef'sky)
Russian mathematician
Born: Moscow, January 15, 1850
Died: Stockholm, Sweden, February 10, 1891

Kovalevsky, the daughter of a general, had the childhood and education of an aristocratic Russian woman of tsarist times—which meant that there was a limit as far as intellectual matters were concerned, as there was (for women) everywhere else in Europe.

Kovalevsky married at eighteen; but that was a device to get away from parental supervision and go to Germany, where she could not attend university lectures (for the crime of being feminine) but where Weierstrass [593], captivated by her obvious talent, tutored her privately.

She worked on partial differential equations, where she managed to improve on the great Cauchy [463]; on integrals, where she improved on Abel [527]; and on the mathematical consideration of Saturn's rings, where she improved on Laplace [347] and Maxwell [692]. She received a Ph.D. *in absentia* from Göttingen and won prizes for her work where the cash value was increased

because of the unusual merit they showed. She was elected to both the Swedish and Russian Academy of Sciences despite her sex and then, with her ability still at its height, she died of pneumonia.

[805] **GAFFKY,** Georg Theodor August (gaf'kee)
German bacteriologist
Born: Hannover, February 17, 1850
Died: Hannover, October 23, 1918

Gaffky, the son of a shipping agent, served as a hospital orderly in the Franco-Prussian War in 1870.

Returning thereafter to his interrupted studies, he obtained his medical degree from the University of Berlin, in 1873. Gaffky accompanied Koch [767] to Egypt and India in 1883 and 1884. In 1884 he made his own chief contribution by isolating a bacillus and demonstrating it to be the causative factor of typhoid fever.

In 1888 he was appointed professor of hygiene at the University of Giessen. He continued to be interested in cholera (the trip to India was for the purpose of studying the disease) and it seemed less exotic when an epidemic of the disease broke out in Hamburg in 1892. He made another trip to India in 1897 and in 1904 was appointed director of the Institute for Infectious Diseases at Berlin.

During World War I he served as adviser to the government on hygiene and public health, dying just too soon to see Germany go down in defeat.

[806] **HEAVISIDE,** Oliver
English physicist and electrical engineer
Born: London, May 18, 1850
Died: Paignton, Devonshire, February 3, 1925

Heaviside was the son of an artist. Like Edison [788], he had no formal ed-

ucation past the elementary level, became a telegrapher, and was hampered
by deafness. With the encouragement of
his uncle (by marriage), Charles Wheatstone [526], he inaugurated a program of
self-education that succeeded admirably.
He could concentrate on it the more
since he never married and lived with his
parents till they died.

He did important work in applying
mathematics to the study of electrical
circuits and extended Maxwell's [692]
work on electromagnetic theory. Perhaps
because of his unorthodox education, he
made use of mathematical notations and
methods of his own that were greeted by
other (and lesser) physicists with disdain. For instance, he used vector notation where many physicists, notably Kelvin [652], did not. It was Kelvin, however, who first brought Heaviside's work
to the notice of the scientific community.

Heaviside was forced to publish his
papers at his own expense because of
their unorthodoxy. After the discovery
of radio waves by Hertz [873], Heaviside
applied his mathematics to wave motion
and published a large three-volume
work, *Electromagnetic Theory*. In it he
predicted the existence of an electrically
charged layer in the upper atmosphere
just months after Kennelly [916] had
done so. This layer is now often referred
to as the Kennelly-Heaviside layer.

Heaviside spent his last years poor and
alone and died, finally, in a nursing
home.

[807] **SHARPEY-SCHÄFER**, Sir Ed-
ward Albert
English physiologist
Born: Hornsey, Middlesex, June
2, 1850
Died: North Berwick, Scotland,
March 29, 1935

Sharpey-Schäfer, the son of a German
immigrant, was born with only the last
half of his name, but at the University of
London, he had William Sharpey as his
teacher in anatomy and physiology. He
was sufficiently impressed to prefix the

latter's name to his own in 1918, in
order to perpetuate it.

He developed the prone-pressure
method of artificial respiration, the one
we have all seen performed in demonstrations until mouth-to-mouth resusci-
tation came into use.

Sharpey-Schäfer's most significant
work was the demonstration, in 1894,
that an extract of the adrenal glands
would act to raise blood pressure. This
led to the isolation of adrenaline by
Takamine [855] seven years later which
in turn helped the evolution of the hormone concept by Bayliss [902] and Starling [954].

In 1916 Sharpey-Schäfer suggested
that the hormone whose existence he
suspected in the secretions of the islets of
Langerhans [791] be named "insulin"
from the Latin word for island. When
the hormone was discovered six years
later by Banting [1152] and Best [1218]
that name was used over the discoverers'
own preference for "isletin."

Outside the regular performance of his
duties as physician and scientist, Sharpey-Schäfer was an indefatigable fighter
for equal opportunities for women in
medicine.

During World War I, he attempted to
fight against anti-German hysteria in England, and he drew down denunciations
on his head from the superpatriots—
even though both his sons died fighting
for Britain in the war.

[808] **BRAUN**, Karl Ferdinand (brown)
German physicist
Born: Fulda, Hesse-Nassau, June
6, 1850
Died: New York, New York,
April 20, 1918

Braun obtained his doctorate at the
University of Berlin in 1872 under
Helmholtz [631], he was appointed professor of physics at the Technical University of Karlsruhe and in 1885 moved
on to the University of Tübingen, then
in 1895 to the University of Strasbourg.

In 1897 he modified the cathode-ray

tube so that the spot of green fluorescence formed by the stream of speeding electrons was shifted in accordance with the electromagnetic field set up by a varying current. Thus was invented the oscillograph, by means of which fine variation in electric currents could be studied and which was the first step, as it turned out, toward television.

As early as 1874 he had noted that some crystals transmitted electricity far more easily in one direction than in the other. Such crystals could therefore act as rectifiers, converting alternating current, which forever doubled on its own tracks, into direct current. The crystals came to be essential to the crystal-set radios until they were replaced by De Forest's [1017] superior triodes.

However, crystal rectifiers came into their own again, with sophisticated modifications, in the form of the solid-state systems devised by Shockley [1348] and his co-workers a half century later.

Braun's improvements in radio technology earned him the 1909 Nobel Prize in physics, which he shared with Marconi [1025]. He visited the United States during World War I in connection with patent litigation. When the United States entered the war, he was detained in New York as an enemy alien and died before the war's end would have made it possible for him to return home.

[809] **RICHET,** Charles Robert (ree-shay')
French physiologist
Born: Paris, August 26, 1850
Died: Paris, December 3, 1935

Richet was the son of a physician and followed in his father's footsteps, obtaining his medical degree in 1877 at the University of Paris. In 1887 he was appointed professor of physiology there.

Richet was versatile, writing on many subjects both in and out of science. As a young man he published a book of poetry under a pseudonym and in later years wrote novels and plays. He was an active pacifist, writing extensively on the

problems and necessity of maintaining peace.

In 1887 Richet conceived the notion of producing an immune serum; that is, of injecting into an animal a particular substance to which it could then produce an antidote. (The injected material is an antigen; the countermaterial produced is an antibody.) If the antigen is a bacterium or a bacterial toxin, then an antibody will exist that will prevent future infections. If serum containing this antibody is then injected into a human being, it may lend him immunity to a particular disease. Richet tried to produce such an immune serum for tuberculosis but failed. Behring [846], working along similar lines, succeeded with diphtheria.

Richet continued work in this direction, however, and about the turn of the century discovered, rather to his surprise, that sometimes a second dose of antigen put an animal into fatal shock. The antibody the animal had produced, far from protecting him, killed him. In 1902 Richet named this phenomenon anaphylaxis, from Greek words meaning "overprotection."

From then on, physicians were warned. Serum therapy had to be conducted in such a way as to prevent this possibility of sensitization that would produce serum sickness. Preliminary tests to determine the degree of sensitization of a particular patient must precede the administration of sera or, sometimes, even of such things as antibiotics. Furthermore, natural sensitization to any of the myriad antigens that abound in nature (in plant pollen, in food) can produce unpleasant reactions when mild doses of the antigen are encountered by the sensitized person. These reactions were termed "allergies," a word introduced in 1906, and the scientific study of allergic phenomena dates from Richet's work.

In 1913, for his work on anaphylaxis, Richet was awarded the Nobel Prize in medicine and physiology. In his later years he grew interested in telepathy and other manifestations of what is now called extrasensory perception. In this, he had the company of other scientists of the time, but nothing noteworthy came of it.

[810] **RIGHI,** Augusto (ree'gee)
Italian physicist
Born: Bologna, August 27, 1850
Died: Bologna, June 8, 1920

Righi studied at the University of Bologna, graduating in 1872. He taught at the University of Palermo, then at the University of Padua, returning to Bologna in 1889 and remaining there till his death.

He was interested in electromagnetic radiations and soon after Hertz's [873] experiments was able to show that the shorter Hertzian waves, at least, displayed the phenomena of reflection, refraction, polarization, and interference, in the same fashion that light did.

This was the final proof that radio waves differed from light, not in nature, but only in wavelengths. Such experiments finally established the existence of the electromagnetic spectrum.

[811] **GOLDSTEIN,** Eugen (golt'shtine)
German physicist
Born: Gleiwitz, Silesia (now Gliwice, Poland), September 5, 1850
Died: Berlin, December 25, 1930

Goldstein worked at the University of Berlin, where he obtained his Ph.D. in 1881 with Helmholtz [631], and then established a laboratory of his own at the Potsdam Observatory. He studied the luminescence produced at the cathode in an evacuated tube, as Plücker [521] had a couple of decades earlier; but in 1876 Goldstein was the first to apply the name "cathode rays" to them.

In 1886 he used a perforated cathode and found that there were rays going through the channels in the direction opposite to that taken by the cathode rays. He called these *Kanalstrahlen* ("channel rays" or, as they were more often called, "canal rays"). In 1895 Perrin [990] showed they consisted of positively

charged particles and in 1907 J. J. Thomson [869] termed them "positive rays." The study of the positive rays led eventually to the recognition by Ernest Rutherford [996] of the existence of the proton.

[812] **LE CHÂTELIER,** Henri Louis
(luh shah-tuh-lyay')
French chemist
Born: Paris, October 8, 1850
Died: Miribel-les-Echelles, Isère, September 17, 1936

Le Châtelier's college training was interrupted by the Franco-Prussian War and when he returned, it was to specialize in mining engineering. (His father had been inspector general of mines for France, so this might be considered a natural decision.) After graduating, he obtained a post as professor of general chemistry at the School of Mines in 1877. He was interested in the chemistry of cement, of ceramics, and of glass. He also studied the chemistry and physics of flames with a view to preventing mine explosions.

This led him to study heat and its measurement. In 1877 he suggested the use of a thermoelectric couple for measuring high temperatures. This consisted of two wires, one of platinum and one of platinum-rhodium alloy, bound together at the ends. If one end is heated, a tiny current is set flowing through the wire, the strength of the current being proportional to the temperature. He also invented an optical pyrometer designed to measure high temperatures by the nature of the light radiated by the hot object.

A study of heat naturally led him into thermodynamics. This brought him to that for which he is best known, the enunciation of a rule, in 1888, that is still called Le Châtelier's principle. This may be stated: "Every change of one of the factors of an equilibrium brings about a rearrangement of the system in such a direction as to minimize the original change."

In other words, if a system in equilibrium is placed under what would ordinarily be increased pressure, it rearranges itself so as to take up as little room as possible. Because of this the pressure does not increase as much as it would seem it should. Again, if the temperature is raised, the system undergoes a change that absorbs some of the additional heat so that the temperature does not go up as much as would be indicated.

This is a very general statement that includes the famous law of mass action, enunciated by Guldberg [721] and Waage [701], and fits in well with Gibbs's [740] chemical thermodynamics. (In fact, so general is that statement that it can be applied, with amusing success, to human behavior.)

Le Châtelier's principle, by forecasting the direction taken by a chemical reaction to a particular change of condition, helped rationalize chemical industries and guide chemists in producing desired products with a minimum of waste. Knowledge of this principle helped Haber [977], for instance, to devise his reaction that would form ammonia from atmospheric nitrogen, a crucial discovery for both peace and war, and one which Le Châtelier himself anticipated in 1901, nearly twenty years before Haber.

Le Châtelier was one of the Europeans who discovered Gibbs, and was the first to translate him into French. He, like Roozeboom [854], devoted himself to working out the implications of the phase rule experimentally.

In later life, he corresponded with Taylor [864] and labored to introduce his time-study methods into French industry.

[813] **BUCHNER,** Hans Ernst Angass
German bacteriologist
Born: Munich, Bavaria, December 16, 1850
Died: Munich, April 8, 1902

Although he is now best known as the brother of Eduard [903] (whose Nobel Prize award he did not live to witness), Hans won victories in the battle of science on his own.

He obtained his M.D. in 1874 and was professor of hygiene at the University of Munich from 1892. In his researches on immunity, he noted that protein in blood serum was of importance in this connection. He was thus a pioneer in the study of gamma globulins, those natural weapons out of which the body fashions antibodies with which to neutralize and render harmless invading microorganisms. He also devised methods for studying anaerobic bacteria, those that grow in the absence of air.

[814] **MILNE,** John
English geologist
Born: Liverpool, December 30, 1850
Died: Shide, Isle of Wight, July 30, 1913

Milne studied at the Royal School of Mines and became a mining engineer. A traveler from youth, he visited Iceland and Labrador, then joined an expedition to Egypt, Arabia, and Siberia as a geologist.

His real chance came in 1875, however, when he accepted an appointment as a professor of geology and mining in the Imperial College of Engineering at Tokyo. He reached Japan after an eleven-month journey across Asia, then remained there for twenty years and had a marvelous opportunity to study earthquakes, for no land is more riven with them than Japan.

In 1880 he invented the modern seismograph. In a sense this was a horizontal pendulum, one end of which was fixed in bed rock. When the earth moved as a result of a quake, this motion would be recorded on a drum (either by a pen or by a quivering ray of light). Milne established a chain of seismographs in Japan and elsewhere, marking the beginning of modern seismology.

When he returned to England (with his Japanese wife) he established a seismological station on the Isle of Wight.

The velocity of earthquake vibrations through the earth's body have told us almost all we know about the earth's interior. In 1906 Milne attempted to determine the velocity of earthquake waves through the deep layers of the earth, with only limited success. Three years later, however, Mohorovičić [871] was to obtain more constructive results.

In addition to various British honors, Milne received the Order of the Rising Sun from the Japanese emperor.

[815] **KAPTEYN,** Jacobus Cornelius (kahp-tine')
Dutch astronomer
Born: Barneveld, January 19, 1851
Died: Amsterdam, June 18, 1922

In 1878 Kapteyn, the son of a schoolmaster, who had graduated from the University of Utrecht, was appointed professor of astronomy at the University of Groningen, and thereafter he spent a dozen years painstakingly measuring and recording the positions and brightnesses of the stars of the southern hemisphere. (These were always less well known than those of the northern hemisphere, which had been visible to the eyes of civilized man for six thousand years, and where 90 percent of the population, and virtually all of the observatories, were to be found.)

Kapteyn used Gill's [763] photographs and after ten years published a catalog of 454,000 stars within 19° of the South Celestial Pole. He used his mass studies of stars to elicit information concerning our galaxy.

For instance, he decided to count stars as Herschel [321] had done a century earlier and to determine, from the number of stars to be found in varying directions, the shape of the galaxy. Telescopes were better than in Herschel's day and the task might have been unbearably tedious had not Kapteyn decided in 1906 that random areas of the sky be selected and the stars within those areas only be counted. It would amount to a straw poll of the heavens and, indeed, Kapteyn may be considered the originator of statistical astronomy.

Many observatories collaborated. In the last year of his life, Kapteyn was able to announce the shape of our galaxy as deduced from these counts. He concluded, as Herschel had before him, that it was a lens-shaped object with our sun

located near the center. His notion of the size of the galaxy, however, was nine times the size of Herschel's estimate, for he believed it to be 55,000 light-years in diameter and 11,000 light-years thick. (A light-year is the distance traveled by light in one year, or 5,880,000,000,000 miles.)

This galactic model clashed, however, with another that was being proposed by Harlow Shapley [1102]. Kapteyn died too soon to see the disagreement resolved in favor of Shapley.

Kapteyn's interest in the stars on a mass basis led him also to study their proper motions. One star studied by Kapteyn, now called Kapteyn's star, has the second most rapid proper motion known. Only Barnard's [883] star moves more quickly. The motions of the stars had first been detected by Halley [238] and by studying the proper motions of various stars, Herschel had been able to show that the sun itself was moving through space. However, down to Kapteyn's time the general feeling had been that the proper motions of the various stars were distributed randomly, that the stars resembled an aimlessly moving swarm of bees.

Kapteyn, however, discovered that some of the stars of the Big Dipper, plus a number of other stars widely scattered over the skies, were all moving in the same direction at about the same velocity. By 1904, in fact, he had found that the stars could be divided into two streams, moving in opposite directions, three fifths of them in one direction, two fifths in the other, a notion later extended to fainter stars by Eddington [1085]. In this way, our galaxy was reduced to a kind of order. Kapteyn himself did not penetrate the meaning of his results; this was done a quarter century later by Oort [1229].

Through the mass study of proper motions Kapteyn was able to detect in any given group of stars the common motion imposed upon all of them by the motion of our own sun. This common motion (like the landscape seeming to move backward when viewed from the windows of a moving train) was smaller the more distant the group of stars, and by this means, Kapteyn was able to determine stellar distances beyond the previous limits possible.

[816] **CHAMBERLAND,** Charles
Édouard (shahn-ber-lahn')
French bacteriologist
Born: Chilly-le-Vignoble, Jura,
March 12, 1851
Died: Paris, May 2, 1908

Chamberland served as an associate of Pasteur [642] from 1875. He worked on the conditions required to kill bacterial spores in order to make certain of the sterility of solutions and equipment. He brought the autoclave into use. It is an airtight heating device which could be used for temperatures above the boiling point, and it quickly became an indispensable item for use in bacteriology laboratories, hospitals, and so on.

He also improved methods of filtering out bacterial cells from solutions, producing filters of unglazed porcelain that were superior to anything then in use. These Chamberland filters made possible the discovery of viruses by Ivanovsky [939] and Beijerinck [817].

[817] **BEIJERINCK,** Martinus Willem
(by'er-ink)
Dutch botanist
Born: Amsterdam, March 16,
1851
Died: Gorssel, January 1, 1931

Beijerinck was the son of a tobacco dealer, who had gone bankrupt when Martinus was two. Beijerinck's earliest scientific interest was botany, but he majored in chemistry at the Delft Polytechnic School, where he had the financial help of an uncle and where Van't Hoff [829] was a close friend. After graduating from college, he taught botany in order to support himself and continued working toward his Ph.D., which he finally obtained in 1877.

As a botanist Beijerinck in the early 1880s became interested in the tobacco mosaic disease, which dwarfed the tobacco plants and mottled their leaves in a mosaic pattern. He searched for a causative bacterium and found none, but the search got him interested in bacteriology. He took a position as bacteriologist for an industrial concern and set about learning more on the subject, traveling about Europe at the expense of the firm.

He succeeded in one respect, for he discovered one of the types of bacteria that live in nodules on leguminous plants and that convert atmospheric nitrogen into useful and soil-fertilizing compounds.

In 1895 he returned to academic life, at the Delft Polytechnic School he had once attended. There he also returned to the tobacco mosaic disease. He pressed out the juice of infected leaves but could still locate no suspicious bacteria, nor could he grow anything in culture media. And yet the juice possessed the capacity of infecting a healthy plant. He passed it through a porcelain filter that could take out any known bacterium, even the smallest, and it was still infective. Nor was it a mere toxin, for he could infect a healthy plant and from that infect another and from that infect another and so on, so that whatever the infective agent was, it grew and multiplied.

Now, Pasteur [642] had found no causative agent for rabies and had speculated on germs too small to see with the microscope, but he confined himself, in this case at least, to speculation. To be sure, Ivanovsky [939] a few years earlier had observed that tobacco mosaic disease could be transmitted by a filtered liquid; but he believed there was a flaw in his filter and that the disease was bacterial. It was Beijerinck who, in 1898, published his observations and boldly stated that tobacco mosaic disease was caused by an infective agent that was not bacterial. He believed the liquid itself was alive and he called the disease agent a "filterable virus"; *virus* is but Latin for "poison."

In this way he discovered the class of disease agents that cause not only ailments of plants and animals, but also polio, mumps, chickenpox, influenza, the common cold, and a number of other diseases among man. It took another generation, however, with a line of research climaxing in that of Stanley [1282] a few years after Beijerinck's death to show that the virus was not liquid but consisted of particles.

[818] **MAUNDER,** Edward Walter
English astronomer
Born: London, April 12, 1851
Died: London, March 21, 1928

Maunder was appointed as assistant in the Royal Observatory at Greenwich in 1873 after passing a civil service test in photography and spectroscopy. Until then, Greenwich had been concerned chiefly with positional astronomy; now it entered into the world of astrophysics.

Maunder worked at the observatory for forty years, dealing largely with photographing the sun and studying sunspots. He interested himself in the history of astronomy, too, and there he came across something that proved more important than any of his current research. He found that through the period from 1645 to 1715 there was a remarkable lack of reports on sunspots, although there were ample reports before 1645 and (of course) after 1715. He suggested that this was due not to faulty reporting but to an actual dearth of sunspots during that period.

This was not taken seriously at the time the report was issued, but in recent years additional researches have confirmed Maunder's findings and now the existence of Maunder minima, periods of many decades in length during which the sun is relatively free of spots, is well accepted.

[819] **BERLINER,** Émile (behr-lee'ner)
German-American inventor
Born: Hannover, Germany, May 20, 1851
Died: Washington, D.C., August 3, 1929

Berliner was educated in Germany, where he worked as an apprentice printer, and in 1870 came to the United States. He worked as chief inspector for the Bell Telephone Company, which was then rapidly exploiting Bell's [789] invention. In 1877 Berliner patented a version of the modern mouthpiece two weeks before Edison [788] patented what was virtually the same thing. Edison retained patent rights but not until after fifteen years of litigation.

In 1904 Berliner scored a more definite victory over Edison: He devised the flat phonograph record in which the needle vibrated from side to side. Its greater compactness allowed it to replace Edison's cylinder (with a needle vibrating up and down) almost at once. And indeed the familiar "platters" of today are of Berliner's design.

In the early decades of the twentieth century, he was one of those who turned their attention to aeronautics, and he did useful work on airplane motors. He also carried on a vigorous campaign against the use of raw milk and in favor of compulsory pasteurization, a campaign that was carried through to victory to the great benefit of the health of Americans.

[820] **LODGE,** Sir Oliver Joseph
English physicist
Born: Penkhull, Staffordshire, June 12, 1851
Died: Lake, near Salisbury, Wiltshire, August 22, 1940

Lodge, the son of a merchant, originally aimed for a business career but, attracted to science by the lectures of Tyndall [626], he entered the University of London. He obtained his doctorate in 1877 and, in 1881, was appointed professor of physics at that institution.

In the 1890s he grew interested in electromagnetic radiation and he conducted experiments similar to those of Hertz [873] and Marconi [1025] but working with shorter radio waves. These made him one of the forerunners of radio communication. He was knighted in 1902 for his work in the field. He had a receptive mind and this, in the early 1900s, made him a champion of the new and radical theories of atomic structure advanced by young men like Ernest Rutherford [996] and Soddy [1052].

As early as 1894, he suggested that radio signals might be emitted from the sun. He was correct, but it was not till half a century had passed that such signals were detected.

After 1910, this same receptive mind involved him increasingly in an attempt to reconcile what seemed to him the divergences between science and religion. This, in turn, led him into a fixed belief in the possibility of communicating with the dead, a belief inspired by the hope of somehow reaching his youngest son, killed during World War I. He became a leader of psychical research, and is one of the prime examples of a serious scientist entering a field that is usually the domain of quacks.

[821] **FITZGERALD,** George Francis
Irish physicist
Born: Dublin, August 3, 1851
Died: Dublin, February 21, 1901

FitzGerald, a nephew of Stoney [664], received his early education from a sister of Boole [595]. In 1866, he entered Trinity College in Dublin, graduating in 1871, and in the final decades of his life served as professor of natural philosophy there. Through his efforts, he greatly advanced the development of technical education in Ireland.

In his youth he made his mark as a scientific conservative, for he was unimpressed by the theory of electromagnetic radiation put forth by Maxwell [692] and even went so far as to publish a paper maintaining that it was impossible to produce lightlike waves by oscillating electric forces. Not many years after this paper was published, Hertz [873] showed it could be done.

Later, FitzGerald's vision improved. When J. J. Thomson [869] demonstrated in the 1890s that the cathode rays consisted of particles far smaller than atoms, FitzGerald was one of the first to hop on the subatomic particle bandwagon and to predict that vast new advances in knowledge of the atoms were about to be made. He was also the first to suggest that the comets were not continuous objects in the ordinary sense, but that even their nuclei were stony aggregates.

He is best known, however, for his explanation of the failure of the famous experiment performed in 1887 by Michelson [835] and Morley [730]. Michelson and Morley had failed to detect any difference in the velocity of two beams of light traveling in different directions even though, because of the earth's supposed motion through the ether, it was thought that such a difference in velocity ought to have existed.

FitzGerald's solution, advanced in 1895, was that the distance covered by the light beam altered with the velocity of motion of the light source in such a way as to allow the beam of light to seem to travel at the same velocity in all directions. Thus, when by ordinary Newtonian mechanics one might expect that a beam of light would move more slowly over a certain distance because of the motion of the light source, the distance contracts just enough to cause the light beam to save the necessary time to make it appear to be moving at only its usual velocity. FitzGerald presented a simple formula to describe the amount of contraction of distance with velocity of motion that would just cancel out what would otherwise be differences in light's velocity. All material objects would have to be contracted as well, but such contraction is only perceptible at vast speeds. Thus, a foot rule would contract to six inches, when velocity had reached the enormous value of 161,000 miles a second. At the speed of light, 186,282 miles a second, contraction would be complete and all objects would have zero length in the direction of motion. Since a negative length would seem to have no meaning, this FitzGerald contraction was the first indication that the velocity of light in a vacuum might be the maximum velocity theoretically possible for any material object.

The FitzGerald contraction seemed to go against common sense but with the growth of understanding of the electrical nature of matter, it became less so. Lorentz [839] a little later, independently advanced the same theory and expanded it, so that it is frequently referred to as the Lorentz-FitzGerald contraction. FitzGerald did not live to see his contraction hypothesis become an integral part of a new world system, the relativity theory, first advanced by Einstein [1064] in 1905.

[822] **REED**, Walter
American military surgeon
Born: Belroi, Virginia, September 13, 1851
Died: Washington, D.C., November 23, 1902

Reed, the son of a minister, entered the University of Virginia in 1866, obtaining a medical degree there in 1869 and a second from Bellevue Medical School in New York in 1870. He entered the Army Medical Corps in 1874. He made bacteriology his specialty and in 1893 was appointed professor of bacteriology in the Army Medical School.

The Spanish-American War made the American army more disease conscious than ever before, because in that one-sided little conflict, Spanish guns succeeded in killing very few American soldiers, but disease felled them in battalions. Reed headed a commission to study the cause and spread of typhoid fever, one of the epidemic diseases involved.

Another was yellow fever, a particularly dreaded disease, which in 1897 Reed proved was not caused by a certain bacterium on which the blame had been placed. In 1899, the war over, Reed was made head of a commission to travel to Cuba (temporarily an American protectorate), where the disease was particularly bad.

His careful studies led him to believe that the disease was not transmitted by bodily contact, or by clothing, bedding, or anything like that. He returned to an idea that had been advanced earlier, that the germ of yellow fever was transmitted by a mosquito. There was no way of testing this theory on animals and there followed a period of high (and grisly) drama in which the doctors of the commission allowed themselves to be bitten by mosquitoes to see if they would catch the disease. Some did and one, Jesse William Lazear [955], died, but Reed proved his point.

Get rid of the Aedes mosquito by tracking down its breeding sites and destroying them. Avoid being bitten by using mosquito netting, and you get rid of yellow fever. Havana was indeed rid of the disease in this way. The Panama Canal was built through the adoption by Gorgas [853] of mosquito-killing techniques. With the focal points of infection in Latin America moderated, the Eastern Seaboard of the United States was freed of the dread of this disease, which periodically had visited such cities as New York and Philadelphia, slaying tens of thousands.

In 1901 Reed proved the causative agent which the mosquitoes carried was a filterable virus of the type discovered by Beijerinck [817] just a few years earlier. Yellow fever thus became the first human disease attributed to a virus. Yellow fever quickly disappeared from Havana, where it had long been endemic. The last yellow fever epidemic the United States has seen struck New Orleans in 1905. Reed did not live to witness it; he had died three years earlier of appendicitis. In 1945 Reed was elected to the Hall of Fame for Great Americans, and the Army General Hospital in Washington, D.C., is named in his honor.

[823] **BALFOUR**, Francis Maitland
Scottish biologist
Born: Edinburgh, November 10, 1851
Died: Mont Blanc, Switzerland, July 19, 1882

Balfour's elder brother, Arthur James, was an important British statesman who held high positions in the government, including that of prime minister from 1902 to 1906. In much less spectacular fashion, Francis Maitland graduated from Cambridge in 1873 and then grew interested in the study of embryology.

Through embryos he traced the connection between different groups of organisms, following the exaggerated notions of Haeckel [707], which were then popular. He noted, for instance, the connection of the vertebrates generally with certain comparatively primitive creatures that lacked vertebrae. These primitive creatures had instead a flexible rod running down their backs, at least in their larval stage if not in their adulthood, and vertebrates showed this same rod (a notochord) in the embryonic portion of their life. Kovalevski [750] was making similar observations.

In 1880 Balfour suggested that all creatures possessing a notochord at some time in their life be grouped in a phylum, Chordata, and that suggestion was accepted. The Vertebrata are a subphylum within Chordata, making up almost all of it, to be sure.

Shortly afterward, Balfour suffered an attack of typhoid fever and in 1882 went to Switzerland in the hope that mountain air would restore his health. He attempted to climb one of the as-yet-unconquered crags of Mont Blanc and never returned. He was only thirty years old.

[824] **FRASCH,** Herman (frahsh)
German-American chemist
Born: Gaildorf, Württemberg,
December 25, 1851
Died: Paris, France, May 1, 1914

Frasch's father was mayor of the town in which young Frasch was born and he could undoubtedly have received the best chemical education in the world in Germany. However, he was one of many who felt the call of the land beyond the Atlantic and in 1868 he arrived in the United States during its post-Civil War prosperity and established a laboratory in Philadelphia. Not many years before, the first oil well had been drilled in Pennsylvania and Frasch was astute enough to get into the field, specializing in petroleum chemistry.

One of the problems of the infant oil industry was the fact that much of the oil was "sour" and unsalable because it contained sulfur compounds and stank to high heaven even after refining. It was Frasch in 1887 who patented a method for removing the sulfur compounds through the use of metallic oxides. The supply of usable petroleum was multiplied and the industry was ready for the coming of the automobile.

Frasch's attention turned to sulfur, the

valuable mineral out of which sulfuric acid, industry's most vital chemical, was manufactured. The island of Sicily held virtually a world monopoly on sulfur; the sulfur deposits were near the surface of the earth and Sicilian labor was cheap and mercilessly exploited. There were notable deposits of sulfur in Louisiana and Texas, but they were deeper underground, and American labor was comparatively dear and accustomed to better-than-Sicilian treatment.

Frasch adapted his petroleum experience to the problem. Why not pump sulfur as one pumps petroleum? To be sure, sulfur is a solid and not a liquid and not even boiling water is hot enough to melt it. But what if superheated water under pressure were sent down? The sulfur would melt and could be forced up to the surface.

In 1894 Frasch had weighed all the factors as far as they could be weighed on paper and decided to gamble with an actual attempt in the field, down in the swamps of Louisiana. He was a crackerjack chemical engineer and he managed to solve each problem that arose (and there were many). Even when he made it work, there was still a problem in the matter of fuel to supply the hot water. If the fuel had to be transported over too great a distance, it would be expensive, and the sulfur would be expensive also—too expensive. Fortunately the famous Texas oil wells began to come in about then and fuel oil was cheap.

By 1902 the Frasch process was practical from end to end. America had a homegrown and, for the foreseeable future, inexhaustible supply of sulfur (and therefore of sulfuric acid). Imports from Sicily ceased and one more step was taken toward America's chemical independence of Europe, a process that was to reach a climax following World War I, which began three months after Frasch's death.

[825] **DEMARÇAY,** Eugène Anatole
(duh-mahr-say´)
French chemist
Born: Paris, January 1, 1852
Died: Paris, 1904

Demarçay first worked in organic chemistry with Dumas [514] among his teachers. During an investigation of compounds of nitrogen and sulfur, an explosion destroyed the sight in one eye, an accident much like that suffered by Bunsen [565] some forty years earlier.

Demarçay went on to the study of spectra and grew to be one of the foremost experts in the field, learning with his one eye to read the complicated line patterns like a book. In 1896 he began the research that led to the discovery of a new rare-earth element, europium.

In 1898, when Madame Curie [965] believed she had isolated a new element (radium), judging by its radioactive properties, she called in Demarçay. He found prominent lines of barium in the sample handed him (barium is very like radium in its chemical properties, and any process intended to separate the one will also separate the other) but in among them were the lines of a new element. The presence of radium was confirmed.

[826] **LINDEMANN,** Carl Louis
Ferdinand von (lin'-duh-mahn)
German mathematician
Born: Hannover, April 12, 1852
Died: Munich, March 6, 1939

Lindemann received his Ph.D. at Erlangen under Klein [800] in 1873. Making use of Hermite's [641] methods, he tackled that well-known quantity, π (pi), the ratio of the circumference of a circle to its diameter and showed, in 1882, that it was a transcendental number. This was of particular importance because it was possible to show that no line equivalent in length to a transcendental number could be constructed in a finite number of steps by use of a straight-edge and compass alone.

It was by the use of these (the proper tools of the geometer, according to Plato [24]) that, for two thousand years, mathematicians had been trying to construct a square equal in area to a given circle ("squaring the circle"). Since π was transcendental and since any method of squaring a circle had to construct a line equivalent to π, Lindemann had finally

shown once and for all that squaring the circle by Platonic methods was impossible, though by other methods it was not. (Nevertheless, the circle-squarers have not given up and will always be with us.)

Lindemann had less luck with another famous mathematical problem. He spent six years or more attempting to prove Fermat's [188] last theorem and in 1907 published a very long paper in which he thought he had succeeded; but it contained a blatant error at the very beginning, one he had somehow overlooked.

He joined the faculty of the University of Königsberg in 1883 and the University of Munich in 1893, retiring in 1923.

[827] **RAMÓN Y CAJAL,** Santiago
(rah-mone' ee kah-hahl')
Spanish histologist
Born: Petilla de Aragon, May 1, 1852
Died: Madrid, October 18, 1934

Ramón y Cajal, like Golgi [764], had a father in the medical profession, but Ramón's own schooling was less aimed in the family direction. He seemed backward in school and it was only after successive apprenticeships to a barber and to a shoemaker that he finally got the chance to study medicine.

After obtaining his degree in 1873 and serving a year in Cuba, he became professor of anatomy at the University of Zaragoza in 1877. He was hampered for a time by serious illnesses—malaria while he served in Cuba (a Spanish possession at the time), tuberculosis at home in Spain.

In the 1880s he learned of Golgi's stain, improved upon it, and went to work on the nervous system. By 1889 he had worked out the connections of the cells in the gray matter of the brain and spinal cord and had demonstrated the extreme complexity of the system. He also worked out the structure of the retina of the eye. He established the neuron theory, which proclaimed the nervous system to consist entirely of nerve cells and their processes, in contradistinction to Golgi, who opposed it.

In 1889, at a scientific meeting in Germany, Ramón y Cajal demonstrated his improved Golgi stain and won the support of Kölliker [600] and Waldeyer [722]. He shared the Nobel Prize in medicine and physiology with Golgi in 1906. He retired in 1922.

[828] **LÖFFLER,** Friedrich August Johannes (lerf'ler)
German bacteriologist
Born: Frankfurt an der Oder, Prussia, June 24, 1852
Died: Berlin, April 9, 1915

Löffler, the son of an army surgeon, obtained his M.D. from the University of Berlin in 1874. He worked for Koch [767] from 1879 to 1884 and applied Koch's methods to the isolation of specific bacteria.

His most important discovery, in 1884, was that of the bacillus of diphtheria. He showed that natural immunity to diphtheria existed among some annimals and this laid the groundwork for Behring's [846] labors in preparing an antitoxin. He also showed in 1898 that hoof-and-mouth disease was caused by a virus, the first animal disease pinned to such a cause.

[829] **VAN'T HOFF,** Jacobus Henricus (vahnt hof)
Dutch physical chemist
Born: Rotterdam, August 30, 1852
Died: Steglitz (part of Berlin), Germany, March 1, 1911

Van't Hoff, the son of a physician, decided on a chemical career against the wishes of his parents. He had his way and after attending college in the Netherlands (where Beijerinck [817] was a friend) he traveled to Bonn, Germany, in 1872 to study under Kekulé [680], who paid him little attention. After that he spent some time in Paris before returning to the Netherlands.

However, he did not wait to complete his education to begin his career. In 1874, at the age of twenty-two, and with his Ph.D. from the University of Utrecht as yet a few months in the future, he published a startling paper on the structure of organic compounds. Chemists had been puzzling for more than half a century over the fact that some organic compounds were optically active while others were not. As long ago as Biot [404] there had been the suggestion that this was due to some sort of asymmetry, but the nature and location of the asymmetry remained a mystery. Pasteur [642] had located the asymmetry in crystals, but that did not help with respect to the optical activity of substances in solution.

Van't Hoff suggested that the asymmetry existed in the molecules themselves. He drew the four valences of the carbon atom (each represented as a short line or "bond"), not two-dimensionally toward the four angles of a square, as Couper [686] had done, but three-dimensionally toward the four angles of a tetrahedron. When the tetrahedral arrangement was considered, matters cleared up. If four different types of groupings were attached to the four carbon bonds, an asymmetric situation resulted and two compounds, mirror images of each other, could be shown to exist. It was just these asymmetric compounds that showed optical activity (rotating the plane of polarized light); others did not. A similar theory was put forth simultaneously by another youngster, Le Bel [787], and the two share the credit.

The theory of the spatial distribution of the carbon bonds was bitterly attacked by some of the more conservative chemists such as Kolbe [610] who thought that atoms and bonds were just convenient fictions and that giving actual directions to carbon bonds was to take them far too literally. Helmholtz [631] also was suspicious of the wild growth in the popularity of the structural formula.

However Van't Hoff's theory explained so much that it was eventually accepted in full and for over half a century served as an adequate guide to structural theory in organic chemistry. To be sure, a more sophisticated view of chemical bonds arose with the work of men such as Pauling [1236] in the 1930s, but the

Van't Hoff theory is still the easiest way to explain optical activity to students.

Van't Hoff's reputation did not suffer unduly from Kolbe's blast, for only a few months afterward he was offered a position as professor of chemistry, mineralogy, and geology at Amsterdam University and started on his duties in 1878. He promptly turned from organic chemistry to the new field of physical chemistry being established by Ostwald [840].

He went to work on thermodynamics and in 1884 published the results of his researches. These consisted among other things of a good statement of the law of mass action and of considerable material on chemical thermodynamics. Here, however, he was unfortunate. Much of his work had (unknown to the French and German leaders in the field) been done a decade and more before by Gibbs [740], Guldberg [721], and Waage [701]. The primary credit went to them rather than to Van't Hoff.

Van't Hoff continued working on chemical thermodynamics, however, and grew interested particularly in the problems of dilute solutions. In 1886 he showed that in some ways the simple laws that govern the behavior of gases could also be applied to the material that was sparsely dissolved in liquid solvents. It was as though the dissolved molecules moved around in the liquid as gas molecules moved around in space. He developed these notions over the next decade and this led to a far better understanding of solutions than had been possible before, although here again he was attacked rather violently, this time by Lothar Meyer [685]. And again the attack did not harm him.

In 1893 he received the Davy medal of the Royal Society. When the Nobel Prizes were established in 1901, the first to receive the award in chemistry was Van't Hoff, for his work on solutions.

In 1896 he transferred his labors from Amsterdam to Berlin, and his last years were spent in studies on the behavior of the mixture of salts found in the Stassfurt deposits, the results of which were important to Germany's chemical industries.

[830] **HALSTED,** William Stewart
American surgeon
Born: New York, New York, September 23, 1852
Died: Baltimore, Maryland, September 7, 1922

Halsted, the son of a prosperous merchant, was privately tutored at first and was then sent to a religious school from which he ran away. Finally, he found stability at Phillips Exeter at Andover, Massachusetts. He graduated from Yale in 1874, where he was primarily interested in sports (serving as captain of the football team, for instance). It was not till his senior year that he became interested in medicine. He bent his ambition toward medical school and obtained his M.D. at Columbia in 1877.

He went on to spend a year in Europe, where he studied under Kölliker [600] among others. He was the first professor of surgery at Johns Hopkins University, joining the faculty in 1886. There he established the first separate surgical school in the United States.

He was one of the first to make use of cocaine injections for local anesthesia following the pioneer work of Freud [865] and Koller [882]. In his work with cocaine, he experimented on himself to determine safety of use and became addicted (the dangers of such drug addiction were not yet understood) and it was only with difficulty, and several operations, that he freed himself of the incubus.

Halsted continued the work of Lister [672] and even went beyond it. In 1890 he became the first surgeon of importance to use rubber gloves during operations. He used them first to protect a nurse against contact dermatitis and then, in June 1890, married her. The use of rubber gloves was a valuable innovation, since rubber can be sterilized more drastically and effectively than the skin of the hands. This marked the transition from antiseptic surgery (killing the germs that are present) to aseptic surgery (not letting the germs get there in the first place). Halsted was particularly noted for the skill of his breast amputations.

His meticulousness persisted outside the operating room: He sent his shirts to Paris to have them laundered.

[831] **MOISSAN,** Ferdinand Frédéric Henri (mwah-sahn´)
French chemist
Born: Paris, September 28, 1852
Died: Paris, February 20, 1907

Moissan was the son of a railway employee. His early schooling was hampered by poverty and at the age of eighteen he was apprenticed to an apothecary. His interest in chemistry was great enough, however, for him to break away two years later and obtain by hard labor the education he believed he needed. In 1879 he qualified as a professional pharmacist and in 1882 he married a loving and charming wife who, by good fortune, had a sympathetic father (also a pharmacist) who was willing to help support Moissan while he devoted himself to chemistry and finally earned his Ph.D. in 1885. He then joined the faculty of the School of Pharmacy in Paris in 1886 and, in 1900, moved on to the Sorbonne.

Moissan's chemistry teacher, Edmond Frémy [582], back in the 1870s had been interested in isolating the element fluorine. Since the days of Davy [421], chemists had realized this element existed and must be similar in properties to chlorine but even more active. Numerous chemists had tried to isolate the gas. Davy himself had tried; so had Gay-Lussac [420] and Thénard [416]. All had failed and most, including Davy, suffered badly from poisoning by fluorine or its compounds; some chemists died. The trouble was that even if fluorine gas could be broken loose from its compounds, it proceeded to combine with almost anything in sight.

Moissan decided to undertake this dangerous task and he, too, suffered the consequences of exposure to the compounds of this violent element. He was only fifty-four when he died and in middle age he dolefully stated a number of times that he believed fluorine had shortened his life by ten years.

In his attempt to isolate fluorine he used platinum, one of the few materials that were reasonably immune to the onslaughts of fluorine, for his apparatus. He tried numerous variations of technique and on June 26, 1886, passed an electric current through a solution of potassium fluoride in hydrofluoric acid in all-platinum equipment. He chilled the solution to −50°C to reduce the activity of fluorine. He isolated a gas in these platinum surroundings, a pale yellow gas that bit savagely at anything but platinum that was brought near it. It was the long-sought fluorine, the most active of all the elements.

Shortly after this dramatic discovery Moissan was appointed professor of pharmacy at the School of Pharmacy and in 1900 received a professorial appointment in the University of Paris, where his lectures were superb. The climactic reward, however, was the Nobel Prize in chemistry, which was awarded him in 1906 for his isolation of fluorine. He won this award, according to report, by only one vote over Mendeléev [705] who, it might well be argued, deserved it more.

Moissan's discovery of fluorine and his invention of an electric furnace by means of which many uncommon elements could be prepared in unprecedented purity, were by no means his most dramatic achievements or the ones for which he is best known. That honor belongs to what most people now consider a fake (though not Moissan's).

He grew interested in trying to prepare carbon in its most beautiful and valuable form, that of diamond. At first he tried to get diamonds from compounds of carbon and his beloved fluorine. When that didn't work, he involved himself in unpleasant, long-drawn-out experiments in which he tried to convert charcoal into diamond by the use of high pressures. We now know that with the pressures and temperatures available to Moissan it was impossible to produce diamonds. The deed was not accomplished for a half century and had to await the equipment devised by Bridgman [1080] for attaining new levels of pressure.

In 1893, nevertheless, it seemed to Moissan he had succeeded. Several tiny impure diamonds were reported by him and a sliver of colorless diamond, over half a millimeter in length, was exhibited.

The suggestion, nowadays, is that one of Moissan's assistants, either in an effort to stop the miserable experiments, or as a practical joke (which was later too embarrassing to own up to), had slipped the sliver into the material being worked with. Others who attempted to make diamonds at that period, but without Moissan's dubious success, were Crookes [695] and Parsons [850].

[832] **RAMSAY,** Sir William (ram'zee)
Scottish chemist
Born: Glasgow, October 2, 1852
Died: High Wycombe, Buckinghamshire, England, July 23, 1916

Ramsay, the son of a civil engineer, was an all-round man. As a youngster he was interested in music and languages and then developed further interests in mathematics and science. He was a man of athletic inclinations. To whatever he turned mind and hand, in that he did well. He was even a first-rate glass blower and made most of the apparatus he later used in handling the gases that brought him fame.

He entered the University of Glasgow in 1866 and in 1871 studied chemistry in Germany under Bunsen [565], among others. He obtained his Ph.D. at the University of Tübingen. In 1880 he became professor of chemistry at University College in Bristol and in 1887 he received a similar position at University College in London, succeeding A. W. Williamson [650]. Although till then chiefly interested in organic chemistry (the constitution of alkaloids, particularly), he grew intrigued, in 1892, by the problem posed by Rayleigh [760] in connection with nitrogen and it was then that he approached the peak of his career.

Rayleigh's problem was that the nitrogen he obtained from air was a trifle denser than the nitrogen he obtained from compounds. Ramsay remembered reading that Cavendish [307], a century

earlier, in a long-neglected experiment, had tried to combine the nitrogen of the air with oxygen and found that a final bubble of air was left over. It followed there might be a trace of some gas in air that was heavier than nitrogen and that did not combine with oxygen. So Cavendish had thought, at least.

Ramsay repeated the experiment in more sophisticated fashion, trying to combine a sample of nitrogen obtained from air with magnesium. He too found a bubble of gas left over. But now Ramsay had something Cavendish had not had—the spectroscope, which Kirchhoff [648] had introduced to chemistry a generation earlier. In 1894 Ramsay heated the gas and he and Rayleigh studied the lines produced. The strongest lines were in positions that fitted no known element. It *was* a new gas, denser than nitrogen and making up about 1 percent of the atmosphere. It was completely inert and would not combine with any other element, so they named it argon, from a Greek word for inert.

Since it combined with no element, it had a valence of 0. This, taken together with its atomic weight, seemed to indicate that it belonged between chlorine and potassium in the periodic table. Chlorine and potassium both had valences of 1, so that the succession of valences was now 1, 0, 1, which was quite in the spirit of Mendeléev [705], the originator of the table.

Moreover, if the periodic table could be accepted as a guide, argon had to be just one of a whole family of inert gases (or noble gases), each with a valence of 0. Such a family of elements, undreamed of by Mendeléev, would nevertheless fit into the periodic table rationally.

Ramsay began the search. In 1895 he learned that in America, samples of a gas taken for nitrogen had been obtained from a uranium mineral. Ramsay repeated the work on a mineral called cleveite, named for Cleve [746], and found that the gas, when tested spectroscopically, showed lines that belonged neither to nitrogen nor argon. Instead, most astonishingly, they were the lines observed in the sun a generation earlier by Janssen [647]. Lockyer [719] had then attributed these to a new element he called helium, and now it turned out that helium existed after all, and right here on earth.

Ramsay and his assistant searched for new gases in minerals. They failed. Then in 1898 they tried fractionating argon carefully after obtaining it from liquid air. They spent months preparing fifteen liters of argon and then they liquefied it and carefully allowed it to boil. The first fractions of gas contained a new light gas they called neon ("new"). The final fractions contained traces of two heavy gases which they named krypton ("hidden") and xenon ("stranger"). The new column in the periodic table was filled, except for the lowest row, and that last place was filled two years later through studies in radioactivity.

Ramsay himself grew interested in radioactivity, because that had been found to be a property of uranium and it was in uranium ores that he had found helium. In 1903 he was able to show, in collaboration with Soddy [1052], that helium was continually produced by naturally radioactive products. When the final inert gas was discovered by Dorn [795]—the radioactive gas, radon—it was Ramsay who weighed a tiny quantity of it and determined its atomic weight.

He was knighted in 1902 and, more important, he received the 1904 Nobel Prize in chemistry for his work on the inert gases.

[833] **FISCHER**, Emil Hermann
German chemist
Born: Euskirchen, Rhenish Prussia, October 9, 1852
Died: Berlin, July 15, 1919

Fischer's father, a successful merchant, wanted him to enter the family business (he was the one surviving son) but young Fischer, who finished at the head of his class at the Bonn high school in 1864, preferred science and easily demonstrated his lack of business talent. His father gave in and Fischer attended the lectures of Kekulé [680] at the University of Bonn and later studied under

Baeyer [718] and Kundt [744] at the University of Strasbourg. Fischer obtained his doctorate in 1874 and went on to devote his professional life to extraordinarily fruitful researches in various branches of organic chemistry.

In 1875 he worked with organic derivatives of hydrazine (a compound of nitrogen and hydrogen) and showed how they could be used to separate and identify sugars that, otherwise, were almost impossible to handle except as impure mixtures. His aptitude for chemistry was so clear by this time that his father decided to be proud of him and saw to it that he remained financially secure. Fischer joined Baeyer, then went to the University of Erlangen in 1882 and to Würzberg in 1885.

During the 1880s Fischer made use of his hydrazine compounds to isolate pure sugars and study their structures. He showed that the best-known sugars contained six carbons and could exist in sixteen varieties, depending on how the carbon bonds were arranged. Each different arrangement was reflected in the way the plane of light polarization was twisted, and he worked out exactly which arrangement of carbon bonds applied to which sugar. In this way the practical observations of Pasteur [642] were combined with the theory of Van't Hoff [829], so that stereochemistry (the study of chemical structure in three-dimensional space) was placed on a sound footing.

Fischer showed there were two series of sugars, mirror images of each other, which he called the D-series and the L-series. He had to pick which mirror image belonged to which possible method of writing the formula and did so arbitrarily. He had a fifty-fifty chance of guessing right, and recent work shows that he did guess right.

The importance of stereochemistry to life is shown in the fact that just about all sugars in living tissue are of the D-series. The L-series virtually never appears in nature. Living tissue can tell them apart, so to speak, and prefers one series to the other.

While doing all this, Fischer also worked with a class of compounds he called purines, and elucidated their structure in detail. This turned out to be important, not just as an academic chemical exercise, but for the connection eventually discovered with the mechanism of life. Purines, as it turned out, are an important part of a group of substances called the nucleic acids, and these, it was discovered in the twentieth century, are the key molecules of living tissues.

In 1892 Fischer moved to the University of Berlin as successor to Hofmann [604] after the latter's death.

In 1902 Fischer received the Nobel Prize for chemistry for his researches in sugars and purines, but this by no means meant that his life's work was finished. He had shifted interest to the complicated molecules of proteins. It was known that proteins were built up out of relatively simple compounds called amino acids, but Fischer showed exactly how these amino acids were combined with each other within the protein molecule. Furthermore, he devised methods for linking one to another, in the same fashion that linkage took place in natural proteins. In 1907 he built up a very simple but quite authentic protein molecule made up of eighteen amino acid units and showed that digestive enzymes attacked it just as they would attack natural proteins.

This was a beginning in the complex field of protein structure, a type of work that was to culminate in the researches of Sanger [1426] and Du Vigneaud [1239] a half century later.

Fischer's final years were embittered by World War I, during which he organized German food and chemical production for war, and in which he lost two of his three sons. In a fit of despondency over the personal and national tragedy, and over the fact that he was suffering from cancer, he killed himself.

[834] BECQUEREL, Antoine Henri
    (beh-krel')
    French physicist
    Born: Paris, December 15, 1852
    Died: Le Croisic, Loire Inférieur,
    August 25, 1908

Becquerel, whose early schooling was as an engineer, obtained his doctorate in 1888 with a thesis on the absorption of light. He was a member of a family of physicists and his father was the A. E. Becquerel [623] who had done important work on fluorescence.

Becquerel, in 1891, succeeded to the post at the Museum of Natural History in Paris that his father and grandfather had held before him. He continued the researches of his father and stumbled across something far more important, which, at a stroke, destroyed the nineteenth-century conception of atomic structure.

The discovery of X rays by Roentgen [774] had intrigued Becquerel, as it had almost every physicist in Europe. Viewing the discovery in the light of his own specialty, he wondered if any fluorescent materials might be emitting X rays. (After all, Roentgen discovered X rays by the fluorescence they brought about.)

In February 1896 Becquerel wrapped photographic film in black paper and put it in sunlight with a crystal of a fluorescent chemical upon it. His reasoning was that if sunlight induced the fluorescence, and if the fluorescence contained X rays, then those X rays would penetrate the paper, as ordinary light and even ultraviolet light could not. (It was the penetrating power of X rays that was the most unusual property they possessed.) Becquerel used a chemical in which his father had been particularly interested—potassium uranyl sulfate. This was a compound containing uranium atoms, and it was this fluorescent material that Becquerel placed on top of his wrapped plates.

Sure enough, when the plate was developed, he found it to be fogged. This showed that radiation had penetrated the black paper, and Becquerel decided that X rays were indeed produced in fluorescence.

Then came a series of cloudy days and Becquerel could not continue his experiments. By March 1 he was restless. He had a fresh plate neatly wrapped in the drawer, with the crystals resting on it, and there was nothing to do. Finally, unable to bear the wait, he decided to develop the plates anyway. Perhaps a little of the original fluorescence persisted and there would be some faint fogging, even though the crystals hadn't been exposed to sunlight for days.

To his amazement, the plate was strongly fogged. Whatever radiation the compound was giving off did not depend on sunlight and did not involve fluorescence. Forgetting the sun, Becquerel began to study the radiation and found it quite like X rays, since it penetrated matter and ionized air. It continued to be given off by the compound in an unending stream, actively radiating in all directions. In 1898 Marie Curie [965] named the phenomenon radioactivity, a name that stuck. For a while the radiation from uranium was called Becquerel rays, a term also introduced by Marie Curie.

By 1899 Becquerel noted that the radiation could be deflected by a magnetic field so that at least part of it consisted of tiny, charged particles. In 1900 he decided the part that was negatively charged consisted of speeding electrons, identical in nature to those of the cathode rays as identified by J. J. Thomson [869].

The only place the electrons radiated by uranium could be coming from was from within the atoms of uranium (which Becquerel identified in 1901 as the radioactive portion of the compound). This was the first clear indication that the atom was not a featureless sphere but that it had an internal structure and that it might contain electrons.

As a result of his discoveries Becquerel was awarded a share in the 1903 Nobel Prize in physics. The Curies also received a share.

[835] MICHELSON, Albert Abraham (my′kul-sun)
German-American physicist
Born: Strelno, Prussia (now Strzelno, Poland), December 19, 1852
Died: Pasadena, California, May 9, 1931

Michelson was four years old when his parents brought him to the United States. The family made its way out to the Far West, which was in the midst of its gold boom, and there they went into business rather than into mining.

In his teens Albert applied for entrance to the United States Naval Academy. He had the backing of the Nevada congressman, who pointed out to President Grant the political usefulness of such a gesture to a prominent Jewish merchant of the New West. At the academy, Michelson shone in science but was rather below average in seamanship. He graduated in 1873 and served as a science instructor at the academy in the latter part of that decade. He was not a particularly good teacher.

In 1878 Michelson began work on what was to be the passion of his life, the accurate measurement of the speed of light. Roemer [232] had been the first to measure this two centuries earlier. Bradley [258], Foucault [619], and Fizeau [620] had done their bit, but Michelson working with homemade apparatus was determined to do better than any of them. Using Foucault's method, but adding some minor improvements, he made his first report on the velocity.

Feeling that he had to study optics before he was qualified to make still further progress, he crossed the ocean and studied in Germany and France. On his return to America he resigned from the navy and became a professor of physics at the Case School of Applied Science (now Case Western Reserve University) in Cleveland. In 1882 he was ready to try again and the result was a measurement of the speed of light at 299,853 kilometers a second (186,320 miles a second), a value that remained the best available for a generation. (When it was bettered, it was Michelson who bettered it.)

In 1881 Michelson was constructing an "interferometer" (with the financial help of A. G. Bell [789]), a device designed to split a beam of light in two, send the parts along different paths, then bring them back together—an experiment Maxwell [692] had suggested six years before. If they had traveled different distances at the same velocity or equal distances at different velocities, the two parts of the beam would be out of phase and would interfere with each other, producing bands of light and dark. (It was these interference fringes that Thomas Young [402] detected when two rays of light met, and which had established the wave nature of light.)

Michelson put his interferometer to use by studying the two halves of a beam of light that were made to travel at right angles to each other. At that time it was considered that light, being a wave, had to be waves of something (just as the ocean waves are waves of water). Consequently it was supposed that all space was filled with a luminiferous ether. (The word "luminiferous" means "light-carrying" and "ether" is a hark-back to the fifth element that Aristotle [29] supposed to be the component of all objects outside the earth's atmosphere.)

It was believed that ether was motionless and that the earth traveled through it. Light sent in the direction of earth's motion ought therefore (or so it seemed) to travel more rapidly than light sent at right angles to it. The two beams of light ought to fall out of phase and show interference fringes. By measuring the width of the fringes it would then be possible to show the earth's exact velocity when compared with the ether. In this way the earth's "absolute motion" could be determined and the absolute motion of all bodies of the universe whose motions relative to the earth were known would also be determined.

His first experiments in 1881, in Helmholtz's [631] laboratory in Berlin, showed no interference fringes, but he continued to try with ever more elaborate precautions against error, until in 1887 he and Morley [730] tried it under circumstances where it seemed they could not fail. Nevertheless, they failed. They could detect no fringes of significant width and therefore no difference in the velocity of light in any direction under any circumstances. (Nor has anyone else since that day.) The Michelson-Morley experiment, as it has always been known, is undoubtedly the most famous experiment-that-failed in the history of science.

(Despite this, the introduction to the physics section in the catalog of the University of Chicago for 1898–1899 implied that the structure of physics was so firmly placed that nothing further remained to be done but to determine the sixth decimal place of various constants —this despite the fact that the Michelson-Morley experiment had knocked physics topsy-turvy. And who was the head of the physics department at the time? Why, Michelson!)

The experiment overturned, particularly, all theories involving the ether (Mach [733] said at once that the ether did not exist) and made it necessary to find some explanation for the invariance of the velocity of light. FitzGerald [821] came up with the most dramatic one, which involved slight changes in the lengths of objects at high velocities, changes which were just sufficient to mask any change in the velocity of light and thus make it seem to be constant. The climax came in 1905 when Einstein [1064] announced his special theory of Relativity, which began by assuming the velocity of light in a vacuum to be a fundamental and unvarying constant, and which wiped out the need for any ether at all by making use of the quantum theory that Planck [887] advanced in 1900. (Michelson, however, could never bring himself to accept relativity.)

There is no doubt at all that the Michelson-Morley experiment served as the kicking-off point for the theoretical aspects of the Second Scientific Revolution, just as the discovery of X rays by Roentgen [774] in 1895 was to kick off its phenomenological aspects.

In 1907 Michelson was awarded the Nobel Prize in physics for his optical studies generally. He was the first American to win a Nobel Prize in one of the sciences.

But Michelson's optical studies are not noted for negative results alone. His interferometer made it possible for him to determine the width of heavenly objects by comparing the light rays from both sides and, from the nature of the interferences fringes, determine how far apart

541

their points of origin are. In this way he measured the angular width of the large satellites of Jupiter. This was no more than a neat trick, however, for that width can be measured by direct observation. However, in 1920, with better telescopes, he turned his efforts to the measurement of the diameter of stars that cannot be measured by direct observation even today. Using a twenty-foot interferometer attached to the 100-inch telescope, he was able to measure the diameter of the giant star Betelgeuse in this fashion, a startling first in astronomy which made the front page of the New York *Times* (a rare feat for a scientific advance in those days).

Meanwhile he had suggested the use of light waves as a standard of length in place of the platinum-iridium bar preserved in a Paris suburb as the International Prototype Meter. At first he thought the bright yellow line of sodium would do, but later his studies showed that the red light radiated by heated cadmium would make a better standard. In 1893 he measured the meter in terms of cadmium-red wavelength. (The use of light waves as a length standard was finally accepted in 1960, though light radiated by the rare gas krypton, unknown in 1893, was accepted as the standard, in place of cadmium red.) In 1892 Michelson became head of the department of physics at the University of Chicago, a position he held till his retirement. From 1923 to 1927 he served as president of the National Academy of Sciences.

In 1923 Michelson returned to the problem of the accurate measurement of the velocity of light. In the California mountains he surveyed a twenty-two-mile pathway between two mountain peaks to an accuracy of less than an inch. He made use of a special, eight-sided revolving mirror, prepared for him by his friend Sperry [907], and by 1927 he had the value 299,798 kilometers per second. He tried again, this time using a long tube that could be evacuated so that the velocity of light in a vacuum could be measured. Light was reflected and re-reflected until it traveled ten miles in

542

that vacuum. Michelson was a sick man now and did not live to make the final measurements, but in 1933, after his death, the final figure was announced. It was 299,774 kilometers per second (186,271 miles per second).

A generation after Michelson's death, the accepted value of the speed of light is 299,792.5 kilometers per second (186,282 miles per second), which lies between the values obtained by Michelson's last two sets of experiments.

As an example of experiments not involving the speed of light, consider Michelson's microscopic observations of the water level in an iron pipe. The tidal changes in level amounted to four microns (less than a six-millionth of an inch) but this sufficed to make it possible to calculate the intensity of the attraction of the sun and moon on the earth as easily as though the tides of the ocean itself were being studied. He showed that the solid earth rose and fell in response to sun and moon, changing its level by thirty-five centimeters, or a little over a foot.

[836] **SCHAEBERLE,** John Martin
(shay'ber-lee)
German-American astronomer
Born: Württemberg, Germany,
January 10, 1853
Died: Ann Arbor, Michigan, September 17, 1924

Schaeberle was taken to the United States by his family when he was still an infant. His career revolved about astronomic instruments after he graduated from the University of Michigan in 1876.

His best-remembered feat was that of detecting the dim companion (13th magnitude) of Procyon in 1896, duplicating the work of Clark [696] in detecting the dim companion of Sirius. This was an indication that such dim stars might not be rare, and by the time W. S. Adams [1045] showed the dim companion of Sirius to be what came to be called a "white dwarf," these were seen to make up a numerous class.

[837] **THOMSON,** Elihu
English-American inventor
Born: Manchester, England,
March 29, 1853
Died: Swampscott, Massachusetts,
March 13, 1937

Thomson was taken to the United
States by his family when he was five
years old and was educated at Central
High School (an elite school) in 1870.

He proved a talented inventor who
ended with something like seven hundred
patents, chiefly in the fields of electricity
and radiology. His inventions led to the
development of successful alternating-
current motors, and in 1890 he devised a
high-frequency electrical generator. He
founded an electrical company that
merged with Edison's [788] company in
1892 to form General Electric.

Outside the field of electricity, he was
the first to suggest the use of helium-
oxygen mixtures in place of the atmospheric nitrogen-oxygen mixtures to minimize the danger of bends in high-pressure work.

[838] **PETRIE,** Sir (William Matthew)
Flinders (pee'tree)
English archaeologist
Born: Charlton, near London,
June 3, 1853
Died: Jerusalem, Palestine, July
28, 1942

Petrie's maternal grandfather, Matthew
Flinders, had been a renowned explorer
of Australia and Tasmania. Petrie was
a sickly child, privately educated. He
early became interested in ancient civilizations, particularly that of Egypt and
most particularly in the nature of the
measurement units used by the ancient
Egyptians.

He felt that one could deduce what
those units had been by studying the ancient monuments. He began with Stonehenge, concerning which he published a
book in 1880, then went on to the love
of his life, the Egyptians. In the course
of his archaeological researches in
Egypt, he uncovered many interesting
relics, including most particularly a stele

of the time of Merneptah, the successor
of Rameses II, which contains the earliest known mention of Israel outside the
Bible. He also excavated Akhetaten, the
capital city of Egypt's monotheist
pharaoh, Ikhnaton. In addition, he did
important work in correlating Mycenean
history with that of Egypt by his digs in
Crete and in Greece.

In 1892 he became professor of Egyp-
tology at University College, London
University, and in 1923 he was knighted.

[839] **LORENTZ,** Hendrik Antoon
(loh'rents)
Dutch physicist
Born: Arnhem, July 18, 1853
Died: Haarlem, February 4, 1928

Lorentz attended Leiden University,
obtaining his doctor's degree, *summa
cum laude,* in 1875 and returned three
years later as professor of theoretical
physics, a post he held until his death.

Lorentz's doctoral thesis dealt with
the theory of electromagnetic radiation,
which Maxwell [692] had advanced a little over a decade before. Lorentz refined
the theory to take account of the manner
of the reflection and refraction of light,
points concerning which Maxwell's own
work had been somewhat unsatisfactory.
He went further in his search into the
implications of Maxwell's work.

According to Maxwell, electromagnetic radiation was produced by the oscillation of electric charges. Hertz [873]
showed this to be true for radio waves,
which in 1887 he formed by causing
electric charges to oscillate. But if light
was an electromagnetic radiation after
the fashion of radio waves, where were
the electric charges that did the oscillating?

By 1890 it seemed quite likely that the
electric current was made up of charged
particles, and Lorentz thought it quite
possible that the atoms of matter might
also consist of charged particles. (The
theories of Arrhenius [894] on the subject of ionization, which had just been
advanced, pointed in that direction.)
Lorentz suggested then that it was the
charged particles within the atom that

oscillated, producing visible light. (To be sure, this vision of oscillating particles was made much more subtle—and hard to picture—by the theoretical work of men like Bohr [1101] and Schrödinger [1117].)

If this was so, then placing a light in a strong magnetic field ought to affect the nature of the oscillations and therefore of the wavelength of the light emitted. This was demonstrated experimentally in 1896 by Zeeman [945], a pupil of Lorentz. By that time the discovery of the electron by J. J. Thomson [869] and of radioactivity by Becquerel [834] made it seem more than ever likely that the atom did indeed contain a structure made up of charged particles, and by 1902, when there seemed no longer doubt of this, Lorentz and Zeeman shared the Nobel Prize in physics.

Lorentz also tackled the negative results of the experiment conducted by Michelson [835] and Morley [730] and came to the same conclusion as FitzGerald [821]. He too postulated that there are contractions of length with motion. It seemed to him, further, that the mass of a charged particle such as the electron depends on its volume; the smaller the volume, the greater the mass. Since the Lorentz-FitzGerald contraction reduced the volume of an electron as it sped along and reduced it the more as it moved more rapidly, it must also increase its mass with velocity. At 161,000 miles a second, the mass of an electron is twice its "rest-mass," according to the Lorentz formulation, and at 186,282 miles a second, the velocity of light, the mass must be infinite since the volume becomes zero. This was another indication that the velocity of light in a vacuum is the greatest velocity at which any material object can travel.

By 1900, mass measurements on speeding subatomic particles did indeed show that Lorentz's equation describing how mass varied with velocity was followed exactly. And in 1905 Einstein [1064] advanced his special theory of Relativity from which the Lorentz-FitzGerald contraction could be deduced and from which it could be shown that the Lorentz mass-increase with velocity

held not only for charged particles, but for all objects, charged and uncharged.

In later life Lorentz ably supervised the enclosure of the Zuider Zee, an ambitious Dutch project to make more agricultural land out of a shallow basin of the sea.

[840] OSTWALD, Friedrich Wilhelm
(ohst'vahlt)
Russian-German physical chemist
Born: Riga, Latvia, September 2, 1853
Died: Leipzig, Saxony, April 4, 1932

Ostwald, the son of a master cooper, was born and educated in the Baltic provinces of the Russian Empire, where the ruling classes were descendants of the German immigrants who had moved in during early modern times.

In his scientific training, he spent seven years on a five-year course because his agile mind was deflected here and there instead of driving steadily forward toward graduation.

At the University of Dorpat (in what is now the Estonian SSR) he grew interested in H.P.J.J. Thomsen's [665] work on thermochemistry. He began studying other physical properties of chemical substances, obtaining his doctor's degree on the subject in 1878. He was appointed professor of chemistry at the University of Riga in 1881, but in 1887 he accepted a professorship at Leipzig and remained in Germany the rest of his life.

Ostwald is considered one of the chief founders of modern physical chemistry and his interest in this field was further stimulated by reading the dissertation of Arrhenius [894]. Arrhenius' views were not popular then but in Ostwald he found a firm friend and helper. Recognizing the importance of Gibbs's [740] work, Ostwald translated the American's papers into German so that they might receive general European appreciation. (Ostwald's grasp of the importance of American research led him in 1905 to accept the invitation to lecture for a year at Harvard as part of a program, then just starting, of a German-American exchange of professors. It was a clear sign that the United States was taking its rightful place, at last, on the research map.)

In 1887 Ostwald, in collaboration with his close friend Van't Hoff [829], had established the first learned journal to be devoted exclusively to physical chemistry. He himself did important work in many branches of physical chemistry, most notably in the field of catalysis. Thus, in 1894 he prepared an abstract of someone else's paper on the heat of combustion of foods, this abstract to appear in his own journal. He disagreed strongly with the conclusions of the man who wrote the paper and therefore casually added comments of his own. In this way he pointed out that the theories of Gibbs made it necessary to assume that catalysts hastened reaction without altering the energy relationships of the substances involved. Catalysts performed their functions, instead, by lowering the energy of activation, the latter being Arrhenius' concept. Ostwald further recognized that the ions, postulated by Arrhenius as electrically charged atoms, could also serve as catalysts. This was particularly true of the hydrogen ions liberated by acids in solution, thus accounting for the acid catalysis of starch breakdown to sugar.

This view of catalysis, still held today, made it useful in industry and in the applications soon to be made to the chemical phenomena in living tissue. (Even biochemistry was bending to the new physical chemical outlook, and Rubner [848], for instance, spent much time measuring the energy relationship involved in the chemical activity of living organisms.)

In 1909 Ostwald was awarded the Nobel Prize in chemistry for his work on catalysis, and he congratulated the committee for selecting that part of his work which he himself thought the best.

Ostwald was firm in his belief that chemists ought to confine their studies to measurable phenomena such as energy changes. In this respect he was a firm follower and admirer of Mach [733]. He believed that thermodynamics was the centrally important facet of chemistry and objected to theories that involved objects that could not be measured. For that reason he refused for a long time to accept the atomic theory as anything more than a convenient fiction; he was one of the last holdouts. It was the analysis by Perrin [990] of the phenomenon of Brownian motion that finally forced him to admit that atoms were responsible for a clearly visible phenomenon that could be easily measured.

In later life he wrote on the philosophy of science and in 1902 founded a journal devoted to that subject. He also tried to work out a new system for mixing and harmonizing colors. After he died, his home was converted into a museum in his memory.

[841] **GRAM,** Hans Christian Joachim
(grahm)
Danish bacteriologist
Born: Copenhagen, September 13, 1853
Died: Copenhagen, November 14, 1938

Gram, the son of a professor of law, obtained his M.D. at the University of Copenhagen in 1878.

His great contribution came in 1884, when he stained bacteria by one of Ehrlich's [845] methods and then treated the stained bacteria with iodine solution and an alcohol wash, which removed the stain from some and not from others. Those bacteria that retained the stain have been called Gram-positive ever since, while those that lost it are Gram-negative. This distinction was used as an important means of classifying bacteria and in recent years has shown interesting correlation with antibiotic activity. For instance, penicillin is active against Gram-positive bacteria for the most part, while streptomycin will attack Gram-negative.

In 1900 Gram was appointed professor of pathology at the University of Copenhagen, retaining the post till his retirement in 1923.

[842] **KOSSEL,** (Karl Martin Leonhard)
Albrecht (kohs'ul)
German biochemist
Born: Rostock, Mecklenburg,
September 16, 1853
Died: Heidelberg, July 5, 1927

It was Kossel's intention to study botany. His father, a merchant, saw no future in that, however, so Kossel studied medicine, obtaining his degree in 1878. At the University of Strasbourg, he came under the influence of Hoppe-Seyler [663], a leading light of the then infant science of biochemistry, and in 1877 he began four years as his assistant. This made a biochemist of him. Later, he worked under Du Bois-Reymond [611].

In 1879 he began to investigate a substance called nuclein, which had been isolated ten years earlier by Miescher [770], one of Hoppe-Seyler's students, and which the master had worked on himself. Until it entered Kossel's hands, however, it remained a poorly defined substance.

Kossel's studies began by showing that nuclein contained a protein portion and a nonprotein portion so that in place of the vague nuclein, one could speak of nucleoprotein, in which the prosthetic group (the nonprotein portion) was "nucleic acid." The protein was much like other proteins, but the nucleic acid was quite unlike any other natural product known until that time. When the nucleic acids were broken down, Kossel found that among the breakdown products were purines and pyrimidines, nitrogen-containing compounds with the atoms arranged in two rings and one ring respectively. (Fischer [833] had worked on the purines.)

Kossel isolated two different purines, adenine and guanine, and a total of three different pyrimidines, thymine (which he was the first to isolate), cytosine, and uracil. He also recognized the existence of a carbohydrate among the breakdown products, but the identification of that portion had to wait another generation for Levene [980].

Spermatozoa have a high content of nucleic acids, and Kossel went on to study the proteins in those cells. They proved to be considerably simpler than proteins in ordinary cells, and Kossel evolved quite an elaborate theory for the build-up of ordinary proteins out of the simple cores present in spermatozoa. In this he had entered a blind alley, for he did not realize (nor did anyone for nearly half a century more) that the crucial compounds in the spermatozoa and in all cells were the nucleic acids rather than the proteins and that the nucleic acids were present in sperm cells in full complexity.

His work, even without his having realized the full importance of nucleic acids, was impressive. He discovered the essential amino acid, histidine, for instance.

He was appointed professor of physiology at the University of Marburg in 1895, and in 1901 he succeeded Kühne [725] as professor of physiology at Heidelberg where he remained till his retirement in 1924. In 1910 he received the Nobel Prize in physiology and medicine for his work on proteins and nucleic acids.

[843] **KAMERLINGH ONNES,** Heike
(ka'mer-ling ohn'es)
Dutch physicist
Born: Groningen, September 21, 1853
Died: Leiden, February 21, 1926

Kamerlingh Onnes, the son of a prosperous manufacturer, had his early schooling in his hometown. He entered the University of Groningen in 1870. The next year he went to Heidelberg, where he studied under Bunsen [565] and Kirchhoff [648]. He returned to Groningen for his doctorate (awarded in 1879 *summa cum laude* for studies on new proofs of the rotation of the earth) and in 1882 was appointed professor of experimental physics at Leiden University. Here he established the Cryogenic Laboratory (now known by his name) at which new depths of temperature were plumbed and which made Leiden famous as the cold-research center of the world.

Kamerlingh Onnes chose low-temperature work because of his interest in the researches of his countryman Van der Waals [726]. It seemed to Kamerlingh Onnes that to study the behavior of gases it was necessary to measure volume, pressure, and temperature very accurately, and that important information could be obtained at very low temperatures. To reach low temperatures, one had to use liquefied gases, and Kamerlingh Onnes' interest shifted to the problem of liquefying gas, in particular, helium, the one gas still defying all efforts at liquefaction in the first decade of the twentieth century.

Kamerlingh Onnes built an elaborate device that would cool helium intensively by means of evaporating liquid hydrogen, after which the Joule-Thomson effect as used by Dewar [759] could be brought into play. The result was that in 1908 liquid helium was produced for the first time and collected in a flask contained in a larger flask of liquid hydrogen, which was in turn contained in a still larger flask of liquid air. It turned out that the liquid helium was at a temperature only 4 degrees above absolute zero. In 1910 he found that by allowing some of it to evaporate, the remainder (still liquid) could be cooled to 0.8 degrees above absolute zero. To the end of his life Kamerlingh Onnes did not succeed in producing solid helium, but a few months after his death, one of his co-workers, Keesom [1042], managed the trick by using not only low temperatures but also high pressures.

There was more to liquid helium than the mere establishment of a new record of cold, or of the final liquefaction of the last gas. Kamerlingh Onnes studied the properties of materials at liquid helium temperatures and in 1911 made the startling discovery that certain metals, such as lead and mercury, underwent a total loss of electrical resistance at such temperatures. In this way the phenomenon of superconductivity was discovered. Kamerlingh Onnes also found that superconductivity could be wiped out, even at those temperatures at which it could exist, by imposing a large enough magnetic field upon the substance.

The phenomenon of superconductivity was not all. Other odd properties were found to exist only in the close neighborhood of absolute zero. A form of liquid helium ("helium II") was found which had properties radically different from those of all other substances. A whole new world of the ultracold opened up. Modern computers can make use of ultra-small switches that will enable a great amount of circuitry to be crammed into a small space. Some of these switches work through superconductivity and must be cooled in liquid helium.

Kamerlingh Onnes received the 1912 Rumford medal of the Royal Society and the next year did even better when he received the Nobel Prize in physics for his liquefaction of helium.

[844] ROUX, Pierre Paul Émile (roo)
French bacteriologist
Born: Confolens, Charente, December 17, 1853
Died: Paris, November 3, 1933

In 1878 Roux was accepted as an assistant at Pasteur's [642] laboratory in Paris. He and Chamberland [816] worked with Pasteur on the attenuation of pathogens so that an inoculation could be produced that would not initiate a serious disease but would bring about immunity. The specific success lay with anthrax.

Roux went on to study diphtheria. He clearly demonstrated that the bacillus, discovered shortly before by Löffler [828], did indeed cause diphtheria and, moreover, that it was not its mere presence that did the trick, but a toxin which it produced.

Once an understanding of the toxin and its role was reached, it was possible to produce an antitoxin that would neutralize the pathogenic effect of the toxin, and this Behring [846] went on to do.

[845] EHRLICH, Paul (air'likh)
German bacteriologist
Born: Strehlen, Silesia (now Strzelin, Poland), March 14, 1854
Died: Bad Homburg, Rhenish Prussia, August 20, 1915

Ehrlich, the son of a prosperous Jewish businessman, did poorly in school. From early youth, however, he was interested in both chemistry and biology and, during his later schooling, attempted to combine the two. In medical school he was abnormally (for those days) interested in chemistry and like Flemming [762] and Koch [767] began to try to apply the new aniline dyes to the problem of staining. Fortunately his teacher, Waldeyer [722], encouraged the young man and in the end Ehrlich discovered several practical bacterial stains and wrote his graduation thesis on the subject. He also learned to stain white blood corpuscles and discovered a new variety called mast cells through their staining characteristics.

After obtaining his medical degree at Leipzig in 1878, Ehrlich discovered a good method of staining the tubercle bacillus and this brought him to the attention of Koch, whose specialty was tuberculosis. In 1882 Ehrlich began work with Koch, but unfortunately he caught a light case of the disease in 1886 and retired to Egypt, where he hoped the dry climate might cure him. It did.

When Ehrlich returned from Egypt in 1889, he joined forces with Behring [846] and Kitasato [870], two other men who had worked with Koch, and in 1890 received a professorial appointment at the University of Berlin. They were attempting to find a cure for diphtheria. It was Behring's idea (similar to Richet's [809] but independent of him) to make use of antibodies produced by animals that had been inoculated with the diphtheria germ, which had itself been discovered a few years earlier by Löffler [828]. Ehrlich, who was a most gifted and intuitive experimenter, worked out the details of technique and dosage and by 1892 a diphtheria antitoxin was produced that worked wonders against that dreaded childhood disease. The achievement won Ehrlich a professorship at the University of Berlin (and won Behring a Nobel Prize).

Ehrlich quarreled with Behring and they parted in anger. But Ehrlich would quarrel at the drop of a hat. Throughout his life he had his own notions about the exact course that research should take and anyone who worked for or with him received detailed instructions as to what to do. Any deviation from these instructions was cause enough for a quarrel. The fact that Ehrlich was almost invariably right did not make his dictatorship easier to take.

In 1896 the German government, impressed by the diphtheria toxin, opened an institute for serum research and Ehrlich was put in charge. He continued to work on serum therapy and evolved a theory, interesting in its time, but now outmoded, of how antibodies function.

However, he kept returning to his stains, which, thanks to the work of men such as Golgi [764] and Gram [841], were becoming more important in microscopic work. Ehrlich reasoned that the value of a stain was that it colored some cells and not others; it colored bacteria, for instance, and made them stand out against a colorless background. Well, a stain could not color bacteria unless it combined with some substance in the bacterium and if it did that it would usually kill the bacterium. If a dye could be found that stained bacteria and not ordinary cells, it might represent a chemical that killed bacteria without harming human beings. Ehrlich would have, in effect, a "magic bullet" that could be taken into the body where it would seek out the parasites and destroy them.

And, indeed, Ehrlich did discover a dye, called trypan red, that helped destroy the trypanosomes that caused such diseases as sleeping sickness.

Ehrlich kept looking for something better. He decided that the action of trypan red was caused by the nitrogen atom combinations it contained. Arsenic atoms resemble nitrogen atoms in chemical properties and, in general, introduce a more poisonous quality into compounds. He began to try all the arsenic-containing organic compounds he could find or synthesize, one after the other. He set his students and associates to work on them, and literally hundreds of chemicals were tried. By 1907 he had reached   dihydroxydiamino-arsenobenzene hydrochloride, which was number

606. It did not work very well against trypanosomes and he left it behind and went on.

In 1908 Ehrlich was awarded a share, along with Mechnikov [775], of the Nobel Prize in medicine and physiology for his work on immunity and serum therapy generally. As was to happen in more than one case, however, his most dramatic achievement came after the Nobel Prize.

In 1909 a new assistant of Ehrlich, practicing the techniques involved in testing arsenicals for trypanosome-killing properties, picked up chemical 606 again. (By now Ehrlich had reached the 900s.) It was still no good for trypanosomes but it turned out to be a remarkably efficient killer for spirochetes, the microorganism that causes syphilis.

Syphilis, more dreaded than trypanosomiasis, was almost a secret disease, especially in those days. Ehrlich therefore pounced upon his assistant's finding at once, confirmed the observation, and in 1910 announced it to the world. He named the chemical salvarsan (although its proper short chemical name is now arsphenamine). For the rest of his life he worked strenuously to see to it that the medical profession used the chemical correctly and had 65,000 units distributed to physicians all over the globe without charge, feeling the cure to be more important than income.

Sometimes doctors did not follow instructions carefully, and incorrect usage led to tragedies that brought on vicious attacks on Ehrlich as a quack and murderer. Ehrlich won through, however (though he was forced to sue the most slanderous ones), and shone the more brightly and permanently as a healer and benefactor of mankind.

Trypan red and salvarsan marked the beginning of modern chemotherapy (a word coined by Ehrlich). Chemicals had been used against disease before Ehrlich and, indeed, since the dawn of history. These, like quinine against malaria, or foxglove against heart disease, were, however, folk remedies, stumbled upon by accident. Ehrlich's chemical cures were deliberately sought after with all the techniques of science.

It was thought, after Ehrlich, that a chemical cure for each infectious disease would now quickly be found, but in this mankind was disappointed. Another quarter century had to pass before Domagk [1183] was to make the next step and throw chemotherapy into high gear.

Ehrlich was buried in the Jewish cemetery in Frankfort. A generation later, the tomb was desecrated by the Nazis, but it was restored after World War II.

[846] **BEHRING,** Emil Adolf von
(bay'ring)
German bacteriologist
Born: Deutsch-Eylau, East Prussia (now Ilawa, Poland), March 3, 1854
Died: Marburg, Rhenish Prussia, March 31, 1917

Behring, the son of a schoolmaster, was slated to be a minister, but one of his teachers recognized his talent and arranged for a free medical education on the promise he would serve in the army. He obtained his M.D. in 1880 and duly became an army surgeon. In 1889 he went to work with Koch [767] at the latter's Institute for Infectious Diseases in Berlin.

There he discovered, in 1890, that it was possible to produce an immunity against tetanus (or lockjaw) in an animal by injecting into it graded doses of blood serum from another animal suffering from tetanus. A fraction of the serum from the immunized animal (which he called the antitoxin) could then be used to confer at least temporary immunity on still another animal. (Richet [809] was trying similar techniques against tuberculosis, but failed where Behring succeeded.)

Behring wondered if this could not be done for diphtheria, a disease that was in those days almost sure death to the children it attacked. The diptheria antitoxin, successfully marketed by 1892, not only conferred immunity, but also helped defeat the disease after it had begun. Although Ehrlich [845] probably did most of the actual work involved in the development, the idea was Behring's and he was given the credit for it. In 1884 it gained him a professorship at the University of Halle and in 1901 it earned for him the first Nobel Prize awarded in medicine and physiology.

However, it may be significant that after Behring and Ehrlich parted in anger, Behring achieved nothing of consequence, while Ehrlich went on to additional triumphs.

[847] POINCARÉ, Jules Henri (pwahn-kah-ray')
French mathematician
Born: Nancy, April 29, 1854
Died: Paris, July 17, 1912

Poincaré has been called by some the last of the universal mathematicians because he managed to do first-class creative work in most branches of mathematics, as well as in astronomy (writing well enough to be considered a literary figure), and because the twentieth-century ramification of mathematics makes it seem unlikely that one man will ever be able to do so again.

His start, however, was inauspicious, for his motor coordination and his eyesight were poor and in some ways he seemed actually retarded. His photographic memory helped him do well at school.

As a teenager, he lived through the horrors of the Franco-Prussian War, as did his first cousin, Raymond Poincaré. The latter gained an enduring anti-German hatred that had ample opportunity to express itself when Raymond served as President of France during World War I. Henri Poincaré, on the other hand, grew interested in mathematics as a teenager, died before World War I, and, in any case, found mathematics to be above nationalism.

Poincaré obtained his doctor's degree in 1879, one of his teachers being Hermite [641], and served at the University of Paris thereafter. He worked on celestial mechanics and his contributions to the three-body problem earned him, in 1889, a prize awarded by King Oscar II of Sweden. His theoretical work on tides

and on rotating fluid spheres amplified and buttressed the work of G. H. Darwin [777] on the tidal hypothesis of the creation of the moon.

He was one of the first to see the significance of the young Einstein's [1064] theory of relativity and in later life wrote profoundly on mathematical creativity. This he considered a matter of fundamental importance (and it would be impossible to disagree with that if we assume, as may well be true, that all creativity of whatever sort is related).

[848] RUBNER, Max
German physiologist
Born: Munich, Bavaria, June 2, 1854
Died: Berlin, April 27, 1932

Rubner, the son of a locksmith, studied medicine at the University of Munich, obtaining his medical degree in 1878. He carried on the work of his teacher, Voit [691], adding to it the painstaking quantitativeness that was coming into fashion in late nineteenth-century Germany. In testing the energy production by humans in large calorimeters, he missed no tricks. He measured the nitrogen content of urine and feces, and carefully estimated the quantity of the various types of foodstuffs in the diet he fed his subjects.

He concluded in 1884 that no one particular type of foodstuff produced energy. The body made use of carbohydrates, fats, and proteins with equal readiness. The nitrogen portion of proteins was split away before it was used for fuel, he maintained, and in this he was proved correct.

In 1891 he succeeded to the chair of hygiene at the University of Berlin, which had been held by Koch [767]; and by 1894 he had discovered that the energy produced from foodstuffs by the body was precisely the same in quantity as it would have been if those same foodstuffs had been consumed in a fire (once the energy content of urea was subtracted). The laws of thermodynamics, in other words, held for living tissue as well as for the inanimate world, and organisms had no magic ways of extracting energy.

Thus was finally confirmed the conjecture advanced by Mayer [587] a half century earlier. This was a serious blow against vitalism (the view that there was one set of laws of nature for living tissue and another for inanimate bodies). Still another blow was to be provided by Buchner [903] three years later.

[849] **CARROLL,** James
English-American physician
Born: Woolwich (now part of London), England, June 5, 1854
Died: Washington, D.C., September 16, 1907

Carroll intended to be a naval engineer, but he left England for Canada in 1869 and then in 1874 enlisted in the U. S. Army. He remained in the army for the rest of his life, became a hospital steward in 1883, attended medical school and gained his M.D. from the University of Maryland in 1891. During the Spanish-American War, he served as acting assistant surgeon.

Carroll was with Reed [822] in the investigation of yellow fever in Cuba. On August 27, 1900, Carroll decided to test the theory that mosquitoes were carriers of yellow fever, something he rather doubted. He allowed a mosquito that had been biting fever victims to bite him and within a few days he had a severe case of yellow fever.

He recovered, fortunately, something his fellow investigator, Lazear [955] did not do, but the good fortune was limited. The disease left as a legacy a damaged heart which killed Carroll seven years later.

[850] **PARSONS,** Sir Charles Algernon
British engineer
Born: London, England, June 13, 1854
Died: on shipboard off Kingston, Jamaica, February 11, 1931

Parsons was the fourth son of the 3d earl of Rosse [513], but he made his mark in a field far removed from his father's astronomy. After studying at the University of Dublin and at Cambridge, he devoted himself to engineering.

In particular, he was interested in improving the utilization of steam power. The steam engine, as designed by Watt [316] a century before, used the energy of steam to set a piston moving back and forth and this reciprocal motion was converted, by appropriate coupling, into the rotational movement of a wheel. It had naturally occurred to men ever since Watt's day that if one could direct a current of stream against the blades set about the rim of a wheel, a rotational movement could be set up directly, producing a far greater velocity of rotation. In the 1880s such high speeds of rotation were highly desirable, since they would be most useful in electric generators of the type Faraday [474] first constructed a half century earlier. In other words the development of a steam turbine would not only produce mechanical energy but also electrical energy.

The problem had its engineering difficulties, for the wheel had to be designed to withstand the mechanical stress of rapid rotation; the metal of which it was constructed had to withstand the heat; and the steam itself could not be allowed to escape prematurely. Parsons solved each of these problems and in 1884 succeeded in producing the first practical steam turbine. Successive improvements in design increased its efficiency and he went into business. In 1894 he was experimenting with ships driven by such engines and in 1897 he was ready for a dramatic show. It was the Diamond Jubilee of Queen Victoria. The British navy was holding a stately review when suddenly past the ships skinned Parson's turbine-powered ship, *Turbinia,* going 35 knots, an unheard-of speed for any ship. It moved, moreover, with scarcely any vibration or noise. A naval vessel was sent after it, but couldn't get near it.

At once the steam turbine was bid for and in 1885 a Chilean battleship was the first to be turbine-equipped. Soon turbines were powering both warships and merchant vessels.

If anything, the steam turbines rotated too rapidly. The rotation was fine for generating electricity, but propellers were driven too quickly for maximum efficiency. In the 1890s and 1900s Parsons worked on devices to gear down the rotation, the turbines rotating at maximum speed but driving the propellers at less than a tenth the speed. He finally succeeded in that too, and the steam turbine was complete. Parsons was knighted in 1911.

In his retirement, Parsons tried unsuccessfully to make artificial diamonds, a popular pastime of the period that also occupied Moissan [831] and Acheson [863].

[851] HAMPSON, William
English inventor
Born: Bebington, Cheshire, 1854
Died: London, January 1, 1926

Hampson, about whose life little is known, seems to have intended to become a lawyer at first, but does not appear to have carried through with this intention.

He became an engineer and inventor instead, and he is best known for having developed methods for producing quantities of liquid air, anticipating the methods used by Linde [758] and Claude [989]. The liquid air supplied by Hampson made it possible for Ramsay [832] to discover neon, for instance. That he did not receive the credit due him may have in part been the fault of Dewar [759], who was not inclined to abandon any credit for anything and who disputed priorities acrimoniously with him on the question of the liquefaction of hydrogen.

[852] EASTMAN, George
American inventor
Born: Waterville, New York, July 12, 1854
Died: Rochester, New York, March 14, 1932

Like Edison [788], Eastman (whose family moved to Rochester while he was still a child) was born poor and had little

chance at schooling. He was working and supporting himself at fourteen.

In 1877 he became interested in photography when he was planning a vacation trip to Santo Domingo and a friend suggested he take along a camera. Eastman foresaw that people would take to a device that would freeze the past, provided the device was simple and straightforward. Photography, he decided, would have to be divorced from the chemical laboratory, at least as far as taking the picture was concerned.

Until Eastman's time, the photographic plate was glass, and an emulsion of chemicals had to be smeared upon it before a photograph could be taken. The emulsion would not keep; it had to be made up on the spot, smeared over the plate, and the picture taken. As long as all that was necessary, photography would be only for a handful of professionals. In 1878 Eastman learned how to mix the emulsion with gelatin, smear it on the plate, and let it dry into a firm gel. Now it would keep for long periods of time and could be used when convenient. By 1880 he was in business.

The glass, however, was still heavy and clumsy. In 1884 Eastman patented photographic "film" in which the gel was smeared on paper. In 1888 he began selling the Kodak camera (he invented the name, a meaningless one, as a catchy trademark), which used such flexible film though the camera weighed about two pounds, even so. The owner pressed buttons to take pictures, then sent the camera to Rochester and eventually received back his photograph and a freshly loaded camera. "You press the button—we do the rest" was Kodak's successful slogan.

(Eventually the owner would need only to give away the roll of film to be developed, and over half a century after the coming of the Kodak, Land [1344] was to make developing as automatic and almost as rapid as taking the photograph.)

In 1889 Eastman got rid of the paper and made the film out of a tougher material, Hyatt's [728] celluloid. This plastic served as solvent for the emulsion and as an independent support. Photography for the masses had come to stay. Eastman's film also made motion pictures possible, for Edison seized upon strips of such film as a carrier for successive "stills" taken in rapid succession.

The great difficulty with celluloid film was its inflammability. It was always a fearful hazard in quantity. For a generation Eastman experimented and by 1924 cellulose acetate, far less inflammable, had replaced celluloid.

As head of a large business, Eastman introduced many enlightened business practices, such as sickness benefits, retirement annuities, and life insurance for his employees, long before such extras became general. He contributed over $100 million to various educational institutions, including $54 million to the University of Rochester and $19 million to Massachusetts Institute of Technology, in order that others might receive the schooling he had never had. He also endowed dental clinics in various European cities.

In 1932, after a long and successful life, and facing a few last years in loneliness and without the prospect of further accomplishment, Eastman killed himself.

[853] **GORGAS,** William Crawford
(gawr′gus)
American army surgeon
Born: Mobile, Alabama, October 3, 1854
Died: London, England, July 3, 1920

Gorgas was the son of a Confederate soldier and his life closely paralleled that of his fellow Southerner Reed [822]. Gorgas also obtained his degree from Bellevue (in 1879) and also entered the army (in 1880). He too was in Havana, from 1898 to 1902, combating the yellow fever menace.

The high point of his life came in 1904 when, after Reed's death, he was sent to Panama. There he placed the mosquito under such effective control that both malaria and yellow fever were wiped out. It was this, more than any en-

gineering feat, that made it possible to bring the building of the Panama Canal to a successful conclusion.

In 1914 the canal was opened and Gorgas was made surgeon general of the U. S. Army. Afterward, he devoted himself to the fight against yellow fever in other parts of the world, notably in Ecuador. In 1950 he was elected to a place in the Hall of Fame for Great Americans.

[854] **ROOZEBOOM,** Hendrik Willem
Bakhuis (roh′zuh-bome)
Dutch physical chemist
Born: Alkmaar, October 24, 1854
Died: Amsterdam, February 8, 1907

Roozeboom worked in a butter factory as a young man, but went on to study chemistry at the University of Leiden, graduating in 1884. He then served as professor of chemistry at the University of Amsterdam, succeeding Van't Hoff [829] in that post in 1886.

Learning of the phase rule from Van der Waals [726], he popularized it throughout Europe. He converted Gibbs's [740] theory into practice. Gibbs had rarely experimented but Roozeboom made all sorts of measurements that served to prove the validity of the phase rule and, in addition, worked out the details of its application to many individual cases.

The modern chemistry of alloys could scarcely exist without an understanding of phase rule as amplified by Roozeboom.

[855] **TAKAMINE,** Jokichi (tah-kah-mee-nee)
Japanese-American chemist
Born: Takaoka, Japan, November 3, 1854
Died: New York, New York, July 22, 1922

In the year of Takamine's birth, Commodore Perry forced Japan to open its doors to the West, and the Japanese people turned out to be apt and ready pupils. Takamine, the son of a physician, was brought up according to the Samurai code, but proved a scientist in quite the Western style. He graduated in 1879 from the Imperial University at Tokyo as a chemical engineer. He interested himself in agricultural chemistry, founding the chemical fertilizer industry in Japan when he built the first superphosphate works in the land in Tokyo in 1887.

In 1890, having married an American woman, he moved to the United States and established a laboratory in Clifton, New Jersey. In 1901 he isolated a substance from the adrenal glands that is now best known by the tradename Adrenalin, or as adrenaline, although its proper chemical name is epinephrine. The hormone concept had not yet been advanced, but eventually it came to be realized that Takamine, unknowingly, had been the first to isolate a pure hormone.

He also isolated a starch-hydrolyzing enzyme from rice which was similar to the diastase that Payen [490] had isolated, as the first known enzyme, nearly a century earlier. He named it Takadiastase and devised methods for its use as a starch-digestant in industrial processes.

In 1912 he negotiated with the mayor of Tokyo for the cherry trees that have ever since bloomed in Washington, D.C.

[856] SABATIER, Paul (sa-ba-tyay')
French chemist
Born: Carcassonne, Aude, November 5, 1854
Died: Toulouse, Haute-Garonne, August 14, 1941

Sabatier, born of a poor family, obtained his doctor's degree in 1880 at the Collège de France, where he served as assistant to Berthelot [674]. In 1882 he joined the faculty of the University of Toulouse, earning a professorial position in 1884 and remaining there the rest of his long life. At first he taught physics and interested himself in physical chemistry. He approached organic chemistry,

in which he was to achieve fame, entirely through the failure of an experiment he had conducted in 1897.

Nickel forms one of its few volatile compounds (that is, compounds that vaporize at quite low temperatures) through combination with carbon monoxide to form nickel carbonyl. This was an interesting compound and Sabatier and an assistant reached over into organic chemistry to see if another volatile nickel compound could not be formed by the addition of the hydrocarbon ethylene. This organic compound had a double bond, like carbon monoxide, and there was a chance its behavior might be similar. However, the experiment failed. When nickel was heated under ethylene, no volatile nickel ethylene compound was formed.

But Sabatier and his assistant saved what gases did form for later analysis and to their surprise found that ethane was present. Ethane's molecule was like ethylene's, plus hydrogen atoms at the double bond. Apparently the nickel had acted as a catalyst, bringing about the addition of hydrogen to ethylene to form ethane.

Sabatier switched to organic chemistry and spent the rest of his career studying catalytic hydrogenations. The work was fruitful. Until then the catalyst routinely used for hydrogen additions had been platinum or palladium, very expensive metals. If the comparatively cheap metal nickel could be used instead, hydrogenations would no longer be confined to the laboratory but could be used in large industrial-scale processes much more easily. Nickel catalysis made possible the formation of edible fats such as margarine and shortenings from inedible plant oils such as cottonseed oil in record quantity and with record economy. Through the fame of this discovery Sabatier might have gone on to the Sorbonne in Paris in 1907 to succeed Moissan [831], but he chose to remain in the South of France.

For his work on catalysis Sabatier received the 1912 Nobel Prize in chemistry, sharing it with Grignard [993].

[857] **RYDBERG,** Johannes Robert
(rid'bar-yeh)
Swedish physicist
Born: Halmstad, November 8,
1854
Died: Lund, Malmöhus, December 28, 1919

Rydberg studied at the University of Lund and received his Ph.D. in mathematics in 1879, and then joined the faculty, reaching professorial status in 1897.

He was primarily interested in spectroscopy and labored to make sense of the various spectral lines produced by the different elements when incandescent (as Balmer [658] did for hydrogen in 1885). Rydberg worked out a relationship before he learned of Balmer's equation, and when that was called to his attention, he was able to demonstrate that Balmer's equation was a special case of the more general relationship he himself had worked out.

Even Rydberg's equation was purely empirical. He did not manage to work out the reason why the equation existed. That had to await Bohr's [1101] application of quantum notions to atomic structure. Rydberg did, however, suspect the existence of regularities in the list of elements that were simpler and more regular than the atomic weights and this notion was borne out magnificently by Moseley's [1121] elucidation of atomic numbers.

[858] **ELSTER,** Johann Philipp Ludwig
Julius
German physicist
Born: Bad Blankenburg, December 24, 1854
Died: Bad Harzburg, Saxony,
April 6, 1920

Elster worked together with Hans Geitel (1855–1923). They were fellow students at Heidelberg and fellow teachers of physics at a secondary school near Brunswick.

Beginning in 1889, they studied the photoelectric effect, by which an electric current was set up on the exposure of certain metals to light. This had been observed for the first time, in a rather primitive fashion, in 1888 by Hertz [873], but Elster and Geitel were the first to produce practical photoelectric cells that could be used to measure the intensity of light.

They also studied the new phenomenon of radioactivity after it had been reported by Becquerel [834] in 1896 and showed that external effects did not influence the intensity of the radiation, which they were the first to characterize as caused by changes that took place *within* the atom.

[859] **NEISSER,** Albert Ludwig
Sigismund (ny'ser)
German physician
Born: Schweidnitz, Silesia (now
Swidnica, Poland), January 22,
1855
Died: Breslau, Silesia (now
Wrocław, Poland), July 30, 1916

Neisser was the son of a physician and naturally gravitated toward medicine as a lifework. In secondary school, Ehrlich [845] was a classmate. Neisser gained his medical degree in 1877 after having proved himself a rather mediocre student.

As a physician, however, he did well. In 1879 he discovered the small bacterium that caused gonorrhea (and was named "gonococcus" by Ehrlich). He then traveled to Norway, where he had the opportunity to examine a number of patients suffering from leprosy and identified the bacillus responsible for that disease. A Norwegian physician, A.G.H. Hansen (1841–1912), seems to have isolated the bacillus some years earlier and there was a dispute over priorities, but even if Neisser were the second to have seen the bacillus, he seems to have been the first to make the connection clear between it and the disease.

He failed, however, in his studies of syphilis, and his attempts at inoculating against the disease may have spread it instead.

[860] **LOWELL, Percival**
American astronomer
Born: Boston, Massachusetts,
March 13, 1855
Died: Flagstaff, Arizona, November 12, 1916

Percival Lowell was a member of that aristocratic Boston family who "speak only to Cabots" while the Cabots "speak only to God." His sister was Amy Lowell, a first-rate poet, and his brother became president of Harvard University.

After graduation with honors in 1876 from the rather inevitable Harvard, he spent some time in business and in travel in the Far East. He was interested in mathematics, however, and had dabbled in astronomy as a boy. He was greatly excited by the "canals" reported by Schiaparelli [714] to exist on Mars.

On his return to the United States he exercised the privilege, as a man of independent wealth, of establishing a private observatory in Arizona where the mile-high dry desert air and the remoteness from city lights made the seeing excellent. The Lowell Observatory was opened in 1894, when Mars was quite close to the earth.

For fifteen years Lowell avidly studied Mars, taking thousands of photographs of it. There was no question that he saw the canals (or thought he did). In fact, he saw far more than Schiaparelli ever did and he drew detailed pictures that eventually included over five hundred canals. He plotted the "oases" at which they met, recorded the fashion in which they seemed to double at times, and noted in detail the seasonal changes, which seemed to mark the ebb and flow of agriculture. All in all, he is the patron saint of the intelligent-life-on-Mars cult.

At the same time Pickering [885] was almost as assiduous in his study of Mars, and though he reported straight markings, they were few and shifting and were not at all like the sharp, well-defined markings of Lowell. Modern astronomers side with Pickering against Lowell and point out, as H. S. Jones [1140] did, for instance, that irregular blotches at the limit of seeing seem to affect the eyes as interconnecting straight lines. The canals are probably an optical illusion, in other words.

Lowell made his mark in another respect as well. Even after Neptune had been discovered by Leverrier [564] and J. C. Adams [615], the discrepancies in the motion of Uranus were not completely understood. It still wandered off its calculated orbit by a tiny amount. Lowell believed this was due to still another planet beyond Neptune. He calculated its possible position in the sky—by its effect on Uranus—and searched with determination for what he called Planet X.

He never found it, but for fourteen years after his death the search continued with better telescopes until it was brought to a successful conclusion by Tombaugh [1299]. The new planet was named Pluto, an appropriate name for the planet farthest from the sun (as far as we now know), and it was no accident that the first two letters of the name are the initials of Percival Lowell.

[861] **TEISSERENC DE BORT,** Léon Philippe (tes-rahn' duh-bawr)
French meteorologist
Born: Paris, November 5, 1855
Died: Cannes, Alpes-Maritimes, January 2, 1913

At first Teisserenc de Bort, the son of an engineer, was employed by the Central Meteorological Bureau at Paris, and he became chief meteorologist in 1892. However, he resigned in 1896 and went into business for himself, so to speak, opening a private observatory near Versailles.

There he was able to conduct experiments with high-flying instrumented balloons to his heart's content, without worrying about official duties. He was one of the pioneers in the use of unmanned balloons, which pierced new heights without endangering human life. He discovered that above seven miles or so the temperature, which drops steadily from sea level to that altitude, remained constant up to the highest points he could reach.

He therefore suggested in 1902, after

years of careful measurement, that the atmosphere was divided into two layers. The lower layer, where temperature changes induced all sorts of air movements, cloud formations, and, in short, weather, he named the troposphere ("sphere of change") in 1908. The upper boundary of this troposphere was the tropopause.

Above the tropopause, Teisserenc de Bort believed there must be a region of changelessness because the impetus of temperature difference was lacking. He suggested that different gases might lie in layers, with lighter gases floating on heavier ones (oxygen at the bottom, nitrogen above that, the newly discovered helium above that, and hydrogen above all). He therefore called the upper region the stratosphere ("sphere of layers").

Teisserenc de Bort's theory of gas layers immediately above the tropopause has not been borne out by the rocket experiments of the mid-twentieth century (though at far greater heights, extremely thin layers of hydrogen and helium are now known to exist), but the name stratosphere remains. Teisserenc de Bort's was the first systematic investigation of the atmospheric heights. In fact, such is the progress of research that the high stratosphere is now considered part of the lower atmosphere.

[862] **CROSS,** Charles Frederick
English chemist
Born: Brentford, Middlesex, December 11, 1855
Died: Hove, Sussex, April 15, 1935

Cross graduated from King's College, London, in 1878.

In 1892 he worked out a method for dissolving cellulose in carbon disulfide and squirting the viscous solution ("viscose" he called it) out of fine holes. As the solvent evaporated, fine fibrous threads of "viscose rayon" were formed.

By 1908 methods were found to squeeze the viscose through a narrow slit to form thin, transparent sheets of "cellophane."

[863] **ACHESON,** Edward Goodrich
American inventor
Born: Washington, Pennsylvania, March 9, 1856
Died: New York, New York, July 6, 1931

Acheson was another of the self-made men in which nineteenth-century America was so rich. When he was in his teens the panic of 1872 made it necessary for him to work and this he did, at anything he could turn his hand to, first at an iron furnace, then in a civil engineering corps. In his spare time he occupied himself in electrical experimentation.

In 1880 he accepted a position in Edison's [788] establishment at Menlo Park, which, for an electrical experimenter, represented the heights. He was Edison's representative in Europe for a while, working with the Edison exhibit at the Paris International Exhibition in 1881 and installing the first electric lights in Italy, Belgium, and the Netherlands. He might have gone to higher posts in the Edison organization, but he preferred to continue his own research.

Acheson grew interested in carbon and, as Moissan [831] was doing in France, tried to devise methods for converting it into its most precious form, diamond. He tried heating carbon intensely, and though he obtained no diamonds, he found something almost as valuable. In 1891 he found that carbon heated with clay yielded an extremely hard substance. He thought the substance was a compound of carbon and alundum (alundum being the common name for a form of aluminum oxide), and so he called it carborundum. Eventually carborundum was found to be silicon carbide, a compound of silicon and carbon. It remained for half a century the hardest known substance, with the exception of diamond itself, and proved extremely useful as an abrasive.

In 1895 Acheson established a factory near Niagara Falls, where he could take advantage of the power generated by Westinghouse's [785] hydroelectric installations, and proceeded to manufacture carborundum commercially.

In 1899, while studying the effects of high temperature on carborundum, he prepared carbon in the form of an unprecedentedly pure graphite. This lacked the beauty of diamond, but for all its dull ugliness it was endlessly valuable for the formation of electrodes and of special lubricants (which Acheson developed in 1906) capable of withstanding high temperatures.

[864] TAYLOR, Frederick Winslow
American engineer
Born: Philadelphia, Pennsylvania, March 20, 1856
Died: Philadelphia, March 21, 1915

Taylor, the son of a lawyer, studied at Phillips Exeter Academy and intended to enter Harvard. Eye trouble, however, aborted his educational plans. He entered the employ of a steel company, instead, and worked his way up, step by step, till he was chief engineer in 1889. While working by day, he studied by night and obtained a degree in engineering from the Stevens Institute of Technology in 1883.

He began to make useful inventions, too, of the ordinary sort, but his most important innovation was to apply the rules of engineering to the human beings working in a plant and not to the machines only. He attempted to rationalize the manner in which people fit into the scheme of production, counting steps, timing motions, working out ways in which waste of time and effort could be eliminated.

He called this "scientific management" and spent the last years of his life as an independent consultant on this subject, organizing matters so as to have people work less to produce more. He was the first "efficiency expert."

[865] FREUD, Sigmund (froit [German]; froid [English])
Austrian psychiatrist
Born: Freiberg (now Pribor, Czechoslovakia), May 6, 1856
Died: London, England, September 23, 1939

Freud was born of Jewish parents and both his grandfather and great-grandfather had been rabbis. When he was four years old, the family business failed and his family moved to Vienna. In that city, which Freud always claimed he hated, he remained to nearly the end of his life.

Freud turned toward medicine, partly to escape from his penchant for general philosophy into something concrete, and in 1873 entered the University of Vienna. He emerged in 1881 with a medical degree. His family remained poor, but Sigmund was his mother's favorite and his family underwent heroic sacrifices on his behalf (sacrifices that Sigmund accepted calmly as his due). He also obtained the help of a Jewish philanthropic society.

In school he grew interested in neurology, working on the nerve tracts and disentangling the relationships of the nerve cells as Golgi [764] and Ramón y Cajal [827] were doing, and certainly with no less skill. He also did pioneer work on the use of cocaine as a local anesthetic, but this he did not carry through and it was left for Koller [882] and Halsted [830] to introduce cocaine to medical practice. He used it for minor pains and praised it highly, which is supposed to have contributed to a wave of cocaine addiction in Europe. (Sherlock Holmes, in the earlier stories, was described as a cocaine addict about this time.)

In 1885 Freud traveled to Paris, where he worked with Jean Martin Charcot [662], a French neurologist, who was interested in hysteria and who, as much as anyone, founded the study of psychiatry as a separate medical specialty dealing with mental disorders. His interest roused, Freud began to turn from the physiological basis of neurology, the cells and nerves, to the psychological aspects, the manner in which mental disorders arise. In 1886 he entered private practice as a neurologist.

A colleague was treating a patient suffering from hysteria by using the technique of hypnotism, which had been introduced into medical practice by Mesmer [314] and made respectable by

Braid [494]. Under hypnosis the patient talked of painful memories that, in the normally conscious state, she did not remember. In 1887 Freud adopted this method of treatment by hypnotism and began to formulate views of the mind as containing both a conscious and an unconscious level. Painful memories, or wishes and desires of which a person was ashamed, might, he believed, be repressed, that is, stored in the unconscious mind. There these memories and desires might still affect a person's attitudes and produce actions which, if solely the conscious mind were taken into account, would seem unmotivated.

In the 1890s Freud abandoned hypnotism as a technique for reaching the unconscious mind. Instead, he began to make use of free association, allowing the patient to talk randomly and at will, with a minimum of guidance. In this fashion the patient was gradually put off guard and matters were revealed that, in ordinary circumstances, would be kept secret even from the patient's own conscious mind. The advantage over hypnotism lay in the fact that the patient was at all times aware of what was going on and did not have to be informed afterward of what he had said.

Ideally, once the contents of the unconscious mind were revealed, the patient's reactions would no longer be unmotivated to himself. With the cause and motivation of his behavior known, he could more easily avoid that behavior. This slow analysis of the contents of the mind was called psychoanalysis and it seemed a translation into psychological terms of the statement in the Gospel of St. John (8:32), "And you shall know the truth and the truth shall make you free."

To Freud, dreams were highly significant, for it seemed to him that they gave away the contents of the unconscious mind (though often in highly symbolized form) in a manner not possible during wakefulness, when the conscious mind was more carefully on guard. In 1900 he published *The Interpretation of Dreams* and the very old practice of dream interpretation, at least

as old as the biblical Joseph, gained a new meaning.

However, the most sensational and controversial aspect of his work was in connection with sex. The Judeo-Christian tradition had thrown an uneasy blanket of "sin" over the question, and while this never stopped the exercise of sex in all its forms, it did inhibit scientific discussion of the subject. The taboo had been broken two decades earlier by Krafft-Ebing [749], but it was Freud who smashed it entirely. In 1905 he published his theories on infantile sexuality and how it could persist into adulthood, bringing about abnormal sexual responses that could invade and influence all other aspects of life. For the first time Freud was really noticed, but the notice consisted in large part of a storm of abuse and derision. Nevertheless his theories slowly became influential.

Beginning in 1902, a group of young men had begun to gather about Freud. They did not always see eye to eye with him and Freud was rather unbending in his views and not given to compromise. Men such as Adler [984] and Jung [1035] later broke away to establish schools of their own.

Freud spent the final quarter century of his life collecting data to support his theories. He lived to see psychoanalysis become an important (if slow and expensive) adjunct of psychiatry. His long life, however, brought him, in his final decade, face to face with Nazi anti-Semitism. In Austria he was reasonably safe for at least five years after Hitler's coming to power in neighboring Germany, protected by his age and his worldwide reputation.

In 1938, however, Nazi Germany invaded and occupied Austria, and nothing would have protected Freud any longer had he remained. With great difficulty, his removal was arranged despite the pathological antagonism of the Nazi mind. One month after the occupation of Austria, the eighty-two-year-old Freud was taken to sanctuary in London, where he spent the final year of his life.

He died, finally, of the cancer of the jaw that had first afflicted him in 1923

559

and for which he underwent repeated operations.

[866] **PEARY,** Robert Edwin (peer'y)
American explorer
Born: Cresson, Pennsylvania,
May 6, 1856
Died: Washington, D.C., February 20, 1920

Peary graduated from Bowdoin College in Maine in 1877 and began his professional life in 1881 as a civil engineer in the U. S. Navy. An early tour of duty carried him to the tropics in connection with the projected Nicaragua Canal (which has never been built). However, his imagination was seized by what he read of Greenland and that island became his life.

The explorations from the fifteenth to the nineteenth centuries had exposed all the world of the temperate and torrid zones and by the 1880s only the polar areas (plus some remote jungle, desert, and mountain fastnesses) were left to be penetrated by man. In 1886 Peary made his first trip to Greenland and penetrated deeper inland than anyone ever had before. It was not until 1891, however, that he organized an expedition for the serious exploration of hitherto-untouched northern Greenland. He explored the northern coast and proved Greenland to be an island. The northernmost section of Greenland (interestingly enough, largely free of the ice cap that covers most of the rest of the island) is called Peary Land in his honor.

In the course of his explorations he discovered what is still the largest known meteorite. It weighed ninety tons and is now at the American Museum of Natural History in New York.

Over the next dozen years, Peary made repeated trips to Greenland, learning to live like the Eskimos, and each time managing to penetrate closer to his ultimate goal, the North Pole. In 1909 he organized an elaborate travel party of which successive members were to turn back at periodic intervals until, at the end, Peary and his black associate, Matthew Hensen, made the final dash. They reached the pole on April 6, 1909.

When Peary returned, he found that an erstwhile associate, Frederick Albert Cook, claimed to have reached the pole in 1908. There was considerable controversy over this (which has not entirely died down even today) but most geographers have accepted Peary as the discoverer (or, more correctly, the attainer) of the North Pole.

In 1911 he was made a rear admiral of the U. S. Navy as a reward for his achievement.

[867] **TESLA,** Nikola
Croatian-American electrical engineer
Born: Smiljan, Croatia (then part of Austria-Hungary, now part of Yugoslavia), July 10, 1856
Died: New York, New York, January 7, 1943

Tesla, the son of a clergyman, was himself first intended for the clergy. He was of Serbian ancestry though born in Croatia.

He developed a taste for mathematics and science, perhaps through the influence of his illiterate mother who was extraordinarily bright and an inventor of implements about the farm and home.

Tesla began his own inventing career in Austria, where he studied engineering at the University of Graz. In 1882 he went to Paris to work for the Continental Edison Company. Then in 1884 he emigrated to the United States, becoming an American citizen in 1891. For a time he was associated with Edison [788] himself.

Edison, somewhat dictatorially, went back on a promise to pay him a sum of money for a particular invention and Tesla broke off relations at once and went into the inventing business for himself. (It should be mentioned that Tesla was a queer chap whom it was almost impossible not to offend and who was seriously neurotic. In later life he bred pigeons, on whom he lavished all the affection he was unable to give human beings.)

As an inventor, Tesla, while not quite in Edison's class (no one ever was), nevertheless did well. In particular, he made alternating current practical. The great difficulty in the electrical industry of the late nineteenth century was that of transporting electricity over wires without too much loss. It was found that electricity at high voltage could be transported efficiently and Tesla worked out transformers that could lift electricity to high voltage for transporting purposes and then drop it to low voltage for use at its destination. However, transformers would only work for alternating current, so Tesla also worked out motors that would run on alternating current.

Edison, meanwhile, had committed himself thoroughly to the use of direct current (d.c.), and a long career of being always right made it impossible for him to endure being wrong. He fought the use of alternating current (a.c.) quite unscrupulously. First he lobbied New York state into adopting a.c. for its newly devised electric chair (and a.c. is indeed more efficient in electrocution than d.c.) and then he pointed with great horror to the electric chair as an example of the deadly nature of a.c.

Tesla, with enduring bitterness, fought back just as hard, enlisting the help of the businessman and inventor George Westinghouse [785], and in the end the transport efficiency of a.c. won out over d.c. and the Edison prestige. In 1912 there was the intention of awarding the Nobel Prize in physics jointly to Tesla and Edison, but Tesla refused to be associated with Edison and the prize went to Lippmann [778], a Swedish inventor of lesser merit than either. Tesla fought a long battle just as bitterly with Marconi [1025] over priority in the invention of radio.

The last quarter century of his life degenerated into wild eccentricity. Even so, his achievements were great and the unit of magnetic flux density has been named the tesla in his honor.

[868] **WILSON,** Edmund Beecher
American zoologist
Born: Geneva, Illinois, October 19, 1856
Died: New York, New York, March 3, 1939

Wilson, the son of a lawyer, entered Antioch College in 1873 and went on to Yale University in 1875, graduating in 1878. He then went to Johns Hopkins, where he obtained his Ph.D. in 1881. By then he had grown fiercely interested in the problems of heredity and went to Europe for still further studies. He studied under Bateson [913] and Huxley [659] in England and under Leuckart [640] and Ludwig [597] in Germany.

Back in the United States, he had his first teaching position at Williams College in 1883, headed the biology department at Bryn Mawr in 1885, and finally gained a professorial position and chairmanship of the zoology department at Columbia in 1891. He was at all times an inspiring teacher.

In his research, he devoted years to the careful study of the exact manner in which the fertilized egg of various types of animals divided in the early stages of embryo formation. His most important work, however, was in connection with the chromosomes that Flemming [762] had first noted.

Once Mendel's [638] theories had been revived by De Vries [792] and others, it had been one of Wilson's students, Sutton [1047], who had first made the connection between Mendelian factors of heredity and chromosomes, but it was Wilson himself who first went into detail. He was the first to note the X and Y chromosomes, seeing that females had an XX perfect pair while the males had an XY. He thus connected chromosomes and sex determination and was quite convinced that chromosomes affected and determined other inherited characteristics as well—which turned out to be so.

[869] **THOMSON,** Sir Joseph John
English physicist
Born: Cheetham Hall, near Manchester, December 18, 1856
Died: Cambridge, August 30, 1940

Thomson, the son of a bookseller, entered a college in Manchester at fourteen, intending to take up engineering, but his father's early death made it impossible to pay the extra fees required, so he grew interested in physics instead. In 1876 he entered Cambridge on a scholarship and there he was to remain for the rest of his life. He finished second in his class in mathematics and in 1884, when he was only twenty-seven, he succeeded Rayleigh [760], on the latter's retirement, as professor of physics. He became director of the Cavendish Laboratory in 1884, succeeding Rayleigh there too, and remained its head for a generation—till 1919. It was largely due to his direction and inspired teaching that England maintained clear leadership in the field of subatomic physics for the first three decades of the twentieth century.

Thomson was initially interested in Maxwell's [692] theories of electromagnetic radiation, and this led him on to the cathode rays as a novel form of radiation that was not electromagnetic in character. Crookes [695] and others had presented evidence that the cathode rays consisted of negatively charged particles, pointing to the deflection of the rays by a magnetic field. The demonstration, however, remained inconclusive because no one could show the rays to be also affected by an electric field, as they would have to be if they were charged particles. Thomson worked with very highly evacuated tubes and was finally able, in 1897, to show cathode-ray deflection in an electric field, the final link in the chain of evidence. The cathode rays were accepted thereafter as particulate in nature.

Furthermore, Thomson measured the ratio of the charge of the cathode-ray particles to their mass. It turned out that if the charge were equal to the minimum charge on ions as worked out by the laws of electrochemistry first expounded by Faraday [474], then the mass of the cathode-ray particles was only a small fraction (now known to be 1/1837) of that of hydrogen atoms. The cathode-ray particles were thus far smaller than atoms and Thomson had opened up the field of subatomic particles.

The cathode-ray particles were accepted as units of electrical current. The name earlier proposed by Stoney [664] for a hypothetical unit of electrical current was electron, and Lorentz [839] applied it to the particles over Thomson's objections. Since Thomson was the one who supplied the final proof for the existence of such particles in cathode rays and since he was the first to offer evidence of their subatomic size, he is usually considered the discoverer of the electron.

Thomson viewed the electron as a universal component of matter and was one of the first to suggest a theory as to the internal structure of the atom. He believed that the atom was a sphere of positive electricity in which negatively charged electrons were embedded (like raisins in pound cake) in just sufficient quantity to neutralize the positive charge. This theory, although a good beginning, was quickly replaced by the far more useful one advanced by Thomson's student Rutherford [996].

In 1906 Thomson was awarded the Nobel Prize in physics for his work on the electron and in 1908 he was knighted. (Subsequently, no fewer than seven of his research assistants were to win Nobel Prizes.)

After 1906 Thomson interested himself in the "channel rays," which Goldstein [811] had discovered. These were streams of positively charged ions, so Thomson named them positive rays. Thomson deflected them by magnetic and electric fields in such a way as to cause ions of different ratios of charge to mass to strike different portions of a photographic plate. In so doing he found in 1912 that ions of neon gas fell on two different spots, as though the ions were a mixture of two types, differing in charge, mass, or both. Soddy [1052] had already suggested the existence of isotopes, that is, of atom varieties of a single element, differing in their mass. Here Thomson had the first indication that ordinary elements might also exist as isotopes. Thomson's pupil Aston [1051] was to carry this research further and he established the fact.

Thomson died on the eve of the Battle of Britain, when England's fortunes seemed lower than at any time in history. He was buried in Westminster

Abbey, near the remains of Newton [231].

[870] **KITASATO,** Baron Shibasaburo
(kee-tah-sah-toh)
Japanese bacteriologist
Born: Oguni, Kumamoto,
December 20, 1856
Died: Nakanojo, Gumma,
June 13, 1931

After graduation from the medical school of the University of Tokyo in 1883, Kitasato, the son of a village mayor, left for Germany to study under Koch [767], with whom he worked from 1885 to 1891. He was a most successful student, for he isolated the bacillus causing tetanus and another causing anthrax in 1889. He collaborated with Behring [846] in his work.

He returned to Tokyo in 1892 and there had ample opportunity to continue the study of disease. An outbreak of bubonic plague in Hong Kong in 1894 gave him the opportunity to isolate the agent causing that disease, and in 1898 the agent causing dysentery. He was made a baron in 1924.

[871] **MOHOROVIČIĆ,** Andrija (moh-hoh-roh-vee'cheech)
Croatian geologist
Born: Volosko, Istria, January 23, 1857
Died: Zagreb, December 18, 1936

Mohorovičić, the son of a shipwright, entered the University of Prague, where he attended lectures by Mach [733]. He received a post at the Royal Nautical School at Bakar, where he taught meteorology.

He grew increasingly interested in seismology. Studying the wave patterns set up by a Balkan earthquake in 1909, Mohorovičić deduced the fact that the earth possessed a layered structure. Waves that penetrated deeper into the earth arrived sooner than waves traveling along the surface, even allowing for the difference in distance traversed. Mo-

horovičić maintained that the earth's outermost crust rested on a layer that is more rigid and in which earthquake waves traveled more quickly. Furthermore, the separation between the two layers does not seem to be gradual, but is sharp. The separation is now called the Mohorovičić discontinuity and it is known to lie from ten to forty miles below sea level. (Americans dodge the Slavic name by speaking of it as the Moho discontinuity.)

The discontinuity is nearest the surface under the deep ocean basins, where, moreover, a great deal of the distance separating it from the sea level is just water. Attempts were considered in the 1960s to penetrate the three or so miles of solid crust under chosen spots in the ocean floor in order to reach this discontinuity and study the nature of the layer below. The name of the penetration planned still bears a piece of the geologist's name, for it is the Mohole.

[872] **JOHANNSEN,** Wilhelm Ludwig
(yoh-han'sun)
Danish botanist
Born: Copenhagen, February 3, 1857
Died: Copenhagen, November 11, 1927

Johannsen, the son of a Danish army officer, could not afford a university education and, in 1872, was apprenticed to a pharmacist but continued his program of self-education in chemistry and biology. In 1881 he worked as an assistant in the chemistry department at Carlsberg under Kjeldahl [801]. He reached professorial rank in 1903 and in 1917 was rector of the university, though still without a formal education.

He is another one of those scientists whose fame in the history of science rest chiefly on the invention of a word.

After Mendel's [638] work had been rediscovered by De Vries [792] in 1900, the former's factors of inheritance became matters of intense importance to biologists. In 1909 Johannsen suggested they be called "genes" from a Greek word meaning "to give birth to." The suggestion was adopted and from it other words such as "genotype" and "genetics" arose.

[873] **HERTZ,** Heinrich Rudolf
German physicist
Born: Hamburg, February 22, 1857
Died: Bonn, January 1, 1894

After starting his studies in engineering, Hertz, a Lutheran who was the son of a Jewish lawyer, abandoned that for physics, studying at the University of Berlin under Helmholtz [631] and Kirchhoff [648]. He obtained his Ph.D. *magna cum laude* in 1880 and stayed on for two years more as Helmholtz's assistant. He maintained a strong friendship with Helmholtz which remained lifelong, for the sadly short-lived Hertz was survived by the older Helmholtz by nearly a year.

Working at the University of Kiel in 1883, Hertz grew interested in the equations governing the electromagnetic field that had been worked out by the then recently deceased Maxwell [692]. The Berlin Academy of Science was offering a prize for certain work in the field of electromagnetics and Helmholtz suggested to his young protégé that he take a stab at it.

Hertz, who by then had a professorial position at a school in Karlsruhe, got to work without too much enthusiasm, but in the course of that work he succeeded, in 1888, in finding something that went far beyond anything for which he had been searching. He had set up an electrical circuit that oscillated, surging into first one, then another, of two metal balls separated by an air gap. Each time the potential reached a peak in one direction or the other, it sent a spark across the gap. (In the course of these experiments, he noted that when ultraviolet light shone on the negative terminal of the gap, the spark was more easily elicited. He did not follow that up, but this was the first observation of the photoelectric effect, which, a generation later, Einstein [1064] was to explain, earning a Nobel Prize thereby.)

With such an oscillating spark, Maxwell's equations predicted, electromag-

netic radiation should be generated. Each single oscillation should produce one wave, so that the radiation would be expected to be of extremely long wavelength. After all, since light travels at 186,282 miles a second, a wavelength formed in an oscillation of a mere thousandth of a second would still be over 186 miles long.

Hertz used, as a device for detecting the possible presence of such long-wave radiation, a simple loop of wire with a small air gap at one point. Just as current gave rise to radiation in the first coil, so the radiation ought to give rise to a current in the second coil. Sure enough, Hertz was able to detect small sparks jumping across the gap in his detector coil. By moving his detector coil to various points in the room, Hertz could tell the shape of the waves by the intensity of spark formation and could calculate the wavelength as 66 centimeters (2.2 feet). This is a million times the size of a wavelength of visible light. He also managed to show that the waves involved both an electric and a magnetic field and were therefore electromagnetic in nature. He thought at first they might travel at only two-thirds the speed of light but this proved an error and was soon corrected.

In this way Hertz verified the usefulness of Maxwell's equations. Hertz's experiments were quickly confirmed in England by Lodge [820], while Righi [810] in Italy demonstrated the relationship of these "Hertzian waves" to light. When Marconi [1025] devised a practical means for using these waves as a form of wireless communication, they came to be called radio waves. (Actually, "radio" is short for "radiotelegraphy"; that is, telegraphy by radiation as opposed to telegraphy by electric currents.)

In 1889 Hertz succeeded Clausius [633] as professor of physics at the University of Bonn. There he worked on cathode rays, which he believed were waves and not particles because they penetrated thin metal films; it did not seem to him particles would be able to do so. He might have lived to see radio become an important factor in human society. However, he did not even witness its beginnings. Nor did he witness the discovery of the electron by J. J. Thomson [869], who showed it to be a particle far smaller than the atom, and therefore one that, not surprisingly after all, could easily penetrate ordinary matter. Hertz died, after a long illness due to chronic blood poisoning, before his thirty-seventh birthday.

[874] WAGNER VON JAUREGG, Julius (vahg'ner-fun-yoo'rek)

Austrian psychiatrist
Born: Wels, Upper Austria, March 7, 1857
Died: Vienna, September 27, 1940

Wagner von Jauregg, the son of a civil servant, obtained a medical education at the University of Vienna, met Freud [865] while still a student, and established a lifelong friendship with him. Wagner von Jauregg found his way into psychiatry somewhat by accident but by 1887 was a qualified teacher in the field, and in 1889 succeeded Krafft-Ebing [749] as a professor of psychiatry at the University of Graz.

Wagner von Jauregg achieved his best-remembered claim to fame when he noticed that patients with advanced syphilis sometimes improved after they had suffered from diseases that were accompanied by high fever. The high temperature apparently damaged the germ causing syphilis. It occurred to Wagner von Jauregg, therefore, that patients far gone in syphilis might deliberately be infected with malaria. The malarial fever could greatly ameliorate the syphilis, while the malaria itself could be controlled by quinine.

He tried this for the first time in 1917 and by and large it worked. The method was widely adopted and in 1927 earned him the Nobel Prize for physiology and medicine.

The malaria treatment of syphilis did not long endure; it has been replaced by antibiotics. However, it was the forerunner of shock treatment for a variety of mental ailments.

[875] PEARSON, Karl

English mathematician
Born: London, March 27, 1857
Died: Coldharbour, Surrey, April 27, 1936

Pearson, the son of a lawyer, studied at Cambridge under Stokes [618], Maxwell [692], and Cayley [629], and in 1879 graduated third in his class in mathematics. He eventually went on to qualify in law, but never practiced. He obtained a professorship in applied mathematics at University College, London, in 1884.

During postgraduate studies in Germany he had attended lectures by Du Bois-Reymond [611] on Darwin's evolutionary thinking, and had grown interested. The writings of Galton [636] on heredity interested him further. He began to apply mathematics to the random processes of heredity and evolution and in so doing served as the founder of modern statistics. Among other things he evolved the chi-square test of statistical significance. His work in this direction was carried on by Fisher [1142].

[876] ROSS, Sir Ronald

English physician
Born: Almora, India (near Nepal), May 13, 1857
Died: London, September 16, 1932

Ross was born of an Anglo-Indian family and first saw England at the age of eight. He received his education in England and obtained his medical degree in 1879. In 1881, however, he entered the Indian Medical Service and returned to India, where he served in a British military campaign in Burma in 1885.

There (in addition to writing novels, plays, and poems) he grew interested in malaria and in the suggestion that mosquitoes might play a role in transmitting it. Despite the hampering effect of his military service he devoted himself to collecting, feeding, and dissecting mosquitoes.

Finally, in 1897, he located Laveran's [776] malarial parasite in the Anopheles mosquito. Ross's discovery meant that it was rational to launch a systematic attack on the breeding places of mosquitoes as a way of wiping out malaria. There was reason for efforts as small as using netting at night and as great as draining swamps.

Ross returned to England and was eventually a professor of tropical medicine, first at Liverpool, then at King's College in London. He was rewarded with the 1902 Nobel Prize in medicine and physiology. He was knighted in 1911.

The attack on insects has continued ever since and a half century after Ross's time, new weapons were discovered by Paul Müller [1216] and others in the form of powerful insecticides.

[877] **ABEL,** John Jacob
American biochemist
Born: Cleveland, Ohio, May 19, 1857
Died: Baltimore, Maryland, May 26, 1938

Abel, the son of a prosperous farmer, got his undergraduate training at the University of Michigan, graduating in 1883. He then went to Germany for his graduate training, remaining there for six years, and studied under men such as Ludwig [597]. He got his Ph.D. in 1888 and his M.D. in 1890. On his return to the United States, he had a professorial appointment first at the University of Michigan, then at Johns Hopkins University.

In 1897 he was the first to isolate an active molecule from the adrenal medulla. He called it epinephrine, though it later came to be better known as by the trade name Adrenalin or as adrenaline. Abel's compound was not, however, the hormone itself, but a somewhat more complicated analogue. It was Takamine [855] who obtained the bare hormone soon afterward.

He was also interested in another hormone, insulin, which had come into particular prominence with the work of Banting [1152]. In 1925 Abel prepared insulin in crystalline form for the first

time. This was an important step in preparing pure and reproducible solutions of this important substance.

Then, too, in 1912, he was the first to work on an artificial kidney and even managed to produce one that could be useful in laboratory work.

[878] **BINET,** Alfred (bee-nay')
French psychologist
Born: Nice Alpes-Maritimes, July 8, 1857
Died: Paris, October 18, 1911

At the time of Binet's birth, Nice was part of the Italian-speaking kingdom of Sardinia, so that Binet was not, strictly speaking, French. However, Nice was ceded to France before Binet's third birthday. In 1871 he went to Paris for his education and studied medicine and law. In the 1880s he grew interested in psychology and in the uses of hypnotism, much as Freud [865] was to be doing in Vienna shortly afterward. In 1891 he became associated with the Sorbonne in Paris, and in 1894 he became director of its psychology laboratory.

Binet, however, was concerned more with the normal workings of the mind than with the abnormal; and, in particular, in measuring human intelligence objectively. Tests of various sorts had always been used to determine the progress a student was making in his studies, but Binet wanted more than that. He wanted to test those facets of human ability that did not depend on specific instructions in one field or another or upon the memorization of facts. He wanted to measure the innate ability of a mind to think and reason.

For this he designed various tests which asked children to name objects, to follow commands, to rearrange disordered things, to copy designs, and so on. In 1905 he and his associates published the first batteries of tests designed to measure intelligence, and in 1908 others were published. The value was tested empirically. If a particular test was passed by some 70 percent or so of the nine-year-olds in the Paris school system, then it represented the nine-year-old level of intelligence.

The tests proved popular and were quickly accepted in France and other countries. Other tests were developed, following the principles pioneered by Binet, and the phrase "intelligence quotient" (usually abbreviated IQ) became popular. It represents the ratio of the mental age to the chronological age. Thus, if a six-year-old can pass a ten-year-old test, his IQ is 10/6 multiplied by a hundred, or 167. Naturally, an IQ of 100 is considered average.

This sort of testing has given rise to the whole battery of personality tests, achievements tests, aptitude tests, and others that now permeate our civilization; and the value of which may perhaps be overestimated.

[879] **KEELER,** James Edward
American astronomer
Born: La Salle, Illinois, September 10, 1857
Died: San Francisco, California, August 12, 1900

Keeler graduated from Johns Hopkins University in 1881. He spent a year in Germany, 1883–1884, studying under Helmholtz [631] among others. After returning to the United States, Keeler accompanied Langley [711] on his expedition to the Rockies to measure the radiation of the sun. After a year of graduate study in Germany, he, like Barnard [883], went to work at Lick Observatory, where he was to rise to the rank of director in 1898.

In 1888 he used Lick's 36-inch telescope to try to confirm Schiaparelli's [714] observation of the Martian canals but failed. In 1895 he took the spectrum of Saturn and its rings and, from the inclination of the spectral lines, measured the rate of rotation of the system. He showed that the rings were not rotating as a unit but that the inner boundary had a considerably shorter period than the outer. This was the first observational evidence that the rings were not solid but consisted of discrete particles, something Maxwell [692] had predicted

from theoretical considerations a half century before.

Keeler measured the radial motion of gaseous nebulae such as that in Orion and showed that their motions were similar to those of stars; thus they were part of the stellar system. He also photographed numerous spiral galaxies and showed that the spiral form was the rule rather than the exception.

[880] **TSIOLKOVSKY,** Konstantin
Eduardovich (tsyul-kuv'skee)
Russian physicist
Born: Izhevsk, Ryazan', September 17, 1857
Died: Kaluga, September 19, 1935

Handicapped by almost total deafness from a streptococcus infection at the age of nine, and by the scientific backwardness of tsarist Russia, Tsiolkovsky, the son of a forester, nevertheless educated himself to the point where he could serve as a teacher and write scholarly papers in chemistry and physics.

In 1881 he worked out the kinetic theory of gases, unaware that Maxwell [692] had already done so more than a decade earlier. By 1895 he was beginning to mention space flight in his papers and in 1898 was referring to the necessity for liquid-fuel rocket engines.

In 1903 he began a series of articles for an aviation magazine in which he went into the theory of rocketry quite thoroughly, and on this his reputation as a pioneer of space flight rests. During the 1920s he suggested some of the devices Goddard [1083] was soon to develop.

He had enormous difficulties. His son committed suicide in 1902, his daughter was arrested for revolutionary activity in 1911, a flood destroyed many of his papers, and he himself went unappreciated. He had his dream, however, and after the 1917 revolution, the authorities began to listen.

Tsiolkovsky wrote of space suits, satellites, and the colonization of the solar system and was the first to suggest the possibility of a space station. In later life he also wrote a science fiction novel, *Outside the Earth,* in which he presented his theories for those who would rather read adventure than equations. By the 1930s he was a well-known figure in the Soviet Union, which was already interested in some sort of space program.

The tombstone on Tsiolkovsky's grave carries the message "Mankind will not remain tied to earth forever," and so it proved. Twenty-two years after his death the Soviet government planned to launch the first man-made satellite on the hundredth anniversary of Tsiolkovsky's birth. The launching was twenty-nine days late, but even so Sputnik I made a wonderful memorial for the man.

[881] **SHERRINGTON,** Sir Charles Scott
English neurologist
Born: London, November 27, 1857
Died: Eastbourne, Sussex, March 4, 1952

Sherrington, the stepson of a physician, was encouraged by his stepfather to undertake a medical career. He obtained his medical degree from Cambridge in 1885 and traveled to Berlin to study under Virchow [632] and Koch [767]. In 1891 he was appointed professor of physiology at the University of London, then Liverpool in 1895, then Oxford in 1913.

He was primarily interested in the workings of the nervous system, and modern knowledge of neurophysiology dates back largely to him—as knowledge of neuroanatomy dates back to Golgi [764] and Ramón y Cajal [827]. Sherrington's first paper in the field was published while he was still at medical school.

In 1894 Sherrington presented evidence that nerves going to muscles were not concerned only with stimulating contraction of the muscle. Some one third to one half of the nerve fibers were sensory, carrying sensations to the brain. In other words, the brain was able to judge the tensions upon the muscles and joints and therefore possessed a sense of position

and equilibrium. This helped explain certain nervous disorders marked by loss of the ability to coordinate muscular movements. He studied the effect of cutting the spinal cord or removing the cerebrum on the muscular control of animals.

By 1906 he had developed a theory of reflex behavior of antagonistic muscles that helped explain the way the body, under the coordinating guidance of the nervous system, behaved as a unit. Through the later years he continued to study reflex action and how it coordinates behavior; how, for instance, a man stands in balance without conscious realization of the manner in which his muscles play against one another to maintain that balance. Sherrington's work, as well as that of Pavlov [802], helped foster the mechanistic philosophies of men such as Loeb [896].

Sherrington also mapped out with greater accuracy than had been done before the motor areas of the cerebral cortex, showing which region governed the motion of which part of the body. During World War I, he spent three months as an unskilled laborer (incognito, so as not to be sent back to his laboratory) in a munitions factory. He was elected president of the Royal Society in 1920, was knighted in 1922, and for his work on the nervous system received a share of the 1932 Nobel Prize in medicine and physiology. He was one of the patriarchs of science, living into his ninety-fifth year.

[882] **KOLLER,** Carl
Austrian-American physician
Born: Schüttenhofen, Bohemia (now Susice, Czechoslovakia), December 3, 1857
Died: New York, New York, March 21, 1944

Koller was an intern at the University of Vienna (from which he had graduated in 1882) when Freud was working with cocaine. Freud [865] suggested its possible use as a pain-relieving agent (rather like the modern aspirin). Koller, however, went a step further and thought of it as an anesthetic during operations. He experimented on animals first and then in 1884 attempted an eye operation while using it.

The operation was successful and marked the beginning of the use of local anesthesia. This was the most important step forward in the field since Morton's [617] work a generation earlier. It made it unnecessary to put the patient altogether under and eliminated the complicated ritual of protecting lung and heart action. Why not only put out of action those few nerve endings in the immediate vicinity of the operation? Local anesthesia is now routine and, indeed, indispensable in dentistry.

Koller emigrated to the United States in 1888, establishing his practice in New York City, and became an American citizen in 1902.

[883] **BARNARD,** Edward Emerson
American astronomer
Born: Nashville, Tennessee,
December 16, 1857
Died: Williams Bay, Wisconsin,
February 6, 1923

Barnard was of a poverty-stricken family. His father died before the child was born and young Edward had only two months of formal schooling. At the age of nine, he was put to work in a portrait studio to help support his family, and he worked there for seventeen years.

He grew interested first in photography, then in astronomy, in which he was encouraged by Newcomb's [713] kindly interest. Barnard began his astronomic findings, as an amateur, by discovering a comet, then made his way into college and finally graduated from Vanderbilt University at the age of thirty but without a degree. By that time, however, he was skilled enough in astronomy to have been placed in charge of the college observatory. He never had the mathematics for theory but he was a peerless observer.

After graduation he joined the Lick Observatory at Mount Hamilton, California. In 1892 he studied a nova that appeared in the constellation Auriga and was the first to note the puff of gaseous matter it had given off (a clear sign that a nova involved some sort of explosion).

In that same year he showed (as did Keeler [879] likewise) that the solar system itself contained material for discovery. Galileo [166] had initiated the telescopic age by discovering four large satellites of Jupiter, and in all the nearly three centuries that had elapsed since, no new satellites of the giant planet had been detected. In 1892 Barnard discovered a fifth. It was closer to Jupiter than the first four and far smaller. It is often called Barnard's satellite, the only satellite to be named in honor of its discoverer. It is also called Jupiter V, since it is the fifth to be discovered. It was named Amalthea by Flammarion [756] after the goat that served as wet nurse for Zeus (Jupiter, in the Latin version) during the god's infancy. It was the last satellite discovered without photography.

About then, he also detected craters on Mars but did not publish this finding since he felt it might be an illusion. It wasn't—but science had to wait three-quarters of a century before Mars probes showed that Barnard's peerless eyes had been right.

In 1895 Barnard became professor of astronomy at the University of Chicago and worked at Yerkes Observatory. There he used the 40-inch telescope that Hale [974] had brought into existence to make photographs of the Milky Way. He and Wolf [927] were the first to realize that the dark patches in the Milky Way were clouds of obscuring gas and dust.

In 1916 Barnard discovered a dim star that had a fast proper motion, the fastest, in fact, ever discovered. It moves the width of the moon in a hundred and eighty years. This may not seem fast to the nonastronomer, but to astronomers it is fast enough to give the star the dramatic name of Barnard's Runaway Star. One of the reasons for its fast proper motion is that it is one of the closest stars to our solar system. It is dim only because it is a red dwarf, cool and small.

In 1914 Barnard developed diabetes. He was childless and after his wife died at the end of 1922, he lost the will to live and died soon after.

[884] **DUBOIS,** Marie Eugène François Thomas (dyoo-bwah′)
Dutch paleontologist
Born: Eijsden, the Netherlands, January 28, 1858
Died: Halen, Belgium, December 16, 1940

Dubois studied medicine and natural history and grew interested in the problem of the "missing link." After Darwin's [554] theories had been published, it occurred to a number of men that evolutionary principles ought to be applicable to the development of the human species. Lyell [502], Huxley [659], and finally Darwin himself wrote on the subject.

For a generation after that, however, the evidence for human evolution continued to rest chiefly on primitive stone tools, the presence of vestigial remnants in the human body, and so on. Of direct fossil evidence there was none.

To be sure, Neanderthal men had been found, in skeleton form, in the 1850s. There was enough of the primitive about those skeletons for men such as Broca [653] to consider them examples of an earlier species of man. However, they were not so primitive that others, Virchow [632], for example, could not maintain they were ordinary men deformed by disease or accident.

What was needed were fossil creatures, so markedly more primitive than man, yet so markedly more advanced than apes as to form a connecting link between man and his apelike ancestors. This link was still missing.

Dubois was on fire with the hope of finding it. He believed that primitive manlike creatures might be found in areas where apes still abounded, that is, either in Africa, home of the gorilla and chimpanzee, or in southeast Asia, home of the orangutan and the gibbon. He was particularly interested in the latter possibility because he was influenced by Haeckel's [707] belief (now considered erroneous) that the gibbon was the ape most closely related to man.

He was serving in the army and in 1889 he had his great chance, for he was commissioned by the government to search deposits in Java (a Dutch possession at the time) for fossils.

He accepted eagerly and, considering everything, had quite unbelievable luck. Within a very few years he had discovered a skullcap, a femur, and two teeth of what was undoubtedly a primitive man. The skullcap was considerably larger than that of any living apes, and yet considerably smaller than that of any living man. The teeth, too, were intermediate between ape and man. Dubois called the creature of which the bones were remnants *Pithecanthropus erectus* ("erect ape-man") and published the details in 1894.

Tremendous controversy was aroused by this discovery, for the evolution of man was a touchy matter and to have it attested to by so dubious a find as a few scraps of bone was hard to take.

However, other and similar finds were made later in China and Africa. The slow accumulation of evidence made it quite certain that missing links had indeed been found. The case for man's evolution was no longer a matter of theory alone.

Dubois was rewarded with a professorship at the University of Amsterdam in 1899. Oddly enough, in his later years, when he was old and cranky with long controversy, he suddenly switched views. With the anthropological world convinced that *Pithecanthropus,* or "Java Man," was a real subman, Dubois suddenly began to maintain stubbornly that the skeletal remains were only those of an advanced fossil ape.

[885] **PICKERING,** William Henry
American astronomer
Born: Boston, Massachusetts, February 15, 1858
Died: Mandeville, Jamaica, January 16, 1938

Pickering graduated from the Massachusetts Institute of Technology in 1879 and after serving on its staff he joined the department of astronomy at Harvard in 1887. With his elder brother, Edward Charles Pickering [784], he established an astronomical observatory in Peru, in 1891.

In 1899 Pickering discovered Phoebe, the outermost of Saturn's satellites, and noted that it revolved about its planet in retrograde fashion (clockwise with respect to a viewer far above earth's north pole, rather than counterclockwise). It was the first satellite discovered by photography. In 1905 he reported a tenth satellite, which he named Themis, but this seems to have been an error.

Much of his work in later life consisted of his observations of the planet Mars, in competition, so to speak, with Percival Lowell [860]. Pickering's opposition to Lowell was not that of a conservative, for as a result of his own detailed studies of the moon, Pickering suspected the existence of forms of life there. That is certainly as startling and as unlikely a conclusion as that of canals on Mars, and both were finally proven untrue in the 1960s by the instruments of the space age.

Pickering also calculated the orbit of a possible trans-Neptunian planet, with results that were close to Lowell's.

[886] **DIESEL,** Rudolf (dee′zel)
German inventor
Born: Paris, France, March 18, 1858
Died: English Channel, September 30, 1913

Diesel was born in France of German parents. On the outbreak of the Franco-Prussian War, the family was rounded up by the French police and sent to London. From there they went to Germany. He was educated both in France and in Germany. He studied engineering in Munich where he passed his examinations with the highest mark on record. During the 1880s he worked as manager of Linde's [758] ice factory. He then returned to Paris, defying nationalist feelings, for he was an ardent pacifist and internationalist.

In the 1890s he experimented with internal combustion engines and by 1897 had perfected his invention of what is now known as the diesel engine. This works in a fashion similar to the Otto [694] engine but does not depend on an

electric spark for ignition of the fuel-air mixture.

Instead, it works on the heat developed by compressing the fuel-air mixture. The energy of the compressive force is converted into heat energy and the temperature of the mixture can be raised in this manner to the point where ignition will take place. His financial backing in this work came from a St. Louis brewer and the first diesel engine was built in the United States.

A diesel engine can use heavier fractions of petroleum than an Otto engine —kerosene rather than gasoline. This means that diesel fuel is cheaper and, being less inflammable, safer. However, the diesel engine is a large and heavy structure and unsuitable for the light passenger cars that Ford [929] was about to make a household word. Nor was it suitable for the airplanes about to be invented by the Wright brothers [961, 995]. The diesel engine, however, proved admirable for heavy transport vehicles so that oil begin to replace coal in locomotives and ships, particularly during the interval between World Wars I and II, and Diesel quickly became a millionaire. Oil, in its various fractions, became the world's prime fuel, largely replacing coal (except in the steel industry) as coal had displaced wood nearly two centuries earlier.

In 1913 the British Admiralty called Diesel in for consultations, but while crossing the Channel on the way to London he fell overboard and drowned. It may even have been suicide, for he was quite neurotic and given to chronic headaches and occasional breakdowns.

Furthermore, it didn't take much foresight to see that each year the danger of a European war was increasing, and that was something Diesel couldn't face.

[887] **PLANCK,** Max Karl Ernst Ludwig
German physicist
Born: Kiel, Schleswig, April 23, 1858
Died: Göttingen, October 3, 1947

Planck was the son of a professor of civil law. His family moved to Munich when Max was nine years old and he obtained his first education there. In his college days he transferred from Munich to Berlin and there, as was true of Hertz [873], studied under Helmholtz [631], Clausius [633], and Kirchhoff [648], receiving his doctorate *summa cum laude* in 1879 (suffering a two-year delay because of illness).

In 1880 he joined the faculty at Munich and five years later received a professorial appointment at Kiel University. In 1889 he replaced Kirchhoff, who had died, at the University of Berlin. He remained there until his retirement in 1926.

Planck's doctoral work was on thermodynamics because of his interest in the works of Clausius. He claimed that Helmholtz did not read his dissertation at all and that though Kirchhoff read it, he disapproved. Clausius himself was not interested. And, indeed, Planck's doctoral work was of minor importance and was perhaps worth no more than these great men indicated by their lack of interest. In time, however, Helmholtz grew to appreciate Planck and was instrumental in getting him his Berlin appointment.

In Berlin, Planck turned to the problem, first raised by his old teacher, Kirchhoff, of the black body, one that absorbs all frequencies of light and therefore, when heated, should radiate all frequencies of light.

But now comes a delicate point. The number of different frequencies in the high-frequency range is greater than the number in the low-frequency range; just as the number of integers higher than a million is greater than the number of integers lower than a million. If a black body radiated all frequencies of electromagnetic radiation equally, then virtually all the energy would be radiated in the high-frequency region; just as, if you were asked to pick *any number at all* you would be almost certain to pick a number over a million because there are so many more numbers to choose from in that region. This situation, with regard to radiation, is referred to as the "violet catastrophe" because the highest frequency radiation in the visible light spectrum is the violet.

In actuality, this does not happen; there is no violet catastrophe and the physical theory of the 1890s could not explain why. Both Wien [934] and Rayleigh [760] tried to work out equations describing how the radiation of the black body was distributed in actual fact. Wien's equation worked pretty well at high frequencies but not at low. Rayleigh's equation worked at low frequencies but not at high.

In 1900 Planck managed to work out a relatively simple equation that described the distribution of radiation accurately over the entire stretch of frequency. His equation was based on a crucial assumption: energy is not infinitely subdivisible. Like matter, it existed in "particles." These particles Planck called quanta (from Latin, meaning "how much?") or, in the singular, quantum.

He further supposed that the size of the quantum for any particular form of electromagnetic radiation was in direct proportion to its frequency. Thus, the violet light at one extreme of the visible spectrum has twice the frequency of the red light at the other extreme. A quantum of that violet light would therefore contain twice the energy of a quantum of red light.

Now then, suppose energy can only be absorbed or emitted in whole quanta. Therefore, when a black body radiates, it is not likely to radiate all wavelengths equally. To radiate low frequency is easy, for only a small quantity of energy must be brought together to form a quantum of low-frequency radiation. However, to radiate higher-frequency radiation requires more energy and it is less probable that the additional energy can be gathered together. The higher the frequency the less probable the radiation. Thus, a body at 600°C radiates mostly in the small-quantum infrared with just enough in the visible red to give it a glow. There is no violet catastrophe because although the high frequencies are many, their quantum-energy requirements make their radiation improbable.

As temperature goes up, the supply of energy is heightened and it becomes more and more probable that higher energy quanta can be radiated. For that reason, as an object heats up, the light radiated turns orange, yellow, and eventually bluish. In this way Wien's law, worked out by observation only, was given a theoretical basis.

The small constant that is the ratio of the frequency of the radiation and the size of the quantum is called Planck's constant and it is symbolized as h. It is now recognized as one of the fundamental constants of the universe.

This theory was so revolutionary that it was not accepted by physicists at once and, in fact, Planck himself did not quite believe it but half-suspected it might be only a piece of mathematical jugglery without any correspondence to anything real in nature. He struggled for years to find a way around his own discovery and would not accept statistical interpretations of thermodynamics introduced by Boltzmann [769].

In 1905 Einstein [1064] first applied the quantum theory to an observable phenomenon that could not be explained by nineteenth-century physics—to the photoelectric effect first noted by Hertz. Planck would not quite believe that either, although he readily accepted Einstein's theory of relativity.

Then, in 1913 Bohr [1101] incorporated the quantum theory into the structure of the atom and explained a great deal that nineteenth-century physics could not. In fact, all of physics before 1900 is now called classical physics and after 1900 it is modern physics. The watershed is the quantum theory. Modern physics could not exist without new forms of mathematical analysis involving quanta, this being referred to as quantum mechanics.

In 1918 the importance of the quantum theory had reached the point where Planck received the Nobel Prize in physics. Einstein and Bohr, for the use they made of it, received the prize a very few years later.

The joy of the Nobel Prize must have been tempered for Planck by the death of a son in action in World War I and the loss, at this same period, of his two daughters in childbirth.

In 1930 Max Planck became president of the Kaiser Wilhelm Society of Berlin, and it was renamed the Max Planck Society. His old age saw his renown in the world of science second only to that of Einstein. Nor was he too old to resist Hitler firmly in the days of Nazi ascendancy. He conceived it his duty to remain in Germany but at no time did he lend his voice and prestige to the Hitler regime in any way. He interceded personally (but unsuccessfully) with Hitler on behalf of his Jewish colleagues and was forced to resign his presidency of the Max Planck Society in 1937 in consequence.

World War II was disastrous for him. His house was destroyed by Allied bombings and his son Erwin was executed in 1944, accused of taking part in the plot against Hitler's life.

Planck lived into his ninetieth year, however, surviving World War II and living to see Nazism destroyed. He was rescued by American forces in 1945, while in flight during the last days of confusion before Germany's final defeat. He was renamed president of the Max Planck Society until a successor could be found. He was returned to Göttingen and there spent his last two years, honored and respected.

[888] **EIJKMAN,** Christiaan (ike'mahn)
Dutch physician
Born: Nijkerk, August 11, 1858
Died: Utrecht, November 5, 1930

Eijkman, the son of a schoolmaster, obtained his medical degree at the University of Amsterdam in 1883, then went to Germany to study under Koch [767]. At first he had been interested in physiology, but after a short stay in the army in the Dutch East Indies he grew interested in bacteriology and began to work in that field after having been invalided home. In 1886, when he was strong enough to return to the East Indies, it was as part of a medical team sent to study the disease beriberi. Koch had been asked to tackle this particular disease but the press of work forced him to refuse the project and he suggested his former pupil Eijkman for the task.

Pasteur's [642] germ theory of disease was, at the time, leading to victory after victory at the hands of such physicians as Koch and Behring [846]. In the 1880s it almost seemed natural to think that all diseases were caused by microorganisms. Consequently, the organism that was responsible for beriberi was sought but in vain. Most of the group returned home with nothing accomplished, but Eijkman remained behind in Batavia (the modern Djakarta) as director of a new bacteriological laboratory medical school for native doctors. In 1896 he solved the problem of beriberi, partly by accident.

A disease broke out among the chickens being used at the laboratory for bacteriological researches. It showed symptoms similar to beriberi. Eijkman pounced upon those chickens, trying to find the germ causing it, trying to transfer the disease from a sick chicken to a healthy one. He failed in both attempts. Then, as suddenly as it had appeared, the disease vanished, and nothing was left on which to experiment.

Eijkman investigated in other directions and found that for a certain period one of the cooks had been using rice from the hospital stores to feed the chickens. The cook was transferred and the succeeding functionary did not think it right to use rice meant for hospital patients on chickens. He went back to commercial chicken feed. The chickens had developed the disease only when they were on the rice.

Eijkman found that he could produce the disease at will by feeding the chickens polished rice of highest quality. By feeding them on unpolished rice, he cured it. Eijkman was thus the first to pinpoint what we now call a "dietary-deficiency disease," that is, a disease caused by the absence from the diet of some essential component that need be present only in traces to prevent the disease.

Eijkman did not appreciate the true meaning of his findings at first. He thought that there was a toxin of some

sort in rice grains which was neutralized by something else in the hulls. In the course of the next decade, however, several people suggested the correct explanation, the most prominent being Hopkins [912]. The missing trace component then received the name "vitamine" from Funk [1093], the word losing its final "e" and becoming "vitamin" a few years later.

Thus, with the turning of the century it was shown that the germ theory of disease, admirable though it was, did not offer a universal explanation for all disorders. There were some diseases that were purely biochemical. About the same time as the concept of a dietary-deficiency disease developed, the researches of Starling [954] and Bayliss [902] opened the way to the understanding of still another variety of biochemical disorder.

Shortly after his triumph, Eijkman was ill again and returned to the Netherlands for good, becoming professor of hygiene at the University of Utrecht. In 1929, with the significance of his finding fully realized, he shared the Nobel Prize in medicine and physiology with Hopkins, though he was by then too ill to travel to Stockholm to accept the prize in person.

[889] **PEANO,** Giuseppe (pay-ah'noh)
Italian mathematician
Born: Cuneo, Piedmont,
August 27, 1858
Died: Turin, April 20, 1932

Peano's uncle was a priest and lawyer who took charge of the boy when he was twelve and saw to his education. In 1876 Peano entered the University of Turin and graduated with high honors in 1880. He gained a professorial appointment at Turin in 1890.

Peano labored to develop the system of symbolic logic beyond the beginnings of Boole [595]. In 1889 he published *A Logical Exposition of the Principles of Geometry* in which he applied symbolic logic to the fundamentals of mathematics, a work Whitehead [911] was to carry further a quarter century later.

Peano built up a system of axioms beginning with undefined concepts for "zero," "number," and "successor." In 1890 he accepted a professorship in mathematics at the University of Turin.

Peano stepped out of mathematics in 1903 in order to invent what he hoped would be an international language (for speakers of the West European languages at any rate) by adopting a form of what might almost be called pig Latin. It made use of Latin stems without inflections, throwing in words from German and English where these seemed advisable.

The result is "Interlingua," which can be read without trouble by anyone speaking a Romance language and without too much trouble by those who speak Teutonic languages provided they are not completely unfamiliar with the Romance languages. Some scientific journals now publish summaries of the papers they contain in Interlingua as a device for reaching as many people as possible with a minimum of translation.

[890] **AUER,** Karl, Baron von Welsbach
(ow'er)
Austrian chemist
Born: Vienna, September 1, 1858
Died: Welsbach Castle, Carinthia,
August 8, 1929

Auer was the son of the director of the Imperial Printing Press in Vienna and had a good education. For his college training he traveled to Heidelberg and studied under Bunsen [565]. There he grew interested in rare earths, particularly in the supposed element didymium, discovered a generation earlier by Mosander [501]. In 1885, after much careful work, he managed to show that didymium (derived from the Greek word for "twin") was twins in actual fact. He isolated the oxides of two separate rare earth elements from didymium, and these he named praseodymium ("green twin," from the color of a prominent spectral line) and neodymium ("new twin").

Auer was the first to find practical uses for the rare earth elements. It occurred to him that gas flames might be made to give more light if they were allowed to heat up some compound that would itself then glow brightly.

He tried many substances that would glow at high heat without melting and finally found that if he impregnated a cylindrical fabric with thorium nitrate to which a small percentage of cerium nitrate (a compound of one of the rare earth elements) was added, he could obtain a brilliant white glow in a gas flame. This "Welsbach mantle" was patented in 1885. It would have greatly improved city lighting had not Edison's [788] electric light done far better and outmoded all forms of gas lighting. The mantle is still used in kerosene lamps and in other limited ways.

Auer, however, improved on Edison's lights in one respect. In 1898 he was the first to introduce a metallic filament in place of Edison's carbonized thread. Auer used the rare metal osmium for the purpose. The metallic filament was longer lasting than the carbon, but osmium, a member of the platinum group, was far too rare to be really useful. However, Auer had pointed the way toward Langmuir's [1072] tungsten filaments a decade later.

Auer's interest in lighting (he chose as his baronial motto, "more light") led him to another discovery related to his beloved rare earth elements. He found that a metallic mixture of these elements (appropriately called "Mischmetal" and consisting chiefly of cerium), when mixed with some iron, was strongly pyrophoric; that is, on being struck, it yielded hot sparks. These sparks could be used to light gas jets and could even be made to allow automatic lighting. In this respect, Auer was the first to improve on the prehistoric invention of flint and steel. The most common use of Mischmetal now is as flints in cigarette lighters.

In 1901 Auer was raised to the hereditary nobility by Francis Joseph I of Austria and was made Freiherr (Baron) von Welsbach.

PUPIN, Michael Idvorsky (poo'-peen [Serbian]; pyoo-peen' [English])
Yugoslavian-American physicist
Born: Idvor, Austria-Hungary
(now part of Yugoslavia),
October 4, 1858
Died: New York, New York,
March 12, 1935

Pupin, the son of illiterate peasants, was encouraged by them to obtain an education. He spent more than a year in Prague, but then went to the United States, arriving there in 1874 as an absolutely penniless, fifteen-year-old immigrant. Working his way upward at anything he could turn his hand to, he finally managed to attend Columbia University, graduating in 1883.

He had intended a general education in the liberal arts, but a book of Tyndall's [626] popular essays on science fired his interest. He went on to obtain his doctorate in Germany under Helmholtz [631], studying also under Kirchhoff [648]. He returned to the United States to join the faculty of Columbia University in 1890.

His inventions were numerous. He devised a fluorescent screen that would react to the impingements of X rays, which could then be observed directly and photographed more easily (a fluoroscope). He also devised a method whereby signals could be transmitted across thin wires over long distances without distortion by loading the line with inductance coils at intervals, these serving to reinforce the signals. This was in accord with a suggestion made earlier by Heaviside [806]. The Bell Telephone Company bought the device in 1901 and it made long-distance telephony practical.

During World War I, Pupin participated actively in the war effort of Serbia, whose quarrel with Austria-Hungary had precipitated the war. At the final peace treaty the section of Austria-Hungary in which Pupin had been born was joined to Serbia to form the greatly enlarged nation of Yugoslavia.

After the war he wrote his autobi-ography, *From Immigrant to Inventor,* which won the Pulitzer Prize in 1924.

HADFIELD, Sir Robert Abbott
British metallurgist
Born: Sheffield, Yorkshire,
November 28, 1858
Died: London, September 30,
1940

Sheffield was a great iron and steel center and Hadfield, born the son of a steel manufacturer, early interested himself in the problem of improving steel. He took over the family firm in 1882 when ill health forced his father's retirement.

Adding manganese seemed to make steel brittle, but Hadfield tried adding more manganese than previous metallurgists had thought advisable. By the time the steel was 12 percent manganese it was no longer brittle. If it was then heated to 1000°C and quenched in water, it became super-hard and could be used for rock-breaking machinery and for metal working. Where ordinary steel used for railroad rails had to be replaced every nine months, manganese-steel rails lasted twenty-two years. It was also used for steel helmets in World War I.

Hadfield patented his manganese-steel in 1883 and that marks the beginning of the triumph of "alloy steel." Other metals were added to steel—chromium, tungsten, molybdenum, vanadium—in search of new alloys with new and useful properties.

By 1913 even a nonrusting "stainless steel" (containing chromium and nickel) had come into use after one experimenter had noticed that a scrap pile containing alloy specimens that had been discarded as worthless included some pieces that had remained bright and shiny after a long period in the open. Similarly Honda [985] devised new magnetic alloys. Steel can now do innumerable jobs that it couldn't do in Bessemer's [575] time. Hadfield was knighted in 1908 and made a baronet in 1917.

During World War I, Hadfield and his wife established a hospital in France.

[893] **BOSE,** Sir Jagadischandra (bose)
Indian physicist
Born: Mymensingh, India (now
Nasirabad, Bangladesh),
November 30, 1858
Died: Giridh, India,
November 23, 1937

Bose, the first Indian scientist to gain
an international reputation, was the son
of a civil servant. He studied at St.
Xavier's School in Calcutta, graduating
in 1879. He then went to England, intending to gain a medical education, but
switched to science instead. He attended
Cambridge, where Rayleigh [760] was
one of his teachers. He returned to India
in 1884 and gained a professorial position at Calcutta in 1887. The Bose Research Institute was founded in Calcutta
in 1917. Bose presided over the dedication and served as director till his death.
He was knighted in 1917.

Bose was best known for his careful
studies of plant growth. He devised very
sensitive instruments capable of recording extremely small movements. These
were capable of magnifying plant growth
ten million times. Bose was thus able to
follow plant responses to a variety of
stimuli.

[894] **ARRHENIUS,** Svante August
(ar-ray'nee-us)
Swedish chemist
Born: Vik (near Uppsala),
February 19, 1859
Died: Stockholm, October 2,
1927

Arrhenius, the son of a surveyor, was
an infant prodigy (he taught himself to
read at three) and a brilliant student,
graduating from high school as the
youngest and brightest in his class. While
attending the University of Uppsala he
began to study how electricity passed
through solutions, an important subject
since the days of Davy [421] nearly a
century earlier.

Faraday [474] had worked out the
laws of electrolysis and from those laws
it seemed that electricity, like matter,
must exist in the form of tiny particles.
Faraday had spoken of "ions" (from a
Greek word for "wanderer"), these
being the particles that carried electricity
through the solution, but there remained
the question as to just what the ions
were. Men like Williamson [650] and
Clausius [633] had suggested they might
be atoms or groups of atoms, but they
did not proceed to make the necessary
points that would explain matters. Arrhenius did.

He considered the fact that some substances, such as salt (sodium chloride),
conducted electricity when in solution
and were "electrolytes," while others,
such as sugar (sucrose), did not and
were "non-electrolytes." Other differences between electrolytes and non-
electrolytes arose in connection with the
freezing point of water.

A substance dissolved in water lowered the water's freezing point somewhat. This lowering was in proportion to
the quantity of substance dissolved, as
had been shown by the work of Raoult
[684]. Doubling the quantity doubled the
lowering.

For different substances in solution,
the lowering was in inverse proportion to
the molecular weight. Thus, ordinary
sugar (sucrose) had a molecular weight
about twice that of grape sugar (glucose). A gram of glucose dissolved in a
liter of water lowered the freezing point
twice as much as a gram of sucrose so
dissolved. Since the glucose molecule
was only half the size of the sucrose
molecule, a gram of glucose would contain twice as many molecules as a gram
of sucrose. It was easy to show, then,
that the amount of lowering of the freezing point was proportional to the number
of particles present in solution, whatever
the dissolved substance. This held, at
least, for non-electrolytes.

What about electrolytes? A fixed
quantity of sodium chloride is composed
of a fixed number of molecules. From
this the amount of lowering of the freezing point could be calculated. However,
as it turned out, the amount of lowering
induced by dissolved sodium chloride
was just twice what it ought to be. One
explanation for this was that each molecule of sodium chloride gave rise to two
particles. This was also true of other

electrolytes—potassium bromide, for instance, or sodium nitrate.

On the other hand, a substance like barium chloride or sodium sulfate produced three times the lowering that one might expect. Each molecule must give rise to three particles.

This anomalous behavior of electrolytes held for other properties that depended upon the number of particles present, as, for instance, the osmotic pressure; that is, the pressure forcing liquid through a semipermeable membrane of the type Graham [547] used in separating crystalloids from colloids.

Arrhenius decided that the only explanation was that sodium chloride did break up into two particles, a sodium and a chlorine, as soon as it was placed in solution. Of course, these solutions did not contain metallic sodium and gaseous chlorine; so what happened must be that the sodium and chlorine carried electric charges, and that was why sodium chloride solutions could transmit an electric current.

The positively charged sodium ion and the negatively charged chloride ion would have properties quite different from the uncharged atoms. In the same way, barium chloride would split into three particles, a doubly charged positive barium ion and two singly charged negative chloride ions.

This turned out to be a revolutionary concept; a bit too revolutionary for most of the chemists of the time. Electrically charged atoms were inconceivable to those who accepted the century-old view of Dalton [389] that atoms were structureless and indivisible. Where would the electric charge come from? And how could a stable substance like sodium chloride break up at once as a result of solution in so mild a substance as water? One of Arrhenius' teachers, Cleve [746], dismissed the young man peremptorily when the latter tried to explain his theory.

Finally, in 1884 Arrhenius prepared his theory of ionic dissociation as part of his Ph.D. dissertation. He underwent a rigorous four-hour examination and was then awarded the lowest possible passing grade by his incredulous examiners.

Fortunately it was a day when a new kind of physical chemistry was on the rise. The two brightest stars of the new discipline, Van't Hoff [829] and Ostwald [840], were intrigued by the new theory as were Clausius [633] and J. L. Meyer [685]. They took up the cudgels on its behalf against such powerful opponents as Mendeléev [705]. Ostwald even traveled to Uppsala just to discuss the matter with the young man. Arrhenius worked with the two in Germany (also with Boltzmann [769]) and for a decade they formed a loud minority view in the world of chemistry. In 1889 Arrhenius contributed to the new physical chemistry again by studying how rates of reaction increased with temperature. He suggested the existence of an energy of activation, an amount of energy that must be supplied molecules before they will react. This is a concept that is essential to the theory of catalysis.

Arrhenius' stock began to go up suddenly in the 1890s, when J. J. Thomson [869] discovered the electron and Becquerel [834] discovered radioactivity. The atom was not structureless after all, it appeared, but was made up of electrically charged particles, notably the negatively charged electron. A negative ion such as a chloride ion could now easily be seen to be a chlorine atom that had obtained one electron more than its fair share, while a positive sodium ion was a sodium atom with an electron missing. If the sodium and chlorine in a sodium chloride molecule were held together by the attraction of electric charges, the somewhat insulating properties of water could make the atoms fall apart, so to speak. If, in doing so, they divided the electrons unequally, a positively charged ion and a negatively charged ion would be formed.

Suddenly Arrhenius' ionic theory made the very best kind of sense. He returned to Sweden from Germany in 1891 and in 1895 he was appointed to a professorship at the University of Stockholm. In 1903, for the same thesis that had barely earned him a passing grade in his doctor's examination, he won the Nobel Prize in chemistry.

This took place only after considerable

discussion within the group awarding the prize as to whether it should be recorded as the prize in chemistry or in physics; some even suggested giving Arrhenius a half share in both prizes. Cleve, who had turned a deaf ear to Arrhenius a score of years earlier, now explained that it was this "in-betweenness" of the work that had obscured its importance to him, and he made up for this by earnestly supporting Arrhenius for the award.

Arrhenius then turned to the large mysteries of science. He studied the application of physical chemistry to the life processes and was one of the forerunners of modern molecular biology. In a book entitled *Worlds in the Making,* published in 1908, he upheld the notion of the universality of life and suggested that life on earth had begun when living spores had reached it across the emptiness of space. He pointed out that spores could withstand the cold and airlessness of space for indefinite periods and he believed that the driving force that carried spores from star to star was the pressure of radiation, a pressure that had recently been measured by Lebedev [952].

The consequence of this theory, he believed, was that life was diffused throughout the universe wherever it could exist at all, a view which has recently been revived in modified form by Crick [1406]. He was particularly interested in the possibility of life on Mars, a point made popular at the time by the work of Schiaparelli [714] and Lowell [860].

Unfortunately, two points, one experimental and one philosophical, militate against the Arrhenius theory of space-wandering spores. The first is that although spores are resistant to cold and vacuum they are not resistant to ultraviolet light and other energetic radiation. Since space (at least in the neighborhood of stars) is riddled with such energetic radiation, the survival of spores is very questionable.

The second objection is that a spore theory does not really explain the origin of life; it merely puts it off. If life did not originate on the earth but on another world and reached us only in the form of already living spores, how did the life originate in the first place on the other world? It took another generation and the work of Urey [1164] and others before scientists believed they could begin to speculate reasonably on the subject of extraterrestrial life.

In his book Arrhenius also argued against the "heat death" of the universe, the ultimate state of maximum entropy envisaged by Clausius. Arrhenius believed processes existed that would decrease entropy and maintain equilibrium. In this he was a kind of forerunner of those like Gold [1437] who imagined a universe undergoing continuous creation.

Arrhenius also pointed out that carbon dioxide in the atmosphere served as a "heat trap," for it allowed the high-frequency sunlight to penetrate freely to the earth's surface but was opaque to the low-frequency infrared radiation which the earth reradiated at night. A slight rise in carbon dioxide content in the atmosphere would raise the earth's temperature markedly and might account for the worldwide mildness in the dinosaur-ridden Mesozoic Era. A slight fall in carbon dioxide content might, in turn, set off an Ice Age. Such a suggestion is still taken seriously and, indeed, may account for the situation on the planet Venus, where the atmosphere was found, by W. S. Adams [1045] a generation later, to be high in carbon dioxide, and where Mariner II, the Venus probe, demonstrated in 1962 that the surface temperature of Venus was about 350°C, far higher than would be expected without a carbon-dioxide "greenhouse effect."

In 1905 after turning down (for the second time) the offer of a professorship in Germany, Arrhenius was appointed director of the Nobel Institute for Physical Chemistry and held that post until shortly before his death.

[895] **POPOV**, Alexander Stepanovich
Russian physicist
Born: Bogoslavsky, Perm,
March 16, 1859
Died: St. Petersburg,
January 13, 1906

Popov, the son of a priest, had plans for the priesthood himself but switched to mathematics. He graduated from the University of St. Petersburg in 1883 and eventually joined its faculty.

Like Marconi [1025] he recognized the importance of H. R. Hertz's [873] discovery of radio waves and began to work on methods of receiving them over long distances the year before Marconi did. He was the first to use an antenna and in 1897 could send a signal from ship to shore for three miles.

In the years following, Popov managed to persuade the Russian navy to begin the installation of radio equipment in its vessels. However, Popov was mainly interested in using his receiver for signals from lightning strokes, in his studies of the physics of thunderstorms, and it was Marconi who took the crucial step of commercializing the radio signal, and the dramatic one of sending it across the ocean.

The Soviet Union, in a fit of nationalist fervor, insists that it was Popov who invented the radio. Though the Soviet Union has a poor case, it is not quite as poor as the nationalist fervor of nations opposed to the Soviet Union makes it out to be.

[896] **LOEB**, Jacques
German-American physiologist
Born: Mayen, Rhenish Prussia,
April 7, 1859
Died: Hamilton, Bermuda,
February 11, 1924

Loeb, the son of a prosperous Jewish businessman, obtained his M.D. at Strasbourg in 1884 and taught first at Strasbourg and then at Wurzburg. After marrying an American philologist, he emigrated to the United States. He arrived in 1891 and joined the faculty of the University of Chicago. In 1902 he transferred to the University of California and in 1910 joined the staff of the Rockefeller Institute for Medical Research (now Rockefeller University) in New York.

Leob was a mechanist at the time when mechanism was reaching new heights, thanks to the work of Sherrington [881] and Pavlov [802] on reflexes.

Loeb tried to show that the tropisms that govern plant behavior (simple reactions toward or away from light, water, gravity, and so on) might be applied to simple animals and that, indeed, it was possible to elaborate such behavior into quite complicated structures. He even suggested that man's morals and ethics were but the products of tropism combinations.

In 1899 he attracted wide attention when he found that an unfertilized sea urchin egg could be made to develop to maturity by proper environmental changes. Such "artificial parthenogenesis" was later extended to frogs. Undoubtedly, part of the interest in this work among laymen was founded on the grisly (but unjustified) thought that the male sex might turn out to be superfluous.

[897] **CURIE**, Pierre
French chemist
Born: Paris, May 15, 1859
Died: Paris, April 19, 1906

Pierre, the son of a physician, was a slow learner as a child and received his early schooling at home. Then he studied at the Sorbonne where he gained his bachelor's degree in 1875 and his master's in 1877. From 1878 he was an assistant teacher in the physical laboratory there.

In 1880 he and his brother observed how an electric potential appeared across crystals of quartz and of Rochelle salt when pressure was applied to them. The potential varied directly with the pressure and the brothers named the phenomenon piezoelectricity, from a Greek word meaning "to press." Conversely, if a rapidly changing electric potential is applied to such a crystal, its faces can be made to vibrate rapidly. In this way the crystal can be used to set up beams of ultrasonic sound, sound waves with frequencies far too high to hear. Crystals with piezoelectric properties form an essential portion of sound-electronic devices such as microphones and record players.

For his doctorate, which he obtained

in 1895, Pierre Curie studied the effect of heat on magnetism and showed that there is a certain critical temperature (still called the Curie point) above which magnetic properties disappear. In that same year he married Marie Sklodowska [965] and after that his scientific career merged with hers. Earlier in life he had said a wife was a hindrance to a scientist, but Marie was surely an exception.

He conducted one dangerous experiment on his own. Becquerel [834] had noted a skin burn after carrying some radium in his pocket. Curie confirmed this in 1901 by deliberately inducing a burn on his arm. He also measured the heat given off by radium as 140 calories per gram per hour. This was the first indication of the huge energies available within the atom; energies that were to make themselves all too evident in nuclear bombs. Thus began an understanding of the dangers of radioactivity, dangers that hang dreadfully over mankind today.

In 1904 he was appointed professor of physics at the Sorbonne, a post to which his wife succeeded when, two years later, his life was snuffed out in a street accident.

[898] **REID,** Harry Fielding
American geophysicist
Born: Baltimore, Maryland,
May 18, 1859
Died: Baltimore, Maryland,
June 18, 1944

Reid, the first American geophysicist, was a great-grandnephew of George Washington on his mother's side. He obtained his Ph.D. at Johns Hopkins University in 1885, and after teaching at Case School of Applied Science (now Case Western Reserve University) and at the University of Chicago, he returned to Johns Hopkins as a professor of physics in 1894 and remained there until his retirement in 1930.

His early interest was in glaciers and their movements and perhaps it was this that led him to consider the earth's crust and its movements. He was part of the scientific committee chosen to investigate the San Francisco earthquake of 1906. His observations of the displacement of the crust that resulted from that disaster led him to propose the "elastic rebound theory." This supposed that faults were preexisting and were not breaks in the crust caused by earthquakes. Rather, pressures along the fault increased until there was a sudden slippage of one side of the fault against the other, the vibrations causing the effects of the earthquake. This theory is still accepted today.

[899] **SMITH,** Theobald
American pathologist
Born: Albany, New York, July 31,
1859
Died: New York, New York,
December 10, 1934

Smith was the son of a tailor, who, together with his wife, were of German birth (the surname being, originally, Schmitt). He graduated from Cornell University in 1881 with honors, then attended Albany Medical College, getting his M.D. in 1883 at the top of his class.

In 1892 he demonstrated that Texas cattle fever was caused by a protozoan parasite that was spread by blood-sucking ticks. This was the first definite indication of the spread of disease by blood-sucking arthropods (ticks in this case, insects in others). It was met with considerable skepticism but it laid the groundwork for the findings of Reed [822], Ricketts [992], and others.

[900] **OSBORNE,** Thomas Burr
American biochemist
Born: New Haven, Connecticut,
August 5, 1859
Died: New Haven, January 29,
1929

Osborne, the son of a banker, graduated from Yale in 1881, made a half-hearted attempt in the direction of a medical career, then went on to graduate work in chemistry. He obtained his Ph.D. in 1885 with a dissertation on inorganic analysis but then took a position at the Connecticut Agricultural Experiment Station, and slowly shifted in the direction of biochemistry.

His study of proteins obtained from different seeds led him finally to a position contradicting Liebig's [532] early feeling that there were only a few different proteins. Proteins, instead, clearly existed in many, many subtly different varieties. For one thing, they were different in amino acid content and Osborne showed that difference in nutritional properties were dependent on differences in amino acid content. He showed, for instance, that lysine and tryptophan could not be synthesized by rats but had to be present in the diet protein.

Osborne also discovered what later came to be called vitamin A but McCollum [1062] published his independent finding three weeks earlier and got the credit. It was Osborne, however, who discovered that cod-liver oil was a rich source of the vitamin, thus condemning a generation of American children to the forced consumption of this nauseating compound.

[901] **HAFFKINE,** Waldemar Mordecai
Wolfe (haf'kin)
Russian-British bacteriologist
Born: Odessa, March 15, 1860
Died: Lausanne, Switzerland,
October 25, 1930

Haffkine was the son of Jewish parents. He attended the University of Odessa, where Mechnikov [775] was one of his teachers. He might have joined the faculty of the university afterward, but conversion to Christianity was the condition and Haffkine refused.

He left Russia and in 1889 was working at the Pasteur Institute in Paris, working under Roux [844]. Haffkine was particularly interested in cholera, epidemics of which frequently visited Europe. In 1892 he prepared an attenuated strain of cholera culture, which he thought might induce immunity without danger, and injected himself with a concentrated strain to make sure it was without danger.

In 1893 he went to India, where cholera was endemic and where it was at the time wreaking havoc. Working under difficult conditions and against the hostility of much of the population (which, like people generally, were suspicious of anything new), he inoculated forty-five thousand people and reduced the deathrate by 70 percent among those inoculated. He also attempted to work up a vaccine against the plague.

Haffkine's work met with constant opposition from British medical officials even though he was honored by Queen Victoria in 1897 and became a British citizen in 1899. When nineteen people who had been inoculated against plague died of tetanus, Haffkine was accused of responsiblity and five years passed before he was exonerated and the responsibility laid at the door of the carelessness in handling one particular vial of vaccine by the local authorities.

[902] **BAYLISS,** Sir William Maddock
English physiologist
Born: Wolverhampton, Staffordshire, May 2, 1860
Died: London, August 27, 1924

Bayliss began medical training at University College, London, but he had no great taste for it and switched to physiological research at Oxford. In 1888 he returned to University College as a faculty member. His father was a prosperous iron manufacturer so Bayliss was free of financial insecurity.

Like Starling [954] he did much work on the heart and, again like Starling, he published an important text in physiology. In 1893 he married Starling's sister, and thereafter he and Starling formed a research team. In particular, he joined with Starling in the discovery of hormones. He received the Copley medal of the Royal Society, the first physiologist to do so in 180 years. He was knighted in 1922.

During World War I he worked on methods for treating wounded soldiers.

In 1903 Bayliss considered himself to have been libeled by an antivivisectionist. Bayliss took the person to court and, with ease, won £2,000 damages, which he donated to his university for the furtherance of research in physiology.

[903] **BUCHNER,** Eduard (bookh'ner)
German chemist
Born: Munich, Bavaria,
May 20, 1860
Died: Focsani, Romania,
August 13, 1917

Eduard Buchner was fortunate in his brother, Hans Buchner [813], ten years his elder. It was Hans who first interested Eduard in chemistry and guided him through the initial stages. Eduard studied chemistry under Baeyer [718] and botany under Nägeli [598]. He obtained his Ph.D. in 1888 and continued as Baeyer's assistant until 1893, when he became professor of chemistry at Kiel University.

Through his brother, who was a bacteriologist, the younger Buchner became interested in the problem of fermentation. This was both the oldest and newest of biochemical problems. It was as old as prehistory in the fermenting of fruit juice to form wine and the leavening of dough to make bread. On the other hand, it was not until the time of Payen [490] and Schwann [563], a little over half a century before, that the chemist had his hands on samples of the actual "ferments," the chemical substances bringing about these changes in organic materials.

There was a question as to the role life played in fermentation. The vitalists had always believed that life obeyed a set of laws peculiar to itself and that the generalizations deduced in the laboratory from the study of inanimate objects did not necessarily apply to living organisms. Their position had been shaken by the synthesis from inorganic materials of an organic substance by Wöhler [515] in 1828, and by the synthesis a generation later of organic materials not found in nature by Perkin [734] and those who followed him.

The vitalists fell back on fermentation. Whereas organic substances prepared in the laboratory made use of strenuous methods (high temperature, harsh solvents, and so on), living tissue made use of the mildest conditions: body temperature, a watery solution neither acid nor alkaline, and so on. The difference, it appeared, lay in the fact that living tissue made use of the so-called ferments as catalysts.

To be sure, Schwann and others had isolated ferments and showed that they could work in the test tube as ordinary nonliving chemicals. However, said the vitalists, these were ferments involved in digestive processes that took place in the alimentary canal and not within the cell. As for the chemical processes that took place within the cell, such as the conversion of sugar to alcohol, these, the vitalists held, were inseparable from life and could not be carried through with a system made up of nonliving materials only. Kühne [725] even suggested that ferments outside the cell be given the special name of "enzymes."

Buchner wondered whether it might not be experimentally demonstrated that alcoholic fermentation was inseparable from life, or at least to present evidence in favor of that view. To do this, it was his intention to grind up yeast cells with sand until not one of them was left alive and to show, if he could, that the production of alcohol from sugar would stop. His superiors viewed this line of experimentation with disapproval and advised against it, but Buchner persisted.

In 1896 he obtained his cell-free yeast juice and filtered it. He then searched for a method to preserve it against bacterial contamination. One method was to add a good thick sugar solution. (In preparing fruit preserves, it is the high concentration of sugar that "preserves" it against bacteria.) He added the sugar and found that before long, bubbles of carbon dioxide were forming. The completely dead yeast juice was rapidly fermenting the sugar, forming carbon dioxide and alcohol, exactly as the intact cells would have done.

Intercellular fermentation and life were therefore not inseparable and Buchner had demonstrated the reverse of what he intended. The last stronghold of the vitalists was breached and overthrown.

The chemical processes within cells were carried on by no "vital force" but by ferments no different in kind from the ferments associated with chemical activity outside the cell. Ferments of all kinds now received Kühne's name of "enzyme."

Buchner's demonstration was assailed by Rubner [848], among others, but Buchner was able to maintain his position and eventually he won out. In 1907 he was awarded the Nobel Prize in chemistry for his feat and in 1909 became professor of chemistry at Breslau. There are vitalists even today, but the viewpoint carries with it now a rather strong tinge of mysticism, and it has little if any influence on the course of science.

Buchner died in the trenches during World War I. He served as a major in the German army and died of a grenade wound on the Romanian front. He was perhaps the outstanding scientist to be thrown away in this fashion on the side of the Central Powers, as Moseley [1121] was the outstanding loss on the Allied side. (In World War II, the powers learned to hoard their scientists more carefully.)

[904] **EINTHOVEN**, Willem (eyent'-hoh-ven)
Dutch physiologist
Born: Semarang, Java (now part of Indonesia), May 22, 1860
Died: Leiden, September 29, 1927

Einthoven's father was a practicing physician serving in the East Indies, which was then a Dutch colony. The father died in 1866, and in 1870 the family returned to the Netherlands and settled in Utrecht. In 1878 Einthoven entered the University of Utrecht and began the study of medicine, though always with considerable interest in physics. He obtained his medical degree in 1885 and was at once appointed to a professorship of physiology at the University of Leiden, serving there the remainder of his life.

The physicist in him provoked his interest in the tiny electric potentials produced in the human body. That these existed had been known ever since the time of Galvani [320] a century earlier, but knowing it and putting the fact to medical use were two different things.

The heart, for instance, when in health worked with an integrated rhythm that must be reflected in the electrical potentials that progressed along its substance. Perhaps a departure from the normal pattern of that progression might be used to diagnose pathological conditions before they could be discovered in any other way. The problem was to detect the small currents with sufficient accuracy.

In 1903 Einthoven developed the first string galvanometer. This consisted of a delicate conducting thread stretched across a magnetic field. A current flowing through the thread would cause it to deviate at right angles to the direction of the magnetic lines of force, the extent of the deviation being proportional to the strength of the current. The delicacy of the device was sufficient to make it possible to record the varying electrical potentials of the heart.

Einthoven continually improved his device and worked out the significance of the rises and falls in potential. By 1906 he was correlating the recordings of these peaks and troughs (the result being what he called an electrocardiogram) with various types of heart disorders. It became a valuable means of diagnosis and led the way to a similar tapping of the electric potentials of the brain by Berger [1014]. Further refinements of technique by Erlanger [1023] and Gasser [1126] elicited still more information about the electrical properties of nerve. For the development of electrocardiography Einthoven was awarded the 1924 Nobel Prize in medicine and physiology.

[905] **BARRINGER**, Daniel Moreau
American mining engineer and geologist
Born: Raleigh, North Carolina, May 25, 1860
Died: 1929

Barringer graduated from Princeton in 1879. He was interested in mining and this drew him out to the mineral-rich West, where he met his destiny in the shape of a crater in Arizona.

This crater is nearly round, almost a mile in diameter and about six hundred feet deep. Most people assumed it was an extinct volcano, but to Barringer it looked as though it had been formed by the impact of a large meteorite. This theory, advanced in 1905, was laughed at to begin with, but closer study has made it seem very likely. There are no signs of recent volcanic activity in the vicinity, whereas a great deal of meteoric material has been obtained all around it.

Barringer began mining operations in the hope of finding the main mass of a large iron meteorite, since this might prove a bonanza. After his death in 1929, his son continued the operations, but so far the main mass eludes the diggers.

The existence of the Great Barringer Meteor Crater made more dramatic the theory that the lunar craters were formed by meteoric bombardment and it is only earth's atmosphere that saves it from all but the largest strikes. There are many signs of ancient meteoric craters formed by such large strikes. The Barringer Crater is remarkable among them only because it is the most recent and because it is in a desert area where the forces of erosion are unusually slow.

[906] **VILLARD,** Paul Ulrich
French physicist
Born: Lyon, September 28, 1860
Died: Bayonne, Basses-Pyrénées, January 13, 1934

Villard obtained his teacher's license in 1884. His moment of glory came in 1900 when he was studying the uranium radiations that had been discovered four years earlier by A. H. Becquerel [834]. Some of these had already been demonstrated to be bent in one direction by a magnetic field and some in another. These consisted of charged particles and were eventually named "alpha rays" and "beta rays" by Rutherford [996].

Villard noted that some radiation was not bent in a magnetic field and was unusually penetrating. These came to be called "gamma rays." They were like X rays in nature but were more energetic and penetrating.

[907] **SPERRY,** Elmer Ambrose
American inventor
Born: Cortland, New York, October 12, 1860
Died: Brooklyn, New York, June 16, 1930

Sperry, the son of a farmer, was raised by his grandparents after his mother, a schoolteacher, died in childbirth. He spent a year at Cornell University in 1879. The next year, at the age of twenty, he had organized his own company to manufacture electrical generating equipment and other heavy devices.

Of his four hundred patents his most famous involves his development of a gyroscopic compass between 1896 and 1910. A turning gyroscope maintains its plane of rotation and resists being turned out of that plane. A gyroscope mounted on gimbals on a ship in such a way that the ship's movements would not force it out of its plane could be used as a true north-south compass, subject to none of the variations of the ordinary magnetic compass and not influenced by surrounding iron and steel. It was the first essential improvement on the compass in a thousand years.

It was first tried on board the battleship *Delaware* in 1911 and was adopted almost at once by the navy. Sperry also developed stabilizers for ships and aircraft and during World War I invented a high-intensity arc searchlight that the armed forces quickly adopted.

[908] **FINSEN,** Niels Ryberg
Danish physician
Born: Tórshavn, Faeroe Islands, December 15, 1860
Died: Copenhagen, September 24, 1904

Born of Icelandic parents, young Finsen had his early schooling at Reykjavik,

Iceland, but he traveled to Denmark (which at the time ruled over both Iceland and the Faeroe Islands) for his professional education. He obtained his medical degree in 1891 at the University of Copenhagen.

Even as an undergraduate he was interested in the effect of light on disease, for he himself suffered from a chronic ailment which, he believed, was benefited by sunlight.

In 1893 he gained considerable attention by claiming that red light was effective in ameliorating the effects of smallpox. By hanging red curtains on the windows of sickrooms, he let in the longer "heat waves" and shut out the shorter "chemical waves."

In 1896 he established a Light Institute at Copenhagen, which was first supported by private sources and then by the Danish government. There he studied the "chemical waves" and found that shortwave light obtained from the sun or from a concentration of powerful electric lights could kill bacteria in cultures and on the skin. He established, moreover, that this was caused by the light itself and was not due to heating effects.

In particular he was able to cure *lupus vulgaris*, a skin disease brought on by the tubercle bacillus, by irradiation with strong shortwave light. For the purpose he designed a large and powerful arc lamp called the Finsen Light.

Some of Finsen's work with light was rather borderline and has since been abandoned, notably the treatment of smallpox with red light. The discovery of the effect of blue and violet light (and particularly of ultraviolet light) on bacteria was valuable, however. It laid the groundwork for therapy with the still more energetic X rays and gamma rays discovered by Roentgen [774] and A. H. Becquerel [834] at just about the time Finsen was experimenting with his chemical rays.

Finsen's contribution was rewarded with the 1903 Nobel Prize in medicine and physiology. He donated half the prize money to the Light Institute. In delicate and failing health for most of his adult life, Finsen died the next year, still a young man.

[909] **GOLDSCHMIDT,** Johann (Hans) Wilhelm
German chemist
Born: Berlin, January 18, 1861
Died: Baden-Baden, May 20, 1923

During the nineteenth century many metals had been obtained from their oxides by heating those oxides with sodium or potassium. This was an expensive procedure. Sainte-Claire Deville [603] had prepared aluminum in this way and he reported that powdered aluminum could then replace sodium or potassium for the purpose.

Goldschmidt, who had studied under Bunsen [561], joined his family's metallurgical business in 1888 and then investigated the problem. In 1898 he described the best manner in which it could be done. Aluminum powder mixed with an oxide will, when ignited, react furiously and develop tremendous heat. In the end pure metal is produced. Pure iron and chromium can be prepared in this fashion, for instance. Because of the great heat developed, the oxide/aluminum mixture (called thermite) can be used in welding and for some purposes it is the best form of welding.

[910] **GUILLAUME,** Charles Édouard (gee-yome´)
Swiss-French physicist
Born: Fleurier, Switzerland, February 15, 1861
Died: Sèvres, near Paris, June 13, 1938

In college Guillaume, the son of a watchmaker, studied mathematics and physics, obtaining his doctor's degree in 1883 in Zürich. In that year he entered the Bureau of International Weights and Measures, which had just been established. He began as an assistant and worked his way up to the directorship, in 1915, retiring in 1936.

In the bureau Guillaume's tasks included making every effort to increase the precision of the standard measures. Thus he redetermined the volume of the liter. A kilogram of pure water is defined as occupying one liter at 4°C and this was supposed to have a volume of exactly 1,000 cubic centimeters. In 1904 his new measurements showed, however, that a kilogram of water took up a volume of 1,000.028 cubic centimeters. Ever since chemists have carefully spoken of milliliters rather than of cubic centimeters.

Guillaume also searched assiduously for some cheap material out of which to construct standards of length and mass. The materials in use were platinum-iridium alloy, very expensive but useful because they did not corrode. In his search he discovered, in 1896, an alloy of iron and nickel, in the ratio of 9 to 5, which changed volume with temperature only very slightly. He gave this alloy the name invar, for "invariable," because of its lack of change.

Invar is of great value in the manufacture of balance wheels and hair springs. The relative lack of change with temperature meant watches and chronometers that kept time so much the better. It was another half century before scientists learned to divorce chronometry from these gross properties of matter, thanks to Townes [1400].

For the discovery of invar, Guillaume was awarded the 1920 Nobel Prize in physics.

[911] **WHITEHEAD,** Alfred North
English mathematician and philosopher
Born: Ramsgate, Kent, February 15, 1861
Died: Cambridge, Massachusetts, December 30, 1947

Whitehead, the son of a clergyman-headmaster, graduated from Cambridge in 1884. For most of his life he taught mathematics in England, at Cambridge till 1911, then at the University of London; but in 1924 he went to the United States as professor of philosophy at Harvard University, remaining in the country the rest of his life.

He was intensely interested in the logical basis of mathematics. From 1910 to 1913, in collaboration with Bertrand

Russell [1005], he published the three-volume work *Principia Mathematica* in which mathematics was built up out of symbolic logic on what seemed to be a definitive way at last. However, owing to the later work of Gödel [1301], it would seem that the adjective "definitive" can never be applied to any system of mathematics.

[912] **HOPKINS,** Sir Frederick Gowland
English biochemist
Born: Eastbourne Sussex, June 30, 1861
Died: Cambridge, May 16, 1947

After an unhappy childhood and youth, Hopkins spent time uncertainly in insurance, analytical chemistry, and a few other miscellaneous activities. In 1888, however, he took advantage of a small inheritance and aimed for medicine. He obtained his doctoral degree and began teaching, in 1894, at Guy's Hospital in London. He then entered the field of biochemical research.

In the late nineteenth century, it was known that gelatin, although a protein, would not support life if it was the sole protein in a rat's diet. In 1900 Hopkins discovered tryptophan, one of the amino acid building blocks of proteins, and showed that it was missing in gelatin. This made it clear that some of the amino acids could not be manufactured in the body and had to be present as such in the diet. He thus originated the concept of the "essential amino acid," which Rose [1114] was to bring to a climax a generation later.

Hopkins then found that of two samples of apparently identical protein, one might support life and one might not. This to him meant that one might contain some substance essential to the body only in traces. In 1906 he made this point in a lecture, saying that rickets and scurvy might be brought about by lack of such necessary trace substances. Eijkman [888] had already done his work on beriberi, and that too could be interpreted in the light of Hopkins's suggestion.

In 1905 he was elected to the Royal

Society and in 1914 appointed professor of biochemistry at Cambridge. (It was a new department.) Nor did his labors cease, for in 1921 he isolated the important substance glutathione from living tissue and showed its role in oxidative processes within cells.

In 1925 he was knighted, and in 1929 he shared the Nobel Prize in medicine and physiology with Eijkman for his enunciation of what later came to be known as the "vitamin concept." From 1930 to 1935 he served as president of the Royal Society.

[913] **BATESON**, William
English biologist
Born: Whitby, Yorkshire, August 8, 1861
Died: Merton, Surrey, February 8, 1926

Bateson obtained his master's degree from Cambridge, where his father held an important position. His first important investigations dealt with Balanoglossus, a wormlike creature, with a larval stage resembling that of echinoderms, such as starfish. (In fact, Johannes Müller [522] had classified the Balanoglossus larva as an echinoderm.) Bateson showed that Balanoglossus possessed in addition to gill slits, a scrap of a notochord and a dorsal nerve chord. This established the creature as a chordate, the phylum introduced by Kovalevski [750] and Balfour [823] that includes the vertebrates and, therefore, man. This was the first indication that chordates were offshoots of a primitive echinoderm stock, a theory now widely accepted.

Bateson was a strong supporter of Mendelian views after Mendel's [638] papers had been rediscovered by De Vries [792]. It was Bateson who translated Mendel's papers into English. In 1905 experiments he conducted on Mendelian inheritance showed that not all characteristics are independently inherited. Some characteristics are inherited together and this gene linkage was eventually explained by Morgan [957] (though Bateson proved reluctant

to accept Morgan's theories when these were first advanced).

About the same time, Bateson proposed that the study of the mechanism of inheritance be termed genetics and thus he added a key term to the vocabulary of science.

Bateson, in 1908, was the first ever to hold a professorial position (at Cambridge) in this new field of genetics.

[914] **NANSEN**, Fridtjof (nahn'sen)
Norwegian explorer
Born: Store-Frøen (near Oslo), October 10, 1861
Died: Lysaker (near Oslo), May 13, 1930

Nansen studied zoology at the University of Christiania (Oslo) but gained fame as an explorer. In 1882 he was serving on a sealing ship and, in Greenland waters, could see the ice cap from a distance. It occurred to him that the ice cap could be crossed. In 1888 he and five others landed on the eastern shore of Greenland and managed to cross it to the inhabited western shore in a six-week trek. It was the first time Greenland had ever been crossed by land.

He then planned to cross the Arctic Ocean by designing a ship that would be lifted, rather than crushed, when the ocean about it froze. His idea was to have the ship (and himself and crew) carried along by the drifting sea ice of the Arctic Ocean to a spot near the North Pole.

His ship *Fram* ("Forward"), with thirteen men aboard, set sail in 1893. It was frozen in and drifted. On March 14, 1895, Nansen left the frozen-in ship and trekked farther northward by dogsled, reaching 86°14' (on April 8) before turning back. It was the most northerly attitude ever reached by human beings up to that point. Nansen got back to Norway, with his ship, in 1896 after a three-year voyage.

After World War I, Nansen interested himself in humanitarian work, in caring for prisoners of war, for those suffering in famines, for the displaced and persecuted. His work in this direction eclipsed even his towering fame as an explorer, and in 1922 he was awarded the Nobel Peace Prize.

[915] **INNES,** Robert Thorburn Ayton
(in'is)
Scottish astronomer
Born: Edinburgh, November 10, 1861
Died: Surbiton, England, March 13, 1933

Innes left school at twelve and was entirely self-taught thereafter. He emigrated to Australia in 1884 and was a merchant there, doing well. His work as an amateur in astronomy was sufficiently notable, however, for him to be offered a post at the Cape Observatory in South Africa by Gill [763].

While there, Innes specialized in scouring the southern skies for binary stars, discovered 1,628 hitherto unknown examples of this class. His best-known discovery came in 1915, however, when he discovered a faint star near Alpha Centauri, which seems to be a third and distant companion of that binary. At its present position in its mighty orbit about that star, it happens to be a little closer to us than its companions are, so that it is the nearest individual star to us (always excluding our own sun). It is often called Proxima Centauri for that reason, "proxima" meaning, in Latin, "nearest."

[916] **KENNELLY,** Arthur Edwin
British-American electrical engineer
Born: Bombay, India, December 17, 1861
Died: Boston, Massachusetts, June 18, 1939

Kennelly, the son of an Irish lawyer, was educated in London and did not attend a university. He grew interested in the expanding field of electricity and became a telegraph operator in his teens, as Edison [788] had been a couple of decades before. At the age of twenty-six Kennelly went to the United States and worked as an assistant to Edison until

1894, when he went into business for himself as a consulting engineer.

Like Heaviside [806] and Steinmetz [944], his importance to the development of electricity was not so much in the construction of novel devices making use of electrical circuits, as in the application of advanced mathematics to the understanding of the behavior of such circuits.

He is best known, however, for a suggestion he made in 1902 arising out of the fact that the wireless messages of Marconi [1025] had reached from England to Newfoundland, working their way around the bulge of the earth. The radio waves ought to have moved in a straight line, as light waves do, and have been unable to travel past the horizon. That radio waves did travel beyond the horizon made it seem to Kennelly that somewhere in the upper atmosphere was a layer of electrically charged particles that, his theories told him, could reflect radio waves. Thus, Marconi's message crossed the Atlantic Ocean by bouncing off the upper atmosphere.

This speculation, a more sophisticated version of something Stewart [678] had suggested twenty years earlier, was independently published some months later by Heaviside and was eventually shown to be founded in fact by Appleton [1158].

In 1902 he was appointed professor of engineering at Harvard and remained there till his retirement in 1930.

[917] **WIECHERT,** Emil (vee'khert)
German seismologist
Born: Tilsit, East Prussia (now Sovetsk, USSR), December 26, 1861
Died: Göttingen, March 19, 1928

Wiechert, the son of a merchant, studied physics at Königsberg University, graduated in 1889, and began lecturing there the following year. In 1897 he moved to Göttingen and established a department of geophysics.

At that time, earthquakes were being studied in detail at last, thanks to the work of John Milne [814], but the seismographs in use were rather primitive. In 1900 he produced an "inverted-pendulum" seismograph, which is essentially what has been used ever since. It was this seismograph that produced records sufficiently accurate to allow some idea of the detailed inner structure of the earth to be worked out. Wiechert suggested the presence of a dense core, for instance, something Beno Gutenberg [1133] was soon to demonstrate convincingly.

[918] **HILBERT,** David
German mathematician
Born: Königsberg, East Prussia (now Kaliningrad, USSR), January 23, 1862
Died: Göttingen, February 14, 1943

Throughout the nineteenth century, particularly after the discovery of non-Euclidean geometries by Lobachevski [484], Bolyai [530], and Riemann [670], mathematicians inspected Euclid's [40] system of axioms closely. It became more and more plain that Euclid did not really start with basic self-evident concepts and actually assumed a great many things in addition without specifically saying so.

Attempts were made to establish a minimum number of unidentified terms and basic definitions, and from these to deduce rigorously the entire structure of mathematics. This is the science of axiomatics, and it was Hilbert and Peano [889] who finally established it.

Hilbert, the son of a judge, obtained his Ph.D. at the University of Königsberg in 1885, and in 1899 he published a book *Foundations of Geometry* in which the first really satisfactory set of axioms for geometry was set forth. He began with points, lines, and planes as undefined concepts. Euclid had tried to define them, without, however, actually doing so. Euclid's definitions had only seemed satisfactory because his readers already had an intuitive knowledge of what it was he was trying to define.

Hilbert was content not to define them but merely to describe certain properties of these objects. Provided they possessed those properties, the formal definition did not matter. He also used certain relationships as "between," "parallel," and "continuous" without defining them. Again, provided the consequences of using those words were clearly set forth, it didn't matter what they actually meant. Hilbert also proved his system of axioms to be self-consistent, something the Greeks had assumed concerning the Euclidean axioms (and correctly) but had not formally proved.

Thus, Euclid's work was finally completed. It was not changed in essence, but its foundation was shifted from intuition to logic.

Hilbert's system of axioms is not the only one possible, but that does not matter. Axioms are no longer considered self-evident truths, but merely self-consistent starting points from which a mathematical structure can be developed. This structure is independent of "reality" (whatever that is), but to be useful it must have some analogy to what seems to us to be the "real world."

Hilbert became professor of mathematics at Göttingen in 1895 and held the post till his retirement in 1930.

In 1925, he fell ill with pernicious anemia, then thought to be incurable. At just that time, however, Minot [1103] was working out the appropriate treatment and Hilbert had eighteen more years of life.

[919] **GULLSTRAND,** Allvar
(gul'strand)
Swedish physician
Born: Landskrona, Malmöhus, June 5, 1862
Died: Uppsala, July 21, 1930

Gullstrand, the son of a physician, studied at Uppsala, Vienna, and Stockholm and received his license to practice medicine in 1888.

He was an ophthalmologist, who studied the physics of the eye in the greatest detail, carrying matters far beyond Helmholtz [631]. His studies on astigmatism, for instance, made it possible to design corrections more efficiently. He designed lenses to improve the vision of eyes from which lenses had been removed because of cataract. He also designed devices for locating foreign bodies in the eye.

For his work on the eye, he received the 1911 Nobel Prize for medicine and physiology.

[920] **LENARD,** Philipp Eduard Anton von (lay'nahrt)
Hungarian-German physicist
Born: Pozsony,   Austria-Hungary (now Bratislava, Czechoslovakia), June 7, 1862
Died: Messelhausen, Baden-Württemberg, May 20, 1947

Lenard, the son of a wealthy winemaker, studied under Bunsen [565] and Helmholtz [631], obtaining his doctor's degree *summa cum laude* at the University of Heidelberg in 1886. After filling a variety of posts including that of assistant to H. R. Hertz [873] in 1893, he returned to Heidelberg in 1907 as professor of theoretical physics, a position he held until his retirement in 1931.

When he was a teenager, Lenard read a paper by Crookes [695] on the subject and became interested in cathode rays, the radiation emitted from the negative electrode in a vacuum, under the influence of a high electric potential. Hertz had discovered that cathode rays could penetrate thin layers of metal and Lenard, who was then his assistant, devised a cathode-ray tube in 1892 with a thin aluminum window through which the cathode rays could emerge into the open air. (Such open-air cathode rays were called Lenard rays for a time.) Lenard studied the properties of these rays carefully, measuring their absorption by different materials, and how they ionized air, making it electrically conducting. For these investigations he received the 1905 Nobel Prize in physics.

Beginning in 1902 he studied the photoelectric effect, work which also dates back to Hertz, the first to observe it. Lenard showed that the electrical effects produced by light falling upon certain metals was the result of the emission by those metals of electrons. The emission of electrons by way of the photoelectric effect, more than anything else, persuaded scientists that atoms contained electrons as part of their structure. Furthermore, since all substances showing the effect gave off identical electrons, it seemed that different atoms might have very similar internal structures.

He also showed that only certain wavelengths of light could bring about electron emission and that, for any particular wavelength, electrons of fixed energies were given off. Increasing the intensity of the light would increase the number of electrons but not their individual energy. His explanations for this were the first to assume that an atom was largely empty space, an assumption that was to be definitely established a few years later by Ernest Rutherford [996]. Lenard believed that electrons and analogous positively charged particles were evenly distributed through the atom. He did not foresee the nuclear atom which Rutherford was to make famous.

It was Einstein [1064] who, in 1905, explained the photoelectric effect, neatly and finally, by the application of the quantum theory of Planck [887].

During World War I, Lenard was caught up in a supernationalism that afflicted a number of scientists at the time, but it was something from which he, unlike many others, never recovered. In fact, it grew only the more extreme and paranoid with Germany's defeat.

Lenard was openly anti-Semitic and wholeheartedly supported the Nazi doctrines, one of only two important scientists (the other being Stark [1024]) to do so. He heatedly denounced "Jewish science," forgetting his debt to Hertz, who was of Jewish descent. He also denounced Einstein and the theory of relativity on purely racial grounds, for he advanced no scientific arguments of merit. His own lack of mathematical ability turned Lenard the more bitterly against the great mathematical theories of relativity and quantum mechanics.

He knew Hitler personally and coached him on the racial interpretation of physics. Most nuclear theory was pictured by Lenard as mere Jewish perversion of science. This helped encourage Hitler to ignore that facet of scientific advance, so that Germany did not develop the nuclear bomb despite its initial lead in the field.

Lenard lived to see the bomb exploded after Nazi Germany had been smashed and Hitler had committed suicide. He may have regretted his own stupidity in the light of events, or he may have been altogether too stupid to do so.

[921] NEF, John Ulric
Swiss-American chemist
Born: Herisau, Switzerland, June 14, 1862
Died: Carmel, California, August 13, 1915

Nef's father, foreman of a textile mill, went to America in 1864 to investigate the possibilities of establishing a mill and remained, bringing his family in 1868. Nef was therefore educated in America, graduating from Harvard with honors in 1884. He did his graduate work in Germany under Baeyer [718], obtaining his doctorate in 1886.

In 1892 he was appointed professor of chemistry at the then new University of Chicago, after having taught at Purdue and at Clark University. He helped transfer the German university traditions in organic chemistry to the United States. He spent considerable time working on the chemistry of isocyanides and fulminates, substances containing rather unusual combinations of carbon and nitrogen atoms. This led him to a consideration of a point of disagreement between Kekulé [680] and Couper [686] on methods of writing the structural formula of organic compounds. Kekulé had held out firmly for a fixity of valence. He felt carbon always had a valence of four. Couper had maintained that it might sometimes have a valence of two.

Nef's studies of his own compounds made it possible for him to demonstrate conclusively that Couper was right. This broadening of the Kekulé system by no means damaged it, but, rather, increased its flexibility and usefulness.

Like Couper, Nef suffered a nervous

breakdown while still comparatively young, though in his case, the illness was not permanently incapacitating.

[922] BRAGG, Sir William Henry
English physicist
Born: Wigton, Cumberland, July 2, 1862
Died: London, March 12, 1942

Bragg, the son of a master mariner turned farmer, was left motherless at seven. He lived with two uncles and worked in a grocery store. He was educated at King William's College on the Isle of Man and there grew interested in mathematics. In 1882 he entered Cambridge, on a scholarship, finishing third in his class in mathematics and passing on to the study of physics under Lord Rayleigh [760] and J. J. Thomson [869]. In 1885 he was offered a professorship at Adelaide University in Australia and accepted it, remaining down under until 1908.

The turning point in his life came in 1903 when he gave a presidential address before the Australasian Association for the Advancement of Science. He chose to lecture on the recent discoveries in radioactivity and atomic structure by A. H. Becquerel [834], the Curies [897, 965], and others and, in so doing, succeeded in interesting himself so profoundly in the subject that he decided to enter the field of radioactive research.

Bragg began by showing, from theoretical considerations, that alpha particles produced by radioactive atoms ought to have a definite energy and therefore a definite range; that is, they ought to travel a definite distance through air or other material before being absorbed. In 1904, making use of some radium, Bragg measured the range of alpha particles emitted and found that there were several ranges, sharply delineated. This lent color to Ernest Rutherford's [996] theories that radioactive elements broke down in stages and that intermediate atoms would produce their own sets of alpha particles. The different ranges observed by Bragg clearly represented alpha particles produced by different intermediates in the radioactive series. This alone was enough to make Bragg's name prominent in the field.

Returning to England in 1909 Bragg accepted a professorship in physics at the University of Leeds, and in 1915 he transferred to University College in London. While at Leeds he heard of the work of Laue [1068] on the diffraction of X rays by crystals and was immediately interested. Bragg's son, William Lawrence Bragg [1141], was a student at Cambridge at the time, and it was he who took the initiative in this direction. Together, they worked out methods for determining the wavelengths of X rays by crystal diffraction, and together they shared the 1915 Nobel Prize in physics (the year after it had been awarded to Laue). The Braggs are the only father-son combination ever to have been honored in this fashion.

Bragg was another of the first-rank scientists who wrote entertainingly about science for the general reader, as in *Concerning the Nature of Things* published in 1925.

During World War I, Bragg headed a research group that invented the hydrophone for the detection of submarines. He was knighted in 1920; later, he succeeded James Dewar [759] as director of the Royal Institution of Great Britain; and in 1935 he was elected president of the Royal Society. During World War II he was appointed chairman of Great Britain's scientific food committee, but did not live to see victory.

[923] **BOVERI,** Theodor (boh-vay′ree)
German cytologist
Born: Bamberg, Bavaria, October 12, 1862
Died: Würzburg, Bavaria, October 15, 1915

Boveri, the son of a physician, studied at the University of Munich and received his Ph.D. *summa cum laude* in 1885. In 1893 he became professor of zoology at the University of Würzburg and remained there, by and large, the rest of his life. He was rather prone to illness and died comparatively young.

His most important work lay with chromosomes, which, as a result of careful investigations, he showed did not form at the time of cell division and then disappear. From the work of Beneden [782], it seemed that sperm and ovum contributed equal amounts of chromosomes to the developing organism, and if they were the storehouses of genetic characteristics they must represent continuing entities, and this Boveri showed to be so. He held, in fact, that the chromosomes were almost sub-cells that maintained an existence independently of the cells, something that seems to be so. He also maintained and produced evidence for the belief that chromosomes did not carry inherited factors generally but that particular chromosomes carried particular facets of inheritance.

He also studied the detail of cell division very carefully and discovered and named the "centrosome," the small structure that seems to orchestrate the process of cell division.

[924] **VERNADSKY,** Vladimir Ivanovich
Russian geochemist
Born: St. Petersburg (now Leningrad), March 12, 1863
Died: Moscow, January 6, 1945

Vernadsky, the son of a professor, studied at the University of St. Petersburg, where he attended the lectures of Mendeléev [705]. In 1897 he gained his Ph.D. and the next year obtained a professorial appointment at Moscow University.

Vernadsky was interested in the overall chemical composition of the earth's crust and is considered the father of modern geochemistry, though that word itself was coined as long before as 1838 by Schönbein [510].

Vernadsky worked in great detail on the structure and chemistry of silicates and aluminosilicates, which make up a major portion of the crust. He studied the manner in which molecules migrated under the influence of geologic processes, and he was the first to recognize that radioactivity released enough heat over the eons to be a powerful driving force in geochemical change. He also was the first to recognize the great contribution made by life processes to geological development—to the nature of the atmosphere, for instance.

[925] **HÉROULT**, Paul Louis Toussaint
(ay-roo′)
French metallurgist
Born: Thury-Harcourt, Calvados, April 10, 1863
Died: off the coast of Antibes, May 9, 1914

Héroult, the son of a tanner, read of Sainte-Claire Deville's [603] work on aluminum while he was still a student. Héroult studied under Le Châtelier [812] who had himself studied under Sainte-Claire Deville. Héroult's own discovery of the electrolytic method of producing aluminum in April 1886 resulted in the development of Europe's aluminum industry, as C. M. Hall's [933] identical process developed America's.

There is an odd coincidence in the fact that Hall and Héroult (both names begin with an H) were united, after a fashion, throughout life. Héroult was born eight months before Hall and died almost eight months before him. Both made themselves famous by discovering the identical process in the same year when both were twenty-three.

It meant prolonged patent litigation, of course, but a more or less amicable agreement was eventually reached.

[926] **LOVE**, Augustus Edward Hough
English geophysicist
Born: Weston-super-Mare, Somersetshire, April 17, 1863
Died: Oxford, June 5, 1940

Love, the son of a surgeon, was educated at Cambridge and became professor of natural philosophy at Oxford in 1899.

In mathematics he was interested in elasticity, the way materials deformed and regained their shape as pressure

upon them changed. It was easy to progress from this to a consideration of how earthquakes set up waves in the body of the earth. The nature and the properties of these waves had been analyzed by Rayleigh [760] in 1885, but Love showed that this earlier theory was insufficient. Love showed an additional type of "Love waves" (as they are now called) could be set up along Earth's surface.

The analysis of the behavior of Love waves made it possible to estimate the thickness of the earth's crust in different places in the earth and yielded the first evidence that the crust was considerably thicker under the continents than under the ocean.

[927] **WOLF**, Maximilian Franz Joseph Cornelius
German astronomer
Born: Heidelberg, June 21, 1863
Died: Heidelberg, October 3, 1932

Wolf, the son of a wealthy physician, obtained his Ph.D. in 1888 at Heidelberg. After two years in Stockholm, he returned to Heidelberg and became a member of the faculty in 1890. He had the advantage of a private observatory that his father had financed. He extended Schwabe's [466] data on the sunspot cycle by gathering all the observations he could find on the subject from the time of Galileo [166]. The cycle was confirmed but was shown to be rather irregular.

His best-known achievement, however, was that of adapting the technique of photography to the wholesale discovery of asteroids. The first asteroid had been discovered by Piazzi [341] a century before, and thereafter they had been picked out one by one by visual observation, so that a man who discovered half a dozen asteroids was most unusual. In 1891, however, Wolf demonstrated how one could take a photograph of a large region of the sky with the telescope following the stars exactly so that their images appeared as points. The asteroids, moving independently, would then appear as short streaks.

His first discovery was Brucia (asteroid 323), and over the space of a generation, Wolf discovered five hundred more asteroids in this way, a third of all those now known to exist.

He discovered Achilles (asteroid 588) in 1906. It was the first of the "Trojan asteroids," a group that travels in Jupiter's orbit, in step with that mighty planet, in such a way that Jupiter, the sun, and the asteroids form an equilateral triangle, a formation shown to be gravitationally stable by Lagrange [317] in 1772, but one that had never before been seen.

Also, as Barnard [883] was simultaneously doing in America, Wolf studied the light and dark nebulae of the Milky Way. He discovered the North American nebula, for instance (so-called because as viewed from the earth it vaguely resembles North America in shape). He was, in addition, the first to detect Halley's comet on its 1909–1910 return to the vicinity of the earth.

[928] **WALDEN,** Paul (vahl'den)
Russian-German chemist
Born: Rosenbeck, Wenden, Latvia, July 26, 1863
Died: Gammertingen, near Siegmaringen, Germany, January 24, 1957

Walden, the son of a farmer, was orphaned as a child. He put himself through school by working as a tutor. He studied and taught at the universities of Riga and St. Petersburg in the Russian empire, but after the Russian Revolution he left the country for Germany. He taught at the University of Rostock from 1919 to 1934.

His most important discovery came in 1895, while he was still teaching at Riga. He found that he could take malic acid, which rotated polarized light in clockwise fashion, and cause it to undergo a change, which he could then undo so as to obtain his malic acid back again. Now, however, the malic acid rotated polarized light in the counterclockwise fashion. Somewhere in the course of

the series of reactions, the compound had been turned inside out, or "inverted." The process has been known as the Walden inversion ever since.

Studies of the Walden inversion have led to important understanding of reaction mechanisms. In such studies it is not only the end products of a chemical reaction that are investigated but also the intermediate stages whereby those products are obtained. Knowledge of these stages has greatly sharpened the tools of the twentieth-century organic chemist.

In later life, he grew interested in the history of chemistry, publishing an important book on the subject in 1947.

[929] **FORD,** Henry
American industrialist
Born: Greenfield Village, Michigan, July 30, 1863
Died: Dearborn, Michigan, April 7, 1947

A farmboy in his youth, Ford, the son of Irish immigrants, early showed no interest in farm work except for what could be performed by machine. He moved to Detroit in 1887, became a machinist's apprentice at sixteen and was for a time chief engineer for an electric light company. He had little education but much drive.

He built his first automobile in 1893. It was a two-cylinder job he drove for a thousand miles and then sold for two hundred dollars. He founded a company for the manufacture of cars of his own design in 1899. The production of standardized parts had been introduced a century earlier by Whitney [386], and in 1908 Ford conceived the notion of bringing the parts to the men rather than vice versa. His "assembly line" began with parts and ended with automobiles, each man along the line standing still and performing a single task.

He placed the automobile within the reach of the average man's wallet and revolutionized the American way of life; more than that, he gave a new push to the Industrial Revolution. His mass production methods were imitated in other industries and in other nations. Even in the Soviet Union, later on, where capitalism was an enemy, the technological methods of capitalism were welcomed, and Ford was almost a hero.

He was inconsistent in many ways. Vaguely pacifist, he was a great producer of war goods. Incredibly shrewd in business, he was naïve to the point of stupidity in intellectual matters. In his social views, he was reactionary, bitterly opposing labor unions and rather admiring Hitler, with whose anti-Semitism he was in sympathy.

[930] **KIPPING,** Frederic Stanley
English chemist
Born: Manchester, August 16, 1863
Died: Criccieth, Caernarvonshire (now Gwynedd), Wales, May 1, 1949

Kipping, the son of a bank official, graduated from the University of London in 1882 and obtained a minor government post as chemist. Upon a friend's advice he decided to go to Germany for graduate instruction and worked under Baeyer [718], whom, however, he claimed he practically never saw. He obtained his Ph.D. *summa cum laude* in 1887. In 1894 he wrote virtually the first textbook restricted to organic chemistry. In 1897 he was elected to the Royal Society and made professor of chemistry at University College in Nottingham.

In 1899 he began the research for which he is best known and which he was to continue for forty years. This was in connection with the organic derivatives of silicon. His interest arose out of his search for stereoisomerism, of the type first explained in connection with the carbon atom by Van't Hoff [829] and Le Bel [787], in atoms other than carbon. (Stereoisomerism was fascinating organic chemists of the time and its study by men such as Walden [928] was yielding exciting results.)

Kipping and Pope [991] had presented evidence of stereoisomerism for nitrogen and other atoms and now Kipping was

on the trail of silicon. Kipping had the advantage of being able to use the new and very versatile type of reaction discovered by Grignard [993] at just about this time and could therefore synthesize a variety of organic compounds containing one or more silicon atoms in their molecule. He published fifty-one papers all told on the subject, the last during the early days of World War II.

In World War II and afterward, the "silicones" grew important as greases, hydraulic fluids, synthetic rubbers, water repellents, and so on. These silicones were substances with complicated molecules containing long chains of silicon atoms alternating with oxygen atoms, with organic groupings attached to each silicon atom. Knowledge concerning them arose out of Kipping's researches.

This is an example of how the organic chemistry of compounds containing elements not usually found in naturally occurring compounds can turn out to be useful to man as well as interesting to chemists. The investigations of Stock [1043] into organic compounds containing boron is another example.

[931] **BAEKELAND,** Leo Hendrik
(bake′land)
Belgian-American chemist
Born: Gent, Belgium, November 14, 1863
Died: Beacon, New York, February 23, 1944

Baekeland, always at the head of his class, graduated from high school at sixteen and like Arrhenius [894] was the youngest and brightest. He attended the University of Gent on a scholarship. He graduated in 1882 and by 1884, when he was still only twenty-one, he had his doctor's degree *maxima cum laude*. His first professorial appointment came in 1887 at the University of Bruges.

About that time he won a three-year traveling fellowship and in 1889 arrived in the United States where, thanks to his hobby of photography, he was at once offered a good job and remained thereafter. By 1891 he had opened an office as an independent consultant and invented a type of photographic paper that could be developed under artificial light.

It was the first commercially successful photographic paper and he sold it to Eastman-Kodak for a million dollars. (Baekeland had planned to ask $50,000 and to go down to $25,000 if necessary, but fortunately for him Eastman [852] spoke first.)

After a short visit to Germany in 1900 Baekeland plunged into a project to evolve a synthetic substitute for shellac in the laboratory he had built in his home in Yonkers, New York. For the purpose he began to investigate those organic reactions that produced gummy, tarlike insoluble residues that ruined glassware and seemed to have no other use. It was Baekeland's intention to form such a residue by reacting phenol and formaldehyde, then find a solvent that would dissolve it. That solution would then be his shellac substitute. He formed the residue easily enough but could find no solvent.

Suddenly it occurred to him to look at matters backward. If the residue was hard and resistant to solvents, couldn't that be a useful combination of properties in itself? He began to concentrate on forming the resinous mass more efficiently and making it still harder and tougher. By using the proper heat and pressure, he obtained a liquid that solidified and took the shape of the container it was in. Once solid, it was hard, water-resistant, solvent-resistant, and an electrical insulator. Moreover, it could be cut with a knife and easily machined.

He waited for several years while he continued to experiment and in 1909 he announced the existence of the substance he named Bakelite after himself. It was not the first plastic; Hyatt [728] and his celluloid deserve that credit. However, Bakelite was the first of the "thermosetting plastics" (one that once set would not soften under heat) and is still one of the most useful a half century later. It was Bakelite that sparked the modern development of plastics.

In 1924 Baekeland served as president of the American Chemical Society.

[932] **CANNON,** Annie Jump
American astronomer
Born: Dover, Delaware, December 11, 1863
Died: Cambridge, Massachusetts, April 13, 1941

Cannon was the daughter of a state senator. She was educated at Wellesley College, graduating in 1884, then returned in 1894 for additional instruction in astronomy. She went on to study it still further at Radcliffe, perhaps at the suggestion of E. C. Pickering [784]. In 1896 she joined the staff at Harvard Observatory and remained there the rest of her life.

She was particularly interested in the task of classifying the large numbers of stellar spectra that had been photographed, and developed a classification system that Harvard used ever since. She showed that with very few exceptions the spectra could be arranged into a continuous series. Her work formed the basis of the *Henry Draper* [723] *Catalogue,* which eventually came to contain the spectral classification of 225,300 stars brighter than ninth or tenth magnitude.

[933] **HALL,** Charles Martin
American chemist
Born: Thompson, Ohio, December 6, 1863
Died: Daytona Beach, Florida, December 27, 1914

Hall, the son of a minister, was educated at Oberlin, from which he graduated in 1885. He, like Perkin [734], was intensely interested in chemistry as a youngster and, again like Perkin, was stimulated by a chance remark of his teacher into making the great discovery of his life. Hall's teacher stated that anyone discovering a cheap way of making aluminum would grow rich and famous. Hall took him at his word, made the discovery, and grew rich and famous.

Aluminum, a very common constituent of the earth's crust, in metallic form is light, strong, and a good conductor of electricity. It has any number of possible uses, but the one trouble was that for over half a century after its discovery there seemed no way of isolating it from its compounds in a cheap and practical way. The closest approach had been that of Sainte-Claire Deville [603] in 1855 and even then aluminum remained a semiprecious metal. Napoleon III of France had his cutlery and his baby's rattle made out of aluminum, and the top of the Washington Monument (which was dedicated in 1885) is a slab of the then expensive metal.

In 1886 Hall, at twenty-two, went to work in his home lab (as Perkin had done a generation earlier) and, using homemade batteries, devised a method of making aluminum by electrolysis after the fashion of Davy [421] and did it only eight months after graduation from college. The key discovery was that of dissolving an aluminum oxide in a molten mineral called cryolite and using carbon electrodes. That same year, working independently, Héroult [925], in France, devised the same method. It is therefore usually called the Hall-Héroult process.

On February 23, 1886, Hall was able to show his teacher the little globules of aluminum he had formed. These globules are still reverently preserved by the Aluminum Company of America, for, indeed, the Hall-Héroult process was the foundation of the huge aluminum industry of today. Within seven years, the price of aluminum dropped from $5 a pound to 70¢ a pound. By 1914 it was down to 18¢ a pound.

Aluminum now is second only to steel (which, thanks to Hadfield [892], developed astonishing new properties of its own) as a construction metal, and where lightness is important, it is first. It is difficult to see how practical aircraft could ever have been developed without a plentiful supply of cheap aluminum. Its uses are numberless, from canoes to house siding to paint to power lines to storm windows. Goldschmidt [909] even managed to use it in a high-temperature device.

In 1911 Hall, very appropriately, received the Perkin medal.

On his death he left no less than five million dollars to his old alma mater, Oberlin.

[934] **WIEN**, Wilhelm (veen)
German physicist
Born: Gaffken, East Prussia (now Primorsk, USSR), January 13, 1864
Died: Munich, Bavaria, August 30, 1928

Wien was the son of a landowner, and though this placed him in a position to afford a good education, it did introduce difficulties, for between 1886 and 1890 he had to interrupt his studies to run the family estate during the sickness of his father. He had the good fortune in his student years to work as assistant to Helmholtz [631], under whom he obtained his Ph.D. in 1886.

In the 1890s Wien began to work with the problem of radiation. A generation earlier Kirchhoff [648] had worked out his theory that hot bodies radiate those wavelengths that they absorb when cold. It followed, then, that a body that absorbed all wavelengths and was therefore perfectly black (a "black body") would radiate all wavelengths when heated. Naturally, as Prévost [356] had pointed out a century before, the amount of radiation rose with temperature. About fifteen years earlier Stefan [715] had used thermodynamics to show exactly how the amount rose.

Wien was interested in the nature as well as the amount of the radiation. He and his colleagues experimented with the practical equivalent of a black body, an enclosed, heated chamber with a small hole in it. Any light of whatever wavelength entering the hole was not reflected but was absorbed within, so out of the hole should stream black-body radiation of all wavelengths.

Through observation of the nature of the radiation emitted and through thermodynamic reasoning, Wien in 1893 showed that the wavelengths of the radiation emitted reach a peak at some intermediate level. The wavelength at this peak varies inversely with temperature. Therefore, as temperature rises, the predominant color shifts toward the blue end of the spectrum. Moderately hot bodies radiate chiefly in the infrared, to which we are visually insensitive, but as the temperature rises, the peak shifts toward the visible red and the heated body begins to glow. As temperature continues to rise, the glow is first a dull red, then a bright red, then yellow-white and finally blue-white. Extremely hot stars radiate mostly in the ultraviolet to which again we are visually insensitive, and superhot objects such as the sun's corona actually radiate in the X-ray region. This shift of peak wavelength with temperature is called Wien's displacement law.

Wien also tried to evolve an equation that would describe the distribution of all wavelengths in black-body radiation for all temperatures, and not just for the peak wavelength. He had to juggle matters a bit but worked out an equation that would fit the observed distribution of the short wavelength (high-frequency) radiation. It would not, however, fit the long wavelength (low-frequency) radiation. On the other hand Rayleigh [760] evolved an equation that fit the long wavelengths and not the short. It was as a result of these shortcomings that Planck [887] was lured at the end of the decade into devising the quantum theory, which placed the entire matter of energy and, indeed, of physics generally, in a new and better light.

Wien then grew interested in X rays and cathode rays, which in the second half of the 1890s were setting the world of physics by its ears and were inaugurating the Second Scientific Revolution. Although his work here was good (he deflected Goldstein's [811] canal rays with a magnet, for instance, and showed them to be positively charged), he was outclassed by others.

In 1900 he succeeded Roentgen [774] at the University of Würzburg and in 1920 succeeded him again at the University of Munich.

In 1911, for his work on black-body radiaton, he received the Nobel Prize in physics.

[935] **MINKOWSKI,** Hermann (ming-kuf'skee)
Russian-German mathematician
Born: Alexotas, Russia, June 22, 1864
Died: Göttingen, Germany, January 12, 1909

Minkowski was born of German parents who returned to Germany in 1872. He earned his Ph.D. at the University of Königsberg in 1885. He taught there for a few years, then went to the University of Zürich, and finally to Göttingen.

When Einstein's [1064] special theory of relativity was first published in 1905, Minkowski was extraordinarily interested. (Einstein had been one of his pupils.) Einstein's paper made it clear that ordinary three-dimensional geometry was not adequate to describe the universe, but it was Minkowski who placed a formal geometric interpretation upon relativity.

He showed in a book, *Time and Space*, published in 1907, that relativity made it necessary to take time into account as a kind of fourth dimension (treated, mathematically, somewhat differently from the three spatial dimensions). Neither space nor time has existence separately, in his view, so that the universe consists of a fused "space-time."

Einstein adopted this notion and went on to develop it to still greater heights in his general theory of relativity nine years later, but by then Minkowski was dead, unfortunately.

[936] **NERNST,** Hermann Walther
German physical chemist
Born: Briesen, West Prussia (now Wabrzezno, Poland), June 25, 1864
Died: Bad Muskau, near Berlin, November 18, 1941

Nernst, the son of a judge, was born only twenty miles from the birthplace of Copernicus [127]. He obtained his doctor's degree *summa cum laude* at the University of Würzburg in 1887 and then, in 1890, became an assistant to Ostwald [840].

He made his first important mark on physical chemistry as a young man of twenty-five when in 1889 he applied the principles of thermodynamics to the electric cell. For the first time since Volta [337] had invented it nearly a century earlier, someone was able to give a reasonable explanation for the electric potential it produced. He evolved a simple equation, commonly called the Nernst equation, relating the potential to various properties of the cell. Nernst's explanation has been replaced by other and better ones but his equation is still useful.

In 1891 he became professor of physical chemistry at Göttingen, and got to work on a new textbook of theoretical chemistry, one that made full use of the thermodynamic notions of men like Ostwald. It was published in 1893.

In that year he also advanced an explanation for the ready ionization of compounds in water, a problem that had puzzled the men who objected to Arrhenius' [894] theories a decade before. Nernst pointed out that water has a high dielectric constant, that it is an electric insulator, in other words. It is difficult for positively charged ions and negatively charged ions to attract each other through the insulating water molecules. They no longer hold each other as tightly as they do in the original pure compound and "fall apart" on solution in water. The separated ions could now carry an electric current. In a solvent of lower dielectric constant, the ions would cling together and there would be neither ionization nor the ability to carry an electric current. J. J. Thomson [869] independently suggested the same idea, which is therefore called the Nernst-Thomson rule.

Nernst became professor of physical chemistry at the University of Berlin in 1905 and a year later announced his most important discovery, usually referred to as the third law of thermodynamics: Entropy change approaches zero at a temperature of absolute zero. From this is deduced the impossibility of attaining absolute zero. One can get as close as patience, expense, and the excellence of equipment and scientific ingenuity permit (and temperatures of only a millionth of a degree above absolute zero have been attained), but the actual temperature bottom can not be touched.

For this Nernst was awarded the 1920 Nobel Prize in chemistry.

Nernst's third law was put into its simplest form by Planck [887] in 1911. Lewis [1037] went on to show that the law could be strictly true only for substances in a crystalline state and this was demonstrated experimentally by Giauque [1178].

Nernst, in 1918, explained how hydrogen and chlorine explode on exposure to light. Light energy, he pointed out, broke the chlorine molecule into two chlorine atoms. The chlorine atom (much more reactive than the molecule) reacted with the hydrogen molecule to form hydrogen chloride and a hydrogen atom. The hydrogen atom reacted with a chlorine molecule to form hydrogen chloride and a hydrogen atom and so on. The reaction could continue for ten thousand to a million steps on the initial molecular break through light. Light, in this way, sets up a "chain reaction." Chain reactions proved useful in explaining many forms of reactions, such as those producing polymers (long-chain molecules). Chain reactions of a completely different sort were eventually found by Hahn [1063] and others to produce nuclear explosions far more devastating than any ordinary chemical explosion could be.

Nernst was also an inventor of sorts but certainly not of the first rank. His most famous invention was a lamp made of ceramic, which could be made to heat to incandescence with a comparatively weak current. However, it had disadvantages and was no competitor at all to Edison's [788] light, but to Edison's astonishment he nevertheless sold the patent for a million marks. (Edison firmly believed all professors were impractical dreamers but Nernst certainly was not.) Nernst also invented an electric piano, which was never heard of again.

He maintained an inventor's attitude toward science, too. He announced that in his opinion Roentgen [774] ought to have patented the X ray he had discovered and made money out of it (which certainly never occurred to Roentgen).

Nernst served his country in World War I and both his sons died in action in that war. Nevertheless, he spent his last years in official disfavor, since two of his daughters had married Jews—which was a considerable crime in the time of Hitler.

[937] **CARVER,** George Washington
American agricultural chemist
Born: near Diamond Grove, Missouri, 1864
Died: Tuskegee, Alabama, January 5, 1943

The exact date of Carver's birth is not known, for he was a black, born at a time and in a place where blacks were still enslaved and were chattels rather than men. Vital statistics were not considered important in their case. The young infant was technically a slave until the passage of the Thirteenth Amendment to the Constitution outlawed slavery in the United States in 1865.

When he was only a few months old, he and his mother were stolen by raiders (slave rustlers) and carried off into Arkansas. The mother was lost forever, but the owner, Moses Carver, was able to get back the baby by trading a three-hundred-dollar racehorse for him. The Carvers adopted him after the law of the land freed him and the child bore his foster father's last name for the rest of his life.

The Carvers tried to get an education for the obviously intelligent youngster, but that was difficult. An elementary education was eked out, at a black school in another town, and when it came time for college, young Carver had to travel north. He was accepted at Simpson College at Indianola, Iowa, in 1889, and was the first black ever to attend that college. He did well, and after graduation, attended Iowa State Agricultural College from which he graduated at the head of his class. In 1892 he earned a master's degree and joined the staff of the school.

But a higher duty called. At Tuskegee, Alabama, the Tuskegee Institute, a black

college, had been founded by Booker T. Washington, and Carver was invited to join the faculty at a salary of $1500 per year, plus room and board—all the school could afford. In 1896 he accepted the call and returned to the South in order to help blacks obtain the higher education there which he himself had been unable to find. To do this, he refused more lucrative offers elsewhere.

He became director of Tuskegee's Department of Agricultural Research, and slowly, with the help of his students, he built up a laboratory out of virtually nothing and rebuilt the played-out land by using muck from nearby swamps and from compost heaps.

It was his mission to do the same all over the South. The traditional crops of the region, cotton and tobacco, had robbed the soil of its minerals and the Southern farmer was in a never-ending cycle of debt and fruitless labor. Carver carried on a campaign, in the end successful, to plant peanuts and sweet potatoes in order to enrich the soil.

Then, to take care of the surplus of peanuts and sweet potatoes, Carver devoted himself to the development of side products. He became a chemical Burbank [799], developing not new plant varieties, but new plant products. From peanuts alone, he developed some three hundred types of synthetic material, including everything from dyes and soap to milk and cheese substitutes. From sweet potatoes came 118 by-products. All his work was given freely to the world and he made no attempt to amass any personal profit.

He continued to regard his work at Tuskegee as of prime importance in bettering the lot of the black and refused flattering offers to join Edison [788] or Ford [929], where he might have grown considerably wealthier and—since he would then be in the North—live somewhat more comfortably. He also refused an offer to go to the Soviet Union as consultant to their cotton industry.

All in all, the South profited enormously from the labor of this black born a slave. In 1939 he was awarded the Roosevelt medal, with a citation reading: "To a scientist humbly seeking the guidance of God and a liberator to men of the white race as well as the black." In 1953, ten years after his death, the plantation on which he was born was made a national monument.

Perhaps his greatest contribution was the clear demonstration provided by his life story of the fact that it is tremendously worth while to educate human beings of any race.

[938] **CORRENS,** Karl Franz Joseph Erich (kawr′ens)
German botanist
Born: Munich, September 19, 1864
Died: Berlin, February 14, 1933

Correns, the son of an artist, married a niece of Nägeli [598] under whom he had studied. Like De Vries [792], he was engaged in a line of research which by 1900 had led him to the independent elucidation of the laws of genetics, then discovered Mendel's [638] earlier work and published his own merely as confirmation.

By the fact of having been anticipated, Correns lost his chance at fame. He served the last two decades of his life, however, as director of the Kaiser Wilhelm Institute for Biology in Berlin, so he did not go entirely without recognition.

Correns was honest enough, furthermore, to publish the correspondence between Mendel and Nägeli, which revealed the shortsightedness of his uncle-in-law. Correns' own unpublished manuscripts were preserved at his institute until they and it were destroyed in the bombing of Berlin in 1945.

[939] **IVANOVSKY,** Dmitri Iosifovich (ee-van-uf′skee)
Russian botanist
Born: Gdov, November 9, 1864
Died: USSR, June 20, 1920

Ivanovsky, the son of a landowner, studied at the University of St. Petersburg, where Mendeléev [705] was one of his teachers, and graduated in 1888. From the start he was interested in tobacco mosaic disease, an infection that damaged the valuable tobacco crop, and the most obvious symptom of which was the mosaic pattern that formed on the leaves of the affected plants.

In 1892 he mashed up infected leaves and forced them through a very fine filter designed to remove all bacteria. He found that the liquid that passed through the filter could still infect healthy plants. He thus had the proof in hand that there was a pathogenic agent smaller than bacteria—an agent that was later to be named a "virus." However, Ivanovsky suspected that there was something wrong with his filters and did not draw the necessary conclusion, leaving it to Beijerinck [817] a few years later to repeat the experiment, accept the conclusion, and receive the credit for the discovery of viruses.

[940] **HARTMANN,** Johannes Franz
German astronomer
Born: Erfurt, Saxony, January 11, 1865
Died: Göttingen, September 13, 1936

Hartmann, the son of a merchant, obtained his Ph.D. at the University of Leipzig in 1891. In 1896 he moved on to the observatory at Potsdam, and there he did the work for which he is best known. In 1904 he studied the spectrum of delta-Orionis and found that although there was a radial shift involving most of its lines, there were calcium lines in their accustomed place, indicating that the calcium at least was stationary with respect to Earth. Since it was unlikely that the entire star was moving and leaving its calcium behind, Hartmann came to the conclusion that there was interstellar matter in the form of dust or gas that included calcium, and that over the vast distances between the star and Earth this gas and dust absorbed enough light to produce detectable dark lines. This was the first indication of the existence of interstellar matter.

[941] **PASCHEN,** Louis Carl Heinrich
Friedrich (pahsh'en)
German physicist
Born: Schwerin, Mecklenburg,
January 22, 1865
Died: Potsdam, February 25, 1947

Paschen was born into a family of military tradition, but he chose an academic life. He studied at the University of Strasbourg under Kundt [744] and received his Ph.D. in 1888, then went on to serve as Hittorf's [649] last assistant. He joined the faculty of the Physical Institute of the Technische Hochschule at Hannover in 1893.

Paschen's chief field of interest was spectroscopy, and in 1895 he carefully studied the spectrum of helium, newly discovered by Ramsay [832], and showed that it was indeed identical with the solar helium discovered by Janssen [647] and Lockyer [719]. In 1908 he discovered a new Paschen series of lines in the hydrogen spectrum.

Paschen was probably the most skillful experimental spectroscopist of his time and he carefully produced the results that bore out the theories of Zeeman [945] and Sommerfeld [976].

He was not a German nationalist, however, and had stuck to his research during World War I, for instance, making no effort to involve himself in war work. Once the Nazis, under Hitler, came to power in 1933, this made it possible for the super-Nazi Stark [1024] to oust Paschen from the presidency of a scientific association and take it over himself. Paschen, forced into retirement, survived World War II and, though he lost his home and possessions in a bombing raid in 1943, lived to see the destruction of the Nazi regime.

[942] **WEISS,** Pierre (wise)
French physicist
Born: Mulhouse, Haut-Rhin,
March 25, 1865
Died: Lyon, October 24, 1940

Weiss, the son of a haberdasher, was born in the province of Alsace, which was annexed by Germany following the Franco-Prussian War. The family remained in Alsace and Weiss was educated in German and Swiss schools but, at the age of twenty-one, decided he wanted to be a Frenchman. After graduating at the top of his class from the Zürich Polytechnikum in 1887, he went to Paris for further education.

His interest was chiefly in magnetism, and in 1907 he worked out an explanation for ferromagnetism. All atoms are made up of charged particles and magnetic properties always accompany electric charge. However, only iron and a few related metals show strong ferromagnetic properties (from *ferrum,* the Latin word for "iron") as opposed to weak paramagnetic properties. Weiss advanced the notion of unusually strong coupling of individual atomic magnets which caused them all to point in the same direction, forming "domains" of cumulative magnetic intensity. Iron consists of these domains, which can point in various directions, but if forced by some external magnetic field to line up in a single direction the metal becomes an overall magnet.

In 1919, when Alsace was returned to France, Weiss established a physics institute at Strasbourg that became a leading center of magnetic research. He retired in 1936 but lived long enough to see German troops in Alsace again in World War II. He fled to Lyon and died there not long after the French surrender brought the nation to its humiliating nadir.

[943] **ZSIGMONDY,** Richard Adolf
(zhig'mun-dee)
Austro-German chemist
Born: Vienna, Austria, April 1,
1865
Died: Göttingen, Germany, September 23, 1929

Zsigmondy, the son of a dentist, earned his Ph.D. in organic chemistry at the University of Munich in 1890. In his postdoctorate years, however, when he worked with Kundt [744], he grew interested in the colors produced by organic solutions of gold, when these were applied to porcelain. This roused his interest in colloid chemistry, a science Graham [547] had founded a generation before.

From 1897 to 1900 he was employed at the Jena glassworks, where he was particularly interested in colloidal gold (gold that was broken up into such fine particles by one means or another that it did not settle out but remained in suspension in water or other solvent, forming deeply colored red or purple liquids). He also produced several types of colored glasses, including a white variety called milk glass that became very popular.

It is the frustration of the colloid chemist that the particles making up the colloid are too small to be seen in an ordinary microscope. Improvements in design are useless because the limitation lies in the nature of light itself. Objects smaller than the wavelengths of visible light (and this includes the colloidal particles) cannot be made out no matter how perfect the microscope lenses are.

However, colloidal particles are large enough to show the Tyndall [626] effect, that is, to scatter light. It occurred to Zsigmondy that this could be taken advantage of. If light was shone through a colloidal solution and if a microscope was adjusted at right angles to the beam of light, then only the scattered light would enter the microscope. Even if the colloidal particles could not be seen in detail, they could at least be made out as points of light that could be counted, and the movements of which could be studied. From this the size of the individual particles and even something about their shape could be deduced.

At the time, most chemists disagreed with Zsigmondy's theory about colloid structure. He was sure an ultramicroscope would prove his point. In 1900, therefore, he quit the glassworks and joined with a physicist to produce such a device. By 1902 the instrument was developed. Zsigmondy used it on colloidal gold preparations and at once it was quite clear that his theories were wrong. He had succeeded in neatly proving the theories of his opponents.

In 1908 he received a professorial appointment at the University of Göttingen and there built up an excellent center for colloidal research. In 1925, in recognition for his work on colloids, he was awarded the Nobel Prize in chemistry.

Zsigmondy's ultramicroscope is still of great importance in colloid studies, but in most fields of research where great magnification is required, it has been outdistanced by the electron microscope devised by Zworykin [1134] a generation later.

[944] **STEINMETZ,** Charles Proteus
(*originally* Karl August)
German-American electrical engineer
Born: Breslau, Germany (now Wrocław, Poland), April 9, 1865
Died: Schenectady, New York, October 26, 1923

A hunchback from birth (a congenital defect from which Steinmetz's father and grandfather also suffered), Steinmetz led a lonely, solitary life, lit only by the flame of his genius and the gentleness of his soul. This loneliness was, in part, deliberate, for he never considered marriage, the reason being his reluctance to pass on his deformity to another generation.

Yet if he could have passed his mentality on as well, it might have been worth it to the world if not to his children. Already in high school his work was such that his proud father, a bookbinder by trade, bound his papers. He might have gone on to a scientific career that would have reflected glory on his nation, but in his youth he was openly a socialist and in conflict, therefore, with the authorities. The fact of his Jewish origin did not make matters easier for him either. He was placed under police surveillance in 1887 and in 1889, shortly before he was to obtain his Ph.D., he fled first to Switzerland and then to the United States; it was Germany's loss and America's gain.

When he took out his American citizenship papers he changed his German first name Karl to the American Charles, adding the middle name Proteus (a Greek demigod with an infinitely changeable body) to indicate the change in name and nationality.

In 1893 the small factory for which he worked was absorbed by the General Electric Company in Schenectady, where he remained for the rest of his life, universally recognized as one of America's foremost electrical geniuses. His eccentricities became famous. "No smoking, no Steinmetz," he growled, when gently informed that smoking was absolutely forbidden on the laboratory grounds. He stayed—and smoked—but smoking remained absolutely forbidden for everyone else.

He loved to work on intricate problems while drifting lazily in a canoe. His softheartedness was also famous. He sat shivering through the winter once rather than disturb a family of mice in the heating equipment.

His greatest achievement was to work out (while still in his twenties) in complete mathematical detail the intricacies of alternating current circuitry, using complex numbers (involving the famous square root of minus one), thus making use of Wallis's [198] two-century-old concept. It was this that made it possible to design alternating current (a.c.) equipment most efficiently. His textbooks slowly spread his theories among the electrical engineering profession and completed the victory of a.c. over direct current (d.c.) that had been begun by Tesla [867]. In addition to this towering work of theory, he is credited with over two hundred patents for inventions in every phase of electrical engineering. He remained a socialist and toward the end of his life ran (unsuccessfully) for state office on the Socialist ticket. He also carried his socialist principles to the almost-unheard-of extreme of refusing more than a modest salary.

The importance of his theoretical work was beyond the grasp of anyone but specialists. However, he also built generators capable of producing electricity at extremely high potential. The study of discharges so produced was of consid-erable importance and it was this "man-made lightning" that made Steinmetz's name most impressive to the layman.

[945] ZEEMAN, Pieter (zay'mahn)
Dutch physicist
Born: Zonnemaire, Zeeland, May 25, 1865
Died: Amsterdam, October 9, 1943

At Leiden University, Zeeman, the son of a Lutheran minister, studied under Kamerlingh Onnes [843] and Lorentz [839]. He gained his Ph.D. in 1893.

Under Lorentz's direction he performed the experiments which showed that a source of light in an intense magnetic field possessed spectral lines that were split into three components. This Zeeman effect (which Faraday [474] had sought and failed to find) confirmed Lorentz's suggestion that the atom consisted of charged particles whose oscillations could be affected by a magnetic field.

The nature of the effect could be used to deduce details concerning the fine structure of the atom and also to deduce other details concerning the magnetic fields of stars. A small thing like a single line becoming a triplet could thus at once enlighten the microcosm and macrocosm.

The initial announcement of Zeeman's discovery attracted little attention, however, till Kelvin [652] publicly noted its importance. He gained a professorial post at the University of Amsterdam in 1900, and in 1902 Zeeman shared the Nobel Prize in physics with his teacher, Lorentz.

[946] NAGAOKA, Hantaro
Japanese physicist
Born: Nagasaki, August 15, 1865
Died: Tokyo, December 11, 1950

Nagaoka graduated from the University of Tokyo in 1887 and then went on for further training to Germany and

Austria-Hungary, after having obtained his Ph.D.

He was interested in atomic structure. It had already been discovered that atoms contained negatively charged electrons and J. J. Thomson [869] had suggested that the atom was a sphere of positively charged matter on the surface of which electrons were placed. Nagaoka rejected this view and felt there was a positively charged object at the center of the atom and that the electrons circled it as planets circled the sun, or as its rings circled Saturn.

This Saturnian model was advanced in 1904 and it showed remarkable prescience. Within two years, Ernest Rutherford [996] showed that there was indeed a central positively charged nucleus in the atom. The notion of electronic satellites, however, was too simple. Once Bohr [1101] applied quantum mechanical considerations to the atom, electrons were found to behave far differently from tiny "planets."

[947] **HARDEN**, Sir Arthur
English biochemist
Born: Manchester, Lancashire, October 12, 1865
Died: Bourne End, Buckinghamshire, June 17, 1940

Harden, the son of a businessman, did his undergraduate work at Owens College in Manchester but went to Germany for further education, obtaining his doctor's degree at the University of Erlangen in 1888. He spent ten years teaching at Owens College and engaged in the writing of textbooks. The turning point of his life came when he grew furiously interested in Buchner's [903] discovery that alcoholic fermentation could be made to proceed without the presence of living cells.

In 1897 he joined the Jenner Institute of Preventive Medicine and began research into alcoholic fermentation. In 1904 he placed an extract of yeast inside a bag made of a semipermeable membrane and placed that bag in pure water. In this way small molecules in the extract pass through the membrane and are gone while large molecules cannot pass through the membrane and remain behind. The process is called dialysis and the technique stems back to the days of Graham [547].

Harden found that when he did this, the activity of the yeast enzyme was lost; it no longer fermented sugar. However, if he added the water outside the dialyzing bag to the material within, activity was restored. The yeast enzyme, it seemed, consisted of two parts, one small-molecular in nature, the other large-molecular.

If the material within the bag was boiled, then activity was lost even if the outer water was added. The large portion of the molecule was therefore, in all probability, protein. The small molecule survived boiling and was, in all probability, not protein. The latter was the first example of a "coenzyme," a small molecule not protein in nature, which is necessary to the working of an enzyme, itself a protein.

The chemical nature of the coenzyme was studied by Euler-Chelpin [1011], among others, and it became clear that the vitamins, whose discovery begins with Eijkman [888], are necessary to life only because they formed portions of coenzymes. Since enzymes, being catalysts, are needed only in small quantities, coenzymes and, therefore, vitamins are also needed in only small quantities. This explains why a substance may be essential to life and yet be necessary only in traces. The same rationale accounts for the fact that minerals like copper, cobalt, manganese, and molybdenum are necessary in traces. They too form part of coenzymes.

Harden noticed another interesting thing. Yeast extract breaks down glucose and produces carbon dioxide quite rapidly at first, but as time goes on the level of activity drops off. The natural assumption is that the enzyme breaks down with time. In 1905, however, Harden showed that this could not be so. If he added inorganic phosphate to the solution, the enzyme went back to work as hard as ever. This was a strange finding, for neither the sugar being fermented, nor the alcohol and carbon dioxide produced, nor the enzyme itself contained phosphorus.

Since the inorganic phosphate disappeared, Harden searched for some organic phosphate formed from it and located it in the form of a sugar molecule to which two phosphate groups had become attached. In the course of fermentation it was formed and then after many other reactions had taken place, the phosphate groups were removed again.

This was the beginning of the study of intermediary metabolism, the search for the numerous compounds formed as intermediates (sometimes very briefly lived ones) in the course of the chemical reactions going on in living tissue. It is now one of the liveliest and most important branches of biochemistry.

Furthermore, Harden's work led the way to the gradual realization by biochemists that phosphate groups play an essential role in every phase of biochemistry. This culminated, a generation later, in the work of the Coris [1192, 1194], who finally worked out the fine details of fermentation, and in the development of the concept of the high-energy phosphate bond by Lipmann [1221].

In 1912, Harden became professor of biochemistry at the University of London. For his work in fermentation he shared the 1929 Nobel Prize in chemistry with Euler-Chelpin. In 1936 Harden was knighted.

[948] **LEISHMAN,** Sir William Boog (leesh'man)
Scottish physician
Born: Glasgow, November 6, 1865
Died: London, England, June 2, 1926

Leishman, the son of a professor, graduated from the University of Glasgow in 1886 and then went into army service, finally reaching the rank of lieutenant-general in 1923. He was shipped overseas to India where he remained

from 1890 to 1897 and where he had ample opportunity to study tropical diseases.

In particular, he grew interested in one called kala-azar and in 1900 detected the disease agent, which turned out to be a protozoon. The disease is now sometimes called leishmaniasis. In 1903 he became professor of pathology at the Army Medical School and during the following decade he developed a vaccine against typhoid fever that was used during World War I and was credited with reducing the incidence of the disease. He was knighted in 1909.

[949] **PLASKETT,** John Stanley
Canadian astronomer
Born: Hickson, Ontario, November 17, 1865
Died: Esquimalt, British Columbia, October 17, 1941

Plaskett, the son of a farmer, was a high school dropout. In 1889 he was a mechanic in the department of physics at the University of Toronto and began to take undergraduate courses and graduated in 1899.

In 1903 Plaskett joined the staff of the new Dominion Observatory in Ottawa, and with his background in mechanics he was able to get the most out of the instruments. He pushed the Canadian Parliament ceaselessly for funds to build a 72-inch reflecting telescope, to be built according to his own design, and he finally had his way.

Using it, after it was put into action in 1918, Plaskett discovered in 1922 that a star which had been thought to be single was actually a binary with each member of the binary unusually massive. Known as Plaskett's twins, for half a century they remained the most massive known stars.

He also noted spectral lines of calcium that did not partake of the usual shift in the stellar spectra and that were the stronger the more distant the star. He maintained, independently of Hartmann [940], that this calcium arose from interstellar matter, and as it turned out he was correct.

[950] **GOMBERG**, Moses
Russian-American chemist
Born: Elizavetgrad (now Kirovograd), Ukraine, February 8, 1866
Died: Ann Arbor, Michigan, February 12, 1947

In 1884 Gomberg and his family were forced to leave Russia, for his father had been accused of anti-tsarist activity. Russia was, in any case, not a comfortable land for members of the Jewish faith in those days.

The family settled in Chicago and young Gomberg, whose high school education had been interrupted, completed it in the new land, then went on to the University of Michigan where he obtained his Ph.D. in 1894.

He traveled to Germany for postdoctorate research, working in Baeyer's [718] institute in Munich and under Viktor Meyer [796] at Heidelberg. Under Meyer he decided to try to prepare tetraphenylmethane, a compound in which four rings of carbon atoms are all attached to a single central carbon atom. Meyer himself had tried to hang all this weight upon a single carbon atom and had failed. He suggested that Gomberg try something else, but the young man had his mind made up and succeeded. He prepared tetraphenylmethane; not much, to be sure, but enough to study.

When he returned to the University of Michigan, he took the next step, which was to prepare hexaphenylethane, in which six rings of carbon atoms are attached to two adjoining carbon atoms in the center, three rings to each carbon atom. Here he failed. He did, however, obtain a compound that was very reactive and that was strongly colored in solution. (Hexaphenylethane, it was quite certain, would, when prepared, be colorless and quite unreactive.)

Gomberg was astonished and in 1900 was forced to conclude that he had half molecules, a single carbon atom with three rings attached, which he called triphenylmethyl. Carbon has four valences, according to the Kekulé [680] scheme of structure, and since in triphenylmethyl only three valences of the central carbon atom are in use, the

608

fourth must hang loose, so to speak. A molecule with such an unfilled valence bond is called a free radical and Gomberg had isolated the first example of this sort of substance.

This was by all odds the crowning achievement of his life (although later on he also developed the first satisfactory antifreeze for automobile radiators). As the twentieth century progressed, it dawned on chemists that free radicals are extremely important in chemical reactions. Most of them are far more fugitive than Gomberg's triphenylmethyl, but the manner in which they are formed and destroyed helps determine the nature of the reaction. One of the virtues of Pauling's [1236] theory of resonance, advanced a generation after Gomberg's discovery, was that it could explain just why triphenylmethyl should be so unusually stable for a free radical, so stable that it could actually be isolated in solution and last long enough to be studied.

In 1927 Gomberg was made head of the department of chemistry at Michigan and he remained in that position until his retirement in 1936.

Gomberg never married and would not allow his graduate students to marry until after they had obtained their degree.

[951] **WASSERMAN**, August von
(vahs'er-mahn)
German bacteriologist
Born: Bamberg, Bavaria, February 21, 1866
Died: Berlin, March 16, 1925

Wasserman, the son of a banker, obtained his medical degree at the University of Strasbourg in 1888 and for a time worked under Koch [767]. His research in immunology reached a climax in 1906, when he developed a diagnostic test for syphilis that is still known as the Wasserman test. This is based on Bordet's [986] discovery of complement fixation.

The subject's serum is allowed to react with certain antigens and if the antibody to the syphilis microorganism (discovered the year before by Schaudinn

[997]) is present the reaction takes place and complement is used up. The key portion of the test is then to test for the presence of complement. Its absence is indicative of syphilis; its presence means that it was not used up and therefore no syphilis, or its antibody, was present.

In 1913 Wasserman was appointed director of the Kaiser Wilhelm Institute in Berlin-Dahlem.

[952] **LEBEDEV**, Pyotr Nicolaievich
(lay'beh-dev)
Russian physicist
Born: Moscow, March 8, 1866
Died: Moscow, April 1, 1912

Lebedev, the son of a merchant, was unable to enter a Russian university, so he obtained his graduate training in Germany under Kundt [744] and Helmholtz [631], obtaining his doctor's degree in 1891. After returning to Russia he was appointed professor of physics at the University of Moscow in 1892 but resigned in 1911 in protest against tsarist oppression of education.

He was interested in the possibility that light might exert pressures. This had been predicted by Maxwell's [692] equations and it was a possible explanation, for instance, of the fact that comets' tails always pointed generally away from the sun whether the comet was approaching the sun or receding. In 1901, using very light mirrors in a vacuum, Lebedev was actually able to observe and measure the pressure exerted by light, again confirming Maxwell's theories, as well as providing a vehicle for Arrhenius' [894] life spores.

[953] **MILLER**, Dayton Clarence
American physicist
Born: Strongsville, Ohio, March 13, 1866
Died: Cleveland, Ohio, February 22, 1941

Miller, the son of a shopkeeper, graduated from Baldwin-Wallace College, obtained his Ph.D. at Princeton University in 1890, and was appointed professor of physics at the Case School (now Case Western Reserve University) in Cleveland, where he remained till his death. Michelson [835] and Morley [730] had conducted their famous experiment on the speed of light the decade before and Miller worked with Morley to check the results under even more delicate conditions. This work, carried out from 1902 to 1904, confirmed the Michelson-Morley results.

However, Miller was unwilling to accept Einstein's [1064] theories that arose out of the experiment and continued to search for some positive evidence of "ether-drift," which would make relativity invalid. In 1921 he thought he had it but that turned out to be a false alarm.

He obtained more positive results inventing a photodeik in 1912, a device whereby the oscillations of sound waves were visualized when they were made to cause vibrations in a mirror that in turn induced vibrations in a spot of reflected light. By this means he was able to study musical sounds in detail and, in effect, to make musicology a science.

[954] **STARLING**, Ernest Henry
English physiologist
Born: London, April 17, 1866
Died: at sea near Kingston, Jamaica, May 2, 1927

Starling, the son of a lawyer, obtained his medical degree in 1890 and in 1900 became professor of physiology at University College in London. In the 1890s he did important work on the functioning of the heart and on the interrelationship of the blood and lymph. In 1912 he published a standard text on physiology.

His most memorable work, however, turned out to have its chief influence in biochemistry. With Bayliss [902] he was studying in 1902 how the pancreas began to secrete its digestive juice as soon as the acid food contents of the stomach entered the intestine. According to Pavlov [802] this was nerve controlled. However, when Starling and Bayliss cut the nerves to the pancreas, it still performed on cue. They discovered that the lining of the small intestine secreted a substance (which they named secretin) under the influence of stomach acid, and it was this secretin that stimulated the pancreatic flow. Eventually Starling suggested a name for all substances discharged into the blood by a particular organ for the purpose of rousing some other organ or organs to activity. This was "hormone," from Greek words meaning to "rouse to activity."

Some years before, Takamine [855] had isolated the first pure substance that eventually was to be recognized as a hormone. The way was open to recognition of the fact that hormone malfunction was a cause of disease. Two decades later, Banting [1152] was to show how this new knowledge could be used to great advantage in medicine.

During World War I, Starling worked on defenses against poison gas, and then served as scientific adviser to the Ministry of Food.

[955] **LAZEAR,** Jesse William (luh-zeer´)
American physician
Born: Baltimore County, Maryland, May 2, 1866
Died: Quemados, near Havana, Cuba, September 25, 1900

Lazear graduated from Johns Hopkins University in 1889 and went on to earn his medical degree at Columbia University in 1892. He joined the staff of Johns Hopkins and studied the malarial parasite. In 1900 he was named acting assistant surgeon in the United States Army and was sent to Cuba with Reed [822]. When the group turned from their vain attempt to find a bacterial agent and began to study mosquitoes, Lazear was put in charge of the insects.

He did not intend to experiment on himself as his fellow investigator, Carroll [849], had done, but when a mosquito lit on his arm, he allowed it to bite him and was dead of yellow fever within a week. Lazear is the classic case of the medical martyr.

[956] **NICOLLE,** Charles Jules Henri (nee-kole´)
French physician
Born: Rouen, Seine-Marne, September 21, 1866
Died: Tunis, Tunisia, February 28, 1936

Nicolle was the son of a physician and he followed in his father's footsteps, obtaining his medical degree in 1893 and then joining the faculty of the medical school in Rouen where his father was a professor. He had taken a course in microbiology at the Pasteur Institute during his education and in that direction lay his important work, though he also tried his hand at novel writing.

In 1902 he was appointed director of the Pasteur Institute in Tunis and it was there, in a colonial area (as was true of so many physicians around the turn of the century, Reed [822] and Leishman [948], for example), that he had a particularly good opportunity to study a certain disease. In this case, it was typhus fever, which Ricketts [992] was to study in the western hemisphere with tragic results.

In Tunis, Nicolle noticed an interesting thing. Typhus was very contagious outside the hospital, spreading on contact. Doctors visiting patients caught it; hospital employees who admitted the patients caught it. However, once the patient was actually in the hospital and under observation, typhus was no longer contagious. Nicolle decided that the crucial point was at the entrance into the hospital, when the patient was stripped of his clothes and scrubbed down with soap and water. Whatever transmitted the disease was in the clothes, then, and was removed from the body by washing. His suspicion fell on the body louse.

He began to work with animals, first chimpanzees, then guinea pigs, and proved the case. As mosquitoes transmitted malaria and yellow fever, so the louse transmitted typhus. Unfortunately it is not as easy to get rid of a tiny body parasite as it is to get rid of the free-flying insect, and typhus remained a great killer in World War I. It was Müller [1216] and his discovery of DDT that turned the trick and just about wiped out typhus among World War II troops.

Nicolle also demonstrated that animals might sometimes carry a disease in mild form, displaying virtually no symptoms yet remaining infective. This explained how diseases remained in existence between epidemics. It was there all the time, and the epidemic was merely the result of a periodic increase in virulence. The reason for such changes in virulence came when men like Beadle [1270] extended the De Vries [792] concept of mutation to microorganisms.

[957] **MORGAN**, Thomas Hunt
American geneticist
Born: Lexington, Kentucky, September 25, 1866
Died: Pasadena, California, December 4, 1945

Morgan, the nephew of a Confederate general and a descendant, through his mother, of Francis Scott Key (who wrote the words to "The Star-Spangled Banner"), graduated from what is now the University of Kentucky in 1886 and obtained his Ph.D. from Johns Hopkins University in 1890. A year later he joined the faculty of Bryn Mawr College, where he came under the influence of Loeb [896]. In 1904 he became professor of experimental zoology at Columbia University.

During his decade at Bryn Mawr, genetics had come into being. Mendel's [638] work had been rediscovered by De Vries [792] and at once several people suggested that the chromosomes' behavior during cell division and egg formation just fit the behavior of the genetic factors according to Mendel. However, there were only some two dozen pairs of chromosomes in the human cell. Surely they could not account for the thousands of characteristics inherited by human children, unless each chromosome contained large numbers of different factors. The separate factors were called genes, from a Greek word meaning "to give birth to."

But since Flemming's [762] work, a

quarter century earlier, made it clear that chromosomes were inherited as units, the characteristics controlled by the genes on each chromosome should be inherited together and not independently. (Mendel had discovered that characteristics *were* inherited independently, but he had dealt with only seven characteristics and each of these, by a stroke of coincidence, had been controlled by genes on separate chromosomes.)

The problem, now, was to check this question of "gene-linkage" experimentally. In 1907 Morgan, who had at first doubted the validity of Mendel's theories, made the necessary advance, the discovery and utilization of a new biological tool. He began work with a tiny insect called Drosophila, the fruit fly. It was a small insect, capable of being bred in large numbers with virtually no trouble; it multiplied like wildfire and its cells possessed only four pairs of chromosomes.

The problem of inheritance was thus reduced to simple terms, and by following the generations, Morgan discovered numerous cases of mutations (which demonstrated De Vries's theory in the animal kingdom as well as in the plant kingdom) and showed that various characteristics were indeed linked, that is, inherited together, as though the genes involved occurred on the same chromosome.

And yet linked characteristics were not eternally linked. Every once in a while each was inherited separately. This was correlated with the fact that pairs of chromosomes occasionally switched portions ("crossing over") so that the integrity of an individual chromosome was not absolute.

These experiments definitely established the chromosomes as carriers of heredity and strongly backed the gene concept. It was even possible to locate the spot on the chromosome at which a particular gene might exist. The greater the length of chromosome separating two genes, the greater the likelihood that crossing over at a random spot would separate the two. By studying the frequency with which two particular linked characteristics were unlinked, the relative positions of the genes could be established. By 1911 the first chromosome maps for fruit flies were being drawn up.

Morgan published a book, *The Theory of the Gene*, in 1926, which may be considered as establishing, extending, and completing the Mendelian scheme as far as the eye and the microscope could carry it. H. J. Muller [1145], one of Morgan's pupils, was to apply another tool, that of the X ray, to the study, but the major advance beyond Morgan had to wait for a quarter of a century and the establishment of molecular biology, through the work of men like Crick [1406] and James Watson [1480]. Morgan was president of the National Academy of Sciences from 1927 to 1931.

For his work Morgan received the 1933 Nobel Prize in medicine and physiology. He also gained another and most peculiar kind of renown. In the Soviet Union, in the days when the notions of Lysenko [1214] were paramount in Soviet biology, Morganism became virtually a dirty word.

[958] **FESSENDEN,** Reginald Aubrey
Canadian-American physicist
Born: Milton, Quebec, October 6, 1866
Died: Hamilton, Bermuda, July 22, 1932

Fessenden, the son of a minister, worked as chief chemist for Edison [788] during the 1880s, then, from 1890 to 1892, for Edison's great rival Westinghouse [785]. Although almost unknown in comparison with Edison or many other nineteenth-century inventors, Fessenden is actually second only to Edison in the number and variety of patents he obtained, holding five hundred by the time of his death.

His most remarkable invention was that of the modulation of radio waves. Radio waves themselves could be sent out in pulses to imitate the dots and dashes of the Morse code. However, it occurred to Fessenden to send out a continuous signal with the amplitude of the waves varied (or "modulated") to make

that variation follow the irregularities of sound waves. At the receiving station, these variations could be sorted out and reconverted into sound.

On December 24, 1906, the first such message was sent out from the Massachusetts coast and wireless receivers could actually pick up music. In this way radio as we know it was born, although many inventions, notably the triode of De Forest [1017], were required before it came fully of age.

Like Armstrong [1143] after him, Fessenden was often engaged in litigation over his patents.

[959] **BROOM,** Robert
Scottish-South African paleontologist
Born: Paisley, Scotland, November 30, 1866
Died: Pretoria, South Africa, April 6, 1951

Broom, the son of a textile designer, attended the University of Glasgow, where he attended the lectures of Kelvin [652], and from which he obtained his medical degree in 1889.

His chief interest was in paleontology, however, and he collected fossils first in Australia and then in South Africa. He made his home in South Africa after 1897.

He was particularly interested in the problem of the mammalian line of descent, whether from reptiles or from amphibians, and if from reptiles, from which variety. In his researches he did much to straighten out the taxonomic relationships of the extinct reptiles.

He is best known for his work on early human evolution, however. He was one of the few paleontologists who accepted the discoveries of Dart [1162] as representing an ancient and early form of hominid, and set about searching for additional remnants of the so-called *Australopithecus* ("southern ape"). In 1936 he found one, an adult skeleton that seemed larger than Dart's find.

Broom accepted evolution but his early religious training forced him to find divine design in it and to find reasons for arguing that, with the development of the human species, evolution had come to an end. Humanity, in other words, represented the sixth and final day of creation, so to speak, and Genesis, if interpreted with sufficient latitude, was still correct. This view did not win over biologists, however.

[960] **WERNER, Alfred** (vehr'ner)
German-Swiss chemist
Born: Mulhouse, Haut-Rhin, December 12, 1866
Died: Zürich, Switzerland, November 15, 1919

Werner was the son of an ironworker. At the time of his birth, Alsace was French, but when he was four it became German as a result of the Franco-Prussian War. Werner died in the year it became French again as a result of World War I.

Werner, the son of a factory inspector, received a German education, though he (like his fellow-townsman, Weiss [942]) and his family remained strongly pro-French in their sympathies. At the age of twenty, after completing a year of service in the German army, Werner moved to Switzerland where he became a Swiss citizen and where he remained the rest of his life.

While he was still in Alsace he installed a home chemistry laboratory in his parents' barn and by eighteen had done creditable original work. He earned his Ph.D. at the University of Zürich in 1890, then did postdoctoral work with Berthelot [674] in Paris. His doctor's thesis dealt with the spatial arrangement of atoms about a central nitrogen atom. Like Kipping [930] and Pope [991] he was interested in extending the views of Van't Hoff [829] and Le Bel [787] to atoms other than carbon. Before he was through, he had surpassed even Pope, producing optically active compounds about such metals as cobalt, chromium, and rhodium.

Beginning in 1891 he developed a coordination theory of molecular structure, the idea of which, according to himself, came to him during his sleep,

waking him at 2 A.M. He rose at once, got to work, and by 5 A.M. the theory was worked out.

Essentially, the theory suggested that the structural relationships between atoms did not need to be restricted to ordinary valence bonds, either ionic as in Arrhenius's [894] concept of simple inorganic molecules, or covalent, as in the organic molecules so well represented by the Kekulé [680] system.

Instead, atoms or groups of atoms could be distributed about a central atom in accordance with fixed geometric principles and regardless of valence.

The coordination theory immensely broadened understanding of chemical structure and much could be explained by it that would have been quite mysterious otherwise. Coordination bonds are sometimes spoken of as secondary valence. Both ordinary and secondary valence were finally united into a single theory by men like Pauling [1236] a generation after Werner.

Werner was forced to work and teach under primitive conditions, in poorly lit basement rooms. Nevertheless, he attracted many students and was a most popular lecturer. As further proof of his worth, he was awarded the 1913 Nobel Prize in chemistry for his coordination theory.

[961] **WRIGHT, Wilbur**
American inventor
Born: Millville, Indiana, April 16, 1867
Died: Dayton, Ohio, May 30, 1912

Wilbur's life was bound up with his brother's [995]. Together they bicycled, glided, and built the airplane, though it was Wilbur who, of the two, was the driving force.

For several years after the first flight, the United States government could not have been less interested, and in 1908 Wilbur took the airplane to France. There his flights aroused tremendous enthusiasm. However, he died of typhoid fever in 1912, having lived to see airplanes begin to take hold of the public fancy, but having died too soon to see it come to be used as an instrument of death.

He was elected to the Hall of Fame for Great Americans in 1955.

[962] **FABRY,** Charles (fah-bree′)
French physicist
Born: Marseille, June 11, 1867
Died: Paris, December 11, 1945

Fabry studied at the École Polytechnique and received his doctorate in 1892. He lectured first at the University of Marseille and, in 1920, became professor of physics at the Sorbonne.

He specialized in optics and in the study of spectra. His most dramatic discovery came in 1913 when he was able to demonstrate the presence of ozone in the upper atmosphere. Although ozone is an excessively small component of the air it is very important. The ozone absorbs most of the ultraviolet radiation of the sun, screening earth's surface from its life-harming effect.

It would seem also that this ozone may have played an important role in the development of life. The original atmosphere of earth did not contain free oxygen, most geophysicists think, and the oxygen now present was first formed by the photosynthetic activity of green plants. As the oxygen formed, the ozone (an energetic form of oxygen) built up in the upper atmosphere, and screened off the ultraviolet. Till then, the energy of the ultraviolet had possibly formed organic molecules in the sea; afterward that process no longer took place and photosynthesis became the only important method for such formation.

[963] **DOUGLASS,** Andrew Ellicott
American astronomer
Born: Windsor, Vermont, July 5, 1867
Died: Tucson, Arizona, March 20, 1962

Douglass graduated from Trinity College (Hartford, Connecticut) in 1889. After college he worked first at Harvard,

then at Lowell Observatory in Arizona, joining in 1906 the faculty of the University of Arizona.

His interest in the sun led him to an interest in climate, and here he was offered a unique opportunity. Ancient wood is well preserved in Arizona's dry climate and it shows a pattern of tree rings, whose variations in width betoken successions of seasons wetter and drier than average. The pattern was quite distinctive, and as he began with living trees, then worked back to recently dead ones, then to older and older ones, he found he could work out a pattern covering many centuries. No sizable section of the pattern fitted any other and he found he could date any piece of wood from the region by noting where its small pattern fit into the larger overall pattern. He could then date the archaeological remnants in which the wood had been found. This system of dendrochronology, developed by 1920, was the first of many delicate methods of dating the near past accurately, culminating in Libby's [1342] carbon-14 method of a generation later.

[964] **PERRINE,** Charles Dillon (peh-rine′)
American-Argentinian astronomer
Born: Steubenville, Ohio, July 28, 1867
Died: Villa General Mitre, Argentina, July 21, 1951

Perrine was a businessman to begin with, but his skill at photography led him into astronomy, and in 1893 he joined the staff of the Lick Observatory.

Like a number of astronomers before him, he was a skilled comet-hunter, but the discoveries for which he was best known were two small satellites of Jupiter, the sixth and seventh, in orbits far outside the four large satellites discovered by Galileo [166] three centuries before. These satellites, first detected in 1904 and 1905, were the first of Jupiter's outer satellites (probably captured asteroids) to be discovered.

In 1909 Perrine was appointed director of the Argentine National Observatory at Córdoba, and he made his home in Argentina thereafter. In the 1930s he incurred the wrath of Argentinian rightists and by 1936 he was forced into retirement.

[965] **CURIE,** Marie Sklodowska (kyoo-ree')
Polish-French chemist
Born: Warsaw, Poland, November 7, 1867
Died: Haute Savoie, France, July 4, 1934

Marie Sklodowska's father was a physics teacher and her mother was the principal of a girls' school, so there seemed every reason for life to augur well for an intelligent girl. However, Poland was under Russian domination at the time and after the unsuccessful Polish revolt of 1863, the Russian fist clenched harder. Her mother died of tuberculosis in Marie's youth and her father lost his position.

Marie was unable to obtain any education past the high school level in repressed Poland. An older brother and sister had left for Paris in search of education and Marie worked to help meet their expenses and to save money for her own trip there, meanwhile teaching herself as best she could out of books. In 1891 her earnings had accumulated to the minimum necessary, and off she went to Paris where she entered the Sorbonne. She lived with the greatest frugality during this period (fainting with hunger in the classroom at one time), but when she graduated, it was at the top of the class.

In 1894 she met a French chemist, Pierre Curie [897], who had already made a name for himself by the discovery of piezoelectricity, that is, the manner in which an electric potential could be made to appear across certain crystals by the application of pressure. On July 25, 1895, they were married in a civil ceremony, for both were anticlerical in their views. Even such fripperies as wedding dresses and gold rings were absent. They invested instead in a pair of bicy-

cles which they used for transportation on their honeymoon trip.

The discovery of X rays by Roentgen [774] and of uranium radiations by A. H. Becquerel [834] galvanized Marie Curie into activity. It was she who named the process whereby uranium gave off rays "radioactivity." She studied the radiations given off by uranium and her reports coincided with those of Ernest Rutherford [996] and Becquerel in showing that there were three different kinds of rays, alpha, beta, and gamma.

Marie Curie then applied her husband's discovery of piezoelectricity to the measurement of radioactivity. The radioactive rays ionized the air and made it capable of conducting electricity. The more intense the radioactivity, the greater the current conducted. This current could be detected by a galvanometer and could be counteracted by the potential set up by a crystal under pressure. The amount of pressure required to just balance the current set up by the radioactive radiations gave a measure of the intensity of the radioactivity. By studying various uranium compounds in this manner, she showed that their radioactivity was in proportion to the amount of uranium they contained, thus narrowing the source of radiation to atoms of that element. In 1898 she showed that the heavy element thorium was also radioactive.

She had, meanwhile, made an interesting discovery in connection with uranium minerals, which she was investigating at Becquerel's suggestion. As measured by her piezoelectric method, some proved to be much more active than could be accounted for by any conceivable content of uranium. At once she decided the ores must contain elements that were more intensely radioactive than uranium. Since all the other elements known to occur in the minerals were also known to be nonradioactive, the excess radioactivity must be due to the presence of elements in quantity too small to be detected, and such elements must therefore be very radioactive indeed. At this point Pierre Curie abandoned his own research and joined his wife as a willing and admiring assistant, remaining so for the final seven years of his life. (In doing this he judged rightly, for though he was an excellent scientist, she was an outstanding one, and undoubtedly the greatest woman scientist who ever lived.)

By July of 1898 the two, working together, had isolated from uranium ore a small pinch of powder containing a new element hundreds of times as radioactive as uranium. This they called polonium after Madame Curie's native land. Nevertheless, polonium did not account for all the intense radioactivity of the ore by any means. Work went on.

In December 1898 they detected the still more radioactive substance and named it radium. However, the quantity was so small it could only be detected, as a trace impurity, by the nature of its radiations and by the spectral characteristics observed for them by Demarçay [825]. What the Curies wanted was to produce radium in visible, weighable quantities so that its extraordinary properties should not remain in dispute. For the purpose, large masses of ore were needed.

These existed. The mines at St. Joachimsthal in Bohemia (then part of Austria-Hungary, now part of Czechoslovakia) had been mined for centuries for their silver and other elements. Waste ore, rich in uranium, lay around in heaps. The Vienna Academy of Sciences lent its good offices and the mine owners were perfectly willing to let the two mad French scientists carry off all this worthless material, or as much as they wanted, without charge, provided only that they pay shipping costs. The Curies paid with their life savings and gladly.

At the physics school where the Curies worked there was an old wooden shed with a leaky roof, no floor, and very inadequate heat. The two obtained permission to work there and for four years (during which Marie Curie lost fifteen pounds) they carefully purified and repurified the tons of ore into smaller and smaller samples of more and more intensely radioactive material. All this time, they had to take care of their baby, Irène, who was destined to become a famous scientist in her own right as Irène Joliot-Curie [1204]. But Marie's burning determination kept the husband-and-wife team going in the face of mountainous difficulties. By 1902 they had succeeded in preparing a tenth of a gram of radium after several thousand crystallizations. Eventually, eight tons of pitchblende gave them a full gram of the salt. Despite their poverty and the obvious chance of wealth, the Curies were idealistic enough to refuse to patent the process.

In 1903 Marie Curie wrote her doctor's dissertation, a Homeric document indeed, and for it, she and Pierre shared the Nobel Prize in physics in that year with Becquerel. (The Curies were too ill at the time to make the trip to Stockholm.) Marie commented on the vast energies poured out continuously by a material such as radium, but the source of that energy remained a mystery until Einstein [1064] in 1905 told how mass could be converted into energy. In 1903 they visited London where they were greeted by the admiring Kelvin [652] and where Pierre gave a guest lecture at the Royal Institution, while Marie was the first woman to attend a session of the organization.

In 1906 Pierre was killed in a traffic accident (he was run over by a horse-drawn vehicle). Marie took over his professorship at the Sorbonne, the first woman ever to teach there (a remarkable thing in the notoriously conservative world of French science), taking up Pierre's lectures at the point where he had left them. Nevertheless, she could not transcend sex prejudice everywhere. When she was nominated for membership in the august French Academy, she lost by one vote—because she was a woman.

Her 1903 Nobel Prize in physics had been for her studies of radioactive radiations. In 1911, for her discovery of two new elements, she was awarded the Nobel Prize in chemistry and, with her husband dead, had to accept it alone. In later years, her daughter Irène and her son-in-law, Frédéric Joliot-Curie [1227], won Nobel Prizes, as did her neighbor and close friend Perrin [990]; a most unusual cluster indeed. (Her fame did not free her of her humanitarian obligations.

During World War I, she drove an ambulance.)

Her work on radioactivity and the dramatic discovery of radium put the finishing touches on the excitement that had begun with Roentgen's discovery of X rays, and the whole subject of radioactivity began to obsess physicists. Other radioactive elements were soon discovered by men like Dorn [795] and Boltwood [987], who followed the trail the brilliant Polish woman had blazed.

Her last decades were spent in the supervision of the Paris Institute of Radium. She had made no attempt to patent any part of the extraction process of radium and it remained in the glamorous forefront of the news for nearly a generation, thanks to its ability to stave off the inroads of cancer under the proper circumstances. But in the end Marie died of leukemia (a form of cancer of the leukocyte-forming cells of the body) caused by overexposure to radioactive radiation.

[966] **IPATIEFF,** Vladimir Nikolaevich (ih-pah'tyef)
Russian-American chemist
Born: Moscow, November 21, 1867
Died: Chicago, Illinois, November 29, 1952

Ipatieff, the son of an architect, was intended for a military career and was therefore sent to a military school, where the instruction in chemistry was rather poor. However, Ipatieff found his instruction in Mendeléev's [705] textbook. He became an officer in the Russian Army in 1887, and in 1889, as a result of a competitive examination, entered the Mikhail Artillery Academy, where he could continue his chemical education under better conditions. Later, he lectured in chemistry at the school.

In 1897 he was allowed to go to Germany, where he studied under Baeyer [718] in Munich, rooming with Gomberg [950] and Willstätter [1009]. Gomberg, who was Russian-born, could speak Russian, which was convenient indeed for Ipatieff. At Munich, the young Russian determined the structure of isoprene, a hydrocarbon that is the basic unit of the rubber molecule. This introduced him to hydrocarbons, which were to be the love of his life.

He went on to study explosives for a few months in France (after all, he was an artillery man) and in 1899 became a professor of chemistry and explosives at the Mikhail Artillery Academy. In 1900 he made his great discovery that organic reactions taking place at high temperatures could be influenced in their course by varying the nature of the substance with which they were in contact. Until then it had been believed that at high temperatures, organic molecules broke into pieces crazily and at random, but Ipatieff learned to direct them. Through the years he worked out the effect of different catalysts and the details of various reactions. Despite the lack of the formal academic prerequisites, his work earned him a Ph.D. at the University of St. Petersburg in 1908.

World War I and the Russian Revolution interrupted his work. He had held important administrative posts during the war, coordinating Russia's chemical industries. The revolutionaries naturally held him under suspicion as a result, but his talents were necessary to the country under any government. He continued to work for the Soviets, hoping to contribute to the rebuilding of Russia from the devastation of war and to aid its strenuous attempt at industrialization. Ipatieff was not, however, in sympathy with Communism and toward the end of the 1920s he began to fear for his safety. In 1930 he attended a chemical conference in Berlin and upon receiving an offer of a job in the United States decided not to return to the Soviet Union.

In Chicago, Illinois, he began the third phase of his life and once again proved successful. Working for the Universal Oil Product Company in Chicago, he applied his catalyzed high-temperature processes to the tailor-making of new hydrocarbon mixtures out of old.

This had become a matter of vital importance, for gasoline, a hydrocarbon mixture, was the power source of the automobile, which, thanks to Henry Ford

[929], was now a factor of prime importance on the social scene. For gasoline to work most efficiently in a motor, it must burn smoothly and evenly. Too rapid burning produced a damaging and wasteful "knock." Certain types of hydrocarbons were less subject to knock than others were, and the less knock a gasoline mixture gave rise to, the higher its "octane rating." Ipatieff showed how poor gasoline could be converted into good "high octane" gasoline. The only comparable victory in the battle against knock was that of Midgley [1132] and his tetraethyl lead.

Ipatieff's work was also important in the development of aviation gasoline for use in airplanes during World War II.

Ten days after his death (soon after his eighty-fifth birthday) his wife died too. They had been married sixty years.

Ipatieff had been expelled from the Soviet Academy of Sciences in 1931 as a traitor, but he was exonerated and posthumously reinstated in 1965.

[967] **SØRENSEN**, Søren Peter Lauritz
(sir'ren-sen)
Danish chemist
Born: Havrebjerg, near Slagelse, Zealand, January 9, 1868
Died: Copenhagen, February 12, 1939

Sørensen, the son of a farmer, obtained his Ph.D. at the University of Copenhagen in 1899, took a post with the Carlsberg Laboratory in Copenhagen, and remained there the rest of his life.

His chief claim to fame is his new way of looking at the concentration of the hydrogen ion. The hydrogen ion, smallest and nimblest of all ions, is always present in any system that contains water, which means it is present in almost all systems that concern the chemist and biochemist. Many reactions vary greatly in speed and even in nature, according to the concentration of the hydrogen ion present.

In 1909 Sørensen suggested that chemists deal with the negative logarithm of that concentration, and introduced the

expression pH for this. A chemist, instead of speaking of a hydrogen ion concentration of 10^{-7} moles per liter, would speak of a pH of 7. This alteration in view changed no facts, of course, but it simplified many mathematical and graphic representations and made it easier to grasp and understand numerous relationships in chemistry and biochemistry.

[968] **RICHARDS,** Theodore William
American chemist
Born: Germantown, Pennsylvania, January 31, 1868
Died: Cambridge, Massachusetts, April 2, 1928

Richards' father was a painter and his mother was a poet, and he himself inherited talents in both directions. In addition, he was interested in music and, of course, in science.

He was educated at Haverford where his first interest was astronomy but poor eyesight caused him to turn to chemistry instead. He graduated in 1885 at the head of his class, then went on to Harvard, where he received his doctor's degree in 1888. In his doctoral thesis he undertook to determine a more accurate value for the ratio of the atomic weight of oxygen to that of hydrogen, a problem also preoccupying Rayleigh [760] across the ocean. After obtaining his degree Richards continued his studies in Germany, studying under Viktor Meyer [796], Ostwald [840], and Nernst [936]. He was offered a professorship at Göttingen, but he returned to the United States in 1894 to take up a professorship in chemistry at Harvard.

His professional life was dedicated to determining with the greatest possible accuracy the atomic weights of the various elements. Over nearly three decades he and his students established the atomic weight of some sixty elements with an accuracy that seemed to represent the limit of what could be done with purely chemical methods. He surpassed even the achievements of Stas [579], lowering the atomic weight of silver, for instance, from Stas's value of 107.93 to the more nearly correct 107.88, and for his atomic weight determinations Richards received the Nobel Prize for chemistry in 1914.

His work brought the age of classical atomic weight determinations to an end, and marked the initiation of a new age as well. In 1913 he began the determination of the atomic weights of lead from different minerals and detected small but definite differences. This provided experimental verification of the predictions of Soddy [1052], who had, shortly before, advanced the theory of isotopes.

The existence of isotopes, thus established by Soddy's physical approach and Richards' chemical one, showed that ordinary atomic weights, though still a matter of importance for chemical calculations, were no longer fundamental physical data. Attention turned to the measurement of the mass of individual atomic species by electromagnetic methods. Atomic weights were more accurately determined in this fashion than they could possibly be by the older chemical methods and Richards' work paled in the face of the new era of atomic physics.

[969] **MILLIKAN,** Robert Andrews
American physicist
Born: Morrison, Illinois, March 22, 1868
Died: Pasadena, California, December 19, 1953

During his undergraduate years at Oberlin College, from which he graduated in 1891, after studying Greek, Millikan had only a mild interest in physics. After his graduation, however, he went through a change of heart. He taught physics at the school for a couple of years (for lack of any formally qualified teacher) while taking his master's degree and fell in love with the subject. He then obtained his doctorate in 1895 at Columbia University where he studied under Pupin [891]. He was the first Ph.D. in physics to come out of Columbia. (The United States was only then, belatedly, beginning to move forward in science education.) After postdoctoral work in Ger-

many under Planck [887] and Nernst [936], he obtained a professorial appointment at the University of Chicago in 1910, and there he worked with Michelson [835].

In 1906 Millikan set about his most famous work, the determination of the size of the electric charge on a single electron. To do this he followed the course of tiny electrically charged water droplets falling through air under the influence of gravity against the pull of a charged plate above. By 1911 he had switched to oil droplets to avoid the effect of evaporation.

Every once in a while such a droplet would attach to itself an ion which Millikan produced in the chamber by exposing it to X rays. With the ion added, the effect of the charged plate above was suddenly strengthened and the droplet would fall more slowly or, perhaps, even rise. The minimum change in motion Millikan felt to be due to the addition of a single electronic charge. By balancing the effects of the electromagnetic attraction upward and the gravitational attraction downward both before and after such an addition, Millikan was able to calculate the charge on the single electron. He also showed that the electric charge existed only as a whole number of units of that charge. It was the final proof of the particulate nature of electricity, a century after Faraday's [474] work had first pointed the way.

This very spectacular (and, once explained, engagingly simple) experiment earned for Millikan the Nobel Prize in physics in 1923. The award also mentioned the careful experimental work he performed to verify the equations deduced theoretically by Einstein [1064] in connection with the photoelectric effect. He also used this work to calculate the value of Planck's constant and got results that checked Planck's own calculations closely.

During World War I he served in the Army Signal Corps with the rank of lieutenant-colonel.

By 1921 Millikan had transferred to the California Institute of Technology, where he remained until his retirement and where he grew interested in the radiation that V. F. Hess [1088] had detected as arising from outer space. In 1925 Millikan named the radiation "cosmic rays," the name used ever since.

Millikan tested the intensity of the radiation in the upper atmosphere by plane and balloon, and below the surface, too, by sinking instruments to the bottom of lakes. This work was carried on with notable results by Millikan's pupil Anderson [1292].

For many years Millikan maintained that cosmic rays were a form of electromagnetic radiation like gamma rays, only more energetic. He believed also that cosmic rays originated in the outskirts of the universe where matter was being created. It was the "birth cry" of matter. Millikan was one of the relatively small number of scientists who actively fought to reconcile religion and science. He was the son of a Congregational minister and was deeply religious himself. Since his thought that matter was still being created had religious significance to him ("The Creator is still on the job," he said), he clung to it, and to the wave nature of cosmic rays, even when the evidence presented by Compton [1159] and others made it quite certain that cosmic rays were particulate in nature and were, for the most part, extremely energetic protons.

Although a conservative Republican in domestic politics, he was no isolationist in the dangerous early years of World War II, but actively promoted aid to the Allies.

[970] **HAYFORD,** John Fillmore
American engineer
Born: Rouses Point, New York, May 19, 1868
Died: Evanston, Illinois, March 10, 1925

Hayford graduated from Cornell University as a civil engineer in 1889. He joined the U. S. Coast and Geodesic Survey and then in 1909 became director of the College of Engineering at Northwestern University in Evanston.

He was primarily interested in geodesy, the careful calculation of the precise shape of the earth. The methods he used in 1900 and thereafter initiated the modern practice of geodesy.

Hayford is best known for his establishment of the principle of isostasy: the idea that elevated regions of the earth's crust (mountain ranges, for instance) are less dense than low-lying regions and, in essence, float on the denser, deeper layers. This is now accepted, with modifications, and has helped greatly with the understanding of the earth's crust as a whole.

[971] **SCOTT,** Robert Falcon
English explorer
Born: Devonport (now part of Plymouth), Devonshire, June 6, 1868
Died: Antarctica, about March 29, 1912

Scott entered the British navy in 1882. As a naval officer he was in successful command of an Antarctic expedition from 1900 to 1904. In 1909, after Peary's [866] discovery of the North Pole, he, like Amundsen [1008], was anxious to reach the South Pole. Here, however, every variety of bad luck assailed him and his expedition. Bad weather delayed them and when they reached the pole on January 17, 1912, after traveling 1842 miles by sledge, they found Amundsen's marker already there.

Bad weather continued on the way back and Scott and his party died in the frozen wasteland of Antarctica.

[972] **SABINE,** Wallace Clement Ware
American physicist
Born: Richwood, Ohio, June 13, 1868
Died: Cambridge, Massachusetts, January 10, 1919

Sabine was the son of a farmer who had held state office and who had been hit hard by the Panic of 1873. He graduated from Ohio University in 1886 and then went on to Harvard, where he did not obtain a Ph.D. but where, in 1890, he joined the faculty, attaining professorial status in 1905.

In 1895 Harvard opened a brand-new building, with a fine lecture room which had only one trifling flaw: the lecturer could not be heard because of excessive reverberation. Sabine was asked to study the problem and he did, even going so far as to photograph sound waves by the changes in light refraction they produced. (The photography of sound waves was developed further by D. C. Miller [953].)

By his studies Sabine founded the science of architectural acoustics and what was until then a hit-and-miss affair became a matter of calculation and forethought. The first structure designed according to his principles was the Boston Symphony Hall, which opened on October 15, 1900. It proved a great success.

Sabine found that he could measure the absorptivity of sound in a particular room in terms of the area of open window, since sound that escaped outdoors was just as lost as sound absorbed by curtains or drapery. He measured the absorptivity of many materials by comparing it with the absorptivity of a standard open window, in terms of duration of reverberation. He found that the duration of reverberation multiplied by the total absorptivity of the room was a constant and that this constant varied in proportion to the volume of the room.

This is Sabine's law and it has formed the basis for the architectural design of acoustically useful rooms—those that have enough reverberation to give strength and body to sound but not so much reverberation as to interfere with hearing.

[973] **LANDSTEINER, Karl**
Austrian-American physician
Born: Vienna, Austria, June 14, 1868
Died: New York, New York, June 26, 1943

Landsteiner, the son of a newspaper publisher, obtained his medical degree at the University of Vienna in 1891. He had a thorough grounding in chemistry, working under Emil Fischer [833], among others. When he turned to bacteriology and immunology afterward, he approached it with a chemical turn of mind.

His key discovery was made in 1900 in connection with the existence of different types of human blood. It had always been a part of folk wisdom that blood differed from individual to individual and that this difference was somehow inherited, but folk wisdom had the details all wrong. Occasional physicians throughout history had tried to make up for possibly fatal blood loss by transferring blood from an animal or a healthy man into the veins of the patient. Sometimes it was helpful, but often death was actually hastened. Most European nations had, by the end of the nineteenth century, prohibited blood transfusions.

By raising folk wisdom to a far more sophisticated level of insight, Landsteiner made transfusions safe. He discovered that human blood differed in the capacity of serum to agglutinate red cells (that is, to cause them to clump together). One sample of serum might clump red cells from person A but not from person B. Another sample of serum might clump red cells from person B but not from person A. Still another sample might clump both, and yet another might clump neither. By 1902 Landsteiner and his group had clearly divided human blood into four blood groups, which he named A, B, AB, and O.

Once this was done, it was a simple task to show that in certain combinations, transfusions were permissible, while in others the incoming red cells would be agglutinated with possibly fatal results. Once patient and donor were blood-typed beforehand, transfusion could be made safe, and, in fact, it at once became an important adjunct to medical practice.

By 1910 it was discovered that these blood groups were inherited according to Mendel's [638] laws and through studies on large populations they could be used as tools by men such as Boyd [1264] to help settle paternity disputes, to study past migrations, and to work out "races" on a basis that was more logical and useful than those used by Retzius [498] a century earlier.

In 1908 Landsteiner was appointed professor of pathology at the University of Vienna. After World War I, during which Austria-Hungary suffered a catastrophic defeat, Landsteiner left Vienna and went to Holland. In 1922 he was invited to join the staff of the Rockefeller Institute for Medical Research (now Rockefeller University) in New York. He accepted, became an American citizen in 1929, and remained in the institute for the rest of his life.

In 1927 his group discovered additional blood groups (M, N, and MN), which, while not important in connection with transfusion, were as useful as the first group in anthropological studies. Then in 1940 he was also involved in the discovery of the Rh blood groups, which proved to have a connection with a disease of newborn infants called erythroblastosis fetalis.

His work on blood groups tends to eclipse, in the public mind, his research on poliomyelitis. He was the first, in 1908, to isolate the poliomyelitis virus and was also the first to use monkeys as an experimental animal in polio research. However, nearly half a century passed before a real weapon against polio was devised by Sabin [1311] and Salk [1393].

In 1930 Landsteiner was awarded the Nobel Prize in medicine and physiology for his discovery of blood groups. He retired from his post at the Rockefeller Institute in 1939 but kept on working anyway, and suffered his fatal heart attack while at his laboratory bench.

[974] **HALE,** George Ellery
American astronomer
Born: Chicago, Illinois, June 29, 1868
Died: Pasadena, California, February 21, 1938

Hale, the son of a manufacturer of elevators who had made possible the skyscrapers of Chicago, graduated from the Massachusetts Institute of Technology in 1890 and, after some work in Europe, organized the Kenwood Observatory in Chicago. There in 1889 he invented the

spectroheliograph, a device that made it possible to photograph the light of a single spectral line of the sun. Thus, he was able to photograph the sun by the light of glowing calcium, and the result was a clear indication of the distribution of calcium in the solar atmosphere. Hale detected calcium clouds he called flocculi. (In 1924 he modified the instrument to allow the sun to be seen by hydrogen light. This showed up the hydrogen-rich prominences in particular and the modified instrument is the spectrohelioscope.)

Hale also detected strong magnetic fields inside sunspots in 1908. This was the first association of magnetic fields with any extraterrestrial body, and it led to the Nobel prize work of Zeeman [945].

To continue his studies, however, Hale felt the need of better observatories and larger telescopes. Hale was a persuasive gentleman and in 1892 talked a hardheaded American street-car magnate, Charles Tyson Yerkes, into putting up the money for a large observatory to be built in Williams Bay, Wisconsin, about eighty miles northwest of Chicago. For it, Hale had Alvan Clarke [696] (who had bought the necessary glass discs for another job and had been stuck with them by a reneging university) build a 40-inch refracting telescope, the largest of the type built before or since. It was completed in 1897 and Yerkes was paid off in fame, for it is the Yerkes telescope at Yerkes Observatory.

Hale was not satisfied. He went on to plan and have built a still larger telescope on Mount Wilson, near Pasadena, California with the help of money from the steel magnate Andrew Carnegie. A 60-inch reflecting telescope was put into action there in 1908 and a 100-inch reflecting telescope in 1917, paid for by the Los Angeles hardware tycoon John D. Hooker. The latter was to remain the largest telescope in the world for a generation.

However, Pasadena and, even more so, Los Angeles, were growing, and the night sky, illuminated by these cities, began to lose its sharpness. (During World War II the blackout of those cities enabled Baade [1163] to do great work with this telescope.) Hale, therefore, chose a site on Mount Palomar, about ninety-five miles southeast of Mount Wilson, where the destroying hand of man had not yet come, and decided to build an even more monstrous telescope there. In 1929 he obtained a grant from the Rockefeller Foundation and began work.

He did not live to see it completed, but in 1948 a 200-inch telescope was finally mounted after fifteen years of the most painstaking labor (with World War II introducing its own sort of troublesome delay). It is, very rightly, named the Hale telescope and it remains one of the largest telescopes in the world. The Soviet Union has constructed a 600-centimeter (236-inch) telescope.

The Mount Palomar Observatory is also blessed with a 48-inch camera of a type invented by Schmidt [1065], the largest devise of this sort in the world. It is, in its way, even more useful than the telescope itself.

During World War I, Hale placed the National Academy of Sciences on a war footing, as the importance of science in warfare was coming to be realized. The prime accomplishment of the academy was the organization of methods of producing helium from natural gas wells. At the time, helium was useful as a noninflammable buoyant gas for use in dirigibles—a gas only the United States could then produce in quantity. However, with dirigibles passing out of the picture before World War II, helium became even more useful and important in connection with low-temperature devices.

[975] **LEAVITT,** Henrietta Swan (lev'it)
American astronomer
Born: Lancaster, Massachusetts,
July 4, 1868
Died: Cambridge, Massachusetts,
December 12, 1921

Leavitt, the daughter of a minister, graduated from the school now known as Radcliffe College in 1892. She joined the staff of Harvard Observatory, under Pickering [885] in 1902. In her meticu-lous determinations of stellar magnitudes, she discovered 2,400 variable stars, doubling the number known in her time.

Her great moment came in 1912, when she was working in the observatory set up by Harvard at Arequipa, Peru. She was then studying the Magellanic clouds (named for Magellan [130]). These are large star collections lying outside our galaxy but not very far away as galactic distances go. All the stars in these clouds are roughly the same distance from us, since variations from point to point within the clouds are small in comparison with the total distance from us.

Leavitt was particularly interested in certain stars that displayed periodic variations in brightness. These are called Cepheids because the first one studied was in the constellation Cepheus.

She noted in 1904 that the longer the period of light variation, the greater the average brightness of the star. In our own galaxy this relationship had been obscured because a short-period star of low brightness might be so close to us that it would appear brighter than a distant long-period star of high real brightness. In the Magellanic clouds, with all stars at about the same great distance from us, this source of confusion was absent.

Even the nearest Cepheid is too far from us to make it easy to determine its distance by the usual parallax method first successfully used by Bessel [439]. However, there were other methods and Hertzsprung [1018] used one to pin down a Cepheid. Once one distance was known, it became possible to learn the distance of the rest by using the period-luminosity curve set up by Leavitt and Shapley [1102]. By comparing the true brightness, as shown by the period of variation, and the apparent brightness, the distance could be worked out.

The Cepheids offered the first method of determining really vast stellar distances and man's knowledge of the universe was greatly enlarged in consequence. A still more tremendous yardstick was soon to be established, however, by Hubble [1136].

[976] **SOMMERFELD,** Arnold Johannes Wilhelm
German physicist
Born: Königsberg, East Prussia (now Kaliningrad, U.S.S.R.), December 5, 1868
Died: Munich, Bavaria, April 26, 1951

Sommerfeld, the son of a physician, studied at the University of Königsberg and, in 1906, succeeded to Boltzmann's [769] post at Munich through Roentgen's [774] influence. His primary interest was in X rays and gamma rays and it was he who set Laue [1068] to work on them.

In 1916 he modified Bohr's [1101] theory to allow the inclusion of elliptical orbits for electrons. In doing so he applied Einstein's [1064] relativity theory to the speeding electrons. Thus both relativity and Planck's [887] quanta found their place in the atom. As a result, one often speaks of the Bohr-Sommerfeld atom.

Sommerfeld, although not Jewish, vigorously opposed growing Fascism and anti-Semitism in Germany after World War I. When Hitler came to power, Sommerfeld was denounced and by 1940 was forced into retirement. He survived Hitler and the war, however.

At the age of eighty-three, when strolling with his grandchildren, he was run down by an automobile.

[977] **HABER,** Fritz (hah'ber)
German chemist
Born: Breslau, Silesia (now Wrocław, Poland), December 9, 1868
Died: Basel, Switzerland, January 29, 1934

Haber, whose mother died when he was born, could not bear to work in his father's dry-salt business, and, like Emil Fischer [833], found that he much preferred chemistry. He studied under Hofmann [604] at the University of Berlin and eventually obtained his doctorate in that field in 1891. In 1898 he gained a professorial appointment at the University of Dahlem, near Berlin.

He was drawn to the relatively new field of physical chemistry, established by men such as Ostwald [840] and Arrhenius [894]. He did work in electrochemistry and in 1909 devised a glass electrode of a type now commonly used to measure the acidity of a solution by detecting the electric potential across a piece of thin glass. It is the most common and convenient method for quickly measuring what Sørensen [967] that very year was to begin calling pH.

Haber was also interested in the chemical processes in a flame such as that of the Bunsen burner. (Part of his education had been under Bunsen [565].) It was the study of gaseous reactions under heat that led him to his greatest fame.

In the early twentieth century, one of the outstanding problems that faced chemists was finding a practical use for atmospheric nitrogen on a large scale. Nitrogen compounds were essential in fertilizers and explosives but the best large-scale source of such compounds was in the nitrate deposits of the desert in northern Chile, a long way from the industrial centers of the world. Yet the atmosphere everywhere in the world was four fifths nitrogen and it formed an inexhaustible supply if only someone could learn to convert the elemental nitrogen into compound form cheaply and on a large scale.

In the very early 1900s Haber investigated the possibility of combining nitrogen and hydrogen under pressure, using iron as a catalyst, to form ammonia. Ammonia could then easily be converted into fertilizer or explosive. By 1908 he was convinced he had something and his work was thought sufficiently well of to earn for him the directorship of the Kaiser Wilhelm Institute for physical chemistry and electrochemistry in 1911.

Bosch [1028] developed the Haber process into a practical method for fixing nitrogen, and in World War I this proved a lifesaver for the German armies. The British navy cut off all imports of nitrates and if imports had been the only source, it is estimated that Germany would simply have run out of explosives by 1916 and been forced to surrender.

However, the atmosphere was at German disposal, thanks to Haber, and the Kaiser's war machine never ran out of ammunition and fought with terrible effect for two more years. In 1918, with the German armies going down to defeat at last, Haber, for the scientific value of his researches rather than for their wartime uses, was awarded the 1919 Nobel prize in chemistry. Many scientists from nations that had fought Germany denounced the award.

And yet the Haber process had uses other than those for war. Using the principle of the process, Bergius [1098] worked out methods for hydrogenating coal to form useful organic compounds.

Haber, an extremely patriotic (even chauvinistic) German, had labored unceasingly during World War I on gas warfare, directing the first use of the poison gas chlorine in 1915 and that of the far worse mustard gas in 1917. Had Germany used the first gas attacks on the large scale that Haber's work made possible, they might well have won the war. As a result of the conservatism and timidity of the German generals, the Allies had their own poison gas in a short time and the weapon was neutralized.

After the war, Haber attempted to pay off the huge indemnity that had been laid upon Germany (which was never paid anyway) by isolating gold from seawater. In this, he failed.

In 1933 Hitler came to power, and Haber faced an unexpected peril. One might have thought that, having saved the German armies in World War I, having organized their gas attacks, having labored for years to pay off reparation, he might have been recognized as a German of Germans. But he was Jewish, and he was therefore forced to leave his post by the very ones who, having driven Germany to defeat in one war despite all that Haber could do, were destined to drive her to far worse defeat in a far worse war.

Haber left for England but apparently did not like the land of the old enemy of the first war. Determined not to spend the winter there, he set out for a research institute in Palestine but had a heart attack in Basel and died, just a few miles from his beloved—and ungrateful—homeland.

[978] **ABEGG,** Richard Wilhelm Heinrich
German chemist
Born: Danzig (now Gdansk, Poland), January 9, 1869
Died: Köslin (now Koszalin, Poland), April 3, 1910

Abegg obtained his doctorate at the University of Berlin in 1891 and, for a time, worked as assistant to Nernst [936]. He was appointed professor of chemistry at the University of Breslau in 1897. He began to concern himself shortly afterward with the effect on chemical valence of the new electronic view of the atom.

It seemed to him that the configuration of electrons in the inert gas atoms (two in the outermost electron shell of helium—to use later terminology—and eight in those of the others) was particularly stable. An element like chlorine that possessed one electron short of the desired eight tended to accept one, while an element like sodium that possessed one over, tended to give it up. A sodium atom would transfer an electron to a chlorine atom, forming a positively charged sodium ion and a negatively charged chloride ion and the two would hold together by electrostatic attraction. In this way a chemical reaction became the transfer of electrons and chemical bonds became the attraction between opposite electric charges.

Abegg died in a balloon accident while still a young man and did not live to see his notions extended by a series of chemists, beginning with Lewis [1037].

[979] **WILSON,** Charles Thomson Rees
Scottish physicist
Born: Glencorse, Midlothian, February 14, 1869
Died: Carlops, Peeblesshire, November 15, 1959

Educated in Manchester, where his family had moved on the death of Wilson's father, a shepherd, in 1873, Wilson entered the field of meteorology and in 1895 began the study of clouds. This was to lead him in most unexpected directions.

Wilson, fascinated by the clouds on top of Ben Nevis (a Scottish peak nearly a mile high and the highest in Great Britain), tried to duplicate the effect on a small scale, while working in J. J. Thomson's [869] laboratory at Cambridge. He allowed moist air to expand within a container. The expansion lowered the temperature of the air so that not all the moisture could be retained, the excess coming out as water droplets to form a mist or cloud.

The droplets of the cloud formed about the dust particles in the air, for if Wilson went to the trouble of using dust-free air, the cloud did not form easily. (Work of the same sort was to lead Schaefer [1309] a half century later to attempts to control weather.) Dust-free moist air remained supersaturated upon expansion and cooling, and clouds did not form until the degree of supersaturation had reached a certain critical point. In the absence of dust, Wilson believed, clouds must form by condensing about ions in the air. The electrical charge of those ions could serve as nuclei whereas ordinary neutral molecules could not.

As soon as Wilson heard of the discovery of X rays by Roentgen [774] and of radioactivity by A. H. Becquerel [834], it occurred to him that ion formation as a result of such radiations might bring about more intensive cloud formations in the absence of dust. This did indeed happen and Wilson's theory of condensation about ions was thus proved.

Wilson experimented for a decade and found that not only did water droplets form about the ions produced by energetic radiation and by speeding particles, but the radiation and particles left a track of such ions as they moved. This track became visible in the form of water droplets that appeared when the chamber was expanded. Charged particles, in particular, left useful tracks, for the tracks curved when the chamber was subjected to a magnetic field and the nature of the curve showed whether the

charge was negative or positive and how massive the particle was. The tracks indicated collisions of particles with molecules or with other particles and offered a guide to events that took place during and after the collision.

By 1911 the Wilson cloud chamber was perfected and offered a way of making the events of the subatomic world visible to the eye in easily interpretable form. For years it proved an indispensable adjunct to nuclear research. Blackett [1207] eventually improved the cloud chamber and Glaser [1472] devised a first cousin to it, a generation later, in the form of the bubble chamber. But Wilson's work was the original inspiration, and the rest was commentary.

Wilson received the 1927 Nobel Prize in physics for his cloud chamber. Its usefulness is further attested to by the fact that Blackett and Glaser earned similar prizes for their improvements.

[980] **LEVENE,** Phoebus Aaron Theodor
Russian-American chemist
Born: Sager, Russia, February 25, 1869
Died: New York, New York, September 6, 1940

Levene's unusual first name is an attempt at adaptation. Levene, born of a Jewish family, originally had Fishel as a first name. For use among Russians, after the family had moved to St. Petersburg in 1873, the Russian name Fyodor was adopted. Then, when the family emigrated to the United States in 1891, it became Phoebus, keeping the initial "f" sound.

Levene's medical education had been interrupted by the emigration. He returned to Russia, completed the course, got his degree, and came to the United States again in 1892.

After attending courses in chemistry at Columbia University, he decided to abandon medicine for chemistry and went abroad again to study under German chemists such as Emil Fischer [833] and Kossel [842]. From Kossel he caught an interest in nucleic acids that was to dominate his scientific life. He then returned to the United States and joined the newly formed Rockefeller Institute (now Rockefeller University) in 1905.

Levene isolated the carbohydrate portion of the nucleic acid molecule and identified it, a feat that had stumped even Kossel. In 1909 Levene showed that the five-carbon sugar, ribose, was to be found in some nucleic acids, and in 1929 he showed that a hitherto unknown sugar, deoxyribose (ribose minus one oxygen atom), was to be found in others. To this day, no other sugars have been found in nucleic acids and, indeed, all nucleic acids are divided into two groups, ribonucleic acid and deoxyribonucleic acid, depending on which sugar they contain. Under the abbreviations RNA and DNA these have become almost the best-known letter combinations in biochemistry, especially after the vast breakthrough in nucleic acid chemistry a generation later with James Watson [1480] and Crick [1406].

Levene worked out the manner in which the components of the nucleic acids were combined into nucleotides (the building blocks of the large nucleic acid molecule) and how these were combined into chains. This work was extended and elaborated later by Todd [1331].

[981] **SPEMANN,** Hans (shpay'mahn)
German zoologist
Born: Stuttgart, Württemberg,
June 27, 1869
Died: Freiburg-im-Breisgau,
Baden, September 12, 1941

Although Spemann, the son of a book publisher, studied medicine, physics, and botany, as well as zoology (physics under Roentgen [639]), it was upon zoology that he centered his professional life. He obtained his doctorate in that subject in 1895 at the University of Würzburg under Boveri [923]. From 1919 until his retirement in 1935, he was professor of zoology at the University of Freiburg.

His outstanding work was done on embryos. One of the most puzzling questions in biology was just how an embryo developed. In the 1880s it had seemed as though the first act of a fertilized ovum, that of dividing in two, determined the plane of bilateral symmetry. If one of the resulting cells was killed with a hot needle, what was left developed into a longitudinal half of an embryo. It seemed that the fertilized ovum was organized within, into precursors of its eventual parts from the very start; even, there was reason to think, from before the moment of fertilization. This was almost a kind of revival of the early theory of preformation that Wolff [313] had laid to rest a century before.

Further experiments showed that if the egg divisions were not killed, but separated, then the individual cells after the first division, or even after the first five divisions, could each develop into a complete (though smaller) embryo. This led to the suggestion that there was some vital force within the cell that directed it toward normal development even when it represented a part rather than the whole of the original fertilized egg.

To Spemann, it seemed that the difference in behavior when a cell was killed but allowed to remain where it was, and when a cell was actually separated, showed that the various cells of an embryo exerted an effect upon their neighbors.

In the 1920s he undertook a series of experiments. He demonstrated that even after an embryo had begun to show definite signs of differentiation, it could still be divided in half with each half producing a whole embryo, although one half was almost all "potential back" and the other almost all "potential belly." This showed that the cells remained plastic quite late in the game and once again knocked out the possibility of preformation.

Furthermore, Spemann found that an area of an embryo develops according to the nature of the neighboring areas. An eyeball develops originally out of the brain material and is joined by a lens that develops out of the nearby skin. If the eyeball is placed near a distant section of the skin, one that would never, in the course of nature, develop a lens, it nevertheless begins to develop one.

There were apparently "organizers" in the embryo (not a mysterious vital force, but definite chemicals) that brought about certain developments in their neighborhood. An area containing an organizer that brought about the development of nerve tissue in a frog embryo could even bring about the development of nerve tissue in a newt embryo. By properly transplanting parts of embryos, a portion on the way toward development as brain will develop as intestine.

In Spemann's time the hormone concept advanced by Starling [954] and Bayliss [902] was well understood, as it was not in the time of his predecessors. It could be seen that embryonic development was under hormonal control, and neither a vital force nor preformation had to be called upon. For his work Spemann was awarded the 1935 Nobel Prize in medicine and physiology.

[982] **PREGL**, Fritz (pray'gul)
Austrian chemist
Born: Laibach, Austria (now Ljubljana, Yugoslavia), September 3, 1869
Died: Graz, December 13, 1930

Pregl attended the University of Graz (in the town to which he and his mother had moved in 1887 after his father's death) and obtained his medical degree in 1894. In 1904 he was appointed to a professorial position there after having done postgraduate work in physical chemistry under Ostwald [840] at Leipzig.

He practiced medicine, performing eye surgery, but his real interest lay in research. In particular he investigated the bile acids, complicated compounds that one could isolate in small quantities from liver bile. He began his work from the medical standpoint but found himself slowly lured into chemistry. It was the smallness of the quantities of material he had to deal with that forced Pregl into the path of fame.

In 1909 he found himself staring at a barely visible amount of a new compound whose molecular structure he had to determine. There was not enough to analyze by usual methods, so he was faced with two alternatives. Either he had to start all over, working on a far larger scale, or he had to invent analytic methods for unprecedentedly small quantities of substances. He chose the latter course and from then on became an analytical chemist.

He obtained a balance that was extremely precise and worked with a glass blower to produce new and tiny pieces of equipment. He put his surgeon's hands to work in delicate manipulations. By 1911 he was demonstrating methods of analysis for the different elements, accurately, with only 7 to 13 milligrams of substance at hand. He drove this further downward and by 1913 could handle as little as 3 milligrams. (Since Pregl's time, microchemists have learned how to work with organic samples of only a few tenths of a milligram in weight.)

Pregl's manipulations made him world-famous. Levene [980] brought his methods to the United States, and in 1923 Pregl was awarded the Nobel Prize for chemistry for his microchemical feats.

[983] **POULSEN**, Valdemar (powl'sin)
Danish inventor
Born: Copenhagen, November 23, 1869
Died: Copenhagen, July 1942

Poulsen was the first to reduce to practice the notion of having sound control the imposition of a varying magnetic field on a length of wire. That varying magnetic field could then be used to reproduce the sound wave.

The idea was a perfectly good one but there were bugs in the practical application thereof that could not easily be ironed out. Poulsen, who patented his device in 1898, could not find the necessary financial backing. His company failed, and it was not till after World War II that the invention was perfected and that tape and wire recording became useful and popular.

[984] **ADLER,** Alfred
Austrian psychiatrist
Born: Penzing, February 7, 1870
Died: Aberdeen, Scotland, May 28, 1937

Adler obtained his M.D. at Vienna in 1895 and began his medical career as an ophthalmologist, but his interest shifted to mental disorders and in 1902 he was one of the first to gravitate toward Freud [865], joining a discussion group which became the first psychoanalytic society.

He was also one of the first to secede, disagreeing with Freud's tendency to base his theories on the sex impulse. By 1911 he had evolved his own theories, in which power, not sex, was the mainspring of action. The child, being a small and powerless item in a world dominated by adults, was painfully conscious of inferiority (Adler popularized the term "inferiority complex") and the rest of his life was spent in an effort to attain "compensation." Adler even viewed sex as primarily an attempt by each of two people to gain power over the other. Sexual abnormality was not the cause of mental disturbance, in his view, but the consequence of it. His version of psychiatric treatment was much briefer than Freud's psychoanalysis and dealt more actively with the patient's overt difficulties.

In 1919 he founded the first child guidance clinics in the Vienna school system. They were closed in 1934 by the reactionary regime of Engelbert Dollfuss.

After 1925 Adler visited the United States frequently. He proved a popular lecturer there and by 1935 decided to settle permanently in the United States. He died while on a lecture tour in Scotland.

[985] **HONDA,** Kotaro
Japanese metallurgist
Born: Aichi-ken Prefecture, February 1870
Died: Tokyo, February 12, 1954

Honda, the son of a farmer, was one of the Japanese scientists who seemed to burst on the world after Japan's industrialization in the late nineteenth century. He was educated at Tokyo Imperial University. Between 1907 and 1911 he did graduate work in Germany and then returned at Tohoku University, becoming its president in 1931.

In 1916 he found that the addition of cobalt to tungsten steel produced an alloy capable of forming a more powerful magnet than ordinary steel.

This opened the way to the new magnetic alloys and eventually thanks to further research by Japanese metallurgists, led to the production of alnico, not only more strongly magnetic, but corrosion-resistant, relatively immune to vibration and temperature change, and cheaper than ordinary steel magnets. Nothing more advanced in the field of magnetism was produced until the mid-twentieth century, with the construction of electromagnets working at liquid helium temperatures and wound with super-conducting wires.

In 1937 Honda was awarded the Cultural Order of the Rising Sun, the Japanese equivalent of the Nobel Prize.

[986] **BORDET,** Jules Jean Baptiste Vincent (bawr-day')
Belgian bacteriologist
Born: Soignies, Hainaut, June 13, 1870
Died: Brussels, April 6, 1961

Bordet obtained his medical degree in 1892 from the University of Brussels and then went on to the Pasteur Institute in Paris, where he worked under Mechnikov [775]. In 1901 he founded the Pasteur Institute in Brussels and served as its director, thus, in effect, going into business for himself.

In 1898 during his stay in Paris, Bordet discovered that if serum is heated to 55°C, the antibodies within it may not be destroyed (as is shown by the fact that the serum will still react with antigens) but its ability to destroy bacteria is gone. Presumably some very fragile component or group of components of the serum must act as a complement for the antibody and make it possible for it to react with the bacteria. Bordet called this component alexin, but Ehrlich [845] named it "complement" and it is so known today.

In 1901 Bordet showed that when an antibody reacts with an antigen, complement is used up, a process called complement fixation, and this has proved of importance in immunological work. In fact, Wasserman [951] devised his well-known diagnostic test for syphilis on the basis of complement fixation.

Bordet went on, in 1906, to discover the bacillus of whooping cough and to devise a method of immunization against that disease. In 1907 he was appointed professor of bacteriology at the University of Brussels and, as a climax to his work on immunology, and with particular reference to his work on complement fixation, he received the 1919 Nobel Prize in medicine and physiology. In 1920 he wrote a treatise on immunology that admirably summarized the knowledge of the time.

He held out, however, against the current of gathering knowledge concerning viruses, refusing to consider that the bacteriophages, discovered by Twort [1055], were actually organisms and long maintaining they were merely toxins.

[987] **BOLTWOOD,** Bertram Borden
American chemist and physicist
Born: Amherst, Massachusetts,
July 27, 1870
Died: Hancock Point, Maine,
August 15, 1927

Boltwood, the son of a lawyer, earned his doctor's degree at Yale in 1897 and spent most of his later life on the faculty of that university.

He turned to the study of radioactivity and in 1904 confirmed something that had been suspected by Ernest Rutherford [996] (with whom Boltwood was to spend a year in 1909) and demonstrated in one particular, at least, by Dorn [795]; that is, the point that the radioactive elements were not independent, but that one might be descended from another to form a radioactive series. In particular, radium was descended from

uranium, and Boltwood discovered an element between, which he called ionium. Ionium turned out eventually to be a variety of thorium and not a truly new element. Boltwood, among others, was on the track of such atomic varieties, a concept finally nailed down by Soddy [1052].

In 1905 Boltwood carried through his radioactive series notion by pointing out that lead was always found in uranium minerals and might be the final stable product of uranium disintegration. In 1907 he was the first to suggest that, from the quantity of lead in uranium ores and from the known rate of uranium disintegration, it might be possible to determine the age of the earth's crust. Such radioactive dating did indeed prove possible eventually, and for the first time geologists did not need tortuous and uncertain reasoning to date the geologic eras. Uranium decay is so slow that it is useless for periods within the era of man's existence on the planet. For this, nonradioactive methods were developed, notably by Douglass [963], but eventually Libby [1342] put radioactivity, in the form of carbon-14, to use here as well.

In 1927, due to the strain of overwork, Boltwood suffered a nervous breakdown and, in a fit of depression, committed suicide.

[988] **IVANOV,** Ilya Ivanovich (ee-vah'nuf)
Russian biologist
Born: Shigry, Kursk province,
August 1, 1870
Died: Alma-Ata, Kazakh SSR,
March 20, 1932

Ivanov, the son of a government clerk, studied at the universities of Moscow and of Kharkov, and did some postgraduate work at the Pasteur Institute in Paris.

His chief interest was reproductive biology and, in particular, the artificial insemination of domestic animals, a practice that had been pioneered by Spallanzani [302]. Spallanzani merely showed that it was possible. Ivanov made of it a practical procedure.

As early as 1901 he founded the world's first center for the artificial insemination of horses. Between 1908 and 1917 about eight thousand Russian mares were artificially inseminated, thus making it possible to use the most vigorous stallions for multiple inseminations.

After the October Revolution, the practice (encouraged by Soviet authorities) was accelerated. By 1932 over 180,000 mares, 385,000 cows, and 1,615,000 ewes had been artificially inseminated and, of course, the practice spread beyond the Soviet boundaries, too.

[989] **CLAUDE**, Georges
French chemist
Born: Paris, September 24, 1870
Died: Saint-Cloud, Seine-et-Oise, May 23, 1960

Claude was particularly interested in liquefying gases. Independently of Linde [625] he devised a method of producing liquid air in quantity in 1902. Earlier, in 1897, he had found that acetylene (which is very inflammable) could be transported safely if dissolved in acetone. This expanded the uses of acetylene. Then, too, during World War I, he produced liquid chlorine for use in poison gas attacks. And in 1917 he developed something very much like the Haber process independently of Haber [977].

He helped supply Ramsay [832] with liquid air in which to conduct his search for the inert gases. Then, when Ramsay had found them, Claude grew interested in them and worked successfully on their separation from air and their production in quantity.

His researches, beginning in 1910, showed that electric discharges through these gases could be made to produce light, and this was the beginning of neon lights, which made Claude rich. The fact that tubes filled with neon or other gas could be twisted into any shape, so that they could spell out words, for instance, made it inevitable that they replace ordinary incandescent bulbs in advertising signs. In the 1930s such tubes were coated internally with fluorescent materials so that a white light was produced

that would be acceptable for homes and factories. After World War II fluorescent lights began to replace the old incandescent bulbs that had come in with Edison [788] three quarters of a century before.

During World War II, Claude was a supporter of the Vichy government. He was convicted as a collaborationist in 1945 after France had been liberated and, despite his age, spent the next five years in prison.

[990] **PERRIN**, Jean Baptiste (peh-ran')
French physicist
Born: Lille, Nord, September 30, 1870
Died: New York, New York, April 17, 1942

Perrin's father died of wounds received in the Franco-Prussian War soon after the infant was born and he was raised by his mother.

He obtained his doctorate in 1897 at the École Normale Supérieure in Paris. He was appointed professor of physical chemistry at the University of Paris in 1910 and remained there for thirty years. He was strongly in favor of Boltzmann's [769] statistical treatment of atomic motions and against the nonatomic views of Ostwald [840] and Mach [733].

During the 1890s he was attracted to the study of cathode rays, which Crookes [695] had shown to be electrically charged. Even so, there remained controversy over whether they were particles (as it seemed they would have to be if they were charged) or whether Crookes's observations were in error and they were actually a form of wave radiation. Perrin settled the matter once and for all in 1895 by showing that the radiation could be made to impart a large negative charge to a cylinder upon which they fell. The cathode rays must, therefore, consist of negatively charged material, and must be particles rather than waves. Almost immediately thereafter, J. J. Thomson [869] was able to determine the mass of the particles and to show that they were much smaller than atoms.

Perrin's other major work was also on particles, but less directly. In 1905 Einstein [1064] had worked out the equations governing Brownian motion on the assumption that it was the result of a bombardment against small suspended particles by the water molecules surrounding it. The way the particle was maintained in suspension against the force of gravity was, according to the equation, partly dependent on the size of the water molecules. In 1908 Perrin set about determining that size by observation.

Through a microscope he counted the number of small particles of gum resin suspended at different heights in a drop of water. He found that the manner in which the numbers dropped off with height fitted in exactly with Einstein's equation and, for the first time, the approximate size of atoms and molecules could be calculated from an actual observation. He described his work in a book he published in 1913, which was well enough written to sell thirty thousand copies. At last, the tiny entities, whose existence had been accepted almost on faith for the century since Dalton [389] had promulgated the atomic theory, took on a patently real existence. Boltzmann was right and even the diehard Ostwald had to admit that atoms were real objects and not just convenient fictions.

In 1941, after France's disastrous defeat by Nazi Germany, Perrin (who had been an active anti-Fascist) left for the United States. There he used his influence to support the De Gaulle movement, which maintained a continuing French resistance outside the country itself. Perrin, over seventy years of age by then, did not live to see his country liberated.

After the war, his remains were returned to France for honored burial.

[991] **POPE,** Sir William Jackson
English chemist
Born: London, October 31, 1870
Died: Cambridge, October 17, 1939

Pope was an actively intelligent youngster who was encouraged by his parents. (They allowed him to set up a small chemical laboratory in his room.) He became a skilled photographer—another hobby—and learned several languages with ease. Nevertheless, though he left school in 1885 with good marks, he had not remained long enough to pick up degrees.

During the 1890s Pope served as assistant to Kipping [930]. In 1899 he produced an optically active compound that contained an asymmetric nitrogen atom, but no asymmetric carbon atoms. This proved that the Van't Hoff [829] theory applied to atoms other than carbon.

In 1901 he became a professor of chemistry at the University of Manchester and went right on with his work. By 1902 he had prepared optically active compounds centered upon asymmetric atoms of sulfur, selenium, and tin. Later, he demonstrated that compounds without asymmetric atoms of any sort, but asymmetric as a whole, through the influence of the steric hindrance first expounded by Viktor Meyer [796], could also be optically active. He thus changed the notion of stereoisomerism from its original narrow coverage to the broad and general concept that now prevails. He received the Davy medal in 1914 and was knighted in 1919.

During World War I, Pope had the rather dubious honor of developing methods for manufacturing mustard gas in quantity. It was the most fearful of the poison gases used in that war and was to stand as a peak in military horror till the development of the nuclear bomb in World War II.

[992] **RICKETTS,** Howard Taylor
American pathologist
Born: Findley, Ohio, February 9, 1871
Died: Mexico City, Mexico, May 3, 1910

Ricketts, the son of a grain merchant, graduated from the University of Nebraska in 1894. By then his family had lost its money in the Panic of 1893 and

Ricketts had to work his way through medical school, and broke down (temporarily) under the strain in his third year.

He gained his medical degree at Northwestern University in 1897 and followed that up with further training in Europe. He joined the faculty of the University of Chicago in 1902, then investigated Rocky Mountain spotted fever and in 1906 showed that it was spread by cattle ticks.

He was the first to locate the microorganism that caused it, and it proved to be a most unusual one. It was smaller than bacteria generally and was not a truly independent organism, for it resembled viruses in being able to grow only within a living cell. It was larger than the ordinary virus, however. It seemed very much like a creature intermediate in position between bacteria and viruses.

Ricketts went on to study typhus, another disease caused by such a microorganism, and as Nicolle [956] was doing in Tunis he showed that it was transmitted by the body louse. In 1911, in Mexico City, while experimenting with the disease, Ricketts contracted it and died. Mexico observed three days of mourning on his behalf. After his death the microorganisms of the type that caused typhus and Rocky Mountain spotted fever were named rickettsia in his honor.

[993] **GRIGNARD,** François Auguste Victor (gree-nyahr')
French chemist
Born: Cherbourg, Manche, May 6, 1871
Died: Lyon Rhône, December 13, 1935

Grignard, the son of a sailmaker, won several prizes for his studies as a youngster, and when he entered the University of Lyon, he studied mathematics. He finally obtained his degree in that subject, although he did not particularly excell in it. He had a poor opinion of chemistry at first, but casual contact with work in a chemical laboratory brought a quick conversion and mathematics had

to do without him. He did not even undertake physical chemistry, where mathematics might have been useful, but plunged into organic chemistry, to which in those days mathematics was a stranger.

Grignard embarked upon a course of experiments in which he was attempting to add a methyl group (consisting of a carbon atom and three hydrogen atoms) to a molecule. The problem was to find the right catalyst. Zinc shavings worked in some cases, but not in the one he was dealing with. Magnesium metal seemed to offer hope but results were irregular and undependable. Frankland [655] had prepared combinations of zinc with organic compounds by using diethyl ether as the solvent, and Grignard wondered if he couldn't do the same with magnesium and if the resulting compounds might not be useful.

It was a lucky stroke of intuition, for the trick worked. Furthermore, this device proved extremely versatile and magnesium-ether in combination with a number of compounds produced a whole series of what are now known as Grignard reagents. A powerful new weapon had been added to the armory of the synthetic chemist.

The Grignard reagents were first announced in 1900 and Grignard presented the work as his doctor's thesis in 1901. In no time at all, many chemists, including Grignard himself, were investigating Grignard reagents in all directions. Within five years, two hundred papers had been published on the subject. The usefulness of the device was such that in 1910 Grignard received a professorship in chemistry at the University of Nancy and at Lyon in 1919. In 1912 he was honored with the Nobel Prize in chemistry, sharing it with Sabatier [856].

When World War I broke out, Grignard was called to service as a corporal, but he was quickly put into chemical war work. He worked out methods for preparing phosgene, a poisonous gas, and for detecting the first traces of mustard gas, another poisonous gas. After the war Grignard returned to organic research.

[994] **BODENSTEIN,** Max (boh'den-shtine)
German chemist
Born: Magdeburg, July 15, 1871
Died: Berlin, September 3, 1942

Bodenstein, the son of a brewer, like Pope [991] started young as a chemist by setting up a laboratory in his room. He attended the University of Heidelberg and did his doctoral research under Viktor Meyer [796], receiving his Ph.D. *summa cum laude* in 1893.

From his doctoral work on, he was chiefly interested in chemical kinetics, the study of the rates of reactions. He concentrated on apparently simple reactions such as the decomposition of hydrogen iodide, or the combination of hydrogen and chlorine.

He found, about 1920, that reactions did not usually proceed in a simple way and, in particular, he was the first to see the necessity of postulating a "chain reaction": one in which the product of a molecular change serves to bring about a similar change in another molecule. Such chain reactions can thus continue with explosive rapidity.

A thorough understanding of chain reactions led to better methods of plastics formation, and the analogous nuclear chain reactions led, of course, to the nuclear bomb.

In 1923 Bodenstein succeeded Nernst [936] (who had originally suggested the possibility of chain reactions) as head of the Institute of Physical Chemistry.

[995] **WRIGHT,** Orville
American inventor
Born: Dayton, Ohio,
August 19, 1871
Died: Dayton, Ohio,
January 30, 1948

Orville and his older brother, Wilbur [961], were sons of a minister and lived the most proper lives imaginable. They neither smoked, drank, nor married and always wore conventional business suits even when tinkering in a machine shop.

Neither had more than part of a high school education, so they were quite in the tradition of the American inventive tinkerers who make instinct, intuition, and endless intelligent effort replace theory—after the fashion of the greatest noneducated intuitive genius of them all, Edison [788].

Orville Wright was a champion bicyclist and so the brothers went into the bicycle repair business, which gave full vent to their mechanical aptitude. Another hobby was gliding, which, in the last decade of the nineteenth century, had become a most daring, yet practical, sport, thanks to Lilienthal [793]. The Wright brothers followed Lilienthal's career, read his publications and those of Langley [711], and felt the stirring hope of manned flight grow. It was Lilienthal's death in 1869 that inspired them to begin their own experimentation, for they thought they could correct the errors that had led the German to his end.

The Wright brothers combined their two hobbies by making every effort to equip a bicycle with wings and place an internal-combustion engine aboard to turn a propeller. They made shrewd corrections in design and invented ailerons, the movable wing tips that enable a pilot to control his plane. That served as their original patent. In addition, they built a crude wind tunnel to test their models; they designed new engines of unprecedented lightness for the power they could deliver; they produced engines, in fact, that weighed only seven pounds per horsepower delivered. Naturally, in any aircraft, lightness is at a premium, and the engine is about the most difficult object to make light. The Wrights' feat in achieving this was an important step in making powered air-flight possible. Their entire eight-year program of research cost them about $1,000.

On December 17, 1903, at Kitty Hawk, North Carolina, Orville made the first airplane flight in history—a powered flight as opposed to mere gliding. He remained in the air for almost a minute and covered 850 feet. There were only five witnesses and this first flight was met with absolute lack of interest on the part of the newspapers. In fact, as late as 1905, the *Scientific American* magazine mentioned the flight only to suggest it was a hoax. In that year, however, the Wrights made a half-hour, 24-mile flight.

Slowly, though, the fact that airplanes existed penetrated the realization of the world. Orville flew for an hour in 1908. The first flight across the English Channel in 1909 stirred the public, and the aerial dogfights of World War I lent a new and spurious glamour to the dreadful business of war. However, it was Lindbergh's [1249] solo flight across the Atlantic in 1927 that made it quite obvious that the airplane was here to stay.

Orville lived to see airplanes drop atomic bombs on Hiroshima and Nagasaki. His brother Wilbur was less, or more, fortunate, depending on one's outlook. Orville was elected to the Hall of Fame for Great Americans in 1965.

[996] **RUTHERFORD,** Ernest, 1st Baron Rutherford of Nelson
British physicist
Born: Brightwater, near Nelson, New Zealand, August 30, 1871
Died: London, October 19, 1937

Rutherford's grandfather was a Scotsman who had migrated to New Zealand in 1842. Rutherford's father was a wheelwright and farmer, and Rutherford himself, the second of twelve children, worked on the farm. He showed great promise at school and in his teens gained a scholarship to New Zealand University, where he finished fourth. (One wonders what happened to the three who beat him.) In the university he became interested in physics and developed a magnetic detector of radio waves. He was completely uninterested in practical applications for his discoveries, however, and even refused to testify as an expert witness in court in a case involving radio transmission—it would have brought him out of his ivory tower.

In 1895 came the turning point, for he received a scholarship to Cambridge University. This was even more of a fortunate break (for Rutherford and for the world) than it seemed, because he had ended only in second place. The first-place winner, however, refused the scholarship because he wanted to stay in New

Zealand and get married. Furthermore, Cambridge had just adopted a rule that allowed acceptance of students from other universities and Rutherford was the very first to qualify under the new regulation. The news reached him, it is said, while he was digging potatoes on his father's farm. He flung down his spade, saying, "That's the last potato I'll dig," postponed his own marriage plans, and left for England.

At Cambridge he worked under J. J. Thomson [869] who quickly came to appreciate this loud, unpolished colonial with the deft hands. (Thomson himself tended to be rather clumsy in his experimentation.) Then after a short period at McGill University in Montreal, Canada, and a trip back to New Zealand to get married, he came to England again.

Hard on the heels of A. H. Becquerel [834], Rutherford began work in the exciting new field of radioactivity. He was one of those who, along with the Curies [897, 965], had decided that the rays given off by radioactive substances were of several different kinds. He named the positively charged ones alpha rays and the negatively charged ones beta rays. These names are still used except that both are now known to consist of speeding particles, so one often speaks of alpha particles and beta particles instead. When in 1900 it was discovered that some of the radiations were not affected by a magnetic field, Rutherford was able to demonstrate them to consist of electromagnetic waves and named them gamma rays.

In collaboration with Soddy [1052] in 1902 and thereafter, Rutherford followed up the lead given by Crookes [695], who had found that uranium formed a different substance as it gave off radiation. By subjecting uranium and thorium to chemical manipulations and following the fate of the radioactivity, Rutherford and Soddy demonstrated that uranium and thorium broke down in the course of radioactivity into a series of intermediate elements. Boltwood [987] was proving the same point in the United States at this time. Soddy was to carry this work forward and advance the notion of isotopes.

Each different intermediate element broke down at a particular rate so that half of any quantity was gone in a fixed period. Rutherford named this fixed period the half life.

Between 1906 and 1909 Rutherford, together with his assistant, Geiger [1082], studied alpha particles intensively and proved quite conclusively that the individual particle was a helium atom with its electrons removed. The alpha particles were like the positive rays that had been discovered by Goldstein [811], and in 1914 Rutherford suggested that the simplest positive rays must be those obtained from hydrogen and that these must be the fundamental positively charged particle. He called it a proton.

For nearly twenty years thereafter it seemed that all atoms were made up of protons and electrons in equal numbers, until Heisenberg [1245] modified the concept into the one we hold today. The electric charge on a proton is positive and that on an electron is negative, and the two charges are just equal in size so that one electron neutralizes one proton, electrically speaking. However, the mass of the proton is 1,836 times the mass of an electron.

Rutherford's interest in alpha particles led to something greater still. In 1906, while still at McGill in Montreal, he began to study how alpha particles are scattered by thin sheets of metal. He continued these experiments in 1908, when he had returned to England and was working at Manchester University. He fired alpha particles at a sheet of gold foil only one fifty-thousandth of an inch thick. Most of the alpha particles passed through, unaffected and undiverted, recording themselves on the photographic plate behind. There were, however, photographic signs of some scattering, even scattering through large angles.

Since the gold foil was two thousand atoms thick, and the alpha particles passed through, for the most part, undeflected, it would seem that the atoms were mostly empty space. Since some alpha particles were deflected sharply, even at right angles and more, it meant that somewhere in the atom was a very massive positively charged region capable of turning back the positively charged alpha particle. (Like charges repel.) From this experiment Rutherford evolved the theory of the nuclear atom, a theory he first announced in 1911. He maintained that the atom contains a very tiny nucleus at its center, which is positively charged and which contains all the protons of the atom and therefore virtually all of its mass. In the outer regions of the atom are the negatively charged electrons which are very light and which interpose no detectable barrier to the passage of the alpha particles.

This view of the atom is the one accepted today, and it replaced the concept of the featureless, indivisible spheres of Democritus [20], which dominated atomistic thinking for twenty-three centuries.

For working out the theory of radioactive disintegration of elements, for determining the nature of alpha particles, for devising the nuclear atom, Rutherford was awarded the 1908 Nobel Prize in chemistry, a classification he rather resented, for he was a physicist and tended to look down his nose at chemists. Yet great achievements still lay ahead.

Rutherford employed a scintillation counter of the type first devised by Crookes to measure the amount of radioactivity being produced. By counting the flashes on the zinc sulfide screen (one flash for each colliding subatomic particle) he and Geiger could tell that a gram of radium would eject 37 billion alpha particles per second. (Rutherford was too impatient to sit there counting flashes, but Geiger, with steady Teutonic patience, had no problem in this respect.) A substance undergoing this number of disintegrations (of any sort, not necessarily of the type that produced alpha particles) is now referred to as a curie of that material, in honor of the Curies. This is a great deal of radioactivity, and it is commoner to deal with material breaking down only a millionth as rapidly, this amount being a microcurie. Nevertheless, Rutherford himself is not forgotten, for a rutherford of radioactivity represents that amount of material which yields one million breakdowns per second.

(Scintillations of the sort used by Rutherford in his scientific work were put to use in industry in the following decade. Zinc sulfide, containing a trace of radium, was used on watch faces to create luminous figures that could be seen at night. This worked well except that the women painting the figures absorbed traces of the radium and came down with serious, slowly fatal cases of radiation sickness. The practice was discontinued and the dangers of radioactivity were made clear.)

In 1917 Rutherford got to work in earnest on quantitative measurements of radioactivity. He allowed alpha particles from a bit of radioactive material to shoot through a cylinder into which he could introduce certain gases. When he introduced oxygen, the number of scintillations fell off as the gas absorbed some of the alpha particles before they could reach the zinc sulfide screen.

With hydrogen in the cylinder, particularly bright scintillations were produced. This was because the nucleus of the hydrogen atom consisted of single protons and these were knocked forward by the alpha particles. When the protons collided with the screen, the bright scintillations were produced.

And yet, when nitrogen was introduced into the cylinder, although the alpha particle scintillations were reduced in number, occasional scintillations of the hydrogen type appeared. The conclusion could only be that alpha particles were knocking protons out of the nuclei of the nitrogen atoms. What was left of the nuclei had to be those of oxygen atoms.

Rutherford was thus the first man ever to change one element into another as a result of the manipulations of his own hands. He had achieved the dream of the alchemists. He had also demonstrated the first man-made "nuclear reaction." However, only one alpha particle in about 300,000 interacted with the nuclei, so it wasn't a very practical form of transmutation. By 1924 Rutherford had managed to knock protons out of the nuclei of most of the lighter elements.

Rutherford accepted a professorship of physics at Cambridge in 1919 and, in that year, succeeded J. J. Thomson as director of the Cavendish Laboratory. He was president of the Royal Society from 1925 to 1930. He was knighted in 1914 and was created Baron Rutherford of Nelson (after his birthplace) in 1931. This made it possible for him to take a seat in the House of Lords.

After 1933 he was strongly anti-Nazi in his sympathies and was active in arranging to help Jewish scientists forced out of Germany. He drew the line at personally helping Haber [977], however. Rutherford felt that Haber's development of gas warfare put him outside the pale.

In 1933 he expressed himself as quite doubtful that the vast energy of the atomic nucleus, as made evident in radioactivity, could ever be controlled by man. He called the notion "moonshine." In this he was overly conservative (as he was in his reluctance to accept Einstein's [1064] theory of relativity). However, he died two years before the discovery of uranium fission by Hahn [1063] and so he was not to know how wrong he was in this respect.

He was buried in Westminster Abbey near Newton [231] and Kelvin [652].

[997] **SCHAUDINN**, Fritz Richard
(show'din)
German zoologist
Born: Röseningken, East Prussia,
September 19, 1871
Died: Hamburg, June 22, 1906

Schaudinn, the son of an inspector of stud farms, obtained his doctorate at the University of Berlin in 1894. His researches extended from the fauna of the Arctic (where he traveled in 1898 as a member of an exploratory expedition) to the parasites of tropical disease, where he was the first to show that dysentery was caused by an amoeba and that hookworm infection occurs through the skin.

His short life was crowned in 1905 by the discovery of the organism (*Spirochaeta pallida*) that caused syphilis. This seemed to break the log jam surrounding the disease that had terrorized Europe since (according to legend) it was brought back from the New World by Columbus' [121] sailors four centuries before. A year later, Wasserman [951] devised his diagnostic method for the disease and three years after that, Ehrlich [845] and his team had discovered a specific therapy for the disease. Schaudinn did not live to see this.

[998] **CANNON,** Walter Bradford
American physiologist
Born: Prairie du Chien, Wisconsin, October 19, 1871
Died: Franklin, New Hampshire, October 1, 1945

Cannon graduated from Harvard in 1896 and got his medical degree there in 1900. He was the first to use Roentgen's [774] X rays for physiological purposes. To do this, he devised a bismuth meal, a suspension of material of high atomic weight which was harmless and which was opaque to X rays. After such a meal, the intestinal system would stand out as white against a black background, under X rays, and for the first time men could see the body's soft internal organs on display while the outer skin remained intact. In the days before World War I this created a sensation indeed.

After the war, Cannon studied the manner in which the body met emergency stresses, having been led to this by his study of hemorrhagic and traumatic shock among wounded soldiers. He developed the notion of homeostasis, that is, the effort by the body to maintain a stable internal environment despite fluctuations (within reason) of the outside environment. Primarily responsible for this were the various hormones, particularly adrenaline.

Studying the nerve endings particularly influenced by adrenaline, Cannon discovered that they secreted an adrenaline-resembling compound even under normal nonemergency conditions. Since these nerve endings belonged to what was called the sympathetic nervous system, he called the compound "sympathin."

[999] **TSCHERMAK VON SEYSENEGG,** Erich (cher-mahk'fun-zy'-zuh-nek)
Austrian botanist
Born: Vienna, November 12, 1871
Died: Vienna, October 11, 1962

Tschermak von Seysenegg was the son of a professor of mineralogy at the University of Vienna, who had been ennobled. Tschermak studied at the University of Vienna himself and obtained his Ph.D. in botany in 1896.

In 1898 Tschermak began experiments on the hybridizing of peas and by 1900 had worked out Mendel's [638] laws of inheritance without knowing at first that Mendel had done it thirty-three years before. Like De Vries [792] and Correns [938], he recognized and accepted Mendel's priority and published his own work only as confirmation.

[1000] **LANGEVIN,** Paul (lahnzh-van')
French physicist
Born: Paris, January 23, 1872
Died: Paris, December 19, 1946

Langevin, the son of an appraiser, was a great-great-grandnephew of Pinel [338] on his mother's side.

In the late 1890s Langevin went to Cambridge to study under J. J. Thomson [869] and then he returned to the Sorbonne for his Ph.D. in 1902 under Pierre Curie [897]. In 1904 he obtained a professorship in physics at the Collège de France.

He popularized Einstein's [1064] theories for the French public as Eddington [1085] did for the English and American publics. He also considered paramagnetism and diamagnetism, phenomena displayed by substances that are weakly attracted and weakly repelled (respectively) by a magnetic field. Faraday [474] had noticed the phenomenon in 1845 and coined the words. However, in 1905 Langevin first interpreted it in the modern manner on the basis of the electron's electric charges within the atom.

The work for which he is most renowned was the use of ultrasonic wavelengths (sound frequencies too high to be heard). These could be produced by Pierre Curie's piezoelectric effect. Radio circuits had been developed in the first decades of the twentieth century that could shift potentials quickly enough to make crystals vibrate fast enough to produce sound waves with frequencies in the ultrasonic range.

Such ultrasonic sound could far more easily be reflected from small objects than ordinary sound could, and it was Langevin's intention during World War I to develop this into a device for the detection of submarines ("echo location"). Actually, by the time he had it working, the war was over, but the principle forms the basis of modern sonar. In sonar, ultrasonic sound waves are now used for the detection not only of submarines but of the contours of the ocean bottoms, of the presence of schools of fish, and so on.

Langevin was an outspoken anti-Nazi and, during the war, suffered an eclipse under the puppet Vichy regime. For a time he was imprisoned, but he escaped to Switzerland, was restored to his posts in 1944, and lived to see his homeland free again.

[1001] **TRAVERS,**   Morris   William (trav′erz)
English chemist
Born: London, January 24, 1872
Died: Stroud, Gloucestershire, August 25, 1961

Travers, the son of a physician, graduated from University College, London, in 1893. He intended to become an organic chemist but in 1894 he began work with Ramsay [832] and shared in the exciting labor of isolating the noble gases. Making use of a large quantity of liquid air supplied them by Hampson [851], Travers located krypton in May 1898.

That same year, Travers obtained his doctoral degree, and in 1903 he accepted a professorial post at University College. From 1927 to 1937 he was at Bristol University. In 1956 Travers published a biography of Ramsay.

[1002] **URBAIN,** Georges (ür-bahn′)
French chemist
Born: Paris, April 12, 1872
Died: Paris, November 5, 1938

Urbain, the son of a chemistry professor, was a latter-day Renaissance man, for in addition to his work in chemistry, he indulged in painting, sculpture, and music in a reasonably proficient manner.

He worked for Friedel [693] and received his Ph.D. from the University of Paris in 1899. His outstanding scientific work was conducted on the rare earth elements. In 1907, just ahead of Auer [890], he isolated the last of the stable rare earths, which he named lutetium, after the village that stood on the site of Paris in Roman times.

In 1911 he thought he had isolated still another element, which he called celtium and which he believed fitted under zirconium in the periodic table. When Urbain heard in 1914 of Moseley's [1121] method of characterizing elements by the X rays they could be made to emit, he traveled to Oxford in order to bring the young Englishman a mixture of rare earths for analysis. Without trouble Moseley identified the rare earths in the mixture; orthodox chemical methods would have been long, painstaking, and uncertain. Furthermore a sample that Urbain believed to contain celtium proved to be nothing more than a mixture of known rare earths. (The true element located under zirconium was found by Hevesy [1100] a decade later.)

Urbain was terribly impressed with all this and helped popularize the work of the so-soon-to-be-dead Moseley throughout the world of chemistry.

[1003] **MOULTON,** Forest Ray (mohl′-tun)
American astronomer
Born: Le Roy, Michigan, April 29, 1872
Died: Wilmette, Illinois, December 7, 1952

Moulton graduated from Albion College in 1894 and earned his Ph.D. in

1899 at the University of Chicago. He spent the remainder of his professional life there.

He collaborated with Chamberlin [766] in advancing the planetesimal theory of the origin of the solar system. When the smaller satellites of Jupiter were discovered by Nicholson [1151] and others in the early decades of the twentieth century, Moulton suggested they might be captured asteroids. This theory is now widely accepted among astronomers.

[1004] **SITTER,** Willem de
Dutch astronomer
Born: Sneek, Friesland, May 6, 1872
Died: Leiden, November 20, 1934

Sitter, the son of a judge, obtained his doctorate at the University of Gröningen, where he had studied under Kapteyn [815]. Then, at the invitation of Gill [763], he spent the period from 1897 to 1899 at the Cape Observatory in South Africa.

He became professor of astronomy at the University of Leiden in 1908 and its director in 1919. He was one of the first to become seriously interested in Einstein's [1064] theory of relativity. It was he whose reports reached Eddington [1085] in England and popularized the theory there, paving the way for the English expedition to test general relativity during the eclipse of 1919.

Sitter did not agree with Einstein's conception of the universe in one respect. Because light was bent by gravitational forces, any ray of light eventually curved and curved and reached its starting point once more: the universe consisted of "curved space." To Einstein, at first, the radius of curvature was constant, and the universe was static, not changing in size. Sitter maintained that the general theory could more properly be interpreted to show that the curvature was constantly growing less and that the curved universe was constantly expanding like a growing bubble. The spectra of the distant galaxies, as interpreted by

Hubble [1136], bore this out and in the end Einstein too was converted to Sitter's view.

Sitter calculated the universe to have a radius of two billion light-years and to contain eighty billion galaxies, but this, like all earlier estimates of the size of the universe since prehistoric times, proved to be overconservative.

[1005] **RUSSELL,** Bertrand Arthur William Russell, 3d Earl
English mathematician and philosopher
Born: Trelleck, Monmouthshire, May 18, 1872
Died: Penrhyndeudraeth, Merionethshire, February 2, 1970

Russell's parents died by the time he was four, and his grandfather John Russell took charge. This grandfather had been prime minister of Great Britain from 1846 to 1852 and from 1865 to 1866, and was created 1st Earl Russell in 1861. He died in 1878 and Bertrand was left with his grandmother.

Young Bertrand led a lonely, unhappy childhood in the puritanical home of his grandparents. He entered Cambridge in 1890, where George Darwin [777] was one of his teachers and where Whitehead [911] grew interested in the young man.

Bertrand Russell inherited the earldom from his elder brother in 1931 but preferred not to use the title. This was all of a piece with his strong and unconventional liberal views, which led him to fight for women's suffrage, for instance. Through much of his life he had been a militant pacifist (which is not the contradiction in terms it seems) and for this lost his college post during World War I and spent some months in jail in 1918. He ran for Parliament (unsuccessfully) on the Labour ticket in 1922.

His views on social problems were equally unconventional. From 1927 to 1932 he ran a school for children in which advanced notions of discipline (or, rather, lack of it) were used. In 1940, when, during a temporary stay in the United States, he was appointed to the staff of the City College of New York, his published views on sex were used by the clergy and the Hearst press to arouse a storm of disapproval against him. His appointment was pusillanimously withdrawn as a result by a state court order.

During the stressful times before World War II, Russell retreated from pacifism, but with the coming of the nuclear race and the cold war of the 1950s, he returned to his earlier views with greater force than ever. In his nineties this militant patriarch led the forces of neutralism in England and constantly defied the government, confident that it would not choose to jail him (although it did for a short while in 1961).

Russell heard Peano [889] lecture in mathematics in 1900 and grew interested in the basic logic of mathematics. In 1902 he made his first mark in this direction when he wrote to Frege [797], pointing out what has since become a famous logical paradox and asking how Frege's new system of mathematical logic would handle it. Frege was forced to admit that his system fell short and so added a footnote to his two-volume work that nullified all that had gone before.

Russell then went on to try to answer his own question by setting up a still better system of logic on which to base mathematics. This effort reached its climax in the publication from 1910 to 1913 in collaboration with Whitehead of *Principia Mathematica,* a name reminiscent of Newton's [231] great work. This was the most ambitious and nearly successful effort to make all of mathematics completely rigorous, but as Gödel [1301] was to show twenty years later, all such efforts were doomed to failure.

Russell wrote numerous books and in 1950 he received the Nobel Prize in literature.

[1006] **TSVETT,** Mikhail Semenovich
Russian botanist
Born: Asti, Italy, May 14, 1872
Died: Voronezh, June 26, 1919

Tsvett, born of a Russian father (a civil servant) and an Italian mother, lost his mother soon after birth. He studied at Geneva University in Switzerland and in 1896 went to St. Petersburg, Russia, to do research. In 1902 he settled in Warsaw, then part of the Russian empire. The German invasion of Russia in 1915 pushed the institute with which he was associated eastward and he finally came to rest in Voronezh.

His name, often spelled Tswett (the German "w" is pronounced "v"), means "color" in Russian, which is an interesting coincidence in view of the nature of his most important scientific achievement.

Tsvett's major work was on plant pigments and in 1903 he had his great inspiration. He let a mixture of the pigments trickle down a tube of powdered alumina. The different substances in the pigment mixture held to the surface of the powder with different degrees of strength. As the mixture was washed downward, the substances separated, those holding with less strength being washed down farther. In the end, the mixture was separated into colored bands. The fact of separation was "written in color" and Tsvett named the technique chromatography (which means "written in color" in Greek). His report, in Russian, roused no interest and his work was forgotten until the method was reintroduced by Willstätter [1009] after Tsvett's death.

[1007] **CURTIS,** Heber Doust
American astronomer
Born: Muskegon, Michigan,
June 27, 1872
Died: Ann Arbor, Michigan,
January 9, 1942

Curtis was educated at the University of Michigan, earning his master's degree in 1893. He became a professor of Latin and Greek at Napa College in California and there he grew interested in a telescope, was won over to astronomy, and in 1896 transferred his professorship to that subject.

In 1898 he began to work at Lick Observatory and in 1902 he earned his doctorate in astronomy at the University of Virginia.

In the course of his work, he studied nebulae, which he thought to represent "island universes" as Kant [293] had believed. His best argument was that there seemed to be numerous very faint novas in some of those nebulas, far more numerous than could be expected and far fainter than if they were objects within our own galaxy.

In this view, he collided head on with Shapley [1102], who accepted the observations of Adriaan van Maanen (1884–1946) that nebulae rotated more quickly than they should be seen to do if they were indeed very distant. Van Maanen's observations were mistaken but Shapley didn't know that.

In 1920 Curtis and Shapley met in a great debate before the National Academy of Sciences, and at the time it was held that Curtis had the better of it. Certainly as the 1920s wore on, it became clear that Curtis was correct and Shapley was mistaken, and in this way the universe of the galaxies was for the first time spread out before human eyes in its full glory.

[1008] **AMUNDSEN,** Roald Engelbregt
Gravning (ah'moon-sen)
Norwegian explorer
Born: Borge, Østfold, July 16, 1872
Died: near Spitsbergen, June 16, 1928

Amundsen interrupted a medical education to join the Norwegian navy and by 1897 was engaged in an Antarctic expedition conducted under Belgian auspices. This was the first expedition to winter in the Antarctic.

As the twentieth century opened, he was exploring the Arctic and in 1903 made his way by sea from the Atlantic to the Pacific along the Arctic coast of North America (the famous Northwest Passage). He sailed secretly, by the way, to avoid his creditors. In 1904 he located the site of the North Magnetic Pole. It took him three years to complete this journey.

When the news of the attainment of the North Pole by Peary [866] reached him, it seemed to Amundsen that the most important remaining unreached area of the planet was the South Pole. At the beginning of 1911 he reached the Antarctic continent and waited for the Antarctic summer season (December through February). In October 1911 he began his dash for the pole, reaching it on December 14 and returning safely, beating Scott [971] by a month.

He then added to his laurels by flying from Spitsbergen to Alaska by dirigible in 1926, passing over the North Pole as he did so. He had failed in three previous attempts. There were some unpleasant disputes afterward as to whether he, or a colleague, deserved the credit.

He died on another flight over the Arctic in June 1928, in a search for survivors of a shipwreck.

[1009] **WILLSTÄTTER,** Richard (vil'-shtet-er)
German chemist
Born: Karlsruhe, Baden, August 13, 1872
Died: Locarno, Switzerland, August 3, 1942

Willstätter, the son of a well-to-do Jewish textile merchant, received his education at the University of Munich, where he studied under Baeyer [718] and obtained his doctorate in 1894. He served as Baeyer's private assistant for a time thereafter.

His most important research was in connection with plant pigments after he had obtained a professorial position at the University of Zürich in Switzerland in 1905. The plant pigments were interesting for two reasons. The first was that one of them, chlorophyll, was the means whereby the energy of sunlight was converted into foodstuffs, so that upon it all life (except for some microorganisms) depended. The second was that the pigments formed so complex a group of similar substances that the problem of their separation was an almost unbearably attractive (if desperately frustrating) challenge.

The problem had already been solved in its essence by Tsvett [1006] in 1906, who had introduced the technique of chromatography. However, Tsvett's report had been published in Russian and it attracted little attention. Willstätter reintroduced the technique and through him and others like Kuhn [1233] it became important. In fact, when two decades later the method was adapted for use with filter paper by Martin [1350] and Synge [1394], it became the universally used technique for separating mixtures. Willstätter worked out the way in which the magnesium atom was placed in the chlorophyll molecule and showed that the iron atom was held in similar fashion in heme, the colored portion of the hemoglobin molecule.

Willstätter was honored with the 1915 Nobel Prize in chemistry for his work on plant pigments.

After 1911 Willstätter returned to professorial posts in Germany. During World War I, he went into war work at the plea of his good friend Haber [977] and designed an effective gas mask. In 1916 he succeeded Baeyer as professor of chemistry at Munich.

He interested himself in the 1920s in enzymes. It seemed to him that enzymes were not protein in nature (as most chemists suspected they were) for he purified enzyme solutions to the point where they still possessed catalytic properties and yet reacted negatively to the most delicate tests for protein. For ten years his views held sway in this respect but he was wrong, as was demonstrated by Sumner [1120] and Northrop [1148]. Enzymes, it turned out, *were* protein.

Willstätter resigned his professorial post at the University of Munich in 1925 in protest against the anti-Semitism increasingly manifest there. With the coming of Hitler in 1933 he remained in Germany, however, believing his place was there. His life was in continual danger, and in 1939, he recognized that to remain longer was suicide. He left for Switzerland in March of that year and there spent the last years of his life.

[1010] **DUGGAR,** Benjamin Minge
(dug′er)
American botanist
Born: Gallion, Alabama,
September 1, 1872
Died: New Haven, Connecticut,
September 10, 1956

Duggar, the son of a country doctor, entered the University of Alabama at not quite fifteen. He obtained his Ph.D. from Cornell in 1898, then did further work in Germany and Italy.

His great discovery came at a time when the average scientist is long retired. In 1948, when he was seventy-six years old, he discovered and introduced aureomycin, the first of the tetracycline antibiotics—a family that, next to penicillin perhaps, represents the most useful and least dangerous of the antibiotics.

[1011] **EULER-CHELPIN,** Hans Karl August Simon von (oi′ler-khel′pin)
German-Swedish chemist
Born: Augsburg, Bavaria,
Germany, February 15, 1873
Died: Stockholm, Sweden,
November 7, 1964

Euler-Chelpin was the son of a German army officer and was distantly related to Euler [275]. He was interested in painting, but he veered from that to chemistry. He graduated from the University of Berlin in 1895, where he studied under Planck [887] and Emil Fischer [833]. He then worked with Nernst [936] and afterward with Arrhenius [894] and Van't Hoff [829]. In 1906 Euler-Chelpin left Germany to become a professor at the University of Stockholm and there he remained, retiring in 1941.

He worked on enzymes, coenzymes, and vitamins, contributing to the determination of the structure of several of the vitamins. In particular, he was the first, through a line of experimentation beginning in 1923, to work out the structure of Harden's [947] coenzyme. For this he shared with Harden the 1929 Nobel Prize in chemistry.

[1012] **D'HÉRELLE,** Félix Hubert (day-rel')
Canadian-French bacteriologist
Born: Montreal, Canada, April 25, 1873
Died: Paris, France, February 22, 1949

D'Hérelle was born in Canada of a French father and a Dutch mother, and continued this French-Dutch combination by studying medicine at Paris and then at Leiden.

While working at the Pasteur Institute in 1916, he was culturing bacteria when he noticed places in the culture where there were no bacteria. Something was destroying them. By 1917 he was convinced he had discovered a virus that infested and destroyed bacterial cells. He called the virus "bacteriophage" ("bacteria eater").

This had been noticed a little earlier by Twort [1055], but Twort did not follow up on the discovery and D'Hérelle did.

[1013] **SIDGWICK,** Nevil Vincent
English chemist
Born: Oxford, May 8, 1873
Died: Oxford, March 15, 1952

Sidgwick was educated at Oxford and, except for some graduate work in Germany (where, for a short time, he studied under Ostwald [840]), he remained at Oxford as a member of the faculty for all his professional life.

He did his chief work in the 1920s on the electronic concept of valence. As advanced by Abegg [978] and Lewis [1037] it did not, even at its widest application, apply to Werner's [960] coordination compounds. Sidgwick investigated this, making use of Bohr's [1101] concept of the atom, and its electron shells, which had now been published. Sidgwick showed that the Lewis concept of electron sharing applied outside the realm of organic chemistry and, in particular, that the pair of shared electrons might both come from the same atom to form a coordinate bond. These coordinate bonds played a special role in coordina-

tion compounds and even in ordinary organic compounds at times when the nitrogen atom was involved.

(Sidgwick had long specialized in the organic chemistry of nitrogen. His book on the subject, first published in 1910, was a classic and he expanded it into a bulky two-volume work in 1947.)

[1014] **BERGER,** Hans
German psychiatrist
Born: Neuses (near Coburg), Bavaria, May 21, 1873
Died: Jena, June 1, 1941

Berger, the grandson of a well-known German poet, gained his medical degree in 1897 and taught at the University of Jena from 1900. He was the first, in 1929, to devise a system of electrodes that, when applied to the skull and connected to an oscillograph, would give a recording of the rhythmic shifting of electric potentials, commonly called brain waves. His first human subject in these experiments was his young son.

He studied the rhythms, and labeled the most prominent as "alpha waves" and "beta waves." Out of this discovery the technique of electroencephalography was born. It has been useful in the diagnosis of epilepsy and it is quite possible that, with growing understanding of the brain, electroencephalography will yet serve as a guide to the fine workings of the nervous system.

[1015] **LOEWI,** Otto (loi'vee)
German-American physiologist
Born: Frankfurt-am-Main, June 3, 1873
Died: New York, New York, December 25, 1961

Loewi, the son of a wealthy Jewish wine merchant, studied medicine at the University of Strasbourg and obtained his medical degree there in 1896. Thereafter he worked some years in London under Starling [954]. In 1905 he went to Austria, where he held professorial positions first at the University of Vienna, then, after 1909, at the University of Graz.

His chief work was in connection with nerve action. It had been known since the time of Galvani [320] over a century earlier that the nerve impulse was electrical in nature. Loewi, however, demonstrated that chemical phenomena were also involved. In 1921, working with the nerves attached to a frog's heart, he showed that chemical substances were set free when the nerve was stimulated. The fluid containing the substance could be used to stimulate another heart directly without the intervention of nerve activity.

The idea for the experiment occurred to him at 3 A.M. on two successive nights. The first night he wrote it down and went back to sleep. In the morning he could not read what he had written. The second night he went straight to his laboratory and got to work. By 5 A.M. he had established the point.

Loewi called the substance he had discovered Vagusstoff ("vagus material") because he obtained it by stimulating the vagus nerve. The material was soon shown by Dale [1034] to be acetylcholine and, as a result, the two men, Loewi and Dale, shared the 1936 Nobel Prize in medicine and physiology.

Two years later Hitler's Germany invaded and absorbed Austria. Loewi was placed under arrest. Fearing death was inevitable, he managed to persuade a guard to allow him to mail a postcard to the scientific journal *Naturwissenschaften* detailing some of his current work. Fortunately death was avoided. He was allowed to leave the country provided he turn over his Nobel Prize money to the Nazis.

He went first to England and in 1940 to the United States. There he joined the faculty of the New York University College of Medicine, becoming an American citizen in 1946 and spending the remainder of his life in his new home.

[1016] **CARREL,** Alexis (ka-rel´)
    French-American surgeon
    Born: Lyon, June 28, 1873
    Died: Paris, November 5, 1944

Carrel, the son of a textile manufacturer, who died when Alexis was five, studied at the University of Lyon and obtained his medical degree in 1900.

He quickly proved himself a deft surgeon. He was inspired with interest in the field of blood-vessel repair by the assassination, in 1894, of the French president, Carnot (the nephew of Sadi Carnot [497]). In that incident, the bullet severed a major artery and, conceivably, his life could have been saved if the artery had been quickly repaired.

Carrel developed a technique whereby blood vessels could be delicately sutured, that is, sewn together end to end. He did this successfully in 1902, requiring as few as three stitches for the job.

For some reason, however, he temporarily lost interest in the field and in 1904 went to Canada with the idea of becoming a cattle rancher. But science would not let him be and he went on to the United States. In 1906 he joined the Rockefeller Institute for Medical Research (now Rockefeller University) in New York, remaining there until his retirement in 1939.

Carrel's surgical research in his early years at Rockefeller was directed toward the replacement or transplantation of organs. For this to be successful, it was necessary to insure a proper blood supply in an organ's new location, and Carrel's blood-vessel techniques were exactly what was required.

At about this time Landsteiner's [973] discovery of blood groups had made blood transfusion practical, and such blood-vessel suturing was useful for the purpose. With the development of anticoagulants, suturing proved unnecessary for transfusion, but it remained vital to many surgical operations which now became much more practical. Carrel was awarded the 1912 Nobel Prize in medicine and physiology for this work.

In itself, such suturing still did not make possible the transplantation or replacement of organs. However, Carrel then went on to attempt to keep organs or portions of organs alive by means of perfusion, that is, by passing blood or blood substitutes continuously through the organ by way of its own blood vessels. He kept a piece of embryonic chicken heart alive and growing (it had to be periodically trimmed) for over thirty-four years—much longer than the normal life-span of a chicken—before the experiment was deliberately terminated, and this appealed dramatically to public fancy. To make the process more efficient, he worked with Lindbergh [1249] in the early 1930s to design a perfusion pump that was germ-proof, a so-called "artificial heart."

Carrel served with the French army during World War I and devised an antiseptic fluid, essentially a solution of sodium hypochlorite, that kept down the death rate from infected wounds. His experiences in World War II were to be less happy.

His philosophy as expressed in his book *Man, the Unknown* (published in 1935) was rather authoritarian and visualized a world run by an intellectual elite. He was out of sympathy with western notions of democracy.

He returned to France in 1939 just before the outbreak of World War II and during the opening year of the war was employed by the French government in the field of public health. France was defeated in 1940 and a portion of the nation was placed under the control of a government centered in the town of Vichy, one which was subservient to the Germans. Carrel seemed in sympathy with the Vichy government and worked for it.

When France was liberated, he was dismissed from his posts. He was not tried for "collaboration," however. For one thing, he died within a matter of months.

[1017] DE FOREST, Lee
American inventor
Born: Council Bluffs, Iowa,
August 26, 1873
Died: Hollywood, California,
June 30, 1961

De Forest grew up in Alabama, where his father, a minister, had come in 1879 to serve as a principal of a school for blacks. The family was, of course, os-

tracized for this crime and young Lee found his friends only among black children. He did not seem to suffer unduly from this fact.

De Forest's father wanted him to enter the ministry, too, but the young man wanted science. He graduated from Yale in 1896 and obtained his Ph.D. in 1899, after some time spent in military service in the Spanish-American War, during which he saw no action.

While yet at school, where he studied under Gibbs [740], he became interested in the new field of wireless telegraphy being opened up by Marconi [1025]. Indeed, his Ph.D. dissertation was probably the first in the United States to deal with radio waves.

In 1901 he devised methods of speeding up the transmission of wireless signals and his system was used in 1904 for the first instance of news reporting (of the Russo-Japanese War) in this manner.

His greatest invention, however (and he had three hundred patents before he was done), was the triode. The Edison effect, noticed first by Edison [788], had been investigated by Fleming [803] and in 1904 made the basis of a rectifier. In 1906 De Forest inserted a third element, called the grid, making the instrument a triode (three electrodes) rather than a diode.

The stream of electrons moved from the filament to the plate at a rate that varied markedly with the charge placed on the grid. A varying but very weak electric potential on the grid could be converted into a similarly varying but much stronger electron flow in the filament-plate combination. In De Forest's hands Fleming's instrument became an amplifier as well as a rectifier.

The triode is the basis of the familiar radio tube, which made radios and a whole variety of electronic equipment practical by magnifying weak signals without distortion. In 1910 De Forest had taken Fessenden's [958] system of broadcasting voice and used his triodes to broadcast the singing of Enrico Caruso. In 1916 he established a radio station and was broadcasting news.

In the end De Forest sold his radio tube (or audion as he called it) to

American Telephone and Telegraph Company for $390,000 (a bargain at the price), but in the days of its first development, he had his hard times. At one point he was placed under arrest for using the mails to defraud, when he was merely trying to raise cash to finance this invention. Like many inventors he was not a particularly successful businessman. Frequently engaged in litigation, he lost fortunes as often as he made them.

His triode, however, remained in undisputed command of the 90-billion-dollar electronic industry it created for a generation until Shockley's [1348] transistor put it in the shade.

In the early 1920s De Forest worked out a "glow lamp," which could convert the irregularities of a sound wave into similar irregularities of an electric current, which would in turn create similar irregularities in the brightness of the lamp filament. The filament brightness could be photographed along with a motion picture and the varying brightness of the sound track could then be reconverted into sound. In 1923 De Forest demonstrated the first sound motion picture and within five years "talkies" began to take over.

All in all, De Forest was granted more than three hundred patents, the last in 1957 when he was eighty-four years old.

Because of the invention of the triode, De Forest is sometimes called the father of radio and he wrote an autobiography with that title. However, few inventions have had so many fathers.

[1018] HERTZSPRUNG, Ejnar
Danish astronomer
Born: Frederiksberg, October 8, 1873
Died: Roskilde, October 21, 1967

Hertzsprung, the son of a minor government official, was educated as a chemical engineer and worked in St. Petersburg from 1899 to 1901. He returned to Copenhagen in 1902 as an amateur astronomer and in 1909 he was appointed lecturer of astrophysics at Göttin-

gen because of the favorable impression his work made on Schwarzschild.

Hertzsprung had first advanced the notion of "absolute magnitude," comparing the brightness of the stars by placing them, in imagination, at a standard distance of ten parsecs ("luminosity"), where a parsec is the distance at which a star has a parallax of one second, or 3.25 light-years.

He went on to note the relationship of color and luminosity among stars as early as 1905. He specialized in photography (doing good work in estimating stellar magnitude from photographs and in photographing double stars accurately) so he published his notions in a journal of photography in a semipopular way. His article lay there unnoticed for nearly a decade. H. N. Russell's [1056] independent discovery of the fact was announced more formally and as a result both astronomers share equally in the credit.

In 1911 Hertzsprung noted that the Pole star varied slightly in brightness and was a Cepheid and in 1913 he was the first to estimate the actual distances of some Cepheid variables. This, together with the work of Leavitt [975], allowed Shapley [1102] to work out the proper shape of our galaxy.

Hertzsprung was full professor at Leiden in 1935. He retired in 1945 and returned to Denmark to die in the fullness of his years, one of the patriarchs of science.

[1019] SCHWARZSCHILD, Karl
(shvahrts'shild)
German astronomer
Born: Frankfurt-am-Main, October 9, 1873
Died: Potsdam, May 11, 1916

Schwarzschild was the son of a prosperous Jewish businessman. He grew interested in astronomy as a child, was encouraged by his culture-centered family, and wrote and published his first astronomical paper (on the orbits of double stars) when he was sixteen.

He studied at the universities of Strasbourg and of Munich, and received his

Ph.D. *summa cum laude* in 1896. In 1901 he accepted a professorial position at Göttingen.

Schwarzschild developed the use of photography for measuring the brightness of stars, particularly of variable ones. As a result of using this technique, he suggested that periodic variable stars behaved so because of periodic temperature changes, and this led to the further work of Eddington [1085] on Cepheid variables.

He volunteered for military service when World War I began and was serving on the Russian front with the artillery in 1916 when he heard of Einstein's [1064] work on general relativity. He was the first to offer a solution to Einstein's field equations, and he was the first to calculate gravitational phenomena in the neighborhood of a star with all its mass concentrated in a point. This was what came to be called a black hole a half century later, and the concept of the Schwarzschild radius as the boundary of such a black hole is still accepted. He died soon afterward of a rare metabolic disorder.

Schwarzschild, throughout his working life, attached great importance to lecturing and writing on popular astronomy.

[1020] **COOLIDGE,** William David
American physicist
Born: Hudson, Massachusetts, October 23, 1873
Died: Schenectady, New York, February 3, 1975

Coolidge, a distant cousin of President Calvin Coolidge, graduated from Massachusetts Institute of Technology in 1896 on borrowed money, then went to Germany on a scholarship for graduate work, obtaining his Ph.D. *summa cum laude* at Leipzig in 1899. In 1905 he joined the General Electric Company where he remained till his retirement in 1944, eventually becoming director of research, and vice president.

One of the great technological problems of the early twentieth century was that of finding a satisfactory fiber for use in electric light bulbs. Edison [788] had

introduced carbon fibers, but these were brittle and difficult to handle. Some high-melting metal, in the form of wire, would be much better.

Tungsten is the metal with the highest melting point (about 3410°C) but it is also brittle and there was no reasonable way of drawing it into wires. At least there wasn't till Coolidge got to work. In 1909 he patented a technique for manufacturing ductile tungsten, which could be drawn out into fine wires, and it is such wires that, to this day, are to be found in light bulbs, radio tubes, and other devices.

Coolidge also made use of a tungsten block as anode in an X-ray tube in 1913 and the resultant version (the "Coolidge tube") shifted X-ray production from the laboratory into common use in industry and medicine.

During World War I, in collaboration with Langmuir [1072], he developed the first successful submarine-detection system. In World War II he was engaged in atomic bomb research at Hanford, Washington.

He shared with Chevreul [448] the distinction of being a scientist-centenarian.

[1021] **COBLENTZ,** William Weber
American physicist
Born: North Lima, Ohio, November 20, 1873
Died: Washington, D.C., September 15, 1962

Coblentz, the son of a farmer, was graduated from Case Institute of Technology in 1900 and obtained his Ph.D. in 1903 from Cornell. In 1905 he founded the radiometry section of the National Bureau of Standards, which he then headed for forty years.

He was particularly interested in radiation beyond the visible spectrum and showed that different atomic groupings absorbed characteristic and specific wavelengths in the infrared. His instruments were too crude to convert this finding into a method of analysis, but before he had ended his long life, the advance of technology had brought the infrared spectrophotometer into being.

This measured and recorded the extent of absorption of different wavelengths in the infrared so that from the rise and fall of the inked stylus, the various atomic groupings in a given molecule could be detected with extraordinary delicacy and without damage to the molecule itself.

[1022] **HARKINS,** William Draper
American chemist
Born: Titusville, Pennsylvania, December 28, 1873
Died: Chicago, Illinois, March 7, 1951

Harkins was born near the site where oil was first obtained by drilling, and his father was one of the pioneers in this field. Harkins obtained his Ph.D. at Stanford University in 1900, then traveled to Germany for advanced work under Haber [977]. After teaching for some years at the University of Montana, he took a post at the University of Chicago in 1912 and remained there for the rest of his life.

He grew interested in nuclear chemistry and showed daring foresight, predicting the existence of the neutron and of heavy hydrogen. He was particularly interested in the slight deviations from the whole number in the mass of atomic nuclei, introducing what he called the packing fraction, which signified the amount of energy consumed in packing the nucleons into the nucleus. He used Einstein's [1064] equation relating mass and energy to show that if four hydrogen atoms were converted into a helium nucleus, some mass would be lost (saved in the packing, so to speak), which would appear as energy.

He suggested this as the mechanism whereby stars gained energy and this has turned out to be essentially correct. The hydrogen-to-helium conversion is, in essence, the basis for fusion power and the hydrogen bomb. The latter development, however, Harkins did not quite live to see.

He was one of the first to consider the problem of the relative proportions of the elements in the universe as a whole,

basing his calculations on considerations of nuclear stability, the more stable nuclei being the more common.

[1023] **ERLANGER,** Joseph
American physiologist
Born: San Francisco, California, January 5, 1874
Died: St. Louis, Missouri, December 5, 1965

Erlanger, the son of a German immigrant, attended the University of California and graduated in 1895, having majored in chemistry. He continued his education at Johns Hopkins medical school where he received his medical degree in 1899. In 1900 he joined the physiology department of Johns Hopkins. He next went to the University of Wisconsin's newly organized medical school as head of the physiology department and there Gasser [1126] was one of his students. Finally he headed the physiology department of Washington University, St. Louis, in 1910 (keeping this position till his retirement in 1948). Gasser joined him there.

In the 1920s they did their work on the electrical properties of nerve fibers. They achieved great delicacy of measurement, not by making still more sensitive detectors as Einthoven [904] had done, but by making use of Braun's [808] oscillograph to amplify the currents detected. In this way they determined how different fibers conducted their impulses at different rates, velocity of impulse varying directly with the thickness of fiber. For their work Erlanger and Gasser shared the 1944 Nobel Prize in medicine and physiology.

[1024] **STARK,** Johannes (shtahrk)
German physicist
Born: Schickenhof, Bavaria, April 15, 1874
Died: Traunstein, Bavaria, June 21, 1957

Stark studied at the University of Munich and joined the physics department at Göttingen in 1900.

He worked with the canal rays that had been discovered by Goldstein [811] and managed to observe a Doppler [534] effect in them in 1905.

In 1913 he showed that a strong electric field would cause a multiplication in spectral lines. This is an analogue of the effect of a magnetic field, discovered by Zeeman [945]. The Stark effect could be explained by quantum mechanics and thus served as another piece of support for quantum theory. For his work Stark received the 1919 Nobel Prize in physics.

Stark, like Lenard [920], was one of the few German scientists of note who wholeheartedly supported Hitler and his racial theories. He turned violently and irrationally against both quantum theory and relativity, spoke and wrote reams of nonsense about "Aryan science," and was all the Nazis could hope for in a scientist. He snapped vindictively at the heels of Sommerfeld [976] and Heisenberg [1245], terming them "white Jews."

He served as president of the Reich Physical-Technical Institute from 1933 to 1939 and was sufficiently active as a Nazi to be tried and convicted by a denazification court in 1947.

He was sentenced to four years' imprisonment, a far milder punishment than would have been true had he been in the judge's seat.

[1025] MARCONI, Marchese Guglielmo
Italian electrical engineer
Born: Bologna, April 25, 1874
Died: Rome, July 20, 1937

Marconi came of a well-to-do family and was privately tutored. He studied physics under well-known Italian professors but without formally enrolling in any university.

In 1894 he came across an article on the electromagnetic waves discovered eight years earlier by H. R. Hertz [873] and it occurred to him that these might be used in signaling. By the end of the year he was ringing a bell at a distance of thirty feet.

He made use of Hertz's method of producing the radio waves and of a device called the coherer to detect them. The coherer consisted of a container of loosely packed metal filings, which ordinarily conducted little current, but which conducted quite a bit when radio waves fell upon it. In this way radio waves could be converted into an easily detected electrical current.

Gradually, Marconi improved his instruments, grounding both the transmitter and receiver, and using a wire, insulated from the earth, which served as an antenna or aerial to facilitate both sending and receiving. In the use of the aerial he was anticipated by Popov [895].

As time went on, he sent signals across greater and greater distances. In 1895 he sent one from his house to his garden and later for the distance of a mile and a half. In 1896, when the Italian government showed itself uninterested in his work, he went to England (his mother was Irish and he could speak English perfectly) and sent a signal nine miles. He then applied for and obtained the first patent in the history of radio.

In 1897, again in Italy, he sent a signal from land to a warship twelve miles away, and in 1898 (back in England) he covered eighteen miles.

By then he was beginning to make his system commercial. The aged Kelvin [652] paid to send a Marconigram to the even more aged Stokes [618] and that was the first commercial wireless message. Marconi also used his signals to report the yacht races at Kingstown Regatta that year.

He obtained a key patent (number 7,777) in 1900 and then, in 1901, Marconi reached the denouement of his drama. His experiments had already convinced him that the Hertzian radio waves would follow the curve of the earth instead of radiating straight outward as electromagnetic waves might be expected to do. (The explanation came the next year from Kennelly [916] and Heaviside [806] as suggestions that were demonstrated to be correct by Appleton [1158].) For this reason he made elaborate preparations for sending a radio signal from the southwest tip of England to

Newfoundland, using balloons to lift his antennae as high as possible.

On December 12, 1901, he succeeded, to the openly expressed admiration of Edison [788] (though Rayleigh [760] seemed to think it was a fraud). This might be considered as good a date as any for the invention of radio, although it was still only useful for sending signals in Morse code. It was left to Fessenden [958] to facilitate the transmission of sound-wave signals on radio-wave carriers. In 1904 a demonstration of radio operation was a big hit at the St. Louis World's Fair.

In 1909 Marconi shared the Nobel Prize in physics with Braun [808] and in later years experimented extensively with the use of short-wave radio for signaling.

He was in charge of Italy's radio service during World War I, and perfected the "radio beam" along which a pilot could fly blind.

Marconi interested himself in politics, too. He served as one of the Italian delegates to the peace conference that concluded the war. After that, he was an enthusiastic supporter of Mussolini's Fascist government. In 1929 he was made a noble, with the rank of marchese, by the Italian government.

Radio came to be used as the chief means of public entertainment until largely replaced a generation later by television. Private communications, however, required the privacy of the telephone wire, particularly after the improvement in the process introduced by Pupin [891].

When Marconi died, he was given a state funeral by the Italian government.

[1026] **DEBIERNE,** André Louis (duh-biehrn′)
French chemist
Born: Paris, 1874
Died: Paris, August 1949

Debierne, a student of Friedel [693], was a close friend of Pierre and Marie Curie [897, 965] and was associated with their work. In 1899, for instance, he discovered the radioactive element actinium, as a result of continuing the

work with pitchblende that the Curies had initiated.

After the tragic death of Pierre Curie in 1906, Debierne helped Marie Curie carry on and worked with her in teaching and research.

In 1910 he and Marie Curie prepared radium in metallic form in visible amounts. They did not keep it metallic, however. Having demonstrated the metal's existence as a matter of scientific curiosity, they reconverted it into compounds with which they might continue their researches.

[1027] **GOLDBERGER,** Joseph
Austrian-American physician
Born: Girált, Austria-Hungary (now Giraltovce, Czechoslovakia), July 16, 1874
Died: Washington, D.C., January 17, 1929

Goldberger, the son of a Jewish immigrant, was taken to the United States at the age of six. He was educated in the City College of New York, and obtained his medical degree from Bellevue Hospital Medical College in 1895. He entered the U. S. Public Health Service in 1899 and was sent to Cuba and Mexico to investigate yellow fever and typhus, both of which he contracted.

In 1913 he was caught up in the growing field of vitamin research and spent most of the rest of his life investigating pellagra, endemic in the southern part of the United States. Funk [1093] had speculated that pellagra might be caused by inadequate diet, and Goldberger and his associates noted that it struck wherever the diet was monotonous and limited and did not include much in the way of milk, meat, or eggs. Addition of these items to the diet relieved the condition.

In 1915 he conducted a dramatic experiment on prisoners in a Mississippi jail. Volunteers (who were promised pardons in return) were placed on a limited diet, lacking meat or milk. After six months they developed pellagra, which could be relieved by adding milk and meat to the diet. Goldberger's study group went to great lengths to try to contract pellagra by contact with the patients, their clothing, and their excretions. They failed. Pellagra was not infectious; it was a dietary deficiency disease. Goldberger spoke of a P-P factor ("pellagra-preventive"), but the vitamin involved was proved by Elvehjem [1240] to be nicotinic acid or, as it is also called, niacin.

Cancer ended Goldberger's unusual life; unusual even outside science, for in 1906 he had married a Gentile and made a happy (though rather impoverished) life of it. And this was at a time when mixed marriages of this sort were quite uncommon.

[1028] **BOSCH,** Karl (boshe)
German chemist
Born: Cologne, August 27, 1874
Died: Heidelberg, April 26, 1940

Bosch, the son of an engineer, obtained his Ph.D. from the University of Leipzig in 1898, majoring in chemistry and studying under Wislicenus [716]. He had training as an engineer, too. In 1909 he undertook the development of the Haber [977] process, turning it from a laboratory demonstration into an industrial operation. For one thing, Haber had used a carbon-steel container for the reacting gases. This reacted with hydrogen and in time grew brittle and eventually, subjected as it was to high temperature and pressure, broke down. Bosch substituted alloy steel, which held up well.

Under his direction a huge ammonia plant at Oppau was built and it was still under construction when World War I broke out. In 1931 he received the Nobel Prize in chemistry, along with Bergius [1098], not for having contributed so vitally to the German war effort, of course, but for his investigations of the type of high-pressure reactions that made it possible to produce ammonia from nitrogen. It is important to remember that the Haber process (or "Haber-Bosch process," as it is sometimes called) is as important to the production of fertilizer as explosive.

In 1935 he succeeded Planck [887] as

head of the Kaiser Wilhelm Society. Bosch managed to continue his work under the Nazi regime without bowing to Nazi principles (he openly honored Haber, for instance, after that man's death in exile) and died before the horrors of war turned back in full force upon Germany itself.

[1029] **BLAKESLEE,** Albert Francis
American botanist
Born: Geneseo, New York, November 9, 1874
Died: Northampton, Massachusetts, November 16, 1954

Blakeslee obtained his Ph.D. from Harvard in 1904. His important contribution came in 1937 when, as director of the Carnegie Station for Experimental Evolution, he found that the alkaloid colchicine, obtained from the autumn crocus, can produce mutations in plants. To be sure, it does not do this by altering genes, as Muller's [1145] X rays do; instead, it allows the chromosomes to double in number without allowing the cell itself to divide, so that cells are produced with multiple numbers of chromosomes (polyploidy). Nevertheless, this discovery did represent the first directly chemical interference with the mechanics of heredity. Other chemicals, such as nitrogen mustards, were soon discovered that produced mutations by inducing chemical changes within the chromosomes, so that the field of chemical mutagens was opened wide.

He retired in 1942 to a post at Smith College, which he held till his death.

[1030] **KROGH,** Schack August Steenberg (krawg)
Danish physiologist
Born: Grenå, Jutland, November 15, 1874
Died: Copenhagen, September 13, 1949

Krogh, the son of a brewer, was educated at the University of Copenhagen, where he intended to study medicine but shifted his interest to physiology. He obtained his master's degree in 1899.

He was particularly interested in the physical mechanisms involved in respiration, following the path of oxygen, nitrogen, and carbon dioxide in and out of the body. In 1908 he gained a professorial position at the University of Copenhagen and there his studies of respiration led him to suggest that the capillaries (the tiniest blood vessels) of the muscles were open during muscular work and partially closed during rest. He went on to demonstrate this and to show the importance of such capillary control to the economy of the body.

For this work, he was awarded the Nobel Prize in physiology and medicine in 1920. He went on thereafter to show that this capillary control was brought about by the action of both muscles and hormones.

After Denmark was occupied by Nazi Germany in 1940, Krogh was forced to go underground and then to escape to Sweden. He remained there till the end of the war, then returned to liberated Denmark.

[1031] **WEISMANN,** Chaim (vytse'-mahn)
Russian-British-Israeli chemist
Born: Motol' (near Pinsk), Russia, November 27, 1874
Died: Rehovoth, Israel, November 9, 1952

Weizmann, the son of a Jewish lumber transporter, journeyed to Germany for his higher education, obtaining his doctorate *magna cum laude* in 1900 at the University of Freiburg. He then lectured on chemistry at the University of Geneva.

In 1904 he went to England to join the faculty of the University of Manchester as a reader in biochemistry. England suited him and he remained, becoming a British subject in 1910.

The coming of World War I put Great Britain (and all the warring nations, in fact) in dire need of explosives. Great Britain had nitrates available from Chile (as Germany had not), thanks to her control of the sea, but nitrates were not everything. Gunpowder, a mixture of carbon and inorganics, had given way to Dewar's [759] cordite, which made use of organic nitrates that had to be synthesized in quantity. Fortunately Great Britain's new subject Weizmann had in 1911 discovered a way to put a particular strain of bacterium to work synthesizing the compound acetone, in the course of its fermentation of grain. Acetone supplied the essentials for the manufacture of cordite.

In peacetime the fermentation could be modified and made to yield butyl alcohol to use, for instance, in lacquers. Weizmann's process was the forerunner of the deliberate use of microorganisms for a wide variety of syntheses. A generation later such compounds as penicillin and vitamin B_{12} were produced by microorganisms cultivated for the purpose.

Thus, Weizmann relieved the British explosives pinch, while his fellow religionist Haber [977] was doing the same for Germany. Weizmann's reward was quite different, however. He was a convinced and fiery Zionist and it was partly owing to him that the British government was induced to put forth the Balfour Declaration in 1917 agreeing to the reestablishment of a Jewish national state in Palestine. In 1919 he headed a Jewish delegation to the peace conference that followed World War I.

From 1921 he was president of the World Zionist Organization and deeply involved with other organizations dedicated to the establishment of such a state and to the consideration of the gathering problems of Jews everywhere. A generation was to pass—a tragic one that was to see bitter Arab-Jewish clashes in Palestine as well as the barbarity of Hitler and his followers—before the Balfour Declaration was implemented.

In 1932 he became president of the Hebrew University in Jerusalem. Then, in 1948, when the state of Israel was founded, Weizmann became its first president, though his age and poor health made it impossible to be very active. Nevertheless, he remained in the post until his death. He was one of the very few research scientists ever to serve as head of a state.

[1032] **MONIZ,** Antonio Caetano de Abreu Freire Egas (mawn'eess)
Portuguese surgeon
Born: Avanca, November 29, 1874
Died: Lisbon, December 13, 1955

Moniz received his early education from his uncle, a cleric. He went on to study medicine at the University of Coimbra, getting his degree in 1899, and was appointed to a professorial position there in 1902. In 1911 he became the first professor of neurology at the University of Lisbon. His chief interest in those years was in the visualization of the blood vessels, of the brain particularly. He did this by injecting into the blood a substance opaque to X rays and then taking an X-ray photograph.

Moniz was active in public affairs, serving a number of years in the Portuguese legislature prior to World War I and spending some time in prison after the revolution of 1908. He rose to the post of minister of foreign affairs in 1917 and led the Portuguese delegation to the Paris Peace Conference in 1918.

After a duel in 1919, he retired from politics.

His greatest fame came in connection with his interest in the foremost region of the brain, the prefrontal lobe. It had no clear-cut functions and was one of the so-called silent areas of the brain. It seemed reasonable to suppose that it served as one of the coordinating centers in the brain, an area where associations were made, where routes, so to speak, were set up among the nerve cells accumulating life's experiences and thoughts.

It seemed to Moniz that where a mental patient was at the end of his rope, and ordinary psychiatry and ordinary physical therapy did not help, it might be possible simply to sever the prefrontal lobes and cut the patient off from some of the nerve patterns he had built up. They might very well be undesirable

and pathological ones and their loss might be to the good.

The operation was first carried through in 1935 and in a number of cases it did seem to help. Moniz had, in this manner, opened a new field of medical specialization, that of psychosurgery, and he was awarded a share of the 1949 Nobel Prize in medicine and physiology as a result. The operation has, however, remained a last resort and has never gained more than a very limited popularity. It virtually died out after the discovery of tranquilizers and other drugs which could be used to treat emotional disturbances.

[1033] **MICHAELIS,** Leonor (mih-khah-ay'lis)
German-American chemist
Born: Berlin, Germany, January 16, 1875
Died: New York, New York, October 9, 1949

Michaelis obtained his medical degree at the University of Berlin in 1896 and for a while thereafter worked under Ehrlich [845], developing useful cell stains.

His chief interest lay in the application of physical chemical principles to biochemical reactions. For instance, he dealt with the variations in hydrogen ion concentration (which, at about that time, was reduced to an elegant representation by Sørensen [967]) and the influence of those variations on reactions.

Virtually all reactions in living tissue are catalyzed by enzymes and it was the still mysterious enzymes that Michaelis turned to. Kühne [725] had given them a name a generation before, but their actual nature remained unknown for a quarter century to come because Willstätter [1009] made a wrong decision in that connection.

Michaelis, however, did not care what an enzyme was as long as he could understand how it worked. He applied the rules of chemical kinetics (a branch of physical chemistry dealing with the rates of reactions) and in 1913 evolved an

equation that seemed to describe how
the rate of an enzyme-catalyzed reaction
varied with the concentration of the substance taking part in the reaction. This is
called the Michaelis-Menten equation
after himself and his assistant.

To work out this equation he postulated the formation of a union between
the enzyme and the reacting substance
prior to the reaction, a union for which
no direct evidence existed for nearly another half century.

The equation took the curse off enzymes, in a manner of speaking. They
were brought down from the status of a
mysterious name and nothing more to a
level where at least they were amenable
to the same mathematical treatments
that ordinary chemicals were—and
therefore, presumably, were ordinary
chemicals.

In 1929 Michaelis went to the United
States, where he remained for the rest of
his life. Of lesser importance to science
than his enzyme work, but of more immediate importance to practical life was
his discovery that keratin is soluble in
thioglycolic acid. Keratin is the chief
constituent of hair and the discovery
opened the way to the development of
the home permanent.

[1034] **DALE,** Sir Henry Hallett
English biologist
Born: London, June 9, 1875
Died: Cambridge, July 23, 1968

Dale, the son of a businessman, graduated from Trinity College, Cambridge, in
1898 and, after considerable hesitation
as to the direction he wished his life to
take, he earned his medical degree at
Cambridge in 1909. Earlier he had
worked under Starling [954] and had, at
that time, met Loewi [1015].

In his work on a fungus called ergot
during the 1910s Dale isolated a compound called acetylcholine. Dale's studies
showed that it produced effects on organs similar to those brought about by
nerves that belonged to the parasym-
pathetic system. Once he heard of
Loewi's Vagusstoff it was possible to
show that this was acetylcholine.

Dale was knighted in 1932 and shared
in the 1936 Nobel Prize in medicine and
physiology with Loewi. Between 1940
and 1945 he served as president of the
Royal Society.

[1035] **JUNG,** Carl Gustav (yoong)
Swiss psychiatrist
Born: Kesswil, near Basel, July
26, 1875
Died: Küsnacht, near Zürich,
June 6, 1961

The son of a clergyman, Jung found
his early interest in archaeology. Medicine was only his second choice. After
obtaining his medical degree at Zürich in
1902, he worked in a mental hospital
where he had more opportunity to study
psychotic states than Freud [865] ever
had. In 1906 he began to develop word-
association tests, which, by forcing a person to make a quick response, tapped
the unconscious mind before the conscious mind could raise a protective wall.

In 1907 he met Freud, whose early
works he had read, and for a few years
he was an enthusiastic disciple of the
older man. By 1912 he too, like Adler
[984] before him, had broken away. He
thought Freud's explanations in terms of
infantile sexuality were adequate perhaps
for neuroses like hysteria, but inadequate
for more serious disorders such as
schizophrenia, in which Jung was particularly interested at the time.

Jung's interest in archaeology and
primitive myths reflected itself in the formulation of the term "collective unconscious." The child is born with a mind
containing an imprint from quite primitive times; the deeper unconscious levels
can be interpreted in terms of mythology, which has been created out of just
such levels in the past. His theories are
more difficult to understand than those
of Freud and Adler and his influence has
been correspondingly smaller. He popularized the concepts "introvert" and "extrovert."

He became professor of psychology at
the Federal Polytechnic University in
Zürich in 1933 and shifted to Basel in

1943. In this period, many of his remarks, filled with vague Teutonishness, gave rise to suspicions that he was pro-Nazi.

[1036] **SHERMAN,** Henry Clapp
American biochemist
Born: Ash Grove, Virginia, October 16, 1875
Died: Rensselaer, New York, October 7, 1955

Sherman obtained his doctorate at Columbia University in 1895 and served on Columbia's faculty thereafter. His primary interest was in nutrition and through the early decades of the century he studied the calcium and phosphorus requirements of the body, as McCollum [1062] was also doing. Sherman showed that both were needed in an appropriate ratio and that rickets could be induced on a low-phosphorus diet even when calcium was more than ample.

His most important work lay in the development of quantitative biological methods for assaying the vitamin content of food. Beginning with an animal on a basic diet, complete but for a particular vitamin, he measured its rate of growth as various foods were added to the diet. That rate of growth was a measure of the quantity of the excluded missing vitamin in each food.

[1037] **LEWIS,** Gilbert Newton
American chemist
Born: West Newton, Massachusetts, October 25, 1875
Died: Berkeley, California, March 23, 1946

Lewis, the intellectually precocious son of a lawyer, moved with his family to Lincoln, Nebraska, in 1884 and began his college career at the University of Nebraska, then transferred to Harvard in 1895. He obtained his doctorate at the latter institution in 1899, working under Richards [968]. He then spent a year in the Philippines and went through the usual course of advanced studies in Germany, studying under Ostwald [840] and Nernst [936]. He joined the faculty of Massachusetts Institute of Technology in 1905, and in 1912 he accepted a post on the faculty of the University of California, where he remained till his death.

There he introduced thermodynamics into the curriculum in the early decades of the twentieth century. Furthermore, a textbook he wrote with Merle Randall, entitled *Thermodynamics and the Free Energy of Chemical Substances,* published in 1923, became the undoubted classic in the field. More than any other single book, this introduced, clarified, and expanded Gibbs's [740] chemical thermodynamics for the benefit of the student of chemistry. In the book Lewis introduced a variety of new concepts including that of "activity," which was more useful in working out rates of reactions and questions of equilibria than was the older "concentration." It modified and made more accurate, for instance, Guldberg [721] and Waage's [701] law of mass action.

Meanwhile, the "nuclear atom" concept introduced by Ernest Rutherford [996] cried out for application to the question of atomic valence. The visualization by Kekulé [680] and Couper [686] of valence bonds as short dashes begged the question as to the nature of those bonds. In 1904 Abegg [978] was the first to try to explain valence bonds in terms of electrons, but his explanation applied only to the simple electrolytes.

In 1916 Lewis tried to relate the electrons of the atom to the nonelectrolytic links present in organic compounds. He suggested that a bond between two elements could be formed not only through the transfer of electrons, as in Abegg's view, but through the sharing of electrons. Each bond in organic compounds represented the sharing of one pair of electrons, the final result being that all atoms achieved the stable electronic configuration of the inert gas atom. Similar notions were independently advanced by Langmuir [1072]. Sidgwick [1013] advanced the thesis still further, and a generation after Abegg's first attempt Pauling [1236] combined the electronic bond notion with the quantum mechanics that followed the theories of Schrödinger [1117] and De Broglie [1157]. (Lewis also worked out a theory of acid-base action founded on the behavior of electron pairs.)

In the very early 1930s Lewis was engaged in the search for hydrogen's heavy isotope, whose existence was strongly suspected. In this he was anticipated in 1932 by Urey [1164]. Lewis was not far behind, however, and in 1933 was the first to prepare a sample of water in which all the hydrogen atoms consisted of this heavy isotope ("heavy hydrogen" or "deuterium"), which had an atomic weight of 2 rather than the 1 of the usual hydrogen atom.

Such water was called heavy water and a decade later it played an important role as a "moderator" of neutrons, slowing them down and making them more effective in setting up a chain reaction and smoothing the path to the atomic bomb.

[1038] **SLIPHER,** Vesto Melvin (sly'fer)
American astronomer
Born: Mulberry, Indiana, November 11, 1875
Died: Flagstaff, Arizona, November 8, 1969

Slipher graduated from Indiana University in 1901, and he received his Ph.D. there in 1909. He joined the Lowell Observatory at Lowell's [860] request in 1906 and became assistant director in 1915 and director in 1926. He held the latter post till his retirement in 1952.

His work extended from the solar system to the bounds of the universe. Within the solar system he was the first to obtain good photographs of Mars, and his photographs of the absorption spectra of Jupiter and Saturn were used by Wildt [1290] to demonstrate that the atmospheres of these giant planets were rich in ammonia and methane. In 1933 Slipher himself showed that the atmosphere of Neptune contained methane. He had reached out farther still, for, a

few years earlier, he had directed the research that led Tombaugh [1299] to the discovery of Pluto.

Beyond the solar system he was particularly interested in the nebulae. In 1912 he was the first to apply the Doppler-Fizeau [534, 620] effect to the Andromeda nebula, which at the time was not yet recognized as an extragalactic object. He reported it to be approaching the earth at 125 miles a second. He continued the same work on other nebulae and the Andromeda was found to be an exception. All but one of the others were receding from the earth, and at rates far higher than the radial velocities of ordinary stars. Since a motion of recession is indicated spectrally by a shift of absorption lines toward the red end of the spectrum, the phrase "the red shift" became famous among astronomers studying the new world of galaxies that Hubble [1136] was uncovering. Hubble used it to establish the concept of the expanding universe.

[1039] **DIELS,** Otto Paul Hermann
(deels)
German chemist
Born: Hamburg, January 23, 1876
Died: Kiel, March 7, 1954

Diels, the son of a professor of classical philology at the University of Berlin, was educated at that university and obtained his Ph.D. there in 1899, having done his work under Emil Fischer [833]. He joined the faculty as a professor of chemistry at once. In 1916 he transferred to the University of Kiel, remaining there till his retirement in 1945, after having seen two of his sons killed on the eastern front in World War II, and his home and laboratories destroyed in bombing raids.

For any organic chemist, the synthesis of a new and important compound is a delightful success. In 1906 Diels achieved this when he isolated the unusual substance carbon suboxide (C_3O_2).

Even more important, however, is the discovery of a technique of atomic combination that may be put to use in the course of many different kinds of syntheses.

Diels, together with a young assistant, Kurt Alder [1254], discovered such a technique in 1928. Properly it may be known as the diene synthesis, but it is customary to give a reaction the name of its discoverers and it is commonly called the Diels-Alder reaction.

In essence the reaction involves a method of joining two compounds so as to form a ring of atoms. Diels investigated the potentialities of the reaction, using it to synthesize a variety of compounds. It was also used by others to synthesize alkaloids, polymers, and other complex molecules. Woodward [1416], for instance, was to use it in his synthesis of cortisone.

For the discovery of this technique Diels and Alder shared the 1950 Nobel Prize in chemistry.

[1040] **BÁRÁNY,** Robert (bah'rahn-yuh)
Austrian physician
Born: Vienna, April 22, 1876
Died: Uppsala, Sweden, April 8, 1936

Bárány, the son of a bank official, graduated from the University of Vienna in 1900, then went on to study medicine. In 1903 he began work in the University of Vienna ear clinic.

There he found ways to apply the knowledge that had been gained of the inner ear as a means of regulating the equilibrium sense. He studied disorders of equilibrium by such means as following eye movements, and by stimulating each inner ear separately by irrigating one ear with hot liquid, the other with cold.

When World War I began in 1914, Bárány volunteered for military service in the Austrian army in order to be able to work on any brain wounds that might come his way. He was taken prisoner by the Russians, which was not part of his plan, of course, and in 1915, while he was prisoner of war, he was awarded the Nobel Prize for medicine and physiology

for his work on the ear. After 1916 he taught at the University of Uppsala.

[1041] **YERKES,** Robert Mearns (yur'-keez)
American psychologist
Born: Breadysville, Pennsylvania, May 26, 1876
Died: New Haven, Connecticut, February 3, 1956

Yerkes, the son of a farmer, was educated at Ursinus College, Collegeville, Pennsylvania, and at Harvard, where he obtained his Ph.D. in psychology in 1902.

He spent his working life studying the intelligence of various animals and soon realized that in studying the mental processes of those animals closest to human beings in the evolutionary scheme—the great apes—he might find information of use in understanding human mental processes. It was not till 1929, however, that he was able to establish an experimental station in Florida for the study of primates. In that same year, with his wife he published a book, *The Great Apes,* which was long the standard texts on these animals.

During World War I he was in charge of psychological testing of army personnel and administered tests to 1,726,000 men.

He retired in 1944.

[1042] **KEESOM,** Willem Hendrik (kay'-sum)
Dutch physicist
Born: Texel, North Holland, June 21, 1876
Died: Oegstgeest, March 24, 1956

Keesom, the son of a farmer, was educated at Amsterdam University, and studied under Van der Waals [726] among others. He obtained his doctoral degree in 1904, then served as an assistant of Kamerlingh Onnes [843] at the University of Leiden. He gained a professorial post at the University of

Utrecht in 1918, and in 1923 returned to Leiden. There he became director of the Kamerlingh Onnes laboratory.

He continued to work on liquid helium and was the first person to produce solid helium by applying external pressure in combination with temperatures of less than 3°K.

He also made it clear that there are two forms of liquid helium: helium I and helium II, the latter remaining liquid at ordinary pressures down to absolute zero itself and the dividing line coming at about 2°K. Helium II has very unusual properties. The heat capacity changes abruptly and all internal friction disappears so that it is "superfluid."

Keesom retired in 1945.

[1043] **STOCK,** Alfred (shtuk)
German chemist
Born: Danzig (now Gdansk, Poland), July 16, 1876
Died: Karlsruhe, Baden-Württemberg, August 12, 1946

Stock, the son of a bank executive, studied at the University of Berlin under Emil Fischer [833] and obtained his doctorate in 1899, *magna cum laude.* He then spent a year in Paris as an assistant to Moissan [831].

In 1909 Stock began the study of boron hydrides (compounds of boron and hydrogen). He managed to synthesize a mixture of these compounds together with silicon hydrides. Carefully, he separated the boron hydrides and studied each. At the time this was without practical application, but with the dawning of the space age a half century later, boron hydrides became glamorous indeed as possible rocket fuel additives to increase the push that forced rockets upward into the upper atmosphere and space. In addition the boron hydrides are of theoretical interest since the boron atoms are attached to too many hydrogen atoms if one follows the structures drawn according to the Kekulé [680] system. However, the resonance theory of Pauling [1236] accounts for the structures nicely.

In the 1920s Stock varied his interests by an investigation into mercury poisoning, from which he suffered most of his adult life. Mercury is volatile enough to release small quantities of its vapor into the air, and these vapors are cumulatively poisonous over considerable periods of time. Many chemists, such as Berzelius [425], Faraday [474], Wöhler [515], and Liebig [532], may have suffered from mercury poisoning, not always knowing it. As a result of Stock's investigation, modern chemists treat the innocent-seeming little globules of mercury (always lying around in corners and cracks in laboratory floors) with more animosity than they used to, and take more care to remove them.

The last decade of his life was made miserable by difficulties with the Nazi government and by his progressive illness. As World War II drew to its end, he fled the advancing Russians to a small town on the Elbe River and there died.

[1044] **KETTERING,** Charles Franklin
American inventor
Born: Loudonville, Ohio, August 29, 1876
Died: Loudonville, Ohio, November 25, 1958

Kettering, the son of a farmer, graduated from Ohio State University in 1904 with a degree in electrical engineering. In 1909 he founded the Dayton Engineering Laboratories Company (Delco), which eventually merged with other companies to form General Motors.

Kettering's greatest achievement was the invention of an electric self-starting system, which was introduced for the first time in the 1912 Cadillac. This did away with the necessity of cranking an engine into motion by manual effort (dangerous if the engine caught before you were ready) and brought the automobile within the physical capacity of everyone.

In collaboration with Midgley [1132], he discovered tetraethyl lead as a cure for engine knock and developed a quick-drying lacquer that hastened automobile production.

In 1919 he became head of the General Motors Research Corporation. He was involved in the discovery of Freon and in the improvement of the engine developed by Diesel [886] to the point where it became standard on railroads, buses, and trucks.

[1045] ADAMS, Walter Sydney
American astronomer
Born: Kessab, near Antioch, Turkey, of American parents, December 20, 1876
Died: Pasadena, California, May 11, 1956

Adams was the son of an American missionary couple working in the Middle East. He spent his infancy there and was brought to the United States in 1885. He attended Dartmouth College, graduating in 1898. After further education in Germany he began his role as astronomer in the United States, under Hale [974], rising by 1923 to the directorship of the Mount Wilson Observatory.

Chiefly interested in stellar spectra, in 1914 he proved that from the spectra alone it was possible to tell whether a star was a giant or a dwarf. In fact, he deduced a star's luminosity from its spectrum. By comparing this luminosity with its apparent brightness, he calculated the star's distance. This method, miscalled spectroscopic parallax, was usable to distances far greater than those for which the true stellar parallax, first used by Bessel [439], could be applied. Spectroscopic parallax made it possible for Hertzsprung [1018] to deduce the distance of some Cepheid variables so that the period-luminosity curve, so important for the knowledge of distances beyond our own galaxy, could be prepared by Shapley [1102].

In 1915 Adams' attention was attracted by the Companion of Sirius. This had been discovered by Bessel, who deduced its large mass (comparable to that of our own sun) from the wobbling motions its gravity imposed on the star Sirius. The Companion was actually seen by Alvan Clark [696], and from its dimness he and everyone else assumed it to be a dying, cooling star. Adams, however, managed to study its spectrum despite the glare of nearby Sirius and found it to be a hot star, hotter than our sun.

To be so hot it would have to be more luminous (per unit surface area) than the sun. Since it was so dim, that could only mean it had very little surface area. In fact, it could be little more voluminous than the earth itself. Yet Bessel's calculations as to its mass still held.

For a star to be so small and yet so massive, it must have a density about forty thousand times greater than that of water, or two thousand times greater than that of platinum. Had such a discovery been made twenty years earlier, it would have seemed utter nonsense. By 1915, however, the new picture of the atom advanced by Ernest Rutherford [996] was just coming into acceptance, and the ordinary atom in the condition in which it existed on the earth was recognized to be mostly empty space. In superdense stars such as the Companion of Sirius, the atoms had broken down and the constituent subatomic particles were crushed together in what was called degenerate matter. Such stars came to be referred to as white dwarfs.

Other white dwarfs were discovered and in the 1920s Eddington [1085] pointed out that they must have superintense gravitational fields, large enough to produce a shift in spectral absorption lines toward the red in accordance with the theory of general relativity proposed by Einstein [1064]. In 1925 Adams searched for this shift and found one. It was not exactly the size predicted by Einstein but it was close enough to be considered a check of the theory.

In 1932 Adams' spectroscopic work proved of service within the solar system, for he showed that the atmosphere of Venus was rich in carbon dioxide.

[1046] WINDAUS, Adolf (vin'dows)
German chemist
Born: Berlin, December 25, 1876
Died: Göttingen, June 9, 1959

80. Maria Mitchell (seated)

81. HEINRICH SCHLIEMANN

82. HEBER DOUST CURTIS

83. ANTHONY HEWISH

84. CHARLES ADOLPHE WURTZ

85. Satyendranath Bose (center)

Windaus obtained his Ph.D. at the University of Freiburg in 1899 and then taught at Göttingen. He intended to be a physician but a year's work with Emil Fischer [833] converted him to chemistry.

In 1907 he synthesized histamine, a compound with important physiological properties. For his researches on cholesterol (and therefore steroid) structure (a subject that had been his concern from the days of his doctoral research), he was awarded the 1928 Nobel Prize in chemistry. Thus, for two years in a row, the chemistry prize went to a steroid chemist.

It was Windaus who discovered that vitamin D consisted of a steroid molecule in which a bond was broken by the action of sunlight. This provided the rationale for the irradiation process whereby the vitamin D content of such foods as milk and bread are increased by exposure to ultraviolet light.

He was also the first, in 1932, to locate a sulfur atom in the molecule of vitamin B_1 (thiamin), an important step in working out the structure of that important compound.

[1047] **SUTTON,** Walter Stanborough
American geneticist
Born: Utica, New York, April 5, 1877
Died: Kansas City, Kansas, November 10, 1916

Sutton was the son of a farmer who, with his family, moved to Kansas when young Walter was ten years old. Sutton entered the University of Kansas in 1896 and planned to be an engineer but the death of a younger brother as a result of typhoid turned his attention to biology. He did graduate work at Columbia University but never got his Ph.D.

In 1902, however, even without his doctorate he published a paper of tremendous importance to genetics. He was able to show that all the chromosomes existed in pairs and pointed out that it was very likely that they were the hereditary factors that Mendel [638] had postulated in his work, which had been re-discovered just two years before. In 1903, in another paper, he maintained that chromosomes carried the genes, that each sex cell contained one chromosome of each pair, the one included being decided by random factors.

After two years of work in the oil industry, Sutton returned to the academic life, obtained his M.D. at Columbia in 1907, and then practiced as a surgeon till his death, before his fortieth birthday, of a ruptured appendix.

[1048] **WIELAND,** Heinrich Otto (vee'-lahnt)
German chemist
Born: Pforzheim, Baden, June 4, 1877
Died: Munich, Bavaria, August 5, 1957

Wieland, the son of a chemist, obtained his doctor's degree at the University of Munich in 1901 and spent most of his later life teaching at that university.

His research led him into various regions of organic chemistry, but his most important studies, begun in 1912, involved the bile acids. These had been studied by Pregl [982], but where Pregl had branched off into analysis, Wieland kept firmly to the mark.

Three bile acids had just been isolated and Wieland began by showing how closely related they were in basic structure and the detailed manner in which they differed. The molecular skeleton he showed to be steroid in nature, related to the well-known molecule cholesterol, which was being studied by Wieland's friend Windaus [1046].

After World War I, Wieland grew interested in the oxidations that proceeded within living tissue. He maintained, as a result of his experiments over a number of years, that the crucial reaction in living tissue was dehydrogenation. This was the term used for the removal of hydrogen atoms from foodstuffs, two at a time. It was this, he maintained, and not the addition of oxygen, that was enzymatically catalyzed. He was opposed by Warburg [1089], who, as a result of his own experiments, maintained that it was the addition of oxygen that was crucial and that this addition was catalyzed by enzymes containing iron atoms.

As it turned out this was a particularly fruitful controversy, for both parties were right. Together they made a good start toward working out the respiratory chain in tissues, the route by which the body slowly converted organic molecule to water and carbon dioxide, producing available energy in the process.

Meanwhile, the steroids, of which cholesterol and the bile acids were examples, grew to seem of greater and greater importance to life. At least one of the vitamins, vitamin D, was closely related to steroids and, among the hormones, those controlling sexual development and reproduction were steroids. As a result, Wieland, who was recognized as one of the chief elucidators of the steroid structure, was awarded the 1927 Nobel Prize in chemistry.

During World War II, Wieland was openly anti-Nazi and some of his students were involved in the 1944 treason trials. Wieland survived the war and Nazism, however, by a dozen years.

[1049] **BARKLA,** Charles Glover
English physicist
Born: Widnes, Lancashire, June 27, 1877
Died: Edinburgh, Scotland, October 23, 1944

Barkla studied at University College, Liverpool, where one of his teachers was Oliver Lodge [820]. While still a student Barkla substituted for Lodge as lecturer when necessary. After graduation Barkla spent time at Cambridge under Thomson [869] (where he was also a prominent member of a choral group, singing baritone), returning in 1902 to Liverpool as a faculty member.

In 1907 he moved to the University of London and, in 1913, at Edinburgh he began his investigations into the X rays discovered a few years earlier by Roentgen [774]. Barkla noticed that X rays were scattered by gases and that the extent of scattering was proportional to the density of the gas and therefore to its molecular weight. From this he deduced that the more massive the atom, the greater the number of charged particles it contained, for the charged particles did the scattering. This was the first indication of a connection between the number of electrons in an atom and its position in the periodic table, a move toward the concept of the atomic number.

In 1904 Barkla further showed, from the manner in which X rays were scattered, that they consisted of a particular kind of wave. They were transverse waves like those of light and not longitudinal waves like those of sound, as Roentgen himself had thought.

Barkla began his most important work in 1906. He showed that when X rays were scattered by particular elements, they produced a beam of characteristic penetrance. (At the time, there was no way of measuring the wavelength of X rays, so Barkla had to draw his deductions from the amount of absorption of a particular beam by an aluminum sheet of standard thickness.) If the elements were studied according to their order in the periodic table, the "characteristic X rays" they produced were more and more penetrating. It was these characteristic X rays that Moseley [1121] soon used to bring the notion of the atomic number to completion.

Barkla went on to recognize two types of such X rays, a more penetrating set which he called K radiation and a less penetrating set which he called L radiation. This was the first step toward learning the distribution of electrons within the atom, a matter which Siegbahn [1111] and Bohr [1101] were soon to illuminate.

For his work on X rays Barkla was awarded the 1917 Nobel Prize in physics.

[1050] **BEEBE,** Charles William (bee′-bee)
American naturalist
Born: Brooklyn, New York, July 29, 1877
Died: Simla Research Station, near Arima, Trinidad, June 4, 1962

Beebe graduated from Columbia University in 1898 and then in 1899 began work at the New York Zoological Gardens in the Bronx. He was particularly interested in birds and built up one of the finest ornithological collections in the world. As a youngster he had been fascinated by the extraordinary voyages of Jules Verne (he was by no means the only scientist who received an initial inspiration from science fiction) and he engaged in a lifetime of extraordinary voyages of his own.

He served as a combat aviator during World War I, traveled all over the world, and wrote fascinating books about his experiences. While modern naturalists from Linnaeus [276] to Andrews [1091] have achieved fame through their wanderings over the face of the earth, Beebe's chief renown came with a journey of less than a mile—straight down. The desire to probe deeply in the ocean arose out of his interest in corals, which he wanted to study in their native haunts.

Divers, however well protected, can only go down a few hundred feet beneath sea level. Submarines can do little better. Beebe decided, however, to build a shell of thick metal and conquer the pressures of the deep by brute force. He had to sacrifice maneuverability and be content to dangle from a surface ship (and if the cable holding his shell were to break, that would be the end).

Such a shell of steel, with thick quartz windows, was built in the early 1930s. President Franklin D. Roosevelt, a friend of Beebe's, helped to design the device, suggesting a spherical shape as opposed to Beebe's original desire for a cylinder.

In 1934 Beebe and a companion, Otis Barton, descended to a record depth of 3028 feet, well over half a mile. The dive, made near Bermuda, was the first penetration by man of depths beyond the surface layer of the ocean. The steel sphere was called a bathysphere ("sphere of the deep").

Beebe did not think his trip had proved of much scientific value and abandoned such attempts after making over thirty dives. However, he paved the way for Piccard's [1092] bathyscaphe ("ship of the deep"), which a quarter of a century later was to make even more spectacular plunges into the depths.

[1051] **ASTON,** Francis William
English chemist and physicist
Born: Harborne, near Birmingham, September 1, 1877
Died: Cambridge, November 20, 1945

Aston, the son of a merchant, finished high school at the top of his class in science and mathematics in 1893 and went on to study chemistry at the University of Birmingham, where he worked under Frankland [655]. In 1910 he went to Cambridge to work under J. J. Thomson [869]. World War I (during which he served as an aeronautical engineer) interrupted, but he returned in time to help Thomson in the latter's experiments on deflecting positively charged ions in magnetic fields. These experiments made it appear that atoms of a particular element might not all have the same weight, despite Dalton's [389] original assumption of a century earlier.

In order to decide the matter, Aston improved Thomson's apparatus in 1919 and designed it so that all ions of a particular mass would focus in a fine line on the photographic film. Working with neon he showed that there were two lines, one indicating a mass of 20 and the other a mass of 22. From the comparative darkness of the two lines, Aston calculated that the ions of mass 20 were ten times as numerous as those of 22. If all the ions were lumped together they would have an average mass of 20.2 and that was, indeed, the atomic weight of neon. (Later, a third group of neon ions of mass 21, occurring in only tiny concentration, was discovered.)

Working with chlorine Aston found two types of atoms, with masses of 35 and 37 in the ratio of 3 to 1. A weighted average came out to 35.5, which was the atomic weight of chlorine. By the end of 1920 it seemed quite clear to Aston that all atoms had masses that were very close to integers if the mass of hydrogen

was taken as 1. The only reason that
particular elements had atomic weights
that were not integers was that they were
mixtures of different atoms of different
integral weights. Thus, the hypothesis
first advanced by Prout [440] a century
earlier was vindicated after all, as Marignac [599] had foreseen it might be, although it had been "killed" over and
over again through the nineteenth century. (Prout's hypothesis had, indeed,
been vindicated by Moseley's [1121]
atomic numbers the previous decade, but
Aston's work was the more direct evidence.)

Aston's mass spectrograph (so called
because it divided the elements into lines
like that of a spectroscope, with the
different lines marking off differences in
mass) showed that most stable elements
were mixtures of isotopes, differing in
mass but not in chemical properties. This
strongly confirmed Soddy's [1052] isotope concept, which that physicist had
been able to apply to radioactive elements only. Using his device, Aston was
able to discover 212 of the 287 stable
isotopes.

A more refined mass spectrograph,
built in 1925, enabled Aston to show
that the "mass numbers" of the individual isotopes were actually very slightly
different from integers, sometimes a little
above, sometimes a little below. These
slight mass discrepancies, it turned out,
represented the energy that went into
binding the component particles of the
nucleus together and were called, by
Harkins [1022], "packing fraction" or
"binding energy." When one type of
atom was changed into another, the
difference in binding energy could make
itself felt in devastating fashion if
enough atoms made the change. Two
decades later, just such a wholesale
change in atoms was found in connection with an isotope discovered by
Dempster [1106], and the nuclear bomb
was a reality.

Aston was awarded the 1922 Nobel
Prize in chemistry for his mass spectrograph and the knowledge it had given
rise to. Unlike Ernest Rutherford [996],
Aston envisaged a future in which the

energy of the atom would be tapped by
man, and in his Nobel acceptance speech
he spoke of the dangers involved in such
an eventuality. But such forethought remained the province of only a few scientists and science fiction writers. (Nevertheless, he lived just long enough—by
three months—to see the dropping of the
first nuclear bombs on Japanese cities.)

Aston's business acumen, by the way,
had enabled him to accumulate a large
estate which, on his death, he left, for
the most part, to Trinity College.

[1052] **SODDY**, Frederick
English chemist
Born: Eastbourne, Sussex, Sep-
tember 2, 1877
Died: Brighton, Sussex, Septem-
ber 22, 1956

After studying at Oxford and graduating in 1898 at the head of his class in
chemistry, Soddy, the son of a merchant,
went to Canada in 1899. There he
worked under Ernest Rutherford [996]
at McGill University. While there, he
and Rutherford worked out an explanation of radioactive disintegration. They
suggested (as Boltwood [987] was also
suggesting) that each radioactive element, beginning with uranium or
thorium, breaks down to form another
element as it emits a subatomic particle.
The new element in turn breaks down,
and so on, until lead is formed. There
are three series of such consecutive
breakdowns now known. A fourth is
possible, and although it does not exist in
nature, it was created in the laboratory a
generation after Soddy's work.

Soddy returned to England in 1902
and worked with Ramsay [832]. He then
showed another facet of radioactive
transformation, for he demonstrated
spectroscopically that helium was formed
in the course of uranium breakdown.

In the process of radioactive disintegration, some forty to fifty different elements (as judged by the difference in radioactive properties) were detected, and
there were no more than ten or twelve
places at the end of the periodic table

where they could possibly be put. No chemist desired to throw out Mendeléev's [705] extremely useful table, if that could possibly be avoided, so some way of allowing for the large number of intermediates had to be found.

Soddy suggested that different elements produced in radioactive transformations were capable of occupying the same place in the periodic table and on February 18, 1913, he called these elements isotopes, from Greek words meaning "same place." Furthermore, he indicated the positions in which individual isotopes might be found by suggesting that the emission of an alpha particle causes the emitting element to become a new element with an atomic number decreased by two. The emission of a beta particle raises the atomic number by one. In this way, all the radioactive intermediates could be placed.

In the next few years it became quite clear that isotopes were really different versions of a single chemical element. The isotopes differed in the mass of the nucleus and therefore had different radioactive characteristics (since these depended on the nature of the nucleus). On the other hand, all isotopes of a particular element had the same number of electrons in the outer regions of the atom and so had the same chemical properties (since these depended on the number and distribution of the electrons of the atom).

By 1914 Soddy had demonstrated quite conclusively that lead was the final stable element into which the radioactive intermediates were converted. (Boltwood had suggested this might be so a decade before.) It turned out that lead found in rocks that contained uranium or thorium did not have the same atomic weight as lead found in nonradioactive rocks. This was shown clearly by T. W. Richards [968]. The different samples of lead were the same chemically, and this pointed up the fact that isotopes differed in the mass of the atom but not in the chemical properties.

Within five years the existence of isotopes in many elements that were neither radioactive nor formed by radioactivity was shown by J. J. Thomson [869] and, particularly, by Aston [1051].

For his discovery of isotopes Soddy was awarded the 1921 Nobel Prize in chemistry. He had accepted a professorship at Oxford two years earlier, and there he remained until his retirement in 1936. The retirement was brought on at a relatively early age through his grief at the death of his wife. Also, he did not get on well at the university, for he was not apparently a very tactful person.

He was enraged by the abomination of World War I and, in particular, by the death of Moseley [1121] and developed radical ideas in consequence. As an example, he was a firm believer in odd economic theories such as Solvay's [735] technocracy and wrote angry books on the subject.

[1053] **JEANS,** Sir James Hopwood
English mathematician and astronomer
Born: Ormskirk, Lancashire, September 11, 1877
Died: Dorking, Surrey, September 17, 1946

Jeans, the son of a journalist, was a precocious, unhappy child, interested in clocks. He was second in his class in mathematics at Cambridge. After graduation in 1898 he taught mathematics there and from 1905 to 1909 lectured at Princeton University in the United States.

Jeans applied his mathematics to astronomy with fruitful results. He studied the behavior of rapidly spinning bodies and, in particular, their methods of breaking up under the stress of centrifugal force. He showed that the nebular hypothesis of Laplace [347] was untenable, at least in the form presented by the French astronomer a century before.

The nebular hypothesis had, in any case, been under attack for some time because, for one thing, the planets contain 98 percent of the angular momentum of the solar system. (To put it as simply as possible, the planets move rapidly in their orbits while the sun rotates

665

rather slowly.) If the solar system had begun as a whirling cloud of gas, how could all that circular or near circular motion be concentrated in the outer edges that became the planets, and so little reserved for the large central mass that became the sun?

Chamberlin [766] had suggested that the sun had had a close encounter with a passing star and that the debris lifted into space by the mutual gravitational attraction had formed the planets. He had made some attempt to make this account for the distribution of angular momentum, but it was Jeans in 1917 who advanced the most detailed analysis.

The passing star, according to Jeans, had drawn a huge cigar-shaped lump of matter out of the sun. As the invader passed, its gravitational attraction gave the cigar-shaped matter a sideways pull, imparting to it a great deal of angular momentum. The thick part of the cigar produced the large planets Jupiter and Saturn, while the outer parts produced the smaller planets beyond and within the orbits of the two giants.

This theory maintained popularity for a generation. Since near collisions of two stars are extremely unlikely because of the vast distance between stars, such a theory of planetary origins would indicate that solar systems were very rare. In fact, it seemed quite likely that our sun (and the invader) might be the only stars in our galaxy to possess a planetary system.

However, a new version of the nebular hypothesis arose out of the shambles that Jeans had made of Laplace's suggestion. The new version was presented along new and more sophisticated lines by men like Weizsäcker [1376] in the last couple of years of Jeans's life. Contemporary thought, which quite discredits the various theories of catastrophic origin of the solar system, would make it seem that planetary systems are common indeed. In 1928, the year in which he was knighted, Jeans speculated that matter was constantly being formed (at a very slow rate) in the universe. This speculation was to be elevated into a serious theory by men like Gold [1437] and Hoyle [1398].

From 1919 to 1929 Jeans was secretary of the Royal Society and in 1934 he was appointed professor of astronomy at the Royal Institution in London. However, Jeans was known more for his writings on astronomy for the layman than for his serious contributions to the subject. From 1928 he devoted himself entirely to such writings. His most popular books, perhaps, were *The Universe Around Us* (1929) and *Through Space and Time* (1934).

[1054] **AVERY**, Oswald Theodore
Canadian-American physician
Born: Halifax, Nova Scotia, October 21, 1877
Died: Nashville, Tennessee, February 20, 1955

Avery, the son of a clergyman who emigrated to the United States in 1887, obtained his medical degree from Columbia University in 1904 and joined the staff of the Rockefeller Institute (now Rockefeller University) in New York in 1913.

His field of research involved the pneumococci—the pneumonia-causing bacteria. Bacteriologists had been studying two different strains of pneumococci grown in the laboratory—one with a smooth coat (S), and the other lacking the coat and therefore rough in appearance (R). Apparently the R strain lacked some enzyme needed to make the carbohydrate capsule. It was discovered that if an extract of the S strain was mixed with live R strain and the whole injected into a mouse, the mouse's tissue would eventually contain live S strain. The S extract (thoroughly nonliving) apparently contained a factor of some sort that supplied the necessary enzyme to the R strain and converted it into an S strain.

Everyone was sure the factor was protein in nature. In 1944, however, Avery and his associates studied the S extract and were able to show that the factor was pure deoxyribonucleic acid (DNA) and that no protein was present. This was a key development. Until then, DNA had been thought to be a relatively unimportant adjunct of the proteins that served as the basis of genetics. Now it seemed that it was DNA that was the real thing.

This led directly to a new assault on DNA and the discovery of its structure and its mode of replication by Crick [1406] and James Dewey Watson [1480].

[1055] **TWORT,** Frederick William
English bacteriologist
Born: Camberley, Surrey, October 22, 1877
Died: Camberley, March 20, 1950

Twort, the son of a physician, obtained a medical degree in 1900. As a professor of bacteriology at the University of London, Twort discovered in 1915 a type of virus that infested and killed bacteria. The discovery was made independently a couple of years later by D'Hérelle [1012], who named the viruses bacteriophages ("bacteria eaters"). There were some rather unsavory disputes concerning precedence, but it was the bacteriophages themselves that proved important, whoever discovered them.

Although they made the tiniest cells their prey, they were themselves larger and more complicated in structure than the average virus, and therefore more interesting to study. In the decade following Twort's death, the bacteriophages, studied by men like Fraenkel-Conrat [1355], yielded a number of the secrets of viral structure and action.

[1056] **RUSSELL,** Henry Norris
American astronomer
Born: Oyster Bay, New York, October 25, 1877
Died: Princeton, New Jersey, February 18, 1957

Russell, the son of a minister who had emigrated from Canada, was educated at Princeton University, obtaining his doctorate in 1900. After postdoctoral work in England, he returned to teach at Princeton in 1905 and in 1912 became the director of the university's observatory. In 1921 he began an association with Mount Wilson Observatory that continued till his retirement.

In 1914 Russell published his observations of a certain regularity he had discovered in the relationship between the brightness of stars, their color, and their spectral class. It was to be expected that red stars were cooler than yellow stars, which were in turn cooler than blue-white stars. The work of Wien [934] twenty years earlier had made that clear.

In that case, then, red stars, as the coolest and least luminous, ought to be the dimmest. Some were. Other red stars, however, were quite bright. The only way a cool red star could be very luminous is to suppose it to be very large so that although its surface radiates little light per unit area, there is a great deal of radiating area, giving rise to a large total radiation. Thus there were red giants and red dwarfs. Russell could find no red star of intermediate size. To a less marked extent, there were yellow giants and yellow dwarfs, our own sun being a yellow dwarf.

In fact, if the spectral class (which dictates the color of the star) is plotted against the luminosity, the stars fall in a diagonal line, from the red dwarfs of spectral class K, at the lower right, to the blue-whites of spectral class O at the upper left, with the giant and supergiant stars making a horizontal line at the top.

This same fact had been discovered some years earlier by Hertzsprung [1018], so the plot is usually called the Hertzsprung-Russell diagram. It is very tempting, from this diagram, to deduce that stars are following a definite life cycle. The simplest picture, and the one presented by Russell, and before him by Lockyer [719] in 1890, is that as a quantity of gas contracts, it begins to heat up and radiate in the red, at which time it is a red giant. It continues to contract and heats further, becoming a smaller, but hotter and brighter yellow giant, then a still smaller but still hotter and brighter blue-white star. In doing this, the star is pictured as traveling along the horizontal bar on top of the Hertzsprung-Russell diagram.

Thereafter, it descends the diagonal line, cooling down as it shrinks further, becoming a yellow dwarf, then a red dwarf, and finally a black cinder. From this viewpoint, our sun is past its best days and is on its way down to extinction, though still good for billions of years.

This was the first reasonably good attempt to work out the evolutionary life cycle of stars. It came, however, before the nuclear mechanisms of stellar energy formation had been worked out a quarter century later by men like Bethe [1308]. Once that was done, Russell's evolutionary scheme proved far too simple and was abandoned. Nevertheless, the diagonal line of stars in the diagram still has its significance even in modern schemes of stellar evolution and is referred to as the Main sequence.

In 1929 Russell analyzed the sun's spectrum and worked out its composition in detail. Rather surprisingly the sun proved to be largely hydrogen with helium, oxygen, nitrogen, and neon the most important of the minor constitutents. Stars generally proved to be mostly hydrogen and the universe itself is thought to be mainly hydrogen and helium in a 9–1 ratio.

Russell, in 1927, published an astronomy text that, for the first time shifted the main emphasis from the solar system and celestial mechanics to the stars and astrophysics.

[1057] **WATSON,** John Broadus
American psychologist
Born: Greenville, South Carolina,
January 9, 1878
Died: New York, New York,
September 25, 1958

Watson obtained his Ph.D. at the University of Chicago in 1903 and joined its faculty that same year. In 1908 he was appointed professor of experimental and comparative psychology at Johns Hopkins.

Watson carried on intensive experi-

ments in animal behavior and was extremely interested in the conditioned responses described by Pavlov [802]. In studying animals, there is no question of penetrating motivation, of making use of introspection to enter the unconscious; only the actual behavior can be observed. Watson transferred this view to the study of human psychology.

He took a position directly contrary to Freud [865] and the various schools descended from that Austrian's psychoanalytic teachings. In 1913 Watson published an article that served to found the behaviorist school of psychology. Watson believed that human behavior was explainable in terms of conditioned responses and relegated even heredity to a minor role. Animals, including the human being, were viewed as intensely complicated machines, who reacted according to their nerve-path "wiring," these nerve paths being altered, or conditioned, by experience. These views are far too extreme for most psychologists today, but no doubt they serve as a useful corrective for the ultra-Freudians and Jungians who tend to rise on wings of words into the semimystical. In addition, the observations of men such as Gesell [1070] do lend a certain mechanistic patina to the development of human children.

In 1924 Watson left the academic world for an executive position in an advertising firm. However, advertising is certainly applied psychology, if anything is, so the move was by no means as radical as it might seem.

[1058] **NIEUWLAND,** Julius Arthur
(nyoo'land)
Belgian-American chemist
Born: Hansbeke (near Gent),
Belgium, February 14, 1878
Died: Washington, D.C., June 11,
1936

Nieuwland was brought to the United States by his parents when he was three years old. The family settled in South Bend, Indiana, and young Nieuwland, after an education in the parochial school system, attended the University of Notre Dame from which he graduated in 1899. He studied for the priesthood, to which he was ordained in 1903. This did not prevent him from also studying chemistry and botany, and he was awarded his doctor's degree in 1904 at Catholic University.

His scientific life shows a progress from botany to chemistry, for he was professor of botany at Notre Dame from 1904 to 1918, and professor of chemistry there from 1918 to his death. It is for his chemical researches, however, that he is best remembered.

His doctoral dissertation dealt with the reactions of acetylene and that remained his prime interest. One of the products he had obtained in the course of this doctoral research was divinylchlorarsine, a compound he described but with which he refused to work because of its extremely poisonous nature. Perhaps his intuition guided him here, for when its properties were further studied over a decade later, it gained considerable notoriety. It was renamed Lewisite, after the army chemist who devised methods of preparing it, and it proved a worse poison gas than any of those used in World War I. Fortunately, it was not prepared in quantity until the very month of the Armistice, and what had been made ready was eventually destroyed at sea.

In 1906 Nieuwland, in continuing his studies on acetylene, detected a strange odor. For fourteen years he tracked down that odor and in 1920 identified the compounds giving rise to it. He found that acetylene, a compound with a molecule containing two carbon atoms, could be made to combine with itself to form a four-carbon molecule and a six-carbon molecule. These larger molecules could continue to add on two-carbon units (polymerizing) forming a giant molecule that had some of the properties of rubber.

This attracted the attention of chemists at Du Pont, with whom Nieuwland worked closely thereafter. Under the leadership of Carothers [1190], who was later to prepare nylon, it was found that if a chlorine atom was added at the four-

carbon stage, the final polymer was much more like rubber. It was, in fact, what is now called neoprene, one of the early synthetic rubbers. When Japan cut off the supply of natural rubber during the tragic months after Pearl Harbor, it was synthetic rubber that kept essential facets of the American economy rolling. Neither Nieuwland nor Carothers long survived the development of neoprene, however, or lived to see its consequences.

[1059] **WHIPPLE,** George Hoyt
American physician
Born: Ashland, New Hampshire, August 28, 1878
Died: Rochester, New York, February 1, 1976

Whipple graduated from Yale University in 1900 and received his medical degree in 1905 from Johns Hopkins University. After a stay in the Panama Canal Zone and some years of training and teaching at Johns Hopkins he went to California in 1914 as professor of medicine at the University of California. In 1921 he went to the University of Rochester where he organized its new medical school, serving as its first dean, and retaining that position till 1953.

He was primarily interested in bile pigments, as were Pregl [982] and Wieland [1048], but for Whipple the problem led in a third direction. Since bile pigments are formed in the body from hemoglobin, Whipple thought he ought to tackle the methods by which hemoglobin was handled by the body, beginning with its formation.

He therefore began a series of experiments in 1917 in which he bled dogs to introduce an anemia, and then followed the manner in which new red blood corpuscles were formed. He kept dogs on various kinds of diet to see what effect that would have on corpuscle formation and found that liver was the most potent item of those he tried. This paved the way for the successful treament of pernicious anemia by Minot [1103] and Murphy [1154] and so he shared with them the 1934 Nobel Prize in medicine and physiology.

[1060] **MEITNER,** Lise (mite'ner)
Austrian-Swedish physicist
Born: Vienna, November 7, 1878
Died: Cambridge, England, October 27, 1968

Meitner, the daughter of a lawyer, was of Jewish descent but was baptized in infancy and was raised as a Protestant. She grew interested in science when she read of the Curies' [897, 965] discovery of radium in 1902. She studied at the University of Vienna under Boltzmann [769], among others, obtaining her doctorate in 1906.

She visited Berlin in 1907 in order to attend the lectures of Max Planck [887] and stayed to join Otto Hahn [1063] in a research collaboration that lasted thirty years. She had to battle a comically stupid prejudice against women scientists on the part of the German professors. Emil Fischer [833] allowed her to work for him only after she promised never to enter laboratories where males were working (though eventually he gave in and allowed her to enter the sacred precincts). During World War I she patriotically served as a nurse in the Austrian army.

During the first years of Hitler's regime, she was safe from harm, though of Jewish descent, because she was an Austrian national. After the Nazi absorption of Austria in 1938, however, she was forced to leave Germany. Through the help of Debye [1094] and Coster [1135], she managed to enter the Netherlands without a visa. She then went to Bohr [1101] in Denmark and finally to Stockholm, where Bohr helped get her a position with Siegbahn [1111].

She was more firmly convinced than Hahn of the actuality of uranium fission and it was from Stockholm, in January 1939, that she published the first report concerning it. She visited the United States after World War II, then returned to Sweden, becoming a Swedish citizen in 1949.

She moved on to Cambridge in 1960,

and in 1966 she was awarded a share of the Fermi Award issued by the Atomic Energy Commission. She was the first woman to win the award.

She died just short of her ninetieth birthday, and outlived her long-time friend and associate, Hahn, by just three months. Her devotion to science had been total. She never married.

[1061] **BRØNSTED,** Johannes Nicolaus (brun'sted)
Danish chemist
Born: Varde, Jutland, February 22, 1879
Died: Copenhagen, December 17, 1947

Brønsted's father (who died when Brønsted was thirteen) had been a civil engineer and at first Brønsted himself was slated for the same profession. However, he was interested in chemistry and in college switched to that subject. In 1908 he earned his doctorate at the Copenhagen Polytechnic Institute and was selected for a new professorship of chemistry instituted at the University of Copenhagen.

Brønsted interested himself in chemical thermodynamics, his fundamental contributions rivaling those of G. N. Lewis [1037]. He also produced experimental work that confirmed the theories of Debye [1094] concerning ionic substances in solution.

Brønsted's studies of how acids and bases catalyzed reactions, begun in 1921, forced him to clarify just what acids and bases were. The classic definition was that acids were substances that gave up hydrogen ions in solution, while bases gave up hydroxyl ions. Since the properties of acids and bases were in so many respects opposed to each other, Brønsted believed that it would make far more sense to supply definitions that were opposed to each other.

In 1923, therefore, Brønsted suggested that if acids were substances that gave up a hydrogen ion in solution, bases must be substances that took up a hydrogen ion in solution. This left the hydroxyl ion a strong base, since it certainly reacted with the hydrogen ion, taking it up to form water. However, the base concept was most usefully broadened to include many substances other than hydroxyl ion.

In fact, the connection between acids and bases was clarified, since every acid, in giving up a hydrogen ion, became a base, with the capacity of taking up a hydrogen ion once more to form the acid again. Thus, rather than a set of acids and a set of bases with no necessary connection, there was one set of conjugate acid-base systems.

The new view is the one most commonly used in chemical thinking now, although Lewis introduced a still broader concept of acids and bases.

After World War II, during which Brønsted distinguished himself by his firm anti-Nazi attitude, he was elected to the Danish parliament in 1947 but died before he could take his seat.

[1062] **McCOLLUM**, Elmer Verner
American biochemist
Born: near Fort Scott, Kansas, March 3, 1879
Died: Baltimore, Maryland, November 15, 1967

McCollum studied at the University of Kansas, graduating in 1903, then going on to earn his doctorate at Yale University in 1906. He joined the faculty of the University of Wisconsin in 1907, but went to Johns Hopkins University in 1917 as professor of biochemistry, the first faculty member in its School of Hygiene and Public Health. There he remained till his retirement in 1946.

McCollum's prime interest was in diet and he continued the attempt, earlier carried on by men like Hopkins [912], to find a way to nourish and support animals on a mixture of simple substances. (He popularized the use of the white rat as an experimental animal.) Through his early years at Wisconsin he failed, even though he tried to flavor his mixture in various ways, just in case it was the insipidity of the food rather than its chemical insufficiency that bothered the experimental animals. Some admixture of nat-

ural food, however, continued to be required no matter what he did.

The work of Eijkman [888] was filtering into the biochemical consciousness at the time and Hopkins' notion of the vitamin concept was reinforced by Funk [1093]. It began to appear that it was not the natural food that was required to supplement the diet, but the vitamin content thereof, additional simple substances essential to life in very small quantities. McCollum started trying to locate these.

In 1913 McCollum and his colleagues discovered that a factor essential to life was present in some fats. This had to be chemically different from the factor studied by Eijkman, which was soluble in water. McCollum spoke of fat-soluble A and water-soluble B and this soon became vitamin A and vitamin B, the first of a host of lettered vitamins. These letters survived a quarter of a century until increasing knowledge of the chemical nature of the vitamins allowed the use of proper chemical names. The letters are still used in popular articles and discussions.

Later, McCollum contributed to the discovery of other fat-soluble vitamins, such as vitamin D in 1922, and vitamin E still later. (The letter C was already assigned to the factor whose absence caused scurvy, and whose existence in the citrus fruits used by Lind [288] cured the disease a century and a half earlier.)

Knowledge of the water-soluble vitamins was being extended in the 1920s also, by men like Goldberger [1027]. Methods for assaying various foods for vitamin content, so that diets could be rationalized in the light of the new knowledge, were developed by Sherman [1036].

McCollum also did important work in the field of trace minerals. These were inorganic elements which, like the organic vitamins, were necessary to life in small quantities. McCollum showed that a deficiency of calcium in the body would eventually produce tetany, that is, muscular spasm. He also showed that the body required no phosphorus-containing organic materials, of the type first reported by Harden [947], in the diet. It could manufacture all such compounds from simple inorganic phosphates. McCollum also experimented on the importance of fluorine, zinc, and manganese to life.

[1063] **HAHN**, Otto
German physical chemist
Born: Frankfurt-am-Main, March 8, 1879
Died: Göttingen, July 28, 1968

Hahn, the son of a glazier, was a mediocre student in college. Despite his father's wish that he become an architect, he grew interested in chemistry. He studied under Baeyer [718] at Munich, and it was not until he had entered graduate school that he found himself. He obtained his Ph.D. in 1901 at the University of Marburg, and did so *magna cum laude*. He then continued his studies abroad.

He worked with Ramsay [832] in London in 1904. Ramsay persuaded him to stay in research and in 1905 he went on to work with Ernest Rutherford [996] in Canada, succeeding Soddy [1052], who, in fair exchange, had returned to England to work with Ramsay. In 1906 Hahn returned to Germany, worked with Emil Fischer [833], achieved professorial rank in 1910, and served in World War I, working on poison gas under Haber [977]. In 1928 he became director of the Kaiser Wilhelm Institute for Chemistry.

During the early period of his research he helped work out some of the intermediate stages in the radioactive breakdown of thorium. Then, in 1917, with his longtime associate Meitner [1060], he discovered the new element protactinium. In 1921 the two also discovered nuclear isomers, atoms with nuclei that did not differ in content of subatomic particles but only in energy content and type of radioactive breakdown.

However, Hahn's real fame came fifteen years later in connection with the bombardment of uranium with neutrons, a project that had first been undertaken by Fermi [1243], in the mid 1930s. The results obtained by Fermi had

been confusing, though it was suspected that artificial elements more complicated than uranium had been formed. Hahn and Meitner, among others, investigated the situation. They treated the bombarded uranium with barium, which carried down a certain fraction of strongly radioactive material. This made them suspect that one of the products of neutron-bombarded uranium was radium, which was chemically very similar to barium and would be expected to accompany barium in any chemical manipulations. However, no radium could be obtained in those barium-treated fractions.

By 1938 Hahn, working with Fritz Strassman [1251], began to wonder if it was not barium itself—radioactive barium, of course, formed from the uranium in the course of its bombardment by neutrons—that was being carried down by the barium he had added. However, the barium atom was much lighter than the uranium atom, so much lighter that it could have been formed only through the breaking in half of the uranium atom. Such a breaking in half (uranium fission) was unheard of in nuclear work and Hahn hesitated to publish this suggestion. He published his findings in January 1939 but he carefully did not interpret them as representing fission. As a chemist he did not wish to fly in the face of physical dogma.

Meitner, now in exile (and feeling perhaps that she had little to lose), having received the news from Hahn himself, took the plunge and published the suggestion of fission a month later.

For his discovery of fission Hahn received the 1944 Nobel Prize in chemistry. Very fortunately for the world, the Nazi government of Germany remained blind to the potentialities of fission and Hahn was left pretty much to himself and to minor experimentation during the course of World War II. In 1946, the war being over, Hahn became president of the West German Max Planck Society, holding this position till his retirement in 1960.

The news of fission had, however, been brought to the United States by

Bohr [1101] and, thanks to Szilard [1208], American research got under way, culminating in the development of the atomic bomb.

In 1945, after the end of the European phase of World War II, Hahn, who had taken no part in war research this time, was taken into custody by American forces, along with Laue [1068], Heisenberg [1245], and Weizsäcker [1376]. It was while he was in custody that Hahn received the news of the dropping of the atomic bomb on Hiroshima.

Hahn conceived his personal responsibility to be great and, for a while, even considered suicide. The fission bomb diminished, however, when compared with the fusion bomb whose theoretical basis had been forecast by Harkins [1022]. In 1966 he was granted a share of the Fermi award issued by the Atomic Energy Commission of the United States. He was the first foreigner to win this award.

After his death (as the result of an accidental fall), element number 105 was named hahnium in his honor.

[1064] **EINSTEIN**, Albert
German-Swiss-American physicist
Born: Ulm, Germany, March 14, 1879
Died: Princeton, New Jersey, April 18, 1955

Einstein was the son of a chemical engineer. Although Jewish, Einstein received his earliest education in a Catholic grammar school in Munich, Bavaria, to which city his family moved while he was still quite young. Like Newton [231], with whom he is often compared (and certainly he is the only scientist since Newton's time who can bear the comparison), he showed no particular intellectual promise as a youngster. As a matter of fact, he was so slow in learning to speak that by the time he was three there was some feeling that he might prove retarded.

In 1894 his father (who had failed in business) left for Milan, Italy, while Albert stayed behind to finish his high school studies. However, he did very badly in Latin and Greek and was interested only in mathematics, so he left school by invitation of the teacher who said, "You will never amount to anything, Einstein." The young man thus became the most unusual dropout in the history of science. His uncle, Jakob, another engineer, then began giving him mathematical puzzles that continued to feed his interest in this direction.

After an Italian vacation (taken to avoid qualifying for military service in Germany—for he was a pacifist from the start) he began his college work in Switzerland. This was not without difficulty, for only in mathematics was he really qualified for entrance. Nor did he enjoy the experience. He cut most of the lectures, preferring to concentrate on independent reading in theoretical physics. That he could pass his courses at all was due to the excellent lecture notes of a friend.

Once graduated, he tried to find a teaching post but that wasn't easy, for he was not a Swiss citizen and he was Jewish besides. In 1901, thanks to the influence of the father of the same friend whose lecture notes Einstein had used, Einstein accepted a position as a junior official at the patent office at Berne, Switzerland, and in that year became a Swiss citizen.

Therefore, without any academic connections, he began his work and for it, fortunately, he required no laboratory but only a pencil, some paper, and his mind. The year 1905 was his *annus mirabilis,* for it saw the publication of five of his papers in the German Yearbook of Physics, involving three developments of major importance (and in that same year, he earned his Ph.D.).

One paper dealt with the photoelectric effect, whereby light falling upon certain metals was found to stimulate the emission of electrons. Lenard [920] had in 1902 found that the energy of the emitted electrons did not depend on the intensity of the light. A bright light might bring about the emission of a greater number of electrons, but not of more energetic ones. There was no satisfactory explanation for this in terms of classical physics.

Einstein, however, applied to the problem the quantum theory worked out five years earlier by Planck [887] and disregarded since. Einstein maintained that a particular wavelength of light, being made up of quanta of fixed energy content, would be absorbed by a metallic atom and would force out an electron of fixed energy content and no other. Brighter light (more quanta) would then bring about the emission of more numerous electrons, but all still of the same energy content. Light of shorter wavelength, however, would have more energetic quanta and would bring about the emission of more energetic electrons. Light that had wavelengths longer than a certain critical value would be made up of quanta so weak as to bring about no electron emission at all. The energy content of such long wavelength photons would be insufficient to break electrons away from the atoms of which they formed a part. This "threshold wavelength" would be different for different metals, of course.

Planck's theory was thus, for the first time, applied to a physical phenomenon (other than the black-body problem that had occasioned its development in the first place) that it could explain and classical physics could not. This went a long way, perhaps even all the way, toward establishing the new quantum mechanics. For this feat Einstein was eventually awarded the 1921 Nobel Prize in physics, and yet it was not his greatest work of that year.

In his second paper of 1905, published two months after the first, Einstein worked out a mathematical analysis of Brownian motion, first observed by Brown [403] three quarters of a century earlier. Einstein showed that if the water in which the particles were suspended was composed of molecules in random motion, according to the requirements of the kinetic theory of Maxwell [692] and Boltzmann [769], then the suspended particles would indeed jiggle as they were observed to do. Svedberg [1097] had suggested this molecular explanation

of Brownian motion three years earlier, but it was Einstein who worked matters out in mathematical detail.

All objects in water (or in any liquid or gas) are continually bombarded from all sides by molecules. Through the workings of chance, the number of molecules striking any object of ordinary size from one angle is about the same as the number from another angle, the differences in number that do exist being insignificant in comparison with the truly vast total numbers involved. For that reason there is no overall effect (or at least no detectable one) upon objects of ordinary size.

As an object grows smaller, the total number of molecules bombarding it decreases and small differences in bombardment from this direction or that grow appreciable. Grains of pollen or particles of dye are small enough to be pushed first this way by a slight excess of molecules striking in that direction, then in another, then in still another. The motion is quite random, attesting to the random motion of the molecules themselves.

The larger the average size of the molecules, the larger the body for which this difference in bombardment can produce detectable effects. Therefore, the equation deduced by Einstein to describe Brownian motion could be used to work out the size of molecules and of the atoms that compose them. Three years later Perrin [990] conducted experiments on Brownian motion which confirmed Einstein's theoretical work and which gave the first good values of atomic size. The atomic theory of Dalton [389] was a hundred years old by then and had been accepted by all but a few diehards such as Ostwald [840], and yet this was the first time the effect of individual molecules could be directly observed. Even Ostwald gave in.

Einstein's greatest accomplishment of the year involved a new outlook on the universe, replacing the old Newtonian view, which had reigned supreme for two and a quarter centuries.

Einstein's work climaxed the famous experiment of Michelson [835] and Morley [730], who had been unable to detect any difference in the velocity of light with changes in its direction through the ether. Einstein later claimed he had not yet heard of the experiment in 1905, but that he was troubled by a certain lack of symmetry in Maxwell's equations concerning electromagnetic effects. Whatever the case, he began with the assumption that the measured velocity of light in a vacuum is always constant despite any motion of its source or of the individual measuring the light. Furthermore, he canceled out the ether as unnecessary by assuming that light traveled in quanta and therefore had particle-like properties and was not merely a wave that required some material to do the waving. This particle-like form of light was named a photon a decade later by Compton [1159]. It represented a retreat from the extreme wave theory of light, moving back toward Newton's old particle theory and taking up an intermediate position that was more sophisticated, and more useful, than either of the older theories.

Einstein also pointed out that without the ether there was certainly nothing in the universe that could be viewed as at "absolute rest," nor could any motion be considered an "absolute motion." All motion was relative to some frame of reference chosen, usually, for its convenience, and the laws of nature held unchanged for all such frames of reference. His theory, because of the "all motion is relative" idea, is therefore called relativity. In this particular paper he dealt only with the special case of systems in uniform nonaccelerated motion, so it is called the special theory of relativity.

He showed that from this simple assumption of the constancy of the velocity of light and the relativity of motion, the Michelson-Morley experiment could be explained and Maxwell's electromagnetic equations could be kept. He showed also that the length-contraction effect of FitzGerald [821] and the mass-enlargement effect of Lorentz [839] could be deduced, and that the velocity of light in a vacuum was therefore the

maximum speed at which information could be transferred.

All sorts of peculiar (in appearance) results followed. The rate at which time passed varied with velocity of motion; one had to give up notions of simultaneity, for one could no longer say, under certain conditions, whether A happened before B, after B, or simultaneously with B. Space and time vanished as single entities and were replaced by a fused "space-time." All this was against "common sense" but common sense is based on a limited experience with objects of ordinary size moving at ordinary velocity. Under such conditions the difference between Einstein's theory and the ordinary Newtonian view (which is "common sense") becomes indetectably small. In the vast world of the universe as a whole and the tiny world within the atom, however, common sense is no guide; there *is* a detectable difference between the two views; and it is Einstein's view and not Newton's that is the more useful.

In the special theory of relativity, Einstein worked out an interrelationship of mass and energy in a famous equation that goes: $E=mc^2$, where E is energy, m mass, and c the velocity of light. Since the velocity of light is a huge quantity, a small amount of mass (multiplied by the square of the velocity) is equivalent to a large amount of energy.

With mass and energy thus interpreted as different aspects of the same phenomenon, it was no longer sufficient to speak of Lavoisier's [334] conservation of mass or of Helmholtz's [631] conservation of energy. Instead there was the greater generalization of the conservation of mass-energy. Or, if one still speaks simply of the conservation of energy, it must be understood that mass is but one more aspect of energy.

This new view at once explained the energies given off by radioactive elements as a consequence of the slight loss of mass involved, a loss so slight as to be indetectable by ordinary chemical procedures. The interrelationship of mass and energy was quickly confirmed by a variety of nuclear measurements and has, ever since, proved fundamental in atomic studies. Once only did its usefulness seem to flag and then Pauli [1228] postulated the existence of the neutrino to save it.

The value of the new generalization in everyday affairs, and not merely in the highly esoteric work of the atomic physicists, was overwhelmingly shown when the conversion of mass to energy on a large scale made possible the devastation by atomic bombs a generation later, a denouement to which Einstein was to contribute directly, and which he was to find horrifying.

Despite this triple thunderbolt of papers, it was four more years before Einstein could finally obtain a professorship (and a poorly paying one) at the University of Zürich. His reputation continued to grow, however, and in 1913 a position was created for him at the Kaiser Wilhelm Physical Institute in Berlin, thanks to Planck, who was greatly impressed by the young Einstein. For the first time Einstein was to be paid generously enough to make it possible for him to devote his life to science.

World War I broke out but Einstein was little affected, since he was at the time a Swiss citizen. However, when many German scientists signed a nationalistic pro-war proclamation, Einstein was one of the few to sign a counterproclamation calling for peace.

Einstein was then working on the application of his theory of relativity to the more general case of accelerated systems and in so doing worked out a new theory of gravitation of which Newton's classic theory was but a special case. He published it in 1915 in another tremendous paper usually referred to as the "General Theory of Relativity." The equations set up in this theory allowed grand conclusions to be drawn about the universe as a whole and Sitter [1004] was to use those equations to better effect than Einstein himself.

In the general theory, Einstein pointed out three places where his theory predicted effects that were not like those predicted by Newton's theory. The phenomena concerned could be measured and in that way a decision between the two theories could be reached.

First, Einstein's theory allowed for a shift of the position of the perihelion of a planet, a shift that Newton's theory did not allow. Only in the case of Mercury (closest to the sun and its gravitational influence) was the difference large enough to be noticeable. And, as a matter of fact, the motion that Leverrier [564] had detected and tried to explain by supposing the existence of an infra-Mercurian planet, was explained on the spot by Einstein's theory. This, however, was not so impressive as it might be since Einstein knew about the discrepancy of Mercury's motion to begin with and could have "aimed" his theory at it.

Secondly, however, Einstein pointed out that light in an intense gravitational field should show a red shift. This had never been looked for or observed so the coast was clear for a fair test. Only extreme gravitational fields could show a shift large enough to measure at the time and, at Eddington's [1085] suggestion, W. S. Adams [1045] demonstrated the existence of this Einstein shift in the case of the white-dwarf companion of Sirius, which had the intensest gravitational field then known.

(In the 1960s, with improvement in measuring devices, the much smaller Einstein shift of the light of our own sun was measured and found to match Einstein's prediction. In addition, the shift in gamma-ray wavelength, worked out by Mössbauer [1483] in the late 1950s, was essentially an Einstein shift and it too has been measured and found to be in accord with the prediction.)

Thirdly and most dramatically, Einstein showed that light would be deflected by a gravitational field much more than Newton predicted. There was no way of testing this in the midst of World War I. However, with the war over (and Germany, but not Einstein, defeated) the opportunity arose on March 29, 1919, when a solar eclipse was scheduled to take place at just the time when more bright stars were in the vicinity of the eclipsed sun than would be there at any other time of year.

The Royal Astronomical Society of London made ready for two expeditions, one to northern Brazil and one to Principe Island in the Gulf of Guinea off the coast of West Africa. The positions of the bright stars near the sun were measured. If light was bent in its passage near the sun, those stars would be in positions that differed slightly from those they occupied six months before, when their light passed nowhere near the sun as they rode high in the midnight sky. Again the comparison of positions backed Einstein.

Einstein was now world-famous. Ordinary people might not understand his theories and might only grasp dimly what it was all about but there was no question that they understood him to be *the* scientist. No scientist was so revered in his own time since Newton. This, however, was not to save Einstein from the malevolent forces that were beginning to sweep Germany.

In 1930 Einstein visited California to lecture at the California Institute of Technology and was still there when Hitler came to power. There was no point in returning to Germany, and he took up permanent residence in Princeton, New Jersey, at the Institute for Advanced Studies where, a year before, he had already been offered a post. In 1940 he became an American citizen.

The final decades of his life were spent in a vain hunt for a theory that would embrace both gravitation and electromagnetic phenomena (the unified field theory) but this, to his increasing distress, eluded him and, so far, it has eluded everyone else. Nor did Einstein succeed in accepting all the changes that were sweeping the world of physics, despite his own role as intellectual revolutionary. He would not accept Heisenberg's [1245] principle of uncertainty, for instance, for he could not believe that the universe would be so entirely in the grip of chance. "God may be subtle," he once said, "but He is not malicious."

In 1930 he had argued that the uncertainty principle implied that time and energy could not be simultaneously determined with complete accuracy. He presented a "thought experiment" to show that this was not so and that time and energy *could* be determined simultaneously to any degree of accuracy. The next day, however, Bohr [1101], having spent a sleepless night, pointed out an error in Einstein's argument. Now the time-energy uncertainty is accepted.

With the beginning of World War II, Einstein was instrumental in achieving something he did not want. Uranium fission had been discovered in 1939 by Hahn [1063] and Meitner [1060], and Szilard [1208] could see quite well what that implied. Szilard did not want the horrors of nuclear bombs to be released on mankind but, on the other hand, the possibility that Hitler might come into possession of such bombs had to be reckoned with.

Einstein, as the most influential scientist in the world, was persuaded by Szilard to write a letter to President Franklin D. Roosevelt, urging him to put into effect a gigantic research program designed to develop a nuclear bomb. The result was the Manhattan Project, which, in six years, did develop such a bomb, the first being exploded at White Sands near Alamogordo, New Mexico, on July 16, 1945. By that time Hitler had been defeated, so the second and third bombs were exploded over Japan the next month.

The nuclear bombs remained to threaten postwar mankind, and six countries—the United States, the Soviet Union, Great Britain, France, China, and India—now have such weapons. To the end of his life Einstein fought stubbornly for some world agreement to end the threat of nuclear warfare. He also expressed his strong opposition to the temporary aberration of McCarthyism that swept the United States in the early 1950s. His ability to revolutionize physics was greater, however, than his ability to change man's heart, and at the time of his death the peril was greater than ever before. In death, he remained as unostentatious as in life. He was cremated without ceremony and his ashes were scattered at some undisclosed place.

Element number 99, discovered after his death, was named einsteinium in his honor, shortly after his death.

[1065] **SCHMIDT,** Bernhard Voldemar
Russian-German optician
Born: Neissaar Island, Estonia,
March 30, 1879
Died: Hamburg, Germany, December 1, 1935

Schmidt was born at a time when Estonia was part of the Russian empire (as it is of the USSR today). He lost his right arm in an accident when he was a boy and he received little schooling but succeeded in educating himself in optics.

As telescopes grow larger, the field they can enlarge grows smaller. If one tries to keep the field both large and enlarged, distortion creeps in about the edges. In 1930 Schmidt devised a special corrector plate, a small glass object with a complicated shape which could be placed near the focus of a spherical mirror. The corrector plate bent the light waves in such a way as to eliminate distortion, and even wide fields could be enlarged without distortion or aberration.

An instrument outfitted with such a mirror and corrector plate is called a Schmidt telescope or a Schmidt camera. Used in conjunction with a conventional telescope it can guide the work of that telescope, for otherwise the astronomer would be looking at the heavens through a tiny peephole and large surveys would take up prohibitive amounts of time.

Schmidt was an alcoholic who literally drank himself to death and whose last year of life was spent in a mental hospital.

[1066] **RICHARDSON,** Sir Owen
Willans
English physicist
Born: Dewsbury, Yorkshire,
April 26, 1879
Died: Alton, Hampshire, February 15, 1959

After an education at Cambridge, Richardson, the son of a salesman of industrial tools, came to the United States in 1906 and remained at Princeton as a professor of physics in the years before World War I.

During those years he studied how electrons and ions were given off by heated substances. It was because of this phenomenon that Edison [788] had been able to detect an electric current across a vacuum under certain conditions. The phenomenon had been used by John Fleming [803] to devise a rectifier and by De Forest [1017] to construct a triode. It was Richardson, though, who worked out the theory of electron and ion emission in detail and made possible the rapid improvement and development of radio tubes, television tubes, and so on.

He was honored with the 1928 Nobel Prize in physics as a result. He had returned to England in 1913 and there he taught at King's College until 1944, then at the University of London until his retirement. He was knighted in 1939.

[1067] **ROUS,** Francis Peyton (rows)
American physician
Born: Baltimore, Maryland, October 5, 1879
Died: New York, New York, February 16, 1970

Rous studied at Johns Hopkins University and obtained his medical degree in 1905.

In 1909 he joined the Rockefeller Institute for Medical Research (now Rockefeller University) and almost at once a poultry breeder wandered in with a sick Plymouth Rock chicken that he wanted examined. It had a tumor and when it died, Rous, among other things, decided to test whether it might contain a virus. (He was sure it didn't.)

He mashed up the tumor and passed it through a filter that would keep out all infectious agents but viruses. He found, however, that this "cell-free filtrate" was infectious and would produce tumors in other chickens. He did not dare call it a virus in the report he published in 1911, but a quarter century later, when virus research began to explode with success, there was nothing else to call it. The "Rous chicken sarcoma virus" was the first of the "tumor viruses."

In 1966 he was awarded a share of the Nobel Prize for medicine and physiology for this work. The interval of fifty-five years between work and award set a record, as did the age of the recipient—eighty-seven and still actively at work. Indeed, he remained at his desk till past his ninetieth birthday.

[1068] **LAUE**, Max Theodor Felix von (low'uh)
German physicist
Born: Pfaffendorf (near Coblenz), Prussia, October 9, 1879
Died: Berlin, April 23, 1960

Laue, the son of an army official, spent his youth on the move as his father's assignments brought him to various places. The schools he attended were many, but it was the high school at Strasbourg that crystallized his interest in science. He entered the University of Strasbourg in 1899 and devoted himself to theoretical physics. He obtained his doctor's degree there in 1903 and in 1905 returned to the university as Planck's [887] assistant, and between the two men a close friendship was established.

In 1909 Laue joined the faculty at the University of Munich, where he began his work on X rays. Since the discovery of X rays by Roentgen [774] in the previous decade, controversy had flourished as to the exact nature of the radiation. Some held it to consist of particles, as was true of cathode rays; some (including Roentgen himself) opted for longitudinal waves like those of sound; and some suggested that X rays were transverse electromagnetic waves like those of light. The work of Barkla [1049] had made it almost certain that the third alternative was the correct one. However, until the actual wavelength of X rays could be measured it was difficult to close the books.

The wavelength of ordinary light could be measured by the extent of the diffraction of a particular monochromatic beam by a ruled grating in which the marks were separated by known distances. The shorter the wavelength of the light, the closer the grating had to be ruled for efficient determination. The trouble was that all the evidence indicated that the wavelength of X rays was very much shorter than that of ordinary light and in order to diffract the X rays, a grating would have to be ruled far more finely than the techniques then available could manage.

It occurred to Laue that there was no need to manufacture such a grating. A crystal consisted of layers of atoms that were spaced just as regularly but far more closely than the ruled scratches of any man-made grating. A beam of X rays aimed at a crystal ought then to be diffracted as ordinary light would be by an ordinary grating. However, because the crystal had "lines" of atoms in various directions, the results would be more complicated. There would be beams located at varying distances and angles from the center, those distances and angles depending on the structure of the crystal.

In 1912 having transferred to the University of Zürich in that year, Laue tried the experiment on a crystal of zinc sulfide and it worked perfectly. The pattern was obtained and recorded on a photographic plate. It was the final point in favor of the electromagnetic view of X rays and the results were twofold. First, it offered a method of measuring the wavelengths of X rays by beginning with a crystal of known structure and measuring the amount of diffraction. (This the Braggs [922, 1141] accomplished almost at once.) Second, by using X rays of known wavelength it was possible to study the atomic structure of crystals, where such structure was unknown. It could even, as it turned out, be used to study polymers, with their giant molecules showing the necessary internal regularities to diffract X rays. In 1953 such work reached a climax with Wilkins' [1413] X-ray diffraction studies of nucleic acids.

Laue was awarded the 1914 Nobel Prize in physics for his work. In 1919 he became professor of theoretical physics at the University of Berlin, a post he kept until he resigned in 1943 in protest against the Nazis. (As early as 1939 he seized the occasion of a visit to Switzerland to make his anti-Nazi stand plain, by denouncing Hitler's policy of refusing to allow Germans to accept Nobel Prizes.) After the war he returned as director of the Max Planck Institute for Physical Chemistry.

He died in an automobile accident in his eighty-first year.

[1069] **WOOLLEY,** Sir Charles Leonard
English archaeologist
Born: London, April 17, 1880
Died: London, February 20, 1960

Woolley, the son of a minister, was educated at Oxford, and became an archaeologist, though that was not his first intention since he had been aiming at becoming a schoolmaster.

He began digging in the Middle East as early as 1907 but work was interrupted by World War I, of course, during the course of which he served as an intelligence officer with the British army in Egypt.

After the war, he began digging in Iraq (then under British control) and, particularly, at the site of the ancient Sumerian city of Ur, from which Abraham (according to the Bible) had emigrated to Canaan. It was Woolley's work, his uncovering of the artifacts of the earliest of the great civilizations (for it was the Sumerians who had been the first, shortly before 3000 B.C., to devise a system of writing), that placed Sumeria in the world's consciousness during the 1920s.

It created a sensation greater than the world of archaeology had seen since the work of Schliemann [634] a half century before. This was particularly so because Woolley's work cast light upon the Bible rather than upon the *Iliad*. He discovered, for instance, geological evidence of a great flood, which had clearly given rise to the biblical tale of the Flood, though the real one had been confined to the Tigris-Euphrates Valley.

In the 1930s and 1940s, he labored to uncover the relics of a Hurrian kingdom in northern Syria. He was knighted in 1935.

[1070] **GESELL,** Arnold Lucius (geh-zel')
American psychologist
Born: Alma, Wisconsin, June 21, 1880
Died: New Haven, Connecticut, May 29, 1961

Gesell's mother was a schoolteacher. He graduated from the University of Wisconsin in 1903 and obtained his doctorate (in psychology) from Clark University in 1906. He joined the faculty of Yale University in 1911 (obtaining a medical degree from the university in 1915), and remained there for the rest of his life.

He was interested at first in retarded children, but since retardation is a relative matter, he gradually grew interested in the mental development of children generally. Gesell and his group went into the matter in a large way, taking motion pictures of more than twelve thousand children. Their findings tended to show that children developed mentally in as set and orderly a pattern as they developed physically. It was easy to believe that the mental development followed closely the physical development of the nervous system, and the mind seemed more closely an aspect of the body and less a thing in itself.

His books, describing his findings, have been extremely popular with parents wishing to judge the relative progress of their offspring.

[1071] **WEGENER,** Alfred Lothar (vay'-guh-ner)
German geologist
Born: Berlin, November 1, 1880
Died: Greenland, November 1930

Wegener, the son of a director of an orphanage, obtained his Ph.D. in astronomy at the University of Berlin in 1905. Like Peary [866], he became a Greenland specialist. He took part in four different expeditions to that Arctic island, and died on the fourth.

He was impressed, as others had been before him, by the similarity of the coast lines of South America and Africa. It is easy to imagine that the South American bulge on its east coast can just fit into the indentation on the west coast of Africa.

It also seemed that the New World and the Old World were drifting apart. At least, based on nineteenth-century longitude determinations, it would seem that Greenland (Wegener's specialty) had moved a mile away from Europe in a century, that Paris and Washington were moving apart by fifteen feet each year, and that San Diego and Shanghai were approaching by six feet each year.

In 1912 Wegener therefore proposed that originally the continents had formed a single mass (Pangaea or "All-earth") surrounded by a continuous ocean (Panthalassa or "All-sea"). This large granite mass broke into chunks that slowly separated, floating on a basalt ocean, and, over hundreds of millions of years, took up the pattern of the fragmented continents we now have.

In this fashion Wegener undertook to explain the changing pattern of glaciations, for, of course, the relative positions of the poles with respect to the continents changed. He also used his hypothesis to explain patterns of species similarities, wherein related species were found in widely separated parts of the world, and so on.

It was quite a plausible theory and made converts. However, counterevidence appeared. The apparent movement of Greenland was found to be based on faulty determinations, and the better determinations of the twentieth century showed no movements of land masses at all. Nevertheless, additional evidence on the structure of the continental shelves, the nature of the mid-oceanic rift, plus the discovery of a fossil amphibian in Antarctica have all worked to make "continental drift" more and more attractive to geologists.

Wegener also took part in the controversy over the lunar craters as to whether they arose through volcanic action or through meteoric bombardment. He tried an ingenious experiment: dropping powdered plaster onto a smooth layer of powdered cement. He was able to produce miniature replicas of lunar craters so faithfully that he all but convinced astronomers that the meteoric hypothesis was correct.

[1072] **LANGMUIR,** Irving (lang'-myoor)
American chemist
Born: Brooklyn, New York, January 31, 1881
Died: Falmouth, Massachusetts, August 16, 1957

Langmuir, the son of an insurance executive, spent three years of his youth at school in Paris, then returned to the United States and graduated from Pratt Institute in 1898. He obtained a degree in metallurgical engineering at Columbia University in 1903, and in 1906 a Ph.D. in chemistry at the University of Göttingen in Germany, where he worked under Nernst [936]. After returning to the United States, Langmuir taught chemistry at the Stevens Institute of Technology and then joined the staff of the General Electric Company at Schenectady, New York, in 1909. He remained there until his retirement in 1950.

At General Electric his first task was to extend the life of the light bulb, then very short. The tungsten filaments just coming into use were enclosed in vacuum. The presence of air would mean the rapid oxidation of tungsten once heated and it was thought that to lengthen the life one must improve the vacuum.

Langmuir's studies, however, showed that in a vacuum, tungsten atoms slowly evaporated from the wire at the white-hot temperature of the glowing bulb. The wire grew thinner and eventually broke. The rate of evaporation was decreased in the presence of a gas—one, naturally, with which tungsten would not combine. Thereafter, light bulbs were filled with nitrogen (and, later, with the still less reactive argon) and lifetimes were multiplied. (Nevertheless, the incandescent bulb was not the end of progress in lighting, as Claude [989] was demonstrating in France.)

Langmuir then studied the effect of hot metal surfaces on all sorts of gases. It led him in many directions that had nothing to do with electric lighting, but General Electric had already profited enough from him for a lifetime and they gave him complete freedom to do as he chose.

In the mid-1920s, for instance, Langmuir proceeded to develop an atomic hydrogen blowtorch that could produce temperatures almost as hot as the surface of the sun. He did this by allowing a stream of hydrogen to be blown past hot tungsten wires (the connection with his incandescent bulb work is obvious). Under those conditions the hydrogen molecule is broken into its constituent atoms. As the jet of gas leaves the tungsten filament, the hydrogen atoms recombine to form hydrogen molecules, and the heat of this combination producing temperatures near 6000°C.

His interest in the vacuums within the old electric light bulbs led him to devise methods of producing high-vacuum tubes, which proved essential to radio broadcasting. He also invented a high-vacuum mercury pump.

His work on the gas films that formed on metal wires led him to consider how atoms formed bonds with each other. With the independent work of G. N. Lewis [1037], this was the beginning of the modern theory of electronic bonds, in which the dashes of Kekulé [680] are replaced by paired dots, signifying electrons. He also devised a theory of catalysis based on the formation of gas films on platinum wires.

He found that certain substances will form films on water that are one molecule thick and was the first to study such monomolecular films. This led to methods of cutting down glare on glass surfaces, for instance. For his work in surface chemistry, Langmuir received the 1932 Nobel Prize in chemistry, the first American industrial scientist to do so.

In later life, the most startling contribution to come out of his laboratories was his work with Schaefer [1309] and Vonnegut [1391] on "rainmaking." This is the first (if, as yet, only very shakily

successful) attempt on the part of man to do more about the weather than just talk.

[1073] **HESS,** Walter Rudolf
Swiss physiologist
Born: Frauenfeld, Thurgau,
March 17, 1881
Died: Zürich, August 12, 1973

Hess was originally an ophthalmologist, but he grew interested in physiology, studied it at the University of Bonn, and in 1917 was appointed professor of physiology at the University of Zürich.

In order to study in detail the autonomic nervous system, that portion of the system that controls the various automatic functions of the human body, he used fine electrodes to destroy tiny, specific sections of the brain of cats and dogs. In this manner, he located the autonomic centers in the hypothalamus and medulla oblongata so exactly that by stimulating the proper portion of the brain of a cat he could make it behave as it would on the sudden sight of a threatening dog—with no dog in sight.

For the deeper understanding of the brain's functioning that this led to, Hess shared the 1949 Nobel Prize for physiology or medicine with Egas Moniz [1032].

[1074] **STAUDINGER,** Hermann
(shtow'ding-er)
German chemist
Born: Worms, Hesse, March 23,
1881
Died: Freiburg-im-Breisgau, September 8, 1965

Staudinger, the son of a professor, obtained his doctorate at the University of Halle in 1903. He taught at the Technical Institute of Karlsruhe, where he was associated with Haber [977] until 1912.

Most of his professional life was spent at the University of Freiburg, where after 1951 he was professor emeritus. He did work in many branches of organic chemistry, but his outstanding labors were on the nature of polymers.

These are made up of large molecules, which are in turn built up out of a series of small units, something like beads on a string. Starch and cellulose are natural polymers built up out of glucose molecules from which water has been subtracted; while proteins are built up out of amino acids from which water has been subtracted. Staudinger showed, in work beginning in 1926, that the various plastics being produced were similar polymers with the simple units being arranged in a straight line and that they weren't, as many had suspected, merely disorderly conglomerates of small molecules.

The consequences of such studies were important enough, in the light of the vast proliferation of plastics after World War II, to earn for Staudinger the 1953 Nobel Prize in chemistry, two years after his retirement.

[1075] **KARMAN,** Theodore von
(kahr'mahn)
Hungarian-American physicist
Born: Budapest, Hungary, May 11, 1881
Died: Aachen, Germany, May 7, 1963

Karman was the son of a professor of education who had been knighted by Emperor Francis Joseph I of Austria-Hungary for his reorganization of Hungarian education. Among Karman's ancestors was Rabbi Judah Löw of Prague who, in legend, had devised the famous automaton called the Golem.

Karman was educated at the Royal Polytechnic University in Budapest after his father had deliberately guided him toward engineering, distrusting the youngster's great proficiency in pure mathematics. He served on the faculty of the university for some years, then went to Göttingen for his postdoctorate work and then to the University of Paris. In Paris in 1908 he saw the flight of one of the early airplanes and grew interested in aeronautical engineering, something that occupied him the rest of his life. He analyzed fluids in motion, and turbulence, and established the theory of

aeronautics that, until then, had been in the hands of trial-and-error engineers.

Karman and his student laid the groundwork for the designs that lead to supersonic flight. This was while he was in the United States, to which he had been invited in 1930 and where he decided to stay as the advance of Nazism was casting its shadow over Germany. He taught at California Institute of Technology and was largely responsible for its emergence as a top aeronautical research center. He became an American citizen in 1936.

[1076] **FISCHER,** Hans
German chemist
Born: Höchst-am-Main (now part of Frankfurt), July 27, 1881
Died: Munich, Bavaria, March 31, 1945

Fischer, the son of a dye chemist, obtained his doctorate in chemistry in 1904 at the University of Marburg and then took up medicine, obtaining his M.D. at the University of Munich in 1908. Trained in both disciplines, he became assistant to Emil Fischer [833] (no relation) at the University of Berlin. In 1916 he received his first professorial appointment, at the University of Innsbruck, succeeding Windaus [1046], who had moved on to Göttingen.

However, it was only in 1921, when Fischer accepted a position at the University of Munich, that his research really began to move. He got to work on the chemical structure of heme, that portion of hemoglobin (the red coloring matter of blood) not amino acid in nature. Painstakingly he and the students working under him took it apart into simpler components and discovered that it was made up of four pyrrole rings (consisting of four carbon atoms and a nitrogen atom each) arranged in a larger ring. Little by little the finer points were straightened out and by 1929 he had located every last atom in the heme molecule. From the standpoint of pure virtuosity, it was an extraordinary example of solving an organic jigsaw puzzle by careful work and reasoning, one not to be outdone until Sanger [1426] and his group took on the structure of insulin a generation later.

For this work Fischer was awarded the 1930 Nobel Prize in chemistry.

He went on to tackle chlorophyll, the green coloring matter of plants, on which Willstätter [1009] had expended so much effort. Chlorophyll has a molecular constitution quite like that of heme but there were subtle differences that were not easy to track down. Fischer devoted the 1930s to the task and eventually succeeded, working out the complete structure of the chlorophyll molecule. The red of blood and the green of leaves had both given up their secrets to him.

He remained in Germany during World War II and died a month before his country's defeat, committing suicide in despair after mass air raids on Munich had destroyed his laboratory.

[1077] **FLEMING,** Sir Alexander
Scottish bacteriologist
Born: Lochfield, Aryshire, August 6, 1881
Died: London, England, March 11, 1955

Fleming, the seventh of eight children of a farmer, was educated at Kilmarnock Academy, but after graduation, the fact that his father had died while he was young and that his family was poor, forced him to go to work in London as a shipping clerk. In 1900 he joined the army, but he was too late to see service in the Boer War. In 1902 he earned a scholarship and that, combined with a legacy from an uncle, allowed him to begin medical studies at the University of London. He made a brilliant mark as a medical student and took his degree in 1906.

In World War I he served in the British army's medical corps, ending with the rank of captain. When the war was over, he obtained a professorial position at the Royal College of Surgeons in 1919.

From the start he was interested in bacteriology, particularly the chemother-

apy of disease. He pioneered the introduction of Ehrlich's [845] Salvarsan in Great Britain.

During the war he had begun a line of research that culminated in 1922 in the discovery of a protein called lysozyme. This is found in tears and mucus and has bacteria-killing properties. (The art of bacteria-killing led into other interesting byways. Twort [1055], during those same years, uncovered a special sort of parasite that was quite deadly to bacteria.)

Fleming's chief discovery, however, came by accident. In 1928, when he was appointed professor of bacteriology at the school where he had been a medical student, he left a culture of staphylococcus germs uncovered for some days. He was through with it and was about to discard the dish containing the culture when he noticed that some specks of mold had fallen into it. That in itself was nothing, but about every speck the bacterial colony had dissolved away for a short distance. Bacteria had died and no new growth had invaded the area. (Tyndall [626] had briefly noted a similar observation a half century earlier.)

Fleming isolated the mold and eventually identified it as one called *Penicillium notatum,* closely related to the common variety often found growing on stale bread. Fleming decided that the mold liberated some compound that, at the very least, inhibited bacterial growth. He called the substance, whatever it was, penicillin.

He cultured the mold and attempted to grow various types of bacteria in its neighborhood. Some grew well; others would not approach the mold past a certain distance. Apparently penicillin affected some germs and not others. Fleming further experimented on the effect of the chemical on white blood cells. It was, after all, no trick to find something that was poisonous to bacteria. If it was also poisonous to human cells, nothing was gained. However, penicillin did not affect the white blood cells at all at concentrations that were highly deleterious to bacteria.

Unfortunately Fleming came to the

end of his rope. He was no chemist and could not isolate or identify the substance; nor did he arouse much interest in the descriptions he published of these unusual results.

The coming of World War II altered matters. The discovery of new antibacterials would be of the highest importance in the treatment of wounded soldiers and Florey [1213] and Chain [1306] set to work isolating penicillin. They succeeded, and it proved to be as successful as Fleming's first experiments had shown it would be. Penicillin was the first important example of what Waksman [1128] was soon to call the antibiotics. However, the delay between Fleming's experiments and their fulfillment allowed the development of the sulfa drugs through the work of Domagk [1183], and it was the sulfa drugs (not, strictly speaking, antibiotics) that initiated the age of the wonder drugs.

With the value of penicillin proved to the hilt, Fleming was knighted in 1944 and, along with Florey and Chain, awarded the 1945 Nobel Prize in medicine and physiology.

[1078] **DAVISSON**, Clinton Joseph
American physicist
Born: Bloomington, Illinois, October 22, 1881
Died: Charlottesville, Virginia, February 1, 1958

Davisson, the son of a paperhanger, entered the University of Chicago on a scholarship in 1902 and attracted the favorable attention of Millikan [969]. With Millikan's recommendation he entered Princeton for graduate work in physics and obtained his doctorate in 1911, working under the supervision of Richardson [1066] on the emission of ions by heated materials. After he had obtained his degree, he married Richardson's sister.

Davisson worked at the Carnegie Institute of Technology (now Carnegie-Mellon University) in Pittsburgh from 1911 to 1917, except that he spent the summer of 1913 in England working with J. J. Thomson [869]. When the United States entered World War I, he obtained leave of absence to join the company now known as the American Telephone and Telegraph Company (the Bell System) and remained there. (He tried to enlist, but was turned down for reasons of health.)

Davisson was interested in De Broglie's [1157] theory of the wave nature of electrons, first announced in 1924, but Davisson probably never suspected that he was going to demonstrate that wave nature experimentally. He did it by accident.

In 1925 he was studying the reflection of electrons from a metallic nickel target enclosed in a vacuum tube. The tube shattered by accident and the heated nickel promptly developed a film of oxide that made it useless as a target. To remove the film, he had to heat the nickel for an extended period. Once this was done, he found that the reflecting properties of the nickel had changed.

Investigation showed that whereas the target had contained many tiny crystal surfaces before heating, it contained just a few large crystal surfaces afterward. Davisson followed this out to its logical conclusion and prepared a single nickel crystal for use as a target. Now he found that the electron beam was more than reflected. It was diffracted as well. But diffraction is characteristic of waves, not particles, and in this manner the wave nature of electrons was proved and De Broglie's theory was confirmed. Additional confirmation was received that same year by the independent and different work of G. P. Thomson [1156].

As a result Davisson and Thomson shared the 1937 Nobel Prize in physics.

[1079] **BARKHAUSEN**, Heinrich
(bahrk'how-zen)
German physicist
Born: Bremen, December 2, 1881
Died: Dresden, February 20, 1956

Barkhausen, the son of a judge, obtained his Ph.D. in 1907 and in 1911 became professor of communications engineering at the University of Dresden.

Barkhausen's main contribution to physics arose over the magnetization of iron. As iron is subjected to a continuously increasing magnetic field, its magnetization increases by little jerks rather than smoothly. These jerks are actually accompanied by noise, which can be heard as a series of clicks when magnified through a loudspeaker.

This Barkhausen effect was explained eventually when it came to be realized that iron consists of a series of minute domains within which all the tiny atomic magnets are lined up. Separate domains are strong magnets but each is canceled by the next, so that ordinary iron is not magnetized. As the domains are subjected to a strong magnetic field, however, they all line up and the iron, generally, becomes a magnet. As the domains line up, one rubs against its neighbor and the vibrations thus set up account for the noise.

This arrangement by domains is characteristic of ferromagnetic substances, that is, those substances capable of forming strong magnets—of which iron is chief.

[1080] **BRIDGMAN,** Percy Williams
American physicist
Born: Cambridge, Massachusetts,
April 21, 1882
Died: Randolph, New Hampshire,
August 20, 1961

Bridgman, the son of a newspaper reporter, had his scientific life entirely bound up with Harvard. After an education in the public schools of Newton, Massachusetts, he entered Harvard in 1900, earning successive degrees there up to his Ph.D. in 1908. Immediately after obtaining his doctorate he joined the faculty, attaining a professorial position in 1913 and remaining until his retirement in 1954.

Even as a candidate for the doctor's degree, Bridgman was already working in the field of high pressures. In 1905 the equipment with which he was work-

ing failed under the pressures he wanted to use and he turned his attention to the design of equipment that would not fail. In the early apparatus it had been the seals at the joints that had given. Bridgman therefore designed seals that squeezed tighter together as the pressure increased so that only the strength of the material making up the chamber was the limit of permissible pressure. Quite early in the game he reached a pressure of 20,000 atmospheres (128 tons to the square inch).

By using stronger materials and by putting pressure on his container from the outside, he kept reaching higher and higher pressures up to 400,000 atmospheres. Through use of these higher pressures, he was able to study new forms of solids. This was valuable not only in itself, but also for the light it threw on substances and processes deep within the earth. A dramatic consequence was announced in 1955 when, with Bridgman as a consultant, research workers at General Electric were able finally to form synthetic diamonds by the use of a combination of high pressure and high temperature. For his work Bridgman had received the 1946 Nobel Prize in physics.

Bridgman was a poor lecturer but he was an important philosopher of science, writing thoughtful books on the nature of physics. In 1961, almost eighty years old, with over half a century of success behind him, and incurably and painfully ill, Bridgman shot himself to death, writing a note stating it was the last day he would be physically able to do so. He pointed out that it was indecent of society to turn its back and force him to do it without help or sympathy.

[1081] **FRANCK,** James
German-American physicist
Born: Hamburg, August 26, 1882
Died: Göttingen, May 21, 1964

Franck, the son of a Jewish banker, studied chemistry at the University of Heidelberg, then physics at the University of Berlin, where he obtained his

Ph.D. in 1906 and where he began a life-long friendship with Born [1084]. During World War I, he fought valiantly for Germany as a volunteer, winning an Iron Cross. Afterward, he worked under Haber [977].

In 1920 he received a professorial appointment at the University of Göttingen. While there, he and Gustav Hertz [1116] did the work that earned them the 1925 Nobel Prize in physics. This consisted of bombarding gases and vapors with electrons of different energies. When the energy was not enough to allow the absorption of a full quantum of energy, the electron rebounded elastically and there was no light emission. When the energy was enough, a quantum was absorbed and light was emitted. This fitted in well with Planck's [887] quantum theory and showed that the inner structure of the atom was quantized.

At the time, the Bohr [1101] theory was the only one in the field, so the Franck-Hertz experiments were considered as bolstering it, but, of course, it equally supports the later and better theories of a quantized atom, such as Schrödinger's [1117] theory.

In 1933 Franck resigned his university position in protest against the policies of the new Nazi government, and in 1934 he was forced to flee Hitler's anti-Semitism. He first joined Bohr in Copenhagen, then went to the United States, where he taught at Johns Hopkins University and later at the University of Chicago. He became an American citizen and worked on the atomic bomb project during World War II.

He strenuously opposed dropping the atomic bomb on Japan and favored a demonstration before representatives of the United Nations instead, in the hope that this would encourage a ban of the bomb instead of its use. In a petition to the secretary of war in 1945, Franck and others accurately forecast the nuclear stalemate that would follow a failure to ban the bomb. The petition was ignored. After the war Franck recast his Nobel medal, which had been dissolved eleven years before so that it might be carried safely out of Germany. He also made annual visits to Göttingen in his later years and it was during one of these that he died.

[1082] **GEIGER,** Hans Wilhelm
(gigh'ger)
German physicist
Born: Neustadt-an-der-Haardt
(now Neustadt-an-der-
Weinstrasse), Rhineland-
Palatinate, September 30, 1882
Died: Potsdam, September 24,
1945

Geiger, the son of a professor of philology, obtained his Ph.D. in 1906 at Erlangen. A fellowship took him to England, where he was Ernest Rutherford's [996] capable assistant in his work on alpha particle scattering, but with the opening of World War I, he returned to Germany to serve in the artillery.

His name is now most famous in connection with the Geiger counter, a device for detecting energetic subatomic particles, invented in 1913. This is a cylinder containing a gas under a high electric potential, one not quite high enough to overcome the resistance of the gas. If the high-energy subatomic particle enters, it ionizes one of the gas molecules. This ion is pulled toward the cathode with great energy and in the process, as a result of collisions, it ionizes some more atoms, which in turn begin to move and ionize others. In short, there is an "avalanche" of ionization, which conducts a momentary electric current that can be recorded as a clicking sound. The clickings of such a Geiger counter record the particles entering, and electronic devices are now used to count the particles automatically.

In 1925 Geiger received a professorial appointment at the University of Kiel, in 1929 one at the University of Tübingen, and in 1936 one at Berlin-Charlottenburg.

He participated briefly in Germany's abortive attempt to develop an atomic bomb during World War II. In June 1945 Geiger fled the Russian occupation to Potsdam and died less than two months after the American atomic bomb fell on Hiroshima.

[1083] **GODDARD,** Robert Hutchings
American physicist
Born: Worcester, Massachusetts, October 5, 1882
Died: Baltimore, Maryland, August 10, 1945

Goddard, the son of a machine shop owner, was raised in Boston, a sickly boy whose thoughts turned inward toward what seemed fantasy in those days. His family returned to Worcester when he was sixteen and he went to the Polytechnic Institute there, graduating in 1908. He received his Ph.D. in physics at Clark University in Worcester in 1911. He taught at Princeton but returned to Clark in 1914 and remained there for nearly thirty years.

He had a mind daring enough for a science fiction writer, and he was firmly grounded in science, to boot. While still an undergraduate, he described a railway line between Boston and New York in which the trains traveled in a vacuum under the pull of an electromagnetic field and completed their trip in ten minutes. He called it "Traveling in 1950," but, alas, the railroad trip still took four hours and more when 1950 actually rolled around.

He also grew interested in rocketry as a teenager thanks to his reading of H. G. Wells. Already in 1914 he had obtained two patents involving rocket apparatus and by 1919 all this had ripened to the point where he published a small book entitled *A Method of Reaching Extreme Altitudes.* In this he had been anticipated by Tsiolkovsky [880], but Goddard went a step further and began to experiment with ordinary gunpowder rockets.

In 1923 Goddard tested the first of a new type of rocket engine, one using gasoline, and liquid oxygen as the motive force. This was his first revolutionary advance over previous solid-fuel rockets. (Of course, early rockets were used mostly in Fourth of July celebrations and similar affairs, but there had

been a time in the first half of the nineteenth century when they were used in warfare. The U.S. national anthem speaks of "the rockets' red glare.")

In 1926 Goddard sent up his first rocket. His wife took a picture of him standing next to it before it was launched. It was about four feet high, six inches in diameter, and was held in a frame like a child's jungle gym. This, nevertheless, was the grandfather of the monsters that a generation later were to rumble upward from the Transcaspian, from Florida, and from California.

Goddard managed to get a few thousand dollars from the Smithsonian Institution and in July 1929 sent up a larger rocket near Worcester, Massachusetts. It went faster and higher than the first. More important, it carried a barometer, a thermometer, and a small camera to photograph the proceedings. It was the first instrument-carrying rocket.

Unfortunately Goddard already had a small reputation as a crackpot and, like Langley [711] before him, had earned an editorial in the good, gray New York *Times,* berating him for his scientific folly. The noise of this second rocket brought calls to the police. Officials ordered him to conduct no more rocket experiments in Massachusetts.

Fortunately Lindbergh [1249] interested himself in Goddard's work. He visited Goddard and was sufficiently impressed to persuade Daniel Guggenheim, a philanthropist, to award Goddard a grant of $50,000. With this, Goddard set up an experimental station in a lonely spot near Roswell, New Mexico. Here he built larger rockets and developed many of the ideas that are now standard in rocketry. He designed combustion chambers of the appropriate shape, and burned gasoline with oxygen in such a way that the rapid combustion could be used to cool the chamber walls.

From 1930 to 1935 he launched rockets that attained speeds of up to 550 miles an hour and heights of a mile and a half. He developed systems for steering a rocket in flight by using a rudderlike device to deflect the gaseous exhaust, with gyroscopes to keep the rocket headed in the proper direction. He patented the device of a multistage rocket. He accumulated a total of 214 patents, in fact.

But the United States Government never really became interested in his work. This lack of interest was made easier by the fact that Goddard was a rather withdrawn and suspicious person who preferred to work in isolation.

Only during World War II did the government finance him, and then only to have him design small rockets to help navy planes take off from carriers. (One of Goddard's early inventions was also perfected as the World War II weapon known as the bazooka.)

In Germany, meanwhile, rockets were being developed as powerful war weapons. When German rocket experts were brought to America after the war and were questioned about rocketry, they stared in amazement and asked why American officials did not inquire of Goddard, from whom they had learned virtually all they knew.

American officials could not do so because Goddard had been neglected during his lifetime and died of throat cancer before that neglect could be made up for. He had lived long enough to learn of the German rockets, and even to see one, but did not live to see the United States step into the space age. However, if the space age could be said to have been manufactured by any one man, that one man was Goddard.

In 1960 the United States Government issued a grant of one million dollars for the use of his patents—half to Goddard's estate and half to the Guggenheim Foundation. The Goddard Space Flight Center in Maryland is named in his honor.

[1084] **BORN**, Max
German-British physicist
Born: Breslau, Silesia (now Wrocław, Poland), December 11, 1882
Died: Göttingen, January 5, 1970

Born was the son of a professor of anatomy. He was educated in various German universities, obtaining his Ph.D. at Göttingen in 1907. Later, he studied at Cambridge under J. J. Thomson [869]. He lectured at the University of Chicago in 1912 at the invitation of Michelson [835]. In 1915 he accepted a professorship at the University of Berlin, one that was intended to relieve Planck [887] of his teaching duties. In 1921 he moved on to Göttingen.

Born, like Schrödinger [1117], Heisenberg [1245], and Dirac [1256], performed his most notable work in hammering out the mathematical basis of quantum mechanics. Born gave electron waves a probabilistic interpretation: the rise and fall of waves could be taken to indicate the rise and fall in probability that the electron would behave as though it existed at those particular points in the "wave packet."

Like Schrödinger he got out of Germany as soon as Hitler came to power, moving over to Cambridge in 1933. He became professor of natural philosophy at the University of Edinburgh in 1936 and a British subject in 1939. After his retirement in 1953 he returned to Germany and in 1954 was awarded the Nobel Prize in physics for his work on quantum mechanics, sharing it with Bothe [1146].

[1085] **EDDINGTON,** Sir Arthur Stanley
English astronomer and physicist
Born: Kendal, Westmoreland, December 28, 1882
Died: Cambridge, November 22, 1944

Eddington, the son of a headmaster, was of Quaker origin and, like Dalton [389], remained a firm Quaker throughout his life. He was an infant prodigy and distinguished himself in mathematics at Cambridge (where Whitehead [911] was one of his teachers), being first in his class in 1904. In 1906, he became chief assistant at the Greenwich Observatory and in 1913 was appointed professor of astronomy at Cambridge. In 1914, he became director of Cambridge Observatory. He did not serve in World War I for, as a Quaker, he qualified as a conscientious objector.

Eddington's major contribution to astronomy arose from his theoretical investigation of the interior of stars. The density of the sun—and presumably of stars generally—is considerably lower than the earth's and there were reasons to believe that the sun was gaseous throughout. The question arose, then, of what kept the gas from contracting, under the tremendous force of stellar gravity, into a tiny, compact mass—something like the white dwarfs that W. S. Adams [1045] had just discovered.

Eddington decided that the expansive force of heat and radiation pressure countered the contracting force of gravity. Since the pressure of the stellar matter increased rapidly with depth, the radiation pressure countering it must also increase and the only way that could happen was because of a rise in temperature. Eddington, in the early 1920s, showed quite convincingly that the rise in temperature required was such that its value in the sun's interior must reach into the millions of degrees.

This made it difficult to see how the solar system could start catastrophically with material pulled out of the sun by a passing star, as Chamberlin [766] and Jeans [1053] would have it. Matter at the temperature of the sun's surface might conceivably condense, but matter from the sun's interior, at the temperatures Eddington showed that interior must have, could only expand violently into a thin gas. It could never condense into planets.

The temperatures of millions of degrees in the sun's interior were to prove important the following decade when the nuclear processes powering the sun and other stars were worked out by Bethe [1308].

The more massive a star, Eddington went on to show, the greater the pressures in its interior, and the greater the countering temperatures and radiation pressure, consequently the more luminous the star. Thus, in 1924, Eddington announced the mass-luminosity law.

It followed, too, that as the mass of a star increased, the expansive force of radiation pressure increased very rapidly.

At masses greater than fifty times that of the sun, the force of radiation pressure would be large enough to blow the star apart, which is why very massive stars do not exist. (To be sure, there are extremely large stars from the standpoint of volume, but these are very rarefied and the masses are not past Eddington's limit. Some stars, at the edge of stability, pulsate, and these are the Cepheid variables. Eddington worked out a theoretical explanation for the behavior of such Cepheids that still passes muster today.)

Chandrasekhar [1356] later gave the disruptive force of radiation pressure an important role in stellar evolution.

Eddington was among the first, along with Bertrand Russell [1005] and Whitehead, to appreciate the importance of the relativity theories of Einstein [1064]. He was one of the observers of the total eclipse in 1919, which went a long way toward establishing those theories. Eddington himself was so busy changing plates on that expedition, however, that he did not actually see the eclipse. His treatise on relativity, published in 1923, was considered by Einstein to be the best presentation of the subject in any language.

Eddington, like Jeans (with whom he maintained a firm professional enmity), was the author of a number of books on astronomy for the layman in the 1920s and 1930s, notably *The Expanding Universe,* published in 1933. A whole generation of youngsters was introduced to Einstein via Eddington. He was knighted in 1930.

[1086] **BURT,** Sir Cyril Lodowic
English psychologist
Born: Stratford-on-Avon,
Warwickshire, March 3, 1883
Died: London, October 10, 1971

Burt, who was educated at Oxford, taught there and at Cambridge, and the universities of Liverpool and London. He developed the art of psychological testing and of statistic study of those testing results. He studied identical twins particularly and labored to show that intelligence was inherited at least to some degree and that people could be divided into groups of which some were, on the average, more intelligent than others. For instance, men were more intelligent than women, Gentiles more intelligent than Jews, Englishmen more intelligent than Irishmen, upper-class Englishmen more intelligent than middle-class Englishmen, who were in turn more intelligent than lower-class Englishmen.

In every case, the results fit the natural prejudice of an upper-class Englishman. There were a number who objected to the results, but those who supported Burt took the attitude that the truth was the truth even if the results didn't fit the liberal dogma. Burt was knighted, honored, revered, and died in the odor of sanctity.

After his death, investigation of his work made it clear, beyond the shadow of a doubt, that he had literally made up his figures and adjusted them to suit his prejudices. What he had done was not only incorrect; it was shameful; the worst crime a scientist can commit—and he did so in an area where the world could least afford it. It had just emerged from the incredible racist crimes of Adolf Hitler and his Nazis, with its false science labeling people as "superior" and "inferior."

[1087] **HAWORTH,** Sir Walter Norman
(hahrth)
English chemist
Born: Chorley, Lancashire,
March 19, 1883
Died: Birmingham, March 19,
1950

Haworth, the son of a prosperous businessman, was educated at the University of Manchester, where Perkin's [734] son was one of his teachers. He graduated in 1906, then went on for further education at the University of Göttingen, studying under Wallach [790] and obtaining his Ph.D. in 1910.

After working for the government during World War I, he was appointed professor of organic chemistry at the Uni-

versity of Durham, then in 1925 went on to the University of Birmingham.

Much of his research work was done on the structure of the sugars, where he filled in whatever Emil Fischer [833] had left undone. Haworth devised a form of representing the sugar molecules in ring form (rather than placing the carbon atoms in a straight line) which more accurately presented the molecular structure and which was more useful in describing chemical reactions in which the sugar was involved. These are still called Haworth formulas. He worked on vitamin C, which is related in structure to the simple sugars, and was one of the first (in 1934) to synthesize it. He suggested the name "ascorbic acid" for the vitamin, a name now universally accepted. He shared in the 1937 Nobel Prize in chemistry with Karrer [1131].

He worked on the atomic bomb project during World War II and was knighted in 1947.

[1088] **HESS,** Victor Franz
Austrian-American physicist
Born: Schloss Waldstein, Styria,
Austria, June 24, 1883
Died: Mount Vernon, New York,
December 17, 1964

Hess, the son of a forest warden, obtained his Ph.D. from the University of Graz in 1906. He was on the faculty of the Vienna Academy of Sciences for a number of years and received a professorial appointment at Graz in 1920, which he quickly interrupted for a two-year leave of absence in the United States.

During this time Hess was interested in locating the source of the background radiation that showed up in the form of ionizations in the atmosphere, even within containers that were shielded. It was believed that small quantities of radioactive material were present everywhere in the soil and air and that these gave rise to the radiation.

Hess was one of those who in 1911 and thereafter sent up balloons carrying electroscopes, as high as six miles. (Electroscopes are simple instruments in which two gold leaves or, better still, two quartz fibers, both electrically charged, repel each other. Where radiation ionizes the air within the electroscope, the charge is carried off and the leaves or fibers slowly come together. From the rate of coming together the quantity of ionization, and therefore of radiation, can be measured.) He made ten balloon ascents himself, five of them at night.

The balloon experiments were supposed to show that a shielded electroscope was less affected in the heights, away from the radioactivity of the soil. Hess, however, found to his surprise that at these great heights, the radiation was markedly greater, up to eight times as great, in fact, as at the surface of the earth. Others had observed this too, but Hess was the first to take the results at face value and suggest that the radiation came from outer space. Millikan [969] named the radiation "cosmic rays."

Cosmic rays were important not only for the information they gave, or might give, concerning astrophysical processes and the history of the universe, but also for the fact that they represented a particularly concentrated form of energy. Cosmic rays formed new particles, therefore, which could be encountered, until very recently, in no other way. It was during cosmic-ray research, for instance, that Anderson [1292] discovered the positron and Powell [1274] the pi-meson.

Hess received the 1936 Nobel Prize in physics for his discovery, sharing it with Anderson.

Shortly before Hitler's absorption of Austria, Hess who, though himself a Catholic, had a Jewish wife, saw what was to come and emigrated first to Switzerland and then to the United States. In 1938 he joined the faculty of Fordham University (where he stayed until his retirement in 1956) and in 1944 became an American citizen.

After World War II, he was deeply engaged in the measurement of radioactive fallout from nuclear bombs. He was one of those nuclear physicists who strongly opposed nuclear tests.

692

[1089] **WARBURG,** Otto Heinrich
(wahr′boorg)
German biochemist
Born: Freiburg-im-Breisgau,
Baden, October 8, 1883
Died: Berlin-Dahlem, August 1,
1970

Warburg, the son of a physics professor, studied chemistry under Emil Fischer [833] and obtained his doctorate in 1906 with work on polypeptides, which at that time was Fischer's absorbing interest. Warburg turned toward medicine, however, obtaining his medical degree in 1911, and thereafter concentrated on tissue respiration.

During World War I, Warburg served as an officer on the Russian front and was wounded in action.

The problem of respiration had taken on its modern form a century and a quarter earlier when Lavoisier [334] had demonstrated the nature of combustion and argued that respiration, like combustion, was an oxidation requiring the free oxygen of the air. Hemoglobin was later found to carry the oxygen to the cells, but what did the oxygen do there? The details were missing.

Warburg in 1923 devised a method for preparing thin slices of still-respiring tissue and measuring the uptake of oxygen by the decrease in pressure in a small flask, this decrease being determined by the change in level of a fluid in a thin U-shaped tube attached to the flask. Carbon dioxide was absorbed by a small well of alkaline solution within the flask. Such a Warburg manometer to which Warburg flasks were attached proved a powerful tool for studying respiration.

Through his studies in 1925 and afterward, Warburg began to suspect that a group of enzymes called cytochromes were involved in the reactions that consumed oxygen within the cells. These had been detected by their absorption of light a generation earlier. Observing that carbon monoxide molecules attached themselves to the cytochromes, Warburg further suspected that they contained iron atoms. Indeed, they eventually proved to contain heme groups of the type present in hemoglobin. The heme groups of hemoglobin carried the oxygen to the cells, in other words, and the heme groups of the cytochromes (proteins quite distinct from the one forming part of hemoglobin) grasped the oxygen and put it to work.

For this new insight into the details of respiration, Warburg was awarded the 1931 Nobel Prize in medicine and physiology.

There was still the question, however, of what exactly the oxygen did when it was "put to work." It was coming to be known that the small molecules absorbed after digestion (glucose and fatty acids, for instance) lost hydrogen atoms, two at a time, and that these were attached to oxygen atoms to form water. Some biochemists, notably Wieland [1048], believed that it was these dehydrogenations that were the key reactions, the ones catalyzed by enzymes, and that the role of oxygen was rather minor. Warburg held out for his oxygen activation by enzymes in a Homeric battle that both sides won, for both sides were right. Enzymes controlled both the dehydrogenations and the oxidations.

Warburg went on to study the dehydrogenation reactions during the 1930s. He isolated a flavoenzyme, for instance, which, in addition to protein, contained a molecular grouping that eventually proved to be very similar to one of the vitamins. He also worked with coenzyme I, Harden's [947] coenzyme, and helped show its similarity to what proved to be another vitamin, Goldberger's [1027] P-P factor, in fact. Before the end of the decade, work like this had helped clarify the actual functioning of the vitamins. They were no longer merely mysterious trace essentials in food as they had seemed all through the generation since Eijkman [888]. They were components of enzymes, portions of catalysts controlling important metabolic actions.

Warburg bent his method of studying respiration to the attack on cancer. In the heyday of Koch's [767] exploitation of Pasteur's [642] germ theory of disease, it had been believed that all diseases, cancer included, were caused by germs. With the advancement of the vitamin concept by Hopkins [912] and the hormone concept by Starling [954], it came to be realized that serious diseases could arise from flaws and shortcomings in the mechanisms of body chemistry (the body's metabolism, in other words) without assistance from outside. Since no germ could be found that caused cancer and since cancer did not seem to be contagious, the view grew in the first few decades of the twentieth century that it too was a disease of metabolism. To be sure, Rous [1067] had located a tumor virus but even he scarcely dared mention the word "virus" in connection with cancer.

Warburg studied the respiratory mechanisms of cancerous tissue as opposed to normal tissue and found that oxygen uptake was distinctly less in the former. Tissue can extract energy by the dehydrogenation of substances without the use of molecular oxygen. This is inefficient and only a temporary device where oxygen cannot be supplied in sufficient quantity, as when muscles are laboring under an intense workload. Such oxygen-free respiration, which had been noted in yeast by Pasteur over half a century before, is called glycolysis. Cancer tissue, then, tends to glycolyze more than normal tissue does.

Warburg's work on cancer made it possible for him to survive in Nazi Germany despite the fact that he was half-Jewish. In 1941 he was removed from his post but Hitler (who feared the possibility of throat cancer) personally ordered him back to cancer research. However, when in 1944 it seemed he might be nominated for a second Nobel Prize, the chance fell through, for Nazi policy at the time forbade Germans to accept such prizes.

Warburg's discoveries unfortunately did not lead to a breakthrough on the cancer problem. Little else of significance has been discovered about the distinctive metabolic pattern of cancer cells in the generation since Warburg's discovery. In fact, even the question of the cause of cancer grew puzzling as the connection with viruses was outlined more clearly by men like Bittner [1277].

[1090] **SMITH,** Philip Edward
American endocrinologist
Born: De Smet, South Dakota,
January 1, 1884
Died: Florence, Massachusetts,
December 8, 1970

Smith, the son of a minister, attended Pomona College in California (where his family had moved when he was six) and graduated in 1908 at the head of his class. He did his graduate work at Cornell University, getting his Ph.D. in histology in 1912. During his graduate work he grew interested in the pituitary gland. He retained that interest all his working life.

He demonstrated the overriding importance of the pituitary. He developed methods for removing the pituitary without any damage to the brain and showed that such "hypophysectomy" resulted in the cessation of growth and the atrophy of other endocrine glands, such as the thyroid, the adrenal cortex, and the reproductive glands.

During the 1920s he had professorial positions, first at the University of California, then Stanford, and then Columbia.

[1091] **ANDREWS,** Roy Chapman
American zoologist
Born: Beloit, Wisconsin,
January 26, 1884
Died: Carmel, California,
March 11, 1960

Andrews was educated at Beloit College, graduating in 1906 and joining the staff of the American Museum of Natural History in New York that same year.

One of his first jobs was to bring in the skeleton of a dead whale beached on Long Island. For a decade he concerned himself with whales and whaling.

He then became interested in fossils and beginning in 1916 scoured the far reaches of the world for them. His expeditions into the little-known depths of central Asia resulted in his most dramatic find—fossilized dinosaur eggs. This, more than any single discovery, seemed to lend life to these reptilian monsters.

He also discovered fossil bones of the Baluchitherium ("beast of Baluchistan," where the bones were discovered), the largest known land mammal ever to have lived. Its shoulders were as high in the air as the head of a tall giraffe. Andrews was director of the American Museum of Natural History from 1935 until his retirement in 1942.

[1092] **PICCARD,** Auguste (pee-kahr')
Swiss physicist
Born: Basel, January 28, 1884
Died: Lausanne, March 24, 1962

Auguste Piccard was one of a pair of twins (the other was Jean Félix) born to the head of the department of chemistry at the University of Basel. Piccard studied mechanical engineering at Zürich, while his twin brother studied chemical engineering. Both earned doctoral degrees and achieved professorial ranks. Auguste collaborated with Einstein [1064] in the design of instruments for electrical measurements. In 1922 he joined the faculty of the Polytechnic Institute in Brussels, Belgium, where he remained until his retirement in 1954.

Piccard was interested in cosmic rays and the ion-filled layers of the upper atmosphere and he was anxious to explore the high reaches. A half century before, man had climbed, as far as he could safely manage, in balloons equipped with open gondolas. Since then, thanks mainly to the initiative of Teisserenc de Bort [861], instrumented but unmanned balloons had been used.

Piccard was dissatisfied with this situation. It occurred to him that if one built a sealed aluminum gondola, a man could live comfortably in it at any height to which the balloon could carry him, and manned observations (always superior, somehow, to unmanned ones, however sophisticated the instrumentation) would be possible. In 1931 he and a fellow aeronaut, Paul Küpfer, rose from Augsburg, Germany, to an altitude of 51,775 feet in an eighteen-hour flight. This flight, to a height of nearly ten miles, was half again as high as man had ever risen before and marked the first penetration of the stratosphere by a human being. In the United States in 1932 Piccard made another and somewhat higher flight with his twin brother. He made twenty-seven balloon ascensions altogether before he retired from this line of work.

Piccard's pioneering paved the way for still more remarkable feats once balloons came to be made out of new plastic materials which were at once lighter than the older materials and less permeable to helium. The American balloon *Explorer II* reached an altitude of 72,395 feet (13½ miles) in 1935 and by the decade of the 1960s, heights of 101,000 feet (19 miles) had been attained. By then, however, rocketry had come into its own and manned rocket flights had carried human beings 150 miles, and more, above the earth's surface.

Having penetrated the stratosphere, Piccard restlessly aimed his energies in the opposite direction. He had met Beebe [1050] at the 1933 Chicago World's Fair and that had sparked him. In the late 1930s he designed a ship that could be maneuvered in the great depths. This bathyscaphe ("ship of the deep") was designed something like a dirigible. The upper portion was a cigar-shaped float, containing gasoline to give the vessel buoyancy. The lower portion was a steel sphere something like Beebe's bathysphere.

For the bathyscaphe to sink, it is only necessary to fill a couple of tanks in the float with sea water. The bathyscaphe carries tons of small iron pellets, which can be jettisoned gradually to slow a descent or to bring about an ascent.

World War II intervened. Work on the first bathyscaphe was not begun until 1946 and the ship was not completed until 1948. It was tested thoroughly, and in 1954 two French naval officers descended to a depth of 13,287 feet (2½ miles) off the Mediterranean coast of Africa. It set a new record, since it penetrated more than four times deeper than Beebe had a quarter century earlier.

Piccard built a second bathyscaphe, *Trieste*, which was bought by the United States Navy in 1948. On January 23, 1960, with two men aboard (one of them Piccard's son), the *Trieste* descended into the Marianas Trench, about two hundred and ten miles southwest of Guam in the Marianas Islands. This was the deepest known spot in the Pacific, thought to be at 33,600 feet. The *Trieste* reached a bottom even lower than that, dropping down to 35,800 feet (6¾ miles) below sea level. Thus, the ocean depths have been sounded by man probably close to the very limit, and until man learns to penetrate the crust itself to great depths, no human being can better this mark.

[1093] **FUNK,** Casimir (foonk)
Polish-American biochemist
Born: Warsaw, Poland (then part of Russia), February 23, 1884
Died: New York, New York, November 20, 1967

Funk, the son of a physician, was educated in various places in western Europe, obtaining his doctor's degree in 1904 at the University of Berne in Switzerland. He worked in Paris, Berlin, and London, but came to the United States in 1915 and was naturalized in 1920.

He returned to Poland in 1923 to accept the directorship of the State Institute of Hygiene in Warsaw but when World War II broke out in 1939, he came to the United States for good.

In 1912 Funk once again advanced the concept, earlier proposed by Hopkins [912], that diseases such as beriberi, scurvy, pellagra, and rickets were caused by lack of substances that were needed in the diet in small quantities.

He suggested a name for these substances, a name that arose as follows. His investigation of Eijkman's [888] antiberiberi factor had shown him that it was an amine; that is, that it contained the amine group ($-NH_2$) in its molecule. Funk erroneously supposed that all similar substances were amines and so he named the factors vitamines ("lifeamine"). When some years later it turned out that not all the factors were amines, the final "e" was dropped and the word became "vitamin."

In the same year, Funk isolated nicotinic acid in rice polishings, but finding

695

that it did not counter beriberi he let it go. It was left to men like Warburg [1089] and Elvehjem [1240] to discover its importance in connection with pellagra.

[1094] **DEBYE,** Peter Joseph Wilhelm
(dee-bigh′)
Dutch-American physical chemist
Born: Maastricht, Netherlands,
March 24, 1884
Died: Ithaca, New York, November 2, 1966

Debye's training at the University of Aachen was originally in the field of electrical engineering. He received a degree in that subject in 1905. However, he turned to physics and in 1910 received his Ph.D. at the University of Munich, working under Sommerfeld [976]. He accepted a professorship in theoretical physics at the University of Zürich in 1911, succeeding Einstein [1064] in that post. Later he taught at the universities of Leipzig and Berlin.

His fields merged in a way, however, for his first important work was in a theoretical treatment of dipole moments, which measure the effect of an electrical field on the orientation of those molecules that carry a positive electric charge on one portion of their structure and a negative one on another. (The unit of dipole moment is called a debye in his honor.)

In 1916 Debye extended the work of the Braggs [922, 1141] and showed that X-ray analysis could be used not only for intact crystals but also for powdered solids, which were mixtures of tiny crystals oriented in all possible directions.

Most spectacularly, perhaps, Debye extended the work of Arrhenius [894] on ionic dissociation in solution. According to Arrhenius, electrolytes (including most inorganic salts) dissociated into positively and negatively charged ions, when dissolved, but the dissociation was not necessarily complete. Debye, on the other hand, maintained that most salts (such as sodium chloride, for instance) had to ionize completely, since X-ray analysis showed that they existed in ionic form in the crystal before ever they were

dissolved. He suggested, however, that each positive ion was attended by a cloud of ions in which the negatively charged ones were preponderant, while each negative ion was attended by a cloud of predominantly positive ones. Each type of ion suffered a braking "drag" for which the ions of opposite charge were responsible and this made the solution seem incompletely ionized when it wasn't. He worked out the mathematics representing the phenomenon in 1923 and the so-called Debye-Hückel theory (named for himself and a colleague) is the key to the modern interpretation of the properties of solutions.

Debye received the 1936 Nobel Prize in chemistry for his work on dipolar moments in particular. In 1935 Debye had become director of the Kaiser Wilhelm Institute for Physics at Berlin (which he renamed the Max Planck Institute), but his position during World War II became increasingly difficult.

In 1939 the Nazi government ordered him to become a German citizen. He refused and returned to the Netherlands. In 1940, just two months before his native land was invaded by Hitler's armies, he left for the United States to deliver a guest lecture at Cornell University. There he stayed, taking up a position as professor of chemistry and head of the department at Cornell University, remaining until his retirement in 1952. He became an American citizen in 1946.

[1095] **MEYERHOF,** Otto Fritz (my′er-
hofe)
German-American biochemist
Born: Hannover, April 12, 1884
Died: Philadelphia, Pennsylvania,
October 6, 1951

Meyerhof, the son of a Jewish merchant, obtained his medical degree at the University of Heidelberg in 1909. He was interested in psychology and psychiatry at first, but a meeting with Warburg [1089] drew him toward physiology and biochemistry. In 1918 he joined the faculty of the University of Kiel and devoted himself to the biochemistry of muscle.

It was known that muscle contained glycogen, the substance Bernard [578] had discovered in liver over half a century before. Hopkins [912] and his co-workers had shown, the decade before, that working muscle accumulated lactic acid. Meyerhof, in a series of careful experiments, showed that there was a quantitative relationship between the glycogen that disappeared and the lactic acid that appeared and that in the process oxygen was not consumed. What was taking place, then, was anaerobic glycolysis ("glycogen-breakdown without air"). Meyerhof also showed that when muscle rested after work, some of the lactic acid was oxidized (molecular oxygen being then consumed to pay off what the physiologists called the "oxygen debt"). The energy so developed made it possible for the major portion of the lactic acid to be reconverted to glycogen.

Meyerhof's work initiated the labors, carried on later by the Coris [1192, 1194], that worked out the detailed steps whereby glycogen is converted to lactic acid and this is therefore known as the "Embden-Meyerhof pathway" after himself and a co-worker. For this work Meyerhof was awarded the 1922 Nobel Prize in medicine and physiology, sharing it with Hill [1108].

Under the Hitler regime Meyerhof's position in Germany grew increasingly uncomfortable. In 1938 he left for France, and in 1940, when that country fell to the Germans, he was forced to flee again, this time to the United States, where he joined the faculty of the University of Pennsylvania in Philadelphia. In 1948 he qualified for citizenship and the last three years of his life were therefore spent as an American.

[1096] **BLACK,** Davidson
Canadian anthropologist
Born: Toronto, Ontario, July 25, 1884
Died: Peking, China, March 15, 1934

Black, the son of a lawyer, chose a medical career and obtained his M.D. at the University of Toronto in 1909. After teaching at Western Reserve University (now Case-Western Reserve University) in Cleveland as an anatomist, he grew interested in anthropology. He worked in England and the Netherlands in the field and then decided it must be Asia that was the home of early ancestors of humanity.

In 1920, he took a post at the Peking Union Medical College in order to advance his investigations. Twenty-five miles west of Peking at Chou K'ou-tien, in 1927, he located a single human molar. From this tooth alone, he deduced the existence of a small-brained ancestor he called *Sinanthropus pekinensis* ("China man of Peking"), which came to be popularly known as Peking man.

Other teeth were found then in 1929 and 1930, skulls were found, together with other bones, tools, and remains of campfires. Peking man, very much like Dubois's [884] Java man, is now considered an example of *Homo erectus,* ancestral to *Homo sapiens.*

[1097] **SVEDBERG,** Theodor H. E.
(svayd-bare'y)
Swedish chemist
Born: Fleräng, near Valbo, August 30, 1884
Died: Stockholm, February 25, 1971

Svedberg, the son of a civil engineer, studied at the University of Uppsala, graduated and joined its faculty in 1907, becoming professor of physical chemistry in 1912.

Svedberg was chiefly interested in the chemistry of colloids and during his student years he prepared colloidal suspensions of metals by setting up electric arcs between metal electrodes under water. As was the case for that other colloid chemist, Zsigmondy [943], Svedberg invented a new tool for studying them.

Colloid particles are so small that the incessant banging of water molecules is enough to keep them from settling out. If only gravitational force were more intense than it is, molecular collisions of the solvent would not be enough and the colloidal particles would then settle out, the largest ones fastest.

It is, of course, impossible with present-day techniques to alter the gravitational field itself, but Svedberg could make use of an effect that resembled gravitation—the centrifugal effect. Centrifuges were already being used to separate milk from cream and blood corpuscles from blood plasma. However, cells and fat droplets are relatively large. To force the much tinier colloid particles out of solution, much stronger centrifugal effects were necessary. For the purpose Svedberg developed the ultracentrifuge in 1923. (Such an ultracentrifuge can be made to whirl so fast that an effect equivalent to hundreds of thousands of times normal gravity is developed.)

Colloidal particles did indeed settle out. From the rate of settling, the size of the particles and even the shape could be deduced, while a mixture of two different types of particles could be separated.

This turned out to be most important in the case of protein molecules. The protein molecule is a giant of the molecular world and, all by itself, is of colloidal size. For that reason, proteins, even though going completely into solution, remain colloidal in their properties. The individual protein molecules settle out neatly in the ultracentrifuge, however, and it was in this way that the molecular weight of the larger proteins could be determined (from the rate of settling) for the first time. Later, the technique proved useful for other giant molecules too, such as the synthetic polymers whose molecular properties were studied by Staudinger [1074].

For this and for his other work on colloids Svedberg was awarded the 1926 Nobel Prize for chemistry. In later years he collaborated with his student Tiselius [1257] in working out modern methods of electrophoresis that have proved at least as important as ultracentrifugal methods in studying proteins. Svedberg was director of the Institute for Physical Chemistry at Uppsala.

[1098] **BERGIUS,** Friedrich Karl Rudolf (behr'gee-oos)
German chemist
Born: Goldschmieden, Silesia (now part of Poland), October 11, 1884
Died: Buenos Aires, Argentina, March 30, 1949

Bergius's father was head of a chemical factory, and so Bergius was following in family tradition by becoming interested in industrial chemistry. He studied under Nernst [936] and Haber [977], gaining his doctorate at the University of Leipzig in 1907.

From Haber he developed an interest in reactions under pressure and worked out methods of treating coal and heavy oil with hydrogen to form gasoline, being guided in part by data that had been gathered by Ipatieff [966]. He first accomplished this in 1912, but the evolution from laboratory demonstration to practical industrial process took twelve years. He also discovered methods of breaking down the complicated molecules of wood to simpler molecules, which could, in turn, be made to undergo chemical reactions that produced alcohol and sugar. For his work on high-pressure processes he shared with Bosch [1028] the 1931 Nobel Prize in chemistry.

Germany, during World War II, used the Bergius processes to supply herself with gasoline and to make a certain amount of edible material out of wood. After the war Bergius did not wish to remain in defeated Germany. He moved first to Austria, then Spain, and finally to Argentina, where he served the government of that country as technical adviser. However, he died about a year after he arrived in Argentina.

[1099] **RORSCHACH,** Hermann (rawr'-shahkh)
Swiss psychiatrist
Born: Zürich, November 8, 1884
Died: Herisau, April 2, 1922

Rorschach, the son of an art teacher, took his medical training at the University of Zürich, and was drawn into psychiatry by his interest in Jung's [1035] theories.

Rorschach the man is buried almost entirely in the technique he devised for diagnosing psychopathological conditions.

This involved the use of ten symmetrical inkblots, which the patient was asked to interpret. From the interpretations (the Rorschach test) it was presumably possible to tell a great deal about the patient.

This technique has proved very popular, although it is difficult to tell how much validity there can be to it.

[1100] **HEVESY**, György (heh'veh-shee)
Hungarian-Danish-Swedish
chemist
Born: Budapest, August 1, 1885
Died: Freiburg-im-Breisgau,
Germany, July 6, 1966

Hevesy came of a wealthy family and he called himself "von" Hevesy in Germany. He was educated in Hungary and in Germany. He received his Ph.D. in 1908 from the University of Freiburg. He worked with Haber [977] for a while, then traveled to England for work with Ernest Rutherford [996].

He served in the Austro-Hungarian army in World War I, but in the chaos of defeat left for Bohr's [1101] laboratory in Copenhagen in 1920.

Hevesy's two great contributions were both made in 1923 and the less dramatic was by far the more important.

The search for new elements, it seemed, was petering out in the twentieth century. Dozens had been discovered in the nineteenth but the field was narrowing. Mendeléev's [705] periodic table had been rationalized by the X-ray studies of Moseley [1121] and the theories of atomic structure that Bohr had put forth. From this rationalization one could see that there was an opening for an as yet undiscovered element corresponding to atomic number 72.

Bohr suggested that the undiscovered element be sought for in ores of the metal zirconium, just above atomic number 72 in the periodic table. In January of 1923 the new element was found by Hevesy and a colleague. Its newness was verified by X-ray analysis in the manner worked out by Moseley, and it was named hafnium, from the Latinized name of Copenhagen. So much for the more dramatic discovery.

Hevesy was also interested in using radioactive atoms to study living systems. Radioactive atoms could be detected easily, even when present only in small traces, through the energetic radiations they threw out in all directions. Hevesy began by using a radioactive isotope of lead, obtained from thorium breakdown products. Working under Rutherford, he had failed to find any chemical difference between radioactive and ordinary lead, and now he planned to make use of this lack of difference.

In 1918 he used it to determine the solubility of lead salts, since the presence of even minute traces of radioactive lead in water could be detected easily and he could then assume that ordinary lead dissolved to the same extent that radioactive lead did. Then, again, by watering plants with solutions containing the radioactive isotope, he was able in 1923 to follow the absorption and distribution of lead in great detail.

It might have been fair to assume that what was true of lead would be true of substances in general, but it was not. Lead is not a normal component of living systems (indeed it is highly poisonous) and it would be unsafe to generalize from lead-poisoned plants to all plants. However, the principle had been established. If an isotope could be found which, except for its radioactivity, was a normal component of living tissue, then one might follow its trail of radiation with a feeling that it did represent the normal pathways, both physiological and chemical, within the organism.

After the discovery of artificial radioactivity by the Joliot-Curies [1204, 1227], just such isotopes were developed and the principle of isotopic "tracers" was firmly established. Indeed, without such tracers it is hard to see how the network of metabolic reactions within living tissue could possibly have been straightened out to the extent that it now is.

Hevesy's use of radioactive tracers for the first time made no splash in 1923, but by the time a pair of decades had passed, the importance of the step was manifest.

In 1926 Hevesy moved to Germany, accepting a professorship at the University of Freiburg. When Hitler came to power, Hevesy went back to Copenhagen, and when the Nazis occupied Denmark in 1940, Hevesy managed to escape to Sweden in 1942. There he taught at the University of Stockholm. While there he was awarded the 1943 Nobel Prize in chemistry. In 1959 he received the Atoms for Peace Award.

Eventually, he returned to Germany and there he died.

[1101] **BOHR,** Niels Henrik David
Danish physicist
Born: Copenhagen, October 7,
1885
Died: Copenhagen, November
18, 1962

Bohr, the son of a physiology professor, entered the University of Copenhagen in 1903, where he studied physics and was also a crackerjack soccer player. (His younger brother was even better and made the 1908 Danish Olympic soccer team, which took a second place.)

Bohr received his doctorate there in 1911. The next year, he obtained a grant to travel abroad in order to further his education and went at once to Cambridge, where he worked under J. J. Thomson [869], and then to Manchester, where he worked under Ernest Rutherford [996]. He married in 1912 (and eventually had five sons) and in 1916 he returned to the University of Copenhagen as professor of physics.

Rutherford had put forth the notion of the nuclear atom; that is, of an atom containing a tiny massive nucleus at its center with a cloud of light electrons located on the periphery. It seemed to Bohr, while yet at Cambridge, that if this internal structure of the atom were combined with the quantum theory put out

by Planck [887] a little over a decade before, then perhaps it would be possible to explain how substances emitted and absorbed radiant energy. This absorption and emission was of vital importance in spectroscopy for it accounted for the spectral lines that had been discovered by Fraunhofer [450] a century earlier and put to use by Kirchhoff [648] a half century after that. Through all the past century, however, scientists had been content to measure the position of the lines without attempting to explain why a line should be located in one place rather than another.

Bohr attempted to rectify this omission and happened to come across Balmer's [658] formula for the hydrogen spectrum. He began, then, to consider the hydrogen atom, which was the simplest of all. In 1913 he had his scheme. He suggested that the single electron of the hydrogen atom did *not* radiate electromagnetically as it oscillated within the atom as Lorentz [839] had suggested in 1895. At first thought it would seem it must, according to the equation of Maxwell [692], from which it appeared that electromagnetic radiations were produced whenever an electric charge such as that on an electron was accelerated, as when the electron moved in a closed orbit. Nevertheless, Bohr maintained that radiation was not emitted as long as it stayed in orbit. (The apparent contradiction was resolved the next decade when De Broglie [1157] showed that the electron was not merely a particle but a wave form and Schrödinger [1117] worked out a theory where the electron was not revolving about the nucleus but was merely a "standing wave" formed about it. The electron in a particular orbit was therefore not accelerating and did not have to radiate.)

Radiation was emitted, Bohr pointed out, when the electron changed its orbit and approached closer to the nucleus. On the other hand, when radiation was absorbed, the electron was driven into an orbit farther from the nucleus. Thus, electromagnetic radiation was produced by shifts in "energy levels" in subatomic particles and not by oscillations or accelerations of those particles. This seemed to divorce the world of the atom from the ordinary world about us and it became increasingly difficult to picture atomic structure in "common-sense" terms.

For instance, the electron couldn't take on just any orbit. It could have an orbit only at fixed distances from the nucleus and each orbit had a certain fixed amount of energy. As it changed from one orbit to another, then, the amount of energy liberated or absorbed was fixed; and this amount consisted of whole quanta. In this way Planck's quantum theory was interpreted as a manifestation of the discontinuous electron positions within an atom.

Bohr was even able to choose orbital energies in such a way as to account for the lines in the hydrogen spectrum, showing that each one marked the absorption of quanta of energy just large enough to lift the electron from one particular orbit to another farther from the nucleus. (Or to mark the emission of a quantum of energy just large enough to drop the electron from one particular orbit to another nearer the nucleus.) In particular the regularities of the hydrogen spectrum, first noted by Balmer, were easily accounted for. To describe the discrete energies which electrons might possess, Bohr made use of Planck's constant divided by 2π. This is symbolized as $\hbar$ and referred to as "h bar."

Bohr's model of the hydrogen atom proved to be insufficiently complex to account for the fine detail of the spectral lines, however. He had postulated only circular orbits, but Sommerfeld [976] went on to work out the implications of the existence of elliptical orbits as well. Then orbits at various angles were also included.

Regardless of the modifications necessary Bohr's scheme was the first reasonably successful attempt to make the internal structure of the atom explain spectroscopy and to use spectroscopic data to explain the internal structure of the atom. Not all the older generation was enthusiastic. Rayleigh [760], Zeeman [945], and Thomson were dubious but Jeans [1053], to Bohr's everlasting grati-

tude, was firmly on his side. It was Thomson's opposition to the new atom that sparked Bohr's shift to Rutherford, by the way.

Of course, Bohr won out smashingly in the end. For his new theory, he received the 1922 Nobel Prize in physics. The theory received experimental support from the work of Franck [1081] and G. Hertz [1116], who in their turn were awarded Nobel Prizes.

Bohr was unable to work out satisfactory models for atoms more complex than hydrogen, but he was among those who pointed out that where more than one electron existed in the atom, they must exist in "shells"; and he pointed out that it was the electron content of the outermost shell that determined the chemical properties of the atoms of a particular element. Pauli [1228] brought this notion to fulfillment.

The picture of the electron as both a particle (as in his own theory) and a wave (in Schrödinger's) induced Bohr in 1927 to put forth what has been called the principle of complementarity—that a phenomenon can be looked upon in each of two mutually exclusive ways, with both outlooks nevertheless remaining valid in their own terms. This principle has been eagerly adopted by some contemporary biologists and used as a vehicle for a new kind of vitalism. The suggestion is made that living systems can be interpreted, on the one hand, according to physical and chemical laws governing the components of a cell and, on the other, according to vitalistic laws, governing the cell or organism as a whole. According to this view there would be elements of life forever unamenable to ordinary investigation by the physical sciences. It seems doubtful, though, that this new variety of vitalism will be any more successful in the long run than the other varieties strewn in the boneyards of history.

In Copenhagen, during the 1920s and 1930s, Bohr headed an institute for atomic studies that was supported by the Carlsberg brewery (the greatest service offered by beer to theoretical physics since the time of Joule [613]). It proved a magnet for theoretical physicists from everywhere. The concentration of scientific talent in Copenhagen made it, for that period, almost a new Alexandria.

When Hitler came to power in Germany in 1933, Bohr took what action he could on behalf of his colleagues in that terrorized land, doing his best to get Jewish physicists to safety. (Bohr's own mother was of Jewish descent but it is quite certain that Bohr's gentle, humane soul required no self-serving motivation.)

In 1939 Bohr visited the United States to attend a scientific conference and brought with him the news that Lise Meitner [1060] was about to announce Hahn's [1063] view that uranium undergoes fission when bombarded with neutrons (uncharged particles—hence the name—that Chadwick [1150] had discovered earlier that decade). This broke up the conference as scientists rushed home to confirm the Hahn-Meitner suggestion. It was confirmed, all right, and events were put in motion that culminated in the atomic bomb. Bohr went on to develop a theory of the mechanism of fission, one in which the nucleus was viewed as behaving something like a drop of fluid. Bohr predicted that the particular isotope, uranium-235, discovered a few years earlier by Dempster [1106], was the one that underwent fission and in this he was quickly proved right.

Bohr returned to Denmark and was still there when Hitler's army suddenly occupied the nation in 1940. In 1943, to avoid imprisonment (for he certainly did not cooperate with the German occupation), and at the urgent encouragement of Chadwick, he escaped amidst considerable peril to Sweden. There he helped to arrange the escape of nearly every Danish Jew from death in Hitler's gas ovens. On October 6, 1943, he was flown to England in a tiny plane, in which he nearly died from lack of oxygen. Before Bohr left Denmark he dissolved the gold Nobel medals of Franck and Laue [1068]—which had been given him for safekeeping—in a bottle of acid. (His own had been donated for Finnish war relief.)

He went on to the United States, where until 1945 he worked on the atomic bomb project at Los Alamos. His anxiety about the consequences of the bomb and his desire to share the secret with other allies in order to secure international control at the earliest possible time roused the bitter anger of Winston Churchill, who was on the edge of ordering Bohr's arrest.

After the war, he returned to Copenhagen, precipitated the gold from the acid, and recast the medals. It was symbolic of the passing of one evil, but another had come, that of the threat of nuclear war.

Bohr labored unremittingly on behalf of the development of peaceful uses of atomic energy, organizing the first Atoms for Peace Conference in Geneva in 1955. In 1957 he was awarded the first Atoms for Peace award.

[1102] SHAPLEY, Harlow
American astronomer
Born: Nashville, Missouri, November 2, 1885
Died: Boulder, Colorado, October 20, 1972

Shapley, the son of a farmer, had little schooling at first and worked as a reporter. He labored to save money and to study in order to make a university education possible. In 1903 he enrolled at the University of Missouri, from which he graduated in 1910, and then obtained his doctorate at Princeton University in 1913 working under H. N. Russell [1056]. In 1914 he joined the Mount Wilson Observatory in California and in 1921 was appointed to succeed E. C. Pickering [784] as director of the Harvard Observatory, a post he held till 1952. He was professor emeritus at Harvard after 1956.

Between 1915 and 1920 Shapley used the 100-inch telescope at Mount Wilson to make a particular study of the globular clusters. These are immense densely packed aggregations of stars, some containing as many as a million member bodies. About a hundred such clusters were known at the time. Far from being evenly distributed over the sky, they were concentrated in the direction of Sagittarius. One-third of them, in fact, occur within the boundaries of that one constellation.

Shapley had at his disposal the Cepheid yardstick worked out by Leavitt [975] a few years earlier and he applied the period-luminosity curve to the Cepheid stars in each globular cluster in 1914. From the period of those Cepheids and from their apparent brightness, he could calculate their distances. In this way he determined the distance of the various clusters and found that they were distributed in a sphere, roughly speaking, about a center in the constellation Sagittarius. (He also suggested that Cepheids varied through pulsations, or variations in diameter. This was further worked out by Eddington [1085].)

It seemed sensible to suppose that those globular clusters, if they assumed a spherical arrangement about some point, would do so about the center of our galaxy, and this center, judging from the arrangement of the clusters, was 50,000 light-years from the sun. Shapley suggested this galactic model in 1918. (Later work by Oort [1229] reduced this figure to 30,000; and the smaller figure is now accepted.)

Earlier astronomers, from Herschel [321] to Kapteyn [815], had assumed the sun to be near the center of our galaxy, since the Milky Way (the mass of faint stars seen in the direction of the long axis of the galaxy) was about equally bright in all directions. Shapley, however, pointed out that dark dust clouds (many of which are clearly visible in the Milky Way) obscured the bright center and left us with a clear optical view only of our own neighborhood in the outskirts of the galaxy. (A generation later, radio astronomy was to confirm this.)

Shapley's work, which triumphed over what was, to begin with, bitter opposition, was the first to present a picture of our galaxy that gave a relatively true idea of its size. All previous estimates had been far too small. And just as Copernicus [127] had dethroned the earth from its supposed position as center of the universe, so Shapley deposed the sun from its supposed position as center of the galaxy. The latter discovery was less epoch-making, but it did mark the real beginning of galactic astronomy, a field soon considerably advanced by Hubble [1136].

After World War II, he was active in the cause of civil liberties and peace and clashed frequently with such obscurantists as Senator Joseph McCarthy.

[1103] **MINOT**, George Richards (my'-nut)
American physician
Born: Boston, Massachusetts, December 2, 1885
Died: Brookline, Massachusetts, February 25, 1950

Minot, the son of a physician, was educated at Harvard University as an undergraduate and a graduate student, receiving his medical degree in 1912. After work at Johns Hopkins he returned to Boston in 1915, serving at Massachusetts General and Peter Bent Brigham hospitals, as his father, uncle, and grandfather had done before him.

Minot was interested in blood disorders and particularly in pernicious anemia, in which the red blood corpuscle count declines progressively, with an invariably fatal end. In the early 1920s G. H. Whipple [1059] had reported experiments in which liver in the diet had had a strong effect in raising red blood corpuscle counts in anemia (though pernicious anemia was not studied) and this set Minot to thinking.

He had already decided that pernicious anemia might be a dietary deficiency disease resulting from the lack of a vitamin, since it was always accompanied by a lack of hydrochloric acid in the stomach secretions. Perhaps digestion failed and less than normal quantities of a particular vitamin were absorbed. There seemed no harm in trying liver in the diet, since liver was known to be rich in vitamins.

In 1924 he and his assistant Murphy

[1154] began feeding pernicious anemia patients liver, and by 1926 forty-five of them were on such a diet. It worked amazingly well and pernicious anemia has been an eminently treatable disease ever since. In a way, Minot thus repaid a debt to medicine. He himself was a diabetic who would surely have died a quarter century earlier than he did had Banting's [1152] isolation of insulin not come along just in time to save him.

In 1928 Minot was appointed professor of medicine at Harvard Medical School and in 1934 he, Whipple, and Murphy all shared the Nobel Prize in medicine and physiology. Minot was quite right in suspecting a vitamin deficiency to be at the root of pernicious anemia. This was to be proved two decades after his work by men like Folkers [1312].

[1104] **WILLIAMS**, Robert Runnels
American chemist
Born: Nellore, India (of American parents), February 16, 1886
Died: Summit, New Jersey, October 2, 1965

Williams, the son of a Baptist missionary, was not taken to the United States till he was ten. He obtained his master's degree at the University of Chicago in 1908, then spent some time teaching in the Philippine Islands. He returned to the United States in 1915, and his later years were spent chiefly at the Bell Telephone Laboratories, from which he retired in 1945.

In the 1930s he brought to completion the effort, begun by Eijkman [888] and Funk [1093] a generation earlier, to isolate and identify the anti-beriberi factor (thiamin). In 1934 Williams perfected methods of isolating about a third of an ounce of the material from a ton of rice polishings. By 1936 he had worked out its molecular structure and proved that structure by synthesizing the compound.

In the decades following, synthetic methods have enabled the United States to produce twenty-five tons or more of the vitamin each year. Synthetic vitamins have become big business, and dependence on natural sources for thiamin and many other vitamins is no longer necessary for those who choose to invest in vitamin pills.

[1105] **KENDALL**, Edward Calvin
American biochemist
Born: South Norwalk, Connecticut, March 8, 1886
Died: Princeton, New Jersey, May 4, 1972

Kendall was educated at Columbia University, gaining all his degrees there through his doctorate, which he obtained in 1910 with Sherman [1036] as one of his teachers. While working at St. Luke's Hospital in New York in the early 1910s he grew interested in the thyroid gland. Starling [954] and Bayliss [902] had introduced the hormone concept the previous decade and it seemed clear that the thyroid produced a hormone. In the late nineteenth century the thyroid had been shown to be responsible for the overall rate of metabolism of the body, so that the human engine raced, so to speak, when the thyroid was overactive and slowed to a crawl when it was underactive. Surely this was done through the mediation of a hormone.

In the 1890s the thyroid gland had been shown to contain unusual quantities of iodine, an element not previously known to occur as an essential component of tissue, and over the next decade an iodine-containing protein, thyroglobulin, had been obtained from thyroid. It was Kendall's intention to narrow down the search for the actual thyroid hormone by breaking up the large thyroglobulin molecule and finding, if he could, an active fragment.

In 1916 (by which time Kendall had joined the staff of the Mayo Foundation in Rochester, Minnesota) he achieved his aim and isolated what he called thyroxine. Over the next decade its structure was determined and found to be comparatively simple, that of a single amino acid. Furthermore, it was most closely related to the common amino acid, tyrosine, its most unusual characteristic being that its molecule contained four iodine atoms.

Thyroid hormone became an important item in the medical armory, along with the insulin isolated by Banting [1152] and Best [1218] the decade after Kendall's feat. The hormone concept became more than mere theory; it offered a route for practical therapy.

The road of research led to other hormone-producing glands and the adrenals long resisted the probing quest. The adrenal gland is an organ made up of two parts. The inner part, the medulla, manufactures epinephrine (adrenaline) and that was no problem, for Takamine [855] had isolated that even before the hormone concept was advanced. The outer part, the cortex, however, manufactured a wide variety of substances and the problem was to identify their structure and function. Work toward this end was done in Kendall's laboratory and in that of Reichstein [1201] in Switzerland.

During the 1930s Kendall isolated no fewer than twenty-eight different cortical hormones or corticoids, of which four showed effects on laboratory animals. He named the corticoids by letter and the four effective ones were compounds A, B, E, and F.

Research in the corticoids received a strong stimulus during World War II. A rumor made the rounds that the Germans were buying up adrenal glands in Argentine slaughterhouses and that extracts of the glands were enabling Nazi pilots to fly and fight at heights of forty thousand feet. The rumor was untrue, but it helped push American investigation of the adrenals and, in fact, give it top priority among medical problems. By 1944 Compound A was synthesized, and in 1946 Compound E was. Their molecular structures were proved in that fashion.

The importance of the corticoids in medicine (even if not in making supermen out of Nazi pilots) was underscored shortly afterward by Hench [1188], one of Kendall's collaborators, who successfully used Compound E in relieving the symptoms of rheumatoid arthritis. In 1950 Kendall, Hench, and Reichstein all

shared the Nobel Prize in medicine and physiology as a result. In 1952 Kendall became professor of chemistry at Princeton University.

[1106] **DEMPSTER,** Arthur Jeffrey
Canadian-American physicist
Born: Toronto, Ontario, August 14, 1886
Died: Stuart, Florida, March 11, 1950

Dempster was educated at the University of Toronto. He went to Germany for advanced work, but World War I made it impossible for him to remain and in 1914 he moved to the United States. He became an American citizen in 1918, having earned his Ph.D. in 1916 at the University of Chicago. He became professor of physics at the University of Chicago in 1927. His work with the mass spectrograph (he built his first one in 1918) was second only to that of Aston [1051].

In 1935 he discovered an isotope that Aston had missed, one that was destined to be the most famous isotope of all, the rare uranium-235. It was out of that achievement that within the decade and thanks to the work of men like Hahn [1063], Fermi [1243], and Oppenheimer [1280], the first nuclear bomb was to arise.

[1107] **ROBINSON,** Sir Robert
English chemist
Born: Bufford, near Chesterfield, Derbyshire, September 13, 1886
Died: Great Missenden, near London, February 8, 1975

Robinson, the son of an inventor and manufacturer, was educated at the University of Manchester with the original notion of entering his father's business. His ambition soon soared beyond that, however. He obtained his doctorate in 1910, and in 1912 traveled far from home for his first professorial position, which was in organic chemistry at the University of Sydney in Australia. In 1915 he returned to England and taught at a number of schools, ending, in 1929, at Oxford.

As the techniques of organic synthesis developed, the chemists' quest ventured further and further up the slopes of complexity and reached the alkaloids. These are nitrogenous compounds, produced by plants, possessing molecular structures consisting of rings of atoms (including nitrogen as well as carbon) in rather complex relationships. As a whole, they are the most complicated "one-piece" molecules known to chemists. The larger giant molecules, such as those of proteins and starch, are made up of individual units, indefinitely repeated, the individual units being smaller and far less complex than most alkaloids.

The importance of the alkaloids, aside from pure curiosity as to their molecular structure, lies in their profound physiological effects upon the animal body even in small proportions. These effects can be poisonous or, in proper dosage, stimulating or analgesic. They can conceivably have any number of effects that can be put to good use. Nicotine, quinine, strychnine, morphine, and cocaine are all well-known alkaloids.

Robinson studied the alkaloids painstakingly and his greatest success was to work out the structure of morphine (all but for one dubious atom) in 1925 and the structure of strychnine in 1946. The latter structure was later confirmed by Woodward [1416], who synthesized the molecule. Robinson was knighted in 1939 and served as president of the Royal Society from 1945 to 1950.

Robinson did work also on steroids and on certain plant coloring matters called flavones. It was for his work on alkaloids, however, that he received the 1947 Nobel Prize in chemistry.

[1108] **HILL,** Archibald Vivian
English physiologist
Born: Bristol, Gloucestershire, September 26, 1886
Died: Cambridge, June 3, 1977

Hill was educated at Cambridge, where he was first interested in mathematics, finishing third in his class in that

subject. However, he studied under a man who had collaborated with Hopkins [912] in the discovery of lactic acid in muscle.

Influenced by his teacher, Hill investigated the workings of muscles. He did not attempt to work out the chemical details of muscle action but, instead, aimed for the determination of the quantity of heat produced. This was difficult enough. The heat production was so small and so transient that its measurement had stumped the ingenuity of Helmholtz [631]. Hill made use of thermocouples, which swiftly and delicately recorded heat changes in the form of tiny electric currents, and adapted them for his purpose with great patience and ingenuity. He could measure a rise of $0.003°C$ during a period of a few hundredths of a second.

He found as early as 1913 that heat was produced after the muscle had done its work, and he showed that molecular oxygen was consumed then, but not during the muscle's contraction. His results jibed exactly with those of Meyerhof [1095], with whom he shared the 1922 Nobel Prize in medicine and physiology.

During World War II, Hill represented Cambridge University in Parliament, as an Independent Conservative, and was a member of the War Cabinet Scientific Advisory Committee.

[1109] **TRUMPLER,** Robert Julius
Swiss-American astronomer
Born: Zürich, Switzerland, October 2, 1886
Died: Oakland, California, September 10, 1956

Trumpler, the son of an industrialist, after an education in Switzerland and in Germany (obtaining his Ph.D. in the latter country in 1910), came to the United States in 1915 and spent his professional career at the University of California, joining the staff of Lick Observatory, where he remained till his retirement in 1951.

In 1930 he showed that the light of the more distant globular clusters was dimmer than was to be expected from their sizes. The more distant the cluster, the more marked this departure from the expected brightness. What's more, the more distant the cluster, the redder it seemed.

The easiest way of explaining this was to suppose that incredibly thin wisps of dust filled interstellar space and that over vast distances there was enough dust to dim and redden the light of the farther clusters. By taking this dimming effect into account, the size of the galaxy was shown to be smaller than expected, since the dimness of the distant clusters was not due to distance alone. Where Shapley [1102] had thought the galactic center to be 50,000 light-years away, a 30,000-light-year figure seemed now more accurate.

[1110] FRISCH, Karl von
Austrian-German zoologist
Born: Vienna, Austria, November 20, 1886

Von Frisch obtained his Ph.D. from the University of Munich in 1910. He served at the Zoological Institutions of Rostock, then Breslau, and finally Munich in 1925.

The destruction of the Munich Institution during the bombings of World War II led him to shift to the University of Graz in Austria for a while, but again he returned to Munich in 1950.

He is best known for his research on bees. Making use of Pavlov's [802] conditioned reflexes he forced bees to "tell" him of such highly personal matters as the colors they saw. (He had already ascertained in this manner in 1910 that fish could distinguish differences in color and intensity of light and that they had an acute sense of hearing.)

Beginning in 1911, he conditioned bees to go to certain locations for their food and then would alter the color of those locations to see if the conditioning to one color would stop them from flying to another. Conditioned to black, they would fly to red with equal readiness, but not to a place radiating ultraviolet which still looked black to human eyes. They could see ultraviolet, but they could not see red.

Von Frisch also interpreted the manner in which the bee communicated its findings to its colleagues of the hive. Having obtained honey from a new source, the returning bee would "dance," moving round and round, or side to side. The number of the evolutions and their speed gave the necessary information as to the location of the new source. Von Frisch also showed that, in flight, bees could orient themselves by the direction of light polarization in the sky.

In 1973 he was awarded a share of the Nobel Prize for physiology and medicine for his work, receiving it at the age of eighty-seven and thus tying the mark of Rous [1067] in this respect.

[1111] SIEGBAHN, Karl Manne Georg
(seeg′bahn)
Swedish physicist
Born: Örebro, December 3, 1886
Died: Stockholm, September 26, 1978

Beginning in 1914, Siegbahn, who obtained his Ph.D. at the University of Lund in 1911, turned his attention to X rays. Barkla [1049] and Moseley [1121] had been forced to work comparatively crudely with the X rays produced by different elements. Siegbahn developed improved techniques whereby the wavelengths of the X rays produced could be determined accurately.

In this way he discovered groups of X rays less penetrating and longer in wavelengths than the characteristic X rays studied by Moseley. In short, he produced veritable X-ray spectra for each element. From these different groups of X rays, it was possible to support strongly the view of Bohr [1101] and others that the electrons in the various atoms were arranged in "shells." The different bands of X rays were labeled K, L, M, N, O, P, and Q in order of increasing wavelengths and the electron shells were similarly lettered in order of increasing distance from the atomic nucleus.

In 1924 Siegbahn, shortly after having joined the faculty of the University of Uppsala, even managed to refract X rays

707

by means of a prism, showing another similarity of this form of radiation to light. In that same year, he was awarded the Nobel Prize in physics for his development of X-ray spectroscopy. Siegbahn was director of the Institute of Experimental Physics of the Swedish Royal Academy of Sciences in Stockholm from 1937 until his retirement in 1964.

[1112] **KÖHLER,** Wolfgang (koi'ler)
Russo-German-American
psychologist
Born: Revel (now Tallinn),
Estonia, January 21, 1887
Died: Enfield, New Hampshire,
June 11, 1967

Köhler's birthplace was then (as now, since the Soviet takeover of Estonia) part of Russia. He was educated, however, in Germany, obtaining his doctorate at Friedrich-Wilhelm University, Berlin, in 1909. He became a lecturer at the University of Frankfurt in 1911.

During World War I he found himself in the Canary Islands controlled by neutral Spain and was unable to return home over an ocean controlled by Germany's enemies. He amused himself in his involuntary exile by studying the behavior of hens and chimpanzees.

He found striking examples of the ability of the chimpanzees to make use of what, in human beings, would be called reason. In one case, a chimpanzee, after trying in vain to reach bananas with a stick that was too short, suddenly picked up another that had deliberately been left nearby, joined them, and so brought the fruit within reach. In another, a chimpanzee piled one box on another to reach bananas. In neither case was training, experience, or imitation involved; there seemed, rather, the flash of insight—something that was shown to be, for the first time, not limited to Genus Homo.

To Köhler it seemed that learning involved the entire pattern of a process, made plain by such sudden insights, rather than a plodding progression from portion to portion of the process. He was one of the founders of the Gestalt school

of psychology; "Gestalt" being the German word for "pattern."

In 1921 Köhler obtained a professorial position at the University of Berlin.

When Hitler came to power in Germany, Köhler fearlessly expressed his anti-Nazi views and by 1935 it was clear that if he stayed longer it would only be to enter a concentration camp. He left for the United States and took a post at Swarthmore College. He became an American citizen in 1946. In 1956 he moved on to Princeton and in 1958 to Dartmouth.

[1113] **KEILIN,** David (ky'lin)
Russian-British biochemist
Born: Moscow, March 21, 1887
Died: Cambridge, England, February 27, 1963

Keilin was born of Polish parents, temporarily residing in Moscow. His college education was conducted in the West, at Liège, Belgium, and in Paris, where he earned his Ph.D. at the Sorbonne in 1917. By then he had been invited to Cambridge, where he remained for the rest of his life.

He began his career as an entomologist, working on the life cycles of flies. In 1924, however, he was studying the absorption spectrum of the muscles of the horse botfly and noticed four absorption bands that disappeared when the cell suspension was shaken in air but reappeared afterward.

He concluded that there was a respiratory enzyme within cells that absorbed oxygen and, presumably, catalyzed its combination with other substances. He called it cytochrome. With further investigation he was able to show that cellular respiration involved a chain of enzymes that passed hydrogen atoms from one compound to another until, by way of cytochrome, those hydrogen atoms were combined with oxygen. This fit well with the work of Warburg [1089].

Cytochrome turned out to be an iron-containing enzyme and Keilin went on to investigate other iron-containing enzymes such as catalase and peroxidase, which also were in one way or another involved with oxygen.

[1114] **ROSE,** William Cumming
American biochemist
Born: Greenville, South Carolina,
April 4, 1887

Rose obtained his Ph.D. at Yale in
1911 and took his postdoctoral work in
Germany. His first professorial appointment was at the University of Texas in
1913. In 1922 he joined the staff of the
University of Illinois, remaining there
until his retirement in 1955.

Rose's special area of research involved the role of the amino acids in nutrition. From about the turn of the century it had been realized that some proteins were more valuable nutritionally
than others, thanks to the work of men
like Hopkins [912]. Rats lost weight and
eventually died, for instance, if their
only source of proteins was the zein of
corn. They resumed growth and recovered health, however, if a bit of casein,
the protein of milk, was added to their
diet before it was too late.

It was suspected that the difference lay
in the nature of the amino acid building
blocks in the two proteins. Rose began
experimenting, therefore, with diets in
which there was no intact protein, only a
mixture of free amino acids. He found
that rats would thrive on casein that had
been broken down to amino acids but
lost weight if the various known amino
acids were mixed in the proportions in
which they were thought to be present in
casein.

Either it was important for casein to
remain intact (which seemed incredible,
since it was broken down in the digestive
process before absorption) or it contained an unknown amino acid that was
essential to nutrition. Rose accepted the
latter explanation and buckled down to
the search. He succeeded in 1935 in
finding threonine, the last of the nutritionally significant amino acids to be discovered.

Adding threonine to his artificial mixture of amino acids gave Rose what he
wanted—a diet on which rats could live.
He then tried diets from which one
amino acid or another was absent. Sometimes the subtraction of a particular
amino acid made no difference; the ani-

mal could manufacture it out of the
remaining amino acids in its diet. At
other times, the subtraction of a particular amino acid resulted in loss of body
nitrogen, tissue wastage, and other unpleasant symptoms. That amino acid
could not be formed from the others by
the animal and, in its absence, protein
could not be synthesized. (For protein to
be synthesized, all necessary amino acids
must be present.)

Amino acids which had to be present
in the diet were called essential amino
acids. By 1937 Rose had shown that of
the twenty or so amino acids that were
present in nearly every protein molecule,
only ten were dietarily essential to the
rat. Threonine was one.

In the 1940s Rose advanced a notch in
the animal kingdom and began similar
nutritional experiments with graduate
students, feeding them on carefully controlled diets in which free amino acids
were the only nitrogen source. Here only
eight amino acids proved essential. The
amino acids, arginine and histidine, essential in the rat, were not essential in
the adult human being. The case of histidine was quite surprising since there
had been reasons for assuming it would
prove essential. Repeated experiments
confirmed the finding and by the early
1950s it was accepted.

Rose even calculated the minimum
daily requirement for each of the essential amino acids. His work thus placed
the problem of protein nutrition, which
had occupied nutritionists since the time
of Magendie [438] a century before, on
a firm and rational basis at last.

[1115] **HOUSSAY,** Bernardo Alberto
Argentinian physiologist
Born: Buenos Aires, April 10,
1887
Died: Buenos Aires, September
21, 1971

Houssay, the son of French immigrants to Argentina, was educated at the
University of Buenos Aires, from which
he received his medical degree in 1911
and where he had already achieved
professorial status in 1910.

As a medical student he grew interested in the pituitary gland, a small hormone-producing structure suspended from the base of the brain. It was shown by him (independently of P. E. Smith [1090]) and, later, by Li [1382] to have numerous crucial functions in the body. In particular, Houssay showed that it affected the course of sugar metabolism. The anterior lobe of the pituitary seemed to produce at least one hormone that had an effect opposite to that of the insulin first isolated by Banting [1152] and Best [1218].

Removal of the pituitary from a diabetic animal reduced the severity of the diabetes, since such insulin as is formed is not countered by the pituitary secretion. On the other hand, injection of pituitary extracts increased the severity of diabetes, or produced a diabetic condition where one did not exist before. For his demonstration of the complex interlocking of hormonal effects, Houssay shared the 1947 Nobel Prize in medicine and physiology with the Coris [1192, 1194].

Some years before, however, Houssay had fallen out with Juan Domingo Perón, then dictator of Argentina. In 1943 he had been dismissed from his university post, along with 150 other educators, for taking too firm a pro-American stand at a time when Argentina was flirting with the German Nazis. Now, on Houssay's receiving the Nobel Prize, the controlled Argentinian press, rather than rejoicing at this first award of the science prize to a Latin-American, complained that the award was politically motivated as a blow to Perón. Houssay responded that one must not confuse little things (Perón) with big things (the Nobel Prize).

He continued his research work on a private basis and in 1955, after Perón had been driven into exile, he was reinstated.

[1116] **HERTZ,** Gustav Ludwig
German physicist
Born: Hamburg, July 22, 1887
Died: Berlin, October 30, 1975

A nephew of Heinrich Hertz [873], Gustav Hertz obtained his doctorate at the University of Berlin. He fought on the German side in World War I and was severely wounded.

He worked with Franck [1081] to establish the quantized nature of the atom's internal structure and shared with him the 1925 Nobel Prize in physics. In 1928 he was appointed professor of physics at the Technical University, Berlin-Charlottenburg.

Since he was of Jewish descent, he was forced, after Hitler came to power, to resign his post in 1934. Nevertheless, he remained in Germany through World War II, and even survived. He was taken by the advancing Soviet Army and from 1945 worked in the Soviet Union and in East Germany. In 1955 he was appointed professor of physics at the University of Leipzig in East Germany until his retirement in 1961.

[1117] **SCHRÖDINGER,** Erwin (shroi´-ding-er)
Austrian physicist
Born: Vienna, August 12, 1887
Died: Alpbach, January 4, 1961

Schrödinger, the only son of a prosperous factory owner, was taught at home as a youngster. He then attended the University of Vienna and obtained his Ph.D. in 1910. In World War I he served as an artillery officer on the southwest front. More fortunate than Moseley [1121], he survived unharmed. In 1918 he made up his mind to abandon physics for philosophy, but the city in which he had hoped to obtain a university post was lost to Austria in the peace treaties. Schrödinger therefore remained a physicist.

After the war Schrödinger went to Germany and by 1921 had a professorial appointment at the University of Stuttgart. As soon as Schrödinger learned of the matter waves postulated by De Broglie [1157] (reading of it in a footnote in one of Einstein's [1064] papers) and the concept of the electron as having wave properties, it occurred to him that the picture of the atom as built up by Bohr

[1101] could be modified to take those waves into account. Once this was done, the Bohr atom might even be improved.

In Schrödinger's atom the electron can be in any orbit, around which its matter waves can extend in an exact number of wavelengths. This produced a standing wave and therefore did not represent an electric charge in acceleration, so that the electron, as long as it remained in its orbit, need not radiate light and did not violate the conditions of Maxwell's [692] equations.

Furthermore, any orbit between two permissible orbits where a fractional number of wavelengths would be required is impermissible. This accounts for the existence of discrete orbits, with nothing possible in between, as a necessary consequence of the properties of the electron, and not as a mere arbitrary deduction from spectral lines.

Schrödinger, along with others like Dirac [1256] and Born [1084], worked out the mathematics involved in this concept. The relationships that were derived (sometimes referred to as wave mechanics and sometimes as quantum mechanics) placed Planck's [887] quantum theory on a firm mathematical basis a quarter century after it was first promulgated. The key relationship in the mathematical fabric is referred to as the Schrödinger wave equation.

Schrödinger's work on the subject was published in 1926 and it was later shown that the matrix mechanics of Heisenberg [1245], advanced in 1925, and Schrödinger's wave mechanics were equivalent, in that everything explained by one was explained by the other. Psychologically, wave mechanics was more attractive because it offered the mind a picture of the atom, however ungraspable that picture might be.

In 1933 Schrödinger was awarded the Nobel Prize in physics for his work on wave mechanics, sharing it with Dirac.

In 1928 Schrödinger had succeeded Max Planck as professor of theoretical physics at the University of Berlin, but in the same year that he earned the Nobel Prize, Hitler came to power. Schrödinger did not wish to remain, and left for his native Austria. Although not

Jewish (and therefore not directly threatened) he made no secret of his detestation of the Nazis and their anti-Semitic policy. He once interfered with storm troopers bent on a pogrom. He nearly got himself killed for his pains.

When Austria was absorbed by Nazi Germany in 1938, he went to England and in 1940 became professor at the School for Advanced Studies in Dublin, Ireland. He was joined there by Dirac, his fellow adventurer in the realms of wave mechanics. In 1956 Schrödinger returned to Vienna and lived out the rest of his life there.

[1118] **PANETH,** Friedrich Adolf
(pan'et)
German-British chemist
Born: Vienna, Austria, August 31, 1887
Died: Mainz, Germany, September 17, 1958

Paneth, the son of an eminent physiologist, obtained his Ph.D. from the University of Vienna in 1910. He visited Great Britain, where he worked with Soddy [1052] and Ernest Rutherford [996], then taught at various universities in Germany.

In 1933 the coming to power of Hitler made it advisable for him to leave Germany for Great Britain. He returned to Germany only in 1953.

In 1913 he had worked with Hevesy [1100] in the use of radium D as a tracer in determining the solubility of lead salts. Paneth went on to use the technique for studying the unstable hydrides of lead and bismuth. The technique for studying compounds that existed only evanescently made it possible for him to demonstrate the existence of free radicals in the course of organic reactions.

During the 1920s he worked out methods for determining trace amounts of helium in rocks. This made it possible to determine their age, since uranium in rocks very slowly liberated helium. In particular, Paneth used the technique for measuring the age of meteorites and this was an important step toward determining the age of the solar system and setting that at its presently accepted figure of 4,600 million years.

[1119] **RUŽIČKA,** Leopold Stephen
(roo'zheech-kah)
Croatian-Swiss chemist
Born: Vukovar, Croatia (Yugoslavia), September 13, 1887
Died: Zürich, Switzerland, September 26, 1976

Ružička's education and professional life was variedly Teutonic, for though of Slavic extraction, he was born in an area which at the time of his birth was part of the German-controlled nation of Austria-Hungary. Ružička attended high school in Germany and college in Switzerland (where he became a citizen in 1917).

He obtained his doctorate under Staudinger [1074]. His first teaching position was at the University of Utrecht in the Netherlands and in 1929 he became a professor of chemistry at the State Technical College in Zürich.

In the mid-1930s he synthesized several of the sex hormones, but ten years earlier he had done something that, to theoretical chemists, was more startling. He had analyzed the active compounds in musk and civet, two substances very important in the perfume industry, and showed that they consisted of rings of atoms. But what rings! One contained sixteen carbon atoms, the other seventeen. This was quite startling as, for a half century or so, Baeyer's [718] theory that rings composed of more than six atoms were too unstable to exist, had been generally accepted.

Ružička's discovery paved the way for a more liberal and useful interpretation of atomic ring structures. Baeyer's theory applied, strictly speaking, to rings of atoms in a single plane, but it was possible, after all, for rings of atoms to "pucker" out of the plane. For this and for his investigations of a class of compounds called terpenes, the study of which had been pioneered by Wallach [790], Ružička shared the 1939 Nobel Prize in chemistry with Butenandt

[1265], who received it for his work on the sex hormones.

[1120] **SUMNER,** James Batcheller
American biochemist
Born: Canton, Massachusetts, November 19, 1887
Died: Buffalo, New York, August 12, 1955

In 1904, when he was seventeen, Sumner, the son of a well-to-do cotton manufacturer, suffered a serious accident while hunting and his left arm had to be amputated. Since he was left-handed, he had to retrain himself to use his right hand. He did that well, becoming an expert tennis player, for instance.

Sumner became a chemist against the advice of his teachers, who thought that the fact he had but one arm would be a handicap (as indeed it would be if scientific research was purely a matter of dexterous fingering). Sumner persisted and attended Harvard, graduating in 1910 and obtaining his doctorate in 1914. He then accepted a position as assistant professor of biochemistry at Cornell University Medical College.

His chief interest was enzymes, and at the time he began his researches the question of the nature of enzymes had been thrown into confusion. It had for a long time been assumed, without direct evidence, that enzymes were proteins. Willstätter [1009] had produced negative evidence to the effect that enzymes were *not* proteins; that is, he had developed enzyme preparations that yielded no positive response to any test for protein he used. (The tests weren't delicate enough.)

In 1926 Sumner was extracting the enzyme content of jack beans. The enzyme involved was one that catalyzed the breakdown of urea to ammonia and carbon dioxide, so Sumner called it urease. In performing his extraction Sumner found that he obtained a number of tiny crystals that had precipitated out of one of his fractions. He isolated the crystals, dissolved them, and found he had a solution with concentrated urease activity. He prepared more crystals and found

that try as he might, he could not separate the enzyme activity from the crystals. The crystals were the enzyme and
all his tests further agreed on the fact
that the crystals were also proteins.
Urease, in short, was the first enzyme
prepared in crystalline form, and the first
enzyme shown incontrovertibly to be a
protein.

The impression made at the time by
the unknown Sumner against the evidence presented by the Nobel laureate
Willstätter was at first very small. In
1929, however, he traveled to Stockholm
to work on urease with Euler-Chelpin
[1011] and Svedberg [1097] and by 1930
the much more elaborate researches of
Northrop [1148] on crystalline enzymes
made it quite plain that Sumner was right
and Willstätter was wrong.

Sumner, in consequence, received the
1946 Nobel Prize in chemistry, sharing it
with Northrop and with Stanley [1282].

[1121] **MOSELEY,** Henry Gwyn-Jeffreys
English physicist
Born: Weymouth, Dorsetshire,
November 23, 1887
Died: Gallipoli (Gelibolu), Tur-
key, August 10, 1915

Moseley's father had been a naturalist
on the *Challenger* expedition that had
been the first to explore the ocean deeps,
and was a professor of human and comparative anatomy. He died when his son
was only four. Young Moseley's bent,
however, was not toward the life sciences but toward physics. He studied at
Eton and Oxford, to both of which he
won scholarships. (He was one of the
very few important scientists to have
come from Oxford rather than Cambridge. He chose Oxford in order to
remain near his mother.)

For a time he did research under
Ernest Rutherford [996] where he was
the youngest and most brilliant of Rutherford's brilliant young men.

When Laue [1068] and the Braggs
[922, 1141] demonstrated how X rays
could be refracted by crystals, Moseley
seized upon the technique as a manner
of determining and comparing the wave-

lengths of the characteristic X-ray radiation of the various elements, a type of radiation Barkla [1049] had discovered a
few years earlier.

In doing so, Moseley clearly demonstrated what Barkla had suspected: the
wavelength of the characteristic X rays
decreased smoothly with the increasing
atomic weight of the elements emitting
them. This Moseley attributed to the increasing number of electrons in the atom
as atomic weight increased, and to the
increasing quantity of positive charge in
the nucleus. (This nuclear charge was
later found to be a reflection of the number of positively charged protons contained within the nucleus.)

This discovery led to a major improvement of Mendeléev's [705] periodic
table. Mendeléev had arranged his table
of elements in order of atomic weight,
but this order had had to be slightly
modified in a couple of instances to keep
the table useful. Moseley showed that if
it was arranged in order of nuclear
charge (that is, according to the number
of protons in the nucleus, a quantity that
came to be known as the atomic number) no modifications were necessary.

Furthermore, in Mendeléev's table any
two neighboring elements might conceivably be separated by any number of in-
tervening elements, for no minimum
difference in atomic weights among the
elements had been established. Working
with the atomic number changed things
completely, however. The atomic number had to be an integer, so that between
iron, with an atomic number of 26, and
cobalt, with an atomic number of 27, no
new and undiscovered elements could
possibly exist. It also meant that from
hydrogen, the simplest known element at
the time, to uranium, the most complex,
only ninety-two elements could exist.
Furthermore, Moseley's X-ray technique
could locate all the holes in the table
representing still-undiscovered elements,
and exactly seven such holes remained in
1914, the year Moseley developed the
concept of the atomic number. In addition to all this, if a new element filling
one of these holes was reported, Moseley's X-ray technique could be used to
check the validity of the report, as was

done in the case of Urbain's [1002] report on the so-called celtium, and of Hevesy's [1100] hafnium.

In this respect, X-ray analysis was a new and sophisticated technique for chemical analysis. It departed from old methods involving weighing and titration and used far more delicate methods involving measurement of light absorption, of alteration in electrical potential, as in Heyrovsky's [1144] polarimetry, and so on.

Moseley's work did not significantly alter Mendeléev's table, in other words, but it certainly nailed the elements it contained into position.

World War I had broken out at this time and Moseley enlisted at once as a lieutenant of the Royal Engineers. Nations were still naïve in their understanding of the importance of scientists to human society and there seemed no reason not to expose Moseley to the same chances of death to which millions of other soldiers were being exposed. Rutherford tried to get Moseley assigned to scientific labors but failed. On June 13, 1915, Moseley shipped out to Turkey and two months later he was killed at Gallipoli as part of a thoroughly useless and badly bungled campaign, his death having brought Great Britain and the world no good (except for what cold comfort could be obtained out of the fact that he had willed his money to the Royal Society). In view of what he might still have accomplished (he was only twenty-seven when he died), his death might well have been the most costly single death of the war to mankind generally.

Had Moseley lived it seems as certain as anything can be in the uncertain world of scientific history, that he would have received a Nobel Prize in physics. Siegbahn [1111], who carried on Moseley's work, received one.

[1122] **VAVILOV**, Nikolay Ivanovich (vah-vee'luf)
Russian botanist
Born: Moscow, November 25, 1887
Died: Saratov, January 26, 1943

Vavilov, the son of an owner of a shoe factory, graduated from the Moscow Agricultural Institute in 1911. In 1913 he went to England, where he studied under Bateson [913], but returned to Russia with the outbreak of World War I. (An eye problem kept him out of the army.)

Both in England and in Russia he worked on plant immunity and tried to explain it on an evolutionary basis. He searched for specific strains of wheat that were resistant to the various damaging wheat diseases. He went further in attempting to produce new strains of grain by judicious crossing that would have various desirable characteristics. In doing this he made full use of Mendel's [638] genetic laws, of course.

This meant he fell afoul of Lysenko [1214]. Vavilov had praised Lysenko's early work, but Lysenko denounced Vavilov's adherence to Mendelism. Vavilov resisted and what might have been a scientific controversy became a political one when Joseph Stalin sided with Lysenko. Lysenko did not hesitate to take advantage of this: On August 6, 1940, Vavilov was arrested, accused of a variety of ridiculous charges, and sentenced to death. On second thought, the sentence was reduced to ten years' imprisonment; but in the turmoil of World War II he was evacuated to Saratov, was maltreated, and died.

In 1955, after Stalin's death, Vavilov was rehabilitated and posthumously honored, while Lysenko remains a symbol of scientific oppression.

[1123] **GOLDSCHMIDT,** Victor Moritz
Swiss-Norwegian geochemist
Born: Zürich, Switzerland, January 27, 1888
Died: Oslo, Norway, March 20, 1947

Goldschmidt's father was a physical chemist of considerable reputation and obtained a post as professor of chemistry at the University of Oslo, succeeding Waage [701] in 1905. He brought his family with him and arrived shortly before Norway succeeded in establishing its independence from Sweden. In a few years the family became Norwegian citizens.

Goldschmidt entered the university himself, majoring in the earth sciences. He earned his Ph.D. in 1911 with a thesis in which he applied the phase rule— recently popularized by Roozeboom [854]—to the mineralogical changes that took place in the earth's crust.

Goldschmidt spent years studying the minerals of Norway, then in 1929 took a post at the University of Göttingen. By working out the chemical consequences of the properties of the elements and by making use of new knowledge of atomic and ionic sizes, Goldschmidt was able to predict in what sort of minerals which elements ought to appear so that mineralogy was no longer a purely descriptive science. Goldschmidt was pioneering in geochemistry as Beno Gutenberg [1133] was pioneering in geophysics.

The stay at Göttingen was cut short by Hitler's coming to power, however, since Goldschmidt was Jewish. In 1935 he returned to Norway. Nor did that remain a safe haven, for in 1940 Norway was occupied by Germany and Goldschmidt had to leave for England in 1942, traveling by way of Sweden. He carried a capsule of cyanide in his mouth in case there was no other way of evading the Nazis. This was only after periods of imprisonment in concentration camps (from which he managed to escape) had ruined his health.

In June 1946 he returned to Oslo, but life was essentially over. He died of cancer within a year.

[1124] **STERN**, Otto (shtehrn [German]; stern [English])
German-American physicist
Born: Sohrau, Germany (now Zory, Poland), February 17, 1888
Died: Berkeley, California, August 17, 1969

Stern, the son of a prosperous Jewish grain merchant, studied physical chemistry at the University of Breslau and received his doctorate in 1912. He spent two years thereafter working for Einstein [1064] before striking out for himself. His first professorial appointment came in 1914 at the University of Frankfurt. He served later at Rostock and at Hamburg.

About 1920 Stern began to work with molecular beams; that is, he allowed gases to escape from a container through a tiny hole into a high vacuum. The escaping molecules met virtually no molecules with which they could collide in the vacuum, so that they formed a straight beam of moving particles. Although these molecules (and sometimes he also used metallic atoms) are neutral overall, they are made up of charged particles, a positively charged nucleus and negatively charged electrons. As a result they should behave in some ways like tiny magnets. By studying these beams in a magnetic field through the 1920s and into the early 1930s, Stern was able to confirm that they did act as magnets. He made some measurements of these properties that helped to confirm Planck's [887] quantum theory. His pupil Rabi [1212] carried matters further.

Stern also demonstrated that these molecular beams showed wave properties, as De Broglie's [1157] theories predicted. At the time, Davisson [1078] had already proved De Broglie's theories in the case of electrons, but Stern carried matters into the far more massive range of atoms and molecules.

In 1933 Stern was compelled to leave Germany when Hitler came to power. In the United States he accepted a post as professor of physics at Carnegie Institute of Technology (now Carnegie-Mellon University) at Pittsburgh, remaining there until his retirement in 1945. In 1943 he was awarded the Nobel Prize in physics for his work on molecular beams.

[1125] **FRIEDMANN**, Alexander Alexandrovich (freed'mahn)
Russian mathematician
Born: St. Petersburg (now Leningrad), June 29, 1888
Died: Leningrad, September 16, 1925

Friedmann was the son of a composer, and, on his mother's side, the grandson of a Czech composer. He graduated from St. Petersburg University in 1910. He was interested in meteorology at first and during World War I he was at the front in connection with the Russian air force.

He grew interested in Einstein's [1064] general theory of relativity, and was the first to work out a mathematical analysis of the notion of an expanding universe in 1922, thus removing the "cosmological term," which Einstein had inserted and later described as the greatest mistake of his life. Friedmann's model of the universe was the first to make it seem that its beginning would have had to be something like the "big bang" that Lemaître [1174] and Gamow [1278] would then bring into the mainstream of cosmological thinking.

He died of typhoid fever while still in his thirties.

[1126] **GASSER,** Herbert Spencer
American physiologist
Born: Platteville, Wisconsin, July 5, 1888
Died: New York, New York, May 11, 1963

Gasser, the son of an Austrian immigrant who became a physician, was graduated from the University of Wisconsin in 1910 and he began his medical education at the new medical school being organized by the university, taking his physiology course under Erlanger [1023]. He completed his training at Johns Hopkins and obtained his medical degree in 1915.

After the interruption of World War I, during which he served in the Chemical Warfare Service, he joined the faculty of Washington University and worked with Erlanger on nerve potentials, becoming professor of pharmacology in 1921. For this work he shared with Erlanger the 1944 Nobel Prize in medicine and physiology. In 1931 he was appointed head of the physiology department at Cornell University Medical School and in 1935 he became director of the Rockefeller Institute (now Rockefeller University), retaining that position until his retirement in 1953.

[1127] **ZERNICKE,** Fritz (tsehr'nih-kee)
Dutch physicist
Born: Amsterdam, July 16, 1888
Died: Naarden, near Amsterdam, March 10, 1966

Zernicke, the son of a headmaster, obtained his Ph.D. at the University of Amsterdam in 1915 under Kapteyn [815]. He then joined the faculty of the University of Groningen, where he remained the rest of his life.

His great contribution was the development, in 1934, of the phase-contrast microscope. This microscope slightly alters the phase of diffracted light as compared with direct light so that the different objects in the cell appear to take on color even though they are colorless in an ordinary microscope. Intracellular objects become clearly visible without staining, and therefore without killing, the cell.

After World War II phase-contrast microscopes became popular and Zernicke was awarded the 1953 Nobel Prize in physics.

[1128] **WAKSMAN,** Selman Abraham
Russian-American microbiologist
Born: Priluki, Russia, July 22, 1888
Died: Hyannis, Massachusetts, August 16, 1973

Waksman, of Jewish descent, left Russia as a high school graduate and arrived in the United States in 1910. He attended Rutgers University, graduating in 1915, and became an American citizen in 1916. He went to the University of California for further study, obtaining his doctorate there in 1918, then returned to Rutgers to join the faculty.

He was particularly interested in the microorganisms dwelling in the soil, a study that took a sudden new direction in 1939 when Dubos [1235], who had been one of Waksman's students, discovered a bacteria-killing agent in a soil microorganism. This helped stimulate a new look at Fleming's [1077] penicillin, especially since World War II had broken out and new methods of handling infection would be badly needed for wounded soldiers.

Waksman, in 1941, coined the term "antibiotic" ("against life") for the chemicals, obtained from microorganisms, which killed bacteria, and he began to look for such chemicals. Dubos' agent and penicillin were both effective only toward Gram [841] -positive bacteria and did not affect Gram-negative ones. Waksman was therefore particularly interested in some substance that would combat the latter group. He happened to have a pet mold, so to speak, of the Streptomyces family, one that he had been studying ever since the first days of his graduate work. From it, in 1943, he finally isolated an antibiotic effective against Gram-negative bacteria and marketed it as Streptomycin. It was first successfully used on a human being on May 12, 1945.

For this discovery Waksman was awarded the 1952 Nobel Prize in medicine and physiology. He turned the prize money over to a research foundation at Rutgers. Streptomycin is a little too toxic for convenience, but its finding initiated a strenuous and systematic search among soil microorganisms for additional antibiotics and it was not long before the tetracyclines were discovered by Duggar [1010].

[1129] **BYRD,** Richard Evelyn
American explorer
Born: Winchester, Virginia,
October 25, 1888
Died: Boston, Massachusetts,
March 11, 1957

Of a distinguished Virginia family (his older brother was Virginia's longtime senator Harry F. Byrd), Richard E. Byrd forecast his career when he made a trip around the world, unattended, at the age of twelve. He graduated from the U. S. Naval Academy in 1912 but retired from active service in 1916 because of an injury suffered on the playing field. During World War I, he became an air pilot and in 1921 crossed the Atlantic Ocean in a dirigible. In 1925 he took part in his first polar expedition and in 1926 was the first to fly over the North Pole by airplane.

He then turned to the Antarctic. The attainment of the South Pole by Amundsen [1008] and by Scott [971], though great feats, was only a beginning. The entire continent of Antarctica remained untouched, the largest blank spot remaining on the map of the world, five million square miles of uninhabited land.

In 1928 Byrd established his camp, Little America, on the ice off Antarctica's shoreline and flew over the South Pole by plane. He was made a rear admiral by act of Congress as a result and in 1933 to 1935 conducted a still more extensive expedition to Antarctica, observing and mapping many areas of the frozen continent. During 1934 he spent five months alone in Antarctica.

A third, fourth, and fifth expedition followed, the last in 1955, when he was in his late sixties. No one man did more to map Antarctica. It is pleasant to record that despite his many forays into the polar areas he died at home, unlike Amundsen and Scott. He died on the eve of the Geophysical Year, which opened a concentrated scientific attack on the Antarctic continent.

[1130] **RAMAN,** Sir Chandrasekhara Venkata (rah'man)
Indian physicist
Born: Tiruchirappalli (Trichinopoly), Madras, November 7, 1888
Died: Bangalore, November 21, 1970

Raman was the descendant of a long line of landholders, and the son of a physics professor. His education took place entirely within India and he graduated from the Presidency College in Madras in 1904 at the age of sixteen. He obtained his master's degree, with highest honors, in 1907. Since there was virtually no chance of a scientific education in India at the time, and ill health prevented him from seeking further education in England, Raman took a job with the civil service after passing a competitive examination for the post in 1903. Like Einstein [1064] under similar

717

circumstances, he labored at science in his spare time; he helped found the Indian Association for the Cultivation of Science in 1909. Eventually he came to the attention of the University of Calcutta, which in 1917 offered him a professorship in physics.

After Compton's [1159] discovery of the Compton effect, Heisenberg [1245] in 1925 predicted that a similar effect ought to be found in the case of visible light. Raman had already been investigating light scattering and had come to the same conclusion before Heisenberg had made his suggestion and even before Compton's work.

In 1928 he definitely showed that scattered light had weak components of changed wavelength so that photons of visible light, like those of X rays, had particulate properties. Furthermore, the exact wavelengths produced in the scattering depended on the nature of the molecules doing the scattering. For this reason, Raman spectra proved to be most useful in determining some of the fine details of molecular structure.

As a result of this discovery Raman was knighted by the British Government in 1929, and in 1930 was awarded the Nobel Prize in physics. He was the first Asian to win a Nobel Prize in one of the sciences and he used the money to buy several hundred diamonds for laboratory use. In 1947 he became the director of the Raman Research Institute at Bangalore in India.

Throughout his life, Raman, remembering his own early struggle, labored ceaselessly to build up scientific research and education in India, training more than five hundred young Indians to hold important positions in science and education at home and abroad.

[1131] **KARRER**, Paul
Swiss chemist
Born: Moscow, Russia, April 21, 1889
Died: Zürich, June 18, 1971

Karrer was born in Russia of Swiss parents, his father being a dentist who was practicing there. The family re-

turned to Switzerland in 1892. There Karrer attended the University of Zürich, serving as assistant to Alfred Werner [960]. In 1911, after obtaining his Ph.D., he journeyed to Frankfurt-am-Main, where he worked with Ehrlich [845], returning to Zürich as a professor in 1918 and succeeding Werner in 1919. He remained there till his retirement in 1959.

Karrer worked on a large variety of problems in organic chemistry, but he is most famous for his achievements in connection with vitamins. In the early 1930s he was one of those who most advanced the study of the carotenoids, the yellow-orange-red coloring matters in such food items as carrots, sweet potatoes, egg yolk, and tomatoes, and in such nonedible objects as lobster shells and human skin. He isolated several new varieties and proved the structure of the best-known examples.

Most important of all, he showed in 1931 that vitamin A is related to carotenoids in structure (in fact, it resembles half a molecule of a typical carotenoid). This was finally established by the actual synthesis of vitamin A by Karrer and his group. Others, such as Kuhn [1233], also worked out schemes of synthesis.

Karrer synthesized other vitamins too: vitamin B_2 (riboflavin) in 1935 and vitamin E (tocopherol) in 1938. Such work (considering the complications of the structure of most vitamins) requires considerable virtuosity in the chemist, but it is not merely a chemical jigsaw puzzle to be solved for amusement only. Synthesis is the final step in proving molecular structure, and this synthesis in particular led to a better understanding of the role of the vitamin in metabolism, as men like Elvehjem [1240] were about to show.

For his work Karrer received the 1937 Nobel Prize in chemistry, sharing it with Haworth [1087].

[1132] **MIDGLEY**, Thomas, Jr.
American chemist
Born: Beaver Falls, Pennsylvania, May 18, 1889
Died: Worthington, Ohio, November 2, 1944

At Cornell, Midgley, the son of an inventor, took his degree in mechanical engineering, receiving his degree in that field in 1911.

Working for the Dayton Engineering Company from 1916, he grew interested in finding something to prevent fuel knock. Midgley thought a red dye might cause the fuel to absorb heat more smoothly and thus prevent knock. He tried iodine and that held down the knock, but it was not the color that did it, for colorless ethyl iodide was even better.

Midgley decided he needed to know chemistry and educated himself for years in that subject. He narrowed down his search by using the periodic table of Mendeléev [705] and considering only elements near those already proved to exist in compounds with antiknock properties. In 1921 he came across tetraethyl lead. It is still the best antiknock known.

In the late 1920s a new problem came up. Home refrigeration was blossoming, but the most common refrigerants were ammonia, methyl chloride, and sulfur dioxide, all poisonous. What was needed was something neither poisonous nor inflammable and yet was a gas easily liquefied by pressure alone. In 1930 Midgley prepared difluorodichloromethane (Freon). He demonstrated its safety to an audience of chemists by taking in a deep lungful and letting it trickle out over a lighted candle, which was put out. Freon is now universally used in home refrigerators, freezers, and air conditioners.

In 1940 Midgley was paralyzed by an attack of polio. He worked up a harness with pulleys to enable him to get out of bed but in 1944 tragically strangled himself in that harness.

[1133] **GUTENBERG,** Beno
German-American geologist
Born: Darmstadt, Germany,
June 4, 1889
Died: Los Angeles, California,
January 25, 1960

Gutenberg, the son of a soap manufacturer, obtained his Ph.D. in 1911 at the University of Göttingen. He came to the United States in 1930 and became an American citizen in 1936. While in the United States he taught at the California Institute of Technology.

Gutenberg worked on the speed of propagation of earthquake waves. He was the first to explain satisfactorily the existence of the "shadow zone" where earthquake waves are not felt. This zone forms a band encircling the earth at a fixed distance from the epicenter of the earthquake. Gutenberg in 1913 postulated the existence of a core at the center of the earth about 2,100 miles in radius. Earthquake waves entering it are refracted away from the shadow zone. From the fact that transverse waves do not penetrate the core at all, it was assumed to be liquid. From considerations of density and from the composition of many meterorites, the suggestion has been widely accepted among geologists that this liquid core is iron-nickel (in the proportion of 9 to 1) in composition. The sharp boundary between the core and the rocky mantle that lies above it is called the Gutenberg discontinuity.

[1134] **ZWORYKIN,** Vladimir Kosma
(zwawr'ih-kin)
Russian-American physicist
Born: Mourom, Russia, July 30,
1889

Zworykin, the son of a river-boat merchant, received a degree in electrical engineering from the St. Petersburg Institute of Technology in 1912. He traveled to France to do graduate work under Langevin [1000], but on the outbreak of World War I, he returned to Russia. During the war, he served as a radio officer with the Russian forces. The coming of the Russian Revolution sent him away again, this time permanently.

In 1919 he arrived in the United States, and was naturalized in 1924. He worked for Westinghouse Electric Company and attended the University of Pittsburgh, where he obtained a Ph.D. in 1926. Zworykin was fascinated by the cathode-ray tube; he realized that the motion of its electron beams was so fast

719

that an appropriately varying magnetic field could cause it to scan (that is, pass its beam over every part of) a picture in a small fraction of a second. He patented the idea in 1928 and became director of research at the Radio Corporation of America (RCA) in 1929 and vice-president in 1947.

By 1938 he had developed the first practical television camera, which he called the iconoscope. In the iconoscope the rear of the camera is coated with a large number of tiny cesium-silver droplets. Each emits electrons as the light beam scans it, in proportion to the brightness of this light, and the electrons in a television tube are controlled by the electrons in the iconoscope. As the electrons in the tube scan its fluorescent screen, the original scene scanned by the iconoscope is reproduced.

Refinements and improvements were later added by RCA (four million dollars' worth, in fact) and in the end television proved a practical home device. Even with the delays introduced by World War II, it took over in the 1950s, superseding radio and the movies as the premier entertainment medium.

Zworykin also grew interested in an allied instrument, one that had been built by German physicists in crude form. It was designed to alter electron beams magnetically, not for scanning purposes, but in order to focus them. De Broglie's [1157] theories had shown that electrons possessed associated matter waves with a wavelength far smaller than that of ordinary light waves. Since the amount by which any object can be magnified depends on the wavelength of the radiation with which it is viewed, electrons could be used for far higher magnifications than light beams could.

Zworykin's modification of the instrument made it into a practical and useful electron microscope. By 1939 he had a model that could make enlargements fifty times as great as those of the best optical microscopes. This device allowed the biologist and the biochemist to enter the world of viruses and protein molecules, which, for the first time, man now was able to see.

[1135] **COSTER,** Dirk
Dutch physicist
Born: Amsterdam, October 5, 1889
Died: Groningen, February 12, 1950

Coster obtained his Ph.D. at the University of Leiden in 1922, then went to the University of Copenhagen for postdoctoral work.

At Copenhagen, in collaboration with Hevesy [1100], Coster used his own experience in Moseley's [1121] method of X-ray analysis to discover the element hafnium. The next year he accepted a professorship of physics at the University of Groningen, and there he remained for the rest of his professional life.

He died of a progressive spinal disease that slowly reduced him to paralysis.

[1136] **HUBBLE,** Edwin Powell
American astronomer
Born: Marshfield, Missouri, November 20, 1889
Died: San Marino, California, September 28, 1953

Hubble, the son of a lawyer, was interested in law to begin with and, as a Rhodes scholar at Oxford in 1910, took his degree in that field. His interest, however, had already begun to turn to astronomy under the influence of Millikan [969] and Hale [974]. Finding himself irresistibly attracted to it still, he abandoned law and worked at Yerkes Observatory from 1914 to 1917.

During World War I he served in France, volunteering as an infantry private and rising to the rank of major. In 1919 he took a post he had been offered before he had gone off to war and began work at the Mount Wilson Observatory, where he had at his disposal the 100-inch telescope, and where he remained for the rest of his life.

His interest turned to the patches of luminous fog or nebulae, some of which had first been systematically observed by Messier [305] a century and a half before and which were still like so many question marks in the sky. By this time, the dimensions of our galaxy (the vast group of stars of which our sun is one) had been correctly worked out by Shapley [1102], but the question still remained whether anything beside the Magellanic Clouds, which had been studied by Leavitt [975], lay outside the galaxy.

Suspicion turned to the nebulae. Some of these were undoubtedly clouds of dust and gas illuminated by stars shining within them, and were definitely part of our galaxy. The luminosity of others, however, like the Andromeda nebula (M31 on the Messier list), could not be attributed to a content of visible stars. If stars were there, they were a large mass of extremely dim ones, producing an effect like that in our Milky Way. Since the Andromeda nebula was dimmer than the Milky Way, it would have to be much farther.

Some novas had been located in the Andromeda nebula but, until Hubble's time, never any ordinary stars. In 1924 Hubble and his giant telescope (the largest of its day) were finally able to enlarge the nebulosity to the point of making out stars within it. Hubble went on to show that some of the stars were, indeed, Cepheid variables. Using the period-luminosity law of Shapley and Leavitt, he concluded that the Andromeda nebula was some 800,000 light-years away, eight times the distance of the farthest star of our own galaxy. (Twenty years later, this was found to be an underestimate.) There was no question that the Andromeda nebula lay beyond our own galaxy.

Other nebulae were placed farther still, their distance ranging out into the billions of light-years. In this way Hubble founded the study of the universe beyond our own galaxy and gave the first indication of the existence of what he called "extragalactic nebulae" (objects we now know to exist in the tens of billions). Shapley later made the logical suggestion that the extragalactic nebulae be called galaxies, emphasizing the fact that our own galaxy (sometimes called the Milky Way Galaxy) was only one of many.

Hubble went on to classify the galaxies according to shape and to make suggestions as to the possible course of their evolution. The grandest result of his researches was his analysis in 1929 of the radial velocities of the galaxies, which had been measured by Slipher [1038]. Hubble suggested that the speed at which a galaxy receded from us was directly proportional to its distance. This could best be explained by supposing that the universe was steadily expanding, as Sitter [1004] had already theorized. If it was, the distance between all galaxies was steadily increasing. And in that case, all the galaxies would seem to be receding from an observer no matter which galaxy served as his observation point.

Furthermore, at some vast distance from ourselves, the velocity of recession should attain the speed of light and neither light nor any other form of communication could reach us from any of those galaxies or others still more distant. This distance would represent the effective Hubble radius of that portion of the universe that we can come to know. The Hubble radius of the universe has been estimated at 13 billion light-years. To put it another way, the knowable universe is a sphere with a diameter of 26 billion light-years.

If Hubble's suggestion was correct, then the speed of recession could be used to determine the distance of a nebula (a yardstick even mightier than Leavitt's Cepheids). From the distance, the true size of the galaxy could then be determined. When this was done, the various galaxies all proved to be markedly smaller than our own Milky Way Galaxy. Furthermore, in 1931 Hubble studied the globular clusters of the Andromeda galaxy (no longer "nebula"), which resembled those of our own galaxy in being distributed about the galactic center—this being strong evidence in favor of the assumption that Shapley used to determine the size and shape of our own galaxy. Hubble found that the Andromeda clusters were markedly smaller than our own.

This unusual size of our own galaxy proved an illusion, based on an error of the period-luminosity curve, which Baade [1163] was to correct a decade later.

Reversing the expanding universe would bring all the galaxies together about two billion years ago, if Hubble's original figures are accepted. This length of time was too short for geologists, who were certain that the earth itself had been in existence for at least three billion years. This discrepancy, too, was corrected by Baade, and in favor of the geologists.

All the vast cosmogonic schemes of today, schemes designed to account for the origin and development of the universe, must take into account and explain the expansion of the universe or, at the very least, explain why it seems to expand, if the fact itself is denied. The simplest explanation is that the universe expands because at some time in the far past it exploded, the "big bang" theory favored by Lemaître [1174] and Gamow [1278].

Hubble's work on the recession of the galaxies has been carried on by Humason [1149].

When the United States entered World War II, Hubble, an active anti-Nazi, tried to join the army again but was persuaded that he could do more in war-related research.

When the 200-inch telescope was installed at Mount Palomar, Hubble was given the honor of being the first to use it.

[1137] **ADRIAN,** Edgar Douglas
Baron
English physiologist
Born: London, November 30, 1889
Died: London, August 4, 1977

Adrian was educated at Trinity College, Cambridge, obtaining his medical degree there in 1915. He served as a physician in the British armed forces during World War I, then returned as a member of the faculty at Trinity, gaining a professorship in 1937 and becoming master of the college in 1951.

He worked on nerve impulses from sense organs, measuring changes in the electropotential with greater delicacy than had been managed by earlier researchers. Eventually, he was able to detect and measure the impulses from single nerve fibers, and for this he shared with Sherrington [881] the 1932 Nobel Prize for physiology or medicine. Afterward, he worked on the electropotential of the brain itself, contributing to an understanding of epilepsy and to the possible location of cerebral lesions.

He was elected president of the Royal Society in 1950 and was raised to the peerage in 1955 as Baron Adrian of Cambridge.

[1138] **HOLMES,** Arthur
English geologist
Born: Hebburn on Tyne, Durham, January 14, 1890
Died: London, September 20, 1965

Holmes studied at Imperial College of Science in London under Rayleigh [760] but turned from physics to geology by the time of his graduation in 1910.

His lifework was that of making use of radioactive transformation to estimate the age of the rocks, in line with the suggestion of Boltwood [987]. Holmes clearly showed that radioactive heat completely invalidated Kelvin's [652] estimate of a short-lived earth. To begin with, Holmes found rocks that were 1,600 million years old, more than sixty times the age Kelvin had allowed. By the time he had worked out his final scale, an age of 4,600 million years had been accepted for the earth, and, thanks to the work of Paneth [1118] on meteorites, for the solar system generally.

[1139] **BUSH,** Vannevar
American electrical engineer
Born: Everett, Massachusetts, March 11, 1890
Died: Belmont, Massachusetts, June 28, 1974

Bush, the son of a minister, was educated in the Boston area, doing his undergraduate work at Tufts University and obtaining his doctorate at the Massachusetts Institute of Technology and

Harvard University in 1916. He taught at Tufts for a few years but in 1919 accepted a professorial position at M.I.T.

In 1925 Bush and his colleagues constructed a machine capable of solving differential equations. Kelvin [652] had worked out the theory for such a machine a half century before, but .Bush was the first to construct one and to carry forward the abortive attempts of Babbage [481], a half century earlier still, to build a computer. Bush's machine was, in fact, the first analogue computer, and more elaborate versions were built at M.I.T. over the next decade and a half. From 1939 to 1955 he was president of the Carnegie Institution of Washington.

During World War II further important advances were made both in theory and practice. Norbert Wiener [1175] developed the science of cybernetics, which guided men in the construction of computers, while electronic switches (much faster) replaced mechanical ones. The first electronic computer (Eniac) was built in 1946, and since then extremely advanced and sophisticated computers of all varieties have been built in considerable number. It is through such devices that scientists can make routine calculations that would ordinarily take prohibitive time. (As trivial examples, pi can be calculated to 10,000 places in a matter of a few hours, and election results can be predicted quickly from initial voting figures. More significantly, perhaps, the calculations required to work out the orbit of Mars, which took Kepler [169] four years, according to his own report, were repeated by computer in 1964 in eight seconds!)

Industries are using computers and allied instruments to control and guide production and administration with a minimum of human interference. This trend (usually referred to as automation) threatens a Second Industrial Revolution with consequences as unsettling and, perhaps, unforeseen as those of the first two centuries earlier.

In 1940 Bush was made chairman of the National Defense Research Committee, acting as coordinator of scientific research in connection with national de-

fense. (A year later the Japanese were to bomb the United States into World War II.) Among other things Bush was in charge of the research on uranium, in which the United States Government grew interested after Einstein [1064] sent his letter to President Roosevelt.

This area of research grew broader and more important and in 1942 Bush wrote an optimistic report, which resulted in the establishment, on August 13, 1942, of what became popularly known as the Manhattan Project after the war. It was this scientific organization that developed and exploded the first atomic bomb not quite three years after its organization.

[1140] **JONES,** Sir Harold Spencer
English astronomer
Born: London, March 29, 1890
Died: London, November 3, 1960

Jones, the son of an accountant, was educated at Cambridge, where he earned his bachelor's degree in 1911 and his doctorate in 1925. From 1913 to 1923 he was assistant to the astronomer royal at Greenwich and thereafter spent a decade at the observatory in South Africa where, nearly a century earlier, Henderson [505] had determined the distance of Alpha Centauri. Jones's ambition was much more modest: He wanted to determine the distance of the sun.

Through the 1920s he made delicate measurements of the manner in which the moon occulted stars, measurements from which the solar distance could be deduced. However, his major effort came in 1931, in connection with the asteroid Eros.

Galle [573] nearly a century before had first suggested that the parallax of asteroids be measured to help determine the scale of the solar system. At the time, however, the only known asteroids were too far to yield parallaxes with sufficient accuracy. Eros, however, was discovered in 1898 and found to have an orbit that carried it closer to the earth than any object then known except the moon. In 1931 it was scheduled to approach to within 16 million miles of the earth, two-thirds the distance of Venus at its closest and only half the distance of Mars.

A long, detailed program was set up. Fourteen observatories in nine countries took part. Seven months were spent on the project and nearly three thousand photographs were taken. The position of Eros was determined on each one of them. Ten years of calculations, under the leadership of Jones (who in 1933 had been appointed astronomer royal), followed. In 1942 Jones finally published the result as 93,005,000; and the distance of the sun had been established with greater accuracy than ever before, to one part in ten thousand, in fact.

Jones was knighted in 1943 for this. His mark was not improved until the late 1950s when pulses of radar were sent out to strike Venus and bounce back. From the time lapse between pulse and echo, still more accurate figures for the scale of the solar system were obtained.

Under Jones, the Greenwich Observatory moved from the time-honored headquarters it had occupied since Flamsteed's [234] time two and a half centuries earlier. The growth of London had engulfed Greenwich with smog and pollution and made the site unfit for astronomical work. After World War II, therefore, the observatory was moved to Sussex, and Jones moved with it, staying till his retirement in 1955.

[1141] **BRAGG,** Sir William Lawrence
　　　　Australian-English physicist
　　　　Born: Adelaide, Australia, March
　　　　31, 1890
　　　　Died: Ipswich, England, July 1,
　　　　1971

William Lawrence Bragg was the son of William Henry Bragg [922] and was born while his father was teaching at Adelaide University. He was an infant prodigy and, like his father, he studied mathematics and physics, entering the University of Adelaide at the age of fifteen and getting an honors degree at eighteen. He then entered Trinity Col-

lege, Cambridge, where he studied under Wilson [979].

While still a student he was intrigued by the work of Laue [1068], who had diffracted X rays by passing them through a crystal. Although he was at Cambridge and his father at Leeds, they labored together on the problem (after discussing the subject during a summer vacation).

They worked out the mathematical details involved in the diffraction, showed how to calculate wavelengths of the X rays, and deduced certain facts concerning crystal structure from the manner of the X-ray diffraction. For instance, it was possible to show that crystals of substances such as sodium chloride contained no actual molecules of sodium chloride but only sodium ions and chloride ions arranged with geometric regularity. In the case of sodium chloride, each sodium ion was equidistant from six chloride ions while each chloride ion was equidistant from six sodium ions. There was no particular connection between one individual sodium ion and one individual chloride ion.

This had a profound effect on theoretical chemistry and led, for instance, to Debye's [1094] new treatment of ion dissociation.

The results of the experiments were published in 1915 under the joint names of father and son, and they shared the Nobel Prize in physics for that year. The son achieved the unusual feat of becoming a Nobel Prize winner at the age of twenty-five, the youngest ever to receive such an award. He lived to celebrate the fifty-fifth anniversary of the award, also a record.

After the war, during which he served in the artillery, Bragg proposed the notion of "ionic radii," which was to prove quite fruitful in connection with Pauling's [1236] theory of resonance.

In 1919 William Lawrence Bragg accepted a professorship of physics at Manchester University. In 1938 he became professor of physics at Cambridge and director of the Cavendish Laboratory, succeeding Rutherford [996] in that post and remaining there till 1953. In later years he was particulary interested in lecturing on science to young people.

He was knighted in 1941 and retired in 1965.

[1142] **FISHER,** Sir Ronald Aylmer
English biologist
Born: London, February 17, 1890
Died: Adelaide, Australia, July 29, 1962

Fisher was the son of an auctioneer and the surviving member of a pair of twins. He graduated from Cambridge in 1912 and channeled his mathematical talents and interests into the field of statistics and, through that, genetics.

He placed on a much firmer footing methods for sampling in order to achieve full randomization, and methods for varying different factors in an experiment ("analysis of variance"). Fisher particularly considered the statistical nature of inheritance according to Mendel's [638] laws and showed that it fit Darwin's [554] doctrine of natural selection. He labored to make sense out of blood group inheritance and clarified the manner of inheritance of the Rh blood-group series.

He was knighted in 1952. In 1959, upon his retirement, he emigrated to Australia.

[1143] **ARMSTRONG,** Edwin Howard
American electrical engineer
Born: New York, New York, December 18, 1890
Died: New York, February 1, 1954

In his teens, Armstrong read the story of Marconi [1025] and his experiments in popular books of science, and before he was twenty he was building his own radio transmitter and broadcasting signals with it. He went on to Columbia University and earned a degree in electrical engineering in 1913, studying under Pupin [891]. In 1912, while still but in his third year at Columbia, he devised the "regenerative circuit," which supplied radio with its first amplifying receiver and reliable transmitter.

During World War I, Armstrong, then a Signal Corps officer, grew interested in methods of detecting airplanes. Existing systems, developed by Fessenden [958], detected them by the sound waves they emitted but Armstrong believed it might be more sensitive and efficient to detect the electromagnetic waves set up by their ignition systems. Those waves were too high in frequency to be received easily, so Armstrong devised a circuit that lowered the frequency, then amplified that. He named it a superheterodyne receiver.

Actually, this was developed too late to play a role in the war (although it was used in radar equipment in World War II), but it could be used for reception of any radio waves, and with it radio sets became easy to use. It was no longer necessary to be an electrical engineer to tune in radio signals. With superheterodyning added to the radio, it could be done by the twist of a dial. Radio sets became hugely popular.

Armstrong returned to Columbia after the war and found himself a millionaire. However, there was long and messy litigation with De Forest [1017] over who owned the patent for the regenerative circuit. Armstrong lost the case after fourteen years and two appeals to the Supreme Court, but the scientific community seemed to feel the judgment was in error.

Armstrong's greatest triumph was still ahead of him. In 1934 he became professor of electrical engineering at Columbia and in 1939, after six years of labor, he defeated the problem of static.

In ordinary radio sets, signals are carried by systematic alteration of the amplitude of the carrier signal, the alteration following the variation in amplitude of the sound waves being transmitted. This is amplitude modulation, or AM. Unfortunately, thunderstorms and electrical appliances also modulate the amplitude of the carrier wave, doing it randomly. This random modulation is, of course, converted into random sound at the receiver; in other words, static.

Armstrong devised a method of trans-

725

mitting a signal by systematic alteration of the *frequency* of the carrier signal. This is frequency modulation, or FM, and it virtually eliminated static. FM radio came into popularity after World War II, particularly for programs of serious music, and it is also used in the sound circuits of television sets. Unfortunately FM will work only for carrier waves of high frequency and these cannot be transmitted much beyond the horizon. The area of reception for a given FM transmitting station is therefore limited—and again there was patent litigation.

Armstrong, a contentious man, made a great deal of money but lost it all in unfortunate business and legal misadventures. He was increasingly certain there was a conspiracy against him and in 1954, in a fit of depression or despair, he jumped to his death from his apartment window.

[1144] **HEYROVSKÝ,** Jaroslav (hay-rof'skee)
Czech physical chemist
Born: Prague, Czechoslovakia (then part of Austria-Hungary), December 20, 1890
Died: Prague, March 27, 1967

Heyrovský, the son of a professor of law, studied at the University of Prague and then, between 1910 and 1913, in London. He was on holiday in Prague when World War I broke out, so he could not return to London.

He served in the Austro-Hungarian army, but managed to obtain his Ph.D. in 1918. He did postdoctoral work in London, where he worked under Ramsay [832] and in 1926 joined the staff of the University of Prague, reaching the rank of professor of physical chemistry in 1926.

Beginning in 1918, and inspired by a question asked of him on his doctoral examination, Heyrovský worked out a device whereby an electric potential could be put across mercury electrodes that were so arranged that a small drop of mercury was repeatedly falling

through a solution to a mercury pool below. An electric current flowed through the solution and as the potential was heightened, the current reached a plateau that depended on the concentration of certain ions in the solution. By measuring this plateau, one could determine the concentration of those ions in a solution of unknown composition. The theory had been worked out a generation earlier by Nernst [936], but now Heyrovský had put it to work as "polarography," a word he coined in 1925. It proved a very delicate analytical tool.

The Polarographic Institute was founded by Czechoslovakia in 1950 and Heyrovský, who had managed to continue his work even during the German occupation (thanks to the protection of a courageous German co-worker), was made its director. The technique was not properly appreciated at first and it was not till 1959 that Heyrovský was awarded the Nobel Prize in chemistry.

[1145] **MULLER,** Hermann Joseph
American biologist
Born: New York, New York, December 21, 1890
Died: Indianapolis, Indiana, April 5, 1967

Muller founded what was probably the first high school science club at Morris High School in the Bronx, New York. He entered Columbia University on a scholarship in 1907 and carried on through to his doctorate in 1916.

In 1911 he began work, under T. H. Morgan [957], on the genetics of the fruit fly and had ample opportunity to see how mutations appear. Muller, however, was impatient with waiting; he believed that geneticists did not necessarily have to.

When he began independent research he sought methods of hastening the rate of mutation. He found in 1919, for instance, that raising the temperature increased the number of mutations. Furthermore, this was not the result of a general "stirring up" of the genes. It always turned out that one gene might be affected while its duplicate on the other chromosome of the pair (chromosomes occur in pairs) was not. Muller decided, consequently, that changes on the molecular or submolecular level were involved, changes that were hastened by heat.

It occurred to him to try X rays. They were more energetic than gentle heat, and on striking a chromosome they would certainly have an effect on a point. By 1926 he could see that he had hit home. X rays greatly increased the mutation rate. This served several useful purposes. First, it increased the number of mutations that geneticists could study in a given time. Second, it showed that there was nothing mystical about a mutation; it was but the result of a chemical change that man could himself initiate. (In fact, Blakeslee [1029] was soon to show that ordinary chemicals, and not just radiation, could bring about mutations.) This pointed the way toward the work of molecular biologists like Crick [1406] a quarter century later.

Eventually Muller received the honor due him: He was awarded the 1946 Nobel Prize in medicine and physiology.

In the early 1930s Muller went to Germany but left with the rise of Hitler. (Muller was of part-Jewish descent.) He then went to the USSR at the invitation of Vavilov [1122] but left in 1937, after openly opposing Lysenko's [1214] views on genetics.

Muller's studies of mutations had convinced him that the vast majority were deleterious. To be sure, in the course of evolution the few useful ones survive and the deleterious ones tend to die out, but for this to continue, there must not be too many deleterious ones. If the mutation rate is increased, the absolute numbers of imperfect individuals may become too great for species survival. Muller therefore began to work in two areas.

First, he tirelessly warned against needless X-ray therapy and diagnosis in medicine. It was well known that exposure to hard radiation could cause cancer —which, from his standpoint, was a mutation in which a normal cell became cancerous. However, Muller was concerned about ordinary mutations, too,

and wanted to see that gonads were effectively shielded in all those exposed to X rays under either medical or industrial circumstances. After World War II, Muller was particularly active in pointing up the danger of a rising mutation rate because of radioactive fallout from nuclear bomb tests and in 1955 joined seven other scientists including Einstein [1064] in a plea to outlaw nuclear bombs.

Second, Muller, like a latter-day Galton [636], but with far more genetic information at his disposal, pushed for some sort of eugenic measures to improve the genetic health of the human species. One imaginative notion that he strongly supported was the establishment of sperm banks so that the genetic endowment of gifted men could be widely spread through space and time.

[1146] **BOTHE,** Walther Wilhelm Georg
Franz (boh'tuh)
German physicist
Born: Oranienburg, near Berlin,
January 8, 1891
Died: Heidelberg, February 8,
1957

Bothe, the son of a merchant, obtained his education at the University of Berlin, studying under Planck [887] and obtaining his doctorate in 1914. He taught at Berlin after graduation with some time off for service during World War I (most of which he spent as a prisoner of war in Russia), then went on to professorial positions at Giessen and at Heidelberg, where he worked with Geiger [1082]. In 1934 he became director of the Max Planck Institute for Medical Research.

In 1929 he devised a method of studying cosmic rays by placing two Geiger counters one above the other and setting up a circuit that would record an event only if both counters recorded virtually simultaneously. This would happen only if a cosmic ray particle, streaking down from above, shot vertically through both counters. Other particles would be coming from some other direction and would pass through one counter and not the other, or, if coming from the right direction would be insufficiently energetic to go through both.

Such "coincidence counting" turned out to be very useful in measuring short intervals of time. Such times, a billionth of a second and less, were still long enough to allow much to happen on a subatomic scale. He used this technique to demonstrate that the laws of conservation of energy and of momentum were as valid for atoms as for billiard balls.

For devising this method of coincidence counting and for the research results obtained with it, Bothe received a share, along with Born [1084], of the 1954 Nobel Prize in physics.

Even a successful scientist is not always successful. In 1930 Bothe had reported that strange radiations were emerging from beryllium exposed to bombardment with alpha particles. He did not, however, interpret the meaning of his results properly. Neither did the Joliot-Curies [1204, 1227], who repeated the experiment, and it was left to Chadwick [1150] to discover the neutron.

In 1944 Bothe constructed Germany's first cyclotron, an instrument first devised by Lawrence [1241] in the previous decade.

[1147] **JEFFREYS,** Sir Harold
English astronomer
Born: Fatfield, Durham, April 22, 1891

Jeffreys studied at St. John's College at Cambridge and is best known for his collaboration with Jeans [1053] in working out the tidal hypothesis for the origin of the earth.

Where men such as Helmholtz [631] and Kelvin [652] had spoken of the earth's age in terms of tens of millions of years, Jeffreys was among the first to raise the ante to several billions.

He also demonstrated that the giant outer planets, Jupiter, Saturn, Uranus, and Neptune, have frigid surface temperatures, and are not, as some thought, still warm from interior heat.

He was knighted in 1953.

[1148] **NORTHROP,** John Howard
American biochemist
Born: Yonkers, New York,
July 5, 1891

Northrop was the son of a zoology instructor at Columbia University, one who was killed in a laboratory explosion. This did not prevent the son from following a scientific career. He obtained his Ph.D. in 1915 at Columbia and then joined the Rockefeller Institute for Medical Research (now Rockefeller University) working under Loeb [896].

After Sumner's [1120] discovery of crystalline urease, Northrop began the work that broke the back of the enzyme controversy. By 1930 he had crystallized pepsin, the protein-splitting digestive enzyme in gastric secretions. In 1932 he announced the crystallization of trypsin and in 1935 that of chymotrypsin, both protein-splitting digestive enzymes of the pancreatic secretions. He purified them and studied them carefully and since then dozens of enzymes have been crystallized by a number of researchers and all have proved to be proteins.

With the work of Sumner and Northrop, enzymes ceased altogether to be mysterious substances but came to possess a known chemical nature. Northrop shared with Sumner and with Stanley [1282] the 1946 Nobel Prize in chemistry.

[1149] **HUMASON,** Milton La Salle
American astronomer
Born: Dodge Center, Minnesota,
August 19, 1891
Died: Mendocino, California,
June 18, 1972

Humason entered astronomy by the back door, beginning his career as a janitor at the Mount Wilson Observatory.

Working with Hubble [1136] who recognized his talent, and continuing in the investigation of distant galaxies, Humason measured the speed of recession of about eight hundred galaxies, some as distant as 200 million light-years. In 1956 he and others, making use of new data, refined Hubble's law (that the speed of recession of a galaxy is proportional to distance) in order to allow a greater speed of recession in the far past. This would fit in with the "big bang" theory of Lemaître [1174] and Gamow [1278] and not with the continuous creation theory of Thomas Gold [1437].

Early in his career, in 1919, he engaged in a search for a planet beyond Neptune at the request of Pickering [885]. He failed through an odd and frustrating accident. It later turned out that the image of Pluto, the sought-for planet, had actually been obtained but had fallen on a small flaw in the photographic plate. The discovery had to wait eleven additional years for Tombaugh [1299].

[1150] **CHADWICK**, Sir James
English physicist
Born: Manchester, Lancashire, October 20, 1891
Died: Cambridge, July 24, 1974

Chadwick was educated at the University of Manchester and after graduating in 1911 worked under Ernest Rutherford [996], who was teaching there at the time. In 1913 he was awarded the same scholarship that had brought Rutherford from New Zealand to England eighteen years before. Chadwick allowed it to carry him to Germany, where he intended to work with Geiger [1082]. Unfortunately World War I broke out and he found himself an enemy alien interned for the duration.

In 1919 he was back in England, doing research at Cambridge. He worked with Rutherford again on the bombardment of elements with alpha particles. In 1920 he used the data gained in these experiments to calculate the positive charge on the nuclei of some atoms and his results fitted nicely into the theory of atomic numbers worked out by Moseley [1121].

During the 1920s two subatomic particles were known: the electron, discovered by J. J. Thomson [869], and the proton, discovered by Rutherford. The protons were all located in the nucleus, but if the nucleus contained enough protons to make up its mass, it would have too large a positive charge. Thus, the helium nucleus has a mass equal to four protons, but a charge equal only to two protons. It was thought, therefore, that the nucleus must contain a few electrons to neutralize some of the proton charge. The electrons would not affect the mass much since they were extremely light particles. It was even thought that the electrons would act as a "cement" to hold the protons together, for without the electrons the similarly charged protons would repel each other and fly apart. According to this viewpoint, the helium nucleus would contain four protons and two electrons for a mass of 4 and a positive net charge of 2.

There were theoretical reasons, however, for dissatisfaction with the theory of the proton-electron nucleus, and there were also theoretical reasons for suspecting that an uncharged particle might exist. In the 1920s Rutherford and Chadwick made several attempts to locate such a particle but failed. The difficulty was that uncharged particles did not ionize molecules of air and it was through this ionization that subatomic particles were most easily detected.

Between 1930 and 1932, however, some physicists, including Bothe [1146] and the Joliot-Curies [1204, 1227], noted that when certain light elements such as beryllium were exposed to alpha particles, some kind of radiation was formed which showed its presence by ejecting protons from paraffin. The proper interpretation was not made, unfortunately.

It was Chadwick in 1932 who repeated these experiments and showed that the best way of explaining the effects was to suppose that the alpha particles were knocking neutral particles out of the nuclei of the beryllium atom and that these neutral particles (each about as massive as a proton) were in turn knocking protons out of paraffin. In this way, the neutral particle (a neutron) was discovered.

The neutron proved to be by far the

most useful particle for initiating nuclear reactions and Chadwick received the 1935 Nobel Prize in physics. At that time it was yet to be discovered that among the reactions initiated by neutrons was uranium fission. This Hahn [1063] and Meitner [1060] were to show three years later.

With the discovery of the neutron it was realized that the nuclei of atoms did not have to contain any electrons. Instead, as Heisenberg [1245] soon suggested, the nucleus was made up of protons and neutrons. Thus, the helium nucleus contained two protons and two neutrons for a total mass of 4 and a total positive charge of 2. Different isotopes of a particular element all contained the same number of protons (and therefore the same number of electrons in the periphery—and it was on the electron number and arrangement that the chemical properties depended) but possessed different numbers of neutrons. Thus, of the two varieties of chlorine atoms, one contained 17 protons and 18 neutrons for a total mass of 35, while the other contained 17 protons and 20 neutrons for a total mass of 37. The two isotopes would be distinguished as chlorine-35 and chlorine-37. Thus, finally, the isotope theory of Soddy [1052] and Aston [1051], advanced two decades before, was rationalized.

The proton-neutron view of the nucleus met all the theoretical requirements but one: What kept all the positive-charged protons crowded together into the tiny nucleus? For an explanation of this, it was necessary to wait just a few years for the calculations of Yukawa [1323].

In 1935 Chadwick became professor of physics at the University of Liverpool. He remained out of Germany in World War II, fortunately, and served instead as head of Great Britain's phase of the atomic bomb project, spending some time in America. Indeed, he began work toward an atomic bomb shortly after Meitner announced the fact of fission and well before the United States was stirred to action.

He was knighted in 1945.

[1151] **NICHOLSON,** Seth Barnes
American astronomer
Born: Springfield, Illinois,
November 12, 1891
Died: Los Angeles, California,
July 2, 1963

Nicholson, the son of a geologist, attended Drake University in Des Moines, Iowa, then went on to take his Ph.D. in 1915 at the University of California. That year he joined the staff of Mount Wilson Observatory at Pasadena, remaining there until his retirement in 1957.

Nicholson carried out delicate measurements of astronomical temperatures. In 1927, for instance, he discovered that the surface temperature of the moon dropped nearly 200 Centigrade degrees during its eclipse by the shadow of the earth. Such a precipitous drop indicates that stored heat from deeper layers reaches the surface only very slowly and has given rise to the belief that the moon is covered with a layer of loose dust, the vacuum between the dust particles being an excellent heat insulator. He also measured the surface temperature of Mercury, finding a maximum of 410°C.

Nicholson joined the select company of Galileo [166] and Barnard [883] as the discoverer of satellites of Jupiter. He discovered one in 1914, while still a graduate student, two in 1938, and a fourth in 1951. The four discovered by Nicholson are small objects (probably captured asteroids) very distant from Jupiter. So are additional satellites discovered by others in the twentieth century. These brought the total number of Jupiter's moons to more than a dozen.

[1152] **BANTING,** Sir Frederick Grant
Canadian physiologist
Born: Alliston, Ontario,
November 14, 1891
Died: Near Musgrave Harbour,
Newfoundland, February 21,
1941

At the University of Toronto, Banting, the son of a farmer, began studies for the ministry, then transferred to the study of medicine. He obtained his medical degree in 1916 and served for the remainder of World War I as a medical officer overseas. He was wounded at Cambrai and in 1918 was awarded the Military Cross for heroism under fire.

After a short period of medical practice, Banting grew interested in diabetes mellitus, a disease in which the chief biochemical symptom was the presence of abnormally high glucose levels in the blood and the eventual appearance of glucose in the urine. At the time, this disease meant slow, but sure, death.

A generation earlier, suspicion had arisen that the pancreas was somehow connected with it, for removal of the pancreas in experimental animals brought about a diabetes-like condition. Once the hormone concept had been propounded by Starling [954] and Bayliss [902], it seemed logical to suppose that the pancreas produced a hormone that controlled the manner in which the body metabolized its glucose molecules. An insufficient supply of this hormone caused glucose to pile up and led to diabetes.

Of course, the chief function of the pancreas was to produce a digestive juice. Nevertheless, there were numerous little patches of cells within the pancreas (called Islets of Langerhans after the man who had first described them a half century earlier) which differed from the rest of the gland. These might well be the source of the hormone. The hormone had even received a name, insulin, from the Latin word for "island."

There had already been successful isolations of hormones—notably Kendall's [1105] isolation of thyroxine, the thyroid hormone—so it occurred to a number of people to attempt to isolate insulin from the pancreas. If that could be done, the isolated hormone might be administered to human diabetics, who could then survive the disease indefinitely while medication continued. All attempts to isolate insulin failed, however, for the digestive enzymes in the pancreas broke up the insulin molecule (a protein) as soon as the pancreas was mashed up.

In 1920 Banting read an article describing how tying off the duct through which the pancreas delivered its digestive

secretion into the intestines caused the pancreatic tissue to degenerate. This gave Banting the key idea. The Islets of Langerhans, not being involved in producing the digestive secretions, should not degenerate. If the rest of the pancreas did, then there would be no digestive enzymes left to break up the insulin, which would still be present in full.

In 1921 he went to the University of Toronto with his idea, and, after some trouble, persuaded a professor of physiology, John J. R. Macleod, to grant him some laboratory space and assign him a co-worker, who turned out to be Best [1218]. After that, Macleod went off on a summer vacation.

Together, Banting and Best tied off the pancreatic ducts in a number of dogs and waited seven weeks. The pancreases had by then become shriveled and useless to the dogs as digestive organs but the Islets of Langerhans were still in fine shape. From such pancreases, they extracted a solution that could then be supplied to the dogs who had been made diabetic by the removal of the pancreas. The extract quickly stopped the symptoms of diabetes. Banting and Best called the hormone "isletin" but Macleod, who now decided to take an interest, insisted on the older "insulin."

The experiments were completed in 1922, and in 1923 Banting and Macleod were awarded the Nobel Prize in medicine and physiology, the first Nobel Prize awarded to Canadians. Millions of diabetics have, since that time, been able to live reasonably normal lives. Among these were Eastman [852] and Minot [1103], as well as George V of England and the writer H. G. Wells.

Banting was furious, however, that the prize had been shared with Macleod, who had merely given them laboratory space, and not with Best, who had borne his fair share of the labor. It was only with difficulty that Banting was persuaded to accept the prize and when he did so, he gave half his share of the money to Best.

Banting was voted an annuity by the Canadian Parliament in 1923 and the Banting Research Foundation was established for him. A Banting-Best professorship was established at the University of Toronto and in 1934 Banting was knighted.

With the coming of World War II, Banting was once again involved in medical war work. He served as a major in the Canadian Army, but was less fortunate this time. He died in a plane crash over Newfoundland.

[1153] **STURTEVANT,** Alfred Henry
  (stur'tuh-vant)
  American geneticist
  Born: Jacksonville, Illinois,
  November 21, 1891
  Died: Pasadena, California,
  April 5, 1970

Sturtevant was the son of a mathematics teacher turned farmer. The family moved to southern Alabama in 1899. In 1908 Sturtevant entered Columbia University, where it was possible for him to live with his older brother, who was teaching Latin and Greek at Barnard. Sturtevant's brother encouraged the young man to study genetics, and this he did to such effect that in 1910 he was able to work in T. H. Morgan's [957] laboratory. He obtained his Ph.D. in genetics under Morgan in 1914, and for some years worked with Muller [1145]. In 1928 he obtained a professorship in genetics at the California Institute of Technology, remaining there till his death.

Sturtevant's best-known advance was the principle of mapping the position of genes on a chromosome by the frequency with which crossing over separated them. The greater the frequency the farther apart the genes. He published details of the technique in 1913. The four chromosomes of the fruit fly were soon mapped in detail in this way. Sturtevant presented a map of the fourth and smallest of the chromosomes in 1951.

[1154] **MURPHY,** William Parry
  American physician
  Born: Stoughton, Wisconsin,
  February 6, 1892

Murphy studied at the University of Oregon, graduating in 1914. After a spell of teaching, he went on to medicine and obtained his medical degree from Harvard University in 1920.

At Peter Bent Brigham Hospital he worked with Minot [1103] in developing the liver treatment for pernicious anemia and shared with him and Whipple [1059] the 1934 Nobel Prize in medicine and physiology.

[1155] **WATSON-WATT,** Sir Robert
  Alexander
  Scottish physicist
  Born: Brechin, Angus, April 13,
  1892
  Died: Inverness, December 6,
  1973

Watson-Watt was educated at the University of St. Andrews and taught there from 1912 to 1921. Even then he was interested in the reflection of radio waves.

That they were reflected was known, for it was their reflection from ionized layers in the upper atmosphere that made long-distance broadcasting possible, as Kennelly [916] and Heaviside [806] had made clear. The reflection was sharper as wavelength decreased, and in 1919 Watson-Watt had already taken out a patent in connection with radiolocation by means of shortwave radio.

Though the technology is rather complicated, the principle is simple. Radio waves travel at an accurately known velocity, the velocity of light. A pulse of very shortwave radio waves (now called microwaves) can be sent out and, upon striking an obstacle and being reflected, will return to the sender. The difference in time between emission and reception can then be converted into distance; and, of course, the direction from which the reflection is obtained is the direction of the obstacle.

By 1935 Watson-Watt, as a result of continued experiments, had patented improvements that made it possible to follow an airplane by the radio-wave reflections it sent back. The system was called "radio detection and ranging" (to "get a range" on an object is to determine its distance) and this was abbreviated to "ra. d. a. r." or "radar."

Research was continued in secrecy and by the fall of 1938, the time of the Munich surrender to Hitler, radar stations were in operation. By the time of the Battle of Britain in 1940, radar made it possible for the British to detect oncoming German planes as easily by night as by day, and in all weathers, including fog. The German planes found themselves consistently outguessed and, with all due respect to the valor of the British airmen, it was radar that won the Battle of Britain.

The principles of radar had been worked out in Germany too, during the 1930s. However, it is reported that Hitler and Goering decided that it was fit only for defensive warfare and that since the German armed forces would never have to stand on the defensive, radar might be ignored. By the time they learned better, it was fortunately too late.

American electrical engineers had been working on radar systems as early as 1931, but Watson-Watt's labors and the wartime pressures had given Great Britain the lead. In 1941 Watson-Watt visited the United States and helped the Americans complete the job and set up radar systems of their own. In 1942 he was knighted. American radar at Pearl Harbor in 1941 detected the oncoming Japanese planes, but the warning was tragically ignored.

Radar, of course, has developed myriad peacetime uses since World War II (including even its use in the detection of storms and the mapping of the surface of Venus).

[1156] **THOMSON,** Sir George Paget
English physicist
Born: Cambridge, May 3, 1892
Died: Cambridge, September 10, 1975

Thomson, the only son of J. J. Thomson [869], was educated at Cambridge,

graduating in 1913 and beginning research under his father. World War I came, and after time spent in the army and in war work on aerodynamics, he returned to physics, doing some work under Millikan [969] in the United States, and was appointed professor of natural philosophy at the University of Aberdeen in 1922.

In 1927, very shortly after Davisson [1078] had published his work, Thomson published his own independent observation on electron diffraction. He achieved his results by passing fast electrons through metallic foil (using thin gold foil of a type developed by Frédéric Joliot-Curie [1227] in 1927), much as Laue [1068] had passed X rays through a crystal. Thomson obtained the same sort of diffraction pattern with electrons that Laue had obtained with X rays and that was strictly in accordance with De Broglie's [1157] theory. Consequently he shared the 1937 Nobel Prize in physics with Davisson.

In 1930, he accepted a post at the University of London. During World War II, Thomson was chairman of the British Commission on Atomic Energy. In 1943 he was knighted, and in 1952 he became master of Corpus Christi College, Cambridge.

[1157] **DE BROGLIE,** Louis Victor
Pierre Raymond, Prince (broh′-glee′)
French physicist
Born: Dieppe, Seine-Marne, August 15, 1892

De Broglie was born into a noble French family, his ancestors having served the French kings in war and diplomacy as far back as the time of Louis XIV. His great-great-grandfather died on the guillotine during the French Revolution.

De Broglie was educated at the Sorbonne. It was only after obtaining his degree in history that he entered the French army in World War I, became involved in radio communication there, and decided to turn to science. (During the war, his role as a radio engineer had kept him stationed in the Eiffel Tower.)

He went back to his education with the new aim in mind and in 1924 obtained his doctorate with a thesis dealing with the quantum theory. It was in the year before that, however, that, inspired by the need for a symmetric inverse of the Compton [1159] effect—if waves were particles, why might not particles be waves?—he did his great work.

By a rather simple combination of the formula of Einstein [1064], which related mass and energy, and that of Planck [887], which related frequency and energy, he showed in 1923 that with any particle there ought to be an associated wave. The wavelength of such waves (which are not electromagnetic in nature, and have since come to be called matter waves) is inversely related to the momentum of the particle, which in turn depends on its mass and velocity.

The wavelength is so small for any sizable body such as a baseball, or even a proton, that it would seem hopeless to try to detect it. For a body as light as an electron, however, the wavelength ought to be as large in magnitude as some of the X-ray wavelengths and that should be detectable. As a matter of fact, Davisson [1078] and G. P. Thomson [1156] managed to detect it in 1927.

This particle-wave dualism for the electron matched the wave-particle dualism for the photon as worked out by Compton. Einstein's contention that matter was but a form of energy and that the two were interconvertible made more common sense when it could be seen that particles were always wavelike, and waves always particle-like. Mass and energy then came to seem much the same in structure after all and Einstein's view was no longer astonishing.

Schrödinger [1117] used the new wave concept of the electron to build a picture of atom structure in which the jumping electron particles of Bohr [1101] gave way to standing electron waves. Similarly, the static electrons of Lewis [1037] gave way, in connection with chemical bond formation, to the reasonating electron waves of Pauling [1236].

De Broglie was consequently awarded the 1929 Nobel Prize in physics. In 1945 he became technical adviser to the French atomic energy commission.

[1158] **APPLETON,** Sir Edward Victor
English physicist
Born: Bradford, Yorkshire,
September 6, 1892
Died: Edinburgh, Scotland,
April 21, 1965

Appleton, the son of a millworker, had an early ambition to become a professional cricket player but won a scholarship which took him to Cambridge and to science. At Cambridge, Appleton studied under J. J. Thomson [869] and Ernest Rutherford [996], which in itself was a good start for a bright young man. Appleton served as a radio officer during World War I, which interrupted his studies but introduced him to the problem of the fading of radio signals.

After the war he looked into the problem in earnest and was helped by the fact that by 1922 commercial broadcasting had started in Great Britain, so there were plenty of powerful signals to play with. Appleton found that fading took place at night and he wondered if this might not be due to reflection from the upper atmosphere, a reflection that took place chiefly at night. If so, such reflection might set up interference since the same radio beam would reach a particular spot by two different routes: one, direct, and two, by bouncing off the layers of charged particles postulated by Kennelly [916] and Heaviside [806] twenty years earlier. If so, the two beams might arrive out of phase, with partial cancellation of the wave.

Appleton began to experiment by using a transmitter and receiver that were about seventy miles apart and by altering the wavelength of the signal and noting when it was in phase so that the signal was strengthened and when out of phase so that it was weakened. From this he could calculate the minimum height of reflection. In 1924 he found that the Kennelly-Heaviside layer was some sixty miles high.

At dawn the Kennelly-Heaviside layer broke up and the phenomenon of fading was no longer particularly noticeable. However, there was still reflection from charged layers higher up. By 1926 he had determined these to be about one hundred and fifty miles high and they are sometimes called the Appleton layers.

Further experiments over the next few years detailed the manner in which these charged layers altered in behavior with the position of the sun and with the changes in the sunspot cycle. These studies initiated the modern investigation of the layer of air above Teisserenc de Bort's [861] stratosphere. Because of the high content of ions, the air above the stratosphere is often called the ionosphere, a name first suggested by Watson-Watt [1155]. The ionosphere became a prime object of study when rocket research became practical a generation after Appleton's discovery.

By 1924 Appleton had become a professor of physics at the University of London, and in 1936 he was appointed professor of natural philosophy at Cambridge, succeeding Wilson [979]. During World War II he was in charge of British atomic bomb research, and in 1941 he was knighted.

In 1944 he became vice-chancellor of Edinburgh University, but the climax of his career came in 1947 when he was awarded the Nobel Prize in physics.

[1159] **COMPTON,** Arthur Holly
American physicist
Born: Wooster, Ohio, September 10, 1892
Died: Berkeley, California, March 15, 1962

Compton, the son of a Presbyterian minister, graduated from Wooster College (where his father was dean) in 1913 and obtained his Ph.D. at Princeton University in 1916, taught physics at the University of Minnesota for a year, then served an additional two years as engineer for the Westinghouse Lamp Company in Pittsburgh. In 1919 he spent a year at Cambridge University, studying under Ernest Rutherford [996]. When he returned to the United States the next year, it was to become the head of the physics department at Washington University in St. Louis, Missouri. In 1923 he moved on to the University of Chicago.

Compton carried further the researches of Barkla [1049] involving the scattering of X rays by matter. Barkla had been able to ascertain the nature of the scattered X rays only by very rough measurements of absorbability. Compton, however, had the technique of the Braggs [922, 1141] at his disposal and was able to measure the wavelengths of the scattered X rays accurately.

When he did this, he found in 1923 that some of the X rays had, in scattering, lengthened their wavelength. (This was named the Compton effect in his honor.) A few years later, Raman [1130] was to make a similar discovery in connection with visible light.

Compton was able to account for this by presuming that a photon of light struck an electron, which recoiled, subtracting some energy from the photon and therefore increasing its wavelength. This made it seem that a photon acted as a particle and it was Compton who suggested the name "photon" for the light quantum in its particle aspect. Thus, after more than a century, the particulate nature of light, as evolved by Newton [231], was revived. However, the particulate nature was rendered much more sophisticated by the theories of Planck [887] and Einstein [1064] and it did not obliterate the wave phenomena established by such nineteenth-century physicists as Young [402], Fresnel [455], and Maxwell [692].

What it amounted to was that Compton brought to fulfillment the view that electromagnetic radiation had both a wave aspect and a particle aspect, and that the aspect that was most evident depended on how the radiation was tested. De Broglie [1157] was at the same time showing that this held true also for ordinary particles such as electrons. This famous duality impresses some people as a "paradox" that implies the universe is too mysterious to be penetrated by reason. Actually, it is perfectly understandable, for instance, that a man should have, let us say, two different aspects, one as a husband and one as a father, and that each aspect becomes prominent according to circumstances. It is no more paradoxical or mysterious that photons or electrons should have more than one aspect.

For his discovery of the Compton effect, Compton received the Nobel Prize in physics in 1927, sharing it with Wilson [979].

About 1930 Compton turned his attention to cosmic rays. Millikan [969], who was the outstanding man in the field at the time, believed that cosmic rays were electromagnetic in nature, like gamma rays but even more energetic. If this were so, then cosmic rays ought to remain unaffected by the earth's magnetic field and ought to strike all portions of the earth's surface about equally. If, on the other hand, cosmic rays consisted of charged particles as Bothe [1146] maintained, for instance, then they ought to curve in the earth's magnetic field, and more ought to be detected in polar regions as one approached the magnetic poles, and less in tropic regions.

Compton became a world traveler for this research, conducting a series of painstaking measurements, which showed that a "latitude effect" did exist. Cosmic rays were indeed affected by the magnetic field so that they must consist, at least in part, of charged particles. Despite Millikan's continued adherence to the electromagnetic view, further research has consistently strengthened the particle view until now there is no reasonable doubt of it. (Compton, so often linked with Millikan in any discussion of cosmic ray research, was like Millikan in being an outspokenly religious scientist.)

During World War II, Compton was one of the top scientists in the Manhattan Project that developed the atomic bomb, and he remained on the best terms with the military. He directed the research on methods of producing plutonium and, ultimately, approved the use of the atomic bomb over Japan.

After the war, he returned to Washington University as chancellor in 1945, serving till 1953.

[1160] **HALDANE,** John Burdon
Sanderson
English-Indian geneticist
Born: Oxford, England, November 5, 1892
Died: Bhubaneswar, India, December 1, 1964

Haldane, the son of a noted physiologist, entered science as an assistant to his father, at the tender age of eight. He studied the humanities at Oxford, but his heart remained in science. He served in World War I, the horrors of which disillusioned him with conventional pieties and made of him an outspoken atheist.

After the war, he worked as a biochemist at Cambridge. He was particularly interested in genetics and in 1932 was the first to estimate the rate of mutation of a human gene.

He became best known for his experiments on himself designed (sometimes in horrendous fashion) to study the behavior of the human body under stress. For instance in 1942 he and a companion spent forty-eight hours in a tiny submarine to check whether a particular system for purifying the air supply would work. He also subjected himself to extremes of temperature, carbon dioxide concentration, and so on.

In the 1930s he became a Communist, was quite outspoken about it and even served as editor of the London *Daily Worker* for a time and became a prolific writer of science popularization. He was active in aiding refugees from Nazi Germany and helped Chain [1306] get a position with Florey [1213]. He left the Communist Party (though remaining a Marxist) as a result of his disillusionment with the Lysenko [1214] ascendancy in the Soviet Union, something that was bound to disturb any reasonable geneticist.

His dissatisfaction with British policy, however, remained strong enough to force him into self-exile to India in 1957.

As a further gesture of turning his back on his homeland, he accepted Indian citizenship.

[1161] **LARSON,** John Augustus
Canadian-American psychiatrist
Born: Shelbourne, Nova Scotia,
December 11, 1892

Larson graduated from Boston University in 1914 and obtained his Ph.D. at the University of California in 1920. His interest in criminology led him to study medicine and he obtained his M.D. from Rush Medical College in 1928. He served as psychiatrist at prisons, hospitals, and health centers.

It occurred to him that lying involves an effort that telling the truth does not, and that the fear of being caught lying ought to elicit an involuntary flow of adrenaline that could be detectable by the changes in body properties it brought about.

He therefore devised a machine, the "polygraph," which could simultaneously and continuously record the pulse rate, breathing rate, blood pressure, and perspiration secretion. Such changes would, or should, be greater when a lie was told than when the truth was told. The instrument was promptly named a "lie detector." It is not infallible, but it has proved useful.

[1162] **DART,** Raymond Arthur
Australian-South African
anthropologist and surgeon
Born: Brisbane, Australia,
February 4, 1893

Dart was educated in Australia and got his medical degree in 1917. He went to South Africa in 1923 and remained there afterward. His professional life was largely that of surgeon and anatomist, but his fame arose from a nonmedical discovery.

In 1924 a small skull that, except for its size, looked human, was discovered in a limestone quarry in South Africa. Dart was then working at the University of Witwatersrand in Johannesburg and the skull was taken to him. He recognized it as a primitive precursor of *Homo sapiens* and called it *Australopithecus* ("southern ape").

The discovery was a controversial one and Dart and others, such as Broom [959], were forced to start a systematic hunt for similar fossil relics. They found a number, enough to prove that the first skull was no mistake. The australopithecines are now a well-established part of the developing hominids, which include, as non-African specimens, the "Java Man" discovered by Dubois [884] and the "Peking Man" of East Asia.

The findings of still earlier fossil relics of prehuman creatures in eastern Africa make it appear fairly certain that man's ancestors developed from the primitive primate stock in that continent.

[1163] **BAADE,** Walter (bah'duh)
German-American astronomer
Born: Schröttinghausen,
Westphalia, March 24, 1893
Died: Göttingen, June 25, 1960

Baade, the son of a teacher, was intended for the Protestant ministry, but in high school, he decided he wanted to be an astronomer. He obtained his Ph.D. at Göttingen in 1919, a hip ailment having exempted him from service in World War I. After eleven years on the staff at the University of Hamburg, Baade went to the United States in 1931. It was there at Mount Wilson and Palomar observatories that he made his great contributions to astronomy.

In 1920, to be sure, he had made the interesting discovery of the asteroid Hidalgo, whose orbit carries it as far out as the orbit of Saturn. It was then, and is now, the farthest known asteroid. By an odd coincidence, Baade in 1948 discovered the asteroid Icarus, the orbit of which carries it to within 18 million miles of the sun, closer than Mercury and therefore the innermost known asteroid. Obviously, as Kuiper [1297] and Nicholson [1151] were also to show, discoveries remain to be made within the solar system, even though Baade referred to the asteroids, with a kind of good-natured contempt, as "vermin in the sky."

Outside the solar system, Kuiper in 1941 found a patch of nebulosity in about the position of Kepler's [169] nova.

It was in 1942, however, that Baade made his most notable contribution. As an "enemy alien," he could not engage in war work, so he was forced to continue in pure science. He took advantage of the wartime blackout of Los Angeles, which cleared the night sky at Mount Wilson, to make a detailed study of the Andromeda galaxy with the 100-inch telescope. He was able to resolve some of the stars in the inner regions of the galaxy for the first time. Before then, Hubble's [1136] efforts at resolution had only obtained a view of the blue-white giants of the spiral arms. Baade noted that the brightest stars of the galactic interior were not blue-white, but reddish.

To Baade it seemed that there were two sets of stars of different structure and history. He called the bluish stars of the galactic outskirts Population I and the reddish stars of the interior Population II. Population I stars are relatively young and are built up out of the dusty surroundings of the spiral arms. Population II stars are old and are built up in the dust-free regions of the nuclei.

When the 200-inch telescope came into operation after World War II, Baade continued his investigations and located over three hundred Cepheids in the Andromeda galaxy. He found that Cepheid variable stars occurred both among the Population I and Population II stars, but that the period-luminosity curve worked out for them by Shapley [1102] and Leavitt [975] applied only to Population II. It was Population II that occurred in globular clusters and in the Magellanic clouds so that the distances worked out within our own galaxy, and as far as the Magellanic clouds outside the galaxy, were all right.

However, the distances of the outer galaxies, as worked out by Hubble, were based on Population I Cepheids, and for these, Baade in 1952 worked out a new period-luminosity curve in which

the stars for a given period proved much more luminous. This meant that the Andromeda galaxy must be far more distant than Hubble had thought if the blue-white Cepheids in its spiral arms were as dim as they seemed. The Andromeda galaxy was not 800,000 light-years distant, then, but over 2 million light-years away. The entire universe increased its volume twentyfold.

Now if time is imagined as running backward, it would take the galaxies (moving at their observed velocities) 5 or 6 billion years to come together into contact, rather than the 2 billion years that would have been required in Hubble's smaller universe. This gave the geologists, who knew the earth's solid crust to be better than 3 billion years old, ample time for earth's evolution. (Actually, the universe shows signs of being far older than 6 billion years, though our own solar system is almost certainly no older. The present figure most often accepted for the age of the universe is 15 billion years.)

Baade's discovery also meant that the Andromeda galaxy and the other galaxies, being so much farther than had been thought, must also be that much larger in order to appear as bright as they seem from the earth. Our own galaxy was no longer an outsize example, much larger than all others, but was of average size. It was smaller than the Andromeda galaxy, for instance. As Copernicus [127] had dethroned the earth and Shapley the sun, so Baade dethroned our galaxy from its position of preeminence.

With the scale of the universe growing ever grander, attention began to switch from individual galaxies to groups and clusters of galaxies, a field of research in which Zwicky [1209] achieved prominence.

The construction of radio telescopes, following Jansky's [1295] initial discovery of radio radiation from outer space, offered a new tool for the investigation of great distances. One of the strongest radio sources in the sky, for instance, could be localized to no object within the range of the 200-inch telescope. In 1959 Baade found a distorted galaxy in the constellation Cygnus that proved to be the source.

The radio waves emitted by the galaxy could be distinctly detected at a distance of 260 million light-years. It was seen that with radio telescopes of practical size, distances could be penetrated that could not be reached by any optical telescope of practical size. The age of the radio exploration of the universe began in earnest.

In 1958 Baade returned to Göttingen in Germany, and there the enlarger of the universe died.

[1164] **UREY,** Harold Clayton
American chemist
Born: Walkerton, Indiana, April 29, 1893
Died: La Jolla, California, January 5, 1981

Urey was the son of a schoolteacher who was also a lay minister. His father died in 1899. His mother remarried and his stepfather was also a clergyman.

He studied at Montana State University, majoring in zoology and graduating in 1917. Work during World War I turned his attention to high explosives and through that to chemistry generally. He obtained a scholarship and went on to a Ph.D. in 1923 at the University of California, where he worked with Lewis [1037]. In 1923 he traveled to Copenhagen and spent a year in Bohr's [1101] laboratory. After joining the Johns Hopkins faculty in 1924, he went on to Columbia University in 1929.

In 1931 Urey tackled the problem of heavy hydrogen. There had been suggestions that there might be a form of hydrogen with atoms twice the mass of the ordinary hydrogen atom, almost from the moment that Soddy [1052] had advanced the isotope theory. Accurate measurements of the mass of the hydrogen atom, however, revealed that any heavy isotope, if present at all, could only be there in very small concentration.

It seemed to Urey that the vapor pressure of ordinary hydrogen ought to be greater than heavy hydrogen's. That meant that if a quantity of liquid hydrogen was vaporized, the ordinary hydrogen atoms would be more easily removed and the last bit of liquid would be richer in heavy hydrogen than the original had been. Atoms of heavy hydrogen, with a more massive atomic nucleus, would have lone electrons with energy levels slightly different from those in ordinary hydrogen atoms. This would mean that, if heated, their spectral lines would be at wavelengths slightly different from those of ordinary hydrogen. Perhaps through the evaporation of liquid hydrogen, the concentration of the heavy form might be increased to the point where it could be detected spectroscopically.

Urey consequently evaporated four liters of liquid hydrogen by slow stages down to a single cubic centimeter and then investigated the spectrum of that final bit. Sure enough, the ordinary absorption lines of hydrogen were accompanied by faint lines that were in exactly the positions predicted for heavy hydrogen. The name deuterium was given to the heavy isotope.

Once the existence of the isotope was proved, it did not take long for water containing high proportions of deuterium (so-called heavy water) to be prepared, notably through the work of Lewis. Biochemically significant compounds could then be prepared with deuterium in place of hydrogen and, thanks to the pioneer work of Schoenheimer [1211], the use of isotopic tracers in working out the intricate pattern of chemical reactions within living tissue was initiated.

Urey was awarded the 1934 Nobel Prize in chemistry for his feat. Since he refused to travel to Sweden that year because his wife was pregnant, he delivered his Nobel lecture the next year.

Urey began to investigate methods of separating isotopes of other elements and was the first to put to use the fact that heavier isotopes tended to react a bit more slowly than their lighter twins. By taking advantage of differences in such reactivity and by devising procedures whereby these differences could constantly be built up, he was able in the late 1930s to prepare high concentrations of such isotopes as carbon-13 and nitrogen-15, which are found in natural carbon and nitrogen but ordinarily only in small concentration. Schoenheimer put these to profitable use in biochemical research also.

Experience with isotope separation turned out to be useful indeed in the early 1940s when the United States' development of the atomic bomb required methods of separating the rare isotope uranium-235 (needed for the bomb) from the much more common uranium-238. After World War II, hydrogen-2 (Urey's own deuterium) turned out to be of key importance to the development of the even more horrible hydrogen bomb.

In 1945 Urey joined the faculty of the University of Chicago and in 1952 that of the University of California. Urey was one of the scientists most concerned with the developing danger to mankind represented by the nuclear weapons that owe so much to his own isotopic research. In the postwar years he busied himself with geophysics, a study that, it would seem, could not be turned to destructive purposes.

Here, too, his interest in isotopes proved useful. Isotopes of a given element differ in speed of reactivity, the more massive being somewhat slower to react. This difference changes in extent, slightly, with change in temperature. Thus, the proportion of oxygen isotopes in a seashell depends on the temperature of the ocean at the time the shell was formed. By working with fossil shells, Urey and his co-workers were able to prepare a history of changing ocean temperatures over long geologic periods.

Urey also worked out detail theories of planetary formation based on situations such as those postulated by Weizsäcker [1376], in which the planets are viewed as having been built up by accumulating smaller fragments. Urey was one of those who maintained that the planets were formed by processes that retained comparatively low temperatures throughout and, like Otto Struve [1203], suspected life to be common in the universe.

Urey also believed that the early atmosphere of the earth was a reducing one, rich in hydogen, ammonia, and methane —something like the atmosphere of the giant outer planets today. It was in his laboratories in 1953 that Miller [1490] conducted his startling experiments relating to the possible origin of life under such conditions.

Urey took firm stands on political and social issues. He was against war, against nuclear power, and denounced Senator Joseph McCarthy at a time when it was rather dangerous to do so.

[1165] **SIMON,** Sir Franz Eugen Francis
German-British physicist
Born: Berlin, Germany, July 2, 1893
Died: Oxford, England, October 31, 1956

Simon was born into a well-to-do family. He served in the German army for four years during World War I, reaching the rank of lieutenant in the field artillery. He then studied at the University of Berlin and attained his Ph.D. in physics in 1921 under Nernst [936]. He earned a professorial appointment at Berlin in 1927 and went on to Breslau in 1931.

He was lecturing at Berkeley as a visiting professor when Hitler came to power. Simon knew better than to return to Germany under those conditions and went to Oxford instead, where he remained until his death.

Simon was interested in low-temperature physics. The method used to get liquid gases, right down to Kamerlingh Onnes's [843] liquefaction of helium, was by the use of the Joule-Thomson effect, but that had reached as low a temperature as was practical.

During his stay at Oxford, Simon worked out methods for withdrawing heat by lining up paramagnetic molecules at very low temperatures and then allowing their orientation to randomize, abstracting further heat from their surroundings and lowering the temperature still farther. He went on to do the same with nuclear spins, a harder task but one that reached still farther toward the unattainable absolute zero. Just before Simon's death, his group reached a low of

20 millionths of a degree above absolute zero.

Simon used his low temperatures to demonstrate more firmly than ever before the validity of the third law of thermodynamics, which had been advanced by his old teacher, Nernst.

Simon was knighted in 1955.

[1166] **NODDACK,** Walter Karl Friedrich
German chemist
Born: Berlin, August 17, 1893
Died: Bamberg, Bavaria, December 7, 1960

Noddack was educated at the University of Berlin, and he obtained his Ph.D. under Nernst [936] in 1920.

In 1922 he began a long search for two elements (atomic numbers 43 and 75) that still remained undiscovered. Associated with him in this endeavor were Ida Tacke [1187] and Otto Berg.

Three years of careful fractionation of ores in which the missing elements might be found finally resulted in the detection of element 75 in May 1925. It was named rhenium after the Rhine River. It was the last stable element to be discovered. All elements discovered since, including element 43 (and, it is believed, all elements likely to be discovered in the future), are radioactive.

Noddack, Tacke, and Berg also announced the discovery of element 43 and called it "masurium" after a region in East Prussia. This, however, turned out to be an error.

In 1926 Noddack and Tacke married and together they continued research on rhenium.

[1167] **SZENT-GYÖRGYI,** Albert
(shent-jee-awr'jee)
Hungarian-American biochemist
Born: Budapest, Hungary, September 16, 1893

Szent-Györgyi's full name is Albert Szent-Györgyi von Nagyrapolt, and the odd Hungarian spelling of the middle portion should not be allowed to obscure the fact that in English it would be simply Saint George. He was born into a family of noted scientists but was himself an indifferent student at first. He was receiving top honors by the time he finished high school, however.

Szent-Györgyi spent the early years of World War I in the Austrian army, was decorated for bravery, but seeing no sense to the war, deliberately wounded himself and returned to his studies. He obtained his medical degree in 1917 at the University of Budapest.

The Austrian defeat in 1918 impoverished the family and Szent-Györgyi followed the call of further education abroad. During the 1920s he studied under Michaelis [1033] in Berlin and under Kendall [1105] at the Mayo Clinic in the United States. He obtained his Ph.D. at Cambridge University in 1927 and in 1932 he returned to Hungary as president of the University of Szeged.

In 1928, while still at Cambridge and working in Hopkins's [912] laboratory, Szent-Györgyi isolated a substance from adrenal glands (whose function he was investigating). This substance easily lost and regained hydrogen atoms and was therefore a hydrogen carrier. Since its molecule seemed to possess six carbon atoms, Szent-Györgyi named it hexuronic acid ("hex" is "six" in Greek). He also obtained it from cabbages and oranges, both rich in vitamin C. This caused him to suspect it might actually be the vitamin. In this, however, he was anticipated, for in 1932 King [1193] reported the isolation of vitamin C and found it to be identical to hexuronic acid. He reported this only two weeks before Szent-Györgyi could make a similar announcement.

The 1930s were the golden decade of vitamin research, with men like Williams [1104] performing prodigies, and Szent-Györgyi doing his bit too. He studied how ascorbic acid was used in the body and noted a rich source for it in Hungarian paprika (the town of Szeged, where he worked, was the center of the paprika-growing area). In 1936 he isolated certain flavones, which had the property of altering the permeability of capillaries—the ease, that is, with which substances could pass through the capillary walls. Whether these are actually vitamins is doubtful but, for a time at least, they were referred to as vitamin P.

Szent-Györgyi also studied the oxygen uptake of minced muscle tissue, using Warburg's [1089] methods. If the system was untouched, the rate of oxygen uptake would die down, as some substance within the tissue was used up. Szent-Györgyi tried adding substances that might conceivably be located on the pathway of the overall chemical change involved in oxygen uptake, the change from lactic acid to carbon dioxide. In 1935 he found that any of four closely related four-carbon compounds—malic acid, succinic acid, fumaric acid, and oxaloacetic acid—would serve to restore activity. Since each would do it alone, it followed that the body could interconvert them and that perhaps all four were on the pathway. Krebs [1231] continued this line of research and used Szent-Györgyi's discovery, plus his own added material, to work out the Krebs cycle.

For all this work, particularly that on vitamin C, Szent-Györgyi was awarded the 1937 Nobel Prize in medicine and physiology.

He kept on working thereafter. He began to study the chemical mechanisms of contracting muscle. He found the muscle protein to consist of two loosely bound portions, actin and myosin, and named the union "actomyosin." He worked out mechanisms whereby adenosine triphosphate (ATP), a compound possessing Lipmann's [1221] high-energy phosphate bonds, initiated changes leading to muscle contraction. His views are not conclusive, however, and the subject is still wide open.

During World War II, Szent-Györgyi was active in the anti-Nazi underground, and incurred considerable danger, from which he was saved only by Swedish (fortunately un-neutral) aid. After the war, however, Hungary was occupied by Soviet forces and Szent-Györgyi felt he had earned some repose. In 1947 he emigrated to the United States and became an American citizen in 1955. In the United States he joined the staff of

the Marine Biological Laboratories at Woods Hole, Massachusetts.

In the 1960s his attention turned to the thymus gland, which in 1961 had been shown to be involved in the initial establishment of the body's immunological capabilities. Szent-Györgyi isolated several substances from thymus that seem to have some controlling effect on growth. His old age has seen no lessening in his fiery concern for humanity as he spoke out loudly and forcefully against the madness of war.

[1168] ÖPIK, Ernst Julius
Soviet astronomer
Born: Port Kunda, Estonia (then part of Russia, now part of the USSR), October 23, 1893

In 1916 Öpik joined the staff of the Tashkent Observatory in Uzbekistan and in 1924 he moved to the Astronomical Observatory in Tartu Estonia. After World War II he worked in Germany, in Ireland, and at the University of Maryland in the United States.

His work has been primarily with meteors and in the early 1920s he worked out the theory of their entry into the atmosphere and of the effect upon them of atmospheric resistance and atmospheric heating. It is an example of how difficult it is to keep ivory-tower theory from becoming of practical use, when we consider that these considerations of "ablation"—the effect of heating on a heat-resisting substance and the manner in which it is peeled away as a result—has proved to be of great importance in connection with the design of nose cones and heat shields for ballistic missiles and rocket ships.

[1169] DOISY, Edward Adelbert
American biochemist
Born: Hume, Illinois, November 13, 1893

Doisy was educated at the University of Illinois, graduating in 1914. He obtained his doctorate at Harvard University in 1920 after a two-year delay owing to service in World War I. He joined the faculty of the St. Louis University School of Medicine in 1923 and remained there during his professional life. The university's department of biochemistry was named in his honor in 1955.

In 1929 he was the first to prepare estrone, a female sex hormone, in crystalline form. In 1939 the group he headed worked out the chemical constitution of two varieties of vitamin K and for this he shared with Dam [1177] the 1943 Nobel Prize in medicine and physiology.

[1170] BOSE, Satyendranath
Indian physicist
Born: Calcutta, January 1, 1894
Died: Calcutta, February 4, 1974

Bose, the son of an accountant, was educated at Presidency College in Calcutta, where Jagadischandra Bose [893] (no relation) was among his teachers. He obtained his master's degree in mathematics in 1915 at the top of his class.

A paper of his in 1924 came to the attention of Einstein [1064], who praised it enthusiastically for its handling of Planck's [887] quantum theory. This gave Bose entry to western Europe and in France he worked with Langevin [1000].

Einstein generalized Bose's paper and worked out a type of quantum statistics useful in considering subatomic particles that is still called Bose-Einstein statistics. Another variety worked out two years later by Fermi [1243] based on Dirac's [1256] exclusion principle was worked out in 1926. This is Fermi-Dirac statistics.

Subatomic particles, depending on whether they follow one set of statistics or the other, are called "bosons" or "fermions." The photon and other exchange-particles, for instance, are bosons.

[1171] OPARIN, Alexander Ivanovich
Soviet biochemist
Born: north of Moscow, March 3, 1894

Oparin graduated from Moscow University in 1917, and was professor of plant biochemistry there after 1929.

Oparin is best known for his book *The Origin of Life on Earth,* published in 1936. The question of the origin of life on the primordial earth through the blind and random processes of physics and chemistry had been speculated upon by scientists even as far back as Darwin [554] but few were willing to spend time on a subject concerning which so little could be known (it seemed) and over which so much controversy was sure to arise.

Such theories, which treated the origin of life in mechanistic fashion, were bound to offend the religious, but Oparin lived in a nation that, after 1917, was officially atheistic. He had nothing to fear from governmental piety. Postulating the presence of a methane/ammonia atmosphere and a source of energy in the sun, Oparin reasoned out the steps by which life might gradually have come into being.

He opened the door and biochemists of the West gratefully stepped through. The work of men such as Miller [1490] and Ponnamperuma [1457] was the result.

The Soviet government established a biochemical institute in Oparin's honor in Moscow in 1935. In 1946 Oparin became its director.

[1172] OBERTH, Hermann Julius
Austro-German engineer
Born: Hermanstadt, Transylvania (then part of Hungary, now part of Romania), June 25, 1894

Oberth, the son of a physician, studied medicine but was interrupted by World War I, during which he served in the Austro-Hungarian army. He was wounded and during a period of enforced idleness he grew interested in the problem of astronautics, becoming one of the pioneers of the field along with Tsiolkovsky [880] and Goddard [1083].

His experiments were dismissed by the Austro-Hungarian war ministry as folly, and after the war, in 1922, when he tried to get a Ph.D. at Heidelberg with a dissertation on rocket design, it was rejected. Eventually, Oberth published that dissertation, partly at his own expense, as *The Rocket Into Interplanetary Space* in 1934. The book achieved considerable popularity.

In 1938 Oberth joined the faculty of the Technical University of Vienna and he became a German citizen in 1940. During World War II he worked with von Braun [1370] at Peenemunde. After the war he worked in Italy and then in the United States. He retired in 1958 and returned to Germany.

[1173] **KAPITZA**, Peter Leonidovich
(ka'pih-tsuh)
Soviet physicist
Born: Kronshtadt, July 8, 1894

Kapitza, the son of a tsarist general, graduated in 1919 from the Petrograd Polytechnic Institute, then for his graduate work traveled to England in 1921 where, as it turned out, he was to spend fourteen years. During that interval he worked in Ernest Rutherford's [996] laboratory, pioneering in the production of large (though temporary) magnetic fields, and was elected a member of the Royal Society, the first foreigner to be so elected in two centuries.

In 1934, after one of his annual visits to the Soviet Union to see his mother, he did not return. Rutherford suspected it was a forced detention, but Kapitza remained in the Soviet Union thereafter, apparently voluntarily.

His most renowned work was in connection with the extremely low temperatures of liquid helium, a field first opened up by Kamerlingh Onnes [843]. Kapitza was one of those who studied the unusual properties of helium II (that is, helium in the form that exists at temperatures below $2.2°K$, that is, within $2.2°$ of absolute zero). He showed helium II conducted heat so well (eight hundred times as rapidly as copper, the best conductor at ordinary temperatures) because it flowed with remarkable ease. Helium II flows even more easily than a

gas, having a viscosity only one thousandth that of hydrogen at normal temperature and pressure (and hydrogen is the least viscous gas).

Kapitza's work on helium II was published in Moscow in 1941. This work on extremely low temperatures was then carried onward by Landau [1333].

During World War II, Kapitza attempted to rescue his old friend Bohr [1101] from Denmark but the British were there first. Kapitza quietly refused to work on Soviet nuclear weapon research and was kept under virtual house arrest for seven years. After Stalin's death, however, he became extremely active in space research.

In the 1950s Kapitza also turned his attention, in part, to ball lightning, a puzzling phenomenon in which plasma (high-energy gas, with its atoms and molecules broken up into electrically charged fragments) maintains itself for a much longer period than seems likely. Kapitza's analysis involves standing waves; that is, trains of waves that reinforce each other and remain in being over appreciable periods of time.

He was allowed to visit England in 1966 and the United States in 1969 to receive awards. For his work on low-temperature physics, Kapitza shared in the 1978 Nobel Prize in physics.

[1174] **LEMAÎTRE**, Abbé Georges
Édouard (luh-meh'tr)
Belgian astronomer
Born: Charleroi, July 17, 1894
Died: Louvain, June 20, 1966

Lemaître studied at the University of Louvain and was a civil engineer when World War I broke out in 1914. He served in the Belgian army as an artillery officer and, like De Broglie [1157], grew interested in physics and mathematics by way of war.

He returned to Louvain to work toward his Ph.D., then turned toward still another vocation and was ordained a priest in 1922.

He went on to study astrophysics at Cambridge in England and at the Massachusetts Institute of Technology in the

United States. He obtained his Ph.D. from the latter institution in 1927. He then returned to Belgium, where he was appointed professor of astrophysics at the University of Louvain, where he had done his undergraduate work.

In 1927, also, he worked out his theories of cosmogony, making use of the dramatic concept of the expanding universe that had recently been popularized by the studies of Hubble [1136] on the recession of the galaxies, and which had been postulated from purely theoretical considerations by Sitter [1004].

The most startling aspect of Abbé Lemaître's theories was his suggestion that if one extrapolated backward in time, the galaxies could be pictured as drawing closer and closer together until at the beginning they existed crushed together in a kind of "cosmic egg" or "superatom" that contained all the matter in the universe. This exploded in a "big bang" and the recession of the galaxies is what remains now, billions of years later, of that original super-explosion. Lemaître's suggestion went largely unnoticed, however, until his paper was brought to the attention of scientists by Eddington [1085].

From Hubble's picture of the size of the universe, and from the known velocities of the galaxies, it would seem that the moment of the "big bang" was 2 billion years in the past. This was an impossibly short time because radioactive disintegration studies of the type first proposed by Boltwood [987] made it seem quite certain that the earth's solid crust was older than that, and an earth older than the universe seemed ridiculous.

Baade's [1163] expansion of the scale of the universe a quarter of a century later put the "big bang" much farther in the past. The most commonly accepted figure eventually came to be 15 billion years.

The "big bang" theory of creation was further elaborated by Gamow [1278] and won out over the "continuous creation" theory of astronomers like Gold [1437] and Hoyle [1398], largely because background microwave radiation was de-tected by Penzias [1501] and R. W. Wilson [1506].

At the time of his death, Lemaître was president of the Pontifical Academy of Sciences at Rome.

[1175] **WEINER,** Norbert (wee'ner)
American mathematician
Born: Columbia, Missouri, November 26, 1894
Died: Stockholm, Sweden, March 18, 1964

Norbert Wiener was, as a child, a remarkable prodigy. He was the son of a renowned immigrant Russian-Jewish scholar in the field of languages and literature who drove his unusual son forward in rather a merciless fashion. Wiener began reading when he was three, entered Tufts University at the age of eleven, and earned his doctorate in mathematics at Harvard University in 1913 before his nineteenth birthday. He then studied under Bertrand Russell [1005] at Cambridge and Hilbert [918] at Göttingen. When the United States entered World War I in 1917, he tried to enlist but his poor eyesight made him unusable.

During World War II, Wiener was involved (as a mathematician) in work connected with antiaircraft defense. To shoot down an airplane one must know the speed and direction of the airplane's movements, the speed and direction of the wind, the speed of the projectile aimed at the airplane, and other factors as well. All this must be taken into account rapidly in aiming the antiaircraft gun and unless the result is computed very quickly, the gun might just as well be aimed by guesswork. To do more than guess, better computers than Bush's [1139] were absolutely necessary, and Wiener grew interested in working out the mathematical basis of the communication of information, and of control of a system in the light of such communication. By 1948 he had summarized his work in a book entitled *Cybernetics.* (He coined the word from a Greek term for "steersman.") The basic theories involved in cybernetics apply equally to the human nervous system and to man-made computers. Wiener was himself a thorough anti-vitalist, denying any basic distinction between life and nonlife, be-tween man and machine. In 1947 he an-nounced he would contribute no further to any form of military research, and spent the rest of his life trying to alert humanity to the significance and prob-lems of the coming age of automation.

[1176] VIRTANEN, Artturi Ilmari
(vihr'tuh-nen)
Finnish biochemist
Born: Helsinki, Finland (then part of Russia), January 15, 1895
Died: Helsinki, November 11, 1973

Virtanen obtained his Ph.D. at the University of Helsinki in 1919 and stud-ied thereafter in Germany, in Swit-zerland, and with Euler-Chelpin [1101] in Sweden. He then joined the faculty of Helsinki in 1924, achieving professorial rank in 1931.

During the 1920s Virtanen studied methods of preserving green fodder and discovered that by properly acidifying it, those reactions producing deterioration were stopped without damage to any of the nutritional qualities of the fodder. By making it that much more economi-cal to feed cattle during long winter months (a particularly important consid-eration in northern regions like Scan-dinavia) human nutrition is, of course, also benefited. In 1945 Virtanen was honored with the Nobel Prize in chemis-try.

[1177] DAM, Carl Peter Henrik
Danish biochemist
Born: Copenhagen, February 21, 1895
Died: Copenhagen, April 18, 1976

Dam, the son of a pharmaceutical chemist, obtained his doctorate in 1934 from the University of Copenhagen. However, during the course of his educa-tion, he studied under Pregl [982] in Austria in 1925 and under Schoenheimer [1211] in Germany. After obtaining his degree, Dam worked with Karrer [1131] in Switzerland in 1935.

Dam served on the faculty of the Uni-versity of Copenhagen from 1923 on, and attained professorial rank in 1929. In 1929 he studied how hens synthesize cholesterol. In his experiments, he fed his hens on a synthetic diet and noted that they developed small hemorrhages under the skin and within the muscles. These looked like the hemorrhages that develop in scurvy, so he added lemon juice to the diet, using a therapy first ad-vanced by Lind [288] a century and a half earlier. It did not help.

Dam tried other food additives, adding one or another of the vitamins that, since Eijkman's [888] time, had been found to be essential in trace quantities in the diet. None worked and he was forced to the conclusion that a vitamin, hitherto unknown, was involved. Since it seemed to be necessary to the proper clotting, or coagulation, of the blood, he named it "vitamin K," for "Koagulation" (the German spelling).

Within a few years several biochem-ists, notably a group led by Doisy [1169], had isolated vitamin K and worked out its formula. Its importance to blood clotting has made it useful in surgical operations, where the amount of bleeding can be reduced by its adminis-tration. In particular, newborn infants are deficient in vitamin K and are there-fore in danger of hemorrhage.

Ordinarily the intestinal tract of such infants is, however, quickly infested with bacteria that, in the course of their own metabolism, produce vitamin K, which is then absorbed and used by the child. In the modern, aseptic hospital, the period of danger, before bacterial infestation corrects matters, is extended somewhat, and it is usually considered wise to inject vitamin K into the mother (and hence indirectly into the child) shortly before birth takes place.

In 1940 Dam crossed the Atlantic in order to give a series of lectures in the United States and Canada. While there, Hitler's Nazi armies invaded and occu-pied Denmark. Dam therefore remained in the United States during the war, working chiefly at the University of Rochester. During this period of exile, he and Doisy shared the 1943 Nobel Prize in medicine and physiology. In absentia he was appointed professor of biochemistry at the Polytechnic Institute in Copenhagen. In 1946 he returned to liberated Denmark and in 1956 became head of the Danish Public Research Institute.

[1178] **GIAUQUE,** William Francis (jee-oké)
American chemist
Born: Niagara Falls, Ontario, Canada (of American parents), May 12, 1895

Giauque's academic life was spent at the University of California where, influenced by Lewis [1037], he grew interested in thermodynamics. He was first a student there, graduating with highest honors in 1920 and obtaining his Ph.D. in 1922. He then joined the faculty and was a full professor of chemistry by 1934.

In 1929 he discovered that oxygen was a mixture of three isotopes. Of these, the most common had an atomic weight which, by ordinary standards, was not quite 16. The other two, rather rare, had weights of 17 and 18. The weighted average of these isotopes was 16.00000 (used as atomic weight standard by chemists for a century ever since the time of Berzelius [425]).

This led to some important consequences. Physicists thought it made more sense to use the oxygen-16 isotope as atomic weight standard and set its weight at exactly 16, while chemists continued to set the weighted average of the three isotopes at exactly 16. This set up a conflict between the "physical atomic weight" and the "chemical atomic weight." These differed slightly. Finally in 1961 chemists and physicists united behind a new standard in which the most common isotope of carbon was set equal to exactly 12. This established the principle of using a single isotope as standard, but gave values that were almost exactly those that had been used by chemists all along.

Oxygen-18 could be used as an isotopic tracer for those reactions involving the oxygen atom. It was used for this purpose quite extensively, and it was by means of this tracer that nearly twenty years after Giauque's discovery it was found that the oxygen liberated by plants during photosynthesis (a liberation first detected by Priestley [312] a century and a half earlier) came from water and not from carbon dioxide.

Meanwhile, Giauque had also applied himself to the problem of low temperatures. The usual methods of achieving low temperatures by evaporation were used by Kamerlingh Onnes [843] a generation earlier to liquefy helium and to attain temperatures near 1°K. Temperatures as far down as 0.4°K had been reached but that seemed to be the limit.

In 1926, however, Giauque came up with a suggestion (which was also made independently and at the same time by Debye [1094] and by Simon [1165]) that at that low temperature a magnetic salt be prepared with its molecules all lined up under the influence of a magnetic field. Once that was done, and the salt brought to the lowest possible temperature in a container surrounded by liquid helium, the magnetic field might be removed. The molecules would then fall out of alignment and in order to do that, they would have to absorb heat from the surrounding helium. The temperature would then fall farther.

By following this suggestion, temperatures within thousandths of a degree of absolute zero were obtained, and the region of ultimate cold was open to more intensive study. For this, Giauque was honored with the award of the 1949 Nobel Prize in chemistry.

[1179] **MINKOWSKI,** Rudolph Leo B.
German-American astronomer
Born: Strassburg (then part of Germany), May 28, 1895
Died: Berkeley, California, January 4, 1976

Minkowski obtained his Ph.D. in physics at the University of Breslau in 1921 but by 1935 Germany was too

Nazified a land in which to remain. He came to the United States with the help of Baade [1163], became an American citizen in 1940, and worked in various California observatories.

He joined Baade in the study of supernovas, which they divided into two kinds on the basis of spectral characteristics.

They also labored to pinpoint the radio sources that Reber [1368] had mapped and to associate them with some definite optical objects. Thus, in 1951, a radio source located by Reber in the constellation of Cassiopeia, was successfully associated by Minkowski and Baade with wisps of gas that were clearly the remnant of a long-past supernova. Minkowski also collaborated with Baade in identifying the radio source in the constellation of Cygnus, as arising from a distant galaxy.

In 1951, he discovered the Earth-grazing asteroid Geographos, which he named for the National Geographic Society–Palomar Observatory, where he was working at the time.

[1180] **TAMM,** Igor Yevgenyevich
Russian physicist
Born: Vladivostok, July 8, 1895
Died: Moscow, April 12, 1971

Tamm, the son of an engineer, graduated from Moscow State University in 1918. Just before World War I he had studied in Edinburgh. Back in Russia he participated actively in the Revolution of 1917 but did not formally join the Communist Party.

During the 1920s and early 1930s he worked out the manner of light dispersion in solid bodies on the basis of quantum mechanics, but it was his explanation (together with Frank [1340]) of the Cherenkov [1281] radiation in 1937 that eventually earned him a share in the 1958 Nobel Prize in physics.

After World War II he was one of those working on techniques looking toward the control of the fusion reaction of the hydrogen bomb, in order that it might be turned to peaceful uses. In 1950 he suggested the use of the "pinch effect" to hold hot plasma (electrically

charged atom fragments) in place by a magnetic field.

After 1924 he served on the faculty of the Moscow State University, achieving a professorship in 1927.

[1181] **COURNAND,** André Frédéric (kour-nan')
French-American physiologist
Born: Paris, September 24, 1895

Cournand obtained his M.D. at the University of Paris in 1930 and in that year came to the United States and became an American citizen in 1941. He taught at the College of Physicians and Surgeons at Columbia University. He was the first to make use of Forssmann's [1283] technique of cardiac catheterization clinically and as a result shared with him and with D. W. Richards [1184] the 1956 Nobel Prize for physiology and medicine.

[1182] **RHINE,** Joseph Banks
American parapsychologist
Born: Waterloo, Pennsylvania, September 29, 1895
Died: Hillsborough, North Carolina, February 20, 1980

Rhine was educated at the University of Chicago, from which he obtained his Ph.D. in 1925. After teaching botany at West Virginia University, he joined the faculty of Duke University in Durham, North Carolina, in 1928 and remained there till his retirement in 1965.

Rhine attempted to investigate experimentally those phenomena that may be interpreted as resulting from the ability of human beings to perceive information other than through the known sense organs. This is extrasensory perception, usually abbreviated as ESP. His book, *Extrasensory Perception,* published in 1934, established the field in its present form.

That ESP exists is a matter of common belief. Many people have experienced phenomena that made it seem they were directly aware of another person's thoughts (telepathy). Cases in which events are perceived at a great distance (clairvoyance), or before they occur (precognition), or where objects are made to move by thought alone (telekinesis) are constantly being reported. However, these cases are very often explainable in less romantic fashion than as ESP and, not unusually, prove the result of honest mistake or even downright fraud. The relatively few cases that remain unexplained would, in all likelihood, be understood if enough data were obtained and enough time spent on the investigation. Most scientists are reluctant to spend time on matters that seem almost certain to come to nothing.

Rhine ran exhaustive tests on students, who were set to guessing the symbols on cards they could not see. The percentage of correct guesses they might be expected to make by pure chance could easily be estimated, and if the percentage was consistently higher than that for any one student (and it occasionally was), the intervention of ESP seemed a reasonable explanation. Thus, the person guessing the card might be reading the mind of the person holding it; and perhaps might be doing so unconsciously.

Rhine seemed quite convinced that as a result of his researches, conducted over a period of a generation, one may consider the existence of ESP proved, and that there is a whole field of knowledge (parapsychology or psionics) to be investigated.

However, the majority of scientists are reluctant to admit the existence of ESP on the basis of the work done by Rhine and others. Many think the tests were insufficiently controlled. The existence of ESP seems to be so far outside the elaborate scientific structure built up in the nearly four centuries since Galileo [166] that considerable evidence will have to be accumulated before most scientists will be satisfied.

Then, too, parapsychology has been exploited by occult practitioners. As has often happened in the history of science, notably in the cases of Mesmer [314] and Gall [371], it is not the offbeat results of the scientist himself that bring on hostility, so much as the extreme

views of many of his followers. It may be, as in the case of Mesmer and Gall, that what is valuable in Rhine's work will eventually be understood and accepted.

[1183] **DOMAGK,** Gerhard (doh'mahkh)
German biochemist
Born: Lagow, Brandenburg (now Poland), October 30, 1895
Died: Burberg, Württemburg-Baden, April 24, 1964

Domagk, the son of a teacher, had his education at the University of Kiel interrupted at its very beginning by World War I. He volunteered and served throughout the war, being wounded in 1915 and transferred to the Medical Corps. Thereafter, he returned to the university and obtained his medical degree in 1921. In the late 1920s he entered industry, working for I. G. Farbenindustrie, the great German dye firm.

Domagk began a systematic survey of new dyes with a view to detecting possible medical applications for some of them. (He was, after all, a physician by training.) One of the dyes was a newly synthesized orange-red compound with the trade name Prontosil. In 1932 Domagk found that injections of the dye had a powerful effect on streptococcus infections in mice.

This was extremely exciting. A generation earlier, Ehrlich [845] and others had discovered chemotherapeutic agents for several diseases, but those diseases had, like trypanosomiasis, been caused by protozoa, or, like syphilis, by rather uncommon bacteria. The more common, smaller bacteria had remained untouched by purely chemical attack.

The effect of Prontosil held good for humans, as Domagk discovered in the most direct way. His young daughter, Hildegarde, had been infected by streptococci following the prick of a needle. No treatment did any good until Domagk in desperation injected large quantities of Prontosil. She recovered dramatically and by 1935 the world had learned of the new drug. It gained further fame when it was used to save the life of Franklin D. Roosevelt, Jr., son of the President of the United States, who was also dying of an infection.

It was not long before it was recognized by Bovet [1325] that not all the molecule of Prontosil was needed for the antibacterial effect to be evident. A mere portion of it, sulfanilamide, a compound well known to chemists for a generation, was the effective principle.

The use of sulfanilamide and related sulfa compounds inaugurated the era of the wonder drug. A number of infectious diseases, notably some varieties of pneumonia, suddenly lost their terrors.

Shortly thereafter, the researches of Dubos [1235] revealed that not only synthetic compounds, but also natural compounds produced by microorganisms would serve as antibacterials. This in turn brought into prominence the neglected work of Fleming [1077] on penicillin, and the new medical age was launched.

In 1939 Domagk was awarded the Nobel Prize in medicine and physiology for his discovery. In October he accepted. However, Hitler was in a rage with the committee awarding the prizes, for the 1935 Nobel Prize for peace had been awarded to Karl von Ossietzky, a German who was in a concentration camp. Hitler refused to allow Germans to accept Nobel Prizes. Under the threat of arrest by the Gestapo (he was actually jailed for a week), Domagk was forced in November to withdraw his acceptance.

The money that accompanied the prize could be kept for him only one year, after which it reverted to the Nobel Foundation funds; however, one could be patient with the medal and the honor. In 1947, with Hitler dead and Nazism shattered, Domagk visited Stockholm and accepted the prize. After World War II he worked on the chemotherapy of tuberculosis and cancer.

[1184] **RICHARDS,** Dickinson Woodruff
American physician
Born: Orange, New Jersey, October 30, 1895

Richards graduated from Yale University in 1917, then went on to the College of Physicians and Surgeons at Columbia University, where he obtained his M.D. in 1923. He taught there from 1928. He studied the technique of cardiac catheterization introduced by Forssmann [1283] and, along with Cournand [1181], improved and made use of it. As a result he, Forssmann, and Cournand shared the 1956 Nobel Prize for physiology and medicine.

[1185] **LINDBLAD,** Bertil
Swedish astronomer
Born: Örebro, November 26, 1895
Died: Stockholm, June 26, 1965

Lindblad, the son of an army officer, obtained his Ph.D. at Uppsala in 1920 and taught at the University of Stockholm. He became director of the Stockholm Observatory in 1927.

In 1926 Lindblad carefully studied the apparent motions of the various stars and analyzed the rotation of the galaxy in the light of his results. He decided that while the central core of the galaxy might rotate as a unit, the outskirts (in which the sun itself is located) revolve more and more slowly as distance from the center increases.

This was confirmed in greater detail by Oort [1229] the next year.

Lindblad also labored to determine the absolute magnitude (the actual brightness after distance is taken into account) of many stars.

[1186] **MILNE,** Edward Arthur (miln)
English physicist
Born: Hull, Yorkshire, February 14, 1896
Died: Dublin, Ireland, September 21, 1950

Milne, the son of a headmaster, entered Cambridge after World War I had begun. Defective eyesight kept him out of active service but he worked on war-related scientific matters. In 1924 he was granted a professorial post at the University of Manchester and went on in 1929 to become a professor of mathematics at Oxford. During World War II he took leave to work on problems similar to those that had engaged him in the earlier war.

In pure science he did much work in the 1920s on the solar atmosphere. He worked out methods for determining the temperature of the sun at varying depths and showed that particles could be ejected from the sun at speeds of up to one thousand kilometers per second. This was the birth of the notion of the "solar wind," which Rossi [1289] was to observe thirty years later.

He was also the first to relate stellar explosions and stellar collapse, which was to bear fruit in the work of Chandrasekhar [1356].

In 1932 he worked out a variation of Einstein's [1064] general relativity, which was called "kinematic relativity," and he introduced the "cosmological principle" (now generally accepted), which stated that from any galaxy the general appearance of the universe would remain the same.

[1187] **NODDACK,** Ida Eva Tacke
German chemist
Born: Wesel, Rhenish Prussia,
February 25, 1896

Ida Noddack (née Tacke) obtained her doctorate in 1921 and worked with Walter Noddack [1166] at the University of Berlin. Both were engaged in the search for missing elements 43 and 75. Together they discovered the latter, which was named rhenium, after the Rhine River on whose shores Tacke was born, and mistakenly announced the discovery of the former as well.

In 1926 the two were married and continued their work together. In 1934, when Fermi [1243] reported his first observations in the neutron bombardment of uranium, Ida Noddack suggested the possibility of fission. Her remark was ignored then, but five years later it became apparent that her suggestion was valid.

[1188] **HENCH,** Philip Showalter
American physician
Born: Pittsburgh, Pennsylvania,
February 28, 1896
Died: Ocho Rios, Jamaica,
March 30, 1965

Hench obtained his medical degree at the University of Pittsburgh in 1920, then went on to the University of Minnesota, from which it was an easy leap to the Mayo Clinic, which he first joined in 1921 and where he remained until his retirement in 1957.

Hench was particularly interested in rheumatoid arthritis, a painful and crippling disease. Its symptoms were relieved during pregnancy and during attacks of jaundice, so he conjectured that it was not a germ disease, but a disorder of metabolism. He tried a number of chemicals, including hormones, in an effort to discover something that would bring relief. Since his colleague Kendall [1105] was so interested in the corticoids, Hench kept his eye on them.

In the mid-1940s, when corticoids were synthesized and reasonable quantities were available for the first time, he began to experiment with Compound E, which had been given the name cortisone.

World War II, during which he served as a colonel in the Army Medical Corps, delayed matters till 1948. Then, to his pleased surprise, tests showed that cortisone worked well, and as a result he along with Kendall and Reichstein [1201] received the 1950 Nobel Prize in medicine and physiology. Although cortisone has turned out to be a tricky material, to be used only with great care and judgment, it is another potent weapon in the modern armory of hormone therapy.

[1189] **SEMENOV,** Nikolay Nikolaevich
(sih-myoh'nof)
Soviet physical chemist
Born: Saratov, April 15, 1896

Semenov was educated at the University of St. Petersburg, which he entered in 1913, and from which he graduated in

1917, by then renamed the University of Petrograd, in the midst of the disorders of war and revolution. He remained in research institutions in Leningrad (still another new name for St. Petersburg), attaining professorial rank in 1928. In 1944 he joined the staff of Moscow State University.

During the 1920s he worked on chain-reaction mechanisms and on the theory of thermal explosions. He developed the theory of branched chain reactions. In 1956 he shared the Nobel Prize in chemistry with Hinshelwood [1200].

He was the first Soviet citizen to win a Nobel Prize.

[1190] **CAROTHERS,** Wallace Hume
American chemist
Born: Burlington, Iowa, April 27, 1896
Died: Philadelphia, Pennsylvania, April 29, 1937

Carothers' father rose to be vice-president of a small commercial college in Des Moines and in 1914 young Carothers entered that college to study accounting. He was interested in science, however, and in 1915 entered a college in which he could study that subject. The second was also a small institution and in it he was forced to teach chemistry, since the only chemistry teacher had left during World War I and it was impossible to get another.

He did his graduate work at the University of Illinois, where he obtained his Ph.D. in 1924. He tried his hand at teaching both there and at Harvard University, but teaching did not appeal to him. It was research that interested him.

In 1928 the Du Pont company was planning to initiate a program in basic research and hired Carothers to run it.

Carothers was interested in the study of polymers, molecules with long chain-like molecules. He investigated synthetic rubbers with Nieuwland [1058], for instance, and developed neoprene. In 1930 Carothers began work with diamines and dicarboxylic acids, joining them in linkages that were similar to those in silk and forming synthetic fibers. In the process, he confirmed Staudinger's [1074]

theories of polymer structure, which held such substances to consist of long-chain molecules.

In 1931 Carothers found one fiber that, after stretching, became even stronger than silk. He had discovered one variety of the type of fiber that was to be called nylon.

Carothers, subject to deep depressions, particularly after the death of a beloved twin sister in 1936, died a suicide when he had just turned forty-one and did not live to see what was to come of nylon. In 1938 it began to be used for toothbrush bristles but its production for the general public was delayed by World War II, during which it was put to military use only. After the war, however, it appeared in an almost endless variety of ways both as a fiber and as a solid material, wherever toughness and strength combined with lightness was needed.

The coming of nylon marked the beginning of a new era of synthetic fibers that burst upon the world after World War II, when chemists like Ziegler [1215] and Natta [1263] learned methods for directing more accurately the detailed structure of the large molecules being formed. In this area, information concerning chemical reaction mechanisms, gathered by men such as Hinshelwood [1200] and Semenov [1189], was particularly useful.

[1191] **MULLIKEN,** Robert Sanderson
American chemist
Born: Newburyport, Massachusetts, June 7, 1896

Mulliken, the son of a professor of chemistry at Massachusetts Institute of Technology, followed in his father's footsteps, studying chemistry and graduating from M.I.T. in 1917. He went on to the University of Chicago, where he gained his Ph.D. in 1921.

His chemical interests lay in molecular structure, but with the development of quantum mechanics in the 1920s it became clear that the intimate details of the molecule would not be worked out by classical chemical methods but required the mathematical techniques of the new physics. Mulliken shifted from chemistry to physics, therefore, and in 1926 was an associate professor of physics at New York University. In 1928 he moved on to the University of Chicago, where he remained until 1965, when he joined the Institute of Molecular Biophysics at Florida State University.

Mulliken discarded the earlier notion that electrons circled nuclei in orbits somehow analogous to those met with in astronomy. Instead, he accepted the Schrödinger [1117] view of the electron as a kind of standing wave forming a cloud of electronic matter about or between nuclei. The electron existed in "orbitals."

This new view made it far easier to understand interactions between molecules, and in 1966 Mulliken received the Nobel Prize in chemistry.

[1192] **CORI,** Gerty Theresa Radnitz
Czech-American biochemist
Born: Prague, Austria-Hungary
(now Czechoslovakia), August
15, 1896
Died: St. Louis, Missouri, October 26, 1957

Gerty Radnitz entered the medical school of the University of Prague in 1914. There she met Carl Cori [1194] as a classmate. After both had obtained their medical degrees in 1920, they married. She shared the labor of research with him, and eventually, the 1947 Nobel Prize in medicine and physiology. As a husband-and-wife team in research, they were equaled only by the Curies [897, 965] and the Joliot-Curies [1204, 1227]. The similarity in names between the Curies and the Coris is a curious coincidence.

[1193] **KING,** Charles Glen
American biochemist
Born: Entiat, Washington, October 22, 1896

King attended Washington State College, graduating in 1918, and obtained his doctorate at the University of Pittsburgh in 1923. He served on the faculty of the University of Pittsburgh till 1942

and, later, on that of Columbia University.

The high point in King's career came in 1932, when a long series of investigations culminated in the isolation of vitamin C. Its structure was quickly determined and it was synthesized by men like Haworth [1087] and Reichstein [1201] in 1933.

[1194] **CORI,** Carl Ferdinand
Czech-American biochemist
Born: Prague, Austria-Hungary
(now Czechoslovakia), December
15, 1896

Cori's father was a zoologist and the director of the Marine Biological Station in Trieste (then, like Prague, a part of Austria-Hungary) and Cori was educated in that city. His medical training, however, was at the University of Prague and he obtained his medical degree there in 1920. In the same year he married Gerty Theresa Radnitz [1192], a classmate, who became his lifelong partner in research.

During World War I, Cori served in the Austrian Sanitary Corps on the Italian front. After the war the Coris spent some years in a shattered Austria, then in 1922 emigrated to the United States, becoming American citizens in 1928. They worked on cancer research in Buffalo first, but in 1931 they joined the faculty of Washington University Medical School in St. Louis, Missouri, where Cori eventually came to head the department of biological chemistry.

During the 1930s the Coris investigated how glycogen, the carbohydrate stored in liver and muscle, broke down in the body and was resynthesized. Meyerhof [1095], two decades earlier, had made it quite plain that in working muscle, glycogen was converted to lactic acid, but the Coris were after the details of the conversion.

They isolated a hitherto unknown compound from muscle tissue; glucose-1-phosphate is the proper name, though it is often called Cori ester, in their honor. Glycogen, it turned out, did not break down to glucose molecules by the addition of water molecules at the links between the glucose units in the chainlike glycogen structure (as would seem the most direct and simplest route). Instead, inorganic phosphate was added at those links to form phosphate-containing Cori ester.

If glycogen were hydrolyzed to glucose, there would have been a pronounced energy loss and this energy would have had to be restored for the glycogen to be re-formed from glucose. Glycogen synthesis, under those circumstances, would have been difficult. The formation of glucose-1-phosphate instead involved little energy change and the balance between glycogen and glucose-1-phosphate could therefore be easily shifted in either direction.

The glucose-1-phosphate was changed to the allied compound glucose-6-phosphate and this in turn underwent other changes through a whole series of phosphate-containing compounds. Painstakingly the Coris detected these and fitted them into the proper niches of the breakdown course. One of the intermediates proved to be fructose-1, 6-diphosphate, the ester first discovered by Harden [947] a generation earlier.

With the elucidation of the role of the high-energy phosphates by Lipmann [1221] a few years afterward, the part played by these phosphate-containing compounds in converting the chemical energy of carbohydrates into forms usable by the body was clarified.

The Coris, for their work on glycogen breakdown, shared with Houssay [1115] the 1947 Nobel Prize in medicine and physiology.

[1195] **ENDERS,** John Franklin
American microbiologist
Born: West Hartford, Connecticut, February 10, 1897

Ender's education at Yale was interrupted by World War I, during which he served as a flying instructor. He graduated in 1920. Though his father was a successful and wealthy businessman, Enders had no talent for business himself, and after a halfhearted attempt in real estate he entered Harvard University for graduate work. He nearly obtained a

doctorate in English, but contact with medical students helped him find that he preferred the medical sciences to literature and it was in bacteriology that he finally obtained his doctorate in 1930. After that he served on the faculty of Harvard University Medical School.

Enders grew interested in viruses, and like other virologists he recognized that many difficulties originated from the fact that one could not culture viruses outside an organism. Bacteria could be cultured in test tubes on nutrient broths; by rationalizing the methods of such culture, Koch [767] and his followers had done great things. Viruses, however, could not be treated so conveniently, though an important advance came when it was found they could be grown in live chick embryos. (Remove a small section of the shell of a fertilized hen's egg and you have your "nutrient broth.")

Enders realized, however, that the living cells in which viruses might grow need not necessarily be parts of intact organisms, embryonic or otherwise, or even intact organs. With his co-workers, Weller [1397] and Robbins [1410], Enders in 1948 grew mumps virus in mashed-up chick embryos, bathed in blood. This sort of thing had been tried before but had failed because bacteria also grew in the tissues and made the preparation impossible to work with.

However, Enders had the key, now. Fleming's [1077] penicillin was available, thanks to the work of Florey [1213] and Chain [1306], and by the addition of penicillin to the mashed tissue, bacterial growth was stopped while viral growth remained unaffected.

The group then turned to poliomyelitis, the dreaded crippling disease that destroyed nerves and left bodies paralyzed for life. Research in polio had been hampered by the fact that the virus could only be grown in living nerve tissue of men or monkeys.

Enders had some polio virus on hand and thought it would be interesting to see if this virus, like that of mumps, could be made to grow on embryonic tissue scraps laced with antibiotic. In 1949 he obtained tissue from human embryos (stillborn) and successfully grew polio virus upon it. The virus was made to grow on other types of tissue scraps as well.

Once this was done, polio virus could be studied easily and in quantity. The way was opened for the type of research that led to the development of antipolio vaccines by Salk [1393] and Sabin [1311] in the 1950s.

For their work on virus cultures, Enders, Weller, and Robbins shared the 1954 Nobel Prize in medicine and physiology.

[1196] **LYOT**, Bernard Ferdinand
(lee-oh′)
French astronomer
Born: Paris, February 27, 1897
Died: on a train near Cairo,
Egypt, April 2, 1952

Lyot, the son of a surgeon, obtained his doctorate at the University of Paris.

His specialty was instrumentation. He devised techniques for taking pictures in rapid succession and blending them in such a way as to minimize the effect of the emulsion grain and in this way photographed Mars with unprecedented clarity.

In 1924 he improved methods for detecting and studying polarized light and showed that the polarization characteristics of moonlight could arise from a surface coating of volcanic ash; by 1929 similar studies of Venus convinced him that its cloud layer was composed of water.

His most remarkable instrumental victory, however, was his invention, in 1930, of the coronagraph. This focused the light of the sun on an opaque disc and cut out all scattered light from the atmosphere and from the lens itself. Mounting a telescope in the clear air of the Pyrénées, Lyot managed to observe the inner corona, at least, in broad daylight. Astronomers no longer had to wait for total eclipse to study the coronal spectral lines.

By 1937 Lyot's photographs showed the corona to be rotating at about the same speed as the solar disc itself. Close attention to its spectral lines showed that the postulated unknown element "coronium" did not exist and that the lines attributed to it were produced by highly ionized atoms of such metals as iron. In fact, in 1942 it was shown that coronal temperatures were in the range of 1,000,000°C, and still later rocket observations showed that the high-temperature corona emitted X rays.

He died of a heart attack on his way back from Khartoum, Sudan, where he had been observing a solar eclipse.

[1197] **HASSEL**, Odd
Norwegian physical chemist
Born: Oslo, May 17, 1897

Hassel obtained his Ph.D. at the University of Berlin in 1924 and joined the faculty of the University of Oslo in 1925.

In 1930 he began studies on the three-dimensional shape of cyclohexane and its derivatives, compounds with a ring of six carbon atoms. He showed that the ring could exist in two three-dimensional shapes (called "boat" and "chair") and that this affected the nature of the reactions of such compounds.

Once the Germans occupied Norway in 1940, Hassel stopped publishing in German journals but used Scandinavian journals instead, so that his work was not widely read. He suffered two years of imprisonment by the Germans from 1943 to 1945, along with other faculty members of the University of Oslo.

After World War II his work on three-dimensional structures ("conformational analysis") became known. By this time Barton [1427] was working on the subject independently. Hassel and Barton shared the 1969 Nobel Prize for chemistry.

[1198] **COCKCROFT**, Sir John Douglas
English physicist
Born: Todmorden, Yorkshire,
May 27, 1897
Died: Cambridge, September 18,
1967

Cockcroft, the son of a textile manufacturer, was educated at Manchester College of Technology, taking his degree in electrical engineering. He served as an artilleryman in World War I, and managed to survive the Battle of the Somme. After the war he entered Cambridge University, where in 1928 he received his Ph.D.

He studied under Ernest Rutherford [996] and for a time worked with Kapitza [1173] on magnetic fields at liquid helium temperatures.

His interest turned to nuclear physics and his training in electrical engineering stood him in good stead, for he occupied himself with the problem of accelerating particles in an electric field.

During the 1920s the only particles that could be used for bombarding and breaking down the atomic nucleus (a process popularly termed "atom-smashing") were alpha particles emitted by naturally radioactive elements. Rutherford had done wonders with them and had exploited them to the limit, but it was now necessary to go beyond that and find particles of still higher energies.

Cockcroft, with the assistance of Walton [1269], devised an instrument in 1929 that could build up voltages (a voltage multiplier) and, in so doing, accelerate protons (which are easy to obtain by ionizing hydrogen atoms) to energies higher than those of natural alpha particles. His inspiration, here, lay in Gamow's [1278] theoretical work on particle bombardment.

In April 1932 Cockcroft and Walton bombarded lithium with such protons and produced alpha particles. It was clear that what they had done was to combine lithium and hydrogen to form helium. This was the first nuclear reaction brought about through artificially accelerated particles and without the aid of any form of natural radioactivity. The voltage multiplier was quickly outmoded by the cyclotron invented by Lawrence [1241], but the principle had been established and Cockcroft and Walton were awarded the 1951 Nobel Prize in physics as a result.

Both during and after World War II, Cockcroft was engaged in work having to do with the development first of radar, then of the atomic bomb. He supervised the construction of nuclear reactors in Canada, for instance. And, as it

happened, his very first artificially induced nuclear reaction, that of lithium with hydrogen, proved to be of great importance in the development of the hydrogen bomb.

In 1939 Cockcroft took up a professorial post at Cambridge and in 1946 he was head of the Atomic Energy Research Establishment at Harwell. In 1960 he became master of the newly founded Churchill College at Cambridge.

He was knighted in 1948 and in 1961 received the Atoms for Peace award.

[1199] **WITTIG,** Georg Friedrich Karl
        German chemist
        Born: Berlin, June 16, 1897

Wittig studied at the University of Tübingen, but this was interrupted by military service during World War I. After the war he graduated from the University of Marburg in 1923 and received his Ph.D. there in 1926. As a teacher he moved up the ranks of universities till he attained a professorship at Heidelberg in 1956.

He worked chiefly with phosphorus-containing organic compounds, studying those that contained a negative charge on one or another of the carbon atoms, a "carbanion." This balanced the work of H. C. Brown [1373] on boron-containing organic compounds, and those that contained a positive charge ("carbonium atoms"). As a result, Wittig and Brown shared the 1979 Nobel Prize for chemistry.

[1200] **HINSHELWOOD,** Sir Cyril Norman
        English physical chemist
        Born: London, June 19, 1897
        Died: London, October 9, 1967

Hinshelwood was the son of an accountant. His professional life was spent at Oxford, both as student (winning a scholarship in 1919 and obtaining his doctorate there in 1924) and as member of the faculty. He became professor of chemistry there in 1937, succeeding Soddy [1052].

His interest was primarily in kinetics, the study of the rate at which chemical reactions proceed. In analyzing this rate, one could deduce the mechanisms by which the reactions took place. Even in so seemingly simple a reaction as that of hydrogen and oxygen to form water, a complex chain of events had to take place, in which the hydrogen molecules (made up of a pair of atoms) had to split apart into "atomic hydrogen." A hydrogen atom could then combine with an oxygen molecule, liberating a free oxygen atom, which could combine with a hydrogen molecule, liberating a free hydrogen atom, and so on.

Such "chain reactions" could be used to explain the formation of large-polymer molecules and many other chemical events. It could also by used to explain the fact that at a certain temperature, a mixture of hydrogen and oxygen would explode. Nernst [936] had made use of such mechanisms in connection with the light-catalyzed reaction of hydrogen and chlorine.

In 1928 Hinshelwood showed that below this temperature the chain reaction was stopped at the walls of the vessel before it had a chance to reach explosive rates, and above the temperature it was not. Semenov [1189] had come to a similar conclusion the year before. Hinshelwood and Semenov, for their work on reaction mechanisms, shared the 1956 Nobel Prize in chemistry.

Hinshelwood was knighted in 1948 and served as president of the Royal Society from 1955 to 1960. He retired in 1965.

[1201] **REICHSTEIN,** Tadeusz (rikhe´-shtine)
Polish-Swiss chemist
Born: Włocławek, Poland, July 20, 1897

Reichstein's father was an engineer who, during Reichstein's childhood, worked in Kiev in the Ukraine. In 1905 the family left Russia (which had just lost a war and was suffering the upheavals of an abortive revolution), moving first to Berlin and then to Zürich, Switzerland. In 1914 they became Swiss citizens.

Reichstein received his doctorate in 1922 under Staudinger [1074] in the State Technical College at Zürich. In 1931 he was appointed assistant to Ružička [1119], a fellow naturalized Swiss citizen, and a fellow student under Staudinger.

Reichstein was one of those who in 1933 succeeded in synthesizing ascorbic acid (vitamin C) shortly after that vitamin's identification by King [1193], Haworth [1087] having also succeeded independently that same year. His chief labors, however, were during the 1930s, when he and his colleagues isolated the various corticoids just as Kendall [1105] was doing in the United States. For this he shared the 1950 Nobel Prize in medicine and physiology with Kendall and Hench [1188].

[1202] **WYCKOFF,** Ralph Walter Graystone
American crystallographer
Born: Geneva, New York, August 9, 1897

Wyckoff graduated from Hobart College in his hometown in 1916 and went on to gain his Ph.D. at Cornell University in 1919.

He became early interested in the use of X rays in determining crystal structure after the fashion of the Braggs [922, 1141]. He went on to other methods of dealing with submicroscopic structures, working with ultracentrifuges and electron microscopes.

Following an idea of R. C. Williams [1339], he developed the technique of spraying a thin film of metal obliquely over objects in an electron microscope field. A metal-free area would form in the shaded region behind each object, and this area would, by its shape and size, tell something about the height and shape of the particle. Electron microscopy thus became three-dimensional, so to speak.

He carried through the laboratory

preparation of a vaccine against a virus disease (equine encephalitis).

In 1959 he accepted a post as professor of physics at the University of Arizona.

[1203] STRUVE, Otto (stroov)
Russian-American astronomer
Born: Kharkov, Russia, August 12, 1897
Died: Berkeley, California, April 6, 1963

Struve was the fourth in a dynasty of noted astronomers. His great-grandfather was F.G.W. von Struve [483], who had been one of the first to measure the parallax of a star. Struve's university education was interrupted by World War I. He served in the field artillery with the Russian army on the Turkish front during World War I, then went on to graduate with honors from Kharkov University in 1919.

The post-Revolutionary disorders in what had now become the USSR drove Struve (who fought with the counter-revolutionary "Whites") first to Turkey in 1920, then to the United States in 1921. He obtained his Ph.D. at the University of Chicago in 1923 and became an American citizen in 1927. He taught at the University of Chicago, remaining there till 1947.

Struve dealt with every phase of stellar astronomy, working out contemporary notions of the evolutionary processes within stars. He discovered interstellar matter, the thin gas that spreads between the stars. First he noted calcium, which had prominent spectral lines, then the much more important hydrogen, which was soon to be so significant in the work of radio astronomers such as Oort [1229].

Struve was one of those who turned from the view of men like Jeans [1053] that planetary systems were excessively rare. He devised mechanisms, instead, whereby such systems were normal developments in stellar evolution. Thus, he noted that some stars rotated rapidly; others, like our own sun, quite slowly. The slow stars, he felt, were slow be-

cause they had lost angular momentum to planets and were therefore centers of stellar systems.

Combined with the geochemical work of men such as Urey [1164], it began to seem more and more likely that life itself (even intelligent life, perhaps) was common in the universe.

In 1950 he accepted a professorship at the University of California and in 1959 became director of the National Radio Astronomy Observatory at Green Bank, West Virginia. Struve was childless, and with his death the Struve astronomical dynasty came to an end.

[1204] JOLIOT-CURIE, Irène
French physicist
Born: Paris, September 12, 1897
Died: Paris, March 17, 1956

Irène was the elder daughter of Pierre and Marie Curie [897, 965] and was educated privately for years, though she finally attended the Sorbonne. She was brought up without religion. During World War I she served as an army nurse.

While working as her mother's assistant, she met Frédéric Joliot [1227], another assistant, who was also an atheist. Finding their views thoroughly comfortable and compatible, they were married in 1926 and had a happy life together.

When ill health forced her mother to retire, Irène succeeded to her post. In their work, she and her husband were a unit, sharing the triumph of the 1935 Nobel Prize in chemistry, just too late for her famous mother to witness it, for Marie Curie had died the year before. Irène also shared in her husband's perils during the period of the German occupation of France. It was not till 1944 that she and her children were smuggled into Switzerland.

In 1936 Irène had served a short period in the cabinet of Léon Blum and after World War II was active in movements considered Communist-influenced. In 1954 her application for membership in the American Chemical Society was rejected because of the society's disapproval of her politics. She died, like her mother, of leukemia, brought on undoubtedly by her years of work with hard radiation.

[1205] **BJERKNES,** Jacob Aall Bonnevie
(byerk′nes)
Norwegian-American meteorologist
Born: Stockholm, Sweden (of Norwegian parents), November 2, 1897
Died: Los Angeles, California, July 7, 1975

Bjerknes's father, Vilhelm Bjerknes (himself the son of a professor of mathematics), was a Norwegian physicist who taught at the University of Stockholm from 1895 to 1907. During the nineteenth century, Norway was under the Swedish crown, but in 1905 it gained its independence. Two years later, the elder Bjerknes transferred to the University of Oslo in Norway's capital. It had been his own alma mater and the younger Bjerknes was educated there too, gaining his doctorate in 1924.

The two men, father and son, organized a network of weather-observing stations all over Norway during World War I. From the reports received, they worked out the theory of polar fronts, which serves as the basis of modern weather forecasting.

They showed by 1920 that the atmosphere is made up of air masses that are more or less sharply differentiated in temperature between warm tropical air masses and cold polar air masses. The sharp boundaries between them they called "fronts" from an analogy with the battle lines that had so impressed themselves on the minds of men during the war just ended. During the 1920s and 1930s the manner in which the masses fought it out were analyzed.

In 1939 the younger Bjerknes came to the United States and the next year (unable to return to a Norway that had been occupied by the Nazis) obtained a professorial position at the University of California. He was naturalized as an American citizen in 1946.

Meanwhile, World War II occasioned a new meteorological discovery. American bombers, flying high across the Pacific on their way toward Japan, sometimes found themselves virtually motionless. They had entered a stream of rapidly moving air, blowing from west to east. This was the jet stream.

There are two of these, one in the northern hemisphere and one in the southern, at a height of from six to nine miles. The usual velocity of the wind is from 100 to 200 miles per hour, though speeds of 350 miles and more have been recorded. They make winding girdles about the earth, following the paths between the polar and tropical air masses and therefore usually marking the regions of greatest storminess.

The changing course of the jet streams from day to day is now also taken into account in plotting the movements of the air masses and in attempting to predict future events in the changing weather pattern.

In 1952 Bjerknes made use of pictures of cloud covers taken by rockets as a new aid to weather analysis. Thus, meteorology entered the space age.

[1206] **NORRISH,** Ronald George Wreyford
English chemist
Born: Cambridge, November 9, 1897
Died: Cambridge, June 7, 1978

Norrish's education at Cambridge (via a scholarship) was interrupted by World War I, during which he served as a lieutenant in the artillery. He returned to Cambridge after the war, graduating in 1921 and receiving a Ph.D. in 1924. He remained on the faculty of Cambridge, reaching professorial status in 1937 and retiring in 1965.

Between 1949 and 1955 he and his coworker Porter [1443] began to investigate very fast chemical reactions. Working with a gaseous system at equilibrium, they illuminated it with ultra-short flashes of light. This introduced a momentary disequilibrium and the time taken to reestablish equilibrium was then measured. In this way, chemical changes taking place in but a billionth of a second could be studied.

As a result, Norrish and Porter shared half the 1967 Nobel Prize in chemistry, the other half going to Eigen [1477] for his independent but similar work.

[1207] **BLACKETT,** Patrick Maynard
Stuart Blackett, Baron
English physicist
Born: London, November 18, 1897
Died: London, July 13, 1974

Blackett entered a naval school in 1910, at thirteen, to train as a naval officer. The outbreak of World War I came just in time to make use of him and he was at sea throughout the war, taking part in the Battle of Jutland.

With the war over, however, he resigned from the navy and went to Cambridge, where he studied under Ernest Rutherford [996] and obtained his master's degree in 1923. In 1933 he became professor of physics at the University of London, moving on to Manchester in 1937.

It was Blackett who first turned to the wholesale use of the Wilson [979] cloud chamber. Rutherford had observed scintillation effects on a screen of zinc sulfide and had interpreted those as indicating that he had succeeded in converting nitrogen to oxygen through the bombardment of the former with alpha particles. Blackett felt the need for more direct evidence of this.

In the early 1920s, therefore, he went to work with the cloud chamber. He bombarded nitrogen within the cloud chamber with alpha particles and expanded the chamber periodically in order to catch any tracks that might be formed. He took over 20,000 photographs, catching a total of more than 400,000 alpha particle tracks. Of these tracks, just eight involved a collision of an alpha particle and a nitrogen molecule. From the forked tracks that resulted, it was possible to show that Rutherford's contention that elements had been transmuted was correct. These first photographs of a nuclear reaction in

progress, taken in 1925, were immensely impressive, and if anything was needed to dramatize the Wilson cloud chamber this was it.

Blackett turned the cloud chamber to other uses as the 1930s approached. He almost discovered the positron but Anderson [1292] was a few months ahead of him there. He also studied cosmic rays, and here an idea struck him.

There was no way of knowing when an interesting event was taking place in the cloud chamber, so that the chamber had to be expanded at random and as often as possible in the hope of catching something. In 1932, therefore, Blackett placed a Wilson cloud chamber between two Geiger [1082] counters. Any cosmic ray particle passing through both Geiger counters had to pass through the cloud chamber. Blackett arranged the circuits so that the surge of current set up in the two counters operated the cloud chamber. In this case, the chance of a significant photograph in these "coincidence counters" was enormously increased.

In 1935 Blackett showed that gamma rays, on passing through lead, sometimes disappear, giving rise to a positron and an electron. This was the first clear-cut case of the conversion of energy into matter. This confirmed the famous $E = mc^2$ equation of Einstein [1064] as precisely as did the more numerous examples, earlier observed, of the conversion of matter to energy (and even more dramatically).

During World War II, Blackett worked on the development of radar and the atomic bomb. His strong backing of Watson-Watt [1155] was one of the crucial factors in the decision to back radar development and that proved the salvation of Britain. Blackett worked under George Thomson [1156] in the atomic bomb project and urged that such research be centered in the United States for efficiency and security.

After the war, however, he was one of those most vociferously concerned with the dangers of nuclear warfare. In 1948 he was awarded the Nobel Prize in physics for his work with and upon the Wilson cloud chamber.

In 1963 he became head of the physics department at the Imperial College of Science and Technology and in 1965 he was elected president of the Royal Society. In 1969 he was made a life peer and became Lord Blackett.

[1208] **SZILARD,** Leo (zee'lahrd)
Hungarian-American physicist
Born: Budapest, Hungary, February 11, 1898
Died: La Jolla, California, May 30, 1964

Szilard, the son of a Jewish engineer, obtained his doctorate at the University of Berlin in 1922 and joined its faculty thereafter. When Hitler came to power, however, Szilard, mindful of his Jewish origins, lost no time in leaving Germany, and went to England.

While in England he went into the field of nuclear physics and in 1934 conceived the idea of a nuclear chain reaction, in which a neutron induced an atomic breakdown, releasing two neutrons, which break down two more atoms, and so on. He even applied for a patent for the process, keeping it secret, in part, because he foresaw its importance in nuclear bombs. However, the reaction he had in mind involved the breakdown of beryllium to helium and this did not, in fact, form a practical chain reaction.

Nevertheless, when uranium fission was discovered by Hahn [1063] and announced by Meitner [1060] in 1939, Szilard saw that here was a chain reaction that *would* be practical. He had gone to the United States in 1937 and now he realized the importance of getting a practical nuclear bomb before Hitler did. The newspapers had publicized the early fission experiments without really knowing what they were talking about and Szilard's blood ran cold. He persuaded America's physicists not to publish their work in the field to avoid giving the Germans any ideas.

That summer he, Wigner [1260], and Teller [1332] (all Hungarian refugees) persuaded Einstein [1064] to send his famous letter (written by Szilard, actually) to President Franklin D. Roosevelt, and this set in motion the Manhattan Project that was to prepare the first nuclear bomb.

Szilard worked with Fermi [1243] in Chicago on the development of the first self-sustained nuclear reactor, their innovation being the use of graphite as a moderator to slow neutrons to a velocity where they were most efficiently captured. (The French, under Frédéric Joliot-Curie [1227], were trying to use heavy water for the purpose.)

In 1943 Szilard became an American citizen. Once the atomic bomb was ready for use, Szilard was one of the large group of scientists who, in revulsion at their own work, pleaded that the bomb not be used or else used only over uninhabited territory as a demonstration. The military, and some scientists such as Compton [1159], thought otherwise, however, and President Harry S Truman made the fateful decision that visited nuclear destruction upon the Japanese cities of Hiroshima and Nagasaki.

Szilard veered away from nuclear physics after the war, accepting a post as professor of biophysics at the University of Chicago in 1946. He labored unceasingly to ban nuclear warfare and even nuclear testing and to turn nuclear power to peaceful uses only. In 1959 he received the Atoms for Peace award.

[1209] **ZWICKY,** Fritz (tsvik'ee)
Swiss astronomer
Born: Varna, Bulgaria (of Swiss parents), February 14, 1898
Died: Pasadena, California, February 8, 1974

Zwicky studied at the Federal Institute of Technology in Zürich, Switzerland, obtaining his doctorate in 1922. He went to the United States in 1925 and taught at the California Institute of Technology and worked at the Mount Wilson and Palomar observatories.

One of Zwicky's fields of interest was supernovas. The distinction between these and ordinary novas was first advanced by him and Baade [1163] in 1934.

Ordinary novas had been observed in

plenty by astronomers, but in 1885 a nova had been observed in the Andromeda galaxy (or nebula, as it was then called) which attained the magnitude of 7, so that it was nearly visible to the naked eye. In the 1920s, when the distance of the Andromeda galaxy was set at 800,000 light-years by Hubble [1136], it was realized that the nova must have been as bright as many millions of ordinary stars to appear so luminous at such a distance. A supernova, then, is a star that blew up in one grand flash, whereas an ordinary nova merely puffs away perhaps one percent of its mass and then returns to its ordinary way of stellar life. The extremely bright novas observed by Tycho Brahe [156] and Kepler [169] must have been supernovas within our own galaxy as was the nova of 1054, which ended as Rosse's [513] Crab nebula.

Since Kepler's time, however, no supernova had appeared in our galaxy and Zwicky searched the outer galaxies for any that might be bright enough for spectral studies. His researches showed that in any given galaxy, only two or three supernovas appear every thousand years. The connection of supernovas and white dwarfs has been illuminated by Chandrasekhar [1356].

Zwicky also investigated clusters of galaxies. In 1942 he studied the large cluster of galaxies in the constellation Coma Berenices and showed that their distribution resembled statistically the distribution of molecules in a gas at temperature equilibrium. Thus, the largest and the smallest seem to join hands.

[1210] **ASTBURY,** William Thomas
English physical biochemist
Born: Stoke-on-Trent,
Staffordshire, February 25, 1898
Died: Leeds, Yorkshire, June 4, 1961

Astbury did his research at Cambridge under William Henry Bragg [922] from 1921. In 1928 he joined the faculty of the University of Leeds.

In 1930 he was studying the structure of wool and subjected it to X-ray diffrac-

tion determinations (the work that had made Bragg famous) both in the stretched and unstretched form. The X-ray diffraction pattern changed and with that Astbury began to try to work out the structure of protein molecules generally from such studies. In 1937 he made the first X-ray diffraction studies of nucleic acid.

Astbury's determinations of structure were wrong, but they were a respectable first attempt and they led on to the work of Pauling [1236] in proteins and James Dewey Watson [1480] and Crick [1406] in nucleic acids.

[1211] **SCHOENHEIMER,** Rudolf
(shern'high-mer)
German-American biochemist
Born: Berlin, May 10, 1898
Died: New York, New York,
September 11, 1941

Educated in Germany and receiving his Ph.D. at the University of Berlin, in 1923, Schoenheimer was another of those German-Jewish scientists to whom the coming of Hitler meant that safety lay only in exile. He emigrated to the United States in 1933 and obtained a position at Columbia University's College of Physicians and Surgeons.

In 1935 Schoenheimer introduced the use of isotopic tracers in biochemical research. Hevesy [1100] had been the first to make use of isotopes more than a decade earlier, to be sure, but he had worked with lead isotopes, atoms of types that were foreign to living tissue, and isotope work had languished since. By 1935, however, deuterium, the heavy isotope of hydrogen, had become available in reasonable quantity, thanks to the work of Lewis [1037] and Urey [1164]. Here was an isotope of an element naturally found in living tissue.

Schoenheimer made use of fat molecules that contained deuterium atoms in place of some of the hydrogen atoms. These were incorporated into the diet of laboratory animals, whose tissues treated the deuterized fat much as they would ordinary fat. Analysis of the body fat of the animals for deuterium content threw new and startling light on hitherto obscured facets of biochemistry.

It was believed at the time, for instance, that the fat stores of an organism were usually immobile; that the molecules composing it just lay there, so to speak, until such time as famine demanded their use. In times of reasonable nourishment, it was thought, the body made use of newly digested fat pouring in from the alimentary tract.

However, when Schoenheimer fed rats on his deuterized fat and analyzed the fat stores, he found that at the end of four days the tissue fat contained nearly half of the deuterium that had been fed the animal. In other words, ingested fat was stored and stored fat was used. There was a rapid turnover and the body constituents were not static, but changed constantly and dynamically.

Schoenheimer then made use of a heavy isotope of nitrogen, soon after it was first prepared in quantity by Urey, and tagged amino acids with it. In a series of experiments he traced the heavy nitrogen within the amino acids of the organism after it had been ingested as part of a single amino acid. He found that here, too, there was constant action. Molecules were rapidly changing and shifting, even though the overall movement might be small.

Schoenheimer's work was the first to catch body chemistry in action, so to speak, and he was undoubtedly the father of isotopic tracer research in biochemistry. However, in 1941, during the darkest days of World War II, Schoenheimer committed suicide.

He did not live to see the defeat of Germany, nor the coming, in quantity, of radioactive isotopes after World War II; isotopes which, in the hands of men like Calvin [1361], were to serve as a still more delicate tool for revealing the details of chemical mechanisms within living tissue.

[1212] **RABI,** Isidor Isaac (rah'bee)
Austrian-American physicist
Born: Rymanów, Austria (now in Poland), July 29, 1898

Rabi was taken to the United States at the age of one. He did his undergraduate work at Cornell University on a scholarship, majoring in chemistry, and graduated in 1919. After a few fruitless years as a chemist, he decided it was physics he really enjoyed. He returned to school and obtained his Ph.D. at Columbia University in 1927. From 1927 to 1929 he made the European rounds, studying with a number of prominent physicists, including Bohr [1101], Sommerfeld [976], Pauli [1228], Heisenberg [1245], and Stern [1124].

Stern's work particularly impressed him. When Rabi returned to the United States he obtained a faculty position at Columbia University in 1929 and began work on molecular beams on his own. In 1933 and thereafter he instituted improvements in the study of molecular beams that made it possible to measure magnetic properties of atoms and molecules with great accuracy. This finding was important in connection with the development of the maser (acronym for "microwave amplification by stimulated emission radiation") by Townes [1400]. As an analytic technique, it was to be outdone by the nuclear magnetic resonance of Purcell [1378].

In 1944, the year after Stern's Nobel Prize, Rabi himself won the Nobel Prize in physics.

During World War II, Rabi worked on radar and on the atomic bomb and after the war served as chairman of the advisory committee to the Atomic Energy Commission from 1952 to 1956. In 1964 he became the first University Professor —without departmental ties—in Columbia's history.

[1213] **FLOREY,** Howard Walter Florey, Baron
Australian-English pathologist
Born: Adelaide, Australia, September 24, 1898
Died: Oxford, England, February 21, 1968

Florey attended the University of Adelaide and obtained his medical degree there in 1921. He then traveled to England as a Rhodes Scholar, studying at Oxford (under Sherrington [881]) and Cambridge. He received a Ph.D. at Cambridge in 1927. He went on to teach pathology, first at the University of Sheffield in 1931 and then, beginning in 1935, at Oxford.

Domagk's [1183] discovery in the mid-1930s of the antibacterial activity of Prontosil had raised the issue of chemotherapy with new urgency. Dubos' [1235] isolation of the first antibiotic in 1939 stimulated matters even further and the coming of World War II gave the fight against infection important military incentives.

Florey had been working on lysozyme, an antibacterial agent discovered by Fleming [1077], and that led naturally to a consideration of Fleming's neglected work on penicillin. In collaboration with Chain [1306], Florey set about trying to isolate the actual antibacterial agent from the mold studied by Fleming. Rather quickly he obtained a yellow powder from moldy broth that contained the agent.

During World War II, an intense course of research in Great Britain and the United States succeeded in preparing ever purer samples of penicillin. Initial studies of antibacterial activity were made with preparations containing only 1 percent of penicillin. Even so, these were encouraging. In 1941 penicillin was used on nine cases of human bacterial infection with dramatically successful results.

Penicillin was first used for war casualties in Tunisia and Sicily in 1943, and very successfully, too. By 1945 preparations were prepared in a concentration sufficient to display antibacterial activity even after a fifty-millionfold dilution and half a ton per month was being prepared.

Under war pressure, the chemical structure of penicillin was worked out by means of X-ray diffraction studies. The X rays were scattered in complicated fashion indeed from so complex a molecule, and for the first time electronic computers were used to work out the tedious mathematics involved; this foreshadowed the even greater computer vic-

tories in this field a decade later in connection with Hodgkin [1352] and her determination of the structure of vitamin B_{12}.

With the problem of structure beaten, methods of quantity production were devised. After the war, penicillin became an important medical workhorse, and it is still the most used of the antibiotics. Unlike some of the antibiotics discovered subsequently, penicillin has a very low toxicity.

Florey was knighted in 1944 for his work, and in 1945 he shared the Nobel Prize in medicine and physiology with Fleming and Chain. In 1958 synthetic penicillin analogues were formed by letting the mold form the basic ring structure and then adding different groups to that structure in the test tube. Such synthetic penicillins could be used against bacteria unaffected by the natural product.

In 1960 Florey was elected president of the Royal Society and in 1962 provost of Queen's College, Oxford. In 1965 he was given a life peerage and became Baron Florey of Adelaide.

[1214] **LYSENKO,** Trofim Denisovich
(lee-syen′ko)
Soviet biologist
Born: Karlovka, Poltava Oblast, Ukraine, September 29, 1898
Died: Kiev, Ukraine, November 20, 1976

Lysenko graduated from the Poltava School of Horticulture in 1921 and from the Kiev Institute of Agriculture in 1925.

After 1928 Lysenko was concerned with the cultivation of new varieties of plant forms, as Burbank [799] was a half century earlier. Like Burbank (but with far less cause, considering the half-century advance in genetic knowledge), Lysenko maintained that acquired characteristics could be inherited. He believed for instance that he could alter the genetic constitution of strains of wheat by properly controlling the environment. He denounced violently those geneticists, notably Mendel [638], Weismann [704], and T. H. Morgan [957], who had maintained that inherited characteristics were inborn and not affected by environmental change.

Lysenko was adroit enough to so arrange his arguments as to make them seem to fit Soviet economic and philosophic theories. (Even if they did, of course, that would in no way affect their scientific truth or falsity.) The Soviet leader Joseph Stalin, increasingly arbitrary in his old age, was foolish enough to think that he could profitably take a hand in scientific disputes. At a gathering of agricultural scientists, Lysenko's views, with the powerful support of Stalin, were accepted, and geneticists who disagreed, notably Vavilov [1122], were forced to disagree in silence.

With Stalin's death in 1953, Lysenko's views, essentially worthless, receded somewhat into the background. Nevertheless, serious damage had been done to Soviet biology and to the world image of Soviet science that was not repaired until the launching of Sputnik I in 1957. Then for a time Soviet science came to be overestimated as seriously, perhaps, as it had earlier been underestimated.

Lysenko retained some influence during the period of dominance of Nikita Khrushchev, but with the latter's fall in 1964 the end seemed to come. In 1965 Lysenko was removed from his post as director of the Institute of Genetics, which he had headed since 1940, and was roundly attacked by other scientists. It was an interesting way to celebrate the centennial of Mendel's publication of his genetic laws.

[1215] ZIEGLER, Karl (tsee'gler)
German chemist
Born: Helsa, near Kassel, Hesse-Nassau, November 26, 1898
Died: Muhlheim-Ruhr, August 12, 1973

Ziegler, the son of a minister, obtained his Ph.D. at the University of Marburg in 1920 and then taught first at Frankfurt and then at Heidelberg.

He was early interested in metallic-organic compounds, searching for improvements on the famous compounds developed by Grignard [993]. Unexpectedly, these metallic-organic compounds proved of importance in the synthesis of polymers. Throughout the 1930s and 1940s, plastics had been manufactured out of polymers that were produced in rather hit-or-miss fashion. That is, molecules were put together in such a way as to produce random orientation. Polyethylene, for instance, was formed by putting the two-carbon compound, ethylene, into long chains, end to end. But branches would form in the chain, weakening the final product and giving it a low melting point.

In 1953 Ziegler discovered that he could use a resin, to which ions of metals such as aluminum or titanium were attached, as a catalyst in the production of polyethylene. Chains without branching were then formed. As a result, the new polyethylene was tougher than the old and melted at a considerably higher temperature.

Similar catalysts are now being used, thanks to the work of Natta [1263], to orient molecules into long chains in which small side-chains of carbon atoms all point the same way—instead of in different directions at random—with the result that plastics and other polymers with new and useful properties can now be designed. As a result, Ziegler and Natta shared the 1963 Nobel Prize in chemistry.

[1216] MÜLLER, Paul Hermann
(myoo'ler)
Swiss chemist
Born: Olten, Solothurn Canton, January 12, 1899
Died: Basel, October 13, 1965

Müller, the son of a civil servant, was a practicing chemist by the time he returned to school for his degrees. He was educated at the University of Basel, obtaining his doctorate in 1925. He accepted a position thereafter with a dye firm.

In 1935 he began a research program designed to discover an organic compound that would kill insects quickly, yet would have little or no poisonous effect on plants or on mammals, and would be cheap, stable, and without unpleasant odor.

To be sure, there were a number of insecticides already on the market; but some were arsenic compounds that were dangerous to all forms of life and that accumulated (dangerously) in the soil. Others, less deadly to vertebrates, were also not very deadly to insects. It did not seem at all likely that Müller would find the combination of properties for which he was seeking, but if he did the value to agriculture would be inestimable.

In his search Müller concentrated on certain types of chlorine-containing compounds, for some examples of these types seemed to show promise. In September 1939, the month World War II broke out, Müller tried dichlorodiphenyltrichloroethane (DDT is the common abbreviation), a compound that had first been synthesized in 1873. It worked!

Switzerland put it to use at once in fighting the Colorado potato beetle. In 1942 it began to be produced commercially in the United States and the next year it had its first important use in connection, directly, with human beings. In late 1943, soon after it had been captured by Anglo-American forces, Naples had a typhus epidemic. Typhus epidemics had altered the course of World War I on the Russian and Balkan fronts, and it might well have done so again in World War II by stopping the Allied offensive in Italy faster than Nazi guns.

However, Nicolle [956] had shown that typhus was contagious only through the transmitting bite of the body louse and in January 1944 DDT was brought into play against the creature. The population of Naples was sprayed en masse and the lice died. For the first time in history, a winter epidemic of typhus (when the multiplicity of clothes, not removed very often, made louse infestation almost certain and almost universal) was stopped in its tracks. A similar epidemic was stopped in Japan in late 1945 after the American occupation.

Müller received the 1948 Nobel Prize in medicine and physiology for his discovery.

With the end of the war, DDT came into use for agricultural purposes. Insect raids upon man's food (or potential food) were decreased. Unfortunately, DDT-resistant strains of insects rapidly made their appearance, but to counter that, other insecticides were synthesized. The battle is by no means an easy one, but where insecticides are used intelligently and with caution, the insect menace is under far better control than ever before. However, it is also possible to use insecticides unwisely, with consequent damage to desirable species of animals and, for that matter, even to man.

Within a quarter century of its first great victories, therefore, DDT was being gravely studied as a possible serious pollutant of the environment. Its use was restricted or banned in various places and anxious looks are being turned on the study of ecology (the interrelationship of forms of life with each other and with the inanimate environment) and the effect upon it of man's chemical ingenuity and carelessness.

[1217] **THEILER,** Max (ty'ler)
South African–American microbiologist
Born: Pretoria, South Africa, January 30, 1899
Died: New Haven, Connecticut, August 11, 1972

Theiler attended the University of Capetown, but in 1920, midway in his studies, he persuaded his father (a Swissborn veterinarian) to send him to London. There he found he would have to start his college courses over again and rather than do that he spent four years in a hospital, absorbing practical instruction.

In 1922 Theiler arrived in the United States, having accepted a post at the Harvard University Medical School. He transferred to the Rockefeller Foundation in New York in 1930.

In the 1920s Theiler began research on yellow fever. Reed [822] had conquered it in one way by showing that wiping out the appropriate mosquito prevented its being transmitted. This, however, was only second best, for it was impractical to expect to wipe out all the mosquitoes. Artificially acquired immunity by vaccination, after the methods of Jenner [348] and Pasteur [642], would be better.

To work out some sort of vaccine, Theiler had to cultivate the yellow fever virus. He found that he could infect monkeys with yellow fever, then pass the virus into mice. In mice, it developed as encephalitis, a brain inflammation. He could pass the virus from mouse to mouse and then, eventually, back to monkeys. But then it was an attenuated virus, producing only the feeblest yellow fever attack but inducing full immunity to the most virulent strains of the virus. He used himself and his colleagues as guinea pigs to test its protective qualities against such full-strength virus.

This vaccine was much used by the French in Africa during the 1930s and 1940s. A still safer vaccine, produced by selecting nonvirulent strains of virus from among those passed along from chick embryo to chick embryo in nearly two hundred transplants, was prepared in 1937. This second vaccine became standard in South America.

For this work, Theiler, still without academic degrees, was awarded the 1951 Nobel Prize in medicine and physiology.

In 1964 he accepted a post as professor of microbiology at Yale University and held that till his retirement in 1967.

[1218] BEST, Charles Herbert
American-Canadian physiologist
Born: West Pembroke, Maine,
February 27, 1899
Died: Toronto, Ontario, March
31, 1978

Best, the son of a Canadian-born physician, attended the University of Toronto, graduating in 1921 after taking time out to serve in the Canadian artillery during World War I. (He qualified for Canadian citizenship by so doing.) He then went on to medical studies.

It was as a medical student that he put in a summer with Banting [1152] and helped isolate insulin. His motivation, in part, arose from the fact that a favorite aunt of his had recently died of diabetes.

He obtained his medical degree in 1925, and although he had missed out on a share of the Nobel Prize (to Banting's great indignation) he has received his fair share of the acclaim.

He remained connected with the University of Toronto, directed the Banting-Best Department of Medicine Research after Banting's death, and became the head of the physiology department in 1929. He did work on the anti-allergic enzyme histaminase, and on the blood-clotting agent heparin.

With Norman B. Taylor, he wrote a best-selling textbook on physiology, which went through eight editions in his lifetime.

[1219] VAN VLECK, John Hasbrouck
American physicist
Born: Middletown, Connecticut,
March 13, 1899
Died: Cambridge, Massachusetts,
October 27, 1980

Van Vleck graduated from the University of Wisconsin in 1920 and obtained his Ph.D. at Harvard in 1922. He taught at Harvard, the University of Minnesota, and the University of Wisconsin. He returned to Harvard in 1934 and remained there thereafter.

His chief field of research lay in the magnetic properties of individual atoms, based on a quantum mechanical consideration of the electronic distribution within the atom. During the 1930s he evolved a theory that took into account the influence on each electron of neighboring electrons. It is still the dominating theory in the field and for it he obtained a share of the 1977 Nobel Prize for physics.

[1220] BÉKÉSY, Georg von
Hungarian-American physicist
Born: Budapest, Hungary, June 3,
1899
Died: Hawaii, June 13, 1972

Békésy, the son of a diplomat, studied at the University of Bern in Switzerland, graduating in 1920. He went on to further studies at the University of Budapest, gaining his doctorate in 1923. He then worked for the Hungarian telephone system for nearly a quarter of a century thereafter, doing research in acoustics. He served also on the faculty of the University of Budapest.

His work went on undisturbed by World War II, but at its close, with Soviet forces occupying the land, he no longer thought it wise to remain in Hungary. He left in 1946 for Sweden, then in 1947 went to the United States.

After his arrival he worked at Harvard University and then, in 1966, accepted a professorial position at the University of Hawaii.

He devised an audiometer to test the hearing function. In addition, he suggested a theory of hearing to replace one first proposed by Helmholtz [631].

The immediate organ of hearing is contained in a spiral tube called the cochlea, located in the inner ear. It is divided into two sections by a basilar membrane.

The basilar membrane is made up of some 24,000 parallel fibers stretched across its width. These fibers are progressively wider as one moves along the cochlea to its tip.

Helmholtz had thought that each fiber had its natural period of vibration and responded to a sound that vibrated in that natural period. Every ordinary sound is made up of a combination of pure vibrations and such a sound sets up vibrations in a combination of fibers. The nerve messages sent by the various vibrating fibers would then be combined and interpreted by the brain as a sound of a particular pitch, loudness, and quality.

Békésy, however, conducted careful experiments with an artificial system designed to mimic all the essentials of the cochlea and found that sound waves passing through the fluid in the cochlea set up wavelike displacements in the basilar membrane. It is the shape of the wave, varying with pitch, loudness, and quality that gives the brain the material to work with.

As a result, Békésy was awarded the

1961 Nobel Prize in medicine and physiology, the first physicist ever to win the prize in this category.

[1221] LIPMANN, Fritz Albert
German-American biochemist
Born: Königsberg, Germany
(now Kaliningrad, Soviet Union),
June 12, 1899

After studying at the universities of Königsberg and of Munich, Lipmann obtained his medical degree at the University of Berlin in 1922 and his Ph.D. there in 1927. He spent three years thereafter in Meyerhof's [1095] laboratory in Heidelberg and a year with Levene [980] in New York.

The growth of the Nazi movement made life in Germany increasingly uncomfortable for him and in 1932 he transferred the scene of his labors to Copenhagen, Denmark. In 1939 he emigrated to the United States and became an American citizen in 1944. He worked for two years with Du Vigneaud [1239] at Cornell, then served on the staff of the Massachusetts General Hospital through 1957, after which he joined the Rockefeller Institute for Medical Research (now Rockefeller University) in New York.

Lipmann rationalized the role of phosphate esters in carbohydrate metabolism. The existence of these esters had first been noted by Harden [947] and had been worked out in greater detail by Meyerhof and by the Coris [1192, 1194], but in 1941 Lipmann supplied a vital point. He noted that phosphate esters, on breaking down and losing their phosphate group, might yield a relatively small amount of energy (low-energy phosphate) or a considerably higher amount (high-energy phosphate). He was able to distinguish the characteristic structures of each variety.

He went on to show that the course of carbohydrate metabolism involved the fixing of phosphate groups onto organic molecules in low-energy configuration, followed by changes in the molecule that would convert it into a high-energy configuration. The high-energy configuration would then serve as the "small change" energy bits utilized by the body.

This concept has been strengthened in the decades since. The energy content of the various foodstuffs, as molecules are broken down, is pumped into phosphate-containing compounds, changing the low-energy configuration into the high-energy. The most versatile of the high-energy configurations is a compound called adenosine triphosphate, usually referred to as ATP, which has been found to be concerned with body chemistry at almost every point where energy is required.

In 1947 Lipmann discovered a compound that controlled the transfer of two-carbon groups from one molecule to another. He called it coenzyme A and showed that the B vitamin known as pantothenic acid (first discovered in 1933, with a structure first worked out in 1940) made up part of the molecule. In fact, pantothenic acid in small quantities is essential to life, precisely because it forms part of coenzyme A.

The work of Krebs [1231] had shown that lactic acid was broken down to carbon dioxide and water by way of a two-carbon compound that entered what came to be known as the Krebs cycle. Lipmann thought it quite likely that this two-carbon compound entered the cycle with the help of coenzyme A and by 1951 was able to demonstrate this. The two-carbon compound combined with coenzyme A, in fact, to form acetylcoenzyme A.

Acetylcoenzyme A turned out to be a veritable crossroads of body chemistry. Carbohydrates, fats, and most portions of the protein molecule had to pass through it in order to be broken down for energy purposes and it was through acetylcoenzyme A that carbohydrate, for instance, could be converted into fat.

For his work on coenzyme A, Lipmann shared the 1953 Nobel Prize in medicine and physiology with Krebs.

[1222] **CLAUDE**, Albert
    Belgian-American cytologist
    Born: Longlier, Belgium, August 24, 1898

Claude received his M.D. from the University of Liège in 1928. He then went on to work at the Rockefeller Institute (now Rockefeller University) in New York and became an American citizen in 1941.

He pioneered the use of the electron microscope in the study of cells and by 1945 had produced the first studies of the intimate anatomy of the cell on a finer scale than would have been thought possible a decade before. He probed the mitochondria and discovered the endoplasmic reticulum, which serves as the structural background of the cell, holding the organelles in place.

For this he shared the 1974 Nobel Prize for physiology and medicine with Palade [1380] and De Duve [1418].

[1223] **BURNET**, Sir Frank Macfarlane
    Australian physician
    Born: Traralgon, Victoria, September 3, 1899

Burnet was educated at Geelong College in Victoria and obtained his medical degree in 1923 at the University of Melbourne. He did further work in England at the University of London, where he obtained his Ph.D. in 1927. He then returned to Australia, working at the Walter and Eliza Hill Institute for Medical Research in Melbourne, and after 1944 serving as professor of experimental medicine at the University of Melbourne.

Burnet's great concern was virus diseases, and through this he began to consider the mechanism of immunity. Immunity results from the formation of antibodies in response to some foreign substance, usually a protein. The antibody, by combining with the protein, vitiates its harmful effects. The protein eliciting the formation of an antibody may be part of a microorganism or not. It may be a food component or a tissue graft. Where antibodies are formed against essentially harmless proteins in food or other materials (producing distressing symptoms in the process) the process is described as an allergy.

The proteins of every human being

(identical twins excepted) are strange to every other human being. If skin, or some internal organ, is grafted from one person to another, the receiving person produces antibodies that combine with the graft and prevent it from "taking." Surgical procedures that could be very helpful, even life-saving, to a patient are thus brought to nothing by the patient's own chemical mechanisms.

It seemed to Burnet that the ability of a human being to form antibodies against the proteins of another human being might not be inborn. Antibodies against disease develop only after exposure to the microorganisms causing the disease. Allergies develop only after sensitization to a particular protein. Should not resistance to the proteins of another individual likewise be developed only in the course of life; perhaps very early in life, to be sure; in the embryonic stage, for instance?

Burnet made this suggestion in 1949 and the idea was acted on, with success, by Medawar [1396]. For this Burnet was knighted in 1951, and he and Medawar shared the 1960 Nobel Prize in medicine and physiology.

Burnet's suggestion was more pointed than ever when it was discovered in 1961 that the ability to form antibodies lodged with the thymus gland at birth and was not distributed through the tissues until some time after birth.

[1224] **DOBZHANSKY,** Theodosius
Russian-American geneticist
Born: Nemirov, Ukraine, January 25, 1900
Died: Davis, California, December 18, 1975

Dobzhansky, the son of a teacher of mathematics, entered the University of Kiev in 1917 and remained firmly at his studies during the chaos of the Russian Revolution and the civil war, graduating in 1921. He taught at Kiev, then moved on to Leningrad.

In 1927 Dobzhansky went to Columbia University to work with T. H. Morgan [957] and went with him to the California Institute of Technology. He obtained

a teaching position there and became a U.S. citizen in 1937. He returned to Columbia in 1940, accepted a position at the Rockefeller Institute (now Rockefeller University) in 1962, and, after his retirement in 1971, moved on to the University of California at Davis.

Since the rediscovery of Mendelian genetics by De Vries [792] and others in 1900, geneticists had been trying to fuse genetics with Darwin's [554] evolution by natural selection. The assumption had been that there were normal genes and periodic mutations (which were mostly deleterious and quickly weeded out), with the very occasional beneficial mutation serving to produce an evolutionary change.

Dobzhansky showed this was not so and in 1937 published a book entitled *Genetics and the Origin of Species,* in which Mendel and Darwin were neatly put together. Dobzhansky showed that mutations were common and were frequently viable so that there was no such thing as a "normal" gene, merely different varieties that all maintained themselves in varying amounts depending on chance and on local conditions. Natural selection had a great deal to work on, but the work was complex and anything but clearcut.

Dobzhansky also worked on the manner in which new species formed and on the manner in which humankind had evolved.

[1225] **RICKOVER,** Hyman George
Polish-American naval officer
Born: Makov, Poland (then part of Russia), January 27, 1900

Rickover was taken to the United States in 1904. His education was climaxed by graduation from the U. S. Naval Academy in 1922. He became a qualified submariner in 1930 and then studied engineering at Columbia University, earning his master's degree.

In 1946 Rickover (then a captain), with some other officers, went to Oak Ridge, Tennessee, to investigate the possibility of adapting a nuclear reactor to power production on naval vessels.

Largely through Rickover's drive, energy, and persistence, the project was carried through to completion. The U.S.S. *Nautilus,* launched in 1955, was the first of the nuclear submarines.

Rickover's scorning of convention, however, did not make him popular with old-line admirals of lesser ability, and it was only after considerable hesitation (and the application of popular pressure) that Rickover was promoted to vice admiral in 1959.

Although the nuclear submarine is primarily a war weapon, it has also served science. Its fuel supply lasts for months and it does not need to surface to charge batteries. In 1958 the *Nautilus* crossed the Arctic Ocean underwater from the Pacific to the Atlantic, thus initiating the study of the Arctic depths. Nuclear submarines also serve as an interesting method of keeping men closely confined over long periods of time—with results that may be useful in solving the psychological problems that will undoubtedly accompany prolonged space flight.

Rickover was awarded the 1964 Fermi award by the Atomic Energy Commission. It amounted to only $25,000 on that occasion for the cash value of the award had been pettishly reduced by half because of Congressional response to the fact that Oppenheimer [1280] had been granted the award the year before.

[1226] **LONDON,** Fritz Wolfgang
German-American physicist
Born: Breslau, Germany (now Wrocław, Poland), March 7, 1900
Died: Durham, North Carolina, March 30, 1954

London, the son of a Jewish professor, received his Ph.D. *summa cum laude* in 1921 from the University of Munich. The dissertation was on philosophy, but he returned to Munich in 1925 to work on theoretical physics under Sommerfeld [976] and later worked with Schrödinger [1117]. The coming to power of Hitler drove London out of Germany in 1933. After some years in Great Britain and France, he was appointed to a profes-

sorial position at Duke University in North Carolina and remained there the rest of his life.

In 1927 he had worked out a quantum mechanical treatment of the hydrogen molecule, which provided a strong theoretical basis for the study of molecules generally in terms of the new physics, and which laid the groundwork for the resonance theory of Pauling [1236].

[1227] **JOLIOT-CURIE,** Frédéric
(zhoh-lyoh-kyoo-ree')
French physicist
Born: Paris, March 19, 1900
Died: Paris, August 14, 1958

Joliot-Curie was born Jean Frédéric Joliot. He was the son of a merchant who had taken an active part on the side of the radicals in the Paris Commune of 1870. He was brought up without religion and remained an atheist all his life.

He added his wife's name to his own when he married Irène Curie [1204], the daughter of Pierre and Marie Curie [897, 965], not willing (since the Curies had no sons) to let a name so famous in science be wiped out in favor of his own.

He had obtained a degree in engineering from the School of Physics and Chemistry in Paris in 1923. In 1925 he attracted the attention of Langevin [1000], through whose recommendation he became special assistant to Marie Curie and in 1926 married her daughter. After 1931, the Joliot-Curies worked together as the Curies had done before them, and like the Curies they worked on radioactivity. Frédéric concentrated on the chemical aspects (and obtained his Ph.D. in that subject in 1930). Irène on the physical.

On two different occasions, they missed great discoveries by a hair. In 1932 they were within an ace of discovering the neutron but lost out to Chadwick [1150]. Then in 1933 they had the positron almost at their mercy and lost out to Anderson [1292].

In 1934, finally, lightning struck. They were studying the effect of alpha particles on light elements such as aluminum. They knocked protons out of the aluminum nuclei in the course of the bombardment, very much as Ernest Rutherford [996] had been doing in similar experiments for fifteen years. However, at one point the Joliot-Curies discovered that after they had ceased alpha particle bombardment, and protons ceased being emitted by the target, another form of radiation continued.

The Joliot-Curies decided that as a result of the bombardment of aluminum, they had formed phosphorus. Nor was this phosphorus the ordinary form. Their reasoning showed it had to be an isotope that did not occur in nature and that had to be radioactive. After they had stopped their bombardment, the new radioactive isotope of phosphorus they had formed kept right on breaking down. This was the source of the continuing radiation.

What the Joliot-Curies had done was to discover "artificial radioactivity." It was now realized that radioactivity was not at all a phenomenon confined to the very heaviest elements like uranium and thorium. Any element could be radioactive if the proper isotope was prepared. Since that day in 1934 over a thousand different radioactive isotopes have been prepared, at least one (and sometimes a dozen or more) for every known element. These artificial radioactive isotopes (also called radioisotopes) have proved far more useful in medicine, industry, and research than any of the naturally radioactive materials.

For this work the Joliot-Curies were awarded the Nobel Prize in chemistry in 1935, the third Nobel Prize to go to the Curie family, although Marie Curie failed by a year to live to see her daughter and son-in-law so honored.

Just as World War II started, Joliot-Curie discovered that in uranium fission, neutrons were produced. He therefore began work on the development of an explosive chain reaction, research which, in the United States, was eventually to produce a nuclear bomb. Joliot-Curie might have got there first, but for the war.

The German conquest of France in 1940 interrupted him. The Joliot-Curies managed to smuggle the heavy water (the only sizable quantity in the world) necessary for atomic bomb research out

of the country and out of the grasp of the Germans. (Their uranium was hidden, then reclaimed after the war and used to build France's first nuclear reactor in 1948.) The Joliot-Curies themselves remained behind in order to help organize resistance to Hitler. In 1944 Joliot-Curie helped Langevin to escape to Switzerland, then did the same for his wife and finally went into hiding himself.

After the war Joliot-Curie returned to work on a nuclear reactor and was made head of the French atomic energy commission by Charles de Gaulle. In 1948 the reactor was completed and it worked. It had been built in France, independently of the Anglo-American know-how. However, as it turned out, Joliot-Curie was an admitted Communist, having joined the party during World War II after the Nazis had executed Langevin's son-in-law. He was therefore removed from his position in 1950 and was replaced by his friend Perrin [990]. In 1951 he was awarded the Stalin Peace Prize, and for the rest of his life he remained an outspoken Communist.

[1228] PAULI, Wolfgang
Austrian-American physicist
Born: Vienna, Austria, April 25, 1900
Died: Zürich, Switzerland, December 14, 1958

Pauli, the son of a professor of colloid chemistry, was a youthful prodigy and his godfather had been Mach [733]. While still a teenager, he was writing formidably lucid articles on relativity that were admired by Einstein [1064] himself.

He studied under Sommerfeld [976] at the University of Munich and obtained his doctor's degree there in 1921. After postdoctorate work with Bohr [1101] at Copenhagen and with Born [1084] at Göttingen, he joined the faculty of the University of Hamburg in 1923 and the Zürich Institute of Technology in 1928.

He was impossibly clumsy with his hands and was a poor and stumbling lecturer; but it was his brain that was nonpareil. In 1925 he announced his exclusion principle. His teachers, Bohr and Sommerfeld, had worked out the energy levels of the electrons within atoms. These could be expressed as quantum numbers, which could be stated according to certain simple rules. There were three quantum numbers altogether. Pauli, after long consideration of the Zeeman [945] effect, capped the structure by allowing for a fourth. This fourth quantum number could be interpreted as supposing that in any particular energy level, two and only two electrons could be permitted, one spinning clockwise and one spinning counterclockwise.

Once this was allowed, it was possible to arrange the electrons of the various elements in shells and subshells. If the chemical properties of an element were assumed to depend on the number of electrons in the outermost shell, then Mendeléev's [705] periodic table was accounted for. The various elements in the first column (lithium, sodium, potassium, rubidium, cesium) are all similar chemically, because all have a single electron in the outermost shell. They have different numbers of shells inside that outermost one so that they have different atomic weights and vary in chemical detail. In the broad strokes, however, they are similar. The same holds for other rows of the periodic table, which thus completed the rationalization that had begun with Moseley's [1121] discovery of the atomic number.

For this important discovery Pauli received rather belated recognition in the form of the award of the 1945 Nobel Prize in physics.

Meanwhile, he had not rested on his oars. In the 1920s it was discovered that atoms emitting beta particles (speeding electrons) did so with less energy than they should. Some energy was apparently being destroyed and the law of conservation of energy might have to be abandoned. This, physicists did not want to do without overwhelming cause (though Bohr is reported to have been on the point of doing so).

In 1931 Pauli suggested that when a beta particle was emitted, another particle, without charge and perhaps without mass either, was also emitted and that this second particle carried off the missing energy. In the next year Fermi [1243] named Pauli's postulated particle the neutrino, which is Italian for "little neutral one."

Without charge and without mass, the neutrino is practically indetectable. For nearly a quarter of a century, it was the mere ghost of a particle and many scientists thought uneasily that it was simply a "gimmick" to save the energy bookkeeping and preserve the law of conservation of energy. In 1956 the neutrino was finally detected and proved to exist by a very elaborate experiment involving a nuclear power station (which did not exist in 1931).

Pauli lived to see his conjecture proved.

The neutrino, for all its evanescence, can have huge effects. In 1962, for instance, a theory was advanced wherein supernovas exploded through reactions involving neutrino formation.

In the 1930s Pauli was often in the United States and, with the coming of the war, he made his home there and joined the Institute of Advanced Study at Princeton, becoming an American citizen in 1946.

[1229] **OORT,** Jan Hendrik (awrt)
Dutch astronomer
Born: Franeker, April 28, 1900

Oort was the son of a physician and the grandson of a professor of Hebrew. He studied under Kapteyn [815] at the University of Groningen, obtaining his doctorate in 1926. He spent his professional life at Leiden Observatory, entering it in 1924 and becoming its director in 1945.

He had been Kapteyn's last student so it was rather fitting that he continued his teacher's studies of the motion of the stars in mass.

In so doing he was able to reduce Kapteyn's two star streams to something even more orderly, for he could show in 1927 that our galaxy was rotating about its center (something Lindblad [1185] was independently demonstrating). Since the galaxy is not a solid mass, but consists of individual bodies, it does not rotate all in one piece. Instead, the stars nearer the galactic center move faster than those farther from the center, just as the inner portions of Saturn's rings move faster than the outer, and just as the inner planets of the solar system revolve about the sun at a more rapid velocity than the outer ones.

It follows that those stars nearer the galactic center than our own sun, gain on us; in turn, our sun gains on the stars farther from the center than we are. There are Kapteyn's two streams, one group moving ahead and one falling behind, which in 1927 Oort reinterpreted by this picture of a rotating galaxy. From the motion of the stars near us, Oort was able to show that the center about which they were revolving lay in the constellation Sagittarius and in this he disagreed with Kapteyn and agreed with Shapley [1102]. In 1930, however, making allowance for Trumpler's [1109] discovery of dust clouds, which absorbed sunlight and made distant star clouds look fainter and therefore more distant than they really were, he scaled down the size of the galaxy. He calculated the distance of the galactic center at 30,000 light-years instead of Shapley's 50,000, and in this respect it is Oort's figure that is now accepted.

It could be shown, too, that the sun completes its revolution about the galactic center in about 200,000,000 years. From this period of revolution and from the distance of the sun from the galactic center, it could further be shown that the mass of our galaxy is about equal to the mass of 100,000,000,000 stars the size of our sun.

Knowledge concerning the general structure of our galaxy dates from this work of Oort, who has gone on to specialize in the details of galactic structure. After the discovery by Jansky [1295] of radio-wave emission from outer space, the key tool in studying the galaxy came to be radio telescopy. Radio waves could penetrate the dust clouds that remained opaque to ordinary light, so that by radio telescope the galactic center (forever hidden to our ordinary vision) could be studied.

The best means for such study was worked out during World War II, amid the hardships of the German occupation of the Netherlands. With the land prostrate, the observatory closed, instruments unavailable, nothing was left but the unconquerable mind. One of Oort's group, Van de Hulst [1430], spent his time carrying through calculations in 1944 that made it seem as though the electron and proton making up a hydrogen atom ought, once in several million years or so, spontaneously to switch orientation with respect to each other and, in so doing, emit radio-wave radiation at a wavelength of 21 centimeters (about 8 inches). The amount radiated by any ordinary quantity of hydrogen would be far too small to detect, of course, but the quantities of hydrogen thinly spread between the stars ought to amount, in total, to a mass large enough to radiate a detectable amount.

With the war over, and Holland free once more, it became possible to attempt to confirm this purely theoretical deduction. In 1951 Oort and his group did just this. They detected "the song of hydrogen." The pattern traced out by this "song" has allowed astronomers to follow the spiral structure of the galactic arms where the concentration of hydrogen is highest. For this reason the decade of the 1950s saw the spiral structure of our galaxy mapped out in some detail.

Oort in 1950 propounded an ingenious theory concerning the origin of comets. He suggests that the comets make up a vast cloud of minor planets enveloping the sun in a huge asteroid belt at a light-year's distance or thereabouts. Small numbers of these are continually being hurled into the solar system proper through the gravitational perturbations of the nearer stars. About 20 percent of the original supply of comets, Oort estimates, have been hurled inward thus.

[1230] **GABOR,** Dennis
     Hungarian-British physicist
     Born: Budapest, Hungary, June 5, 1900
     Died: London, England, February 9, 1979

Gabor obtained his doctoral degree in Germany in 1927, but with the coming to power of Hitler he left for England, where he served as a professor of physics at the University of London. In 1967 he went to the United States to work at the Columbia Broadcasting System Laboratories at Stamford, Connecticut.

While in England he worked on the electron microscope and got the idea of holography. In ordinary photography, a beam of reflected light falls on a photographic film and a two-dimensional photograph of a cross section of that beam is taken.

Suppose instead that a beam of light is split in two. One part strikes an object and is reflected with all the irregularities that this object would impose on it. The second part is reflected from a mirror with no irregularities. The two parts meet at the photographic film, and the interference pattern is photographed. If light is then shone through the film, it takes on the interference characteristics and produces a three-dimensional image with far more information than the flat photograph. Gabor worked out the theoretical backing of holography in 1947, but it was not reduced to a practical working technique till 1965.

As a result, Gabor received the 1971 Nobel Prize for physics.

[1231] **KREBS,** Sir Hans Adolf
German-British biochemist
Born: Hildesheim, Hannover,
Germany, August 25, 1900
Died: Oxford, November 22, 1981

Krebs, the son of a Jewish physician, received his education at several German universities, obtaining his medical degree in 1925 from the University of Hamburg. He practiced as an ear, nose, and throat specialist, but was drawn to research. He worked as an assistant to Warburg [1089] from 1926 to 1930.

Thereafter, he grew interested in the breakdown of amino acids, the building blocks of proteins. Amino acids might be used for the construction of proteins, but under many circumstances they could be broken down for energy. In the latter case the first step was to remove the ni-

trogen atoms they contained (deamination), and it was Krebs who first observed the process.

The nitrogen atoms were eliminated from the body in the form of urea (the artificial synthesis of which by Wöhler [515] a century earlier had initiated modern organic chemistry). In 1932 Krebs worked out the manner in which urea was formed, by way of the breakdown and regeneration of a portion of the molecule of the amino acid arginine. The urea cycle has been more detailed in the generation since; but its main skeleton is still as Krebs laid it out.

With the advent of Hitler, Krebs could no longer remain in Germany. He went to England in 1933, studied at Cambridge, and by 1934 joined the faculty of the University of Sheffield, moving on to Oxford University in 1954.

Krebs, working under Hopkins [912], took up the matter of carbohydrate metabolism. Meyerhof [1095] and the Coris [1192, 1194] had dealt with those changes that carried the glycogen of the liver down to lactic acid. That portion of the change, however, did not involve the absorption of oxygen and produced only a comparatively small amount of energy. The lactic acid must somehow be broken down to carbon dioxide and water and in the process must take up oxygen. Warburg, Krebs's old superior, had measured oxygen uptake, but that alone had yielded no insight into the details of the change.

Szent-Györgyi's [1167] finding, that once oxygen uptake rates declined they could be restored by any one of four four-carbon acids, was a beginning. Krebs went on to locate two six-carbon acids, including the well-known citric acid, that did the same thing. All must be involved in the chain that led from lactic acid to carbon dioxide and water. By 1940 the manner in which all these compounds fit together was worked out by Krebs.

The result was a cycle; that is, a regenerating series of chemical changes. The lactic acid, a three-carbon compound, was broken down to a two-carbon compound, the exact nature of which was later worked out by Lipmann

[1221]. This two-carbon compound combined with the four-carbon oxaloacetic acid (one of Szent-Györgyi's four-carbon compounds) to form the six-carbon citric acid.

The citric acid underwent a series of changes that converted it to oxaloacetic acid once more. In the process of those changes it lost carbon dioxide and gave up hydrogen atoms that combined (through a series of complicated steps) with atmospheric oxygen. It was the combination of hydrogen and oxygen that yielded energy for the body.

Once the citric acid had been converted back to oxaloacetic acid, the latter was ready to take up another two-carbon fragment and go through the procedure once more. At each turn of this Krebs cycle one two-carbon compound was ground up into carbon dioxide and water.

The Krebs cycle has turned out to be the major energy producer in living organisms (though, of course, not the only one). Fat molecules are broken down into the same two-carbon compound into which carbohydrate molecules are broken down, so that the Krebs cycle represents the final stage of energy production from fats, too. When protein is consumed for energy purposes, fragments enter the Krebs cycle at various stages, most but not all entering at the two-carbon compound stage.

For his work Krebs shared the 1953 Nobel Prize in physiology and medicine with Lipmann. He was knighted in 1958.

[1232] **GRANIT,** Ragnar Arthur
Finnish-Swedish physiologist
Born: Helsinki, Finland, October 30, 1900

At the time of Granit's birth, Finland was part of the Russian empire, but in 1918 it had gained the status of an independent nation.

Granit earned his medical degree at the University of Helsinki in 1927. After several years in the United States, where he met Hartline [1276] and Wald [1318], and in Great Britain, where he studied under Sherrington [881], Granit moved to Sweden, permanently, in 1940.

Like Hartline, Granit worked on individual nerve cells of the retina of the eye and was the first to show that single nerve fibers could distinguish between different wavelengths of light. He shared, with Hartline and Wald, the 1967 Nobel Prize in medicine and physiology.

[1233] **KUHN,** Richard (koon)
Austrian-German chemist
Born: Vienna, Austria, December 3, 1900
Died: Heidelberg, Germany, July 31, 1967

Kuhn, after serving in the Austro-Hungarian army in World War I, studied at the University of Vienna, then Munich, and obtained his Ph.D at the latter institution in 1922 under the direction of Willstätter [1009]. In 1929 he received a professorial appointment at the University of Heidelberg.

The direction of his later research was much like that of Karrer [1131]. Kuhn and his group synthesized both vitamin A and vitamin B_2 almost simultaneously with Karrer. He was one of the first, in 1938, to isolate vitamin B_6 (pyridoxine) in pure form, beginning with 14,000 gallons of skim milk.

In 1938, a year after Karrer's Nobel award, Kuhn too received the Nobel Prize in chemistry. Hitler, offended by a Nobel Peace award to Carl von Ossietzky, a man in a Nazi concentration camp, refused to allow Germans to accept such awards. Kuhn was forced to reject the prize and it was only after World War II that he could be properly honored.

[1234] **UHLENBECK,** George Eugene
(oo'len-bek)
Dutch-American physicist
Born: Batavia, Java (now Djakarta, Indonesia), December 6, 1900

Uhlenbeck, born in what was then part of the colonial empire of the Netherlands, was educated in the homeland, obtaining his Ph.D. in 1927 at the University of Leiden. He then went to the

United States. He joined the faculty of the University of Michigan in 1927, then, during World War II, worked on radar research at the Massachusetts Institute of Technology. In 1961 he went to the Rockefeller Institute (now Rockefeller University) in New York City.

It was while he was still a student at Leiden that he made his most notable contribution. Soon after Pauli [1228] had demonstrated the necessity of a fourth quantum number to describe the electrons in a given atom completely, Uhlenbeck and his colleague Goudsmit [1255] demonstrated that it could be interpreted neatly in terms of particle spin. They showed furthermore that the unit of electron spin was half a common quantum unit so that the electron may be said to have a spin of $+\frac{1}{2}$ or $-\frac{1}{2}$.

Eventually, similar spins (equal to $\frac{1}{2}$ or some multiple thereof) were found to exist for almost all other particles.

[1235] **DUBOS,** René Jules (dyoo-bohs′)
French-American microbiologist
Born: Saint Brice, Haute-Vienne, February 21, 1901

Dubos received his early education (in agricultural sciences) in France. He arrived in America in 1924 and obtained his doctorate three years later from Rutgers University in New Brunswick, New Jersey (Waksman [1128] was teaching microbiology there). Dubos's doctoral thesis dealt with soil microorganisms and that remained his field of research thereafter.

Upon receiving his degree Dubos joined the Rockefeller Institute for Medical Research (now Rockefeller University) in New York and in 1938 became an American citizen. Like Waksman, Dubos was interested in the antibacterial substances produced by microorganisms. In 1939 he isolated such a substance from *Bacillus brevis* and named it tyrothricin. This was found to be a mixture of several polypeptides (with molecules consisting, like proteins, of chains of amino acids, but only of comparatively short chains).

Dubos's compounds were not very effective in themselves but their discovery aroused interest in Fleming's [1077] penicillin and led Waksman to isolate streptomycin and other men to produce the broad-spectrum tetracyclines of the late 1950s.

[1236] **PAULING,** Linus Carl
American chemist
Born: Portland, Oregon, February 28, 1901

Pauling, the son of a druggist, grew interested in chemistry at the age of thirteen, thanks to a friend with a home chemistry laboratory. He attended Oregon State College, graduating in 1922. He obtained his Ph.D. in 1925 at the California Institute of Technology and remained there throughout his academic career, becoming a professor in 1927. In 1926 he went to Europe for a year and a half to study under Sommerfeld [976].

Before he was thirty, Pauling had revolutionized thinking concerning the structure of molecules. Lewis [1037], Pauling's long-time friend, had introduced Ernest Rutherford's [996] nuclear atom into the chemical structure of molecules, but to do so he had pictured a static atom, with motionless electrons placed at the corners of a cube. Meanwhile, though, De Broglie [1157] had revealed the wave characteristics of particles and it was necessary to view electrons as wave forms without fixed positions. London [1226] had then pioneered this view in connection with the hydrogen molecule.

Pauling began with De Broglie's quantum mechanics and worked out a theory whereby electrons, as wave forms, interacted in pairs to form a stabler and less energetic system in combination than either had been separately. This combination could only take place if the atoms, of which the electrons formed part, remained in close proximity. To separate the atoms, one had to add energy to break the electron combination. In this way the chemical bond between atoms was accounted for and Kekulé's [680] system of depicting molecules was rationalized.

But Pauling's picture was clearer than

Kekulé's, for Pauling could show that a particular bond might have some charge separation associated with it. A bond could therefore be partially ionic, thus restoring a bit of Berzelius [425]. Much that had been mysterious in organic chemistry and had been accepted simply as empirical fact, could now be shown to make sense in Pauling's more elaborate view.

Pauling further showed that certain compounds were stabilized by the interaction of electrons over systems of bonds that were alternately double and single. The electron waves were, so to speak, "smeared out" over a relatively extended region. This theory of "resonance" explained the unusual properties of benzenes, accounted for Gomberg's [950] free radicals, and performed many other tasks that could not be touched without it.

In 1939 Pauling published his views in a book entitled *The Nature of the Chemical Bond*, which he dedicated to Lewis. It proved to be one of the most influential chemical texts of the twentieth century.

Pauling went on to apply his notions of molecular structure to the complex molecules of living tissue. He was one of the first to advance the suggestion, in the early 1950s, that protein molecules were arranged in helices (that is, in spiral staircase form); a similar structure advanced soon afterward by Crick [1406] and James Dewey Watson [1480] in connection with nucleic acids was to prove a thunderous breakthrough in the field of genetics. (Pauling might have anticipated Crick and Watson, had he had better X-ray diffraction data available to him.)

At that time Pauling also studied certain blood diseases and worked out useful theories as to the structures of abnormal hemoglobin, thus introducing the notion of a molecular disease, one caused by the abnormal structure of, in this case, a protein molecule.

In 1954 Pauling was awarded the Nobel Prize in chemistry for his work on molecular structure.

After World War II Pauling was in the forefront of the fight against the nuclear danger overshadowing the world. He vigorously fought nuclear testing by the United States and the Soviet Union alike, being quite certain that the very survival of civilization and even of life depends on nuclear disarmament. For this he was awarded the 1962 Nobel Peace Prize, making him the second person in history (after Marie Curie) to win two Nobel Prizes.

In 1970 Pauling made another sort of headline with his contention that large doses of vitamin C were effective in the prevention of the common cold.

[1237] **MENZEL,** Donald Howard
American astronomer
Born: Florence, Colorado, April 11, 1901
Died: December 14, 1976

Menzel graduated from the University of Denver in 1920 and gained his Ph.D. at Princeton in 1924. From 1932 Menzel served on the Harvard faculty and from 1954 to 1966 was director of the Harvard Observatory.

In his later years he took up the thankless task of combating one of the most popular of the pseudo-scientific fallacies that periodically afflict mankind; that of "flying saucers" or "unidentified flying objects" (UFO's). Combating the enthusiastic proponents of the theory that flying saucers represent dangerous (or beneficent) invasions from outer space, Menzel, with the assistance of Mrs. Lyle Gifford Boyd, published an urbane analysis of the various reports that effectively demolished them.

In retirement Menzel was given the task of supervising the assignment of names to the lunar features discovered on the other side of the moon (and on our side) by the probes that have circled our satellite and landed upon it.

[1238] **HINTON,** Christopher Hinton, Baron
English nuclear engineer
Born: Tisbury, Wiltshire, May 12, 1901

Hinton, the son of a schoolmaster, spent his teenage years as an engineer with a railway. He attended Cambridge University on a scholarship and graduated in 1926. During World War II he worked with chemical explosives.

Thanks to the work of Szilard [1208] and Fermi [1243], nuclear explosives had been developed in the United States and Hinton was placed in charge of a project designed to harness uranium fission to peaceful purposes. In this, Hinton was successful. The Soviet Union had built a small nuclear station for the production of electric power in 1954, but the world's first large-scale station of this sort was Calder Hall, built under Hinton's guidance. Calder Hall was put into action in 1956 and Hinton was knighted in 1957 and created a life peer in 1965. He took the title of Baron Hinton of Bankside.

[1239] **DU VIGNEAUD,** Vincent (dyoo-veen'yoh)
American biochemist
Born: Chicago, Illinois, May 18, 1901
Died: Scarsdale, New York, December 11, 1978

Du Vigneaud graduated from the University of Illinois in 1923 and obtained his Ph.D. at the University of Rochester in 1927. After some time at Illinois with Rose [1114], he accepted a professorial position at George Washington University School of Medicine in Washington, D.C., transferring to Cornell University Medical College in New York City in 1938.

Du Vigneaud's interest lay chiefly in the amino acids and, of his numerous achievements, three stand out.

In the late 1930s his studies of the amino acid methionine and of related compounds made it possible to trace how the body shifted a methyl group $(-CH_3)$ from compound to compound. By such shifts, the body sometimes completes the construction of a complicated molecule, slipping in the last carbon atom, so to speak, by way of the active

methyl group of the methionine molecule.

In 1940 Du Vigneaud identified a compound called biotin as being what had earlier been referred to as vitamin H. Working on tiny quantities of biotin with the sure instinct of the chemical detective, Du Vigneaud deduced its rather complicated two-ring structure in 1942. Chemists at Merck Laboratories synthesized the compound in 1943, according to Du Vigneaud's specifications, and it turned out to be biotin indeed.

Most exciting of all, however, was his work on the hormones produced by the posterior lobe of the pituitary gland. For years he had been working on one called oxytocin. He had broken it down into fragments, studied those fragments, and deduced that oxytocin was a small protein molecule made up of only eight amino acids. (The average protein molecule contains several hundred amino acids.)

By 1953 Du Vigneaud had even worked out the exact order in which the amino acids appeared in the chain, as Sanger [1426] was doing for the much more complicated molecule of insulin. The simplicity of oxytocin made it possible for Du Vigneaud to go beyond Sanger's work, for in 1954 he put together the eight amino acids in the order he had deduced and found that he did have oxytocin with all the properties of the natural material. It was the first protein hormone ever synthesized and pointed the way to similar victories over more complicated proteins. For this deed Du Vigneaud was awarded the 1955 Nobel Prize in chemistry.

[1240] **ELVEHJEM,** Conrad Arnold (el'veh-yem)
American biochemist
Born: McFarland, Wisconsin, May 27, 1901
Died: Madison, Wisconsin, July 27, 1962

Elvehjem, the son of a farmer, spent his professional life at the University of Wisconsin. He was educated there, graduating in 1923 and obtaining his doctorate in 1927. He joined the faculty in 1925, was head of the biochemistry department in 1944, dean of the graduate school in 1946, and president of the university in 1958.

In the 1930s Elvehjem's interest turned to the vitamins, a subject occupying much biochemical attention in that decade. The molecular structure of the vitamins was yielding to chemical analysis and so was the molecular structure of the coenzymes. Men like Euler-Chelpin [1011] and Warburg [1089] had shown that Harden's [947] coenzyme and closely related coenzymes contained nicotinic acid as part of the molecular structure. Funk [1093] had, as long ago as 1912, isolated nicotinic acid from rice polishings. He, however, had tried its effect on beriberi and failed.

Yet its proved occurrence in a molecule as vital to the body's workings as a coenzyme now restored interest in it. Since Funk's finding, it had been amply proved, thanks to the work of Goldberger [1027], that pellagra too was a dietary-deficiency disease. Funk himself had suggested that pellagra might be such a disease. Would nicotinic acid help there?

In 1937 Elvehjem, working with dogs suffering from blacktongue, the canine analogue of pellagra, administered 30 milligrams of nicotinic acid to one. Improvement was phenomenal and further doses brought on complete recovery.

This was more than a matter of simply proving that nicotinic acid was a vitamin and an antipellagra factor. Biochemical knowledge had reached the point where one could now say that pellagra was a set of symptoms that arose from the failure of certain enzymes to function normally. The particular enzymes that failed were those that made use of coenzymes containing nicotinic acid as part of the structure. The body could not manufacture nicotinic acid from simpler compounds and had to have it supplied, ready-made, in the diet.

In this way the rationale of vitamin requirements was worked out. Since then, many of the B vitamins have been connected with specific coenzymes; for instance, pantothenic acid was shown to be

a portion of Lipmann's [1221] coenzyme A, and riboflavin (vitamin B_2) was shown by Theorell [1267] to form part of other coenzymes.

Elvehjem's later work was on trace minerals, like zinc and cobalt, a field of research that was to reach a climax a decade later with the work of Folkers [1312]. Such minerals are also essential to life in small quantities and, like the vitamins, perform their functions as component parts of enzymes.

[1241] LAWRENCE, Ernest Orlando
American physicist
Born: Canton, South Dakota, August 8, 1901
Died: Palo Alto, California, August 27, 1958

Lawrence, the son of an educator and the grandson of a Norwegian immigrant, was educated at the University of South Dakota, graduating in 1922. He was not a particularly good student outside science and his early ambition was to enter medicine. A physics teacher at the University of Minnesota roused Lawrence's interest in that field, however. He went on to obtain his Ph.D. in physics from Yale in 1925 and joined its faculty. In 1928 he transferred to the University of California, and he remained there, becoming full professor in 1930.

One of the big problems in the nuclear physics of the 1920s was improving methods of bombarding atomic nuclei. At first the only available projectiles were the alpha particles used by Ernest Rutherford [996]. These, however, had a double positive charge and approached the positively charged atomic nucleus only with difficulty. In 1928 Gamow [1278] had suggested that protons be used instead. These were hydrogen ions, which were very easily available, and they could be imparted the necessary energies by being accelerated in an electric field. Since they possessed only a single positive charge, they would be less strongly repelled by the atomic nuclei they approached than alpha particles would be.

Various devices for imparting the acceleration were invented, the first actually put into action being Cockcroft [1198] and Walton's [1269] voltage multiplier. A far more spectacular particle accelerator was devised by Van de Graaff [1246]. The key device, however, was supplied by Lawrence.

It seemed to Lawrence that instead of trying to give protons or other charged particles one enormous "kick" by building up huge potentials, it might pay to have them move in circles and give them a small kick each time round. The small kicks would build up indefinitely.

In 1930, therefore, he built a small device in which protons were made to travel between the poles of a large magnet that deflected their paths into circles. At each turn they received another push of electric potential. This made them move faster and therefore in a path that, under the constant force of the magnet, curved less sharply. Their path was a sort of spiral that brought them closer and closer to the rim of the instrument. By the time the charged particles finally shot out of the instrument, altogether, they had accumulated high energies indeed.

Lawrence called the instrument a cyclotron. The first cyclotron was a small one, but larger ones were quickly built. By the time the 1930s came to an end, thirty-five huge cyclotrons had been built, twenty more were under construction, and Lawrence was awarded the 1939 Nobel Prize in physics.

The cyclotrons, according to original design, reached their limits by 1940, but modifications and improvements, introduced by men like McMillan [1329], carried the energies to still higher levels. The advances in the understanding of nuclear physics in the last generation could scarcely have taken place without the use of the cyclotron and related instruments.

During World War II Lawrence was busily engaged at Oak Ridge in one of the less successful attempts to separate quantities of uranium-235 from ordinary uranium, for incorporation into the "atomic pile" being built in Chicago by Fermi [1243]. He was one of those scientists who, like Compton [1159] and

unlike Franck [1081] and Szilard [1208], favored the use of the atomic bomb against Japanese cities and never felt any particular concern about the social aspects of the new weapon.

After the war, he spent the final years of his life on nuclear research and in 1957 he won the Fermi award, the highest scientific honor the United States could offer.

After his death, element 103, discovered in 1961, was named lawrencium in his honor.

[1242] **HUGGINS,** Charles Branton
Canadian-American surgeon
Born: Halifax Nova Scotia, September 22, 1901

Huggins graduated from Acadia University in 1920 and then went to the United States for his medical education. He obtained his M.D. from Harvard in 1924. After internship and residency, he joined the faculty of the University of Chicago Medical School in 1927 and remained there, becoming a naturalized American citizen in 1933.

In 1941 Huggins showed that prostatic cancer in males could be controlled by the administration of female sex hormone. This was the first indication that a major type of cancer could be controlled by purely chemical means. For this he shared with Rous [1067] the 1966 Nobel Prize in physiology and medicine.

[1243] **FERMI,** Enrico (fehr'mee)
Italian-American physicist
Born: Rome, Italy, September 29, 1901
Died: Chicago, Illinois, November 28, 1954

Fermi received his doctor's degree *magna cum laude* at the University of Pisa in 1922, just a few months before Benito Mussolini seized power in Italy. Fermi did postdoctorate work in Germany thereafter, under Born [1084], but returned to Italy in 1924 and by 1926 was a professor of physics at the University of Rome, busily working out theories as to the behavior of electrons in solids.

Fermi grew interested in the neutron, as soon as that particle was discovered in 1932 by Chadwick [1150]. Neutral particles seemed to be his forte, for it was he who named the neutrino, which Pauli [1228] had postulated. Fermi went on to work out some of the mathematics involved in neutrino emission. He also worked out the nature of what is now called the weak interaction, which is only a trillionth as strong as the electromagnetic interaction. Fermi's work in this respect guided Yukawa [1323] in his elucidation of the strong interaction.

The importance of the neutron was that with it many new types of nuclear reactions could be initiated. For one thing, the uncharged neutron was not repelled by the positively charged atomic nucleus, as positively charged alpha particles and protons were. For that reason, it was not necessary to build up neutron energies through the use of the accelerators such as those constructed by Cockcroft [1198], Van de Graaff [1246], and Lawrence [1241] for charged particles. Indeed, neutrons were more effective when they possessed less energy.

Fermi discovered this when he noted that neutrons were particularly effective in initiating nuclear reactions if they passed through water or paraffin first. The light atoms in those compounds absorbed some of the neutron's energy with each collision and slowed them to the point where they moved with only the normal speed of molecules at room temperature. Such "thermal neutrons" stayed in the vicinity of a particular nucleus a longer fraction of a second and were therefore more easily absorbed than fast neutrons.

When a neutron is absorbed by the nucleus of a particular atom, the new nucleus sometimes emits a beta particle and becomes an atom of the next higher element. It occurred to Fermi, therefore, in 1934 to bombard uranium with neutrons (fateful decision) in an attempt to form an artificial element above uranium in the periodic table. (No such transuranium element was known to occur in

nature.) Fermi thought for a while that he had actually obtained his new element, which he called uranium X. To Fermi's consternation, this possibility was prematurely disclosed by his superior and was loudly publicized by the Fascist press, anxious to advertise "Italian science" and to boast of a "Fascist victory."

Actually, Fermi was right to a certain extent, as McMillan [1329] was to show five years later. In the main, though, he was wrong. When Hahn [1063] investigated the problem, it was eventually found that Fermi had a much bigger tiger by the tail than he had suspected. He was, without knowing it, playing with uranium fission. Nevertheless, for his work on neutron bombardment, particularly with thermal neutrons, he received the 1938 Nobel Prize in physics, months before Meitner [1060] let the fission-cat out of the bag.

However, these were increasingly bad times for the Fermis. Fermi was anti-Fascist and at the Nobel Prize ceremonies he did not wear the Fascist uniform or give the Fascist salute. Both would have been ridiculously out of place, but the controlled Italian press saw fit to castigate Fermi for these omissions. Besides, Fermi's wife was Jewish, and as Hitler's influence became more pronounced in Italy, anti-Jewish laws were passed. From Stockholm, where Fermi accepted the prize, he and his family sailed to the United States, there to remain permanently. (He had been able to ready himself for this eventuality because Bohr [1101] had quietly hinted to him that he might win the prize.) He became professor of physics at Columbia University.

Once in America, Fermi and others, like Szilard [1208], began to wonder if, in uranium fission, neutrons could be emitted that would then cause other uranium atoms to undergo fission, producing more neutrons and still more fission and so on. Such a nuclear chain reaction would produce incredible amounts of energy in a split second, all from one neutron, which might be supplied from the stray quantities that were in the air all the time, thanks to cosmic rays.

When it was decided to establish the Manhattan Project and try to build a structure in which such a chain reaction might take place, Fermi was placed in charge of the actual building. He was, after Pearl Harbor, an "enemy alien" (he was not naturalized as an American citizen until 1944) but sanity prevailed and this was not allowed to interfere.

Uranium and uranium oxide were piled up in combination with graphite blocks. The graphite served to slow neutrons to thermal velocities, and at those slow velocities neutrons were more easily absorbed by the uranium, and fission was more easily induced. (Fermi's discovery of the decade before paid off here.) The structure was called an atomic pile because the blocks were piled up one atop the other and because the word "pile" used by itself gave no hint of the nature of the work. However, it was the first nuclear reactor, to use the correct term.

The atomic pile worked. It contained cadmium rods to absorb neutrons until such time as the fission reaction was to be initiated. That moment came at 3:45 P.M. on December 2, 1942, in the squash court of the University of Chicago; when the cadmium rods were slowly withdrawn, the chain reaction became self-sustaining and the atomic age began. It was announced (among those in the know) by a cryptic telegram sent out by Compton [1159] that read, "The Italian navigator has entered the new world." And, indeed, Fermi had accomplished a feat as earthshaking as that performed by that other Italian navigator, Columbus [121], four and a half centuries before, and with far greater potentialities for good and evil. In a little over two and a half years, such a fission reaction, arranged to build up to explosive violence, leveled two Japanese cities, with horrible loss of life, and ended World War II. Four years after that, the Soviet Union, under the leadership of Kurchatov [1261], duplicated the American feat and the specter of nuclear war rose to plague a terrified mankind.

In 1945 Fermi accepted a profes-sorship at the Institute for Nuclear Studies at the University of Chicago, and under him a group of graduate students formed who included Gell-Mann [1487], Chamberlain [1439], Lee [1473], and Yang [1451].

Fermi died young of stomach cancer; element 100, discovered the year after his death, was named fermium in his honor.

He lived long enough to see the development by Teller [1332] and others of a far greater and deadlier nuclear weapon than the fission bomb. Like Oppenheimer [1280] he opposed the development of this more deadly H-bomb (or fusion bomb), although he had earlier approved the use of the fission bomb over Japan. He did not live to see his nuclear reactor put to other than explosive uses by Rickover [1225] and Hinton [1238].

[1244] **OLIPHANT**, Marcus Laurence Elwin
Australian physicist
Born: Adelaide, South Australia, October 8, 1901

Oliphant graduated with honors in 1927, from the University of Adelaide, then went to Cambridge for his Ph.D., which he earned in 1929.

Not long after the discovery of deuterium (hydrogen-2) by Urey [1164], Oliphant began to work with deuterons, the nuclei of the deuterium atom. He found, in 1934, that if he bombarded deuterium itself with deuterons, he formed a hitherto unknown atom of a still more complicated form of hydrogen, hydrogen-3. This new hydrogen isotope, called tritium, turned out to be feebly radioactive, the only radioactive form of hydrogen known.

This work on hydrogen-isotope interactions led, by the way, to work on hydrogen fusion and, eventually, to the development of the hydrogen bomb (and someday, one hopes, to useful fusion reactors as well).

In 1943 Oliphant proposed a design for an accelerator more powerful than those then existing. Such accelerators—proton synchrotrons—were eventually built in the 1950s and 1960s and are now the most powerful tools of the sort that physicists have.

[1245] **HEISENBERG**, Werner Karl
(hy'zen-behrg)
German physicist
Born: Würzburg, December 5, 1901
Died: Munich, February 1, 1976

Heisenberg's father was a student of the humanities who became a professor specializing in Byzantine history.

As a teenager after World War I, Heisenberg seemed far removed from the usual stereotype of the scholarly youngster. He engaged in street fights against the Communists in Munich and in later years was an enthusiastic mountain climber. Nevertheless, his serious interest was in science.

At the University of Munich he studied under Sommerfeld [976], obtaining his Ph.D. in 1923. He worked as assistant to Born [1084] at Göttingen and under Bohr [1101] in Copenhagen.

Having worked with Bohr and Sommerfeld, it would have been odd if he had not been interested in the Bohr-Sommerfeld atoms. So were other physicists, such as De Broglie [1157] and Schrödinger [1117], who were trying to present a more subtle picture of the atom than that offered by Bohr, by treating the electrons as wave forms rather than as simple particles.

Heisenberg, however, abandoned all attempts at pictorialization. He believed that one should confine oneself to observable phenomena and not to imaginary pictures. In this, he followed Mach's [733] line of thinking of half a century earlier.

The atoms devised by Bohr and others were intended to explain the positions of the spectral lines. Why not, therefore, begin with those lines and devise a mathematical relationship to account for them? This, Heisenberg did in 1927 during a vacation on a North Sea island where he had gone to escape the discomfort of hay fever. He made use, with Born's help, of matrix algebra, evolving a system called matrix mechanics. This consisted of an array of quantities which, properly manipulated, gave the wavelengths of the spectral lines. It was equivalent, however, to Schrödinger's wave mechanics announced only months later (as Neumann [1273] was eventually to show) and physicists found themselves more comfortable with the latter, which did allow some visualization.

Heisenberg's studies of nuclear theory led him to predict that the hydrogen molecule could exist in two forms: ortho-hydrogen, in which the nuclei of the two atoms spun in the same direction, and para-hydrogen, in which they spun in opposite directions. In 1929 this was confirmed. Eventually his theory helped in the devising of methods for cutting down the evaporation rate of liquid hydrogen, and this in turn proved important when large quantities of such liquid hydrogen were needed, a generation later, as rocket fuel.

More startling still was the enunciation of another deduction in 1927, that of the uncertainty principle. This states that it is impossible to make an exact and simultaneous determination of both the position and the momentum (mass times velocity) of any body. The more exact one determination was, the less exact must the other be. The uncertainties of the two determinations, when multiplied, yielded a value approximately that of Planck's [887] constant.

This had the effect of weakening the law of cause and effect, which, except to a very few scientific philosophers, had been an unquestioned and unstudied anchor of science since the days of Thales [3] and the Ionian philosophers. Heisenberg's uncertainty principle destroyed the purely deterministic philosophy of the universe. Laplace [347] had maintained that the entire history of the universe, past and future, could be calculated if the position and velocity of every particle in it were known for any one instant of time; and it was precisely these two pieces of information that could not be simultaneously known at any one instant of time. Even Einstein [1064], that revolutionary thinker, found himself uncomfortable with this new way of looking at the universe. Heisenberg was awarded the 1932 Nobel Prize in physics for his enunciation of the uncertainty principle.

After the discovery of the neutron by Chadwick [1150] in 1932, Heisenberg at once pointed out that from a theoretical standpoint a nucleus consisting of protons and neutrons was far more satisfactory than one consisting (as had been thought for a decade and more) of protons and electrons. He maintained that the protons and neutrons would be held together in the narrow confines of the nucleus by means of exchange forces. What those forces might be, however, was not worked out until Yukawa [1323] tackled the problem.

Heisenberg was one of the few top-notch scientists who found themselves able to work under the Nazis. He even accepted high positions under them—though it must be pointed out that refusal of a position offered by them might well have been tantamount to suicide.

During World War II Heisenberg was in charge of German research on the atomic bomb. Before success could be achieved, the war came to an end. Heisenberg was director of the Max Planck Institute at Berlin, but after the war he moved into West Germany and became director of the Max Planck Institute for Physics at Göttingen.

[1246] VAN DE GRAAFF, Robert Jemison (van'duh-graf)
American physicist
Born: Tuscaloosa, Alabama, December 20, 1901
Died: Boston, Massachusetts, January 16, 1967

Van de Graaff attended the University of Alabama, graduating in 1922 as a mechanical engineer. After some years at the Sorbonne in Paris, where he attended the lectures of Madame Curie [965], he was awarded a Rhodes Scholarship and studied at Oxford, where he obtained his Ph.D. in 1928. After his return to America he worked first at Princeton University, then in 1931 joined the staff of the Massachusetts Institute of Technology.

He is best known for his high-voltage electrostatic generator, the first model of which was built in 1931. (Van de Graaff had worked out the principle two years earlier by using tin cans, a silk ribbon, and a small motor.)

Actual models look like half dumbbells standing on end and slowly build up giant potentials that can accelerate particles to high energies. It made a dramatic display in the 1930s, producing potentials so high as to be able to give rise to spectacular bolts of "man-made lightning." For practical purposes, however, it was outdistanced by Lawrence's [1241] cyclotron.

[1247] VAN DE KAMP, Peter
Dutch-American astronomer
Born: Kampen, Netherlands, December 26, 1901

After an education at the University of Utrecht, Van de Kamp went to the United States in 1923 and obtained his Ph.D. from the University of California in 1925. In 1937 he became the director of Sproul Observatory at Swarthmore College near Philadelphia. In 1942 he was naturalized an American citizen.

Under his direction, astronomers at Sproul Observatory detected the first planets discovered outside our own solar system. In 1943 small irregularities of one of the stars of the 61 Cygni system showed the existence of a nonluminous component eight times the mass of Jupiter. In 1960 a planet of similar size to that component was located circling about the small star Lalande 21185. In 1963 a smaller planet, only 1.5 times Jupiter's mass, was found to be circling Barnard's [883] Star.

Barnard's Star is second closest to ourselves, Lalande 21185 third closest, and 61 Cygni twelfth closest. That three planetary systems should exist in our immediate neighborhood is extremely unlikely unless planetary systems are common indeed, as theories of star formation like Weizsäcker's [1376] indicate.

785

[1248] **MORGENSTERN,** Oskar
German-American economist
Born: Görlitz, Silesia, January 24,
1902
Died: Princeton, New Jersey, July
26, 1977

Morgenstern taught economics at the
University of Vienna, achieving professorial rank in 1935. However, Nazi Germany absorbed Austria in 1938 and
Morgenstern had to leave. He went to
the United States and became an American citizen in 1944. He taught economics at Princeton University, where
he remained for the rest of his life, attaining professorial rank there in 1941.

He was eager to apply mathematics to
economics and, more broadly, to human
strategies of all kinds—whether business,
war, or scientific research—in order to
maximize gains and minimize loss. He
recognized that these principles applied
to games as well, even something as simple as matching coins, and thus formulated what became known as game
theory. He collaborated with von Neumann [1273], a fellow refugee, to write
*Theory of Games and Economic Behav-
ior* in 1944.

[1249] **LINDBERGH,** Charles Augustus
American aviator
Born: Detroit, Michigan, Febru-
ary 4, 1902
Died: Kipahulu, Hawaii, August
26, 1974

Lindbergh, the son of a Minnesota
congressman, entered the University of
Wisconsin in 1920 but interrupted his
education as a mechanical engineer two
years later to join a flying school. He
bought his own plane and became an airmail pilot in 1925.

At the time, a $25,000 prize was being
offered to whoever made the first non-
stop flight across the Atlantic Ocean
from New York to Paris. Lindbergh obtained the backing of some St. Louis
businessmen, purchased a monoplane,
which he named "The Spirit of St.
Louis," and on May 20–21, 1927, accomplished the flight in thirty-three and
a half hours.

He became a hero of heroes at once as
the United States exploded into vast
demonstrations of worship. But the flight
was more than a stunt. It, and the publicity attending it, served an important
purpose. In the quarter century since the
Wright Brothers [961, 995] flew their
plane, aeronautics had remained little
more than a matter of stunting and
thrills, as ballooning had been a century
before in the time of Charles [343] and
Gay-Lussac [420]. There had been
dogfights in World War I and some airmail service; but the general public did
not take airplanes seriously as a means
of transportation.

Lindbergh's flight, however, brought
the airplane into public consciousness
with a vengeance. The way was paved
for the expansion of commercial flight.
By the time another quarter century had
passed, jet plane travel had arrived, the
people of the world achieved a new mobility, and the railroad after a century of
domination since Stephenson's [431]
time, entered the gray years of decline.

Following the golden days of his solo
flight, Lindbergh served science by working with Carrell [1016] in designing an
artificial heart for use in perfusing tissues. He was also in the news twice in
less happy fashion. In 1932 his first son,
aged two, was kidnaped and murdered in
a crime that made as great a sensation as
had Lindbergh's flight five years before.
In the late 1930s he was one of the leading isolationists, fighting against participation of the United States in World
War II.

[1250] **BRATTAIN,** Walter Houser
American physicist
Born: Amoy   (now   Hsiamen),
China   (of   American   parents),
February 10, 1902

Brattain spent his youth on a cattle
ranch and graduated from Whitman College (in Walla Walla, Washington) in
1924 and obtained his Ph.D. at the University of Minnesota in 1929. He joined
the staff of Bell Telephone Laboratories

in that year as a research physicist and during World War II worked on the magnetic detection of submarines.

He shared the 1956 Nobel Prize in physics with Shockley [1348] and Bardeen [1334].

In 1967 he accepted a professorial position at Whitman, his old alma mater.

[1251] **STRASSMAN,** Fritz (shtrahs'-mahn)
German chemist
Born: Boppard, Rhine, February 22, 1902

Strassman, a ninth child, was educated at Technological Institute at Hannover.

When Meitner [1060] left Germany in 1938 under Nazi pressure, Strassman took her place and worked with Hahn [1063] on the problem of uranium fission. Neither was sympathetic to the Nazis but they maintained silence and were left to themselves.

Strassman's contribution to the working out of an understanding of uranium fission was recognized in 1966 when he shared with Hahn and Meitner in the Fermi Prize for that year.

In 1946 he gained a professorial position at the University of Mainz and in 1953 was made head of the chemistry department of the Max Planck Institute for Chemistry.

[1252] **KASTLER,** Alfred
German-French physicist
Born: Guebwiller, Alsace, May 3, 1902

When Kastler was born, Alsace was part of Germany, but the region was transferred to France after World War I. Kastler began his teaching career in Alsace, held faculty positions in the provinces and in 1941 became a professor at the University of Paris.

In 1950 he developed a system of "optical pumping" whereby atoms were illuminated with frequencies of light they were capable of absorbing. Momentarily they attained a high energy state then emitted light again. Kastler used both visible light and radio waves and from the manner of emission could deduce facts concerning atomic structure in a manner more elegant than was true of the heavier-handed earlier techniques of Rabi [1212], for instance.

The technique led directly to the development of masers and lasers and when Townes [1400] earned his Nobel Prize in 1964 for his work on the maser there was some dissatisfaction in France over the ignoring of Kastler. This was made up for when Kastler was awarded the 1966 Nobel Prize in physics.

[1253] **LWOFF,** André Michael (luh-wawf')
French microbiologist
Born: Aulnay-le-Château, Allier, May 8, 1902

In 1927 Lwoff (of Russian-Polish descent) received a doctorate in medicine and another in science, then joined the staff of the Pasteur Institute. He was active in the French underground during World War II, and became an officer of the Legion of Honor. After 1959 he taught microbiology at the Sorbonne.

It had already been known through the work of Beadle [1270] that genes were involved in the formation of enzymes. In the late 1940s and the 1950s Lwoff and his co-workers, Monod [1347] and Jacob [1438], showed that some genes were regulatory in function, activating or inhibiting other genes.

For this the three men shared the 1965 Nobel Prize in medicine and physiology.

Lwoff also showed that virus-DNA can be incorporated into cellular genes and be passed on in cell division. This is a form of mutation that could play a role in evolution.

[1254] **ALDER,** Kurt
German chemist
Born: Königshütta, Silesia (now Chorzów, Poland), July 10, 1902
Died: Cologne, June 20, 1958

Alder, the son of a teacher, received his early education in his hometown, which became part of Poland after World War I. Alder and his family then left for Germany.

After graduating from the University of Berlin, Alder went on for his Ph.D. at the University of Kiel, working under Diels [1039]. He obtained his degree in 1926 and two years later they worked out what is now called the Diels-Alder reaction and together they shared in the 1950 Nobel Prize in chemistry.

In 1934 Alder had accepted a professorial position at Kiel and after 1940 was professor of chemistry at the University of Cologne.

[1255] **GOUDSMIT,** Samuel Abraham
Dutch-American physicist
Born: The Hague, Netherlands, July 11, 1902
Died: Reno, Nevada, December 4, 1978

Goudsmit's professional life closely paralleled that of Uhlenbeck [1234]. Together the two men studied at the University of Leiden and obtained Ph.D.s in 1927. Goudsmit worked with Uhlenbeck to demonstrate that Pauli's [1228] fourth quantum number could be interpreted as particle spin.

Like Uhlenbeck, Goudsmit also went to the United States in 1927 and worked at the University of Michigan and, during World War II, at Massachusetts Institute of Technology.

In 1944 Goudsmit was one of those sent by the government to Europe to study the gradually increasing areas being liberated by the western Allies in order to find out what progress the Germans might be making in atomic bomb research.

In 1948 Goudsmit joined the physics staff at Brookhaven National Laboratory.

[1256] **DIRAC,** Paul Adrien Maurice
(dih-rak')
English physicist
Born: Bristol, Gloucestershire, August 8, 1902

Dirac, the son of a Swiss immigrant schoolteacher, studied electrical engineering at Bristol University but, finding it difficult to get a job, switched to mathematics upon graduating in 1921 and eventually obtained his Ph.D. at Cambridge in 1926, having made a mathematical physicist out of himself. By 1932 he was Lucasian Professor of Mathematics at Cambridge (Newton's [231] old post). Later, he married Wigner's [1260] sister.

During the late 1920s Dirac, like Schrödinger [1117], worked on the further development of the mathematical studies begun by De Broglie [1157], in which particles like the electron were considered to have wave properties.

Certain equations worked out by Dirac indicated that an electron could have two different types of energy states, one positive and one negative. This could be made to apply to the electric charge. Since the electron was negatively charged, there ought to be a similar particle positively charged.

Naturally the first thought was that this other particle was the proton. However, the proton, although it did have a positive charge equal in size to the electron's negative charge, was nothing like the electron otherwise. For one thing, it was 1,836 times as massive.

In 1930 Dirac suggested that there must be a positive twin of the electron— one with the positive charge of a proton but a mass just equal to that of the electron. Naturally, the same equations held for the proton, so there should be a particle with a negative charge like that of the electron but with the mass of the proton. (Oppenheimer [1280] contributed importantly to this view.)

These oppositely charged particles have come to be called antiparticles. Dirac's theory, although it seemed farfetched when first published, was quickly confirmed by Anderson's [1292] discovery of the antielectron (better known as the positron) two years later.

For the antiproton, a quarter of a century had to pass, but that was finally detected by Segrè [1287]. Furthermore, particles not known in 1930 have been found accompanied by antiparticles and Dirac's work has been upheld in every respect. There are even visions of forms of matter made up of antiparticles only, as matter is made up of particles. It is conceivable that whole galaxies may be composed of such antimatter, but as yet no direct evidence for such a situation exists.

For his work on wave mechanics and for his theory of antiparticles Dirac shared the 1933 Nobel Prize in physics with Schrödinger. In 1940 he went to the Dublin Institute for Advanced Studies while retaining his seat at Cambridge. After his retirement, he accepted a post as professor of physics at Florida State University.

[1257] **TISELIUS,** Arne Wilhelm
Kaurin (tih-say'lee-us)
Swedish chemist
Born: Stockholm, August 10, 1902
Died: Uppsala, October 29, 1971

Tiselius, the son and grandson of mathematicians, lost his father when he was only four. He attended the University of Uppsala, earning his doctor's degree in 1928. For a number of years he served as assistant to Svedberg [1097] and in 1930 he joined the faculty of the university. In 1934 he spent a year at Princeton in the United States.

While with Svedberg he became interested in the phenomenon of electrophoresis (that is, the movement of charged particles in suspension or solution, under the influence of an electric field). Colloidal particles usually carry electric charges at various points on their surface. Added up, these yield a net charge which may be positive, negative, or zero, and which may be varied by adding acid or base to the solution. When an electric current is sent through the solution, the charged colloidal particles will travel toward either the negative or positive electrode, or will stand still, depending on the nature of the net charge. The rate at which they will travel will depend on the size of the net charge, the distribution of the individual charges, and several other factors.

Now protein molecules in colloidal solution carry electric charges and will move in an electric field. It is very unlikely that two different proteins, however similar, would have just the same distribution of charge. And if the charge distribution was different, they would travel at different rates and separate.

This had all been known before, but in 1937 Tiselius made electrophoresis a particularly practical method for studying protein mixtures by devising a special tube arranged like a rectangular U within which the proteins could move and separate. The Tiselius tube consisted of portions fitted together at specially ground joints that could be separated to isolate one of a mixture of proteins in one chamber.

In addition, by the use of proper cylindrical lenses, it was possible to follow the process of separation by observing changes in the bending of light (changes in the "index of refraction," in other words) passing through the suspension, as the protein concentration changed. These changes could be photographed as a wavelike pattern that could be used to calculate the quantity of each protein present in the mixture.

Failure to separate into components under electrophoresis was good evidence of the purity of a protein preparation, particularly if there continued to be no separation when the acidity of the solution was changed.

Electrophoresis was applied particularly to the study of proteins of the blood, which could be separated into an albumin fraction and various globulin fractions. It might seem that by "fingerprinting" the blood in this way valuable diagnostic aid could be obtained, but unfortunately the blood protein mixture held surprisingly close to normal under all sorts of abnormal conditions, although in a few cases there was a significant change.

In 1938 Tiselius was appointed director of the newly formed Institute of Biochemistry and for his work on electrophoresis, particularly in connection with blood, he was awarded the 1948 Nobel Prize in chemistry.

In 1947 he became vice-president of the Nobel Foundation.

[1258] **BROUWER,** Dirk (brow'er)
Dutch-American astronomer
Born: Rotterdam, Netherlands,
September 1, 1902
Died: New Haven, Connecticut,
January 3, 1966

Brouwer, the son of a government employee, studied at the University of Leiden under De Sitter [1004] and obtained his Ph.D. in 1927. He then went to the United States on what might have been a temporary postdoctoral visit but received an offer from Yale University. He joined its faculty in 1928 and gained a professorial position in 1941 together with the directorship of the Yale Observatory. He became an American citizen in 1937.

Brouwer worked on general orbital problems and in 1951 published a paper on the coordinates of the five outer planets from 1653 to 2060. The work is noteworthy because it represented the first use of a high-speed electronic computer in solving an astronomical problem. From this time on, such computer use became common, and even essential, in many branches of science.

Brouwer was elected to the National Academy of Sciences in 1951.

[1259] **SPEDDING,** Frank Harold
American chemist
Born: Hamilton, Ontario, Canada
(of American parents), October
22, 1902

Spedding, the son of a professional photographer, graduated from the University of Michigan in 1925, taking his degree in chemical engineering. He went on to the University of California, where he earned his Ph.D. in physical chemistry in 1929 under Lewis [1037]. After teaching at Cornell, he moved on to Iowa State University in 1937.

While working under Lewis, Spedding grew interested in the rare-earth elements, a group of fourteen metals so similar in properties that they are very difficult to separate and purify. Through the 1940s, Spedding developed an ion-exchange procedure for their separation. This involved a column of resinous material that had the ability to seize metallic ions. The tendency to carry through this seizure varied from one metal to another; sufficiently so, even for metals as similar among themselves as the rare earths, as to make clear separation possible. Entirely because of this, individual rare-earth elements of high purity, virtually unobtainable before, became quite cheap afterward.

When atomic bomb research moved into high gear in the early 1940s, unprecedentedly pure uranium was required in large quantities. Spedding developed the necessary methods for that and in November 1942 his laboratory produced two tons of pure uranium as a contribution toward the first "atomic pile."

After the war Spedding continued work on purifying substances and even made use of ion-exchange methods to separate isotopes of individual elements, producing almost pure nitrogen-15 by the hundreds of grams.

[1260] **WIGNER,** Eugene Paul
Hungarian-American physicist
Born: Budapest, Hungary,
November 17, 1902

Wigner, the son of a businessman, was educated as a chemical engineer (he was a classmate of Neumann [1273] in high school) and obtained his doctorate at the University of Berlin in 1925. He taught in Berlin and, until 1930, in Göttingen, where he worked with Hilbert [918].

In 1930 he was invited (along with Neumann) to the United States, where he obtained a position as professor of mathematical physics at Princeton University and became an American citizen in 1937.

In 1936 Wigner (a brother-in-law of Dirac [1256]) had worked out the theory of neutron absorption, a theory that proved useful indeed when it was time to build a nuclear reactor to make use of neutron absorption. He worked out the theory of conservation of parity, which, two decades later, Lee [1473] and Yang [1451] were to show did *not* apply in certain types of nuclear reactions. Wigner also showed that nuclear forces did not depend on electric charge, so that protons and neutrons within the nucleus had similar properties in that respect. This was a concept most useful to Yukawa's [1323] meson theory.

Wigner cooperated with Szilard [1208] to alert the United States Government to the need for developing a nuclear bomb, and then worked with Fermi [1243] and Szilard in Chicago to develop one. He also helped design the atomic installations at Hanford, Washington.

After the war, he was director of research at the Clinton Laboratories at Oak Ridge for a time. In 1960 he received the Atoms for Peace award and in 1963 shared the Nobel Prize in physics with Goeppert-Mayer [1307] and Jensen [1327].

[1261] **KURCHATOV**, Igor Vasilevich
Soviet physicist
Born: Sim, Ufimskaya,
January 12, 1903
Died: Moscow, February 7,
1960

Kurchatov graduated in 1923 from the Crimean University in Simferopol, then joined the staff of Leningrad's Physico-Technical Institute in 1925. In 1933 he grew interested in nuclear physics and in 1934 he obtained his Ph.D. in physics. He demonstrated branching in nuclear reactions and discovered the existence of nuclear isomers. In 1938 he was appointed head of the Nuclear Physics Laboratory of the institute.

The Soviet Union was well aware of the potentiality of Hahn's [1063] discovery of fission and the disaster of German invasion did not keep the nation from exerting what effort it could in the direction of nuclear weapons. In February 1943 Kurchatov went to Moscow to assume leadership of this research. The Soviet Union was less well equipped scientifically than the United States and suffered much from the disorganization and destruction of World War II.

Nevertheless, on Christmas Eve 1946, the Soviet Union put its first self-sustaining reactor into action and in 1949,

much sooner than many in America had expected, it developed an atomic bomb of its own.

More surprisingly still, Kurchatov's group went on to develop a hydrogen bomb in 1952, the same year as the United States, and then to build an experimental nuclear station for the production of power for civilian use in 1954, some years before the United States did the same.

Kurchatov worked in anonymity and it was not until 1956 that he was revealed as the guiding spirit of Soviet nuclear research. He was elected to the Supreme Soviet (the analogue of the U. S. Congress, but a purely honorary position under the Soviet system of government) in 1950 and was reelected in 1954.

His ashes are entombed in the wall of the Kremlin.

[1262] **ECCLES**, Sir John Carew
(ek'ulz)
Australian physiologist
Born: Melbourne, January 27,
1903

Eccles graduated from Melbourne University in 1925 and went on to Oxford as a Rhodes Scholar, obtaining his Ph.D. there in 1929. At Oxford he worked with Sherrington [881] on reflexes and on the nature of transmission across the synapses.

The work of Loewi [1015] and Dale [1034] made it seem likely that the impulse crossed the synapse through chemical mediation rather than electrical. Eccles studied the action at synapses by means of microelectrodes inserted within the nerve cells themselves. He was able to work out the chemical changes in considerable detail and for this shared with Hodgkin [1387] and A. F. Huxley [1419] the 1963 Nobel Prize for medicine and physiology.

In 1937 Eccles had returned to Australia, teaching there and, for a period of time, in New Zealand. In 1958 he was knighted and in 1966 went to the United States to work at the Institute for Biomedical Research in Chicago.

[1263] **NATTA,** Giulio
Italian chemist
Born: Imperia, near Genoa,
February 26, 1903
Died: Bergamo, May 2, 1979

Natta, the son of a judge, obtained a Ph.D. in chemical engineering in 1924 at the Polytechnic Institute in Milan, where in later years he became director of the Industrial Chemistry Research Center. In 1938 the Italian government made him director of research in the problems of preparing synthetic rubber.

Upon hearing of Ziegler's [1215] development of metal-organic catalysts for polymer formation, Natta at once began working with propylene (ethylene to which a small one-carbon "methyl group" is attached). Within ten weeks he had found that in the polymer that resulted all the methyl groups faced in the same direction, rather than being distributed randomly in different directions.

Such "isotactic" polymers (the name was proposed by Natta's wife) proved to have useful properties and could now be manufactured at will. As a result, Natta shared, with Ziegler, the 1963 Nobel Prize in chemistry.

[1264] **BOYD,** William Clouser
American biochemist
Born: Dearborn, Missouri,
March 4, 1903

Boyd attended Harvard University, graduating in 1925. He joined the staff of Boston University School of Medicine in 1926 and remained there till his retirement in 1968. He obtained his Ph.D. at Boston University in 1930.

Boyd has concerned himself with the various blood groups that have been discovered by Landsteiner [973] and others, and their distribution throughout the human race. No one blood group can be used to distinguish an individual of one segment of the human population from an individual of another, but average distributions are significant when large numbers of men are compared.

During the 1930s Boyd and his wife,

Lyle, traveled to various parts of the earth, blood-typing the populations. From the data so obtained and from similar data obtained from others, Boyd in 1956 was able to divide the human race into thirteen groups. Most of these follow, roughly, the divisions arrived at by rule-of-thumb or by consideration of such characteristics as skin color. One surprise is the existence of an early European race characterized by the presence of unusually high frequencies of the Rh-minus gene. This was largely displaced by modern Europeans, but the older group has persisted in the mountain fastnesses of the western Pyrénées and is known to us as the Basques.

Blood group frequencies offer a method of racial distinction that does not involve visible characteristics and cannot, therefore, be used as a handy index for racism. Unaffected by environmental considerations, they do not suffer the disadvantages of Retzius' [498] craniometry. Furthermore, blood groups are mixed freely down the generations, since men and women are not influenced in their choice of mate by any consideration of blood groups (as they might be by visible characteristics).

Blood group frequencies can also be used to trace the course of prehistoric migrations, or even some that are not prehistoric. For instance, blood type B is highest among the inhabitants of central Asia and falls off as one progresses westward and eastward. That it occurs at all in western Europe is thought by some to be the result of the periodic incursions of central Asian nomads into Europe. Of these, the Hunnish invasions of the fifth century A.D. and the Mongolian invasions of the thirteenth are the most spectacular.

[1265] **BUTENANDT,** Adolf Friedrich
Johann (boo'te-nahnt)
German chemist
Born: Bremerhaven-Lehe (now
Wesermünde), March 24, 1903

Butenandt did his undergraduate work at the University of Marburg and then in

1927 obtained his Ph.D. at the University of Göttingen, where he worked under Windaus [1046]. Three years later he was director of the organic chemical laboratories there.

Butenandt's outstanding work lay in the isolation and identification of the structure of the sex hormones. The first such hormone to be isolated was estrone, which Butenandt obtained in 1929 from the urine of pregnant women. It is one of several substances, secreted by ovarian cells in small quantities, that are responsible for the development of sexual maturity in the woman.

In 1931 Butenandt isolated androsterone, an important male sex hormone produced by cells of the testicles. It accomplishes for men in its way what estrone accomplishes for women. Butenandt began with but 15 milligrams (about a two-thousandth of an ounce) of androsterone; but using the microanalytical methods developed by Pregl [982], he was able to make two analyses of the elements and to prepare a modification of the compound that he could also analyze. This was enough to make it possible for Butenandt to deduce a formula for the compound.

In 1934 Ružička [1119] synthesized a compound with Butenandt's suggested structure from another and somewhat similar compound. The synthetic product was found to have all the properties of androsterone, so that Butenandt's detective work was shown to be correct.

In 1934 Butenandt isolated progesterone, another female sex hormone, one of vital importance to the chemical mechanisms involved in pregnancy.

Butenandt was made director of the Kaiser Wilhelm Institute for Biochemistry at Berlin in 1936 and in 1939 he shared the Nobel Prize in chemistry with Ružička. As was the case with Domagk [1183], another German to win a Nobel Prize that year, and Kuhn [1233], who had won it the year before, Butenandt was forced by the Nazi government to refuse the prize. It was not until 1949, with both World War II and Hitler finished, that he could accept. After the war he taught at the University of Tübingen and after 1956 at the University of Munich. In 1960 he succeeded Hahn [1063] as president of the Max Planck Society.

[1266] **PINCUS,** Gregory
American biologist
Born: Woodbine, New Jersey, April 9, 1903
Died: Boston, Massachusetts, August 22, 1967

Pincus graduated from Cornell in 1924 and then went to Harvard, where he obtained his doctorate in 1927. He did postdoctorate work in England and Germany. From 1944 on, he was associated with the Worcester Foundation of Experimental Biology at Shrewsbury, Massachusetts, which was established that year by himself and Hudson Hoagland.

Interested particularly in reproductive physiology, he contributed to the discovery of a method of so altering female physiology by means of synthetic hormones as to keep her infertile without altering her capacity for sexual enjoyment. This is a situation that takes place naturally during pregnancy and the synthetic hormone duplicates that condition.

In pill form, the compound becomes an oral contraceptive that is far more convenient and less undignified than any other means of divorcing sex from impregnation. In the first few years of its use, the pill accelerated a revolution toward greater sexual freedom. It may also succeed in lowering the birth rate in time to prevent the absolute disaster that increasing overpopulation will otherwise inevitably bring down upon the human race.

[1267] **THEORELL,** Axel Hugo Teodor
(tee'o-rell)
Swedish biochemist
Born: Linköpin, Östergötland, July 6, 1903

Theorell, the son of a physician, obtained a medical degree in 1930 from the Caroline Institute in Stockholm, but an attack of polio forced him to abandon medical practice. In 1932 he obtained a professorial position at Uppsala, and in that year too he was the first to isolate the muscle protein myoglobin in crystalline form.

He studied enzymes catalyzing oxidation reactions, particularly those resembling Warburg's [1089] yellow enzyme. For a time he worked on ultracentrifugation with Svedberg [1097]. In 1935 he showed that the coenzyme associated with that enzyme had a structure like riboflavin (vitamin B_2), to which a phosphate group was attached. Another connection between vitamins and coenzymes, after the fashion of Elvehjem [1240], had been established.

In 1937 he was appointed director of the biochemical department of the Nobel Medical Institute in Stockholm and there he studied the oxidative protein cytochrome c. He showed just how the iron-bearing portion was attached to the rest of the molecules.

For his work on oxidation enzymes, Theorell was awarded the 1955 Nobel Prize in medicine and physiology.

[1268] **LEAKEY,** Louis Seymour Bazett
English anthropologist
Born: Kabete, Kenya, August 7, 1903
Died: London, October 1, 1972

Leakey, the son of a missionary, was born and brought up in Kenya, which was then one of Great Britain's African colonies. His interest in his place of birth continued and at Cambridge he took his Ph.D. in African prehistory. He then spent the rest of his professional life exploring East Africa for traces of the ancestry of *Homo sapiens.*

After World War II he and his second wife, Mary, discovered an almost complete skull of *Proconsul africanus,* the earliest ape discovered up to that time. (The name is "before Consul" since Consul was a popular chimpanzee in the London zoo at the time.)

Beginning in 1959, the Leakeys worked painstakingly in the Olduvai

Gorge in what is now Tanzania. There is 1960 Mary Leakey found the skull of an early australopithecine, which was first called *Zinjanthropus,* and their son, Jonathan, discovered the first remains of *Homo habilis,* a hominid that was dated 1,700,000 years old, the earliest clear example of the genus yet discovered.

From the work of the Leakeys it seems clear that the hominids (primates more closely related to human beings than to the apes) originated in East Africa, and their fossil record has been pushed far back in time.

[1269] **WALTON,** Ernest Thomas Sinton
Irish physicist
Born: Dungarvan, Waterford County, October 6, 1903

Walton, the son of a clergyman, was educated at Trinity College, Dublin. As a graduate student at Cambridge from 1927, he collaborated with Cockcroft [1198] in the work that resulted in his share of the 1951 Nobel Prize in physics.

In 1934 he returned to Dublin and in 1947 he was head of the physics department at its university. In 1952 he was appointed chairman of the School of Cosmic Physics at the Dublin Institute for Advanced Studies.

[1270] **BEADLE,** George Wells
American geneticist
Born: Wahoo, Nebraska, October 22, 1903

Beadle attended the University of Nebraska, graduating in 1926, and there his interest in genetics was first kindled. He went on to obtain his doctorate at Cornell University in 1931 and then spent two years at the California Institute of Technology, doing research in genetics under Morgan [957].

Beadle taught at various institutions in the United States and abroad. He was at Stanford University from 1937 to 1946, when he joined the faculty of the California Institute of Technology. In 1961 he took the post of chancellor at the

University of Chicago and became the sixth president of the institution the following year.

Beadle's most important work began in 1941 when with Tatum [1346] he began work with an organism even simpler than Morgan's fruit flies. This was a mold called *Neurospora crassa*. In the wild state, this mold will grow on a nutrient medium containing sugar as the only organic compound (except for a small quantity of biotin, which is also needed). For its supply of other elements such as nitrogen, phosphorus, and sulfur, Neurospora can make do with inorganic salts.

If the molds are subjected to X-ray irradiation, however, mutations will form, as Muller [1145] had demonstrated in connection with other organisms fifteen years before. Some of these mutations have lost the ability to form some particular organic compound necessary to growth. It may not form the amino acid lysine, for instance, or arginine, and will grow, therefore, only if such an amino acid is added to the nutrient medium.

Beadle found that it was not always necessary to add the missing compound itself to the medium. A different, but similar, compound might do. This meant that the similar compound could be converted into the necessary one. By trying a variety of similar compounds and noting which would promote growth and which would not, Beadle could deduce the sequence of chemical reactions that led to the formation within the mold of the necessary compound.

He could also tell where in the sequence there came a "break," at which point a reaction existed that the mold could no longer handle. He found that two different mutant strains, each of which could not form, let us say, arginine, would perhaps suffer the chemical "break" in the sequence of reactions at two different points. A cross between those two strains would then produce a mold that could form arginine, each member of the cross having supplied what the other had lacked. (The genetic crossing of microorganisms was studied in detail by Lederberg [1466].)

Beadle concluded that the charac-

teristic function of the gene was to supervise the formation of a particular enzyme; that a mutation took place when a gene was so altered that it could no longer form a normal enzyme or, perhaps, any enzyme. When this happened, some particular reaction would not take place, a sequence of chemical reactions was broken, and a radical change might occur in the physical characteristics of the organism.

All the genetic studies conducted by men like Morgan and Muller were—it would seem—but the study of the visible symptoms produced by the changing enzymatic makeup. Furthermore, it seemed to Beadle that his results could best be explained by assuming that each gene supervised the production of one and only one enzyme.

The prime purpose of genetics was shifting from the qualitative study of physical characteristics and their inheritance to the chemical study of the gene and its mode of producing enzymes. After the early 1940s it became more and more plain that the gene was a molecule of the deoxyribonucleic acid (DNA) studied by Levene [980] and Todd [1331]. This meant that nucleic acids were stepping to the center of the biochemical stage. Any doubts were removed by the work of Crick [1406] and Watson [1480] a decade later.

For their work Beadle, Tatum, and Lederberg shared the 1958 Nobel Prize in medicine and physiology.

He retired in 1968.

[1271] **LORENZ,** Konrad (loh'rents)
Austrian zoologist
Born: Vienna, November 7, 1903

Lorenz, the son of a surgeon, was interested in animals from childhood, keeping numerous pets, and studying animal behavior with considerable meticulous detail. He kept this up even during his college days. He spent a year at Columbia University, then returned to Austria and obtained his M.D. at the University of Vienna in 1928. So much for his father's wishes—he went on to study zoology to suit his own and obtained a Ph.D. in that subject in 1933.

He continued to study bird behavior and in 1935 described "imprinting," the manner in which at a certain critical point in early life, soon after hatching, young birds learn to follow a parent, a foster parent, even a human being or inanimate object. Once this has taken place, it affects their behavior to some extent all their life. He is considered the founder of ethology, the study of animal behavior in natural environments. He studied the inheritance of instincts and how those influenced even complex animal behavior. This led to the study of the evolution of behavioral patterns, in addition to and on the same basis as bodily structure and function.

In 1937 he joined the faculty at Vienna and in 1940 obtained a professorial post. During World War II he served as a physician in the German army and was captured and held as a prisoner of war by the Soviets. He returned to Austria in 1948 and took up his academic life once more. In 1966 he published *On Aggression,* in which he considered the inborn nature of human warlike behavior.

In 1973 he shared in the Nobel Prize for physiology and medicine.

[1272] **ONSAGER,** Lars
Norwegian-American chemist
Born: Oslo, Norway, November 27, 1903
Died: Coral Gables, Florida, October 5, 1976

Onsager completed his college education in Norway and in 1926 studied in Zürich under Debye [1094]. In 1928 he went to the United States, where he taught at Johns Hopkins. He then went to Yale to earn his Ph.D. in 1935. He joined the faculty there, becoming a full professor in 1945, the year in which he became a naturalized American citizen.

As a professor, Onsager occupied the J. Willard Gibbs Chair for Theoretical Chemistry and his work was worthy of Gibbs [740]. While still a graduate chemist, Onsager began working out the

rather recondite relationships between heat and electrical potential in irreversible processes.

He made use of his theories during World War II to work out the theoretical basis for the gaseous-diffusion method of separating uranium-235 from the more common uranium-238, a step essential to the development of nuclear bombs and nuclear power.

For this work he received the 1968 Nobel Prize in chemistry.

[1273] **NEUMANN,** John von
Hungarian-American mathematician
Born: Budapest, Hungary, December 3, 1903
Died: Washington, D.C., February 8, 1957

Von Neumann, the son of a Jewish banker, was an infant prodigy who at the age of six could divide two eight-digit numbers in his head. He left Hungary in 1919, during the disorders that followed the defeat of Austria-Hungary in World War I, and studied at various universities in Germany and Switzerland. In the mid-1920s he was at the University of Göttingen, where he met Oppenheimer [1280] and in 1926 he obtained his doctorate at the University of Hamburg.

In 1930 he, along with Wigner [1260], went to the United States. He taught mathematical physics at Princeton University, where Oppenheimer was to join him after World War II. In 1933 he became a professor at the newly founded Institute for Advanced Study at Princeton, remaining there for the rest of his life.

Von Neumann did important work in many branches of advanced mathematics. For one thing, he made a thorough study of quantum mechanics and showed in 1944 that Schrödinger's [1117] wave mechanics and Heisenberg's [1245] matrix mechanics were mathematically equivalent.

Even more important was his development of a new branch of mathematics called game theory. He had written on the subject as early as 1928, but his complete book *The Theory of Games and Economic Behavior* did not appear until 1944. This branch of mathematics is called game theory because it works out the best strategies to follow in simple games, such as coin-matching. However, the principles will apply to far more complicated games such as business and war, where an attempt is made to work out the best strategy to beat a competitor or an enemy. Even scientific research may be considered a game in which man pits his wits against the impersonal universe.

Von Neumann also applied his mathematical abilities to directing the construction of giant computers, which in turn performed high speed calculations that helped in the production of the H-bomb and in reducing it to a size small enough to be fired by missile.

(Some visualize a future in which war is fought not only by the pressing of buttons, but by means of a computer working out the equations of game theory and itself pushing the buttons.)

When Oppenheimer, who had opposed the development of the H-bomb, was being investigated in 1954, during the years when much American thinking was dominated by the views of Senator Joseph R. McCarthy, Von Neumann testified to his old friend's loyalty and integrity (though disagreeing with his views). Von Neumann's countryman Teller [1332] testified against Oppenheimer.

In 1955 he was appointed to the Atomic Energy Commission and in 1956 he received the Fermi award.

[1274] **POWELL**, Cecil Frank
English physicist
Born: Tonbridge, Kent, December 5, 1903
Died: near Bellano, Italy, August 9, 1969

Attending Cambridge on a scholarship, Powell, the son of a gunsmith, obtained his Ph.D. in 1927, second in his class in physics. He went on to do research under C.T.R. Wilson [979] and Ernest Rutherford [996].

Powell's center of interest was Wilson's cloud chamber and he spent years studying the mobility of ions in gases. The connection here is that it is about ions that water droplets condense, making visible tracks in the cloud chamber.

However, Powell finally helped develop a method that sidetracked the cloud chamber altogether. The difficulty of the cloud chamber is that the only time that tracks form is when the chamber is expanded. This expansion may be made automatic when certain events occur, as Blackett [1207] had arranged. Nevertheless, there are always events going on when the chamber is not being expanded and which are therefore not recorded.

Powell arranged for particles to strike a photographic emulsion, producing a line of dark specks. Instead of making tracks in a cloud chamber and photographing them, he skipped the first step and the particles photographed themselves directly. The method had been used before, not very successfully, but Powell during the 1930s made it worth while, particularly as new and more sensitive emulsions were prepared.

After World War II, still better emulsions came into use and Powell decided to put them to the test by taking some to mountain heights and sending others up in balloons to see how they would be affected by cosmic ray particles. In 1947 rather startling results were obtained from photographic plates exposed on the Bolivian Andes. Particles with curvatures indicating an intermediate size were recorded.

One such particle, discovered by Anderson [1292] a decade earlier and named a meson, had first been considered a proof of the theories of Yukawa [1323] concerning the structure of the atomic nucleus. However, Anderson's meson on further study, proved not to fit the role.

The new meson discovered by Powell was somewhat heavier than Anderson's meson, so the two were given different names. Powell's was called a pi-meson or pion, while Anderson's was named a mu-meson or muon.

The pi-meson was found to represent in all respects the particle that had been predicted by Yukawa, and for this Powell was awarded the 1950 Nobel Prize in physics. He taught at the University of Bristol beginning in 1948.

After World War II he was active in movements for peace and for scientific cooperation among all nations. He was the founder of the Pugwash Movement, which had this for its aim.

[1275] SNELL, George Davis
American geneticist
Born: Bradford, Massachusetts,
December 19, 1903

Snell graduated from Dartmouth in 1926 and obtained a doctoral degree in genetics from Harvard in 1930. He joined the Jackson Laboratory in 1935.

His field of interest, beginning in 1944, was that of tissue transplantation and the conditions that affect the acceptance or rejection of the transplant by the organism receiving it. He showed that genetic factors were important, the transplant being accepted if the mice affected were of the same strain, but rejected if they were not. He located specific gene sites that were concerned in the matter of acceptance or rejection.

For his work he received a share of the 1980 Nobel Prize for physiology and medicine.

[1276] HARTLINE, Haldan Keffer
American physiologist
Born: Bloomsburg, Pennsylvania,
December 22, 1903

Hartline graduated from Lafayette College in Easton, Pennsylvania, in 1923 and obtained his M.D. from Johns Hopkins in 1927. After travels abroad and various teaching positions within the United States, he joined the faculty of Rockefeller University in New York in 1953.

Early in his career he was interested in the metabolism of nerve cells and gradually zeroed in on the working of the individual cells in the retina of the eye. Like

Granit [1232], he wanted to study the workings of individual retinal cells. For the purpose he used tiny electrodes and managed to isolate and study individual fibers in the eyes of horseshoe crabs and frogs. Thus, the fine workings of the sense of sight began to yield to investigation.

For this work, Hartline shared the 1967 Nobel Prize in physiology and medicine with Wald [1318] and Granit.

[1277] BITTNER, John Joseph
American biologist
Born: Meadville, Pennsylvania,
February 25, 1904
Died: Minneapolis, Minnesota,
December 14, 1961

After attending St. Stephen's College in New York state, Bittner went on to obtain his Ph.D. in 1930 from the University of Michigan.

Through the 1930s Bittner worked at Bar Harbor, Maine, where carefully inbred strains of mice were kept for research on cancer. Some strains were highly resistant to cancer and rarely developed it, while others were so prone to it that almost every individual developed the disease.

Bittner's observations, published in 1936, established an odd fact. If the young mice of a cancer-resistant strain were transferred to the breast of a foster mother of a cancer-prone strain, the young developed cancer in the course of their lives. If, on the other hand, young mice of a cancer-prone strain were fed at the breast of a foster mother of a cancer-resistant strain, they did not usually develop cancer.

Apparently this particular type of cancer in these particular animals was infectious and the mother's milk carried the infectious agent. The Bittner milk factor was isolated in 1949. At least, particles were found in the milk of cancer-prone mother mice that did not exist in the milk of cancer-resistant mother mice.

These particles were virus-sized and, like viruses, contained nucleic acid. It seemed reasonable to suspect them of being viruses. This was certainly the strongest evidence that at least some cancers were virus-caused since Rous [1067] had initiated the controversy a generation earlier.

[1278] **GAMOW,** George (gay'mov)
Russian-American physicist
Born: Odessa, Russia, March 4, 1904
Died: Boulder, Colorado, August 19, 1968

Gamow, the grandson of a tsarist general and the son of a teacher, grew interested in astronomy when his father gave him a small telescope on his thirteenth birthday.

He attended the University of Leningrad, studying under Friedmann [1125], and obtained his Ph.D. there in 1928. One of his classmates was Landau [1333]. In the year of his Ph.D., Gamow worked out the theory of alpha-decay, suggesting the existence of a tunneling effect that Esaki [1464] was to make good use of three decades later.

Gamow then worked at various universities in western Europe, including a stay with Bohr [1101] and then with Ernest Rutherford [996], meeting Landau, who was also on his travels, at both places. He ended up in the United States in 1934. He made this country his permanent home, teaching at George Washington University until 1956, when he joined the faculty of the University of Colorado.

In the 1930s, Gamow collaborated with Teller [1332] in work on theoretical nuclear physics, but his best-known work elaborates the ideas of Bethe [1308] and Lemaître [1174].

In working out the consequences of the nuclear reactions postulated by Bethe as powering a star and serving as the source of its radiant energy, Gamow showed that as a star's hydrogen (its basic fuel) is used up, the star grows hotter. For the first time the general assumption that the sun was slowly cooling was contravened. Instead, it was very slowly heating up and life on earth would be destroyed some day, not through freezing but through baking.

This marked the beginning of a new understanding of stellar evolution.

Again, Gamow, in 1948, worked out the method by which the explosion of Lemaître's "cosmic egg" would lead to the formation of the various elements of the universe in a very short time, although his is by no means the only theory of the exact mechanism of the creation of the elements.

He predicted the residual background radiation that was detected by Penzias [1501] and Wilson seventeen years later.

Gamow was perhaps the most articulate supporter of Lemaître's "big bang" theory of creation as far as the general public was concerned for he was as formidable a popularizer as was his great antagonist Hoyle [1398].

In an entirely different field, biochemistry, Gamow in 1954 suggested that the nucleic acids acted as a "genetic code" in the formation of enzymes (following the path Beadle [1270] had first laid out). Gamow was the first to maintain that the code was made up of triplets of nucleotides. His details were wrong, but the concept was proved by 1961 to be correct.

In addition to his first-rate science, Gamow proved to be one of the most effective and consistently charming popularizers of science. This second career began in 1937 with his *Mr. Tompkins in Wonderland.*

[1279] **ELSASSER,** Walter Maurice
German-American physicist
Born: Mannheim, Baden, Germany, March 20, 1904

Elsasser obtained his Ph.D. at the University of Göttingen in 1927 and then joined the faculty of the University of Frankfurt. Like so many other scientists, he left Germany in 1933 with the advent of Hitler and after three years in Paris went to the United States in 1936, joined the staff of the California Institute of Technology, and became an American citizen in 1940.

He worked on radar during World War II and served with several universities afterward. In 1960 he joined the

University of New Mexico as chairman of the department of physics. Elsasser has concerned himself with the origin of the earth's magnetic field.

Since the days of Gilbert [155] the earth has been considered a magnet and the presence of an iron core would make it seem that it actually contained a permanent iron magnet. However, the iron core is liquid and above the Curie [897] point, so that it cannot really be an ordinary magnet.

Elsasser suggested in 1939 that the earth's rotation sets up eddy currents in the liquid core, which thus becomes an electromagnet if not an ordinary one. Latest rocket research seems to bear this out, at least indirectly. The moon, which probably lacks an iron core, was shown by the Soviet Lunik satellites to have no magnetic field. According to data from the Venus probe Mariner II obtained in December 1962, Venus, which probably does have an iron core, rotates so slowly that it does not set up eddy currents and, in consequence, lacks a magnetic field.

In 1962 Elsasser accepted a post as professor of geophysics at Princeton University.

[1280] **OPPENHEIMER,** J. Robert
American physicist
Born: New York, New York,
April 22, 1904
Died: Princeton, New Jersey,
February 18, 1967

Oppenheimer, the son of a German-Jewish immigrant, was born into a family of wealth and culture and early showed a precocious intelligence. He was educated at the Ethical Culture School in New York and graduated at the top of his class. In 1922 he entered Harvard, where he studied under Bridgman [1080] and graduated in three years with record grades. He did postgraduate work in England, where he met Thomson [869], Ernest Rutherford [996], and Born [1084]. He obtained his Ph.D. at the University of Göttingen, where he met Neumann [1273], in 1927. In 1928 he joined the faculty of the California Institute of Technology.

In 1930 he showed that the proton could not be Dirac's [1256] "antielectron" and paved the way for the discovery, two years later, of the true antielectron, the positron, by Anderson [1292].

In 1935 Oppenheimer explained how a speeding deuteron (the nucleus of a heavy hydrogen atom, consisting of a proton and neutron in close association) splits up as it approaches a positively charged atomic nucleus. The proton portion, also positively charged, is repelled and veers off. The uncharged neutron continues onward. In this way deuteron bombardment is often the equivalent of neutron bombardment, with this difference: Deuterons, being charged, can be accelerated to high energies in electric fields, while neutrons, being uncharged, cannot. Oppenheimer also contributed to an understanding of the "cascade process" in which a cosmic ray particle produced secondary particles, each of which produced still more, and so on, to form a "cosmic ray shower."

In 1943 Oppenheimer was placed in charge of the laboratories at Los Alamos, New Mexico, where the first atomic bomb was designed and constructed, and near which it was exploded. From 1947 to 1953 he was chairman of the general advisory committee to the Atomic Energy Commission, and in 1947 he joined the Institute of Advanced Studies at Princeton University, a post he held until his retirement in 1966.

After World War II Oppenheimer fought hard for international control of the bomb and was reluctant indeed to press onward to the still further horrors of the hydrogen bomb (though he had approved the use of the fission bomb against Japan). His view was overruled by President Truman in 1949.

In 1954, at the very height of that period in American history marked by the influence of Senator Joseph R. McCarthy, Oppenheimer was labeled "a loyal citizen but not a good security risk" by the Atomic Energy Commission. The equivocal testimony of Teller [1332], who had been ardently in favor of developing the H-bomb, seems to have been the crucial factor in convicting Oppenheimer of this charge, and Oppenheimer was therefore denied access to classified information. Henry Smyth, one of the commissioners, dissented strongly. The Atomic Energy Commission pursued an ambivalent attitude by giving him the 1963 Fermi award for his contribution to nuclear research. President Kennedy intended to award it personally, but he was assassinated and President Johnson made the award.

In the inevitable controversy that followed, Congress reduced the cash award from $50,000 to $25,000 thereafter.

[1281] **CHERENKOV,** Pavel Alekseyevich
Soviet physicist
Born: Voronezh, July 15, 1904

Cherenkov, born of a peasant family, graduated from Voronezh University in 1928 and after 1930 worked at the Institute of Physics of the Soviet Academy of Science.

His important discovery involved the velocity of high-energy particles. The greater the energy of a subatomic particle, the more rapidly it travels; nevertheless it can never move more rapidly than the velocity of light in a vacuum.

However, light traveling through a transparent medium, like water, travels more slowly than in a vacuum. A high-energy particle passing through such a medium may well exceed the velocity of light in that medium. When it does, it throws back a "wake" of light, which is termed Cherenkov radiation.

Cherenkov observed the radiation first in 1934, and Frank [1340] and Tamm [1180] explained the cause of it in 1937. The Cherenkov radiation has been used to activate a counter so that very high-energy particles can be detected while other particles are allowed to pass unnoticed. These devices are known as Cherenkov counters. The volocity of the particle can be calculated from the direction in which the light is given off. Such counters have been useful, for instance, in the discovery of the antiproton by Segrè [1287].

For this discovery, Cherenkov, Frank, and Tamm shared the 1958 Nobel Prize in physics.

[1282] **STANLEY,** Wendell Meredith
American biochemist
Born: Ridgeville, Indiana, August 16, 1904
Died: Salamanca, Spain, June 15, 1971

In Earlham College Stanley played football and looked upon that as his great interest. He planned to be a football coach, in fact. However, while visiting the University of Illinois, he was so incautious as to get into a discussion with a professor of chemistry. This opened his eyes to a new interest and he went to Illinois for graduate work in chemistry. He never became a football coach.

Stanley obtained his Ph.D. from the University of Illinois in 1929. After postdoctorate studies in Germany with Wieland [1048], he went to work for the Rockefeller Institute for Medical Research (now Rockefeller University) in 1931, and in 1946 he joined the faculty of the University of California where he remained for the rest of his life.

In the early 1930s Northrop [1148] excited the chemical world by substantiating the work of Sumner [1120] through the crystallization of pepsin and other enzymes. That mysterious entity the enzyme was thus reduced to something palpable and known—a protein molecule. What about that equally mysterious entity, the virus? It had first been detected by Beijerinck [817] a generation before, but had remained an impalpable something in solution ever since.

Stanley set about preparing a large quantity of tobacco mosaic virus by growing tobacco and infecting it. He mashed up the infected leaves and then put the mash through the usual procedures used by chemists to crystallize proteins, since he was reasonably certain the virus was a protein molecule. In 1935 he obtained fine needlelike crystals which he isolated and found to possess all the infective properties of the virus, and in high concentration.

This was hard for many to accept. A crystalline enzyme was one thing, for an enzyme was an incontrovertibly nonliving substance. A virus, however, can reproduce itself within cells and that is at least one important criterion of life, perhaps even the key criterion. To crystallize an object that possessed some of these criteria seemed truly to poise the virus on the boundary between life and nonlife. There was a tendency to argue that the virus was one or the other, and considerable heat was generated.

Many other viruses have since been crystallized and all have been found to be nucleoproteins. The work of men like Fraenkel-Conrat [1355] has clearly shown that the nucleic acid portion of the nucleoprotein and not the protein portion is the key to virus activity. For this reason the problem of viruses has merged with that of genes (also nucleoprotein in nature) and, beginning with the work of Crick [1406] and Watson [1480], with that of nucleic acids in general.

For his feat Stanley shared the 1946 Nobel Prize in chemistry with those other crystallizers Sumner and Northrop. During World War II Stanley worked on the influenza virus and on the preparation of vaccines against the disease.

In 1948 he established a virus laboratory at the University of California, serving as its head till his retirement in 1969. He died while attending a virus conference in Salamanca.

[1283] **FORSSMANN,** Werner
German surgeon
Born: Berlin, August 29, 1904
Died: Schopfheim, West Germany, June 1, 1979

Forssmann was captured by American forces during World War II and spent some time in a prison camp. He was a surgeon before that episode, however, and he continued his surgical work after he was released.

He was the first to work out a practical system for cardiac catheterization. He inserted a catheter in a vein in the elbow (*his own* elbow), a catheter that was opaque to radiation so that its course could be followed by an X ray, and maneuvered it safely along the vein till it reached the heart. This made it possible, in theory, to study the structure and function of an ailing heart and make more accurate diagnoses without surgery.

The technique was ignored, however, till Cournand [1181] and D. W. Richards [1184] further improved it. All three then shared the 1956 Nobel Prize for physiology and medicine in consequence.

[1284] **FRISCH,** Otto Robert
Austrian-British physicist
Born: Vienna, Austria, October 1, 1904
Died: September 22, 1979

Frisch, a nephew of Lise Meitner [1060], obtained his Ph.D. at the University of Vienna in 1926. He went on to teach at Berlin and at Hamburg, but as soon as Hitler came to power in 1933, he made his way to England.

From 1934 to 1939 he was at Bohr's [1101] laboratory in Copenhagen, and when his aunt fled Germany and evolved the suggestion that uranium was undergoing fission under neutron bombardment, Frisch collaborated in the paper that resulted. He hastened to bring the matter to Bohr's attention even before publication. Bohr took the news to the United States and the rest is history.

After World War II, Frisch made a name for himself as a science writer for the layman on atomic physics.

[1285] **NÉEL,** Louis Eugène Félix (nay-ell')
French physicist
Born: Lyon, November 22, 1904

Néel obtained his doctorate at the University of Strasbourg in 1932, then remained on the faculty of the university till 1945, after which he moved on to the University of Grenoble.

He interested himself primarily in the magnetic properties of solids. Where ferromagnetic substances (such as iron, notoriously) have all the atoms with their north magnetic poles pointing in the same direction if the temperatures are not too high, he pointed out, there are also "antiferromagnetic" substances, where alternate rows of atoms have opposite magnetic orientation so that there is no overall magnetism. In some cases, though, the alternation is stronger in one direction than the other, so that there is a net magnetism which he called "ferrimagnetism."

In this way, he was able to explain some of the magnetic properties of the rocks of the earth's crust, and synthetic ferrites could be prepared with properties suitable for use in computer memories.

Néel, as a result, shared the 1970 Nobel Prize for physics with Alfven [1335], whose studies of magnetism were in space, as Néel's were of the earth's crust.

[1286] **HERZBERG,** Gerhard
German-Canadian physical chemist
Born: Hamburg, Germany, December 25, 1904

Herzberg obtained his doctoral degree at the Darmstadt Institute of Technology in 1928. In 1935 he fled Germany, which had fallen under the brutal tyranny of Hitler, and went to Canada.

He studied with great care the spectra of gases, especially the simple two-atom molecules of hydrogen, oxygen, nitrogen, and carbon monoxide. He showed the relationship of the details of the spectra to their structure and could detect the presence of evanescent atom groupings that are intermediates in chemical reactions. He could also identify the spectra of certain atom combinations in interstellar gas. For his work he received the 1971 Nobel Prize for chemistry.

[1287] **SEGRÈ,** Emilio (say-gray')
Italian-American physicist
Born: Tivoli, Latium, February 1, 1905

Segrè, the son of an industrialist, obtained his Ph.D. at the University of

Rome under Fermi [1243] in 1928. He had originally planned to be an engineer but Fermi's influence drew him to physics and in 1932 he had a professorial post at the University of Rome.

He was soon involved in Fermi's work on the neutron bombardment of uranium and in 1936 he accepted a post at the University of Palermo. There he grew particularly interested in the element with atomic number 43. In the 1930s this was the lightest element still undiscovered. Ten years earlier, Noddack [1166] had claimed the discovery but that claim remained unconfirmed.

To Segrè it seemed that if element 43 could not be found, it could be made through neutron bombardment. He visited the University of California and in 1937 Lawrence [1241] gave him a sample of molybdenum (element number 42) that had been bombarded by deuterons, a process that, as Oppenheimer [1280] showed, was equivalent to neutron bombardment. Such bombardment might be expected to produce small quantities of an element with an atomic number one higher than that of molybdenum—that is, element number 43.

Segrè took the sample back to Italy and subjected the bombarded molybdenum to chemical analysis, tracing the fate of the radioactivity that had been induced in it. In this way he located small quantities of element number 43. The element was named technetium, from the Greek word for "artificial," because it was the first new element artificially produced.

In 1938 Segrè, during another visit to the United States, was removed from his Palermo post by Italy's Fascist government. Segrè shrugged and remained in the United States, becoming a citizen in 1944.

He continued his work at the University of California and in 1940 was one of those who first synthesized another undiscovered element, atomic number 85. It was named astatine, from a Greek word meaning "unstable." Both technetium and astatine are radioactive elements with no stable isotopes. Technetium is the lightest element lacking stable nuclei.

After World War II, Segrè became professor of physics at the University of California in 1946 and took part in the search for the antiproton. Dirac [1256] had predicted the existence of antiparticles. The positron, which is the antiparticle of the electron, was discovered early in the game by Anderson [1292], for it required energies in the gamma-ray range for its manufacture. Over twenty years had passed and the antiproton remained undiscovered. However, the antiproton was 1836 times as massive as the positron and required for its formation particles with energies 1836 times as great as that of the typical gamma ray.

There were cosmic rays that were energetic enough but these were few and far between. It was only when the bevatron (a large and powerful descendant of Lawrence's cyclotron) was constructed at the University of California that sufficiently energetic particles were obtainable in quantity. In 1955 Segrè, in collaboration with Owen Chamberlain [1439], reported the formation of antiprotons through the impact of very high-energy protons on copper atoms.

For this feat Segrè and Chamberlain were awarded the 1959 Nobel Prize in physics.

[1288] **VON EULER,** Ulf Svante
Swedish physiologist
Born: Stockholm, February 7, 1905

Von Euler obtained his M.D. at Karolinska Institute in 1930 and remained on its faculty thereafter. He discovered noradrenalin and showed that it served as the chemical intermediary for neurotransmission in the sympathetic nervous system. As a result, he shared the 1970 Nobel Prize for physiology and medicine with Axelrod [1374] and Katz [1359].

[1289] **ROSSI,** Bruno Benedetto
Italian-American physicist
Born: Venice, April 13, 1905

Rossi, the son of an electrical engineer, studied at the universities of Padua and Bologna, obtaining his Ph.D. at the latter institution in 1927. He then taught at Italian universities until 1938. In that year the Mussolini regime had fallen under Hitler's thumb and Rossi was forced to leave Italy.

He traveled first to Bohr's laboratory in Copenhagen, the Mecca of all physicists, then to England and finally, in 1939, to the United States, where he worked at the University of Chicago. During World War II he was at Los Alamos engaged in the atomic bomb project, and after the war he moved on to the Massachusetts Institute of Technology.

In 1930, while he was still in Italy, he took up the problem of the nature of cosmic rays. Compton [1159] had shown they consisted of particles, but what was the nature of those particles? What kind of electric charge did they carry? Rossi pointed out that the earth's magnetic field ought to deflect them to the east if they were positively charged, but to the west if they were negatively charged. Studies of east-west distribution made it plain that the cosmic ray particles were positively charged; and this led, in turn, to their recognition as high-energy protons (and more complicated atomic nuclei).

Indeed, it was also Rossi who, in 1931, showed the enormous energies of cosmic ray particles by demonstrating that they could penetrate a yard or more into solid lead.

When the age of rocketry dawned, Rossi eagerly took advantage of the chance of studying cosmic rays in their primary manifestation, before they struck earth's atmosphere and were obscured by the production of secondary particles through collisions with air molecules. His rocket experiments helped make astronomers aware of the constant stream of particles flowing out from the sun in all directions, up to and past the earth's orbit—the so-called solar wind.

In addition, he was interested to see if the X rays emitted by the sun's super-hot corona were reflected from the moon. In the search for such reflected X rays, detectors borne by rockets recorded X rays

86. THEODOSIUS DOBZHANSKY

87. HANTARO NAGAOKA

88. Salvador Edward Luria

89. Max Delbruck

90. Dennis Gabor

91. ROSALYN SUSSMAN YALOW

92. SHELDON LEE GLASHOW (LEFT) AND STEVEN WEINBERG

93. ANDREY DMITRIYEVICH SAKHAROV

arriving from deep space, thus giving rise to the discovery of "X-ray stars."

[1290] **WILDT,** Rupert (vihlt)
German-American astronomer
Born: Munich, Germany, June 25, 1905
Died: Orleans, Massachusetts, January 9, 1976

Wildt obtained his Ph.D. at the University of Berlin in 1927. He came to the United States in 1935 and became an American citizen in 1941.

Working at the University of Göttingen, and later at Yale University in the United States, Wildt specialized in atmospheres of all sorts. In 1932 he identified certain absorption bands, observed by Slipher [1038] in the spectra of Jupiter and the other outer planets, as belonging to ammonia and methane. It has since been recognized that the atmospheres of those planets are chiefly hydrogen and helium (which yield no easily observed absorption bands), but certainly ammonia and methane are important minor components.

Wildt took into account this atmospheric composition, plus the overall density of each planet, and the equatorial bulging due to its speed of rotation and the distribution of densities within its structure, and out of it attempted to deduce a picture of the general structure of these outer planets. Essentially, for Jupiter and the others, he pictured a deep and dense atmosphere, underneath which is a thick shell of ice overlying an interior of rock and metal. This model was approached cautiously by astronomers, and it has since been abandoned as a result of the data sent back by the Pioneer and Voyager Jupiter probes in 1973 and thereafter.

In 1937 Wildt speculated that the cloudy cover of Venus might consist of droplets of formaldehyde, since water seemed to be absent. Venus probes from 1962 onward confirmed that surface water is absent on Venus but the clouds do contain water. However, they also contain sulfur and sulfuric acid, so those clouds are anything but benign.

[1291] **CHARGAFF,** Erwin
Austrian-American biochemist
Born: Czernowitz, Austria (now Chernovtsy, USSR), August 11, 1905

Chargaff obtained his Ph.D. at the University of Vienna in 1928 and worked in Berlin from 1930 to 1933. The coming of Hitler was his signal to leave Germany. He spent two years in Paris, then in 1935 left for the United States, where he worked at the Columbia University College of Physicians and Surgeons.

The development of paper chromatography in 1944 by Martin [1350] and Synge [1394] was, initially, to separate the amino acids and estimate the quantity of each in a particular protein molecule. However, the technique could easily be modified to suit all sorts of mixtures and in the late 1940s Chargaff was one of those who set about determining the quantity of each of the nitrogenous bases present in a particular nucleic acid molecule.

He tested a wide variety of such molecules and showed that in general the number of adenine units in each was equivalent to the number of thymine units, while the number of guanine units was equivalent to the number of cytosine units.

This was used, most fruitfully, by Crick [1406] and James Dewey Watson [1480] in working out the Watson-Crick model of DNA structure.

[1292] **ANDERSON,** Carl David
American physicist
Born: New York, New York, September 3, 1905

Anderson studied at the California Institute of Technology, obtaining his Ph.D., *magna cum laude,* in 1930. He remained at the Institute, working with Millikan [969] on cosmic rays, and was a member of the faculty thereafter, becoming professor of physics in 1939 and chairman of the division in 1962.

In the course of his cosmic ray studies, Anderson devised a cloud chamber with a lead plate dividing it. Ordinarily the particles associated with cosmic rays are so energetic that their curvature in even a strong magnetic field is not very pronounced. The lead partition, while not stopping such particles altogether, did subtract sufficient energy so that the paths on the far side assumed a distinct curvature, and more could be learned from a curved track than from a straight one.

In August 1932, while studying photographs of tracks in such a cloud chamber, Anderson came across some that looked exactly like the tracks of an electron, except that they curved the wrong way. They were precisely what one might expect from electrons carrying a positive charge rather than a negative one. Indeed, it seemed to Anderson that this must be the positively charged electron toward which the mathematics of Dirac [1256], two years earlier, had pointed the way. Anderson suggested the name positron for the new particle, and this was accepted. He also suggested negatron as a name for the ordinary electron, but this never caught on. In making his discovery, Anderson just nosed out Blackett [1207] and the Joliot-Curies [1204, 1227], who were also on the track of the positron.

Nor was the positron the only new particle located by Anderson in the course of his cosmic ray work. In 1935, while making cloud chamber exposures on Pike's Peak in Colorado, he observed a new track that was less curved than an electron track and more curved than a proton track. The most direct interpretation of the track was that it belonged to a particle of intermediate mass, of a type that had been theoretically predicted a short time before by Yukawa [1323]. The observed particle proved to be 130 times as massive as an electron and therefore about ¼ as massive as a proton. Anderson suggested the name mesotron for it. The name was accepted but was quickly shortened to meson.

Both positron and meson, formed out of the superabundance of energy associated with cosmic ray particles, are short-lived indeed. The positron reacts with the first electron it approaches. The two cancel each other out, so to speak, matter being destroyed and the equivalent amount of energy, in the form of a pair of gamma rays, being created. The change exactly matches that predicted by Einstein's [1064] famous $E=mc^2$ equation. Later it was found by Blackett that the process could be reversed; gamma rays could be converted into an electron-positron pair, destroying energy and creating mass in its place.

As for the meson, that broke down in a matter of millionths of a second. A positively charged meson broke down to positrons and neutrinos, while a negatively charged one broke down to electrons and neutrinos. Anderson was awarded the 1936 Nobel Prize in physics for his discoveries, sharing it with Hess [1088], whose discovery of cosmic rays led quite directly to Anderson's achievements. In 1963 it was discovered that neutrinos formed in association with Anderson's mesons (later called mu-mesons) were not quite like the neutrinos of those associated with the electron. Thus, the mysterious particle first predicted by Pauli [1228] turned out to exist in two forms, and since to each there had to correspond one of Dirac's antiparticles, there were also two different antineutrinos—four no-charge, no-mass particles altogether.

In one respect, Anderson's meson proved a disappointment. It did not readily interact with atomic nuclei. If it was truly the particle of intermediate mass predicted by Yukawa, it should so interact. In the next decade, however, Powell [1274] discovered a slightly more massive meson, which proved to be Yukawa's predicted particle. Anderson's meson, in fact, was shown in 1961 to be a duplicate of the electron in every property but mass. It was nothing but a very heavy electron, so to speak.

[1293] **OCHOA**, Severo
Spanish-American biochemist
Born: Luarca, Spain, September 24, 1905

Ochoa, the youngest son of a lawyer, attended the University of Málaga, graduating in 1921. He studied medicine at the University of Madrid and obtained his medical degree *cum laude* in 1929. In 1936 he left Spain, spending a year in Germany studying under Meyerhof [1095] and three in England. He went to the United States in 1940 and was naturalized in 1956. After 1942 he served on the faculty of New York University College of Medicine, where he became chairman of the department of biochemistry in 1954.

Ochoa did considerable work on the chemical mechanisms of the body. In particular he studied how molecules of carbon dioxide are incorporated into compounds and how they are liberated. His work, along with that of Lipmann [1221], helped identify the "two-carbon fragment" that is one of the key compounds in the metabolic pattern.

Ochoa's chief fame, however, arose in connection with his work on nucleic acid. Thanks to the work of Watson [1480] and Crick [1406], biochemists in the 1950s were flocking to nucleic acids as, a decade before, they had gathered round coenzymes and as, two decades before, they had swarmed over vitamins.

The nucleic acid is a large and complicated molecule made up of long chains of individual phosphate-containing units called nucleotides. Nucleic acids had been shown by Levene [980] to exist in two varieties, RNA and DNA, each being made up of four different types of nucleotides.

The body was clearly capable of building nucleic acids out of nucleotides and to do this, enzymes were necessary. In 1955 Ochoa isolated such an enzyme from a strain of bacteria and allowed it to react with nucleotides to which a second phosphate unit had been added, nucleotides of the variety which, if they were strung together, would be expected to form molecules of RNA.

The result of incubating the nucleotides in the presence of the enzyme was a startling rise in viscosity. The solution grew thick and jellylike, a pretty good sign that long, thin molecules of RNA

had been formed. Ochoa's synthetic RNA differed from the natural in an interesting fashion. In natural RNA, nucleotides of each of the four varieties existed, but Ochoa could begin with one variety of nucleotide and build up a synthetic RNA consisting of that one variety endlessly repeated. In the next year Kornberg [1422] extended Ochoa's work and synthesized DNA.

As a result Ochoa and Kornberg shared the 1959 Nobel Prize in medicine and physiology.

[1294] **MOTT,** Sir Nevill Francis
English physicist
Born: Leeds, Yorkshire, September 30, 1905

Mott obtained his master's degree at Cambridge in 1930, having studied under Bohr [1101] and Ernest Rutherford [996]. He gained a professorial position at the University of Bristol in 1933 and in 1954 returned to Cambridge.

He worked on theoretical considerations of the scattering of beams of particles by atomic nuclei and on the transition of certain substances between states in which an electrical current was conducted and not conducted. In particular, he and his assistant, P. W. Anderson [1458], worked on the semiconducting properties of amorphous, glassy substances, a potentially cheaper and more convenient raw material for solid-state devices than ultra-pure metals and semimetals.

For this work he and Anderson both received shares in the 1977 Nobel Prize for physics, along with Van Vleck [1219]. Mott was knighted in 1962.

[1295] **JANSKY,** Karl Guthe
American radio engineer
Born: Norman, Oklahoma,
October 22, 1905
Died: Red Bank, New Jersey,
February 14, 1950

Jansky was educated at the University of Wisconsin, where his father was on the faculty. Out of college, and after a year as instructor there, he took a job in 1928 with Bell Telephone Laboratories. There in 1931 he tackled the problem of static. The noisy crackling of static interfered chronically with radio reception (and with radio-telephony, as in ship-to-shore calls, which is where Bell Telephone came in). Static had a number of causes, including thunderstorms, nearby electric equipment, and aircraft passing overhead.

Jansky, however, detected a new kind of weak static from a source that, at first, he could not identify. It came from overhead and moved steadily. At first, it seemed to Jansky, it moved with the sun. However, it gained slightly on the sun, to the extent of four minutes a day. But this is just the amount by which the vault of the stars gains on the sun. Consequently, the source must lie beyond the solar system. By the spring of 1932 Jansky had decided the source was in the constellation of Sagittarius, the direction in which Shapley [1102] and Oort [1229] placed the center of our galaxy. He published his findings in December 1932. When Bell issued a press release on the subject, it made the front page of the New York *Times*.

This represented the birth of radio astronomy, in which astronomers learned to receive and interpret microwaves (the shortest radio waves) rather than light waves. Its usefulness was that microwaves penetrated dust clouds that light waves could not so that a radio telescope could detect the galactic center, which, as a result of obscuring dust clouds, ordinary telescopes could never see.

Jansky himself did not continue the development of the science. He made a few observations after his initial work, but that was all. He was more interested in his engineering and was willing to leave the universe to others. Despite the fact that his discovery was well publicized, astronomers did not take up the challenge for several years, although Whipple [1317] presented a discussion of Jansky's observation. An amateur astronomer, Reber [1368], carried on actual work singlehandedly.

It was the development of microwave

techniques in connection with radar during World War II that made radio astronomy expand and flourish after that war.

Jansky died of a heart ailment while still a young man but he lived long enough to see radio astronomy come out of the doldrums and begin to emerge as a prime tool of the new astronomy. In his honor the unit of strength of radio-wave emission is now called the jansky.

[1296] **BLOCH,** Felix
Swiss-American physicist
Born: Zürich, Switzerland, October 23, 1905

After an education in Zürich originally aimed at engineering, Bloch did his graduate work at the University of Leipzig in Germany, earning his Ph.D. in 1928 and receiving his first professorial appointment in Leipzig in 1932. He left Germany the next year, however, when Hitler came to power, and then worked at institutions in Holland, Denmark, and Italy, going to the United States in 1934 and making it his permanent home. He became an American citizen in 1939.

He became an associate professor of physics at Stanford University in that year and during World War II worked at Los Alamos on the atomic bomb project.

After the war Bloch returned to pure physics and particularly to the study of the magnetic fields of atomic nuclei. This had been investigated by Stern [1124] and Rabi [1212], but they had worked with beams of gaseous atoms or molecules. Bloch devised a method of determination on liquids and solids and, with Alvarez [1363], measured the magnetic moment of the neutron.

Purcell [1378] working independently also devised such a method, a slightly different one. For this work, Bloch and Purcell shared the 1952 Nobel Prize in physics.

Bloch's work on the magnetic properties of atomic nuclei also led to the development of a subtle method of chemical analysis called "nuclear magnetic resonance."

In 1954 and 1955 Bloch served as the

first director-general of CERN, the multinational laboratory for nuclear science at Geneva.

[1297] **KUIPER,** Gerard Peter (koy'per)
Dutch-American astronomer
Born: Harenkarspel, Netherlands, December 7, 1905
Died: Mexico City, Mexico, December 23, 1973

Kuiper was educated at the University of Leiden, from which he graduated in 1927 and where he earned his Ph.D. in 1933. He came to the United States that year and became a naturalized citizen in 1937. After 1936 he served on the faculty of the University of Chicago and worked at the Yerkes Observatory.

His best-known discoveries are in connection with our solar system. In 1948, for instance, he detected carbon dioxide in the atmosphere of Mars, but also showed (by infrared studies) that the Martian polar caps were ice and not frozen carbon dioxide as some had thought. (Recent Mars-probe data may indicate Kuiper was wrong here after all.)

His search for other atmospheres led him to the discovery that Titan, the largest satellite of Saturn, possesses an atmosphere containing methane and ammonia. It is the only satellite now known to possess an atmosphere. His theories led him to suspect that Triton, the satellite of Neptune, may also possess an atmosphere, but its distance prevents that point from being settled. No other satellite is both massive enough and cold enough for an atmosphere.

Kuiper expanded the satellite picture of the solar system by discovering two new small ones in the far reaches of the system (the thirtieth and the thirty-first). In 1948 he discovered a satellite of Uranus, the smallest and closest to that planet, and its fifth. He named it Miranda. In 1949 he discovered a second satellite of Neptune, a small one with an eccentric orbit. He named it Nereid.

Kuiper's studies also brought him to the conclusion that Pluto, the outermost planet, at the very edge of the solar system, is smaller than had been supposed. It is, it would seem, only 3,700 miles in diameter, about the size of Mars. He also determined its period of rotation to be about 6.4 days.

In 1951 he advanced a theory in which planets were formed by condensation of gaseous "protoplanets"; the satellites in this view were independent condensations. This has largely replaced George Darwin's [777] dramatic view of the moon as born of the earth. Kuiper's work sparked a rebirth of interest in the astronomy of the solar system, an interest that grew enormously as the space age dawned and seemed to bring our sister worlds within physical reach.

In the mid-sixties, he was naturally deeply involved in the programs by which rocket devices explored the moon's surface at close range.

[1298] **MORGAN,** William Wilson
American astronomer
Born: Bethesda, Tennessee, January 3, 1906

Morgan studied at the University of Chicago, graduating in 1927 and obtaining his Ph.D. in 1931. He then worked at that university's Yerkes Observatory.

In the late 1940s Morgan made a detailed study of the large blue-white stars of the galaxy. These ionized hydrogen gas in their neighborhood and, by detecting the spectral emissions of this gas, Morgan was able to work out portions of the actual spiral structure of our own galaxy, a structure that had till then been assumed but not demonstrated.

This structure was elaborated still further by means of the radio emissions of non-ionized hydrogen, predicted by Van de Hulst [1430] even as Morgan was doing his work.

[1299] **TOMBAUGH,** Clyde William
(tom'boh)
American astronomer
Born: Streator, Illinois, February 4, 1906

Tombaugh's family was too poor to send him to college, but young Clyde was fascinated by astronomy and worked eagerly with a 9-inch telescope built out of parts of old machinery lying about his father's farm.

In 1929 he managed to get a job as an assistant at Lowell Observatory, where the tradition of Percival Lowell [860], dead for thirteen years, still lingered, and where the search for a planet beyond Neptune, Lowell's Planet X, still continued under the guidance of Slipher [1038].

Tombaugh tackled the job with vigor. If the new planet existed, it would be so dim that any telescope that would bring it into view would also bring into view floods of dim stars. The planet would be distinguishable by its motion, to be sure, but it would be so distant from the sun and from the earth that its visible motion would be only slight.

Tombaugh used a technique whereby he could take two pictures of the same small part of the sky on two different days. Each of these would have from 50,000 to 400,000 stars on it. Despite all those stars, the two plates should be identical if the spots of light were stars and only stars. If the two plates were focused on a given spot on a screen in rapid alternation, none of the stars should seem to move. If one of the "stars" were really a planet, however, one that had moved against the starry background during the interval between photographs, it should shift position, and as the plates are alternately thrown upon the screen, that one star would seem to dart back and forth.

On February 18, 1930, after almost a year of painstaking comparisons, Tombaugh found a "star" in the constellation Gemini that flickered. From the slowness of its motion, he was sure it was trans-Neptunian. A month of observation followed and then the new planet was announced on March 13, 1930, the seventy-fifth anniversary of Lowell's birth. It was named Pluto, a significant name on two counts. First, the god of the nether darkness was an appropriate title for a planet swinging farthest out from the light of the sun, and second, the first two letters of its name are the intials of Percival Lowell.

Once again the solar system had been enlarged, as a century before it had been enlarged by Leverrier [564] and Adams [615] and a century and a half before by Herschel [321]. Nor has any object beyond Pluto been discovered in the generation since Tombaugh's feat, though Oort [1229] has speculated as to a trans-Plutonian asteroid belt that gives rise to the comets, whose composition Whipple [1317] was to clarify. Within the solar system, puzzles also remain, such as the mystery, which Wildt [1290] attempted to penetrate, of what lies below the opaque upper regions of the atmospheres of the giant outer planets.

As for Pluto, it has turned out to be an odd planet, with an orbit more eccentric and more inclined to the ecliptic than any of the other planets. It is far smaller than the other outer planets, as Kuiper [1297] showed, and there are astronomers who now suspect it is not a true planet but was once a satellite of Neptune, which, through some catastrophic change, was jarred into an independent orbit of its own.

After the discovery, Tombaugh was rewarded with a scholarship to the University of Kansas and was finally able to get his college education. He obtained his bachelor's degree in 1936 and his master's in 1939.

[1300] **TOMONAGA**, Shinichiro
Japanese physicist
Born: Kyoto, March 31, 1906
Died: Tokyo, July 8, 1979

Tomonaga, the son of a noted philosopher, graduated from Kyoto University in 1929, having been a classmate of Yukawa [1323]. He studied in Germany under Heisenberg [1245] for a time, then returned to Japan to obtain his doctorate at Kyoto in 1939.

He taught at Tokyo University through World War II and, after its conclusion, worked out the theoretical basis for quantum electrodynamics as, simultaneously and independently, Feynman [1424] and Schwinger [1421] were doing in the United States. All three shared the 1965 Nobel Prize in physics.

Tomonaga was appointed president of the Tokyo University of Education in 1956.

[1301] **GÖDEL**, Kurt (ger'del)
Austrian-American mathematician
Born: Brünn, Austria-Hungary
(now Brno, Czechoslovakia),
April 28, 1906
Died: Princeton, New Jersey,
January 14, 1978

Gödel studied at the University of Vienna, obtaining his Ph.D. in 1930. He then joined its faculty.

In 1931 he published a paper that marked the culmination of the search for a new mathematical certainty, a search that had been going on for a full century, since Lobachevski [484] and Bolyai [530] had shattered the old certainty of Euclid [40].

With the establishment of non-Euclidean geometries, it had been realized that Euclid's revered axioms were insufficient. Men like Hilbert [918] had established new and far better axiom systems for geometry. Other mathematicians had used the symbolic logic of Boole [595] to try to establish axioms that would serve as a rigorous starting point for all of mathematics. Frege's [797] attempt had been frustrated by Bertrand Russell [1005], whose own attempt, with Whitehead [911], had been the most ambitious of all.

But two decades after the Russell-Whitehead structure had been published, Gödel advanced what has come to be called Gödel's proof. He translated the symbols of symbolic logic into numbers in a systematic way and showed that it was always possible to construct a number that could not be arrived at by the other numbers of his system.

What it amounted to was this: Gödel had shown that if you began with any set of axioms, there would always be statements, within the system governed by those axioms, that could be neither proved nor disproved on the basis of those axioms. If the axioms are modified in such a way that that statement could then be either proved or disproved, then another statement can be constructed that cannot be either proved or disproved, and so on forever.

In still other words, the totality of mathematics cannot be brought to complete order on the basis of any system of axioms. Every mathematical system, however complex, will always contain unresolvable paradoxes of the sort that Russell used to upset Frege's system.

Gödel had ended the search for certainty in mathematics by showing that it did not and could not exist, just as Heisenberg [1245] had done for the physical sciences with his uncertainty principle five years earlier.

Gödel formed a connection with the Institute for Advanced Studies at Princeton shortly after his paper was published. In 1940 he made the United States his permanent home and in 1948 he was naturalized an American citizen.

[1302] **BOK**, Bart Jan
Dutch-American astronomer
Born: Hoorn, North Holland,
April 28, 1906

Bok received his Ph.D. at the University of Groningen in 1932. By that time he had already spent time in the United States, and he became an American citizen in 1938. He spent some twenty years thereafter on the faculty of Harvard University. From 1966 to 1974 he was at the University of Arizona.

He is best known for his observation in the 1940s of certain comparatively small, compact, opaque, and isolated dust clouds. He suggested these—now called Bok globules—were stars in the process of formation. Most astronomers think he is right and some estimate that in our galaxy about ten stars are formed each year on the average.

[1303] **EWING**, William Maurice
American geologist
Born: Lockney, Texas, May 12, 1906
Died: Galveston, Texas, May 4, 1974

Ewing was educated at Rice Institute (now Rice University) in Houston,

Texas, graduating in 1926 and obtaining his Ph.D. in 1931. After teaching at Pittsburgh University and Lehigh University, he joined the faculty of Columbia University in 1944. From 1972 until his death, he was connected with the University of Texas at Galveston.

After World War II, Ewing and his associates were engaged in numerous oceanic expeditions in the course of which the ocean bottoms were explored not merely by plumb lines, in the nineteenth-century fashion, but by all the resources of twentieth-century technology: ultrasonic reflection, gravity measurements, the punching out of long cores from the bottom, and so on.

By these methods, modern oceanography has revealed the ocean bottom to be as various a structure as the land surface, with rugged mountain ranges, mysterious flat-topped mounts (guyots), pebble-strewn regions, and other curiosity-rousing details. In particular, mid-ocean ridges like long mountain ranges have been discovered that dwarf those on the continents. The best known is the mid-Atlantic ridge, winding down the center of the Atlantic Ocean. Ewing showed in 1956 that this ridge continued around Africa into the Indian Ocean and around Antarctica into the Pacific, forming a world-girdling system. Later, he showed there was a chasm or fault running down the center of the Atlantic ridge and speculated that the earth might be increasing its size. Later, it seemed more plausible that upwelling material through the rift was causing the sea bottom to spread, forcing the continents apart in some places and together in others. The flaw in Wegener's [1071] scheme was corrected. The continents did *not* drift through the underlying rock that was too stiff to allow it. The continents, fixed in the rock and forming crustal plates, were forced apart or together with the plates they were on by forces in the earth's mantle.

Ewing also suggested in 1952 that the presence of submarine canyons (deep rifts in the continental shelf, or relatively shallow ocean region, rimming the continents) was not caused by rivers running across the area at a time when the sea level was much lower, but by turbulent undersea flows of mud and sediment.

Through the 1950s Ewing and his group accumulated evidence for a new theory explaining the cause of the periodic ice ages as resulting not from a period of cooling, but from one of warming. During the interglacial period, he maintained, the Arctic Ocean is free of ice cover and serves as a source of water vapor, which is deposited on the Siberian and Canadian shores as snow. The snow accumulates, the temperature drops, the glaciers move down from the north, and eventually the Arctic Ocean freezes over.

Once it does, the source of snow is choked off, the glaciers begin to retreat, and the temperature rises, until as now the glaciers are mostly gone from the lowlands (though still lingering on Antarctica and Greenland) while the Arctic Ocean remains frozen over. If warming continues to the point where the Arctic sea ice melts, the Arctic will then contribute water vapor to the polar atmosphere and the cycle will begin again.

As to why the recurrent ice ages are only a recent feature of earth's history (within the last few hundred thousand years) and did not appear for hundreds of millions of years before, there is the possibility that the North Pole has only been located in the landlocked Arctic in recent eras. Before then, it might have been located in the open Pacific where the great volume of circulating sea water would not permit ice formation and where there would be no nearby land surface to receive snow.

[1304] **HESS,** Harry Hammond
American geologist
Born: New York, New York,
May 24, 1906
Died: Woods Hole,
Massachusetts, August 25, 1969

Hess graduated from Yale in 1927 and obtained his Ph.D. at Princeton in 1932. He commanded a submarine base in World War II and reached the rank of rear admiral in the Naval Reserve.

His most glamorous work was done in connection with the oceans. For all the thousands of years that man has been floating, sailing, or steaming across its surface, the land that lies under the waters has remained a mystery. It is only in recent decades that new means of exploring the depths have revealed that land.

In 1945 Hess plumbed the greatest depth of the ocean—something like seven miles deep. He also studied the isolated mountains rising from the ocean floor ("sea-mounts"). Back in 1837 Charles Darwin had suggested that coral atolls were built up at a speed matching the natural sinking of the island. If this were so, it followed that some islands might (for the isostatic reasons suggested by Dutton [753]) sink without coral formation and might now lie under the sea.

Hess discovered, in 1946, that hundreds of flat-topped sea-mounts underlie the Pacific Ocean, all probably sunken islands. These he named guyots in honor of the Swiss-American geographer A. H. Guyot [552].

In 1962, building on the findings of Ewing [1303], he presented evidence to the effect that the Atlantic seabed was spreading. This "sea-floor spreading" is crucial to the new science of "plate tectonics" that is itself central to the new geology.

From 1934 Hess was on the faculty of Princeton, becoming head of the geology department in 1950. After 1965 he was an adviser to the National Aeronautics and Space Administration and helped plan the first landing on the moon, which took place a month before his death.

[1305] **CRAIG,** Lyman Creighton
American chemist
Born: Palmyra, Iowa, June 12, 1906

Craig graduated from Iowa State University in 1928 and obtained his Ph.D. there in 1931. After 1933 he was on the staff of Rockefeller University in New York.

Craig pioneered in the careful fractionation of complex mixtures by a variety of methods. His greatest feat of iso-

lating a rare item from a complicated mixture came in 1960, when he and his colleagues succeeded in isolating and purifying parathormone, the active principle of the parathyroid gland.

[1306] **CHAIN,** Ernst Boris
German-English biochemist
Born: Berlin, Germany, June 19, 1906
Died: Ireland, August 12, 1979

Chain, the son of a chemist, was educated in Berlin, obtaining his Ph.D. in 1930 from the Friedrich-Wilhelm University. The even tenor of his life was interrupted by the coming to power of Hitler in early 1933. Chain saw the inevitable and left at once for England. There he worked under Hopkins [912] at Cambridge. In 1935 he was invited to Oxford by Florey [1213].

There he came across Fleming's [1077] work on penicillin while investigating Fleming's other discovery, lysozyme. He brought it to Florey's attention and, together, they began work on the substance, for which Chain conducted the first chemical assay. For this, Chain shared in the 1945 Nobel Prize in medicine and physiology with Florey and Fleming. Chain also discovered penicillinase, an enzyme that catalyzed the destruction of penicillin. After World War II, in 1948, Chain took the post of scientific director at a health institute in Rome, lured by the thought of working with better equipment than he was able to obtain in Great Britain. By 1961, however, he was wooed back to the University of London, where a new laboratory was constructed for him.

[1307] **GOEPPERT-MAYER,** Marie
(ger′pert-may′er)
German-American physicist
Born: Kattowitz (now Katowice, Poland), June 28, 1906
Died: San Diego, California, February 20, 1972

Marie Goeppert, born of many generations of professors, received her Ph.D. at the University of Göttingen in 1930 under Born [1084]. She moved to the United States that same year and became an American citizen in 1933. She married a physical chemist, Joseph Mayer, whom she had met in Göttingen, and, like Irène Curie, [1204] used a hyphenated name thereafter.

She was, along with her husband, at Princeton and Columbia, and then in 1945 she joined the staff of the University of Chicago. While there, in 1948, she suggested that the atomic nucleus consisted of protons and neutrons arranged in shells, as electrons were arranged in the outer atom. This theory, which was supported by Fermi [1243], made it possible to explain why some nuclei were more stable than others, why some elements were rich in isotopes, and so on.

At about the same time, Jensen [1327] advanced the same notion independently, and in 1950 they collaborated on a book on the subject. Both she and Jensen accordingly shared the 1963 Nobel Prize in physics with Wigner [1036].

In 1960 she joined the faculty of the University of California at San Diego and remained there the rest of her life.

[1308] **BETHE,** Hans Albrecht (bay'-tuh)
German-American physicist
Born: Strassburg (now in Bas-Rhin, France), July 2, 1906

At the time of Bethe's birth, Alsace-Lorraine was part of Germany; it is now part of France. Bethe, the son of a university professor, was educated at the universities of Frankfurt and Munich, obtaining his Ph.D. at Munich in 1928 under Sommerfeld [976]. He worked under Ernest Rutherford [996] at Cambridge and Fermi [1243] at Rome, then taught physics at Munich and Tübingen until 1933. In that year Hitler came to power and Bethe thought it the better part of valor to leave Germany. He taught in England until 1935 and then accepted a post at Cornell University in the United States.

During his stay in England, Bethe worked out the manner in which high-energy particles, subjected to deflection by an electromagnetic field, emitted radiation. This was of particular importance in cosmic ray studies.

In the United States he was one of the scientists engaged in the development of the atomic bomb. In the postwar years he served on the American delegation in Geneva during the long negotiations with the Soviet Union on the control of nuclear bomb tests.

Bethe's chief contribution to science was working out the details of the nuclear mechanisms that power the stars, which he achieved in 1938, when Weizsäcker [1376] was independently reaching similar conclusions in Germany.

Bethe made use of the knowledge of subatomic physics that had been collecting in the forty years since Becquerel's [834] discovery of radioactivity and Eddington's [1085] conclusions about the temperatures of the stellar interiors.

Bethe's mechanism resembled that suggested by Perrin [990] in a qualitative way as long before as 1921. It began with the union of a hydrogen nucleus (that is, a proton) with a carbon nucleus. This initiated a series of reactions at the end of which the carbon nucleus was regenerated and four hydrogen nuclei (protons) had been converted to a helium nucleus (alpha particle). Hydrogen was thus the "fuel" of the star and helium the "ash," while carbon played the role of catalyst.

Stars like the sun were mostly hydrogen, so that there was ample fuel to last for billions of years, while the quantity of helium already present indicated that there had been prior existence for billions of years. Later Bethe evolved a second scheme involving the direct union of hydrogen nuclei to form helium (in a number of steps) as a mechanism that could proceed at lower temperatures.

Bethe's nuclear mechanisms finally answered the question that some three quarters of a century earlier had so concerned Helmholtz [631] and Kelvin [652]: Where do the sun and stars obtain their energy? When hydrogen is converted into helium (whether directly or by way of the catalytic influence of carbon) nearly 1 percent of the mass of the hydrogen is converted into energy. Even a little bit of mass is equivalent to a great deal of energy and so mass loss is ample to account for all the sun's vast and eon-long radiation of energy. To be sure, at the rate the sun radiates energy it must be losing 4,200,000 tons of mass every second, but the total mass of the sun's hydrogen is so great that this loss of mass must remain imperceptible even over millions of years.

In 1961 Bethe was honored with the Fermi award (established in 1956) for his part in the development and use of atomic energy. In 1967 he received the Nobel Prize for physics.

In his later years, Bethe became an active proponent of the continued peaceful exploitation of nuclear energy.

[1309] **SCHAEFER,** Vincent Joseph
American physicist
Born: Schenectady, New York, July 4, 1906

Schaefer's education was very largely on the practical side. He worked in the machine shop at the General Electric Company in his hometown of Schenectady, then thought the outdoors would suit his personality better. He graduated from the Davey Institute of Tree Surgery in 1928 and practiced that profession for a while. Economic necessity drove him back to General Electric and the indoors, however, and there he was noticed by Langmuir [1072], whose assistant he became in 1933. He rose to a research associate in his own right in 1938.

In the 1940s Langmuir and Schaefer were studying the war-intensified problem of airplane wings icing up at high altitudes, creating great hazard. Just what factors caused the formation of ice or snow? This was of particular interest to Schaefer, who, as might be expected of an outdoorsman, was a ski enthusiast and snow lover.

To experiment on this subject, Schaefer used a refrigerated box kept at −23°C within which, it was hoped, water vapor could be condensed around dust particles into ice crystals. Finding what types of particles could be added artificially to hasten the crystal formation proved a baffling problem.

In July 1946, during a hot spell, it was difficult to keep the temperature within the box low enough for the requirements of the experiments. Schaefer therefore dropped some solid carbon dioxide (dry ice) into the box in order to force down the temperature. However, as soon as the dry ice hit the interior of the box, the water vapor within condensed into ice crystals. The box was filled with a miniature snowstorm.

Schaefer was soon ready to try a full-scale experiment. On November 13, 1946, he was flown by airplane over a cloud layer obscuring Pittsfield, Massachusetts, about fifty miles southeast of Schenectady. Six pounds of pellets of dry ice were dumped into those clouds and a snowstorm started. It was the first man-made precipitation in history.

Since that day, rainmaking has passed from the medicine man's ritual to the meteorologist's technique. Dry ice gave way to the more convenient silver iodide, thanks to Vonnegut [1391], and there are few droughts in the United States now that do not bring on some effort at rainmaking.

It is arguable whether rainmaking is truly effective—whether rain that is produced might not have fallen anyway. There is also the ticklish question of the legal responsibility in case a change in weather is construed by some to have been damaging to their economic or personal interests. Nevertheless, Mark Twain's comment that "Everyone talks about the weather but nobody does anything about it" has been refuted.

[1310] **PRELOG,** Vladimir
Yugoslavian-Swiss chemist
Born: Sarajevo (then part of Austria-Hungary), July 23, 1906

Prelog was educated in Prague and at one time studied under Ružička [1119]. In 1935 he joined the faculty of the University of Zagreb in Yugoslavia; but in 1941, when the German army invaded the country, he fled to Switzerland, where he remained afterward.

Using X-ray diffraction techniques he determined the structure of several antibiotics. He also worked out systematic rules for determining whether a particular asymmetric compound is "dextra" or "levo," that is, has a certain structure or the mirror image of that structure. For this he was awarded a share of the 1975 Nobel Prize for chemistry.

[1311] **SABIN,** Albert Bruce
Polish-American microbiologist
Born: Bialystok, Russia (now Poland), August 26, 1906

Like Salk [1393] of Polish-Jewish descent, Sabin arrived in the United States in 1921 and was naturalized in 1930. He attended New York University, going to dental school at first, but becoming interested in microbiology and shifting to medicine. He obtained his medical degree in 1931 and in 1939 became professor of pediatrics at the University of Cincinnati Medical School.

During World War II he served as a medical officer in the army, fighting against such diseases as encephalitis. After the war, however, he turned to poliomyelitis which had concerned him in his younger days, when, a decade before Enders [1195], he attempted to grow polio virus outside intact organisms.

Sabin was not convinced that the Salk technique of using dead virus was adequate. He believed that only living virus could be counted on to produce the necessary antibodies over a long period. Furthermore, living virus could be taken by mouth, since they would multiply and invade the body of their own accord, and would not, like the Salk vaccine, have to be injected by needle. The trick was to find virus strains of each of the three types of polio (each producing its own variety of antibody) that were too feeble to produce the disease itself.

When Sabin thought he had the proper strains, judging by animal experiments, he tried them on himself first, then on prison volunteers. By 1957 he had live vaccines of each polio type that he considered satisfactory. The Sabin vaccine proved popular in the Soviet Union and it was widely used there and in other East European nations. It was not till 1960, however, that the vaccine came into use in the United States.

[1312] **FOLKERS,** Karl August
American chemist
Born: Decatur, Illinois, September 1, 1906

Folkers graduated from the University of Illinois in 1928 and went on to obtain his Ph.D. in 1931 at the University of Wisconsin. After postdoctorate work at Yale University, Folkers became an industrial chemist, finding his niche at Merck & Company in 1934. There he rose in rank until he was director of fundamental research by 1956.

Merck is a pharmaceutical house, and a particularly important field of interest for such a firm during the vitamin-centered 1930s was the possibility of preparing synthetic vitamins. Through the 1930s Folkers and the rest of the Merck group helped establish the chemical structure (by synthesis) of various members of the B-vitamin group, including pyridoxine, biotin, and pantothenic acid.

Their most startling work, however, came in connection with the antipernicious anemia factor that had been located in liver by Minot [1103] and Murphy [1154], while Folkers was still a college student. Feeding liver in large quantities to patients with pernicious anemia was life-saving, to be sure, but could become a form of torture, since liver doesn't wear well as a constant article of diet. Obviously if the vitamin could be administered without the surrounding liver, matters would be greatly improved.

Through the 1930s attempts were made to isolate the factor, which was suspected of being one of the B vitamins and was, in fact, given the name vitamin B_{12}. Liver extracts rich in vitamin B_{12} were obtained, but progress was slowed by the difficulty of assaying the extracts for vitamin potency. For twenty years after

816

the Minot-Murphy discovery, the only way of making such an assay was to feed the various extracts and fractions to patients with pernicious anemia and then to observe the rate at which a certain type of immature red blood cell, the reticulocyte, was formed in response.

In 1948 it was discovered at Merck that certain bacteria required vitamin B_{12} for growth. If those bacteria were supplied a nutrient medium containing all required factors but vitamin B_{12}, their rate of growth would then be in proportion to any added quantity of vitamin B_{12}. In this way, the vitamin content of any extract could quickly be determined without trouble to human patients.

The process of purification was speeded enormously and soon red crystals were obtained that proved to be the vitamin itself. Folkers and his group accomplished the isolation at Merck, just as another group, in England, was accomplishing it as well (and without the advantage of bacterial assay).

Vitamin B_{12} turned out to be an amazing compound in a number of ways. It is required by the body in far smaller quantities than ordinary vitamins are, and it has such a complicated molecule that the final determination of its structure was made by measurements of electron densities, measurements that proved so complicated that a modern computer was required to complete the interpretation. This was carried through in 1956 by D. C. Hodgkin [1352].

Two surprising points were made in connection with the structure. First, a cyanide group was included in the molecule and second, a cobalt atom. The compound was named cyanocobalamine, the first naturally occurring compound found to contain cobalt. This explained why cobalt is a trace element necessary to life.

A person with pernicious anemia does not suffer necessarily from any lack of cyanocobalamine in his diet, since the small amounts required are present in any normal diet. And if they weren't, they would be formed by the intestinal bacteria as long as a trace of cobalt was present in the diet. The pernicious anemic, however, lacks a particular substance in the gastric juice without which he cannot absorb the large molecule of the vitamin. In this area, research still continues.

In a sense, the isolation of cyanocobalamine (which is now produced in quantity from bacterial cultures, is routinely included in vitamin pills, and has removed pernicious anemia from the list of medical problems) marks the climax of the vitamin research that began a half century earlier with Eijkman [888].

What remains to be done is of biochemical rather than medical importance; the various vitamins must be placed in their respective metabolic niches. This is being rapidly accomplished for the B vitamins, beginning with the work of Elvehjem [1240] in the 1930s, and even the vitamins outside that group are beginning to fall into place, a notable example being Wald's [1318] work with vitamin A.

Folkers was involved in matters other than vitamins. After World War II, antibiotics moved into the forefront of pharmaceutical problems and in 1948 Folkers' group was among those who worked out the chemical structure of Waksman's [1128] streptomycin.

In 1963 he became president of the Stanford Research Institute in Menlo Park, California.

[1313] **DELBRÜCK,** Max
German-American microbiologist
Born: Berlin, September 4, 1906
Died: Pasadena, California, March 9, 1981

Delbrück obtained his Ph.D. from the University of Göttingen in 1930, did postdoctoral work in Copenhagen under Bohr [1101], and then worked in Berlin with Hahn [1063] and Meitner [1060]. He left Germany after Hitler came to power, reaching the United States in 1937 and becoming an American citizen in 1945. He joined the faculty of the California Institute of Technology.

While he was still in Berlin his interest had begun shifting from nuclear physics to genetics, and in California he grew absorbed in bacteriophages, the comparatively large viruses that infest bacterial cells. He discovered an improved method of culturing bacteriophages and found that once a bacterial cell was infected by a single bacteriophage, that cell broke up in half an hour, leaving a hundred bacteriophages behind, each ready to infect another bacterial cell.

Delbrück and Hershey [1341] independently discovered in 1946 that the genetic material of different viruses could be combined to form a virus different from either. This founded the study of bacterial genetics and led a generation later to the achievements of microbiologists such as Berg [1470] and their work with recombinant DNA.

For their findings, Delbrück and Hershey shared, with Luria [1377], the 1969 Nobel Prize for physiology and medicine.

[1314] **LELOIR,** Luis Frederico
Argentinian biochemist
Born: Paris, France, September 6, 1906

Leloir was educated at the University of Buenos Aires and remained on the faculty there. He studied the synthesis and breakdown of complex sugars, discovering sugar nucleotides that serve as intermediates, and liver enzymes that are essential to the process. As a result, he received the 1970 Nobel Prize for chemistry.

[1315] **LEY,** Willy (lay)
German-American engineer
Born: Berlin, Germany, October 2, 1906
Died: New York, New York, June 24, 1969

Ley studied at the University of Berlin and might have become a zoologist but in 1925 discovered a book on rocketry that caught his imagination. He wrote a popularized version of his own that met with wide acclaim and for over forty years afterward he remained the most successful popular writer on rocketry in the world.

Nor was he content merely to write. He helped found the German Rocket Society in 1927, the first group of men—with the solitary exception of Goddard [1083]—to experiment with rockets. Wernher von Braun [1370] was introduced into the organization by Ley, who was also consultant for the science fiction movie *Frau im Mond* in which the countdown from ten to zero was introduced.

When Hitler came to power, Ley was soon in trouble. Fiercely anti-Nazi, he was not content to pursue his rocket studies regardless of the political atmosphere as did Von Braun. Ley came to the United States in 1935 and became a naturalized American citizen in 1944.

In the United States, Ley was intimately involved on the one hand with the strong science fiction literary movement and on the other with his serious interest in rocketry. He, more than anyone else, prepared the climate within the United States for the space effort.

In the end, however, he died just three weeks before Armstrong [1492] touched down on the moon. Like Moses, he led the way but could not enter the Promised Land.

[1316] **EDLÉN,** Bengt
Swedish physicist
Born: Gusum, November 2, 1906

Edlén obtained his doctorate at Uppsala in 1934, and remained on its faculty with professorial rank till 1943, when he moved on to the University of Lund.

He was particularly interested in the analyses of spectra in the extreme ultraviolet range and used his findings to deal with particularly hot stars that would be expected to produce large quantities of radiation in that range.

Rather unexpectedly, he found it possible to use his studies on the sun itself. To be sure, its surface is only 6,000°K in temperature but its surface is the coolest part of itself. Not only is it hotter in its depths, but while the total heat declines as one moves upward from the surface, it is distributed among particles, the total number of which per unit volume decreases even more rapidly, so that the heat per particle, or temperature, rises. In 1940 Edlén maintained that the solar corona has a temperature in the million-degree range and this was eventually well confirmed.

[1317] **WHIPPLE,** Fred Lawrence
American astronomer
Born: Red Oak, Iowa, November 5, 1906

Whipple studied at the University of California, graduating in 1927 and obtaining his Ph.D. in 1931. He joined the faculty of Harvard University in the latter year and remained there afterward.

He was particularly interested in the mavericks of the solar system, its comets and meteoroids. Whipple suggested, in 1949, that the comets are composed largely of frozen hydrogen-containing compounds (ammonia, methane, and so on) cemented together, perhaps, by conglomerates of silicates, or ordinary rock.

This is reminiscent of the general composition of the outer planets, as Wildt [1290] had made clear, and if the comets originate in a far-flung asteroid belt beyond the outer planets, as Oort's [1229] theory holds, it is reasonable to suppose this to be their composition. At an approach to the sun, some of the hydrogen-containing "ices" are vaporized and, with silicate dust, are swept back by the solar wind to form the cometary tail.

Whipple, as a science fiction enthusiast, must have found it a dream come true to be intimately involved in the man-made satellite project of the late 1950s. He was director of the Smithsonian Astrophysical Observatory after 1955 and headed the optical tracking system in the United States, a system that mobilized hundreds of observers (professional and amateur) to trace the satellites that began streaking across the sky in late 1957.

[1318] **WALD,** George
American chemist
Born: New York, New York, November 18, 1906

Wald graduated from New York University in 1927 and obtained his Ph.D. at Columbia University in 1932. After working under Karrer [1131] in Zürich, and at the University of Chicago, he joined the faculty of Harvard University in 1934 and remained there afterward.

His chief interest was in the chemistry of vision. The rods of the retina, which function in dim light, contain a pigment (visual purple, or rhodopsin) that, Wald showed, consists of a protein (opsin) in combination with a compound called retinene. Retinene is very similar in structure to vitamin A and is formed from vitamin A in the body. When light strikes rhodopsin, the protein and the retinene separate; they recombine in the dark.

For more than a quarter century Wald and his group worked out the details of these changes with precision. In the process of light-dark changes, some retinene is irreversibly altered and drizzles away, so to speak. More is formed out of the more stable vitamin A. Where the diet is deficient in vitamin A over an extended period, the body's stores of that compound are used up and there is no way of forming additional retinene. The rods will no longer function normally and the eye will not respond to dim light. It is for this reason that one of the symptoms of vitamin A deficiency (though not the only one) is night blindness.

For this work Wald shared the 1967 Nobel Prize in physiology and medicine. Still later, and rather unexpectedly as the result of an impromptu speech he made, he emerged into nationwide fame as a spokesman for the peace movement and youth rebellion that swept the United States during the Vietnam War.

[1319] **GOLDMARK,** Peter Carl
Hungarian-American physicist
Born: Budapest, December 2, 1906
Died: Westchester County, New York, December 7, 1977

Goldmark studied at the University of Vienna and obtained his Ph.D. there in 1931. He came to the United States in

1933 and became an American citizen in 1937.

He worked at the Columbia Broadcasting System Laboratories from 1936 to 1971 and became president of the laboratories in 1954.

He is notable for two advances that have intimately affected the lives of many millions the world over. In 1948 he developed the long-playing (LP) record, which turned 33⅓ times per minute rather than the till then regulation 78. A single LP record could hold six times the amount of music of the old kind. Earlier, in 1940, he had developed the first color television system used in commercial broadcasts. He also contributed to the scanning system that made it possible for viewers on Earth to receive photographs taken of and relayed from the moon.

[1320] **WILKINS,** Robert Wallace
American physician
Born: Chattanooga, Tennessee, December 4, 1906

Wilkins received his medical degree from Harvard University Medical School in 1933 and served on the faculty of Boston University Medical School after 1940.

He is best known for his introduction into the United States of a drug derived from the root of an Indian shrub. It had been used in India in the treatment of high blood pressure and beginning in 1950 Wilkins used it for this purpose at the Massachusetts Memorial Hospital. In 1952 he reported on its sedative and tranquilizing effect and the drug, which was named reserpine, was the first of the tranquilizers.

The tranquilizers have the advantage over earlier sedatives, like barbiturates, in that they produce their calming effect without diminishing alertness or bringing on sleep. Tranquilizers are popular with many people for the reduction (real or fancied) of tensions (real or fancied), but they serve more important uses, too. They are an important adjunct in psychiatric treatment, for, although they are in no sense a cure for any mental disease, they do calm violent patients without the use of harsh physical restraints, and calmed patients are more easily reached by the psychiatrist. Their overuse as a crutch has led to problems of addiction that are by no means trivial.

[1321] **ZINN,** Walter Henry
Canadian-American physicist
Born: Kitchener, Ontario, December 10, 1906

After graduation from Queen's University, Zinn went to the United States in 1930 (he was naturalized in 1938) and obtained his Ph.D. at Columbia University in 1934.

In 1939 he was one of those American physicists who quickly confirmed Meitner's [1060] theory of uranium fission, and during World War II he worked on the development of the nuclear bomb. It was he who withdrew the control rod in the first nuclear reactor in 1942 and made it self-sustaining. After the war he became director of the Argonne National Laboratories in Chicago.

He specialized in the design of nuclear reactors and in 1951 built the first experimental breeder reactor in Idaho. Where ordinary reactors obtain their energy through the fission of uranium-235, a breeder reactor, in the process of obtaining this energy, converts uranium-238 to additional uranium-235. Generally, breeder reactors produce or breed more fuel than they consume. Such reactors make all the uranium and thorium resources of the earth available for use as nuclear fuel.

In 1959 Zinn became vice president of Combustion Engineering.

[1322] **RUSKA,** Ernst August Friedrich
German electrical engineer
Born: Heidelberg, December 25, 1906

Ruska qualified as an engineer at the University of Berlin in 1931 and earned a doctor's degree in 1934.

By then he had already made his mark in the world of science. Since electrons possess a wave aspect (as De Broglie [1157] had reasoned and Davisson [1078] had demonstrated) they ought to be capable of being treated in a fashion analogous to light waves. Since electrons were electrically charged, they could be manipulated by magnetic fields and focused much as light waves were focused by lenses. Why not, then, an "electron microscope"?

Since the shorter the length of waves being used, the greater the magnification, and since electron waves were much shorter than the waves of ordinary light, it followed that electron microscopes ought to be much more powerful than ordinary optical microscopes. And so they were.

Even the first crude instrument, built in 1932 by Ruska and a collaborator, Max Knoll, was capable of magnifying 400 times. The electron microscope did not actually become practical, however, until the later, improved model of Hillier [1401].

[1323] **YUKAWA**, Hideki (yoo-kah'-wah)
Japanese physicist
Born: Kyoto, January 23, 1907
Died: Kyoto, September 8, 1981

Yukawa was educated at Kyoto University, where his father was a professor of geology, graduating in 1929. He did his graduate work at Osaka University, earning his Ph.D. there in 1938, while serving on its faculty.

In the middle 1930s Yukawa addressed himself to the problem of what holds the nucleus of an atom together. After Chadwick [1150] discovered the neutron in 1932, Heisenberg [1245] had pointed out that the atomic nucleus must be made up of protons and neutrons only. If this was so, then only positive electric charges were to be found in the nucleus and these should exert a strong repulsion among themselves, particularly when as close to each other as they must be in the nucleus. Heisenberg had suggested the existence of "exchange forces" but had not pinpointed what those exchange forces might be.

Yukawa reasoned that ordinary electromagnetic forces involved the transfer of photons and that within the nucleus there must be a "nuclear force" involving the transfer of some other entity. Such a nuclear force, if it existed, must be very short-range. That is, over distances not greater than the span of the nucleus (about a ten-trillionth of a centimeter), the force must be very strong, strong enough to overcome the repulsive forces between the positive charges of the various protons. However, the force must decrease very rapidly with distance, for outside the nucleus at the distance of even the nearest electrons it could no longer be detected.

Yukawa evolved a theory whereby such a force evidenced itself by transfers of particles among the neutrons and protons of the nucleus. These particles possessed mass, and the shorter-range the force, the greater the mass would have to be. For a force evidencing itself only across the width of the nucleus, the mass of the particle being transferred would have to be about two hundred times that of the electron and about one-ninth that of a proton or neutron.

In 1935, when Yukawa published his theories, no such intermediate-sized particle was known. The very next year, however, C. D. Anderson [1292] discovered one, and it came to be called a meson. For a while it seemed as though Yukawa's theory had been substantiated, and so it was, to the extent that a particle of intermediate size could exist. (The particle was very short-lived, to be sure, but Yukawa's theory had predicted that.)

Unfortunately Anderson's meson (the mu-meson or muon) did not interact with atomic nuclei to any great extent and Yukawa's theory required such interaction. However, in 1947 a second, slightly heavier meson (the pi-meson) was discovered by Powell [1274] and this second meson fulfilled all requirements. Yukawa was deemed worthy of the 1949 Nobel Prize in physics, the first Japanese to win a Nobel award.

In 1936 Yukawa had also predicted that a nucleus could absorb one of the innermost of the circling electrons and that this would be equivalent to emitting a positron. Since the innermost electrons belong to the "K shell," this process is termed "K capture." This prediction was verified in 1938.

In 1948 Yukawa, at the invitation of Oppenheimer [1280], visited the Institute for Advanced Study at Princeton, then lectured at Columbia University until 1953, when he returned to Kyoto University.

[1324] **VEKSLER,** Vladimir Iosifovich
Soviet physicist
Born: Zhitomir, Ukraine, March 4, 1907
Died: Moscow, September 22, 1966

Veksler, the son of an engineer, graduated from the Moscow Energetics Institute in 1931.

He was an important figure in high-energy experimental physics and in the development of particle accelerators. In 1945 he suggested a method for designing a cyclotron that would allow for relativistic changes in the mass of accelerating particles and thus achieve greater energies. McMillan [1329] independently proposed the same method a few years later.

Synchrocyclotrons were built along these lines in the late 1940s, and as a result in 1963 Veksler shared with McMillan the Atoms for Peace award.

[1325] **BOVET,** Daniele (boh-vay')
Swiss-French-Italian pharmacologist
Born: Neuchâtel, Switzerland, March 23, 1907

Bovet, the son of a professor of pedagogy, was educated at the University of Geneva, obtaining his doctorate in 1929, and did his important work at the Pasteur Institute in Paris.

This began with the announcement of the discovery of Prontosil by Domagk [1183] in 1935. Prontosil (a trade name) was effective against streptococci in the body, but, added to streptococci

cultures in test tubes, it had no effect. To Bovet and his colleagues at the Pasteur Institute, it seemed clear that this was best explained by supposing that Prontosil was changed into something else in the body and that it was the "something else" that handled the bacteria. The easiest way of changing Prontosil was to break its molecule into several fragments. One of these was a well-known compound, sulfanilamide. This was tested at the Pasteur Institute in 1936 and proved to be as effective in the test tube as in the body. In 1937 Bovet became head of the therapeutic chemistry laboratory at the Pasteur Institute.

Also in 1937 Bovet discovered compounds that neutralized some of the unpleasant symptoms of allergic manifestations, such as a stuffed or runny nose. Since these symptoms are thought to arise through the production in the body of a compound called histamine, a drug that counters the symptoms is an antihistamine. Bovet's first clear-cut chemical antihistamine was pyrilamine, introduced in 1944. Numerous antihistamines have been developed since, and while none of them cures an allergy, they tend to suppress the symptoms and make life more bearable for the sufferer.

During the early 1950s it occurred to some drug manufacturers that allergic manifestations resembled some of the symptoms of colds and antihistamine drugs were therefore widely touted as cold relievers (not cold cures). For a while they proliferated into a national fad, as a few years afterward the tranquilizers, first introduced by Wilkins [1320], were to do.

Thirdly, Bovet developed a method of using curare in surgery. Curare is an alkaloid found in the root of several South American shrubs. It paralyzes the muscles (including those of the heart, so that it is a quick poison) and is, indeed, the prototype of the "mysterious South American poison" so beloved by mystery writers. With the proper modification and in the proper doses, it relaxes the muscles without killing. Such relaxation, in conjunction with anesthesia, is very useful in surgery.

For his work on antihistamines and on

curare, Bovet was awarded the 1957 Nobel Prize in medicine and physiology.

In 1947 he had accepted a post as head of a pharmacological laboratory at a research institution in Rome and eventually became an Italian citizen.

[1326] **TINBERGEN,** Nikolaas
Dutch zoologist
Born: The Hague, April 15, 1907

Tinbergen received his Ph.D. from the University of Leiden in 1932 and taught there until 1949, at which time he moved to Oxford.

In 1936, he met Lorenz [1271], grew interested in ethology, and worked particularly with the instincts and behavior of sea gulls. He noted that animals fighting others of the same species tend to suspend aggression when the loser adopts a posture indicating surrender. For that reason quarrels over food and mates rarely lead to death or even serious wounding; such quarrels merely decide who wins and who loses in an all-but-harmless ritualistic fashion. Tinbergen suspects that the use of long-range weapons that increasingly divorces fighters from those with whom they fight has acted to cancel out the possibility of surrender and increases the death and destruction of human warfare.

In 1973 he shared the Nobel Prize for physiology and medicine with Lorenz and Karl von Frisch [1110].

[1327] **JENSEN,** Johannes Hans Daniel
German physicist
Born: Hamburg, June 25, 1907

Jensen, a gardener's son, obtained his Ph.D. at the University of Hamburg in 1932, joined the faculty in 1936, and was then director of the Institute for Theoretical Physics at that university. In 1949 he took up a professorial post at Heidelberg.

He advanced the notion of nuclear shells in 1949 independently of Goeppert-Mayer [1307] and in 1955 coauthored a book on the subject with her. They shared the 1963 Nobel Prize in physics with Wigner [1260].

[1328] **MAUCHLY,** John William
American engineer
Born: Cincinnati, Ohio, August 30, 1907
Died: January 8, 1980

Mauchly obtained his Ph.D. at Johns Hopkins University in 1932, then went on to teach physics at Ursinus College in Collegeville, Pennsylvania, in 1933. He took a post at the University of Pennsylvania in 1941 and there he taught electrical engineering.

In 1944, in partnership with Eckert [1431], he established a company for design and manufacturing of electronic digital computing machinery. He produced the first practical electronic digital computer, ENIAC, in 1946. It was an enormous, energy-guzzling device but it was a wonder in its time and represented a coming-to-life of Babbage's [481] dream.

Almost at once the electronic computer began to improve and grow more versatile, more compact, and more inexpensive. Mauchly helped develop the first UNIVAC in 1951, the first data processor to use magnetic tape.

Then came the solid state devices, pioneered by Shockley [1348], which proceeded to change computers out of all recognition before their first decade had been completed.

[1329] **McMILLAN,** Edwin Mattison
American physicist
Born: Redondo Beach, California, September 18, 1907

McMillan, the son of a physician, graduated from California Institute of Technology in 1928 and obtained his Ph.D. in 1932 at Princeton University. In that year he joined the faculty of the University of California.

There he was involved in the early work with Lawrence [1241] on the cyclotron. By the 1940s the cyclotron had grown so large and the speeding particles had been driven into so great a velocity that their mass increased noticeably. This is the "relativistic mass increase," the increase of mass with velocity that was first predicted by Lorentz [839] and then shown by Einstein [1064] to be a natural consequence of the assumptions upon which the theory of relativity was based.

The increase of mass slowed the particles slightly and threw out of synchronization the little pushes that were supposed to continue to speed up the particles. As a result, the energy that could be imparted to a charged particle could not be raised above a certain maximum and so the cyclotrons of the early 1940s had reached their limits.

In 1945 McMillan was one of those who devised a method whereby the increasing mass could be allowed for. The periodic pushes of the electric field then remained in synchronization and synchrocyclotrons were built that could reach higher energy levels than ordinary cyclotrons. (Similar devices were designed in Great Britain and the Soviet Union where the same advance in technique was made independently.)

The energies of charged particles are measured in electron volts. Energies in the many million-electron-volt range (MEV) were reached in the 1940s. In the 1950s further improvements, suggested by Kerst's [1367] betatron, were introduced and the most powerful particle accelerators, the proton synchrotrons, were devised. The billion-electron-volt range (bev) was reached and the bevatron, used by Segrè [1287] to form antiprotons, carries that fact in its name, for it reaches energies of 5 or 6 bev. Instruments put in action in Geneva and in Brookhaven, Long Island, in the early 1960s, produce particles with energies of over 30 bev.

McMillan's most dramatic discovery, however, had come before World War II. When Fermi [1243] first began bombarding uranium with neutrons, he was trying to form the element beyond uranium, the element with atomic number 93. He thought he had been able to detect such an element, but this was an error. The work of Hahn [1063] showed that uranium fission was taking place instead.

In 1940 McMillan and Abelson [1383], experimenting with fission, discovered a beta-particle activity with a

half life of 2.3 days. When they traced this down, they announced on June 8, 1940, that it was element number 93 (produced in very small quantities by a uranium reaction with neutrons that did not involve fission). Since uranium had been named for the planet Uranus by Klaproth [335], the new element 93, lying beyond uranium, was named neptunium for Neptune, the planet beyond Uranus. This was the first of the transuranium elements.

Since the particular neptunium isotope that had been discovered emitted beta particles, it had to become an element that was higher in the periodic table by one, according to the rules worked out by Soddy [1052]. In 1940 element 94 was detected and named plutonium after Pluto, the planet beyond Neptune. One of the moving spirits in this new phase of the investigation was Seaborg [1372].

McMillan had left the university for war work on radar, sonar, and, of course, the atomic bomb. Seaborg carried on after the war, isolating numerous still-higher transuranium elements. McMillan, after the war, went on to work with high-energy accelerators, as already mentioned, and after 1946 he was professor of physics at the University of California. McMillan and Seaborg shared the 1951 Nobel Prize in chemistry for their work on the new elements beyond uranium. For his discovery of the synchrocyclotron, McMillan received the 1963 Atoms for Peace award, sharing it with Veksler [1324], who had made the same discovery independently.

[1330] **DUNNING,** John Ray
American physicist
Born: Shelby, Nebraska, September 24, 1907
Died: Key Biscayne, Florida, August 25, 1975

Dunning, the son of a grain merchant who was also an amateur radio engineer, graduated from the Nebraska Wesleyan University with highest honors in 1929 and went on to get his Ph.D. from Columbia University in 1934. After that, he spent a year in Europe meeting with the great nuclear physicists and returned to join the physics department at Columbia. He built that institution's first cyclotron in 1936. He became dean of the Faculty of Engineering and Applied Science at Columbia in 1950.

He was one of those who were at the meeting, in 1939, at which Bohr [1101] announced Meitner's [1060] theory on uranium fission. Of the number of physicists who instantly went to work to confirm that theory, Dunning was the first, by a hair, to succeed.

Bohr, furthermore, reasoned from theory that of the two natural uranium isotopes, it would be uranium-235 (much the rarer of the two) that underwent fission. In early 1940 Dunning managed to separate small quantities of uranium-235 and the common variety, uranium-238, and showed that Bohr was right and that it was the former that underwent fission.

Dunning went on to develop the gas-diffusion method of separating the uranium isotopes in quantity. It was the first successful method and is still the most useful. In recognition of this work, the Atomic Energy Commission paid Dunning $30,000 in lieu of patent royalties.

[1331] **TODD,** Alexander Robertus,
Baron
Scottish chemist
Born: Glasgow, October 2, 1907

Todd graduated from the University of Glasgow in 1929, then studied at the University of Frankfurt-am-Main and at Oxford University. He obtained a doctorate at the former in 1931 and at the latter institution, under Robinson [1107], in 1933. In 1934 he joined the faculty of the University of Edinburg and in 1938 accepted a professorship of chemistry at the University of Manchester.

At Manchester, Todd concerned himself with the chemistry of the nucleic acids and the nucleotides. Here he took up where Levene [980] had left off. Levene had deduced the formulas of the nucleotides (the small units out of which the large nucleic acid molecules were built up) and Todd proceeded to synthe-

size all the naturally occurring nucleotide components of the nucleic acids. In doing so, he found that the structures as prescribed by Levene did indeed produce compounds that were identical with those obtained from nucleic acids. This confirmed Levene's deductions.

In 1944 Todd went on to Cambridge University and, while there, synthesized naturally occurring compounds related to the nucleotides. In 1947 he synthesized the compounds adenosine diphosphate and adenosine triphosphate (ADP and ATP), which are of crucial importance in the handling of energy by the body, as Lipmann [1221] showed. In the 1950s he synthesized several coenzymes with nucleotide-like structure.

Todd's work on these compounds made certain the general chemistry of the nucleic acids. The way was clear for M. H. F. Wilkins [1413], James Dewey Watson [1480], and Crick [1406], who, in the 1950s, were then able to work out the fine detail of nucleic acid structure.

Todd was knighted in 1954 and for his work on nucleotides was awarded the 1957 Nobel Prize in chemistry. In 1962 he was created a life peer as Baron Todd of Trumpington.

[1332] **TELLER,** Edward
Hungarian-American physicist
Born: Budapest, Hungary, January 15, 1908

Teller, the son of prosperous Jewish parents, obtained his Ph.D. at the University of Leipzig in Germany in 1930. While a student, he lost his right foot in a streetcar accident.

He did postdoctorate work, almost inevitably, with Niels Bohr [1101] in Copenhagen, then lectured at Göttingen. He, like his countryman Szilard [1208], left because of Hitler. He went first to Denmark, then England, and finally to the United States, where he arrived in 1935. He was naturalized in 1941, and during World War II was engaged in work on the uranium-fission bomb (the so-called atomic bomb or A-bomb) at Los Alamos, New Mexico.

In the early 1950s, when some scientists, notably Oppenheimer [1280], shrank from the development of the hydrogen-fusion bomb (the H-bomb) in view of the power of the nuclear weapons that already existed, Teller was one of those who argued most strenuously in favor of such development. Furthermore, he devised something (the details of which are shrouded in the mists of security) that made the device practical. For that reason, he is called the father of the H-bomb.

The first H-bomb explosion took place in 1952 on a Pacific island. The Soviet Union quickly followed with an explosion of its own and in a decade the force of these bombs was escalated to 50 megatons; that is, to the equivalent of 50 million tons of TNT, or 2500 times the power of the bomb exploded over Hiroshima.

Teller's evidence went furthest in denying Oppenheimer his security clearance in 1954, and this cost Teller considerable loss of respect among a large portion of the scientific community, who were also bothered by the fact that he seemed not frightened by the weapon he fathered. He minimized the effect of fallout, advocated testing in the atmosphere, and argued that a nuclear war need not be disastrous.

In this he stood opposed to the large group of scientists, of whom Pauling [1236] was perhaps the most distinguished, who were by no means as calm in the face of the thermonuclear danger.

In 1956 Teller became professor of physics at the University of California and in 1962 he received the Fermi award.

[1333] **LANDAU,** Lev Davidovich
Soviet physicist
Born: Baku, Azerbaijan, January 22, 1908
Died: Moscow, April 1, 1968

Landau, the son of an engineer father and a physician mother, studied at the University of Baku and moved on to the University of Leningrad (the city and university having been newly renamed

after Lenin's death). He entered the university in 1924 and graduated in 1927.

After a professorial appointment at the University of Kharkov, he traveled abroad, visiting Born [1084] at Göttingen and attending lectures given by Heisenberg [1245] in Leipzig.

He then spent some years in Copenhagen, which Niels Bohr [1101] had singlehandedly converted into a Mecca for theoretical physicists, and went on to Cambridge, where he studied under Ernest Rutherford [996]. In 1931 Landau returned to the Soviet Union. He received his doctorate at Kharkov in 1934.

In 1935 he pioneered the mathematical treatment of magnetic domains, small regions in substances such as iron, in which all the atomic magnets are lined up in a given direction. It is this that gives rise to ferromagnetism, the strongest variety of magnetism. In 1937 he was appointed head of a section at the Institute for Physical Problems in Moscow, where Kapitza [1173] was working, and Landau's interest turned to low-temperature phenomena, too.

In 1938 he was arrested as a German spy by an increasingly repressive Stalin regime and was released only by the personal intervention of Kapitza. In 1941 Landau produced a theoretical treatment of the properties of helium II in terms of quantum mechanics, which he modified in 1947 and which is the most satisfactory to date. In the 1950s he turned to helium-3, a rare isotope of helium, and predicted startling properties for it, too, at very low temperatures. The verification of these properties is a current goal in extreme low-temperature work. For his studies in this direction Landau was awarded the 1962 Nobel Prize in physics. This came at a time of personal tragedy.

On January 7, 1962, Landau was nearly killed in an automobile accident near Moscow, breaking eleven bones and fracturing his skull. After that, he hovered between life and death. Indeed, the story is that he passed the line ordinarily separating life and death several times but was brought back by drastic methods each time.

Finally, in October 1964, he was released from the hospital, but he never really recovered and, inevitably, death finally came.

[1334] **BARDEEN,** John
American physicist
Born: Madison, Wisconsin, May 23, 1908

Bardeen graduated from the University of Wisconsin in 1928 and obtained his Ph.D. under Wigner [1260] at Princeton University in 1936. He was Wigner's second American doctoral candidate. He taught at the University of Minnesota from 1938 to 1941, then, after working for the navy as a physicist during World War II, he joined the Bell Telephone Laboratories in 1945.

He shared with Shockley [1348] and Brattain [1250] the glory of the discovery of the transistor and the 1956 Nobel Prize in physics. After 1951 he was professor of physics at the University of Illinois, working on superconductivity.

For the theories he developed explaining various aspects of superconductivity, he shared the Nobel Prize in physics in 1972. He was the first person to win two Nobel Prizes in physics.

[1335] **ALFVÉN,** Hannes Olof Gösta
Swedish astrophysicist
Born: Norrköping, Sweden, May 30, 1908

Alfvén's work is primarily in the matter of magnetic fields and how plasmas react with them. (Plasma is matter that is hot enough for the atoms to break down into charged fragments.) In 1939 he published a theory of magnetic storms and the aurora. In it he calculated the motions of particles along magnetic lines of force, which could be used to deal with some aspects of sunspots and cosmic rays.

His work on magnetohydrodynamics (the movement of plasma in magnetic fields) is fundamental to the attempts made in the last thirty years to confine plasma at ultra-high temperatures and generate controlled fusion reactions. In addition, magnetohydrodynamics finally explained the problem that had smashed Laplace's [347] nebular hypothesis by showing how, through electromagnetic interaction, the major portion of the angular momentum of the solar system could be concentrated in the comparatively insignificant fraction of the total mass that makes up the planets.

For his work on magnetohydrodynamics, Alfvén shared the 1970 Nobel Prize for physics with Néel [1285].

[1336] **KOZYREV,** Nikolai Alexandrovich (koh-zee′rev)
Soviet astronomer
Born: St. Petersburg (now Leningrad), 1908

Kozyrev graduated from the University of Leningrad in 1928 and by 1931 had taken a post at the astronomical observatory at Pulkovo, ten miles south of the city. In 1937 he was imprisoned for some reason and not released till 1948.

Kozyrev's most dramatic observation came in 1958 in connection with the moon.

The moon, ever since Galileo's [166] first telescopic observations, had generally been considered a cold, dead world, where no change took place or was possible, except for that which was impressed from without (as by meteoric bombardment).

Kozyrev, however, managed to catch the formation of a cloud or mist in the crater Alphonsus, and a spectrum taken of the area at that time made it appear that a cloud of carbon particles had been emitted.

This was the first observation of something like volcanic activity on the moon and heightened the interest with which mankind was approaching the day when human beings would walk our satellite.

[1337] **BAWDEN,** Sir Frederick Charles
English plant pathologist
Born: North Tawton, Devonshire, August 18, 1908

Obtaining his master's degree from Cambridge in 1930, Bawden began work in plant pathology at once. He was particularly interested in plant viruses.

In 1937 Bawden and his associates found that the tobacco mosaic virus, one of the simplest of those super-simple living things whose existence was first made known by Beijerinck [817], contained ribonucleic acid (RNA). This was the first indication that nucleic acids, found in all cells, was found also in subcellular life.

Nucleic acids have been found in all clearly identifiable viruses since and are accepted as a universal (and perhaps the most basic) component of life.

[1338] **AMBARTZUMIAN,** Victor Amazaspovich (am′bahr-tsoo′-mee-an)
Soviet astronomer
Born: Tiflis (Tbilisi), Georgian SSR, September 18, 1908

Ambartzumian, the son of a teacher of literature, graduated from the University of Leningrad in 1928. He taught at that institution till 1944, when he left for Erivan in the Armenian SSR to head the Byurakan Observatory there.

Ambartzumian was interested in the theory of stellar origins and worked out the manner in which gigantic catastrophes might take place in the course of the evolution of stars and galaxies.

When Baade [1163] and Minkowski [1179] first identified the radio source in Cygnus as associated with what looked like a closely connected pair of galaxies, it seemed that a galactic collision was taking place there and that this sort of catastrophe might be common enough to account for the numerous extra-galactic radio sources.

In 1955, however, Ambartzumian presented convincing evidence that this was wrong. He suggested instead vast explosions within the cores of galaxies—somewhat analogous to supernovas on a galactic scale. With the discovery of examples of galaxies that were clearly exploding, notably the case of M-82 by Sandage [1469], this hypothesis seems to have become rather firmly established.

[1339] **WILLIAMS,** Robley Cook
American biophysicist
Born: Santa Rosa, California, October 13, 1908

Williams graduated from Cornell in 1931 and got his Ph.D. there in 1935. Teaching at the University of Michigan first, he went to the University of California in 1950.

Greatly interested in astronomy, despite the fact that he taught in the department of biophysics (later renamed as that of molecular biology), Williams noted the manner in which the lunar mountains became much more visible when sunlight struck them obliquely. Their shadows made their heights and shapes plain. It occurred to him that if tiny objects were sprayed with a thin film of opaque metal from an oblique direction, they would cast shadows of metal-free regions and they too would gain three-dimensional visibility.

Working with the electron microscopist Wyckoff [1202], Williams developed this technique and the electron microscope became a much more versatile and information-yielding instrument.

[1340] **FRANK,** Ilya Mikhaylovich
Soviet physicist
Born: St. Petersburg (now Leningrad), October 23, 1908

Frank, the son of a professor of mathematics, graduated from Moscow University in 1930 and in 1944 received a professorial post at that institution. His explanation (with Tamm [1180]) of the cause of Cherenkov [1281] radiation earned him a share in the 1958 Nobel Prize in physics.

[1341] **HERSHEY,** Alfred Day
American microbiologist
Born: Owosso, Michigan, December 4, 1908

Hershey obtained his Ph.D. in 1934 from Michigan State University, taught at Washington University till 1950, then went on to Cold Spring Harbor, New York, from which he retired in 1975.

His interest lay in bacteriophages. In 1945, he demonstrated the occurrence of spontaneous mutations both in bacteriophages and the bacterial cells on which they preyed, something that Luria [1377] also accomplished independently. In 1946 he showed that the genetic material of different viruses could spontaneously combine to produce the effects of a mutation, something that Delbrück [1313] showed independently.

In 1952 he showed that it was the nucleic acid of the bacteriophage that entered the cell, which indicated that it was the nucleic acid, and not the protein associated with it, that carried the genetic message. This pointed up the revolutionary importance of the findings of James Dewey Watson [1480] and Crick [1406] the following year on nucleic acid replication.

For their work, Hershey, Delbrück, and Luria shared the 1969 Nobel Prize for physiology and medicine.

[1342] **LIBBY,** Willard Frank
American chemist
Born: Grand Valley, Colorado, December 17, 1908
Died: Los Angeles, California, September 8, 1980

Libby, the son of a farmer, attended the University of California, graduating in 1931 and obtaining his Ph.D. in 1933. He then joined its faculty.

During World War II, Libby was at Columbia University working on the atomic bomb project under Urey [1164], developing methods for separating uranium isotopes, and that shifted his attention toward nuclear physics. In 1945, after he had transferred to the Institute of Nuclear Studies at the University of Chicago, a thought occurred to him in connection with the isotope carbon-14. That isotope had been isolated in 1940 and had been found to have an unexpectedly long half life of over five thousand years.

It had just been shown that carbon-14 was continually being formed by cosmic rays colliding with atmospheric nitrogen, which meant that traces of carbon-14 should always be found in the carbon dioxide of the air. Libby reasoned that since carbon dioxide was continually being incorporated into plant tissues, plants ought always to contain tiny amounts of carbon-14; tiny, but enough to detect by modern devices. Furthermore, since animal life depended on plant life in the last analysis, carbon-14 should also be found in animals; indeed, in all living creatures and in all the carbon-containing products of life.

After an organism died, no more carbon-14 would be incorporated into its tissues, and what was already present would begin to break down without replacement, and at a known rate. From the amount of carbon-14 left in old pieces of wood and textile, in mummies and parchment, as compared with the amount in living (or recently dead) samples of similar objects, the age (up to as much as 45,000 years) could be determined. By 1947 Libby had perfected the technique.

Using the carbon-14 dating method, much can be deduced about the earth's very recent history. Archaeological remains, being dated, show that the last retreat of the ice-age glaciers occurred more recently than anyone had suspected —10,000 years ago rather than 25,000. The date of the coming of the Indians to the Americas has been studied; such objects as the Dead Sea Scrolls have been dated without guesswork, and so on. It was a sparkling display of what physical science could do for archaeology, and by and large such dating bore out what archaeologists had deduced by their own more laborious methods.

In 1946 Libby showed that cosmic rays also produced tritium (radioactive hydrogen-3). Traces of this were always present in the atmosphere and therefore in water. Techniques involving the measurement of tritium concentration could be used in dating well water, wine, and so on.

Libby served as a member of the United States Atomic Energy Commission from 1954 to 1959, then returned to the University of California. He was awarded the 1960 Nobel Prize in chemistry for his carbon-14 dating technique.

In the early 1960s Libby, along with Teller [1332], was in the news as a strong advocate of homemade fallout shelters for use in case of a nuclear war. He maintained, further, that these could be built easily and cheaply. He built a model shelter of his own as an object lesson, but the lesson boomeranged when an ordinary fire made it necessary for him to evacuate both house and shelter.

[1343] **ARTSIMOVICH,** Lev Andreevich
Soviet physicist
Born: Moscow, February 25, 1909
Died: USSR, March 1, 1973

Artsimovich graduated from the University of Minsk in 1928. After World War II he worked on isotope separation in connection with the nuclear bomb. This, in turn, led him into work on controlled nuclear fusion, which occupied him during the last third of his life.

His work was instrumental in the development of the Tokamak, which is now the favored instrument for the confinement of ultra-high temperature plasma in the United States as well as the Soviet Union; and it is the possible route whereby controlled fusion may be attained in the next decade or so.

[1344] **LAND,** Edwin Herbert
American inventor
Born: Bridgeport, Connecticut, May 7, 1909

Land attended Harvard College and in the mid-1930s, while still an undergraduate, came up with an ingenious idea. It was known that certain organic crystals polarized light passing through them, just as Bartholin's [210] Iceland spar did. The trouble was that it was difficult to get an organic crystal large enough to be useful. It struck Land that a large crystal was not necessary, but that myriad tiny crystals would do the trick if all were lined up in the same direction. Land left school to work at this idea. He never obtained his degree, but, on the other hand, he collected half a dozen honorary ones.

In 1932 he devised methods of aligning the crystals and of then embedding them in clear plastic, which, when set, served nicely to keep them from drifting out of alignment. The result was given the trade name Polaroid, and in 1937 Land organized the Polaroid Corporation. Polaroid quickly replaced Nicol [394] prisms in polarimeters and came in handy, too, in safety glass, in spectacles, and wherever it was desirable to cut down the transmission of reflected sun glare. (Such reflections are largely polarized, as Malus [408] had discovered a century earlier.)

Other inventions followed, including a system of viewing objects so as to yield a three-dimensional effect. Land developed a new system of color photography which produced a full range of color effects out of two different colors (one of which may be white). This seemed to call for a modification of the Young [402]-Helmholtz [631] theory of color vision, which called for three basic colors out of which the total range might be built.

Land's most ingenious and successful invention was the Polaroid Land Camera in 1947. This is a device that produces developed photographs within seconds after snapping. The camera has a double roll of film, consisting of ordinary negative film and a positive paper, with sealed containers of chemicals between. The chemicals are released at the proper moment and develop the positive print automatically.

[1345] **GREENSTEIN,** Jesse Leonard
American astronomer
Born: New York, New York, October 15, 1909

Greenstein was educated at Harvard University, gaining his Ph.D. in 1937. He then worked at Yerkes Observatory. During World War II he worked on specialized optical instruments for military use and afterward traveled westward to the California Institute of Technology, where, by 1965, he was chairman of the Division of Physics, Mathematics and Astronomy.

He was particularly interested in the constitution of stars and in the variations from one to another. The variations, which make one star rich in a particular element or isotope and another poor, must reflect differences in the composition of the original clouds out of which the stars were formed, or differences in subsequent histories, and Greenstein's studies have helped deepen knowledge of stellar evolution.

He worked with M. Schmidt [1488] in elucidating the nature of the quasars.

[1346] **TATUM,** Edward Lawrie
American biochemist
Born: Boulder, Colorado, December 14, 1909
Died: New York, New York, November 5, 1975

Tatum attended the University of Wisconsin, where his father was head of the Department of Pharmacology. He graduated in 1930 and obtained his Ph.D. in 1934.

He joined the faculty of Stanford University in 1937 and there worked on Neurospora with Beadle [1270], this work earning him a share of the 1958 Nobel Prize in medicine and physiology. In 1957 he joined the staff of the Rockefeller Institute for Medical Research (now Rockefeller University) in New York, where he worked with Lederberg [1466].

[1347] **MONOD,** Jacques Lucien (moh-noh')
French biochemist
Born: Paris, February 9, 1910
Died: Cannes, May 31, 1976

Monod, whose mother was an American, obtained his doctorate at the University of Paris in 1941 and remained on its faculty till 1945 when he joined the Pasteur Institute. There he was associated with Lwoff [1253] and Jacob

[1438], and for work done on regulatory gene action shared with them the 1965 Nobel Prize for medicine and physiology.

In 1970 he published *Chance and Necessity,* in which he insisted, uncompromisingly, on chance as the architect of all things.

[1348] **SHOCKLEY,** William Bradford
English-American physicist
Born: London, England, February 13, 1910

Shockley, the son of a mining engineer, graduated from the California Institute of Technology in 1932 and obtained his Ph.D. from the Massachusetts Institute of Technology in 1936. In the latter year he joined the technical staff of Bell Telephone Laboratories.

There, Shockley and his co-workers Bardeen [1334] and Brattain [1250] came across an interesting fact in the course of their researches. It had long been known that certain crystals could act as rectifiers; that is, they would allow current to pass in one direction but not in the opposite. Alternating current, passing through such crystals, was rectified, and only the surges in one direction were transmitted, so that what emerged was a varying direct current.

Such rectification is needed if radios are to run on alternating current. Crystals were first used for the purpose, which is why early radios were known as crystal sets. The development of the radio tube by Fleming [803] and De Forest [1017] gave radio men a much more efficient and less troublesome rectifier and crystals went out of fashion.

But now the wheel turned full circle and Shockley discovered that germanium crystals containing traces of certain impurities were far better rectifiers than the crystals used a generation earlier, and had definite advantages over the tubes used since.

The impurities either contributed additional electrons that would not fit in the crystal lattice and drifted toward the positive electrode under an electric potential (but not toward the negative); or else the impurities were deficient in electrons, so that the "hole" where an electron ought to be, but was not, would drift toward the negative electrode under an imposed potential (but not toward the positive). In either case, current would pass through in only one direction.

In 1948 Shockley found how to combine "solid-state rectifiers" of these two types in such a way as to make it possible not only to rectify but also to amplify a current; in short, to do all that a radio tube could do. The device was called a transistor, because it transferred current across a resistor.

During the 1950s, as techniques for the manufacture of transistors were standardized and the product was made more uniform and reliable, transistors began to replace tubes. They were much smaller than tubes, so that radios could be reduced in size and would begin operating without a preliminary warm-up. (Transistors, unlike the filaments within tubes, did not have to be brought to a high temperature before operation could start.)

Giant computers, after being "transistorized," also shrank drastically in size. This process of miniaturization was strongly motivated through the latter half of the 1950s by the necessity of cramming as much instrumentation as possible into artificial satellites whose mass had to be reduced to a minimum if they were to be lifted into space without prohibitive expenditure of fuel and energy.

Solid-state devices continued to shrink until, as the 1980s opened, the equivalent of the huge computers of the 1950s could be fit into a shirt pocket and were correspondingly inexpensive. The intense computerization of society came to seem inevitable, and it all began with the transistor.

Shockley, Bardeen, and Brattain were awarded the 1956 Nobel Prize in physics for their discovery of the transistor. In 1955 Shockley became director of research for the Weapons Systems Evaluation Group in the United States Department of Defense and, in 1963, became

professor of engineering science at Stanford University.

In the 1970s he won a certain notoriety by maintaining the importance of genetic factors in intelligence in such a way as to imply the innate mental inferiority of blacks. This was greeted by a storm of disapproval from many quarters.

In 1980 Shockley laid himself open to some ill-natured jests when he revealed he had contributed some of his seventy-year-old sperm cells for the purpose of freezing them for eventual use in the insemination of women of high intelligence.

[1349] WALTER, William Grey
        American-British neurologist
        Born: Kansas City, Missouri,
        February 19, 1910

Walter was educated in England, graduating from Cambridge University in 1931. He grew particularly interested in the electroencephalographic measurements—the "brain waves" first demonstrated by Berger [1014]—and found one that he suggested is associated with the learning process.

More spectacularly, he developed an automatic device that is so wired as to react in fashions that one usually associates with living creatures. It is a small turtlelike object, which he calls a "testudo" (Latin for "turtle") with a photoelectric cell for an eye, a sensing device to detect touch, and motors that enable it to turn, to move forward, and to move backward.

In the dark, it wheels about. When it touches an obstacle, it backs off a bit, turns slightly, and moves forward again; repeating the process till it gets around the obstacle. When its photoelectric eye sees a light, it moves straight toward it until the light gets too bright and then it backs away. When its batteries run down, however, the now "hungry" testudo can crawl close enough to the light to make contact with a recharger placed near the light bulb. Once recharged, it becomes more sensitive to the light and backs away again.

This "robot animal" seems to presage the more elaborate robotic imitations of humanity so beloved by science fiction writers.

As the 1980s opened, in fact, devices are used in industry that are so computerized they can carry through complex operations that, until very recently, required human beings. These are termed "robots," although they are not yet in the least either animal or human in appearance. The study of "robotics" (a term first used by Isaac Asimov in 1942) is now well established.

[1350] **MARTIN,** Archer John Porter
English biochemist
Born: London, March 1, 1910

Martin, the son of a physician, was educated at Cambridge University, where he earned all his degrees, through a Ph.D. in 1936. During the 1930s he worked in the nutritional laboratories at the university and through that his attention turned to the proteins.

The fact that the protein molecule was made up of a connected chain of amino acids had been demonstrated by Emil Fischer [883], but the characterization of a particular protein by breaking down the molecule to fragments and then determining the precise number of each amino acid present, was a difficult matter indeed. It had defeated a generation of biochemists. The amino acids were so alike that a complete separation by ordinary chemical methods was impractical.

Chromatography as developed by Willstätter [1009] had sufficed to separate the very similar plant pigments, but something on a smaller scale was desperately needed for the amino acids. It occurred to Martin and his co-worker, Synge [1394], that chromatography might be tried on porous filter paper.

A drop of amino acid mixture could be allowed to dry near the bottom of a strip, and a particular solvent (into which the bottom edge of the strip could be dipped) could then be allowed to creep up the strip by capillary action. As the creeping solvent passed the dried mixture, the various amino acids would creep up with the solvent but at varying rates, depending on the solubility of each amino acid in the solvent and in water. In the end, the amino acids would be separated. Their position could be detected by some suitable physical or chemical means and matched against the position of samples of known amino acids treated in the same way. The quantity of amino acid in each spot could also be determined.

This technique of paper chromatography was developed in 1944, proved an instant success, and was fruitfully applied to all varieties of mixtures. It was paper chromatography that determined the number of particular amino acids in protein molecules and even allowed Sanger [1426] to work out the exact order in which they occurred in the insulin molecule. It was paper chromatography, combined with the use of isotopic tracers, that enabled Calvin [1361] to work out the scheme of photosynthesis.

Martin and Synge were awarded the 1952 Nobel Prize in chemistry for the development of this technique.

Meanwhile, for some years Martin had been speculating on the possibility of separating gases by chromatographic means and in 1953 perfected such gas chromatography. This has already proved itself to be as useful as paper chromatography and as powerful a tool for the chemist.

[1351] **PIERCE,** John Robinson
American electrical engineer
Born: Des Moines, Iowa, March 27, 1910

Pierce, the son of a businessman, graduated from the California Institute of Technology in 1933 and obtained his Ph.D. there in 1936, passing on at once to the Bell Telephone Laboratories, where he was put to work on vacuum tubes. During World War II he developed at Bell a klystron-oscillator universally used in American radar receivers.

Pierce, like Wernher von Braun [1370] and some other spacemen of their generation, is a science fiction enthusiast (and, in fact, has written for science fiction magazines under the pseudonym J. J. Coupling). The concept of satellites girdling the earth and acting as reflectors for radio waves was first proposed by the astronomer and science fiction writer Arthur C. Clarke in 1948, and Pierce found the concept not too strange a one to work toward, even at a time when artificial satellites existed only in science fiction.

If such satellites succeeded, communication could become worldwide under conditions that would make a transoceanic telephone call as simple as a local call. In 1957 satellites began to be placed in orbit and on August 12, 1960, Pierce's efforts paid off when Echo I was sent up. It was an aluminum balloon, one hundred feet in diameter, which was inflated only after it had settled safely into its orbit. It served as a passive reflector for radio waves and, as such, performed its function perfectly.

Since then, the matter has progressed rapidly and communications satellites are now routinely used in television and in long-distance communication.

In 1971 Pierce accepted a position on the faculty of the California Institute of Technology.

[1352] **HODGKIN,** Dorothy Crowfoot
English biochemist
Born: Cairo, Egypt (of English parents), May 12, 1910

Dorothy Hodgkin, daughter of an archaeologist, was born abroad while her father was on his travels, and she and her family continued this tradition of visiting odd corners of the world in the course of their professional life. Of her three children, one was teaching in Algeria, one in Zambia, while another was working in India at the time Hodgkin reached the climax of her career with a Nobel Prize award. Hodgkin herself was then in Ghana.

Her education, however, was in England, where she graduated from Somerville College, Oxford, in 1932 and where Robert Robinson [1107] was one of her teachers. She went on then to obtain her

Ph.D. at Cambridge University in 1937.

For her doctoral labors, she studied the X-ray diffraction of crystals of the digestive enzyme pepsin. That fixed the direction of her interests and she spent her later professional life on the determination of complex organic structures through X-ray diffraction.

During World War II she tackled the structure of penicillin in this fashion at a time when Florey [1213] and Chain [1306] were desperately trying to work out its structure. Hodgkin made use of an electronic computer in working out the X-ray data and this helped materially in the final structure determination, which was accomplished by 1949. It was the first use of the electronic computer in direct application to a biochemical problem.

Hodgkin went further. In the early 1950s she tackled the molecular structure of cyanocobalamin (vitamin B_{12}), recently isolated by Folkers [1312]. Its molecule was four times as large as that of penicillin and its structure was, in some ways, unique. Again, an electronic computer was called into play, but even so, it took years, for computer work, combined with the more ordinary chemical evidence concerning the breakdown products of cyanocobalamin, to work out the structure in full detail.

By 1955 the back of the problem had been broken and in 1964 Hodgkin was awarded the Nobel Prize for chemistry.

[1353] **COUSTEAU,** Jacques-Yves
(coo-stoh')
French oceanographer
Born: St. André-de-Cubzac, June 11, 1910

Cousteau was educated at the Brest Naval Academy and throughout his life seems to have been much more at home underwater than on land.

He was with the French underground during World War II, and even during that hard time Cousteau managed to work at his life's absorption and to invent the Aqualung. This was a device that supplied air under pressure for the diver. It was self-contained and did not require the heavy suit and the lifeline that the armored diver needed.

Equipped with an Aqualung, men with finned devices on their feet could probe the water under the surface with freedom and mobility. This makes possible the modern sport of scuba diving. "Scuba" stands for "*s*elf-*c*ontained *un*derwater *b*reathing *a*pparatus." Cousteau has used the device for exploration and has produced dramatic motion pictures of underwater life, which millions have seen on television.

He has also designed underwater structures that can house men for prolonged periods of time. Men have stayed in such devices, forty feet below the surface, for weeks, and some optimists forecast man's colonization of the continental shelf before very long.

[1354] **FLORY,** Paul John
American chemist
Born: Sterling, Illinois, June 19, 1910

Flory obtained his Ph.D. at Ohio State University in 1934. He then worked with Carothers [1190] and helped develop nylon and the artificial rubber neoprene. He taught at Cornell University and at the Mellon Institute (now Carnegie-Mellon University), and in 1961 moved to Stanford University as professor of chemistry. He retired in 1975.

He worked on the analysis of "macromolecules," the large molecules made up of repeated units, and studied the ways in which the repetitions could be controlled so that new plastics and other synthetics could be manufactured and so that desired properties could be designed into them, so to speak. For his work he received the 1974 Nobel Prize for chemistry.

[1355] **FRAENKEL-CONRAT,** Heinz
(freng'kel-kon'rat)
German-American biochemist
Born: Breslau, Germany (now Wrocław, Poland), July 29, 1910

Fraenkel-Conrat, son of a famous gynecologist, obtained his medical degree at the University of Breslau in 1933, then left Germany with the advent of Hitler. In 1936 he obtained a Ph.D. in biochemistry at the University of Edinburgh and went to the United States, which he made his permanent home, becoming a naturalized citizen in 1941. He was at the University of California after 1951.

Fraenkel-Conrat's most startling piece of research was in connection with the viruses. In the 1940s it had been shown that viruses were nucleoprotein in character, containing, that is, both protein and nucleic acid. It had also been shown that solutions of nucleic acid alone could change certain physical characteristics of bacterial strains. This rather startled biochemists, who for the first time turned their attention to nucleic acids as the possible carriers of genetic information.

In 1955 Fraenkel-Conrat, working with bacteriophages, developed gentle techniques for teasing apart the nucleic acid and protein of a virus, without seriously damaging either portion, and then putting them together again. At least some of the virus molecules, thus reformed, retained their infectivity and were, therefore, as alive as they ever were by the only criterion by which scientists could judge viral life. This work strengthened the evidence accumulated in the early 1950s that viruses consisted of a hollow protein shell with a nucleic acid molecule within.

Fraenkel-Conrat further showed that whereas the isolated protein was completely dead and showed no properties that could be associated with life, the isolated nucleic acid retained a faint infectivity. The protein, in other words, might be instrumental in getting the nucleic acid into the cell, but it was the nucleic acid itself that was the infective agent—a point strongly supported by other evidence.

Within the infected cell, the nucleic acid (which entered alone, and without its encompassing protein shell) not only brought about the manufacture of additional molecules of nucleic acid like itself, but also the manufacture of protein shells characteristic of itself and not like the proteins naturally produced by the invaded cell. The manner in which the fine structure of the nucleic acid dictated the production of protein molecules of a particular fine structure is termed the "genetic code."

There was no doubt by the late 1950s that the basic properties of life were the consequence of the activity of nucleic acid molecules, and the detailed chemistry of nucleic acids therefore became the prime target of biochemists. It is because of this that the breakthrough by Wilkins [1413], Crick [1406], and James Dewey Watson [1480], two years before Fraenkel-Conrat's experiments, assumed such overwhelming importance.

[1356] **CHANDRASEKHAR,** Subrahmanyan (chan-drah-seek′hahr) Indian-American astronomer
Born: Lahore, India (now in Pakistan), October 19, 1910

Chandrasekhar was educated at Madras University in India, graduating in 1930. He obtained his Ph.D. at Cambridge University in 1933 where he studied under Dirac [1256]. He went to the United States in 1936 and was naturalized in 1953. In the United States he joined the faculty of the University of Chicago and worked at Yerkes Observatory under Otto Struve [1203].

Chandrasekhar was chiefly interested in the structure of the white dwarf stars, whose unusual properties were first discovered by Adams [1045]. In these stars most of the constituent atoms have broken down into collections of subatomic particles—plasma—and the whole compressed to the point where the overall density is thousands of times that of ordinary matter. (Even ordinary stars contain limited quantities of such degenerate matter, as it is also called, in their interior. Plasma received its name from Langmuir [1072] in 1923. He came across it in his study of neon lights.)

Chandrasekhar showed that the more massive a white dwarf star, the more compactly it must be compressed by its own gravitational field. Since it could

only be compressed to a certain amount (the subatomic particles having a finite volume of their own), such a star could not be more massive than a certain amount, an amount which turned out, according to his calculations, to be 1.5 times the mass of the sun. This is known as Chandrasekhar's limit.

It has been shown by Hoyle [1398] and others that when the ordinary nuclear processes that power a star fail, the star collapses into a white dwarf. (This collapse, it was suggested in 1961, is brought about by the loss of energy through massive emission of neutrinos, which builds up very suddenly in the super-hot interior of stars in the pre-white dwarf stage.)

Chandrasekhar suggested that when a star with a mass greater than 1.5 times that of the sun reaches that stage and collapses, it could do so only by exploding and blowing off some of its excess mass. It was this that resulted in supernovas of the type being studied by Zwicky [1209]. This means that our sun can never go supernova, being insufficiently massive. This is cold comfort, however, since if it were to become a red giant (as it would have to before collapsing) life on Earth would be wiped out in short order even if there were no explosion.

[1357] **ROBERTS,** Richard Brooke American biophysicist
Born: Titusville, Pennsylvania, December 7, 1910
Died: April 4, 1980

Roberts received his Ph.D. at Princeton in 1937, then joined the faculty of Carnegie Institution in Washington.

He worked both on cellular components and on nuclear physics, but his most important finding came in 1939, when he contributed most to the discovery that uranium fission did not release all the neutrons it produced at one time. Some came off at measurably later times as "delayed neutrons."

This was crucial because it meant that when a fission reactor reached the critical point where it might go out of control, enough of the neutrons were delayed to keep the rate of fission small enough to give time for the insertion of the control rods. In other words, delayed neutrons are an important element of safety in nuclear reactors, and without them, nuclear reactors might not be practical at all.

[1358] **SHEMIN,** David
American biochemist
Born: New York, New York, March 18, 1911

Shemin graduated from the City College of New York in 1932, then went on to Columbia University for graduate work, getting his Ph.D. in 1938. He spent most of his professional career on the Columbia faculty, but shifted to Northwestern University in 1968.

He was one of those who made use of carbon-14, after its discovery by Kamen [1385] to follow the pathway of chemicals as they changed within the body in response to the many reactions taking place there. The carbon-14 left a trail of energetic particles wherever it went. By following that trail, Shemin worked out the scheme of synthesis of heme, the important iron-containing compound that gives blood its red color and (in combination with a protein—the whole being hemoglobin) serves to carry oxygen from lungs to tissues.

[1359] **KATZ,** Sir Bernard
German-British physiologist
Born: Leipzig, Germany, March 26, 1911

Katz obtained his M.D. at the University of Leipzig in 1934, but by that time Hitler was in control of Germany, and Katz very wisely left for Great Britain. He continued his education at the University of London and received his Ph.D. in 1938. He worked on the electrical impulses that moved along nerves and, in particular, on the transmission of those impulses from nerve to muscle. He showed the manner in which this was mediated by the diffusion of sodium and potassium ions into and out of nerve and

muscle cells in such a way as to set up and remove electrical potentials. For this work he shared the 1970 Nobel Prize for physiology and medicine with Axelrod [1374]. He was knighted in 1969.

[1360] **LYNEN,** Feodor (lee′nen)
German biochemist
Born: Munich, Bavaria, April 6, 1911
Died: Munich, August 6, 1979

Lynen studied at the University of Munich, obtaining his Ph.D. in 1937 under Wieland [1048]. The connection became even closer when he married Wieland's daughter that year. He joined the faculty at Munich in 1941 and in 1956 became head of the Institute of Cell Chemistry there.

Lynen's most important work was in connection with coenzyme A, which Lipmann [1221] had postulated as the carrier of the two-carbon fragment. Lynen's work helped elucidate the rather complicated structure of the coenzyme. He was the first to isolate "acetylcoenzyme A," the combination of the coenzyme A and the two-carbon fragment.

As a result, he shared with K. Bloch [1369] the 1964 Nobel Prize for medicine and physiology.

[1361] **CALVIN,** Melvin
American biochemist
Born: St. Paul, Minnesota, April 8, 1911

Calvin, the son of Russian immigrants, graduated from the Michigan College of Mining and Technology in 1931 and earned his Ph.D. at the University of Minnesota in 1935. He spent two years at the University of Manchester in England, then in 1937 joined the faculty of the University of California and remained there afterward, becoming director of the Lawrence Radiation Laboratory in 1946.

In 1949 he became interested in working out the chemical details of the process of photosynthesis, whereby the green plant takes carbon dioxide out of the air, combines it with water, and forms starch, discharging molecular oxygen (a by-product of the reaction) into the air. This is the most important single biochemical process on earth, since it is on the food thus formed by the plant that all animal life (including man) lives, and it is the oxygen formed that all animal life (including man) breathes.

Unfortunately the reaction cannot so far be imitated in the test tube, with nonliving substances, so that fragments of the process cannot be studied in detail. Instead, living cells must be used and the process studied as a whole. Furthermore, the photosynthetic reactions proceed so rapidly that it is almost impossible to stop the process midway. Calvin and his group made use of radioactive carbon dioxide, containing the isotope carbon-14, in order to get around these difficulties.

They allowed plant cells to make use of this carbon dioxide for no more than seconds of time, then mashed up the cells and separated the contents by means of the paper chromatographic method worked out earlier in the decade by Martin [1350] and Synge [1394]. Those substances containing radioactive carbon (easily detected) must represent compounds manufactured in the very earliest stages of photosynthesis.

Progress was slow; but little by little, Calvin and his group discovered and isolated the intermediate products, deduced how they must fit together, and built up a scheme of photosynthesis that made sense, thus capping a line of research that had begun with Helmont [175] three centuries earlier.

By 1957 the main strokes were filled out with detail and Calvin was awarded the 1961 Nobel Prize in chemistry as a result.

[1362] **GOLDHABER,** Maurice
Austrian-American physicist
Born: Lemberg, Austria (now Lvov, USSR), April 18, 1911

Goldhaber studied at the University of Berlin till 1933. The advent of Hitler made a further stay there highly un-

desirable and he went to England where, at Cambridge University, he obtained his Ph.D. in 1936.

While there, he collaborated with Chadwick [1150] in the determination of the structure of the deuteron (the nucleus of the atoms of Urey's [1164] deuterium). It turned out to consist of a proton and a neutron. He went on to study a number of neutron-bombardment reactions, a type of study similar to that which led Fermi [1243] in the direction of the atomic bomb. In doing so, he supplied evidence for the neutron's being slightly more massive than the proton.

In 1938 Goldhaber went to the United States where he joined the faculty of the University of Illinois (becoming an American citizen in 1944). While there he discovered, in 1940, that beryllium would function as a "moderator"; that is, it would slow fast neutrons and make it more readily possible for uranium to undergo fission. The atomic bomb project had not yet begun and secrecy had not yet been clamped down. Entirely voluntarily, however, Goldhaber felt the necessity of keeping his discovery quiet, and voluntarily withheld publication till after World War II.

In 1950 Goldhaber joined Brookhaven National Laboratory.

[1363] **ALVAREZ,** Luis Walter
American physicist
Born: San Francisco, California, June 13, 1911

Alvarez, the son of a well-known physician, attended the University of Chicago for both his undergraduate and graduate work, obtaining his Ph.D. in 1937. He then moved on to the University of California, where he achieved professorial status in 1945. He remained there throughout his career.

During World War II he worked on radar and on the atomic bomb.

His most important labors involved the use of Glaser's [1472] bubble chamber, which Alvarez developed to enormous sizes and with which he detected and studied extremely short-lived "resonance particles." There were numbers of these and the necessity for explaining their existence led to the theories of Gell-Mann [1487] and Ne'eman [1465]. For this work Alvarez was awarded the 1968 Nobel Prize in physics.

In 1980, quite by accident, he noted an unusually high concentration of iridium at a certain layer of a sedimentary core studied in Italy. It turned out the layer had been laid down 65 million years ago at the end of the Cretaceous and the time of the disappearance of the dinosaurs.

This high concentration of iridium (and other metals) has turned up in widely different places on Earth and has led to the speculation that the dinosaurs, and all large animals, were wiped out in the wake of the collision with Earth of an asteroid ten kilometers wide, an occurrence that released so much dust into the stratosphere as to block all radiation of the sun for three years. As a result, vegetation was so reduced as to plunge animals into extinction.

[1364] **MUELLER,** Erwin Wilhelm
German-American physicist
Born: Berlin, June 13, 1911
Died: Washington, D.C., May 17, 1977

Mueller graduated from the Technical University at Berlin in 1935, working under Gustav Hertz [1116]. He worked in Berlin for nearly two decades thereafter, but in 1952 came to the United States and has since been at Pennsylvania State University. He was naturalized in 1962.

Mueller is best known for his field-emission microscope, which he first conceived in 1936. Essentially this involves a very fine needle tip in a high vacuum. This tip can be made to emit electrons, which shoot outward in straight lines (radiating from the curved needle tip) and strike a fluorescent screen. What appears on the screen, then, is a vastly magnified picture of the needle tip. Magnifications of up to one million diameters are achieved so that the field-emission microscope is the most powerful ever built, an unimaginably far cry

from the days of Malpighi [214] and Leeuwenhoek [221].

Ions rather than electrons can also be made to shoot off the needle tip. For this purpose the needle is kept at liquid hydrogen temperatures and helium, absorbed on the needle surface, is emitted as helium ions.

The image produced by the ions on the screen can distinguish individual atoms; some of these images, taken as early as 1955, are already classics in scientific photography.

By 1967 not only could atoms be seen in this way but chemicals could be identified. Through them the atoms first postulated by Democritus [20] twenty-three centuries earlier and first introduced to modern chemistry by Dalton [389] a century and a half earlier have finally been seen, at least to the extent that their orderly positions in certain substances can be made out.

So far, field-emission microscopy is applicable only to a limited number of high-melting metals and alloys, but it is of great use in studying gas adsorption and crystal imperfections. A few fairly large organic molecules, such as that of phthalocyanine, have been made visible.

[1365] **STEIN,** William Howard
American biochemist
Born: New York, New York, June 25, 1911
Died: New York, New York, February 2, 1980

Stein graduated from Harvard University in 1933 and obtained his Ph.D. from Columbia University in 1938. He then joined the Rockefeller Institute (now Rockefeller University), where he achieved the status of full professor in 1955.

He is best known for devising chromatographic methods for analyzing amino acids and small peptides in the complex mixture resulting from the hydrolysis of proteins. He developed an automatic amino acid analyzer and used his methods for the determination of the complete structure of the enzyme ribonuclease. In this he was assisted by

Moore [1379] and, as a result, Stein and Moore shared the 1972 Nobel Prize for chemistry.

[1366] **WHEELER,** John Archibald
American physicist
Born: Jacksonville, Florida, July 9, 1911

Wheeler obtained his Ph.D. at Johns Hopkins University in 1933, spent two years at Copenhagen, and joined the faculty of Princeton in 1938, where he remained until he retired.

After World War II he participated in the theoretical work that finally led to the explosion of the first hydrogen bomb in 1952. He then grew interested in those aspects of general relativity that seemed to suggest the possibility of gravitational collapse. To Wheeler it seemed that, under certain conditions, the collapse could not be stopped and would continue until any mass, however large, would shrink down to a point, or "singularity." In the course of such shrinkage the gravitational field at the surface of the shrinking mass would become so intense that the escape velocity would be greater than the velocity of light, which would mean that nothing, not even light, could escape. Wheeler invented the term "black hole" for such a collapsed mass.

Black holes have become one of the most fascinating aspects of astrophysics and Wheeler has remained in the forefront of theoretical thinking on the subject, matched only by Hawking [1510].

[1367] **KERST,** Donald William
American physicist
Born: Galena, Illinois, November 1, 1911

Kerst obtained his Ph.D. in 1937 at the University of Wisconsin, then joined the faculty of the University of Illinois.

His main achievement involved the acceleration of electrons. The electrons are so much lighter than protons that to give them sufficient momentum to induce nuclear transformations, they must be whirled at velocities that would produce so great a relativistic mass increase that an ordinary cyclotron would not work. For that reason, some new method of acceleration had to be devised for electrons.

The result was the betatron, first put to successful use by Kerst in 1940. In it the speeding electrons (or beta particles, whence the name) were whirled in circles rather than in spirals, while the magnetic field was increased in time to the increasing mass of the particles.

During World War II Kerst worked at Los Alamos on the atomic bomb project, but afterward he returned to the betatron, building a huge one for the University of Illinois in 1950.

[1368] **REBER,** Grote
American radio engineer
Born: Wheaton, Illinois, December 22, 1911

Reber entered radio astronomy as a hobby. At fifteen he was already an enthusiastic radio "ham." When he heard of Jansky's [1295] discovery, he, and he alone, fired up. Even as a student at the Illinois Institute of Technology, he tried to take up where Jansky left off. For instance, he tried to bounce radio signals off the moon. (He failed, but the Army Signal Corps, with far more resources at its disposal, managed to do this after World War II.)

In 1937 he built the first radio telescope, in his back yard. The reflector (or "dish") receiving the radio waves was thirty-one feet in diameter. In 1938 he began to receive and for several years was the only radio astronomer in the world. He discovered points in the sky that emitted stronger-than-background radio waves. Such "radio stars," he found, did not coincide with any of the visible stars. One of them was later identified by Baade [1163] a decade later as what seemed to be a distant pair of colliding galaxies.

Reber published his findings in 1942. Oort [1229] in the Netherlands grew interested, and once World War II was over, radio astronomy rapidly gained in importance. In 1947 Reber gave his radio telescope to the National Bureau of Standards. Still later, he shifted observation posts to Hawaii, then to Australia. If Jansky gave birth to radio astronomy, Reber nursed it singlehanded through its infancy. With Lovell [1386] it came to maturity.

[1369] **BLOCH,** Konrad Emil
German-American biochemist
Born: Neisse, Silesia (now Nysa, Poland), January 21, 1912

Bloch studied chemical engineering in Germany but in 1934 left that Nazi-controlled land for Switzerland and then, in 1936, went to the United States, becoming an American citizen in 1944. He did his graduate work at Columbia University, switching to biochemistry and working under Schoenheimer [1211]. He obtained his Ph.D. in 1938 and, after teaching at Columbia and at the University of Chicago, joined the faculty of Harvard University in 1954 as professor of biochemistry.

While still at Columbia, he began to apply isotopic techniques to the elucidation of the manner in which cholesterol was built up in living tissue. Cholesterol is the most common member, in the animal body, of a family of compounds of rather complex structure. It includes a characteristic four-ring combination in its molecule, the structure of which was worked out by Wieland [1048].

Bloch made use of a two-carbon compound, sodium acetate, which was not only labeled with a heavy isotope of carbon but with a heavy isotope of hydrogen as well. Little by little, over the years that followed, Bloch traced the fate of those isotopes and worked out the manner in which the "two-carbon fragment" was built up into long-chain fatty acids and into cholesterol, too.

The reaction required an input of energy and Lynen [1360] helped explain that when, in 1951, he showed that the two-carbon fragment performed its function in combination with coenzyme A, as Lipmann [1221] had suspected. As a re-

sult, Bloch and Lynen shared the 1964 Nobel Prize for medicine and physiology.

[1370] **BRAUN,** Wernher Magnus Maximilian von
German-American rocket engineer
Born: Wirsitz, Germany (now Wyrzysk, Poland), March 23, 1912
Died: Alexandria, Virginia, June 16, 1977

The son of a baron, Von Braun was educated in Zürich, Switzerland, and in Berlin. He obtained his Ph.D. in 1934 at the University of Berlin. As an adolescent Von Braun had grown interested in rocketry through his reading of science fiction and of a book on the subject by Oberth [1172]. In 1930 he joined a group of German enthusiasts, including Ley [1315], who were experimenting with rockets. Some eighty-five rockets were fired, one reaching an altitude of a mile.

In 1932 the German army took over the program. Hitler came to power the next year and by 1936 was building a rocket research center in Peenemünde on the Baltic, a place where Von Braun's grandfather had been accustomed to go duck hunting. In 1938 a rocket with an eleven-mile range had been built. This all became deadly serious, for World War II soon began and rocketry had a crucial military purpose.

Von Braun himself joined the Nazi party in 1940 and under his leadership the first true missile, carrying its own fuel and oxygen, was shot off in 1942, reaching a height of sixty miles. In 1944 Von Braun was briefly imprisoned till Hitler was persuaded the rocket program could not continue without him.

That same year, on September 7, the missile came into combat use, too late, fortunately to win the war for Hitler. The weapon was the famous V-2 (the V stood for *vergeltung,* meaning "vengeance"). In all, 4,300 V-2s were fired during the war, and of these, 1,230 hit London. Von Braun's missiles killed

2,511 English people and seriously wounded 5,869 others.

At the close of the war, Von Braun and many colleagues fled westward to surrender to the Americans. In the process, Von Braun's arm was broken when his driver fell asleep at the wheel and smashed the car. Von Braun was quickly taken to the United States (he became an American citizen in 1955) and he at once placed his talents at the service of his new employer.

In 1947 he was allowed to return to Germany to marry his eighteen-year-old second cousin.

He was the leader of the group at Huntsville, Alabama, that placed America's first satellite (Explorer I) into orbit on January 31, 1958, after four months of post-Sputnik American agony. He might have preceded Sputnik if he had been given the go-ahead, but he was as hindered by American policy under Eisenhower as he had been hampered by German policy under Hitler. In 1962 Von Braun's team began construction of the Saturn 5 rocket that eventually carried men to the moon.

[1371] **FOX,** Sidney Walter
American biochemist
Born: Los Angeles, California, March 24, 1912

Graduating from the University of California in 1933, Fox went on to earn his Ph.D. at the California Institute of Technology in 1940. After 1955 he taught at institutions in Florida and was associated with the National Aeronautics and Space Administration after 1960.

Fox was interested in the evolution of life but from what might almost be described as a biological rather than a biochemical standpoint. He departed from the usual procedure of men such as Miller [1490] and Ponnamperuma [1457] of moving from one chemical to the next a step at a time and attempted to study the development of cells.

A mixture of amino acids subjected to considerable heat (as might be found on the steaming ocean and in exposed rocks of a volcanic primordial earth) becomes

a protein-like polymer which Fox gave the name "proteinoid." Dissolved in water, these form tiny spheres that share some properties with cells. Indeed, Fox's speculation is that cells might be formed directly in this fashion from amino acids.

It is not beyond the bounds of possibility, of course, that cell formation and nucleic acid formation proceed in parallel fashion and that the two combine at some point.

[1372] **SEABORG,** Glenn Theodore
American physicist
Born: Ishpeming, Michigan, April 19, 1912

Seaborg, the son of a machinist, received his education at the University of California, beginning as a literature major, but changing to science in his third year, under the impact of an inspiring teacher. He graduated in 1934 and obtained his Ph.D. in 1937 under Lewis [1037]. He joined the faculty of the university in the latter year, rising through various grades until appointed chancellor of the university at Berkeley in 1958.

Seaborg joined McMillan [1329] in 1940 in work on the elements beyond uranium, and helped isolate plutonium. He took over the direction of this research after McMillan left in 1941 (and after he himself did work in connection with preparing plutonium for use in an atomic bomb at the University of Chicago) and studied the chemistry and physics of neptunium and plutonium in detail. He and his group went on to discover further elements.

In 1944 they identified americium (atomic number 95) and curium (atomic number 96), the former being named in honor of America, the latter for the Curies [897, 965]. In 1949 berkelium (atomic number 97) and californium (atomic number 98) were identified and named in honor of Berkeley, California, where the university is located.

Seaborg and his group recognized that the transuranium elements resembled each other, much as the rare earth elements did. In fact, starting with actinium (atomic number 89) a second set of rare earth elements could be considered to exist. The two sets are distinguished by calling the old one, which begins with lanthanum (atomic number 57) the lanthanides, while the new set is called the actinides. Mendeléev's [705] three-quarter-century-old periodic table thus received one more modification, one which had, by the way, been predicted by Niels Bohr [1101] some years before.

As a result of his work with the transuranium elements, Seaborg shared the 1951 Nobel Prize in chemistry with McMillan.

The discovery of new actinides continued. In 1952 came einsteinium (atomic number 99) and in 1953 fermium (atomic number 100), commemorating Einstein [1064] and Fermi [1243] shortly after their deaths.

Since then, element number 101 was discovered in 1955 and named mendelevium in honor of Mendeléev. Element number 102 was discovered in 1957 and named nobelium in honor of the Nobel Institute in Stockholm, where much of the work had been done, and therefore indirectly in honor of Nobel [703]. In 1961 element number 103 was identified and named lawrencium in honor of Lawrence [1241], who was now dead. With lawrencium the list of actinides was complete. Since then elements 104 and 105 have also been isolated and named rutherfordium and hahnium, respectively, after Ernest Rutherford [996] and Hahn [1063].

Seaborg was also one of the group that in 1942 isolated the isotope uranium-233, which can be prepared from thorium and which, like the better-known uranium-235, can undergo fission. It is, consequently, a valuable nuclear fuel, and the thorium reserves of the world may be added to the uranium reserves as potential fuel for mankind.

In 1961 he was appointed to the chairmanship of the United States Atomic Energy Commission. The increasing consciousness of environmental pollution has made the AEC suspect among younger scientists and Seaborg therefore became a controversial figure. In 1970

he was elected president of the American Association for the Advancement of Science but only after much opposition.

[1373] BROWN, Herbert Charles
English-American chemist
Born: London, May 22, 1912

Brown was taken to the United States by his parents when he was only two years old. He was educated at the University of Chicago, where he obtained his Ph.D. in 1938.

He worked with the hydrides of boron and aluminum, discovering sodium borohydride, which turned out to be a useful reducing agent in chemical procedures. He explored boron-containing organic compounds, preparing new classes of these, and for this work he received a share of the 1979 Nobel Prize for chemistry.

[1374] AXELROD, Julius
American biochemist and pharmacologist
Born: New York, New York, May 30, 1912

Axelrod obtained his Ph.D. at George Washington University in 1955. Much of his professional life has been spent with the National Institutes of Health. He has worked on the action of drugs and hormones, on the chemical side of the transmission of the nerve impulse, and on the action of the pineal gland in particular. For his work he received a share, with Katz [1359], of the 1970 Nobel Prize for physiology and medicine.

[1375] TURING, Alan Mathison
English mathematician
Born: London, June 23, 1912
Died: Wilmslow, Cheshire, June 7, 1954

Turing attended Cambridge University and was elected a fellow of King's College, Cambridge, in 1935. Between 1936 and 1938 Turing worked at Princeton

University in New Jersey and while there dealt with the theoretical concept of the so-called Turing machine, a computer capable of the most general computations. He showed that there are some problems it could not solve, a conclusion reminiscent of the work of Gödel [1301].

During World War II he served with the British Department of Communications, but after the war he became interested in electronic computers and designed the first British computers of this sort, not long after the work of Mauchley [1328] and Eckert [1431]. He was particularly interested in the possibility that computers could be designed to mimic the human process of thinking ("artificial intelligence") and felt that that could be done. He also tried to work out the mathematical basis for the development of strongly nonsymmetric living systems from what seem to be a symmetric egg cell.

He died prematurely of potassium cyanide poisoning, which was considered to have been suicide at the inquest although it is possible that it was the result of an accident.

[1376] **WEIZSÄCKER,** Carl Friedrich, Baron von (vites'ek-er)
German astronomer
Born: Kiel, June 28, 1912

Weizsäcker, who obtained his Ph.D. in 1933 at the University of Leipzig, in 1938 evolved independently the same mechanism for the origin of stellar energy as Bethe [1308] had.

In 1944 Weizsäcker went on to make further astronomical headlines by returning to a form of the nebular hypothesis for the origin of the solar system. It was something like that originally proposed by Kant [293] and Laplace [347] but much more sophisticated. He suggested that the original dust cloud out of which the solar system was formed did not rotate as a single system (as was supposed in the Kant-Laplace theory) but as a system of vortices. These vortices fell into gradually larger systems with increasing distance, the increase in size just matching the law of planetary distances worked out by Bode [344]. At the boundaries between sets of vortices, particles concentrated and fused into planetesimals and eventually into planets.

This theory avoided the glaring difficulties of the various catastrophic theories of Jeans [1053] and others. Once World War II was over and normal scientific communication was restored, Weizsäcker's ideas were brought to the attention of the rest of the world by Gamow [1278] and proved instantly popular.

To be sure, the theory had numerous difficulties and has been modified by taking magnetic forces into account in an attempt to remove them. As a result, the weight of astronomic thought has swung away from catastrophe and toward nebula.

If Weizsäcker's theory, or anything like it, is correct, then the formation of a set of planets is a normal part of the evolution of stars and the universe is rich in planetary systems. Van de Kamp's [1247] observations do, indeed, tend to confirm this. This raises the strong possibility that there may be myriad inhabited planets and even intelligent life forms (other than ourselves) in the universe.

[1377] **LURIA,** Salvador Edward (luree'ah)
Italian-American microbiologist
Born: Turin, Italy, August 13, 1912

Luria obtained his medical degree at the University of Turin in 1935. He went to the United States in 1940 and was naturalized in 1947.

In the United States, he met Delbrück [1313], and since Luria had already been working on bacteriophages at the Pasteur Institute in Paris, they struck up a close relationship. In 1942 Luria obtained the first good electron micrograph of a bacteriophage, showing clearly that it consisted of a round head and a thin tail, rather like an extremely small sperm cell. In 1945 he showed the occurrence of spontaneous mutations both in bacteriophages and the bacterial cells on which they preyed, something that Hershey [1341] showed independently.

For their work, Luria, Hershey, and Delbrück shared the 1969 Nobel Prize for physiology and medicine.

[1378] PURCELL, Edward Mills
American physicist
Born: Taylorville, Illinois, August 30, 1912

Purcell graduated from Purdue University in 1933. After further studies in Germany he entered Harvard University, where he attained his Ph.D. in 1938. He served on the Harvard faculty thereafter, becoming professor of physics there in 1949.

Purcell shared the 1952 Nobel Prize in physics with F. Bloch [1296] for his determination of the nuclear magnetic moments of substances in the liquid and solid state. This made the extremely delicate technique of nuclear magnetic resonance (NMR) possible.

By that time, however, he had also done significant work in radio astronomy. In 1951 he was one of those who detected the 21-centimeter microwave emission of neutral hydrogen atoms in interstellar space, the radiation of which Oort's [1229] group had predicted, from theoretical considerations, during World War II.

[1379] MOORE, Stanford
American biochemist
Born: Chicago, Illinois, September 4, 1913

Moore graduated from Vanderbilt University in 1935 and obtained his Ph.D. at the University of Wisconsin in 1938. In 1939 he joined the Rockefeller Institute (now Rockefeller University), where he worked with Stein [1365] on the chromatographic analysis of amino acids and peptides and the determination of protein and enzyme structure. As a result of this work, he and Moore shared the 1972 Nobel Prize for chemistry.

[1380] PALADE, George Emil (pah-lah'dee)
Romanian-American physiologist
Born: Iaşi, Romania, November 19, 1912

Palade received his medical degree at the University of Bucharest in 1940. He held a professorial post there during World War II. After the war, with Soviet forces occupying Romania, Palade left. He arrived in the United States in 1946 and was naturalized in 1952.

At the Rockefeller Institute for Medical Research (now Rockefeller University) in New York City, Palade has spent his time peering into the cell with a finer probe than has ever before been used. The ordinary microscope in the hands of men like Robert Brown [403] and Flemming [762] had revealed first the nucleus within the cell and then the chromosomes within the nucleus. The coming of Zworykin's [1134] electron microscope had made it possible to study the fine structure of the organelles (little bodies of definite structure and function) within the cell.

The relatively large mitochondria attracted the first attention and proved to be organized batteries of enzymes that brought about the oxidation of fat and sugar molecules, with consequent production of energy. They were the "powerhouses" of the cell.

Also present were far smaller bodies usually referred to as microsomes (meaning, simply, "small bodies"), which were thought of at first as merely mitochondria fragments. Palade's studies of intact cells by electron microscope, however, showed they were more than that. They were independent bodies with chemical compositions quite different from the mitochondria.

By 1956 he had shown that the microsomes were rich in ribonucleic acid (RNA) and they were therefore renamed ribosomes. Quickly it was realized that the ribosomes were the site of protein manufacture and cellular physiology thus merged with the eclectic science of molecular biology.

For his electron-microscopic work,

Palade was awarded a share of the Nobel Prize for physiology and medicine in 1974.

[1381] **FLEROV,** Georgii Nikolaevich
Soviet physicist
Born: March 2, 1913

Flerov, who had been educated at the Leningrad Industrial Institute of Science, was among those Russians who early began the investigation of nuclear fission. In 1941 he discovered that uranium did not undergo fission only when bombarded with neutrons. It also did so (excessively slowly) even without outside interference, in what has come to be called "spontaneous fission." Spontaneous fission is an important method of breakdown among the transuranium elements formed through nuclear bombardment since the 1940s.

Flerov has worked on these transuranium elements, too, and in 1965 he announced the formation of an isotope of element 104, the most complicated element formed to that date. The element has been unofficially named kurchatovium in honor of Kurchatov [1261]; but Flerov's work has not yet been confirmed and the name remains unofficial. American scientists, forming 104 by other methods, have suggested the name rutherfordium instead.

[1382] **LI,** Choh Hao (lee)
Chinese-American biochemist
Born: Canton, China, April 21, 1913

Li graduated from the University of Nanking in 1933. He emigrated to the United States in 1935 and took up graduate studies at the University of California, where he earned his Ph.D. and then joined the faculty. He is now director of the Hormone Research Laboratories there.

Li's professional life has been spent almost entirely on the study of the hormones of the pituitary gland, a study that had been initiated earlier by men like Houssay [1115]. Li and his group iso-

lated a number of protein hormones from the pituitary; one of them was adrenocorticotrophic hormone, better known by the initials ACTH. This stimulates the activity of the adrenal cortex, increasing the output of the corticoids. For that reason administration of ACTH achieves, indirectly, what the administration of a corticoid such as cortisone achieves directly. When Hench [1188] discovered the ameliorative effect of cortisone on rheumatoid arthritis, he found a similar effect for ACTH and that, too, gained fame with the lay public as a wonder drug.

Other pituitary hormones serve to stimulate the activity of such glands as the thyroid and the gonads. The pituitary seems to be a general coordinator for the hormones produced elsewhere and to serve, almost, as the "master gland" of the body.

The protein hormones, like those of the pituitary, resist chemical characterization more than the hormones of simpler structure, like adrenalin, thyroxine, and the various steroid hormones. Nevertheless, with the development of Sanger's [1426] technique for determining the order of amino acids in a protein chain, the protein hormones began to give ground.

In 1956, for instance, Li and his group showed that the molecule of ACTH was made up of thirty-nine amino acids in a specific order and, furthermore, the entire chain of the natural hormone was not essential to its action. Fragments consisting of little more than half the chain possessed major activity.

That the chemical structure was significant was also shown by the fact that melanocyte-stimulating hormone (MSH), also obtained by Li from the pituitary, which produced some effects similar to those produced by ACTH, also possessed an amino acid chain, which in spots duplicated the order in ACTH.

Li studied the growth hormone, perhaps the most remarkable of the pituitary hormones, for it controls the overall growth rate of the body, producing circus giants when present in excess, and midgets when present in inadequate quantities. Whereas ACTH from swine or cattle is effective on human beings, growth hormone from such creatures is not. Li isolated human growth hormone in 1956 and showed that its structure is quite different from other species tested. Its molecule is made up of 256 amino acids, so that it is far more complicated than the other pituitary hormones. However, it is quite likely that not all of this long chain is required for its activity. In 1970 Li synthesized human growth hormone.

[1383] **ABELSON,** Philip Hauge
American physical chemist
Born: Tacoma, Washington,
April 27, 1913

Abelson graduated from Washington State College in 1933 and obtained his Ph.D. at the University of California in 1939 under Lawrence [1241]. While still a student, he had produced uranium fission but had not recognized the significance of what he had done at first. He was on the point of doing so when Hahn [1063] and Meitner [1060] managed to forestall him.

In 1940, when chemists were beginning to concern themselves with the problem of separating uranium into its isotopes (since the rare isotope uranium-235 was involved in the fission reaction), Abelson made an important suggestion. He pointed out that uranium hexafluoride was a volatile liquid and its vapors were the easiest way of obtaining uranium atoms in the gaseous state. Those molecules of uranium hexafluoride that contain uranium-235 are almost 1 percent lighter than the molecules containing the more common uranium-238. If part of the volume of gas is heated, the lighter molecules tend to concentrate in the hot region. By using this principle (thermal diffusion), samples of enriched uranium (containing more than the normal quantity of uranium-235) were prepared. In 1940, also, Abelson assisted McMillan [1329] in initiating the study of the transuranium elements and in discovering neptunium.

In 1962 he became editor of *Science* and he was one of that substantial group of scientists who had serious reservations as to the expensive crash program carried through the 1960s for placing a man on the moon.

[1384] **CHANCE,** Britton
American biophysicist
Born: Wilkes-Barre, Pennsylvania,
July 24, 1913

Chance was educated at the University of Pennsylvania, graduating in 1936 and obtaining his Ph.D. in 1940. He has since been on the faculty of the university and has been a full professor of biophysics since 1949.

Chance has tackled the problem of enzyme mechanisms. Nearly half a century earlier, Michaelis [1033] had evolved a theory to the effect that in the course of the action of an enzyme upon a substrate (that is, upon the compound or compounds involved in the enzyme-catalyzed reaction) the enzyme and substrate form a more or less loosely bound combination, the enzyme-substrate complex.

The discovery of this complex explained how the rate of enzyme-catalyzed reactions changed with certain alterations of the conditions of the reaction. However, although most enzyme chemists accepted the existence of this complex, it remained a purely theoretical model, with no direct observational evidence to testify as to its presence.

In the 1940s Chance worked with peroxidase, an enzyme that catalyzed the oxidation of numerous organic compounds by hydrogen peroxide. Peroxidase has a heme group (a complex iron-containing compound best known for its occurrence in hemoglobin) as part of the molecule and this absorbs certain wavelengths of light strongly. The particular wavelengths absorbed shift with even small changes in the chemical nature of the molecule.

When Chance added hydrogen peroxide to a solution of peroxidase, he could follow the changes in light absorption and noted that they came and went just as one would expect if an enzyme-substrate complex was being formed, then

847

broken, in the manner predicted by Michaelis.

In this way Chance deduced the mechanism of peroxidase action in minute detail. The mystery was further stripped from the activity of enzymes, which was of greater interest to biochemists as the connection between enzymes and nucleic acids was becoming clear during the 1950s.

[1385] **KAMEN,** Martin David
Canadian-American biochemist
Born: Toronto, Ontario, August 27, 1913

Kamen was educated in the United States, graduating from the University of Chicago in 1933 and going on for his Ph.D. in 1936. He became a naturalized American citizen in 1938.

Kamen was interested in the isotopes of the light elements that were of particular interest to biochemists. Oxygen and nitrogen had no radioactive isotopes long-lived enough to be useful and it was thought that the same held true for carbon. In 1940, however, Kamen isolated carbon-14, which turned out, surprisingly, to have a half life of 5,700 years. It quickly became and remained the most useful of all isotopes in biochemical research and was even turned to historical and archaeological use by Libby [1342].

Kamen had already worked with oxygen-18, a stable but rare oxygen isotope in connection with photosynthesis. He showed that in the combination of carbon dioxide and water, in that fundamental light-catalyzed process the oxygen that was liberated comes from the water molecule and not from carbon dioxide. With the discovery of carbon-14, men such as Calvin [1361] could leap ahead in the further investigation of the details of photosynthesis.

[1386] **LOVELL,** Sir Alfred Charles Bernard
English astronomer
Born: Oldland Common, Gloucestershire, August 31, 1913

Lovell, the son of a lay preacher, was educated at the University of Bristol, graduating in 1933 and obtaining his doctorate in 1936. He joined the faculty of Manchester University as a lecturer in physics at once. He was then interested in the ionosphere and worked on cosmic ray studies with Blackett [1207].

During World War II he was occupied with radar research, and in 1946 he was one of those who showed that radar echoes could be obtained from daytime meteor showers, invisible to ordinary sight.

After the war he grew interested in radio astronomy. In 1951 he became the first professor of radio astronomy at Manchester University and began work toward the building of a giant, fully steerable radio telescope. The building of this 250-foot "big dish" at Jodrell Bank Experimental Station represented an epic effort in constuction that took six years. The turret rack of a battleship was, at Blackett's suggestion, used to move the dish. It was finished (or nearly finished) just in time to track Sputnik I, a task that rescued him from the angry inquiries into the value of spending money for such an instrument.

Since then the Jodrell Bank radio telescope has been the most useful instrument anywhere in the world for tracking satellites. Though it will inevitably be surpassed in the future, it will remain the first of the great radio telescopes to grow out of Reber's [1368] homemade job. Lovell was knighted in 1961.

[1387] **HODGKIN,** Alan Lloyd
English physiologist
Born: Banbury, Oxfordshire, February 5, 1914

Educated at Cambridge, Hodgkin worked on radar during World War II, then joined the Cambridge faculty in 1945.

Hodgkin grew interested, in the late 1930s, in the mechanism of the nerve impulse. For the purpose of investigation, he made use of the giant axon of the squid, a single nerve fiber that was, on occasion, as much as a millimeter in diameter.

He and his co-worker, A. F. Huxley [1419], were able to insert fine pipettes inside the axon, without damaging it, and thus test the ionic composition within and immediately outside the cell. By 1952 they had shown that the interior of the cell was rich in potassium ion and the exterior in sodium ion.

At the moment when a nerve impulse passes, the situation changes. Sodium ion first floods into the cell and, a little while later, potassium ion moves out. Once the impulse has passed, sodium ion is pumped out of the cell, somehow, so that the fiber may be ready to carry another impulse.

For working out the importance of the "sodium pump," Hodgkin and Huxley shared the 1963 Nobel Prize for physiology and medicine with Eccles [1262]. (Hodgkin married the daughter of Rous [1067], who, two years later, also won a a Nobel Prize.)

[1388] **DULBECCO**, Renato
(dull-beck'o)
Italian-American virologist
Born: Cantanzaro, Italy, February 22, 1914

Dulbecco earned his medical degree at the University of Turin in 1936. He went to the United States in 1947, became an American citizen in 1953, and began teaching at the California Institute of Technology. He has also been associated with the Salk Institute and the University of California at San Diego Medical School.

His most important work has been on cancer viruses and how they might possibly bring about the chemical change within the cells that lead to cancer. Since the cell is such an enormously complicated interplay of innumerable chemical reactions, Dulbecco introduced the technique of placing within the cell not intact viruses but individual virus genes of known function in order to study the chemical changes that this produced. The promise of this technique earned

him a share in the 1975 Nobel Prize for physiology and medicine.

[1389] **PERUTZ,** Max Ferdinand
Austrian-British biochemist
Born: Vienna, Austria, May 19, 1914

Perutz was educated at the University of Vienna, but the gathering cloud of Nazism, just to the north in Hitler's Germany, and the deteriorating picture in Austria itself, caused him to leave for England in 1936. There he worked at Cambridge University, becoming interested in X-ray diffraction of proteins, with the aid and encouragement of W. L. Bragg [1141]. Perutz obtained his Ph.D. in 1940, but was interned as an enemy alien during World War II.

After the war Perutz organized the laboratory of molecular biology at Cambridge and took as his own problem the working out of the detailed structure of hemoglobin.

In 1953 the break came. The heavier an atom the more efficiently it diffracts X rays. Perutz, therefore, added a single atom of a heavy metal like gold or mercury to each molecule of protein and found he had altered the overall diffraction picture significantly. This now gave Perutz something to go on and eased the process of deduction from diffraction picture to atom position.

Perutz assigned myoglobin to Kendrew [1415] and both produced the results of their research in 1960 and shared in the 1962 Nobel Prize in chemistry.

[1390] **SPITZER,** Lyman, Jr.
American astronomer and physicist
Born: Toledo, Ohio, June 26, 1914

Spitzer graduated from Yale in 1935, then spent a year at Cambridge, England, under Eddington [1085]. Returning to the United States, he obtained a Ph.D. under H. N. Russell [1056] in 1938. He remained on the Yale faculty (except for work on undersea warfare during World War II) till 1947 when he went to Princeton as head of the astronomy department.

Spitzer was particularly interested in the formation of new stars out of the clouds of dust and gas in interstellar space under the influence of the weak magnetic fields that permeate its vast environment.

The combination of high-temperature gas ("plasma") and magnetic fields led him into research on fusion power. In order to force hydrogen gas to fuse into helium, liberating vastly more energy than even uranium fission does, the hydrogen must be raised to temperatures of 100 million degrees or so. To contain gas so ferociously hot, a merely material container will not do.

Spitzer was one of the first to suggest that a magnetic field might be the answer; and he devised a figure-eight-shaped design (called a "stellarator") for such a field. It has remained an important tool in the continuing drive toward controlled hydrogen fusion.

Spitzer was one of those scientists who early grew enthusiastic over the possibility of rockets as a scientific tool. In 1947 he was already speculating on artificial satellites on which telescopes and other astronomic instruments might be mounted.

[1391] **VONNEGUT,** Bernard
American physicist
Born: Indianapolis, Indiana, August 29, 1914

Vonnegut (whose brother is the highly regarded science fiction novelist, Kurt Vonnegut) attended the Massachusetts Institute of Technology, graduating in 1936 and obtaining his Ph.D. in 1939. At M.I.T. he studied icing conditions, then joined the General Electric Research Laboratories in 1945 to continue this work with Schaefer [1309].

After dry ice was found effective as a cloud-seeder, Vonnegut took up the problem of finding some crystals that might serve in place of dry ice. He decided that fine crystals of silver iodide were of the proper shape to serve as "seeds" and experiment proved him correct.

Silver iodide replaced dry ice, for it had several advantages. It could keep indefinitely at room temperature, as dry ice could not. Furthermore, silver iodide crystals need not necessarily be liberated by plane. By taking advantage of updrafts they can be liberated on the ground and wafted upward into the cloud layers. (Dry ice would evaporate en route.) To be sure, silver iodide is rather an expensive chemical, but it has been estimated that two pounds would suffice to seed the clouds over the entire United States.

In 1952 Vonnegut joined the staff of Arthur D. Little, Inc.

[1392] **VAN ALLEN,** James Alfred
American physicist
Born: Mount Pleasant, Iowa,
September 7, 1914

Van Allen, the son of an attorney, graduated from Iowa Wesleyan College (in his home town) in 1935. During his sophomore year there, he was already making measurements of cosmic ray intensities. After graduation he attended the State University of Iowa, where he obtained his Ph.D. in 1939. Since 1951 he has been head of the physics department at the State University of Iowa.

During World War II, Van Allen, serving as a naval officer, developed the proximity fuze. This was a device that could be attached to an explosive weapon such as an antiaircraft shell. It emits radio waves that are reflected from the target. When the target is approached within a certain distance the reflected waves become intense enough to detonate the explosive contained in the shell. In effect this meant that direct hits were not necessary and the effectiveness of antiaircraft fire was multiplied many times. Even more important than the immediate wartime usefulness of the proximity fuze was the practice it gave Van Allen in miniaturization, since a great deal of electronic equipment had to be packed into a small space to make the fuze efficient.

This was needed even more intensely after the war, for in Germany crucial advances in weaponry had been made during the early 1940s. The rockets that had fascinated Goddard [1083] during the decades preceding World War II fascinated others as well. The most successful group of rocketeers were developed in Germany and of these an important member was Wernher von Braun [1370]. During the war, these men developed the V-2 rocket for Hitler's armies.

After the war the reserves of unused V-2s fell into American hands, and under Van Allen's leadership these were turned to research use. Equipment designed to test cosmic ray intensity was included in the payload and results were telemetered (that is, turned into appropriate coded changes in radio signals) back to earth from the hundred miles and more of height reached by the V-2s. Here, Van Allen's experience in miniaturization stood him in good stead, for it was necessary to cram as much equipment as possible into the very limited area in the payload that the rocket could lift far into the outer regions of the atmosphere.

The V-2s were an amazing production, but they were only the first of the missiles, the model-T, as it were. The United States took to designing new and better missiles and these were pressed into the program of research of phenomena in the upper atmosphere as well. In 1952 Van Allen began to make use of rockoons, combinations of balloons and rockets, the idea of which had occurred to him in 1949. A rocket would be lifted into the stratosphere by a balloon and from there would fire off, on signal from the ground. With most of the atmosphere below it, air resistance was eliminated and a small rocket could reach heights that only a large rocket, fired from the ground, could reach.

Van Allen became professor of physics at the University of Iowa in 1954 and then he and his associates began to talk of something new. A payload sent out into space by rocket could be given a velocity and direction of flight that would take it into an orbit about the earth where it would remain for extended periods. It would, in effect, be a man-made satellite. Slowly, government officials

were won over to the scientific importance of such an enterprise. In 1955 President Dwight D. Eisenhower officially announced that within two years such an artificial satellite would be launched.

This was to be in conjunction with the International Geophysical Year (usually abbreviated IGY), which was to run from July 1, 1957, to December 31, 1958, during one of those peaks of solar sunspot activity first brought to the attention of scientists by Schwabe [466] a century before. This was to be a program of research designed on a vast international scale, a truly global effort, in which not only the globe itself (including its glaciers, its polar regions, and its atmosphere) but even nearby space were to be explored.

It all turned out to be an extremely successful affair, too successful in some respects for American peace of mind. The Soviet Union took a major part in the IGY and announced that it too would place satellites in orbit. The United States government, public, and even scientists paid little attention to this, however. Little was known about Soviet efforts in science and, specifically, in rocket research, and much was thought to be known concerning Soviet backwardness.

It therefore came as a shock to all segments of American society when the Soviet Union proved as good as its word and sent up the first artificial satellite (Sputnik I—"sputnik" being the Russian word for "satellite") on October 4, 1957. The Soviets had scheduled it for the centenary of the birth of Tsiolkovsky [880], and said as much in advance, and were only a month late. They sent up the second artificial satellite (Sputnik II), carrying a dog, a month later.

Although the United States went through an unedifying period of panic, the event proved salutary. It is doubtful if the public, or Congress, for that matter, would have been willing to endure the expense involved in space exploration, did they not view it in the ignoble light of an item in the cold war with the Soviet Union.

Van Allen was on a ship in the South

Pacific, on his way toward Antarctica, when the news of the Soviet satellite came through. He hurried back to the United States to participate in American efforts to hasten its own satellites. The American Vanguard program, designed to send up the satellites announced by Eisenhower, proved an expensive fiasco for the most part (though it did score one important success). The army, however, using Von Braun (whom the United States inherited from the defunct Nazi war machine) finally sent up Explorer I, the first American satellite, on January 31, 1958. Its payload was much smaller than that of the Sputniks, but this was made up for by Van Allen's miniaturization, which packed the smaller payload with a surprising quantity of sophisticated instrumentation.

The age of space, which opened with Sputnik I, was to bring the promise of technological advance of breathtaking magnitudes, as in the communications satellites pioneered by Pierce [1351]. It was also to bring new information about the earth itself, as O'Keefe [1412] was to show. It was to promise improved weather forecasting through observations of the cloud cover and atmospheric movements of the planet as a whole, as seen from space. It even brought back new information concerning other worlds, such as the map of the other side of the moon, first sent back in October 1959 by a Soviet "lunar probe," and information concerning Venus sent back by an American "Venus probe" in December 1962.

One piece of startling information in the early years of the space age came from the first Explorers of 1958 and the work of Van Allen. Van Allen's interest in cosmic rays made it certain that Explorer I carried instruments designed to check the cosmic ray count (and that of other energetic particles) of nearby space. The counters reached a surprisingly high level, then went dead. The same was true of a more rugged counter on Explorer III, which was launched in March 1958.

Van Allen's previous work led him to suspect that the counters had stopped working not because the particle count had fallen to zero, but because it had gone too high for the counter to handle. He designed a counter with a lead shield that would only accept a small fraction of the particles (like a man wearing tinted glasses to ward off light that is too bright). Such a counter went up with Explorer IV on July 26, 1958, and the results were conclusive. There was far more high-energy radiation in nearby space than anyone had dreamed.

The regions of high-energy radiation encircle the earth in the neighborhood of the equator, curving in toward the polar regions, which are themselves relatively free. These belts of radiation are popularly called the Van Allen radiation belts, though in the early 1960s the term magnetosphere was accepted as the formal name.

From the shape of the magnetosphere it seemed likely that the particles making it up were trapped in the earth's magnetic field, spiraling about the magnetic lines of force from pole to pole (magnetic lines which Elsasser [1279] attributed to events far in the earth's interior). This was tested in August 1958 by exploding an atomic bomb several hundred miles above the earth's surface, in an experiment referred to as Project Argus. The distribution of the charged particles produced by the bomb showed conclusively that the magnetic field was the determining factor in the formation of the magnetosphere and that, indeed, gave the belts this name. Other such high-altitude tests, backed by Van Allen at first, succeeded in 1962 in producing changes in the magnetosphere, a result generally deplored by the scientific community.

The magnetosphere and, even more so, the sudden and unpredictable increases in radiation intensity produced by solar flares, seemed to pose a difficult problem as far as the manned exploration of space is concerned. The orbital flight of Gagarin [1502] and those who followed him showed that man is reasonably safe in the immediate neighborhood of the earth, and, twelve years later, Armstrong [1492] touched down on the moon.

[1393] **SALK,** Jonas Edward
American microbiologist
Born: New York, New York, October 28, 1914

Salk, the son of a Polish-Jewish garment worker, graduated from the College of the City of New York in 1934 and went on to obtain a medical degree in 1939 from New York University College of Medicine. Through the 1940s he served on the faculty first of the University of Michigan School of Public Health, then of the University of Pittsburgh School of Medicine.

After the Enders [1195] group had shown the way to culture polio virus and make quantities available for experimentation, Salk began his attempts to kill the virus in such a way as to make it incapable of causing the disease but capable of producing antibodies that would then be active against living polio virus.

By 1952 he had prepared a vaccine he dared try on children who had recovered from polio and who would therefore be resistant to infection. The vaccine increased the antibody content of the children's blood and so seemed effective. He then tried it on children without a history of polio and was again successful. In 1954 the vaccine was prepared in quantity.

By 1955 the news of the Salk vaccine broke and there was certainly the biggest medical brouhaha since Jenner [348] first discovered smallpox vaccination a century and a half earlier. The newspaper headlines and the wild publicity resulted in the overhasty use of some vaccine samples that were prepared with insufficiently stringent precautions. Some two hundred cases of polio were caused by vaccine injections, with eleven deaths.

The vast majority of inoculations did no harm, however, and greater care prevented such sad events in succeeding years. With the Sabin [1311] vaccine as another weapon in the armory, poliomyelitis had, within a decade, ebbed to only a twentieth of its previous incidence.

In 1963 Salk became director of the Salk Institute for Biological Studies at San Diego, California.

[1394] **SYNGE,** Richard Laurence Millington (sing)
English biochemist
Born: Liverpool, October 28, 1914

Like Martin [1350], Synge, the son of a stockbroker, studied at Cambridge University, graduating in 1936 and obtaining his Ph.D. in 1941. He spent the years from 1936 to 1939 in Hopkins's [912] laboratory.

He is chiefly known for his collaboration with Martin in the development of paper chromatography, work for which he shared with Martin the 1952 Nobel Prize in chemistry.

Since 1948 he has been at the Rowett Research Institute in Scotland. He used paper chromatography to work out the exact structure of the very simple molecule (for a protein) of Gramicidin S. This led directly to the work of Sanger [1426].

[1395] **HOFSTADTER,** Robert
American physicist
Born: New York, New York, February 5, 1915

Hofstadter was educated at the College of the City of New York, from which he graduated *magna cum laude* in 1935. He did graduate work at Princeton University, receiving his Ph.D. in 1938. During World War II he worked on Van Allen's [1392] proximity fuze for the National Bureau of Standards. After serving on the faculty of Princeton University, Hofstadter accepted a position as professor of physics at Stanford University in 1950, becoming head of the department in 1954.

At Stanford he had an opportunity to make use of the university's large "linear accelerator." This accelerated particles by moving them, with successive pushes, in a straight line, rather than in a spiral as was the case with Lawrence's [1241] cyclotron, or in a circle as with Kerst's [1367] betatron. The relativistic mass increase does not affect the situation in straight-line acceleration so that a linear accelerator can be used to produce very high-energy electrons in less complicated fashion than the betatron can. (On the other hand, linear accelerators have the disadvantage of taking up tremendous quantities of space; it can easily be two miles long, or more. For this reason, although it is one of the earliest types of particle accelerator invented, the "linac" is built less frequently than the various members of the cyclotron family.)

Hofstadter studied the scattering effects imposed on high-energy electrons by atomic nuclei and from those effects deduced information about the structure of the nucleus. The more energetic the electrons, the closer they approached the nucleus before bouncing or veering off, and the more sharply details could be deduced.

By 1960 he was using electrons energetic enough to enable him to "see" within individual protons and neutrons. In 1961 he announced that the protons and neutrons were made up of a central core of positively charged matter, about which were two shells of mesonic material. In the proton, the meson shells were both positively charged. In the neutron, one of the shells was negatively charged in such a way that the overall charge was zero.

From his observations Hofstadter further deduced the possible existence of mesons more massive than those already known; these included what he called the rho-meson and the omega-meson. Both were shortly detected and were found to be very short-lived. The omega-meson lasts for only 0.0000000000000000000-0001 second before breaking down.

In a way Hofstadter's work represents another step in the steady progression toward more and more fundamental knowledge. Chemistry attained a deeper and better understanding when Dalton [389] divined that matter consists of atoms and Mendeléev [705] discovered the order underlying the elements built up of those atoms. Better understanding, still, came when the structure of the atoms themselves was deduced and clarified by men like Ernest Rutherford [996]. With the mid-twentieth century,

however, the list of known subatomic particles had grown lengthy and the relationships among them uncertain. It was time for a still more fundamental order to be uncovered and Hofstadter's work was headed in this direction, as was Gell-Mann's [1487].

For his work Hofstadter received the 1961 Nobel Prize in physics, sharing it with Mössbauer [1483].

[1396] **MEDAWAR,** Sir Peter Brian
English biologist
Born: Rio de Janeiro, Brazil (of British parents), February 28, 1915

Medawar studied at Oxford University, graduating in 1939 and obtaining his doctorate in 1948. By that time he was serving as a professor of zoology at the University of Birmingham. He transferred to the University of London in 1951. Acting on Burnet's [1223] suggestion, Medawar inoculated the embryos of mice with tissue cells from another strain, hoping that the embryos had not yet gained the ability to form antibodies against it. If so, then by the time the embryo entered independent life and could form antibodies, the "foreign" proteins might no longer be treated as foreign. This turned out to be the case. Once the embryo mice entered independent life, they were able to accept skin grafts from those strains of mice with which they had been inoculated in embryo. For this discovery Medawar shared the 1960 Nobel Prize in medicine and physiology with Burnet.

[1397] **WELLER,** Thomas Huckle
American microbiologist
Born: Ann Arbor, Michigan, June 15, 1915

Weller was the son of a professor of pathology at the University of Michigan, and there he received his college education, graduating in 1936. He then entered Harvard University Medical School and obtained his medical degree in 1940.

During World War II he served as a medical officer in Puerto Rico, but with the end of the war he returned to Harvard and joined Enders' [1195] group. He shared the 1954 Nobel Prize in medicine and physiology with Enders and Robbins [1410].

He was also the first to discover how to grow the German measles virus in the laboratory and how to isolate the chicken pox virus.

[1398] **HOYLE,** Sir Fred
English astronomer
Born: Bingley, Yorkshire, June 24, 1915

Hoyle obtained his master's degree from Cambridge University in 1939, and during World War II worked on radar development. He returned to Cambridge in 1945 and is a professor of astronomy there.

He has accepted Gold's [1437] continuous creation theory and expounded it in several books for laymen. (In this respect, he is a worthy successor to those other astronomer-writers, Jeans [1053] and Eddington [1085]. In fact, Hoyle has gone further and is perhaps the most eminent of those contemporary scientists who have written science fiction under their own names.)

Hoyle has described a scheme of nuclear reactions within stellar interiors, which goes far past the hydrogen-to-helium mechanism elaborated by Bethe [1308]. Hoyle suggests that the helium nucleus itself, once the temperature reaches a high-enough point, "burns" further to produce nuclei of carbon and oxygen. Still more "burning" produces magnesium, sulfur, and other elements up to iron. Iron is the limit, for in its atoms the energy content is at a minimum and it cannot take part in energy-yielding nuclear reactions.

A point is then reached, according to Hoyle, where gravitation is no longer countered by radiation pressure and the star collapses catastrophically, in a matter of minutes, to the white dwarf stage. Such lower elements as remain in the star's outer layers "ignite" to form a supernova explosion (if the star is massive enough) and the energy released forms the heavy atoms beyond iron. Out of the thin gas strewn through space by supernovas, "second-generation stars" rich in the heavier atoms are formed.

In 1946 Hoyle suggested that the sun was originally a double star and that the companion had blown itself up, leaving the planets behind, richer in the heavier elements than the remaining sun is.

He also suggested, in the late 1970s, that interstellar dust clouds and comets might include actual life forms and that cometary pollution, so to speak, may be the cause of sudden pandemics on earth. This is not taken seriously by most scientists.

[1399] **BARGHOORN,** Elso Sterrenberg
(barg-hawrn)
American paleontologist
Born: New York, New York, June 30, 1915

Barghoorn obtained his Ph.D. from Harvard University in 1941 and, after his early teaching stints, joined the faculty of Harvard in 1946 and became a full professor of botany in 1955.

He has been particularly interested in fossil plants, and the work for which he is best known is his analysis of tiny bits of carbonized material in ancient rocks, which seem to be the remains of ancient and primitive fossil cells. If Barghoorn's notions of this "pre-Cambrian" life are correct, and many scientists think they are, then the record of life has been traced back for over 3 billion years, or to the point where the earth was not yet 1.5 billion years old.

[1400] **TOWNES,** Charles Hard
American physicist
Born: Greenville, South Carolina, July 28, 1915

Townes, the son of an attorney, attended Furman University in his hometown, graduating *summa cum laude* in

1935. He obtained his master's degree at Duke University, but traveled west to the California Institute of Technology for his Ph.D., which he earned in 1939. He spent World War II and some years thereafter working for Bell Telephone Laboratories on the design of radar bombing systems.

In 1948 he met Rabi [1212], who suggested he come to Columbia University, a suggestion much to Townes's liking. Townes joined the physics department of the university and since 1950 has been a full professor there.

Radar technology involves the emission and reception of microwaves, that portion of the electromagnetic spectrum that falls between infrared waves and radio waves. At Columbia, Townes followed up this interest in the most general fashion.

Townes felt the strong need for a device that would generate microwaves in great intensity. Ordinary mechanical devices could be used to generate the much longer radio waves, but for those same devices to produce microwaves would require such small-scale construction as to remove the design from the realm of the possible.

It struck Townes in 1951 (while sitting on a park bench in Washington, D.C., early one morning and waiting for a restaurant to open so he might eat breakfast) that something sufficiently small could be found if one turned to molecules rather than to any electronic circuit. Molecules had various fashions of vibration and some of the vibrations would be equivalent to radiation in the microwave region, if the vibrations could be converted into radiation. The ammonia molecule for instance vibrated 24,000,000,000 times a second under appropriate conditions and this could be converted into microwaves with a wavelength of 1¼ centimeters.

Suppose he got ammonia molecules "excited" by pumping energy into them through heat or electricity. Suppose, next, that he exposed such excited molecules to a beam of microwaves of the natural frequency of the ammonia molecule, even a very feeble beam of such microwaves. An individual molecule struck by such a microwave would be stimulated to emit its own energy in the form of such a microwave, which would strike another molecule and cause it to give up its energy. The very feeble incident beam of microwaves would act as the igniter of a cascade, a chain reaction, that would in the end produce a flood of microwaves. All the energy originally used to excite the molecule would be converted into one particular kind of radiation.

Townes thought of all this on the park bench, putting down some quick calculations (in the romantic tradition of science) on the back of an old envelope. By December 1953 he and his students finally constructed a gadget that worked, and produced the necessary beam of microwaves. The process was described by the phrase "microwave amplification by stimulated emission of radiation." This was abbreviated to the word "maser." (Such acronyms are becoming more and more popular in technology.)

The maser turned out to have a number of interesting uses. The steady, undeviating vibration of the ammonia molecules, as measured by the steady, undeviating frequency of the microwaves, could be used to measure time, so that the maser turned out to be an "atomic clock" far more accurate than any mechanical timepiece ever invented.

Masers could also be used to send their microwave beams in different directions. If an ether existed, then the earth moved through this ether, then the frequency should alter with direction. The test was attempted in January 1960, and there was no difference in wavelength. The Michelson [835]-Morley [730] experiment of three quarters of a century earlier was thus confirmed under conditions of unprecedented accuracy, for a deviation in frequency of one part in a trillion would have been detected. Einstein's [1064] theory of relativity was upheld by this, and also by the Mössbauer [1483] effect, which had just been discovered.

Townes felt a more versatile instrument could be built if gaseous ammonia was replaced by molecules of a solid and if the new knowledge of solid-state physics pioneered by Shockley [1348] was taken advantage of. In the late 1950s, such solid-state masers were indeed built by Townes and by others. Such masers could amplify microwaves while introducing unprecedentedly low quantities of random radiation ("noise"), which meant that ultra-weak signals could be amplified far more efficiently than by any other known means of amplification. The almost vanishingly weak reflected signals from Pierce's [1351] Echo I satellite were successfully amplified in this fashion in 1960, as were radar reflections from the planet Venus.

Meanwhile, in 1957 Townes began speculating on the possibility of devising a maser that would deliver infrared or even visible light, instead of microwaves. With his brother-in-law, he published a paper on the subject in 1958. In 1960 such a device was put together for the first time by Maiman [1479]—a pink ruby rod that emitted intermittent bursts of red light. The light was coherent; that is, it did not spread outward but maintained a narrow beam almost indefinitely. Such a beam reaching out to the moon, a quarter of a million miles away, would still have spread so little as to be only a couple of miles wide. There would be so little dissipation of energy that it was quite practical to think of reflecting such maser beams from the moon's surface and mapping that surface in far more efficient style than was possible with an ordinary telescope. The large energies that could be packed into a narrow beam of light could also be made useful in medicine, as in certain eye operations, and in chemical analysis, where small bits of a substance could be vaporized and then subjected to spectroscopic study.

The light was also more monochromatic than any light previously produced by man. All the light rays were of precisely the same wavelength. This meant that such beams could be modulated to carry messages, much as ordinary radiowave carriers are modulated in ordinary radio communication. The advantage of using light waves for the purpose was that at light's high frequency there is far more room for carrier waves in a given band than in the low frequency radiowave spectrum.

The visible-light masers are called "optical masers" or "lasers" (acronym for "light amplification by stimulated emission of radiation").

For this, Townes was awarded the 1964 Nobel Prize for physics, sharing it with Prokhorov [1409] and Basov [1452] who independently worked out the theory.

[1401] **HILLIER,** James
Canadian-American physicist
Born: Brantford, Ontario, August 22, 1915

Hillier graduated from the University of Toronto in 1937 and obtained his Ph.D. there in 1941. Shortly before the doctorate came through officially, he emigrated to the United States, and became an American citizen in 1945.

While still at the university, he constructed, with his collaborator, Albert F. Prebus, an electron microscope along the lines advanced earlier by Ruska [1322]. The new model, however, built in 1937, was much improved. It magnified 7,000 times and produced resolutions sharp enough to be of use in the laboratory. It was the forerunner of over two thousand electron microscopes existing in the world a generation later, some of them capable of magnifying 2,000,000 times and of making visible the most intimate details within the cell, down to large single molecules.

[1402] **SUTHERLAND,** Earl Wilbur, Jr.
American physician and pharmacologist
Born: Burlingame, Kansas, November 19, 1915
Died: Miami, Florida, March 9, 1974

Sutherland received his M.D. in 1942 from Washington University Medical

School in St. Louis. There was then an interlude because of World War II, after which he worked in the laboratory of C. F. Cori [1194] and served on the faculty, attaining professorial status in 1950. In 1953 he went on to Case Western Reserve University in Cleveland and while there, in 1956, he isolated cyclic AMP, an intermediate in the formation of ATP, the vital compound that Lipmann [1221] had uncovered.

Cyclic AMP turned out to play an important role in many chemical reactions in the body, and for it, Sutherland received the 1971 Nobel Prize for physiology and medicine.

[1403] **ANFINSEN,** Christian Boehmer
American biochemist
Born: Monessen, Pennsylvania,
March 26, 1916

Anfinsen obtained his Ph.D. at Harvard University in 1943, and he has been affiliated with a number of institutions in the United States, Sweden, and Israel. His chief research interest has been in the relationship between the structure and function of enzymes and other proteins. He wrote an influential book, *The Molecular Basis of Evolution,* in 1959. For his work, he received a share of the 1972 Nobel Prize for chemistry.

[1404] **SHANNON,** Claude Elwood
American mathematician
Born: Gaylord, Michigan, April
30, 1916

Shannon graduated from the University of Michigan in 1936, then went on to earn a Ph.D. in mathematics at the Massachusetts Institute of Technology in 1940. He joined the staff of Bell Telephone Laboratories in 1941.

At the Bell Telephone Laboratories he worked on the problem of most efficiently transmitting information. For a century, ever since the development of Morse's [473] telegraph, messages in rapidly increasing numbers had been flowing in all direction over wires and cable or through the open air by means of fluctuating electric currents or modulated electromagnetic radiation. A large number of different systems of transmitting these messages were used and it was important to know which was most efficient and if the efficiency could be increased still further.

Shannon turned his efforts toward a fundamental understanding of the problem and by 1948 had evolved a method of expressing information in quantitative form. The fundamental unit of information is a yes-no situation. Either something is or is not. This can be expressed in binary notation as either 1 or 0. Under these circumstances, 1 and 0 are binary digits, a phrase that can be shortened to "bits." Thus, the unit of information is the bit.

More complicated information can be viewed as built up out of combinations of bits. The game of "Twenty Questions" for instance shows how quite complicated objects can be identified in twenty bits or less, using the rules of the game. Something much more elaborate, such as is seen by the human eye, can also be measured in bits (many more than twenty, of course) since each cell of the retina might be viewed as recording "light" or "dark" ("yes" or "no") and it is the combination of these yes-no situations that makes up the complete picture. (The situation is slightly more complicated, but no different fundamentally, if color and other variables are included.)

Shannon's publication in 1949 showed how this quantitation of information could be analyzed by strict mathematical methods. It was possible to measure the likelihood of information being garbled through loss of bits, distortion of bits, addition of extraneous bits, and so on. One could speak with precision of such things as redundancy and noise and even entropy. This branch of mathematics is called information theory. It has proved useful not only in circuit design, computer design, and communications technology; it is being applied to biology and psychology, to phonetics, and even to semantics and literature.

Since 1956 Shannon has been on the faculty of Massachusetts Institute of Technology.

[1405] **DICKE**, Robert Henry
American physicist
Born: St. Louis, Missouri, May 6, 1916

Dicke, who obtained his Ph.D. at the University of Rochester in 1941, has been on the physics faculty of Princeton University since 1946.

He is best known for his scalar-tensor field theory, perhaps the most carefully thought out and ambitious alternative presented to Einstein's [1064] theory of general relativity. Einstein's theory, however, remains the simplest mathematically and of the alternatives seems to be the most nearly in accord with observations. The observational differences that can distinguish between Einstein's theory and others such as Dicke's, however, remain so delicate that a final choice remains difficult to establish.

Dicke also carried further Gamow's [1278] suggestion of a radio-wave residue of the initial big bang and was instrumental in establishing the importance of the observances of Penzias [1501] and R. W. Wilson [1506] in this respect as strong evidence that the big bang had indeed taken place.

[1406] **CRICK**, Francis Harry Compton
English biochemist
Born: Northampton, June 8, 1916

Crick was educated at University College in London and went on to obtain his Ph.D. at Cambridge University in 1953. He was a physicist to begin with and worked in the field during World War II, when he was involved in radar research and in magnetic mine development.

The war years, however, had seen the beginnings of a revolution in biochemistry. Martin [1350] and Synge [1394] had developed paper chromatography, which made it easy to separate complex biochemical mixtures into their components. The development of the nuclear reactor meant that radioisotopes were going to be available in quantity and could be used to tag one particular compound or another. (This work was indeed to come to great results, Calvin's [1361] work being an example.)

At the same time, biochemists were coming to realize that nucleic acids, rather than proteins, were the instruments whereby physical characteristics were inherited and it was the deoxyribonucleic acid (DNA) of the chromosomes that were the key chemicals of life.

The orthodox chemistry of the nucleic acids had been worked out by Todd [1331], but something more was needed. The fine details of structure within the intact giant molecule of DNA were sought and the well-established methods of chemistry were insufficient for the purpose. The new methods and instrumentation of physics were required.

At the time, under the leadership of Perutz [1389], a veritable galaxy of physics-minded scientists was turning to biochemistry at Cambridge and their refined probings established the science of molecular biology, a fusion of biology, chemistry, and physics.

One method of studying the internal structure of large molecules is X-ray diffraction. Wilkins [1413] studied DNA in this manner and by 1953 his data yielded specific information on the type of regularities that were to be found in the molecule. The problem was how best to interpret those regularities in atomic terms.

Crick was one of the physicists who turned to biochemistry or, rather, to molecular biology, and with him was a young American, James Dewey Watson [1480]. Together they considered Wilkins' X-ray diffraction data. Pauling [1236] had in 1951 brought forth convincing evidence to the effect that molecules of fibrous proteins, such as the collagen of connective tissue, existed in the form of a helix (the shape, that is, of what is usually called a spiral staircase). It was easy to assume that the nucleic acids were similarly constructed, but that alone was not enough. It would be ideal if one could find a structure that would fit the X-ray diffraction data and would also explain the key fact about DNA; to wit, that it was capable of replication.

Ever since the time of Flemming [762], three quarters of a century earlier, it had been known that chromosomes formed replicas of themselves during mitosis, and when Mendel's [638] work was rediscovered in 1900 it was quickly seen that such chromosome replication was the key to heredity and to the science of genetics. Since the chromosome came to be seen as essentially a string of DNA molecules, it meant that the molecule of DNA itself must be forming a replica of itself.

Crick and Watson took into consideration the work of men like Chargaff [1291], which showed that within the nucleic acid molecule there was a definite relationship among the nitrogenous bases. There are four such bases in the DNA molecule—adenine, guanine, thymine, and cytosine—and it seemed that the number of units of adenine was always roughly equal to the number of thymine units, while that of guanine was equal to cytosine. (The ratio between those two pairs could, however, be almost anything.)

Crick and Watson, in a classic paper published in 1953, therefore suggested that the DNA molecule consisted of a double helix, each helix made up of the sugar-phosphate backbone known to exist, thanks to Todd's work, in the nucleic acid molecule. The nitrogenous bases extended in toward the center of the helix from each of the two backbones and approached each other.

The nitrogenous bases are of different sizes and if the double helix is to be of uniform width, an adenine unit can approach only a thymine or a cytosine, but never a guanine; a thymine could approach an adenine or guanine but never a cytosine; and so on. The conditions of uniform width would be met if it were assumed that an adenine base from one backbone always approached a thymine from the other; while a guanine from one backbone always approached a cytosine from the other. That would neatly account for the fact that the numbers of thymine and adenine were equal and the numbers of guanine and cytosine were equal.

Furthermore, it was now reasonable to suggest that in the process of replication, the two strands of the double helix unwound. Each single helix could then serve as a model for its complement. Wherever an adenine existed, a thymine could be selected as its neighbor and vice versa. Wherever a guanine existed, cytosine could be selected as its neighbor and vice versa. In this way, helix 1 would form a new helix 2, and helix 2 would form a new helix 1. The end result would be two 1–2 double helixes, where only one had existed previously.

When first advanced, the Watson-Crick model was nothing more than a device plucked out of air to fit the observed data. However, a decade of furious experimental work in many laboratories followed and every painstakingly gathered piece of evidence seemed to confirm the model. It is now generally accepted by biochemists.

Crick named his house at Cambridge the Golden Helix, and for him and for the world of science the helix was indeed golden. Crick, Watson, and Wilkins shared the 1962 Nobel Prize in medicine and physiology, while in that same year the prize in chemistry went to other members of the Cambridge group, Perutz [1389] and Kendrew [1415]. Four years before, the chemistry prize had gone to Sanger [1426], still another member of the group. Molecular biology was indeed a kind of "wave of the future."

The new look of the DNA molecule opened fruitful avenues of research. The work of Fraenkel-Conrat [1355], was showing, clearly enough, that the nucleic acid molecule not only formed a replica of itself but was also capable of bringing about the formation of a specific protein. The mechanism by which it could do so (the genetic code) was tougher to elucidate than that of mere replication. Men like Hoagland [1447], Ochoa [1293], and Crick himself had been working assiduously at it, and as the 1960s opened, considerable and heartening progress was being made.

Crick spent 1959 and 1960 in the United States, lecturing at Harvard, Rockefeller, and at Johns Hopkins universities.

In 1980, Crick advanced notions of the seeding of life on planets, including possibly Earth, that are reminiscent of Arrhenius' [894] earlier theories.

[1407] **FRIEDMAN**, Herbert
American astronomer
Born: New York, New York,
June 21, 1916

The son of an art dealer, Friedman graduated from Brooklyn College in 1936. He went on to Johns Hopkins University, where he obtained his Ph.D. in 1940. He has been working in government centers since. ·

Immediately after World War II, when captured V-2 rockets were made available for American research, Friedman began to occupy himself with the study of X rays in outer space. This was virgin territory, for X rays produced by heavenly bodies cannot penetrate earth's atmosphere.

In 1949 he demonstrated that the sun emits X rays and by 1956 had showed that the solar flares were one source. In 1958, during rocket observations while an eclipse was in progress, he showed that X rays were being produced by the sun's corona, which was not surprising in view of the high temperature of the corona. By 1960 he had actually taken an X-ray photograph of the sun.

In 1963, rocket experiments by Rossi [1289] indicated the presence of X-ray sources other than the sun, and Friedman at once began to search the heavens intensively for "X-ray stars." Many have been discovered and this roused interest in their possible identity as "neutron stars," super-dense objects made up of neutrons in contact so that all the mass of a star like our sun would be condensed into a body a few miles across. Zwicky [1209] had predicted their possible existence.

[1408] **SHKLOVSKII**, Iosif Samuilovich
Soviet astrophysicist
Born: July 1, 1916

Shklovskii graduated from Moscow University in 1938 and has served on its faculty since. He is best known for his synchrotron-emission theory of radio sources. He first proposed this in 1953 in connection with the Crab nebula, suggesting that high-energy particles emitted by it, caught in the magnetic field and following curved pathways, emitted radio waves. He applied this in general fashion to other radio sources.

Shklovskii, along with Sagan [1504] and Drake [1491], has been interested in the search for extraterrestrial intelligence.

[1409] **PROKHOROV**, Alexander Mikhailovich
Soviet physicist
Born: Australia (of Russian parents), July 11, 1916

Prokhorov graduated from Leningrad University in 1939. As was true of almost all Russians in the terrible decade that followed, his career was interrupted by the war with Germany. He served in the Red Army from 1941 to 1944. With the war victoriously concluded, he went on to get his doctorate in 1946.

About the time Townes [1400] was working out the principle of the maser, Prokhorov and Basov [1452] were doing the same in the Soviet Union. Townes was the first actually to build such a device but the Soviet accomplishment in theory was significant.

In 1959 Prokhorov was awarded the Lenin Prize for his work on the maser and in 1964 he and Basov shared the Nobel Prize for physics with Townes.

[1410] **ROBBINS**, Frederick Chapman
American microbiologist
Born: Auburn, Alabama, August 25, 1916

Robbins, the son of a plant physiologist, graduated from the University of

Missouri in 1936, and then like Weller [1397] obtained his medical degree from Harvard University Medical School in 1940. Again like Weller he served as a medical officer during World War II (in the Mediterranean area rather than the Caribbean). After the war, he too joined Enders' [1195] group.

In 1948 he married the daughter of Nobel Prize winner John Howard Northrop [1148]. It isn't every son-in-law of a Nobel laureate who can match the feat. But Joliot-Curie [1227] did it, and Robbins did it too, when he shared with Enders and Weller the 1954 Nobel Prize in medicine and physiology. In 1952 he joined the faculty of Western Reserve University in Cleveland, Ohio.

[1411] DAUSSET, Jean (doh-say')
French physician
Born: Toulouse, Haute-Garonne, October 10, 1916

Dausset received his M.D. from the University of Paris in 1945. Once the war was over he did postgraduate work at Harvard Medical School, then returned to France, where he was placed in charge of the national blood transfusion center.

In 1952 Dausset discovered that the blood serum from patients who had received many blood transfusions could cause the white cells and the platelets (but not the red blood corpuscles) of other individuals to agglutinate. In other words, patients develop antibodies to the blood they accept eventually. The nature and amount of these antibodies could be used to predict the compatibility of tissues intended for grafting and was useful in organ transplantation.

For this, Dausset shared the 1980 Nobel Prize for physiology and medicine with Snell [1275] and Benacerraf [1442].

[1412] O'KEEFE, John Aloysius
American physicist
Born: Lynn, Massachusetts, October 13, 1916

O'Keefe attended Harvard University, graduating in 1937, then went on for

graduate work at the University of Chicago, from which he obtained his Ph.D. in 1941. He has been with the National Aeronautics and Space Administration (NASA) since 1958.

O'Keefe's greatest achievement came in connection with Project Vanguard. This was the United States' first satellite program, one which, for a variety of reasons, was not successful. On March 17, 1958, however, it did succeed in placing a small three-pound satellite (Vanguard I) in orbit. This was small even for an American satellite and the Soviets (who had succeeded in placing large satellites in orbit) were amused.

However, the satellite was sent high enough to avoid atmospheric friction and to secure an orbit that would persist for centuries. Its small radio transmitter (the only instrument it carried) was powered by solar battery and was expected to last for years. Its orbit, followed over many revolutions, yielded considerable information concerning the fine details of earth's shape.

For instance, the pull of the earth's equatorial bulge seemed to be not quite symmetrical, and it varied a bit depending on whether the satellite was north or south of the equator. O'Keefe analyzed the motions of the satellite and showed that the southern half of the equatorial bulge was up to fifty feet farther from the earth's center than the northern part. (To detect fifty feet in four thousand miles is indeed an achievement.) At the same time, the North Pole, counting from sea level, is one hundred feet farther from the center than the South Pole (sea level) is.

The earth has, in consequence, been termed pear-shaped, though actually its pear-shapedness is not sufficient to be detected by any but the most refined techniques. O'Keefe points out that this asymmetry could not be maintained against the smoothing-out effect of earth's gravitational field, unless the underlying rock of earth's mantle was considerably more rigid than had earlier been supposed. This may have an important effect on theories of how mountain ranges originate.

[1413] **WILKINS,** Maurice Hugh Frederick
New Zealand-British physicist
Born: Pongaroa, New Zealand,
December 15, 1916

Wilkins, the son of a physician, was taken to England when he was six. He obtained his Ph.D. from the University of Birmingham in 1940 and was early interested in astronomy and in the history of the telescope. During World War II he was one of the British scientists cooperating with the Americans in their work on the development of the atomic bomb. In those years he worked at the University of California.

After the war he turned away from nuclear physics, partly out of a revulsion against the bomb, a revulsion that struck other physicists too, notably Urey [1164]. A book by Schrödinger [1117] on the nature of life turned his attention to biological problems and he developed the desire to attack them by physical methods.

Laue [1068] and the Braggs [922, 1141] had shown, a generation earlier, that X rays could be diffracted by the regular spacing of atoms in a crystal and that from the manner of the diffraction the positioning of the atoms within a crystal could be deduced. The same (in more complicated fashion) could be done for a large fibrous molecule built up of repetitions of chemical units. (Fibrous molecules generally are built up of such repetitions.) From the details of the diffraction can be determined the size of the units, the spacing between them, and other facts.

Wilkins prepared DNA fibers from a viscous solution of that compound and subjected them to X-ray diffraction. From the data so obtained, Crick [1406] and James Dewey Watson [1480] were able to deduce their celebrated Watson-Crick model of DNA structure and all three shared the 1962 Nobel Prize in medicine and physiology.

[1414] **PRIGOGINE,** Ilya
Russian-Belgian physical chemist
Born: Moscow, January 25, 1917

Prigogine was born just before the Russian Revolution broke out. When he was a child, he was taken by his family, who were fleeing the disorders that followed, to Western Europe. Eventually, they settled in Belgium. He studied at the Free University of Brussels where he eventually became a professor of physical chemistry.

Prigogine applied himself to the problem of the second law of thermodynamics, first enunciated in its full form by Clausius [633] nearly a century before. The second law asserts that the spontaneous change is in the direction of increasing disorder. And yet there are phenomena that seem to move spontaneously toward increasing order—the phenomenon of life particularly. To be sure, life cannot be considered by itself, and as part of a larger entity including energy supply from the sun particularly, overall change is in the direction indicated by the second law. Nevertheless, there is a problem as to how life maintains order within this total entity and Prigogine produced mathematical models to show how this could be done within the requirements of the second law.

For this he received the 1977 Nobel Prize for chemistry.

[1415] **KENDREW,** John Cowdery
English biochemist
Born: Oxford, March 24, 1917

Kendrew was educated at Cambridge University, graduating in 1939, and after work with the Ministry of Aircraft Production during World War II returned to that university to obtain his Ph.D. in 1949. There he came under the aegis of Perutz [1389], who was building a team of molecular biologists that also included Crick [1406].

The problem in which Perutz and Kendrew were interested was the fine structure of the protein molecule. Emil Fischer [833] had worked out the basic amino acid skeleton of the molecule half a century before, and during the 1950s Sanger [1426] was working out his methods of determining the order of the

863

amino acids in the skeleton. It remained, however, to see how the amino acid chain was arranged within the protein molecule as it actually existed.

For this purpose the most suitable technique seemed to be X-ray diffraction, which could be used to detect overall regularities in a large molecule, as Wilkins [1413] was doing in the case of nucleic acid. Here, however, something more was required: the exact position of each atom.

Perutz took hemoglobin as his own prey and handed the simpler molecule of myoglobin (rather like hemoglobin but only a quarter the size) to Kendrew. The hemoglobin molecule contains something like 12,000 atoms, but half of these are hydrogen atoms, small enough not to affect the X rays. This still leaves 6,000 atoms, each capable of affecting the X rays, a tremendously complicated situation. The smaller molecule of myoglobin still disposes of 1,200 such atoms; not as bad, but bad enough.

For several years the X-ray diffraction pictures were studied and analyzed. The complicated patterns could be analyzed only by high-speed computers of types that only became available in the late 1950s. Kendrew's simpler molecule of myoglobin fell into place by 1960. Every atom could then be pinpointed, and a three-dimensional picture of the myoglobin molecule could be drawn accurately. Pauling [1236] had shown a decade earlier that fibrous proteins possessed a helical chain. Now Kendrew could show that globular proteins as represented by myoglobin, which did not tend to form fibers, nevertheless had molecules in which the helix was the basic structure.

Perutz's hemoglobin quickly followed and Perutz and Kendrew consequently shared the 1962 Nobel Prize in chemistry.

[1416] **WOODWARD,** Robert Burns
American chemist
Born: Boston, Massachusetts, April 10, 1917
Died: Cambridge, Massachusetts, July 8, 1979

Woodward was a chemist from boyhood. Like Perkin [734] and Hall [933], he had a chemistry laboratory at home as a teenager. He entered Massachusetts Institute of Technology at sixteen and would have flunked out at seventeen had the faculty not recognized what they had. They organized a special program for him and allowed him complete freedom. In 1936, when his class was graduating with bachelor's degrees, Woodward, at twenty, had earned his Ph.D. He entered Harvard University immediately afterward as a postdoctoral fellow and accepted a position on the faculty in 1938 (when he was still only twenty-one). He remained at Harvard thereafter, becoming a full professor in 1950.

The early promise of his school years bore its first remarkable fruit when in 1944 he and William von Eggers Doering succeeded in synthesizing quinine. It was total synthesis, meaning that they had started with compounds that could in turn be synthesized from the elements carbon, hydrogen, oxygen, and nitrogen. At no stage in the synthesis was it necessary to make use of some intermediate that could be obtained only from living or once-living organisms.

It was the synthesis of quinine that Perkin had been attempting to bring about, nearly a century before, when he stumbled upon the aniline dyes.

Woodward continued to perform amazing feats of synthesis in the decades that followed. The most complicated nonpolymeric molecules (those not built up of numbers of simple units joined into long chains) fell before him. In 1951 he synthesized such steroids as cholesterol (a fatty substance found, usefully, in the myelin coating of nerves and, most dangerously, on the interior surface of atherosclerotic arteries), and cortisone, the steroid hormone whose importance in the treatment of rheumatoid arthritis had been discovered by Hench [1188] a few years earlier.

In 1954 he synthesized strychnine, a fearfully complicated (and poisonous) alkaloid with a molecule built up of seven intricately related rings of atoms. In the same year he synthesized lysergic acid, a compound that had recently been found to influence mental function. In 1956 he synthesized reserpine, the first of the tranquilizing drugs, which R. W. Wilkins [1320] had introduced to Western medicine a few years before.

In 1960 Woodward synthesized chlorophyll, the plant pigment whose workings Calvin [1361] had pieced out over the previous decade and in 1962 he headed a group who, after three years of labor, synthesized a tetracycline antibiotic.

Woodward's accomplishment was a contemporary climax to the long trail of organic syntheses begun by Wöhler [515] a century and a half before, and for this reason he was granted a National Medal of Science Award in 1964 and the Nobel Prize for chemistry in 1965.

[1417] **CORNFORTH,** Sir John Warcup
Australian-British chemist
Born: Sydney, Australia, September 7, 1917

Cornforth studied at the University of Sydney, then went to Oxford University, where he received his Ph.D. in 1941. He worked thereafter with Robinson [1107] and went on to study the structure of enzyme-substrate complexes. Enzymes catalyze the chemical changes of particular compounds (substrates) and in doing so temporarily combine with those substrates. When the union is broken, the substrate has undergone its chemical change. Cornforth, making use of hydrogen isotopes, determined such structures and for this received a share of the 1975 Nobel Prize for chemistry. He was knighted in 1977.

[1418] **DE DUVE,** Christian René
Belgian cytologist
Born: Thames Ditton, England, October 2, 1917

De Duve was born of Belgian parents who had escaped to England when the German army invaded Belgium in World War I, and he maintained his Belgian citizenship. He graduated from the University of Louvain in 1941, when Bel-

gium was once more occupied by the Germans.

He worked both in Belgium and in the United States and probed the cellular interior with the electron microscope, discovering the "lysozymes," organelles that handle the cell's ingested nutrients, breaking down the larger particles. As a result he shared the 1974 Nobel Prize for physiology and medicine with his fellow electron-microscopists, Claude [1222] and Palade [1380].

[1419] **HUXLEY,** Andrew Fielding
English physiologist
Born: London, November 22, 1917

Huxley, a grandson of T. H. Huxley [659], graduated from Cambridge University in 1938 and obtained his master's degree there in 1941.

He collaborated with A. L. Hodgkin [1387] in working out the "sodium pump" mechanism of nerve impulse transmission and shared with him and with Eccles [1262] in the 1963 Nobel Prize in physiology and medicine.

Since 1960 he has been a professor of physiology at University College in London.

[1420] **RAINWATER,** Leo James
American physicist
Born: Council, Idaho, December 9, 1917

Rainwater received his college education at the California Institute of Technology, then went on to Columbia University, where he obtained his Ph.D. in 1946. He remained there on the faculty and by 1952 was a full professor.

In 1949 he heard Townes [1400] speculate on the possibility that the assumption that the nucleus was spherical in shape might be an oversimplification. Rainwater therefore began to consider the possibility that the protons and neutrons on the outer rim of the nucleus might be subjected to centrifugal effects that might create nuclear asymmetries.

Aage Bohr [1450] was then at Columbia and, on returning to Copenhagen, he and Mottelson [1471] worked out the theory in more detail and presented experimental detail that confirmed it. As a result Rainwater, Bohr, and Mottelson shared the 1975 Nobel Prize for physics.

[1421] **SCHWINGER,** Julian Seymour
American physicist
Born: New York, New York,
February 12, 1918

Schwinger was a child prodigy who burned his way through grade school and entered the College of the City of New York at the age of fourteen. He later transferred to Columbia University and graduated in 1936, going on to his Ph.D. in 1939.

He then worked under Oppenheimer [1280] at the University of California. He joined the faculty of Harvard in 1945 and by 1947 was a full professor, one of the very few to achieve such a status at that university while still in his twenties.

Schwinger's theoretical work led to the formulation of quantum electrodynamics and, as a result, he shared with Feynman [1424] and Tomonaga [1300], who had done similar work independently, in the 1965 Nobel Prize in physics.

[1422] **KORNBERG,** Arthur
American biochemist
Born: Brooklyn, New York,
March 3, 1918

Kornberg attended the College of the City of New York on a scholarship and graduated in 1937. He then studied medicine at the University of Rochester on another scholarship and obtained his medical degree in 1941, after which he served in the Coast Guard for a while. He has been associated with a number of universities and is now the head of the biochemistry department at Stanford University.

In 1956 he formed synthetic molecules of DNA by the action of an enzyme upon a mixture of nucleotides, each of

which carried three phosphate groups. For this he shared the 1959 Nobel Prize in medicine and physiology with Ochoa [1293].

[1423] **REINES,** Frederick
American physicist
Born: Paterson, New Jersey,
March 16, 1918

Reines obtained his Ph.D. at New York University in 1944. He worked at Los Alamos till 1959, then moved on to Case Institute of Technology (now Case Western Reserve University) and in 1966 went on to the University of California.

His great interest was in the neutrino, that tiny, elusive particle first postulated by Pauli [1228] as necessary to straighten out the arithmetic of nuclear reactions. Only by including a particle of certain properties could various conservation laws be upheld. The trouble was that those particular properties made it react with ordinary particles so incredibly rarely that it was easy to decide it would never be detected.

Reines, in the early 1950s, chased after it nevertheless, in collaboration with Cowan [1434]. He made use of a nuclear reactor as a particularly rich source of neutrinos. Just because a neutrino *almost* never reacted with ordinary particles, didn't mean *quite* never. Reines set up a detection system that would concentrate on one particular reaction a neutrino might bring about and that would detect the gamma rays produced at just the right energies and time intervals and none other.

In this way, neutrinos were finally detected in 1956, a quarter century after they had been postulated.

Since then, Reines has been setting up large vats of perchloroethylene deep underground (where neutrinos can easily penetrate, but few other particles can) in order to pick up neutrinos emitted by the sun. Some have been detected but, at best, only about a third as many as were expected.

Careful examination of the experimental procedure seemed to show that there was really a "mystery of the missing neutrinos" and astronomers were perturbed. Plans for improved detectors were advanced.

In the late 1970s Reines tackled the matter from a new direction. There were three different kinds of neutrinos known: the electron-neutrino, the muon-neutrino, and the tauon-neutrino. There was no way known to distinguish them by definable differences in properties. There had been suggestions that the neutrinos might not be zero-rest-mass particles as had been supposed almost from the first. If each had a tiny but different mass, that would represent the missing distinction between them. It meant they would oscillate from one form to another so that the electron-neutrinos from the sun would be fewer than expected because some would be converted to muon-neutrinos and tauon-neutrinos en route. In addition, so many neutrinos exist that even with minute individual rest-masses they would make up more than 99 percent of the universe and would supply the necessary mass to make sure the universe would someday cease its expansion and contract again.

In 1980 Reines announced experiments that indicated the neutrino had mass. Soviet work meanwhile suggested the mass was $1/10,000$ that of an electron, which was enough. Further investigation is, of course, required.

[1424] **FEYNMAN,** Richard Philips
American physicist
Born: New York, New York,
May 11, 1918

Feynman graduated from Massachusetts Institute of Technology in 1939 and earned his doctorate at Princeton University in 1942. Like all physicists of his generation he was involved in nuclear bomb research during World War II and was present at the explosion of the first bomb at Alamogordo. He joined the faculty of Cornell University in 1945 and went on to California Institute of Technology in 1950.

In 1948 Feynman developed "quantum electrodynamics," in which the behavior of electrons was worked out mathematically with far greater precision than was the case previously. Schwinger [1421] and Tomonaga [1300] did similar work independently and all three shared the 1965 Nobel Prize in physics.

Feynman is renowned for his excellence as a lecturer and for his ability to handle the bongo drums at parties.

[1425] **MATTHIAS,** Bern Teo
German-American physicist
Born: Frankfurt-am-Main, Germany, June 8, 1918
Died: La Jolla, California, October 27, 1980

Matthias moved from Germany to Switzerland when Hitler gained control of Germany and in 1943 obtained his Ph.D. in physics at the Federal Institute of Technology in Zürich, studying under Pauli [1228]. In 1947 he went to the United States and was naturalized in 1951. He was associated with Bell Laboratories and the University of California after 1961.

Matthias was chiefly interested in superconductivity and is supposed to have established the superconductive properties of more elements and compounds than anyone in the world since the discovery of the phenomenon by Kamerlingh Onnes [843].

One of the most important aspects of his research was that of finding something that would be superconductive at as high a temperature as possible, so that liquid helium would not be required for the property. If superconductivity at temperatures about $20°K$ were found, then it could be maintained by the much cheaper and easier-to-handle liquid hydrogen. As the total number of superconductive materials rose from 30 to more than 1,000 (chiefly through Matthias' work) increasingly higher temperatures were achieved. In 1954 Matthias discovered a superconducting alloy in which three atoms of niobium were joined to one of tin, and which remained super-conductive up to a temperature of 18.3°K.

He died of a heart attack at sixty-two. Had he lived out a normal lifetime he might well (in the opinion of many) have obtained a Nobel Prize.

[1426] **SANGER,** Frederick
English biochemist
Born: Rendcombe, Gloucester-shire, August 13, 1918

Sanger, the son of a physician, graduated from Cambridge University in 1939 and earned his Ph.D. there in 1943. He worked thereafter in the laboratory that was soon to be graced by such additional biochemical giants as Crick [1406], James Dewey Watson [1480], Kendrew [1415], and Perutz [1389].

Sanger's interest lay in the determination of the exact structure of the amino acid chain of protein molecules. Martin [1350] and Synge [1394] had just introduced paper chromatography, which made it possible to tell how many of each amino acid were in the molecule of a particular protein. The next step was to tell the exact position of each amino acid in the molecular chain.

In order to do this, Sanger began to break down molecules only part way, leaving small chains of amino acids intact. In 1945 he discovered a compound called 2, 4-dinitrofluorobenzene (commonly called Sanger's reagent) which would attach itself to one end of a chain of amino acids but not the other. By attaching his reagent to one of the small chains he produced, and then breaking that chain down all the way to amino acids, Sanger could tell which amino acid had been at the vulnerable end by separating them by paper chromatography and noting which amino acid had the reagent attached to it.

Sanger began work on the important molecule of insulin, which had been isolated a quarter century earlier by Banting [1152] and Best [1218]. It is made up of some fifty amino acids, distributed among two interconnected chains. Slowly he identified the short amino acid chains he obtained from it, working out the

order of the amino acids in the short chains by means of his reagent and by other methods.

Then he deduced the longer chains could give rise to just those short chains he had discovered and no others. Little by little he built up the structure of longer and longer chains until by 1953, after eight years of hard work, the exact order of the amino acids in the whole insulin molecule had been worked out. It was a stunning achievement.

With Sanger's work as a guide, other chemists have worked out the exact structure of other and still more complicated compounds, as, for example, Li's [1382] group, which worked out the structure of the pituitary hormone, ACTH. Du Vigneaud [1239] determined the structure of the comparatively simple amino acid chains of oxytocin and vasopressin and was even able to synthesize them thereafter.

It was quite clear that Sanger had scored a breakthrough in protein chemistry that was to lead to still greater triumphs and he was awarded the 1958 Noble Prize in chemistry. And, indeed, by 1964 chemists had succeeded in synthesizing the entire insulin molecule.

Sanger's work only located the amino acids in a chain that could be drawn, abstractly, as a straight line. Building on his work, Kendrew and Perutz went even further, in 1960, locating the actual position of each amino acid in the three-dimensional structure of an intact molecule of proteins like myoglobin and hemoglobin.

Sanger then turned to the sequence determination of nucleotides in nucleic acids, a macromolecule even more important and complex than the protein molecule. By 1977 he and his colleagues had worked out the entire sequence of the DNA molecule in a small virus, which contained 5,375 nucleotide pairs sufficient to code the production of nine different proteins.

For this he received a share of the 1980 Nobel Prize for chemistry, which makes him one of the rare double laureates, along with Bardeen [1334] and Pauling [1236].

[1427] **BARTON,** Sir Derek Harold
Richard
English chemist
Born: Gravesend, Kent, September 8, 1918

Barton obtained his Ph.D. in organic chemistry at the Imperial College, London, in 1942, and joined the faculty of the institution in 1945. While a visiting professor at Harvard University in 1949, he began to work on the relationship of the three-dimensional structure of organic compounds in relation to their chemical properties. The preparation of models of steroids, terpenes, and other complex molecules of biochemical significance showed distinct shapes that could vary considerably with minor changes in orientation of particular atoms. This placed an entirely new light on many aspects of organic chemistry and won for Barton a share of the 1969 Nobel Prize for chemistry. He was knighted in 1972.

[1428] **RYLE,** Sir Martin
English astronomer
Born: England, September 27, 1918

Ryle, the son of a physician, worked on radar during World War II. After the war, he received a fellowship at the Cavendish Laboratory in Cambridge, where he worked on radio astronomy. Under his leadership the Cambridge radio astronomy group compiled catalogues of radio sources, the latest being the *Third Cambridge Catalogue.* It has proved essential to the discovery of the quasars, so that the first ones discovered were given names that began with "3C" for the Third Cambridge.

Ryle became professor of radio astronomy in 1959, was knighted in 1966, and was appointed astronomer royal in 1972.

He devised ingenious systems for increasing the sharpness with which radio telescopes could "see" radio sources. The most important of these was called "aperture synthesis." He used two radio telescopes and changed the distance between them. The variation in the signals they received could then be analyzed by computers to give the sharpness one would expect of a single radio telescope as wide as the maximum distance between the two actual telescopes. In this way, and in other ways, Ryle could achieve a resolution of radio sources equal to the best that could be done with light sources by optical telescopes. Instruments like this made it possible for Hewish [1463] to discover pulsars.

As a result, Ryle and Hewish shared the 1974 Nobel Prize for physics.

[1429] **FISCHER,** Ernst Otto
German chemist
Born: Müchen-Solln, November 10, 1918

Fischer, the son of a physics professor and born the day before the armistice that ended World War I, found his own education delayed by World War II. It was not till 1952 that he obtained his Ph.D. at the Technische Hochschule of Munich. After 1957 he served there as a full professor.

In 1951, he began work on a newly isolated substance, ferrocene, which was of unknown structure. He showed that it consisted of two five-membered carbon rings in parallel, with an iron atom in between, with bonding between itself and all ten carbon atoms to some extent. This was a completely new type of metal-organic compound, and in 1973 Fischer shared the Nobel Prize for chemistry with Wilkinson [1445], who had made the same discovery independently.

[1430] **VAN DE HULST,** Hendrik
Christoffell
Dutch astronomer
Born: Utrecht, November 19, 1918

Van de Hulst's chance came during the sad years of World War II when the German occupation of the Netherlands forced most Dutchmen into the shadows and made ordinary scientific research impossible. With the instruments of astronomy not at hand, Van de Hulst's young and restless mind turned to pen and paper.

He considered the behavior of cold hydrogen atoms and worked out the manner in which the magnetic fields associated with the proton and the electron in the hydrogen atom were oriented to each other. They could line up in the same direction or in opposite directions. Every once in a while, the atom could flip from one configuration to another and in so doing it would emit a radio wave 21 centimeters in length.

Any single hydrogen atom ought to do so only once in 11 million years or so, on the average, but there were so many such atoms in space that a continuing drizzle of 21-centimeter radiation should result.

After the war was over, radio astronomers sought for such radiation and, by 1951, F. Bloch [1296] and Purcell [1378] had detected it. The use of such radiation has made it possible to map the spiral arms of the galaxy with detail that would be impossible from a consideration of the stars alone.

[1431] ECKERT, John Presper, Jr.
American engineer
Born: Philadelphia, Pennsylvania,
April 9, 1919

Eckert attended the University of Pennsylvania from 1941 to 1946. There he met Mauchly [1328] and with him designed the pioneer electronic computers, ENIAC in 1946 and UNIVAC in 1951. These quickly became obsolete but they ushered in a change that is likely to alter the world beyond recognition more quickly than any previous technological change has done.

[1432] HILLARY, Sir Edmund Percival
New Zealand explorer
Born: Auckland, New Zealand,
July 20, 1919

Hillary was a beekeeper in his younger days, and during World War II he served in the South Pacific with the New Zealand Air Force.

He began mountain climbing as a hobby. To any mountain climber, the goal of goals is Mount Everest, the highest mountain on earth, and Hillary's eyes eventually fixed upon it.

Almost every spot on the earth's surface had been reached by mid-twentieth century, including the North Pole by Peary [866] and the South Pole by Amundsen [1008] and Scott [971] nearly half a century before. Yet there remained localized spots untrodden by man—the depths of jungles, deserts, and ice sheets, and most spectacularly the peaks of the highest mountains. Six vertical miles was far harder to manage by foot in the 1950s than thousands of horizontal miles.

Hillary took part in the great preparations for an attempt to climb Mount Everest in the early 1950s, and it was this expedition, meticulously arranged, that finally succeeded where others had failed. On May 29, 1953, Hillary and a native guide finally made it and stood on the highest bit of land anywhere on the face of the globe. For this feat he was knighted later in the year. Although there remain mountains that still have not been scaled, the conquest of Everest makes it certain that the rest require only time and the necessary effort.

In 1960, when Piccard's [1092] bathyscaphe penetrated the deepest known abyss of the ocean, there remained no extreme on earth's surface that had not felt the presence of man. Outer space itself was the new frontier and soon Gagarin [1502] was to make man's presence felt there, too.

During the course of the International Geophysical Year (1957–58), Hillary contributed another feat, almost as dramatic. The exploration of Antarctica was a prime target of the IGY, and Hillary was one of the leaders of the expedition that for the first time in history crossed by land the entire Antarctic continent from sea to sea. Hillary reached the South Pole on January 4, 1958, the first to reach it by land since Amundsen and Scott. In 1960 Hillary began a search for the "abominable snowman," a manlike creature reputed to haunt the Himalayan heights. He failed to find one.

[1433] **BONDI,** Sir Hermann
Austrian-British mathematician
Born: Vienna, November 1, 1919

Bondi left Austria after the Nazi occupation made life intolerable and went to Great Britain, where he remained thereafter, obtaining his master's degree from Cambridge University in 1944.

He is best known for his work on the steady-state ("continuous creation") theory of the universe in conjunction with Hoyle [1398] and Gold [1437], though he has also done important work on general relativity. He was knighted in 1973.

[1434] **COWAN,** Clyde Lorrain
American physicist
Born: Detroit, Michigan, December 6, 1919

Cowan obtained his Ph.D. at Washington University in 1949, after having served as a captain in the air force during World War II. In 1948 he joined the faculty of Catholic University in Washington, D.C.

He is best known for his collaboration with Reines [1423] in the detection of the neutrino in 1956.

[1435] **LIPSCOMB,** William Nunn, Jr.
American chemist
Born: Cleveland, Ohio, December 9, 1919

Lipscomb attended the University of Kentucky, graduating in 1941, then went on to California Institute of Technology, where, working under Pauling [1236] he obtained his Ph.D. in 1946. That year he joined the faculty of the University of Minnesota, going on to Harvard University in 1959.

He was particularly interested in boranes, the compounds of boron and hydrogen, which Stock [1043] had introduced to chemical thinking a half century before. Lipscomb made use of the X-ray diffraction techniques that Pauling had used, as well as Pauling's theory of resonance, and tackled the complex cage-like structures of the boranes. The difficulty lay in the fact that there were two few electrons to allow the conventional theories of electron-bonding to work. Lipscomb, however, showed that two electrons, ordinarily thought of as binding two atoms together, could bind three atoms under appropriate conditions. This not only explained the borane structure but served to indicate the possibility of a whole class of new compounds.

For this work, Lipscomb was awarded the 1976 Nobel Prize for chemistry.

[1436] **BLOEMBERGEN,** Nicolaas
(bloom'ber-gen)
Dutch-American physicist
Born: Dordrecht, Netherlands, March 11, 1920

Bloembergen was educated at the University of Utrecht, attaining his master's degree in 1943. Those were hard times and in that year the occupying Nazis shut down the Dutch universities. It was not till after the war that he could continue and he got his Ph.D. in 1948.

By then, he had already done some studying at Harvard University and in 1952 he undertook permanent residency in the United States, qualifying for citizenship in 1958. He has been on the Harvard faculty since 1951.

Bloembergen grew interested in the maser developed by Townes [1400]. The first masers discharged their stored energy in a quick emission and then there was a pause while sufficient energy was stored for a second one. Discharge was intermittent. Bloembergen, in 1956, designed a maser in which energy was on three levels rather than two, so that one of the upper levels could be storing while another was emitting. In this way, he designed the first continuous maser.

[1437] **GOLD,** Thomas
Austrian-British-American astronomer
Born: Vienna, Austria, May 22, 1920

Gold was one of those who fled from Hitler-dominated Central Europe while there was yet time. As in so many other cases, this was a loss for the Germans and a gain for the West. Gold settled in England for two decades, attending Cambridge University, from which he graduated in 1942 and where he obtained his master's degree in 1945. In 1956 he went to the United States and after a year at Harvard University accepted a professorial position at Cornell University.

Gold's chief fame is in cosmology, that branch of astronomy that deals with the overall structure of the universe. Thanks to the work of Hubble [1136], man's vision had expanded beyond the Milky Way into a vast space of countless galaxies. Some of these were bound together (at least temporarily) in clusters, but in the large view the galaxies and galactic clusters were moving away from each other, the relative velocity of one galaxy with reference to another being proportional to the distance between them. This was the "expanding universe" for which justification could be found in the equations of Einstein's [1064] general theory of relativity.

In order to interpret the structure of the universe, astronomers make use of what is called the cosmological principle, which says in effect that in the very large view the universe is homogeneous; viewed from any point, the vista of the galaxies would be just as it seems viewed from our special point on earth. (If this principle is not accepted, then everything we see might be interpreted as a purely local condition, and we could draw no conclusions about the universe as a whole. There would, in short, be no cosmology.)

It seemed to a few astronomers including, notably, Gold, that the cosmological principle ought to hold in time as well as in space; not only ought the universe to seem the same from any point in space,

but also at any time in the past or future. But the concept of the expanding universe seemed to preclude that, since in the past, the galaxies would have had to be closer together and in the future will have to be farther apart.

In 1948 Gold and others suggested that as the galaxies separated, new matter slowly formed in the vast reaches of space between them. By the time the distance between two neighboring galaxies had doubled, enough matter had formed between them to make up a new galaxy, so that the density with which galaxies filled space remained unchanged. Furthermore, this did not increase the total number of galaxies, for the farther a galaxy receded from a given reference point (say, ourselves), the faster it moved, until it reached the speed of light and we could no longer see it. It had, effectively, moved out of our universe. In this way, old galaxies moved out of the universe and new galaxies were born, but the overall picture did not change with time.

This "steady state" universe implies continuous creation, for matter (presumably in the form of hydrogen atoms) must be created continuously out of nothing to make it work. The rate at which this takes place is far too small to detect, for in order to form new galaxies at a rate just sufficient to make up for the recession of the old ones, it has been calculated that not more than five hundred atoms of hydrogen need be formed in every cubic kilometer of space per year. At this rate the total quantity of matter formed in the volume occupied by the planet earth during its entire five-billion-year period of existence would amount to not more than a seventh of an ounce.

The continuous creation theory has been publicized most ardently by Hoyle [1398] and has been opposed most intransigently by Gamow [1278], who supports the big bang theory of Lamaître [1174] and pictures a universe of galaxies steadily moving apart under the impact of the initial explosion, like an expanding wisp of gas, and nothing more.

The continuous creation theory implies a violation of the laws of thermodynamics, for matter (and therefore energy) is created out of nothing, while the overall entropy of the universe does not increase, as a century of physicists since Clausius [633] have maintained, but remains constant. However, the laws of thermodynamics are not deduced from first principles but are merely abstractions from human experience and human experience is confined to a small section of the universe indeed. The laws of thermodynamics might well, therefore, not apply to the universe as a whole.

There are ways of testing these competing cosmological theories. In continuous creation there are old galaxies and young galaxies with, perhaps, different properties, while in the big bang, all galaxies are of the same age. In continuous creation the universe expands at a constant rate—unchanging with the passage of time. Therefore the velocity of galactic recession increases smoothly with distance, and even the most distant galaxies would behave as expected from the studies of nearby galaxies. In the big bang theory, the expansion of the universe is fading off with time as the impetus of that first explosion diminishes. This means that the galaxies close to us are receding as one might expect, but as one considers galaxies farther and farther away, one is staring at light that originated longer and longer ago in the past, when the universe was expanding more rapidly than it is today. Therefore, distant galaxies would seem to be receding more rapidly than one would expect from studies of nearby galaxies. The more distant the galaxy the greater the discrepancy.

Such distinctions are so fine that, based on those alone, there might be no clear-cut distinction one way or the other. However, the discovery of quasars through the work of Schmidt [1488], and the microwave background by Penzias [1501] and Wilson [1506], have all but wiped out the possibility that the universe can be "steady state." Even the notion of perpetual expansion embodied in the steady-state universe is called into question by the possibility that the neutrino has mass, as Reines [1423] has suggested.

On a less cosmic note, however, Gold has scored a distinct victory. When Hewish [1463] discovered pulsars, it was Gold who in the early 1970s suggested they were neutron stars and pointed out that in that case their rate of pulsation should be slowing at a slow but measurable rate. Measurements proved Gold to be precisely right in this, and the neutron-star interpretation of pulsars was accepted.

[1438] **JACOB,** François (zhah-kohb′)
French biologist
Born: Nancy, Meurthe-et-Moselle, June 17, 1920

Jacob's education was interrupted by World War II, during which he served with the Free French forces from 1940 to 1945. He was badly wounded, has a 90 percent disability pension, and was decorated with the Croix de Guerre.

After the war he resumed his medical studies and got his M.D. at the University of Paris in 1947 and an Sc.D. in 1954. In 1950 he joined the Pasteur Institute where he was associated with Lwoff [1253] and Monod [1347], and for work done on regulatory gene action, shared with them the 1965 Nobel Prize for medicine and physiology.

Jacob and Monod proposed the existence of the "messenger-RNA" that served to carry the DNA blueprint from the nucleus to Palade's [1380] ribosomes, which were the cytoplasmic site of protein formation.

[1439] **CHAMBERLAIN,** Owen
American physicist
Born: San Francisco, California, July 10, 1920

Chamberlain, the son of a radiologist, attended Dartmouth College, graduating in 1941 and worked on the atom bomb project from 1942 to 1946. He obtained his Ph.D. at the University of Chicago in 1949, working under Fermi [1243], then joined the faculty of the University of California, becoming professor of physics in 1958.

There he collaborated with Segrè [1287] in the detection of the antiproton. For this he shared the 1959 Nobel Prize in physics with Segrè.

[1440] **FRANKLIN,** Rosalind Elsie
English physical chemist
Born: London, July 25, 1920
Died: London, April 16, 1958

Franklin, born of a banking family, graduated from Cambridge University in 1941, and then worked with Norrish [1206] on chromatographic techniques. Between 1947 and 1950 she worked at a laboratory in Paris where she learned X-ray diffraction techniques, and in 1951 she began to work on DNA under Wilkins [1413].

She made careful X-ray diffraction photographs of DNA under different conditions of humidity and saw that they were consistent with a helical form of the molecule. What's more, she recognized that the phosphate groups must be on the outside of the helix.

Nevertheless, her native caution caused her to progress slowly and she remained doubtful DNA would actually take up a helical form under all conditions, assuming that a helix was a special case under special conditions.

However, when Watson [1480] saw her X-ray diffraction photographs, through the help of Wilkins and apparently without the consent of Franklin, he and Crick [1406] saw in them all the confirmation they needed for their own double-helix structure of the DNA molecule.

Franklin went on to work with tobacco mosaic virus and to show the manner in which the nucleic acid molecule existed inside a helical array of repeated protein units on the outside.

She died early of cancer, four years before Watson, Crick, and Wilkins were awarded a Nobel Prize. Her own contribution to the double-helix structure of nucleic acids has been consistently underestimated and some blame it on the anti-woman prejudices of the English scientific establishment.

[1441] **MITCHELL,** Peter Dennis
English chemist
Born: Mitcham, Surrey, September 29, 1920

Mitchell obtained his Ph.D. at Cambridge University in 1950. His professional labors have involved themselves with a careful study of the mitochondrion, which is the energy-handling organelle of the cell. It contains a number of enzymes that pass hydrogen ions from one compound to another, with the energy developed serving to convert adenosine diphosphate into adenosine triphosphate. Mitchell showed the manner in which the enzymes involved were fixed to the membrane of the mitochondrion in such a way that they acted as an efficient bucket brigade for hydrogen ions. For his work, he received the 1978 Nobel Prize for chemistry.

[1442] **BENACERRAF,** Baruj (ben-uh-cer'af)
Venezuelan-American geneticist
Born: Caracas, Venezuela, October 29, 1920

Benacerraf went to the United States in 1939 and was naturalized in 1943. He received his M.D. from the Medical College of Virginia in 1945. In 1956 he joined the faculty at the Medical School of New York University and worked with Edelman [1486] on the structure of antibodies.

Benacerraf felt that it was important to obtain purer antibodies and he tried to obtain these by subjecting experimental animals to synthetic antigens. The animal would then produce an antibody to that antigen alone. In doing this, Benacerraf discovered that the response of the animal varied with its genetic strain, and located genes that controlled those responses. This proved valuable in the study of autoimmune diseases, that is, those in which an organism (including human beings) produces antibodies that attack the body's own tissue, a kind of suicide attempt at the molecular level.

For his work, Benacerraf received a

share of the 1980 Nobel Prize for physiology and medicine.

[1443] PORTER, George
English chemist
Born: Stainforth, Yorkshire, December 6, 1920

Porter studied at the University of Leeds, then served as a naval radar officer during World War II. He went on to Cambridge after the war, where he earned his Ph.D.

At Cambridge, during the early 1950s, Porter was a faculty member of the department of physical chemistry, which was headed by Norrish [1206]. Together they worked on ultra-fast chemical reactions, which earned the two, together with Eigen [1477], shares in the 1967 Nobel Prize in chemistry.

In 1955 Porter took a position with the University of Sheffield and in 1964 with the Royal Institution in London.

[1444] SAKHAROV, Andrey Dmitriyevich
Soviet physicist
Born: Moscow, May 21, 1921

Sakharov, the son of a physicist, himself entered the field, obtaining his Ph.D. in 1947. He worked on the hydrogen bomb, fulfilling the role in the Soviet Union that Teller [1332] had in the United States.

Sakharov then went on, however, to take up the role of Oppenheimer [1280] and began to fear the consequences of nuclear weaponry. He opposed atmospheric testing of nuclear bombs and in 1968 spoke out forcefully in favor of nuclear arms reduction. In other ways he showed himself at odds with Communist orthodoxy and began to favor greater tolerance of political dissent. He himself became the Soviet Union's most forceful and fearless dissenter since he was relatively immune because of his great services to the nation and because of his fame abroad.

He was awarded the 1975 Nobel Prize

for peace, which displeased Soviet hardliners as much as Pauling's [1236] award of that prize a dozen years before had displeased American hard-liners. The Soviet Union went further, however, and taking a leaf out of Hitler's book, refused to allow Sakharov permission to go to Oslo to accept the prize. Since then he has been harassed in other ways and has been isolated and placed under a kind of house imprisonment in a provincial city.

[1445] WILKINSON, Sir Geoffrey
English chemist
Born: England, July 14, 1921

Wilkinson received his Ph.D. at the University of London, and was teaching at Harvard University in 1951 when he grew interested in ferrocene. Working independently of E. O. Fischer [1429] he showed that ferrocene was a "sandwich compound" with an iron atom between two parallel carbon rings. For this he shared with Fischer the 1973 Nobel Prize in chemistry.

In 1955 Wilkinson returned to the University of London and assumed a faculty position there. He was knighted in 1976.

[1446] YALOW, Rosalyn Sussman
American biophysicist
Born: Bronx, New York, July 19, 1921

Yalow graduated from Hunter College, New York City, in 1941 and received her Ph.D. from the University of Illinois in 1945. The next year she received a professorial appointment at Hunter and in 1950 initiated a long-term association with the Veterans Administration Hospital in the Bronx.

Yalow, with her colleague Solomon Berson (who died in 1972), worked out the technique of "radioimmunoassay," which can locate antibodies and other biologically active substances that are present in the body in quantities so minute that they are detectable in no other way. This is done by making use of a substance that would combine with the biologically active material in question, where the substance contains a radioactive item. An excessively minute amount of combination takes place but the radioactive atom can nevertheless be detected and the extent of combination thus determined. This greatly increased the delicacy with which numerous significant tests can be conducted for purposes of medical diagnosis and in the course of medical treatment. For her work, Yalow shared in the 1977 Nobel Prize for physiology and medicine.

[1447] **HOAGLAND,** Mahlon Bush
American biochemist
Born: Boston, Massachusetts, October 5, 1921

Hoagland obtained his medical degree at Harvard University Medical School in 1948 and is now in the department of bacteriology in that school. Hoagland is one of many who, in the late 1950s, studied how nucleic acids bring about the formation of protein molecules.

Since the DNA of the chromosomes always remains in the nucleus and proteins are formed in the cytoplasm, there must be an intermediary, and the logical candidate is another variety of nucleic acid, ribonucleic acid (RNA), which is found in both nucleus and cytoplasm. RNA was found to make up Palade's [1380] ribosomes, on which the protein molecule is constructed.

The DNA molecules of the chromosomes carry the genetic code in the particular pattern of nitrogenous bases (adenine, guanine, cytosine, and thymine, usually referred to by the abbreviations A, G, C, and T) that make up the molecule. Each triple combination or triplet, such as AGC, or GGT, represents, it is thought, a specific amino acid. This code is transferred to an RNA molecule (messenger-RNA), as suggested by Jacob [1438] and Monod [1347], which travels into the cytoplasm and joins a ribosome.

Hoagland was able to locate a variety of small RNA molecules (transfer-RNA) in the cytoplasmic fluid, each of which had the ability to combine with one specific amino acid and no other. Each molecule of transfer-RNA had as part of its structure a characteristic triplet that joined to a complementary triplet on the messenger-RNA after the fashion first suggested by Crick [1406] and James Dewey Watson [1480]. Since each transfer-RNA clicked into a specific place with a specific amino acid attached, a protein molecule was built up, amino acid by amino acid, according to the design that originally existed in the DNA molecules of the chromosome.

In this fashion the chromosomes of a particular cell produce a particular battery of enzymes (all protein molecules, of course) that guide the chemistry of that cell and, in the long run, produce all the physical characteristics studied by geneticists. The actual identification of a particular triplet with a particular amino acid (the heart of the problem of the genetic code) was accomplished by 1961 through the work of Nirenberg [1476].

[1448] **KHORANA,** Har Gobind
Indian-American chemist
Born: Raipur, India, January 9, 1922

Khorana's education was an exercise in globe-trotting. He obtained his bachelor's degree (1943) and his master's (1945) at the University of Punjab in India, then went to England for his doctorate, which he gained in 1948 at the University of Liverpool. For postdoctoral work he went to Switzerland, then taught in British Columbia, Canada, and finally joined the faculty of the University of Wisconsin in 1960. He is now a naturalized American citizen.

Khorana had worked early in his career with Todd [1331] and later became interested in the matter of the genetic code. Nirenberg [1476] had made the first dent in that and Khorana went on from there, introducing new techniques of comparing DNA of known structure with the RNA it would produce and showing that the separate nucleotide triplets, which were the "letters" of the code, did not overlap.

Independently of each other, he and Nirenberg worked out almost the entire genetic code and the two shared, along with Holley [1449], the 1968 Nobel Prize for medicine and physiology.

[1449] **HOLLEY,** Robert William
American chemist
Born: Urbana, Illinois, January 28, 1922

Holley graduated from the University of Illinois in 1942 and went on to obtain his doctorate at Cornell University in 1947. During World War II he worked at Cornell Medical School on the project that involved the synthesis of penicillin. In 1948 he took a post with the New York State Agricultural Experiment Station at Geneva, and by 1964 was a professor of biochemistry at Cornell.

Interested in the mechanism of the formation of proteins by nucleic acids, he set about trying to work out the structure of naturally occurring nucleic acids by methods similar to those of Sanger [1426] on proteins. The smallest of the natural nucleic acid molecules were the various transfer-RNA units. By 1962 he had produced highly purified preparations of three varieties of these and in March 1965 he had worked out the complete structure of one of them.

From this he shared with Nirenberg [1476] and Khorana [1448] the 1968 Nobel Prize for medicine and physiology.

[1450] **BOHR,** Aage Niels
Danish physicist
Born: Copenhagen, Denmark, June 19, 1922

Bohr is the son of Niels Bohr [1101]. He worked with his father on the atomic bomb project during World War II and obtained his Ph.D. at the University of Copenhagen. He gained a professorial position there in 1956 and on his father's death in 1962 took over the directorship of the Bohr Institute in Copenhagen, a position he held till 1970.

In 1951 he and his associate, Mottel-

son [1471], worked out the mathematical details of nuclear structure in accordance with a theory of Rainwater [1420] by which the atomic nucleus was not necessarily spherical. The possibility of an asymmetric nucleus, depending on the motions of the protons and neutrons within it, allowed a better understanding of such matters as controlled nuclear fusion and gained Bohr, Mottelson, and Rainwater equal shares in the 1975 Nobel Prize for physics.

[1451] **YANG,** Chen Ning
Chinese-American physicist
Born: Hofei, China, September 22, 1922

In 1929 Yang's family (his father was a mathematician) moved to Peiping, but in later years had to move again to stay out of the way of the Japanese invaders.

Like Lee [1473], Yang studied at the National Southwest Associated University. He obtained his master's degree in 1944 and in 1945 went to the United States on a scholarship. He was anxious to study under Fermi [1243] and went to Columbia University for the purpose. Finding that Fermi had moved on to the University of Chicago, Yang did so also and obtained his Ph.D. there, under Fermi, in 1948. Yang then went to the Institute of Advanced Studies and, unlike Lee, remained there, becoming a professor in 1955. He, with Lee, disproved the necessary existence of parity conservation and shared with him the 1957 Nobel Prize in physics.

In 1965, Yang became professor of physics at the State University of New York at Stony Brook.

[1452] **BARNARD,** Christiaan Neethling
South African surgeon
Born: Beaufort, Cape Province, November 8, 1922

Barnard obtained his medical degree at the University of Capetown in 1946.

His climb to world prominence came very suddenly on December 3, 1967,

877

when he performed the first successful heart transplant in history. It proved also the most enduring, for his patient lived on for a year and a half, much longer than any of the other heart recipients who benefited by repetitions of the operation all over the world, once Barnard had shown the way.

Despite the flash of popularity that heart transplants underwent, they, like Moniz' [1032] prefrontal lobotomy, faded away as the benefits seemed dubious and the ethical problems enormous. It seems rather likely that the future lies with artificial hearts rather than with transplanted ones.

[1453] **BASOV**, Nikolai Gennadievich
Soviet physicist
Born: Leningrad, December 14, 1922

Basov graduated from the Moscow Engineering and Physics Institute in 1950 and in 1956 obtained his doctorate. He works at the Lebedev Institute, where he has been deputy director since 1958.

He and Prokhorov [1409], for their work on the theoretical basis of the maser, shared the 1964 Nobel Prize for physics with Townes [1400].

[1454] **FITCH**, Val Logsden
American physicist
Born: Merriman, Nebraska, March 10, 1923

Fitch planned a chemical career at first, but while in the army during World War II he was sent to Los Alamos to work on the nuclear bomb project, and that focused his interest on physics. After the war he went to McGill University, graduating in 1948, and then took his Ph.D. at Columbia University in 1954. He joined the faculty of Princeton University in that year and became a professor of physics in 1960.

He collaborated with Cronin [1497] in the study of the decay of neutral K-mesons that demonstrated the violation

of CP symmetry and, as a result, he and Cronin shared the 1980 Nobel Prize for physics.

[1455] **FRANKLIN**, Kenneth Linn
American astronomer
Born: Alameda, California, March 25, 1923

Franklin obtained his Ph.D. at the University of California in Berkeley in 1953. He has been with the Hayden Planetarium in New York since 1956. He is best known for his discovery, in early 1955, that the planet Jupiter is a radio wave source. Since then Jupiter probes have indeed shown that surrounding Jupiter is an immense magnetic field and that from it and from Jupiter's turbulent atmosphere radio-wave radiation can and does originate.

[1456] **GAJDUSEK**, Daniel Carleton
American physician
Born: Yonkers, New York, September 9, 1923

Gajdusek's parents were Hungarian immigrants. He graduated from the University of Rochester *summa cum laude* in 1943 and earned his M.D. from Harvard University in 1946. After postdoctorate work at California Institute of Technology, he became a globe-trotter, spending time in Teheran, Iran, and in Australia.

In Australia, in 1955, he learned of a tribe in New Guinea that suffered from a usually fatal disease called kuru that seemed peculiar to them. Upon investigation, he decided it might be an infectious neurological disease that tribesmen caught because there was a ritualistic eating of human brains as part of the funeral rites for those who died.

One puzzling fact was that the infection did not show up, sometimes, for years. Gajdusek implanted filtered brain material from kuru victims into healthy chimpanzees and found that symptoms did not appear for months. The conclusion was finally reached that kuru was caused by a slow-acting virus, and similar viruses may be responsible for other diseases such as multiple sclerosis and Parkinson's disease. In short, a new classification of infectious disease was uncovered and for his work Gajdusek received a share in the 1976 Nobel Prize for physiology and medicine.

[1457] PONNAMPERUMA, Cyril (pon-am-per-u'ma)
Sri Lankese-American biochemist
Born: Galle, Sri Lanka, October 16, 1923

Educated first in India, then in England, Ponnamperuma went to the United States in 1959 and finally earned his Ph.D. at the University of California in 1962. He became an American citizen in 1966.

He is one of the most ardent investigators into the mechanisms of the primordial origin of life after the fashion of S. L. Miller [1490]. He has concentrated on producing compounds related to the nucleic acids, and has shown that nucleotides and dinucleotides can be formed by random processes alone. He has also demonstrated the formation of ATP, a related compound essential to the handling of energy within the cell. Once ATP is formed through the ultimate agency of solar energy, it could be used as the immediate source of energy by the developing living molecules.

[1458] ANDERSON, Philip Warren
American physicist
Born: Indianapolis, Indiana, December 13, 1923

Anderson received his Ph.D. at Harvard University in 1949, after having Van Vleck [1219] as one of his teachers. As a visiting professor in Cambridge University, he worked with Mott [1294] on the properties of semiconductors. He also worked on superconductivity, extending the theories of Bardeen [1334] to include the effects introduced by the presence of impurities in superconducting materials. For his work, he shared

the 1977 Nobel Prize for physics with Van Vleck and Mott.

[1459] DYSON, Freeman John
English-American physicist
Born: Crowthorne, England, December 15, 1923

Dyson graduated from Cambridge University in 1945, went to the United States in 1951, and became an American citizen in 1957. He taught first at Cornell University and then in 1953 moved on to the Institute for Advanced Study at Princeton, New Jersey.

He did important work on the theory of quantum electrodynamics but he is best known for his imaginative speculations on the possibility of extraterrestrial civilizations. He points out, for instance, that an advanced civilization might build absorbing structures in a globular sphere about a star to catch all its radiation, making use of it and then discarding it as degraded heat into interstellar space. For that reason, an ordinary star that dimmed in the visible light range and became an infrared star in a very brief period on the astronomic scale would surely indicate the presence of an advanced civilization in its planetary system.

[1460] GUILLEMIN, Roger (geel-man')
French-American physiologist
Born: Dijon, France, January 11, 1924

Guillemin obtained his M.D. at Lyon in 1949 and his Ph.D. in physiology at Montreal in 1953. In that year he went to the United States to initiate a long connection with Baylor College of Medicine in Houston, Texas, and he became an American citizen in 1963.

Guillemin, with his co-worker Schally [1474], worked on the problem of whether the pituitary gland, which governs the activity of many other glands, is itself controlled by substances produced by the hypothalamus, a section of the brain.

When Schally left Baylor in 1962,

both kept on working on the problem, and in 1968 and 1969 they succeeded and isolated the pituitary-affecting substance. It turned out to be a fairly simple molecule present in excessively small quantities in the body itself. It can be used in the treatment of pituitary disorders.

As a result, Guillemin and Schally shared the 1977 Nobel Prize for physiology and medicine with Yalow [1446].

[1461] **CORMACK,** Allan MacLeod
South African–American physicist
Born: Johannesburg, South
Africa, February 23, 1924

Cormack intended to be an astronomer at first and obtained his master's degree at the University of Capetown in 1945 with that end in view. He went to Cambridge University for two more years of study and then returned to Capetown, where he found himself involved with medical physics.

There he was struck by the inadequacy of ordinary X-ray pictures of an essentially globular object such as the skull. A two-dimension photograph is obtained with no three-dimensional resolution. For that a number of different photographs from different angles must be taken and even then the results are meager.

He devised a "computerized axial tomography (CAT) scanner" in which short pulses of radiation are sent out as the emitter rotates about the patient's head (or other part of the body). These are received by electronic detectors, rather than photographic plates, which also rotate. The results are analyzed by computer to give a three-dimensional picture of the object being studied. The CAT scanner has greatly increased the accuracy of diagnosis of disorders of the brain and other organs since it was introduced in 1973, its only disadvantage being the great expense of producing and using the instrument.

The instrument was designed and worked out after Cormack had gone to the United States in 1956 (where he eventually joined the physics faculty at

Tufts University in Massachusetts, and where he became an American citizen in 1966).

For his work on the CAT scanner, Cormack received a share of the 1979 Nobel Prize for physiology and medicine.

[1462] **HEEZEN,** Bruce Charles
American oceanographer and geologist
Born: Vinton, Iowa, April 11, 1924
Died: near Reykjanes, Iceland, June 21, 1977

Having graduated from the State University of Iowa in 1948, Heezen went on to Columbia University where he earned his Ph.D. in 1957. He led the more-or-less glamorous life of an oceanographer, sailing across the oceans of the world in an attempt to learn more about them and about the land that lies beneath them.

In collaboration with Ewing [1303], he produced a picture of a rugged sea-floor as mountainous as the dry land, or more so. He discovered the Mid-Oceanic Ridge, a gigantic mountain chain that girdles the world, underlying the various oceans. The best-known portion is the Mid-Atlantic Ridge, which curves down the length of the Atlantic.

[1463] **HEWISH,** Antony
English astronomer
Born: Fowey, Cornwall, May 11, 1924

Hewish was educated at Cambridge University and after World War II returned there to work with Ryle [1428].

In 1967 Hewish made use of 2,048 separate radio-receiving devices spread out over an area of 18,000 square meters, which were designed to catch rapid changes in radio-emission intensities on the part of stellar radio sources.

In July 1967 observations began and within a month a young graduate student, Jocelyn Bell, noted bursts of radio-wave radiation from a place midway between the stars Vega and Altair—bursts at much smaller intervals and much more regular than had been expected.

Hewish investigated matters, reported the details in February 1968, and called it a "pulsating star," or "pulsar" for short. He had checked other observations carried through earlier and had by then located three other pulsars. Soon they were being discovered by the dozens.

Gold [1437] suggested they were rapidly rotating neutron stars not more than 8 kilometers across or so, but as massive as the sun, and that, if so, the rotation should be slowing and the pulses coming at lengthening intervals at a predicted rate. Observations showed Gold to be correct.

For the discovery, Hewish shared with Ryle the 1974 Nobel Prize for physics.

[1464] **ESAKI, Leo**
Japanese physicist
Born: Osaka, March 12, 1925

Esaki, an architect's son, attended the University of Tokyo, graduating in 1947. It had been his hope to do research in nuclear physics, but Japan at the time was just rising out of the devastation it had brought upon itself in World War II, and it lacked the necessary particle accelerators that, beginning with the work of Lawrence [1241], had become essential to the field.

By default, Esaki entered the field of solid-state physics which had suddenly sprung to new life, thanks to the work of Shockley [1348]. Working with tiny crystal rectifiers (semiconductor diodes) he found that there were occasions when the resistance decreased with current intensity, instead of increasing as was expected. This was caused by a "tunnel effect," an ability on the part of electrons to penetrate barriers that were perhaps a hundred atoms thick. The barrier-crossing electrons can be put to use for switching purposes and Esaki tunnel diodes were ultra-small and ultra-fast.

This discovery, made in 1957, was advanced by Esaki in his Ph.D. thesis, a degree he earned at Tokyo University in 1959. In that year, Esaki went to the United States and took a position with International Business Machines. For his discovery, he received a share of the 1973 Nobel Prize in physics.

[1465] **NE'EMAN, Yuval**
Israeli physicist
Born: Tel-Aviv, May 14, 1925

Ne'eman graduated from the Israel Institute of Technology in 1945 and thereafter was caught up in the postwar Jewish rebellion against British forces in Palestine. He eventually rose to the rank of colonel in the Israeli army.

After Israel won its independence, Ne'eman eventually found time to complete his education. He went on to study in France and finally to earn a Ph.D. at the University of London in 1962 (he was at that time serving as military attaché to the Israeli Embassy in that city).

It was in 1961, while still in London, that, almost simultaneously with Gell-Mann [1487] (and independently), he worked out a method of grouping baryons in such a way as to show that they fell, quite logically, into families.

Since 1963 Ne'eman has been head of the physics department at Tel-Aviv University.

[1466] **LEDERBERG, Joshua**
American geneticist
Born: Montclair, New Jersey,
May 23, 1925

Lederberg graduated from Columbia College in 1944 and went on to do postgraduate work at Yale University during Tatum's [1346] three years on the faculty there. Lederberg obtained his Ph.D. in 1947.

He, with Tatum, showed that different strains of bacteria could be crossed in such a way as to make the genetic material intermingle. In short, bacteria were capable of sexual reproduction. This greatly expanded the type of genetic work that could be performed with bacteria and earned for Lederberg a share of the 1958 Nobel Prize in medicine and physiology.

In 1952 Lederberg showed that bacteriophage virus particles could transfer genetic material from bacterium to bacterium. This phenomenon he named transduction. He taught at the University of Wisconsin from 1947 to 1954, then accepted a post as professor of genetics at Stanford University.

[1467] **BLUMBERG,** Baruch Samuel
American physician
Born: New York, New York, July 28, 1925

Blumberg received his M.D. from Columbia University in 1951, then went on to obtain a Ph.D. at Oxford University in 1957. Later he joined the faculty of the University of Pennsylvania.

He has spent time working in various far-flung portions of the world and grew interested in the manner in which certain disorders seemed to be confined more or less to certain ethnic groups. Studying these special disorders, he discovered a protein in the blood of Australian Aborigines that resembled one found in those suffering from hepatitis. He recognized the protein as part of a virus that caused hepatitis infection. He developed a method for detecting the protein and this gave biochemists a way of checking blood being used for transfusion and cutting down the incidence of hepatitis infection caused by the procedure.

For this discovery, Blumberg shared with Gajdusek [1456] the 1976 Nobel Prize for physiology and medicine.

[1468] **SALAM,** Abdus
Pakistani-British physicist
Born: Jhang Maghiana, Pakistan (then part of India), January 29, 1926

Salam was educated at the Government College, Lahore, Pakistan, then went to England where he obtained his Ph.D. from Cambridge University in 1952. Independently of Glashow [1500] and Weinberg [1502], he worked on the theory of weak interactions and on the possibility of producing a mathematical treatment that would describe both them and the electromagnetic interactions. As a result, Salam shared the 1979 Nobel Prize for physics with Glashow and Weinberg.

[1469] **SANDAGE,** Allan Rex
American astronomer
Born: Iowa City, Iowa, June 18, 1926

Sandage graduated from the University of Illinois in 1948 and obtained his Ph.D. at the California Institute of Technology in 1953. He became a member of Mount Wilson and Mount Palomar observatories in 1952. His astrophysical researches have taken him into the far reaches of space and time.

Thus, his investigations of the spectral characteristics of certain globular clusters have led him to maintain that they, and therefore the universe generally, must be no less than 25 billion years old. His studies of very distant objects have caused him to speculate that the universe does not merely expand, but expands and contracts over and over again with a period of perhaps 80 billion years.

Perhaps his most dramatic discovery came in 1963 in connection with galaxy M-82, which was a suspicious object because it was a strong radio source. Sandage photographed it through the 200-inch telescope, using a special filter that would let through light associated with hot hydrogen.

The photograph showed the galaxy to be undergoing an enormous explosion in its core. Jets of hydrogen up to a thousand light-years long were streaming outward in all directions and, apparently, the explosion would have had to be continuing for 1.5 million years. This was a dramatic demonstration in favor of the theoretical work of Ambartzumian [1338].

[1470] **BERG,** Paul
American biochemist
Born: New York, New York, June 30, 1926

Berg obtained his Ph.D. from Western Reserve University (now Case Western Reserve University) in 1952. After two years of postdoctorate work in Copenhagen, he joined the faculty of Washington University in St. Louis in 1955 and in 1959 moved on to Stanford University.

Berg studied methods for cutting the nucleic acid molecules of genes in specific places according to the techniques of Nathans [1482] and Smith [1496] and then of recombining them in different fashion. This initiated the technique of recombinant DNA (DNA standing for "deoxyribonucleic acid"). It meant that new genes and, therefore, new viruses, or new bacteria would be formed in place of the old—new organisms with new properties. It meant that microorganisms might be devised that would synthesize compounds of use to man—such as insulin—or with properties that would be useful—such as being able to live on oil waste, or to concentrate certain minerals from the sea.

It also meant the possibility that microorganisms with new pathogenic abilities might be formed and that animals or humans would be struck with deadly disease which they had no natural immunities to. Berg and others in the field suggested in 1975 that research in recombinant DNA be carefully regulated. Since then, however, the dangers have been found to be exaggerated and some relaxation of controls has taken place.

For his work, Berg won half the 1980 Nobel Prize for chemistry, the other half being shared by Sanger [1426] and Gilbert [1498].

[1471] **MOTTELSON,** Ben Roy
American-Danish physicist
Born: Chicago, Illinois, July 9, 1926

Mottelson obtained his Ph.D. at Harvard University and obtained a fellowship to the Bohr Institute. There he met Aage Bohr [1450] and a strong professional relationship was built up. Mottelson eventually became a Danish citizen and worked with Bohr on the shape of the atomic nucleus, for which he and

Bohr, along with Rainwater [1420], received shares of the 1975 Nobel Prize for physics.

[1472] **GLASER,** Donald Arthur
American physicist
Born: Cleveland, Ohio, September 21, 1926

Glaser graduated from the Case Institute of Technology (now Case Western Reserve University) in Cleveland in 1946 and went on to the California Institute of Technology, where he earned his Ph.D. in 1949. He joined the faculty of the University of Michigan in that year, and moved on to the University of California in 1959.

While at the University of Michigan, Glaser turned his attention to the Wilson [979] cloud chamber. Though useful to nuclear physicists, it did have its flaws, despite the improvements introduced by a generation and a half of physicists. It contained a gas and this is a rarefied form of matter so that any particle passing through it could only form a relatively small number of ions. For that reason, rare or short-lived nuclear events could be missed.

It occurred to Glaser that the situation ought to be reversed. Instead of allowing supercooled vapor to condense about ions, forming drops of liquid in an ocean of gas, as was true in the cloud chamber, one ought to allow superheated liquid to boil about ions, forming drops of gas in an ocean of liquid. (The story goes that he had this revelation while watching bubbles form in a glass of beer.)

In 1952 Glaser constructed his first "bubble chamber," only a few inches in diameter. He used ether as his liquid, but greater efficiency came with lower temperatures and soon he switched to liquid hydrogen. Within a decade, huge bubble chambers, six feet in diameter and containing 150 gallons of liquid hydrogen, were in operation.

Bubble chambers have indeed proved to be far more sensitive than cloud chambers. They are particularly useful for the high-energy particles which, striking more targets per unit distance in liquid than in gas, are more quickly slowed, and form shorter and more highly curved paths that can be studied in their entirety. In 1960 Glaser was awarded the Nobel Prize in physics for this invention and promptly announced that he was shifting his focus of interest from nuclear physics to molecular biology.

[1473] **LEE,** Tsung-Dao
Chinese-American physicist
Born: Shanghai, China, November 24, 1926

Lee studied at the National Southwest Associated University in K'un-ming, China, and in 1946, before receiving his degree, was taken to the United States by a teacher. The University of Chicago would permit an undergraduate to work toward a Ph.D. and no other university would. Lee therefore attended the University of Chicago and, working under Teller [1332], obtained his Ph.D. in 1950.

While at the University, he met his countryman Yang [1451], whom he had known briefly in K'un-ming. Lee went on to work at the University of California. He and Yang met again at the Institute for Advanced Study in Princeton, New Jersey, in 1951; and though Lee went on to Columbia University in 1953, they maintained contact and held weekly meetings.

Together they studied the strange case of the K-mesons (discovered in the early 1950s and included among the "strange particles" with which Gell-Mann [1487] worked), which seemed to break down in two different ways. The difference was such that it was thought two different K-mesons were involved, and yet, except for the breakdown, the K-mesons seemed identical.

It had been thought, ever since Wigner [1260] worked out the mathematics for it in 1927, that something called conservation of parity existed. This was equivalent to saying that the universe made no distinction between right and left. If you stepped into a looking-glass house in which left and right were interchanged, the laws of nature would remain unchanged. You would have no way of detecting which was reality and which was looking glass.

The double breakdown of the K-meson involved this. It was as though one K-meson broke down in a real way, the other in a looking-glass way. If it was the same particle breaking down either way then the conservation of parity did not hold and nature would be able to distinguish right from left.

It finally occurred to Lee and Yang that perhaps there was only one K-meson and perhaps the conservation of parity really didn't hold. If there was a difference between left and right and nature could tell reality from looking glass, then it would be possible to explain the double breakdown. At least perhaps it was so for the special "weak interactions" in which strange particles and neutrinos were involved.

Lee and Yang reached this conclusion in 1956 and within months a friend of theirs (also of Chinese birth) who was an experimental physicist—Lee and Yang were theoreticians—designed and carried through an experiment which showed that, indeed, parity was not conserved in weak interactions.

This broke like a bomb on the world of nuclear physics and men like Pauli [1228], who in his time had proposed, with equal daring, the neutrino, now found it difficult to accept the new development. Nevertheless, the truth of the matter was quickly and amply confirmed and Lee and Yang shared the 1957 Nobel Prize in physics. They were the first scientists of Chinese birth to win a Nobel Prize.

The breakdown of parity conservation has made possible new and better views of the neutrino, for instance. These were advanced by Lee and Yang and also, independently, by Landau [1333].

In 1960 Lee returned to the Institute for Advanced Studies.

In 1963 Lee moved back to Columbia to assume the first Enrico Fermi professorship in physics there.

[1474] **SCHALLY,** Andrew Victor
Polish-American biochemist
Born: Vilna, Poland (now Vil-
nius, Lithuanian SSR), November 30, 1926

Schally's family fled Poland at the
time of the German invasion in 1939,
and Schally eventually studied at the
University of London, graduating in
1949. He went on to Canada, obtaining
his Ph.D. in biochemistry at McGill University in 1957, in which year he went to
the United States, joining Guillemin
[1460] at the Baylor College of Medicine
and working with him on the task of
finding the chemical controls of the pituitary gland and locating additional pituitary hormones. In 1962 he moved on to
the Veterans Administration Hospital in
New Orleans but continued the work.
Success meant a share with Guillemin
and Yalow [1446] in the 1977 Nobel
Prize for physiology and medicine.

[1475] **O'NEILL,** Gerard Kitchen
American physicist
Born: Brooklyn, New York, Feb-
ruary 6, 1927

O'Neill graduated from Swarthmore
College in 1950 and obtained his Ph.D.
from Cornell University in 1954. In that
year he joined the faculty of Princeton
University, where he has remained since.
He has worked with particle physics
for the most part and has developed
storage rings designed to raise two
groups of particles to high energies, then
smash them into a head-on collision for
still higher energies.
He is best known, however, for having
devised and publicized, in the 1970s,
carefully drawn-up plans for the design
and establishment of space structures,
particularly of space settlements for the
housing of tens of thousands of individuals in an Earth-like environment.

[1476] **NIRENBERG,** Marshall Warren
American biochemist
Born: New York, New York,
April 10, 1927

Nirenberg did his undergraduate work
at the University of Florida, graduating
in 1948, then went on to the University
of Michigan where he obtained his Ph.D.
in 1957. After that, he went to the National Institutes of Health.
As the 1960s opened, the outstanding
problem in biochemistry was that of the
genetic code. Crick [1406] and others
had worked out the structure of DNA
and the broad mechanism of the production of proteins was known, too. Each
combination of three nucleotides along
the DNA chain corresponded to a particular amino acid, which was put into
place in a protein chain by means of the
work of messenger-RNA, transfer-RNA,
and ribosomes, as the research of Hoagland [1447] had shown. Now the question was: Which DNA triplet corresponded to which amino acid?
Nirenberg broke through in 1961. He
made use of a synthetic RNA to serve in
the role of messenger-RNA. The synthetic RNA, formed according to the
method of Ochoa [1293], consisted of
but a single nucleotide, uridylic acid, so
that its structure was . . . UUUUUU
. . . The only possible nucleotide triplet
in it was UUU and when it formed a
protein containing the amino acid, phenylalanine, only, it was clear the UUU
corresponded to phenylalanine and the
first item in the "dictionary" was worked
out.
Others joined the hunt at once and new
correlations between triplets and amino
acids were worked out. Before the decade was over the dictionary was complete. In 1968 Nirenberg shared the
Nobel Prize for medicine and physiology
with Khorana [1448] and Holley [1449]
as a result.

[1477] **EIGEN,** Manfred
German physicist
Born: Bochum, Ruhr, May 9,
1927

Eigen, the son of a musician (and no
mean musician himself), studied at the
University of Göttingen. He had barely
reached eighteen on the last day of

World War II, but in its last desperate days, Germany was drafting children and Eigen served briefly with an antiaircraft gun crew. He then returned to Göttingen where he earned his doctorate in 1951.

In 1953 he joined the Max Planck Institute for Physical Chemistry, where he eventually became director.

Like Norrish [1206] and Porter [1443], he studied ultra-short chemical reactions by very briefly disturbing equilibria. Where the former used light flashes impinging on gaseous systems, Eigen used brief changes in temperature, pressure, or electrical fields on liquid systems.

In consequence, Eigen shared, with the other two, the 1967 Nobel Prize in chemistry.

[1478] PARKER, Eugene Newman
American physicist
Born: Houghton, Michigan, June 10, 1927

Parker gained his Ph.D. at California Institute of Technology in 1951. He joined the faculty of the University of Utah in 1951 and moved on to the University of Chicago in 1955.

He worked with the movement of high-energy particles in magnetic fields, particularly in the environment of space, and predicted that charged particles would be emitted by the sun in all directions, following the lines of force of its magnetic field. This prediction, made in 1959, was verified by the Mariner 2 Venus probe in 1962. The phenomenon, now known as the "solar wind," accounts for the manner in which comets' tails point away from the sun, for the existence of charged particles in the magnetic fields of Earth and Jupiter, for certain properties of the moon's surface, and so on.

[1479] MAIMAN, Theodore Harold
American physicist
Born: Los Angeles, California
July 11, 1927

Maiman, the son of an electrical engineer, worked his way through college by repairing electrical appliances. He graduated from the University of Colorado in 1949, then did graduate work at Stanford where he earned his Ph.D. in 1955.

Working at the Hughes Research Laboratories in Miami, Florida, he grew interested in Townes's [1400] maser. Townes had predicted that the maser principle, which was originally designed for microwave (very short radio waves) emission, could, under proper circumstances, be applied to waves even as short as those of visible light.

Maiman set himself the task of accomplishing this, making use of the three-level principle worked out by Bloembergen [1436]. He designed a ruby cylinder with its ends carefully polished flat and parallel, and covered with silver coatings. Energy was fed into it from a flash lamp and in May 1960 it emitted its first flash of light.

The light so emitted was monochromatic (of a single wavelength) and coherent (all the waves in a single direction). Such coherent light could form a beam that would traverse thousands of miles without spreading so far as to become useless, and it could be concentrated into so small a spot as to deliver energy with a temperature equivalent to or much greater than that of the surface of the sun.

This was an example of "light amplification by stimulated emission of radiation"; or, to use its acronym, it was the first "laser."

[1480] WATSON, James Dewey
American biochemist
Born: Chicago, Illinois, April 6, 1928

Watson, a child prodigy and radio "quiz kid," entered the University of Chicago at the age of fifteen and graduated in 1947. He obtained his Ph.D. in 1950 at the University of Indiana. He had intended to work in ornithology, but the presence of Muller [1145] at the school turned his attention toward biochemistry and genetic problems.

After a year at the University of Copenhagen, allowing him to work on the effects of radiation on viruses, he changed his mind and interests. He went to Cambridge University in 1951 to work on what he considered more fundamental problems. His grant was revoked but he forged ahead anyhow.

With Crick [1406] he labored on the structure of DNA, and it was Watson who had the brainstorm of constructing a model with the bases inside and backbone outside, thus making a double helix possible. This fit perfectly with the physical data of Wilkins [1413] and the chemical data of Chargaff [1291]. After his return to the United States, Watson spent two years at the California Institute of Technology, then joined the faculty of Harvard University in 1955. He shared with Crick and Wilkins the 1962 Nobel Prize in medicine and physiology.

In 1968 Watson published a sprightly, informal account of his DNA research entitled *The Double Helix*. It scored quite a success and made his name more famous with the general public than the research itself and the Nobel Prize had succeeded in doing. In that year, he became head of the Laboratory of Quantitative Biology at Cold Spring Harbor, New York.

[1481] **HAWKINS,** Gerald Stanley
English-American astronomer
Born: Norfolk, England, April 20, 1928

Hawkins received his Ph.D. from the University of Manchester in 1952. He went to the United States in 1954 and was naturalized in 1964, working both at Harvard and Boston universities in those years.

He is best known for his book *Stonehenge Decoded,* published in 1965, in which he suggested that Stonehenge performed the function of a prehistoric observatory, keeping track of the movements of the sun and moon, making it possible to sight and predict solstices and lunar eclipses. While Hawkins' views did not go unchallenged, his work initiated a sharp increase in interest in the astro-

nomical observations of prehistoric peoples.

[1482] **NATHANS,** Daniel
American microbiologist
Born: Wilmington, Delaware, October 30, 1928

Nathans received his M.D. from Washington University in 1954 and has been on the faculty of Johns Hopkins University since 1962. He, in collaboration with H. O. Smith [1496], also of Johns Hopkins, studied enzymes that were capable of breaking up the DNA molecule in specific sites. This made it possible to work with known fractions of the nucleic acid that were still large enough to contain genetic information. This work, carried through in 1971, led eventually to recombinant-DNA work in which nucleic acids could be taken apart and put together again in other fashions. As a result, Nathans and Smith shared in the 1978 Nobel Prize for physiology and medicine.

[1483] **MÖSSBAUER,** Rudolf Ludwig
(murss'bow-er)
German physicist
Born: Munich, Bavaria, January 31, 1929

Mössbauer grew up and was educated in Munich, receiving his degrees at the Institute of Technology, including the Ph.D. in 1958. In the same year, he announced what is now known as the Mössbauer effect.

Under ordinary conditions, atoms recoil as they emit gamma rays, and the energy of the gamma ray and therefore its wavelength depend in part on the amount of recoil. The amount of recoil of a light object like an atom is large and varies to a considerable degree from atom to atom. Gamma rays are therefore emitted with a considerable spread in energy and wavelength.

Under particular conditions investigated by Mössbauer, however, a crystal as a whole may take up the recoil. The recoil of this relatively massive body is then vanishingly slight and virtually does not affect the energy of the gamma rays, which are consequently emitted with an exceedingly narrow spread of wavelengths. This is the Mössbauer effect.

Gamma rays of just the wavelength emitted by the atoms of such a crystal will be strongly absorbed by the atoms of another crystal of the same type. If the wavelength alters even slightly, absorption drops considerably.

This proved useful almost at once in connection with the theory of general relativity propounded by Einstein [1064] nearly half a century earlier. The predictions of general relativity had been checked in only three ways (none others being available). There was the advance of Mercury's perihelion, first studied in detail by Leverrier [564]; there was the bending of light measured by Eddington [1085] at the eclipse of 1919; and there was the red shift of the light of a white dwarf star, as measured by W. S. Adams [1045]. All these tests were astronomical in nature and had to be taken as they were found.

Now, making use of the sharply defined gamma rays of the Mössbauer effect, it could be possible for the first time to test the theory of general relativity in the laboratory under conditions that could be varied to suit the experimenter. According to Einstein's theory the wavelength of electromagnetic radiation should increase as a gravitational field was intensified. This should include gamma rays as well as visible light.

The gravitational field was intensified (though only slightly) in the basement of a building as compared with the roof, since the basement was closer to the center of the earth, and that is all that is required. If a beam of gamma rays is shot downward from roof to basement, its wavelength increases by a vanishingly small quantity, to be sure, but sufficient to produce a measurable drop in absorption by the crystal exposed to them.

In 1960 the experiment was performed first in England then in the United States. The loss of absorption indicated a lengthening of wavelength with increase in gravitational intensity just like that predicted by relativity. Einstein's theory

was once more verified and more convincingly than ever before.

In 1961 Mössbauer received the Nobel Prize in physics, sharing it with Hofstadter [1395]. At the time the prize was awarded, Mössbauer was working at the California Institute of Technology, but in 1964 he returned to Munich to take up a post as professor of physics at the Technische Hochschule.

[1484] GIAEVER, Ivar
Norwegian-American physicist
Born: Bergen, Norway, April 5, 1929

Giaever was trained as an electrical engineer in Trondheim and worked as a patent examiner for the Norwegian government. In 1954 he emigrated to Canada, took a job with the General Electric Company, was transferred to Schenectady, New York, and earned his Ph.D. in 1964 at Rensselaer Polytechnic Institute. He became an American citizen in 1963.

He worked on Esaki's [1464] tunneling effect, introducing a new factor by making use of a superconducting metal as well as a normal one. This led not only to a better understanding of tunneling but to some interesting points about superconductivity. As a result, Giaever shared the 1973 Nobel Prize in physics with Esaki and Josephson [1509].

[1485] ARBER, Werner
Swiss microbiologist
Born: Granichen, Aargau, June 3, 1929

Arber was educated at the Swiss Federal Institute of Technology in Zürich, the University of Geneva, and the University of Southern California. From 1960 to 1970 he was on the faculty of the University of Geneva and then moved to the University of Basel, where he is professor of microbiology.

Arber was interested in the phenomenon noted by Luria [1377] to the effect that bacteriophages not only induce mutations in the bacterial cells they infest but undergo mutations themselves. Arber collected evidence to show that bacterial cells could defend themselves against bacteriophage onslaughts through the presence of a "restriction enzyme" that restricted the growth of bacteriophages by splitting the DNA of the bacteriophage and thus rendering it largely or entirely inactive.

By 1968 Arber had gathered enough information about the restriction enzymes to be able to show that a particular enzyme of this sort split only those DNA molecules that contain a certain sequence of nucleotides characteristic of bacteriophages. It was this work, which was extended by Nathans [1482] and Smith [1496], that led on to recombinant-DNA techniques of men such as Berg [1470].

Arber, Nathans, and Smith shared the 1978 Nobel Prize for physiology and medicine.

[1486] **EDELMAN,** Gerald Maurice
American biochemist
Born: New York, New York, July 1, 1929

Edelman obtained his M.D. at the University of Pennsylvania in 1954 and his Ph.D. at Rockefeller University in 1960. He has been associated with Rockefeller University since. His work has centered upon the elucidation of the chemical structure of antibodies and for this he received a share of the 1972 Nobel Prize for physiology and medicine.

[1487] **GELL-MANN,** Murray (gell′-mann)
American physicist
Born: New York, New York, September 15, 1929

Gell-Mann, the son of an Austrian immigrant, entered Yale University in 1944 on his fifteenth birthday. After graduating in 1948 he went on to Massachusetts Institute of Technology and obtained his Ph.D. in 1951. He spent some time at the Institute for Advanced Research and

then in 1952 went to the University of Chicago, where he worked under Fermi [1243].

In 1955 Gell-Mann joined the faculty of the California Institute of Technology and in 1956 (when not yet twenty-seven) was made a full professor.

By now he had plunged into the world of subatomic particles, which in the 1950s had become a jungle. After Chadwick [1150] had discovered the neutron and Heisenberg [1245] had placed it in the atomic nucleus, the question arose as to what held protons and neutrons together. Yukawa [1323] solved that with his meson theory, but too many mesons were discovered. Powell's [1274] pi-meson does the job envisioned by Yukawa, but Anderson's [1292] mu-meson was, and has remained, a mystery. In addition, the 1950s saw the discovery of heavier mesons still, the K-mesons, which were about half the mass of a proton. And particles even heavier than the protons were discovered, the various hyperons, in prolific quantities.

The K-mesons and the hyperons were created by strong interactions and it was thought that they should break down by strong interactions, too. Instead they broke down by weak interactions. The difference lies in this, that although a weak interaction takes place in a fraction of a billionth of a second, that time is, nevertheless, a billion or more times longer than the time required for a strong interaction. In other words a K-meson may endure a trillionth of a second before breaking down, instead of enduring a trillionth of a trillionth of a second. To a nuclear physicist, this seemed strange and so K-mesons and hyperons came to be called "strange particles."

Gell-Mann addressed himself to the problem of determining the reason for the strangeness and in 1953 he (and a Japanese physicist, independently) published his results.

He began with the theory of charge independence. By this view the proton and neutron differ only in the presence of a positive charge on the former and no charge on the latter. If that was ignored the two particles would be indistinguishable. Other particles could similarly be grouped into clusters of two or three, differing among themselves only in the nature of the electrical charge and nothing more. There were reasons for giving each group a charge center, representing a kind of average charge. For instance, the proton has a charge of +1, and the neutron a charge of 0; their charge center is therefore +½.

For the K-mesons and the hyperons, the actual charge center is not where expected; it is displaced. A quantity equal to twice the displacement was named by Gell-Mann the "strangeness number." For neutrons, protons, and pi-mesons, the strangeness number is 0. For the various strange particles, it is never 0. For some, it is +1, for some −1, and for some −2.

This strangeness number is conserved; that is, in any particle interaction, the total strangeness number of the particles before the interaction and the total number of those after the interaction were the same. This conservation could be used to explain the unexpected long life of the strange particles.

This removed one area of puzzlement, or at least lessened it. Another, in the same area of weak interactions, was removed, or at least lessened, by the abolition of parity conservation by Lee [1473] and Yang [1451].

Gell-Mann went on in 1961 to group the many mesons, nucleons, and hyperons (all together named the "hadrons") according to certain fixed rules which he whimsically called the "Eight-Fold Way," with reference to certain Buddhist teachings. Certain particles, of peculiar properties, would be included in such groups and Gell-Mann predicted their existence as once Mendeléev [705] predicted the existence of new elements under similar circumstances. One, in particular, Gell-Mann called an "omega-minus" particle and this was indeed detected in 1964.

To account for his particle families, Gell-Mann postulates unusual particles carrying fractional electric charges (an unheard-of situation till then). He calls them "quarks" from a phrase in *Finnegans Wake* by James Joyce (more whimsy). Quarks are now considered fundamental particles and, in a number of varieties, are in the forefront of the cutting edge of nuclear physics.

[1488] **SCHMIDT,** Maarten
Dutch-American astronomer
Born: Groningen, Netherlands,
December 28, 1929

Schmidt obtained his Ph.D. at the University of Leiden in 1956, later emigrated to the United States. He established himself at the California Institute of Technology and at the Mount Wilson and Mount Palomar observatories in 1959.

In the early 1960s he grew interested in certain radio sources that Sandage [1469] had managed to pinpoint to what looked like individual stars. The spectra of these radio-emitting stars were completely strange. Not only Sandage but Greenstein [1345] too tried to make sense of them and failed.

Then in 1963 it suddenly occurred to Schmidt that the unfamiliarity of the spectra was the result of an enormous red shift and that the lines were familiar ones that ought to be in the ultraviolet section of the spectrum. This turned out to be correct and the enormous red shift indicated the objects to be very distant, a billion light-years away and more.

In that case, they could not be stars but must be objects far more luminous than ordinary galaxies. They were called "quasi-stellar objects"; that is, objects with a star-like appearance; and the phrase was quickly abbreviated to "quasars."

These very distant, very luminous objects pose enormous problems for astronomers since there is no easy way of accounting for their nature.

[1489] **COOPER,** Leon N.
American physicist
Born: New York, New York,
February 28, 1930

Cooper obtained his Ph.D. at Columbia University in 1954, and from 1958 has been on the faculty of Brown University. He collaborated with Bardeen [1334] and Schrieffer [1495] on the development of the currently accepted theory of superconductivity. Part of that theory involves the action of pairs of electrons, which are termed "Cooper electron pairs" in Cooper's honor. Cooper shared with the other two the 1972 Nobel Prize for physics.

[1490] **MILLER,** Stanley Lloyd
American chemist
Born: Oakland, California,
March 7, 1930

Miller obtained his Ph.D. at the University of Chicago in 1954. He worked under Urey [1164], whose attention had turned toward geochemistry, toward the formation of the planets, and toward the deduction of the primordial conditions of the just formed earth. It seemed natural to wonder how life first formed.

For nearly a century it had been assumed that Pasteur [642] had laid to rest forever the bogey of "spontaneous generation," but it had to be remembered that Pasteur had only disproved spontaneous generation under the specialized conditions of his experiment. He kept sterile solutions as long as four years without life developing, but what if he kept it a billion years? And instead of a flask full, what if he had an ocean full of solution? And instead of the air of our atmosphere bathing the solution what if it was the air of a completely different primordial atmosphere?

After all, from the mere fact that we are here, we are forced to assume that once upon a time at least one case of spontaneous generation took place (assuming, further, that one eliminates supernatural creation from consideration).

It was Miller's task to try to duplicate, in a very small. way, the conditions of the primordial earth. Urey thought that the primordial atmosphere on earth was something like Jupiter's today (according to the findings of Wildt [1290]); that is, consisting mainly of hydrogen, with strong admixtures of ammonia and methane. Ammonia would dissolve readily in the primordial ocean and small quantities of methane and ammonia would find their way there, too. The interaction of water, hydrogen, methane and ammonia to form more complicated compounds would require an input of energy, but that was there in the form of solar ultraviolet at the very least.

Later on, the earth would lose the hydrogen it was not massive enough to hold. At a later stage in planetary development, photosynthetic reactions would fill the atmosphere with free oxygen that would form ozone in the upper layers and cut off most of the ultraviolet. At the time that life was first forming, however, there would be no free oxygen and plenty of hydrogen and ultraviolet.

Miller therefore began with carefully purified and sterilized water and added an "atmosphere" of hydrogen, ammonia, and methane. He circulated this through his apparatus past an electric discharge, which represented an energy input that, it was hoped, would mimic the effect of solar ultraviolet. He kept this up for a week then separated the components of his water solution. He found simple organic compounds among those components and even a few of the simpler amino acids. This work was carried further by men like Calvin [1361] and Sagan [1504].

The moral was obvious. The original ocean and atmosphere could have served as source material for a wide variety of organic molecules. In the absence of life, these molecules would not be consumed and broken down again by ravenous cells but would accumulate into a "soup." Slowly these compounds would grow more and more complex until a nucleic acid capable of replication, after the fashion described by Crick [1406] and James Dewey Watson [1480], would be developed. This may seem like asking a good deal of chance. But if in one week, and in one small setup, Miller could get amino acids, how much could be done in a billion years?

Miller is now a professor of chemistry at the University of California.

[1491] **DRAKE,** Frank Donald
American astronomer
Born: Chicago, Illinois, May 28,
1930

Drake obtained his Ph.D. at Harvard University in 1958 and then worked at the National Radio Astronomy Observatory at Green Bank, West Virginia. After a year at the Jet Propulsion Laboratories in Pasadena, California, in 1963, he joined the faculty of Cornell University.

He has carefully studied and analyzed radio signals from space, whether from Jupiter or the galactic center. He is best known, perhaps, for his alertness to the possibility of radio signals that might indicate the existence of civilizations elsewhere than on Earth. He is responsible, along with Sagan [1504], for the plaques carried on Pioneer 10 and Pioneer 11, the Jupiter probes that were launched in 1972 and 1973 and will eventually move out of the solar system and wander endlessly through interstellar space. These plaques contained a drawing of a man and a woman and various pieces of information designed to indicate the source of the plaques—Earth's identity and location in the universe. They are the first artifacts that will ever leave the solar system and it may still be wandering and recognizable long after all the accomplishments of humanity on Earth itself will be gone like a forgotten dream.

[1492] **ARMSTRONG,** Neil Alden
American astronaut
Born: Wapakoneta, Ohio, August 5, 1930

Armstrong has been in the air almost all his adult life. He was a licensed pilot at sixteen and was flying planes in the Korean War when he was twenty. He flew seventy-eight missions and was shot down twice.

After graduating from Purdue University in 1955, he joined NASA and was one of the test pilots of the X-15 rocket plane, flying more than 1,100 hours. He reached heights of 200,000 feet and flew at speeds of 4,000 miles per hour. He also flew the huge B-29 bombers.

In 1962 he became an astronaut and was command pilot of Gemini 8 in March 1966 when he performed the first successful docking of two vehicles in space.

The climax of his life, however, came at 4:18 P.M. Eastern Daylight Time on July 20, 1969, when, as commander of the Apollo 11 spacecraft, he and Edwin Aldrin took the lunar module down to the very surface of the moon near the southwestern edge of the Sea of Tranquillity. Armstrong was then the first human being in history to set foot upon that surface. He said, "That's one small step for a man, one giant leap for mankind."

They remained on the moon for 21 hours, 37 minutes, and splashed down on Earth at 12:51 P.M. Eastern Daylight Time on July 24, eight days after takeoff.

Indeed, as a steppingstone in space exploration, it was the most significant moment since Gagarin's [1502] first orbital flight only eight years before; and in the history of exploration generally, possibly since Columbus' [121] first voyage nearly five centuries earlier.

[1493] **RICHTER,** Burton
American physicist
Born: New York, New York,
March 22, 1931

Richter obtained his Ph.D. at the Massachusetts Institute of Technology, then went on to Stanford University. There he specialized in the high-energy studies of elementary particles. He supervised the building of the world's first pair of electron storage rings in which two streams of high-energy electrons could collide head on, thus doubling the effective energy of collision. In the 1960s he designed the Stanford Positron-Electron Accelerating Ring, which produced head-on collisions of matter and antimatter resulting in a still further escalation of energy.

The use of the energy lay in the new field of quarks. When Gell-Mann [1487] advanced the concept of quarks, two quarks were all that were needed to ex-

plain the existence of neutrons and protons. These were termed "up quarks" and
"down quarks." A third quark, the
"strange quark," was needed to account
for strange particles.

However, as the nature of quarks was
delved into, it seemed they ought to exist
in pairs. If a third quark existed, a
fourth must as well, and it was dubbed
the "charmed quark."

In 1974 Richter, thanks to the enormous energies he had available, produced what he called a "psi particle"
which from its properties had to include
in its makeup a charmed quark. As it
happened, Ting [1507], working at the
Brookhaven National Laboratory on
Long Island, happened upon what he
called a "J particle" independently and
almost simultaneously. It was identical
with the psi particle, and the two discoveries were announced jointly.

As a result Richter and Ting shared
the 1976 Nobel Prize for physics, since
the discoveries offered strong evidence in
favor of the current quark theories.

[1494] **MILLER,** Jacques Francis Al-
bert Pierre
French-Australian physician
Born: Nice, France, April 2, 1931

Miller earned his medical degree, with
top honors, at the University of Sydney.
He taught in England and in the United
States, and in 1966 returned to Australia.

In 1962, while at the University of
London, he demonstrated the importance
of the thymus gland (an organ prominent in young animals and withering
away in adults—and until then without
known function) in organizing the system of immunity in animals. If the
thymus gland is removed at a sufficiently
early stage, a young animal is unable to
develop antibody resistance to foreign
molecules.

This may be of importance in the era
of organ transplantations, which dawned
in the 1960s and reached a climax with
the work of Barnard [1452], where the
greatest difficulty is dealing with the

body's rejection of the alien organ even
though that organ is vital to its own existence.

[1495] **SCHRIEFFER,** John Robert
(shree'fer)
American physicist
Born: Oak Park, Illinois, May 31,
1931

Schrieffer received his Ph.D. in physics
at the University of Illinois in 1957, and
he has been on the faculty of the University of Pennsylvania since 1962 as a
professor of physics. He was associated
with Bardeen [1334] and Cooper [1489]
on the theory of superconductivity currently accepted by physicists and shared
with them the 1972 Nobel Prize for
physics.

[1496] **SMITH,** Hamilton Othanel
American microbiologist
Born: New York, New York, Au-
gust 23, 1931

Smith obtained his M.D. from Johns
Hopkins University in 1956 and joined
the faculty of the school in 1967. In
1970 Smith discovered an enzyme that
broke a molecule of DNA at one specific
site. This was elaborated by Smith's colleague Nathans [1482] and it became
possible to tailor-make nucleic acid fragments, so to speak, and study their properties and ability to pass along genetic
information. It also led to recombinant-
DNA work in which nucleic acids could
be taken apart and put together in other
forms. As a result Smith and Nathans
shared in the 1978 Nobel Prize for physiology and medicine.

[1497] **CRONIN,** James Watson
American physicist
Born: Chicago, Illinois, Septem-
ber 29, 1931

Cronin obtained his Ph.D. at the University of Chicago in 1955, then joined
the staff at Brookhaven National Laboratory. He joined the faculty of Princeton

University in 1958, attaining professorial rank in 1965, then returned to the University of Chicago as professor of physics in 1971.

Cronin's work was on the grand symmetries of nature. When Lee [1473] and Yang [1451] showed that the law of conservation of parity did not always hold, that was combined with the law of conservation of charge conjugation and people talked of "CP symmetry."

In 1964, however, Cronin and Fitch [1454] showed that CP symmetry was not always obeyed. Certain particles, called the neutral K-mesons, in their decay on very rare occasions violated CP symmetry. This meant that one had to move to a still more general conservation law entitled "CPT symmetry" in which T stands for time. In those cases where CP symmetry fails, T must also fail in such a way as to make up for it. This means that time reversal does not always reverse events exactly on the subatomic level.

As a result Cronin and Fitch shared the 1980 Nobel Prize for physics.

[1498] **GILBERT,** Walter
American microbiologist
Born: Boston, Massachusetts,
March 21, 1932

Gilbert obtained his master's degree at Harvard University in 1954 and then went on to Cambridge University for further study, gaining his Ph.D. in physics in 1957. He then joined the Harvard faculty as a physicist, winning professorial status in 1968, but grew interested in molecular biology.

Gilbert found ways of breaking the nucleic acid molecule at certain points by chemical reagents, of analyzing the fragments so obtained, and from this, of deducing the exact nature of the original long chain. This duplicated, independently, the work Sanger [1426] was doing in Cambridge. As a result, Gilbert and Sanger shared half the 1980 Nobel Prize for chemistry, the other half going to Berg [1470] for splitting and recombining nucleic acids.

[1499] **BARTLETT,** Neil
English chemist
Born: Newcastle, Northumberland, September 15, 1932

Bartlett was educated at King's College in Newcastle and obtained his Ph.D. there in 1957. In 1958 he moved on to the University of British Columbia in Canada, where he served on the faculty.

There Bartlett was working with the fluorides of metals related to platinum. (Fluorides in general had come into prominence in the 1940s because of the importance of uranium hexafluoride in the development of the atomic bomb.) Platinum hexafluoride proved to be an unusually active chemical, so active that from theoretical calculations it seemed possible that it might react with xenon.

Xenon is one of the noble gases discovered by Ramsay [832] over half a century before and all those gases were commonly thought to be so inert as to be incapable of any chemical reactions at all. Xenon, however, the heaviest stable gas of this family, is the least inert. It might, it just *might,* react with a very active chemical.

Bartlett tried, and succeeded. He formed xenon platinofluoride ($XePtF_6$) in 1962. Soon afterward, other chemists, flooding into the new and exciting field, formed other noble gas compounds, not only of xenon, but of its sister elements, radon and krypton as well.

The newspapers hailed this as an unexpected revolution in chemistry that had overturned chemical thinking, but they overdid this a little. Actually, the new discoveries fit in closely with chemical theory and had been predicted by Pauling [1236] thirty years before.

In 1966 Bartlett accepted a position as professor of chemistry at Princeton University.

[1500] **GLASHOW,** Sheldon Lee
American physicist
Born: New York, New York, December 5, 1932

Glashow obtained his Ph.D. in physics at Harvard University in 1958, and after

894

some time in Copenhagen, at California Institute of Technology, Stanford University, and the University of California, returned to Harvard in 1966 and became a full professor there in 1967.

He, like Weinberg [1502] (the two were classmates at the Bronx High School of Science and, as undergraduates, at Cornell University), worked on a theory of subatomic particles that placed both the electromagnetic interaction and the weak nuclear interaction under the same mathematical roof. This was the first step toward a "grand unified theory" of interactions that Einstein [1064] had spent half his life laboring toward uselessly. The theory was supported by observational data sufficiently for Glashow and Weinberg to share the 1979 Nobel Prize for physics with Salam [1468].

[1501] **PENZIAS,** Arno Allan
German-American physicist
Born: Munich, Bavaria, April 26, 1933

Penzias, born of a Jewish family, saw the light of day only ten weeks after Hitler took control of Germany. Life was precarious indeed but the family managed to get out eventually and arrived in the United States in 1940. He graduated from City College of New York in 1954 and obtained his Ph.D. at Columbia University in 1958. He then joined the Bell Telephone Laboratories.

He and R. W. Wilson [1506] were trying to determine the characteristics of any radio-wave emission that might come from the outer regions of the galaxy where a gaseous halo might exist. They made use of a big horn-shaped antenna originally built to detect radio reflections from the Echo satellite. They refined it and, in May 1964, pointed it at the sky and found an excess of radio-wave radiation they could not explain. When they had accounted for all possible sources of error (including pigeon droppings inside the antenna) they found there was a distinct radiation above and beyond all natural causes

coming from all directions in equal quantities.

They turned to Dicke [1405], who, as it happened, had been following up a suggestion made by Gamow [1278] nearly two decades before that the big bang would have left a residue of radio waves coming from every direction, the waves becoming longer as the universe expanded and cooled.

The characteristics of the radiation detected by Penzias and Wilson fit what Dicke thought should result from the big bang if the average temperature of the universe were now 3°K. This "echo" of the big bang virtually killed Hoyle's [1398] steady-state universe. Penzias and Wilson therefore shared in the 1978 Nobel Prize for physics along with Kapitsa [1173].

[1502] **WEINBERG,** Steven
American physicist
Born: New York, New York, May 3, 1933

Weinberg was a classmate of Glashow [1500] at the Bronx High School of Science and at Cornell University. He went on to Princeton University for his Ph.D., attaining it in 1957, whereas Glashow went to Harvard. He too made the rounds of universities as a researcher and teacher, and like Glashow, Weinberg eventually came to Harvard in 1973.

Both worked on the unification of the electromagnetic and the weak nuclear interactions and both were successful enough to win shares of the 1979 Nobel Prize for physics along with Salam [1468].

[1503] **GAGARIN,** Yuri Alekseyevich
(gah-gah'rin)
Russian cosmonaut
Born: near Gzhatsk, Smolensk region, March 9, 1934
Died: near Kirzhach, Vladimir region, March 27, 1968

Under the lash of World War II the fighting nations developed airplanes capable of unprecedented speeds. The propeller reached its limit, for it could turn no faster without flying apart, but toward the end of the war a stream of burning gas, hurtling backward, pushed "jet planes" forward, by Newton's [231] third law, more rapidly than ever.

After the war, planes approached the speed of sound (740 miles an hour) or Mach 1, as it is called in honor of Mach [733], who first analyzed the behavior of air at those velocities. Air molecules get out of the way of an onrushing plane at a speed that depends on their elasticity and it is upon this elasticity that the speed of sound depends. A plane approaching the speed of sound is getting close to the point where it is moving faster than the air molecules can dodge. Air begins to pile up and it becomes difficult to control the plane.

Painstaking design on the basis of wind-tunnel studies overcame this difficulty and on October 14, 1947, an American Bell X-1 plane "broke the sound barrier." For the first time a human being traveled faster than the speed of sound with reference to the Earth's surface.

On December 12, 1953, the fiftieth anniversary of that first half-minute flight of the Wright Brothers [961, 995], a speed of Mach 2½ (that is, 2½ times the speed of sound) was attained. By the 1960s the rocket plane X-15 was climbing to heights of fifty miles and attaining speeds of over Mach 5.

But by that time, satellites were being placed into orbit and traveling at speeds approaching Mach 25. It was only a matter of time before men were placed in them. In the Soviet Union and in the United States men were undergoing training for the purpose. They were called cosmonauts in the Soviet Union and astronauts in the United States.

One of the Soviet cosmonauts was Gagarin, the son of a carpenter, who was born on a collective farm. His early education was interrupted by the necessity of escape from the invading Germans. After the war, however, he attended a vocational school and was trained in foundry work.

His interest in flying led him to a Soviet air force school from which he graduated with honors as an air force lieutenant in 1957. After serving as a test pilot, he joined the group of cosmonauts in training for orbital flight and it was upon him that the choice fell in 1961.

On April 12, 1961, Gagarin became the first man placed in orbit about the earth and returned alive. He remained in orbit 89.1 minutes, rising as high above the surface as 187.66 miles and traveling at a velocity that reached 17,400 miles an hour.

Thus, only three and a half years after the opening of the space age, with the orbiting of Sputnik I, man was in space. Within eight years of Gagarin's adventure, so rapid is progress, Armstrong [1492] was on the moon. Gagarin, however, did not live to see that, since he died in a tragic airplane crash the year before the moon landing.

After his death his birthplace, Gzhatsk, was renamed Gagarin.

[1504] SAGAN, Carl (say'gan)
American astronomer
Born: New York, New York, November 9, 1934

Sagan obtained his Ph.D. at the University of Chicago in 1960.

He is primarily interested in planetary surfaces and atmospheres, a field that rose out of the doldrums with Kuiper's [1297] researches and the advent of rocketry. Thus, he worked out a greenhouse model for the atmosphere of Venus, accounting for the otherwise puzzling high temperature of the planet. He also found evidence for elevation differences on the surface of Mars and for organic molecules in the atmosphere of Jupiter.

Further in the periphery of his interests but possessing added glamour is the question of the probabilities of life on other planets and of the origin of life on ours. (It is not surprising that he is another of those scientists who are fond of reading science fiction.) He has been one of a group trying to form compounds from a system that mimics the conditions of the primordial earth, attempting to pass beyond the amino acids and into the building blocks of the nucleic acids. In 1963 he succeeded in detecting the formation of adenosine triphosphate (ATP), the prime energy-store of living tissue. Thus, it seems quite reasonable to visualize the formation of a chemical energy-store in the oceans, building up steadily at the expense of solar energy and serving as a ready source of energy for the production of complex nucleic acids and proteins; in short, for the production of life.

In 1968 he transferred his operations to Cornell University, where he is an associate professor of astronomy and the director of its Laboratory for Planetary Studies. In 1969 he accepted a position of editor of the astronomical journal *Icarus*.

Sagan's daring and imaginative approach to astronomy has left its mark on the field. He was one of the driving forces behind planetary exploration that placed the Vikings on the surface of Mars and the Voyagers sending back photographs of Jupiter and Saturn, together with their satellite systems in the 1970s. He also lent life to the field of SETI (acronym for "search for extraterrestrial intelligence") and is perhaps the strongest single proponent of the view that "we are not alone."

In the 1970s he blossomed out also as the most successful science popularizer in history. His book *The Dragons of Eden* (not even about astronomy) was a best-selling Pulitzer Prize winner. In 1980 his television series, "Cosmos," and the book that was published as a spinoff achieved an absolutely unprecedented peak in quality and popularity.

[1505] **TEMIN,** Howard Martin
American oncologist
Born: Philadelphia, Pennsylvania, December 10, 1934

Temin obtained his Ph.D. in 1959 at California Institute of Technology, working under Dulbecco [1388]. He then moved on to the University of Wisconsin, where his investigations of cancer cells led him to question the assumption that genetic information flowed exclusively in a one-way movement from the DNA of chromosomes to the RNA of the cytoplasm to enzymes. It seemed possible that there were loops in the progression and that some enzymes could affect the workings of DNA. He located such an enzyme, called "reverse transcriptase," and Baltimore [1508], working independently, also located the enzyme. As a result, Temin and Baltimore shared the 1975 Nobel Prize for physiology and medicine with Dulbecco.

[1506] **WILSON,** Robert Woodrow
American radio astronomer
Born: Houston, Texas, January 10, 1936

Wilson graduated from Rice University with honors in 1957 and went on to obtain his Ph.D. at California Institute of Technology in 1962. Most of his career has been spent at the Bell Laboratories.

He is best known for his collaboration with Penzias [1501] in detecting the radio-wave background that is the distant echo of the long-ago big bang. Since then he has detected carbon monoxide and other molecules in the interstellar dust clouds, thus contributing to the fast-growing information being gathered on the chemical constitution of these dust clouds from their radio-wave emissions.

Because of his work, he shared with Penzias the 1978 Nobel Prize for physics.

[1507] **TING,** Samuel Chao Chung
American physicist
Born: Ann Arbor, Michigan, January 27, 1936

Ting was the son of a Chinese student working at the University of Michigan. He was taken by his family back to China; but after the victory of the Chinese Communists, the family moved to

Taiwan, the only portion of the land to remain free of Communist control. In 1956 Ting returned to the University of Michigan to follow in his father's footsteps as a student. By 1962 he had earned his Ph.D. there. He taught at Columbia University and then from 1967 at Massachusetts Institute of Technology.

Working at the Brookhaven National Laboratory in 1974, Ting discovered a particle that from its properties had to include in its makeup the postulated but not yet discovered "charmed quark." This was an important finding, since it at once lifted to a much higher degree of probability the theory of quarks that physicists were working with. The finding had been simultaneously made by Richter [1493] at Stanford University, and the two shared the 1976 Nobel Prize for physics as a result.

[1508] **BALTIMORE,** David
American biochemist
Born: New York, New York,
March 7, 1938

Baltimore received his Ph.D. from Rockefeller University in New York. Since 1972 he has been a professor at Massachusetts Institute of Technology. Independently of Temin [1505], Baltimore isolated an enzyme, "reverse transcriptase," which he showed could affect the working of DNA, thus complicating the transmission of genetic information but making it more responsive to the needs of the cell. For this, Baltimore and Temin shared the 1975 Nobel Prize for physiology and medicine with Dulbecco [1388].

[1509] **JOSEPHSON,** Brian David
Welsh physicist
Born: Cardiff, Wales, January 4,
1940

Josephson was educated at Cambridge University and in 1962, while still a graduate student there, he studied Esaki's [1464] tunneling effect. Whereas Giaever [1484] had considered the elec-

tric current flow across an insulator when one metal was superconducting, Josephson dealt with the situation where both were superconducting.

Making use of Bardeen's [1334] theory of superconductivity, Josephson predicted a flow of current which could oscillate under certain circumstances and would be affected by the presence of magnetic fields. Subsequent measurements showed this Josephson effect existed and this was a strong confirmation of the superconductivity theory of Bardeen. It also offered a method for measuring the intensity of weak magnetic fields in space with hitherto unattainable accuracy.

Josephson shared the 1973 Nobel Prize in physics with Esaki and Giaever.

[1510] **HAWKING,** Stephen William
English physicist
Born: Oxford, January 8, 1942

Hawking, educated at both Oxford and Cambridge universities (receiving his Ph.D. at the latter) is one of the most formidable intellects engaged in elucidation of the deepest problems in cosmology. He has labored to combine both general relativity and quantum theory in working out the theories of black holes, those fascinating objects that involve complete gravitational collapse.

He has produced two interesting suggestions concerning black holes, both of which yet require observational evidence (as indeed almost everything about black holes does). First, he has shown the possibility that black holes of any mass-range can have been produced at the time of the big bang, so that small "mini black holes" might exist in space now in undetermined numbers and at undetermined locations.

Second, he has shown from quantum mechanical considerations that black holes can "evaporate" with rates that increase the less massive they are. For ordinary star-sized black holes, evaporation is insignificant and can scarcely balance the influx of matter under almost all circumstances. For small black holes, evaporation is a significant factor and mini black holes that are small enough might evaporate so quickly as to explode, leaving behind telltale gamma radiation.

Hawking's tragedy is that early in life he was struck by amyotrophic lateral sclerosis, a progressive wasting disease for which there is no known cure. He has been reduced to virtual immobility and helplessness but trapped within the dying body is a brilliant mind and an apparently indomitable spirit.

ABOUT THE AUTHOR

ASIMOV, Isaac (ă'zih-mov)
  Russian-American biochemist and science writer
  Born: Petrovichi, USSR, January 2, 1920

Isaac Asimov, the son of a Jewish immigrant candy-store keeper, was taken to the United States by his parents in 1923 and has been a naturalized American citizen since 1928. He was educated at Columbia University, graduating in 1939 and remaining for further work in chemistry under such men as Sherman [1036], Urey [1164], and King [1193]. World War II interrupted his studies; while it lasted he worked as a chemist at the United States Navy Yard in Philadelphia and, later, served as a member of the armed forces. He returned to Columbia in 1946, earning his Ph.D. in 1948 under Charles R. Dawson.

In 1949, through the recommendation of Boyd [1264], he accepted a position on the faculty of Boston University School of Medicine, where he has remained. He is now professor of biochemistry at that school though he has not taught actively since 1958.

In 1929 Asimov made his first acquaintance with science fiction in *Amazing Stories,* a magazine edited at that time by T. O'Conor Sloane, whose grandson and namesake at Doubleday asked Asimov to prepare this *Biographical Encyclopedia.*

His encounter with science fiction was fateful in three ways: It interested him permanently not only in science fiction itself, but in science as well and in writing. At the age of twelve, he was already seeking out obscure corners where he might set down interminable stories in five-cent copybooks. He progressed to typewriter and bond paper and in 1938 decided to try for publication.

After his first submission and instant rejection by John W. Campbell, Jr.—to whose continuing encouragement he owes so much that followed—it took him four months and seven more rejections to make his first sale. That first sale was a short story, "Marooned off Vesta," which appeared in the March 1939 issue of *Amazing Stories.* Since then he has sold hundreds of stories and articles to science fiction magazines.

He did not appear in hard covers until 1950, when Doubleday & Company published his first science fiction novel, *Pebble in the Sky.* Doubleday has published over 80 of Asimov's books.

Dr. Asimov's first effort in science was *Biochemistry and Human Metabolism,* a textbook on biochemistry for medical students written in collaboration with two other members of the department at Boston University. It was published in 1952 by Williams and Wilkins (third edition, 1957).

Asimov, influenced by the work of Ley [1315] and of L. Sprague de Camp, then decided he wanted to write science for the general public. In this ambition, he has received the cooperation of several publishers. His books have dealt with mathematics, astronomy, physics, chemistry, and biology, as well as such nonscientific subjects as mythology, geography, the Bible, Shakespeare, and humor. The *Biographical Encyclopedia of Science and Technology,* in its first edition, was his sixty-first book. Nor has he stopped. In October 1969 his hundredth book (appropriately entitled *Opus 100*) was published by Houghton-Mifflin.

In March 1979 he published his two hundredth book, *In Memory Yet Green,* the first volume of a large two-volume autobiography—the self-indulgent product of a man who cheerfully admits that nothing much has ever happened to him, but insists he can hide that fact by clever writing. To avoid saddening his publishers, he let Doubleday publish the autobiography, and on the same day, Houghton-Mifflin published *Opus 200,* which Asimov also called his two hundredth book.

With this new edition of the *Biographical Encyclopedia* he is approaching the 250 mark.

INDEX

NOTE: *The following index contains subjects, plus names of individuals other than those whose biographies are included in the book. The number references are to the numbered biographies and* not *to the page number.*

Abacus, 456
Aberration, light, 258
Ablation, 1168
A, B, O blood groups, 973
Abominable snowman, 1432
Abrasive, 863
Absolute magnitude, 1018
Absolute motion, 835, 1064
Absolute rest, 1064
Absolute scale, 652
Absolute temperature, 497
Absolute zero, 244, 343, 561, 625, 652, 726, 843, 936, 1165, 1178
Academia Secretorum Naturae, 150
Academy, 24, 29
Accademia dei Lincei, 150, 163
Accademia del Cimento, 206
Acceleration, 231
Accelerators, particle, 1198, 1241, 1244, 1246, 1324, 1329, 1395, 1475
Accommodation, lens, 173, 402
Acetic acid, 76, 610
Acetone, 190, 989, 1031
Acetylcholine, 1015, 1034
Acetylcoenzyme A, 1221, 1360
Acetylene, 515, 989, 1058
Acetylsalicylic acid, 610
Achilles, 927
Acid-base indicators, 212
Acid-base systems, 1061
Acids, 420, 421
    nature of, 1061
    organic, 329
Acorn worm, 750
Acoustics, 370, 972
Acquired characteristics, inheritance of, 336, 704, 799, 1214
ACTH, 1382, 1426
Actin, 1167
Actinides, 1372
Actinium, 1026
Action at a distance, 104
Activation, energy of, 894

Activity, 1037
Actomyosin, 1167
Actuarial tables, 481
Adams, John, 333
Addison's disease, 482
Adenine, 842, 1291, 1406
Adenosine diphosphate (ADP), 1331, 1441
Adenosine triphosphate (ATP), 1221, 1331, 1402, 1441, 1457, 1504
ADP, 1331, 1441
Adrenal cortex, 482, 1105
Adrenal glands, 141, 855, 1105, 1167
Adrenalin, 855, 877
Adrenaline, 807, 855, 998
Adrenal medulla, 877
Adrenocorticotrophic hormone (ACTH), 1382, 1426
Advancement of Learning, 163
Aerial, radio, 1025
Aeronautical engineering, 1075
Aether, 29
Affinities, chemical, 315
Africa, circumnavigation of, 12, 111
Agar-agar, 767
Agassiz, Lake, 551
Age of Reason, 231, 261, 272, 314, 333, 370, 387
Agglutination, blood, 973
Aggression, 1326
Agnosticism, 659
Agricultural chemistry, 421, 525
Ailerons, 995
Air, 5
    compressibility of, 60, 212
    liquid, 758, 832, 851, 989
    temperature and, 45, 203, 244
Airbrake, 785
Air masses, 1205
Airplane, 711, 713, 1249
    invention of, 961, 995
Air pressure, 207
Air pump, 189, 212, 223, 235, 583
Albedo, 299

Albert (Prince, Great Britain), 474, 581, 604, 734
Alchemia, 162
Alchemy, 76, 162, 260
  medicine and, 131
  origins of, 67
Alcibiades, 21
Alcohol, ethyl, 103, 650, 668
Aldehyde, 668
Alexander I (Tsar, Russia), 450
Alexander I Island, 426
Alexander III the Great (King, Macedon), 29, 31, 33, 34, 67
Alexander VI (Pope), 122, 130
Alexin, 986
Alfonsine Tables, 100, 127, 143
Algae, 675
Algebra, 79
  abstract, 472, 481
  fundamental theory of, 415
  symbols of, 153, 183
Algebraic numbers, 641
Algol, 381, 757
Al-Hakim (Caliph), 85
Alienist, 338
Alizarin, 718, 734, 752
Alkaloids, 437, 454, 1107
Allergies, 137, 809, 1223
Alloys, 854
Alloy steel, 892, 1028
Almagest, 64, 90, 118, 119
Al-Mudadid (Caliph), 80
Alnico, 985
Alp Arslan (Sultan), 87
Alpha Centauri, 284
  distance of, 505
Alpha particles, 996, 1146, 1227, 1278
  elements and, 1052
  neutrons and, 1150
  scattering of, 996
Alpha rays, 695, 906, 965, 996
  range of, 922
Alpha waves, 1014
Alternating currents, 785, 837, 867, 944
Alternation of generations, 651
Aluminum, 417, 515, 665, 737, 741, 1215, 1227
  production of, 603, 925, 933
Aluminum chloride, 741
Aluminum oxide, 863, 933
Aluminum powder, 909
Alundum, 863
AM (amplitude modulation), 1143
Amalthea, 883
Amber, 61, 155

Amoeba, disease and, 997
America, discovery of, 121
American Association for the Advancement of Science, 462
Americium, 1372
Amines, 602
Amino acids, 379, 388, 438, 1074
  abiogenic formation of, 1490
  breakdown of, 1231
  essential, 1114
  linkages between, 833
  nutritional properties of, 900
  protein structure and, 1239
  separation of, 1350, 1365, 1379
Ammonia, 312, 346, 735, 812, 1132
  formation of, 977, 1028
  liquid, 758
  masers and, 1400
  planetary atmospheres and, 1038, 1290
Ammonium chloride, 76, 490
Ammonium cyanate, 515
Ammonium sulfate, 162
Ampere, 407
Amphioxus, 750
Amplifier, 803
Amplitude modulation (AM), 1143
Amyntas II (King, Macedon), 29
Anabolism, 578
Anaerobic bacteria, 813
Anaerobic glycolysis, 1095
Analogue computer, 1139
Analysis, chemical, 315
Analysis, mathematical, 153
Analysis of variance, 1142
Analytical Mechanics, 317
Analytic geometry, 183
Analytic Theory of Heat, 393
Analytic trigonometry, 246
Anaphylaxis, 809
Anatomy, 34, 146, 251
  comparative, 148, 396
Andromeda galaxy, 171, 305, 1163, 1209
  distance of, 1136
  radial motion of, 1038
Andromeda nebula (*see* Andromeda galaxy)
Androsterone, 1265
Anemia, 208, 1059
  pernicious, 482, 1059, 1103, 1154, 1312
Anemometer, 487
Aneroid barometer, 233
Anesthesia, 421, 435, 494, 558, 567, 576, 594, 617
  local, 830, 865, 882
Anesthetic, 617

Angiosperms, 403
Ångström unit, 585
Angular momentum, 777
  solar system and, 1053, 1335
Aniline, 604, 734
Aniline purple, 734
Animal photography, 683
Animals, classification of, 213, 336, 396
Animal spirit, 611
Anne (Queen, Great Britain), 231
Anode, 474, 487
Anopheles mosquito, 876
Antarctica, 426, 512, 1129
  crossing of, 1432
Antenna, radio, 1025
Anthracene, 752
Anthrax, 642, 767, 870
Antibacterials, 1183
Antibiotics, 874, 1077, 1128, 1213
Antibodies, 809, 813, 1010, 1223
  structure of, 1442, 1486
Anticyclone, 636
Antielectrons, 1256, 1280, 1292
Antiferromagnetism, 1285
Antifreeze, 950
Antigens, 809
Antihistamines, 1325
Antiknock compounds, 1132
Antimatter, 1256
Antimony, 82
Antineutrinos, 1292
Antiparticles, 1256
Antiprotons, 1256, 1287, 1329
  detection of, 1439
Antiquity of Man, The, 502, 554
Antisepsis, 607, 642, 672, 830
Antitoxin, diphtheria, 844, 845, 846
Antitoxin, lockjaw, 846
Apes, 761, 1041
Aphasia, 653
Aphids, 291
Appendicitis, 134, 465
Appendix, perforated, 365
Appleton layers, 1158
Aqua regia, 162
Aqueducts, 62
Arabic numerals, 79, 84, 89, 95, 118
Arachnids, 336
Archaeological dating, 963
Archaeology, 634
Architecture, 55
Arc lamp, 421
Arctic Ocean, 914
Arcturus, 238

Arginine, 1114, 1231, 1270
Argon, 307
  discovery of, 760, 832
  light bulbs and, 1072
Ariel, 509
Arithmetic, 79
  fundamental theorem of, 415
Aromatic compounds, 628, 752
Arsenic, 96
  chemotherapy and, 845
Arsphenamine, 845
Arteries, 11, 36, 43
  pulsation of, 42
Arthur of Brittany, 578
Artificial heart, 1016
Artificial insemination, 302, 988
Artificial intelligence, 1375
Artificial radioactivity, 1227
Artificial respiration, 807
Artificial satellites, 1317, 1351, 1370, 1392
  tracking of, 1386
Ascorbic acid (vitamin C), 1087, 1167
  synthesis of, 1201
Asepsis, 830
Asimov, Isaac, 1349
Asklepios, 1, 22
Asparagine, 379
Aspirin, 610
Assassins, 76
Assembly line, 929
Astatine, 1287
Aster, 762
Asteroids, 341, 372, 523, 573, 763, 1163
  collision with Earth of, 1363
  origin of, 713
  parallax of, 1140
  perturbations of, 586
  photography and, 927
Asthma, 137
Astigmatism, 402, 523, 605, 919
Astrology, 52, 106, 119, 134, 137, 156, 159,
    164, 169
Astronautics, 1172
Astronomia Nova, 169
Astronomic unit, 763
Astronomy, prehistoric, 1481
Astrophysics, 589
Asymmetric compounds, structure of, 1310
Atlantic cable, 621, 652
Atlantis, 24, 218
Atlas, 144
Atmosphere, depth of, 85
  layers of, 861
  lower, 861
  pressure of, 192

primordial, 1164
refraction of, 52
upper, 962, 1155, 1158
Atomic bomb (see Nuclear bomb)
Atomic clock, 1400
Atomic hydrogen blowtorch, 1072
Atomic numbers, 857, 1051, 1052, 1121, 1228
Atomic pile, 1241, 1259
Atomic theory, 389, 733
Atomic volume, 685
Atomic weights, 389, 412, 425, 440, 485, 579, 599, 668, 730, 760, 968, 1051
 specific heat and, 441
Atomism, 15, 20, 29, 35, 38, 53, 60, 182, 212, 268, 364, 769, 840, 1064
Atoms, 389
 electron waves and, 1117, 1157, 1191
 internal structure of, 834, 839, 869, 946, 996, 1111
 magnetic properties of, 1219
 size of, 628, 990, 1064
 visualization of, 1364
Atom-smashing, 1198
ATP (adenosine triphosphate), 1221, 1331, 1402, 1441, 1504
 abiogenic formation of, 1457
Audiometer, 1220
Audion, 1017
Aureomycin, 1010
Aurora borealis, 182, 290, 585
Auscultation, 429
Australia, 300, 331
 animals of, 643
Australopithecus, 959, 1162
Autoclave, 816
Autoimmune diseases, 1442
Automation, 316, 1139
Automobile, 635, 694, 708, 929
Autonomic nervous system, 1073
Aviation gasoline, 966
Aviation medicine, 702
Avogadro's hypothesis, 412, 553, 568
Avogadro's number, 412
Axiomatics, 889, 918
Axioms, 889
Axis, tipping of, 18
Azote, 334, 368

Bacco in Toscana, 211
Bacillus brevis, 1235
Bacteria, 304
 anaerobic, 813
 chemotherapy and, 1183
 classification of, 675

destruction of, 1012, 1055
 discovery of, 221
 disease and, 767
 filtering of, 816
 reproduction of, 1466
 staining of, 767, 841
Bacterial genetics, 1313
Bacteriology, 675
Bacteriophages, 986, 1012, 1055, 1313, 1485
 nucleic acid and, 1341
 structure of, 1377
Baeyer's strain theory, 718
Baffin Bay, 178
Baily's beads, 406
Bakelite, 728, 931
Balance, organs of, 755
Balanoglossus, 750, 913
Balfour, Arthur J., 823, 1031
Ball lightning, 1173
Balloons, 191, 309, 343, 362, 364, 404, 737
 dirigible, 737
 high-altitude, 1092
 invention of, 325
 unmanned, 861
Baluchitherium, 1091
Banana, 160
Barbiturates, 1320
Barbituric acid, 718
Barium, 1063
 isolation of, 421
 radium and, 825
Barium platinocyanide, 774
Barkhausen effect, 1079
Barnard's star, 883
 planets of, 1247
Barometer, 189, 192, 207, 244
 aneroid, 233
Basal metabolic rate (BMR), 691
Basalt, 296
Basilar membrane, 1220
Basques, 1264
Bassi, Laura, 302
Bathyscaphe, 1050, 1092
Bathysphere, 1050
Bats, 302
Battery, electric, 337, 361, 470, 709
Bazooka, 1083
Becquerel rays, 834
Bees, 1110
Beet sugar, 279
Behaviorism, 1057
Bell, Jocelyn, 1463
Bellingshausen Sea, 426
Bends, 702, 837

Benzene, 190, 474, 734, 796, 1236
structure of, 680
Benzene ring, 628
Benzoic acid, 515
Beriberi, 888, 1093, 1240
Bering Island, 250
Bering Sea, 250
Bering Strait, 250
Berkeley, George, 263
Berkelium, 1372
Bernard of Clairvaux, 88
Bernoulli, Jacob (or Jacques), 268
Bernoulli, Johann (or Jean), 268
Bernoulli's principle, 268
Berson, Solomon, 1446
Beryllium, 515, 1146, 1362
discovery of, 379
neutrons and, 1150
Bessel's functions, 439
Beta particles, 996
Beta rays, 906, 965, 996
elements and, 1052
energy of, 1228
Betatron, 1329, 1367, 1395
Beta waves, 1014
Betelgeuse, diameter of, 835
Bevatron, 337, 1329
Biela's comet, 434
Bielids, 434
Bifocal glasses, 272
Big bang, 1125, 1136, 1149, 1174, 1278, 1437, 1501
Bile, 214
Bile acids, 1048
Bile pigments, 457, 1059
Binary notation, 233, 1404
Binary stars, 294, 321
spectroscopic, 757
Binding energy, 1051
Binomial nomenclature, 276
Binomial theorem, 231, 527
Biochemistry, 175, 663, 674
Biology, 336
Biotin, 1239
Birds, 443
Birth rate, 201
Bismarck, Otto von, 632, 638
Bismuth meal, 998
Bits, 1404
Bittner milk factor, 1277
Black body radiation, 648, 678, 760, 887, 934
Black hole, 1019, 1366
evaporation of, 1510
Blanc, Mont, 322

Blast furnaces, 575
Blasting gelatin, 703
Bligh, William, 331
Blind spot, 203
Bliss, Nathaniel, 310
Blood, air and, 219
circulation of, 43, 65, 122, 140, 142, 146, 174, 214
gases in, 597
proteins of, 1257
transfusion of, 219, 227, 973, 1016, 1411
white corpuscles in, 775
Blood groups, 973
race and, 1264
Blood-letting, 42, 429, 469
Blood pressure, 249, 500, 597, 683
Blood vessels, 36
repair of, 1016
X rays and, 1032
Blowpipe, 292, 339
Blum, Léon, 1204
BMR (basal metabolic rate), 691
Bode's law, 301, 341, 344
Bode-Titius law, 344
Bohr-Sommerfeld atom, 976
Bok globules, 1302
Bolívar, Simón, 525
Bolometer, 711
Bonaparte, Napoleon (see Napoleon I)
Bone, 339
Bone structure, 237
Boniface VIII (Pope), 103
Bonner Durchmusterung, 508
Bookkeeping, double-entry, 120
Boranes, 1435
Borax, 490
Borgia, Cesare, 122
Boric acid, 490
Boron, 420, 421
Boron hydrides, 1043
Bose-Einstein statistics, 1170
Bosons, 1170
Boston Symphony Hall, 972
Botany Bay, 331
Boyd, Lyle G., 1237
Boyle's law, 203, 212, 561
Brain, 11, 29, 106, 146, 371
convolutions of, 43
mapping of, 731, 761, 881
paralysis and, 278
Brain surgery, 653
Bread, 903
Breeder reactor, 1321
Brewster's law, 433
Bright's disease, 465

Broca's convolution, 653
Bromine, 438, 796
  discovery of, 529
Bronze Age, 53, 460
Brougham, Henry, 402
Brownian motion, 403, 990, 1064
Brucia, 927
Brucine, 454
Bubble chamber, 979, 1363, 1472
Bubonic plague, 767, 870
Buckingham, George Villiers, duke of, 163
Bunsen burner, 565, 648, 977
Buoyancy, principle of, 47
Butler, Samuel, 704
Butyl alcohol, 1031
Byrd, Harry F., 1129
Byron, George Gordon, Lord, 481

Cadmium, 835
  discovery of, 411
Caesar, Julius, 54, 55
Caffeine, 493
Calcar, Jan Stephen van, 146
Calcium, 421
  interstellar, 940, 949, 1203
  sun and, 974
Calcium carbide, 515
Calcium carbonate, 298
Calcium deficiency, 1062
Calcium ions, 717
Calcium oxide, 298, 428
Calculating machines, 207, 233, 481
Calculus, 47, 198, 231, 233, 263
Calculus of variations, 317
Calendar, lunar, 23
  solar, 54
Californium, 1372
Caligula, 85
Callisthenes, 29
Callisto, 166
Caloric, 334, 360
Calorimeter, 674, 691
Calvin, John, 142
Cambrian era, 442
Camera, pinhole, 117, 150
Canal rays, 811, 1024
Canals, Martian, 499, 681, 714, 860
Cancer, 1089, 1242, 1277
  viruses and, 1067, 1277, 1388
Candide, 233
Candles, 448
Canning, 359
Cannizzaro reaction, 668
Canopus, 52
Capillaries, 214

control of, 1030
Capillarity, 768
Capillary action, 245
Capillary electrometer, 778
Carbanions, 1199
Carbohydrates, 440
  metabolism of, 1221, 1231
Carbolic acid, 672
Carbon, 515, 863
  conducting properties of, 312
  electric lights and, 677
  isotopes of, 1164, 1178, 1342, 1385
  steel and, 252
  valence of, 680, 921, 950
Carbon-12, 1178
Carbon-13, 1164
Carbon-14, 963, 987, 1358, 1361
  half life of, 1385
Carbon-14 dating, 1342
Carbon dioxide, 298, 312, 375, 389, 421,
    474, 735, 1231
  blood content of, 770
  diamond and, 334
  discovery of, 175
  greenhouse effect and, 894
  liquefaction of, 580
  planetary atmospheres and, 1045, 1297
  solid, 1309
Carbon filament, 788
Carbonium ions, 1199
Carbon monoxide, 103, 389, 578, 856
  cytochromes and, 1089
  liquid, 698
Carbon powder, 789
Carbon rings, 729, 1119
Carbon suboxide, 1039
Carborundum, 863
Cardiac catheterization, 1181, 1184, 1283
Carnegie, Andrew, 974
Carnot, M. F. S., 1016
Carolingian Renaissance, 77, 78
Carotenoids, 1131
Carver, Moses, 937
Cascade process, 1280
Casein, 1114
Caspian Sea, 280
Cassini's division, 209, 586
Cast iron, 575
Castor, 209
Catabolism, 578
Catalase, 1113
Cataldi, P. A., 202
Catalysis, 380, 650, 840
Catalysts, organic, 490
Catalytic action, 650

Catapults, 45, 46
Cataract, optic, 57, 919
Catastrophism, 291, 396
Catherine I (Empress, Russia), 275
Catherine II the Great (Empress, Russia), 169, 275, 286, 289, 313, 317
Cathode rays, 474, 487, 649, 664, 695, 774, 811, 834, 869, 873, 920, 934
    particulate nature of, 990
Cathode-ray tube, 808, 1134
CAT scanner, 1461
Causality, 15
Cedar tree, 148
Celestial Mechanics, 347, 392, 404, 545
Cell differentiation, 313
Cell division, 538, 598, 651, 704, 722, 762
Cellophane, 862
Cell pathology, 632
Cells, 223
    chromosomes in, 782
    staining of, 762, 764, 845
    synthetic dyes and, 762
Cells, electric, 568
Cell staining, 762, 764, 845
Cell Substance, Nucleus and Cell Division, 762
Cell theory, 400, 537, 538, 563
Celluloid, 728
    photography and, 852
Cellulose, 430, 490, 743, 1074
Cellulose acetate, 852
Celsius scale, 271
Celtium, 1002, 1121
Center of gravity, 47
Centrifugal effect, 1097
Centrifuges, 1097
Centrosome, 923
Cepheid variables, 975, 1018, 1019, 1085, 1102
    Andromeda galaxy and, 1136
    distance of, 1045
    populations of, 1163
Cerebellum, 43
Cerebral cortex, 731
Cerebrospinal fluid, 438
Cerebrum, 43
Ceres, 341, 344
Cerium, 335, 425
    discovery of, 390
Cerium nitrate, 890
Cesium, 565, 648
Chain reaction, chemical, 936, 994, 1200
    branched, 1189
Chain reaction, nuclear, 1208
Chamberland filters, 816

Chance and Necessity, 1347
Chandrasekhar's limit, 1356
Channel rays, 869
Characteristic X rays, 1049
Charcoal, 490
Chardonnet silk, 743
Charge conjugation, conservation of, 1497
Charles I (King, England), 174, 198
Charles II (King, England), 172, 198, 201, 202, 208, 212, 213, 231, 234, 235
Charles III (King, Spain), 382
Charles IV (King, Spain), 364
Charles V (Holy Roman Emperor), 126, 130, 133, 144, 146
Charles IX (King, France), 139
Charles X (King, France), 396, 416, 463, 571
Charles XIV (King, Sweden), 425
Charles's law, 343
Charmed particles, 1493, 1507
Chatelet, Marquis de, 274
Chemical analysis, 982
Chemical bonds, electrons and, 978, 1013, 1037, 1236
Chemical History of a Candle, The, 474
Chemical kinetics, 994, 1033
Chemical nomenclature, 319, 334, 366
Chemical potential, 674, 740
Chemical reactions, electrons and, 978
    fast, 1206, 1443, 1477
Chemical Society, 547
Chemical thermodynamics, 721, 740, 829, 1061
Chemistry, 67
    agricultural, 421, 525
    quantitative, 334
Chemistry Applied to the Arts, 368
Chemotherapy, 845
Cherenkov radiation, 1180, 1281, 1340
Chicken pox virus, 1397
Childbed (puerpueral) fever, 205, 607
Child psychology, 780
Children, development of, 1070
Chimborazo, Mount, 397
Chimpanzees, 1112
Chi-square test, 875
Chladni figures, 370
Chlorine, 329, 474
    bleaching and, 346
    discovery of, 421
    isotopes of, 1051, 1150
    liquid, 989
    poison gas attacks and, 977
Chloroform, 435, 567, 617

Chlorophyll, 454, 493, 699, 1009, 1076, 1416
Chloroplast, 699
Cholera, 570, 576, 612, 767, 805, 901
Cholesterol, 1046, 1048
  synthesis of, 1369, 1416
Chordata, 478, 750, 823, 913
Christian IV (King, Denmark), 156
Christian V (King, Denmark), 232
Christina (Queen, Sweden), 183, 191, 207, 218
Chromatic aberration, 231, 240, 273
Chromatin, 722, 762
Chromatography, 1006, 1009
  paper, 1291, 1350, 1361, 1394, 1406, 1426
Chromium, 382, 909
  discovery of, 379
Chromosomes, 704, 722, 762, 768, 782, 868, 923, 957, 1406
  mapping of, 1153
  mutations and, 1029
  pairs of, 1047
Chromosphere, 446, 719
Chronology, 48, 154
Chronometer, 259
Churchill, Winston, 1101
Chymotrypsin, 1148
Cicero, 24, 27, 47, 52
Cigarette lighters, 890
Cilia, 537, 560
Cinchonine, 454
Citric acid, 1231
Citrus fruits, scurvy and, 288
Civet, 1119
Clairvoyance, 1182
Clapeyron-Clausius equation, 507
Clarke, Arthur C., 1351
Classical physics, 692, 774, 887, 1064
Cleanthes, 41
Clement IV (Pope), 99
Cleopatra VII (Queen, Egypt), 40, 207
Clepsydra, 46
Clinical thermometer, 720
Clitoris, 149
Clock, longitude and, 259
  pendulum, 166, 181, 204, 215
Cloud chamber, 979, 1207, 1274, 1472
Clouds, 979
  interstellar, 765
Coal, hydrogenation of, 977, 1098
  plant origin of, 365
Coal gas, 363
Coal mines, 236
Coal tar, 222, 409, 604, 752

Cobalt, 260
  vitamin B_{12} and, 1312
Cocaine, 830, 865, 882
Cochlea, 631, 1220
Cod-liver oil, 900
Cody, William F., 690
Coelenterata, 640, 659
Coenzyme A, 1221, 1240, 1360
Coenzymes, 947, 1011
  vitamins and, 1240, 1267
Coffee, 160
Coherent light, 1479
Coherer, 1025
Coincidence counters, 1146, 1207
Colchicine, 1029
Coleridge, Samuel Taylor, 130, 421
Collective unconscious, 1035
Colloids, 547, 1097
  light-passage through, 626
Colorado potato beetle, 1216
Color blindness, 389
Color perception, 402
Color photography, 692, 778, 1344
Color television, 1319
Columbium, 383, 388
Coma Berenices, 44
Combining volumes, law of, 420, 425, 668
Combustion, 241, 334
  heat of, 334, 347, 528
Comets, 180, 194
  breakup of, 434
  discovery of, 305, 352, 372, 376, 434, 639, 671
  distance of, 156
  gravity and, 238
  meteors and, 434
  motion of, 191
  orbits of, 238
  origin of, 1229
  pandemics and, 1398
  return of, 189
  short-term, 326
  spectrum of, 646, 671
  structure of, 671, 821, 1317
  tails of, 133, 952
Commodus, 65
Communications satellites, 1351
Commutative law, 545
Comparative anatomy, 396
Comparative embryology, 669, 707
Compass, gyroscopic, 907
Compass, magnetic, 104, 155
  variations of, 121, 184
Compensation, 984
Complement, 951, 986

Complementarity, principle of, 1101
Complex numbers, 944
Compound A, 1105
Compound E, 1105, 1188
Compton effect, 1159
Computerized axial tomography (CAT)
  scanner, 1461
Computers, 481
Computers, electronic, 843, 1139, 1175,
  1328, 1431
  analogue, 1139
  astronomy and, 1258
  digital, 1328
  memory of, 1285
  solid-state devices and, 1348
  vitamin B_{12} and, 1352
Comte, Auguste, 648
Concerning the Nature of Things, 922
Concertina, 526
Conciliator, 106
Condenser, electrical, 272
Conditioned reflexes, 802, 1057, 1110
Conductors, electrical, 253, 262
Cone, 30
Conformational analysis, 1197, 1427
Conic sections, 49
Conservationism, 443
Constellations, 170
Continued fractions, 202
Continuity of the germ plasm, 704
Continuous creation, 1149, 1174, 1398,
  1433, 1437
Contraceptives, oral, 1266
Control rods, 1357
Conventions, scientific, 423
Convergent series, 226
Conversations on the Plurality of Worlds,
  239
Cook, Frederick A., 866
Coolidge, Calvin, 1020
Coolidge tube, 1020
Cooper electron pairs, 1489
Coordination theory, 960
Copper, 470
Copper arsenite, 329
Copper carbonate, 364
Copper plating, 413
Copper sulfate, 413
Coral reefs, 554, 1304
Corals, 252, 491
Cordite, 510, 673, 759, 1031
Core, Earth's, 584, 917, 1133
Cori ester, 1194
Coriolis forces, 480
Corona, solar, 712

  temperature of, 1196, 1316
  X rays and, 1407
Coronagraph, 1196
Coronium, 719, 1196
Corrector plate, 1065
Corticoids, 1105, 1188
  isolation of, 1201
Cortisone, 1188
  synthesis of, 1039, 1416
Cosimo II (Grand Duke, Tuscany), 211
Cosmic egg, 1174, 1278
Cosmic rays, 969, 1088, 1274, 1292
  detection of, 1146
  particulate nature of, 1159, 1289
  showers of, 1280
Cosmogony, 777, 1174
Cosmological principle, 1186
Cosmological term, 1125
"Cosmos," 1504
Cotton gin, 386
Cottonseed oil, 856
Coulomb, 474
Coulomb's law, 318
Coumarin, 734
Counter-earth, 19
Coupling, J. J., 1351
Cowcatcher, 481
Cowpox, 348
CP symmetry, 1454, 1497
CPT symmetry, 1497
Crab nebula, 513, 1408
Cranial index, 498
Craniometry, 653
Craters, lunar, 724, 1071
  names of, 185
Creatine, 612, 661
Creatinine, 661
Critias, 21
Critical temperature, 580, 698
Critique of Pure Reason, 293
Cromwell, Oliver, 172, 197, 208, 220
Crookes tube, 695
Cross hairs, 195
Crossing-over, 957, 1153
Crust, Earth's, 871
  magnetic properties of, 1285
  plates of, 1303
  thickness of, 926
Crustaceans, 336
Cryogenics, 474
Cryolite, 665, 933
Crystallization, 485
Crystallography, 332
Crystalloids, 547
Crystals, 162, 225

asymmetry of, 642
  mirror images of, 642
  structure of, 1141
  ultrasonic sound and, 897
  X rays and, 1068
Crystal sets, 808
Cube, duplication of, 25
Cubic centimeters, 910
Cubic equations, 135
Cuneiform, 511, 559
Curare, 270, 1325
Curie, 996
Curie point, 897
Curium, 1372
Cyanates, 532
Cyanocobalamin, 1312
  structure of, 1352
Cybernetics, 316
Cybernetics, 1175
Cyclic AMP, 1402
Cyclohexane, 1197
Cyclotron, 1241, 1246, 1329, 1395
Cystine, 388
Cytochrome C, 1267
Cytochromes, 1089, 1113
Cytology, 768
Cytoplasm, 768
Cytosine, 842, 1291, 1406

Daedalus, 1
Daguerrotype, 467, 511
Daltonism, 389
Dalton's law, 389
Daniell cell, 470
Darius I (King, Persia), 9, 559
David, Jacques L., 443
Davy lamp, 421, 431
DDT, 1216
  typhus fever and, 956
Deaf-mutes, 286
Death rate, 201
Debye, 1094
Debye-Hückel theory, 1094
Decimal fractions, 158
Decimal point, 159
De Corporis Humani Fabrica, 146
Deep sea, life in, 590
Deferent, 50
Definite proportions, law of, 364, 389, 425,
  515
Defoe, Daniel, 265
De Gaulle, Charles, 990, 1227
Degenerate matter, 1045
Degrees of freedom, 740
Dehydrogenations, 1048, 1089

Deimos, 681
D'Elhuyar, Juan José, 367
De Magnete, 155
Demography, 201
De Motu Animalium, 191
De Natura Rerum, 53
Denatured alcohol, 547
Dendrochronology, 963
De Nova Stella, 156
Deoxyribonucleic acid (*see* DNA)
Deoxyribose, 980
Dephlogisticated air, 312, 334
De Re Metallica, 132
Descent of Man, The, 554
Descriptive geometry, 340
Determinants, 541
Deuterium, 1037, 1164, 1211, 1244
Deuteron, 1244, 1280
  structure of, 1362
Devonian era, 442, 477
Dewar flasks, 759
Diabetes mellitus, 205, 448, 1115, 1152
Dialogue on the Two Chief World Systems,
  166
Dialysis, 547, 947
Diamagnetism, 1000
Diamonds, 334, 375
  synthetic, 831, 850, 863, 1080
Diane de Poitiers, 134
Diastase, 490
Diatomaceous earth, 703
Dichlorodiphenyltrichloroethane (DDT),
  1216
Dickens, Charles, 474
*Dictionary of Practical and Theoretical
  Chemistry,* 361
Didymium, 501, 890
Dielectric constant, 936
Diels-Alder reaction, 1039, 1254
Diene synthesis, 1039
Diesel engine, 886
Dietary-deficiency disease, 888, 1027
Diffraction, light, 199, 402
Diffusion, gas, 547
Difluorodichloromethane (Freon), 1132
Digestion, 43, 191, 196, 578
  chemistry of, 252
  nerve control of, 802
Digestive juice, 725
Digitalis, 327
Dimensional analysis, 393
Diminishing returns, law of, 387
Dinosaur eggs, 1091
Dinosaurs, 396, 468, 539, 690
  extinction of, 1363

Dione, 209
Dionysius II (King, Syracuse), 24
Diophantine equations, 66
Diphtheria, 419, 809, 828, 844, 845, 846
Dipole moments, 1094
Dirigibles, 737, 974
Discourse on Method, 183
Disease, 22
  bacteria and, 767
Disraeli, Benjamin, 554
Dissection, 11, 42, 43, 110, 134, 146
Distances, stellar, 975
Distillation, 59
Divinylchlorarsine, 1058
DNA (deoxyribonucleic acid), 980, 1054, 1270
  enzymes affecting, 1505, 1508
  genetic code and, 1448, 1476
  protein formation and, 1447
  replication of, 1406, 1480
  structure of, 1406
  synthetic, 1422
Doering, William von Eggers, 1416
Dog whistle, 636
Dolomite, 353
Dollfuss, Engelbert, 984
Dolphins, 29
Domagk, Hildegarde, 1183
Domains, magnetic, 942, 1079
Donati's comet, 671
Doppler effect, 534
Doppler-Fizeaux effect, 1038
Double bonds, 661
Double Helix, The, 1480
  DNA and, 1406
Double refraction, 210, 231, 394, 404, 408, 455
Double stars, 185, 209, 483
Dowsing, 413
Dragons of Eden, The, 1504
Draper point, 566
Dreams, 865
Drinking water, 687
Drosophila, 957
Drug addiction, 830, 865
Dry ice, 1309, 1391
Dry plate photography, 677
D-series, 833
Duodenum, 42
Dust, clouds and, 979
Dyes, synthetic, 706, 734
  cells and, 762
Dynamite, 703
Dynamo, 666
Dysentery, 870, 997

Dysprosium, 736

e, 164, 275, 555, 641
Ear, 631
  inner, 1040
Earth, age of, 169, 231, 277, 297, 502, 531, 652, 987
  circumference of, 204
  circumnavigation of, 124, 130
  core of, 1133, 1279
  curvature of, 4
  internal heat of, 297
  interior of, 814, 1133
  iron core of, 584
  magnetic field of, 155, 459, 546, 678, 1279
  mass of, 307
  moon's tidal influence on, 777
  motion of, 19, 41, 127
  origin of, 277
  primordial atmosphere of, 1490
  rotation of, 28, 119, 270, 293, 480, 619, 777
  shape of, 267, 270, 283, 970, 1412
  size of, 48, 52
  spherical form of, 29, 33, 75, 99, 121
  surface changes of, 296, 297
  zones of, 56, 58
Earth (mineral), 373
Earthquakes, 550, 898, 917
  cause of, 223, 294
Earthquake waves, 753, 814, 871, 1133
Earthshine, 166
Easter, 23
  dating of, 75
Eccentricity, 169
Echinodermata, 336, 640, 913
Echo I, 1351, 1400
Echolocation, 1000
Eclipse, 3, 14
  solar, 406, 647, 719, 1064, 1085
  stellar, 381
Ecliptic, obliquity of, 18, 48
Ecology, 707, 1216
Edison effect, 788, 803
Edward III (King, England), 111
Edward VII (King, Great Britain), 474
Efficiency expert, 864
Egg incubator, 252
Eggs, 704
  cellular nature of, 669
  dinosaur, 1091
  mammalian, 478
Egypt, archaeology of, 838
Einsteinium, 1064, 1372

911

Einstein shift, 1064, 1483
Eisenhower, Dwight D., 1370, 1392
Electric cell, 936
Electric chair, 867
Electric circuits, mathematics of, 806
Electric current, 337
Electric fishes, 611
Electric force, distance and, 318
Electric furnace, 831
Electric generator, 837
Electric impulse, velocity of, 648
Electricity, animal, 320
  element isolation and, 421
  flow of, 337, 461
  galvanic, 320
  particulate nature of, 474, 664
  positive and negative, 266, 272
  transport of, 867
Electric lights, 788, 863, 1020
Electrics, 155
Electric shock, 257, 269
Electrocardiogram, 904
Electrochemistry, 474, 649
Electrode, 474
Electrodynamics, 407
Electroencephalography, 1014
Electrolysis, 361, 474
  laws of, 474, 894
Electrolytes, 474, 684, 894, 1094
Electromagnetic interaction, 1243
Electromagnetic radiation, 692, 810, 839,
  873, 969, 1025
  electrons and, 1101
Electromagnetic spectrum, 810
Electromagnetic theory, 692, 806
Electromagnetic Theory, 806
Electromagnetism, 407, 446
  discovery of, 417
Electromagnets, 436, 503, 985
Electrometer, 322
  capillary, 778
Electronic charge, 969
Electronic computer, 1139
Electron microscope, 1134, 1202, 1222,
  1322, 1339, 1380, 1401, 1418
Electron orbits, 1101, 1117
Electron-positron formation, 1207
Electrons, 272, 583, 613, 664, 695
  acceleration of, 1367
  atomic magnetism and, 1219
  bombardment of gases by, 1081
  charge of, 618, 969
  chemical bonding and, 978, 1013, 1037,
    1236
  diffraction of, 1156

discovery of, 869
distribution of, 1049, 1111
Edison effect and, 803
emission of, 1066
energy levels of, 976, 1101, 1228
ions and, 894
nucleus and, 1150
orbits of, 976
photoelectric effect and, 920, 1064
radioactivity and, 834
radio tube and, 1017
valence and, 978, 1013
wave nature of, 1078, 1084, 1101, 1117
Electron shells, 1101, 1111, 1228
Electron spin, 1228, 1234
Electron-volts, 337
Electron waves, 1117, 1157, 1191
Electrophoresis, 1097, 1257
Electrophorus, 337
Electrophysiology, 611
Electroscopes, 1088
Electrostatic capacitance, 474
Electrostatic generator, 1246
Electrostatics, 189, 257, 266, 272, 407
Electrotherapy, 591
Elementary Treatise on Chemistry, 334
Elements, chemical, 212
  Greek, 3, 17
  list of, 334
  missing, 705
  periodic table of, 685, 705, 727
  relationships among, 427
  similarities among, 622
  spectral lines and, 648
  valence of, 474
Elephantiasis, 771
Elevator, 122, 569
Elixir of life, 76
Elizabeth I (Queen, England), 155, 163
Ellipses, 169
Elliptical functions, 541
Elliptical integrals, 358
Embden-Meyerhof pathway, 1095
Embryo, 981
  chick, 489
Embryology, 148, 151, 313, 478, 489, 600
  comparative, 478, 707
Emerson, Ralph Waldo, 543
Enceladus, 321
Encke's comet, 376, 434, 475
Encyclopedia, 286, 289, 309
Endocrine glands, 482
Endoplasmic reticulum, 1222
Endothermic, 674
Energy, 402, 625

conservation of, 298, 587, 613, 631, 1064
  human, 848
  Krebs cycle and, 1231
  mass and, 1064, 1207
  particles of, 887
Engine, internal combustion, 635, 694, 708, 995
Engine knock, 1044, 1132
Eniac, 1139, 1328, 1431
Entropy, 633, 692
Enzymes, 490, 563, 725, 903, 1009
  crystalline, 1120, 1148
  genes and, 1270
  iron-containing, 1113
  proteins as, 1120, 1148
  reaction mechanism of, 1033
  respiratory, 1113
  trace minerals and, 1240
Enzyme-substrate complex, 1384, 1417
Eocene, 487
Epicycle, 50
Epidemics, 208
Epigenesis, 478
Epilepsy, 22, 1014
Epinephrine, 855, 877, 1105
Equilibrium, 1040
Equine encephalitis, 1202
Equinoxes, precession of, 50
Equivalent weights, 474, 668
Eras, geologic, 442
Erbium, 501
Erebus, Mount, 512
Erlenmeyer flask, 661
Ernst August (Elector, Hannover), 670
Eros, 763
  parallax of, 1140
Erythronium, 382, 451
ESP (extrasensory perception), 1182
Essay on Population, 387
Essay on the Principle of Population, An, 554
Essential amino acids, 912, 1114
Essex, Robert Devereux, earl of, 163
Ester, 457
Estrone, 1169
  isolation of, 1265
Ethane, 856
Ether, diethyl, 543, 594, 617, 650, 993
Ether, luminiferous, 455, 463, 618, 835, 1064, 1400
Ether-drift, 953
Ethics, 21
Ethology, 1271, 1326
Ethylene, 389, 856
Ethylene glycol, 602

Ethyl iodide, 1132
Etymologies, 72
Eugenics, 636, 1145
Eugenius IV (Pope), 116
Euphonium, 370
Euripides, 14
Europa, 166
Europium, 825
Eustachian tube, 11, 141
Evaporated milk, 524
Everest, Mount, 1432
Evolution, behavioral, 1271
  biological, 17, 29, 276, 277, 286, 291, 308, 336, 502, 539, 624, 631, 652
  human, 502, 554, 643, 659, 884, 959, 1096, 1268
  mutations and, 792
  natural selection and, 297, 387, 554, 562, 643, 1224
  stellar, 606, 777, 1056, 1203, 1278, 1345, 1356, 1398
Exchange forces, 1245, 1323
Exchange particles, 1170
Exercitatio de Motu Cordis et Sanguinis, 174
Exothermic, 674
Expanding universe, 1004, 1038, 1125, 1136, 1174, 1423, 1437
Expanding Universe, The, 1085
Experimental physiology, 578
Experimentation, 99, 104, 163
Explorer I, 1370, 1392
Explorer III, 1392
Explorer IV, 1392
Explosions, chemical, 1200
Explosives, 977
Exponents, 198
Extragalactic nebulae, 1136
Extrasensory Perception, 1182
Extraterrestrial civilizations, 1459, 1491, 1504
Extrovert, 1035

Fahlberg, Constantine, 781
Fahrenheit scale, 254
Falconry, 97
Falling bodies, 38, 122, 158, 166
Fallopian tubes, 149
Fallout shelters, 1342
Farad, 474
Faraday, 474
Farsightedness, 605
Fat, tissue, 1211
Fats, 440

chemistry of, 448
synthesis of, 674
Fatty acids, 448
Faults, crustal, 898
Ferdinand II (King, Spain), 99, 121, 123
Ferdinand III (Holy Roman Emperor), 189
Ferdinand (Duke, Brunswick), 415
Fermat's last theorem, 188, 410, 826
Fermentation, 222, 642, 903
Ferments, 725, 903
Fermi-Dirac statistics, 1170
Fermions, 1170
Fermium, 1243, 1372
Ferrimagnetism, 1285
Ferrites, 1285
Ferrocene, 1429, 1445
Ferromagnetism, 942, 1079, 1285, 1333
Fertilization, plant, 354
Fertilizers, 302, 532, 977
artificial, 588
Fever, 592
Fibers, artificial, 677, 743, 1190
Field-emission microscope, 1364
Fifth degree, equation of the, 527, 571
Filaments, electric light, 677, 788, 890,
1020, 1072
Film, photographic, 852
Filterable virus, 817
Fingerprints, 636
Finnegans Wake, 1487
Fire, 10
discovery of, 55
First International Chemical Congress, 668,
680
Fission, nuclear, 1060, 1063, 1064, 1101,
1187, 1208, 1227, 1238, 1243, 1244,
1251, 1284, 1321, 1330, 1362
FitzGerald, Edward, 87
FitzGerald contraction, 821, 835, 1064
Flatworms, 517
Flavoenzymes, 1089
Flavones, 1107
Flies, 1113
Fluorescence, 618, 623, 834
Fluorescent lights, 989
Fluorine, 582
discovery of, 831
Fluoroscope, 774, 891
Flying saucers, 1237
FM (frequency modulation), 1143
Foci, elliptical, 169
Fodder, preservation of, 1176
Follicle, ovarian, 478
Food, preservation of, 359
Forces, 166, 231

Fossils, 96, 122, 147, 213, 225, 333, 690,
748, 1091
classification of, 396
micro-organismic, 491, 1399
strata and, 395
Foster, George C., 727
Foucault's pendulum, 619
Foundations of Geometry, 918
Fourier's theorem, 393
Foxglove, 327
Fractions, 66
Francis I (Emperor, Austria), 323, 371
Francis I (King, France), 122, 134, 148
Francis II (King, France), 139
Francis Joseph I (Emperor, Austria), 890,
1075
Franklin stove, 272
Frasch process, 824
Frau im Mond, 1315
Fraunhofer lines, 450, 618, 619
Frederick I (King, Prussia), 221, 233
Frederick I (King, Sweden), 242, 260
Frederick II (King, Denmark), 156
Frederick II the Great (King, Prussia), 267,
275, 279, 289, 293, 299, 317, 321, 329,
356, 397
Frederick III (Holy Roman Emperor), 118
Frederick (Prince of Wales), 253
Frederick William I (King, Prussia), 241
Frederick William III (King, Prussia), 439
Frederick William IV (King, Prussia), 508,
541, 551, 670
Free association, 865
Free energy, 674, 740
Free radical, 950, 1118, 1236
Freezing point, depression of, 894
Freon, 1044, 1132
Frequency modulation (FM), 1143
Friedel-Crafts reaction, 693, 741
From Immigrant to Inventor, 891
Fronts, weather, 1205
Fructose, 663, 691
Fructose-1, 6-diphosphate, 1194
Fruit fly, 957
Fuel cells, 568
Fulbert, 88
Fulminates, 532
Fumaric acid, 1167
Fusion bomb (see Hydrogen bomb)
Fusion, nuclear, 1180, 1335, 1390

Gadolinium, 373
discovery of, 599
Gahnite, 339
Galaxies, 321, 1136

clusters of, 1163, 1209
distance of, 1163
exploding, 1338, 1469
radio sources and, 1179
speed of recession of, 1149
spiral, 879, 1007
Galaxy (*see also* Milky Way), 281
center of, 1102, 1109, 1229
rotation of, 1185, 1229
size of, 815, 1102, 1229
spiral structure of, 1229, 1298, 1430
Gallium, 739
discovery of, 736
Galvanized iron, 320
Galvanometer, 320, 422, 436
string, 904
Game theory, 1248, 1273
Gamma globulins, 813
Gamma rays, 906, 908, 965, 996, 1159,
1292, 1423
matter from, 1207
Mössbauer effect and, 1483
Ganymede, 166
Garfield, James A., 789
Garibaldi, Giuseppe, 668, 727
Gas, 175
Gas-diffusion method, 1272, 1330
Gases, blood, 597
diffusion of, 547
electron bombardment of, 1081
high-pressure, 751
kinetic theory of, 692
liquefaction of, 474, 580, 698, 779, 783,
843
perfect, 726
spectra of, 1286
transportation of, 785
Gas laws, 698, 726
Gas lighting, 363
Gas masks, 490, 1009
Gasoline, 886, 966
coal conversion to, 1098
Gastric juice, 444, 902
Gas warfare, 977
Gaussia, 415
Gaussian curve, 496
Gay-Lussac's law, 343, 420
Geiger counter, 1082
Geissler tubes, 521, 583, 695
Gelatin, 438, 691, 912
photography and, 852
Gene-linkage, 957
General Anatomy, 400
General History of Nature, 293
General theory of relativity, 564, 794, 935,

1045, 1064, 1125, 1186, 1405, 1483
Generator, electric, 474
Genes, 872, 957, 1047
enzymes and, 1270
mapping of, 957, 1153
regulatory, 1253
transplant rejection and, 1275
viruses and, 1282
Genetic code, 1278, 1355, 1406, 1447,
1448, 1476
Genetics, 598, 872, 913
bacterial, 1313
DNA and, 1054
laws of, 638, 938
Genetics and the Origin of Species, 1224
Geneva nomenclature, 553
Genghis Khan, 105
Genotype, 872
Geochemistry, 374, 924, 1123
Geocoronium, 719
Geodesy, 970
Geographos, 1179
Geology, 297, 322
life and, 924
Geomagnetic poles, 415
Geometric isomerism, 716
Geometry, descriptive, 340
n-dimensional, 556, 629
non-Euclidean, 247, 415, 484, 530, 670,
800
projective, 456, 800
Geophysics, 397, 1123
George I (King, Great Britain), 233, 242
George II (King, Great Britain), 32
George III (King, Great Britain), 253, 259,
273, 288, 308, 312, 321, 331, 360
George IV (King, Great Britain), 384
George V (King, Great Britain), 1152
George (Prince, Denmark), 234
Georgium Sidus, 321
German Chemical Society, 604
Germanium, 739
transistors and, 1348
German measles virus, 1397
German Rocket Society, 1315
Germ layers, 478, 591, 750
Germ plasm, 704
Germ theory of disease, 419, 557, 642, 767,
888
Gerontology, 448
Gestalt psychology, 1112
Geysers, 565
Gibbon, 884
Gilbert, Joseph H., 588
Gin, 196

Girardin, Saint Marc, 578
Glaciers, 449, 453, 551, 766
Gladstone, William, 554
Glass, 450
Glass electrode, 977
Glauber's salt, 190
Gliders, 793, 995
Globular clusters, 1102, 1109, 1163, 1469
Glow lamp, 1017
Glucose, 364, 380, 430, 663, 691, 1074
  diabetes and, 448, 1152
Glucose-1-phosphate, 1194
Glucose-6-phosphate, 1194
Glutathione, 912
Glycine, 515
Glycogen, 578, 1095, 1231
  breakdown of, 1194
  formation of, 691
Glycolysis, anaerobic, 1095
Gmelin's test, 457
Gobi desert, 742
Gödel's proof, 1301
Godwin, Francis, 197
Goering, Hermann, 1155
Goiter, 525
Gold, 977
  colloidal, 943
Goldbach's conjecture, 256
Gold foil, 996, 1156
Golgi bodies, 764
Goniometer, 388
Gonococcus, 859
Gonorrhea, 859
Gout, 208
Governor, centrifugal, 316
Graafian follicles, 228
Grafting, tissue, 1223
Graf Zeppelin, 737
Graham's law, 547
Gramicidin S, 1394
Gram-negative bacteria, 841
Gram-positive bacteria, 841
Granite, 777
Graphite, 863, 1243
  moderator effect of, 1208
Gratings, refraction, 798
Gravitation, law of universal, 231
Gravitational acceleration, 794
Gravitational constant, 231, 307
Gravitational red shift, 1064
Gray matter, 371
Great Apes, The, 1041
Great Barringer Meteor Crater, 905
Great Hercules Cluster, 305
Great Train Robbery, The, 788

Greek fire, 74
Greene, Nathanael, 386
Greenhouse effect, 894
Greenland, 866, 1071
  crossing of, 914
Gregorian calendar, 83, 152, 156, 198, 232, 258
Gregory XIII (Pope), 152, 156
Gresham's law, 127
Grid, 1017
Grignard reagents, 993
Group theory, 571
Grove cell, 568
Growth hormone, 1382
Guanidine, 661
Guanine, 842, 1291, 1406
Guano, 397
Guide for the Perplexed, 92
Guillotin, Joseph, 314
Gulf Stream, 272, 548
Guncotton, 510, 703
Gunnery, 166
Gunpowder, 99, 510
Gustavus II Adolphus (King, Sweden), 189
Guyots, 1304
Gymnosperms, 403, 651
Gynecology, 567
Gypsum, 334
Gyroscope, 619, 907

Haber process, 1028
Haber-Bosch process, 1028
Hadrons, 1487
Hafnium, 1121
  discovery of, 1100, 1135
Hahnium, 1063, 1372
Hairsprings, 223
Hale telescope, 974
Half life, 996
Hall (crater), 681
Hall, James N., 331
Halley's comet, 119, 238, 283, 289, 439, 475, 573, 927
Hall-Héroult process, 933
Handbook of Chemistry, 457
Handbook of Organic Chemistry, 732
Hannibal, 47
Hansen, A. G. H., 859
Harden's coenzyme, 1011, 1089
Harmonic analysis, 393
Harun al-Rashid (Caliph), 76
Haversian canals, 237
Hawaiian Islands, 300
Hayes, Rutherford B., 503
H-bomb (see Hydrogen bomb)

Hearing, 1220
Hearst, William R., 1005
Heart, 17, 36, 106
   artificial, 1016
Heartbeat, 219, 717
Heart transplant, 1452
Heat, 298, 334, 346
   flow of, 356, 393
   measurement of, 613
   mechanical equivalent of, 360
   motion and, 360
Heat as a Mode of Motion, 626
Heat-death of the universe, 633, 692, 894
Heat radiation, 715
Heavy hydrogen, 1022, 1037, 1280
   isolation of, 1164
Heavy water, 1037, 1164, 1227
   moderator effect of, 1208
Hegel, G. W. F., 800
Heliometer, 264, 439
Heliotrope, 415
Helium, 759
   age of the earth and, 1118
   alpha particles and, 996
   bends and, 837
   discovery of, 647, 719, 832
   isotopes of, 1333
   Joule-Thomson effect and, 726
   liquefaction of, 843
   liquid, 1042
   nuclear structure of, 1150
   production of, 974
   solid, 843, 1042
   spectrum of, 941
   sun and, 1308
Helium I, 1042
Helium II, 843, 1042, 1333
   heat conduction of, 1173
   superfluidity of, 1173
Helium-3, 1333
Héloise, 88
Heme, 1009, 1384
   structure of, 1076
   synthesis of, 1358
Hemoglobin, 578, 663, 1009, 1059, 1076, 1084
   abnormal, 1236
   amino acid structure of, 1415, 1426
Hemorrhage, 1177
Henle's loop, 557
Henry, 503
Henry II (King, England), 89
Henry II (King, France), 134, 139
Henry III (King, England), 99
Henry III (King, France), 139, 157

Henry IV (King, France), 153
Henry Draper Catalogue, 932
Hensen, Matthew, 866
Heparin, 1218
Hepatitis, 1467
Heredity, 636
Hering, Ewald, 755
Herodotus, 3, 9, 12
Hertzian waves, 873
Hertzsprung-Russell diagram, 1056
Hesperia, 714
Hesperornis, 690
Hess's law, 528
Hexaphenylethane, 950
Hexuronic acid, 1167
Hidalgo, 1163
Hieroglyphics, 187, 402
Hieron II (King, Syracuse), 47
Hieronymus, 47
High-energy phosphate bond, 947
High octane gasoline, 966
High pressure, 751
Hindenburg, 737
Hippuric acid, 515
Histaminase, 1218
Histamine, 1046
Histidine, 842, 1114
Histology, 400, 600
History, 9
History of Plants, 136
Hitler, Adolf, 273, 865, 887, 920, 929, 936, 941, 976, 977, 1009, 1015, 1024, 1031, 1060, 1064, 1068, 1081, 1084, 1086, 1088, 1089, 1094, 1095, 1100, 1101, 1112, 1116, 1117, 1118, 1123, 1124, 1145, 1155, 1165, 1177, 1183, 1208, 1211, 1226, 1227, 1231, 1233, 1265, 1289, 1291, 1306, 1308, 1313, 1332, 1370, 1389, 1444
Hofmann degradation reaction, 604
Hofmann violets, 604
Holmes, Oliver W., Jr., 558
Holmes, Sherlock, 865
Holmium, 746
Holography, 1230
Homeostasis, 998
Home permanent, 1033
Hominids, 1268
Homo erectus, 1096
Homo habilis, 1268
Homo sapiens, 276, 1096, 1268
Homunculi, 313
Honorius IV (Pope), 101
Hoof-and-mouth disease, 828
Hooker, John D., 974

Hoover, Herbert, 132
Hormones, 807, 954, 1152
  isolation of, 855
  pituitary, 1239, 1382
Horse, evolution of, 748
Horsepower, 316
Hothouses, 470
Hubble radius, 1136
Hugh Capet (King, France), 84
Human evolution, 1096
Humboldt Current, 397
Humors, 22
Huns, 1264
Hydraulic press, 207
Hydrazine, 833
Hydrocarbons, 966
Hydrochloric acid, 162, 190, 421
  stomach and, 440, 1103
Hydrodynamics, 268
Hydrofluoric acid, 831
Hydrogen, 334, 421, 977
  balloons and, 325, 343
  discovery of, 307
  heavy, 1022, 1037
  interstellar, 1203
  isotopes of, 1164, 1211, 1244
  Joule-Thomson effect and, 726
  liquid, 698, 759, 779, 851, 1245
  microwave radiation of, 1229, 1378, 1430
  palladium and, 547
  platinum and, 427
  solid, 759
  spectral lines of, 658, 941
  steel and, 1028
  sun and, 585, 974, 1308
  universe and, 1056
Hydrogen-2, 1244
Hydrogen-3, 1244, 1342
Hydrogenation, catalytic, 856
Hydrogen atom, 1101
Hydrogen bomb, 1022, 1164, 1180, 1243,
  1244, 1261, 1273, 1332, 1366, 1444
Hydrogen bromide, 474
Hydrogen chloride, 312, 741
Hydrogen cyanide, 329, 420
Hydrogen fluoride, 582
Hydrogen fusion, 1022, 1308
Hydrogen ions, 840, 967
  catalytic properties of, 1061
Hydrogen molecules, 1245
  quantum mechanics and, 1226
Hydrogen peroxide, 416, 1384
Hydrogen sulfide, 474
Hydrophobia, 642
Hydrostatics, 158

Hygiene, 612
Hygrometer, 244, 322, 470
Hypatia, 69
Hyperbolic functions, 299
Hyperion, 509, 660
Hyperons, 1487
Hypnotism, 314, 494, 662, 865
Hypothalamus, 1460
Hysteria, 865

i, 275
Iapetus, 209
Iatrochemistry, 131
Icarus, 1163
Ice, 783
Ice Ages, 551, 766, 1303
Iceland spar, 210, 394, 408, 455
Iconoscope, 1134
Ideal gas, 726
Identical twins, 636
Iguanodon, 468
Ikhnaton, (King, Egypt), 838
Iliad, 479, 634, 1069
Illumination, electrical, 421, 788, 863, 1020
Imaginary numbers, 137, 198, 545
Immunity, 1223
Immunization, 642, 809
Immunology, 348
Impossibility, proof of, 415, 527
Imprinting, 1271
Index of refraction, 1257
Indigo, 718, 734
Indium, 506, 654
Induction, electrical, 474, 503, 536
Industrial chemistry, 368
Industrial Revolution, 316, 616
Inert gases, 832
Inertia, 122
Infectious disease, 570, 576
Inferiority complex, 984
Infinitesimals, 186
Infinity, 772
Information theory, 1404
Infrared radiation, 321, 711, 765
  properties of, 504
Infrared spectrophotometer, 1021
Inheritance, laws of, 792, 999
Ink, 114
Inner ear, 1040
Innocent XII (Pope), 214
Inoculation, smallpox, 270, 306, 348
Inorganic compounds, 515
Insecticides, 876, 1216
Insect mimicry, 656
Insects, 223, 224, 1216

plant fertilization and, 354
respiration of, 291
Insemination, artificial, 302, 988
Insensible perspiration, 165
Insulators, electrical, 253, 262
Insulin, 791, 807, 1115, 1218
amino acid structure of, 1426
crystalline, 877
discovery of, 1152
Integers, 645, 772
Intelligence, inheritance of, 1086, 1348
measurement of, 878
Intelligence quotients, 878
Interference, light, 402
Interferometer, 835
Interlingua, 889
Intermediary metabolism, 691, 947
Intermediates, reaction, 1286
Internal combustion engine, 635, 694, 708,
886, 995
International Geophysical Year, 1392, 1432
Interpretation of Dreams, The, 865
Interstellar matter, 940, 949, 1109, 1203,
1286
Introduction to Natural Philosophy, 361
Introvert, 1035
Invar, 910
Inversion, optical, 928
Invertase, 663
Invertebrates, 750
classification of, 336
Investigation of the Laws of Thought, An,
595
Io, 166
Iodine, 420, 438, 529, 796
antiknock and, 1132
discovery of, 414
goiter and, 525
thyroid gland and, 786, 1105
Ion-exchange resins, 1259
Ionic radii, 1141
Ionium, 987
Ionization, theory of, 649, 894
Ionosphere, 1158
Ions, 487, 649, 894
clouds and, 979
IQ tests, 878
Iridium, 1363
discovery of, 375
Iron, 575, 909
anemia and, 208
cytochromes and, 1089
Earth's core and, 584
enzymes and, 1113
heme and, 1009

magnetic properties of, 942, 1079
solar corona and, 1196
Iron Age, 53, 460
Iron-nickel alloy, 910
Irradiation, 1046
Irrational numbers, 641, 688, 772
Isabella (Queen, Spain), 99, 121
Isagoge in artem analyticam, 153
Isis, 423
Island universes, 293, 1007
Isletin, 807, 1152
Islets of Langerhans, 791, 1152
Isomers, 532, 716
nuclear, 1261
optical, 642
structural formulas of, 680
Isomorphism, 485
Isoprene, 966
Isostasy, 523, 753, 970
Isotopes, 695, 869, 968, 996, 1051, 1052
nuclear structure and, 1150
radioactive, 100, 1227
Isotopic tracers, 1164, 1211
Ivan IV (Emperor, Russia), 85
Ivan VI (Emperor, Russia), 275
Ivory, 728

Ja'far al-Sadiq, 76
James I (King, England), 155, 156, 163,
169, 174
James II (King, England), 231
James VI (*see* James I)
Jansky, 1295
Java Man, 884, 1096, 1162
Jeffries, John, 362
Jet streams, 1205
John I (King, Portugal), 111
John II (King, Portugal), 121, 130
John VIII (Byzantine Emperor), 116
John XXII (Pope), 109
John of Gaunt (Duke, England), 111
Johnson, Lyndon B., 1280
Joseph, 1, 865
Joseph II (Emperor, Austria), 323
Josephson effect, 1509
Joule, 613
Joule-Thomson effect, 613, 652, 698, 726,
758, 759
Joyce, James, 1487
J particles, 1493
Julian calendar, 23, 54, 83, 99, 119, 152,
156
Julian Day, 154
Julius II (Pope), 140
Jupiter, 185

atmosphere of, 1038, 1290
diameter of, 258
mass of, 439
radio wave radiation from, 1455
red spot of, 466
rotation of, 209
satellites of, 166, 171, 209, 232, 696, 835, 883, 964, 1003, 1151
structure of, 1290
surface temperature of, 1147
Trojan asteroids and, 927
Jupiter probes, 1491
Jupiter V, 883
Jussieu, Bernard, 345
Jussieu, Joseph, 345
Justinian I (East Roman Emperor), 24

Kala-azar, 948
Kaleidoscope, 433
Kamchatka, 250
Kapteyn's star, 815
Karl Theodor (Elector, Bavaria), 360
K capture, 1323
Kelvin scale, 652
Kennedy, John F., 1280
Kennelly-Heaviside layer, 806, 1158
Kepler's laws, 169, 231
Keratin, 1033
Kerosene, 886
Ketone, 457
Key, Francis Scott, 957
Khrushchev, Nikita, 1214
Kidneys, 465
Kidney stones, 298
Kieselguhr, 703
Kinematic relativity, 1186
Kinetic energy, 215, 480, 613, 652
Kinetic theory of gases, 547, 633, 692, 726, 769
Kinetogenesis, 748
Kingsley, Charles, 69
Kirchhoff's law, 648
Kirkwood gaps, 586
Kjeldahl flask, 801
Klystron-oscillator, 1351
K-mesons, 1473, 1487
Kolbe reaction, 610
Kosmos, 397, 466
K radiation, 1049
Krebs cycle, 1167, 1221, 1231
Krypton, 835
compounds of, 1499
discovery of, 832, 1001
K shell, 1323
Kublai Khan, 105

Kurchatovium, 1381
Kuru, 1456
Kymograph, 597

Lacquers, 1031
Lactic acid, 631, 716, 1194, 1231
glycolysis and, 1095
muscle and, 1108
Ladislas V (King, Hungary), 118
Lalande *21185,* 309
planet of, 1247
Lamarckism, 336
Lambert, 299
Land camera, 1344
Langley, 711
Language, international, 889
Lanthanides, 1372
Lanthanum, 501
Lasers, 1252, 1400
invention of, 1479
Latent heat, 298
Latitude, 27
line of, 33
Latitude and longitude, 50
Latitude effect, 1159
Laudanum, 131, 208
Laughing gas, 421
Lavoisier, Marie-Anne, 334, 360
Lawrencium, 1241, 1372
Lead, 709
atomic weight of, 968
isotopes of, 1052, 1100
radioactivity and, 987
superconductivity of, 843
Lead acetate, 67
Least action, principle of, 267
Least squares, method of, 415
Leblanc process, 328
Le Châtelier's principle, 812
Lecithin, 663
Lectures on Experimental Philosophy, 503
Leiden jar, (*see* Leyden jar)
Leishmaniasis, 948
Lenard rays, 920
Lenin, Nikolai, 1333
Lens, optic, 151, 402
Lenses, achromatic, 273
Lenz's law, 536
Leo X (Pope), 122
Leo, XIII (Pope), 75
Leopold I (Holy Roman Emperor), 222
Leopold II (King, Belgium), 579
Leopold (Prince, England), 567
Leprosy, 859
Leukemia, 632, 774, 965

Lever, 38, 47
Lewisite, 1058
Leyden jar, 257, 269, 272, 320, 337
Lice, disease and, 767, 956, 992, 1216
Lie detector, 1161
Life, age of, 1399
  geological development and, 924
  origin of, 626, 894, 1171, 1371, 1457,
    1490
Life expectancy, 201, 215
Light, 94, 150, 349
  aberration of, 258
  chemical reactions and, 936
  coherent, 1479
  diffraction of, 199, 402
  disease and, 908
  electric, 788
  gravitational deflection of, 1064
  magnetism and, 839, 945
  oscillation and, 839
  particulate nature of, 231, 1159
  polarized, 394, 1344
  pressure of, 952
  reflection of, 60
  refraction of, 177, 231
  scattering of, 626, 760, 1130
  shift with velocity of, 620
  temperature rise and, 934
  velocity of, 232, 619, 620, 692, 835, 839,
    1281
  wavelength of, 402
  wave nature of, 215, 402, 446, 455
Light, electric, 677
Lighthouses, 455
Lightning, 272
  man-made, 944, 1246
Lightning rods, 272
Light waves, standard measures and, 835
Light-year, 439
Limelight, 428
Limes, 288
Linac, 1395
Lincoln, Abraham, 554
Linear accelerator, 1395
Lines of force, magnetic, 474, 523, 692,
  1335
Liquid air, 832, 851, 989
Liquid-fuel rockets, 1083
Liquid hydrogen, 851
Little America, 1129
Liver, diet and, 1059, 1103
Lockjaw, 846
Locomotion, animal, 683
Locomotive, 399
  invention of, 431

Logarithms, 159, 164, 169, 172
Logic, 29
  symbolic, 233, 549, 595, 797, 889
*Logical Exposition of the Principles of
  Geometry, A*, 889
Long division, 164
Longevity, 775
Longitude, 27
  determination of, 138, 178, 234, 259, 310
  meridians of, 144
Longitudinal waves, 402
Long-playing records, 1319
Lorentz-FitzGerald contraction, 821, 839
Lorenzo the Magnificent (Florence), 122
Louis IV (Holy Roman Emperor), 109
Louix IX (King, France), 104
Louis XII (King, France), 122
Louis XIV (King, France), 209, 215, 227,
  233, 235, 246, 253, 273, 396, 397, 551,
  1157
Louis XV (King, France), 261, 266, 277,
  286, 289, 303, 305
Louis XVI (King, France), 312, 317, 343
Louis XVIII (King, France), 340, 347, 364,
  368, 396, 404, 571
Louis Philippe I (King, France), 397, 420,
  425, 432, 463, 571, 642
Love waves, 926
Lovelace, Ada Augusta, Countess of, 481
Löw, Judah, 1075
Lowell, Amy, 860
Low temperature, 843
L radiation, 1049
LSD, 421
L-series, 833
Lucas, Henry, 231
Ludwig I (King, Bavaria), 461
Luminescence, 774
Luminosity, stellar, 1018, 1045
Lunar probe, 1392
Lunar Society, 308, 312, 316, 327, 363
Lupus vulgaris, 908
Lutetium, 1002
Luther, Martin, 114
Lyceum, 29, 31, 38
Lymph, 218
Lymphatic vessels, 218
Lysergic acid, 1416
Lysine, 900, 1270
Lysozyme, 1077, 1213
Lysozymes, 1418

M-82, 1469
Machine gun, 609, 745
Machines, simple, 60

Mach numbers, 733
Mach's principle, 733
Macromolecules, 1354
Magellan, Strait of, 130
Magellanic clouds, 130, 479, 975, 1163
Magic, 150, 163
Magnesium, 565
  catalytic action of, 993
  chlorophyll and, 1009
  discovery of, 421
Magnetic declination, 158
Magnetic dip, 161
Magnetic domains, 942, 1333
Magnetic poles, 104
Magnetic storms, 290
Magnetic variations, 238
Magnetism, 3, 104, 155
  animal, 314, 494
  heat and, 897
  light and, 839, 945
  molecular beams and, 1124
  superconductivity and, 843
Magnetohydrodynamics, 1335
Magnetosphere, 1392
Magnetostriction, 613
Magnets, strong, 985
Magnitude, absolute, 1018
Malaria, 208, 764, 771, 776, 853
  syphilis and, 874
  transmission of, 876
Malic acid, 928, 1167
Malik Shah (Sultan), 87
Maltose, 691
Mammals, descent of, 959
Mammoth, 519
Mamun (Caliph), 79
Man, evolution of, 458, 502, 554, 643, 653
Manganese, 339
Manganese dioxide, 427
Manganese-steel, 892
Manhattan Engineer District (see
  Manhattan Project)
Manhattan Project, 1064, 1139, 1159, 1208,
  1243
Man in the Moone, 197
Manned space flight, 1392, 1503
Man, the Unknown, 1016
Manual of the Steam Engine, 625
Manure, 532
Maps, 4, 9, 27, 33, 48, 144
  geologic, 395, 405
Marat, Jean Paul, 334
Marcellus, 47
Marcus Aurelius, 65
Margarine, 856

Maria, lunar, 194
Maria Theresa, (Empress, Austria), 302,
  306
Mariner 2, 1279, 1478
Mariotte's law, 203
Markovnikov rule, 729
Mars, 763
  atmosphere of, 1297
  canals of, 499, 681, 714, 860
  color of, 606
  craters on, 883
  ice caps of, 1297
  life on, 756, 860
  map of, 499, 714, 724
  markings on, 215
  motion of, 156, 169
  parallax of, 209, 217
  photographs of, 1038
  rotation of, 209
  satellites of, 681, 696
  surface of, 1504
Marsupials, 303, 331
Masers, 1212, 1252, 1400, 1409, 1453
  continuous, 1436
Masochism, 749
Mass, 231
  conservation of, 334, 1064
  energy and, 1064
Mass action, law of, 346, 701, 721, 829
Mass-energy, conservation of, 1064
Mass-luminosity law, 1085
Mass numbers, 1051
Mass spectrograph, 1051
Mast cells, 845
Masurium, 1166
Mathematics, 3
  Egyptian, 2
  fundamentals of, 797, 889, 911, 1005
  purity of, 24
Matrices, 629
Matrix mechanics, 1117, 1245, 1273
Matter, formation of, 1053
  interstellar, 1109
Matter waves, 1157
Matthias (Holy Roman Emperor), 169
Maunder minima, 818
Maurice of Nassau, 158
Maurice of Saxony (Duke), 132
Maury Hall, 548
Mauve Decade, 734
Mauveine, 734
Maxim gun, 745
Maximilian I (King, Bavaria), 450
Maximilian I (Holy Roman Emperor), 126
Maximilian (Emperor, Mexico), 548

Maxwell's demon, 692
Maxwell's equations, 692, 1064
Mayer, Joseph, 1307
McCarthy, Joseph R., 1102, 1164, 1273, 1280
McKinley, William, 711
Measles, 208
Measures, standard, 486
Méchain, Perre F. A., 350
Mechanical energy, 613
  conservation of, 233
Mechanical equivalent of heat, 587, 613
Medici, Giulio de, 122
Megatherium, 396
Meister, Joseph, 642
Melanocyte-stimulating hormone (MSH), 1382
Melbourne, Lord, 474
Membranes, semipermeable, 773
Mendelevium, 705, 1372
Mental disorders, 338, 494
Mercator projection, 144
Mercuric oxide, 312
Mercury (element), 470
  freezing of, 282
  gas collection over, 312
  polarography and, 1144
  superconductivity of, 843
  thermometer and, 254
Mercury (planet), 54, 127
  mass of, 475
  motion of, 28
  perihelion advance of, 564, 1064
  phases of, 194
  rotation of, 586, 714
  surface temperature of, 1151
  transit of, 169, 182
Mercury poisoning, 1043
Merneptah, 838
Mersenne numbers, 181
Mesmerism, 314
Mesons, 1260, 1274, 1292, 1323, 1454
Mesotron, 1292
Messenger-RNA, 1438, 1447, 1476
Metabolism, 165, 515, 563
  intermediary, 691, 947
Meteor Crater, Great Barringer, 905
Meteorites, 14, 370, 404, 424, 584, 866, 905
  age of, 1118
Meteorographica, 636
Meteorological Observations and Essays, 389
Meteorology, 389
Meteors, 1168
  comets and, 434
  radar and, 1386

Meteor swarm, 615
Methane, 337, 389, 515
  planetary atmospheres and, 1038, 1290
Methionine, 1239
Method of Reaching Extreme Altitudes, A, 1083
Methods of Chemical Nomenclature, 334
Methyl chloride, 1132
Metonic cycle, 23
Metric system, 270, 317, 350, 388, 486, 506
Meyerbeer, Giacomo, 499
Mho, 461
Michaelis-Menten equation, 1033
Michelson-Morley experiment, 730, 821, 835, 953, 1064, 1400
Microcurie, 996
Micrographia, 223
Micrometer, 195
Microorganisms, classification of, 304
  soil, 1128
Microphones, 897
Microphotographs, 619
Microscope, 166, 214, 221, 223, 265
  achromatic, 273, 445, 447
  field-emission, 1364
  oil-immersion, 447
  phase-contrast, 1127
Microsomes, 1380
Microtome, 452
Microwave background radiation, 1174, 1405, 1437, 1501, 1506
Microwaves, amplification of, 1400
Mid-Atlantic Ridge, 1303, 1462
Mid-Oceanic Ridge, 1462
Milk glass, 943
Milky Way, 96, 293, 299, 321, 1102
  nature of, 20, 166, 281
Milky Way Galaxy, 1136
Miller indices, 518
Milliliters, 910
Mimas, 321
  Saturn's rings and, 586
Mimeograph, 788
Mineralogy, 292
  medicine and, 132
Minerals, classification of, 315, 355
  hardness of, 401
Miniaturization, 1348, 1392
Mini black holes, 1510
Minor planets, 341
Miocene, 487
Mira, 167
Miranda, 1297
Mirrors, parabolic, 85
Mirrors, telescope, 619

Mischmetal, 890
Missing link, 884
Mr. Tompkins in Wonderland, 1278
Mitochondria, 1222, 1441
  structure of, 1380
Mixed ethers, 650
Mizar, 185, 660
M, N blood groups, 973
Moas, 539
Möbius strip, 471
Moderator, nuclear, 1037, 1208, 1362
Mohole, 871
Mohorovičić discontinuity, 871
Mohs scale, 401
Mold, 1077
Molecular Basis of Evolution, The, 1403
Molecular beams, 1124, 1212
Molecular biology, 957, 1380, 1406
Molecular structure, 680, 686
  coordination theory and, 960
Molecular weight, 668, 684, 773
Molecules, 412, 514, 668
  asymmetry of, 642, 829
  light absorption by, 765
  structure of, 1236
Molybdenum, 342
Momentum, conservation of, 198
Mongolia, 742
Mongols, 1264
Monomolecular films, 1072
Monotheism, 6
Montcalm, Louis Joseph de, 303
Moon, 1336
  craters of, 100, 156, 185
  density of, 777
  distance of, 41, 50, 284
  far side of, 282
  life on, 885
  light reflection by, 3
  man on, 1492
  map of, 194, 499
  maria on, 194
  markings on, 96
  mass of, 283
  motion of, 275, 283, 347
  mountains on, 1339
  nature of, 14, 20
  orbit of, 7, 200, 231
  parallax of, 50
  photographs of, 566, 606
  rotation of, 777
  size of, 41
  surface of, 1196
  surface temperature of, 1151

  tides and, 39, 51, 52
  water on, 185
Morphine, 437, 438
  structure of, 1107
Morphology, 349
Morse code, 473, 958, 1025
Mortality tables, 238
Mosquitoes, malaria and, 771, 876
  yellow fever and, 822, 849, 955
Mössbauer effect, 1400, 1483
Motion, absolute, 835
Motion, laws of, 108, 231
Motion pictures, 788, 852
  sound, 1017
Motorcycle, 708
Motors, alternating-current, 837
  electric, 474, 503
Mountain-climbing, 147, 322, 397, 794
Mountains, 6, 33, 687
Mouthpiece, telephone, 819
Moving bodies, forces upon, 166
MSH (melanocyte-stimulating hormone), 1382
Muhammad, 76
Multiple sclerosis, 1456
Multiplication sign, 172
Mu-mesons, 1292
Mumps virus, 1195
Muon, 1274
Muscle, action of, 191, 278, 631, 1108, 1167
Museum, Alexandrian, 40, 69
Music of the spheres, 24, 169
Musk, 1119
Mussolini, Benito, 1025, 1243, 1289
Mustard gas, 991
Mutagens, 1029
Mutations, 598, 631, 704, 792, 957, 1224
  chemical, 1029
  rate of, 1160
  viruses and, 1253
  X rays and, 1145, 1270
Myasthenia gravis, 205
Myoglobulin, 1267
  amino acid makeup of, 1426
  structure of, 1389, 1415
Myosin, 1167
Mysticism, 314

Naphthalene, 409
  structure of, 661
Napier's bones, 159
Napoleon I, 127, 233, 238, 303, 309, 317, 318, 319, 320, 321, 332, 337, 340, 346, 347, 348, 353, 359, 360, 363, 364, 366,

368, 370, 371, 375, 384, 393, 396, 397, 404, 407, 408, 415, 420, 421, 434, 443, 446, 455, 456, 458, 463, 474, 477, 483, 490, 493, 497, 508, 561
Napoleon III, 328, 446, 463, 490, 497, 514, 516, 533, 564, 575, 578, 619, 668, 933
Natural History (Buffon), 277
Natural History (Pliny), 61
Natural History of Invertebrates, 336
Naturalist's Voyage on the Beagle, A, 554
Natural Questions, 89
Natural selection, 17, 286, 554, 562, 598, 643, 1224
Nature of the Chemical Bond, The, 1236
Nature philosophy, 417, 423, 539, 707
Nausiphanes, 35
Nautical Almanac, 310
Nautilus, 385
Naval hygiene, 288
N-dimensional geometry, 556, 629
Neanderthal man, 653, 884
Nebular hypothesis, 293, 347, 1053, 1376
Nebulas, 879
  dark, 883
Nebulium, 719
Negative numbers, 137
Negative, photographic, 479, 511
Negatron, 1292
Nelmes, Sarah, 348
Neodymium, 890
Neon, 832
  isotopes of, 869, 1051
Neon lights, 989
Neoplatonism, 70
Neoprene, 1058, 1190, 1354
Neptune, 309, 326, 344, 415, 860
  atmosphere of, 1038
  Bode's law and, 301
  discovery of, 523, 535, 564, 573, 615, 639
  satellites of, 509, 1297
  surface temperature of, 1147
Neptunism, 355, 374
Neptunium, 1329, 1372
Nereid, 1297
Nernst-Thomas rule, 936
Nerva, 62
Nerve cells, 764
Nerve impulse, 611, 1023, 1137, 1359, 1387
  speed of, 631, 1023
  transmission of, 1288, 1374
Nerve potentials, 1126
Nerves, 42, 43, 278, 438
  sensory, 881
Neuroanatomy, 881
Neurology, 278

Neuron, 722
Neuron theory, 600, 722, 827
Neurophysiology, 881
Neurospora crassa, 1270
Neutral K-mesons, 1454, 1497
Neutrinos, 1064, 1228, 1243, 1292, 1356
  detection of, 1423, 1434
  mass of, 1423
  varieties of, 1423
Neutron absorption, 1260
Neutrons, 1022, 1146, 1227, 1280
  delayed, 1357
  discovery of, 1150
  magnetic moment of, 1296
  mass of, 1362
  nuclear structure and, 1245, 1307
  slowing of, 1037
  thermal, 1243
  uranium and, 1063, 1243
Neutron stars, 1407, 1437
  rotating, 1463
New Almagest, 156, 185
New Atlantis, The, 163
New System of Chemical Philosophy, 389
New Zealand, 300
Niacin, 1027
Nicholas I (Emperor, Russia), 397, 483, 491
Nickel, 856
  discovery of, 292
  electron waves and, 1078
Nickel carbonyl, 856
Nicol prism, 394, 1344
Nicotinic acid, 1027, 1093, 1240
Night-blindness, 1318
Niobium, 383
Niobium-tin alloy, 1425
Nitric acid, 76, 734
Nitrobenzene, 485
Nitrocellulose, 510, 673, 677, 743
Nitrogen, 334, 368, 812, 977
  bends and, 702
  density of, 760, 832
  discovery of, 351
  elimination of, 1231
  fixing of, 817
  isotopes of, 1164, 1259
  light bulbs and, 1072
  liquid, 698, 758
  organic, 801
  plant nutrition and, 689
  stereochemistry and, 960
Nitrogen-15, 1164, 1259
Nitrogen balance, 588, 691

Nitrogen compounds, 977
  asymmetry of, 991
Nitrogen fixing, 525
Nitrogen mustards, 1029
Nitrogen trichloride, 421, 441
Nitroglycerine, 574, 673, 703
Nitrous oxide, 421
Nobelium, 703, 1372
Nobel prizes, 703
Noble gas compounds, 1499
Noble gases, 665, 832
Non-electrolytes, 894
Non-Euclidean geometry, 247, 530, 670, 800
Noradrenalin, 1288
Nordhoff, Charles B., 331
North America nebula, 927
Northeast Passage, 700
North magnetic pole, 512, 1008
North Pole, 866, 1129
North Star, 39
Northwest Passage, 178, 1008
Notochord, 478, 750, 823
Novas, 156, 166, 169, 883, 1209
  Andromeda galaxy and, 1136
Novum Organum, 163
Nuclear atom, 996
  quantum theory and, 1101
Nuclear bomb, 897, 920, 1051, 1063, 1064,
  1081, 1088, 1101, 1106, 1150, 1158,
  1159, 1198, 1207, 1241, 1255, 1259,
  1260, 1272, 1280, 1308, 1332, 1362,
  1372
Nuclear energy, 897, 996
Nuclear fission, 1060, 1063, 1064, 1101
Nuclear force, 1323
Nuclear fusion, 1343
Nuclear isomers, 1063, 1261
Nuclear magnetic presonance, 1212, 1296,
  1378
Nuclear reactions, 996, 1207
  branching of, 1261
  man-made, 1198
Nuclear reactors, 1208, 1225, 1227, 1238,
  1260, 1321, 1357
Nuclear shells, 1307, 1327
Nuclear structure, 1260
  neutrons and, 1245
Nucleic acids, 663, 770, 833, 842, 980,
  1282, 1331
  analysis of, 1498
  bacteriophage and, 1341
  composition of, 1291
  life and, 1355, 1406
  nucleotide analysis of, 1426

synthesis of, 1293
  virus and, 1337, 1355
Nuclein, 770, 842
Nucleoplasm, 768
Nucleoprotein, 842, 1282
Nucleotides, 980, 1278, 1331
  abiogenic formation of, 1457
Nucleus (atomic), charge on, 1121, 1150
  magnetic field of, 1296
  shape of, 1420, 1450, 1471
  structure of, 1150, 1307, 1323
Nucleus (cell), 403, 538, 600
Numbers, algebraic, 641
  complex, 944
  imaginary, 545
  irrational, 7, 26, 40, 641, 688, 772
  rational, 772
  real, 772
  theory of, 415
  transcendental, 358, 555, 641, 826
  transfinite, 772
Nutation, 258
Nutrition, 438
Nylon, 1058, 1190, 1354

Oberon, 321
Oblate spheroid, 270
Ocean, 548
  floor of, 1303, 1304
  life in the depths of, 682
  primordial temperatures of, 1164
Ocean currents, 397
Ocean depths, 1050
Oceanography, 548
Ockham's razor, 109
Octane rating, 966
Oersted, 417
Oersted, Anders, 417
Ohm, 461
Ohm's law, 461, 520
Oil (*see* Petroleum)
Olberia, 372
Olbers' comet, 372
Olbers' paradox, 372
Old Ironsides, 558
Oleic acid, 448
Olybrius, 71
Omega-meson, 1395
Omega-minus particle, 1487
Omicron Ceti, 167
On Aggression, 1271
On the Consolation of Philosophy, 71
On the Motive Power of Fire, 497
On the Origin of Species, 554, 624, 636,
  638, 656, 659, 802

Open-hearth method, 644
Operations research, 481
Ophthalmology, 605
Ophthalmometer, 631
Ophthalmoscope, 481, 631
Opium, 131, 208, 437
Opsin, 1318
Optical activity, 787, 829, 960, 991
Optical inversion, 928
Optical isomers, 642
Optical masers, 1400
Optical pumping, 1252
Opticks, 231
Optic nerves, 522
Optics, 40, 85, 169
Opus Majus, 99
Orangutan, 276
Orbitals, 1191
Orbits, planetary, 341, 358, 415
  shapes of, 169
Organic acid, 668
Organic analysis, 514, 532
Organic chemistry, 440, 674
Organic compounds, 515
  properties of, 601
  structure of, 514, 553, 829
  synthesis of, 674, 734
Organisms, classification of, 29, 213
Organizers, embryo, 981
Organometallic compounds, 655
Organ transplantation, 1016
Origin of Life on Earth, The, 1171
Orinoco River, 397
Orion nebula, 180, 215, 646
  radial motion of, 879
Orthobenzoyl sulfimide, 781
Orthogenesis, 598
Ortho-hydrogen, 1245
Oscar II (King, Sweden), 847
Oscillograph, 808
Osmium, 890
  discovery of, 375
Osmosis, 542, 547, 773
Osmotic pressure, 773, 894
Ossietzky, Karl von, 1183
Otto II (Holy Roman Emperor), 84
Otto engine, 694, 886
Outlines of Astronomy, 479
Outside the Earth, 880
Ovary, 42, 228
Overpopulation, 1266
Overtones, 631
Oxaloacetic acid, 1167, 1231
Oxygen, 580
  atomic weight of, 412, 760

combustion and, 334
  density of, 760
  discovery of, 312, 329
  enzymes and, 1113
  isotopes of, 1164, 1178, 1385
  liquid, 623, 698, 758, 759, 760
  tissue respiration and, 1089
Oxygen debt, 1095
Oxygen-16, 1178
Oxygen-17, 1178
Oxygen-18, 1178, 1385
Oxy-hydrogen blowpipe, 428
Oxytocin, 1239
  amino acid arrangement of, 1426
Ozone, 580
  discovery of, 510
  liquid, 759
  upper atmosphere and, 962

Pacific Ocean, 128
  exploration of, 300
  naming of, 130
  moon and, 777
Packing fraction, 1022, 1051
Paleontology, 396, 519
Palladium, 547, 856
  discovery of, 388
Pallas, 372, 388
Palmitic acid, 448
Panama Canal, 822, 853
Pancreas, 578
  insulin production by, 1152
  structure of, 791
  secretions of, 954
Pancreatic juice, 560, 725
Pangaea, 1071
Panthalassa, 1071
Pantothenic acid, 1221, 1240
Paper, 63
  photographic, 931
Paper chromatography, 1291, 1350, 1361,
  1394, 1406, 1426
Parachute, 122, 309, 362
Paraffin, 1150
Para-hydrogen, 1245
Parallax, 50
  spectroscopic, 1045
Paramagnetism, 1000, 1165, 1178
Paranoia, 749
Parapsychology, 1182
Parasitology, 517, 640
Parathyroid glands, 539, 1305
Parathormone, 1305
Parity, conservation of, 1260, 1451, 1473
Parkinson's disease, 365, 1456

Parr, Thomas, 174
Parsec, 1018
Parthenogenesis, 291
    artificial, 896
Partial pressures, law of, 389
Particle accelerators, 1198, 1241, 1244,
    1246, 1324, 1329, 1395, 1475
Particles (subatomic), spin of, 1228, 1255
    wave nature of, 1157
Particle-wave dualism, 1157, 1159
Pascal's principle, 207
Paschen series, 941
Pasteurization, 359, 642, 819
Pathology, 134, 251
Paul VI (Pope), 166
Paving, street, 369
Peabody, George, 690
Peanuts, 937
Peary Land, 866
Pedro II (Emperor, Brazil), 789
Pedro III (King, Aragon), 103
Peking man, 1096, 1162
Pellagra, 1027, 1093
    nicotinic acid and, 1240
Pemmican, 524
Pendulum, 166
    latitude and, 217
Penicillin, 841, 1010, 1031, 1077, 1128,
    1183, 1213, 1306
    virus culture and, 1195
Penicillin analogues, 1213
Penicillinase, 1306
Penicillium notatum, 1077
Pensées, 207
Pepsin, 563
    crystallization of, 1148
Perchloroethylene, 1423
Percussion powder, 435
Perfect gas, 726
Perfumes, 790
    synthetic, 734
Perfusion, blood, 597
Pericles, 14, 16
Periodic table, 427, 705, 727, 832, 1049,
    1052, 1121, 1228, 1372
Period-luminosity curve, 975
Peristalsis, 134
Permafrost, 280
Permian era, 477
Pernicious anemia, 482, 1059, 1103, 1154,
    1312
Perón, Juan Domingo, 1115
Peroxidase, 1113, 1384
Perpetual motion, 122, 158
Perry, Matthew C., 855

Perspective, laws of, 117
Perturbations, planetary, 231, 275, 317,
    347, 415
Peter I the Great (Emperor, Russia) 221,
    233, 238, 242, 248, 250, 255, 256, 275
Peter I Island, 426
Peter II (Emperor, Russia), 256
Petersburg Academy, 275
Petri, Julius Richard, 767
Petroleum (oil), 132, 824, 886
    drilling for, 614
pH, 967, 977
Phagocytes, 775
Pharmacology, 438
Pharmacopeia, 59
Phase-contrast microscope, 1127
Phase rule, 740, 854
Phases, 740
Phenol, 672
Philip II (King, Macedon), 29
Philip II (King, Spain), 146, 153, 159
Philip III (King, Spain), 259
Philippe Égalité, 328
Philosopher, 7
Philosopher's stone, 76, 131, 175
Philosophiae Naturalis Principia
    Mathematica, 231, 233, 234, 238, 240,
    261, 274, 545, 625, 788
Phipps, James, 348
Phlegm, 219
Phlogiston, 241, 279, 307, 312, 334, 351,
    360, 413
Phobos, 681
Phoebe, 885
Phonograph, 788, 819
Phosgene, 993
Phosphate esters, 1221
Phosphate ions, 947
Phosphates, 1062, 1194, 1221
Phospholipids, 663
Phosphoric acid, 547
Phosphorus, 212, 279
    bone and, 339
    discovery of, 216
    iron ore and, 575
    isotopes of, 1227
Phosphorus oxychloride, 602
Photochemistry, 566
Photodeik, 953
Photoelectric effect, 858, 887, 920, 1064
Photographic paper, 931
Photography, 384, 413, 467, 479, 511, 565,
    566, 577, 589, 723, 765, 832
    color, 692, 778, 1344
    dry-plate, 677

sound and, 972
stellar, 763
Photoheliograph, 589
Photometry, 264
Photons, 1159, 1170
Photosynthesis, 306, 454, 699, 1178, 1385
chemistry of, 1361
Phrenology, 371, 731
Phyla, 396
Physical chemistry, 840
Physical Geography of the Sea, 548
Physical organic chemistry, 601
Physicist, 487
Physics, classical, 592
Physiology, 134, 522
Pi, 299, 358
transcendental nature of, 826
value of, 47, 55, 153, 202, 572, 1139
Piazzia, 341
Piezoelectricity, 897, 965
Pi-meson (pion), 1274, 1323
Pinch effect, 1180
Pineal gland, 183, 225
Pion, 1274
Pioneer *10*, 1491
Pioneer *11*, 1491
Piperidine, 417
Pitchblende, 335, 1026
Pithecanthropus erectus, 884
Pituitary gland, 1090, 1115, 1382, 1460, 1474
posterior lobe of, 1239
Pius V (Pope), 166
Planck, Erwin, 887
Planck's constant, 887, 1245
Planetary spheres, 27, 29, 32, 118, 156
Planetary tables, 119, 127, 143, 156, 350
Planetesimals, 766, 1003
Planetoids (*see* Asteroids), 341
Planets, 301
extra-solar, 1247
motion of, 7, 27, 37
orbits of, 1258
Planet X, 860, 1299
Plankton, 491, 746
Plant growth, 893
Plant immunity, 1122
Plant nutrition, 689
Plant physiology, 249
Plants, 34
breeding of, 799
classification of, 213, 276, 345, 396, 418
sex in, 29, 160
species of, 31
Plasma, 1173, 1180, 1335, 1356, 1390

Plaster of Paris, 82
Plastics, 728, 931, 1074
Plate tectonics, 1304
Platinum, 364, 375, 711, 812, 856
catalytic properties of, 421, 427
electric lights and, 677
fluorine and, 831
melting of, 428
working of, 388
Platinum hexafluoride, 1499
Platinum-iridium alloy, 910
Platinum wire, 788
Pliocene, 487
Plotinus, 70
Plutarch, 41, 47
Pluto, 1149
discovery of, 860, 1299
rotation of, 1297
Plutonium, 1329, 1372
Pneumococci, 1054
Pneumonia, 1054
Poincaré, Raymond, 847
Poise, 500
Poiseuille's law, 500
Poison gas, 991, 993, 1058, 1063
Poisson's distribution, 432
Polar fronts, 1205
Polarimetry, 404, 642
Polarized light, 394, 408, 433, 455, 716, 1196, 1344
rotation of, 404, 642, 928
Polarography, 1144
Polaroid, 1344
Pole star, 1018
Poliomyelitis, 973
vaccine against, 1311, 1393
Poliomyelitis virus, 1195
Polonium, 965
Polycrates, 7, 8
Polyethylene, 1215
Polygons, regular, 415
Polygraph, 1161
Polymerization, 1058
Polymers, 1074, 1190, 1215
isotactic, 1263
synthetic, 1097
Polypeptides, 1235
Polyploidy, 1029
Pompey, 52
Pons-Brookes's comet, 376
Pons-Winnecke comet, 376
Pope, Alexander, 231, 249
Popular Astronomy (Flammarion), 756
Popular Astronomy (Mädler), 488
Population increase, 387

Positional notation, 95
Positive, photographic, 479
Positive rays, 811, 869, 996
Positrons, 1227, 1256, 1280
  discovery of, 1292
Potash, 414, 421
Potassium, 420, 603, 909
  discovery of, 421
Potassium carbonate, 414
Potassium chlorate, 346, 427
Potassium ferrocyanide, 457
Potassium fluoride, 831
Potassium ions, 717, 1359
  nerve impulse and, 1387
Potassium nitrate, 414
Potassium uranyl sulfate, 834
Potential energy, 613
Pound, James, 258
P-P factor, 1027, 1089
Praseodymium, 890
Prebus, Albert F., 1401
Pre-Cambrian life, 1399
Precession of the equinoxes, 127, 231
Precognition, 1182
Prefrontal lobotomy, 1032
Pressure, atmospheric, 192
Pressure, high, 751, 1080
Pressure cooker, 235
Prime meridian, 234
Prime mover, 316
Prime numbers, 40, 48
Principia Mathematica (Newton) (*see
  Philosophiae Naturalis Principia
  Mathematica*)
Principia Mathematica (Russell and
  Whitehead) 911, 1005
Principles of Chemistry, The, 705
Principles of Geology, The, 502
Principles of Psychology, The, 754
Printing, 114
Probability, 188, 207, 215, 246, 347, 432
Proconsul africanus, 1268
Procyon, companion of, 439, 836
  proper motion of, 238
Progesterone, 1265
Progression, mathematical, 25
Project Argus, 1392
Projective geometry, 456, 800
Project Vanguard, 1412
Prominences, solar, 589, 719
Prontosil, 1183, 1213, 1325
Proper motion, 646
Propylene, 1263
Prostate gland, 42
Prostatic cancer, 1242

Protactinium, 1063
Protamine, 770
Proteinoids, 1371
Proteins, 379, 388, 438, 440, 531, 1074
  amino acid structure of, 833
  classification of, 663
  enzymes as, 1120, 1148
  incomplete, 691
  molecular weight of, 773, 1097
  separation of, 1257
  structure of, 1210, 1236, 1239, 1389,
    1406, 1426
  variety of, 900
Protons, 996, 1256, 1280
  mass of, 996
  shells of, 1307
Proton synchrotrons, 1244, 1329
Protoplanets, 1297
Protoplasm, 452, 542, 657
Protozoa, 491, 517, 537
  discovery of, 221
  disease and, 776, 948, 997
Proust's law, 364
Prout's hypothesis, 440, 579, 760, 1051
Proxima Centauri, 505, 915
Proximity fuze, 1392, 1395
Prussic acid, 420
Przhevalsky's horse, 742
Pseudosphere, 484
Psi particles, 1493
Psychiatry, 865
Psychic research, 754, 760, 820
Psychoanalysis, 755, 865
Psychology, 754
  child, 780
  experimental, 697
Psychopathia Sexualis, 749
Psychophysics, 520, 733
Psychosomatic disease, 272, 314
Psychosurgery, 1032
Pterodactyls, 396, 690
Ptolemy I (King, Egypt), 38, 40
Ptolemy III (King, Egypt), 44, 48
Puerperal fever, 205, 607
Pugwash movement, 1274
Pulleys, 47
Pulsars, 1428, 1437, 1463
Pulse rate, 165, 683
Purines, 833, 842
Purkinje effect, 452
Pyramids, 3
Pyridoxine, 1233
Pyrilamine, 1325
Pyrimidines, 842

Pyrometer, 470
  optical, 812
Pyroxylin, 581, 728
Pyrrole rings, 1076
Pythagorean theorem, 7, 40

Quanta, 887
Quantum electrodynamics, 1300, 1421,
  1424, 1459
Quantum mechanics, 877, 1024, 1084, 1117,
  1226, 1236, 1273
Quantum numbers, 1228
Quantum theory, 648, 835, 887, 1081
  nuclear atom and, 1101
  photoelectric effect and, 1064
Quarks, 1487, 1493, 1507
Quartz, 618
Quasars, 1437, 1488
Quasistellar objects, 1488
Quaternions, 545
Quinine, 208, 454, 493, 604
  structure of, 734
  synthesis of, 1416

Rabies, 642, 817
Races, human, 357, 973
  blood groups and, 1264
Racism, 357, 498, 636
Radar, 1155, 1207, 1351, 1386
  Venus and, 1140
Radial velocity, 646
Radiation pressure, 894, 1085
Radiation sickness, 996
Radicals, 425
Radio, 820, 1017, 1143
  crystal set, 808
  invention of, 895, 1025
Radioactive series, 987, 1052
Radioactivity, 613, 652, 832, 858, 965, 979,
  996
  artificial, 1227
  danger of, 897
  discovery of, 834
  energy of, 897, 1064
  geochemical change and, 924
  volcanoes and, 753
Radio astronomy, 1295, 1368
Radioimmunoassay, 1446
Radioisotopes, 1100, 1227
Radiometer, 695
Radio sources, 1179
Radio stars, 1368
Radio-telephony, 1295
Radio telescope, 1163, 1368, 1386, 1428
Radio tubes, 1017, 1072

Radio waves, 820, 839, 895
  atmospheric reflection of, 1155, 1158
  discovery of, 873
  modulation of, 958
Radium, 987, 1063
  alpha particles and, 996
  breakdown of, 795
  discovery of, 825, 965
  metallic, 1026
Radium D, 1118
Radon, 795, 832
  compounds of, 1499
Railways, 431
Rainbow, 5, 85
Rainfall, 297
Rainmaking, 1072, 1309, 1391
Raman spectra, 1130
Rameses II (Egypt), 838
Randall, Merle, 1037
Rankine scale, 625
Raoult's law, 684
Rare earths, 335, 373, 501, 746, 890, 1002,
  1372
  separation of, 1259
Rational numbers, 772
Rayleigh's equation, 887
Rayon, 743
  viscose, 862
Reactions, chemical, 1206, 1443, 1477
Real numbers, 772
Reaumur porcelain, 252
Reaumur scale, 252
Recombinant-DNA, 1313, 1470, 1482,
  1485, 1496
Record players, 897
Rectifiers, 803, 808, 1348
Red blood corpuscles, 224, 445, 578, 1103
Red giant, 1356
Red shift, 646, 1038
  gravitational, 1045, 1064
Reflex action, 469, 881
Reflexes conditioned, 802, 1057, 1110
Refraction gratings, 450, 798
Refrigerants, 1132
Refrigerator, 758
Regenerative circuit, 1143
Regenerative furnace, 644
Relativity, theory of, 794, 821, 835, 839,
  935, 976, 1045, 1064, 1125, 1187, 1400,
  1405, 1483
Relay, electrical, 503
Replication, DNA, 1406
Reserpine, 1320
  synthesis of, 1416
Resistance, electrical, 461

Resonance, theory of, 553, 950, 1141, 1236, 1435
Resonance particles, 1363
Respiration, 230, 1030
  artificial, 807
  tissue, 1089
Respiration rate, 770
Respiratory chain, 1048
Respiratiry enzyme, 1113
Respiratory quotient, 561
Rest-mass, 839
Restriction enzyme, 1485
Retina, 42, 1232, 1276
  rods in, 1318
Retinene, 1318
Retrograde motion, 127
Reverberation, 972
Reverse transcriptase, 1505, 1508
Reversible reaction, 650, 674
Reversing layer, 712
Rh blood groups, 973, 1142, 1264
Rhea, 209
Rhenium, 1166, 1187
Rheumatoid arthritis, 1105, 1188
Rhodium, 812
  discovery of, 388
Rhodopsin, 1318
Riboflavin, 1131, 1240, 1267
Ribonuclease, 1365
Ribonucleic acid (RNA), 980, 1337, 1380
Ribose, 980
Ribosomes, 1380, 1438, 1447, 1476
Richard I (King, England), 92, 93
Rickets, 912, 1036, 1093
Rickettsia, 992
Ringer's solution, 717
Rings, Saturn's, 209, 215, 464, 586, 692, 879
RNA (Ribonucleic acid), 980, 1337, 1380
  genetic code and, 1448
  protein formation and, 1447
Robespierre, Maximilien, 393
Robinson Crusoe, 265
Robotics, 1349
Robots, 1349
Roche's limit, 627
Rocket into Interplanetary Space, The, 1172
Rockets, 231, 880, 1083, 1172, 1315, 1370, 1392, 1407
Rocks, age of, 1138
  volcanic, 287
Rocky Mountain spotted fever, 992
Roentgen, 774
Roosevelt, Franklin D., 1050, 1064, 1139, 1208

Roosevelt, Franklin D., Jr., 1183
Rorschach test, 1099
Ross Ice Shelf, 512
Ross Sea, 512
Rous chicken sarcoma virus, 1067
Royal Society, 163, 197, 198, 212, 221, 223, 231
Rubber, 270, 312, 516
  synthetic, 1058
Rubber gloves, 830
Rubidium, 565, 648
Rubies, synthetic, 582
Rudolf II (Holy Roman Emperor), 156, 169
Rudolphine Tables, 169, 200
Rusting, 241, 334
Ruthenium, 495
Rutherford, 996
Rutherfordium, 1372, 1381

Sabine's law, 972
Sabin vaccine, 1311
Saccharin, 781
Sadism, 749
St. Martin, Alexis, 444
Saint Vitus's dance, 208
Saladin, 92
Salicylic acid, 610
Salk vaccine, 1393
Saltpeter, 334, 414
Salvarsan, 845, 1077
Samarium, 736
Sandwich compound, 1445
San Francisco earthquake, 898
Sanger's reagent, 1426
Satellites, 169
  artificial, 1351, 1370, 1392
  tracking of, 1317, 1386
Saturn, atmosphere of, 1038
  mass of, 439
  rings of, 209, 215, 464, 586, 692, 879
  rotation of, 681
  satellites of, 209, 215, 321, 509, 885, 1297
  surface temperature of, 1147
Saturn 5 rocket, 1370
Scalar-tensor theory, 1405
Scaliger, Julius Caesar, 154
Scandium, 739
  discovery of, 747
Scarlet fever, 208
Sceptical Chemist, The, 212
Scheele's green, 329
Scheelite, 329
Schiller, Friedrich von, 452

Schizophrenia, 1035
Schmidt camera, 1065
Schwann cells, 563
Schwarzschild radius, 1019
Science, 789
Science, art and, 117, 122, 126
Science fiction, 756, 880, 1050, 1051, 1083, 1315, 1317, 1351, 1398, 1502
Scientific American, 995
Scientific Revolution, 114, 121, 127, 166, 231
Scientist, 474, 487
Scintillation counter, 996
Scott, Walter, 351
Screw of Archimedes, 47
Screw propeller, 533
Scuba diving, 1353
Scurvy, 288, 912, 1093
Sea anemones, 345
Sea-floor spreading, 1303, 1304
Sea-mounts, 1304
Seashells, 6
Seaweed, 414
Second-generation stars, 1398
Second Industrial Revolution, 1139
Second law of thermodynamics, 497, 507, 633, 652, 692, 769, 1414
Second Scientific Revolution, 774, 835, 934
Secretin, 954
Seebeck effect, 398
Seismograph, 550, 814, 917
Seismology, 294, 814
Selenium, 194
Selenographia, 194
Seleucus I (Seleucid Emperor), 43
Self-induction, 503
Self-pollination, 354
Self-starter, automobile, 1044
Semicircular canals, 755
Semiconductor diodes, 1464
Semiconductors, 1458
   glassy, 1294
Semipermeable membranes, 773
Sensation, 492
Senses, untrustworthiness of, 13, 16
Sensory nerves, 522
Septimius Severus, 65
Serum sickness, 809
Sewing machine, 616
Sex, 865
Sex cells, 768
Sex hormones, 1119, 1169
   female, 1242
   isolation of, 1265
Sex impulse, 984

Sexual selection, 554
Sforza, Ludovico, 120, 122
Shadow zone, 1133
Shakespeare, William, 163
Sharks, 29
Sharpey, William, 807
Shelburne, Lord, 312
Shellac, 931
Shock, electric, 257
Shock treatment, 874
Siberia, 250, 280
Sic et Non, 88
Sidereus Nuncius, 166
Sieve of Eratosthenes, 48
Sight, sense of, 1276
Sigismund III (King, Poland), 165
Silane, 515
Silicon, 515, 863
   discovery of, 425
   stereoisomerism and, 930
Silicon carbide, 863
Silicones, 930
Silicon hydrides, 1043
Silliman's Journal, 424
Silurian era, 477
Silver, 968
Silver chloride, 413
Silver iodide, 1309, 1391
Sinanthropus pekinensis, 1096
Sines, 1118
   table of, 83
Singularity, 1366
Sinkiang, 742
Sirius, 238
   companion of, 439, 696, 1045, 1064
   recession of, 646
Sixtus IV (Pope), 119
61 Cygni, 341
   distance of, 439
   planets of, 1247
Skeleton, vertebrate, 423
Skeleton keys, 481
Skull, 659
Sky, 626, 760
   map of, 27
   spherical, 4
Skyscrapers, 569
Sleeping pills, 718
Sleeping sickness, 767, 845
Slide rule, 172
Small intestine, 578
Smallpox, 348
Smith, J. E., 276
Smithsonian Institution, 503
Smokeless powder, 510, 673, 759

Smyth, Henry, 1280
Soap, 328
Soda, 421
Soda water, 312
Sodium, 602, 603, 909
  discovery of, 421
Sodium acetate, 1369
Sodium bicarbonate, 735
Sodium borohydride, 1373
Sodium carbonate, 328, 665
Sodium chloride, 735
Sodium hypochlorite, 1016
Sodium ions, 1359
  nerve impulse and, 1387
Sodium pump, 1387, 1419
Sodium sulfate, 190
Sodium thiosulfate, 467, 479
Soft drinks, 312
Soil microorganisms, 1128
Solar energy, 631
Solar flare, 667
Solar prominences, 974
Solar system, age of, 1118, 1138, 1147
  origin of, 766, 1003, 1053, 1147, 1335,
    1376
  stability of, 317, 347
Solar wind, 1186, 1289, 1478
Solenoid, 407, 436
Solids, regular, 24, 26, 169
Solid state devices, 808, 1328, 1348
Solid-state physics, 1464
Solomon Islands, 303
Solutions, 829
Solvay process, 735
Somnium, 169
Sonar, 1000
Sound, 7
  absorptivity of, 972
  mechanical reproduction of, 788, 789
  pitch of, 25
  radio and, 958
  transmission of, 370
  vacuum and, 187, 189, 212
  velocity of, 182, 370, 744
  wave motion of, 38, 972
Southey, Robert, 421
South Pole, 971, 1008, 1129
Space, 733, 1004
Space flight, 880
Space settlements, 1475
Space station, 880
Space suits, 880
Space-time, 935, 1064
Special theory of relativity, 835, 839, 935,
  1064

Specific heat, 298
  atomic weights and, 441
Spectacles, 99, 115
Spectral lines, 388, 450, 618, 619, 646, 695,
    857, 941
  coronal, 712, 1196
  electric field and, 1024
  elements and, 648
  magnetism and, 945
  regularity of, 658
Spectra, photography of, 646, 784
Spectra, stellar, 1045
  classification of, 606, 932
  photography of, 723
Spectroheliograph, 974
Spectrohelioscope, 667
Spectroscopic binaries, 757
Spectroscopy, 565, 606
  elements and, 506
Spectrum, solar, 231, 585, 711
Speedometer, 481
Spermaceti, 448
Spermatozoa, 302, 704, 842
  cellular nature of, 669
  discovery of, 221
Sperm banks, 1145, 1348
Spherical trigonometry, 83
Sphygmograph, 683
Spinal cord, 36, 65, 134, 469, 478, 881
Spinoza, Benedict, 212, 215
Spinthariscope, 695
Spiral galaxies, 513, 879
Spiritualism, 428, 448, 540, 676, 695
Spirochetes, 845, 997
Spontaneous fission, 1381
Spontaneous generation, 175, 211, 285, 302,
    626, 632, 642, 1490
Spores, bacterial, 675
  killing of, 816
  space and, 894
Sports, 792
Springs, 223
Sputnik I, 880, 1214, 1386, 1392, 1503
Sputnik II, 1392
Square-cube law, 166
Squaring the circle, 826
Squid, giant axon of, 1387
Stainless steel, 892
Stalin, Josef V., 1122, 1173, 1214, 1333
Standard measures, 486, 518, 835, 910
Staphylococcus, 1077
Star catalogues, 309, 439, 508, 546, 815
Starch, 430, 490, 1074
  hydrolysis of, 380
Star clusters, 321

Stark effect, 1024
Star maps, 48, 50, 112, 234, 238, 284
  photographic, 784
Star populations, 1163
Stars, binary, 294, 321
  birth of, 1302
  close encounters of, 1053
  clusters of, 1102
  collapse of, 1186
  color of, 1056
  composition of, 646
  density of, 1085
  diameter of, 835
  distance of, 99, 127, 156, 169, 215, 258,
    294, 439, 1045
  evolution of, 606, 1056
  interior of, 1085
  magnitude of, 50, 679
  motion of, 1229
  names of, 170
  nature of, 115
  parallax of, 258, 321, 439
  photographs of, 464, 596, 660, 763
  planets of, 1247
  populations of, 1163
  proper motions of, 238
  pulsating, 1085, 1463
  radial motion of, 646
  rotation of, 1203
  second generation, 1398
  spectra of, 606, 784
  streams of, 815
  variable, 381, 508, 975
Star-Spangled Banner, 957
Stassfurt deposits, 829
Static, radio, 1143, 1295
Statics, 47, 158
Statistics, 201, 496, 875
  genetics and, 1142
Steady-state universe, 1149, 1174, 1398,
  1433, 1437
Steam engine, 60, 235, 236, 243, 363, 497,
  507, 644, 850
  invention of, 316
Steam heat, 316
Steamship, 330, 385
Stearic acid, 448
Steel, 252
  alloy, 892, 985
  smelting of, 575, 644
Stefan-Boltzmann law, 715, 769
Stellarator, 1390
Step pyramid, 1
Steric hindrance, 796
Stereochemistry, 796, 833

Stereoisomerism, 930, 991
Stereoscope, 433
Steroids, 1046, 1048, 1107
Stethoscope, 429
Stickney, Angelina, 681
Stickney (crater), 681
Stigmata, 291
Stoichiometry, 378
Stokes's law, 618
Stomach, 444
Stone Age, 53, 460
  divisions of, 630
Stonehenge Decoded, 1481
Storage battery, 709
Storage rings, 1475, 1493
Storm winds, 462
Strangeness number, 1487
Strange particles, 1473, 1487
Strata, 395
Stratosphere, 861
  humans in, 1092
Streptomycin, 841, 1128, 1312
Strong interaction, 1243
Strontium, 421
Strychnine, 438, 454, 493
  structure of, 1107
  synthesis of, 1416
Stuart, Charles, 263
Subatomic particles, 521, 869, 1082
  families of, 1465, 1487
Submarine detection, 1020
Submarines, 385, 1250
  nuclear, 1225
Succinic acid, 1167
Sucrose, 663, 691
Sugar, 490
  composition of, 420
Sugar beets, 490
Sugar phosphates, 947
Sugars, 364
  optical activity of, 833
  separation of, 833
  structure of, 833, 1087
Sulfa drugs, 1077
Sulfanilamide, 1183, 1325
Sulfur, 1046
  petroleum and, 824
  rubber and, 516
Sulfur dioxide, 312, 1132
  liquefaction of, 340
Sulfuric acid, 107, 162, 709
  catalytic effect of, 650
Sulla, 29
Sumeria, 1069
Sun, 1102

calcium and, 974
composition of, 648, 1056
distance of, 41, 176, 209, 475, 763, 1140
energy source of, 631, 1022, 1308
galactic revolution of, 1229
hydrogen in, 1308
mass-loss of, 1308
nature of, 14
neutrinos from, 1423
photographs of, 589, 606
planetary center, 41, 51
radio waves from, 820
real motion of, 321, 508
rotation of, 166, 667
size of, 41, 52
surface appearance of, 647
temperature of, 1186
Sundial, 4
Sun, New York, 479
Sunspot cycle, 466, 564, 589
Earth's magnetic field and, 546
Sunspots, 166, 173, 321, 459, 818
magnetic fields and, 974
position of, 667
spectra of, 719
temperature of, 503
Superconductivity, 843, 1334, 1425, 1458,
1489, 1495, 1509
Superfluidity, 1042
Superheterodyne receiver, 1143
Supernovas, 1209, 1356, 1398
Superphosphate, 855
Supersonic flight, 1075, 1503
Surgery, 139
Survival of the fittest, 624
Sweat glands, 248
Sweet potatoes, 937
Swift, Jonathan, 221
Sydenham's chorea, 208
Symbolic logic (*see* Logic)
Symbols, chemical, 425
Sympathetic nervous system, 1288
Sympathin, 998
Synapses, nerve, 764, 1262
Synchrocyclotrons, 1324, 1329
Synthesis, 610
Synthetic DNA, 1293
Synthetic dyes, 604, 706, 734
Synthetic perfumes, 734
Synthetic RNA, 1293
Syphilis, 131, 859, 874
cause of, 997
chemotherapy of, 845
test for, 951, 986
Systema Naturae, 276

Tabulae Prutenicae, 143
Takadiastase, 855
Talbotype, 511
Talking pictures, 1017
Tamerlane, 112
Tantalum, 383
discovery of, 391
Tape recording, 983
Tautomerism, 676
Taxonomy, 418
Taylor, Norman B., 1218
Technetium, 1287
Technocracy, 735, 1052
Teeth, 539
Telegraph, 540, 788
invention of, 473, 503
Telegraph Plateau, 548
Telekinesis, 1182
Telepathy, 1182
Telephone, 652, 789
long-distance, 891
Telescopes, 166, 169, 321
glass mirrors of, 723
invention of, 168
large, 513, 696, 974, 1065
reflecting, 226, 231, 619
Television, 818, 1134
color, 1319
Television camera, 1134
Telluric helix, 622
Tellurium, 335
discovery of, 323
Temperature, 934
absolute, 497
measurement of, 812
Temperature scales, 625, 652
Terbium, 501
Terpenes, 790
Tesla, 867
Testicles, 228
Tetanus, 846, 870
Tetany, 1062
Tethys, 209
Tetracycline antibiotics, 1010, 1416
Tetraethyl lead, 966, 1044, 1132
Tetrahedron, 829
Tetraphenylmethane, 950
Texas cattle fever, 899
Textile machinery, 311
Thallium, 695
Thénard's blue, 416
Theodoric the Ostrogoth, 71
Theon, 69
*Theory of Games and Economic Behavior,
The,* 1248, 1273

Theory of numbers, 188
Theory of the Earth, 297
Theory of the Gene, 957
Thermal neutrons, 1243
Thermite, 909
Thermochemistry, 347, 528, 665
Thermodynamics, 497, 740, 812, 840, 1037
  chemical, 721, 740, 829, 1061
  electric cell and, 936
  living tissue and, 848
  second law of, 497, 507, 633, 652, 692,
    769, 1414
  third law of, 936, 1165
Thermodynamics and the Free Energy of
  Chemical Substances, 1037
Thermoelectric couple, 812
Thermoelectricity, 398
Thermometer, 244
  clinical, 165, 720
  gas, 166
  maximum-minimum, 351
  mercury, 254
  Réaumur, 252
  sealed, 193
Thermopile, 504
Thiamin, 1046
  isolation of, 1104
Thioglycolic acid, 1033
Thiophene, 796
Third Cambridge Catalogue, 1428
Third Law of Thermodynamics, 936, 1165
34 Tauri, 321
Thorium, 1372
  breakdown of, 1063
  discovery of, 425
  isotopes of, 987
  radioactivity of, 965
Thorium nitrate, 890
Threonine, 1114
Threshold wavelength, 1064
Through Space and Time, 1053
Thule, 39
Thulium, 746
Thymine, 842, 1291, 1406
Thymus gland, 1167, 1223, 1494
Thyroglobulin, 1105
Thyroid gland, 786, 1105
Thyroxine, 1105
Tibet, 742
Ticks, disease and, 899, 992
Tidal forces, 627
  lunar, 777, 835
Tides, 39, 51, 52, 75
Time, 935
  velocity and, 1064

Time and Space, 935
Times, New York, 711, 835, 1083, 1295
Time-study methods, 812
Time zones, 738
Tin tetrachloride, 162
Tire, rubber, 637
Tissue transplantation, 1275
Tissues, 400
Titan, 215
  atmosphere of, 1297
Titania, 321
Titanium, 335, 1215
  discovery of, 377
Titian, 146
Titration, 420
Titus, 61
Tobacco mosaic disease, 817, 939
Tobacco mosaic virus, 1282, 1337
  structure of, 1440
Tocopherol, 1131
Tokamak, 1343
Tonsillectomy, 57
Tools, prehistoric, 324, 458
Topology, 471
Torpedo fish, 29
Torsion balance, 294, 318, 794
Trace minerals, 947, 1062
  enzymes and, 1240
Tracers, isotopic, 1100, 1211, 1358
Tracheotomy, 419
Tranquilizers, 1032, 1320
Transcendental numbers, 358, 555, 641, 826
Transduction, 1466
Transfer-RNA, 1447, 1476
Transfinite numbers, 772
Transformers, electric, 474, 867
Transfusion, blood, 219, 227, 973, 1016,
  1411
Transistors, 1348
  invention of, 1334
Transmutation, 67, 103, 212, 231, 260, 334
Transplants, tissue, 1016, 1396, 1411, 1452,
  1494
Transport numbers, 649
Transuranium elements, 1329, 1372, 1381,
  1383
Transverse waves, 402
Treatise on Crystallography, A, 518
Tree rings, 963
Trichinosis, 539
Trieste, 1092
Trigonometric functions, 172
Trigonometric tables, 145
Trigonometry, 3, 50
Triodes, 808, 1017

Triphenylmethyl, 950
Triple bonds, 661
Tritium, 1244, 1342
Triton, 564, 1297
  discovery of, 509
Trojan asteroids, 927
Trojan system, 317
Tropical medicine, 771, 776
Tropisms, 699, 896
Tropopause, 861
Troposphere, 861
Troy, 634
Truman, Harry S, 1208, 1280
Trypanosomes, 845
Trypan red, 845
Trypsin, 725
  crystallization of, 1148
Tryptophan, 900, 912
Tsetse fly, 767
Tube, radio, 1017
Tuberculosis, 767, 809, 845
Tungsten, 367, 890
Tungsten wires, 1020, 1072
Tunicates, 750
Tunnel effect, 1278, 1464, 1484
Tunnels, 8
Turbine, steam, 850
Turbinia, 850
Turing machine, 1375
Twain, Mark, 1309
Two-carbon fragment, 1221, 1231, 1293, 1369
Tyler, John, 533
Tyndale, William, 626
Tyndall effect, 626, 943
Typhoid fever, 205, 805
  vaccine against, 948
Typhus fever, 137, 956, 992, 1216
Tyrosine, 661, 1105
Tyrothricin, 1235

UFO (unidentified flying objects), 1237
Ultracentrifuge, 1097
Ultramicroscope, 626, 943
Ultrasonic sound, 302, 897, 1000
Ultraviolet radiation, 388, 413, 618, 894
  ozone and, 962
  vitamin D and, 1046
Umbriel, 509
Uncertainty principle, 1064, 1245
Undefined concepts, 918
Unidentified flying objects (UFO), 1237
Unified field theory, 1064, 1468, 1500, 1502
Uniformitarianism, 297, 502
United States Weather Bureau, 503, 738

Units of measurement, 415, 540
Univac, 1328, 1431
Universal gravitation, law of, 231
Universe, 20
  age of, 1136, 1163
  closed, 1423
  composition of, 646, 1056
  expanding, 1004, 1038
  size of, 1004, 1163
  steady state, 1149, 1174, 1398, 1433, 1437
Universe Around Us, The, 1053
Ur, 1069
Uracil, 842
Uranium, 987
  fission of, 1060, 1063, 1064, 1101, 1187, 1208, 1227, 1238, 1243, 1251, 1284, 1321
  helium and, 832
  isotope-separation of, 1330, 1383
  isotopes of, 1106, 1164, 1241, 1272, 1321, 1330, 1372
  neutron bombardment of, 1063, 1243, 1329
  purification of, 1259
  radioactivity and, 695, 834, 965
  spontaneous fission of, 1381
Uranium-233, 1372
Uranium-235, 1101, 1106, 1164, 1241, 1321, 1330, 1372
  separation of, 1272
Uranium-238, 1164, 1272, 1321, 1330
Uranium breakdown, 1052, 1118
Uranium fission, 1060, 1063, 1064, 1101, 1187, 1208, 1227, 1238, 1243, 1251, 1284, 1321
Uranium hexafluoride, 1383
Uranium oxide, 1243
Uranium pile, 1243
Uranium X, 1243
Uranometria, 170
Uranus, 326, 335, 341, 344
  discovery of, 321
  mass of, 546
  motion of, 564, 615
  orbit of, 392, 439
  satellites of, 321, 509, 1297
  surface temperature of, 1147
Urban VIII (Pope), 166
Urea, 515, 691, 1120
Urea cycle, 1231
Urease, 1120
Urine, 515, 691

V-2 rockets, 1370, 1392, 1407

Vaccination, 348, 435, 642, 771
Vacuum, 38, 192, 212
  electric lights and, 577
  outer space and, 192
  production of, 189, 583
  sound and, 187, 189
Vagina, 149
Valence, theory of, 474, 655, 680, 705, 832
  electrons and, 1013, 1037
Vanadium, 382, 515
  discovery of, 451
Van Allen radiation belts, 1392
Vanderbilt, Cornelius, 785
Vanguard I, 1392, 1412
Variable star, 381, 508, 975
Variation, natural, 554, 799
Varieties of Religious Experience, 754
Vasopressin, 1426
Vector analysis, 556
Vega, 464
  parallax of, 483
Veins, 151
Venn circles, 710
Venus, 7
  atmosphere of, 282, 1045, 1504
  clouds of, 1196, 1290
  magnetic field of, 1279
  mass of, 283
  motion of, 28
  phases of, 166
  radar and, 1140
  surface of, 1155
  surface temperature of, 894
  transit of, 169, 200, 238, 255, 295, 310,
    475, 523, 763, 765
Venus probes, 1279, 1392, 1478
Verne, Jules, 1050
Vernier, 179
Vertebrata, 823
Vertebrate paleontology, 690
Vertebrates, 336
Vespasian, 61
Vesta, 372
Vestiges, 554
Vesuvius, Mount, 56, 302
  eruption of, 61
Victoria (Queen, Great Britain), 474, 479,
    567, 581, 604, 613, 734, 789, 850, 901
Violet catastrophe, 887
Virus diseases, 817
Viruses, 642, 816, 817, 822, 986
  cancer and, 1277
  crystallization of, 1282
  culture of, 1195
  discovery of, 939

  genes and, 1282
  mutation and, 1253
  nucleic acid and, 1337, 1355
  tumor, 1067
  vaccines against, 1202
Viscose, 862
Viscosity, 618
Vision, chemistry of, 1318
Visual purple, 1318
Vitalism, 515, 597, 611, 631, 642, 674, 680,
    848, 903, 1101
Vitamin A, 790, 900, 1062
  structure of, 1131
  synthesis of, 1233
  vision and, 1318
Vitamin B, 1062
Vitamin B_1, 1046
Vitamin B_2, 1240, 1267
  synthesis of, 1131, 1233
Vitamin B_6, 1233
Vitamin B_{12}, 1031, 1213
  structure of, 1312, 1352
Vitamin C, 1062, 1087
  isolation of, 1167, 1193
  synthesis of, 1201
Vitamin D, 790, 1046, 1048, 1062
Vitamin-deficiency diseases, 912
Vitamin E, 1062
  synthesis of, 1131
Vitamin H, 1239
Vitamin K, 1169
  discovery of, 1177
Vitamin P, 1167
Vitamins, 288, 1027, 1093
  assay of, 1036
  coenzymes and, 947, 1240, 1267
  discovery of, 888
  synthetic, 1312
Vivisection, 42, 761, 902
Volcanoes, 353, 355, 405
  radioactivity and, 753
Volt, 337, 407
Voltage multiplier, 1198
Voltaic pile, 337, 361
Vonnegut, Kurt, 1391
Voyager I, 586
Vulcan, 564
Vulcanism, 355
Vulcanized rubber, 516

Walden inversion, 928
Wallace's line, 643
Wallenstein, Albrecht von, 169
Warburg manometers, 1089
Warburg's yellow enzyme, 1267

Washington, Booker T., 937
Washington, George, 333, 362, 429, 443, 784, 898
Wasserman test, 951, 986
Water, 412
  density of, 332
  electrolysis of, 361, 413
  freezing of, 212, 894
  hydrogen and, 307
Water clock, 46
Water cycle, 137
Water of crystallization, 547
Watt, 316
Wavelength, light, 402
Wave mechanics, 1117, 1245, 1256, 1273
Wave-particle dualism, 1157, 1159
Waves, electron, 1078, 1084
Wax, 448
Waxpaper, 788
Weak interaction, 1243, 1468, 1473
Weather forecasting, 189, 544, 738, 1205
Weather-mapping, 636
Weber, 540
Weber-Fechner law, 492
Webster, Daniel, 576
Wedgwood, Emma, 554
Wedgwood, Josiah, 554
Welding, 909
Wellington, Duke of, 474
Wells, H. G., 1152
Welsbach mantle, 890
Wheatstone bridge, 526
White blood corpuscles, 775, 845, 1077
White dwarf, 836, 1045, 1064, 1356
White lead, 76
White matter, 371
Wien's displacement law, 887, 934
Wilberforce, Samuel, 659
William II (Emperor, Germany), 680
William IV (King, Great Britain), 389
Williamson synthesis, 650
Wind, plant fertilization and, 354
Wind tunnel, 995
Wine, 903
Wire recording, 983
Wool, 1210
Worlds in the Making, 894
Wolffian body, 313
Wolfram, 367
Wolframite, 367
Wollastonite, 388
Wonderful One-Hoss Shay, The, 558
Word-association tests, 1035
Wordsworth, William, 231, 421

Work, 497
Wrought iron, 575
Wurtz reaction, 602

Xanthippe, 21
X chromosome, 868
Xenon, 832
  compounds of, 1499
Xenon platinofluoride, 1499
Xenophon, 21
X-ray diffraction, 1068, 1141
  borane structure and, 1435
  cyanocobalamin and, 1352
  nucleic acid structure and, 1406, 1413, 1440
  penicillin and, 1213
  protein structure and, 1210, 1389, 1415
X rays, 332, 618, 695, 703, 774, 834, 891, 906, 908, 934, 957, 979, 1032, 1094, 1156
  characteristic, 1002, 1049, 1121
  diagnosis with, 998
  groups of, 1111
  mutations and, 1145, 1270
  scattering of, 1049, 1159
  solar, 1289, 1407
  wavelength of, 922, 1068, 1111
X-ray stars, 1289, 1407
X-ray tube, 1020

Y chromosome, 868
Year, length of, 18, 32, 83
Yeast, 563, 903
  dialysis of, 947
Yellow fever, 822, 849, 853, 955
  vaccine against, 1217
Yellow fever virus, 1217
Yerkes, Charles Tyson, 974
Young-Helmholtz theory, 402, 631
Young's modulus, 402
Ytterbium, 599
Yttrium, 501

Zein, 1114
Zeppelin, 737
Zero, 73, 79, 95
Zinc, 470, 993
  discovery of, 131
  organic compounds of, 655
Zinc carbonate, 411
Zinc sulfide, 695, 996, 1068
Zinjanthropus, 1268
Zircon, 335
Zirconium, 335, 1100

Zodiacal light, 209
Zoo, 97
Zoological Philosophy, 336
Zoonomia, 308

Zoser, 1
Zuider Zee, 839
Zwingli, Ulrich, 147

ROGER BACON

ROBERT BOYLE

COPERNICUS

GUGLIELMO MARCONI

ANDREAS VESALIUS

MARIE CURIE